NINTH EDITION

A
WORLD
OF IDEAS

ESSENTIAL READINGS
FOR
COLLEGE WRITERS

LEE A. JACOBUS

University of Connecticut

BEDFORD/ST. MARTIN'S

Boston ◆ *New York*

For Bedford/St. Martin's

Developmental Editor: Alicia Young
Senior Production Editor: Anne Noonan
Senior Production Supervisor: Dennis Conroy
Executive Marketing Manager: Molly Parke
Editorial Assistants: Charlotte Christy and Bethany Gordon
Copyeditor: Mary Lou Wilshaw-Watts
Permissions Manager: Kalina K. Ingham
Senior Art Director: Anna Palchik
Cover Design: Donna Lee Dennison
Cover Art: Cover Art © Estate of Robert Rauschenberg/
   Licensed by VAGA, New York, NY
Composition: Cenveo Publisher Services
Printing and Binding: RR Donnelley and Sons

President, Bedford/St. Martin's: Denise B. Wydra
Presidents, Macmillan Higher Education: Joan E. Feinberg and Tom Scotty
Editor in Chief: Karen S. Henry
Director of Marketing: Karen R. Soeltz
Production Director: Susan W. Brown
Associate Production Director: Elise S. Kaiser
Managing Editor: Elizabeth M. Schaaf

Manufactured in the United States of America.

7   6   5
f

For information, write: Bedford/St. Martin's, 75 Arlington Street, Boston,
MA 02116 (617-399-4000)

ISBN 978-1-4576-0436-2

Acknowledgments

PREFACE

Among the pleasures of editing *A World of Ideas* are the discussions I have had over the years with students and teachers who have used the book in their writing classes. A student once wrote to tell me that the book meant a great deal to her and that her experience with it impelled her to wonder what originally inspired me to assemble the first edition. I explained that my teaching of first-year writing has always inclined toward ideas that serious writers and thinkers have explored and contemplated throughout the ages; early on, I could not find a composition reader that introduced students to the important thinkers whose writing I believe should be basic to everyone's education. As a result of that need, *A World of Ideas* took shape and has continued to grow and develop through nine editions, attracting a wide audience of teachers and students who value the thought-provoking ideas that affect the way we interpret the world.

In preparing the ninth edition of *A World of Ideas,* I have benefited, as usual, from the suggestions of hundreds of users of earlier editions. The primary concern of both teachers and students is that the book remain centered on the tradition of important ideas and on the writers whose work has had a lasting influence on society. To that end, I have chosen writers whose ideas are central to our most important and lasting concerns. A new edition offers the opportunity to reevaluate old choices and make new ones that expand and deepen what has always been the fundamental purpose of this composition reader: to provide college students in first-year writing courses with a representative sampling of important ideas examined by men and women who have shaped the way we think today.

The selections in this volume are of the highest quality. Each was chosen because it clarifies important ideas and can sustain discussion and stimulate good writing. Unlike most composition readers, *A World of Ideas* presents substantial excerpts from the work of each of its authors. The selections are presented as they originally appeared; only rarely are they edited and marked with ellipses. They average fifteen to twenty pages in length, and their arguments are presented completely, as the authors wrote them. Developing a serious idea in writing takes time and a willingness to experiment. Most students are willing to read deeply into the work of important thinkers to grasp their ideas better because the knowledge yielded by the effort is vast and rewarding.

Additionally, this edition of *A World of Ideas* is also presented in a new format—a combination of the print book and e-Pages, online materials that include one reading per chapter as well as color versions of all the works of art in the "Visualizing" features. The readings that appear in e-Pages are "favorites" that have appeared in past editions of *A World of Ideas*; making them accessible online allows us to give your students more material without increasing the cost or size of the text. The e-Page versions of the "Visualizing" works of art are in full color, giving students the opportunity to view these images in richer detail and thus to better appreciate their subtleties, the particulars of which often lend these paintings much of their significance.

A Text for Readers and Writers

Because students perceive writers such as Plato and Thoreau as serious and important, they take more seriously the writing course that uses texts by these authors: such students learn to read more attentively, think more critically, and write more effectively. But more important, this may be a student's only opportunity to encounter the thinkers whose ideas have shaped civilization. No other composition reader offers a comparable collection of important readings along with the supportive apparatus students need to understand, analyze, and respond to them.

Classic Readings.   *A World of Ideas* draws its fifty-six selections (forty-eight in print and eight in e-Pages) from the writing of some of the world's most important thinkers. Those writers with selections that remain from the eighth edition are Hannah Arendt, Aristotle, Francis Bacon, Carl Becker, Andrew Carnegie, Marcus Tullius Cicero, Charles Darwin, René Descartes, Frederick Douglass, Ralph Waldo Emerson, Sigmund Freud, John Kenneth Galbraith, Howard Gardner, Germaine Greer, Thomas Jefferson, Carl Jung, Martin Luther King Jr., Lao-tzu, Niccolò Machiavelli, Karl Marx, Margaret Mead, John Stuart Mill, Iris Murdoch, Friedrich Nietzsche, Plato, Robert B. Reich, Jean-Jacques Rousseau, Adam Smith, Elizabeth Cady Stanton, Henry David Thoreau, Mary Wollstonecraft, and Virginia Woolf.

A Focus on Eight Great Ideas.   *A World of Ideas'* unique structure highlights seminal ideas as developed by great thinkers throughout history and facilitates cross-disciplinary comparisons. Each of the eight parts of the book focuses on one great idea—democracy, government, ethics and morality, wealth and poverty, education, gender and culture, language, and discoveries and the mind. Part introductions ground students in the history of each idea and connect the philosophies of individual writers.

"Evaluating Ideas: An Introduction to Critical Reading."   This introduction demonstrates a range of methods students can adopt to participate in a meaningful dialogue with each selection. This dialogue—an active, questioning approach to texts and ideas—is one of the keys to critical reading. In the introduction, a portion of Machiavelli's "The Qualities of the Prince" is annotated to help students follow the key ideas of the piece and to model for students a critical reading process that they can adapt to other essays in the book. The introduction encourages students to mark what they think are the most interesting and important ideas in an essay and highlight or underline all sentences that they might want to quote in an essay of their own.

"Writing about Ideas: An Introduction to Rhetoric."   In the ninth edition, this section, which now immediately follows "Evaluating Ideas: An Introduction to Critical Reading," has been much expanded, with an emphasis on developing thesis statements, using rhetorical methods of development, and thinking critically to construct a strong argument. Many new examples based on current selections in the ninth edition help students find fruitful approaches to the material. This section explains how a reader can make annotations while reading critically and then use those annotations to write effectively in response to the ideas presented in any selection in the book. "Writing about Ideas" draws on the annotations of the Machiavelli selection illustrated in "Evaluating Ideas: An Introduction to Critical Reading." A sample student essay on Machiavelli, using the techniques taught in the context of reading and writing, gives students a model for moving from a critical response to a selection to writing their own material. In addition, this section helps students understand how they can apply some of the basic rhetorical principles discussed throughout the book.

Selection Headnotes.   Each selection is preceded by a detailed headnote on the author's life and work and by comments about the primary ideas presented in the reading. The most interesting rhetorical aspects of the selection are identified and discussed to help students see how the writer's rhetorical techniques can achieve specific effects.

Prereading Questions.   To emphasize critical thinking, reading, and writing, prereading questions precede every selection. The content of the selections is challenging, and these prereading questions can help students in first-year writing courses overcome minor difficulties in understanding the author's meaning. These brief questions are designed to help students focus on central issues during their first reading of each selection.

Extensive Apparatus.   At the end of each selection is a group of discussion questions designed for use inside or outside the classroom. Questions for Critical Reading focus on key issues and ideas and can be used to stimulate general class discussion and critical thinking. Suggestions for Critical Writing help students practice some of the rhetorical strategies employed by the author of a given selection. These suggestions ask for personal responses, as well as complete essays that involve research. A number of these assignments, labeled "Connections," promote critical reading by requiring students to connect particular passages in a selection with a selection by another writer, either in the same part of the book or in another part. The variety of connections is intriguing—Lao-tzu with Machiavelli, Aristotle with Andrew Carnegie, Adam Smith with Thomas Jefferson, Julius K. Nyerere with the framers of the Constitution, Francis Bacon with Howard Gardner, Kwame Anthony Appiah with Iris Murdoch and Michael Gazzaniga, Susanne K. Langer with Noam Chomsky, James Baldwin with Jonathan Kozol, Judith Butler with Margaret Mead, and many more.

The "Visualizing" Feature Encourages Students to Apply Great Ideas to Great Works of Art.   Immediately preceding the selections in each part, a well-known painting is accompanied by a commentary that places the work historically and aesthetically and prepares students to make thoughtful connections between the work and the thinkers who follow. For example, "Visualizing Gender and Culture" features Mary Cassatt's painting *In the Loge* along with a brief caption and a discussion of the work's exploration of gender roles. The Seeing Connections questions that follow each of the readings ask students to relate a given text to the work of art. Other featured works of art include, but are not limited to, Howard Chandler Christy's painting *Scene at the Signing of the Constitution of the United States* for "Visualizing Democracy," Eugène Delacroix's *Liberty Leading the People* for "Visualizing Government," Salvador Dalí's *The Persistence of Memory* for "Visualizing Discoveries and the Mind," and Wosene Worke Kosrof's *The Color of Words IX*—from his series *WordPlay*—for "Visualizing Language."

Instructor's Resource Manual. I have prepared an extensive manual, *Resources for Teaching A WORLD OF IDEAS*, that contains further background on the selections, examples from my own class-room responses to the selections, and more suggestions for classroom discussion and student writing assignments. Sentence outlines for the selections—which have been carefully prepared by Michael Hennessy, Carol Verberg, Ellen Troutman, Ellen Darion, and Jon Marc Smith—can be photocopied or downloaded from the book's companion Web site, **bedfordstmartins.com/worldofideas**, and given to students. The idea for these sentence outlines came from the phrase outlines that Darwin created to precede each chapter of *On the Origin of Species*. These outlines may be used to discuss the more difficult selections and to provide additional guidance for students. At the end of the manual, brief bibliographies are provided for all fifty-five authors. These bibli-ographies may be photocopied or downloaded and distributed to stu-dents who wish to explore the primary selections in greater depth.

New in the Ninth Edition

The ninth edition offers a number of new features to help students engage and interact with the texts as they learn to ana-lyze ideas and develop their own thoughts in writing.

Selections and Images Available in e-Pages. As mentioned above, the new edition features online readings—"favorites" from past editions such as Ralph Waldo Emerson's "On Education" and Stephen L. Carter's "The Separation of Church and State"—and full-color versions of the art-work included in the book. Students receive access automatically with the purchase of a new book. If the activation code printed in the inside cover of the student edition is revealed, it might be expired. Students can purchase access at the Student Site. Instructors don't need an access code; they can access the e-Pages at the Student Site. They can also use the free tools accompanying the e-Pages to upload a syllabus, readings, and assignments to share with the class. Visit **bedfordstmartins.com /worldofideas/epages** for more information.

New Essential Readings. The selections in *A World of Ideas* explore the key ideas that have defined the human experience and shaped civiliza-tion. Of the fifty-six selections, twenty-six are new to this edition, includ-ing works by Aristotle, James Madison, the Founding Fathers, Alexis de Tocqueville, Julius K. Nyerere, Benazir Bhutto, Stephen L. Carter, Kwame Anthony Appiah, Michael Gazzaniga, Milton and Rose Fried-man, Hsün Tzu, Maria Montessori, John Dewey, Carter G. Woodson, Jonathan Kozol, Howard Gardner, Ralph Waldo Emerson, Judith Butler,

Karen Horney, Susanne K. Langer, Mario Pei, James Baldwin, Bill Bryson, Neil Postman, Noam Chomsky, and Alexander Pope.

Three New Foundational Ideas.   The selections in the three new parts—"Democracy," "Education," and "Language"—cover considerable historical periods and attitudes toward their subjects. All three of these new sections contain ideas that affect every one of us in a number of important ways. Democracy, for example, is in many respects one of the most important ideas of modern times. With political struggles unfolding in developing countries, whose citizens are voting for the first time and writing their own constitutions, few documents could be more important for students to know well than the U.S. Constitution, which appears in this book for the first time. Likewise, the work of James Madison and others in the *Federalist Papers* points toward political struggles ongoing in modern democracies. The section on education introduces students to ideas by Hsün tzu, Maria Montessori, John Dewey, and Carter G. Woodson that are still relevant to our schools. The section on language introduces some of the modern ideas about language being "hardwired" in our brains, and it explores some theories of language origin and the development of words from authors such as Mario Pei and Susanne K. Langer.

More "Connections" Questions.   Throughout the book, students are asked to make connections and comparisons between writers addressing the same great idea within the same great idea topic and between writers addressing different ideas, helping to stimulate comparative critical thinking and writing.

Increased Coverage of Developing Theses and Arguments.   "Writing about Ideas: An Introduction to Rhetoric" now immediately follows "Evaluating Ideas: An Introduction to Critical Reading" at the beginning of the book, and this section has been expanded to provide support for developing thesis statements, using rhetorical methods of development, and using critical thinking to develop a strong argument. New student writing examples based on selections in the ninth edition help students understand how to approach the material and discuss it meaningfully.

Digital Resources for *A World of Ideas*

A World of Ideas offers more than just a great text. Online you'll find both free and affordable premium resources to help students get even more out of the book and your course. You'll also find convenient instructor resources, such as downloadable sample syllabi, classroom activities, and even a nationwide community of teachers. To learn more about or order any of the products below, contact your Bedford/St. Martin's sales representative, e-mail sales support (sales_support@bfwpub.com), or visit the Web site at bedfordstmartins.com.

Take Advantage of What the Web Can Do with New e-Pages for A World of Ideas. Favorite readings from past editions give your students even more important thinkers to help them explore ideas, and color images from the "Visualizing" features give your students a better look at works of art that relate to great ideas. To access this feature, go to **bedfordstmartins.com/worldofideas/epages**.

A Fully Updated Student Site Gives Students More Ways to Explore **A World of Ideas.** At **bedfordstmartins.com/worldofideas,** students will find links to full-text documents of historical and philosophical interest, more information on each selection's author and his or her ideas, and the book's e-Pages, which are accessible through a code included in the book. Instructors will find the helpful instructor's manual, which includes a sentence outline for every selection.

Let Students Choose Their Format. Students can now purchase *A World of Ideas* in popular e-book formats for computers, tablets, and e-readers. For more details, visit **bedfordstmartins.com/ebooks.**

VideoCentral is a growing collection of videos for the writing class that captures real-world, academic, and student writers talking about how and why they write. *VideoCentral* can be packaged for free with *A World of Ideas.* An activation code is required. To order *Video-Central* packaged with the print book, use **ISBN 978-1-4576-4342-2.**

Re:Writing Plus gathers all of the Bedford/St. Martin's premium digital content for composition into one online collection. It includes hundreds of model documents, the first ever peer-review game, and *VideoCentral. Re:Writing Plus* can be purchased separately or packaged with the print book at a significant discount. An activation code is required. To order *Re:Writing Plus* packaged with *A World of Ideas,* use **ISBN 978-1-4576-4338-5.**

Teaching Central (bedfordstmartins.com/teachingcentral) offers the entire list of Bedford/St. Martin's print and online professional resources in one place. You'll find landmark reference works, sourcebooks on pedagogical issues, award-winning collections, and practical advice for the classroom—all free for instructors.

Bits (bedfordbits.com) collects creative ideas for teaching a range of composition topics in an easily searchable blog. A community of teachers—leading scholars, authors, and editors—discuss revision, research, grammar and style, technology, peer review, and much more. Take, use, adapt, and pass the ideas around. Then, come back to the site to comment or share your own suggestion.

Bedford Coursespacks allow you to easily integrate our most popular content into your own course management system. For details, visit **bedfordstmartins.com/coursepacks**.

Acknowledgments

I am grateful to a number of people who made important suggestions for earlier editions, among them Shoshana Milgram Knapp of Virginia Polytechnic and State University and Michael Hennessy of Texas State University–San Marcos. I want to thank Jon Marc Smith of Texas State University–San Marcos and Chiara Sulprizio of the Loyola Marymount University for assisting with the instructor's manual for the eighth edition. I also remain grateful to Michael Bybee of St. John's College in Santa Fe for suggesting many fascinating pieces by Eastern thinkers, all of which he has taught to his own students. Thanks to him, this edition includes Lao-tzu.

Like its predecessors, the ninth edition is indebted to a great many creative people at Bedford/St. Martin's, whose support is invaluable. I want to thank Charles Christensen, former president, whose concern for the excellence of this book and whose close attention to detail were truly admirable. I appreciate as always the advice of Joan E. Feinberg, copresident of Macmillan Higher Education, and Denise Wydra, president of Bedford/St. Martin's, whose suggestions were timely and excellent. Nancy Perry, editorial director, Custom Publishing, New York; Karen Henry, editor in chief, English; and Steve Scipione, executive editor, offered many useful ideas and suggestions as well, especially in the early stages of development, and kept their sharp eyes on the project throughout. My editor for the eighth edition, Maura Shea, is the professional's professional. My editor for the current edition, Alicia Young, has been a steady guiding hand, discussing material with me and providing help where necessary and when timely. She has been an inspiration in dealing with sometimes intractable problems and responding with encouragement and the kind of help only the best editors can provide.

Assisting her were a number of hardworking individuals, including Charlotte Christy and Bethany Gordon. Anne Noonan, production editor, also helped with innumerable important details and suggestions. Mary Lou Wilshaw-Watts, copyeditor, improved the prose and watched out for inconsistencies. Thanks also to several staff members and researchers: Jenn Kennett cleared text permissions, Donna Dennison found the cover art and designed the cover, and Linda Finigan secured all the new photographs. In earlier editions, I had help from Diane Kraut, Maura Shea, Sarah Cornog, Rosemary Winfield, Michelle Clark, Professor Mary W. Cornog, Ellen Kuhl, Mark Reimold, Andrea Goldman, Beth Castrodale, Jonathan Burns, Mary Beth McNulty, Beth Chapman, Mika De Roo, and Greg Johnson. I feel I had a personal relationship with each of them. I also want to thank the students—quite a few of them—who wrote me directly about their experiences reading the first eight editions. I have attended carefully to what they told me, and I am warmed by their high regard for the material in this book.

Earlier editions named hundreds of users of this book who sent their comments and encouragement. I would like to take this opportunity to thank them again. In addition, the following professors were generous with criticism, praise, and detailed recommendations for the ninth edition: D. Michelle Adkerson, Nashville State Community College; Geraldine Cannon Becker, University of Maine at Fort Kent; Aaron Bradford, Folsom Lake College and Pasadena City College; David Elias, Eastern Kentucky University; Jim Ewing, Fresno City College; Michele Giargiari, Bunker Hill Community College; Susan Gorman, Massachusetts College of Pharmacy and Health Sciences; Deana Holifield, Pearl River Community College; Shelley Kelly, College of Southern Nevada; Christina Lovin, Eastern Kentucky University; Pam Mathis, North Arkansas College; Aggie Mendoza, Nashville State Community College; Sandra Pyle, Point Park University; Robert Royar, Morehead State University; Sam Ruddick, Bunker Hill Community College; Ron Schwartz, Pierce College; Michele Singletary, Nashville State Community College; Jon Marc Smith, Texas State University–San Marcos; Roberta Stagnaro, San Diego State University; Andrea Van Nort, United States Air Force Academy; Paul Walker, Murray State University; Martha Willoughby, Pearl River Community College; and our reviewers at Chaffey College, Pasadena City College, and Monmouth University who wish to remain anonymous. I want to mention particularly the past experiences I had visiting Professor Elizabeth Deis and the faculty and students of Hampden-Sydney College in connection with their writing and humanities programs. Professors James Kenkel and Charlie Sweet were gracious in welcoming me to Eastern Kentucky University for workshops and classes using *A World of Ideas*. These were delightful and fruitful experiences that helped me shape the book. I am grateful to all who took part in these workshops.

TO THE STUDENT

When the first edition of *A World of Ideas* was published, the notion that students in first-year composition courses should be able to read and write about challenging works by great thinkers was a radical one. In fact, no other composition reader at the time included selections from such important thinkers as Hannah Arendt, Aristotle, Friedrich Nietzsche, Karl Marx, Plato, Charles Darwin, or Mary Wollstonecraft. I had expected a moderate response from a small number of people. Instead, teachers and students alike sent me a swarm of mail commending the book for the challenge it provided and the insights they gained.

One of the first letters I received was from a young woman who had read the book after she graduated from college. She said she had heard of the thinkers included in *A World of Ideas* but in her college career had never read any of their works. Reading them now, she said, was long overdue. Another student wrote me an elaborate letter in which he demonstrated that every one of the selections in the book had been used as the basis of a *Star Trek* episode. He sagely connected every selection to a specific episode and convinced me that whoever was writing *Star Trek* had read some of the world's most important thinkers. Other students have written to tell me that they found themselves using the material in this book in other courses, such as psychology, philosophy, literature, and history, among others. In many cases, these students were the only ones among their peers who had read the key authors in their discipline.

Sometimes you will have to read the selections in *A World of Ideas* more than once. Works by influential thinkers, such as Jean-Jacques Rousseau, James Baldwin, Judith Butler, Adam Smith, Sigmund Freud, Francis Bacon, Iris Murdoch, and Noam Chomsky, can be very challenging. But do not let the challenge discourage you. In "Evaluating Ideas: An Introduction to Critical Reading," I suggest methods for annotating and questioning texts that are designed to help you keep track of what you read and to help you master the material. In addition, each selection is accompanied by a headnote on the author's life and work, comments about the primary ideas presented in the selection, and a host of questions to help you overcome minor difficulties in understanding the author's meaning. Some students have written to tell me that their first reading of the book was off-putting, but most of them have written later to tell me how they eventually overcame their initial fear that the selections would be too difficult for them. Ultimately, these students agreed with me that this material is important enough to merit their absolute attention.

The purpose of *A World of Ideas* is to help you learn to write better by giving you something really significant to think and write about. The selections not only are avenues into some of the most serious thought on their subjects but also are stimulating enough to sustain close analysis and to produce many good ideas for writing. For example, when you think about democracy, it helps to know what Aristotle said about it while Athens enjoyed it, just as it is important to know what the United States Constitution says that puts democracy into law. Elizabeth Cady Stanton defends the rights of women in her "Declaration of Sentiments and Resolutions," pointing always to the social injustices that she documents. Frederick Douglass speaks from the perspective of a former slave when he cries out against the injustice of an institution that existed in the Americas for hundreds of years. And a hundred years after Douglass, the Reverend Martin Luther King Jr. sent his "Letter from Birmingham Jail," still demanding justice for African Americans and freedom seekers everywhere. The questions of ethics that still haunt us are treated by Iris Murdoch in relation to religion and by Kwame Anthony Appiah in relation to situational and virtue ethics, each of which concentrates on the relation of ones' character to one's ethical behavior. All these writers place their views in the larger context of a universal dialogue on the subject of justice. When you write, you add your own voice to the conversation. By commenting on the selections, expressing and arguing a position, and pointing out contradictions or contrasts among texts, you are participating in the world of ideas.

Keep in mind that I prepared *A World of Ideas* for my own students, most of whom work their way through college and do not take the idea of earning an education lightly. For that reason, I felt I owed them the opportunity to encounter the very best minds I could put them in touch with. Anything less seemed to me a missed opportunity. I hope you, like so many other writing students, find this book both educational and inspiring.

CONTENTS

PART ONE

DEMOCRACY

– 51 –

VISUALIZING DEMOCRACY

HOWARD CHANDLER CHRISTY, Scene at the Signing of the Constitution
of the United States [IMAGE; AVAILABLE IN COLOR IN E-PAGES]

57

*In 1939, the House of Representatives commissioned Christy—a
renowned American artist—to paint a portrait of one of the most
auspicious moments in his country's history: the signing of the
Constitution of the United States.*

*Having lived in Athens during the period of its democracy, Aristotle
had considerable insight into the political structures that existed*

**For readings that go beyond the printed page,
see bedfordstmartins.com/worldofideas/epages.**

in ancient Greece. His analysis of the choice between democracy—rule by the people—and oligarchy—rule by a wealthy few—remains relevant to this day.

This landmark document of United States history was the result of the founding fathers meeting in Philadelphia in 1787 to ratify a constitution that established a strong federal government that took into account special issues of the states.

The Federalist Papers, *written by James Madison, John Jay, and Alexander Hamilton before the ratification of the Constitution, argued for a federal government to help consolidate the interests of the states. Here, Madison establishes means by which the federal government can balance powers so as to avoid tyranny.*

Tocqueville, a French aristocrat, traveled extensively in the United States in the 1830s and was struck by the sense of equality expressed by nearly every American he encountered. His Democracy in America *remains one of the most profound and astute commentaries on American democracy.*

In an essay written in 1941, at democracy's lowest hour in the West, Becker reminds us that "Democracy is in some sense an economic luxury," but that we must nonetheless recognize its value and persist in its defense.

Nyerere, the first president of Tanzania, tells us that there was no room for the adversarial structure of two political parties when his country was emerging from recent colonial control. Unity was

PART TWO

GOVERNMENT

– 195 –

e bedfordstmartins.com/worldofideas/epages

 bedfordstmartins.com/worldofideas/epages

PART THREE

ETHICS AND MORALITY

– 293 –

VISUALIZING ETHICS AND MORALITY

JOSEPH WRIGHT OF DERBY, An Experiment on a Bird in the Air Pump
[IMAGE; AVAILABLE IN COLOR IN E-PAGES]

298

 bedfordstmartins.com/worldofideas/epages

P A R T   F I V E

EDUCATION

– 533 –

VISUALIZING EDUCATION
NORMAN ROCKWELL, The Problem We All Live With
[IMAGE; AVAILABLE IN COLOR IN E-PAGES]
539

This Rockwell painting—his most requested reproduction—depicts Ruby Bridges' first day of school in New Orleans on November 14, 1960. Federal marshals escorted Ruby to protect her from angry protesters who opposed the integration of the previously all-white school.

ⓔ   bedfordstmartins.com/worldofideas/epages

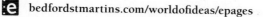 bedfordstmartins.com/worldofideas/epages

PART SIX

GENDER AND CULTURE

– 645 –

VISUALIZING GENDER AND CULTURE
MARY STEVENSON CASSATT, In the Loge
[IMAGE; AVAILABLE IN COLOR IN E-PAGES]

650

Mary Cassatt, who left the United States to become an important impressionist painter in France, puts forth a bold statement about the complexities of gender and class expectations in her painting In the Loge *(1878).*

In this excerpt from one of the first great works of feminism, Wollstonecraft argues that the laws, property rights, and class distinctions of her day are mechanisms of control that deny women their liberty and demean their lives.

Mill, one of the most distinguished philosophers of the Victorian age, cries out against a social system that denies education and opportunity to women. He clarifies the subjection of women in marriage and argues against wasting the talent of half of society, talent that he says is in great demand in the modern industrial age.

In this excerpt from A Room of One's Own, *her book-length essay on the role of women in history and society, Woolf imaginatively reconstructs the environment of Shakespeare's hypothetical sister and demonstrates how little opportunity she would have had in the sixteenth century.*

The anthropologist Margaret Mead attacks the idea that there is a biological basis for what we may think of as a masculine or a feminine temperament. She illustrates her argument with examples from a number of societies whose views about masculinity and femininity are quite at odds with any that we might recognize in our own experience.

:e bedfordstmartins.com/worldofideas/epages

PART SEVEN

LANGUAGE

– 761 –

:e bedfordstmartins.com/worldofideas/epages

The Persistence of Memory *is one of the most well-known paintings of the twentieth century. Dali's surrealistic masterpiece represents a dream state, an expedition into the unconscious interior of the mind.*

[e] bedfordstmartins.com/worldofideas/epages

EVALUATING IDEAS
An Introduction to Critical Reading

The selections in this book demand a careful and attentive reading. The authors, whose works have changed the way we view our world, our institutions, and ourselves, make every effort to communicate their views with clarity and style. But their views are complex and subtle, and we must train ourselves to read them sensitively, responsively, and critically. Critical reading is basic for approaching the essays in this book. Indeed, it is fundamental for approaching any reading material that deserves serious attention.

Reading critically means reading actively: questioning the premises of the argument, speculating on the ways in which evidence is used, comparing the statements of one writer with those of another, and holding an inner dialogue with the author. These skills differ from the passive reception we employ when we watch television or read light-weight materials. Being an active, participating reader makes it possible for us to derive the most from good books.

Critical reading involves most of the following processes:

- *Prereading* Developing a sense of what the piece is about and what its general purposes seem to be.

- *Annotating* Using a pencil or a pen to mark those passages that seem important enough to return to later. Annotations establish a dialogue between you and the author.

- *Questioning* Raising issues that you feel need to be taken into consideration. These may be issues that you believe the author has treated either well or badly and that you feel are important. Questioning can be part of the annotation process.

- *Reviewing* Rereading your annotations and underlinings in order to grasp the entire "picture" of what you've just read. Sometimes writing a summary of the piece as you review makes the meaning even clearer.

1

- *Forming your own ideas* Reviewing what you have read, evaluating the way that the writer presents the issues, and developing your own views on the issues. This is the final step.

THE PROCESS OF CRITICAL READING

Prereading

Before you read a particular selection, you may find it useful to turn to the beginning of the part in which it appears. There you will find an introduction discussing the broader issues and questions central to all the selections in the part. This may help you focus your thoughts and formulate your opinions as you read the essays themselves.

Begin any selection in this book by reading its headnote. Each headnote supplies historical background on the writer, sets the intellectual stage for the ideas discussed in the essay, and comments on the writer's main points. The second part of each headnote introduces the main rhetorical or stylistic methods that the writer uses to communicate his or her thoughts. In the process of reading the headnote, you will develop an overview that helps prepare you for reading the essay.

This kind of preparation is typical of critical reading. It makes the task of reading more delightful, more useful, and much easier. A review of the headnote to Niccolò Machiavelli and part of his essay "The Qualities of the Prince" (p. 219) will illustrate the usefulness of such preparation. This essay appears in Part Two—"Government"—so the content can already be expected to be concerned with styles of government. The introduction to Machiavelli provides the following points, each followed here by the number of the paragraph in which it appears:

Machiavelli was an Italian aristocrat in Renaissance Italy. (1)

Machiavelli describes the qualities necessary for a prince—that is, any ruler—to maintain power. (2)

A weak Italy was prey to the much stronger France and Spain at this time. (2)

Machiavelli recommends securing power by whatever means necessary and maintaining it. (3)

His concern for moralizing or acting out of high moral principle is not great. (3)

He supports questionable means of becoming and remaining prince. (3)

Machiavelli does not fret over the means used to achieve his ends and sometimes advocates repression, imprisonment, and torture. (3)

Machiavelli has been said to have a cynical view of human nature. (4)

His rhetorical method is to discuss both sides of an issue: cruelty and mercy, liberality and stinginess. (8)

He uses aphorisms to persuade the reader that he is saying something wise and true. (9)

With these observations in mind, the reader knows that the selection that follows will be concerned with governance in Renaissance Italy. The question of ends versus means is central to Machiavelli's discussion, and he does not idealize people and their general goodness. Yet because of Machiavelli's rhetorical methods, particularly his use of aphorism,[1] the reader can expect that Machiavelli's argument will be exceptionally persuasive.

Thus, as a critical reader, you will be well advised to keep track of these basic statements from the headnote. You need not accept all of them, but you should certainly be alert to the issues that will probably be central to your experience of the essay. Remember: it is just as reasonable to question the headnote as it is to question the essay itself.

Before reading the essay in detail, you might develop an overview of its meaning by scanning it quickly. In the case of "The Qualities of the Prince," note the subheadings, such as "On Those Things for Which Men, and Particularly Princes, Are Praised or Blamed." Checking each of the subheadings before you read the entire piece might provide you with a map or guide to the essay.

Each passage is preceded by two or three prereading questions. These are designed to help you keep two or three points in mind as you read. Each of these questions focuses your attention on an important idea or interpretation in the passage. For your reading of Machiavelli, the questions are as follows:

1. Why does Machiavelli praise skill in warfare in his opening pages? How does that skill aid a prince?

2. Is it better for a prince to be loved or to be feared?

In each case, a key element in Machiavelli's argument is the center of each question. By watching for the answer to these questions,

---

[1] **aphorism** A short, pithy statement of truth.

you will find yourself focusing on some of the most important aspects of the passage.

Annotating and Questioning

As you read a text, your annotations establish a dialogue between you and the author. You can underline or highlight important statements that you feel help clarify the author's position. They may be statements to which you will want to refer later. Think of them as serving one overriding purpose: to make it possible for you to review the piece and understand its key points without having to reread it entirely.

Your dialogue with the author will be most visible in the margins of the essay, which is one reason the margins in this book are so generous. Take issue with key points or note your assent—the more you annotate, the more you free your imagination to develop your own ideas. My own methods involve notating both agreement and disagreement. I annotate thoroughly, so that after a quick second glance I know what the author is saying as well as what I thought of the essay when I read it closely. My annotations help me keep the major points fresh in my mind.

Annotation keeps track both of what the author says and of what our responses are. No one can reduce annotation to a formula—we all do it differently—but it is not a passive act. Reading with a pencil or a pen in hand should become second nature. Without annotations, you often have to reread entire sections of an essay to remember an argument that once was clear and understandable but after time has become part of the fabric of the prose and thus "invisible." Annotation is the conquest of the invisible; it provides a quick view of the main points.

When you annotate,

- Read with a pen or a pencil.
- Underline key sentences—for example, definitions and statements of purpose.
- Underline key words that appear often.
- Note the topic of paragraphs in the margins.
- Ask questions in the margins.
- Make notes in the margins to remind yourself to develop ideas later.
- Mark passages you might want to quote later.
- Keep track of points with which you disagree.

Some sample annotations follow, again from Niccolò Machiavelli's "The Qualities of the Prince." A sixteenth-century text in translation, *The Prince* is challenging to work with. My annotations appear in the form of underlinings and marginal comments and questions. Only the first few paragraphs appear here, but the entire essay is annotated in my copy of the book.

A Prince's Duty Concerning Military Matters

The prince's profession should be war.

A prince, therefore, must not have any other object nor any other thought, nor must he take anything as his profession but war, its institutions, and its discipline; because that is the only profession which befits one who commands; and it is of such importance that not only does it maintain those who were born princes, but many times it enables men of private station to rise to that position; and, on the other hand, it is evident that when princes have given more thought to personal luxuries than to arms, they have lost their state. And the first way to lose it is to neglect this art; and the way to acquire it is to be well versed in this art.

Examples

Francesco Sforza became Duke of Milan from being a private citizen because he was armed; his sons, since they avoided the inconveniences of arms, became private citizens after having been dukes. For, among the other bad effects it causes, being dis-

Being disarmed makes you despised. Is this true?

armed makes you despised; this is one of those infamies a prince should guard himself against, as will be treated below: for between an armed and an unarmed man there is no comparison whatsoever, and it is not reasonable for an armed man to obey an unarmed man willingly, nor that an unarmed man should be safe among armed servants; since, when the former is suspicious and the latter are contemptuous, it is impossible for them to work well together. And therefore, a prince who does not understand military matters, besides the other misfortunes already noted, cannot be esteemed by his own soldiers, nor can he trust them.

He must, therefore, never raise his thought from this exercise of war, and in peacetime he must

*Training: action/
mind*

*Knowledge of
terrain*

Two benefits

train himself more than in time of war; this can be done in two ways: one by <u>action, the other by the mind</u>. And as far as actions are concerned, besides <u>keeping his soldiers well disciplined and trained,</u> he must always be out hunting, and must accustom his body to hardships in this manner; and he must also <u>learn the nature of the terrain, and know how mountains slope, how valleys open, how plains lie,</u> and understand the nature of rivers and swamps; and he should devote much attention to such activities. <u>Such knowledge is useful in two ways:</u> first, one learns to know one's own country and can better understand how to defend it; second, with the knowledge and experience of the terrain, one can easily comprehend the characteristics of any other terrain that it is necessary to explore for the first time; for the hills, valleys, plains, rivers, and swamps of Tuscany, for instance, have certain similarities to those of other provinces; so that by knowing the lay of the land in one province one can easily understand it in others. And a prince who lacks this ability lacks the most important quality in a leader; because this skill teaches you to find the enemy, choose a campsite, lead troops, organize them for battle, and besiege towns to your own advantage.

[There follow the examples of Philopoemon, who was always observing terrain for its military usefulness, and a recommendation that princes read histories and learn from them. Three paragraphs are omitted.]

On Those Things for Which Men, and Particularly Princes, Are Praised or Blamed

Now there remains to be examined what should be the <u>methods and procedures of a prince</u> in dealing with his subjects and friends. And because I know that many have written about this, I am afraid that by writing about it again I shall be thought of as presumptuous, since in discussing this material I depart radically from the procedures of others. But since my intention is to write something useful for anyone who understands it, it seemed more suitable to me to search after the effectual truth of the matter rather than its imagined one. And many writers have imagined for themselves republics and principalities that have never been seen nor known to exist in reality; for there is such a gap between how one lives and how one ought to live that anyone who abandons what is done for what ought to be done learns his ruin rather than his preservation: for <u>a man who wishes to make a vocation of being good at all times will come to ruin among so many who are not good.</u> Hence it is necessary for a <u>prince</u> who wishes to maintain his position <u>to learn how not to be good,</u> and to use this knowledge or not to use it according to necessity.

Those who are good at all times come to ruin among those who are not good.

Prince must learn how not to be good.

Leaving aside, therefore, the imagined things concerning a prince, and taking into account those that are true, I say that all men, when they are spoken of, and particularly princes, since they are placed on a higher level, are judged by some of these qualities which bring them either <u>blame or praise</u>. And this is why one is considered generous, another miserly (to use a Tuscan word, since "avaricious" in our language is still used to mean one who wishes to acquire by means of theft; we call "miserly" one who excessively avoids using what he has); one is considered a giver, the other rapacious; one cruel, another merciful; one treacherous, another faithful; one effeminate and cowardly, another bold and courageous; one humane, another haughty; one lascivious, another chaste; one trustworthy, another cunning; one harsh, another lenient; one serious, another frivolous; one religious, another unbelieving; and the like. And I know that everyone will admit that it would be a very praiseworthy thing to find in a prince, of the qualities mentioned above, those that are held to be good, but since it is neither possible to have them nor to observe them all completely, because human nature does not permit it, <u>a prince must be prudent enough to know how to escape the bad reputation of those vices that would lose the state for him, and must protect himself from those that</u>

Note the prince's reputation.

Prince must avoid reputation for the worst vices.

*Some vices may
be needed to
hold the state.
True?*

will not lose it for him, if this is possible; but if
he cannot, he need not concern himself unduly if he
ignores these less serious vices. And, moreover, he
need not worry about incurring the bad reputation
of those vices without which it would be difficult to
hold his state; since, carefully taking everything into
account, one will discover that something which
appears to be a virtue, if pursued, will end in his
destruction; while some other thing which seems to
be a vice, if pursued, will result in his safety and his
well-being.

*Some virtues
may end in
destruction.*

Reviewing

The process of review, which takes place after a careful reading,
is much more useful if you have annotated and underlined the text
well. To a large extent, the review process can be devoted to account-
ing for the primary ideas that have been uncovered by your annotations
and underlinings. For example, reviewing the Machiavelli annotations
shows that the following ideas are crucial to Machiavelli's thinking:

- The prince's profession should be war, so the most successful
  princes are probably experienced in the military.
- If they do not pay attention to military matters, princes will lose
  their power.
- Being disarmed makes the prince despised.
- The prince should be in constant training.
- The prince needs a sound knowledge of terrain.
- Machiavelli says he tells us what is true, not what ought to be true.
- Those who are always good will come to ruin among those who
  are not good.
- To remain in power, the prince must learn how not to be good.
- The prince should avoid the worst vices in order not to harm his
  reputation.
- To maintain power, some vices may be necessary.
- Some virtues may end in destruction.

Putting Machiavelli's ideas in this raw form does an injustice to his
skill as a writer, but annotation is designed to result in such summary
statements. We can see that there are some constant themes, such as
the insistence that the prince be a military person. As the headnote

tells us, in Machiavelli's day Italy was a group of rival city-states, and France, a larger, united nation, was invading these states one by one. Machiavelli dreamed that one powerful prince, such as his favorite, Cesare Borgia, could fight the French and save Italy. He emphasized the importance of the military because he lived in an age in which war was a constant threat.

Machiavelli anticipates the complaints of pacifists—those who argue against war—by telling us that those who remain unarmed are despised. To demonstrate his point, he gives us examples of those who lost their positions as princes because they avoided being armed. He clearly expects these examples to be persuasive.

A second important theme pervading Machiavelli's essay is his view on moral behavior. For Machiavelli, being in power is much more important than being virtuous. He is quick to admit that vice is not desirable and that the worst vices will harm the prince's reputation. But he also says that the prince need not worry about the "less serious" vices. Moreover, the prince need not worry about incurring a bad reputation by practicing vices that are necessary if he wishes to hold his state. In the same spirit, Machiavelli tells us that there are some virtues that might lead to the destruction of the prince.

Forming Your Own Ideas

One of the most important reasons for critically reading the texts in this book is to enable you to develop your own positions on issues that these writers raise. Identifying and clarifying the main ideas is only the first step; the next step in critical reading is evaluating those ideas.

For example, you might ask whether Machiavelli's ideas have any relevance for today. After all, he wrote nearly five hundred years ago and times have changed. You might feel that Machiavelli was relevant strictly during the Italian Renaissance or, alternatively, that his principles are timeless and have something to teach every age. For most people, Machiavelli is a political philosopher whose views are useful anytime and anywhere.

If you agree with the majority, then you may want to examine Machiavelli's ideas to see whether you can accept them. Consider just two of those ideas and their implications:

- Should rulers always be members of the military? Should they always be armed? Should the ruler of a nation first demonstrate competence as a military leader?
- Should rulers ignore virtue and practice vice when it is convenient?

In his commentary on government, which is also included in Part Two, Lao-tzu offers different advice from Machiavelli because his assumptions are that the ruler ought to respect the rights of individuals. For Lao-tzu the waging of war is an annoying, essentially wasteful activity. Machiavelli, on the other hand, never questions the usefulness of war: to him, it is basic to government. As a critical reader, you can take issue with such an assumption, and in doing so you will deepen your understanding of Machiavelli.

If we were to follow Machiavelli's advice, then we would choose American presidents on the basis of whether or not they had been good military leaders. Among those we would not have chosen might be Thomas Jefferson, Abraham Lincoln, and Franklin Delano Roosevelt. Those who were high-ranking military men include George Washington, Ulysses S. Grant, and Dwight D. Eisenhower. If you followed Machiavelli's rhetorical technique of using examples to convince your audience, you could choose from either group to prove your case.

Of course, there are examples from other nations. It has been common since the 1930s to see certain leaders dressed in their military uniforms: Benito Mussolini (Italy), Adolf Hitler (Germany), Joseph Stalin (the Soviet Union), Idi Amin (Uganda), Muammar al-Qaddafi (Libya), Saddam Hussein (Iraq). These were all tyrants who tormented their citizens and their neighbors. That gives us something to think about. Should a president dress in full military regalia all the time? Is that a good image for the ruler of a free nation to project?

Do you want a ruler, then, who is usually virtuous but embraces vice when it is necessary? This is a very difficult question to answer. President Richard Nixon tried to hide the Watergate break-in scandal, President Ronald Reagan did not reveal the details of the Iran-Contra scandal, President Bill Clinton lied about his relations with Monica Lewinsky, and George W. Bush misrepresented intelligence to invade Iraq. Yet all these presidents are noted for important achievements while in office. How might Machiavelli have handled these problems differently? How much truthfulness do we expect from our presidents? How much do we deserve?

These are only a few of the questions that are raised by my annotations in the few pages from Machiavelli examined here. Many other issues could be uncovered by these annotations and many more from subsequent pages of the essay. Critical reading can be a powerful means by which to open what you read to discovery and discussion.

Once you begin a line of questioning, the ways in which you think about a passage begin expanding. You find yourself with more ideas of your own that have grown in response to those you have been reading about. Reading critically, in other words, gives you an enormous return on your investment of time. If you have the chance to investigate your responses to the assumptions and underlying premises of passages such as Machiavelli's, you will be able to refine your thinking even further. For example, if you agree with Machiavelli that rulers should be successful military leaders for whom small vices may be useful at times, and you find yourself in a position to argue with someone who feels Machiavelli is mistaken in this view, then you will have a good opportunity to evaluate the soundness of your thinking. You will have a chance to see your own assumptions and arguments tested.

In many ways, this entire book is about such opportunities. The essays that follow offer you powerful ideas from great thinkers. They invite you to participate in their thoughts, exercise your own knowledge and assumptions, and arrive at your own conclusions. Basically, that is the meaning of education.

WRITING ABOUT IDEAS
An Introduction to Rhetoric

Writing about ideas has several functions. First, it helps make our thinking available to others for examination. The writers whose works are presented in this book benefited from their first readers' examinations and at times revised their work considerably as a result of such criticism. Writing about ideas also helps us refine what we think—even without criticism from others—because writing is a self-instructional experience. We learn by writing in part because writing clarifies our thinking. When we think silently, we construct phrases and then reflect on them; when we speak, we both utter these phrases and sort them out in order to give our audience a tidier version of our thoughts. But spoken thought is difficult to sustain because we cannot review or revise what we said an hour earlier. Writing has the advantage of permitting us to expand our ideas, to work them through completely and possibly to revise in the light of later discoveries. It is by writing that we truly gain control over our ideas.

GENERATING TOPICS FOR WRITING

Filled with sophisticated discussions of important ideas, the selections in this volume endlessly stimulate our responses and our writing. Reading the works of great thinkers can also be chastening to the point of making us feel sometimes that they have said it all and there is no room for our own thoughts. However, the suggestions that follow will assist you in writing your response to the ideas of an important thinker.

Thinking Critically: Asking a Question.   One of the most reliable ways to start writing is to ask a question and then to answer it. In many ways, that is what the writers in this book have done again and again. James Madison begins his "Federalist No. 51" (p. 109) with a simple question: "To what expedient then shall we finally resort, for maintaining in practice the necessary partition of power among the several departments, as laid down in the constitution?" This question gives him the focus he wants in establishing the principle that the power of a federal government must not be concentrated in the hands of the president, the Congress, or the judiciary. His essay essentially answers his question. Adam Smith asks what the principles of accumulating wealth really are (p. 441) and proceeds to examine the economic system of his time in such detail that his views are still valued. He is associated with the capitalist system as firmly as Marx is with the communist system. John Kenneth Galbraith asks questions about why poverty exists in a prosperous nation such as the United States (p. 499). When Charles Darwin begins his meditation on the power of natural selection (p. 897), he starts with the most obvious question: "How will the struggle for existence . . . act in regard to variation? Can the principle of selection, which we have seen is so potent in the hands of man, apply in nature?" His previous discussion concerns the ways in which people can create variation in dogs by selecting for desirable traits, just as they do for variations in horses, livestock, flowers, and all vegetables used for food. If people can create variability, what happens when nature does it? Such questioning is at the center of all critical thinking.

As a writer stimulated by other thinkers, you can use the same technique. For example, turn back to the Machiavelli excerpt annotated in "Evaluating Ideas: An Introduction to Critical Reading" (p. 5). All the annotations can easily be turned into questions. Any of the following questions, based on the annotations and our brief summary of the passage, could be the basis of an essay:

- Should a leader be armed?
- Is it true that an unarmed leader is despised?
- Will those leaders who are always good come to ruin among those who are not good?
- To remain in power, must a leader learn how not to be good?

One technique is to structure an essay around the answer to such a question. Another is to develop a series of questions and to answer each of them in various parts of an essay. Yet another technique is to use the question indirectly—by answering it, but not in an obvious way. In "Why the Rich Are Getting Richer and the Poor, Poorer" (p. 513), for example, Robert B. Reich answers a question we may not have asked. In the process he examines the nature of our current economy to see what it promises for different sectors of the population. His answer to the question concerns the shift in labor from manufacturing to information, revealing that "symbolic analysts" have the best opportunities in the future to amass wealth.

Many kinds of questions can be asked of a passage even as brief as the sample from Machiavelli. For one thing, we can limit ourselves to our annotations and go no further. But we also can reflect on larger issues and ask a series of questions that constitute a fuller inquiry. Out of that inquiry we can generate ideas for our own writing.

Two important ideas are isolated in our annotations. The first is that the prince must devote himself to war. In modern times, this implies that a president or other national leader must put matters of defense first — that a leader's knowledge, training, and concerns must revolve around warfare. Taking that idea in general, we can develop other questions that, stimulated by Machiavelli's selection, can be used to generate essays:

- Which modern leaders would Machiavelli support?
- Would Machiavelli approve of our current president?
- Do military personnel make the best leaders?
- Should our president have a military background?
- Could a modern state survive with no army or military weapons?
- What kind of a nation would we have if we did not stockpile nuclear weapons?

These questions derive from "The prince's profession should be war," the first idea that we isolate in the annotations. The next group of questions comes from the second idea, the issue of whether a leader can afford to be moral:

- Can virtues cause a leader to lose power?
- Is Machiavelli being cynical about morality, or is he being realistic (as he claims he is)? (We might also ask if Machiavelli uses the word *realistic* as a synonym for *cynical*.)
- Do most American leaders behave morally?
- Do most leaders believe that they should behave morally?
- Should our leaders be moral all the time?
- Which vices can we permit our leaders to have?
- Are there any vices we want our leaders to have?
- Which world leaders behave most morally? Are they the ones we most respect?
- Could a modern government govern well or at all if it were to behave morally in the face of immoral adversaries?

One reason for reading Machiavelli is to help us confront broad and serious questions. One reason for writing about these ideas is to help clarify our own positions on such important issues.

Using Suggestions for Writing.   Every selection in this book is followed by a number of questions and a number of writing assignments. The questions are designed to help clarify the most important issues raised in the piece. Unlike the questions derived from annotation, their purpose is to stimulate a classroom discussion so that you can benefit from hearing others' thoughts on these issues. Naturally, subjects for essays can arise from such discussion, but the discussion is most important for refining and focusing your ideas. The writing assignments, on the other hand, are explicitly meant to provide a useful starting point for producing an essay of five hundred to one thousand words.

A sample suggestion for writing about Machiavelli follows:

> Machiavelli advises the prince to study history and reflect on the actions of great men. Do you support such advice? Machiavelli mentions a number of great leaders in his essay. Which leaders would you recommend a prince should study? How do you think Machiavelli would agree or disagree with your recommendations?

Like most of the suggestions for writing, this one can be approached in several ways. It can be broken down into three parts. The first question is whether it is useful to study, as Machiavelli does, the performance of past leaders. If you agree, then the second question asks you to name some leaders whose behavior you would recommend studying. If you do not agree, you can point to the performance of some past leaders and explain why their study would be pointless today. Finally, the third question asks how you think Machiavelli would agree or disagree with your choices.

To deal successfully with this suggestion for writing, you could begin by giving your reasons for recommending that a political leader study "the actions of great men." George Santayana once said, "Those who cannot remember the past are condemned to repeat it." That is, we study history in order not to have to live it over again. If you believe that a study of the past is important, the first part of an essay can answer the question of why such study could make a politician more successful.

The second part of the suggestion focuses on examples. In the sample from Machiavelli in "Evaluating Ideas," we omitted the examples, but in the complete essay they are very important for bringing Machiavelli's point home. Few things can convince as completely as examples, so the first thing to do is to choose several leaders to work with. If you have studied a world leader, such as Indira Gandhi, Winston Churchill, Franklin Delano Roosevelt, or Margaret Thatcher, you could use that figure as one of your examples. If you have not done so, then use the research library's sections on history and politics to find books or articles on one or two leaders and read them with an eye to establishing their usefulness for your argument. An Internet search can help you gather information efficiently. Consult the Internet resources created specially for this book at **www .bedfordstmartins.com/worldofideas.** The central question you would seek to answer is how a specific world leader could benefit from studying the behavior and conduct of a modern leader.

The third part of the suggestion for writing—how Machiavelli would agree or disagree with you—is highly speculative. It invites you to look through the selection to find quotations or comments that indicate probable agreement or disagreement on Machiavelli's part. You can base your argument only on what Machiavelli says or implies, and this means that you will have to reread his essay to find evidence that will support your view.

In a sense, this part of the suggestion establishes a procedure for working with the writing assignments. Once you clarify the parts of the assignment and have some useful questions to guide you, and once you determine what research, if any, is necessary, the next step is to reread the selection to find the most appropriate information to help you write your own essay. One of the most important activities in learning how to write from these selections is to reread while paying close attention to the annotations that you've made in the margins of the essays. It is one way in which reading about significant ideas differs from reading for entertainment. Important ideas demand reflection and reconsideration. Rereading provides both.

DEVELOPING IDEAS IN WRITING

Questioning the Text

In many ways, the authors of the selections that follow respond to important questions. Sometimes, as with Darwin's essay, there is one question that controls the entire piece, but in many of the selections there is a range of questions that seem to arise from other questions. That is the nature of inquiry, and it helps not only to shape the essay but also to focus our attention as we read it. By observing the nature of the texts that you read and the ways in which questions function as touchstones for the author, you can soon see how valuable the act of questioning can be for you as a writer. The selections in this book are often controversial and demand a response. When you question a text, you are responding to it and your response can be used to develop ideas of your own that can be the basis for your own writing.

Useful Questions.   The following questions can be applied to virtually any important material that you read.

- What are the most important ideas presented in this selection?
- Is this article an argument or is it simply an observation of fact?
- What is the main point being presented here?
- What seems to be the author's purpose in writing this piece?
- Is the author's purpose explicit?
- What claim or claims does the author make?
- What specifically supports the author's claims?
- Does the author omit arguments and evidence that might contradict the claims?
- Does the author satisfactorily analyze and reject contradictory arguments?
- To what extent is there a bias for or against a position in the author's argument?
- What assumptions does the author make about his subject matter?
- Has the author provided clear support for the argument in terms of evidence, example, or expert testimony?
- Which details in the argument are the most important? Are they convincing?
- How significant is this argument for me personally? For society generally?

Questioning Freud.   At the beginning of "The Oedipus Complex" (p. 915) by Sigmund Freud, three questions suggest points that the reader might use to focus attention on the essay:

- What is the Oedipus complex?
- How does it express itself in dreams?
- How do the examples of *Oedipus Rex* and *Hamlet* illustrate the Oedipus complex?

But these questions are not the same ones you might ask yourself after reading the essay. The most important question you would probably ask is

- Is Freud right? Is there such a thing as an Oedipus complex?

Freud himself is answering a question indirectly: What is the cause of neurosis in the people he has psychoanalyzed? In response, he says that most mental illness arises from the role parents play in a person's childhood. Psychoneurotic children experience an unconscious love for their opposite-sex parent and a hatred for their same-sex parent. In the Greek drama, for which the complex is named, Oedipus kills his father and marries his mother. In the Elizabethan drama by Shakespeare, Hamlet has an unnatural concern for his mother and kills the king, his stepfather. Here is how Freud opens his discussion:

> In my experience, which is already extensive, the chief part in the mental lives of all children who later become psychoneurotics is played by their parents. Being in love with the one parent and hating the other are among the essential constituents of the stock of psychical impulses which is formed at that time and which is of such importance in determining the symptoms of the later neurosis. It is not my belief, however, that psychoneurotics differ sharply in this respect from other human beings who remain normal—that they are able, that is, to create something absolutely new and peculiar to themselves. It is far more probable—and this is confirmed by occasional observations on normal children—that they are only distinguished by exhibiting on a magnified scale feelings of love and hatred to their parents which occur less obviously and less intensely in the minds of most children. (para. 1)

Sample Questions. Here are a few questions that naturally arise from reading Freud's opening paragraph:

- Is Freud's claim that parents play a major role in the neuroses of their children?
- Do children seem to grow up hating one parent and loving the other?
- Does my experience help support Freud's views, or does it contradict them?
- When they grow up, are psychoneurotics who suffer from the Oedipus complex likely to kill one of their parents?
- Could Freud's "occasional observations" of children confirm the wide-ranging claim that he makes?
- How do normal children seem to differ from neurotic children?

Once you have read the entire passage, you will formulate other questions that should help you develop ideas of your own as to whether or not what Freud says makes good sense to you. *Oedipus complex* is a term that is used often, and sometimes used irresponsibly, so it is important for you to decide how valid Freud's thinking is. Once you have read Freud's entire discussion—an argument that employs important examples to support its claim that parents play a major role in the neuroses of their children—you will want to consider the examples carefully. Here are some questions that might be useful after reading the essay:

- Does a discussion of fictitious characters help us understand a cause of neurosis?
- Is Hamlet a neurotic who fits Freud's description?
- Did Oedipus's parents cause his problems?
- Is Oedipus a neurotic?
- If Oedipus and Hamlet are clearly neurotic, does that prove Freud's theory?

You could probably add more questions to these two lists, and if you do, you will be helping yourself not only to better understand the selection but also to better approach writing something of your own about the piece.

A Sample Beginning for a Brief Essay on Freud. The following paragraphs are the beginning of an essay in response to Freud's theory of the Oedipus complex. A few of the questions above are implied in this sample.

My Oedipus Complex

Freud's theory of the Oedipus Complex is a bit unsettling for me. I grew up knowing that I loved my father more than I loved my mother. It was not a really major difference, but it was noticeable to my younger brother, who says he can relate to our mother more than to our father. According to Freud, that seems to be the pattern of the Oedipus complex, but neither I nor my brother have mental problems. Should I be worried? Should my brother be worried? I hope not, but I'm not entirely sure. After reading about Oedipus and Hamlet, I realize that they are extreme cases, what Freud says is on "a magnified scale." There is nothing magnified about my relation with my dad, who drove me to school and met my roommates and took us to dinner and then went home. My mother stayed home with my brother, Tim, and that's what usually happens.

But there have been some things that I see now may be problems that my brother may have that I don't have. For example, Tim no longer goes with Dad to fish or to hunt in spring and fall. Now I can see how disappointed Dad has been to see that Tim does not want to do some of the same things he does. Mom likes to go to plays, which I don't usually have time for, so Tim goes with her, and I think he really enjoys them. Dad and I would rather go to a movie, and when I was in middle school we used to see action adventure films that Mom didn't like. Dad and I are more interested in the same kinds of things than are Tim and Mom, who like different things. Is this normal, or should I be worried that sometime in the future Tim will suddenly explode and let go on Dad? Or that I will on Mom? Should I be frightened?

–Alice F.

The rest of the essay examines Alice's and Tim's relationships with their parents and compares them with Freud's examples. Alice aimed at establishing what she thought were normal patterns of behavior toward parents by questioning some of her roommates and by discussing how the literary examples Freud chose were convincing on one level but how they needed to be balanced with Alice's own experience.

Questioning Galbraith.   Alice's essay was primarily a response to a theory that she was trying to understand in personal terms. The following is an examination of a social problem that faces many countries.

John Kenneth Galbraith in "The Position of Poverty" (p. 507) establishes some positions that he uses to clarify how poverty works in a modern society. He argues that in a society in which the majority is poor, politicians will support reform and major help for those in poverty. But in a society such as ours, in which the poor are a minority, politicians will not support reform but will instead focus on the concerns of the majority. Galbraith's point is that we are an affluent society, and thus our political focus is more on the welfare of the rich than on that of the poor.

Then, he meditates on the way in which an affluent society will respond to poverty. One key paragraph points to his hopes:

An affluent society that is also both compassionate and rational would, no doubt, secure to all who needed it the minimum income essential for decency and comfort. The corrupting effect on the human spirit of unearned revenue has unquestionably been exaggerated as, indeed, have the character-building values of hunger and privation. To secure to each family a minimum income, as a normal function of the society, would help ensure that the misfortunes of parents, deserved or otherwise, were not visited on their children. It would help ensure that poverty was not self-perpetuating. Most of the reaction, which no doubt would be adverse, is based on obsolete attitudes. When poverty was a majority phenomenon, such action could not be afforded. A poor society, as this essay has previously shown, had to enforce the rule that the person who did not work could not eat. And possibly it was justified in the added cruelty of applying the rule to those who could not work or whose efficiency was far below par. An affluent society has no similar excuse for such rigor. It can use the forthright remedy of providing income for those without. Nothing requires such a society to be compassionate. But it no longer has a high philosophical justification for callousness. (para. 17)

Sample Questions. Certain issues in this paragraph are important enough to sustain a considerable response because they concern some of the basic views held by many people in developed countries. As a start, consider the questions that this paragraph raises:

- What does it mean for a society to be compassionate and rational?
- Who would receive a minimum income? How would it be distributed?
- Should people who do not work be given an income?
- Could our society afford to pay the poor?
- If it did pay the poor not to work, would fewer people choose to work?
- Would paying poor people without jobs encourage the children of the poor not to work?
- Would the poor be more likely to improve their position if they knew the society could not or would not help them?
- Does giving people handouts create long-term dependency that may be passed on to the children of the poor?

A Sample Beginning for a Brief Essay on Galbraith. Galbraith argues earlier in his essay that as our society is affluent it has a responsibility to the poor in large part because it can easily afford to help and by doing so could possibly eradicate poverty. Of course, not everyone agrees with this view, and there are strong arguments on both sides of the issue. In the beginning of the following brief essay, some other specific questions lead the author to a consideration of Galbraith's views:

- Is Galbraith's suggestion a form of socialism?
- Would Galbraith's suggestion result in a society's becoming less affluent?
- What are the chances that the poor would become resentful of rather than grateful to the society?
- How would following Galbraith's suggestion affect the values associated with individualism, as opposed to those associated with collectivism?

The paragraphs below establish the view of an opinionated writer who has given thought to Galbraith's suggestion and boldly questions the text.

Paying the Poor

John Kenneth Galbraith's view is that society ought to "secure to all who needed it the minimum income essential for decency and comfort" (para. 17). This view is idealistic but hardly possible to put into action. For one thing, Galbraith sounds like Karl Marx, who said, "From each according to his ability and to each according to his needs." Marx was talking about communism, and that experiment has failed with disastrous results. He suggested that people who had means should give some of their wealth to those who did not have means. What he ignored is that the means of any society — its wealth — had to be created by someone, and that usually signifies that wealthy people did the creating. What happened in Russia is that the society became the opposite of what Galbraith says our society is. It was not an affluent society. If we do what Galbraith says, then maybe we too would become a nonaffluent society.

I have two problems with what Galbraith says. First, I think that the thing that makes our society affluent is initiative. The individual values that tend to produce wealth might be smothered if the individual knew that his or her wealth was going to people who were not earning a living. The second problem I see is that if people know they are going to get a paycheck from the government, they will probably not even try to do anything for themselves. They will become dependents and drag down the society. In his essay, Andrew Carnegie says that "civilization took its start from the day that the capable, industrious workman said to his incompetent and lazy fellow, 'If thou dost not sow, thou shalt not reap,' and thus ended primitive Communism by separating the drones from the bees" (para. 7). Many of the poor are incompetent, and some are lazy, but Galbraith is right in saying that there are some social forces that increase poverty. So while something has to be done to prevent starvation, giving people paychecks for no work is not the way.

–Kevin S.

This writer took issue with Galbraith from the start, all the while admitting that something had to be done to help the poor. His views are more in line with Andrew Carnegie's because he admired the way Carnegie worked to improve society by creating libraries and other socially beneficial institutions. But in Andrew Carnegie's time, jobs were plentiful and the causes of poverty were somewhat different from what they might be today. The overall society was less affluent, but there was a brand-new population of the superwealthy, and Carnegie was in some measure speaking directly to them.

Both Alice and Kevin asked questions about their respective texts, and in doing so, each of them established a foundation on which a successful essay could be built.

Creating a Thesis Statement

One of the most important steps in writing an essay is creating your thesis. Sometimes you will be able to approach your first draft with a thesis in mind, and sometimes you will not discover your thesis until you have reread the selection you are responding to as well as your own first draft.

Your thesis statement is an assertion that will be made good by the specifics of your piece of writing. The specifics may include references to facts, to the opinions of other important writers, or to your analysis of the text itself. What would not be among the specifics would be your own unsupported opinion. Your thesis statement makes a claim that you back up with careful use of evidence and testimony.

Your thesis may come at the beginning of your essay, as is typical, or it may appear in the middle or at the end. Some professional writers spread their thesis throughout the essay as a series of claims, but the best way to start a brief essay is by telling your reader what you are asserting and how you plan to support those assertions.

In the selections in this book you will find several different kinds of thesis statements that demonstrate the range and complexity of theses.

- *A thesis that states a position* In "The Origin of Civil Society" (p. 237), Jean-Jacques Rousseau opens with one of the most famous assertions in history: "Man is born free, and everywhere he is in chains." This dramatic assertion precedes his discussion of how social order developed from its primitive beginnings to the circumstances of the kinds of governments he observes in his own world. Defending this position is his job in this essay.

- *A thesis that establishes a cause* Henry David Thoreau offers a cause for his refusal to obey certain laws: "The government itself, which is only the mode which the people have chosen to execute their will, is equally liable to be abused and perverted before the people can act through it." This is only one of several thesis statements Thoreau makes in the first paragraph of "Civil Disobedience" (p. 301), an essay explaining why he rejects certain laws. Behind this assertion is his earlier statement: "That government is best which governs not at all." The rest of his essay is a discussion of his complaints against the laws he cannot ethically obey while still maintaining his own moral position.

- *A thesis that states an opinion* In "The Gospel of Wealth" (p. 481), Andrew Carnegie asserts, "The problem of our age is the proper administration of wealth, so that the ties of brotherhood may still bind together the rich and poor in harmonious relationship." Carnegie's first sentence expresses his opinion that the "administration of wealth" is the "problem of our age." With so many problems of any age, this statement will need a great deal of support from Carnegie's analysis of the recent events and the circumstances of his time.

- *A thesis that analyzes circumstance* For this example, we turn to a passage by Virginia Woolf: "But for women, I thought, looking at the empty shelves, these difficulties were infinitely more formidable. In the first place, to have a room of her own, let alone a quiet room or a sound-proof room, was out of the question, unless her parents were exceptionally rich or very noble, even up to the beginning of the nineteenth century." This statement, Woolf's famous "A Room of Her Own" declaration in "Shakespeare's Sister" (p. 689), comes very deep in her essay (para. 12), after her careful discussion of the history of Shakespeare's time and her analysis of the difficulties any woman of genius would have had trying to become a noted author of important books or plays.

- *A thesis that defines a condition* Germaine Greer's "Masculinity" (p. 725) begins with her thesis statement, "Masculinity is to maleness as femininity is to femaleness. That is to say that maleness is the natural condition, the sex if you like, and masculinity is the cultural construct, the gender." She offers a definition that will need a good deal of example and reference to authorities and their conclusions regarding the possibility that masculinity is a social construct, not a natural condition.

- *A thesis that establishes a conclusion* In "The Personal and the Collective Unconscious" (p. 927), Carl Jung explores the unconscious mind through dream analysis and waits until the end to state his thesis, which he feels is a reasonable conclusion to his discussion: "I have therefore advanced the hypothesis that at its deeper levels the unconscious possesses collective contents in a relatively active state. That is why I speak of the collective unconscious." The collective unconscious, he says earlier in the piece, contains archetypal patterns that most people in a given culture will experience in their dreams. In the larger body of his work, he asserts that these archetypes are universal and inherited as part of our mental biology.

Your Thesis Statement.   Generally, your own thesis statement will be more direct and assertive than those of the writers in this book. One of the best ways for you to start is by creating a thesis statement that establishes your writing aims. A good modern thesis statement tells your reader what to expect from your essay and controls the scope and focus of your writing, making it easier for you and your reader to know what you are trying to say and when you are finished saying it.

Your thesis identifies your subject and what you want to say about it. Put in a slightly different way, your thesis identifies what is to be argued, explained, or focused on in your writing. It may tell your reader what your approach is and give a hint of your conclusions. In a sense, it acts as a signpost for your writing, guiding your reader throughout the rest of your essay.

Suggestions for Formulating a Thesis.   Most of the time, creating a strong, clear thesis before writing is not a luxury but a necessity. Good writers realize that as it develops a thesis statement is dynamic, not carved in stone, not static and permanent. Just as every aspect of your writing is subject to review and revision, the thesis is capable of being recast, again and again, especially if you change your position as you argue your case. In that situation, your changed position would dictate that a new thesis statement be written.

You have several choices regarding the form of your thesis statement. For one, you may wish to break it into several sentences or craft it as a self-contained, single sentence. Further, you may choose to state your thesis plainly and openly—especially if your primary purpose is to be clear in what you are writing—or you may choose to imply it. To some extent, the choice of whether or not to use a strong thesis statement depends on your purpose as a writer. A clearly formulated thesis statement is most useful when your purpose is to persuade or to inform. An implied thesis is more commonly used in an expressive piece of writing in which the end purpose of informing or persuading is either secondary or omitted. Whatever your purpose, the concept of the thesis statement should be regarded as dynamic. There is not just one kind of thesis any more than there is just one place to state it.

Sample Theses.   A thesis needs defense, elaboration, example, support, and development. For that reason, the thesis is not always a declarative factual statement. Rather, it is a statement that permits you to explore the issues that interest you and identify the key elements that will constitute your essay. A thesis can be stated in a single sentence or in a group of sentences or phrases. The point is that it shows what your concerns are and how you plan to approach discussing them.

The following sample thesis statements are appropriate for brief essays. They all stake some kind of claim and have the potential to be developed into full-length pieces of writing.

- Because of his willingness to break the law in a cause that he felt was just, it is clear that Henry David Thoreau would have championed the cause of Elizabeth Cady Stanton.
- While Friederich Nietzsche may be correct in saying that our concept of morality is anti-nature, what he neglects to consider is that humans do not live in a state of nature: we live in a civilization that would collapse without morality.
- Margaret Mead says that gender-linked temperaments develop because society reinforces them and essentially imposes them on individuals. That may be true to some extent, but my observations, and those of Judith Butler, suggest that there is a significant genetic factor that has to be taken into account.
- Andrew Carnegie would be very pleased with the distribution of wealth in our country today because it is approximately the same as it was in his time. He would have specifically approved of the decisions of Bill Gates and Warren Buffett to give away

their wealth posthumously to benefit the public. Here are my suggestions for how their money should be spent.

- The question of whether or not democracy will become unsuccessful again, as Carl Becker suggests may happen, is extremely important to consider because some of the same conditions that deprived Athens of its democracy seem to be at work today. I want to examine several of those conditions and explain why they are threats to our democracy.

- The writer who I feel is most in sympathy with Iris Murdoch's views on morality and religion is Martin Luther King Jr. King, even more often than Murdoch, refers to religion and the Bible, which essentially agrees with Murdoch's view on the existence of evil. By examining the details of King's writing, I will show how close he is to Murdoch's position on morality.

Supporting Your Thesis.   Each of these statements is flexible enough to appear at the beginning of an essay, within the first paragraph or somewhere deeper in the piece. Each has the advantage of implying what is to follow. In the first case, the writer's job is to analyze Thoreau's views in order to connect them with Stanton's. The fact that they both lived at the same time will help with the argument, but the challenge is to show that Thoreau felt women should enjoy the equality that Stanton felt was the only just position that society could take. The writer's thesis needs support to make it effective. Here are some points from Thoreau's essay that support the thesis:

- When Stanton declares that laws forbidding women to take prominent places in society are unnatural and therefore have no force, Thoreau plainly agrees, having himself written that unjust laws exist and that we have a choice of whether to obey them.

- Stanton calls for change and Thoreau agrees with her when he says, "Abolitionists should at once effectually withdraw their support, both in person and property, from the government of Massachusetts, and not wait till they constitute a majority of one before they suffer the right to prevail through them" (para. 20). Stanton's view is that the time for action is now, not later, and in that, Thoreau agrees.

- Thoreau begins his essay by quoting John L. O'Sullivan, "That government is best which governs least." Stanton might agree with that idea but amend it to say, "That government is best that governs all equally." Thoreau would certainly applaud that idea.

These examples are happy ones in that they help the writer shape the remainder of the essay. However, every thesis statement represents a claim, and in order to make the claim stick, the writer has to provide warrants that support the claim. In other words, what are the truths that warrant a writer's claim that Henry David Thoreau would have been likely to support Elizabeth Cady Stanton? The rest of the essay must answer that question.

A successful thesis must be accompanied by

- Evidence that supports the thesis, either from the selection or from outside sources, either factual or drawn from the opinions of experts,

- Statements and testimony from authoritative texts that address the thesis concept,

- Careful and balanced analysis of the text of the author in question,

- Discussion and analysis of counterarguments that might alter the thesis.

No matter how it is supported, you must realize that your thesis statement is dynamic: it can change. The best thesis statements will establish your purpose and restrict the scope of your essay. A good thesis statement will also reveal some of your conclusions and clarify your approach to your subject. And ultimately, the whole purpose of the thesis is to give you—and your reader—a clear sense of direction for your writing.

METHODS OF DEVELOPMENT

Every selection in this book—whether by Francis Bacon or Margaret Mead, Frederick Douglass or Karl Marx—employs specific rhetorical techniques that help the author communicate important ideas. Each introduction identifies the special rhetorical techniques used by the writer, partly to introduce you to the way in which such techniques are used.

Rhetoric is a general term used to discuss effective writing techniques. For example, an interesting rhetorical technique that Machiavelli uses is illustration by example, usually to prove his points. Francis Bacon (p. 879) uses the technique of enumeration by partitioning his essay into four sections. Enumeration is especially useful when the writer wishes to be very clear or to cover a subject point by point, using each point to accumulate more authority in the discussion. Martin Luther King Jr. (p. 375) uses the technique of allusion, reminding the religious leaders who were his audience that St. Paul wrote similar letters to help early Christians better understand the nature of their faith. By alluding to the Bible and St. Paul, King effectively reminds his audience that they all were serving God.

A great many more rhetorical techniques may be found in these readings. Some of the techniques are familiar because many of us already use them, but we study them to understand their value and to use them more effectively. After all, rhetorical techniques make it possible for us to communicate the significance of important ideas. Many of the authors in this book would surely admit that the effect of their ideas actually depends on the way they are expressed, which is a way of saying that they depend on the rhetorical methods used to express them.

Most of the rhetorical methods used in these essays are discussed in the introductions to the individual selections. Several represent exceptionally useful general techniques. These are methods of development and represent approaches to developing ideas that contribute to the fullness and completeness of an essay. You may think of them as techniques that can be applied to any idea in almost any situation. They can expand on the idea, clarify it, express it, and demonstrate its truth or effectiveness. Sometimes a technique may be direct, sometimes indirect. Sometimes it calls attention to itself, sometimes it works behind the scenes. Sometimes it is used alone, sometimes in conjunction with other methods. The most important techniques are explained and then illustrated with examples from the selections in the book.

Development by Definition.   Definition is essential for two purposes: to make certain that you have a clear grasp of your concepts and that you communicate a clear understanding to your reader. Definition goes far beyond the use of the dictionary in the manner of "According to Webster's, . . ." Such an approach is facile because complex ideas are not easily reduced to dictionary definitions. A more useful strategy is to offer an explanation followed by an example. Because some of the suggestions for writing that follow the selections require you to use definition as a means of writing about ideas, the following tips should be kept in mind:

- Definition can be used to develop a paragraph, a section, or an entire essay.

- It considers questions of function, purpose, circumstance, origin, and implications for different groups.

- Explanations and examples make all definitions more complete and effective.

Many of the selections are devoted almost entirely to the act of definition. For example, in "The Position of Poverty" (p. 499)," John Kenneth Galbraith begins by defining the two kinds of poverty that he feels characterize the economic situation of the poor—case poverty and insular poverty. He defines case poverty in this paragraph:

> Case poverty is commonly and properly related to some characteristic of the individuals so afflicted. Nearly everyone else has mastered his environment; this proves that it is not intractable. But some quality peculiar to the individual or family involved—mental deficiency, bad health, inability to adapt to the discipline of industrial life, uncontrollable procreation, alcohol, discrimination involving a very limited minority, some educational handicap unrelated to community shortcoming, or perhaps a combination of several of these handicaps—has kept these individuals from participating in the general well-being. (para. 7)

When he begins defining insular poverty, however, he is unable to produce a neat single-paragraph definition. He first establishes that insular poverty describes a group of people alienated from the majority for any of many reasons. Next, he spends five paragraphs discussing what can produce such poverty—migration, racial prejudice, and lack of education. When working at the level of seriousness that characterizes his work, Galbraith shows us that definition works best when it employs full description and complex, detailed discussion.

An essay on the annotated selection from Machiavelli might define a number of key ideas. For example, to argue that Machiavelli is cynical in suggesting that his prince would not retain power if he acted morally, we would need to define what it means to be cynical and what moral behavior means in political terms. When we argue any point, it is important to spend time defining key ideas.

Martin Luther King Jr., in "Letter from Birmingham Jail" (p. 375), takes time to establish some key definitions so that he can speak forcefully to his audience:

> Let us consider a more concrete example of just and unjust laws. An unjust law is a code that a numerical or power majority group compels a minority group to obey but does not make binding on itself. This is *difference* made legal. By the same token, a just law is a code that a majority compels a minority to follow and that it is willing to follow itself. This is *sameness* made legal. (para. 17)

This is an adequate definition as far as it goes, but most serious ideas need more extensive definition than this passage gives us. And

King does go further, providing what Machiavelli does in his essay: examples and explanations. Every full definition will profit from the extension of understanding that an explanation and example will provide. Consider this paragraph from King:

> Let me give another explanation. A law is unjust if it is inflicted on a minority that, as a result of being denied the right to vote, had no part in enacting or devising the law. Who can say that the legislature of Alabama which set up that state's segregation laws was democratically elected? Throughout Alabama all sorts of devious methods are used to prevent Negroes from becoming registered voters, and there are some counties in which, even though Negroes constitute a majority of the population, not a single Negro is registered. Can any law enacted under such circumstances be considered democratically structured? (para. 18)

King makes us aware of the fact that definition is complex and capable of great subtlety. It is an approach that can be used to develop a paragraph or an essay.

The following excerpt is by a student writer whose an essay is developed using the method of definition. Using Jean-Jacques Rousseau's distinction between natural liberty and civil liberty (p. 237), the writer tries to establish exactly what those different kinds of liberties are.

> Jean-Jacques Rousseau makes an interesting distinction between two kinds of liberty. The first is connected with the origin of society, which Rousseau takes to be the family, and it is called natural liberty. I take this to mean the kind of liberty we feel when we are alone in nature, or when we live in the country in a very remote place. Natural liberty is the freedom we feel when we alone determine what is permitted in terms of behavior and what is not. On the other hand, the second kind of liberty is called civil liberty and that is the kind of liberty we experience when we live in a city or a group. In the second case, everyone has to give up a bit of individual freedom in order to "fit in" to society. In today's society we can see interesting examples of both kinds of liberty.
>
> —Rashida G.

In this case, the writer goes on to discuss aspects of Libertarian politics and how they connect with ideas that Rousseau developed. She also uses her personal experience of a train ride during which other passengers behaved in ways that annoyed her but that they felt entitled to. Ultimately, she discusses the idea of liberties in conflict with each other.

Development by Comparison. Comparison is a natural operation of the mind. We rarely talk for long about any topic without comparing it with something else. We are fascinated with comparisons between ourselves and others and come to know ourselves better as a result of such comparisons. Machiavelli, for example, compares the armed with the unarmed prince and shows us, by means of examples, the results of being unarmed.

Comparison usually includes the following:

- A definition of two or more elements to be compared (by example, explanation, description, or any combination of these),
- Discussion of shared qualities,
- Discussion of unique qualities,
- A clear reason for making the comparison.

Virginia Woolf's primary rhetorical strategy in "Shakespeare's Sister" (p. 689) is to invent a comparison between William Shakespeare and a fictional sister that he never had. Woolf's point is that if indeed Shakespeare had had a sister who was as brilliant and gifted as he was, she could not have become famous like her brother. The Elizabethan environment would have expected her to remain uneducated and to serve merely as a wife and mother. In the sixteenth century, men like William Shakespeare could go to London and make their fortune. Women, in comparison, were prisoners of social attitudes regarding their sex. As Woolf tells us,

> He was, it is well known, a wild boy who poached rabbits, perhaps shot a deer, and had, rather sooner than he should have done, to marry a woman in the neighborhood, who bore him a child rather quicker than was right. That escapade sent him to seek his fortune in London. He had, it seemed, a taste for the theatre; he began by holding horses at the stage door. Very soon he got work in the theatre, became a successful actor, and lived at the hub of the universe, meeting everybody, knowing everybody, practicing his art on the boards, exercising his wits in the streets, and even getting access to the palace of the queen. Meanwhile his extraordinarily gifted sister, let us suppose, remained at home. She was as adventurous, as imaginative, as agog to see the world as he was. But she was not sent to school. She had no chance of learning grammar and logic, let alone of reading Horace and Virgil. She picked up a book now and then, one of her brother's perhaps, and read a few pages. But then her parents came in and told her to mend the stockings or mind the stew and not moon about with books and papers. (para. 7)

Woolf's comparison makes it clear that the social circumstances of the life of a woman in Shakespeare's time worked so much against her personal desires and ambitions that it would be all but impossible for her to achieve anything of distinction on the London stage — or in any other venue in which men dominated. Even though a woman was monarch of England, it was a man's world.

A natural comparison can be made between Sigmund Freud's "The Oedipus Complex" (p. 915) and Carl Jung's "The Personal and Collective Unconscious" (p. 927). The following writer begins his essay trying to work out the comparison because he sees that these selections tend to reinforce each other even though Freud and Jung were often in disagreement.

> Even though Carl Jung seems to be treating the idea of the unconscious differently from Sigmund Freud, I think that they have more in common than they seem to. For example, when Jung talks about the collective unconscious containing archetypes that are supposed to be universal, Freud seems to be talking about just such an archetype. His discussion of the Oedipus complex seems to me to be the pattern he describes — of the child loving one parent and hating the other — to be a basic archetype of human behavior. I may be wrong, but if it is not an archetype, what is it? Both Sophocles and Shakespeare, almost two thousand years apart, came up with basically the same idea. Jung does not refer to Freud's examples, but he sees archetypes the way Freud does. They both think the archetypes are built in to us as people.
>
> —Brian J.

Development by Example. Examples make abstract ideas concrete. When Machiavelli talks about looking at history to learn political lessons, he cites specific cases and brings them to the attention of his audience, the prince. Thomas Jefferson in the Declaration of Independence (p. 259) devotes most of his text to examples of the unacceptable behavior of the English king toward the colonies. Elizabeth Cady Stanton (p. 269) follows his lead and does the same, beginning her list of examples of gender discrimination with the assertion that "The history of mankind is a history of repeated injuries and usurpations on the part of man toward woman, having in direct object the establishment of an absolute tyranny over her. To prove this, let facts be submitted to a candid world" (para. 3). Then she lists the facts just as did Jefferson. Every selection in this book offers examples either to convince us of the truth of a proposition or to deepen our understanding of a statement.

Examples need to be chosen carefully because the burden of proof and of explanation and clarity often depends on them. When the sample suggestion given earlier for writing on Machiavelli's essay asks who among modern world leaders Machiavelli would approve, it is asking for carefully chosen examples. When doing research for an essay, it is important to be sure that your example or examples really suit your purposes.

Examples can be used in several ways. One is to do as Charles Darwin (p. 897) does and present a large number of examples that force readers to a given conclusion. This indirect method is sometimes time-consuming, but the weight of numerous examples can be effective. A second method, such as Machiavelli's, also can be effective. By making a statement that is controversial or questionable and that can be tested by example, you can lead your audience to draw a reasonable conclusion.

When using examples, keep these points in mind:

- Choose a few strong examples that support your point.
- Be concrete and specific—naming names, citing events, and giving details where necessary.
- Develop each example as fully as possible, and point out its relevance to your position.

In some selections, such as Darwin's discussion of natural selection, the argument hinges entirely on examples, and Darwin cites one example after another. Carl Jung (p. 927), however, concentrates on a single example when he begins to explain the nature of the collective unconscious. He establishes that Sigmund Freud's view of the nature of the unconscious mind is centered on the personal and is a result of the repression of material that he calls "incompatible" to the conscious mind of the individual. During childhood bad things happen and we repress them as we grow up. Sometimes these repressions cause psychic damage and sometimes they do not. Usually they surface in dreams that are personal in nature. But Jung is sure that the unconscious is collective and not only personal. As a way of arguing his case, he presents us with an example of a "father complex" that could be virtually universal in nature:

> Casting about in my mind for an example to illustrate what I have just said, I have a particularly vivid memory of a woman patient with a mild hysterical neurosis which, as we expressed it in those

days, had its principal cause in a "father complex." By this we wanted to denote the fact that the patient's peculiar relationship to her father stood in her way. She had been on very good terms with her father, who had since died. It was a relationship chiefly of feeling. In such cases it is usually the intellectual function that is developed, and this later becomes the bridge to the world. Accordingly our patient became a student of philosophy. Her energetic pursuit of knowledge was motivated by her need to extricate herself from the emotional entanglement with her father. (para. 5)

Jung develops this example extensively. This paragraph is more than a page and a half long and Jung continues his discussion of the example for another page because he sees it as a key to his argument.

Considering the claim that Robert B. Reich (p. 513) makes about symbolic analysts, the following writer develops his ideas about what work those analysts do and who in his immediate college environment would qualify as symbolic analysts. This paragraph is within an essay that explores the idea of the symbolic analyst and takes the position that Reich is accurate in his analysis.

> Symbolic analysts work with ideas, not with their hands. But as Robert B. Reich says, there are higher and lower symbolic analysts and their economic success will be different depending on who they are. Reich talks about some analysts getting incredibly rich, and I think he means analysts like Mark Zuckerberg, who worked with computer symbols and came up with the idea for Facebook. Some of my friends who major in computer science expect that they may be able to develop ideas that will make them rich or at least help them find good jobs as coders. But there are other symbolic analysts like my friends who major in history. They also analyze symbols, but I'm not sure there will be a good market for their talents even though they know a lot and enjoy what they do. I think they might have to get an MBA or a law degree, both of which would make them symbolic analysts who can earn a living.
>
> –Hector D.

Development by Analysis of Cause and Effect. People are interested in causes. We often ask what causes something, as if understanding the cause will somehow help us accept the result. Yet cause and effect can be subtle. With definition, comparison, and example, we can feel that the connections between a specific topic and our main points are reasonable. With cause and effect, however, we need to reason out the cause. Be warned that development by analysis of cause and effect requires you to pay close attention to the terms and situations you write about. Because it is easy to be wrong about causes and effects, their relationship must be examined thoughtfully. After an event has occurred, only a hypothesis about its cause may be possible. In the same sense, if no effect has been observed, only speculation about outcomes with various plans of action may be possible. In both cases, reasoning and imagination must be employed to establish a relationship between cause and effect.

The power of the rhetorical method of development through cause and effect is such that you will find it in every section of this book, in the work of virtually every author. Keep in mind these suggestions for using it to develop your own thinking:

- Clearly establish in your own mind the cause and the effect you wish to discuss.

- Develop a good line of reasoning that demonstrates the relationship between the cause and the effect.

- Be sure that the cause-effect relationship is real and not merely apparent.

In studying nature, scientists often examine effects in an effort to discover causes. Darwin, for instance, sees the comparable structure of the skeletons of many animals of different species and makes every effort to find the cause of such similarity (p. 897). His answer is a theory: evolution. Andrew Carnegie (p. 481), the defender of wealth and modern capitalism, praises the results of the modern industrial model of manufacture. He reminds us that in former times most manufacture was conducted at home and in small shops in an environment that was stable and suffered little change or upheaval.

> But the inevitable result of such a mode of manufacture was crude articles at high prices. To-day the world obtains commodities of excellent quality at prices which even the generation preceding this would have deemed incredible. In the commercial world similar causes would have produced similar results, and the race is benefited thereby. The poor enjoy what the rich could not before afford. What were the luxuries have become the necessaries of life. The laborer has now more comforts than the farmer had a few generations ago. The farmer has more luxuries than the landlord had, and is more richly clad and better housed. The landlord has books and pictures rarer, and appointments more artistic, than the King could then obtain. (para. 4)

Carnegie's examples of laborer, farmer, and landlord stand for the lower, middle, and upper classes in a modern society. He then shows that the modern industrial mode of manufacture has benefited not just one class, but everyone, from the poor to the rich.

Everywhere in this collection authors rely on cause and effect to develop their thoughts. Thomas Jefferson (p. 259) establishes the relationship between abuses by the British and America's need to sever its colonial ties. Karl Marx (p. 453) establishes the capitalist economic system as the cause of the oppression of the workers who produce the wealth enjoyed by the rich. John Kenneth Galbraith (p. 499) is concerned with the causes of poverty, which he feels is an anomaly in modern society. Henry David Thoreau (p. 301) establishes the causes that demand civil disobedience as an effect. John Stuart Mill (p. 669) believes traditional Western values support the subordination of women.

John Kenneth Galbraith's "The Position of Poverty" (p. 499) led the writer of the following paragraph to consider what causes poverty in her immediate environment. She relies on Galbraith's distinctions but sees her world a bit differently from the way Galbraith describes society.

> When I was reading John Kenneth Galbraith's essay "The Position of Poverty," I did not feel that his two distinctions, case poverty and insular poverty, were enough to explain the kind of poverty that I have witnessed in my home community. For one thing, I have worked in the Shoreline Food Bank in the summers and when I'm home during the holiday breaks and I see something different. I'm going to major in economics, so I have been watching the way our local companies ship jobs overseas, and I talk with people who have lost jobs in our area when their company outsources their jobs and they have to come to the food bank to make ends meet. These are not people with special problems, as with case poverty, and they are not all minorities, who suffer from insular poverty. This is a new kind of poverty caused by companies not caring about their workers.
>
> –Sheila B.

This writer is especially sensitive to the issues that Galbraith discusses because her experiences in her community and her professional ambitions help her see poverty as a local problem.

Development by Analysis of Circumstances.
Everything we discuss exists as certain circumstances. Traditionally, the discussion of circumstances has had two parts. The first examines what is

possible or impossible in a given situation. Whenever you try to convince your audience to take a specific course of action, it is helpful to show that given the circumstances, no other action is possible. If you disagree with a course of action that people may intend to follow because none other seems possible, however, you may have to demonstrate that another is indeed possible.

The second part of this method of development analyzes what has been done in the past: if something was done in the past, then it may be possible to do it again in the future. A historical survey of a situation often examines circumstances.

When using the method of analysis of circumstances to develop an idea, keep in mind the following tips:

- Clarify the question of possibility and impossibility.
- Review past circumstances so that future ones can be determined.
- Suggest a course of action based on an analysis of possibility and past circumstances.
- Establish the present circumstances, listing them if necessary. Be detailed, and concentrate on facts.

Martin Luther King Jr. examines the circumstances that led to his imprisonment and the writing of "Letter from Birmingham Jail" (p. 375). He explains that "racial injustice engulfs this community," and he reviews the "hard brutal facts of the case." His course of action is clearly stated and reviewed. He explains why some demonstrations were postponed and why his organization and others have been moderate in demands and actions. But he also examines the possibility of using nonviolent action to help change the inequitable social circumstances that existed in Birmingham. His examination of past action goes back to the Bible and the actions of the Apostle Paul. His examination of contemporary action is based on the facts of the situation, which he carefully enumerates. He concludes his letter by inviting the religious leaders to whom he addresses himself to join him in a righteous movement for social change.

Machiavelli is also interested in the question of possibility, because he is trying to encourage his ideal prince to follow a prescribed pattern of behavior. As he constantly reminds us, if the prince does not do so, it is possible that he will be deposed or killed. Taken as a whole, "The Qualities of the Prince" (p. 219) is a recitation of the circumstances that are necessary for success in politics. Machiavelli establishes this in a single paragraph:

Therefore, it is not necessary for a prince to have all of the above-mentioned qualities, but it is very necessary for him to appear to have them. Furthermore, I shall be so bold as to assert this: that having them and practicing them at all times is harmful; and appearing to have them is useful; for instance, to seem merciful, faithful, humane, forthright, religious, and to be so; but his mind should be disposed in such a way that should it become necessary not to be so, he will be able and know how to change to the contrary. And it is essential to understand this: that a prince, and especially a new prince, cannot observe all those things by which men are considered good, for in order to maintain the state he is often obliged to act against his promise, against charity, against humanity, and against religion. And therefore, it is necessary that he have a mind ready to turn itself according to the way the winds of Fortune and the changeability of affairs require him; and, as I said above, as long as it is possible, he should not stray from the good, but he should know how to enter into evil when necessity commands. (para. 23)

This is the essential Machiavelli, the Machiavelli who is often thought of as a cynic. He advises his prince to be virtuous but says that it is not always possible to be so. Therefore, the prince must learn how not to be good when "necessity commands." The circumstances, he tells us, always determine whether it is possible to be virtuous. A charitable reading of this passage must conclude that his advice is at best amoral.

Many of the essays in this collection rely on an analysis of circumstances. Frederick Douglass (p. 327) examines the circumstances of slavery and freedom. When Karl Marx reviews the changes in economic history in *The Communist Manifesto* (p. 453), he examines the circumstances under which labor functions:

The feudal system of industry, under which industrial production was monopolized by closed guilds, now no longer sufficed for the growing wants of the new market. The manufacturing system took its place. The guild-masters were pushed on one side by the manufacturing middle-class: division of labor between the different corporate guilds vanished in the face of division of labor in each single workshop. (para. 14)

Robert B. Reich (p. 513) examines the circumstances of our contemporary economy. He determines, among other things, that the wages of in-person servers—bank tellers, retail salespeople, restaurant employees, and others—will continue to be low despite the great demand for such workers. Not only are these workers easily replaced, but automation has led to the elimination of jobs—including bank teller jobs made redundant by automatic tellers and by banking with personal computers and routine factory jobs replaced by automation. Under current circumstances, these workers will lose out to the "symbolic analysts" who know how to make their specialized knowledge work for them and who cannot be easily replaced.

The question about the lack of outstanding men in politics that Alexis de Tocqueville raises in "Government by Democracy in America" (p. 121) led the writer of the following excerpt to consider whether what Tocqueville said in 1835 is true today.

> People have been complaining about politicians in Washington, saying that they are not getting anything done and that we don't have the leadership that we did in the 1980s or even in the 1990s. Alexis de Tocqueville says, "the most outstanding men in the United States are rarely summoned to public office." I think he may be right. For example, anyone who runs for a major public office has to expect that the opponents will run attack ads that will do everything to ruin that person's reputation. What person seeking public office is so moral and upright that some dirt can't be found that could be used to make that person look bad? I think, for example, that there have been some politicians who could have won office who refuse to run because of the possibility that they will be hurt and their family hurt in the process. What surprises me is that Tocqueville seems aware of the effects of dirty politics in his own time and now we have even more ways of attacking "outstanding men" running for office.
>
> –Linda R.

Development by Analysis of Quotations. Not all the essays in this collection rely on quotations from other writers, but many do. "Letter from Birmingham Jail" (p. 375), for example, relies on quotations from the Bible. In that piece, Martin Luther King Jr. implies his analysis of the quotations because the religious leaders to whom he writes know the quotations well. By invoking the quotations, King gently chides the clergy, who ought to be aware of their relevance. In a variant on using quotations, Robert B. Reich (p. 513) relies on information taken from various government reports. He includes the information in his text and supplies numerous footnotes indicating the sources, which are usually authoritative and convincing.

When you use quotations, remember these pointers:

- Quote accurately, and avoid distorting the original context.
- Unless the quotation is absolutely self-evident, offer your own clarifying comments.

- To help your audience understand why you have chosen a specific quotation, establish its function in your essay.

When Germaine Greer (p. 725) undertakes her study of the
social construction of masculinity, one of her most interesting rhetorical techniques is to use quotations from a number of sources that
help make her case. For one thing, she sprinkles brief quotations
throughout the essay, such as Bertrand de Jouvenel's "A man feels
himself more of a man when he is imposing himself and making
others the instruments of his will." She does not comment on these
quotations, but simply inserts them for us to ponder. But she also
uses some quotations that she then analyzes, such as the comment
from a U.S. Navy officer that begins with "Warriors kill" (para. 10)
and goes on to declare that men are warriors and women are not.
Greer analyzes the paragraph and uses its own statements to decon-
struct it and show that by its own terms women can function in the
army as well as men can. Greer is an English professor and thus
has considerable experience analyzing texts that make claims that
cannot be substantiated. Her method of textual analysis is accepted
practice among scholars and helps her convince the reader of her
argument.

Kwame Anthony Appiah (p. 397) uses quotations in an interesting variety of ways. He frequently refers to other authorities
and quotes from their work, but in his selection "The Case Against
Character," he does something very unusual and quotes an entire
short story by the fiction writer Lydia Davis. The story is short
enough to be included in his first sentence and it helps illustrate
Appiah's focus on the "virtuous person" and the nature of the virtuous character. His analysis of the story leads to the statement,
"A virtuous act is one that a virtuous person would do, done for the
reasons a virtuous person would do it." In other words, virtuous
acts arise from virtuous character. For comparison, Appiah then
refers to Aristotle's *Ethics* and quotes extensively from Rosalind
Hursthouse's *On Virtue Ethics*, which essentially questions whether
virtue arises from character. Moreover, Appiah goes on to refer to
Aristotle's term *eudaimonia*, which he defines as flourishing and
which other ethicists sometimes define as happiness. Appiah then
examines in depth the concepts implied by that crucial word and
analyzes the ways Aristotle uses it to connect the ethical issues of
virtue with human character in an effort to see if character is the
fundamental issue or not.

In the process of his analysis and discussion of the ethical issues
connected with virtue, Appiah refers to many sources and quotes
them to clarify his argument. He even goes so far as to refer to the

popular film *Schindler's List*, which portrays a German business-man who works for the Nazis building war material while shield-ing more than one thousand Jews from the death camps. Examining the character of Schindler, a man widely regarded as heroic, Appiah says that he "was mercenary, arrogant, hypocritical, and calculating sometimes . . . but not always." The question of virtue needs closer examination.

In your own writing you will find plenty of opportunity to cite passages from an author whose ideas have engaged your attention. In writing an essay in response to Machiavelli, Carl Jung, Germaine Greer, or any other author in the book, you may find yourself quot-ing and commenting in some detail on specific lines or passages. This is especially true if you find yourself disagreeing with a point. Your first job, then, is to establish what you disagree with — and usually it helps to quote, which is essentially a way of producing evidence.

Finally, it must be noted that only a few aspects of the rhetori-cal methods used by the authors in this book have been discussed here. Rhetoric is a complex art that warrants fuller study. But the points raised here are important because they are illustrated in many of the texts you will read, and by watching them at work you can begin to learn to use them yourself. By using them you will be able to achieve in your writing the fullness and purposiveness that mark mature prose.

ESTABLISHING AN ARGUMENT

Most of the selections in this book are constructed as arguments, although they take a variety of forms. Some assume a hostile audi-ence, some a friendly audience. Some assume their subject is con-troversial, some assume they are primarily uncovering the truth, and some are simply being informative by explaining something complex. Machiavelli's selection from *The Prince* argues for a strongman politi-cal leader. In her analysis of Nazism, Hannah Arendt argues that ter-ror is necessary for the state to achieve total domination over the peo-ple. Henry David Thoreau argues for civil disobedience as a means of achieving justice. It is one of the most powerful arguments for justice that any American has written. Martin Luther King Jr.'s "Letter from Birmingham Jail" is itself one of the premier arguments in favor of nonviolent action. Its presentation of reasoned argument is outstand-ing. Andrew Carnegie argues that the wealthy must give their money back to the community in their lifetimes so they can see that their money is well spent.

Karl Marx's *The Communist Manifesto* is still relevant long after the demise of communism. His arguments against globalization are probably the most telling for today's audience. John Kenneth Galbraith's argument in "The Position of Poverty" is that our economy must address the plight of the poor, not the "plight" of the rich. Robert B. Reich also addresses globalization and argues that the people who will prosper in our economy are the "symbolic analysts" who can interpret and master texts. One of the most impressive arguments in the book is Virginia Woolf's insistence that if Shakespeare's imaginary "gifted sister" had the same advantages of education and independence that Shakespeare enjoyed she might have become as accomplished and as well-known. Woolf knew that the mores of the age in which Shakespeare lived denied both education and independence for women and assigned them to supporting roles in the family. What Woolf argued for was equality, something still wanting in her own society. In reality, Woolf is arguing not so much for Shakespeare's sister as for herself and other women in her own age. John Stuart Mill in his essay on the subjection of women in the nineteenth century is arguing much the same case as Woolf is.

Iris Murdoch conducts an experimental argument asking whether religion is essential for morality to be relevant. Can there be morality without religion? By contrast, Nietzsche argues that many forms of morality are denials of our basic nature. He goes so far as to take on the Sermon on the Mount in the Bible, pointing out that it is unnatural to kill the passions, by which he makes "particular reference to sexuality." Nietzsche uses careful analysis of arguments against his position to make his point. Charles Darwin argues with masses of collected evidence to derive an argument in favor of natural selection and, thus, evolution.

Most of the selections use one or more of the three basic forms of argument. **Classical arguments** rely on facts and evidence as well as on logic and reasoning to convince the reader of a specific position. Andrew Carnegie's argument in favor of unequal distribution of wealth is a case in point. He begins by remarking that the Sioux Indians make no distinction between the habitation or the dress of the rich or the poor. He argues that "civilized man" was once in that condition but that with industry and civilization comes wealth and inequality. Carnegie can tolerate these inequities, but he ultimately points to the fact that wealthy people are able to be philanthropists and improve the lot of everyone. And his argument extends to trying to convince the wealthy that they are merely stewards of wealth, not its owners. Their responsibility is to use it wisely for the benefit of society. In fact, Carnegie did exactly that, giving all his money to public service.

Henry David Thoreau refuses to support a government with which he does not agree, particularly when he sees it acting unjustly. As a result, in his classical argument he declares, "That government is best which governs not at all." But he realizes that such a government can exist only when people are so good and so just that they do not need a government.

The second common form, like classical argument, is designed to convince someone of a specific position on a subject. This form, known as the **Toulmin argument**, has three parts:

- Claim: what you are trying to prove (often contained in the thesis statement),
- Support: the data—facts, observations, or conditions—you use to prove your claim, and
- Warrant: an assumption or belief that underlies the claim and is taken for granted.

Thomas Jefferson's claim in the Declaration of Independence is that America deserves to be just that: independent from Britain. The extraordinary volume of support, or data, he presents demonstrates that King George III has become a tyrant and "is unfit to be the ruler of a free people." His warrant is the underlying belief that "all men are created equal" and must be free, not victims of a tyranny. Jefferson has a great deal at stake here. He proposes rebellion and independence from a much more powerful nation and therefore must be convincing, especially to the Americans themselves, most of whom emigrated from Great Britain and felt they owed it allegiance. If other Americans were not convinced by his argument, his life was forfeit.

The third form, the **Rogerian argument,** differs in that it does not appear to try to convince an audience of a specific position that must be accepted. Instead, the Rogerian argument tries to find a common ground on the subject that most people would agree with. Thus, this kind of argument does not seem to be an argument at all. It usually functions by establishing basic positions that most people would find nonthreatening, and in the process, such arguments appear to be simple discussions. That is the case with Judith Butler's essay from *Undoing Gender*. The underlying question in her discussion of the surgical mishaps perpetrated on her case study, David, who had been so badly maimed surgically when young that he was raised as a girl, is whether gender is a socialization or an "essentialism." The argument is not designed to press us toward accepting that gender is established by the society in which we live or that, regardless of society, gender is somehow innate and decreed by biology.

The complexity of David's childhood, including the intervention of those who continued to study his development and who directed much of his growth and tried to craft his sense of self, makes the example very difficult to pin down. That is Butler's point. Because she is not contentious, we are able to consider the example of David without having to accept one view or another. What we come away with is a sense of how very difficult the entire issue of gender assignment is.

Whatever the form, the structure of most argument will follow this pattern:

Beginning of an argument

- Identify the subject and its importance.
- Suggest (or imply) how you plan to argue your case.

Middle of an argument

- Explain the main points of your argument with accompanying evidence.
- Argue each point in turn with the analysis of evidence.
- Rebut arguments against your position.

Conclusion of an argument

- Review the claims basic to your argument.
- Summarize your arguments, what they imply, and what you then conclude.

The following sample essay, "The Qualities of the President," modeled on Machiavelli's "The Qualities of the Prince" (p. 219) is an example of a Rogerian argument. The author reviews examples of the behavior of various kinds of modern leaders and then develops common ground with the reader to foster agreement on the qualities that seem most desirable in a modern president. The writer is not confrontational and does not demand absolute agreement but instead offers an exploration of the subject while nonetheless driving to a reasonable conclusion.

A SAMPLE ESSAY

The following sample essay is based on the first several paragraphs of Machiavelli's "The Qualities of the Prince" that were annotated in "Evaluating Ideas: An Introduction to Critical Reading" (pp. 1–11). The essay is based on the annotations and the questions that were developed from them:

- Should a leader be armed?
- Is it true that an unarmed leader is despised?
- Will those leaders who are always good come to ruin among those who are not good?
- To remain in power, must a leader learn how not to be good?

Not all these questions are addressed in the essay, but they serve as a starting point and a focus for writing. The methods of development that are discussed above form the primary rhetorical techniques of the essay, and each method that is used is labeled in the margin. The sample essay does two things simultaneously: it attempts to clarify the meaning of Machiavelli's advice, and then it attempts to apply that advice to a contemporary circumstance. Naturally, the essay could have chosen to discuss only the Renaissance situation that Machiavelli describes, but to do so would have required specialized knowledge of that period. In this sample essay, the questions prompted by the annotations serve as the basis of the discussion.

The Qualities of the President

Introduction   Machiavelli's essay, "The Qualities of the Prince," has a number of very worrisome points. The ones that worry me most have to do with the question of whether it is reasonable to expect a leader to behave virtuously. I think this is connected to the question of whether the leader should be armed. Machiavelli emphasizes that the prince must be armed or else face the possibility that someone will take over the government. When I think about how that advice applies to modern times, particularly in terms of how our president should behave, I find Machiavelli's position very different from my own.

Circumstance   First, I want to discuss the question of being armed. That is where Machiavelli starts, and it is an important concern. In Machiavelli's time, the late fifteenth and early sixteenth centuries, it was common for men to walk in the streets of Florence wearing a rapier for protection. The possibility of robbery or even attack by rival political groups was great in those days. Even if he had a bodyguard, it was still important for a prince to know how to fight and to be able to defend himself. Machiavelli seems to be talking only about self-defense when he recommends that the prince be armed. In our time, sadly, it too is important to think about protecting the president and other leaders.

Examples   In recent years there have been many assassination attempts on world leaders, and our president, John F. Kennedy, was killed in Dallas in 1963. His brother Robert was killed when he was campaigning for the presidency in 1968. Also in 1968 Martin Luther King Jr. was killed in Memphis because of his belief in racial equality. In the 1980s Pope John Paul II was shot by a would-be assassin, as was President Ronald Reagan. They both lived, but Indira Gandhi, the leader of India, was shot and killed in 1984. This is a frightening record. Probably even Machiavelli would have been appalled. But would his solution — being armed — have helped? I do not think so.

Cause/Effect   For one thing, I cannot believe that if the pope had a gun he would have shot his would-be assassin, Ali Acga. The thought of it is almost silly. Martin Luther King Jr., who constantly preached the value of nonviolence, logically could not have shot at an assailant. How could John F. Kennedy have returned fire at a sniper? Robert Kennedy had bodyguards, and both President Reagan and Indira Gandhi were protected by armed guards. The presence of arms obviously does not produce the desired effect: security. The only thing that can produce that is to reduce the visibility of a leader. The president could speak on television or, when he must appear in public, use a bulletproof screen. The opportunities for would-be assassins can be reduced. But the thought of an American president carrying arms is unacceptable.

Comparison   The question of whether a president should be armed is to some extent symbolic. Our president stands for America, and if he were to appear in press conferences or state meetings wearing a gun, he would give a symbolic message to the world: look out, we're dangerous. Cuba's Fidel Castro often appeared in a military uniform with a gun during his presidency, and when he spoke at the United Nations in 1960, he was the first, and I think the only, world leader to wear a pistol there. I have seen pictures of Benito Mussolini and Adolf Hitler appearing in public in military uniform, but never in business suits. The same was true of the Libyan leader Muammar al-Qaddafi and Iraq's Saddam Hussein. Today when a president or a head of state is armed there is often reason to worry. The current leaders of Russia usually wear suits, but Joseph Stalin always wore a military uniform. His rule in the Soviet Union was marked by the extermination of whole groups of people and the imprisonment of many more. We do not want an armed president.

*Use of
quotations*

Yet Machiavelli plainly says, "among the other bad effects it causes, being disarmed makes you despised . . . for between an armed and an unarmed man there is no comparison whatsoever" (para. 2). The problem with this statement is that it is more relevant to the sixteenth century than to the twenty-first.

Comparison

In our time the threat of assassination is so great that being armed would be no sure protection, as we have seen in the case of the assassination of President Sadat of Egypt, winner of the Nobel Peace Prize. On the other hand, the pope, like Martin Luther King Jr., would never have appeared with a weapon, and yet it can hardly be said they were despised. If anything, the world's respect for them is enormous. America's president also commands the world's respect, as does the prime minister of Great Britain. Yet neither would ever think of being armed. If what Machiavelli said was true in the early 1500s, it is pretty clear that it is not true today.

Definition

All this basically translates into a question of whether a leader should be virtuous. I suppose the definition of *virtuous* would differ with different people, but I think of it as holding a moral philosophy that you try to live by. No one is ever completely virtuous, but I think a president ought to try to be so. That means the president ought to tell the truth, since that is one of the basic virtues. The cardinal virtues — which were the same in Machiavelli's time as in ours — are justice, prudence, fortitude, and temperance. In a president, the virtue of justice is absolutely a must or else what America stands for is lost. We definitely want our president to be prudent, to use good judgment, particularly in this nuclear age, when acts of imprudence could get us blown up. Fortitude, the ability to stand up for what is right, is a must for our president. Temperance is also important; we do not want an alcoholic for a president, nor do we want anyone with excessive bad habits.

Conclusion

It seems to me that a president who was armed or who emphasized arms in the way Machiavelli appears to mean would be threatening injustice (the way Stalin did) and implying intemperance, like many armed world leaders. When I consider this issue, I cannot think of any vice that our president ought to possess at any time. Injustice, imprudence, cowardice, and intemperance are, for me, unacceptable. Maybe Machiavelli was thinking of deception and lying as necessary evils, but they are a form of injustice, and no competent president — no president who was truly virtuous — would need them. Prudence and fortitude are the two virtues most essential for diplomacy. The president who has those virtues will govern well and uphold our basic values.

The range of this essay is controlled and expresses a viewpoint that is focused and coherent. This essay of about one thousand words illustrates each method of development discussed in the text and uses each one to further the argument. The writer disagrees with one of Machiavelli's positions and presents an argument based on personal opinion that is bolstered by example and by analysis of current political conditions as they compare with those of Machiavelli's time. A longer essay could have gone more deeply into issues raised in any single paragraph and could have studied more closely the views of a specific president, such as President Ronald Reagan, who opposed stricter gun control laws even after he was shot.

The range of the selections in this volume is great, constituting a significant introduction to important ideas in many areas. These readings are especially useful for stimulating our own thoughts and ideas. There is an infinite number of ways to approach a subject, but observing how writers apply rhetorical methods in their work is one way to begin our own development as writers. Careful analysis of each selection can guide our exploration of these writers, who encourage our learning and reward our study.

PART ONE

DEMOCRACY

Aristotle
The Founding Fathers
James Madison
Alexis de Tocqueville
Carl Becker
Julius K. Nyerere
Benazir Bhutto
Stephen L. Carter

INTRODUCTION

Democracy . . . is a charming form of government, full of variety and disorder; and dispensing a sort of equality to equals and unequals alike.
— PLATO (424/423–348/347 B.C.E.)

The tyranny of a prince in an oligarchy is not so dangerous to the public welfare as the apathy of a citizen in a democracy.
— CHARLES DE MONTESQUIEU (1689–1755)

Democracy and socialism have nothing in common but one word, *equality*. But notice the difference: while democracy seeks equality in liberty, socialism seeks equality in restraint and servitude.
— ALEXIS DE TOCQUEVILLE (1805–1859)

As I would not be a slave, so I would not be a master. This expresses my idea of democracy.
— ABRAHAM LINCOLN (1809–1865)

It has been said that democracy is the worst form of government except all the others that have been tried.
— WINSTON CHURCHILL (1874–1965)

Democracy cannot succeed unless those who express their choice are prepared to choose wisely. The real safeguard of democracy, therefore, is education.
— FRANKLIN D. ROOSEVELT (1882–1945)

Democracy is good. I say this because other systems are worse.
— JAWAHARLAL NEHRU (1889–1964)

I swear to the Lord/I still can't see/why Democracy means/everybody but me.
— LANGSTON HUGHES (1902–1967)

The idea of democracy has a considerable history. It seems to have begun as a flourishing political system in ancient Greece; it was already a well-known approach to government when Aristotle was writing about it in the fourth century B.C.E. Aristotle's own teacher, Plato, had discussed it in his great book *The Republic* (380 B.C.E.) but was wary of it because he feared the tyranny of the majority. Instead, Plato preferred a government with a philosopher king, someone who was wise and benevolent. But Aristotle disagreed with a good many things that Plato said, and in his view, government by the majority, the people, was more desirable than government by a minority, the rich and successful. His views are carefully developed in his analysis and definition of the systems of government and the classes of people who would be ruled in a democracy. What he says is worth listening to carefully, since he understands the nature of democracy firsthand, having lived when Athens represented the brightest light of democratic government and having witnessed its loss because of Athens's bankrupting and unnecessary wars. Athens was not the only Greek democracy, but it remains for us the model and the original on which all other iterations of democracy are based.

Up until the colonies in America broke away from Great Britain, they had been governed by the king and his administrators in Whitehall and the Royal Court. There were local governors who answered to the king, and each colony had a sense of its own special character, but all the colonies paid taxes and maintained special economic relations with Britain. The idea of establishing a democratic government did not come into being until the colonies rose up against the unfair governance of King George III and fought for their independence.

James Madison, Alexander Hamilton, and John Jay began writing the *Federalist*, now known as the *Federalist Papers*, as essays that were then published in New York newspapers early in 1787, before the convention gathered in Philadelphia for the ratification of the Constitution. In the selection included in this collection, "Federalist No. 51," James Madison discusses the separation of the main sources of power in the federal government. He discusses the executive, the two parts of the legislative, and the judiciary, explaining why they must be independent if all power is not to fall into the hands of one segment of government. He sees that all three elements of government must have power but that they must be able to act without restriction by the other parts of government. This system was novel in its time, and the essays of the *Federalist* were among the most powerful forces that helped the Constitution become the law of the land. Madison himself was among those who provided the first ten amendments, known as the Bill of Rights, that helped satisfy the reluctant among convention attendees.

Late in 1787, ten years after the Declaration of Independence, James Madison and the framers of the United States Constitution gathered to ratify the document that had been carefully and clearly written to create a nation out of a group of states that thought of themselves as independent entities. They had earlier created the Articles of Confederation, but that document had proved useless to the new nation because it made cooperation among the states essentially voluntary, and many states refused to pay their share of the costs of the Revolutionary War as well as the costs of maintaining a central government. In other words, there was no strong federal government—and until the Constitution was ratified, the federal republican form of government in existence today could only be imagined. The Constitution obligated the states to support a central government, but at the same time attended to the special needs of states, such as Virginia, which hesitated to sign due to concerns over maintaining slavery and importing slaves. A great number of compromises, many unhappy and in some ways contrary to the democratic principle, were made in the interests of ratification and formation of a federal government that could preserve the nation.

Alexis de Tocqueville visited the United States in 1831 after a brief career in politics in France. He was born shortly after the French Revolution (1789) and, while himself an aristocrat, was completely aware that in France and elsewhere the old system of government that was dependent on rule by the aristocracy was quickly being replaced. He saw that the common people were moving into a position of power in France, and when he came to the United States, he was surprised that democracy worked in a way that did not oppress the rich or the wellborn. *Equality* is a word that he uses frequently in his famous book, *Democracy in America* (1835). He has much to say about how the system works, but what is most interesting is how much he understood about how democracy worked in America after his few years wandering the nation. He was in touch with the rich, the poor, the Native Americans, the African slaves, and the various social classes among the nation's workers and the nation's politicians. He saw the Senate and the House of Representatives and was surprised at the difference between the men who populated each part of our legislature.

Tocqueville studied the political system with great care and reported on it in enormous detail, not only describing the circumstances that he observed but also offering his own views on the merits of the system and the likelihood that it would last. He was deeply impressed by the feeling that the government was essentially separate from the daily lives of most Americans and that they seemed to conduct themselves with a great deal of independence. As a result of what he saw, he felt the people valued individuality very highly and that the main political power in America was in the hands of the states.

Carl Becker's essay "Ideal Democracy" was written in a time of crisis, during the Great Depression of the 1930s and the rule of absolute dictators such as Benito Mussolini in Italy, Francisco Franco in Spain, Joseph Stalin in Russia, and Adolf Hitler in Germany, all of whom were dealing harshly with their own people while threatening a world war. The presence of these dangerous and murderous dictators made Becker fearful that democracy was under threat throughout Europe and elsewhere, and he feared for the continuation of democracy in the United States. The possibility of a great war was clear to Becker as he wrote, and he feared that with the rise of fascism and communism the prestige of democracy had suffered terribly. In his essay, Becker defines and clarifies the goals of democracy and helps us understand its historical place in world governments.

Julius K. Nyerere, president of Tanzania from 1961 to 1989, took office in Tanganyika, a British colony, at a time when it was essentially a collection of tribes and scattered villages with no history of a central government beyond what had been provided by the colonizing Germans before World War I and the British thereafter. Nyerere was exceptional in that he was the first Tanganyikan to go to a British university. He was educated in Edinburgh and became a teacher in his native country. On the eve of Tanganyika's independence, he took a leadership role and became the country's first president. As president, Nyerere concentrated on providing education, improving the country's infrastructure, and trying to attack the nation's persistent poverty. When Zanzibar was incorporated into Tanganyika, the new nation was renamed Tanzania. In his essay "One-Party Government," Nyerere explains the traditional means by which Africans made political decisions, essentially by holding a conference of peers talk until a consensus was reached. Nyerere regards this as equivalent to a one-party system—people talk, then agree. This, he says, is the African approach to democracy, and he sees it as comparable to the democratic concepts of Aristotle and others.

Benazir Bhutto, twice prime minister of Pakistan, explains in her essay "Islam and Democracy" why the teachings of the Quran, the holy book of Muslims, are receptive to democracy, diversity, equality, and fairness. She recognizes at once that most Westerners will not expect Islam to produce democratic governments because of what the West considers religious restrictions, but she insists that the religion does not limit the possibility of the existence of democracies in Muslim nations. However, she also recognizes that, while Pakistan has a constitution that insists on democracy, there are few if any Muslim democracies. She has a number of theories about why this is so, and she outlines them in her essay. Her greatest fears center on the extremists among Muslims, those who attacked her when she first returned to Pakistan and who, shortly after, would kill her in a suicide bombing. It is especially interesting to read what she said in 2008 now that a number of Muslim nations have experienced upheavals in the name of trying to establish some form of democratic government.

This chapter also contains a selection in e-pages (available online at **bedfordstmartins.com/worldofideas/epages**) from Stephen L. Carter. In his essay "The Separation of Church and State," Carter addresses the relationship of government to religion from the point of view of a lawyer committed to the preservation of religious freedom. He reviews some of the contemporary concerns that inform the debates regarding prayer in public schools and federal funding of religious organizations that perform public service. One important point he makes at the beginning of his essay is that the First Amendment's "establishment clause" separating church and state was designed by the country's founders as a means of protecting religion from the state, not the state from religion. From this basic premise, Carter argues a powerful case.

VISUALIZING DEMOCRACY

Howard Chandler Christy (1873–1952) was primarily an illustrator famous for his pictures of "Christy Girls," images similar to the popular "Gibson Girls" of the 1920s. He came to prominence for his illustrations of the Spanish-American War of 1898, when Teddy Roosevelt charged up San Juan Hill in Cuba; his patriotic posters and advertisements became ubiquitous in the early years of the twentieth century. During World War I, Christy's poster of a girl in a naval uniform saying, "Gee!! I Wish I Were a Man" was famous throughout the country. In 1939, the House of Representatives wanted to commission a painting to celebrate the 150th anniversary of the signing of the Constitution. Christy was a very popular painter with Congress because his work had been uniformly patriotic for decades, and his murals—some featuring racy images of women—were in many famous places, such as the landmark Café des Artistes in New York City (they are still there, despite the café's name having changed to Leopard des Artistes in 2011).

There was some controversy over the expense of the painting and some time was lost in deciding to go ahead with the project. But eventually the money was raised, the research for the painting—which reputedly took more than five years—was brought to an end, and Christy began work in the sail loft of the Washington Navy Yard in early July 1939. Christy's painting, titled *Scene at the Signing of the Constitution of the United States*, is 18 × 26 feet with a frame that brings it to 20 × 30 feet in size, and he presented it in late October 1940. (To see Christy's painting in color, go to **bedfordstmartins.com /worldofideas/epages**.) It now hangs in the east grand staircase of the House of Representatives, the most famous painting in the House.

Christy set about to represent all the signers of the Constitution, although there were more people present at the moment he memorialized than are represented in his painting. His efforts to be historically accurate went so far as to cause him to visit Independence Hall so he could get a sense of what the light had been like when the Constitution was signed. There had been fifty-five delegates at the Convention, but only thirty-nine signed, while three refused to sign and the others had left early. Christy searched for the best early portraits of the signers so he could represent them clearly, and he also researched the furniture present at the signing and managed to get some of the original clothing, such as George Washington's trousers, to help him with accuracy. There were two signers whose portraits he could not find, and in Christy's painting they are obscured by other delegates. Even the flags on the right wall are historically accurate and painted from life.

HOWARD CHANDLER CHRISTY, *SCENE AT THE SIGNING OF THE CONSTITUTION OF THE UNITED STATES,* 1940. 18' × 26'. East grand staircase, House of Representatives, Washington, D.C.

George Washington stands tall on the right, with Richard Dobbs Spaight of North Carolina leaning over the desk signing in front of him. Below, Benjamin Franklin sits prominently, with Alexander Hamilton looking over his shoulder. James Madison is seated between Franklin and William Blount of North Carolina who stands behind Spaight. Thomas Jefferson was not present, but to represent him, Christy included some books from Jefferson's library that Christy borrowed from the rare book collection of the Library of Congress. (For a detailed who's who, go to http:// teachingamericanhistory.org/convention/christy/ and follow the directions.) Christy's painting is the most famous representation of the signing of the Constitution, but it has an odd quality: in his effort to represent every signer, he has composed most of them looking at the viewer, as if posing for a photograph. Artistic license aside, undoubtedly the signers realized how important this moment was for history and their country.

As you read the essays in this part, think about how Christy's painting relates to the authors in this section on democracy. Questions following each selection will ask you to comment on how the author's ideas seem to be illuminated by the painting.

ARISTOTLE
Democracy and Oligarchy

ARISTOTLE (384–322 B.C.E.) is the great inheritor of Plato's influence in philosophical thought. He was a student at the Academy of Plato in Athens from age seventeen to thirty-seven, and by all accounts he was Plato's most brilliant pupil. He did not agree with Plato on all issues, however, and seems to have broken with his master around the time of Plato's death (347 B.C.E.). In certain of his writings, he is careful to disagree with the Platonists while insisting on his friendship with them. In *The Politics*, for example, Aristotle does not give much thought to Plato's theories of the best kind of government described in *The Republic* because they were based on the best person governing the best people. In a sense, those theories omit the possibility of either democracy or oligarchy.

One interesting point concerning Aristotle's career is that, when he became a teacher, his most distinguished student was Alexander the Great, the youthful ruler who spread Greek values and laws throughout the rest of the known world. Much speculation has centered on just what Aristotle might have taught Alexander about politics. The emphasis on the virtue of the warrior class in this segment of the *Politics* suggests that it may have been a great deal. A surviving fragment of a letter from Aristotle to Alexander suggests that he advised Alexander to become the leader of the Greeks and the master of the barbarians.

In his discussion of democracy and oligarchy, Aristotle is careful to present all the qualities that he feels are essential to defining each term. He speaks carefully about distinctions between the rich and the poor in a society, observing that there will always be a small number of wealthy people and a large number of poor people in any community. What Aristotle calls an *oligarchy* is a government run by a small number of people chosen essentially because they are rich.

From the *Politics*.

A *democracy* is governed by the will of the majority, and in most societies, the majority is poor. Aristotle realizes that these definitions are basic and do not cover all the possibilities for either form of government. In the course of his discussion, he reviews many of the possibilities and characteristics of democracy and oligarchy, including that a democracy can work if the rich and the poor are considered equal before the law. Aristotle is careful to point out the importance of the law as being supreme and as helping government by ensuring that the majority avoids excesses and injustice.

Late in this passage, he also considers governments that are variations of democracy and oligarchy, but his view is that these two forms of government are at the root of all variations of government and that it is important to understand them if one is to comprehend the choices society faces in governance. When one reads the *Politics,* it is important to remember that Aristotle experienced a number of different forms of government in Athens. Twenty years before he was born, Athens had been a model democracy for almost a hundred years, but after the Peloponnesian Wars ended in 404 B.C.E., Athens was governed by the Thirty Oligarchs, thirty people chosen by three thousand aristocratic Athenians. That government lasted only a year, and in its place Athens restored a limited form of democracy. Once again, Athens lost its democratic form of government in 322 B.C.E., the same year Aristotle died in exile.

In another of his writings, the *Nichomachean Ethics,* he tells us that the well-ordered state—the pride of the Greek way of life—is of such noble value that other values must take second place to it. Because current thought somewhat agrees with this view, Aristotle sounds peculiarly modern in this passage. Unlike the Christian theorists of the Middle Ages, the theorists of the Islamic insurgence, or the theorists of the Judaic scriptures, Aristotle does not put divinity or godliness first. He is a practical man whose concerns are with the life that human beings know here on earth. When he considers, for instance, the question of whether a man can be happy before he dies (tragedy can always befall the happy man), Aristotle is thoroughly practical and does not point to happiness in heaven as a substitute for happiness on earth.

Aristotle's Rhetoric

Even though Aristotle is the author of the single most influential treatise on rhetoric, this document does not have as eloquent a style as might be expected, which has suggested to some that the manuscript was taken from the lecture notes of a student. But, of course, Aristotle does use certain important techniques that demonstrate his awareness of rhetorical effect. Most characteristically, he dedicates himself entirely to being categorical. He concentrates on the categories of governments, focusing on two but admitting that there may be many more and naming five others (para. 11). In the process of writing, he carefully describes each major category of government and considers its potential for producing a happy state.

In terms of style, Aristotle is at a disadvantage—or perhaps the modern world is—because he addresses an audience who has thought very deeply on the issues of politics. As such, his style is rigorous and complex. Fortunately, nothing he says here is beyond the grasp of the careful reader, although modern readers often expect to be provided with a good many concrete examples to help them understand abstract principles. Aristotle purposely avoids using examples so as not to limit too sharply the truths he aims to impart. He also frequently uses aphorisms to focus the reader's attention, such as when he says that it shouldn't be assumed "that democracy is simply that form of government in which the greater number are sovereign."

Aristotle's most prominent rhetorical technique is definition. His overall goal in this work is to define both democracy and oligarchy. But once having done so, and having considered alternatives to these forms of government, Aristotle returns to categorization by considering the kinds of people who make up the state. In the process of doing so, he uses an analogy comparing the different parts of the state (by which he means the different kinds of people) with "the different species of animals" (para. 4). For him, the different species represent different categories that need to be discussed. In paragraph 4, he identifies husbandmen, who produce food; mechanics; traders engaged in buying and selling; serfs, or laborers; warriors, or those who dispense justice; the wealthy; and magistrates and officers. The interests of all of these people must be served by the state, and while Aristotle examines the distinctions between democracy and oligarchy, he clearly implies that the rights of free Athenians are his concern, not the rights of Athenian slaves. Democracy, in its beginning, already limited its participants according to their capacity to qualify as citizens.

PREREADING QUESTIONS: WHAT TO READ FOR

The following prereading questions may help you anticipate key issues in the discussion of Aristotle's "Democracy and Oligarchy." Keeping them in mind during your first reading of the selection should help focus your attention.

- How does Aristotle define *democracy*?
- What is the best relationship of the wealthy to the poor in government by the majority?
- Which form of government does Aristotle think will contribute most to general happiness?

Democracy and Oligarchy

The reason why there are many forms of government is that every state contains many elements. In the first place we see that all states are made up of families, and in the multitude of citizens there must be some rich and some poor, and some in a middle condition; the rich are heavy-armed, and the poor not. Of the common people, some are husbandmen, and some traders, and some artisans. There are also among the notables differences of wealth and property—for example, in the number of horses which they keep, for they cannot afford to keep them unless they are rich. And therefore in old times the cities whose strength lay in their cavalry were oligarchies, and they used cavalry in wars against their neighbors; as was the practice of the Eretrians and Chalcidians, and also of the Magnesians on the river Maeander, and of other peoples in Asia. Besides differences of wealth there are differences of rank and merit, and there are some other elements which were mentioned by us when in treating of aristocracy we enumerated the essentials of a state. Of these elements, sometimes all, sometimes the lesser and sometimes the greater number, have a share in the government. It is evident then that there must be many forms of government, differing in kind, since the parts of which they are composed differ from each other in kind. For a constitution is an organization of offices, which all the citizens distribute among themselves, according to the power which different classes possess, for example the rich or the poor, or according to some principle of equality which includes both. There must therefore be as many forms of government as there are modes of arranging the offices, according to the superiorities and the differences of the parts of the state. 1

There are generally thought to be two principal forms: as men say of the winds that there are but two—north and south, and that the rest of them are only variations of these, so of governments there are said to be only two forms—democracy and oligarchy. For aristocracy is considered to be a kind of oligarchy, as being the rule of a few, and the so-called constitutional government to be really a democracy, just as among the winds we make the west a variation of the north, and the east of the south wind. Similarly of musical modes there are said to be two kinds, the Dorian and the Phrygian;[1] the other arrangements of the scale are comprehended under one or other of these two. About forms of government this is a very favorite notion. But in either case the better and more exact way is to distinguish, as I have done, the one or two which are true forms, and to regard the others 2

---

[1] **Dorian and Phrygian** Greek musical modes; two different classes of musical scales with intervals different from modern scales.

as perversions, whether of the most perfectly attempered mode or of the best form of government: we may compare the severer and more overpowering modes to the oligarchical forms, and the more relaxed and gentler ones to the democratic.

It must not be assumed, as some are fond of saying, that democracy 3 is simply that form of government in which the greater number are sovereign, for in oligarchies, and indeed in every government, the majority rules; nor again is oligarchy that form of government in which a few are sovereign. Suppose the whole population of a city to be 1,300, and that of these 1,000 are rich, and do not allow the remaining 300 who are poor, but free, and in all other respects their equals, a share of the government—no one will say that this is a democracy. In like manner, if the poor were few and the masters of the rich who outnumber them, no one would ever call such a government, in which the rich majority have no share of office, an oligarchy. Therefore we should rather say that democracy is the form of government in which the free are rulers, and oligarchy in which the rich; it is only an accident that the free are the many and the rich are the few. Otherwise a government in which the offices were given according to stature, as is said to be the case in Ethiopia, or according to beauty, would be an oligarchy; for the number of tall or good-looking men is small. And yet oligarchy and democracy are not sufficiently distinguished merely by these two characteristics of wealth and freedom. Both of them contain many other elements, and therefore we must carry our analysis further, and say that the government is not a democracy in which the freemen, being few in number, rule over the many who are not free, as at Apollonia, on the Ionian Gulf, and at Thera; (for in each of these states the nobles, who were also the earliest settlers, were held in chief honor, although they were but a few out of many). Neither is it a democracy when the rich have the government because they exceed in number; as was the case formerly at Colophon, where the bulk of the inhabitants were possessed of large property before the Lydian War.[2] But the form of government is a democracy when the free, who are also poor and the majority, govern, and an oligarchy when the rich and the noble govern, they being at the same time few in number.

I have said that there are many forms of government, and have 4 explained to what causes the variety is due. Why there are more than those already mentioned, and what they are, and whence they arise, I will now proceed to consider, starting from the principle already admitted, which is that every state consists, not of one, but of many parts. If we were going to speak of the different species

---

[2]**Lydian War** Possibly a reference to the Trojan War, which was in Lydia, now Turkey.

of animals, we should first of all determine the organs which are indispensable to every animal, as for example some organs of sense and the instruments of receiving and digesting food, such as the mouth and the stomach, besides organs of locomotion. Assuming now that there are only so many kinds of organs, but that there may be differences in them—I mean different kinds of mouths, and stomachs, and perceptive and locomotive organs—the possible combinations of these differences will necessarily furnish many varieties of animals. (For animals cannot be the same which have different kinds of mouths or of ears.) And when all the combinations are exhausted, there will be as many sorts of animals as there are combinations of the necessary organs. The same, then, is true of the forms of government which have been described; states, as I have repeatedly said, are composed, not of one, but of many elements. One element is the food-producing class, who are called husbandmen; a second, the class of mechanics who practice the arts without which a city cannot exist;—of these arts some are absolutely necessary, others contribute to luxury or to the grace of life. The third class is that of traders, and by traders I mean those who are engaged in buying and selling, whether in commerce or in retail trade. A fourth class is that of the serfs or laborers. The warriors make up the fifth class, and they are as necessary as any of the others, if the country is not to be the slave of every invader. For how can a state which has any title to the name be of a slavish nature? The state is independent and self-sufficing, but a slave is the reverse of independent. Hence we see that this subject, though ingeniously, has not been satisfactorily treated in the *Republic*.[3] Socrates says that a state is made up of four sorts of people who are absolutely necessary; these are a weaver, a husbandman, a shoemaker, and a builder; afterwards, finding that they are not enough, he adds a smith, and again a herdsman, to look after the necessary animals; then a merchant, and then a retail trader. All these together form the complement of the first state, as if a state were established merely to supply the necessaries of life, rather than for the sake of the good, or stood equally in need of shoemakers and of husbandmen. But he does not admit into the state a military class until the country has increased in size, and is beginning to encroach on its neighbor's land, whereupon they go to war. Yet even amongst his four original citizens, or whatever be the number of those whom he associates in the state, there must be some one who will dispense justice and determine what is just. And as the soul may be said to be more truly part of an animal than the body, so the higher parts

---

[3] **Republic** Plato's political book, written around 380 B.C.E., which preferred a government run by the best people rather than democracy.

of states, that is to say, the warrior class, the class engaged in the administration of justice, and that engaged in deliberation, which is the special business of political common sense — these are more essential to the state than the parts which minister to the necessaries of life. Whether their several functions are the functions of different citizens, or of the same — for it may often happen that the same persons are both warriors and husbandmen — is immaterial to the argument. The higher as well as the lower elements are to be equally considered parts of the state, and if so, the military element at any rate must be included. There are also the wealthy who minister to the state with their property; these form the seventh class. The eighth class is that of magistrates and of officers; for the state cannot exist without rulers. And therefore some must be able to take office and to serve the state, either always or in turn. There only remains the class of those who deliberate and who judge between disputants; we were just now distinguishing them. If presence of all these elements, and their fair and equitable organization, is necessary to states, then there must also be persons who have the ability of statesmen. Different functions appear to be often combined in the same individual; for example, the warrior may also be a husbandman, or an artisan; or, again, the counselor a judge. And all claim to possess political ability, and think that they are quite competent to fill most offices. But the same persons cannot be rich and poor at the same time. For this reason the rich and the poor are regarded in an especial sense as parts of a state. Again, because the rich are generally few in number, while the poor are many, they appear to be antagonistic, and as the one or the other prevails they form the government. Hence arises the common opinion that there are two kinds of government — democracy and oligarchy.

I have already explained that there are many forms of constitution, and to what causes the variety is due. Let me now show that there are different forms both of democracy and oligarchy, as will indeed be evident from what has preceded. For both in the common people and in the notables various classes are included; of the common people, one class are husbandmen, another artisans; another traders, who are employed in buying and selling; another are the seafaring class, whether engaged in war or in trade, as ferrymen or as fishermen. (In many places any one of these classes forms quite a large population; for example, fishermen at Tarentum and Byzantium, crews of triremes at Athens, merchant seamen at Aegina and Chios, ferrymen at Tenedos.) To the classes already mentioned may be added day laborers, and those who, owing to their needy circumstances, have no leisure, or those who are not of free birth on both sides; and there may be other classes as well. The notables again may be divided according to their wealth, birth, virtue, education, and similar differences.

Of forms of democracy first comes that which is said to be based strictly on equality. In such a democracy the law says that it is just for the poor to have no more advantage than the rich; and that neither should be masters, but both equal. For if liberty and equality, as is thought by some, are chiefly to be found in democracy, they will be best attained when all persons alike share in the government to the utmost. And since the people are the majority, and the opinion of the majority is decisive, such a government must necessarily be a democracy. Here then is one sort of democracy. There is another, in which the magistrates are elected according to a certain property qualification, but a low one; he who has the required amount of property has a share in the government, but he who loses his property loses his rights. Another kind is that in which all the citizens who are under no disqualification share in the government, but still the law is supreme. In another, everybody, if he be only a citizen, is admitted to the government, but the law is supreme as before. A fifth form of democracy, in other respects, the same, is that in which, not the law, but the multitude, have the supreme power, and supersede the law by their decrees. This is a state of affairs brought about by the demagogues. For in democracies which are subject to the law the best citizens hold the first place, and there are no demagogues; but where the laws are not supreme, there demagogues spring up. For the people becomes a monarch, and is many in one; and the many have the power in their hands, not as individuals, but collectively. Homer says that "it is not good to have a rule of many," but whether he means this corporate rule, or the rule of many individuals, is uncertain. At all events this sort of democracy, which is now a monarch, and no longer under the control of law, seeks to exercise monarchical sway, and grows into a despot; the flatterer is held in honor; this sort of democracy being relatively to other democracies what tyranny is to other forms of monarchy. The spirit of both is the same, and they alike exercise a despotic rule over the better citizens. The decrees of the demos correspond to the edicts of the tyrant; and the demagogue is to the one what the flatterer is to the other. Both have great power;—the flatterer with the tyrant, the demagogue with democracies of the kind which we are describing. The demagogues make the decrees of the people override the laws, by referring all things to the popular assembly. And therefore they grow great, because the people have all things in their hands, and they hold in their hands the votes of the people, who are too ready to listen to them. Further, those who have any complaint to bring against the magistrates say, "let the people be judges"; the people are too happy to accept the invitation; and so the authority of every office is undermined. Such a democracy is fairly open to the objection that it is not a constitution at all; for where the laws have no authority, there is no constitution. The law ought to be supreme over all, and the magistracies should judge of particulars, and only this should be considered a constitution. So that if democracy be a real form of government, the sort of system in which all things are regulated by decrees is clearly not even a democracy in the true sense of the word, for decrees relate only to particulars.

These then are the different kinds of democracy. 7

Of oligarchies, too, there are different kinds: — one where the prop- 8 erty qualification for office is such that the poor, although they form the majority, have no share in the government, yet he who acquires a qualification may obtain a share. Another sort is when there is a qualification for office, but a high one, and the vacancies in the governing body are filled by co-optation. If the election is made out of all the qualified persons, a constitution of this kind inclines to an aristocracy, if out of a privileged class, to an oligarchy. Another sort of oligarchy is when the son succeeds the father. There is a fourth form, likewise hereditary, in which the magistrates are supreme and not the law. Among oligarchies this is what tyranny is among monarchies, and the last-mentioned form of democracy among democracies; and in fact this sort of oligarchy receives the name of a dynasty (or rule of powerful families).

These are the different sorts of oligarchies and democracies. It 9 should however be remembered that in many states the constitution which is established by law, although not democratic, owing to the education and habits of the people may be administered democratically, and conversely in other states the established constitution may incline to democracy, but may be administered in an oligarchical spirit. This most often happens after a revolution: for governments do not change at once; at first the dominant party are content with encroaching a little upon their opponents. The laws which existed previously continue in force, but the authors of the revolution have the power in their hands.

From what has been already said we may safely infer that there 10 are so many different kinds of democracies and of oligarchies. For it is evident that either all the classes whom we mentioned must share in the government, or some only and not others. When the class of husbandmen and of those who possess moderate fortunes have the supreme power, the government is administered according to law. For the citizens being compelled to live by their labor have no leisure; and so they set up the authority of the law, and attend assemblies only when necessary. They all obtain a share in the government when they have acquired the qualification which is fixed by the law — the absolute exclusion of any class would be a step toward oligarchy; hence all who have acquired the property qualification are admitted to a share in the constitution. But leisure cannot be provided for them unless there are revenues to support them. This is one sort of democracy, and these are the causes which give birth to it. Another kind is based on the distinction which naturally comes next in order; in this, every one to whose birth there is no objection is eligible, but actually shares in the government only if he can find leisure. Hence in such a democracy the supreme power is vested in the laws, because the state has no means of paying the citizens. A third kind is when all freemen have a right to share in the government, but do not actually share, for the reason which has been already given; so that in this form again the law must rule. A fourth kind of democracy is that which comes latest in the history of states. In our own day, when cities have far outgrown their original size, and their revenues have increased, all the citizens have a place in the government, through the great preponderance of the multitude; and they all, including the poor who receive pay, and therefore have leisure to exercise their rights, share in the administration. Indeed, when they are paid, the common people have the most leisure, for they are not hindered by the care of their property, which often fetters the rich, who are thereby prevented from taking part in the assembly or in the courts, and so the state is governed by the poor, who are a majority, and not by the laws. So many kinds of democracies there are, and they grow out of these necessary causes.

Of oligarchies, one form is that in which the majority of the citizens have some property, but not very much; and this is the first form, which allows to any one who obtains the required amount the right of sharing in the government. The sharers in the government being a numerous body, it follows that the law must govern, and not individuals. For in proportion as they are further removed from a monarchical form of government, and in respect of property have neither so much as to be able to live without attending to business, nor so little as to need state support, they must admit the rule of law and not claim to rule themselves. But if the men of property in the state are fewer than in the former case, and own more property, there arises a second form of oligarchy. For the stronger they are, the more power they claim, and having this object in view, they themselves select those of the other classes who are to be admitted to the government; but, not being as yet strong enough to rule without the law, they make the law represent their wishes. When this power is intensified by a further diminution of their numbers and increase of their property, there arises a third and further stage of oligarchy, in which the governing class keep the offices in their own hands, and the law ordains that the son shall succeed the father. When, again, the rulers have great wealth and numerous friends, this sort of family despotism approaches a monarchy; individuals rule and not the law. This is the fourth sort of oligarchy, and is analogous to the last sort of democracy.

There are still two forms besides democracy and oligarchy; one 12 of them is universally recognized and included among the four principal forms of government, which are said to be (1) monarchy, (2) oligarchy, (3) democracy, and (4) the so-called aristocracy or government of the best. But there is also a fifth, which retains the generic name of polity or constitutional government; this is not common, and therefore has not been noticed by writers who attempt to enumerate the different kinds of government; like Plato, in their books about the state, they recognize four only. The term *aristocracy* is rightly applied to the form of government which is described in the first part of our treatise; for that only can be rightly called aristocracy which is a government formed of the best men absolutely, and not merely of men who are good when tried by any given standard. In the perfect state the good man is absolutely the same as the good citizen; whereas in other states the good citizen is only good relatively to his own form of government. But there are some states differing from oligarchies and also differing from the so-called polity or constitutional government; these are termed aristocracies, and in them magistrates are certainly chosen, both according to their wealth and according to their merit. Such a form of government differs from each of the two just now mentioned, and is termed an aristocracy. For indeed in states which do not make virtue the aim of the community, men of merit and reputation for virtue may be found. And so where a government has regard to wealth, virtue, and numbers, as at Carthage, that is aristocracy; and also where it has regard only to two out of the three, as at Lacedaemon, to virtue and numbers, and the two principles of democracy and virtue temper each other. There are these two forms of aristocracy in addition to the first and perfect state, and there is a third form, viz. [namely] the constitutions which incline more than the so-called polity towards oligarchy.

I have yet to speak of the so-called polity and of tyranny. I put 13 them in this order, not because a polity or constitutional government is to be regarded as a perversion any more than the above-mentioned aristocracies. The truth is, that they all fall short of the most perfect form of government, and so they are reckoned among perversions, and the really perverted forms are perversions of these, as I said in the original discussion. Last of all I will speak of tyranny, which I place last in the series because I am inquiring into the constitutions of states, and this is the very reverse of a constitution.

Having explained why I have adopted this order, I will proceed 14 to consider constitutional government; of which the nature will be clearer now that oligarchy and democracy have been defined. For polity or constitutional government may be described generally as a fusion of oligarchy and democracy; but the term is usually applied to those forms of government which incline toward democracy, and the term aristocracy to those which incline toward oligarchy, because birth and education are commonly the accompaniments of wealth. Moreover, the rich already possess the external advantages the want of which is a temptation to crime, and hence they are called noblemen and gentlemen. And inasmuch as aristocracy seeks to give predominance to the best of the citizens, people say also of oligarchies that they are composed of noblemen and gentlemen. Now it appears to be an impossible thing that the state which is governed not by the best citizens but by the worst should be well-governed, and equally impossible that the state which is ill-governed should be governed by the best. But we must remember that good laws, if they are not obeyed, do not constitute good government. Hence there are two parts of good government; one is the actual obedience of citizens to the laws, the other part is the goodness of the laws which they obey; they may obey bad laws as well as good. And there may be a further subdivision; they may obey either the best laws which are attainable to them, or the best absolutely.

The distribution of offices according to merit is a special characteristic of aristocracy, for the principle of an aristocracy is virtue, as wealth is of an oligarchy, and freedom of a democracy. In all of them there of course exists the right of the majority, and whatever seems good to the majority of those who share in the government has authority. Now in most states the form called polity exists, for the fusion goes no further than the attempt to unite the freedom of the poor and the wealth of the rich, who commonly take the place of the noble. But as there are three grounds on which men claim an equal share in the government, freedom, wealth, and virtue (for the fourth or good birth is the result of the two last, being only ancient wealth and virtue), it is clear that the admixture of the two elements, that is to say, of the rich and poor, is to be called a polity or constitutional government; and the union of the three is to be called aristocracy or the government of the best, and more than any other form of government, except the true and ideal, has a right to this name. 15

Thus far I have shown the existence of forms of states other than monarchy, democracy, and oligarchy, and what they are, and in what aristocracies differ from one another, and polities from aristocracies—that the two latter are not very unlike is obvious. 16

Next we have to consider how by the side of oligarchy and democracy the so-called polity or constitutional government springs 17 up, and how it should be organized. The nature of it will be at once understood from a comparison of oligarchy and democracy; we must ascertain their different characteristics, and taking a portion from each, put the two together, like the parts of an indenture. Now there are three modes in which fusions of government may be effected. In the first mode we must combine the laws made by both governments, say concerning the administration of justice. In oligarchies they impose a fine on the rich if they do not serve as judges, and to the poor they give no pay; but in democracies they give pay to the poor and do not fine the rich. Now (1) the union of these two modes is a common or middle term between them, and is therefore characteristic of a constitutional government, for it is a combination of both. This is one mode of uniting the two elements. Or (2) a mean may be taken between the enactments of the two: thus democracies require no property qualification, or only a small one, from members of the assembly, oligarchies a high one; here neither of these is the common term, but a mean between them. (3) There is a third mode, in which something is borrowed from the oligarchical and something from the democratical principle. For example, the appointment of magistrates by lot is thought to be democratical, and the election of them oligarchical; democratical again when there is no property qualification, oligarchical when there is. In the aristocratical or constitutional state, one element will be taken from each — from oligarchy the principle of electing to offices, from democracy the disregard of qualification. Such are the various modes of combination.

There is a true union of oligarchy and democracy when the same state may be termed either a democracy or an oligarchy; those who use both names evidently feel that the fusion is complete. Such a fusion there is also in the mean; for both extremes appear in it. The Lacedaemonian constitution, for example, is often described as a democracy, because it has many democratical features. In the first place the youth receive a democratical education. For the sons of the poor are brought up with the sons of the rich, who are educated in such a manner as to make it possible for the sons of the poor to be educated like them. A similar equality prevails in the following period of life, and when the citizens are grown up to manhood the same rule is observed; there is no distinction between the rich and poor. In like manner they all have the same food at their public tables, and the rich wear only such clothing as any poor man can afford. Again, the people elect to one of the two greatest offices of state, and in the other they share; for they elect the Senators and share in the Ephoralty. By others the Spartan constitution is said to be an oligarchy, because it has many oligarchical elements. That all offices are filled by election and none by lot, is one of these oligarchical characteristics; that the power of inflicting death or banishment rests with a few persons is another; and there are others. In a well attempered polity there should appear to be both elements and yet neither; also the government should rely on itself, and not on foreign aid, and on itself not through the good will of a majority — they might be equally well-disposed when there is a vicious form of government — but through the general willingness of all classes in the state to maintain the constitution.

Enough of the manner in which a constitutional government, and 19 in which the so-called aristocracies ought to be framed.

QUESTIONS FOR CRITICAL READING

1. According to Aristotle, what seem to be the markers of wealth in Athens?

2. What does the presence of heavy armament and of the cavalry imply for rule by oligarchy?

3. Aristotle admits that there are "many forms of government" (para. 1). What, then, is his explanation for primarily considering only two?

4. In paragraph 4, Aristotle says that some classes are more essential to the state than others. What are they, and do you agree?

5. How important is the idea of equality in a democracy? See paragraph 6.

6. In paragraph 9, Aristotle says the law, not individuals, must govern. What are his reasons?

7. Who can vote in Aristotle's democracy?

SUGGESTIONS FOR CRITICAL WRITING

1. The concept of majority rule is central to Aristotle's discussion of democracy. Explain his views on this question and examine what he says about the limitations of majority rule. Does his thinking on majority rule cause you to change your own ideas about it? What are the strengths and weaknesses of majority rule in a modern democracy?

2. In paragraph 4, Aristotle talks about the different elements in the state, referring to nine classes of people: husbandmen, traders, the military, lawyers, and others. Do these different groups still constitute the modern state in the way in which Aristotle describes them? Why does he consider these different elements when talking about government? Do you feel he is justified in doing so? What are the most important different "elements" in the state as you understand them?

3. **CONNECTIONS** Aristotle says, "Because the rich are generally few in number, while the poor are many, they appear to be antagonistic, and as the one or the other prevails they form the government" (para. 4).

Do you find that Aristotle is correct about the relationship between the rich and the poor in our modern democracies? Aristotle implies that when the rich govern, we have an oligarchy, and when the poor govern, we have a democracy. Does this view correlate with your observations about government? Compare Aristotle's view with that of Andrew Carnegie in "The Gospel of Wealth" (p. 481). Why does he raise the issue of class warfare between the rich and the poor? Would Carnegie welcome a benevolent oligarchy?

4. **CONNECTIONS** In paragraph 3, Aristotle discusses the question of how we calculate majority in a democracy in which the majority rules. He points to a variety of such majorities. If the majority in a democracy were to profess a single religion, should then the precepts of that religion guide the entire democracy? Consider Stephen Carter's "The Separation of Church and State" (**bedfordstmartins.com/worldofideas/epages**). How would Carter react to such a suggestion? How would a religious majority, even if it were tolerant of other religions, operate in a democracy in a manner that might restrict religious minorities? What protection does Carter feel minority religions need?

5. In paragraph 6, Aristotle says, "Of forms of democracy first comes that which is said to be based strictly on equality." What does he seem to mean by equality? What, in terms of government, do you think the term *equality* means today? Is it possible to have a democracy without equality? Why would equality be such an important issue in any form of government? What is your definition of *equality*? Do you think equality is possible in a modern state?

6. In discussing some of the dangers of majority rule in a democracy, Aristotle raises the issue of the possibility of creating a demagogue. What does he mean? What is a demagogue, and how could a democracy produce one? What harm might a demagogue cause a democratic state? What examples of modern demagogues speak to the issues Aristotle raises?

7. Aristotle makes a clear distinction between the minority wealthy class and the majority poor class. When only the wealthy have power, the state is an oligarchy. When the poor have power, the state is a democracy. How would Aristotle's theories be altered if he considered a numerous middle class between the rich and the poor? When the middle class is the majority of the population, how does that affect the distinction between democracy and oligarchy? Would a dominant middle class produce a democracy or an oligarchy?

8. **SEEING CONNECTIONS** How might Aristotle have responded to the painting by Howard Chandler Christy of the signing of the Constitution of the United States (p. 57)? How many different "elements" of society are represented in this painting? Would Aristotle have assumed that the government being formed was a democracy or an oligarchy? Research the men who signed the Constitution. How well did they represent the elements of society of the newly formed country?

THE FOUNDING FATHERS
The Constitution of the United States of America

BEFORE THE COMPOSITION and ratification of the Constitution of the United States in 1788, the colonies had bound together in a loose confederation in opposition to England. The Continental Congress was given the responsibilities of conducting the war against England and carrying on relations with foreign nations. In addition, the Articles of Confederation, finally ratified in 1781 when no longer relevant, authorized a postal system and a means of regulating trade. Each state had its own constitution and complied only voluntarily with the requests of the Continental Congress. Several states even refused to pay taxes to fund the war with Britain.

The Constitution took only a year to be written and agreed on by all the states, but the process was extremely difficult and required considerable negotiation and compromise. The issue of greatest importance was the question of how strong the federal government should be. The states were split internally by those who fostered Federalism and those who fostered Anti-Federalism. The Anti-Federalists were worried about their civil rights and the possibilities of corruption in government. They promoted states' rights, whereas the Federalists insisted that the laws enacted by Congress were for all people, not just for the states as separate entities. James Madison, Alexander Hamilton, and John Jay wrote the *Federalist Papers*, a series of eighty-five essays that argued for a form of republicanism that separated the legislative, executive, and judicial branches of government so that there would be a balance of powers. The essays were published in newspapers between 1787 and 1788. After vigorous debate and the addition of the first ten amendments, usually referred to as the Bill of Rights, the Constitution was ratified by all thirteen states.

One of the issues at stake in the debates was the question of slavery and whether it should to be protected by federal law. From 1775 to 1788, Pennsylvania, New York, Rhode Island, Connecticut, and New Jersey either abolished slavery or began the process of abolishing it. The Northwest Territories (what would one day become states such as Ohio and Michigan) were prohibited from maintaining slavery. The fact that the word *slave* or *slavery* never appears in the first seven articles of the Constitution implies how sensitive the subject was for some of the founders. But slaves were taken into account when it came to taxation in Article I, Section 2, because the population of a state determined its representation. For tax purposes, the population of a state included "the whole Number of free Persons, including those bound to Service for a Term of Years, and excluding Indians not taxed, three-fifths of all other Persons." A slave was counted as three-fifths of a person. In that sense, the Constitution defended and enabled slavery by protecting it under property laws.

Another troubling issue facing the framers of the Constitution was the fear that a pure democracy would prove to be a danger that might destroy the new country. Obviously, those who met with the Continental Congress, those who signed the Declaration of Independence, and those who signed and ratified the Constitution were men of means and often had considerable education. They were sometimes considered by their countrymen and -women to be smooth-talking, self-interested elites who did not always act for the common good. In 1786, veteran of the Revolutionary War and western Massachusetts farmer Daniel Shays raised some 2,500 men in revolt against the heavy taxation Massachusetts instituted to pay for the war and other debts. This uprising, called Shays's Rebellion, frightened those concerned with creating the Constitution. Samuel Adams urged the rebels to wait until the next vote, but they were too distressed to be contained. The governor, who had once protested British taxation, put the rebellion down harshly, in part because it represented the threat of a popular (democratic) uprising that challenged the elected government's authority. This rebellion may have had a hand in helping the Federalists establish a republican structure in which democratic voters elect representatives whose votes enact laws. The Senate guaranteed the rights of states by allotting two senators for each state, and the House protected the rights of the most populous states by including proportional representation. The Electoral College was instituted as a hedge against pure democracy: the states choose the electors, who in turn choose the president. The judiciary was to be selected by the Senate, although today the Supreme Court is selected by the president and approved by the Senate.

These basic issues concerning how democracy would work in the new America were on the minds of those who worked to form its government, from the first to the last.

The Rhetoric of the Constitution

The Constitution was the product of compromise and of several different minds and hands. A committee of style was formed to normalize the content of the document, and the result is its structure of three primary and four secondary articles. Article I and its sections describe the nature and powers of Congress. Article II and its sections describe the nature and powers of the presidency, and Article III describes the nature and powers of the Supreme Court. The next four articles describe specific powers conferred on the various branches of government. The first ten amendments outline the rights and responsibilities of citizens in the nation. The form of the Constitution resembles a legal document because it is the law of the land, and its form and structure emphasize its powers.

However, unlike what we might expect to see in a legal document, the Constitution is written in plain English with little or no flourish of any kind. In the eighteenth century, all educated people were tutored rigorously in Latin and Greek. As a result, the literature of that age has a highly Latinized English writing style: polysyllabic words and somewhat obscure vocabulary are commonplace, and long, periodic sentences in which the main idea comes at the very end are the norm. But in the Constitution, most of the words are simple and most of the sentences are short and to the point. Little effort was made to produce a stylish literary document, but great effort was expended to write prose that was clear, intelligible, and unambiguous.

In that sense, the style of the Constitution was designed to communicate with the common man as much as with the country's educated founders. At the time the Constitution was composed, a large portion of the country was uneducated except in the most basic rudiments of reading and writing. If the Constitution had been framed in highly elaborate prose, farmers and tradesmen in the outlying districts (people like Daniel Shays) would not have trusted the document at all. But with its straightforward style and the addition of the first ten amendments, the Constitution was understandable and adopted more quickly than it might otherwise have been.

PREREADING QUESTIONS:
WHAT TO READ FOR

The following prereading questions may help you anticipate key issues in the discussion of the Constitution. Keeping them in mind during your first reading should help focus your attention.

- How do the three branches of government differ?
- What are the legislative powers of Congress?
- The first ten amendments are called the Bill of Rights. What rights do they protect?

The Constitution of the United States of America

(Proposed By Convention September 17, 1789
Effective March 4, 1789)

We the People of the United States, in Order to form a more perfect Union, establish Justice, insure domestic Tranquility, provide for the common defence, promote the general Welfare, and secure the Blessings of Liberty to ourselves and our Posterity, do ordain and establish this Constitution for the United States of America.

Article I.

SECTION 1.

All legislative Powers herein granted shall be vested in a Congress of the United States, which shall consist of a Senate and House of Representatives.

SECTION 2.

The House of Representatives shall be composed of Members chosen every second Year by the People of the several States, and the Electors in each State shall have the Qualifications requisite for Electors of the most numerous Branch of the State Legislature.

No Person shall be a Representative who shall not have attained to the Age of twenty-five Years, and been seven Years a Citizen of the United States, and who shall not, when elected, be an Inhabitant of that State in which he shall be chosen.

[Representatives and direct Taxes shall be apportioned among the several States which may be included within this Union, according to their respective Numbers, which shall be determined by adding to the whole Number of free Persons, including those bound to Service for a Term of Years, and excluding Indians not taxed, three-fifths of all other Persons.]* The actual Enumeration shall be made within three Years after the first Meeting of the Congress of the United States, and within every subsequent Term of ten Years, in such Manner as they shall by Law direct. The Number of Representatives shall not exceed one for every thirty Thousand, but each State shall have at Least one Representative; and until such enumeration shall be made, the State of New Hampshire shall be entitled to choose three, Massachusetts eight, Rhode Island and Providence Plantations one, Connecticut five, New York six, New Jersey four, Pennsylvania eight, Delaware one, Maryland six, Virginia ten, North Carolina five, South Carolina five, and Georgia three.

When vacancies happen in the Representation from any State, the Executive Authority thereof shall issue Writs of Election to fill such Vacancies.

The House of Representatives shall choose their Speaker and other Officers; and shall have the sole Power of Impeachment.

SECTION 3.

The Senate of the United States shall be composed of two Senators from each State, [chosen by the Legislature thereof,]* for six Years; and each Senator shall have one Vote.

Immediately after they shall be assembled in Consequence of the first Election, they shall be divided as equally as may be into three Classes. The Seats of the Senators of the first Class shall be vacated at the Expiration of the second Year, of the second Class at the Expiration of the fourth Year, and of the third Class at the Expiration of the sixth Year, so that one-third may be chosen every second Year; [and if Vacancies happen by Resignation, or otherwise, during the Recess of the Legislature of any State, the Executive thereof may make temporary Appointments until the next Meeting of the Legislature, which shall then fill such Vacancies.]*

No Person shall be a Senator who shall not have attained to the Age of thirty Years, and been nine Years a Citizen of the United States, and who shall not, when elected, be an Inhabitant of that State for which he shall be chosen.

---

* Language in brackets has been changed by amendment.

The Vice President of the United States shall be President of the Senate, but shall have no Vote, unless they be equally divided.

The Senate shall choose their other Officers, and also a President pro tempore, in the Absence of the Vice President, or when he shall exercise the Office of President of the United States.

The Senate shall have the sole Power to try all Impeachments. When sitting for that Purpose, they shall be on Oath or Affirmation. When the President of the United States is tried, the Chief Justice shall preside: And no Person shall be convicted without the Concurrence of two-thirds of the Members present.

Judgment in Cases of Impeachment shall not extend further than to removal from Office, and disqualification to hold and enjoy any Office of honor, Trust, or Profit under the United States: but the Party convicted shall nevertheless be liable and subject to Indictment, Trial, Judgment, and Punishment, according to Law.

SECTION 4.

The Times, Places, and Manner of holding Elections for Senators and Representatives, shall be prescribed in each State by the Legislature thereof; but the Congress may at any time by Law make or alter such Regulations, except as to the Places of choosing Senators.

The Congress shall assemble at least once in every Year, and such Meeting shall be [on the first Monday in December,]* unless they shall by Law appoint a different Day.

SECTION 5.

Each House shall be the Judge of the Elections, Returns, and Qualifications of its own Members, and a Majority of each shall constitute a Quorum to do Business; but a smaller Number may adjourn from day to day, and may be authorized to compel the Attendance of absent Members, in such Manner, and under such Penalties as each House may provide.

Each House may determine the Rules of its Proceedings, punish its Members for disorderly Behavior, and, with the Concurrence of two-thirds, expel a Member.

Each House shall keep a Journal of its Proceedings, and from time to time publish the same, excepting such Parts as may in their Judgment require Secrecy; and the Yeas and Nays of the Members of either House on any question shall, at the Desire of one-fifth of those Present, be entered on the Journal.

Neither House, during the Session of Congress, shall, without the Consent of the other, adjourn for more than three days, nor to any other Place than that in which the two Houses shall be sitting.

SECTION 6.

The Senators and Representatives shall receive a Compensation for their Services, to be ascertained by Law, and paid out of the Treasury of the United States. They shall in all Cases, except Treason, Felony, and Breach of the Peace, be privileged from Arrest during their Attendance at the Session of their respective Houses, and in going to and returning from the same; and for any Speech or Debate in either Houses, they shall not be questioned in any other Place.

No Senator or Representative shall, during the Time for which he was elected, be appointed to any civil Office under the Authority of the United States, which shall have been created, or the Emoluments whereof shall have been increased during such time; and no Person holding any Office under the United States, shall be a Member of either House during his Continuance in Office.

SECTION 7.

All Bills for raising Revenue shall originate in the House of Representatives; but the Senate may propose or concur with Amendments as on other Bills.

Every Bill which shall have passed the House of Representatives and the Senate, shall, before it become a Law, be presented to the President of the United States; If he approve he shall sign it, but if not he shall return it, with his Objections to that House in which it shall have originated, who shall enter the Objections at large on their Journal, and proceed to reconsider it. If after such Reconsideration two-thirds of that House shall agree to pass the Bill, it shall be sent, together with the Objections, to the other House, by which it shall likewise be reconsidered, and if approved by two-thirds of that House, it shall become a Law. But in all such Cases the Votes of both Houses shall be determined by Yeas and Nays, and the Names of the Persons voting for and against the Bill shall be entered on the Journal of each House respectively. If any Bill shall not be returned by the President within ten Days (Sundays excepted) after it shall have been presented to him, the Same shall be a Law, in like Manner as if he had signed it, unless the Congress by their Adjournment prevent its Return, in which Case it shall not be a Law.

Every Order, Resolution, or Vote to which the Concurrence of the Senate and House of Representatives may be necessary (except on a question of Adjournment) shall be presented to the President of the United States; and before the Same shall take Effect, shall be approved by him, or being disapproved by him, shall be repassed by two-thirds of the Senate and House of Representatives, according to the Rules and Limitations prescribed in the Case of a Bill.

SECTION 8.

The Congress shall have Power To lay and collect Taxes, Duties, Imposts, and Excises, to pay the Debts and provide for the common Defense and general Welfare of the United States; but all Duties, Imposts, and Excises shall be uniform throughout the United States;

To borrow Money on the credit of the United States;

To regulate Commerce with foreign Nations, and among the several States, and with the Indian Tribes;

To establish an uniform Rule of Naturalization, and uniform Laws on the subject of Bankruptcies throughout the United States;

To coin Money, regulate the Value thereof, and of foreign Coin, and fix the Standard of Weights and Measures;

To provide for the Punishment of counterfeiting the Securities and current Coin of the United States;

To establish Post Offices and post Roads;

To promote the Progress of Science and useful Arts, by securing for limited Times to Authors and Inventors the exclusive Right to their respective Writings and Discoveries;

To constitute Tribunals inferior to the supreme Court;

To define and punish Piracies and Felonies committed on the high Seas, and Offenses against the Law of Nations;

To declare War, grant Letters of Marque and Reprisal, and make Rules concerning Captures on Land and Water;

To raise and support Armies, but no Appropriation of Money to that Use shall be for a longer Term than two Years;

To provide and maintain a Navy;

To make Rules for the Government and Regulation of the land and naval Forces;

To provide for calling forth the Militia to execute the Laws of the Union, suppress Insurrections, and repel Invasions;

To provide for organizing, arming, and disciplining, the Militia, and for governing such Part of them as may be employed in the Service of the United States, reserving to the States respectively, the Appointment of the Officers, and the Authority of training the Militia according to the discipline prescribed by Congress;

To exercise exclusive Legislation in all Cases whatsoever, over such District (not exceeding ten Miles square) as may, by Cession of particular States, and the Acceptance of Congress, become the Seat of the Government of the United States, and to exercise like Authority over all Places purchased by the Consent of the Legislature of the State in which the Same shall be, for the Erection of Forts, Magazines, Arsenals, dock-Yards, and other needful Buildings; — And

To make all Laws which shall be necessary and proper for carrying into Execution the foregoing Powers, and all other Powers vested by this Constitution in the Government of the United States, or in any Department or Officer thereof.

SECTION 9.

The Migration or Importation of such Persons as any of the States now existing shall think proper to admit, shall not be prohibited by the Congress prior to the Year one thousand eight hundred and eight, but a Tax or duty may be imposed on such Importation, not exceeding ten dollars for each Person.

The Privilege of the Writ of Habeas Corpus shall not be suspended, unless when in Cases of Rebellion or Invasion the public Safety may require it.

No Bill of Attainder or ex post facto Law shall be passed.

[No Capitation, or other direct, Tax shall be laid, unless in Proportion to the Census or Enumeration herein before directed to be taken.]*

No Tax or Duty shall be laid on Articles exported from any State.

No Preference shall be given by any Regulation of Commerce or Revenue to the Ports of one State over those of another: nor shall Vessels bound to, or from, one State, be obliged to enter, clear, or pay Duties in another.

No Money shall be drawn from the Treasury, but in Consequence of Appropriations made by Law; and a regular Statement and Account of the Receipts and Expenditures of all public Money shall be published from time to time.

No Title of Nobility shall be granted by the United States: And no Person holding any Office of Profit or Trust under them, shall, without the Consent of the Congress, accept of any present, Emolument, Office, or Title, of any kind whatever, from any King, Prince, or foreign State.

SECTION 10.

No State shall enter into any Treaty, Alliance, or Confederation; grant Letters of Marque and Reprisal; coin Money; emit Bills of Credit; make any Thing but gold and silver Coin a Tender in Payment of Debts; pass any Bill of Attainder, ex post facto Law, or Law impairing the Obligation of Contracts, or grant any Title of Nobility.

No State shall, without the Consent of the Congress, lay any Imposts or Duties on Imports or Exports, except what may be absolutely necessary for executing it's inspection Laws: and the net Produce of all Duties and Imposts, laid by any State on Imports or Exports, shall be for the Use of the Treasury of the United States; and all such Laws shall be subject to the Revision and Control of the Congress.

No State shall, without the Consent of Congress, lay any Duty of Tonnage, keep Troops, or Ships of War in time of Peace, enter into any Agreement or Compact with another State, or with a foreign Power, or engage in War, unless actually invaded, or in such imminent Danger as will not admit of delay.

Article II.

SECTION 1.

The executive Power shall be vested in a President of the United States of America. He shall hold his Office during the Term of four Years, and, together with the Vice President, chosen for the same Term, be elected, as follows:

Each State shall appoint, in such Manner as the Legislature thereof may direct, a Number of Electors, equal to the whole Number of Senators and Representatives to which the State may be entitled in the Congress: but no Senator or Representative, or Person holding an Office of Trust or Profit under the United States, shall be appointed an Elector.

[The Electors shall meet in their respective States, and vote by Ballot for two Persons, of whom one at least shall not be an Inhabitant of the same State with themselves. And they shall make a List of all the Persons voted for, and of the Number of Votes for each; which List they shall sign and certify, and transmit sealed to the Seat of the Government of the United States, directed to the President of the Senate. The President of the Senate shall, in the Presence of the Senate and House of Representatives, open all the Certificates, and the Votes shall then be counted. The Person having the greatest Number of Votes shall be the President, if such Number be a Majority of the whole Number of Electors appointed; and if there be more than one who have such Majority, and have an equal Number of Votes, then the House of Representatives shall immediately choose by Ballot one of them for President; and if no Person have a Majority, then from the five highest on the List the said House shall in like Manner choose the President. But in choosing the President, the Votes shall be taken by States, the Representation from each State having one Vote; A quorum for this Purpose shall consist of a Member or Members from two-thirds of the States, and a Majority of all the States shall be necessary to a Choice. In every Case, after the Choice of the President, the Person having the greatest Number of Votes of the Electors shall be the Vice President. But if there should remain two or more who have equal Votes, the Senate shall choose from them by Ballot the Vice President.]*

The Congress may determine the Time of choosing the Electors, and the Day on which they shall give their Votes; which Day shall be the same throughout the United States.

No Person except a natural-born Citizen, or a Citizen of the United States, at the time of the Adoption of this Constitution, shall be eligible to the Office of President; neither shall any person be eligible to that Office who shall not have attained to the Age of thirty-five Years, and been fourteen Years a Resident within the United States.

[In Case of the Removal of the President from Office, or of his Death, Resignation, or Inability to discharge the Powers and Duties of the said Office, the Same shall devolve on the Vice President, and the Congress may by Law provide for the Case of Removal, Death, Resignation, or Inability, both of the President and Vice President, declaring what Officer shall then act as President, and such Officer shall act accordingly, until the Disability be removed, or a President shall be elected.]*

The President shall, at stated Times, receive for his Services, a Compensation, which shall neither be increased nor diminished during the Period for which he shall have been elected, and he shall not receive within that Period any other Emolument from the United States, or any of them.

Before he enter on the Execution of his Office, he shall take the following Oath or Affirmation: — "I do solemnly swear (or affirm) that I will faithfully execute the Office of President of the United States, and will to the best of my Ability, preserve, protect, and defend the Constitution of the United States."

SECTION 2.

The President shall be Commander in Chief of the Army and Navy of the United States, and of the Militia of the several States, when called into the actual Service of the United States; he may require the Opinion, in writing, of the principal Officer in each of the executive Departments, upon any Subject relating to the Duties of their respective Offices, and he shall have Power to grant Reprieves and Pardons for Offenses against the United States, except in Cases of Impeachment.

He shall have Power, by and with the Advice and Consent of the Senate, to make Treaties, provided two-thirds of the Senators present concur; and he shall nominate, and by and with the Advice and Consent of the Senate, shall appoint Ambassadors, other public Ministers and Consuls, Judges of the supreme Court, and all other Officers of the United States, whose Appointments are not herein otherwise provided for, and which shall be established by Law: but the Congress may by Law vest the Appointment of such inferior Officers, as they think proper, in the President alone, in the Courts of Law, or in the Heads of Departments.

The President shall have Power to fill up all Vacancies that may happen during the Recess of the Senate, by granting Commissions which shall expire at the End of their next Session.

SECTION 3.

He shall from time to time give to the Congress Information of the State of the Union, and recommend to their Consideration such Measures as he shall judge necessary and expedient; he may, on extraordinary Occasions, convene both Houses, or either of them, and in Case of Disagreement between them, with Respect to the Time of Adjournment, he may adjourn them to such Time as he shall think proper; he shall receive Ambassadors and other public Ministers; he shall take Care that the Laws be faithfully executed, and shall Commission all the Officers of the United States.

SECTION 4.

The President, Vice President, and all civil Officers of the United States, shall be removed from Office on Impeachment for, and Conviction of, Treason, Bribery, or other high Crimes and Misdemeanors.

Article III.

SECTION 1.

The judicial Power of the United States, shall be vested in one supreme Court, and in such inferior Courts as the Congress may from time to time ordain and establish. The Judges, both of the supreme and inferior Courts, shall hold their Offices during good Behavior, and shall at stated Times, receive for their Services, a Compensation, which shall not be diminished during their Continuance in Office.

SECTION 2.

The judicial Power shall extend to all Cases, in Law and Equity, arising under this Constitution, the Laws of the United States, and Treaties made, or which shall be made, under their Authority; — to all Cases affecting Ambassadors, other public Ministers and Consuls; — to all Cases of admiralty and maritime Jurisdiction; — to Controversies to which the United States shall be a Party; — to Controversies between two or more States; — [between a State and Citizens of another State; —]* between Citizens of different States, — between Citizens of the same State claiming Lands under Grants of different States, [and between a State, or the Citizens thereof; — and foreign States, Citizens, or Subjects.]*

In all Cases affecting Ambassadors, other public Ministers and Consuls, and those in which a State shall be Party, the supreme Court shall have original Jurisdiction. In all the other Cases before mentioned, the supreme Court shall have appellate Jurisdiction, both as to Law and Fact, with such Exceptions, and under such Regulations as the Congress shall make.

The Trial of all Crimes, except in Cases of Impeachment; shall be by Jury; and such Trial shall be held in the State where the said Crimes shall have been committed; but when not committed within any State, the Trial shall be at such Place or Places as the Congress may by Law have directed.

SECTION 3.

Treason against the United States, shall consist only in levying War against them, or in adhering to their Enemies, giving them Aid and Comfort. No Person shall be convicted of Treason unless on the Testimony of two Witnesses to the same overt Act, or on Confession in open Court.

The Congress shall have Power to declare the Punishment of Treason, but no Attainder of Treason shall work Corruption of Blood, or Forfeiture except during the Life of the Person attainted.

Article IV.

SECTION 1.

Full Faith and Credit shall be given in each State to the public Acts, Records, and judicial Proceedings of every other State. And the Congress may by general Laws prescribe the Manner in which such Acts, Records and Proceedings shall be proved, and the Effect thereof.

SECTION 2.

The Citizens of each State shall be entitled to all Privileges and Immunities of Citizens in the several States. A Person charged in any State with Treason, Felony, or other Crime, who shall flee from Justice, and be found in another State, shall on Demand of the executive Authority of the State from which he fled, be delivered up, to be removed to the State having Jurisdiction of the Crime.

[No Person held to Service or Labor in one State, under the Laws thereof, escaping into another, shall, in Consequence of any Law or Regulation therein, be discharged from such Service or Labor, but shall be delivered up on Claim of the Party to whom such Service or Labor may be due.]*

SECTION 3.

New States may be admitted by the Congress into this Union; but no new State shall be formed or erected within the Jurisdiction of any other State; nor any State be formed by the Junction of two or more States, or Parts of States, without the Consent of the Legislatures of the States concerned as well as of the Congress.

The Congress shall have Power to dispose of and make all needful Rules and Regulations respecting the Territory or other Property belonging to the United States; and nothing in this Constitution shall be so construed as to Prejudice any Claims of the United States, or of any particular State.

SECTION 4.

The United States shall guarantee to every State in this Union a Republican Form of Government, and shall protect each of them against Invasion; and on Application of the Legislature, or of the Executive (when the Legislature cannot be convened) against domestic Violence.

Article V.

The Congress, whenever two-thirds of both Houses shall deem it necessary, shall propose Amendments to this Constitution, or, on the Application of the Legislatures of two-thirds of the several States, shall call a Convention for proposing Amendments, which in either Case, shall be valid to all Intents and Purposes, as Part of this Constitution, when ratified by the Legislatures of three-fourths of the several States, or by Conventions in three-fourths thereof, as the one or the other Mode of Ratification may be proposed by the Congress; Provided that no Amendment which may be made prior to the Year One thousand eight hundred and eight shall in any Manner affect the first and fourth Clauses in the Ninth Section of the first Article; and that no State, without its Consent, shall be deprived of its equal Suffrage in the Senate.

Article VI.

All Debts contracted and Engagements entered into, before the Adoption of this Constitution, shall be as valid against the United States under this Constitution, as under the Confederation.

This Constitution, and the Laws of the United States which shall be made in Pursuance thereof; and all Treaties made, or which shall be made, under the Authority of the United States, shall be the supreme Law of the Land; and the Judges in every State shall be bound thereby, any Thing in the Constitution or Laws of any State to the Contrary notwithstanding.

The Senators and Representatives before mentioned, and the Members of the several State Legislatures, and all executive and judicial Officers, both of the United States and of the several States, shall be bound by Oath or Affirmation, to support this Constitution; but no religious Test shall ever be required as a Qualification to any Office or public Trust under the United States.

Article VII.

The Ratification of the Conventions of nine States, shall be sufficient for the Establishment of this Constitution between the States so ratifying the Same.

Done in Convention by the Unanimous Consent of the States present the Seventeenth Day of September in the Year of our Lord one thousand seven hundred and Eighty seven and of the Independence of the United States of America the Twelfth In Witness whereof We have hereunto subscribed our Names,

Go. Washington — Presidt: and deputy from Virginia

NEW HAMPSHIRE

John Langdon
Nicholas Gilman

MASSACHUSETTS

Nathaniel Gorham
Rufus King

CONNECTICUT

Wm. Saml. Johnson
Roger Sherman

NEW YORK

Alexander Hamilton

NEW JERSEY

Wil: Livingston
David Brearley

Wm. Paterson
Jona: Dayton

PENNSYLVANIA

B Franklin
Thomas Mifflin
Robt Morris
Geo. Clymer
Thos. FitzSimons
Jared Ingersoll
James Wilson
Gouv Morris

DELAWARE

Geo: Read
Gunning Bedford jun
John Dickinson
Richard Bassett
Jaco: Broom

MARYLAND

James McHenry
Dan of St. Thos. Jenifer
Danl Carroll

VIRGINIA

John Blair
James Madison Jr.

NORTH CAROLINA

Wm. Blount
Richd. Dobbs Spaight
Hu Williamson

SOUTH CAROLINA

J. Rutledge
Charles Cotesworth Pinckney
Charles Pinckney
Pierce Butler

GEORGIA

William Few
Abr Baldwin

Attest William Jackson Secretary
In Convention Monday
September 17th, 1787.
Present
The States of
New Hampshire, Massachusetts, Connecticut, Mr. Hamilton from New York, New Jersey, Pennsylvania, Delaware, Maryland, Virginia, North Carolina, South Carolina, and Georgia.

Resolved,

That the preceeding Constitution be laid before the United States in Congress assembled, and that it is the Opinion of this Convention, that it should afterwards be submitted to a Convention of Delegates, chosen in each State by the People thereof, under the Recommendation of its Legislature, for their Assent and Ratification; and that each Convention assenting to, and ratifying the Same, should give Notice thereof to the United States in Congress assembled. Resolved, That it is the Opinion of this Convention, that as soon as the Conventions of nine States shall have ratified this Constitution, the United States in Congress assembled should fix a Day on which Electors should be appointed by the States which shall have ratified the same, and a Day on which the Electors should assemble to vote for the President, and the Time and Place for commencing Proceedings under this Constitution.

That after such Publication the Electors should be appointed, and the Senators and Representatives elected: That the Electors should meet on the Day fixed for the Election of the President, and should transmit their Votes certified, signed, sealed, and directed, as the Constitution requires, to the Secretary of the United States in Congress assembled, that the Senators and Representatives should convene at the Time and Place assigned; that the Senators should appoint a President of the Senate, for the sole Purpose of receiving, opening and counting the Votes for President; and, that after he shall be chosen, the Congress, together with the President, should, without Delay, proceed to execute this Constitution.

By the unanimous Order of the Convention

Go. Washington-Presidt:
W. JACKSON Secretary.

THE AMENDMENTS TO THE CONSTITUTION OF THE UNITED STATES AS RATIFIED BY THE STATES

Preamble to the Bill of Rights

CONGRESS OF THE UNITED STATES
BEGUN AND HELD AT THE CITY OF NEW YORK, ON
WEDNESDAY THE FOURTH OF MARCH,
ONE THOUSAND SEVEN HUNDRED AND EIGHTY NINE

THE Convention of a number of the States, having at the time of their adopting the Constitution, expressed a desire, in order to prevent misconstruction or abuse of its powers, that further declaratory and restrictive clauses should be added: And as extending the ground of public confidence in the Government, will best ensure the beneficent ends of its institution.

RESOLVED by the Senate and House of Representatives of the United States of America, in Congress assembled, two-thirds of both Houses concurring, that the following Articles be proposed to the Legislatures of the several States, as amendments to the Constitution of the United States, all, or any of which Articles, when ratified by three-fourths of the said Legislatures, to be valid to all intents and purposes, as part of the said Constitution; viz.

ARTICLES in addition to, and Amendment of the Constitution of the United States of America, proposed by Congress, and ratified by the Legislatures of the several States, pursuant to the fifth Article of the original Constitution.

(Note: The first 10 amendments to the Constitution were ratified December 15, 1791, and form what is known as the "Bill of Rights.")

Amendment I.

Congress shall make no law respecting an establishment of religion, or prohibiting the free exercise thereof; or abridging the freedom of speech, or of the press, or the right of the people peaceably to assemble, and to petition the Government for a redress of grievances.

Amendment II.

A well regulated Militia, being necessary to the security of a free State, the right of the people to keep and bear Arms, shall not be infringed.

Amendment III.

No Soldier shall, in time of peace be quartered in any house, without the consent of the Owner, nor in time of war, but in a manner to be prescribed by law.

Amendment IV.

The right of the people to be secure in their persons, houses, papers, and effects, against unreasonable searches and seizures, shall not be violated, and no Warrants shall issue, but upon probable cause, supported by Oath or affirmation, and particularly describing the place to be searched, and the persons or things to be seized.

Amendment V.

No person shall be held to answer for a capital, or otherwise infamous crime, unless on a presentment or indictment of a Grand Jury, except in cases arising in the land or naval forces, or in the Militia, when in actual service in time of War or public danger; nor shall any person be subject for the same offense to be twice put in jeopardy of life or limb; nor shall be compelled in any criminal case to be a witness against himself, nor be deprived of life, liberty, or property, without due process of law; nor shall private property be taken for public use, without just compensation.

Amendment VI.

In all criminal prosecutions, the accused shall enjoy the right to a speedy and public trial, by an impartial jury of the State and district wherein the crime shall have been committed, which district shall have been previously ascertained by law, and to be informed of the nature and cause of the accusation; to be confronted with the witnesses against him; to have compulsory process for obtaining witnesses in his favor, and to have the Assistance of Counsel for his defense.

Amendment VII.

In suits at common law, where the value in controversy shall exceed twenty dollars, the right of trial by jury shall be preserved, and no fact tried by a jury shall be otherwise re-examined in any Court of the United States, than according to the rules of the common law.

Amendment VIII.

Excessive bail shall not be required, nor excessive fines imposed, nor cruel and unusual punishments inflicted.

Amendment IX.

The enumeration in the Constitution, of certain rights, shall not be construed to deny or disparage others retained by the people.

Amendment X.

The powers not delegated to the United States by the Constitution, nor prohibited by it to the States, are reserved to the States respectively, or to the people.

AMENDMENTS 11–27

Amendment XI.

Passed by Congress March 4, 1794. Ratified February 7, 1795.

(Note: A portion of Article III, Section 2 of the Constitution was modified by the Eleventh Amendment.)

The Judicial power of the United States shall not be construed to extend to any suit in law or equity, commenced or prosecuted against one of the United States by Citizens of another State, or by Citizens or Subjects of any Foreign State.

Amendment XII.

Passed by Congress December 9, 1803. Ratified June 15, 1804.

(Note: A portion of Article II, Section 1 of the Constitution was changed by the Twelfth Amendment.)

The Electors shall meet in their respective states, and vote by ballot for President and Vice-President, one of whom, at least, shall not be an inhabitant of the same state with themselves; they shall name in their ballots the person voted for as President, and in distinct ballots the person voted for as Vice-President, and they shall make distinct lists of all persons voted for as President, and of all persons voted for as Vice-President, and of the number of votes for each, which lists they shall sign and certify, and transmit sealed to the seat of the government of the United States, directed to the President of the Senate;—the President of the Senate shall, in the presence of the Senate and House of Representatives, open all the certificates and the votes shall then be counted;—The person having the greatest number of votes for President, shall be the President, if such number be a majority of the whole number of Electors appointed; and if no person have such majority, then from the persons having the highest numbers not exceeding three on the list of those voted for as President, the House of Representatives shall choose immediately, by ballot, the President. But in choosing the President, the votes shall be taken by states, the representation from each state having one vote; a quorum for this purpose shall consist of a member or members from two-thirds of the states, and a majority of all the states shall be necessary to a choice. [And if the House of Representatives shall not choose a President whenever the right of choice shall devolve upon them, before the fourth day of March next following, then the Vice-President shall act as President, as in case of the death or other constitutional disability of the President.—]* The person having the greatest number of votes as Vice-President, shall be the Vice-President, if such number be a majority of the whole number of Electors appointed, and if no person have a majority, then from the two highest numbers on the list, the Senate shall choose the Vice-President; a quorum for the purpose shall consist of two-thirds of the whole number of Senators, and a majority of the whole number shall be necessary to a choice. But no person constitutionally ineligible to the office of President shall be eligible to that of Vice-President of the United States.

Amendment XIII.

Passed by Congress January 31, 1865. Ratified December 6, 1865.

(Note: A portion of Article IV, Section 2 of the Constitution was changed by the Thirteenth Amendment.)

---

* Superseded by Section 3 of the Twentieth Amendment.

SECTION 1.

Neither slavery nor involuntary servitude, except as a punishment for crime whereof the party shall have been duly convicted, shall exist within the United States, or any place subject to their jurisdiction.

SECTION 2.

Congress shall have power to enforce this article by appropriate legislation.

Amendment XIV.

Passed by Congress June 13, 1866. Ratified July 9, 1868.

(Note: Article I, Section 2 of the Constitution was modified by Section 2 of the Fourteenth Amendment.)

SECTION 1.

All persons born or naturalized in the United States and subject to the jurisdiction thereof, are citizens of the United States and of the State wherein they reside. No State shall make or enforce any law which shall abridge the privileges or immunities of citizens of the United States; nor shall any State deprive any person of life, liberty, or property, without due process of law; nor deny to any person within its jurisdiction the equal protection of the laws.

SECTION 2.

Representatives shall be apportioned among the several States according to their respective numbers, counting the whole number of persons in each State, excluding Indians not taxed. But when the right to vote at any election for the choice of electors for President and Vice President of the United States, Representatives in Congress, the Executive and Judicial officers of a State, or the members of the Legislature thereof, is denied to any of the male inhabitants of such State, [being twenty-one years of age,]* and citizens of the United States, or in any way abridged, except for participation in rebellion, or other crime, the basis of representation therein shall be reduced in the proportion which the number of such male citizens shall bear

---

*Changed by Section 1 of the Twenty-sixth Amendment.

to the whole number of male citizens twenty-one years of age in such State.

SECTION 3.

No person shall be a Senator or Representative in Congress, or elector of President and Vice President, or hold any office, civil or military, under the United States, or under any State, who, having previously taken an oath, as a member of Congress, or as an officer of the United States, or as a member of any State legislature, or as an executive or judicial officer of any State, to support the Constitution of the United States, shall have engaged in insurrection or rebellion against the same, or given aid or comfort to the enemies thereof. But Congress may by a vote of two-thirds of each House, remove such disability.

SECTION 4.

The validity of the public debt of the United States, authorized by law, including debts incurred for payment of pensions and bounties for services in suppressing insurrection or rebellion, shall not be questioned. But neither the United States nor any State shall assume or pay any debt or obligation incurred in aid of insurrection or rebellion against the United States, or any claim for the loss or emancipation of any slave; but all such debts, obligations and claims shall be held illegal and void.

SECTION 5.

The Congress shall have the power to enforce, by appropriate legislation, the provisions of this article.

Amendment XV.

Passed by Congress February 26, 1869. Ratified February 3, 1870.

SECTION 1.

The right of citizens of the United States to vote shall not be denied or abridged by the United States or by any State on account of race, color, or previous condition of servitude.

SECTION 2.

The Congress shall have the power to enforce this article by appropriate legislation.

Amendment XVI.

Passed by Congress July 2, 1909. Ratified February 3, 1913.

(Note: Article I, Section 9 of the Constitution was modified by the Sixteenth Amendment.)

The Congress shall have power to lay and collect taxes on incomes, from whatever source derived, without apportionment among the several States, and without regard to any census or enumeration.

Amendment XVII.

Passed by Congress May 13, 1912. Ratified April 8, 1913.

(Note: Article I, Section 3 of the Constitution was modified by the Seventeenth Amendment.)

The Senate of the United States shall be composed of two Senators from each State, elected by the people thereof, for six years; and each Senator shall have one vote. The electors in each State shall have the qualifications requisite for electors of the most numerous branch of the State legislatures.

When vacancies happen in the representation of any State in the Senate, the executive authority of such State shall issue writs of election to fill such vacancies: Provided, That the legislature of any State may empower the executive thereof to make temporary appointments until the people fill the vacancies by election as the legislature may direct.

This amendment shall not be so construed as to affect the election or term of any Senator chosen before it becomes valid as part of the Constitution.

Amendment XVIII.

Passed by Congress December 18, 1917. Ratified January 16, 1919. Repealed by the Twenty-first Amendment, December 5, 1933.

SECTION 1.

After one year from the ratification of this article the manufacture, sale, or transportation of intoxicating liquors within, the importation thereof into, or the exportation thereof from the United States and all territory subject to the jurisdiction thereof for beverage purposes is hereby prohibited.

SECTION 2.

The Congress and the several States shall have concurrent power to enforce this article by appropriate legislation.

SECTION 3.

This article shall be inoperative unless it shall have been ratified as an amendment to the Constitution by the legislatures of the several States, as provided in the Constitution, within seven years from the date of the submission hereof to the States by the Congress.

Amendment XIX.

Passed by Congress June 4, 1919. Ratified August 18, 1920.

The right of citizens of the United States to vote shall not be denied or abridged by the United States or by any State on account of sex.

Congress shall have power to enforce this article by appropriate legislation.

Amendment XX.

Passed by Congress March 2, 1932. Ratified January 23, 1933.

(Note: Article I, Section 4 of the Constitution was modified by Section 2 of this Amendment. In addition, a portion of the Twelfth Amendment was superseded by Section 3.)

SECTION 1.

The terms of the President and the Vice President shall end at noon on the 20th day of January, and the terms of Senators and Representatives at noon on the 3d day of January, of the years in which such terms would have ended if this article had not been ratified; and the terms of their successors shall then begin.

SECTION 2.

The Congress shall assemble at least once in every year, and such meeting shall begin at noon on the 3d day of January, unless they shall by law appoint a different day.

SECTION 3.

If, at the time fixed for the beginning of the term of the President, the President elect shall have died, the Vice President elect shall become President. If a President shall not have been chosen before the time fixed for the beginning of his term, or if the President elect shall have failed to qualify, then the Vice President elect shall act as President until a President shall have qualified; and the Congress may by law provide for the case wherein neither a President elect nor a Vice President shall have qualified, declaring who shall then act as President, or the manner in which one who is to act shall be selected, and such person shall act accordingly until a President or Vice President shall have qualified.

SECTION 4.

The Congress may by law provide for the case of the death of any of the persons from whom the House of Representatives may choose a President whenever the right of choice shall have devolved upon them, and for the case of the death of any of the persons from whom the Senate may choose a Vice President whenever the right of choice shall have devolved upon them.

SECTION 5.

Sections 1 and 2 shall take effect on the 15th day of October following the ratification of this article.

SECTION 6.

This article shall be inoperative unless it shall have been ratified as an amendment to the Constitution by the legislatures of three-fourths of the several States within seven years from the date of its submission.

Amendment XXI.

Passed by Congress February 20, 1933. Ratified December 5, 1933.

SECTION 1.

The eighteenth article of amendment to the Constitution of the United States is hereby repealed.

SECTION 2.

The transportation or importation into any State, Territory, or possession of the United States for delivery or use therein of intoxicating liquors, in violation of the laws thereof, is hereby prohibited.

SECTION 3.

This article shall be inoperative unless it shall have been ratified as an amendment to the Constitution by conventions in the several States, as provided in the Constitution, within seven years from the date of the submission hereof to the States by the Congress.

Amendment XXII.

Passed by Congress March 21, 1947. Ratified February 27, 1951.

SECTION 1.

No person shall be elected to the office of the President more than twice, and no person who has held the office of President, or acted as President, for more than two years of a term to which some other person was elected President shall be elected to the office of President more than once. But this Article shall not apply to any person holding the office of President when this Article was proposed by Congress, and shall not prevent any person who may be holding the office of President, or acting as President, during the term within which this Article becomes operative from holding the office of President or acting as President during the remainder of such term.

SECTION 2.

This article shall be inoperative unless it shall have been ratified as an amendment to the Constitution by the legislatures of three-fourths of the several States within seven years from the date of its submission to the States by the Congress.

Amendment XXIII.

Passed by Congress June 16, 1960. Ratified March 29, 1961.

SECTION 1.

The District constituting the seat of Government of the United States shall appoint in such manner as Congress may direct:

A number of electors of President and Vice President equal to the whole number of Senators and Representatives in Congress to which the District would be entitled if it were a State, but in no event more than the least populous State; they shall be in addition to those appointed by the States, but they shall be considered, for the purposes of the election of President and Vice President, to be electors appointed by a State; and they shall meet in the District and perform such duties as provided by the twelfth article of amendment.

SECTION 2.

The Congress shall have power to enforce this article by appropriate legislation.

Amendment XXIV.

Passed by Congress August 27, 1962. Ratified January 23, 1964.

SECTION 1.

The right of citizens of the United States to vote in any primary or other election for President or Vice President, for electors for President or Vice President, or for Senator or Representative in Congress, shall not be denied or abridged by the United States or any State by reason of failure to pay poll tax or other tax.

SECTION 2.

The Congress shall have power to enforce this article by appropriate legislation.

Amendment XXV.

Passed by Congress July 6, 1965. Ratified February 10, 1967. (*Note: Article II, Section 1 of the Constitution was modified by the Twenty-fifth Amendment.*)

SECTION 1.

In case of the removal of the President from office or of his death or resignation, the Vice President shall become President.

SECTION 2.

Whenever there is a vacancy in the office of the Vice President, the President shall nominate a Vice President who shall take office upon confirmation by a majority vote of both Houses of Congress.

SECTION 3.

Whenever the President transmits to the President pro tempore of the Senate and the Speaker of the House of Representatives his written declaration that he is unable to discharge the powers and duties of his office, and until he transmits to them a written declaration to the contrary, such powers and duties shall be discharged by the Vice President as Acting President.

SECTION 4.

Whenever the Vice President and a majority of either the principal officers of the executive departments or of such other body as Congress may by law provide, transmit to the President pro tempore of the Senate and the Speaker of the House of Representatives their written declaration that the President is unable to discharge the powers and duties of his office, the Vice President shall immediately assume the powers and duties of the office as Acting President.

Thereafter, when the President transmits to the President pro tempore of the Senate and the Speaker of the House of Representatives his written declaration that no inability exists, he shall resume the powers and duties of his office unless the Vice President and a majority of either the principal officers of the executive department or of such other body as Congress may by law provide, transmit within four days to the President pro tempore of the Senate and the Speaker of the House of Representatives their written declaration that the President is unable to discharge the powers and duties of his office. Thereupon Congress shall decide the issue, assembling within forty-eight hours for that purpose if not in session. If the Congress, within twenty-one days after receipt of the latter written declaration, or, if Congress is not in session, within twenty-one days after Congress is required to assemble, determines by two-thirds vote of both Houses that the President is unable to discharge the powers and duties of his office, the Vice President shall continue to discharge the same as Acting President; otherwise, the President shall resume the powers and duties of his office.

Amendment XXVI.

Passed by Congress March 23, 1971. Ratified July 1, 1971.

(Note: Amendment 14, Section 2 of the Constitution was modified by Section 1 of the Twenty-sixth Amendment.)

SECTION 1.

The right of citizens of the United States, who are eighteen years of age or older, to vote shall not be denied or abridged by the United States or by any State on account of age.

SECTION 2.

The Congress shall have power to enforce this article by appropriate legislation.

Amendment XXVII.

Originally proposed September, 25, 1789. Ratified May 7, 1992.

No law, varying the compensation for the services of the Senators and Representatives, shall take effect, until an election of representatives shall have intervened.

QUESTIONS FOR CRITICAL READING

1. In Article I, Section 2, what is the difference between electors and people?
2. Who are the electors? What are their limits? Why are these limits in place? (See also the Twelfth Amendment.)
3. Who has powers of impeachment, and what is the process of impeachment?
4. To what extent is the House representative?
5. What does the Constitution say about who is a citizen of the new nation? Has anything changed regarding citizenship since 1791?
6. What limits are placed on the executive, the office of the presidency?
7. In your view, how strongly does the Constitution promote and protect democracy?

SUGGESTIONS FOR CRITICAL WRITING

1. If you could write the Twenty-eighth Amendment, what would it be? Give your reasons for the amendment and consider how likely it would be to be adopted by the states. What procedure would you follow to get the amendment considered and passed?

2. The Second Amendment says that the right of the people to bear arms "shall not be infringed." Why does the Constitution say that the people have the right to bear arms? If a well-regulated militia is necessary, should not the Constitution demand that every capable citizen be armed and part of the militia? Should people who cannot carry out the responsibility of being part of the militia be given the right to bear arms? What does *infringed* mean? What are its limits and how does the Constitution use the word? To what extent does the responsibility of being part of a militia enter into modern discussions of this amendment?

3. The Twelfth Amendment (ratified in 1804) discusses the privileges and responsibilities of the electors who choose the president and vice president. Examine the details of this amendment and explain its intention as if you were addressing someone who does not understand it. What protections are implied in this amendment? Are the purposes of democracy being served by the amendment? What were the writers of the amendment fearful of when they drafted and ratified it? Do you approve of it? Be sure to consider what was originally written in Article II, Section 1.

4. Individual freedom was very important to the Anti-Federalists, and judging from earlier writings, it was important to the Federalists as well. What protections of individual freedoms are mentioned in the original seven articles of the Constitution? What protections follow in the amendments? What conclusions can you draw from where the most important freedoms are positioned in the document?

5. What issues are omitted from the Constitution? For instance, how are national elections to be conducted and monitored? What religious issues of great importance are omitted from discussion? Is a belief in God central to the Constitution? What moral issues are omitted from the Constitution?

6. In reviewing the original ten amendments designed as the Bill of Rights, which amendment do you feel is most important for protecting freedom? Which is least important? Do you feel that the purpose of these ten amendments is to guarantee our freedoms? Do they have a force behind them to guarantee our democratic government?

7. **CONNECTIONS** James Madison wrote the establishment clause that is the basis for our concept of the separation of church and state in the First Amendment. Madison, like Jefferson, Hamilton, and Franklin, was a Deist. How might his beliefs as a Deist have affected his position on the separation of church and state? Research Deism as it was understood in the eighteenth century in order to answer this question.

Might Madison have been more worried about the power of the state over religion or the power of religion over the state? To what extent does Stephen Carter's "The Separation of Church and State" (**bedfordstmartins.com/worldofideas/epages**) take into account the possibility that Madison might have regarded religion less positively than Carter himself does?

8. **CONNECTIONS**   Aristotle implied that there are different kinds of democracies. How does the democratic government implied in the Constitution differ from the description that Aristotle offers when he defines democracy? In what ways might he be said to have anticipated the kind of government produced by the Constitution?

9. **SEEING CONNECTIONS**   What does Howard Chandler Christy's *Scene at the Signing of the Constitution of the United States* (p. 57) tell you about the makeup of the framers of the Constitution? Based on their appearance, what would you expect their views on producing a democratic government to be? Given that they are clearly people of means and wealth, what surprises did they include in the Constitution? To what extent might a convention of impoverished people have produced a better Constitution? How would it have been different?

JAMES MADISON
Federalist No. 51: On the Separation of Departments of Power

JAMES MADISON (1751–1836), one of the most important members of the convention that formed the Constitution, was born in Virginia and educated at Princeton University in New Jersey. Although he was not technically the author of the Constitution—no one man, as he said, was its author—his theories had a great deal to do with the ultimate formation of a republican government. Of the eighty-five "Federalist" essays (collectively known as the *Federalist Papers*) that were published in New York newspapers between October 1787 and May 1788, Madison wrote twenty-nine. His purpose, along with that of Alexander Hamilton, who wrote fifty-one essays, and that of John Jay, who wrote five, was to argue for ratification of the Constitution by the states' conventions. At the same time, these papers explored the individual theoretical issues that underlay the entire document. The Constitution was ratified on June 21, 1788.

While Madison did not fight in the Revolutionary War because of ill health, he was swept into political activity almost immediately after the Battle of Lexington and became a member of the Virginia State Assembly, where he met Thomas Jefferson. He was elected to the Continental Congress in 1780, at a time when the war seemed uncertain and the financial situation of the Congress was in serious straits. His views were central to the designs of government that began to produce a financial solution—including imposing taxes and paying the national debt—that saved the Confederation, as the union was then called.

Madison inherited a considerable estate in Virginia that grew tobacco, and like more than half of the members of the Constitutional Convention, he owned a large number of slaves. As a member of the Continental Congress, he was on a committee to consider issues related to slavery in the new nation. He opposed a plan that would have delayed abolishing the importation of slaves until 1808, favoring instead a ban on importation beginning in 1788. The twenty years between these dates, he feared, would "produce all the mischief" that could be "apprehended from the liberty to import slaves." He complained of slavery as "that dreadful calamity which has so long afflicted our country" and joined with Jefferson to support the American Colonization Society, for the purpose of purchasing slaves and returning them to Africa.

Once the Constitution was ratified, Madison became a member of the House of Representatives and drafted nine of the first ten amendments in the Bill of Rights. These amendments were designed to reassure the states that individual rights and states' rights would be protected beyond the original document. Later in life, Madison became secretary of state during Jefferson's term as president. In 1803, Madison was instrumental in acquiring the Louisiana Purchase, which more than doubled the size of the nation at the cost of just three cents an acre. Madison was president of the United States from 1809 to 1817 and experienced the burning of the White House by the British during the War of 1812. Madison's wife, the first lady Dolly Madison, was able to collect and remove some of the most important treasures from the White House before the British arrived with their torches. At the time, Madison was with his generals at the front, and he came back to the White House briefly before he, too, had to flee.

Because the war was so difficult to manage, Madison's views on government changed. He realized the need for a national bank, which he had previously argued against, and he realized the need for a much stronger government than he had argued for in his earlier years.

Madison's Rhetoric

Madison had sketched out the Virginia Plan, which the framers of the Constitution used as the basis for their discussions in 1787, but in the process of discussion and revision, the document became less and less Madison's own. He had been on the Committee of Style for the Constitution, but the final document contained very little of Madison's personal expression.

However, his entries in the *Federalist Papers* showcase Madison's personal style as that of an eighteenth-century author. Having studied Greek, Latin, and even Hebrew in college, he had a deep understanding of the English language and its roots. Consequently, Madison's prose in "Federalist No. 51" is subtle, demanding, and very formal. His primary audience was the New Yorkers who comprised the largest Anti-Federalist group of all the states. Naturally, the *Federalist Papers*, when published together, were disseminated widely and affected citizens in all the states, but it is clear that they were aimed primarily at well-educated readers because they were the people most likely to decide for or against ratification.

Madison maintains an argument devoted more to explaining than to convincing his audience. His view is Federalist, as the name of his essay instantly reveals; therefore, his argument must answer some of the worries of Anti-Federalists. With regard to the three parts of government—the legislative, the executive, and the judicial—he claims that there is a "necessary partition of power" that must be maintained if the government is to achieve its ends. He begins by indicating that, while he cannot develop his point in great detail, he has a number of "observations" that should clarify why these branches of government should be independent. The original title of this essay was a continuation of the subject of "Federalist No. 50": "The meaning of the maxim, which requires a separation of the departments of power, examined and ascertained." Basically, the essay is an examination of the question of the separation of powers.

He insists that "all the appointments for the supreme executive, legislative, and judiciary magistracies, should be drawn from the same fountain of authority, the people, through channels having no communication whatever with one another" (para. 2). He recognizes that there may be some difficulties, particularly with the judiciary branch, but feels that issue can be overcome with the appropriate resources. Further, keeping the offices independent from one another in decisions about their pay will remove a conspicuous threat to independence.

Ambition is another threat to the partition of powers, and in paragraph 4 he discusses the nature of politicians, admitting that there must be ways of governing, not just the governed, but the governors as well. Underlying all of Madison's thinking is the concept of balancing powers, usually by ensuring that each branch of government has the power to "check on the other" (para. 5). As he explains, "experience has taught mankind" that depending on the people alone to check the power of any branch of government is not sufficient. Each branch must have power of its own to counter the other branch. This principle is illustrated in the legislative branch, which Madison admits is the most powerful and most important, but by dividing it into two parts, each elected by different means, even the legislature has checks and balances within it.

Having clarified these points, Madison relies on enumeration to examine two "considerations particularly applicable to the federal system of America" (para. 8). Each distinction is itself divided into sections. The first distinction seems to say that people are either governed by one government or by two, a federal and a state government. The expression of the people's power will be different in each case. In the second consideration, Madison compares a hereditary monarchy with the federal system, paying particular attention to how a minority population would prosper in each. He explains with a hypothetical example that the federal system has the single power of the monarch spread over so many different offices "as will render an unjust combination of a majority of the whole very improbable, if not impracticable" (para. 10).

Much of the last paragraph depends on the analysis of circumstances that might be produced in the future government. Madison's paragraphs in the earlier part of the essay are often brief, but this last paragraph is the longest by far, including a remarkable number of considerations all at once: the force of religion, the question of security, the nature of justice, the problem of stronger and weaker factions, and the protection of the weak. All of these are major issues and some, such as the question of how the government might keep factions under control, are treated in their own earlier *Federalist* essay. But seeing them piled up in one paragraph at the end of this essay makes the reader realize the scope of the entire question of government and how difficult it is to consider all issues at once.

Finally, one interesting rhetorical device Madison is known for is his ability to use aphorisms. For example, in this essay one of his most famous sayings appears in paragraph 4: "If men were angels, no government would be necessary." "Justice is the end of government" appears in paragraph 10. Some aphorisms from his other works are "If Tyranny and Oppression come to this land, it will be in the guise of fighting a foreign enemy" and "In no instance have . . . the churches been guardians of the liberties of the people." And perhaps his most important saying is "Knowledge will forever govern ignorance; and a people who mean to be their own governors must arm themselves with the power which knowledge gives."

PREREADING QUESTIONS: WHAT TO READ FOR

The following prereading questions may help you anticipate key issues in the discussion of James Madison's "Federalist No. 51." Keeping them in mind during your first reading should help focus your attention.

- What are the three partitions of power Madison refers to?
- How can each partition keep from being overpowered by the others?
- Why must these three partitions maintain separate powers?

Federalist No. 51: On the Separation of Departments of Power

To what expedient then shall we finally resort, for maintaining in practice the necessary partition of power among the several departments, as laid down in the Constitution? The only answer that can be given is, that as all these exterior provisions are found to be inadequate, the defect must be supplied, by so contriving the interior structure of the government, as that its several constituent parts may, by their mutual relations, be the means of keeping each other in their proper places. Without presuming to undertake a full development of this important idea, I will hazard a few general observations, which may perhaps place it in a clearer light, and enable us to form a more correct judgment of the principles and structure of the government planned by the convention.

In order to lay a due foundation for that separate and distinct exercise of the different powers of government, which, to a certain extent, is admitted on all hands to be essential to the preservation of liberty, it is evident that each department should have a will of its own; and consequently should be so constituted, that the members of each should have as little agency as possible in the appointment of the members of the others. Were this principle rigorously adhered to, it would require that all the appointments for the supreme executive, legislative, and judiciary magistracies, should be drawn from the same fountain of authority, the people, through channels having no communication whatever with one another. Perhaps such a plan of constructing the several departments would be less difficult in practice, than it may in contemplation appear. Some difficulties, however, and some additional expense, would attend the execution of it. Some deviations, therefore, from the principle must be admitted. In the constitution of the judiciary department in particular, it might be inexpedient to insist rigorously on the principle; first, because peculiar qualifications being essential in the members, the primary consideration ought to be to select that mode of choice which best secures these qualifications; secondly, because the permanent tenure by which the appointments are held in that department, must soon destroy all sense of dependence on the authority conferring them.

It is equally evident, that the members of each department should be as little dependent as possible on those of the others, for the emoluments annexed to their offices. Were the executive magistrate, or the judges, not independent of the legislature in this particular, their independence in every other, would be merely nominal.

But the great security against a gradual concentration of the several powers in the same department, consists in giving to those who administer each department, the necessary constitutional means, and personal motives, to resist encroachments of the others. The provision for defense must in this, as in all other cases, be made commensurate to the danger of attack. Ambition must be made to counteract ambition. The interest of the man, must be connected with the constitutional rights of the place. It may be a reflection on human nature, that such devices should be necessary to control the abuses of government. But what is government itself, but the greatest of all reflections on human nature? If men were angels, no government would be necessary. If angels were to govern men, neither external nor internal controls on government would be necessary. In framing a government which is to be administered by men over men, the great difficulty lies in this: you must first enable the government to control the governed; and in the next place oblige it to control itself. A dependence on the people is, no doubt, the primary control on the government; but experience has taught mankind the necessity of auxiliary precautions. 4

This policy of supplying, by opposite and rival interests, the defect of better motives, might be traced through the whole system of human affairs, private as well as public. We see it particularly displayed in all the subordinate distributions of power; where the constant aim is, to divide and arrange the several offices in such a manner as that each may be a check on the other; that the private interest of every individual may be a sentinel over the public rights. These inventions of prudence cannot be less requisite in the distribution of the supreme powers of the state. 5

But it is not possible to give to each department an equal power of self-defense. In republican government, the legislative authority necessarily predominates. The remedy for this inconveniency is, to divide the legislature into different branches; and to render them, by different modes of election, and different principles of action, as little connected with each other, as the nature of their common functions, and their common dependence on the society, will admit. It may even be necessary to guard against dangerous encroachments by still further precautions. As the weight of the legislative authority requires that it should be thus divided, the weakness of the executive may require, on the other hand, that it should be fortified. An absolute negative on the legislature, appears, at first view, to be the natural defense with which the executive magistrate should be armed. 6

But perhaps it would be neither altogether safe, nor alone sufficient. On ordinary occasions, it might not be exerted with the requisite firmness; and on extraordinary occasions, it might be perfidiously abused. May not this defect of an absolute negative be supplied by some qualified connection between this weaker department, and the weaker branch of the stronger department, by which the latter may be led to support the constitutional rights of the former, without being too much detached from the rights of its own department?

If the principles on which these observations are founded be just,   7
as I persuade myself they are, and they be applied as a criterion to the several state constitutions, and to the federal constitution, it will be found, that if the latter does not perfectly correspond with them, the former are infinitely less able to bear such a test.

There are moreover two considerations particularly applicable to   8
the federal system of America, which place that system in a very interesting point of view.

First. In a single republic, all the power surrendered by the peo-   9
ple, is submitted to the administration of a single government; and the usurpations are guarded against, by a division of the government into distinct and separate departments. In the compound republic of America, the power surrendered by the people, is first divided between two distinct governments, and then the portion allotted to each subdivided among distinct and separate departments. Hence a double security arises to the rights of the people. The different governments will control each other; at the same time that each will be controlled by itself.

Second. It is of great importance in a republic, not only to guard   10
the society against the oppression of its rulers; but to guard one part of the society against the injustice of the other part. Different interests necessarily exist in different classes of citizens. If a majority be united by a common interest, the rights of the minority will be insecure. There are but two methods of providing against this evil: the one, by creating a will in the community independent of the majority, that is, of the society itself; the other, by comprehending in the society so many separate descriptions of citizens, as will render an unjust combination of a majority of the whole very improbable, if not impracticable. The first method prevails in all governments possessing an hereditary or self-appointed authority. This, at best, is but a precarious security; because a power independent of the society may as well espouse the unjust views of the major, as the rightful interests of the minor party, and may possibly be turned against both parties. The second method will be exemplified in the federal republic of the United States. Whilst all authority in it will be

derived from, and dependent on the society, the society itself will be broken into so many parts, interests, and classes of citizens, that the rights of individuals, or of the minority, will be in little danger from interested combinations of the majority. In a free government, the security for civil rights must be the same as that for religious rights. It consists in the one case in the multiplicity of interests, and in the other, in the multiplicity of sects. The degree of security in both cases will depend on the number of interests and sects; and this may be presumed to depend on the extent of country and number of people comprehended under the same government. This view of the subject must particularly recommend a proper federal system to all the sincere and considerate friends of republican government: since it shows, that in exact proportion as the territory of the union may be formed into more circumscribed confederacies, or states, oppressive combinations of a majority will be facilitated; the best security under the republican form, for the rights of every class of citizens, will be diminished; and consequently, the stability and independence of some member of the government, the only other security, must be proportionally increased. Justice is the end of government. It is the end of civil society. It ever has been, and ever will be, pursued, until it be obtained, or until liberty be lost in the pursuit. In a society, under the forms of which the stronger faction can readily unite and oppress the weaker, anarchy may as truly be said to reign, as in a state of nature, where the weaker individual is not secured against the violence of the stronger: and as, in the latter state, even the stronger individuals are prompted, by the uncertainty of their condition, to submit to a government which may protect the weak, as well as themselves: so, in the former state, will the more powerful factions or parties be gradually induced, by a like motive, to wish for a government which will protect all parties, the weaker as well as the more powerful. It can be little doubted, that if the state of Rhode Island was separated from the confederacy, and left to itself, the insecurity of rights under the popular form of government within such narrow limits, would be displayed by such reiterated oppressions of factious majorities, that some power altogether independent of the people, would soon be called for by the voice of the very factions whose misrule had proved the necessity of it. In the extended republic of the United States, and among the great variety of interests, parties, and sects, which it embraces, a coalition of a majority of the whole society could seldom take place upon any other principles, than those of justice and the general good: whilst there being thus less danger to a minor from the will of the major party, there must be less pretext also, to provide for the security of the former, by introducing into the government a will not dependent on the latter: or, in other words, a will independent of the society itself. It is no less certain than it is important, notwithstanding the contrary opinions which have been entertained, that the larger the society, provided it lie within a practicable sphere, the more duly capable it will be of self-government. And happily for the *republican cause,* the practicable sphere may be carried to a very great extent, by a judicious modification and mixture *of the federal principle.*

QUESTIONS FOR CRITICAL READING

1. How desirable is it to keep the three parts of government independent? Has it been difficult or easy to do so?

2. Does the fact that, like George Washington and Thomas Jefferson, Madison owned slaves make his concern for freedom and justice any less important to us today?

3. Which of the three offices of government most needs to be fortified against the power of the others?

4. Madison says that the judiciary presents special problems in being independent. What does he mean? (See paragraph 2.)

5. Each state has a constitution of its own. Does this seem to pose a problem to Madison? Or is it a benefit?

6. Madison mentions problems that may be caused by factions (para. 10). What is he worried about?

7. What might be the effect if the three branches of government were not completely independent of each other?

SUGGESTIONS FOR CRITICAL WRITING

1. Argue the case that "[j]ustice is the end of government. It is the end of civil society." Madison says these words in paragraph 10, and until that point in the essay he has hardly mentioned the concept of justice. How important is this notion in the essay? How important is it today? Has the government he recommended done well in providing the people with justice?

2. **CONNECTIONS**   Compare the quality of writing and style in the Constitution with Madison's in "Federalist No. 51." Consider word choice, the nature and structure of the sentences, the organization of parts, the length and complexity of paragraphs, and the clarity of

thought. How do differences of style affect your response to the ideas that each selection contains? What audiences seem to be addressed in each selection? Is the style of each selection appropriate for its audience? Are they both appropriate for you?

3. Decide whether it is true that in a republican form of government the legislative branch has the most power. Does the division of the legislature into two segments, the House of Representatives and the Senate, help diminish legislative dominance over the executive and the judiciary? What is the import of the two different ways the segments are elected? How does that difference affect legislative dominance?

4. The relationship of the majority to the minority is a prime concern of Madison's here and elsewhere in the *Federalist Papers*. He worries that there will be times when the majority will impose its will and act unjustly toward a minority. In paragraph 10, Madison says that one way to protect the rights of a minority is "by creating a will in the community independent of the majority, that is, of the society itself." Is he correct in his judgment? What does it mean to create will in the community, and how could that be done? Do you have a sense that there is a will in our community that helps keep the majority from exercising its will over a minority?

5. Given what you can tell from the news, how well do the three branches of government maintain their independence today? Do they seem to operate the way Madison expected them to, as described in the Constitution? Does there seem to be any danger of one branch of government being overwhelmed by another? By two others? How well does the system work in actually governing the nation?

6. **CONNECTIONS** Stephen Carter's argument in "The Separation of Church and State" (**bedfordstmartins.com/worldofideas/epages**) depends in large measure on his interpretation of the establishment clause of the Constitution. That clause, along with the free exercise clause, appears in the First Amendment, which was written by James Madison. As with all amendments, this one must be interpreted carefully. The establishment clause states that "Congress shall make no law respecting an establishment of religion, or prohibiting the free exercise thereof." Examine Carter's argument and decide whether or not he interprets these clauses in a reasonable manner. How would you interpret these clauses differently? Considering that these clauses are the law of the land, do you feel they are as clear as they should be and that they are respected by the nation as they should be? Do they clearly establish a separation of church and state?

7. **SEEING CONNECTIONS** Examine the painting by Howard Chandler Christy of the signing of the Constitution of the United States (p. 57). If possible, find out as much as you can about the status of each

of the people in the painting—those who ratified the Constitution—and decide whether you think this group would belong to the majority or the minority in the nation at that time. How important would the protection of the minority population from the oppression of the majority population be for them? How would Madison's suggestions for maintaining the independence of the three branches of government help guarantee their freedom from oppression? You may want to refer to Aristotle's definitions of democracy and oligarchy and decide whether Madison is proposing a possible combination of those forms of government.

ALEXIS DE TOCQUEVILLE
Government by Democracy
in America

ALEXIS DE TOCQUEVILLE (1805–1859), a French aristocrat, came to see what democracy had produced in America during
the early decades of the nineteenth century, when the United States
was expanding rapidly westward and developing both agricultural
and industrial strength. His family had lived through the French
Revolution (1789) and its murderous aftermath. His parents came
close to being killed but fled to England for a few years until Napoleon began his wars, which ended in 1814. When they returned to
France, they helped Tocqueville begin a career in law that resulted in
his appointment to a minor position in Versailles. He spent a good deal
of time reading the works of Machiavelli, Montesquieu, Rousseau, and
other major political thinkers and began writing in his early twenties.
Tocqueville went on to enjoy more important offices in government,
including in France's parlement, where he supported the abolish-
ment of slavery. However, the government in France in 1830 became
unstable, and Tocqueville's situation proved difficult. He applied for
a position that allowed him to visit the United States as an inspector
of American prisons.

He chose his best friend, Gustave de Beaumont, to accompany him, and they set out in 1831 to travel across the new nation.
Tocqueville did visit some prisons and comment on them, but soon
he saw his mission shift to the careful observation of the nature of
the government and the people of the United States. Because of the
violence of the French Revolution and the unstable governments that
followed up to the time of his visit, he was profoundly aware that the
world of the aristocracy was crumbling rapidly. Many aristocrats had

---

From *Democracy in America*.

been guillotined during the French revolution and many more had been forced out of the country. The rise of a middle class in France in the first decades of the 1800s signaled a change that Tocqueville knew was permanent and imminent. His studies in the United States resulted in *Democracy in America* (1835; 1840), still one the most important analyses of the function of democracy as it had been imagined by the framers of the Constitution and the authors of the *Federalist Papers*.

Tocqueville arrived at a propitious time. There were twenty-four states in the Union and the population was thirteen million people. Andrew Jackson (1767–1849) had been elected president in 1829 and was probably the most democratic holder of that office. He had not enjoyed the level of education of the presidents before him nor had he been the heir of great landholdings, like James Madison or the scion of a brilliant family, like John Quincy Adams. He had been born in the backwoods of Carolina and somehow began the study of law in his teens. He rose in politics, took a commission in the War of 1812, and became famous for his defeat of the British at New Orleans. He was tough, immediate, and sometimes coarse, but the country adored him.

In this environment, Tocqueville traveled freely across the country and recorded his observations. In the absence of an aristocracy, he marveled at the sense of equality that Americans had. He even went so far as to include a chapter in *Democracy in America* on the equality of women. In it he says, "I think that the social change which places father and son, servant and master and, in general, lower and upper classes on the same level, will gradually raise women to make them the equals of men." But he also observed that Americans had a great sense of industry and a love of materialism. "To clear, cultivate, and transform the realm of this vast uninhabited continent of his, the American must have the daily support of some energetic passion which can only be the love of money. This love of money has, therefore, never been stigmatized in America and, provided that it does not exceed the limits set by the public order, it is held in high esteem."

He was impressed by the apparent absence of the hand of government, the freedom that people enjoyed, and the essential practicality of the nation's inhabitants. He was certain that the power of the federal government would diminish over time and felt there could never be a civil war in America—despite the fact that the Civil War began just twenty-one years after his second volume appeared. His opinion that civil war was unlikely was based on his view that the power of the states outweighed the power of the federal government at that time: "If the sovereignty of the Union were to come into conflict with that of the states, one can readily foresee that it would be defeated; I doubt whether the fight would ever be undertaken in any serious fashion." He felt this even though South Carolina threatened war while he was in America in 1832.

Tocqueville returned to France after almost two years in America. There he married and continued his career, taking part in politics during tumultuous times in France. He supported French incursion into Algeria, which he visited. He also visited Ireland in 1835 and deplored the conditions of the Irish tenant farmers in the period before the great famine of the 1840s. He took a leadership role following the French revolution of 1848 and in branches of the government in the 1850s. His last work, a study of recent French history, appeared after he died in 1859.

Tocqueville's Rhetoric

Because this is a translation from the French, it is difficult for us to appreciate the directness and skill of Tocqueville's style. However, his principles of organization are clear. He considers only a specific number of issues in this chapter from his book. First, he tackles the question of suffrage, or who can vote. He describes it as universal suffrage because any free male citizen could vote in the United States; there were no restrictions, as in Europe, for men of property, though women, African slaves, and Native Americans could not vote. But Tocqueville also notes that there seem to be fewer distinguished men in office than there were fifty years before, when the Constitution was being written. He implies that when everyone can vote—as opposed to just a limited group of electors—the common people do not choose distinguished men. Tocqueville then develops this point by causal analysis, trying to find what it is that causes fewer men of outstanding quality to assume leadership.

He follows with a discussion of the circumstance of the intervals between elections. The shortness of the intervals between elections, he says, keeps "society in a feverish excitement and public affairs in a continuous state of change" (para. 31). But if there is a long period between elections, the ousted party might try to seize power. Further, with the change that new elections bring, he sees an "instability" of American laws (para. 34). He, like Americans, does not see this as a "great weakness" (para. 34).

Then, considering the "arbitrary power of magistrates," he develops his ideas using a comparison between monarchies, limited monarchies, and democracy, with a reference to the power of New England magistrates, by which he means those "entrusted with the execution of the law." In this section, he compares despotism and democracy by using examples of legislation in New England and continues with a discussion of limited monarchies.

One complaint leads him to devote a section to what he sees as the lack of good record keeping by local governments. Tocqueville points to newspapers as being the only institutions that keep a record of social movements and social issues. As a social scientist, he is himself in the process of recording what he sees at work in America and, in a sense, tries to make up for this lack in contemporary government.

Finally, Tocqueville develops his last idea when he discusses the possibility that American democracy may be financially efficient. Again, he relies on comparison to decide whether democracy is inexpensive or overly expensive to maintain. This leads him to consider taxation and to reflect on the Aristotelian issue of classes of people. Tocqueville sees three classes: first are the wealthy, whose fortunes are considerable; second are the middle class, who hold only a slight fortune; and third are the general poor, who live on their labor and do not get rich. Tocqueville's analysis of taxation under the government of each of these classes is fascinating. And like both Aristotle and James Madison, Tocqueville is led to consider the question of government by the majority or the minority. Obviously, this question remains central to ideas about democracy.

PREREADING QUESTIONS:
WHAT TO READ FOR

The following prereading questions may help you anticipate key issues in the discussion of Alexis de Tocqueville's "Government by Democracy in America." Keeping them in mind during your first reading should help focus your attention.

- How does universal suffrage affect the choice of who will govern?
- How might the frequency of elections affect the stability of the laws of the land?
- To what extent is a democratic form of government economically efficient?

Government by Democracy in America

I realize that I am treading on live cinders. Every single word 1
in this chapter is bound to bruise at some point the different parties
which divide my country. Nonetheless I shall speak my thoughts.

In Europe we find it difficult to assess the true character and the per- 2
manent instincts of democracy because in Europe two opposed principles
are in conflict; it is not precisely known how far this is due to the principles themselves or to the passions aroused by the conflict.

This is not the case in America where the people are in an unim- 3
peded dominance with no dangers to fear nor wrongs to avenge.

Therefore, in America, democracy follows its own inclinations. Its 4
behavior is natural and its movements are free. That is where it must be
judged. And who would find such a study more useful and interesting
than ourselves since we are daily carried along by an irresistible movement, walking like blind men toward what may prove to be a tyranny
perhaps or a republic, but surely toward a democratic social state?

Universal Suffrage

I have previously mentioned that all the states of the Union had 5
adopted universal suffrage. It is found in populations at different
stages on the social ladder. I have had the chance to observe its effects
in various places and among races of men whom language, religion,
or customs turn into virtual strangers to each other, in Louisiana as
well as in New England, in Georgia as in Canada. I have noted that
universal suffrage was far from producing in America all the benefits
or all the ills expected from it in Europe and that its results were in
general other than is supposed.

The People's Choice and the Instincts of American Democracy in Its Choices

*In the United States the most outstanding men are rarely called upon
to direct public affairs — Reasons for this — The envy which, in France,
drives the lower classes against the upper classes is not a French instinct but
a democratic one — Why, in America, eminent men often keep away from a
political career of their own volition.*

Many people in Europe believe without saying so, or say so without 6
believing it, that one of the great advantages of universal suffrage is

to summon men worthy of public trust to the direction of public affairs. The people could not possibly govern on their own, so it is said, but they do always sincerely support the welfare of the state and their instinct unfailingly tells them which men are fired by a similar desire and thus are the most competent to wield power.

For my part, I am bound to say, what I have seen in America   7 does not give me any reason to think that this is the case. When I stepped ashore in the United States, I discovered with amazement to what extent merit was common among the governed but rare among the rulers. It is a permanent feature of the present day that the most outstanding men in the United States are rarely summoned to public office and one is forced to acknowledge that things have been like that as democracy has gone beyond its previous limits. The race of American statesmen has strangely shrunk in size over the last half century.

One can point out several reasons for this phenomenon.   8

Whatever one does, it is impossible to raise the intelligence of a   9 nation above a certain level. It will be quite useless to ease the access to human knowledge, improve teaching methods, or reduce the cost of education, for men will never become educated nor develop their intelligence without devoting time to the matter.

Therefore the inevitable limitations upon a nation's intellectual   10 progress are governed by how great or small is the ease with which it can live without working. This limitation is further off in certain countries and nearer in others; for it not to exist at all, however, the people would need to be free of the physical cares of life. It would have to cease to be the people. Thus it is as difficult to imagine a society where all men are enlightened as a state where all the citizens are wealthy; those are two related difficulties. I willingly accept that the bulk of the population very sincerely supports the welfare of the country; I might go even further to state that in general the lower social classes seem to be less likely to confuse their personal interests with this support than the upper classes. But what they always lack, more or less, is the skill to judge the means to achieve this sincerely desired end. A long study and many different ideas indeed are needed to reach a precise picture of the character of one single individual! Would the masses succeed where greatest geniuses go astray? The people never find the time or the means to devote to this work. They have always to come to hasty judgments and to latch on to the most obvious of features. As a result, charlatans of all kinds know full well the secret of pleasing the people whereas more often than not their real friends fail to do so.

Moreover, it is not always the ability to choose men of merit   11 which democracy lacks but the desire and inclination to do so.

One must not blind oneself to the fact that democratic institu-   12 tions promote to a very high degree the feeling of envy in the human heart, not so much because they offer each citizen ways of being equal to each other but because these ways continuously prove inadequate for those who use them. Democratic institutions awaken and flatter the passion of equality without ever being able to satisfy it entirely. This complete equality every day slips through the people's fingers at the moment when they think they have a hold on it; it flees, as Pascal[1] says, in an eternal flight. The people become excited by the pursuit of this blessing, all the more priceless because it is near enough to be recognized but too far away to be tasted. The chance of success enthuses them; the uncertainty of success frustrates them. Their excitement is followed by weariness and bitterness. So anything which exceeds their limitations in any way appears to them as an obstacle to their desires and all superiority, however legitimate, is irksome to their eyes.

Many people suppose that this secret instinct which persuades   13
the lower classes to remove the upper classes as far as they can from the direction of affairs is found only in France; that is wrong. The instinct I am mentioning is not French, it is democratic; political circumstances may have given it a particularly bitter taste, but they do not bring it into being.

In the United States, the people have no especial hatred for the   14
upper classes of society; but they feel little goodwill for them and exclude them from power; they do not fear great talents but have little liking for them. Generally speaking, it is noticeable that anything which thrives without their support has trouble in winning their favor.

While the natural instincts of democracy persuade the people to   15
remove distinguished men from power, the latter are guided by no less an instinct to distance themselves from a political career, where it is so difficult for them to retain their complete autonomy or to make any progress without cheapening themselves. This thought is very naively expressed by Chancellor Kent. This celebrated author I speak of, having sung the praises of that part of the Constitution which grants the appointment of judges to the executive power, adds: "It is probable, in fact, that the most appropriate men to fill these places would have too much reserve in their manners and too much severity in their principles ever to be able to gather the majority of votes at an election that rested on universal suffrage." (Kent's *Commentaries on American Law,* vol. I, p. 273.)

That was what was being printed without contradiction in Amer-   16
ica in the year 1830.

I hold it proved that those who consider universal suffrage as a   17
guarantee of the excellence of the choice made are under a complete delusion. Universal suffrage has other advantages but not that one.

---

[1] **Blaise Pascal (1623–1662)** French mathematician and philosopher.

Causes Which Are Able Partly to Correct
These Instincts of Democracy

Contrary effects on nations as on men of great dangers—Why America saw so many men at the head of affairs fifty years ago—Influence of intelligence and customs upon the people's choices—Example of New England—States of the Southwest—Influence of certain laws upon the people's choices—Election by two stages—Its effect on the composition of the Senate.

When great dangers threaten the state, the people often make a   18
happy choice of those citizens best suited to save them.

It has been noticed that, in the face of imminent danger, a man   19
rarely remains at his normal level; he either rises well above himself or dips well below. The same happens to nations. Extreme dangers, instead of lifting a nation, sometimes end by bringing it low; they arouse its passions without giving them direction and confuse its perceptions without clarification. The Jews were still slitting each other's throats even in the midst of the smoking ruins of the Temple. But more commonly, with nations as with men, extraordinary courage arises from the very imminence of the dangers. Then great characters stand out like those monuments hidden by the darkness of the night and seen suddenly in the glare of a conflagration. Genius no longer disdains to appear on the stage and the people, alarmed by the dangers facing them, momentarily forget their envious passions. At such a time, it is not rare for famous names to emerge from the ballot box. I have said above that statesmen of modern America seem greatly inferior to those who appeared at the head of affairs fifty years ago. Circumstances, as well as laws, were responsible for that. When America was fighting the most just of causes, that of one nation escaping from another's yoke; when it was a question of introducing a new nation into the world, the spirits of all rose to reach the height of the goal to which their efforts aspired. In this general commotion, outstanding men anticipated the nation's call and the people embraced them and adopted them as their leaders. But such events take place at rare intervals and one must judge by the commonplace aspect of things.

If fleeting events sometimes succeed in checking the passions   20
aroused by democracy, the intelligence and customs of the community exercise a no less powerful but more lasting influence upon its inclinations. This is very obvious in the United States.

In New England, where education and freedom are the daugh-   21
ters of morality and religion, and where an already ancient and long-settled society has managed to shape its own maxims and customs, the people, while they have avoided all the superiorities which

wealth and birth have ever created among men, have become used to respecting intellectual and moral superiorities and to submit to them willingly. Therefore, New England democracy makes better choices than elsewhere.

On the other hand, as one goes further south to those states   22
where social ties are less ancient or less secure, where education is not so widespread and where the principles of morality, religion, and freedom are less happily combined, one observes that the aptitudes and virtues of government leaders are increasingly rare.

Lastly, when we get right down to the new states of the Southwest   23
where the body of society, formed yesterday, is still no more than a mass of adventurers and speculators, the observer is dismayed to see into what hands public authority has been entrusted and he wonders what force, independent of legislation and of men, will enable the state to grow and society to prosper.

Certain laws have a democratic character, yet succeed in correct-   24
ing partially democracy's dangerous instincts.

When you enter the House of Representatives in Washington,   25
you are struck by the coarse appearance of this great assembly. Your eye often seeks in vain a single famous man. Almost all its members are unknown people whose names fail to stimulate any mental picture. For the most part, they are village lawyers, businessmen or even men from the lowest classes. In a country where education is almost universal, it is claimed that the representatives of the people cannot always write correctly.

A couple of paces away lies the Senate whose narrow precincts   26
contain a large proportion of America's famous men. There is hardly a single man who does not recall some recent claim to fame. They are eloquent lawyers, distinguished generals, able magistrates, well-known politicians. All the speeches which emanate from this assembly would bring glory to the greatest parliamentary debates of Europe.

How does this curious contradiction come about? Why does the   27
nation's elite gather in this house rather than the other? Why does the first assembly attract so many coarse elements whereas the latter has a monopoly of talents and intelligence? Yet both spring from the people, both are the product of universal suffrage and no voice has so far been raised in America to maintain that the Senate might be antagonistic to popular interests. So how does such a wide difference arise? I know of only one explanation: the election for the House of Representatives is direct; the one for the Senate is in two stages. The whole citizen body appoints the legislature of each state and the federal constitution converts one by one these legislatures into electoral colleges, which return members to the Senate. Thus the senators represent, albeit indirectly, the result of universal suffrage, for the

legislature which appoints senators is not an aristocratic or privileged body deriving its electoral right from itself; it fundamentally depends upon the totality of citizens; it is generally elected by them every year and they are always able to control its choices by adding new members to its ranks. But it is enough that the will of the people has passed through this elected assembly for it to have become refined in some sense and to have emerged clad in a nobler and more beautiful form. Men thus elected, therefore, represent exactly the ruling majority of the nation but they represent only the highest concepts current in the community, the generous instincts which fire its imagination and not the petty emotions which trouble or the vices which disgrace it.

It is easy to see in the future a moment when American republics will be forced to extend the two tiers in their electoral system for fear of perishing wretchedly on the reefs of democracy.   28

I have no scruple in confessing that I see in the two-stage electoral system the only means of placing the advantage of political liberty within the reach of all classes of society. Anyone hoping to turn this means into the exclusive weapon of one party, or anyone fearing such an outcome, seems to me to be making an equal mistake.   29

Influence Which American Democracy has Exercised on Electoral Laws

Elections at long intervals expose the state to violent crises—Frequency of elections keeps up a feverish agitation—Americans have opted for the latter of these disadvantages—Versatility of the law—Opinions of Hamilton, Madison, and Jefferson on this topic.

When elections occur at long intervals, the state runs the risk of being overthrown each time. Then the parties make the utmost efforts to seize a prize which comes so rarely within their grasp and, since the outcome is almost beyond remedy for those candidates who lose, their ambition, pushed to the point of desperation, must be a source of fear. If, by contrast, the equal struggle is soon to be repeated, the losers retain their patience.   30

When elections follow in rapid succession, their frequency keeps society in a feverish excitement and public affairs in a continuous state of change.   31

Thus, on one side, the state risks the onset of unease or, on the other, revolution; the former system damages the quality of government, the latter threatens its existence.   32

Americans have preferred to risk the first of these evils to the second. In this choice they have been guided more by instinct than reason,   33 since democracy pushes its inclination for variety to the edge of passion and the consequence is a strange changeability of legislation.

Many Americans consider the instability of their laws as a neces-   34
sary result of a system whose general effects are useful. Yet there is no
one in the United States, I believe, who wishes to deny this instability
or who does not regard it as a great weakness.

Hamilton, having demonstrated the usefulness of a power which   35
has been able to prevent or, at least, to impede the promulgation of bad
laws, adds: "It may perhaps be said, that the power of preventing bad
laws includes that of preventing good ones, and may be used to the one
purpose as well as the other. But this objection will have little weight
with those who can properly estimate the mischiefs of that inconstancy
and mutability in the laws which form the greatest blemish in the character and genius of our governments." *Form the greatest blemish in the
character and genius of our government* (The Federalist, No. 73).

"The facility," says Madison, "and excess of law-making seem to   36
be the diseases to which our governments are most liable." (*The Federalist,* No. 62).

Jefferson himself, the greatest democrat to emerge from American   37
democracy, has highlighted the same dangers.

"The instability of our laws is really an immense evil," he says.   38
"I think it would be well to provide in our constitution that there shall
always be a twelve-month between the engrossing a bill and passing it:
that it should then be offered its passage without changing a word: and
that if its circumstances should be thought to require a speedier passage, it
should take two-thirds of both houses instead of a bare majority."[2]

Civil Servants under the Control of
American Democracy

*Simplicity of American civil servants—Absence of uniforms—All
officials are salaried—Political consequences of this fact—No public career
in America—Results of this.*

American civil servants remain indistinguishable from the mass   39
of the citizens; they have neither palaces nor guards, nor ceremonial
uniforms. This simple government attire does not stem simply from a
peculiar twist of the American character but from the basic principles
of their society.

In the eyes of democracy, the government is not a blessing but   40
a necessary evil. Some powers must be granted to civil servants

---

[2] **Letter to Madison of 20 December 1787,** M. Conseil's translation.
[Tocqueville's note]

for, without such power, what use would they be? But the external appearance of power is not vital for the conduct of affairs and is unnecessarily offensive to the public.

The civil servants themselves are perfectly aware that they have   41
gained the right to hold a superior position in relation to others, which they derive from their authority only if they place themselves on a level with the whole community through their way of life.

I can imagine no one plainer in his behavior, more approachable,   42
more sensitive to requests than an American civil servant.

I like this unself-conscious approach of democratic government   43
and I perceive something admirably manly in this inner strength which characterizes the office rather than the official, the man rather than the external symbols of power.

As for the influence that uniforms exert, I believe that the impor-   44
tance they have to carry in a century like ours is much exaggerated. I have not noticed American officials in the exercise of their authority greeted with any less respect or regard because they have nothing but their own merit to recommend them.

On the other hand, I very much doubt whether a special gar-   45
ment induces men in public life to respect themselves if they are not naturally disposed to do so, for I cannot believe that they have more regard for their clothes than their person.

When I see some of our magistrates harassing or indulging their   46
wit against litigants or shrugging their shoulders at the defense pleas or smiling smugly as the charges are listed, I should like to try to take their robes from them so as to find out whether, clothed as ordinary citizens, they might recall the natural dignity of the human race.

Not one American public official wears uniform but they all   47
receive a salary. This flows even more naturally than the preceding example from democratic principles. A democracy may surround its magistrates with pomp and cover them with gold and silk without directly compromising the principle of its existence. Such privileges are transitory and belong to the place not the man. But the creation of unpaid offices is to form a class of wealthy and independent officials; that is the core of an aristocracy. If the people still retain the right to choose, the exercise of that right has inevitable limitations.

Whenever a democratic republic converts salaried offices to unpaid   48
ones, I think one may conclude that it is veering toward monarchy. And whenever a monarchy begins to remunerate unpaid offices, it is a sure sign of progression toward a despotism or a republic.

I, therefore, think that to change from salaried to unpaid offices is   49
by itself the instigation of a real revolution.

The complete absence of unpaid offices is for me one of the   50
most obvious indications of the absolute sway American democracy

holds. Services of whatever kind rendered to the public are rewarded so that everyone has not only the right but also the means of performing such services.

If all the citizens of democratic states are able to take up office, 51 all are not tempted to canvas for them. The choice of the electorate is limited not by the qualifications for candidature but by the number and capability of the candidates.

In nations where the principle of election is universally applied, 52 properly speaking no public career exists. Men reach office to some degree by accident and have no guarantee of staying there. This is especially true with annual elections. The result is that in times of calm, public office offers little attraction to ambition. In the United States, men of moderate desires commit themselves to the twists and turns of politics. Men of great talent and passion in general avoid power to pursue wealth; it often comes about that only those who feel inadequate in the conduct of their own business undertake to direct the fortunes of the state.

These reasons, quite as much as any poor decisions of democracy, 53 have to account for the great number of coarse men holding public office. I do not know whether the people of the United States would choose men of superior qualities who might canvas their votes but it is certain that such men do not bid for office.

The Arbitrary Power of Magistrates[3] under the Sway of American Democracy

Why the arbitrary power of magistrates is greater under absolute monarchies and democratic republics than in limited monarchies— Arbitrary power of magistrates in New England.

Under two types of government, magistrates exercise consider- 54 able arbitrary power, namely, under the absolute government of a single individual and under that of democracy.

This same effect issues from almost analogous causes. 55

In despotisms, no one's fate is secure, whether they be public offi- 56 cials or ordinary individuals. The ruler, holding in his hand the lives, fortunes, and sometimes the honor of those he employs, believes he has nothing to fear from them and allows them great freedom of action because he feels sure they will never use it against him.

In despotisms, the ruler is so enamored of his power that he 57 fears the restrictions of his own regulations; he likes to see his agents

---

[3] Here I mean the word *magistrate* in its widest sense: I apply it to all entrusted with the execution of the law. [Tocqueville's note]

acting in an almost random manner so as to be assured that he will never observe in them any inclination which runs against his wishes.

In democracies, since the majority is able to remove power annually from the hands of those entrusted with it, it has no fear of any abuse against itself. Since the majority has the power to indicate its wishes to its rulers from moment to moment, it prefers to leave them to their own efforts rather than bind them to inflexible rules which, by fettering them, would, to some extent, fetter the majority itself.   58

Looking quite closely, one actually discovers that the arbitrary power of democratic magistrates is even greater than it would be in despotic states, where the ruler can punish at any time all the mistakes he perceives. But he could not possibly flatter himself that he has spotted every mistake he ought to punish. On the other hand, in democracies, the sovereign power is both all-powerful and present everywhere. Thus we see that American officials are much freer in the sphere of action allotted to them by law than any European counterpart. Often they are merely shown the goal to be reached while being left free to choose their own means.   59

In New England for example, the formation of the jury list is left to the selectmen of each township; the only rule imposed on them is as follows: they should choose juries from citizens who enjoy electoral rights and whose reputation is excellent.[4]   60

In France, we would consider the life and liberty of men to be in danger, if we entrusted the exercise of such a formidable right to an official, whoever he was.   61

In New England, these same magistrates are able to have the names of drunkards posted in taverns and to prevent the inhabitants of the town from supplying them with wine.[5]   62

Such a moralistic power would appall people in the most absolute of monarchies; here, however, people have no difficulty in obeying.   63

Nowhere has the law left greater scope to arbitrary power than in democratic republics because such power appears not to scare them.   64

---

[4]See the law of 27 February 1813 in the *General Collection of the Laws of Massachusetts,* vol. 2, p. 331. It must be added that the jurors are subsequently drawn by lot from the lists. [Tocqueville's note]

[5]Law of 28 February 1787, ibid., vol. 1, p. 302. Here is the text: "The selectmen in each town shall cause to be posted up in the houses and shops of all taverners, innholders, and retailers, within such towns, a list of the names of all persons reputed common drunkards, common tipplers, or common gamesters, misspending their time and estate in such houses. And every keeper of such house or shop, after notice given him, that shall be convicted before one or more Justices of the Peace, of entertaining or suffering any of the persons in such list, to drink or tipple, or game, in his or her house, or any of the dependencies thereof, or of selling them spiritous liquor, shall forfeit and pay the sum of thirty shillings." [Tocqueville's note]

It may even be said that magistrates become freer as voting rights are wider spread and the duration of the magistracy is shortened.

That is why it is so difficult to convert a democratic republic 65 into a monarchy. Though they are not elected, magistrates normally retain the rights and the habits of elected magistrates. That leads to despotism.

Only in limited monarchies does the law define the sphere of 66 action around public officials while at the same time taking care to guide their every step. This fact is easily explained.

In limited monarchies, power is divided between the people and 67 the prince. Both have a vested interest in the stability of magistrates.

The prince is unwilling to entrust the fate of public officials to the 68 hands of the people for fear that they betray his authority; the people, from their point of view, are afraid that magistrates, being absolutely dependent upon the prince, might serve to oppress their liberty; thus they are, in a sense, left dependent upon no one.

The same reason which persuades prince and people to make offi- 69 cials independent induces them to seek guarantees against the abuse of that independence so that they do not turn it against the authority of the former or the liberty of the latter. Both agree, therefore, upon the necessity of marking out, in advance, a line of conduct for public officials and find it in both their interests to impose upon these officials rules they cannot possibly disregard.

Administrative Instability in the United States

American society often leaves behind fewer records of its proceedings than a family does—Newspapers are the only historical monuments—How extreme administrative instability injures the art of government.

Men reach power for one brief moment before disappearing in a 70 crowd, which changes its appearance daily; the result is that the proceedings of American society often leave behind fewer records than a private family does. In a sense, public administration hands down its records via an oral tradition. Nothing is written or, if it is, it flies off in the slightest gust of wind like Sibylline leaves,[6] to vanish without recall.

The sole historical monuments in the United States are news- 71 papers. If one number is missing, the chain of events is, as it were, broken; the present and the past are no longer connected. I am quite certain that in fifty years time it will be more difficult to gather together authentic documents about the details of American social life than about the administration of medieval France. And if a barbarian invasion happened to take the United States by surprise,

---

[6] **Sibylline leaves:** A reference to the lost books of the Roman tracks, *The Sibylline Books.*

in order to find out anything about the people who lived there one would have to turn to the history of other nations.

Administrative instability has begun to permeate our thinking; I   72
might almost say that today everyone has ended up with a taste for it. No one has any concern for what happened before his time. No methodical system is in force; no collecting of material takes place; no documents are gathered together when it would be easy to do so. When by chance they are in someone's possession, little care is taken of them. Among my papers I have original documents given to me by public administrators to answer some of my inquiries. American society seems to live from hand to mouth like an army in the field. However, the skill of administration is assuredly a science and all sciences, in order to improve, need to group together the discoveries of the different generations as they follow each other. One man, in the brief span of his life, notes one fact, another conceives an idea; one man invents a method, another finds a formula; the human race collects en route these various fruits of individual experiments and formulates the sciences. It is difficult for American administrators to learn anything from each other. Thus they bring to the conduct of society the enlightenment which they discover widespread in that society and not the knowledge which should be their own. So democracy, pushed to the limits, damages the art of government. In this context, it is better suited to a nation whose administrative education is already complete than to a nation uninitiated in public affairs.

Moreover, this does not apply solely to the science of administra-   73
tion. Democratic government, founded upon such a simple and natural idea, nevertheless always implies the existence of a very civilized and educated society.[7] At first sight, it may be imagined as belonging to the earliest ages of the world; a closer examination allows us to discover that it had to come about last.

Public Expenses under the Rule of American Democracy

In all societies citizens divide into a certain number of classes — The instinct of each of these classes in the organization of state finances — Why public expenses must tend to increase when the people govern — What makes the extravagancies of democracy less of a fear in America — Use of public funds under a democracy.

Is democratic government economical? First we must know with   74
what we are comparing it.

The question would be easy to solve if we set out to draw a   75
parallel between a democratic republic and an absolute monarchy.

---

[7] I do not need to say that I am referring here to the democratic government which applies to a nation and not that which applies to a small tribe. [Tocqueville's note]

Public expenses would be much higher in the former than in the latter. But such is the case for all free states compared with those which are not so. Despotism certainly brings ruin to men, more by preventing them from producing than by taking away the fruits of their labors; it dries up the source of wealth while it often respects wealth once acquired. On the other hand, freedom spawns a thousand times more goods than it destroys and, in nations where this is understood, the people's resources always grow more quickly than taxes.

At present, I am concerned to compare nations which are free 76 and to establish the influence of democracy upon state finances in such nations.

Societies, like other organized bodies, are shaped by certain fixed 77 rules which they cannot sidestep and are made up of certain elements found in all places at all times.

It will always be simple to divide each nation theoretically into 78 three classes.

The first is composed of the wealthy. The second will include 79 those who are, in all respects, comfortably off without being wealthy. In the third are locked those who have only little or no property and who live primarily on the work provided by the first two.

The individuals in these various categories may be more or less 80 numerous according to the state of society, but it is impossible for these categories not to exist.

Each one of these classes will bring to the handling of state 81 finances certain instincts peculiar to itself.

Let us suppose that the first alone makes the laws; it will probably 82 concern itself but little with saving public money because a tax on a substantial fortune removes only part of the surplus without affecting it very much.

On the other hand, let us grant that the middle classes alone 83 make the law. You can count on it that they will not raise extravagant taxes because nothing is more disastrous than a heavy tax on a slight fortune.

Government by the middle classes has to be, I do not say the 84 most enlightened of free governments, nor especially the most generous, but the most economical.

Now, let me suppose that the lowest class is exclusively respon- 85 sible for making the law; I see clearly opportunities for an increase rather than a decrease in public expenditure for two reasons:

As most of the voters then have no taxable property, all the 86 money expended in the interests of society can only profit them without ever harming them; those who do have a little property easily find means of fixing taxes so as to fall upon the wealthy and to profit the poor; this is something the wealthy could not possibly pursue were they to be in charge of the government.

Countries where the poor[8] were exclusively responsible for law-   87
making could not therefore expect much economy in public expenses, which will always be extensive, either because taxes cannot touch those who vote for them or because they are assessed so as not to touch them. In other words, democratic government is the only one where those who vote for the tax can evade the obligation to pay it.

It is an empty objection to say that the interest of the people   88
properly understood is to be careful with the fortunes of the wealthy because it would soon feel an ensuing constriction itself. Is it not also to the advantage of kings to make their subjects happy and of the nobility to know when it is appropriate to open their ranks? If a distant advantage could prevail over the passions and needs of the passing moment, neither tyrannical rules nor exclusive aristocracies would ever have come into being.

Again, someone may stop me and say: Who has ever thought of   89
making the poor solely responsible for lawmaking? Who? Those who introduced universal suffrage. Does the majority or the minority make the law? The majority, of course; and if I demonstrate that the poor always make up the majority, am I not right to add that in countries where they have the vote, they alone make the law?

Now, certainly up to this time, in every nation of the world,   90
those with no property or those whose property was too modest to allow them to live comfortably without working always comprised the greatest number. Therefore, universal suffrage really does entrust the government of society to the poor.

The vexing influence occasionally exercised by the power of the   91
people on state finances was very evident in certain democratic republics of the ancient world in which the public treasury was drained away to help the poorest citizens or to provide the people with games and public spectacles. It is true that the representative system was almost unknown in the ancient world. Nowadays, popular passions find it more difficult to thrive in public affairs; however, you can guarantee that in the long run, the delegate will always in the end conform to the opinions of his constituents and support their inclinations as well as their interests.

However, the extravagancies of democracies are less a source of   92
dread as the people become increasingly property-owning because

---

[8] It should be understood that the word *poor* has here, as in the rest of the chapter, a relative meaning, not an absolute one. Poor men in America might often appear rich compared with their European counterparts; nevertheless one would be right to call them poor in comparison with those of their fellow citizens who are richer than they are. [Tocqueville's note]

then, on the one hand, the people need the money of the wealthy less, on the other, they will experience more difficulty in contriving a tax which will not touch the people themselves. In this respect, universal suffrage should be less dangerous in France than in England, where almost all taxable property is concentrated in a few hands. America enjoys a situation more favorable than France because the great majority of citizens own something.

Still more reasons exist for the possible increase of the financial 93 budget in democracies.

Under an aristocratic regime, those men who rule the affairs of 94 state are free from all need because of their own position in society; satisfied with their lot, they look to society for power and reputation; placed, as they are, above the dim mass of citizens, they do not always understand clearly how the general well-being must contribute to their own greatness. Not that they view the sufferings of the poor without pity; but they cannot feel their wretchedness as if they shared it themselves. Provided that the people appear to tolerate their lot, they themselves are satisfied and expect nothing more from the government. Aristocracy thinks more about preservation than improvement.

On the contrary, when public authority is in the hands of the 95 people, they, as the sovereign power, seek out improvements in every quarter because of their own discontent.

The spirit of improvement then infiltrates a thousand different 96 areas; it delves into endless detail and above all advocates those sorts of improvements which cannot be achieved without payment; for its concern is to better the condition of the poor who cannot help themselves.

Furthermore, an aimless restlessness permeates democratic socie- 97 ties where a kind of everlasting excitement stimulates all sorts of innovations which almost always involve expense.

In monarchies and aristocracies, the men of ambition flatter the 98 sovereign's normal taste for renown and power and thereby often drive him to spend a great deal of money.

In democracies where the sovereign power is always in need of 99 funds, its favors can hardly be won except by increasing its prosperity and that can almost never be achieved without money.

In addition, when the people start to reflect upon their own posi- 100 tion, a host of needs arise which they had not felt at first and which cannot be satisfied except by having recourse to state assets. The result is that public expenditure seems to increase with the growth of civilization and that taxes rise as knowledge spreads.

There is one final reason which often makes democratic govern- 101 ment more expensive than any other. Sometimes democracy aims to economize in its expenditure but fails to succeed because it has no skill in managing money. As it frequently changes its mind and still more frequently its agents, its enterprises are badly conducted or remain incomplete. Firstly, the state expends more than is warranted by the scope of the intended aim; secondly, its expenditure is unprofitable.

QUESTIONS FOR CRITICAL READING

1. Tocqueville was amazed "to what extent merit was common among the governed but rare among the rulers" (para. 7). Is this true today?

2. Tocqueville says, "The people could not possibly govern on their own" (para. 6). What in his essay would convince you that his statement is right or wrong?

3. What does Tocqueville say about the effect of universal suffrage on American democracy?

4. What was the role of newspapers in Tocqueville's time? Is it the same today?

5. How does Tocqueville describe civil servants?

6. Is Tocqueville correct when he says, "Whatever one does, it is impossible to raise the intelligence of a nation above a certain level" (para. 9)? What are his concerns about education in the 1830s?

7. What does Tocqueville think about rule by the majority in a democracy?

SUGGESTIONS FOR CRITICAL WRITING

1. Tocqueville feels all nations must contain three classes: the wealthy, whose fortunes are large; the comfortable, whose fortunes are small; and the poor, who have no fortune and must live by their labors alone. Does this breakdown reflect conditions today? How reasonable is Tocqueville's understanding of how these three groups would vote on taxation? Do you think that if it was true in Tocqueville's time it is true today? Would all three classes vote primarily for their own interests?

2. Tocqueville was disturbed by the fact that when he went into the House of Representatives he met no one who was famous or well-known. He felt that universal suffrage was responsible for that. He says that "it is not always the ability to choose men of merit which democracy lacks but the desire and inclination to do so" (para. 11). Do you agree with Tocqueville that universal suffrage works against choosing the most distinguished and accomplished candidate and toward choosing a mediocre candidate? What are his reasons for thinking so?

3. Because elected office is essentially insecure (one may lose an election), Tocqueville says that politics is not a calling that attracts the best men. As he puts it, "In the United States, men of moderate desires commit themselves to the twists and turns of politics. Men of great talent and passion in general avoid power to pursue wealth; it often comes about

that only those who feel inadequate in the conduct of their own business undertake to direct the fortunes of the state" (para. 52). Argue either for or against his position using examples from selections in this book or from your own studies and experience.

4. In the section that discusses civil servants (paras. 39–53), Tocqueville makes a number of statements that may be controversial. Examine that section and explain why he is concerned about the ways in which civil servants are or are not paid and how they present themselves to the general public in the American democracy. How valid do you feel his arguments are?

5. **CONNECTIONS** The framers of the Constitution as well as James Madison in "Federalist No. 51" were concerned with the effects of a pure democracy. Tocqueville is similarly concerned, and in paragraph 89 he asks, "Does the majority or the minority make the law?" What is his conclusion regarding this question and how does his analysis affect his thinking about taxation and the economic efficiency of a democracy? With what parts of Tocqueville's analysis would Madison take issue, and how would he correct his thinking? How well might Madison and Tocqueville have gotten along had they met?

6. In paragraph 72, while meditating on the failure of the new nation to preserve records of its past, Tocqueville says, "No one has any concern for what happened before his time." Explain what you think Tocqueville means by this statement and see if you can validate or invalidate his view by reference to other selections in Part One. Or consider his statement in light of current national circumstances and your own experience and your experiences with other citizens. Is this statement reasonable and reflective of the way people feel today? How concerned are you that it might be true?

7. **CONNECTIONS** Read Stephen Carter's "The Separation of Church and State" (**bedfordstmartins.com/worldofideas/epages**). Religious lobbyists in Washington, D.C. argue for laws that affect the entire population, such as the laws that now ban stem cell research that uses fetal cells. Should Carter consider such lobbying activity a breach of the separation of church and state? Why would he defend such activity? Given Tocqueville's respect for the American democracy he observed, how would he have reacted to the concept of lobbyists furthering religious interests in Congress? Elsewhere in *Democracy in America*, Tocqueville says, "Weird sects appear from time to time striving to open up extraordinary paths to eternal happiness. Religious insanity is very common in the United States" (Vol. 2; Ch. 12). Would Tocqueville be sympathetic to Carter's argument?

8. **SEEING CONNECTIONS** The figures standing in Howard Chandler Christy's painting of the signing of the U.S. Constitution (p. 57) in Philadelphia in 1787 are portrayed as they were almost fifty years before the publication of *Democracy in America*. Does Tocqueville seem to empathize with them? Does his view of democracy seem similar to theirs? Does he seem surprised that this group of men could have conceived of a democracy that functioned as it did in his time? What about it might have surprised him? What, if anything, about it surprised you?

CARL BECKER
Ideal Democracy

CARL LOTUS BECKER (1873–1945), a distinguished historian, was John Wendell Anderson Professor of History at Cornell University for most of his professional life. He was born in Iowa, in Black-hawk County, and studied at the University of Wisconsin – Madison, where he worked with one of the most distinguished and influential theorists of American history, Frederick Jackson Turner. Turner's theories about the effect of the frontier on shaping the development and character of the United States became central to the way historians viewed the nation's growth. Becker took his doctorate at Columbia University, where he worked with James Harvey Robinson, one of the founders of the movement known as "the new history."

The new history movement, of which Becker was one of the most notable members, broadened the meaning of history to include more than simply the political events of the past. The scientific, sociological, cultural, and intellectual achievements of society became central to historians as a result of Robinson's and Becker's work. Robinson and Becker established the New School for Social Research in New York City and Robinson became its first president.

Becker's early work focused on the beginnings of the U.S. experiment with democracy. He saw that the American Revolution was not only about independence but also about changing the basic form of government and abandoning the age-old institution of a king and court who governed without taking into account the will of the people. An early book, *The United States; an Experiment in Democracy* (1920), clarified his thinking on the nature of the Revolution and its purposes. He followed that with *The Declaration of Independence, a Study in the History of Political Ideas* (1922) and *The Struggle for Independence. Part 1: The Eve of the Revolution* (1926).

From *Modern Democracy.*

The next year he published *The Spirit of '76 and Other Essays,* with J. M. Clark and William E. Dodd.

Becker was president of the American Historical Association in 1931 when he delivered "Everyman His Own Historian," a speech that has resonated with historians ever since. In a very carefully reasoned discussion, Becker proposed a view that seemed heretical to most of his audience. What he suggested is that it is difficult to define history in a way that makes it as absolute and as specific as a fact. In his speech, he contrasts facts and interpretations of facts in such a manner so as to conclude that everyone brings personal values, opinions, commitments, and views to all history and, thus, everyone conceives of history in his or her own way. History, in other words, is not absolute, but relative. This was a revolutionary view, anticipating some of the postmodern thought of our own time.

While his scholarly work centered on the founding of the United States, especially the philosophical underpinnings of the signatories of the Declaration of Independence and their commitment to the values that are expressed in that document, Becker's best-known work is *The Heavenly City of the Eighteenth-Century Philosophers* (1932).

The founders of the United States—such as Jefferson, Adams, Franklin, Hamilton, and others—were themselves eighteenth-century thinkers, so Becker's analysis of the thought, political and otherwise, of the French and English philosophers who established reason as their guide was central to his lifelong concerns for the American experiment. When he delivered the lectures at Yale University that eventually became his book on eighteenth-century philosophers, the world faced many menaces. In 1932, the Great Depression threatened the fate of all capitalist nations. Communism on one side and fascism on another had both created dictatorships that endangered liberal thinkers everywhere. Both of these forces were vying for control of the political structure of the United States at the time of its greatest economic weakness.

Becker's intent in his book was to show how the philosophical roots of the American Revolution's determination to create a democracy were not only deep but also strong. The essentially humanistic thought of the eighteenth-century Enlightenment rejected the idea of a "city of God," as proposed in the Middle Ages, just as it rejected the idea of a golden age of Rome or Greece, as proposed in the Renaissance. The Enlightenment instead established reason as one's guide and a humanitarian principle as one's goal. *The Heavenly City of the Eighteenth-Century Philosophers* became widely known and is still read with considerable respect today.

"Ideal Democracy" is the first of three Page-Barbour lectures delivered at the University of Virginia in 1940 and gathered into a book simply titled *Modern Democracy* (1941). Faced with the prospect of a major European war, Becker had begun to rethink some of his positions as expressed in his speech to the American Historical Association and moved toward a less relativistic position. He felt that moral principles should be central to anyone's sense of history, just as they are central to anyone's conception of humanism. His views on ideal democracy are just that, ideal. He followed that lecture with others titled "The Reality" and "The Dilemma." He lived in difficult and threatening times, much like those of the eighteenth-century men who founded our nation.

Becker's Rhetoric

Becker uses a number of rhetorical approaches to clarify his views. The overarching technique is that of definition. His purpose in the entire lecture is to make evident the nature of democracy. He compares it with forms of government that depend on autocracy and the leadership of the few rather than the many. His definition of *democracy* concludes that "[a] democratic government has always meant one in which the citizens, or a sufficient number of them to represent more or less effectively the common will, freely act from time to time, and according to established forms, to appoint or recall the magistrates and to enact or revoke the laws by which the community is governed" (para. 5). But then, he ends Part I of the lecture with a cautionary observation about the fact that in "our time . . . democracy as thus defined has suffered an astounding decline in prestige" (para. 6). We suffer a rhetorical shock finding that once a definition has been produced we fear it may not define our present condition.

Among Becker's other devices is the rhetorical question. He asks at the end of Part I, "What are we to think of this sudden reversal in fortune and prestige? How explain it? What to do about it?" (para. 7). These are difficult questions and not necessarily answered by what follows. They are for us to ponder. Becker uses a form of enumeration by telling us that to survive, democracy needs certain conditions, each of which he describes for us: the need for communication (para. 11), economic security (para. 12), industrial prosperity (para. 13), ending by saying, "Democracy is in some sense an economic luxury" (para. 13). Added to these conditions, Becker reminds us that the citizens themselves must possess qualities that make democracy work: they must be "capable of managing their own affairs" (para. 14); be able to reconcile conflicts of interest; be rational; and, finally, be "men of goodwill."

A further rhetorical device Becker uses is comparison, as when he compares a modern democracy with a Greek city-state, such as Athens, the birthplace of modern democracy (para. 17). The comparison with a private association—which Athens is more like than is our nation—is crucial because the private association usually contains people of similar status, character, and ambitions because it is self-selective. In a Greek city-state, which was small by modern standards, the citizens were linked by ethnicity, clan, and family. But in a modern democracy diversity is the norm, especially in a nation such as the United States was when it was first born. Becker points out the general success of democracy in "new" countries, as opposed to countries like France, England, and Germany.

Using the topic circumstance, Becker reviews history in Part III of the lecture as a way of exploring the question of progress. He describes the inclination of people to postulate utopias, ideal worlds that contrast with the desperate reality they experience, a result, he says, of the pessimism that haunted pre-Christian Europe (para. 22). The achievement of the humanistic eighteenth century made the modern concept of progress possible. As he says, "the eighteenth-century world view, making man the measure of all things, mitigated if it did not destroy this sharp contrast between authority and obedience. God still reigned but he did not govern. He had, so to speak, granted his subjects a constitution and authorized them to interpret it as they would in the supreme court of reason" (para. 27).

Becker ends with testimonials from two authorities backing his basic views. First is a quotation from John Stuart Mill praising his own father's faith in reason as a guide to happiness (para. 30); that is followed by a comment from historian James Bryce clarifying his ideal democracy (para. 31).

It is not surprising that the very issues Becker worries over regarding an ideal democracy in 1941 are just as much of a concern today, despite the obvious changes in our material circumstances.

PREREADING QUESTIONS:
WHAT TO READ FOR

The following prereading questions may help you anticipate key issues in the discussion of Carl Becker's "Ideal Democracy." Keeping them in mind during your first reading of the selection should help focus your attention.

- What is Becker's fullest definition of *democracy*?
- What conditions are necessary for a democratic form of government to flourish?

- What qualities must citizens of a democracy possess if democracy is to take root and survive?

- What are the aims and goals of good government, and how do they relate to the idea of democracy?

Ideal Democracy

I

I often find it difficult, when invited to speak before a university audience, to hit upon a proper subject. But the invitation to deliver the Page-Barbour lectures at the University of Virginia relieved me of that difficulty: the invitation itself, automatically so to speak, conveniently laid the proper subject in my lap. For the University of Virginia is inseparably associated with the name of its famous founder; and no subject, it seemed to me, could be more appropriate for a historian on this occasion than one which had some connection with the ideas or the activities of Thomas Jefferson.

Even so, you will rightly think, I had a sufficiently wide choice. Jefferson entertained so many ideas, was engaged in so many activities! There was, indeed, scarcely anything of human interest that was alien to his curious and far-ranging intelligence. Nevertheless, his name is always associated with a certain general idea, a certain ideal. In devising his own epitaph, Jefferson himself selected, out of all his notable achievements, only three for which he wished to be especially remembered. *Here was buried Thomas Jefferson, author of the Declaration of American Independence, of the Statute of Virginia for Religious Freedom, and Father of the University of Virginia.* These were the things for which he wished to be remembered. Taken together and in their implications, they are the things for which he has been remembered: that is to say, they conveniently symbolize that way of looking at man and the life of man, that social philosophy, which we always think of when we think of him. The word which best denotes this social philosophy is democracy. I feel sure, therefore, that here, in this famous center of learning, you will not think it inappropriate for me to say something, something relevant if that be at all possible, about democracy—a subject so close to Jefferson's heart and so insistently present in all our minds today.

Democracy, like *liberty* or *science* or *progress*, is a word with which we are all so familiar that we rarely take the trouble to ask what we mean by it. It is a term, as the devotees of semantics say, which has no "referent"—there is no precise or palpable thing or object which we all think of when the word is pronounced. On the contrary, it is a word which connotes different things to different people, a kind of conceptual Gladstone bag which, with a little manipulation, can be made to accommodate almost any collection of social facts we may wish to carry about in it. In it we can as easily pack a dictatorship as any other form of government. We have only to stretch the concept to include any form of government supported by a majority of the people, for whatever reasons and by whatever means of expressing assent, and before we know it the empire of Napoleon, the Soviet regime of Stalin, and the Fascist systems of Mussolini and Hitler are all safely in the bag. But if this is what we mean by democracy, then virtually all forms of government are democratic, since virtually all governments, except in times of revolution, rest upon the explicit or implicit consent of the people. In order to discuss democracy intelligently it will be necessary, therefore, to define it, to attach to the word a sufficiently precise meaning to avoid the confusion which is not infrequently the chief result of such discussions.

All human institutions, we are told, have their ideal forms   4
laid away in heaven, and we do not need to be told that the actual institutions conform but indifferently to these ideal counterparts. It would be possible then to define democracy either in terms of the ideal or in terms of the real form—to define it as government of the people, by the people, for the people; or to define it as government of the people, by the politicians, for whatever pressure groups can get their interests taken care of. But as a historian I am naturally disposed to be satisfied with the meaning which, in the history of politics, men have commonly attributed to the word—a meaning, needless to say, which derives partly from the experience and partly from the aspirations of mankind. So regarded, the term democracy refers primarily to a form of government, and it has always meant government by the many as opposed to government by the one—government by the people as opposed to government by a tyrant, a dictator, or an absolute monarch. This is the most general meaning of the word as men have commonly understood it.

In this antithesis there are, however, certain implications, always   5
tacitly understood, which give a more precise meaning to the term. Peisistratus,[1] for example, was supported by a majority of the people, but his government was never regarded as a democracy for all that. Caesar's power derived from a popular mandate, conveyed

---

[1] **Peisistratus (605–525 B.C.E.)** In 560 B.C.E. made himself the tyrant of Athens.

through established republican forms, but that did not make his government any the less a dictatorship. Napoleon called his government a democratic empire, but no one, least of all Napoleon himself, doubted that he had destroyed the last vestiges of the democratic republic. Since the Greeks first used the term, the essential test of democratic government has always been this: the source of political authority must be and remain in the people and not in the ruler. A democratic government has always meant one in which the citizens, or a sufficient number of them to represent more or less effectively the common will, freely act from time to time, and according to established forms, to appoint or recall the magistrates and to enact or revoke the laws by which the community is governed. This I take to be the meaning which history has impressed upon the term democracy as a form of government. It is, therefore, the meaning which I attach to it in these lectures.

The most obvious political fact of our time is that democracy 6 as thus defined has suffered an astounding decline in prestige. Fifty years ago it was not impossible to regard democratic government, and the liberties that went with it, as a permanent conquest of the human spirit. In 1886 Andrew Carnegie[2] published a book entitled *Triumphant Democracy*. Written without fear and without research, the book was not an achievement of the highest intellectual distinction perhaps; but the title at least expressed well enough the prevailing conviction — the conviction that democracy had fought the good fight, had won the decisive battles, and would inevitably, through its inherent merits, presently banish from the world the most flagrant political and social evils which from time immemorial had afflicted mankind. This conviction could no doubt be most easily entertained in the United States, where even the tradition of other forms of government was too remote and alien to color our native optimism. But even in Europe the downright skeptics, such as Lecky,[3] were thought to be perverse, and so hardheaded a historian as J. B. Bury[4] could proclaim with confidence that the long struggle for freedom of thought had finally been won.

I do not need to tell you that within a brief twenty years the pre- 7 vailing optimism of that time has been quite dispelled. One European country after another has, willingly enough it seems, abandoned whatever democratic institutions it formerly enjoyed for some form of

---

[2] **Andrew Carnegie (1835–1919)** Scotch-born steel magnate, once the richest man in the world.
[3] **William Edward Hartpole Lecky (1838–1903)** Prominent Irish historian.
[4] **J. B. Bury (1861–1927)** Another prominent Irish historian.

dictatorship. The spokesmen of Fascism and Communism announce with confidence that democracy, a sentimental aberration which the world has outgrown, is done for; and even the friends of democracy support it with declining conviction. They tell us that democracy, so far from being triumphant, is "at the cross roads" or "in retreat," and that its future is by no means assured. What are we to think of this sudden reversal in fortune and prestige? How explain it? What to do about it?

II

One of the presuppositions of modern thought is that institu-   8
tions, in order to be understood, must be seen in relation to the conditions of time and place in which they appear. It is a little difficult
for us to look at democracy in this way. We are so immersed in its
present fortunes that we commonly see it only as a "close-up," filling the screen to the exclusion of other things to which it is in fact
related. In order to form an objective judgment of its nature and significance, we must therefore first of all get it in proper perspective. Let
us then, in imagination, remove from the immediate present scene to
some cool high place where we can survey at a glance five or six thousand years of history, and note the part which democracy has played
in human civilization. The view, if we have been accustomed to take
democratic institutions for granted, is a bit bleak and disheartening.
For we see at once that in all this long time, over the habitable globe,
the great majority of the human race has neither known nor apparently much cared for our favorite institutions.

Civilization was already old when democracy made its first   9
notable appearance among the small city-states of ancient Greece,
where it flourished brilliantly for a brief century or two and then
disappeared. At about the same time something that might be called
democracy appeared in Rome and other Italian cities, but even in
Rome it did not survive the conquest of the world by the Roman
Republic, except as a form of local administration in the cities of
the empire. In the twelfth and thirteenth centuries certain favorably
placed medieval cities enjoyed a measure of self-government, but in
most instances it was soon replaced by the dictatorship of military
conquerors, the oligarchic control of a few families, or the encroaching power of autocratic kings. The oldest democracy of modern times is the Swiss Confederation, the next oldest is the Dutch
Republic. Parliamentary government in England does not antedate
the late seventeenth century, the great American experiment is
scarcely older. Not until the nineteenth century did democratic government make its way in any considerable part of the world — in the

great states of continental Europe, in South America, in Canada and Australia, in South Africa and Japan.

From this brief survey it is obvious that, taking the experience of mankind as a test, democracy has as yet had but a limited and temporary success. There must be a reason for this significant fact. The reason is that democratic government is a species of social luxury, at best a delicate and precarious adventure which depends for success upon the validity of certain assumptions about the capacities and virtues of men, and upon the presence of certain material and intellectual conditions favorable to the exercise of these capacities and virtues. Let us take the material conditions first.

It is a striking fact that until recently democracy never flourished except in very small states — for the most part in cities. It is true that in both the Persian and the Roman empires a measure of self-government was accorded to local communities, but only in respect to purely local affairs; in no large state as a whole was democratic government found to be practicable. One essential reason is that until recently the means of communication were too slow and uncertain to create the necessary solidarity of interest and similarity of information over large areas. The principle of representation was well enough known to the Greeks, but in practice it proved impracticable except in limited areas and for special occasions. As late as the eighteenth century it was still the common opinion that the republican form of government, although the best ideally, was unsuited to large countries, even to a country no larger than France. This was the view of Montesquieu,[5] and even of Rousseau.[6] The view persisted into the nineteenth century, and English conservatives, who were opposed to the extension of the suffrage in England, consoled themselves with the notion that the American Civil War would confirm it — would demonstrate that government by and for the people would perish, if not from off the earth at least from large countries. If their hopes were confounded the reason is that the means of communication, figuratively speaking, were making large countries small. It is not altogether fanciful to suppose that, but for the railroad and the telegraph, the United States would today be divided into many small republics maneuvering for advantage and employing war and diplomacy for maintaining an unstable balance of power.

If one of the conditions essential to the success of democratic government is mobility, ease of communication, another is a certain

10

11

12

---

[5] **Montesquieu (1689–1755)** Important French thinker of the Enlightenment.

[6] **Jean-Jacques Rousseau (1712–1778)** French philosopher and political thinker of the Enlightenment (see p. 237).

measure of economic security. Democracy does not flourish in communities on the verge of destitution. In ancient and medieval times democratic government appeared for the most part in cities, the centers of prosperity. Farmers in the early Roman Republic and in the Swiss Cantons were not wealthy to be sure, but equality of possessions and of opportunity gave them a certain economic security. In medieval cities political privilege was confined to the prosperous merchants and craftsmen, and in Athens and the later Roman Republic democratic government was found to be workable only on condition that the poor citizens were subsidized by the government or paid for attending the assemblies and the law courts.

In modern times democratic institutions have, generally speaking, been most successful in new countries, such as the United States, Canada, and Australia, where the conditions of life have been easy for the people; and in European countries more or less in proportion to their industrial prosperity. In European countries, indeed, there has been a close correlation between the development of the industrial revolution and the emergence of democratic institutions. Holland and England, the first countries to experience the industrial revolution, were the first also (apart from Switzerland, where certain peculiar conditions obtained) to adopt democratic institutions; and as the industrial revolution spread to France, Belgium, Germany, and Italy, these countries in turn adopted at least a measure of democratic government. Democracy is in some sense an economic luxury, and it may be said that in modern times it has been a function of the development of new and potentially rich countries, or of the industrial revolution which suddenly dowered Europe with unaccustomed wealth. Now that prosperity is disappearing round every next corner, democracy works less well than it did.

So much for the material conditions essential for the success of democratic government. Supposing these conditions to exist, democratic government implies in addition the presence of certain capacities and virtues in its citizens. These capacities and virtues are bound up with the assumptions on which democracy rests, and are available only insofar as the assumptions are valid. The primary assumption of democratic government is that its citizens are capable of managing their own affairs. But life in any community involves a conflict of individual and class interests, and a corresponding divergence of opinion as to the measures to be adopted for the common good. The divergent opinions must be somehow reconciled, the conflict of interests somehow compromised. It must then be an assumption of democratic government that its citizens are rational creatures, sufficiently so at least to understand the interests in conflict; and it must be an assumption that they are men of goodwill, sufficiently so toward each other at least to make those concessions of individual and class interest required for effecting workable compromises. The citizens of a democracy should be, as Pericles[7] said the citizens of Athens were, if not all originators at least all sound judges of good policy.

These are what may be called the minimum assumptions and the necessary conditions of democratic government anywhere and at any time. They may be noted to best advantage, not in any state, but in small groups within the state—in clubs and similar private associations of congenial and like-minded people united for a specific purpose. In such associations the membership is limited and select. The members are, or may easily become, all acquainted with each other. Everyone knows, or may easily find out, what is being done and who is doing it. There will of course be differences of opinion, and there may be disintegrating squabbles and intrigues. But on the whole, ends and means being specific and well understood, the problems of government are few and superficial; there is plenty of time for discussion; and since intelligence and goodwill can generally be taken for granted there is the disposition to make reasonable concessions and compromises. The analogy must be taken for what it is worth. States may not be the mystical blind Molochs[8] of German philosophy, but any state is far more complex and intangible than a private association, and there is little resemblance between such associations and the democracies of modern times. Other things equal, the resemblance is closest in very small states, and it is in connection with the small city-states of ancient Greece that the resemblance can best be noted.

The Greek states were limited in size, not as is often thought solely or even chiefly by the physiography of the country, but by some instinctive feeling of the Greek mind that a state is necessarily a natural association of people bound together by ties of kinship and a common tradition of rights and obligations. There must then, as Aristotle said, be a limit.

> For if the citizens of a state are to judge and distribute offices according to merit, they must know each other's characters; where they do not possess this knowledge, both the elections to offices and the decisions in the law courts will go wrong. Where the population is very large they are manifestly settled by haphazard, which clearly ought not to be. Besides, in overpopulous states foreigners and metics[9] will readily acquire citizenship, for who will find them out?

---

[7] **Pericles (c. 495–429 B.C.E.)** Athenian hero of the Peloponnesian War and builder of the Acropolis.

[8] **Molochs** The forces of evil that demand obedience.

[9] **metics** Resident aliens.

15

16

It obviously did not occur to Aristotle that metics and for-   17
eigners should be free to acquire citizenship. It did not occur to
him, or to any Greek of his time, or to the merchants of the self-
governing medieval city, that a state should be composed of all the
people inhabiting a given territory. A state was rather an incorporated body of people within, but distinct from, the population of
the community.

Ancient and medieval democracies had thus something of the   18
character of a private association. They were, so to speak, purely
pragmatic phenomena, arising under very special conditions, and
regarded as the most convenient way of managing the affairs of people bound together by community of interest and for the achievement
of specific ends. There is no suggestion in Aristotle that democracy
(polity) is intrinsically a superior form of government, no suggestion that it derives from a special ideology of its own. If it rests upon
any superiority other than convenience, it is the superiority which it
shares with any Greek state, that is to say, the superiority of Greek
over barbarian civilization. In Aristotle's philosophy it is indeed difficult to find any clear-cut distinction between the democratic form of
government and the state itself; the state, if it be worthy of the name,
is always, whatever the form of government, "the government of freemen and equals," and in any state it is always necessary that "the freemen who compose the bulk of the people should have absolute power
in some things." In Aristotle's philosophy the distinction between
good and bad in politics is not between good and bad types of government, but between the good and bad form of each type. Any type of
government—monarchy, aristocracy, polity—is good provided the
rulers aim at the good of all rather than at the good of the class to
which they belong. From Aristotle's point of view neither democracy
nor dictatorship is good or bad in itself, but only in the measure that
it achieves, or fails to achieve, the aim of every good state, which is
that "the inhabitants of it should be happy." It did not occur to Aristotle that democracy (polity), being in some special sense in harmony
with the nature of man, was everywhere applicable, and therefore destined by fate or the gods to carry throughout the world a superior
form of civilization.

It is in this respect chiefly that modern democracy differs from   19
earlier forms. It rests upon something more than the minimum
assumptions. It is reinforced by a full-blown ideology which, by
endowing the individual with natural and imprescriptible rights, sets
the democratic form of government off from all others as the one
which alone can achieve the good life. What then are the essential
tenets of the modern democratic faith?

III

The liberal democratic faith, as expressed in the works of   20
eighteenth- and early nineteenth-century writers, is one of the formu-
lations of the modern doctrine of progress. It will be well, therefore,
to note briefly the historical antecedents of that doctrine.

In the long history of man on earth there comes a time when   21
he remembers something of what has been, anticipates something
that will be, knows the country he has traversed, wonders what
lies beyond — the moment when he becomes aware of himself as a
lonely, differentiated item in the world. Sooner or later there emerges
for him the most devastating of all facts, namely, that in an indifferent universe which alone endures, he alone aspires, endeavors to
attain, and attains only to be defeated in the end. From that moment
his immediate experience ceases to be adequate, and he endeavors
to project himself beyond it by creating ideal worlds of semblance,
Utopias of other time or place in which all has been, may be, or will
be well.

In ancient times Utopia was most easily projected into the   22
unknown past, pushed back to the beginning of things — to the time
of P'an Ku[10] and the celestial emperors, to the Garden of Eden, or
the reign of King Chronos[11] when men lived like gods free from toil
and grief. From this happy state of first created things there had obviously been a decline and fall, occasioned by disobedience and human
frailty, and decreed as punishment by fate or the angry gods. The
mind of man was therefore afflicted with pessimism, a sense of guilt
for having betrayed the divine purpose, a feeling of inadequacy for
bringing the world back to its original state of innocence and purity.
To men who felt insecure in a changing world, and helpless in a world
always changing for the worse, the future had little to offer. It could
be regarded for the most part only with resignation, mitigated by individual penance or well doing, or the hope of some miraculous intervention by the gods, or the return of the godlike kings, to set things
right again, yet with little hope that from this setting right there would
not be another falling away.

This pervasive pessimism was gradually dispelled in the West-   23
ern world, partly by the Christian religion, chiefly by the secular
intellectual revolution occurring roughly between the fifteenth and
the eighteenth centuries. The Christian religion gave assurance that
the lost golden age of the past would be restored for the virtuous in

---

[10] **P'an Ku** The first man in Chinese Taoist creation myths.
[11] **King Chronos** King of the lost island of Atlantis, according to Greek legend.

the future, and by proclaiming the supreme worth of the individual in the eyes of God enabled men to look forward with hope to
the good life after death in the Heavenly City. Meantime, the secular intellectual revolution, centering in the matter-of-fact study of
history and science, gradually emancipated the minds of men from
resignation to fate and the angry gods. Accumulated knowledge of
history, filling in time past with a continuous succession of credible
events, banished all lost golden ages to the realm of myth, and enabled men to live without distress in a changing world since it could
be regarded as not necessarily changing for the worse. At the same
time, a more competent observation and measurement of the action
of material things disclosed an outer world of nature, indifferent to
man indeed, yet behaving, not as the unpredictable sport of the gods,
but in ways understandable to human reason and therefore ultimately
subject to man's control.

Thus the conditions were fulfilled which made it possible for   24
men to conceive of Utopia, neither as a lost golden age of the past
nor as a Heavenly City after death prepared by the gods for the virtuous, but as a future state on earth of man's own devising. In a
world of nature that could be regarded as amenable to man's control, and in a world of changing social relations that need not be
regarded as an inevitable decline and fall from original perfection,
it was possible to formulate the modern doctrine of progress: the
idea that, by deliberate intention and rational direction, men can set
the terms and indefinitely improve the conditions of their mundane
existence.

The eighteenth century was the moment in history when men   25
first fully realized the engaging implications of this resplendent
idea, the moment when, not yet having been brought to the harsh
appraisal of experience, it could be accepted with unclouded optimism. Never had the universe seemed less mysterious, more open
and visible, more eager to yield its secrets to commonsense questions. Never had the nature of man seemed less perverse, or the
mind of man more pliable to the pressure of rational persuasion.
The essential reason for this confident optimism is that the marvels
of scientific discovery disclosed to the men of that time a God who
still functioned but was no longer angry. God the Father could be
conceived as a beneficent First Cause who, having performed his
essential task of creation, had withdrawn from the affairs of men,
leaving them competently prepared and fully instructed for the task
of achieving their own salvation. In one tremendous sentence Rousseau expressed the eighteenth-century worldview of the universe
and man's place in it. "Is it simple," he exclaimed, "is it natural that

God should have gone in search of Moses in order to speak to Jean-Jacques Rousseau?"

God had indeed spoken to Rousseau, he had spoken to all men, 26 but his revelation was contained, not in Holy Writ interpreted by Holy Church, but in the great Book of Nature which was open for all men to read. To this open book of nature men would go when they wanted to know what God had said to them. Here they would find recorded the laws of nature and of nature's God, disclosing a universe constructed according to a rational plan; and that men might read these laws aright they had been endowed with reason, a bit of the universal intelligence placed within the individual to make manifest to him the universal reason implicit in things and events. "Natural law," as Volney[12] so clearly and confidently put it, "is the regular and constant order of facts by which God rules the universe; the order which his wisdom presents to the sense and reason of men, to serve them as an equal and common rule of conduct, and to guide them, without distinction of race or sect, toward perfection and happiness." Thus God had devised a planned economy, and had endowed men with the capacity for managing it: to bring his ideas, his conduct, and his institutions into harmony with the universal laws of nature was man's simple allotted task.

At all times political theory must accommodate itself in some 27 fashion to the prevailing worldview, and liberal-democratic political theory was no exception to this rule. From time immemorial authority and obedience had been the cardinal concepts both of the prevailing worldview and of political and social theory. From time immemorial men had been regarded as subject to overruling authority—the authority of the gods, and the authority of kings who were themselves gods, or descended from gods, or endowed with divine authority to rule in place of gods; and from time immemorial obedience to such divine authority was thought to be the primary obligation of men. Even the Greeks, who were so little afraid of their gods that they could hobnob with them in the most friendly and engaging way, regarded mortals as subject to them; and when they lost faith in the gods they deified the state as the highest good and subordinated the individual to it. But the eighteenth-century worldview, making man the measure of all things, mitigated if it did not destroy this sharp contrast between authority and obedience. God still reigned but he did not govern. He had, so

---

[12] **Constantin-François de Chasseboeuf, comte de Volney (1757–1820)** French philosopher and historian.

to speak, granted his subjects a constitution and authorized them to interpret it as they would in the supreme court of reason. Men were still subject to an overruling authority, but the subjection could be regarded as voluntary because self-imposed, and self-imposed because obedience was exacted by nothing more oppressive than their own rational intelligence.

Liberal-democratic political theory readily accommodated itself to this change in the worldview. The voice of the people was now identified with the voice of God, and all authority was derived from it. The individual instead of the state or the prince was now deified and endowed with imprescriptible rights; and since ignorance or neglect of the rights of man was the chief cause of social evils, the first task of political science was to define these rights, the second to devise a form of government suited to guarantee them. The imprescriptible rights of man were easily defined, since they were self-evident: "All men are created equal, [and] are endowed by their Creator with certain inalienable rights, among which are life, liberty, and the pursuit of happiness." From this it followed that all just governments would remove those artificial restraints which impaired these rights, thereby liberating those natural impulses with which God had endowed the individual as a guide to thought and conduct. In the intellectual realm, freedom of thought and the competition of diverse opinion would disclose the truth, which all men, being rational creatures, would progressively recognize and willingly follow. In the economic realm, freedom of enterprise would disclose the natural aptitudes of each individual, and the ensuing competition of interests would stimulate effort, and thereby result in the maximum of material advantage for all. Liberty of the individual from social constraint thus turned out to be not only an inherent natural right but also a preordained natural mechanism for bringing about the material and moral progress of mankind. Men had only to follow reason and self-interest: something not themselves, God and Nature, would do whatever else was necessary for righteousness. 28

Thus modern liberal-democracy is associated with an ideology which rests upon something more than the minimum assumptions essential to any democratic government. It rests upon a philosophy of universally valid ends and means. Its fundamental assumption is the worth and dignity and creative capacity of the individual, so that the chief aim of government is the maximum of individual self-direction, the chief means to that end the minimum of compulsion by the state. Ideally considered, means and ends are conjoined in the concept of freedom: freedom of thought, so that the truth may prevail; freedom of occupation, so that careers may be open to talent; 29

freedom of self-government, so that no one may be compelled against his will.

In the possibility of realizing this ideal the prophets and pro- 30 tagonists of democracy exhibited an unquestioned faith. If their faith seems to us somewhat naive, the reason is that they placed a far greater reliance upon the immediate influence of goodwill and rational discussion in shaping the conduct of men than it is possible for us to do. This difference can be conveniently noted in a passage from the *Autobiography* of John Stuart Mill,[13] in which he describes his father's extraordinary faith in two things — representative government and complete freedom of discussion.

> So complete was my father's reliance on the influence of reason over the minds of mankind, whenever it was allowed to reach them, that he felt as if all would be gained if the whole population were taught to read, if all sorts of opinions were allowed to be addressed to them by word and writing, and if by means of the suffrage they could nominate a legislature to give effect to the opinions they adopted. He thought that when the legislature no longer represented a class interest, it would aim at the general interest, honestly and with adequate wisdom; since the people would be sufficiently under the guidance of educated intelligence, to make in general good choice of persons to represent them, and having done so to leave to those whom they had chosen a liberal discretion. Accordingly, aristocratic rule, the government of the few in any of its shapes, being in his eyes the only thing that stood between mankind and the administration of its affairs by the best wisdom to be found amongst them, was the object of his sternest disapprobation, and a democratic suffrage the principle article of his political creed.[14]

The beliefs of James Mill were shared by the little group of Phil- 31 osophical Radicals who gathered about him. They were, indeed, the beliefs of all those who in the great crusading days placed their hopes in democratic government as a panacea for injustice and oppression. The actual working of democratic government, as these devoted enthusiasts foresaw it, the motives that would inspire men and the objects they would pursue in that ideal democracy which so many honest men have cherished and fought for, have never been better

---

[13] **John Stuart Mill (1806–1873)** English philosopher and champion of utilitarianism, which aims to provide the greatest good to the greatest number.

[14] *Autobiography* (Columbia Press, 1924), p. 74. [Becker's note]

described than by James Bryce[15] in his *Modern Democracies*. In this ideal democracy, says Bryce,

> the average citizen will give close and constant attention to public affairs, recognizing that this is his interest as well as his duty. He will try to comprehend the main issues of policy, bringing to them an independent and impartial mind, which thinks first not of its own but of the general interest. If, owing to inevitable differences of opinion as to what are the measures needed for the general welfare, parties become inevitable, he will join one, and attend its meetings, but will repress the impulses of party spirit. Never failing to come to the polls, he will vote for his party candidate only if satisfied by his capacity and honesty. He will be ready to . . . be put forward as a candidate for the legislature (if satisfied of his own competence), because public service is recognized as a duty. With such citizens as electors, the legislature will be composed of upright and capable men, single-minded in their wish to serve the nation. Bribery in constituencies, corruption among public servants, will have disappeared. Leaders may not always be single-minded, nor assemblies always wise, nor administrators efficient, but all will be at any rate honest and zealous, so that an atmosphere of confidence and good will will prevail. Most of the causes that make for strife will be absent, for there will be no privileges, no advantages to excite jealousy. Office will be sought only because it gives opportunity for useful public service. Power will be shared by all, and a career open to all alike. Even if the law does not — perhaps it cannot — prevent the accumulation of fortunes, these will be few and not inordinate, for public vigilance will close the illegitimate paths to wealth. All but the most depraved persons will obey and support the law, feeling it to be their own. There will be no excuse for violence, because the constitution will provide a remedy for every grievance. Equality will produce a sense of human solidarity, will refine manners, and increase brotherly kindness.[16]

Such is the ideal form of modern democracy laid away in 32 heaven. I do not need to tell you that its earthly counterpart resembles it but slightly. In the next lecture I shall discuss some of the circumstances that brought about so flagrant a discord between democracy as it was ideally projected and democracy as it actually functions today.

---

[15] **James Bryce (1838–1922)** Irish historian who was a trustee for the Carnegie trust in Scotland.

[16] I, 48. [Becker's note]

QUESTIONS FOR CRITICAL READING

1. Becker says freedom of thought and the competition of diverse opinions will reveal the truth. How important is such freedom of thought and diversity for the survival of a democracy?

2. If a primary assumption in a democracy is that people should be capable of managing their own affairs, what is a government's responsibility to those citizens who cannot do so?

3. From what you can tell of contemporary history, how important is "industrial prosperity" to the flourishing of democracy?

4. Most humans never experienced democracy and many today do not aspire to democracy. To what extent does that bring the concept of democracy into question?

5. In paragraph 3, Becker talks about "varieties" of democracies, including fascist Germany and the Soviet "regime of Stalin." These governments seem to have been supported by a majority of their citizens. Were they then true democracies?

6. How true is it that "virtually all forms of government are democratic, since virtually all governments, except in times of revolution, rest upon the explicit or implicit consent of the people" (para. 3)?

7. Does the concept of an ideal democracy need to be viewed in relation to a specific time and place, such as our own time and place? If so, what contemporary issues help us define *democracy* differently from, say, Becker's definition?

8. Becker says that, given the circumstances of history, democracy "has as yet had but a limited and temporary success" (para. 10). What do you feel he means by this statement?

SUGGESTIONS FOR CRITICAL WRITING

1. Becker talks about the problems of the limitations of communication as having inhibited early democracies and having limited them to small self-contained city-states. How has the vast improvement in communications—by means of radio, television, cell phones, instant video, and print media—helped expand the concept of democracy and make it possible on a global scale? Consider the effect of the Internet and the blogosphere on spreading or maintaining democracy in movements such as the Arab Spring. Will modern communications systems make democracy more widespread? Why?

2. Becker says, "Democracy does not flourish in communities on the verge of destitution" (para. 12). Examine the reports in a major newspaper or newsmagazine and see to what extent your research validates

or invalidates this view. Decide whether or not Becker's judgment is accurate or merely prejudiced against desperately poor communities.

3. The question of whether or not democracy has suffered a decline in prestige is still relevant, even though the times in which Becker wrote were quite different from ours. If you think that democracy has suffered a further decline in prestige, write a brief essay that sets out your views on why it has done so. If possible, suggest some ways in which democracy could restore its prestige in the world. If you feel Becker is too pessimistic and that democracy is more prestigious now than when he wrote, defend that position. Try using some of Becker's rhetorical devices: comparison, testimony, and definition.

4. Carefully examine Becker's lecture and consider each effort he makes to come to a satisfactory definition of *democracy*. How many separate definitions do you find, and how do they differ from one another? Using Becker's lecture as a starting point, and taking into account that more than sixty years have elapsed since he gave it, offer your own definition of *democracy*. Use examples from the way you see democracy working today in different countries and different situations. Do you find democracy at work in the institutions you have a daily experience with, such as church, school, businesses, corporations, and clubs?

5. In paragraphs 8, 9, and 10, Becker reviews the historical record concerning the existence and success of democracy over a considerable sweep of history. He concludes that democracy has had a "limited and temporary success." After considering his ideas, do you feel that democracy may in fact become unsuccessful again, as it did in Athens? Why should you or any citizen fear that democracy might fail? What might be done to help prevent such a failure?

6. **CONNECTIONS**   Andrew Carnegie in "The Gospel of Wealth" (p. 481) would praise Becker's view that suggests democracy would not work in a destitute society. To what extent would Carnegie agree with Becker about the virtue and character of democracy? How might Carnegie wish to amend any of Becker's definitions? Becker was a noted liberal and Carnegie a noted conservative. How do their views affect their respective attitudes toward the ideal of democracy? Carnegie is mentioned specifically by Becker in paragraph 6, so it is clear that Becker took Carnegie's views into consideration.

7. **CONNECTIONS**   How would Stephen Carter (**bedfordstmartins .com/worldofideas/epages**) have regarded the concept of separation of church and state in Becker's concept of an ideal democracy? Like Aristotle, Becker says little about religion. Why would these thinkers omit such a serious subject? In what ways might an ideal democracy be threatened by powerful religious interests? Or, in what ways might powerful religious interests make an ideal democracy more secure? If Carter were to write a critique of Becker's position, how might he have encouraged Becker to include religion in an ideal democracy?

8. **SEEING CONNECTIONS**   Given that the fact that Becker was a very careful student of the American Revolution and the subsequent signing of the Constitution, how do you think he might have reacted to Howard Chandler Christy's *Scene at the Signing of the Constitution of the United States* (p. 57)? Write a brief essay that reassures Becker that the groundwork laid by the signers of the Constitution and the document itself will help democracy survive, even through dark hours, such as those that marked the time during which Becker was writing. What, in the visual organization of the paining, would have given him reason to be optimistic about democracy and its future? Is there anything in the painting that would have made him pessimistic about the future of democracy?

JULIUS K. NYERERE
One-Party Government

Julius K. NYERERE (1922–1999) was one of the first presidents of a former colony in East Africa and also one of the most respected leaders in Africa in the latter part of the twentieth century. Nyerere was born in a small village and followed village life until he had the opportunity to go to a local school. From there, he progressed rapidly and became the first Tanganyikan to attend a British university. He eventually earned his master's degree from Edinburgh University and returned to Tanganyika to become a teacher. He was often referred to as Mwalimu (*teacher* in Swahili) Nyerere, even after he stopped teaching. He also helped create the Tanganyika African National Union (TANU) and became its leader in 1954, working toward making Tanganyika—which had been a German colony before World War I and was a British protectorate when the TANU was formed—an independent nation. He achieved his goal beginning in 1961 when Tanganyika gained self-governance from Britain, after which Nyerere became the nation's first president. The country's name was changed to Tanzania in 1964 when it merged with the archipelago of Zanzibar, a group of islands off the east coast of Tanganyika.

Nyerere governed for a little more than twenty years, basing his governing principles on *Ujamaa,* the Swahili term for familyhood. Ujamaa also came to stand for socialism, which was his governing principle while in office. When he stepped down in 1985, he turned over his government without a struggle, which was unusual in Africa at that time. Yet his experiment with socialism was not successful: the economy and infrastructure of Tanzania was described as being in shambles when Nyerere left office. But Nyerere did not regret his decision to rely on socialist ideals because he felt that socialism was essential to help the poor orient themselves to a new independence and the concept of nationalism. When he took

From *Transition* 2 (1961).

office, the nation had over 120 tribes scattered across the country. Creating a sense of unity was chief among his goals.

Nyerere commented about socialism and his refusal to consider it a total failure during a PBS interview in 1996. He said that socialism is people centered and more likely to help the poor. Capitalism, he said, was ruthless and unlikely to promote justice and freedom in a country in its infancy, like Tanzania was. His principles were designed to bring an undeveloped country into the modern world, and without a history of self-sufficiency or a sense of nationhood, Tanzania faced a challenge that Nyerere felt was unique and unlike anything that the developed world, especially Europe, would understand. He created what he called "African socialism," which aimed to solve the problem of poverty and which he felt was central to ushering his nation into the modern world.

Like Benazir Bhutto (p. 177), Nyerere complained that the interests of the West in Africa were not always those that benefited the African people. The Cold War caused the West to back political figures who were often despotic. But even more important, he felt, was the fact that the original colonial powers had created the borders of African nations in a manner that ignored the ethnic makeup of regions, which led to some very unfortunate catastrophes. Ethnic fighting between Hutus and Tutsis in neighboring Rwanda and Uganda killed thousands in 1994 and sent more than a million people into neighboring nations. Nyerere tried to help negotiate between the two groups, but he also demanded that Western powers intervene to prevent the wholesale slaughter of either group. He complained bitterly that there was no help sent from the West.

Nyerere is notable for having left his office to a constitutionally elected successor, although he remained at the head of the party he created. He is also notable for having translated a number of Shakespeare's plays into Swahili and for having written several books discussing the possibilities for democracy in modern Africa. Unlike other African leaders, many of whom were corrupt and lived in opulence, Nyerere was never charged with corruption and left office still a very modest man. He was voted a pension, which sustained him in his later years.

Nyerere's Rhetoric

Nyerere's prose is graceful and clear. He was a natural writer and in this selection establishes an argument in favor of what he felt was a reasonable version of democracy. His primary rhetorical technique is comparison, balancing the Western view that democracy must have a dialogic structure—with two parties opposing one another in order to produce a synthesis that satisfies most of the citizens—with the African view that political parties are unnecessary to democracy. References to authority bolster his argument: he opens his piece by likening African ideas of democracy with those of the Greeks, who did not have the parliamentary structure that, Nyerere says, makes Europeans see democracy as a form of opposition and resolution.

As he establishes his comparison between the two systems he identifies, he also employs the technique of definition. He defines the Greek sense of democracy as "government by discussion among equals" (para. 1), after which he uses a quote to define the African version of democracy as "'[t]he elders sit[ting] under the big tree and talk[ing] until they agree'" (para. 2). This, he insists, is the essential concept of African democracy. He follows with a discussion of the circumstances of European government: "Western parliamentary tradition and Western concepts of democratic institutions" (para. 3). He then offers another definition: "Basically democracy is government by discussion as opposed to government by force" (para. 4). These definitions and distinctions form the basis of his argument. His thesis is that one-party government can be democratic. His support for his thesis lies in large measure in his ability to define democracy in such a way so as to eliminate parliamentary opposition and elevate general agreement among peers after adequate discussion of the issues. He explains that in the tribal tradition "African society was a society of equals" (para. 4). And, as he said earlier, when equals agree on something, that constitutes democracy.

Such an argument demands close examination. Nyerere is quick to establish that he is not arguing that "the two-party system is not democratic" (para. 6). Rather, he says, it is only one form of democracy. He then goes on to comment on the form of government with an interesting hypothetical example: if one political party in Britain were to win all the seats and thus create a one-party government, that party would still consider the nation to be a democracy. In some Western nations, such results have come close to that scenario and the country's government has remained democratic.

As a way of making his position more secure, Nyerere refers to early Anglo-Saxon tradition, establishing the origin of the two-party system as a result of satisfying the needs of the haves and the have-nots. Considering the Aristotelian view that populations consist of the rich and the poor and that several forms of government respond to wealth and the lack of it, this argument is interesting. Nyerere's view is that political parties establish themselves on the basis of wealth. One party wishes to conserve wealth while the other wishes to distribute it; thus, the parties are often in opposition.

The point Nyerere makes is again comparative: in Africa, as opposed to Europe, the people are uniformly impoverished, so there is no basis for a two-party system.

Ending his discussion of the forms of democracy, he points out that in times of emergency in Western democracies, "opposition parties sink their differences and join together" (para. 12), and his point is that "[t]*his is our time of emergency*" and in a time of emergency, "[t]*here can be no room for difference or division*" (para. 11). He underscores the import of both statements by using italics.

The remainder of his discussion treats what he calls the essentials of democracy, or "the freedom and the well-being of the individual" (para. 14). He maintains his emphasis on the individual as he considers the problems inherent in creating a nation that is emerging from colonialism and that is facing possibly "cynical" and "criminal" attempts by foreign governments to scuttle it. He restates his view that the creation of a new nation must be treated as a national emergency, "comparable almost to that of a country at war" (para. 20). However, he ends his essay by saying that there may come a time when "a genuine and responsible opposition" (para. 23) party may be appropriate for an African nation. He says that will depend on the will of the people.

PREREADING QUESTIONS:
WHAT TO READ FOR

The following prereading questions may help you anticipate key issues in the discussion of Julius K. Nyerere's "One-Party Government." Keeping them in mind during your first reading should help focus your attention.

- What is the African democratic tradition?
- Why is the Western democratic tradition of two oppositional parties inappropriate for an African nation?
- What are the basic elements of democratic government?

One-Party Government

The African concept of democracy is similar to that of the ancient   1
Greeks from whose language the word *democracy* originated. To
the Greeks, democracy meant simply "government by discussion

among equals." The people discussed and when they reached agreement the result was a "people's decision."

Mr. Guy Blutton-Brock[1] writing about Nyasaland described traditional African democracy as: "The elders sit under the big tree and talk until they agree." This "talking until you agree" is the essential of the traditional African concept of democracy.

To minds molded by Western parliamentary tradition and Western concepts of democratic institutions, the idea of an organized opposition group has become so familiar, that its absence immediately raises the cry of "Dictatorship." It is no good telling them that when a group of 100 equals have sat and talked together until they agreed where to dig a well (and "until they agreed" implies that they will have produced many conflicting arguments before they did eventually agree), they have practiced democracy. Proponents of Western parliamentary traditions will consider whether the opposition was organized and therefore automatic, or whether it was spontaneous and therefore free. Only if it was automatic will they concede that here was democracy.

Basically democracy is government by discussion as opposed to government by force, and by discussion between the people or their chosen representatives as opposed to a hereditary clique. Under the tribal system whether there was a chief or not, African society was a society of equals, and it conducted its business by discussion.

It is true that this "pure" democracy—the totally unorganized "talking until you agree" can no longer be adequate; it is too clumsy a way of conducting the affairs of a large modern state. But the need to organize the "government by discussion" does not necessarily imply the need to organize an opposition group as part of the system.

I am not arguing that the two-party system is not democratic. I am only saying it is only one form which democracy happens to have taken in certain countries, and that it is by no means essential. I am sure that even my friends in the Labour Party or the Conservative Party in Britain would admit that if their party could succeed in winning all the seats, they would be perfectly happy to form a one-party government. They, the winning party that is, would not be likely to suspect themselves of having suddenly turned Britain into a dictatorship!

Some of us have been over-ready to swallow unquestioningly the proposition that you cannot have democracy unless you have

---

[1] **Arthur Guy Blutton-Brock (1906–1995)** Farmer and missionary who founded nonracial communities in Rhodesia and other African nations. He was a friend of Nyerere and named a national hero of Zimbabwe after his death.

a second party to oppose the party in power. But, however difficult our friends in Britain and America may find it to accept what to them is a new idea—that democracy can exist where there is not formal opposition—I think we in Africa should think very carefully before we abandon our traditional attitude.

It is often overlooked that the Anglo-Saxon tradition of a two-party system is a reflection of the society in which it evolved. Within that society, there was a struggle between the "haves" and the "have-nots"—each of whom organized themselves into political parties, one party associated with wealth and the status quo and the other with the masses of the people and change. Thus the existence of distinct classes in a society and the struggle between them resulted in the growth of the two-party system. But need this be accepted as the essential and only pattern of democracy? 8

With rare exceptions the idea of class is something entirely foreign to Africa. Here, in this continent, the Nationalist Movements are fighting a battle for freedom from foreign domination, not from domination by any ruling class of our own. To us "the other Party" is the Colonial Power. In many parts of Africa this struggle has been won; in others it is still going on. But everywhere the people who fight the battle are not former overlords wanting to reestablish a lost authority, they are not a rich mercantile class whose freedom to exploit the masses is being limited by the colonial powers, they are the common people of Africa. 9

Thus once the foreign power—"the other party"—has been expelled there is no ready-made division, and it is by no means certain that democracy will adopt the same machinery and symbols as the Anglo-Saxon. Nor indeed is it necessarily desirable that it should do so. 10

New nations like Tanganyika are emerging into independence as a result of a struggle for freedom from colonialism. It is a patriotic struggle which leaves no room for differences, and which unites all elements in the country; and the Nationalist Movements—having united the people and led them to freedom—must inevitably form the first government of the new states. Once the first free government is formed, its supreme task lies ahead—the building up of the country's economy so as to raise the living standards of the people, the eradication of disease, and the banishment of ignorance and superstition. This, no less than the struggle against colonialism, calls for the maximum united effort by the whole country if it is to succeed. *There can be no room for difference or division.* 11

In Western democracies it is an accepted practice that in times of emergency opposition parties sink their differences and join 12 together in forming a national government. *This is our time of emergency,* and until our war against poverty, ignorance, and disease has been won—we should not let our unity be destroyed by a desire to follow somebody else's "book of rules."

If these then are the forms of democracy, what are the essentials? 13

First, the freedom and the well-being of the individual. Freedom alone is not enough; there can be a freedom which is merely the freedom to starve. True freedom must be freedom not only from bondage, from discrimination, and from indignity, but also freedom from all those things that hamper a people's progress. It is the responsibility of the government in a democratic country to lead the fight against all these enemies of freedom. To do this the government, once freely elected, must also be free to govern in the best interests of the people, and without fear of sabotage. It is, therefore, also the duty of the government to safeguard the unity of the country from irresponsible or vicious attempts to divide and weaken it, for without unity the fight against the enemies of freedom cannot be won. 14

> *When, then, you have the freedom and well-being of the individual; who has the right freely and regularly to join with his fellows in choosing the government of his country; and where the affairs of the country are conducted by free discussion, you have democracy.*

True democracy depends far more on the attitude of mind which respects and defends the individual than on the forms it takes. The form is useless without the attitude of the mind of which the form is an external expression. As with individuals, so with organized groups, this question of attitude is all-important. It is not enough to ask what attitude will an African government adopt towards an opposition, without also asking what attitude an opposition will adopt towards a popularly elected government. 15

In the past all that was required of government was merely to maintain law and order within the country, and to protect it from external aggression. Today the responsibilities of governments, whether "communist" or "free," are infinitely wide. However nearly its requirements of money and men may be met, no government today finds it easy to fulfill all its responsibilities to the people. 16

These common problems of a modern state are no less formidable in young and underdeveloped countries. The very success of the nationalist movements in raising the expectations of the people, the modern means of communication which put the American and the British worker in almost daily contact with the African worker, 17 the twentieth-century upsurge of the ordinary man and woman—all these deprive the new African governments of those advantages of time and ignorance which alleviated the growing pains of modern society for the governments of older countries.

We must listen to the demands of the common man in Africa, 18 intensified as they are by the vivid contrast between his own lot and that of others in more developed countries, and the lack of means at the disposal of the African governments to meet these demands, the lack of men, the lack of money, above all the lack of time. To all this add the very nature of the new countries themselves. They are usually countries without natural unity. Their "boundaries" enclose those artificial units carved out of Africa by grabbing colonial powers without any consideration of ethnic groups or geographical realities, so that these countries now include within their borders tribal groups which, until the coining of the European Powers, have never been under one government. To those, in the case of East and Central Africa, you must add the new tribes from Asia, the Middle East, and Europe. Here are divisions enough to pose a truly formidable task in nation building.

As if the natural challenge was not enough, with the raising of each 19 new flag come the intrigues of the international diplomacy of rivalry and all that goes with it; the cynical and the criminal attempts by powerful foreign governments to weaken the unity of any country whose government pursues policies which they do not like. Who does not know that foreign nations have again and again poured in money to back up any stooge who will dance to their political tune? As their sole purpose is to confuse the people and weaken the legal government for their own ends, they are quite indifferent to the fact that their chosen puppets have no following at all in the country itself.

It should be obvious, then, why the governments of these new 20 countries must treat the situation as one of national emergency, comparable almost to that of a country at war.

In the early days of nation building as in time of war the oppo- 21 sition, if any, must act even more responsibly than an opposition in a more developed and more stable, a more unified and a better equipped country in times of peace. Given such a responsible opposition I would be the first person to defend its right. But where is it? Too often the only voices to be heard in "opposition" are those of a few irresponsible individuals who exploit the very privileges of democracy—freedom of the press, freedom of association, freedom to criticize—in order to deflect the government from its responsibilities to the people by creating problems of law and order.

The admitted function of any political opposition is to try 22 and persuade the electorate to reject the existing government at the next election. This is "reasonable" in the case of a responsible opposition with a definite alternative policy in which its members sincerely believe; but that sort of mature opposition is rare indeed in a newly independent state. Usually the irresponsible individuals I have mentioned have neither sincerity, conviction, nor any policy at all save that of self-aggrandizement. They merely employ the catchphrases copied from the political language of older, stable countries, in order to engage the sympathy of the unthinking for their destructive tactics. Nor are the tactics they use those of a responsible democratic opposition. In such circumstances the government must deal firmly and promptly with the troublemakers. The country cannot afford, during these vital early years of its life, to treat such people with the same degree of tolerance which may be safely allowed in a long-established democracy.

This does not mean, however, that a genuine and responsible   23
opposition cannot arise in time, nor that an opposition of that kind would be less welcome in Africa than it is in Europe or America. For myself, as I have said, I would be the first to defend its rights. But whether it does or does not arise depends entirely on the will of the people themselves and makes no difference at all to the freedom of discussion and the equality in freedom which together make democracy.

To those who wonder if democracy can survive in Africa my own   24
answer then would be that far from it being an alien idea, democracy has long been familiar to the African. There is nothing in our traditional attitude to discussion, and current dedication to human rights, to justify the claim that democracy is in danger in Africa. I see exactly the opposite: the principles of our nationalist struggle for human dignity, augmented as it were by our traditional attitude to discussion, should augur well for democracy in Africa.

QUESTIONS FOR CRITICAL READING

1. In what sense are the ancient Greek and modern African understandings of democracy similar?

2. Is "discussing a governmental issue and coming to a satisfactory conclusion" a good definition of *democracy*?

3. Why does Nyerere take issue with the two-party system in African democracies?

4. Does the question of the existence of different social classes affect European and African democracies differently? Do you agree with Nyerere's views on class?

5. What kinds of opposition groups does Nyerere complain of? Are such groups also present in Western democracies? How are they handled in the West?

6. What political forces have helped dictatorships survive in Africa?

7. Why is unity such an important issue to Nyerere? Is it an ideal for all democracies?

SUGGESTIONS FOR CRITICAL WRITING

1. Nyerere points out that the Western democracies developed in reaction to class differences between the haves and the have-nots. Therefore, the two-party system in Britain, the United States, and elsewhere reflects this division. How true is this statement? What evidence would help support or refute such a statement? Does Aristotle's consideration of different social classes support Nyerere's view?

2. Do you agree that a one-party system can be democratic in nature? Which of Nyerere's arguments convince or fail to convince you of his thesis—that one-party rule is potentially good? What do you think are the limitations of one-party rule? What are its advantages? Consider the questions of freedom and individual rights as well as unity and national pride as you formulate your answer.

3. Nyerere inherited a nation that was widely diverse. While the general population was Bantu, there were over one hundred different tribes scattered in small villages throughout the country. There were also considerable populations of Asians, Southeast Indians, and Europeans. What seem to be the problems caused by such diversity in relation to establishing a democracy? Why would less diversity make it easier (or more difficult) to establish a democracy in a new country?

4. **CONNECTIONS**   In 1787, the United States faced a problem similar to Nyerere's because it was a colonial society made up of states with different priorities and needs. To what extent do the framers of the Constitution or James Madison in "Federalist No. 51" take into account issues similar to those that concern Nyerere? How different is their attitude toward establishing a democratic government? Does Nyerere account for those differences in his essay?

5. Nyerere says that democracy results "when a group of 100 equals have sat and talked together until they agreed where to dig a well" (para. 3). He also says that "'[t]he elders sit under the big tree and talk until they agree'" (para. 2). Is this really what we mean by democracy? Elders are apparently chosen based on age. But if only the elders talk until they agree, is that representative democracy? In a sense does this not describe what happens in the U.S. Senate, where 104 elected elders sit and talk about legislation? Or does the Senate work differently than a congress of elders does?

6. In paragraph 5, Nyerere says that the model of pure democracy — the system of talking until you agree — can no longer work. Why would he think so? What makes pure democracy so difficult to put into action today in either Africa or the West? What do you think the relationship is between population diversity and pure democracy? What happens when pure democracy is no longer possible? Does Nyerere discuss this problem in a way that gives you confidence in his hopes for a democratic Tanzania?

7. **CONNECTIONS** Nyerere never mentions religion in relation to an African democracy, but he does stress unity in government in contrast with western-style political opposition. One-party government is based on tribal traditions of talking and coming to agreement. What are some of the basic differences and agreements between the views of Nyerere and Carter (**bedfordstmartins.com/worldofideas/epages**)? Would Nyerere find Carter's views on the separation of church and state useful in sustaining new African democracies? Why does Nyerere not mention religion and why is Carter so concerned with it?

8. **SEEING CONNECTIONS** Examine Howard Chandler Christy's *Scene at the Signing of the Constitution of the United States* (p. 57). How would Nyerere use this painting as evidence for his views on the nature of democracy in Africa? Does the painting represent a communion of equals talking among themselves about the Constitution? Do you think the process of ratifying the Constitution was democratic? Should it have been democratic? To what extent would the painting give Nyerere ammunition for his view that one-party government can be democratic?

BENAZIR BHUTTO
Islam and Democracy

BENAZIR BHUTTO (1953–2007) was the first woman prime minister of Pakistan and thus the first woman leader of an Islamic country. She was educated at Harvard University and Oxford University, where much of her academic attention was focused on political science. Her father, Zulfiqar Ali Bhutto (1928–1979), was prime minister of Pakistan, but after an unfair trial he was hanged on charges of murdering a political dissident. He was denied clemency by the dictator General Zia-ul-Haq (1924–1988), who also imprisoned Benazir Bhutto for more than six years in primitive conditions. She was eventually released in 1984 for medical reasons and permitted to travel out of the country.

In 1986, she returned to Pakistan after her younger brother was poisoned. Upon her return, she was met by some one million people and became active in the Pakistan People's Party, which she had founded in 1982. She was elected prime minister in 1988 and held that office until 1990, when she was accused of corruption and replaced. She was elected again in 1993, however, and held the office until 1996. Both of her terms in office were filled with many struggles. She promoted socialist capitalism, fought against regulation, and dealt with numerous struggles within Pakistan as well as with Pakistan's neighbor India. She was in voluntary exile in Dubai in 1998 when Pakistan acquired nuclear armaments to match those of India. Her enemies then accused her of corruption again and sentenced her to three years' imprisonment. However, she maintained her influence with the Pakistan People's Party while she was abroad, and the party declared her its leader in 2002.

She returned to Pakistan in 2007 and was greeted by crowds, but her entourage was quickly attacked by a suicide bomber who killed 136 people. She survived because she had been traveling in an armored

From *Reconciliation: Islam, Democracy, and the West.*

vehicle and ducked at the last moment. President Pervez Musharraf (b. 1943), who had granted Bhutto amnesty so that she could return to the country, declared a state of emergency and had Bhutto held for a time under house arrest. But in December of 2007, with the Pakistan People's Party far ahead in the upcoming 2008 elections, Bhutto appeared at a major rally for the party and was shot by an assassin who, after shooting her, detonated a bomb that killed almost two dozen bystanders.

For most of her time in public service (and while in detention and exile), Benazir Bhutto represented a powerful voice in favor of democracy in Pakistan. She had a large and enthusiastic following. Her most formidable opponents were fundamentalist extremists, including those who, after several tries, ultimately succeeded in silencing her.

Bhutto's Rhetoric

Bhutto wrote much of her book *Reconciliation* only a few months before she was assassinated and during periods of intense political activity and hopefulness for democracy in Pakistan. Yet her writing does not show signs of haste or anxiety. She begins with a review of Islamic religion and its receptiveness to democratic values. She indirectly cites references to Islam's religious book, the Quran, by pointing to the fact that "Muslims believe in the sovereignty of God" (para. 1) but then goes on to point out the responsibilities of humankind on earth to respect the "immutable principles of justice, truth, and equality" (para. 1). In other words, the principles of Islam lead people to create a "just society on earth on which they will be judged in the hereafter" (para. 2).

Knowing, of course, that terrorists had threatened violence for years and indeed had even attacked her, she insists that such actions are irreligious: "They must not sin by taking innocent life, for God alone has the right to give and take life" (para. 2). Thus, terrorists pervert their religion when they kill. Interestingly, Bhutto twice mentions that it is a sin to take innocent life, leaving one to wonder about whether the death of others—those who are far from innocent—can be justified. A fatwa, a religious edict often invoked for the purpose of killing someone, was leveled against her, but she says that such an edict will not protect an assassin on the day of judgment. However, she does not explain the right of a religious leader to issue a fatwa or how it is permitted by Islam.

Bhutto first establishes the principles of her religion and its implementation in secular life and then offers a remarkable piece of testimony to bolster her view that democracy and Islam are compatible: she quotes the preamble of the 1973 Constitution of Pakistan, much of which was written by her father and passed "unanimously" by Pakistan's Parliament. Some of the basic issues are also covered by the U.S. Constitution, but Pakistan's Constitution also includes concerns and issues that do not appear in the U.S. version. Still, the document's design is used to try to convince us that her original premise, her thesis, is sound.

Bhutto makes a clear distinction between the spiritual agenda of Islam and the political agenda of those who are angry at the West; as she says, "[r]eligion is being exploited" (para. 8) by those who become terrorists. She spends some time dealing with the term *secularism*, which she says is a "rhetorical trap" (para. 7) for Muslims. For someone from the West, secularism means a separation from religious issues. But for Muslims that is a nonissue. Their issues are freedom, equal-opportunity education for both sexes, and independence of the judiciary. She uses an interesting rhetorical question, "Who can doubt" (para. 8), when she asserts that Islam has been distorted. Of course, there is much doubt, and a careful analysis of the situation will either remove doubt or reinforce it depending on circumstances.

Bhutto reviews much current history, including the Russian expedition in Afghanistan and the rise of the mujahideen—the warriors who fought and defeated the Russians and who continue to fight Western influences in Afghanistan. Mujahideen literally means "those who wage jihad," or religious war. She fears that extremists may direct themselves toward disabling Pakistan and taking over its nuclear facilities. In speaking of the nuclear capacity of Pakistan, Bhutto says that the Quran promotes education and "encourages knowledge and scientific experimentation" (para. 16).

In the second part of her discussion, she lays out an argument that suggests that the West has somehow made it difficult, if not impossible, for Pakistan and other Muslim countries to fulfill their goal to become democratic. Because the West has colonized countries such as Pakistan and India, it has supported dictators who have made a point of giving the West access to oil and other important resources. While encouraging civil rights in countries where the West has no immediate interests or needs, it tolerates despotism and the deprivation of rights in countries whose resources it needs. This, she says, "has been a major impediment to the growth of democracy in Islamic nations" (para. 21).

She hopes to prove her argument by using the testimony of President George W. Bush (para. 26) supporting "America's belief in human dignity" while at the same time supporting "Pakistan's military dictator, General Musharraf" (para. 27). She follows this with more testimony from an article in the *New York Times Magazine* (para. 28).

Finally, she concludes with evidence from Freedom House's surveys of the level of freedom enjoyed in nations around the world. Freedom House is credentialed by Bhutto's reference to its founders, Eleanor Roosevelt and Wendell Willkie, a Democrat and a Republican who worked together for the common good in an effort to be as politically unbiased as possible. The statistics she reveals are not as encouraging as we might wish, and the difference between Arab and non-Arab Muslims is significant, although she does not explain why such a difference should exist.

Her point, finally, is that the West is somewhat responsible for the lack of democracy in Muslim countries. The religion of Islam is not the root of the problem; however, the exploitation of religion by extremists remains a very significant and ongoing problem. Indeed, Benazir Bhutto paid with her life for the principles she believed in: democracy and equality.

PREREADING QUESTIONS:
WHAT TO READ FOR

The following prereading questions may help you anticipate key issues in the discussion of Benazir Bhutto's "Islam and Democracy." Keeping them in mind during your first reading should help focus your attention.

- Why do some people assume democracy will not work in Islamic countries?

- Why does Bhutto feel democracy and Islam are compatible?

- What does Bhutto say about the role of the West in supporting democracy in Islamic countries?

Islam and Democracy

Some people assert that democracy will not work in an Islamic   1
country because Muslims believe in the sovereignty of God and thus cannot accept man's law. God is Master of the Universe, of the known and unknown. Humans share two relationships: one with God and one with one another. They are custodians of God's trust, the earth, which has been placed in their care, as they are created by God. God has sent his principles to humans through thousands of Prophets, including Moses, Abraham, Jesus, and Mohammad (who is the last messenger), to instruct us how we should conduct

our lives and the principles by which we should conduct our societies. The immutable principles of justice, truth, and equality must not be transgressed if we are to gain entrance to everlasting life in Paradise.

Thus humans must seek and apply knowledge, must use rea- 2
son, must consult and build a consensus for a just society on earth on which they will be judged in the hereafter. They must not sin by taking innocent life, for God alone has the right to give and take life. Anyone who interferes in God's work by taking a life commits the most heinous crime in Islam.

The terrorists who attacked me with two bomb blasts on Octo- 3
ber 19, 2007, when I returned to Pakistan to a historic reception, committed the most heinous crime of murder by taking the lives of 179 innocent people. So too does anyone who attacks innocent people, whether in the World Trade Center, the tubes in London, or the resorts of Bali, Indonesia.

I am told that the terrorists who made the bombs and conspired to 4
kill me took a *fatwa,* or religious edict, to sanctify the terrorist attacks. However, on the Day of Judgment, such an edict will be of no help. God has ordained that each individual will have to account individually for his actions without intercession from any other individual.

Under the Constitution of Pakistan, authored by my father and 5
passed unanimously by Pakistan's Parliament in 1973, the democratic right to Muslim governance is recognized. The Constitution of 1973 states, in its preamble:

> Whereas sovereignty over the entire Universe belongs to Almighty Allah alone, and the authority to be exercised by the people of Pakistan within the limits prescribed by Him is a sacred trust;
>
> And whereas it is the will of the people of Pakistan to establish an order:
>
> Wherein the State shall exercise its powers and authority through the chosen representatives of the people;
>
> Wherein the principles of democracy, freedom, equality, tolerance, and social justice, as enunciated by Islam, shall be fully observed;
>
> Wherein the Muslims shall be enabled to order their lives in the individual and collective spheres in accordance with the teachings and requirements of Islam as set out in the Holy Quran and Sunnah;[1]
>
> Wherein adequate provision shall be made for the minorities freely to profess and practice their religions and develop their cultures;

---

[1] **Holy Quran and Sunnah** The Quran, the holy book of Islam, is Allah's word as revealed to the prophet Muhammad; the Sunnah is a record of the sayings of Muhammad.

Wherein the territories now included in or in accession with Pakistan and such other territories as may hereafter be included in or accede to Pakistan shall form a Federation wherein the units will be autonomous with such boundaries and limitations on their powers and authority as may be prescribed;

Therein shall be guaranteed fundamental rights, including equality of status, of opportunity and before law, social, economic, and political justice, and freedom of thought, expression, belief; faith, worship, and association, subject to law and public morality;

Wherein adequate provision shall be made to safeguard the legitimate interests of minorities and backward and depressed classes;

Wherein the independence of the judiciary shall be fully secured;

Wherein the integrity of the territories of the Federation, its independence and all its rights, including its sovereign rights on land, sea, and air, shall be safeguarded;

So that the people of Pakistan may prosper and attain their rightful and honored place amongst the nations of the World and make their full contribution towards international peace and progress and happiness of humanity:

Now, therefore, we, the people of Pakistan,

Cognisant of our responsibility before Almighty Allah and men;

Cognisant of the sacrifices made by the people in the cause of Pakistan;

Faithful to the declaration made by the Founder of Pakistan, Quaid-i-Azam Mohammad Ali Jinnah,[2] that Pakistan would be a democratic State based on Islamic principles of social justice;

Dedicated to the preservation of democracy achieved by the unremitting struggle of the people against oppression and tyranny;

Inspired by the resolve to protect our national and political unity and solidarity by creating an egalitarian society through a new order;

Do hereby, through our representatives in the National Assembly, adopt, enact, and give to ourselves, this Constitution.

Thus we can see that there is a perfect constitutional template   6 for democratic governance in the Muslim world. But the current poor relations between much of the West and much of the Islamic world may suggest the need for new terminology if we are to realize the vision. The word *secular,* used to denote separation of state and religion in the Western world, often means "atheism," or rejection

---

[2] **Mohammad Ali Jinnah (1876–1948)** Indian politician who struggled since the 1920s to create a separate Muslim state and managed to create Pakistan in 1947.

of God, when translated into other languages, including into Urdu in Pakistan.

Instead of terms such as *secularism*, the director of the Study 7 of Muslim Civilizations at the Aga Khan University in London, Dr. Abdou Filali-Ansary,[3] believes that we should refer directly to the individual building blocks of democracy — free elections, an independent judiciary, respect for women's and minority rights, the rule of law, and fundamental freedoms — to describe the true meaning of a democratic society. We shouldn't be talking secularism, which to Muslims is a clouded, misleading, and sometimes contentious term. Instead of using terms that fall into the rhetorical trap set by extremists to discredit the elements of modern democratic society, we should rather stress elements such as freedom to travel, freedom to work, opportunity for education for both sexes, the independence of the judiciary, and a robust civil society. These issues, more than the term *secularism*, connote the compatibility of Islam and democratic values.

Who can doubt that Islam — as a religion and as a value struc- 8 ture — has been distorted and manipulated for political reasons by militants and extremists and dictators. The establishment of the Afghan mujahideen by Zia[4] in the 1980s is an example. (After all, the jihad in Afghanistan aimed to rid the country of Soviet occupation, not reject modernity, technology, and pluralism, and to establish "strategic depth" in Pakistan. That was a political agenda of Zia.) Islam is now being used for purely political purposes by a group of people who are angry with the West. Religion is being exploited and manipulated for a political agenda, not a spiritual agenda.

The militants seethe with anger, but their anger is always tied to 9 their political agenda. First, they were angry that the West had abandoned three million Afghan refugees and stopped all assistance to them after the Soviets left Afghanistan. Second, they are angry that their offer to the government of Pakistan to send one hundred "battle-hardened mujahideen to help in the Kashmir uprising of 1989 was rejected. Third, they wanted King Fahd[5] of Saudi Arabia to turn to their "battle-hardened mujahideen" to protect Saudi Arabia after Iraqi president Saddam Hussein[6] invaded Kuwait on August 2, 1990.

---

[3] **Abdou Filali-Ansary** Professor of Islamic studies active in the Muslim Reformist tradition.

[4] **Muhammad Zia-ul-Haq (1924–1988)** Dictator of Pakistan from 1979 until his death.

[5] **King Fahd bin Abdul Aziz Al Saud (1923–2005)** Ruler of Saudi Arabia from 1982–2005.

[6] **Saddam Hussein (1937–2006)** Absolute ruler of Iraq from 1979–2003.

He refused. Fourth, they went off to fight in Bosnia when the region was engulfed in war (from 1993 to 1996 I lobbied President Bill Clinton, Prime Minister John Major, and other European leaders to intervene to bring the conflict to an end). Fifth, they tried to exploit the Chechen nationalist movement. Sixth, with the fall of my government, they turned their attention to Kashmir and tried to take over the nationalist Kashmiri movement from 1997 onward.

Muslim extremists systematically targeted historical nationalist   10
movements to gain credibility and launch themselves into the Muslim heartland with a view to piggybacking off nationalist movements to advance their agenda. However, most Muslims were suspicious and not welcoming of their extreme interpretation of Islam. Thus it was only in Afghanistan, already softened by years of resistance by Afghan mujahideen, that Muslim extremists were able to establish the Taliban dictatorship.

Driven out of Afghanistan after the September 2001 attacks on   11
the United States, they returned to Pakistan, where the journey had begun with General Zia-ul-Haq in 1980.

After the United States invaded Iraq, these same extremists   12
turned their attention to that country. Abu Musab al-Zarqawi[7] went off to fight in Iraq. Presumably others did, too. Again they used religious propaganda to kill, maim, and effectively divide one of the richest Muslim countries, Iraq, into a land of carnage and bloodshed. Sunnis and Shias, who had lived peacefully side by side for centuries, began to kill each other, and Iraq began to fall apart. It is quite easy (and typical) for Muslim extremists to blame the Americans for the sectarian civil war that rages in Iraq today, when actually it is a long-standing tension between Muslim communities that has been exacerbated and militarized to create the chaos under which extremists thrive.

Iraq is not the only goal of the extremists. Pakistan too is in great   13
danger. Pro-Taliban forces have taken over the tribal areas of Pakistan. They occupy the Swat Valley. They have been ceded Waziristan by the Musharraf[8] regime. They are moving into the settled areas of Pakistan. Their apparent next goal is the cities of my country, including our capital, Islamabad. They thrive on dictatorship; they thrive on terror; they provoke chaos to exploit chaos.

I returned to Pakistan on October 18, 2007, with the goal of   14
moving my country from dictatorship to democracy. I hoped that

---

[7] **Abu Musab al-Zarqawi (1966–2006)** An al-Qaeda terrorist.
[8] **Pervez Musharraf (b. 1943)** A general who took control of the Pakistani government by coup in 1999 and ruled as president until 2008, when he went into self-imposed exile. He has been threatened with arrest if he returns to Pakistan.

this transition could take place during the scheduled elections of 2008. I feared that otherwise the extremists would march toward Islamabad. Islamabad is near the town of Kahuta, where Pakistan's nuclear program is being carried out.

It is my fear that unless extremism is eliminated, the people of 15 Pakistan could find themselves in a contrived conflict deliberately triggered by the militants (or other "Islamists") who now threaten to take over Pakistan's nuclear assets. Having a large Muslim nation fall into chaos would be dangerous; having the only nuclear-armed Muslim nation fall into chaos would be catastrophic. My people could end up being bombed, their homes destroyed, and their children orphaned simply because a dictator has focused all his attention and all of the nation's resources on containing democrats instead of containing extremists, and then has used the crisis that he has created to justify those same policies that caused the crisis. It may sound convoluted, but there is certainly method to the madness.

This is such a tragedy, especially because Islam is clearly not only 16 tolerant of other religions and cultures but internally tolerant of dissent. Allah tells us over and over again, through the Quran, that he created people of different views and perspectives to see the world in different ways and that diversity is good. It is natural and part of God's plan. The Quran's message is open to and tolerant of women's full participation in society, it encourages knowledge and scientific experimentation, and it prohibits violence against innocents and suicide, despite terrorists' claims to the contrary.

Not only is Islam compatible with democracy, but the message of 17 the Quran empowers the people with rights (democracy), demanding consultation between rulers and ruled (parliament), and requiring that leaders serve the interests of the people or be replaced by them (accountability).

Islam was sent as a message of liberation. The challenge for 18 modern-day Muslims is to rescue this message from the fanatics, the bigots, and the forces of dictatorship. It is to give Muslims back the freedom God ordained for humankind to live in peace, in justice, in equality, in a system that is answerable to the people on this earth accepting that it is God who will judge us on the Day of Judgment.

It is by accepting that temporal and spiritual accountability 19 are two separate issues that we can provide peace, tranquillity, and opportunity. There are two judgments: the judgment of God's creatures in this world through a democratic system and the judgment by God when we leave this world. The extremists and militants who seek to hijack Islam aim to make their own judgments. In their failure lies the future of all Muslims and the reconciliation of Islam and the West.

Islam and Democracy: History and Practice

Conventional wisdom would have us believe that democracy has 　20
failed to develop in the Muslim world because of Islam itself. According to this theory, somehow Islam and democracy are mutually exclusive because Islam is rooted in an authoritarianism that promotes dictatorship. I reject this thinking as convenient and simplistic, grounded
in neither theology nor experience. As a Muslim who has lived under
both democracy and dictatorship, I know that the reasons are far
more complex.

The so-called incompatibility of Islam and democratic governance 　21
is used to divert attention from the sad history of Western political
intervention in the Muslim world, which has been a major impediment to the growth of democracy in Islamic nations.

The actions of the West in the second half of the nineteenth 　22
century and most of the twentieth century often deliberately
blocked any reasonable chance for democratic development in
Muslim-majority countries. It is so discouraging to me that the
actions of the West in the pursuit of its various short-term strategic goals have been counterproductive, often backfiring. Western
policies have often preserved authoritarianism and contained the
growth of nascent democratic movements in the developing world,
specifically in the Islamic world. Western nations' efforts to dis-
rupt democratic tides — initially for economic reasons and then for
political ones — have fueled and exacerbated tensions between the
West and Islam.

Despite often grand rhetoric to the contrary, there has been 　23
little real Western support for indigenous democratic movements.
Indeed, too often there has been outright support for dictatorships.
Both during the Cold War and now in the current battle with international terrorism, the shadow between Western rhetoric and Western actions has sowed the seeds of Muslim public disillusionment
and cynicism. The double standards have fueled extremism and
fanaticism. It accounts, at least in part, for the precipitous drop in
respect for the West in the Muslim world. This trend is true even in
pro-Western Muslim countries such as Turkey. When I was growing up, I thought of Western nations as inspirations for freedom and
development. I still do, but I'm afraid I'm in a shrinking minority of
Muslims.

There is an abundance of other examples that manifest the 　24
inconsistency of Western support for democracy in the Muslim
world: specifically, Western actions that undermined democratic
institutions, democratic movements, and democratically elected

governments in countries that the West considered critical to other policy objectives. The countries range from large to small, from very important to relatively insignificant. What is remarkable is the clear pattern of Western action: perceived pragmatic self-interest trumping the values of democracy, almost without exception. In a nation that is not relatively strategically important, such as Burma, the West will enforce its democratic creed quite enthusiastically, organizing trade embargoes and other forms of political isolation. But in places that are viewed as strategically important for economic or geopolitical factors, the West's commitment to democracy can often be more platitude than policy.

25   I raise this as not just a strategic inconsistency but a true moral dilemma for the West, especially the United States. On one level the West speaks of democracy almost in the context of the values of religion, using rhetoric about liberty being a "God-given" right. And Western nations often take that standard abroad, preaching democratic values like missionaries preaching religion. The problem arises, of course, in its selective application to bilateral foreign policy relationships. I have always believed, and have publicly argued, that the selective application of morality is inherently immoral.

26   If dictatorship is bad, then dictators are bad—not just dictators who are impotent and irrelevant but also those who are powerful allies in fighting common enemies. The West makes human rights the centerpiece of its foreign policy selectively. The West also stands four-square with struggling democracies selectively. In his second inaugural address, President George W. Bush said:

> We will encourage reform in other governments by making clear that success in our relations will require the decent treatment of their own people. America's belief in human dignity will guide our policies, yet rights must be more than the grudging concessions of dictators; they are secured by free dissent and the participation of the governed. In the long run, there is no justice without freedom, and there can be no human rights without human liberty.

27   President Bush's words notwithstanding, Washington supported Pakistan's military dictator, General Musharraf, whom it considered a key ally in the war against terrorism, even as it simultaneously supported democracy in neighboring Afghanistan and in Iraq in the Middle East.

28   I am not the only one, of course, who has pointed to strategic and moral inconsistencies in the application of Western political values

abroad. Recently Noah Feldman wrote in the *New York Times Magazine* that "a republic that supports democratization selectively is another matter. President Bush's recent speech to the United Nations, in which he assailed seven repressive regimes, was worthy of applause — but it also opened the door to the fair criticism that he was silent about the dozens of places where the United States colludes with dictators of varying degrees of nastiness." Feldman specifically cites my homeland of Pakistan as one example but goes on to criticize American support for Hosni Mubarak[9] of Egypt as Mubarak cracks down on the press and other political parties. Feldman adds that "Saudi Arabia — one [of the United States'] most powerful and durable allies — hasn't moved beyond the largely symbolic local council elections that it held two years ago." The United States, berating Burma and Iran for their undemocratic brutality, has had little to say about U.S. allies. Again, the selective application of morality is criticized as immoral in many nations whose people are also striving for democracy.

There is a clear relationship between dictatorship and religious fanaticism that cannot be ignored. Carl Gershman,[10] the president of the National Endowment for Democracy, has referred to it as a relationship between autocrats and the Islamists. To the extent that international support for tyrannies within Islamic states has resulted in the hostility of the people of these countries to the West — and cynicism about the West's true commitment to democracy and human rights — some might say that the West has unintentionally created its own Frankenstein monster.

I cannot dispute that there have been few sustained democracies in the Islamic world. But the responsibility does not lie in the text of the Muslim Holy Book. It is a responsibility shared by two significant elements that have come together in the context of environmental conditions inhospitable to the establishment, nurturing, and maintenance of democratic institutions in Muslim-majority societies.

The first element — the battle within Islam — is the purportedly theological fight among factions of Islam that also often seeks raw political and economic power at the expense of the people. The second element — the responsibility of the West — includes a long colonial period that drained developing countries of both natural and human resources. During this time the West showed a cold indifference toward supporting democracy among Muslim states and

29

30

31

---

[9] **Hosni Mubarak (b. 1928)** President of Egypt (1981–2011).
[10] **Carl Gershman (b. 1943)** President of the National Endowment for Democracy since its founding in 1984.

leaders for reasons that were either economic (oil) or political (anti-communism).

We cannot minimize the fault line that has existed within   32
Muslim nations, a fault line of internal factionalism, disrespect for
minority rights, and interventionist and often dysfunctional military
institutions. These elements have often been accompanied by the
presence of authoritarian political leadership. There is obviously a
shared responsibility for democracy's weakness in Muslim-majority
states, but there can be no disputing the fact that democratic governance in Muslim countries lags far behind that in most other parts
of the world.

A useful context for the history of democracy within Muslim   33
countries is provided by a brief review of current categorizations
of political rights and civil liberties around the world. It will then
be possible to objectively compare the Muslim and non-Muslim
worlds on standards and criteria of democratic development. Central to this analysis is something that I have always believed and
strongly endorse: that freedom and liberty are universal values that
can be applied across cultures, societies, religions, ethnic groups,
and individual national experiences. Democracy is not an inherently Western political value; it is a universal value. Liberty means
as much to someone from Indonesia as it does to someone from
Louisiana.

Freedom House (which was founded at the beginning of World   34
War II by First Lady Eleanor Roosevelt and Wendell Willkie,[11] the
Republican candidate whom her husband had just defeated for the
presidency) is an international nongovernmental organization (NGO)
dedicated to promoting democracy, human rights, and freedom
around the world. Each year it engages scholars from around the
world to categorize governments on a scale of political rights ranging from "totally free" to "not free." This useful analytical tool is
based on analyses of electoral processes, political pluralism and participation, and how the government functions. Countries are scored
on a numerical scale that ranges from one to seven, with the highest number representing the lowest level of freedom. This number is
then used to determine one of three ratings: free, partly free, or not
free. In some cases, additional variables are used to supplement the
data. For example, for traditional monarchies international scholars
are additionally asked if the system provides for genuine, meaningful

---

[11] **Eleanor Roosevelt (1884–1962)** Social activist and wife of President
Franklin Delano Roosevelt; **Wendell Willkie (1892–1944)** Roosevelt's opponent
for the presidency in 1940.

consultation with the people, encourages public discussion of policy choices, and permits petitioning the ruler.

The analysis is especially useful in evaluating political systems   35
in predominantly Muslim monarchies, because it integrates the elements of legitimate secular government with the citizen consultation enshrined in the Quran. The disparities in Freedom House ratings between the Muslim and non-Muslim worlds are dramatic and statistically significant, but not particularly surprising. It is important to remember, of course, that Muslim nations are very different from Western nations in national experience. Specifically, Islamic law generally has a role in government, whether in secular Islamic states such as Kazakhstan or religiously ideological countries such as the Islamic Republic of Iran.

Of the forty-five predominantly Muslim states, only Indonesia,   36
Mali, and Senegal are considered free. Eighteen Muslim nations are considered partly free: Afghanistan, Albania, Bahrain, Bangladesh, Comoros, Djibouti, Gambia, Jordan, Kuwait, Kyrgyzstan, Lebanon, Malaysia, Mauritania, Morocco, Niger, Sierra Leone, Turkey, and Yemen.

Twenty-four predominantly Muslim nations are labeled not free: 37
Azerbaijan, Brunei, Egypt, Palestine, Guinea, Iran, Iraq, Jordan, Kazakhstan, Libya, Maldives, Oman, Pakistan, Qatar, Saudi Arabia, Somalia, Sudan, Syria, Tajikistan, Tunisia, Turkmenistan, United Arab Emirates, Uzbekistan, and Western Sahara.

The mean score for political rights (on a scale of 1 to 7, with 1   38
being the highest level of rights) in the Muslim world is 5.24, compared to 2.82 for the non-Muslim world. The mean score for civil liberties in Muslim countries is 4.78, compared to 2.71 for non-Muslim countries. These are significant differences. I believe that these differences are not the result of theology but rather a product of both Western manipulation and internal Muslim politicization of Islam.

One frequently overlooked detail in the analysis of Freedom   39
House scores is the difference between Arab and non-Arab Muslim-majority countries. In "An 'Arab' More than 'Muslim' Electoral Gap," Alfred Stephan and Graeme Robertson use two different indices of levels of political rights to compare these two types of Muslim-majority countries. The study contrasts the scores of countries in the Freedom House study and also in the Polity IV Indexes relative to GDP from 1972 to 2000, when the competitiveness of an election was questioned. (The Polity IV Project codes and compiles information on the regulation and competitiveness of political participation.)

The authors differentiate between "underachievers" and "over-   40
achievers" in electoral competitiveness, defined by such criteria as

whether the government was selected by reasonably fair elections and whether the democratically elected government actually wields political power.

Stephan and Robertson found that a non-Arab Muslim-majority country was astoundingly "almost 20 times more likely to be 'electorally competitive' than an Arab Muslim-majority country." Of the forty-seven Muslim-majority countries that they studied, the Arab Muslim countries formed "the largest single readily identifiable group among all those states that 'underachieve,'" but the world's thirty-one Muslim-majority non-Arab countries form the largest bloc that "greatly overachieves" in electoral competitiveness. In studying the thirty-eight countries in the world that suffer from extreme poverty, they found " no comparative Muslim gap whatsoever when it comes to political rights." Their findings suggest that the success of democracy within certain states has less to do with whether a country has a Muslim majority than was previously thought by Western analysts. The result shatters the hypothesis that religion is a key variable related to democracy and that Islam and democracy are inconsistent. It relegates the Islam-democracy incompatibility theory to the level of mythology. 41

Democracies do not spring up fully developed overnight, nor is there necessarily a bright line between democratic governance and autocracy. More typical, democracy can be seen on a continuum. Civil society and democratic institutions such as political parties and NGOs tend to develop slowly over time, one critical step at a time. 42

True democracy is defined not only by elections but by the democratic governance that should follow. The most critical elements of democratic governance go beyond just free and fair elections to the protection of political rights for those in political opposition, the open function of a civil society and free press, and an independent judiciary. Far too often in the developing world—including the Islamic developing world—elections are viewed as zero-sum games. The electoral process is democratic, but that's where democracy ends. What follows is tantamount to one-party authoritarian rule. This is the opposite of true democratic governance, which is predicated on shared constitutional power and responsibility. And because democratic governance rests on a continuum of experience, the length of that experience is directly related to the sustainability of democratic governance itself. In other words, the longer democratic governance is maintained, the stronger the democratic system becomes. 43

A democracy that is more than two hundred years old is not in serious danger of interruption or of suspension of constitutional 44 norms. It has a two-century-old firewall of democratic history and practice to protect itself from extraconstitutional abuse of power. A nation without such a long history of democracy and democratic institutions—political parties; a popularly elected, legitimate, sovereign parliament; NGOs; free media; and an independent judiciary—is vulnerable to the suspension of the democratic order. We must think of a new democracy like a seedling that must be nourished, watered, fed, and given time to develop into a mighty tree. Thus, when democratic experiments are prematurely interrupted or disrupted, the effects can be, if not permanent, certainly long lasting. Internal or external interruptions of democracy (both elections and governance) can have effects that ripple and linger over generations.

We must be realistic and pragmatic about democracy. John F. 45 Kennedy once referred to himself as an "idealist without illusions." To me this is a useful description as I think in particular of my country moving from the brutality of dictatorship to the civility of democracy. When confronted with tyranny, one is tempted to go to the barricades directly, when pragmatism would dictate exhausting other potential (and peaceful) remedies. As I have grown in maturity and experience, I remain as strongly committed to the cause but more patient in finding means to achieve goals peacefully.

The colonial experience of many Muslim countries had con- 46 tributed to their difficulties in sustaining democracy. In the absence of adequate support and without the time and commitment needed to build a democratic infrastructure, they failed to strengthen their electoral and governing processes. Many of the countries discussed in this chapter were exposed to democratic values, democratic ideals, and the gradual development of political and social institutions while under colonial rule or shortly thereafter. However, their nascent democratic seeds were often smothered by the strategic interests of Western powers (often working with elements within their own societies) before they flowered into viable democratic systems.

QUESTIONS FOR CRITICAL READING

1. How effective is Bhutto's use of examples? Which example is most powerful?

2. How does Bhutto see the relationship between the spiritual and the worldly obligations of Muslims?

3. When Bhutto says it is a sin to take innocent life, do you think she implies that taking a life that is not innocent is somehow acceptable?

4. What seem to be some of the basic religious beliefs that Bhutto credits as Islamic in the early part of her essay? How different are they from the beliefs of other religions?

5. What does the suggestion that the Quran promotes diversity have to do with the possibility of Islam's supporting democracies?

6. Why would people today feel that Islam might not support a democratic government?

7. How convincing is Bhutto in this selection? Besides the Quran, what other sources does she use to bolster her argument?

SUGGESTIONS FOR CRITICAL WRITING

1. In paragraph 15, Bhutto raises the question of extremists getting control of Pakistan's nuclear plants and their nuclear weapons. How serious is this possibility? How worried does she seem about this possibility? How worried are you? What should be done if there is such a threat, and who should respond to the threat?

2. In paragraph 29, Bhutto says that "the West has unintentionally created its own Frankenstein monster." What does she mean by this statement? Examine her position in the paragraphs before and after this comment (which she has often used in speeches). How well has she supported her argument? What methods has she used to support the argument? Do you feel that she is correct, or are you not convinced?

3. **CONNECTIONS** Compare the preamble of Pakistan's Constitution with the Constitution of the United States. On what issues do the two documents agree? What seem to be the primary differences between these constitutions? What issues are included in Pakistan's Constitution that are not present in the U.S. Constitution? What is important in the U.S. Constitution that is either omitted from or of lesser importance in the Pakistan Constitution? Does the excerpt from Pakistan's Constitution convince you that its intention is to produce a democratic government?

4. Bhutto says that dictators who are favored by the West help extremists, especially by uniting them in their dislike of the United States. How do dictators help the causes of extremists in Muslim countries? Bhutto talks a good deal about Afghanistan and the Taliban. Research the current situation in Afghanistan and its history since the Russian invasion. Then decide whether or not Afghanistan is a good example for Bhutto to use in her complaint that the West must bear a share of the responsibility for the presence of dictators in Muslim countries.

5. What are the realistic choices for the West in its dealings with nations such as Saudi Arabia, which has a great deal of oil but little in the way of civil rights? Women, for instance, cannot drive cars. There are no elections for a president or prime minister nor for a parliament. Before he

was overthrown, Hosni Mubarak ruled Egypt with an iron hand and denied thousands of people their civil rights, but he guaranteed the security of Israel and kept the Suez Canal open for international trade and military shipping. Should the West demand that these nations become democratic and respect human civil rights? If they don't follow through, what should the West do?

6. Read the Quran for evidence to support Bhutto's claim that the Muslim holy book supports diversity, equality of men and women, civil rights, and a democratic approach to government. Argue a case in favor of Bhutto's position or against it. Use testimony from the Quran to bolster your argument.

7. **CONNECTIONS** Bhutto quotes from Pakistan's constitution: "Wherein the principles of democracy, freedom, equality, tolerance, and social justice, as enunciated by Islam, shall be fully observed" (para. 5). Would Carter (**bedfordstmartins.com/worldofideas/epages**) think it possible that a nation with an official religion could separate religion from the state? How could a democracy that did not separate religion from the state continue to be democratic? Would Carter support a state that did not separate religion from government? Would Bhutto? Would you?

8. **SEEING CONNECTIONS** If Benazir Bhutto had looked at *Scene at the Signing of the Constitution of the United States,* by Howard Chandler Christy (p. 57), what would she have thought of the men in the painting? Would she have felt they were sympathic to the values of the Quran that she discusses in the beginning of her selection? Would the painting have given her a sense of hope for the future of Pakistan or other Muslim countries? What might she have felt was missing from the painting? What hopes for the future might she have had after studying the painting?

PART TWO

GOVERNMENT

Lao-tzu
Niccolò Machiavelli
Jean-Jacques Rousseau
Thomas Jefferson
Elizabeth Cady Stanton
Hannah Arendt
Marcus Tullius Cicero

INTRODUCTION

He who exercises government by means of his virtue may be
compared to the north polar star, which keeps its place and all
the stars turn towards it.

−CONFUCIUS (551–479 B.C.E.)

When a government becomes powerful it is destructive, extravagant, and violent; it is an usurer which takes bread from
innocent mouths and deprives honorable men of their
substance, for votes with which to perpetuate itself.

−MARCUS TULLIUS CICERO (106–43 B.C.E.)

All the ills of mankind, all the tragic misfortunes that fill the history books, all the political blunders, all the failures of the great
leaders have arisen merely from a lack of skill at dancing.

−MOLIÈRE (1622–1673)

Society in every state is a blessing, but Government, even in its best
state, is but a necessary evil; in its worst state, an intolerable one.

−THOMAS PAINE (1737–1809)

No government can be long secure without formidable opposition.

−BENJAMIN DISRAELI (1804–1881)

A government is the most dangerous threat to man's rights: it
holds a legal monopoly on the use of physical force against
legally disarmed victims.

−AYN RAND (1902–1982)

At the core of any idea of government is the belief that individuals need an organized allocation of authority to protect their
well-being. However, throughout history the form of that allocation of authority has undergone profound shifts, and each successive type of government has inspired debates and defenses. The
first civilizations in Mesopotamia and Egypt (4000–3000 B.C.E.)
were theocracies ruled by a high priest. Gradually these political systems evolved into monarchies in which a king whose role
was separate from that of the religious leaders held power. During
the sixth century B.C.E. the Greek city-state Athens developed the
first democratic system wherein male citizens (but not women or
slaves) could elect a body of leaders. As these forms of government
developed, so too did the concept of government as the center of
law and administration. However, governments and ideas of governments (actual or ideal) have not followed a straight path. History has witnessed constant oscillations between various forms
and functions of government, from tyrannies to republics. In turn,

these governments and their relation to the individual citizen have been the focus of many great thinkers.

In this section, the thinkers represented have concentrated on both the role and form of government. Lao-tzu reflects on the ruler who would, by careful management, maintain a happy citizenry. Machiavelli places the survival of the prince above all other considerations of government and, unlike Lao-tzu, ignores the concerns and rights of the individual. For Machiavelli, power is the issue, and maintaining it is the sign of good government. Rousseau's emphasis on the social contract focuses on the theory that citizens voluntarily submit to governance in the hope of gaining greater personal freedom.

Whereas governing well concerns most of these thinkers, the forms of government concern others. Thomas Jefferson struggled with the monarchical form of government, as did Rousseau before him, and envisioned a republic that would serve the people. Kings were a threatened species in eighteenth-century Europe, and with Jefferson's aid, they became extinct in the United States. Elizabeth Cady Stanton argued for equality of women using the model of the Declaration of Independence to bolster her position. Hannah Arendt was convinced that the totalitarian governments of the twentieth century needed concentration camps in order to practice total domination.

Lao-tzu, whose writings provide the basis for Taoism, one of three major Chinese religions, was interested primarily in political systems. His work, the *Tao-te Ching*, has been translated loosely as "The Way of Power." One thing that becomes clear from reading his work — especially the selections presented here — is his concern for the well-being of the people in any government. He does not recommend specific forms of government (monarchic, representative, democratic) or advocate election versus the hereditary transfer of power. But he does make it clear that the success of the existing forms of government (in his era, monarchic) depends on good relations between the leader and the people. He refers to the chief of state as *Master* or *Sage*, implying that one obligation of the governor is to be wise. One expression of that wisdom is the willingness to permit things to take their natural course. His view is that the less the Master needs to do — or perhaps the less government needs to intervene — the happier the people will be.

Niccolò Machiavelli was a pragmatic man of the Renaissance in Italy. As a theoretician and as a member of the political court, he understood government from the inside and carefully examined its philosophy. Because his writings stress the importance of gaining and holding power at any cost, Machiavelli's name has become synonymous with political cunning. However, a careful reading of his work as a reflection of the instability of his time shows that his advice to wield power ruthlessly derived largely from his fear that a weak prince would lose the city-state of Florence to France or to another powerful, plundering nation. His commitment to a powerful prince is based on his view that in the long run strength will guarantee the peace and happiness of the citizen for whom independence is otherwise irrelevant. Therefore, Machiavelli generally ignores questions concerning the comfort and rights of the individual.

In contrast, Jean-Jacques Rousseau is continually concerned with the basic questions of personal freedom and liberty. A fundamental principle in "The Origin of Civil Society" is that the individual's agreement with the state is designed to increase the individual's freedoms, not to diminish them. Rousseau makes this assertion while at the same time admitting that the individual forfeits certain rights to the body politic in order to gain overall freedom. Moreover, Rousseau describes civil society as a body politic that expects its rulers—including the monarch—to behave in a way designed to benefit the people. Such a view in eighteenth-century France was revolutionary. The ruling classes at that time treated the people with great contempt, and the monarch rarely gave any thought to the well-being of the common people. Rousseau's advocacy of a republican form of government in which the monarch served the people was a radical view and would find its ultimate expression decades later in the French Revolution.

Thomas Jefferson's views were also radical for his time. Armed with the philosophy of Rousseau and others, his Declaration of Independence advocates the eradication of the monarch entirely. Not everyone in the colonies agreed with this view. Indeed, his political opponents, such as Alexander Hamilton and Aaron Burr, were far from certain such a view was correct. In fact, some efforts were made to install George Washington as king (he refused). In the Declaration of Independence, Jefferson reflects Rousseau's philosophy by emphasizing the right of the individual to "life, liberty, and the pursuit of happiness" and the obligation of government to serve the people by protecting those rights.

Elizabeth Cady Stanton relies on the rhetorical device of parody in her "Declaration of Sentiments and Resolutions." Modeled directly on Thomas Jefferson's Declaration of Independence, Stanton's appeal serves as a reminder that Jefferson spoke only of men's independence, not that of women. Her demands are no less reasonable than Jefferson's, and it is a source of embarrassment to her that she has to redress such an omission after so much time has elapsed since Jefferson's declaration was adopted.

The issues of freedom, justice, and individual rights were all virtually irrelevant in the totalitarian regimes that served as the focus of Hannah Arendt's work. Arendt argued that the fascist states, especially Nazi Germany, and the communist states, especially the Soviet Union, represented a form of government in which individual rights were sacrificed for the good of "the state." In "Total Domination," Arendt argues that the power of totalitarian states depends on the use of terror to enforce the state's ideology. The result is a form of government that eclipses the tyrannical extremes Rousseau and Jefferson sought to eradicate and exceeds even Machiavelli's imaginings of absolute power.

This chapter also contains a selection in e-pages (available online at **bedfordstmartins.com/worldofideas/epages**) from Marcus Tullius Cicero. Cicero presents a dialogue with a character, Philus, whose assignment is to create an argument in favor of injustice. As a great rhetorician and orator, Cicero plays an interesting game in asking someone whose personal views are strongly in favor of justice to argue against it. The procedure is interesting for us because we can see more clearly the virtue of justice by examining in detail the arguments against it. Philus does a creditable job by relying on arguments already developed by another philosopher, Carneades. His appeal is to the strength of the state and the need for the individual to yield to collective values. The result is an argument for injustice that is dangerous because we might be convinced by it.

VISUALIZING GOVERNMENT

Eugène Delacroix (1798–1863) was considered the greatest of the romantic painters of France. His use of color and subject matter moved away from the earlier classicists who dominated the late eighteenth century. He painted subjects from recent history, such as *Massacre at Chios,* which expressed sympathy for the Greek cause in their war of independence from the Turks. His painting *The Barque of Dante* (1822) made him a controversial figure in France, so when he painted *Liberty Leading the People* in his early thirties, he was already a celebrity. There was no classical or mythic figure of liberty to use from ancient Greek or Roman history, so Delacroix looked back only as far as the French Revolution (1798) and in the process mythicized for all time the force of liberty and the responsibility of government to the people it serves.

His painting was a political document in itself. (To see this painting in color, go to **bedfordstmartins.com/worldofideas/epages**.) It presents a heroic female figure, the epitome of mythic Liberty — whose image in various manifestations appears on coins around the world — struggling with authority in an effort to achieve a truly

EUGÈNE DELACROIX, *LIBERTY LEADING THE PEOPLE,* 1830.
Oil on canvas, 8'6" × 10'10", Louvre, Paris

representative government and surrounded by the common people of France. This painting became a rallying cry for reformers
around the world and is widely reprinted in poster form throughout Europe and the Western Hemisphere. It symbolizes the common cause people have to overthrow dictatorship or tyranny. It also
commemorates the revolutionary action of citizens who barricaded
Parisian streets in their fight against a government that they eventually overthrew.

Because of its powerful visual structure—with Liberty in the
center, the tricolor flag of freedom above, and citizens of all social
orders and ages rallying to the cause—this painting may be considered the most dramatic visual argument for democracy and independence of Delacroix's time, or any time.

The Italian historian and art critic Giulio Carlo Argan declared
this the first political painting of modern art. It is an allegorical
representation of the three-day revolution in July 1830 in which
the Bourbon king, Charles X, was overthrown. The Bourbons
were the family who ruled France prior to the French Revolution
(1789). King Louis XVI was executed during the Revolution and

Napoleon became emperor. After his defeat in 1814, Napoleon went into exile and the victorious allies reinstated the throne for the Bourbons with the intention of their respecting a constitutional monarchy on the model of England's. That worked under Louis XVIII, but when his brother Charles X took the throne, he said he would rather "hew wood" than be a king modeled after the king of England. His imperious ways undid most of the positive achievements of the French Revolution, and in 1830, the people rose and demanded his resignation.

The painting is both allegorical and realistic, but there has never been a suggestion that Delacroix represented a specific street or moment during the 1830 July Revolution, despite the suggestion that he himself was involved in the action. His point was that Liberty would come to the barricades wherever and whenever the people's struggle was just. The painting conspicuously includes middle and poorer classes of citizens as a way of emphasizing the people's movement to reject the autocratic government of the Bourbon king. Liberty, a powerful woman carrying the tricolor of the republic (which the Bourbons had abandoned) also carries a bayonetted musket indicating her willingness to fight for a republican form of government. Her Phrygian hat was a style worn often during the revolution of 1789 and itself symbolized liberty. She may also have been a model for the Statue of Liberty, a gift from France to the United States in 1886. The man with the top hat to the left may be a self-portrait of the artist, Delacroix, who was a member of la Garde nationale, or French National Guard, and whose studio was in the neighborhood where much of the fighting occurred. The boy with the two pistols is said to have been a representation from life.

The painting was purchased by the French government as a reminder of the Revolution for the post-Bourbon, "citizen king," Louis-Phillipe. It hung for a while in the palace, but its message of violence in the streets against the government finally condemned it to removal. It was later brought to the Louvre. The painting is massive, a fact apparent even in the accommodating Louvre, and it stands as a reminder that the people have a vested interest in government—that in modern times they cannot be ignored nor barred from speaking out. It is still one of the most visited paintings in the Louvre in Paris and one of the most reproduced of all modern paintings.

As you read the essays in this part, think about how Delacroix's painting, with its principle of government by and for the people at all costs, relates to each writer's philosophy of government. Following each selection, a Seeing Connections question asks you to directly compare the writer's ideas with Delacroix's work.

LAO-TZU
Thoughts from the Tao-te Ching

THE AUTHOR of the *Tao-te Ching* (in English often pronounced "dow deh jing") is unknown, although the earliest texts
ascribe the work to Lao-tzu (sixth century B.C.E.), whose name can
be translated as "Old Master." However, nothing can be said with
certainty about Lao-tzu (lou′ dzu′) as a historical figure. One tradition holds that he was named Li Erh and born in the state of Ch'u
in China at a time that would have made him a slightly older contemporary of Confucius (551–479 B.C.E.). Lao-tzu was said to have
worked in the court of the Chou dynasty for most of his life. When
he decided to leave the court to pursue a life of contemplation,
the keeper of the gate urged him to write down his thoughts before
he went into a self-imposed exile. Legend has it that he wrote the
Tao-te Ching and then left the state of Ch'u, never to be seen again.

Lao-tzu's writings offered a basis for Taoism, a religion officially founded by Chang Tao-ling in about 150 C.E. However, the
Tao-te Ching is a philosophical document as much about good
government as it is about moral behavior. The term *Tao* cannot be
easily understood or easily translated. In one sense it means "the
way," but it also means "the method," as in "the way to enlightenment" or "the way to live." Some of the chapters of the *Tao-te
Ching* imply that the Tao is the allness of the universe, the ultimate
reality of existence, and perhaps even a synonym for God. The text
is marked by numerous complex ambiguities and paradoxes. It
constantly urges us to look beyond ourselves, beyond our circumstances, and become one with the Tao—even though it cannot tell
us what the Tao is.

The *Tao-te Ching* has often been called a feminine treatise
because it emphasizes the creative forces of the universe and
frequently employs the imagery and metaphor of the womb—for

From *Tao-te Ching*. Translated by Stephen Mitchell.

example, "The Tao is called the Great Mother." The translator, Stephen Mitchell, translates some of the pronouns associated with the Master as "she," with the explanation that Chinese has no equivalent for the male- and female-gendered pronouns and that "of all the great world religions the teaching of Lao-tzu is by far the most female."

The teachings of Lao-tzu are the opposite of the materialist quest for power, dominance, authority, and wealth. Lao-tzu takes the view that possessions and wealth are leaden weights of the soul, that they are meaningless and trivial, and that the truly free and enlightened person will regard them as evil. Because of his antimaterialist view, his recommendations may seem ironic or unclear, especially when he urges politicians to adopt a practice of judicious inaction. Lao-tzu's advice to politicians is not to do nothing but to intercede only when it is a necessity and then only inconspicuously. Above all, Lao-tzu counsels avoiding useless activity: "the Master / acts without doing anything / and teaches without saying anything." Such a statement is difficult for modern Westerners to comprehend, although it points to the concept of enlightenment, a state of spiritual peace and fulfillment that is central to the *Tao-te Ching*.

Lao-tzu's political philosophy minimizes the power of the state—especially the power of the state to oppress the people. Lao-tzu takes the question of the freedom of the individual into account by asserting that the wise leader will provide the people with what they need but not annoy them with promises of what they do not need. Lao-tzu argues that by keeping people unaware that they are being governed, the leader allows the people to achieve good things for themselves. As he writes, "If you want to be a great leader, / you must learn to follow the Tao. / Stop trying to control. / Let go of fixed plans and concepts, / and the world will govern itself" (Verse 57); or in contrast, "If a country is governed with repression, / the people are depressed and crafty" (Verse 58).

To our modern ears this advice may or may not sound sensible. For those who feel government can solve the problems of the people, it will seem strange and unwise. For those who believe that the less government the better, the advice will sound sane and powerful.

The Rhetoric of the *Tao-te Ching*

Traditionally, Lao-tzu is said to have written the *Tao-te Ching* as a guide for the ruling sage to follow. In other words, it is a handbook for politicians. It emphasizes the virtues that the ruler must possess, and in this sense the *Tao-te Ching* invites comparison with Machiavelli's efforts to instruct his ruler.

The visual form of the text is poetry, although the text is not metrical or image laden. Instead of thoroughly developing his ideas, Lao-tzu uses a traditional Chinese form that resembles the aphorism, a compressed statement weighty with meaning. Virtually every statement requires thought and reflection. Thus, the act of reading becomes an act of cooperation with the text.

One way of reading the text is to explore the varieties of interpretation it will sustain. The act of analysis requires patience and willingness to examine a statement to see what lies beneath the surface. Take, for example, one of the opening statements:

> The Master leads
> by emptying people's minds
> and filling their cores,
> by weakening their ambition
> and toughening their resolve.
> He helps people lose everything
> they know, everything they desire,
> and creates confusion
> in those who think that they know.

This passage supports a number of readings. One centers on the question of the people's desire. "Emptying people's minds" implies eliminating desires that lead the people to steal or compete for power. "Weakening their ambition" implies helping people direct their powers toward the attainable and useful. Such a text is at odds with Western views that support advertisements for expensive computers, DVD players, luxury cars, and other items that generate ambition and desire in people.

In part because the text resembles poetry, it needs to be read with attention to innuendo, subtle interpretation, and possible hidden meanings. One of the rhetorical virtues of paradox is that it forces the reader to consider several sides of an issue. The resulting confusion yields a wider range of possibilities than would arise from a self-evident statement. Through these complicated messages, Lao-tzu felt he was contributing to the spiritual enlightenment of the ruling sage, although he had no immediate hope that his message would be put into action. A modern state might have a difficult time following Lao-tzu's philosophy, but many individuals have tried to attain peace and contentment by leading lives according to its principles.

PREREADING QUESTIONS:
WHAT TO READ FOR

The following prereading questions may help you anticipate key issues in the discussion of Lao-tzu's "Thoughts from the *Tao-te Ching*." Keeping them in mind during your first reading of the selection should help focus your attention.

- What is the Master's attitude toward action?
- The Tao is "the way"—how are we to understand its meaning? What does it mean to be in harmony with the Tao?
- According to Lao-tzu, why is moderation important in government?

Thoughts from the Tao-te Ching

3

If you overesteem great men,   1
people become powerless.
If you overvalue possessions,
people begin to steal.

The Master leads   2
by emptying people's minds
and filling their cores,
by weakening their ambition
and toughening their resolve.
He helps people lose everything
they know, everything they desire,
and creates confusion
in those who think that they know.

Practice not-doing,   3
and everything will fall into place.

17

When the Master governs, the people   4
are hardly aware that he exists.

Next best is a leader who is loved.
Next, one who is feared.
The worst is one who is despised.

If you don't trust the people,   5
you make them untrustworthy.

The Master doesn't talk, he acts.   6
When his work is done,
the people say, "Amazing:
we did it, all by ourselves!"

18

When the great Tao is forgotten,   7
goodness and piety appear.
When the body's intelligence declines,
cleverness and knowledge step forth.
When there is no peace in the family,
filial piety begins.
When the country falls into chaos,
patriotism is born.

19

Throw away holiness and wisdom,   8
and people will be a hundred times happier.
Throw away morality and justice,
and people will do the right thing.
Throw away industry and profit,
and there won't be any thieves.

If these three aren't enough,   9
just stay at the center of the circle
and let all things take their course.

26

The heavy is the root of the light.   10
The unmoved is the source of all movement.

Thus the Master travels all day   11
without leaving home.
However splendid the views,
she stays serenely in herself.

Why should the lord of the country   12
flit about like a fool?

If you let yourself be blown to and fro,
you lose touch with your root.
If you let restlessness move you,
you lose touch with who you are.

29

Do you want to improve the world?   13
I don't think it can be done.

The world is sacred.   14
It can't be improved.
If you tamper with it, you'll ruin it.
If you treat it like an object, you'll lose it.

There is a time for being ahead,   15
a time for being behind;
a time for being in motion,
a time for being at rest;
a time for being vigorous,
a time for being exhausted;
a time for being safe,
a time for being in danger.

The Master sees things as they are,   16
without trying to control them.
She lets them go their own way,
and resides at the center of the circle.

30

Whoever relies on the Tao in governing men   17
doesn't try to force issues
or defeat enemies by force of arms.
For every force there is a counterforce.
Violence, even well intentioned,
always rebounds upon oneself.

The Master does his job   18
and then stops.
He understands that the universe
is forever out of control,
and that trying to dominate events
goes against the current of the Tao.
Because he believes in himself,
he doesn't try to convince others.
Because he is content with himself,

he doesn't need others' approval.
Because he accepts himself,
the whole world accepts him.

31

Weapons are the tools of violence;   19
all decent men detest them.

Weapons are the tools of fear;   20
a decent man will avoid them
except in the direst necessity
and, if compelled, will use them
only with the utmost restraint.
Peace is his highest value.
If the peace has been shattered,
how can he be content?
His enemies are not demons,
but human beings like himself.
He doesn't wish them personal harm.
Nor does he rejoice in victory.
How could he rejoice in victory
and delight in the slaughter of men?

He enters a battle gravely,   21
with sorrow and with great compassion,
as if he were attending a funeral.

37

The Tao never does anything,   22
yet through it all things are done.

If powerful men and women   23
could center themselves in it,
the whole world would be transformed
by itself, in its natural rhythms.
People would be content
with their simple, everyday lives,
in harmony, and free of desire.

When there is no desire,   24
all things are at peace.

38

The Master doesn't try to be powerful;   25
thus he is truly powerful.

The ordinary man keeps reaching for power;
thus he never has enough.

The Master does nothing,   26
yet he leaves nothing undone.
The ordinary man is always doing things,
yet many more are left to be done.

The kind man does something,   27
yet something remains undone.
The just man does something,
and leaves many things to be done.
The moral man does something,
and when no one responds
he rolls up his sleeves and uses force.

When the Tao is lost, there is goodness.   28
When goodness is lost, there is morality.
When morality is lost, there is ritual.
Ritual is the husk of true faith,
the beginning of chaos.

Therefore the Master concerns himself   29
with the depths and not the surface,
with the fruit and not the flower.
He has no will of his own.
He dwells in reality,
and lets all illusions go.

46

When a country is in harmony with the Tao,   30
the factories make trucks and tractors.
When a country goes counter to the Tao,
warheads are stockpiled outside the cities.

There is no greater illusion than fear,   31
no greater wrong than preparing to defend yourself,
no greater misfortune than having an enemy.

Whoever can see through all fear   32
will always be safe.

53

The great Way is easy,   33
yet people prefer the side paths.

Be aware when things are out of balance.
Stay centered within the Tao.

When rich speculators prosper   34
while farmers lose their land;
when government officials spend money
on weapons instead of cures;
when the upper class is extravagant and irresponsible
while the poor have nowhere to turn—
all this is robbery and chaos.
It is not in keeping with the Tao.

57

If you want to be a great leader,   35
you must learn to follow the Tao.
Stop trying to control.
Let go of fixed plans and concepts,
and the world will govern itself.

The more prohibitions you have,   36
the less virtuous people will be.
The more weapons you have,
the less secure people will be.
The more subsidies you have,
the less self-reliant people will be.

Therefore the Master says: 37
I let go of the law,
and people become honest.
I let go of economics,
and people become prosperous.
I let go of religion,
and people become serene.
I let go of all desire for the common good,
and the good becomes common as grass.

58

If a country is governed with tolerance,   38
the people are comfortable and honest.
If a country is governed with repression,
the people are depressed and crafty.

When the will to power is in charge,   39
the higher the ideals, the lower the results.
Try to make people happy,
and you lay the groundwork for misery.

Try to make people moral,
and you lay the groundwork for vice.

Thus the Master is content   40
to serve as an example
and not to impose her will.
She is pointed, but doesn't pierce.
Straightforward, but supple.
Radiant, but easy on the eyes.

59

For governing a country well   41
there is nothing better than moderation.

The mark of a moderate man   42
is freedom from his own ideas.
Tolerant like the sky,
all-pervading like sunlight,
firm like a mountain,
supple like a tree in the wind,
he has no destination in view
and makes use of anything
life happens to bring his way.

Nothing is impossible for him.   43
Because he has let go,
he can care for the people's welfare
as a mother cares for her child.

60

Governing a large country   44
is like frying a small fish.
You spoil it with too much poking.

Center your country in the Tao   45
and evil will have no power.
Not that it isn't there,
but you'll be able to step out of its way.

Give evil nothing to oppose   46
and it will disappear by itself.

61

When a country obtains great power,   47
it becomes like the sea:

all streams run downward into it.
The more powerful it grows,
the greater the need for humility.
Humility means trusting the Tao,
thus never needing to be defensive.

A great nation is like a great man: 48
When he makes a mistake, he realizes it.
Having realized it, he admits it.
Having admitted it, he corrects it.
He considers those who point out his faults
as his most benevolent teachers.
He thinks of his enemy
as the shadow that he himself casts.

If a nation is centered in the Tao,   49
if it nourishes its own people
and doesn't meddle in the affairs of others,
it will be a light to all nations in the world.

65

The ancient Masters   50
didn't try to educate the people,
but kindly taught them to not-know.

When they think that they know the answers,   51
people are difficult to guide.
When they know that they don't know,
people can find their own way.

If you want to learn how to govern,   52
avoid being clever or rich.
The simplest pattern is the clearest.
Content with an ordinary life,
you can show all people the way
back to their own true nature.

66

All streams flow to the sea   53
because it is lower than they are.
Humility gives it its power.

If you want to govern the people,   54
you must place yourself below them.

If you want to lead the people,
you must learn how to follow them.

The Master is above the people,   55
and no one feels oppressed.
She goes ahead of the people,
and no one feels manipulated.
The whole world is grateful to her.
Because she competes with no one,
no one can compete with her.

67

Some say that my teaching is nonsense.   56
Others call it lofty but impractical.
But to those who have looked inside themselves,
this nonsense makes perfect sense.
And to those who put it into practice,
this loftiness has roots that go deep.

I have just three things to teach: 57
simplicity, patience, compassion.
These three are your greatest treasures.
Simple in actions and in thoughts,
you return to the source of being.
Patient with both friends and enemies,
you accord with the way things are.
Compassionate toward yourself,
you reconcile all beings in the world.

75

When taxes are too high,   58
people go hungry.
When the government is too intrusive,
people lose their spirit.

Act for the people's benefit.   59
Trust them; leave them alone.

80

If a country is governed wisely,   60
its inhabitants will be content.
They enjoy the labor of their hands
and don't waste time inventing
labor-saving machines.

Since they dearly love their homes,
they aren't interested in travel.
There may be a few wagons and boats,
but these don't go anywhere.
There may be an arsenal of weapons,
but nobody ever uses them.
People enjoy their food,
take pleasure in being with their families,
spend weekends working in their gardens,
delight in the doings of the neighborhood.
And even though the next country is so close
that people can hear its roosters crowing and its dogs barking,
they are content to die of old age
without ever having gone to see it.

QUESTIONS FOR CRITICAL READING

1. According to Lao-tzu, what must the ruler provide the people with if they are to be happy? See especially Verse 66.

2. To what extent does Lao-tzu concern himself with individual happiness?

3. How would you describe Lao-tzu's attitude toward the people?

4. Why does Lao-tzu think the world cannot be improved? See Verse 29.

5. Which statements made in this selection do you feel support a materialist view of experience? Can they be reconciled with Lao-tzu's overall thinking in the selection?

6. What are the limits and benefits of the expression: "Practice not-doing, / and everything will fall into place"? See Verse 3.

7. To what extent is Lao-tzu in favor of military action? What seem to be his views about the military? See Verse 31.

8. The term *Master* is used frequently in the selection. What can you tell about the character of the Master?

SUGGESTIONS FOR CRITICAL WRITING

1. The term *the Tao* is used often in this selection. Write a short essay that defines what Lao-tzu seems to mean by the term. If you were a politician and had the responsibility of governing a state, how would you follow the Tao as it is implied in Lao-tzu's statements? Is the Tao restrictive? Difficult? Open to interpretation? How well do you think it would work?

2. Write a brief essay that examines the following statements from the perspective of a young person today:

    The more prohibitions you have,
    the less virtuous people will be.

> The more weapons you have,
> the less secure people will be.
> The more subsidies you have,
> the less self-reliant people will be. (Verse 57)

To what extent do you agree with these statements, and to what extent do you feel they are statements that have political importance? Do people in the United States seem to agree with these views, or do they disagree? What are the most visible political consequences of our nation's position regarding these ideas?

3. Some people have asserted that the American political system benefits the people most when the following views of Lao-tzu are carefully applied:

> Therefore the Master says:
> I let go of the law,
> and people become honest.
> I let go of economics,
> and people become prosperous.
> I let go of religion,
> and people become serene.
> I let go of all desire for the common good,
> and the good becomes common as grass. (Verse 57)

In a brief essay, decide to what extent American leaders follow these precepts. Whether you feel they do or not, do you think that they should follow these precepts? What are the likely results of their being put into practice?

4. Some of the statements Lao-tzu makes are so packed with meaning that it would take pages to explore them. One example is "When they think that they know the answers, / people are difficult to guide." Take this statement as the basis of a short essay and, in reference to a personal experience, explain the significance of this statement.

5. What does Lao-tzu imply about the obligation of the state to the individual it governs and about the obligation of the individual to the state? Is one much more important than the other? Using the texts in this selection, establish what you feel is the optimum balance in the relationship between the two.

6. **CONNECTIONS** How sympathetic might Cicero (**bedfordstmartins .com/worldofideas/epages**) be to Lao-tzu regarding the moderation of action in government? Philus, in Cicero's selection, argues for a government that tolerates some injustice. How does Lao-tzu's vision of government disable such an argument? Would you rather be governed by Lao-tzu's version of government or Philus's? Explain your position regarding these two writers' views of government

7. **CONNECTIONS** Compare Lao-tzu's view of government with that of Machiavelli in the next selection. Consider what seem to be the ultimate purposes of government, what seem to be the obligations of the leader to the people being led, and what seems to be the main work of

the state. What comparisons can you make between Lao-tzu's Master and Machiavelli's prince?

8. **SEEING CONNECTIONS** How would Lao-tzu have described the action in Delacroix's *Liberty Leading the People* (p. 200)? Would he have been sympathetic to the efforts of the French people trying to remove an unpopular king in 1830? To what extent would he have approved of the representation of Liberty holding a musket with a bayonet? Which figure in the painting would Lao-tzu have felt the most sympathy for? What might Lao-tzu's message to Delacroix have been if it had been possible for him to communicate with the painter?

NICCOLÒ MACHIAVELLI
The Qualities of the Prince

NICCOLÒ MACHIAVELLI (1469–1527) was an aristocrat whose fortunes wavered according to the shifts in power in Florence. Renaissance Italy was a collection of powerful city-states, which were sometimes volatile and unstable. When Florence's famed Medici princes were returned to power in 1512 after eighteen years of banishment, Machiavelli did not fare well. He was suspected of crimes against the state and imprisoned. Even though he was not guilty, he had to learn to support himself as a writer instead of continuing his career in civil service.

His works often contrast two forces: luck (one's fortune) and character (one's virtues). His own character outlasted his bad luck in regard to the Medicis, and he was returned to a position of responsibility. *The Prince* (1513), his most celebrated work, was a general treatise on the qualities the prince (that is, ruler) must have to maintain his power. In a more particular way, it was directed at the Medicis to encourage them to save Italy from the predatory incursions of France and Spain, whose troops were nibbling at the crumbling Italian principalities and who would, in time, control much of Italy.

The chapters presented here contain the core of the philosophy for which Machiavelli became famous. His instructions to the prince are curiously devoid of any high-sounding moralizing or any encouragement to be good as a matter of principle. Instead, Machiavelli recommends a very practical course of action for the prince: secure power by direct and effective means. It may be that Machiavelli fully expects that the prince will use his power for good ends—certainly he does not recommend tyranny. But he also supports using questionable means to achieve the final end of becoming and remaining the prince. Although Machiavelli recognizes that there is often a conflict between the ends and the means used to achieve them, he does not fret over the possible problems that may accompany the

From *The Prince*. Translated by Peter Bondanella and Mark Musa.

use of "unpleasant" means, such as punishment of upstarts or the use of repression, imprisonment, and torture.

Through the years, Machiavelli's view of human nature has come under criticism for its cynicism. For instance, he suggests that a morally good person would not remain long in any high office because that person would have to compete with the mass of people, who, he says, are basically bad. Machiavelli constantly tells us that he is describing the world as it really is, not as it should be. Perhaps Machiavelli is correct, but people have long condemned the way he approves of cunning, deceit, and outright lying as means of staying in power.

The contrast between Machiavelli's writings and Lao-tzu's opinions in the *Tao-te Ching* is instructive. Lao-tzu's advice issues from a detached view of a universal ruler; Machiavelli's advice is very personal, embodying a set of directives for a specific prince. Machiavelli expounds on a litany of actions that must be taken; Lao-tzu, on the other hand, advises that judicious inaction will produce the best results.

Machiavelli's Rhetoric

Machiavelli's approach is less poetic and more pragmatic than Lao-tzu's. Whereas Lao-tzu's tone is almost biblical, Machiavelli's is that of a how-to book, relevant to a particular time and a particular place. Yet, like Lao-tzu, Machiavelli is brief and to the point. Each segment of the discussion is terse and economical.

Machiavelli announces his primary point clearly, refers to historical precedents to support his point, and then explains why his position is the best one by appealing to both common sense and historical experience. When he suspects the reader will not share his view wholeheartedly, he suggests an alternate argument and then explains why it is wrong. This is a very forceful way of presenting one's views. It gives the appearance of fairness and thoroughness—and, as we learn from reading Machiavelli, he is very much concerned with appearances. His method also gives his work fullness, a quality that makes us forget how brief it really is.

Another of his rhetorical methods is to discuss opposite pairings, including both sides of an issue. From the first he explores a number of oppositions—the art of war and the art of life, liberality and stinginess, cruelty and clemency, the fox and the lion. The method may seem simple, but it is important because it employs two of the basic techniques of rhetoric—comparison and contrast.

The aphorism is another of Machiavelli's rhetorical weapons. An aphorism is a saying—a concise statement of a principle—that has been accepted as true. Familiar examples are "A penny saved is a penny earned" and "There is no fool like an old fool." Machiavelli tells us, "A man who wishes to make a vocation of being good at all times will come to ruin among so many who are not good."

Such definite statements have several important qualities. One is that they are pithy: they seem to say a great deal in a few words. Another is that they appear to contain a great deal of wisdom, in part because they are delivered with such certainty and in part because they have the ring of other aphorisms that we accept as true. Because they sound like aphorisms, they gain a claim to (unsubstantiated) truth, and we tend to accept them much more readily than perhaps we should. This may be why the speeches of contemporary politicians (modern versions of the prince) are often sprinkled with such expressions and illustrates why Machiavelli's rhetorical technique is still reliable, still effective, and still worth studying.

PREREADING QUESTIONS: WHAT TO READ FOR

The following prereading questions may help you anticipate key issues in the discussion of Niccolò Machiavelli's "The Qualities of the Prince." Keeping them in mind during your first reading of the selection should help focus your attention.

- Why does Machiavelli praise skill in warfare in his opening pages? How does that skill aid a prince?

- Is it better for a prince to be loved or to be feared?

The Qualities of the Prince

A Prince's Duty Concerning Military Matters

A prince, therefore, must not have any other object nor any other thought, nor must he take anything as his profession but war, its institutions, and its discipline; because that is the only profession which befits one who commands; and it is of such importance that not only does it maintain those who were born princes, but many times it enables men of private station to rise to that position; 1

and, on the other hand, it is evident that when princes have given more thought to personal luxuries than to arms, they have lost their state. And the first way to lose it is to neglect this art; and the way to acquire it is to be well versed in this art.

Francesco Sforza[1] became Duke of Milan from being a private   2 citizen because he was armed; his sons, since they avoided the inconveniences of arms, became private citizens after having been dukes. For, among the other bad effects it causes, being disarmed makes you despised; this is one of those infamies a prince should guard himself against, as will be treated below: for between an armed and an unarmed man there is no comparison whatsoever, and it is not reasonable for an armed man to obey an unarmed man willingly, nor that an unarmed man should be safe among armed servants; since, when the former is suspicious and the latter are contemptuous, it is impossible for them to work well together. And therefore, a prince who does not understand military matters, besides the other misfortunes already noted, cannot be esteemed by his own soldiers, nor can he trust them.

He must, therefore, never raise his thought from this exercise   3 of war, and in peacetime he must train himself more than in time of war; this can be done in two ways: one by action, the other by the mind. And as far as actions are concerned, besides keeping his soldiers well disciplined and trained, he must always be out hunting, and must accustom his body to hardships in this manner; and he must also learn the nature of the terrain, and know how mountains slope, how valleys open, how plains lie, and understand the nature of rivers and swamps; and he should devote much attention to such activities. Such knowledge is useful in two ways: first, one learns to know one's own country and can better understand how to defend it; second, with the knowledge and experience of the terrain, one can easily comprehend the characteristics of any other terrain that it is necessary to explore for the first time; for the hills, valleys, plains, rivers, and swamps of Tuscany,[2] for instance, have certain similarities to those of other provinces; so that by knowing the lay of the land in one province one can easily understand it in others. And a prince who lacks this ability lacks the most important quality in a leader; because this skill teaches you to find the enemy, choose a

---

[1] **Francesco Sforza (1401–1466)** Became duke of Milan in 1450. He was, like most of Machiavelli's examples, a skilled diplomat and soldier. His court was a model of Renaissance scholarship and achievement.

[2] **Tuscany** Florence is in the region of Italy known as Tuscany.

campsite, lead troops, organize them for battle, and besiege towns to your own advantage.

Philopoemon, Prince of the Achaeans,[3] among the other praises 4 given to him by writers, is praised because in peacetime he thought of nothing except the means of waging war; and when he was out in the country with his friends, he often stopped and reasoned with them: "If the enemy were on that hilltop and we were here with our army, which of the two of us would have the advantage? How could we attack them without breaking formation? If we wanted to retreat, how could we do this? If they were to retreat, how could we pursue them?" And he proposed to them, as they rode along, all the contingencies that can occur in an army; he heard their opinions, expressed his own, and backed it up with arguments; so that, because of these continuous deliberations, when leading his troops no unforeseen incident could arise for which he did not have the remedy.

But as for the exercise of the mind, the prince must read histories 5 and in them study the deeds of great men; he must see how they conducted themselves in wars; he must examine the reasons for their victories and for their defeats in order to avoid the latter and to imitate the former; and above all else he must do as some distinguished man before him has done, who elected to imitate someone who had been praised and honored before him, and always keep in mind his deeds and actions; just as it is reported that Alexander the Great imitated Achilles; Caesar, Alexander; Scipio, Cyrus.[4] And anyone who reads the life of Cyrus written by Xenophon then realizes how important in the life of Scipio that imitation was to his glory and how much, in purity, goodness, humanity, and generosity, Scipio conformed to those characteristics of Cyrus that Xenophon had written about.

Such methods as these a wise prince must follow, and never 6 in peaceful times must he be idle; but he must turn them diligently to his advantage in order to be able to profit from them in times of

---

[3] **Philopoemon (252?–182 B.C.E.), Prince of the Achaeans** Philopoemon, from the city-state of Megalopolis, was a Greek general noted for skillful diplomacy. He led the Achaeans, a group of Greek states that formed the Achaean League, in several important expeditions, notably against Sparta. His cruelty in putting down a Spartan uprising caused him to be reprimanded by his superiors.

[4] **Cyrus (585?–529? B.C.E.)** Cyrus II (the Great), Persian emperor. Cyrus and the other figures featured in this sentence — Alexander the Great (356–323 B.C.E.); Achilles, hero of Homer's *Iliad*; Julius Caesar (100?–44 B.C.E.); and Scipio Africanus (236–184/3 B.C.E.), legendary Roman general — are all examples of politicians who were also great military geniuses. Xenophon (431–350? B.C.E.) was one of the earliest Greek historians; he chronicled the lives and military exploits of Cyrus and his son-in-law Darius.

adversity, so that, when Fortune changes, she will find him prepared to withstand such times.

On Those Things for Which Men, and Particularly Princes, Are Praised or Blamed

Now there remains to be examined what should be the methods   7
and procedures of a prince in dealing with his subjects and friends. And because I know that many have written about this, I am afraid that by writing about it again I shall be thought of as presumptuous, since in discussing this material I depart radically from the procedures of others. But since my intention is to write something useful for anyone who understands it, it seemed more suitable to me to search after the effectual truth of the matter rather than its imagined one. And many writers have imagined for themselves republics and principalities that have never been seen nor known to exist in reality; for there is such a gap between how one lives and how one ought to live that anyone who abandons what is done for what ought to be done learns his ruin rather than his preservation: for a man who wishes to make a vocation of being good at all times will come to ruin among so many who are not good. Hence it is necessary for a prince who wishes to maintain his position to learn how not to be good, and to use this knowledge or not to use it according to necessity.

Leaving aside, therefore, the imagined things concerning a prince,   8
and taking into account those that are true, I say that all men, when they are spoken of, and particularly princes, since they are placed on a higher level, are judged by some of these qualities which bring them either blame or praise. And this is why one is considered generous, another miserly (to use a Tuscan word, since "avaricious" in our language is still used to mean one who wishes to acquire by means of theft; we call "miserly" one who excessively avoids using what he has); one is considered a giver, the other rapacious; one cruel, another merciful; one treacherous, another faithful; one effeminate and cowardly, another bold and courageous; one humane, another haughty; one lascivious, another chaste; one trustworthy, another cunning; one harsh, another lenient; one serious, another frivolous; one religious, another unbelieving; and the like. And I know that everyone will admit that it would be a very praiseworthy thing to find in a prince, of the qualities mentioned above, those that are held to be good, but since it is neither possible to have them nor to observe them all completely, because human nature does not permit it, a prince must be prudent enough to know how to escape the bad reputation of those vices that would lose the state for him, and must protect himself from those that

will not lose it for him, if this is possible; but if he cannot, he need not concern himself unduly if he ignores these less serious vices. And, moreover, he need not worry about incurring the bad reputation of those vices without which it would be difficult to hold his state; since, carefully taking everything into account, one will discover that something which appears to be a virtue, if pursued, will end in his destruction; while some other thing which seems to be a vice, if pursued, will result in his safety and his well-being.

On Generosity and Miserliness

Beginning, therefore, with the first of the above-mentioned quali-   9
ties, I say that it would be good to be considered generous; nevertheless, generosity used in such a manner as to give you a reputation for it will harm you; because if it is employed virtuously and as one should employ it, it will not be recognized and you will not avoid the reproach of its opposite. And so, if a prince wants to maintain his reputation for generosity among men, it is necessary for him not to neglect any possible means of lavish display; in so doing such a prince will always use up all his resources and he will be obliged, eventually, if he wishes to maintain his reputation for generosity, to burden the people with excessive taxes and to do everything possible to raise funds. This will begin to make him hateful to his subjects, and, becoming impoverished, he will not be much esteemed by anyone; so that, as a consequence of his generosity, having offended many and rewarded few, he will feel the effects of any slight unrest and will be ruined at the first sign of danger; recognizing this and wishing to alter his policies, he immediately runs the risk of being reproached as a miser.

A prince, therefore, unable to use this virtue of generosity in   10
a manner which will not harm himself if he is known for it, should, if he is wise, not worry about being called a miser; for with time he will come to be considered more generous once it is evident that, as a result of his parsimony, his income is sufficient, he can defend himself from anyone who makes war against him, and he can undertake enterprises without overburdening his people, so that he comes to be generous with all those from whom he takes nothing, who are countless, and miserly with all those to whom he gives nothing, who are few. In our times we have not seen great deeds accomplished except by those who were considered miserly; all others were done away with. Pope Julius II,[5] although he made use of his reputation

---

[5] **Pope Julius II (1443–1513)** Giuliano della Rovere, pope from 1503 to 1513. Like many of the popes of the day, Julius II was also a diplomat and a general.

for generosity in order to gain the papacy, then decided not to maintain it in order to be able to wage war; the present King of France[6] has waged many wars without imposing extra taxes on his subjects, only because his habitual parsimony has provided for the additional expenditures; the present King of Spain,[7] if he had been considered generous, would not have engaged in nor won so many campaigns.

Therefore, in order not to have to rob his subjects, to be able to defend himself, not to become poor and contemptible, and not to be forced to become rapacious, a prince must consider it of little importance if he incurs the name of miser, for this is one of those vices that permits him to rule. And if someone were to say: Caesar with his generosity came to rule the empire, and many others, because they were generous and known to be so, achieved very high positions; I reply: you are either already a prince or you are on the way to becoming one; in the first instance such generosity is damaging; in the second it is very necessary to be thought generous. And Caesar was one of those who wanted to gain the principality of Rome; but if, after obtaining this, he had lived and had not moderated his expenditures, he would have destroyed that empire. And if someone were to reply: there have existed many princes who have accomplished great deeds with their armies who have been reputed to be generous; I answer you: a prince either spends his own money and that of his subjects or that of others; in the first case he must be economical; in the second he must not restrain any part of his generosity. And for that prince who goes out with his soldiers and lives by looting, sacking, and ransoms, who controls the property of others, such generosity is necessary; otherwise he would not be followed by his troops. And with what does not belong to you or to your subjects you can be a more liberal giver, as were Cyrus, Caesar, and Alexander; for spending the wealth of others does not lessen your reputation but adds to it; only the spending of your own is what harms you. And there is nothing that uses itself up faster than generosity, for as you employ it you lose the means of employing it, and you become either poor or despised or, in order to escape poverty, rapacious and hated. And above all other things a prince must guard himself against being despised and hated; and generosity leads you to both one and the other. So it is wiser to live with the reputation of a miser, which produces reproach without hatred, than to be

11

---

[6]**present King of France** Louis XII (1462–1515). He entered Italy on a successful military campaign in 1494.

[7]**present King of Spain** Ferdinand V (1452–1516). A studied politician; he and Queen Isabella (1451–1504) financed Christopher Columbus's voyage to the New World in 1492.

forced to incur the reputation of rapacity, which produces reproach along with hatred, because you want to be considered as generous.

On Cruelty and Mercy and Whether It Is Better to Be Loved Than to Be Feared or the Contrary

Proceeding to the other qualities mentioned above, I say that every 12 prince must desire to be considered merciful and not cruel; nevertheless, he must take care not to misuse this mercy. Cesare Borgia[8] was considered cruel; nonetheless, his cruelty had brought order to Romagna,[9] united it, restored it to peace and obedience. If we examine this carefully, we shall see that he was more merciful than the Florentine people, who, in order to avoid being considered cruel, allowed the destruction of Pistoia.[10] Therefore, a prince must not worry about the reproach of cruelty when it is a matter of keeping his subjects united and loyal; for with a very few examples of cruelty he will be more compassionate than those who, out of excessive mercy, permit disorders to continue, from which arise murders and plundering; for these usually harm the community at large, while the executions that come from the prince harm one individual in particular. And the new prince, above all other princes, cannot escape the reputation of being called cruel, since new states are full of dangers. And Virgil, through Dido, states: "My difficult condition and the newness of my rule make me act in such a manner, and to set guards over my land on all sides."[11]

Nevertheless, a prince must be cautious in believing and in act- 13 ing, nor should he be afraid of his own shadow; and he should proceed in such a manner, tempered by prudence and humanity, so that too much trust may not render him imprudent nor too much distrust render him intolerable.

From this arises an argument: whether it is better to be loved 14 than to be feared, or the contrary. I reply that one should like to be both one and the other; but since it is difficult to join them together, it is much safer to be feared than to be loved when one of the two must be lacking. For one can generally say this about men: that they

---

[8] **Cesare Borgia (1476–1507)** He was known for his brutality and lack of scruples, not to mention his exceptionally good luck. He was a firm ruler, son of Pope Alexander VI.

[9] **Romagna** Region northeast of Tuscany; includes the towns of Bologna, Ferrara, Ravenna, and Rimini. Borgia united it as his base of power in 1501.

[10] **Pistoia** (also known as Pistoria) A town near Florence, disturbed in 1501 by a civil war that could have been averted by strong repressive measures.

[11] The quotation is from the *Aeneid* (2.563–64), the greatest Latin epic poem, written by Virgil (70–19 B.C.E.). Dido, a woman general, ruled Carthage.

are ungrateful, fickle, simulators and deceivers, avoiders of danger, greedy for gain; and while you work for their good they are completely yours, offering you their blood, their property, their lives, and their sons, as I said earlier, when danger is far away; but when it comes nearer to you they turn away. And that prince who bases his power entirely on their words, finding himself stripped of other preparations, comes to ruin; for friendships that are acquired by a price and not by greatness and nobility of character are purchased but are not owned, and at the proper moment they cannot be spent. And men are less hesitant about harming someone who makes himself loved than one who makes himself feared because love is held together by a chain of obligation which, since men are a sorry lot, is broken on every occasion in which their own self-interest is concerned; but fear is held together by a dread of punishment which will never abandon you.

A prince must nevertheless make himself feared in such a manner that he will avoid hatred, even if he does not acquire love; since to be feared and not to be hated can very well be combined; and this will always be so when he keeps his hands off the property and the women of his citizens and his subjects. And if he must take someone's life, he should do so when there is proper justification and manifest cause; but, above all, he should avoid the property of others; for men forget more quickly the death of their father than the loss of their patrimony. Moreover, the reasons for seizing their property are never lacking; and he who begins to live by stealing always finds a reason for taking what belongs to others; on the contrary, reasons for taking a life are rarer and disappear sooner.   15

But when the prince is with his armies and has under his command a multitude of troops, then it is absolutely necessary that he not worry about being considered cruel; for without that reputation he will never keep an army united or prepared for any combat. Among the praiseworthy deeds of Hannibal[12] is counted this: that, having a very large army, made up of all kinds of men, which he commanded in foreign lands, there never arose the slightest dissention, neither among themselves nor against their prince, both during his good and his bad fortune. This could not have arisen from anything other than his inhuman cruelty, which, along with his many other abilities, made him always respected and terrifying in the eyes of his soldiers; and without that, to attain the same effect, his other abilities   16

---

[12] **Hannibal (247–183 B.C.E.)** An amazingly inventive military tactician who led the Carthaginian armies against Rome for more than fifteen years. He crossed the Alps from Gaul (France) in order to surprise Rome. He was noted for use of the ambush and for "inhuman cruelty."

would not have sufficed. And the writers of history, having considered this matter very little, on the one hand admire these deeds of his and on the other condemn the main cause of them.

And that it be true that his other abilities would not have been 17
sufficient can be seen from the example of Scipio, a most extraordinary man not only in his time but in all recorded history, whose armies in Spain rebelled against him; this came about from nothing other than his excessive compassion, which gave to his soldiers more liberty than military discipline allowed. For this he was censured in the senate by Fabius Maximus,[13] who called him the corruptor of the Roman militia. The Locrians,[14] having been ruined by one of Scipio's officers, were not avenged by him, nor was the arrogance of that officer corrected, all because of his tolerant nature; so that someone in the senate who tried to apologize for him said that there were many men who knew how not to err better than they knew how to correct errors. Such a nature would have, in time, damaged Scipio's fame and glory if he had maintained it during the empire; but, living under the control of the senate, this harmful characteristic of his not only concealed itself but brought him fame.

I conclude, therefore, returning to the problem of being feared 18
and loved, that since men love at their own pleasure and fear at the pleasure of the prince, a wise prince should build his foundation upon that which belongs to him, not upon that which belongs to others: he must strive only to avoid hatred, as has been said.

How a Prince Should Keep His Word

How praiseworthy it is for a prince to keep his word and to live 19
by integrity and not by deceit everyone knows; nevertheless, one sees from the experience of our times that the princes who have accomplished great deeds are those who have cared little for keeping their promises and who have known how to manipulate the minds of men by shrewdness; and in the end they have surpassed those who laid their foundations upon honesty.

You must, therefore, know that there are two means of fight- 20
ing: one according to the laws, the other with force; the first way is proper to man, the second to beasts; but because the first, in many cases, is not sufficient, it becomes necessary to have recourse to

---

[13] **Fabius Maximus (?–203 B.C.E.)** Roman general who fought Hannibal. He was jealous of the younger Roman general Scipio.

[14] **Locrians** Inhabitants of Locri, an Italian town settled by the Greeks in c. 680 B.C.E.

the second. Therefore, a prince must know how to use wisely the natures of the beast and the man. This policy was taught to princes allegorically by the ancient writers, who described how Achilles and many other ancient princes were given to Chiron[15] the Centaur to be raised and taught under his discipline. This can only mean that, having a half-beast and half-man as a teacher, a prince must know how to employ the nature of the one and the other; and the one without the other cannot endure.

Since, then, a prince must know how to make good use of the   21
nature of the beast, he should choose from among the beasts the fox and the lion; for the lion cannot defend itself from traps and the fox cannot protect itself from wolves. It is therefore necessary to be a fox in order to recognize the traps and a lion in order to frighten the wolves. Those who play only the part of the lion do not understand matters. A wise ruler, therefore, cannot and should not keep his word when such an observance of faith would be to his disadvantage and when the reasons which made him promise are removed. And if men were all good, this rule would not be good; but since men are a sorry lot and will not keep their promises to you, you likewise need not keep yours to them. A prince never lacks legitimate reasons to break his promises. Of this one could cite an endless number of modern examples to show how many pacts, how many promises have been made null and void because of the infidelity of princes; and he who has known best how to use the fox has come to a better end. But it is necessary to know how to disguise this nature well and to be a great hypocrite and a liar: and men are so simpleminded and so controlled by their present necessities that one who deceives will always find another who will allow himself to be deceived.

I do not wish to remain silent about one of these recent instances.   22
Alexander VI[16] did nothing else, he thought about nothing else, except to deceive men, and he always found the occasion to do this. And there never was a man who had more forcefulness in his oaths, who affirmed a thing with more promises, and who honored his word less; nevertheless, his tricks always succeeded perfectly since he was well acquainted with this aspect of the world.

Therefore, it is not necessary for a prince to have all of the   23
above-mentioned qualities, but it is very necessary for him to appear to have them. Furthermore, I shall be so bold as to assert this: that having them and practicing them at all times is harmful; and appearing to

---

[15] **Chiron** A mythical figure, a centaur (half man, half horse). Unlike most centaurs, he was wise and benevolent; he was also a legendary physician.

[16] **Alexander VI (1431–1503)** Roderigo Borgia, pope from 1492 to 1503. He was Cesare Borgia's father and a corrupt but immensely powerful pope.

have them is useful; for instance, to seem merciful, faithful, humane, forthright, religious, and to be so; but his mind should be disposed in such a way that should it become necessary not to be so, he will be able and know how to change to the contrary. And it is essential to understand this: that a prince, and especially a new prince, cannot observe all those things by which men are considered good, for in order to maintain the state he is often obliged to act against his promise, against charity, against humanity, and against religion. And therefore, it is necessary that he have a mind ready to turn itself according to the way the winds of Fortune and the changeability of affairs require him; and, as I said above, as long as it is possible, he should not stray from the good, but he should know how to enter into evil when necessity commands.

A prince, therefore, must be very careful never to let anything   24 slip from his lips which is not full of the five qualities mentioned above: he should appear, upon seeing and hearing him, to be all mercy, all faithfulness, all integrity, all kindness, all religion. And there is nothing more necessary than to seem to possess this last quality. And men in general judge more by their eyes than their hands; for everyone can see but few can feel. Everyone sees what you seem to be, few perceive what you are, and those few do not dare to contradict the opinion of the many who have the majesty of the state to defend them; and in the actions of all men, and especially of princes, where there is no impartial arbiter, one must consider the final result.[17] Let a prince therefore act to seize and to maintain the state; his methods will always be judged honorable and will be praised by all; for ordinary people are always deceived by appearances and by the outcome of a thing; and in the world there is nothing but ordinary people; and there is no room for the few, while the many have a place to lean on. A certain prince[18] of the present day, whom I shall refrain from naming, preaches nothing but peace and faith, and to both one and the other he is entirely opposed; and both, if he had put them into practice, would have cost him many times over either his reputation or his state.

On Avoiding Being Despised and Hated

But since, concerning the qualities mentioned above, I have   25 spoken about the most important, I should like to discuss the others briefly in this general manner: that the prince, as was noted above,

---

[17] The Italian original, *si guarda al fine*, has often been mistranslated as "the ends justify the means," something Machiavelli never wrote. [Translators' note]
[18] **A certain prince** Probably King Ferdinand V of Spain (1452–1516).

should think about avoiding those things which make him hated and despised; and when he has avoided this, he will have carried out his duties and will find no danger whatsoever in other vices. As I have said, what makes him hated above all else is being rapacious and a usurper of the property and the women of his subjects; he must refrain from this; and in most cases, so long as you do not deprive them of either their property or their honor, the majority of men live happily; and you have only to deal with the ambition of a few, who can be restrained without difficulty and by many means. What makes him despised is being considered changeable, frivolous, effeminate, cowardly, irresolute; from these qualities a prince must guard himself as if from a reef, and he must strive to make everyone recognize in his actions greatness, spirit, dignity, and strength; and concerning the private affairs of his subjects, he must insist that his decision be irrevocable; and he should maintain himself in such a way that no man could imagine that he can deceive or cheat him.

That prince who projects such an opinion of himself is greatly 26 esteemed; and it is difficult to conspire against a man with such a reputation and difficult to attack him, provided that he is understood to be of great merit and revered by his subjects. For a prince must have two fears: one, internal, concerning his subjects; the other, external, concerning foreign powers. From the latter he can defend himself by his good troops and friends; and he will always have good friends if he has good troops; and internal affairs will always be stable when external affairs are stable, provided that they are not already disturbed by a conspiracy; and even if external conditions change, if he is properly organized and lives as I have said and does not lose control of himself, he will always be able to withstand every attack, just as I said that Nabis the Spartan[19] did. But concerning his subjects, when external affairs do not change, he has to fear that they may conspire secretly: the prince secures himself from this by avoiding being hated or despised and by keeping the people satisfied with him; this is a necessary matter, as was treated above at length. And one of the most powerful remedies a prince has against conspiracies is not to be hated by the masses; for a man who plans a conspiracy always believes that he will satisfy the people by killing the prince; but when he thinks he might anger them, he cannot work up the courage to undertake such a deed; for the problems on the side of the conspirators are countless. And experience demonstrates that conspiracies have been many but few have been concluded successfully; for anyone who conspires cannot be

---

[19] **Nabis the Spartan** Tyrant of Sparta from 207 to 192 B.C.E., routed by Philopoemon and the Achaean League.

alone, nor can he find companions except from amongst those whom he believes to be dissatisfied; and as soon as you have uncovered your intent to one dissatisfied man, you give him the means to make himself happy, since he can have everything he desires by uncovering the plot; so much is this so that, seeing a sure gain on the one hand and one doubtful and full of danger on the other, if he is to maintain faith with you he has to be either an unusually good friend or a completely determined enemy of the prince. And to treat the matter briefly, I say that on the part of the conspirator there is nothing but fear, jealousy, and the thought of punishment that terrifies him; but on the part of the prince there is the majesty of the principality, the laws, the defenses of friends and the state to protect him; so that, with the good will of the people added to all these things, it is impossible for anyone to be so rash as to plot against him. For, where usually a conspirator has to be afraid before he executes his evil deed, in this case he must be afraid, having the people as an enemy, even after the crime is performed, nor can he hope to find any refuge because of this.

One could cite countless examples on this subject; but I want   27
to satisfy myself with only one which occurred during the time of our fathers. Messer Annibale Bentivoglio, prince of Bologna and grandfather of the present Messer Annibale, was murdered by the Canneschi[20] family, who conspired against him; he left behind no heir except Messer Giovanni,[21] then only a baby. As soon as this murder occurred, the people rose up and killed all the Canneschi. This came about because of the goodwill that the house of the Bentivoglio enjoyed in those days; this goodwill was so great that with Annibale dead, and there being no one of that family left in the city who could rule Bologna, the Bolognese people, having heard that in Florence there was one of the Bentivoglio blood who was believed until that time to be the son of a blacksmith, went to Florence to find him, and they gave him the control of that city; it was ruled by him until Messer Giovanni became of age to rule.

I conclude, therefore, that a prince must be little concerned with   28
conspiracies when the people are well disposed toward him; but when the populace is hostile and regards him with hatred, he must fear everything and everyone. And well-organized states and wise princes have, with great diligence, taken care not to anger the nobles and to satisfy the common people and keep them contented; for this is one of the most important concerns that a prince has.

---

[20] **Canneschi** Prominent family in Bologna.

[21] **Giovanni Bentivoglio (1443–1508)** Former tyrant of Bologna. In sequence he was a conspirator against, then a conspirator with, Cesare Borgia.

QUESTIONS FOR CRITICAL READING

1. The usual criticism of Machiavelli is that he advises his prince to be unscrupulous. Find examples for and against this claim.

2. Why do you agree or disagree with Machiavelli when he asserts that the great majority of people are not good? Does our government assume that to be true too?

3. Politicians—especially heads of state—are the contemporary counterparts of the prince. To what extent should successful heads of modern states show skill in war? Is modern war similar to wars in Machiavelli's era? If so, in what ways?

4. Clarify the advice Machiavelli gives concerning liberality and stinginess. Is this still good advice?

5. Are modern politicians likely to succeed by following all or most of Machiavelli's recommendations? Why or why not?

SUGGESTIONS FOR CRITICAL WRITING

1. In speaking of the prince's military duties, Machiavelli says that "being disarmed makes you despised." Choose an example or instance to strengthen your argument for or against this position. Is it possible that in modern society being defenseless is an advantage?

2. Find evidence within this excerpt to demonstrate that Machiavelli's attitude toward human nature is accurate. Remember that the usual criticism of Machiavelli is that he is cynical—that he thinks the worst of people rather than the best. Find quotations from the excerpt that support either or both of these views; then use them as the basis for an essay analyzing Machiavelli's views on human nature.

3. By referring to current events and leaders—either local, national, or international—decide whether Machiavelli's advice to the prince is useful to the modern politician. Consider whether the advice is completely useless or completely reliable or whether its value depends on specific conditions. First state the advice, then show how it applies (or does not apply) to specific politicians, and finally critique its general effectiveness.

4. Probably the chief ethical issue raised by *The Prince* is the question of whether the desired ends justify the means used to achieve them. Write an essay in which you take a stand on this question. Begin by defining the issue: What does the concept "the ends justify the means" actually mean? What difficulties may arise when unworthy means are used to achieve worthy ends? Analyze Machiavelli's references to circumstances in which questionable means were (or should have been) used to achieve worthy ends. Use historical or personal examples to give your argument substance.

5. **CONNECTIONS** One of Machiavelli's most controversial statements is: "A man who wishes to make a vocation of being good at all times will come to ruin among so many who are not good." How would Lao-tzu respond to this statement? How does the American political environment in the current decade support this statement? Under what conditions would such a statement become irrelevant?

6. **CONNECTIONS** When Machiavelli wrote *The Prince,* Cicero was studied in virtually every school in renaissance Italy. It is likely that Machiavelli would have not only read Cicero but would have valued his ideas highly. Write an essay that demonstrates conclusively that Machiavelli learned important lessons from the argument that Cicero presents in his "mouthpiece" Philus in "The Defense of Injustice" (**bedfordstmartins.com/worldofideas/epages**). What assumptions does Philus make about government that agree with Machiavelli's views about government?

7. **CONNECTIONS** For some commentators, the prince that Machiavelli describes resembles the kind of ruler Hannah Arendt deplores in her essay "Total Domination." Examine Machiavelli's views in terms of how his principles would result in a form of government similar to that which Arendt describes. Is terror a legitimate weapon for Machiavelli's prince? How would Machiavelli rationalize the prince's use of terror, should it become necessary?

8. **SEEING CONNECTIONS** How would Machiavelli respond to Delacroix's *Liberty Leading the People* (p. 200)? This painting represents a ragtag group of citizens armed and attempting to overthrow a "prince," King Charles X of France. The citizens did indeed cause Charles to abdicate in favor of Louis-Philippe, called "the Citizen King" because he was not part of the royal family of the Bourbons who had produced the modern kings of France. How does the event represented in the painting figure in Machiavelli's advice on how a prince should maintain power? Would Machiavelli have welcomed the idea of Liberty being the central figure in a painting like Delacroix's?

JEAN-JACQUES ROUSSEAU
The Origin of Civil Society

JEAN-JACQUES ROUSSEAU (1712–1778) was the son of
Suzanne Bernard and Isaac Rousseau, a watchmaker in Geneva,
Switzerland. Shortly after his birth, Rousseau's mother died, and
a rash duel forced his father from Geneva. Rousseau was then
apprenticed at age thirteen to an engraver, a master who treated
him badly. He soon ran away from his master and found a home
with a Catholic noblewoman who at first raised him as her son
and then, when he was twenty, took him as her lover. In the process Rousseau converted from Calvinist Protestantism to Roman
Catholicism. Eventually, he left Switzerland for Paris, where he won
an important essay contest and became celebrated in society.

Over the course of his lifetime, Rousseau produced a wide variety
of literary and musical works, including a novel, *Emile* (1762), an opera,
The Village Soothsayer (1752), and an autobiography, *The Confessions*
(published posthumously in 1789). *The Social Contract* (1762) was part
of a never-completed longer work on political systems. In many ways
Rousseau wrote in reaction to political thinkers such as Hugo Grotius
and Thomas Hobbes, to whom he responds in the following selection.
He contended that the Dutch philosopher and legal expert Grotius
unquestioningly accepted the power of the aristocracy. He felt Grotius
paid too much attention to what was rather than what ought to be. On
the other hand, Hobbes, the English political philosopher, asserted that
people had a choice of being free or being ruled. In other words, those
who were members of civil society chose to give up their freedom and
submit to the monarch's rule. Either they relinquished their freedom, or
they removed themselves from civil society to live a brutish existence.

Rousseau argued against Grotius by examining the way things
ought to be. He argued against Hobbes by asserting that both the body

From *Social Contract: Essays by Locke, Hume, and Rousseau.* Translated by
Gerald Hopkins.

politic and the monarch were sovereign and that when people created a civil society they surrendered their freedom to themselves as a group. If one person acted as sovereign or lawgiver, then that lawgiver had the responsibility of acting in accord with the will of the people. In a sense, this view parallels some of the views of Lao-tzu in the *Tao-te Ching*.

Popularly referred to as a defender of republicanism, Rousseau looked to the Republic of Geneva, his birthplace, as a model of government. He also idealized the generally democratic government of smaller Swiss cantons, such as Neuchatel, which used a form of town meeting where people gathered face-to-face to settle important issues. Ironically, Geneva put out a warrant for his arrest upon the publication of *The Social Contract* because although it praised Geneva's republicanism, it also condemned societies that depended on rule by a limited aristocracy. Unfortunately for Rousseau, at that time Geneva was governed by a small number of aristocratic families. Rousseau was deprived of his citizenship and could not return to his native home.

Similarly, Rousseau's controversial views were not easily received by those in power in France. After the publication of *Emile* offended the French parliament, Rousseau was forced to abandon his comfortable rustic circumstances—living on country estates provided by patrons from the court—and spend the rest of his life in financial uncertainty. Ironically, in 1789, a decade after his death, Rousseau's philosophy was adopted by supporters of the French Revolution in their bloody revolt against the aristocracy.

Rousseau's Rhetoric

Rousseau's method is in many ways antagonistic: he establishes the views of other thinkers, counters them, and then offers his own ideas. An early example appears in the opening of paragraph 8: "Grotius denies that political power is ever exercised in the interests of the governed, and quotes the institution of slavery in support of his contention. His invariable method of arguing is to derive Right from Fact." Among other things, Rousseau expects his readers to know who Grotius was and what he said. He also expects his readers to agree that Grotius derives "Right from Fact" by understanding that the fact of monarchy justifies it as being right. As Rousseau tells us, that kind of circular reasoning is especially kind to tyrants because it justifies them by their existence.

Rousseau uses analysis and examination of detail as his main rhetorical approaches. Whether he examines the ideas of others or presents ideas of his own, he is careful to examine the bases of the argument and to follow the arguments to their conclusions.

He does this very thoroughly in his section "Of Slavery," in which he demonstrates that slavery is unacceptable no matter which of the current arguments are used to support it, including the widely held view that it was justifiable to enslave captured soldiers on the grounds that they owed their lives to their captors.

Rousseau also makes careful use of aphorism and analogy. His opening statement, "Man is born free, and everywhere he is in chains," is an aphorism that has been often quoted. It is a powerful and perplexing statement. How do people who are born free lose their freedom? Is it taken from them, or do they willingly surrender it? Rousseau spends considerable time examining this point.

The use of analogy is probably most striking in his comparison of government with the family. The force of the analogy reminds us that the members of a family are to be looked after by the family. As he tells us beginning in paragraph 5, the family is the only natural form of society. But instead of stopping there, he goes on to say that children are bound to the father only as long as they need him. Once they are able to be independent, they dissolve the natural bond and "return to a condition of equal independence." This analogy differs from the existing popular view that the monarch was like the father in a family and the people like his children; in fact, the analogy works against the legitimacy of the traditional monarchy as it was known in eighteenth-century France.

Rousseau also refers to other writers, using a rhetorical device known as *testimony:* he paraphrases the views of other authorities and moves on to promote his own. But in referring to other writers, Rousseau is unusually clever. For example, in paragraph 10 he begins with the analogy of the shepherd as the ruler in this fashion: "Just as the shepherd is superior in kind to his sheep, so, too, the shepherds of men, or, in other words, their rulers, are superior in kind to their peoples. This, according to Philo, was the argument advanced by Caligula, the Emperor, who drew from the analogy the perfectly true conclusion that either Kings are Gods or their subjects brute beasts." Caligula was a madman and an emperor guilty of enormous cruelty; from his point of view it may have seemed true that kings were gods. But Rousseau, in citing this questionable authority, disputes the validity of the analogy.

He argues as well against the view that might makes right in "Of the Right of the Strongest." The value of the social contract, he explains, is to produce a society that is not governed by the mightiest and most ruthless and that permits those who are not mighty to live peacefully and unmolested. Thus, those who participate in the social contract give up certain freedoms but gain many more—among them the freedom not to be dominated by physical brutality.

Rousseau concentrates on the question of man in nature, or natural society. His view is that natural society is dominated by the strongest individuals but that at some point natural society breaks down. Thus, in order to guarantee the rights of those who are not the strongest, the political order must change. "Some form of association" is developed "for the protection of the person and property of each constituent member." By surrendering some freedom to the group as a whole—to "the general will"—the individuals in the group can expect to prosper more widely and to live more happily. According to Rousseau, the establishment of a social contract ensures the stability of this form of civil society.

PREREADING QUESTIONS:
WHAT TO READ FOR

The following prereading questions may help you anticipate key issues in the discussion of Jean-Jacques Rousseau's "The Origin of Civil Society." Keeping them in mind as you read should help focus your attention.

- When Rousseau says, "Man is born free, and everywhere he is in chains," does he seem to be referring literally to slaves in chains or more figuratively to people in general?

- How convincing is Rousseau when he claims that the oldest form of government is the family?

- The "Social Contract" is one of Rousseau's chief ideas. What does it seem to mean?

The Origin of Civil Society

Note

It is my wish to inquire whether it be possible, within the civil order, to   1
discover a legitimate and stable basis of Government. This I shall do by considering human beings as they are and laws as they might be. I shall attempt, throughout my investigations, to maintain a constant connection between what right permits and interest demands, in order that no separation may be made between justice and utility. I intend to begin without first proving the importance of my subject. Am I, it will be asked, either prince or legislator that I take it upon me to write of politics? My answer is—No; and it is for that very reason that I have chosen politics as the matter of my book. Were I either the one or the other I should not waste my time in laying down what has to be done. I should do it, or else hold my peace.

I was born into a free state and am a member of its sovereign body.   2
My influence on public affairs may be small, but because I have a right to

exercise my vote, it is my duty to learn their nature, and it has been for me a matter of constant delight, while meditating on problems of Government in general, to find ever fresh reasons for regarding with true affection the way in which these things are ordered in my native land.

The Subject of the First Book

Man is born free, and everywhere he is in chains. Many a man 3 believes himself to be the master of others who is, no less than they, a slave. How did this change take place? I do not know. What can make it legitimate? To this question I hope to be able to furnish an answer.

Were I considering only force and the effects of force, I should 4 say: "So long as a People is constrained to obey, and does, in fact, obey, it does well. So soon as it can shake off its yoke, and succeeds in doing so, it does better. The fact that it has recovered its liberty by virtue of that same right by which it was stolen, means either that it is entitled to resume it, or that its theft by others was, in the first place, without justification." But the social order is a sacred right which serves as a foundation for all other rights. This right, however, since it comes not by nature, must have been built upon conventions. To discover what these conventions are is the matter of our inquiry. But, before proceeding further, I must establish the truth of what I have so far advanced.

Of Primitive Societies

The oldest form of society—and the only natural one—is the 5 family. Children remain bound to their father for only just so long as they feel the need of him for their self-preservation. Once that need ceases the natural bond is dissolved. From then on, the children, freed from the obedience which they formerly owed, and the father, cleared of his debt of responsibility to them, return to a condition of equal independence. If the bond remain operative it is no longer something imposed by nature, but has become a matter of deliberate choice. The family is a family still, but by reason of convention only.

This shared liberty is a consequence of man's nature. Its first law 6 is that of self-preservation: its first concern is for what it owes itself. As soon as a man attains the age of reason he becomes his own master, because he alone can judge of what will best assure his continued existence.

We may, therefore, if we will, regard the family as the basic 7 model of all political associations. The ruler is the father writ large: the people are, by analogy, his children, and all, ruler and people alike, alienate their freedom only so far as it is to their advantage to do so. The only difference is that, whereas in the family the father's love for his children is sufficient reward to him for the care he has lavished on them, in the State, the pleasure of commanding others takes its place, since the ruler is not in a relation of love to his people.

Grotius[1] denies that political power is ever exercised in the inter-   8 ests of the governed, and quotes the institution of slavery in support of his contention. His invariable method of arguing is to derive Right from Fact. It might be possible to adopt a more logical system of rea- soning, but none which would be more favorable to tyrants.

According to Grotius, therefore, it is doubtful whether the term   9 "human race" belongs to only a few hundred men, or whether those few hundred men belong to the human race. From the evidence of his book it seems clear that he holds by the first of these alternatives, and on this point Hobbes[2] is in agreement with him. If this is so, then humanity is divided into herds of livestock, each with its "guardian" who watches over his charges only that he may ultimately devour them.

Just as the shepherd is superior in kind to his sheep, so, too,   10 the shepherds of men, or, in other words, their rulers, are superior in kind to their peoples. This, according to Philo,[3] was the argument advanced by Caligula,[4] the Emperor, who drew from the analogy the perfectly true conclusion that either Kings are Gods or their subjects brute beasts.

The reasoning of Caligula, of Hobbes, and of Grotius is funda-   11 mentally the same. Far earlier, Aristotle,[5] too, had maintained that men are not by nature equal, but that some are born to be slaves, oth- ers to be masters.

Aristotle was right: but he mistook the effect for the cause. Noth-   12 ing is more certain than that a man born into a condition of slavery is a

---

[1] **Hugo Grotius (1583–1645)** A Dutch lawyer who spent some time in exile in Paris. His fame as a child prodigy was considerable; his book on the laws of war (*De jure belli ac Pacis*) was widely known in Europe.

[2] **Thomas Hobbes (1588–1679)** An Englishman known as a materialist philos- opher who did not credit divine influence in politics. He became famous for *Leviathan*, a study of politics that treated the state as if it were a monster (leviathan) with a life of its own.

[3] **Philo (13? B.C.E.–47? C.E.)** A Jew who absorbed Greek culture and who wrote widely on many subjects. His studies on Mosaic law were considered important.

[4] **Caligula (12–41 C.E.)** Roman emperor of uncertain sanity. He loved his sis- ter Drusilla so much that he had her deified when she died. A military commander, he was assassinated by an officer.

[5] **Aristotle (384–322 B.C.E. See p. 6.)** A student of Plato; his philosophical method became the dominant intellectual force in Western thought.

slave by nature. A slave in fetters loses everything—even the desire to be freed from them. He grows to love his slavery, as the companions of Ulysses grew to love their state of brutish transformation.[6]

If some men are by nature slaves, the reason is that they have been made slaves *against* nature. Force made the first slaves: cowardice has perpetuated the species.   13

I have made no mention of King Adam or of the Emperor Noah, the father of three great Monarchs[7] who divided up the universe between them, as did the children of Saturn,[8] whom some have been tempted to identify with them. I trust that I may be given credit for my moderation, since, being descended in a direct line from one of these Princes, and quite possibly belonging to the elder branch, I may, for all I know, were my claims supported in law, be even now the legitimate Sovereign of the Human Race.[9] However that may be, all will concur in the view that Adam was King of the World, as was Robinson Crusoe of his island, only so long as he was its only inhabitant, and the great advantage of empire held on such terms was that the Monarch, firmly seated on his throne, had no need to fear rebellions, conspiracy, or war.   14

Of the Right of the Strongest

However strong a man, he is never strong enough to remain master always, unless he transform his Might into Right, and Obedience into Duty. Hence we have come to speak of the Right of the Strongest, a right which, seemingly assumed in irony, has, in fact, become established in principle. But the meaning of the phrase has never been adequately explained. Strength is a physical attribute, and I fail to see how any moral sanction can attach to its effects. To yield to the strong is an act of necessity, not of will. At most it is the result of a dictate of prudence. How, then, can it become a duty?   15

Let us assume for a moment that some such Right does really exist. The only deduction from this premise is inexplicable gibberish. For to   16

---

[6] **state of brutish transformation** This sentence refers to the Circe episode in Homer's *Odyssey* (10, 12). Circe was a sorceress who, by means of drugs, enchanted men and turned them into swine. Ulysses (Latin name of Odysseus), king of Ithaca, is the central figure of the *Odyssey*.

[7] **the father of three great Monarchs** Adam in the Bible (Gen. 4:1–25) fathered Cain, Abel, Enoch, and Seth. Noah's sons, Shem, Ham, and Japheth, repopulated the world after the Flood (Gen. 6:9–9:19).

[8] **children of Saturn** Saturn is a mythic god associated with the golden age of Rome and with the Greek god Cronus. It is probably the children of Cronus—Zeus, Poseidon, Hades, Demeter, and Hera—referred to here.

[9] **Sovereign of the Human Race** Rousseau is being ironic; like the rest of us, he is descended from Adam (according to the Bible).

admit that Might makes Right is to reverse the process of effect and cause. The mighty man who defeats his rival becomes heir to his Right. So soon as we can disobey with impunity, disobedience becomes legitimate. And, since the Mightiest is always right, it merely remains for us to become possessed of Might. But what validity can there be in a Right which ceases to exist when Might changes hands? If a man be constrained by Might to obey, what need has he to obey by Duty? And if he is not constrained to obey, there is no further obligation on him to do so. It follows, therefore, that the word Right adds nothing to the idea of Might. It becomes, in this connection, completely meaningless.

Obey the Powers that be. If that means Yield to Force, the precept is admirable but redundant. My reply to those who advance it is that no case will ever be found of its violation. All power comes from God. Certainly, but so do all ailments. Are we to conclude from such an argument that we are never to call in the doctor? If I am waylaid by a footpad at the corner of a wood, I am constrained by force to give him my purse. But if I can manage to keep it from him, is it my duty to hand it over? His pistol is also a symbol of Power. It must, then, be admitted that Might does not create Right, and that no man is under an obligation to obey any but the legitimate powers of the State. And so I continually come back to the question I first asked.

Of Slavery

Since no man has natural authority over his fellows, and since Might can produce no Right, the only foundation left for legitimate authority in human societies is Agreement.

If a private citizen, says Grotius, can alienate his liberty and make himself another man's slave, why should not a whole people do the same, and subject themselves to the will of a King? The argument contains a number of ambiguous words which stand in need of explanation. But let us confine our attention to one only—*alienate*. To alienate means to give or to sell. Now a man who becomes the slave of another does not give himself. He sells himself in return for bare subsistence, if for nothing more. But why should a whole people sell themselves? So far from furnishing subsistence to his subjects, a King draws his own from them, and from them alone. According to Rabelais,[10] it takes a lot to keep a King.

---

[10] **François Rabelais (c. 1494–1553)** French writer, author of *Gargantua* and *Pantagruel*, satires on politics and religion.

Do we, then, maintain that a subject surrenders his person on condition that his property be taken too? It is difficult to see what he will have left.

It will be said that the despot guarantees civil peace to his subjects. So be it. But how are they the gainers if the wars to which his ambition may expose them, his insatiable greed, and the vexatious demands of his Ministers cause them more loss than would any outbreak of internal dissension? How do they benefit if that very condition of civil peace be one of the causes of their wretchedness? One can live peacefully enough in a dungeon, but such peace will hardly, of itself, ensure one's happiness. The Greeks imprisoned in the cave of Cyclops[11] lived peacefully while awaiting their turn to be devoured.

To say that a man gives himself for nothing is to commit oneself to an absurd and inconceivable statement. Such an act of surrender is illegitimate, null, and void by the mere fact that he who makes it is not in his right mind. To say the same thing of a whole People is tantamount to admitting that the People in question are a nation of imbeciles. Imbecility does not produce Right.

Even if a man can alienate himself, he cannot alienate his children. They are born free, their liberty belongs to them, and no one but themselves has a right to dispose of it. Before they have attained the age of reason their father may make, on their behalf, certain rules with a view to ensuring their preservation and well-being. But any such limitation of their freedom of choice must be regarded as neither irrevocable nor unconditional, for to alienate another's liberty is contrary to the natural order, and is an abuse of the father's rights. It follows that an arbitrary government can be legitimate only on condition that each successive generation of subjects is free either to accept or to reject it, and if this is so, then the government will no longer be arbitrary.

When a man renounces his liberty he renounces his essential manhood, his rights, and even his duty as a human being. There is no compensation possible for such complete renunciation. It is incompatible with man's nature, and to deprive him of his free will is to deprive his actions of all moral sanction. The convention, in short, which sets up on one side an absolute authority, and on the other an obligation to obey without question, is vain and meaningless. Is it not obvious that where we can demand everything we owe nothing? Where there is no mutual obligation, no interchange of duties, it must, surely, be clear that the actions of the commanded cease to have any moral value? For how can it

20

21

22

23

---

[11] **cave of Cyclops** The cyclops is a one-eyed giant cannibal whose cave is the scene of one of Odysseus's triumphs in Homer's *Odyssey* (9).

be maintained that my slave has any "right" against me when everything that he has is my property? His right being *my* right, it is absurd to speak of it as ever operating to my disadvantage.

Grotius, and those who think like him, have found in the fact 24 of war another justification for the so-called "right" of slavery. They argue that since the victor has a *right* to kill his defeated enemy, the latter may, if he so wish, ransom his life at the expense of his liberty, and that this compact is the more legitimate in that it benefits both parties.

But it is evident that this alleged *right* of a man to kill his ene- 25 mies is not in any way a derivative of the state of war, if only because men, in their primitive condition of independence, are not bound to one another by any relationship sufficiently stable to produce a state either of war or of peace. They are not *naturally* enemies. It is the link between *things* rather than between *men* that constitutes war, and since a state of war cannot originate in simple personal relations, but only in relations between things, private hostility between man and man cannot obtain either in a state of nature where there is no gener- ally accepted system of private property, or in a state of society where law is the supreme authority.

Single combats, duels, personal encounters are incidents which 26 do not constitute a "state" of anything. As to those private wars which were authorized by the Ordinances of King Louis IX[12] and suspended by the Peace of God, they were merely an abuse of Feudalism—that most absurd of all systems of government, so contrary was it to the principles of Natural Right and of all good polity.

War, therefore, is something that occurs not between man and 27 man, but between States. The individuals who become involved in it are enemies only by accident. They fight not as men or even as citi- zens, but as soldiers: not as members of this or that national group, but as its defenders. A State can have as its enemies only other States, not men at all, seeing that there can be no true relationship between things of a different nature.

This principle is in harmony with that of all periods, and with 28 the constant practice of every civilized society. A declaration of war is a warning, not so much to Governments as to their subjects. The foreigner—whether king, private person, or nation as a whole—who steals, murders, or holds in durance the subjects of another coun- try without first declaring war on that country's Prince, acts not as an enemy but as a brigand. Even when war has been joined, the just

---

[12] **King Louis IX (1214–1270)** King of France, also called St. Louis. He was considered an ideal monarch.

Prince, though he may seize all public property in enemy territory, yet respects the property and possessions of individuals, and, in so doing, shows his concern for those rights on which his own laws are based. The object of war being the destruction of the enemy State, a commander has a perfect right to kill its defenders so long as their arms are in their hands: but once they have laid them down and have submitted, they cease to be enemies, or instruments employed by an enemy, and revert to the condition of men, pure and simple, over whose lives no one can any longer exercise a rightful claim. Sometimes it is possible to destroy a State without killing any of its subjects, and nothing in war can be claimed as a right save what may be necessary for the accomplishment of the victor's end. These principles are not those of Grotius, nor are they based on the authority of poets, but derive from the Nature of Things, and are founded upon Reason.

29   The Right of Conquest finds its sole sanction in the Law of the Strongest. If war does not give to the victor the right to massacre his defeated enemies, he cannot base upon a nonexistent right any claim to the further one of enslaving them. We have the right to kill our enemies only when we cannot enslave them. It follows, therefore, that the right to enslave cannot be deduced from the right to kill, and that we are guilty of enforcing an iniquitous exchange if we make a vanquished foeman purchase with his liberty that life over which we have no right. Is it not obvious that once we begin basing the right of life and death on the right to enslave, and the right to enslave on the right of life and death, we are caught in a vicious circle? Even if we assume the existence of this terrible right to kill all and sundry, I still maintain that a man enslaved, or a People conquered, in war is under no obligation to obey beyond the point at which force ceases to be operative. If the victor spares the life of his defeated opponent in return for an equivalent, he cannot be said to have shown him mercy. In either case he destroys him, but in the latter case he derives value from his act, while in the former he gains nothing. His authority, however, rests on no basis but that of force. There is still a state of war between the two men, and it conditions the whole relationship in which they stand to one another. The enjoyment of the Rights of War presupposes that there has been no treaty of Peace. Conqueror and conquered have, to be sure, entered into a compact, but such a compact, far from liquidating the state of war, assumes its continuance.

30   Thus, in whatever way we look at the matter, the "Right" to enslave has no existence, not only because it is without legal validity, but because the very term is absurd and meaningless. The words *Slavery* and *Right* are contradictory and mutually exclusive. Whether we be considering the relation of one man to another man, or of an individual to a whole People, it is equally idiotic to say — "You and

I have made a compact which represents nothing but loss to you and gain to me. I shall observe it so long as it pleases me to do so—and so shall you, until I cease to find it convenient."

That We Must Always Go Back to an Original Compact

Even were I to grant all that I have so far refuted, the champions of   31
despotism would not be one whit the better off. There will always be a vast difference between subduing a mob and governing a social group. No matter how many isolated individuals may submit to the enforced control of a single conqueror, the resulting relationship will ever be that of Master and Slave, never of People and Ruler. The body of men so controlled may be an agglomeration; it is not an association. It implies neither public welfare nor a body politic. An individual may conquer half the world, but he is still only an individual. His interests, wholly different from those of his subjects, are private to himself. When he dies his empire is left scattered and disintegrated. He is like an oak which crumbles and collapses in ashes so soon as the fire consumes it.

"A People," says Grotius, "may give themselves to a king." His   32
argument implies that the said People were already a People before this act of surrender. The very act of gift was that of a political group and presupposed deliberation. Before, therefore, we consider the act by which a People chooses their king, it were well if we considered the act by which a People is constituted as such. For it necessarily precedes the other, and is the true foundation on which all Societies rest.

Had there been no original compact, why, unless the choice were   33
unanimous, should the minority ever have agreed to accept the decision of the majority? What right have the hundred who desire a master to vote for the ten who do not? The institution of the franchise is, in itself, a form of compact, and assumes that, at least once in its operation, complete unanimity existed.

Of the Social Pact

I assume, for the sake of argument, that a point was reached in   34
the history of mankind when the obstacles to continuing in a state of Nature were stronger than the forces which each individual could employ to the end of continuing in it. The original state of Nature, therefore, could no longer endure, and the human race would have perished had it not changed its manner of existence.

Now, since men can by no means engender new powers, but   35
can only unite and control those of which they are already possessed,

there is no way in which they can maintain themselves save by coming together and pooling their strength in a way that will enable them to withstand any resistance exerted upon them from without. They must develop some sort of central direction and learn to act in concert.

Such a concentration of powers can be brought about only as the   36
consequence of an agreement reached between individuals. But the self-preservation of each single man derives primarily from his own strength and from his own freedom. How, then, can he limit these without, at the same time, doing himself an injury and neglecting that care which it is his duty to devote to his own concerns? This difficulty, insofar as it is relevant to my subject, can be expressed as follows:

"Some form of association must be found as a result of which the   37
whole strength of the community will be enlisted for the protection of the person and property of each constituent member, in such a way that each, when united to his fellows, renders obedience to his own will, and remains as free as he was before." That is the basic problem of which the Social Contract provides the solution.

The clauses of this Contract are determined by the Act of Asso-   38
ciation in such a way that the least modification must render them null and void. Even though they may never have been formally enunciated, they must be everywhere the same, and everywhere tacitly admitted and recognized. So completely must this be the case that, should the social compact be violated, each associated individual would at once resume all the rights which once were his, and regain his natural liberty, by the mere fact of losing the agreed liberty for which he renounced it.

It must be clearly understood that the clauses in question can be   39
reduced, in the last analysis, to one only, to wit, the complete alienation by each associate member to the community of *all his rights*. For, in the first place, since each has made surrender of himself without reservation, the resultant conditions are the same for all: and, because they are the same for all, it is in the interest of none to make them onerous to his fellows.

Furthermore, this alienation having been made unreservedly,   40
the union of individuals is as perfect as it well can be, none of the associated members having any claim against the community. For should there be any rights left to individuals, and no common authority be empowered to pronounce as between them and the public, then each, being in some things his own judge, would soon claim to be so in all. Were that so, a state of Nature would still remain in being, the conditions of association becoming either despotic or ineffective.

In short, whoso gives himself to all gives himself to none. And,   41
since there is no member of the social group over whom we do not

acquire precisely the same rights as those over ourselves which we
have surrendered to him, it follows that we gain the exact equivalent of what we lose, as well as an added power to conserve what we
already have.

If, then, we take from the social pact everything which is not   42
essential to it, we shall find it to be reduced to the following terms:
"each of us contributes to the group his person and the powers which
he wields as a person under the supreme direction of the general will,
and we receive into the body politic each individual as forming an
indivisible part of the whole."

As soon as the act of association becomes a reality, it substitutes   43
for the person of each of the contracting parties a moral and collective
body made up of as many members as the constituting assembly has
votes, which body receives from this very act of constitution its unity,
its dispersed *self,* and its will. The public person thus formed by the
union of individuals was known in the old days as a *City,* but now
as the *Republic* or *Body Politic.* This, when it fulfills a passive role, is
known by its members as *The State,* when an active one, as *The Sovereign People,* and, in contrast to other similar bodies, as a *Power.* In
respect of the constituent associates, it enjoys the collective name of
The People, the individuals who compose it being known as *Citizens*
insofar as they share in the sovereign authority, as *Subjects* insofar as
they owe obedience to the laws of the State. But these different terms
frequently overlap, and are used indiscriminately one for the other. It
is enough that we should realize the difference between them when
they are employed in a precise sense.

Of the Sovereign

It is clear from the above formula that the act of association implies   44
a mutual undertaking between the body politic and its constituent
members. Each individual comprising the former contracts, so to speak,
with himself and has a twofold function. As a member of the sovereign
people he owes a duty to each of his neighbors, and, as a Citizen, to the
sovereign people as a whole. But we cannot here apply that maxim of
Civil Law according to which no man can be held to an undertaking
entered into with himself, because there is a great difference between a
man's duty to himself and to a whole of which he forms a part.

Here it should be pointed out that a public decision which can   45
enjoin obedience on all subjects to their Sovereign, by reason of the
double aspect under which each is seen, cannot, on the contrary, bind
the sovereign in his dealings with himself. Consequently, it is against
the nature of the body politic that the sovereign should impose upon

himself a law which he cannot infringe. For, since he can regard himself under one aspect only, he is in the position of an individual entering into a contract with himself. Whence it follows that there is not, nor can be, any fundamental law which is obligatory for the whole body of the People, not even the social contract itself. This does not mean that the body politic is unable to enter into engagements with some other Power, provided always that such engagements do not derogate from the nature of the Contract; for the relation of the body politic to a foreign Power is that of a simple individual.

But the body politic, or Sovereign, in that it derives its being simply and solely from the sanctity of the said Contract, can never bind itself, even in its relations with a foreign Power, by any decision which might derogate from the validity of the original act. It may not, for instance, alienate any portion of itself, nor make submission to any other sovereign. To violate the act by reason of which it exists would be tantamount to destroying itself, and that which is nothing can produce nothing.   46

As soon as a mob has become united into a body politic, any attack upon one of its members is an attack upon itself. Still more important is the fact that, should any offense be committed against the body politic as a whole, the effect must be felt by each of its members. Both duty and interest, therefore, oblige the two contracting parties to render one another mutual assistance. The same individuals should seek to unite under this double aspect all the advantages which flow from it.   47

Now, the Sovereign People, having no existence, outside that of the individuals who compose it, has, and can have, no interest at variance with theirs. Consequently, the sovereign power need give no guarantee to its subjects, since it is impossible that the body should wish to injure all its members, nor, as we shall see later, can it injure any single individual. The Sovereign, by merely existing, is always what it should be.   48

But the same does not hold true of the relation of subject to sovereign. In spite of common interest, there can be no guarantee that the subject will observe his duty to the sovereign unless means are found to ensure his loyalty.   49

Each individual, indeed, may, as a man, exercise a will at variance with, or different from, that general will to which, as citizen, he contributes. His personal interest may dictate a line of action quite other than that demanded by the interest of all. The fact that his own existence as an individual has an absolute value, and that he is, by nature, an independent being, may lead him to conclude that what he owes to the common cause is something that he renders of his own free will; and he may decide that by leaving the debt unpaid   50 he does less harm to his fellows than he would to himself should he make the necessary surrender. Regarding the moral entity constituting the State as a rational abstraction because it is not a man, he might enjoy his rights as a citizen without, at the same time, fulfilling his duties as a subject, and the resultant injustice might grow until it brought ruin upon the whole body politic.

In order, then, that the social compact may not be but a vain for- 51 mula, it must contain, though unexpressed, the single undertaking which can alone give force to the whole, namely, that whoever shall refuse to obey the general will must be constrained by the whole body of his fellow citizens to do so: which is no more than to say that it may be necessary to compel a man to be free—freedom being that condition which, by giving each citizen to his country, guarantees him from all personal dependence and is the foundation upon which the whole political machine rests, and supplies the power which works it. Only the recognition by the individual of the rights of the community can give legal force to undertakings entered into between citizens, which, otherwise, would become absurd, tyrannical, and exposed to vast abuses.

Of the Civil State

The passage from the state of nature to the civil state produces a 52 truly remarkable change in the individual. It substitutes justice for instinct in his behavior, and gives to his actions a moral basis which formerly was lacking. Only when the voice of duty replaces physical impulse and when right replaces the cravings of appetite does the man who, till then, was concerned solely with himself, realize that he is under compulsion to obey quite different principles, and that he must now consult his reason and not merely respond to the promptings of desire. Although he may find himself deprived of many advantages which were his in a state of nature, he will recognize that he has gained others which are of far greater value. By dint of being exercised, his faculties will develop, his ideas take on a wider scope, his sentiments become ennobled, and his whole soul be so elevated, that, but for the fact that misuse of the new conditions still, at times, degrades him to a point below that from which he has emerged, he would unceasingly bless the day which freed him forever from his ancient state, and turned him from a limited and stupid animal into an intelligent being and a Man.

Let us reduce all this to terms which can be easily compared. 53 What a man loses as a result of the Social Contract is his natural liberty and his unqualified right to lay hands on all that tempts him, provided only that he can compass its possession. What he gains is civil liberty and the ownership of what belongs to him. That we may labor under no illusion concerning these compensations, it is well that we distinguish between natural liberty which the individual enjoys so long as he is strong enough to maintain it, and civil liberty which is curtailed by the general will. Between possessions which derive from physical strength and the right of the first-comer, and ownership which can be based only on a positive title.

To the benefits conferred by the status of citizenship might be added that of Moral Freedom, which alone makes a man his own master. For to be subject to appetite is to be a slave, while to obey the laws laid down by society is to be free. But I have already said enough on this point, and am not concerned here with the philosophical meaning of the word *liberty*.

54

Of Real Property

Each individual member of the Community gives himself to it at the moment of its formation. What he gives is the whole man as he then is, with all his qualities of strength and power, and everything of which he stands possessed. Not that, as a result of this act of gift, such possessions, by changing hands and becoming the property of the Sovereign, change their nature. Just as the resources of strength upon which the City can draw are incomparably greater than those at the disposition of any single individual, so, too, is public possession when backed by a greater power. It is made more irrevocable, though not, so far, at least, as regards foreigners, more legitimate. For the State, by reason of the Social Contract which, within it, is the basis of all Rights, is the master of all its members' goods, though, in its dealings with other Powers, it is so only by virtue of its rights as first occupier, which come to it from the individuals who make it up.

55

The Right of "first occupancy," though more real than the "Right of the strongest," becomes a genuine right only after the right of property has been established. All men have a natural right to what is necessary to them. But the positive act which establishes a man's claim to any particular item of property limits him to that and excludes him from all others. His share having been determined, he must confine himself to that, and no longer has any claim on the property of the community. That is why the right of "first occupancy," however weak it be in a state of nature, is guaranteed to every man enjoying the status of citizen. Insofar as he benefits from this right, he withholds his claim, not so much from what is another's, as from what is not specifically his.

56

In order that the right of "first occupancy" may be legalized, the following conditions must be present. (1) There must be no one

57

already living on the land in question. (2) A man must occupy only so much of it as is necessary for his subsistence. (3) He must take possession of it, not by empty ceremony, but by virtue of his intention to work and to cultivate it, for that, in the absence of legal title, alone constitutes a claim which will be respected by others.

In effect, by according the right of "first occupancy" to a man's needs and to his will to work, are we not stretching it as far as it will go? Should not some limits be set to this right? Has a man only to set foot on land belonging to the community to justify his claim to be its master? Just because he is strong enough, at one particular moment, to keep others off, can he demand that they shall never return? How can a man or a People take possession of vast territories, thereby excluding the rest of the world from their enjoyment, save by an act of criminal usurpation, since, as the result of such an act, the rest of humanity is deprived of the amenities of dwelling and subsistence which nature has provided for their common enjoyment? When Nuñez Balboa,[13] landing upon a strip of coast, claimed the Southern Sea and the whole of South America as the property of the crown of Castille, was he thereby justified in dispossessing its former inhabitants, and in excluding from it all the other princes of the earth? Grant that, and there will be no end to such vain ceremonies. It would be open to His Catholic Majesty[14] to claim from his Council Chamber possession of the whole Universe, only excepting those portions of it already in the ownership of other princes.

One can understand how the lands of individuals, separate but contiguous, become public territory, and how the right of sovereignty, extending from men to the land they occupy, becomes at one real and personal—a fact which makes their owners more than ever dependent, and turns their very strength into a guarantee of their fidelity. This is an advantage which does not seem to have been considered by the monarchs of the ancient world, who, claiming to be no more than kings of the Persians, the Scythians, the Macedonians, seem to have regarded themselves rather as the rulers of men than as the masters of countries. Those of our day are cleverer, for they style themselves kings of France, of Spain, of England, and so forth. Thus, by controlling the land, they can be very sure of controlling its inhabitants.

The strange thing about this act of alienation is that, far from depriving its members of their property by accepting its surrender,

58

59

60

---

[13]**Nuñez Balboa (1475–1519)** Spanish explorer who discovered the Pacific Ocean.

[14]**His Catholic Majesty** A reference to the king of Spain, probably Ferdinand II of Aragon (1452–1516).

the Community actually establishes their claim to its legitimate ownership, and changes what was formerly mere usurpation into a right, by virtue of which they may enjoy possession. As owners they are Trustees for the Commonwealth. Their rights are respected by their fellow citizens and are maintained by the united strength of the community against any outside attack. From ceding their property to the State—and thus, to themselves—they derive nothing but advantage, since they have, so to speak, acquired all that they have surrendered. This paradox is easily explained once we realize the distinction between the rights exercised by the Sovereign and by the Owner over the same piece of property, as will be seen later.

It may so happen that a number of men begin to group themselves into a community before ever they own property at all, and that only later, when they have got possession of land sufficient to maintain them all, do they either enjoy it in common or parcel it between themselves in equal lots or in accordance with such scale of proportion as may be established by the sovereign. However this acquisition be made, the right exercised by each individual over his own particular share must always be subordinated to the overriding claim of the Community as such. Otherwise there would be no strength in the social bond, nor any real power in the exercise of sovereignty. 61

I will conclude this chapter, and the present Book, with a remark which should serve as basis for every social system: that, so far from destroying natural equality, the primitive compact substitutes for it a moral and legal equality which compensates for all those physical inequalities from which men suffer. However unequal they may be in bodily strength or in intellectual gifts, they become equal in the eyes of the law, and as a result of the compact into which they have entered. 62

QUESTIONS FOR CRITICAL READING

1. Examine Rousseau's analogy of the family as the oldest and only natural form of government. Do you agree that the analogy is useful and that its contentions are true? Which aspects of this natural form of government do not work to help us understand the basis of government?

2. Rousseau seems to accept the family as a patriarchal structure. How would his views change if he accepted it as a matriarchal structure? How would they change if he regarded each member of the family as absolutely equal in authority from birth?

3. What does it mean to reason from what is fact instead of from what is morally right?

4. What features of Rousseau's social contract are like those of a legal contract? How does a person contract to be part of society?

5. What distinctions can be made among natural, moral, and legal equality? Which kind of equality is most important to a social system?

SUGGESTIONS FOR CRITICAL WRITING

1. When Rousseau wrote, "Man is born free, and everywhere he is in chains," the institution of slavery was widely practiced and justified by many authorities. Today slavery has been generally abolished. How is this statement relevant to people's condition in society now? What are some ways in which people relinquish their independence or freedom?

2. Clarify the difference between your duty to yourself and your duty to society (your social structure—personal, local, national). Establish your duties in relation to each structure. How can these duties conflict with one another? How does the individual resolve the conflicts?

3. Do you agree with Rousseau when he says, "All men have a natural right to what is necessary to them"? What is necessary to all people, and in what sense do they have a right to what is necessary? Who should provide those necessities? Should necessities be provided for everyone or only for people who are unable to provide for themselves? If society will not provide these necessities, does the individual have the right to break the social contract by means of revolution?

4. What seems to be Rousseau's opinion regarding private property or the ownership of property? Beginning with paragraph 59, Rousseau distinguishes between monarchs with sovereignty over people and those with sovereignty over a region, such as France, Italy, or another country. What is Rousseau's view of the property that constitutes a state and who actually owns it? He mentions that the rights of individual owners must give way to the rights of the community in general. What is your response to this view?

5. Rousseau makes an important distinction between natural liberty and civil liberty. People in a state of nature enjoy natural liberty, and when they bind themselves together into a body politic, they enjoy civil liberty. What are the differences? Define each kind of liberty as carefully as you can, and take a stand on whether you feel civil liberty or natural liberty is superior. How is the conflict between the two forms of liberty felt today?

6. **CONNECTIONS**   Rousseau suggests that the family structure is the model for a civil society's government. If that is true, how valid is Philus's argument for injustice in Cicero's "The Defense of Injustice" (**bedfordstmartins.com/worldofideas/epages**)? Does a family structure provide a good enough model for modern government? Is injustice

commonly experienced in a family structure? Is injustice in the family a useful parallel to help us understand injustice in government? Why might Rousseau take issue with Philus's argument? Why should he take issue?

7. **CONNECTIONS** Rousseau's thinking emphasizes the role played by the common people in any civil society. How does that emphasis compare with Machiavelli's thinking? Consider the attitudes each writer has toward the essential goodness of people and the essential responsibilities of the monarch or government leader. In what ways is Rousseau closer in thinking to Lao-tzu than to Machiavelli?

8. **SEEING CONNECTIONS** Rousseau could not have seen Delacroix's painting *Liberty Leading the People* (p. 200), but he would definitely have had a strong opinion about it if he had. Would he have thought the Liberty leading these people was natural liberty or civil liberty? What details in the painting convince you one way or the other? Would Rousseau have approved of the action going on in the painting or would he have condemned it? What are your reasons for believing this? Shape your essay as an argument defending a clear position.

THOMAS JEFFERSON
The Declaration of Independence

THOMAS JEFFERSON (1743–1826) authored one of the most memorable statements in American history: the Declaration of Independence. He composed the work in 1776 under the watchful eyes of Benjamin Franklin, John Adams, and the rest of the Continental Congress, who spent two and a half days going over every word. Although the substance of the document was developed in committee, Jefferson, because of the grace of his writing style, was selected to craft the actual wording.

Jefferson rose to eminence in a time of great political upheaval. By the time he took a seat in the Virginia legislature in 1769, the colony was already on the course toward revolution. His pamphlet "A Summary View of the Rights of British America" (1774) brought him to the attention of those who were agitating for independence and established him as an ardent republican and revolutionary. In 1779 he was elected governor of Virginia. After the Revolutionary War he moved into the national political arena as the first secretary of state (1790–1793). He then served as John Adams's vice president (1797–1801) and was himself elected president in 1800. Perhaps one of his greatest achievements during his two terms (1801–1809) in office was his negotiation of the Louisiana Purchase, in which the United States acquired from France 828,000 square miles of land west of the Mississippi for about $15 million.

One of the fundamental paradoxes of Jefferson's personal and political life has been his attitude toward slavery. Like most wealthy Virginians, Jefferson owned slaves. However, in 1784 he tried to abolish slavery in the western territories that were being added to the United States. His "Report on Government for the Western Territory" failed by one vote. Historians have pointed out that Jefferson probably had an affair with Sally Hemmings, a mixed-race slave, and fathered children with her.

However unclear his personal convictions, many of Jefferson's accomplishments, which extend from politics to agriculture and mechanical invention, still stand. One of the most versatile Americans of any generation, he wrote a book, *Notes on Virginia* (1782); designed and built Monticello, his famous homestead in Virginia; and in large part founded and designed the University of Virginia (1819).

Despite their revolutionary nature, the ideas Jefferson expressed in the Declaration of Independence were not entirely original. Rousseau's republican philosophies greatly influenced the work. When Jefferson states in the second paragraph that "all men are created equal, that they are endowed by their Creator with certain unalienable rights," he reflects Rousseau's emphasis on the political equality of men and on protecting certain fundamental rights (see Rousseau, beginning with para. 39, p. 249). Jefferson also wrote that "Governments are instituted among Men, deriving their just powers from the consent of the governed." This is one of Rousseau's primary points, although it was Jefferson who immortalized it in these words.

Jefferson's Rhetoric

Jefferson's techniques include the use of the periodic sentence, which was especially typical of the age. The first sentence of the Declaration of Independence is periodic—that is, it is long and carefully balanced, and the main point comes at the end. Such sentences are not popular today, although an occasional periodic sentence can still be powerful in contemporary prose. Jefferson's first sentence says (in paraphrase): *When one nation must sever its relations with a parent nation . . . and stand as an independent nation itself . . . the causes ought to be explained.* Moreover, the main body of the Declaration of Independence lists the "causes" that lead to the final and most important element of the sentence. Causal analysis was a method associated with legal thought and reflects Jefferson's training in eighteenth-century legal analysis. One understood things best when one understood their causes.

The periodic sentence demands certain qualities of balance and parallelism that all good writers should heed. The first sentence in paragraph 2 demonstrates both qualities. The balance is achieved by making each part of the sentence roughly the same length. The parallelism is achieved by linking words in deliberate repetition for effect (they are in italicized type in the following analysis). Note how the "truths" mentioned in the first clause are enumerated in the succession of noun clauses beginning with "that"; "Rights" are enumerated in the final clause:

> We hold these truths to be self-evident,
>> *that* all men are created equal,
>> *that* they are endowed by their Creator with certain inalienable Rights,
>> *that* among these are Life, Liberty, and the pursuit of Happiness.

Parallelism is one of the greatest stylistic techniques available to a writer sensitive to rhetoric. It is a natural technique: many untrained writers and speakers develop it on their own. The periodicity of the sentences and the balance of their parallelism suggest thoughtfulness, wisdom, and control.

Parallelism creates a natural link to the useful device of enumeration, or listing. Many writers using this technique establish their purpose from the outset—"I wish to address three important issues . . ."—and then number them: "First, I want to say . . . Second . . . ," and so on. Jefferson devotes paragraphs 3 through 29 to enumerating the "causes" he mentions in paragraph 1. Each one constitutes a separate paragraph; thus, each has separate weight and importance. Each begins with "He" or "For" and is therefore in parallel structure. The technique of repetition of the same words at the beginning of successive lines is called *anaphora*. Jefferson's use of anaphora here is one of the best known and most effective in all literature. The "He" referred to is Britain's king George III (1738–1820), who is never mentioned by name. Congress is opposed not to a personality but to the sovereign of a nation that is oppressing the United States and a tyrant who is not dignified by being named. The "For" introduces grievous acts the king has given his assent to; these are offenses against the colonies.

However, Jefferson does not develop the causes in detail. We do not have specific information about what trade was cut off by the British, what taxes were imposed without consent, or how King George waged war or abdicated government in the colonies. Presumably, Jefferson's audience knew the details and was led by the twenty-seven paragraphs to observe how numerous the causes were. And all are serious; any one alone was enough cause for revolution. The effect of Jefferson's enumeration is to illustrate the patience of the colonies up to this point and to tell the world that the colonies have finally lost patience on account of the reasons listed. The Declaration of Independence projects the careful meditations and decisions of exceptionally calm, patient, and reasonable people.

PREREADING QUESTIONS:
WHAT TO READ FOR

The following prereading questions may help you anticipate key issues in the discussion of Thomas Jefferson's Declaration of Independence. Keeping them in mind during your first reading of the selection should help focus your attention.

- Under what conditions may a people alter or abolish their government?

- Why does Jefferson consider King George a tyrant?

The Declaration of Independence

In Congress, July 4, 1776

The Unanimous Declaration of the Thirteen United States of America

When in the Course of human events, it becomes necessary for one people to dissolve the political bands which have connected them with another, and to assume among the Powers of the earth, the separate and equal station to which the Laws of Nature and of Nature's God entitle them, a decent respect to the opinions of mankind requires that they should declare the causes which impel them to the separation.

We hold these truths to be self-evident, that all men are created equal, that they are endowed by their Creator with certain inalienable Rights, that among these are Life, Liberty, and the pursuit of Happiness. That to secure these rights, Governments are instituted among Men, deriving their just powers from the consent of the governed. That whenever any Form of Government becomes destructive of these ends, it is the Right of the People to alter or to abolish it, and to institute new Government, laying its foundation on such principles and organizing its powers in such form, as to them shall seem most likely to effect their Safety and Happiness. Prudence, indeed, will dictate that Governments long established should not be changed for light and transient causes; and accordingly all experience hath shown, that mankind are more disposed to suffer, while evils are sufferable, than to right themselves by abolishing the forms to which they are accustomed. But when a long train of abuses and usurpations, pursuing invariably the same Object evinces a design to reduce them under absolute Despotism, it is their right, it is their duty, to throw off such Government, and to provide new Guards for their future security. — Such has been the patient sufferance of these Colonies; and such is now the necessity which constrains them to alter their former Systems of Government. The history of the present King of Great Britain is a history of repeated injuries and usurpations, all having in direct object the establishment of an absolute Tyranny over these States. To prove this, let Facts be submitted to a candid world.

He has refused his Assent to Laws, the most wholesome and nec- 3
essary for the public good.

He has forbidden his Governors to pass Laws of immediate and 4
pressing importance, unless suspended in their operation till his Assent should be obtained; and when so suspended, he has utterly neglected to attend to them.

He has refused to pass other laws for the accommodation of large 5
districts of people, unless those people would relinquish the right of Representation in the Legislature, a right inestimable to them and formidable to tyrants only.

He has called together legislative bodies at places unusual, uncom- 6
fortable, and distant from the depository of their Public Records, for the sole purpose of fatiguing them into compliance with his measures.

He has dissolved Representative Houses repeatedly, for opposing 7
with manly firmness his invasions on the rights of the people.

He has refused for a long time, after such dissolutions, to cause 8
others to be elected; whereby the Legislative Powers, incapable of Annihilation, have returned to the People at large for their exercise; the State remaining in the mean time exposed to all the dangers of invasion from without, and convulsions within.

He has endeavored to prevent the population of these States;[1] for 9
that purpose obstructing the Laws for Naturalization of Foreigners; refusing to pass others to encourage their migration hither, and raising the conditions of new Appropriations of Lands.

He has obstructed the Administration of Justice, by refusing his 10
Assent to Laws for establishing Judiciary Powers.

He has made Judges dependent on his Will alone, for the tenure 11
of their offices, and the amount and payment of their salaries.

He has erected a multitude of New Offices, and sent hither 12
swarms of Officers to harass our People, and eat out their substance.

He has kept among us, in times of peace, Standing Armies with- 13
out the Consent of our legislature.

---

[1] **prevent the population of these States** This meant limiting migration to the colonies, thus controlling their growth.

He has affected to render the Military independent of and supe- 14
rior to the Civil Power.

He has combined with others to subject us to a jurisdiction for- 15
eign to our constitution, and unacknowledged by our laws; giving his
Assent to their acts of pretended Legislation:

For quartering large bodies of armed troops among us: 16

For protecting them, by a mock Trial, from Punishment for 17
any Murders which they should commit on the Inhabitants of these
States:

For cutting off our Trade with all parts of the world: 18

For imposing taxes on us without our Consent: 19

For depriving us in many cases, of the benefits of Trial by Jury: 20

For transporting us beyond Seas to be tried for pretended offenses: 21

For abolishing the free System of English Laws in a neighboring 22
Province, establishing therein an Arbitrary government, and enlarging
its Boundaries so as to render it at once an example and fit instrument
for introducing the same absolute rule into these Colonies:

For taking away our Charters, abolishing our most valuable Laws, 23
and altering fundamentally the Forms of our Governments:

For suspending our own Legislatures, and declaring themselves 24
invested with Power to legislate for us in all cases whatsoever.

He has abdicated Government here, by declaring us out of his 25
Protection and waging War against us.

He has plundered our seas, ravaged our Coasts, burnt our towns, 26
and destroyed the lives of our people.

He is at this time transporting large armies of foreign mercenar- 27
ies to complete the works of death, desolation, and tyranny, already
begun with circumstances of Cruelty & perfidy scarcely paralleled in
the most barbarous ages, and totally unworthy the Head of a civilized
nation.

He has constrained our fellow Citizens taken Captive on the 28
high Seas to bear Arms against their Country, to become the execu-
tioners of their friends and Brethren, or to fall themselves by their
Hands.

He has excited domestic insurrections amongst us, and has 29
endeavored to bring on the inhabitants of our frontiers, the merciless
Indian Savages, whose known rule of warfare, is an undistinguished
destruction of all ages, sexes, and conditions.

In every stage of these Oppressions We have Petitioned for 30
Redress in the most humble terms: Our repeated Petitions have been
answered only by repeated injury. A Prince, whose character is thus
marked by every act which may define a Tyrant, is unfit to be the
ruler of a free People.

Nor have We been wanting in attention to our British brethren. 31
We have warned them from time to time of attempts by their legislature to extend an unwarrantable jurisdiction over us. We have
reminded them of the circumstances of our emigration and settlement here. We have appealed to their native justice and magnanim-
ity, and we have conjured them by the ties of our common kindred
to disavow these usurpations, which, would inevitably interrupt our
connections and correspondence. They too have been deaf to the
voice of justice and of consanguinity. We must, therefore, acquiesce
in the necessity, which denounces our Separation, and hold them, as
we hold the rest of mankind, Enemies in War, in Peace Friends.

We, therefore, the Representatives of the United States of Amer- 32
ica, in General Congress, Assembled, appealing to the Supreme
Judge of the world for the rectitude of our intentions, do, in the
Name, and by Authority of the good People of these Colonies, solemnly publish and declare, That these United Colonies are, and
of Right ought to be Free and Independent States, that they are
Absolved from all Allegiance to the British Crown, and that all
political connection between them and the State of Great Britain,
is and ought to be totally dissolved; and that as Free and Independent States, they have full Power to levy War, conclude Peace, contract Alliances, establish Commerce, and to do all other Acts and
Things which Independent States may of right do. And for the support of this Declaration, with a firm reliance on the Protection of
Divine Providence, we mutually pledge to each other our Lives, our
Fortunes, and our sacred Honor.

QUESTIONS FOR CRITICAL READING

1. What laws of nature does Jefferson refer to in paragraph 1?
2. What do you think Jefferson feels is the function of government
   (para. 2)?
3. What does Jefferson say about women? Is there any way you can determine his views from reading this document? Does he appear to favor a
   patriarchal system?
4. Find at least one use of parallel structure in the Declaration (see p. 260
   in the section on Jefferson's rhetoric for a description of parallelism).
   What key terms are repeated in identical or equivalent constructions,
   and to what effect?
5. Which causes listed in paragraphs 3 through 29 are the most serious?
   Are any trivial? Which ones are serious enough to cause a revolution?

6. What do you consider to be the most graceful sentence in the entire Declaration? Where is it placed in the Declaration? What purpose does it serve there?

7. In what ways does the king's desire for stable government interfere with Jefferson's sense of his own independence?

SUGGESTIONS FOR CRITICAL WRITING

1. Jefferson defines the inalienable rights of a citizen as "Life, Liberty, and the pursuit of Happiness." Do you think these are indeed inalienable rights? Answer this question by including some sentences that use parallel structure and repeat key terms in similar constructions. Be certain that you define each of these rights both for yourself and for our time.

2. Write an essay discussing what you feel the function of government should be. Include at least three periodic sentences (underline them). You may first want to establish Jefferson's view of government and then compare or contrast it with your own.

3. Jefferson envisioned a government that allowed its citizens to exercise their rights to life, liberty, and the pursuit of happiness. Has Jefferson's revolutionary vision been achieved in America? Begin with a definition of these three key terms: *life, liberty,* and *the pursuit of happiness.* Then, for each term use examples—drawn from current events, your own experience, American history—to take a clear and well-argued stand on whether the nation has achieved Jefferson's goal.

4. Slavery was legal in America in 1776, and Jefferson reluctantly owned slaves. He never presented his plan for gradual emancipation of the slaves to Congress because he realized that Congress would never approve it. But Jefferson and Franklin did finance a plan to buy slaves and return them to Africa, where in 1821 returning slaves founded the nation of Liberia. Agree or disagree with the following statement and defend your position: the ownership of slaves by the people who wrote the Declaration of Independence invalidates it. You may wish to read the relevant chapters on Jefferson and slavery in Merrill D. Peterson's *Thomas Jefferson and the New Nation* (1970).

5. What kind of government does Jefferson seem to prefer? In what ways would his government differ from that of the king he is reacting against? Is he talking about an entirely different system or about the same system but with a different kind of "prince" at the head? How would Jefferson protect the individual against the whim of the state, while also protecting the state against the whim of the individual?

6. **CONNECTIONS** Write an essay in which you examine the ways in which Jefferson agrees or disagrees with Lao-tzu's conception of human nature and of government. How does Jefferson share Lao-tzu's

commitment to judicious inactivity? What evidence is there that the king subscribes to it? Describe the similarities and differences between Jefferson's views and those of Lao-tzu.

7. **CONNECTIONS** Thomas Jefferson would clearly disagree with Cicero's argument (**bedfordstmartins.com/worldofideas/epages**), even though Jefferson read Cicero and admired him greatly. Assuming that Jefferson read Cicero and examined Philus's argument carefully, how might he react? Write the counterargument that you think Jefferson would have developed against Philus's position. You may choose either Jefferson's rhetorical strategies or Cicero's, or you may argue in a direct fashion.

8. **CONNECTIONS** What principles does Jefferson share with Jean-Jacques Rousseau? Compare the fundamental demands of the Declaration of Independence with Rousseau's conceptions of liberty and independence. How would Rousseau have reacted to this declaration?

9. **SEEING CONNECTIONS** Jefferson wrote in 1776, thirteen years before the French Revolution and the execution of the French king. He was hardly thinking of overthrowing the British government, but rather he was merely establishing the United States as an independent nation. The citizens in Delacroix's *Liberty Leading the People* (p. 200) in 1830 were intent on ridding themselves of a king (as was Jefferson), not killing him. How likely is it that Jefferson might have taken this painting and used it as a poster for the American Revolution (assuming, of course, that it had been available at that time)? What details in the Declaration of Independence reinforce your belief that Jefferson would or would not have been comfortable with the painting?

ELIZABETH CADY STANTON
Declaration of Sentiments and Resolutions

ELIZABETH CADY STANTON (1815–1902) was exceptionally intelligent, and because her lawyer father was willing to indulge her gifts, she was provided the best education a woman in her time in America could expect. Born and raised in Johnstown, New York, she was one of six children, five girls and one boy, Eleazar, in whom all the hopes of the family rested. When Eleazar died after graduating from college, Elizabeth strove to replace him in the admiration of her father. She studied Greek so successfully that she was admitted as the only young woman in the local secondary school, where she demonstrated her abilities — which on the whole were superior to those of the boys with whom she studied.

Nonetheless, she did not win the esteem she hoped for. Her father, although he loved and cared for her, continually told her he wished she had been born a boy. In Johnstown, as elsewhere, women had few rights and rather low expectations. The question of education was a case in point: it was a profound exception for Elizabeth Cady to go to school with boys or even to study what they studied. She had no hopes of following in their paths because all the professions they aimed for were closed to women. This fact was painfully brought home to her when she finished secondary school. All the boys she studied with went on to Union College in Schenectady, but she was barred from attending the all-male institution. Instead, she attended the much inferior Troy Female Seminary, run by a pioneer of American education, Emma Willard (1787–1870).

Troy was as good a school as any woman in America could attend; yet it emphasized a great many traditional womanly pursuits as well as the principles of Calvinism, which Elizabeth Cady came to

From the *History of Woman Suffrage*.

believe were at the root of the problem women had in American society. In the 1830s, women did not have the vote; if they were married, they could not own property; and they could not sue for divorce no matter how ugly their marital situation. A husband expected a dowry from his wife, and he could spend it exactly as he wished: on gambling, carousing, or speculating. Not until 1848, the year of the Seneca Falls Convention, did New York pass laws to change this situation.

Elizabeth Cady married when she was twenty-four years old. Her husband, Henry Stanton, was a prominent abolitionist and journalist. He had little money, and the match was not entirely blessed by Elizabeth's father. In characteristic fashion she had the word *obey* struck from the marriage vows; thus, she had trouble finding a preacher who would adhere to her wishes. And, preferring never to be known as Mrs. Stanton, she was always addressed as Elizabeth Cady Stanton.

Early on, the couple settled in Boston, where Elizabeth found considerable intellectual companionship and stimulation. Good servants made her household tasks minimal. But soon Henry Stanton's health demanded that they move to Seneca Falls, New York, where there were few servants of any caliber and where there were few people of intellectual independence to stimulate her. Her lot in life became much like that of any housewife, and she could not abide it.

After a discussion at tea with a number of like-minded women, she proposed a woman's convention to discuss their situation. On July 14, 1848 (a year celebrated for revolutions in every major capital of Europe), the following notice appeared in the *Seneca County Courier*, a semiweekly journal:

Seneca Falls Convention

WOMAN'S RIGHTS CONVENTION.—A Convention to discuss the social, civil, and religious condition and rights of woman, will be held in the Wesleyan Chapel, at Seneca Falls, N.Y., on Wednesday and Thursday, the 19th and 20th of July, current; commencing at 10 o'clock A.M. During the first day the meeting will be exclusively for women, who are earnestly invited to attend. The public generally are invited to be present on the second day, when Lucretia Mott, of Philadelphia, and other ladies and gentlemen, will address the convention.

On the appointed day, less than a week after the notice, carriages and other vehicles tied up the streets around the Wesleyan Chapel with a large number of interested people. The first shock was that the chapel was locked, and the first order of business was for a man to climb through an open window to unlock the doors. The chapel was filled immediately, but not only with women. Many men were present, including Frederick Douglass, and the women decided that because they were already there, the men could stay.

The convention was a significant success, establishing a pattern that has been repeated frequently since. Elizabeth Cady Stanton, in her declaration, figured as a radical in the assembly, proposing unheard-of reforms such as granting women the vote, which most of the moderates in the assembly could not agree on. For a while the assembly wished to omit the question of the vote, but Stanton by presenting it as her first statement in the declaration, made it clear that without the right to vote on legislation and legislators, women would never be able to change the status quo. Eventually, with the help of Douglass and others, the convention accepted her position, and the women's movement in America was under way.

Stanton's Rhetoric

Because the Seneca Falls Declaration is modeled directly on Jefferson's Declaration of Independence, we cannot get a good idea of Stanton's rhetorical gifts. However, by relying on Jefferson, she exercised a powerful wit (for which her other writing is well known) by reminding her audience that when the Declaration of Independence was uttered, no thought was given to half its potential audience—women. Thus, the Seneca Falls Declaration is a parody, and it is especially effective in the way it parodies its model so closely.

The same periodic sentences, parallelism, and balance are used and largely to the same effect. She employed the same profusion of one-paragraph utterances and exactly the same opening for each of them. Stanton played a marvelous trick, however. In place of the tyrannical foreign King George—Jefferson's "He"—she has put the tyrant man. Because of the power of her model, her declaration gathers strength and ironically undercuts the model.

The most interesting aspect of Stanton's rhetorical structure has to do with the order in which she includes the abuses and wrongs that she asks to be made right. She begins with the vote, just as Jefferson began with the law. Both are essential to the entire argument, and both are the key to change. Whereas Jefferson demands an entirely new government, Elizabeth Cady Stanton ends by demanding the "equal participation" of women with men in the government they have already won.

PREREADING QUESTIONS:
WHAT TO READ FOR

The following prereading questions may help you anticipate key issues in the discussion of Elizabeth Cady Stanton's Declaration of Sentiments and Resolutions. Keeping them in mind during your first reading of the selection should help focus your attention.

- What power has man had over women, according to Stanton?
- What is Stanton's attitude toward just and unjust laws?

Declaration of Sentiments and Resolutions

Adopted by the Seneca Falls Convention, July 19–20, 1848

When, in the course of human events, it becomes necessary for 1
one portion of the family of man to assume among the people of the earth a position different from that which they have hitherto occupied, but one to which the laws of nature and of nature's God entitle them, a decent respect to the opinions of mankind requires that they should declare the causes that impel them to such a course.

We hold these truths to be self-evident: that all men and women 2
are created equal; that they are endowed by their Creator with certain inalienable rights; that among these are life, liberty, and the pursuit of happiness; that to secure these rights governments are instituted, deriving their just powers from the consent of the governed. Whenever any form of government becomes destructive of these ends, it is the right of those who suffer from it to refuse allegiance to it, and to insist upon the institution of a new government, laying its foundation on such principles, and organizing its powers in such form, as to them shall seem most likely to effect their safety and happiness. Prudence, indeed, will dictate that governments long established should not be changed for light and transient causes; and accordingly all experience hath shown that mankind are more disposed to suffer, while evils are sufferable, than to right themselves by abolishing the forms to which they were accustomed. But when a long train of abuses and unsurpations, pursuing invariably the same object, evinces a design to reduce them under absolute despotism, it is their duty to throw off such government, and to provide new

guards for their future security. Such has been the patient sufferance of the women under this government, and such is now the necessity which constrains them to demand the equal station to which they are entitled.

The history of mankind is a history of repeated injuries and usur-   3 pations on the part of man toward woman, having in direct object the establishment of an absolute tyranny over her. To prove this, let facts be submitted to a candid world.

He has never permitted her to exercise her inalienable right to the   4 elective franchise.

He has compelled her to submit to laws, in the formation of   5 which she had no voice.

He has withheld from her rights which are given to the most   6 ignorant and degraded men — both natives and foreigners.

Having deprived her of this first right of a citizen, the elective   7 franchise, thereby leaving her without representation in the halls of legislation, he has oppressed her on all sides.

He has made her, if married, in the eye of the law, civilly dead.   8

He has taken from her all right in property, even to the wages   9 she earns.

He has made her, morally, an irresponsible being, as she can com-   10 mit many crimes with impunity, provided they be done in the presence of her husband. In the covenant of marriage, she is compelled to prom- ise obedience to her husband, he becoming to all intents and purposes, her master — the law giving him power to deprive her of her liberty, and to administer chastisement.

He has so framed the laws of divorce, as to what shall be the   11 proper causes, and in case of separation, to whom the guardianship of the children shall be given, as to be wholly regardless of the happiness of women — the law, in all cases, going upon a false supposition of the supremacy of man, and giving all power into his hands.

After depriving her of all rights as a married woman, if single,   12 and the owner of property, he has taxed her to support a govern- ment which recognizes her only when her property can be made profitable to it.

He has monopolized nearly all the profitable employments, and   13 from those she is permitted to follow, she receives but a scanty remu- neration. He closes against her all the avenues to wealth and distinc- tion which he considers most honorable to himself. As a teacher of theology, medicine, or law, she is not known.

He has denied her the facilities for obtaining a thorough educa-   14 tion, at colleges being closed against her.

He allows her in Church, as well as State, but a subordinate posi-   15 tion, claiming Apostolic authority for her exclusion from the ministry, and, with some exceptions, from any public participation in the affairs of the Church.

He has created a false public sentiment by giving to the world a 16 different code of morals for men and women, by which moral delinquencies which exclude women from society, are not only tolerated, but deemed of little account in man.

He has usurped the prerogative of Jehovah himself, claiming it as 17 his right to assign for her a sphere of action, when that belongs to her conscience and to her God.

He has endeavored, in every way that he could, to destroy her 18 confidence in her own powers, to lessen her self-respect, and to make her willing to lead a dependent and abject life.

Now, in view of this entire disfranchisement of one-half the people 19 of this country, their social and religious degradation—in view of the unjust laws above mentioned, and because women do feel themselves aggrieved, oppressed, and fraudulently deprived of their most sacred rights, we insist that they have immediate admission to all the rights and privileges which belong to them as citizens of the United States.

In entering upon the great work before us, we anticipate no 20 small amount of misconception, misrepresentation, and ridicule; but we shall use every instrumentality within our power to effect our object. We shall employ agents, circulate tracts, petition the State and National legislatures, and endeavor to enlist the pulpit and the press in our behalf. We hope this Convention will be followed by a series of Conventions embracing every part of the country.

[The following resolutions were discussed by Lucretia Mott, 21 Thomas and Mary Ann McClintock, Amy Post, Catharine A. F. Stebbins, and others, and were adopted:]

WHEREAS, The great precept of nature is conceded to be, that "man 22 shall pursue his own true and substantial happiness." Blackstone[1] in his Commentaries remarks, that this law of Nature being coeval[2] with mankind, and dictated by God himself, is of course superior in obligation to any other. It is binding over all the globe, in all countries and at all times; no human laws are of any validity if contrary to this, and such of them as are valid, derive all their force, and all their validity, and all their authority, mediately and immediately, from this original; therefore,

Resolved, That such laws as conflict, in any way, with the true 23 and substantial happiness of woman, are contrary to the great

---

[1] **Sir William Blackstone (1723–1780)** The most influential of English legal scholars. His *Commentaries of the Laws of England* (4 vols., 1765–1769) form the basis of the study of law in England.
[2] **being coeval** Existing simultaneously.

precept of nature and of no validity, for this is "superior in obligation to any other."

Resolved, That all laws which prevent woman from occupying   24
such a station in society as her conscience shall dictate, or which place her in a position inferior to that of man, are contrary to the great precept of nature, and therefore of no force or authority.

Resolved, That woman is man's equal—was intended to be so by   25
the Creator, and the highest good of the race demands that she should be recognized as such.

Resolved, That the women of this country ought to be enlightened   26
in regard to the laws under which they live, that they may no longer publish their degradation by declaring themselves satisfied with their present position, nor their ignorance, by asserting that they have all the rights they want.

Resolved, That inasmuch as man, while claiming for himself intel-   27
lectual superiority, does accord to woman moral superiority, it is pre-eminently his duty to encourage her to speak and teach, as she has an opportunity, in all religious assemblies.

Resolved, That the same amount of virtue, delicacy, and refine-   28
ment of behavior that is required of woman in the social state, should also be required of man, and the same transgressions should be visited with equal severity on both man and woman.

Resolved, That the objection of indelicacy and impropriety, which   29
is so often brought against woman when she addresses a public audience, comes with a very ill-grace from those who encourage, by their attendance, her appearance on the stage, in the concert, or in feats of the circus.

Resolved, That woman has too long rested satisfied in the cir-   30
cumscribed limits which corrupt customs and a perverted application of the Scriptures have marked out for her, and that it is time she should move in the enlarged sphere which her great Creator has assigned her.

Resolved, That it is the duty of the women of this country to   31
secure to themselves their sacred right to the elective franchise.

Resolved, That the equality of human rights results necessarily from   32
the fact of the identity of the race in capabilities and responsibilities.

Resolved, therefore, That, being invested by the Creator with the   33
same capabilities, and the same consciousness of responsibility for their exercise, it is demonstrably the right and duty of woman, equally with man, to promote every righteous cause by every righteous means; and especially in regard to the great subjects of morals and religion, it is self-evidently her right to participate with her brother in teaching them, both in private and in public, by writing and by speaking, by any instrumentalities proper to be used, and in any assemblies proper to be held; and this being a self-evident truth

growing out of the divinely implanted principles of human nature, any custom or authority adverse to it, whether modern or wearing the hoary sanction of antiquity, is to be regarded as a self-evident falsehood, and at war with mankind.

[At the last session Lucretia Mott[3] offered and spoke to the fol-   34
lowing resolution:]

Resolved, That the speedy success of our cause depends upon the   35
zealous and untiring efforts of both men and women, for the overthrow of the monopoly of the pulpit, and for the securing to woman an equal participation with men in the various trades, professions, and commerce.

---

[3]**Lucretia Mott (1793–1880)** One of the founders of the 1848 convention at which these resolutions were presented. She was one of the earliest and most important of the feminists who struggled to proclaim their rights. She was also a prominent abolitionist.

QUESTIONS FOR CRITICAL READING

1. Stanton begins her declaration with a diatribe against the government. To what extent is the government responsible for the wrongs she enumerates?
2. Exactly what is Stanton taking issue with? What are the wrongs that have been done? Do they seem important to you?
3. How much of the effect of the selection depends on the parody of the Declaration of Independence?
4. Which of the individual declarations is most important? Which is least important?
5. Are any of the declarations serious enough to warrant starting a revolution?
6. Why do you think the suggestion that women deserve the vote was so hard to put across at the convention?

SUGGESTIONS FOR CRITICAL WRITING

1. Make a careful comparison between this declaration and Jefferson's Declaration of Independence. What are the similarities? What are the differences? Why would Stanton's declaration be particularly more distinguished because it is a parody of such a document? What weaknesses might be implied because of the close resemblance?

2. Write an essay that is essentially a declaration in the same style Stanton uses. Choose a cause carefully and follow the same pattern that Stanton does in the selection. Establish the appropriate relationship between government and the cause you are interested in defending or promoting.

3. To what extent is it useful to petition a government to redress the centuries of wrongs done to women? Is it the government's fault that women were treated so badly? Is the government able to have a significant effect on helping to change the unpleasant circumstances of women? Is it appropriate or inappropriate for Stanton to attack government in her search for equality?

4. The Declaration of Independence was aimed at justifying a war. Is the question of war anywhere implied in Stanton's address? If war is not the question, what is? Is there any substitute for war in Stanton's essay?

5. Read down the list of declarations and resolutions that Stanton enumerates. Have all of these issues been dealt with in our times? Would such a declaration as this still be appropriate, or has the women's movement accomplished all its goals?

6. Examine the issues treated in paragraph 16, concerning "a different code of morals" for men and women. Explain exactly what Stanton meant by that expression, and consider how different things are today from what they were in Stanton's day.

7. **CONNECTIONS** To what extent do you think Henry David Thoreau (p. 301) would have agreed with Stanton? What aspects of her declaration would he have found most useful for his own position? Would he have urged women to practice civil disobedience on behalf of women's rights, or would he have accepted the general point of view of his time and concerned himself only with the independence of men?

8. **CONNECTIONS** Stanton uses Jefferson's rhetorical model for her "Declaration of Sentiments and Resolutions," which defends the rights of women to contribute to governmental decisions. Write a short essay that represents the way Stanton might have analyzed Cicero's "The Defense of Injustice" (**bedfordstmartins.com/worldofideas/epages**) for the positive virtues of justice revealed in the ironic argument that Philus presents. What, for Stanton, are the most important points that Philus makes? How sympathetic is she to Cicero's ironic project?

9. **SEEING CONNECTIONS** Would the prominence of woman in Delacroix's *Liberty Leading the People* (p. 200) have helped reinforce Stanton's hopes for the liberation of women in her own time? What in the painting would she have reacted positively to and what could she have used in her own declaration of sentiments? Would the painting have made a good advertisement for her cause, or would it have harmed her cause? Imagine the conversation that might have taken place between her and Delacroix had they stood together in front of this painting. What would they have said to each other?

HANNAH ARENDT
Total Domination

HANNAH ARENDT (1906–1975) was born and educated in Germany, earning her doctorate from the University of Heidelberg when she was twenty-two years old. She left Germany for Paris after Hitler came to power in 1933 and early in the development of Nazi ideology. In New York City she worked with Jewish relief groups and in 1940 married Heinrich Bluecher, a professor of philosophy. Arendt joined the faculty of the University of Chicago in 1963 and then taught as a visiting professor at a number of universities, eventually settling at the New School for Social Research in New York.

The Origins of Totalitarianism, from which this selection is excerpted, was first published in 1951 and solidified Arendt's reputation as an important political philosopher. She began work on the book in 1945, after Nazism was defeated in Europe, and finished most of it by 1949, during the period of growing tension between the United States and the Soviet Union that began the Cold War. Much of the book analyzes the politics of ideology in fascist and communist countries. Arendt went on to write a number of other influential works, such as *The Human Condition* (1958) and *Crises of the Republic* (1972), both of which address the problems she saw connected with a decline in moral values in modern society. One of her most controversial books, *Eichmann in Jerusalem* (1963), examines Adolf Eichmann, head of the Gestapo's Jewish section, who was tried and executed in Jerusalem. She observed that the nature of Eichmann's evil was essentially banal—that his crime involved going along with orders without taking the time to assess them critically. Her last work, *The Life of the Mind*, was not completed, although two of its planned three volumes were published posthumously in 1978.

From *The Origins of Totalitarianism*.

"Total Domination" is part of one of the last chapters in *The Origins of Totalitarianism*. The first part of the book sets forth a brief history of modern anti-Semitism because the rise of totalitarianism in Germany was based in large part on Hitler's belief that the Aryan race was biologically and morally more evolved than all other races. In this selection Arendt shows how the totalitarian state derives its power from propagating a set of ideas, or ideology, such as the view that one race is superior to all others. Once that premise is accepted, she demonstrates, then any and all atrocities against people of other races can be permitted and promoted.

In two instances, describing the ideology of German fascism and the ideology of Soviet communism, Arendt demonstrates the ways in which the uncritical acceptance of an ideology provides the core of power for totalitarian states. In the case of Germany, racism led to the theory that if some races are inferior and debased then they must be destroyed for the good of humanity—a theory that was put into brutal practice by the Nazis. Arendt shows how this view derives from a misunderstanding of Darwin's theories of the survival of the fittest (see Darwin's "Natural Selection," p. 897). In the case of the Soviet Union, totalitarianism depended on the "scientific" theory of history put forth by Karl Marx (see Marx's "Communist Manifesto," p. 453) that insisted on class struggle and the need of the most "progressive class" to destroy the less progressive classes. Marx was referred to as the "Darwin of history" in part because his views reflected the same scientific logic as Darwin's theories of biology. According to Arendt, both the Nazi and communist totalitarian regimes claimed those laws of biology or history as the justification for their own brutal acts of terror.

Arendt's Rhetoric

Arendt is a careful rhetorician. She works in a logical fashion to analyze basic principles to see how they control the outcome of events. In this case, the outcome is the totalitarian institution of the concentration camp in which human dignity is destroyed. For the totalitarian government, the terror and torment of concentration camps demonstrate "that everything is possible" (para. 1), even though it might seem impossible to reduce a person to a thing. Total domination, as she states, is designed to reduce the diversity and complexity of humanity to a single reaction to terror and pain.

Interestingly, Arendt can find no economic virtue in maintaining huge numbers of people in concentration camps. Occasionally in the Soviet Union, inmates' labor was of value, but some 60 percent or more of the inmates died under the harsh labor conditions. In Nazi Germany the work done in the concentration camps was of such poor quality that it usually had to be done again. Further, during World War II, German resources that might have been used to fight the war were diverted to the concentration camps, which functioned as extermination centers even while Germany reeled under potential defeat. In other words, the concentration camps were self-defeating in every important way except that they demonstrated to a populace that total domination was possible.

One important rhetorical principle at work in this essay is the essential definition of total domination by the process of describing the circumstances of the concentration camps as well as the rationale for their construction. The Nazis knew, and Hitler had already trumpeted the news to the world in his book *Mein Kampf* (My Struggle), that if a lie was big enough, large numbers of people would believe it even if it stood against common sense. "The Big Lie" has become a common principle of modern political science. Likewise, if the enormity of the crime is great enough, it is not likely that people will believe it actually occurred. Therefore, it should not have been a surprise that the few people who had escaped the camps before the war were not believed. They told their stories, but even future victims of the camps refused to believe they existed. Western governments thought the accounts of the concentration camps were monstrous exaggerations.

Throughout the book from which this passage comes, Arendt insists that the essence of totalitarianism is terror and that without it the totalitarian state collapses. The concentration camps are the "laboratories" in which absolute terror dominates and that represent total domination. Individual liberty and freedom are erased by the terror of total domination, and in this sense the values that Rousseau and Jefferson argue for are irrelevant. In some states, such as the one Machiavelli imagined (p. 219), terror might be useful for controlling the opposition, but in the totalitarian state it controls everyone. As Arendt states, "a victory of the concentration-camp system would mean the same inexorable doom for human beings as the use of the hydrogen bomb would mean the doom of the human race" (para. 14).

PREREADING QUESTIONS:
WHAT TO READ FOR

The following prereading questions may help you anticipate key issues in the discussion of Hannah Arendt's "Total Domination." Keeping them in mind during your first reading of the selection should help focus your attention.

- What is the role of terror in the totalitarian state?
- Why is total domination necessary in a totalitarian state?
- What happens to human beings in concentration camps?

Total Domination

The concentration and extermination camps of totalitarian   1
regimes serve as the laboratories in which the fundamental belief of
totalitarianism that everything is possible is being verified. Compared with this, all other experiments are secondary in importance—
including those in the field of medicine whose horrors are recorded in
detail in the trials against the physicians of the Third Reich—although
it is characteristic that these laboratories were used for experiments of
every kind.

Total domination, which strives to organize the infinite plural-   2
ity and differentiation of human beings as if all of humanity were
just one individual, is possible only if each and every person can
be reduced to a never-changing identity of reactions, so that each
of these bundles of reactions can be exchanged at random for any
other. The problem is to fabricate something that does not exist,
namely, a kind of human species resembling other animal species
whose only "freedom" would consist in "preserving the species."
Totalitarian domination attempts to achieve this goal both through
ideological indoctrination of the elite formations[1] and through
absolute terror in the camps; and the atrocities for which the elite
formations are ruthlessly used become, as it were, the practical
application of the ideological indoctrination—the testing ground in
which the latter must prove itself—while the appalling spectacle of
the camps themselves is supposed to furnish the "theoretical" verification of the ideology.

The camps are meant not only to exterminate people and degrade   3
human beings, but also serve the ghastly experiment of eliminating,
under scientifically controlled conditions, spontaneity itself as an
expression of human behavior and of transforming the human personality into a mere thing, into something that even animals are not;

---

[1] **elite formations** By this term Arendt seems to mean the SS men and camp guards.

for Pavlov's dog,[2] which, as we know, was trained to eat not when it was hungry but when a bell rang, was a perverted animal.

Under normal circumstances this can never be accomplished,   4 because spontaneity can never be entirely eliminated insofar as it is connected not only with human freedom but with life itself, in the sense of simply keeping alive. It is only in the concentration camps that such an experiment is at all possible, and therefore they are not only "*la société la plus totalitaire encore réalisée*"[3] (David Rousset) but the guiding social ideal of total domination in general. Just as the stability of the totalitarian regime depends on the isolation of the fictitious world of the movement from the outside world, so the experiment of total domination in the concentration camps depends on sealing off the latter against the world of all others, the world of the living in general, even against the outside world of a country under totalitarian rule. This isolation explains the peculiar unreality and lack of credibility that characterize all reports from the concentration camps and constitute one of the main difficulties for the true understanding of totalitarian domination, which stands or falls with the existence of these concentration and extermination camps; for, unlikely as it may sound, these camps are the true central institution of totalitarian organizational power.

There are numerous reports by survivors. The more authentic   5 they are, the less they attempt to communicate things that evade human understanding and human experience—sufferings, that is, that transform men into "uncomplaining animals." None of these reports inspires those passions of outrage and sympathy through which men have always been mobilized for justice. On the contrary, anyone speaking or writing about concentration camps is still regarded as suspect; and if the speaker has resolutely returned to the world of the living, he himself is often assailed by doubts with regard to his own truthfulness, as though he had mistaken a nightmare for reality.

This doubt of people concerning themselves and the real-   6 ity of their own experience only reveals what the Nazis have always known: that men determined to commit crimes will find it expedient to organize them on the vastest, most improbable scale. Not only

---

   [2] **Pavlov's dog** Between 1898 and 1930, the Russian psychologist Ivan Petrovich Pavlov (1849–1936) trained a dog to associate the sound of a ringing bell with food. Eventually the dog's reflex was to salivate at the sound of the bell even when there was no food.

   [3] **la société . . . réalisée** "The most totalitarian society yet achieved." David Rousset (1912–1997) survived the concentration camps and wrote *The Other Kingdom* (1947) about his experience.

because this renders all punishments provided by the legal system inadequate and absurd; but because the very immensity of the crimes guarantees that the murderers who proclaim their innocence with all manner of lies will be more readily believed than the victims who tell the truth. The Nazis did not even consider it necessary to keep this discovery to themselves. Hitler circulated millions of copies of his book in which he stated that to be successful, a lie must be enormous — which did not prevent people from believing him as, similarly, the Nazis' proclamations, repeated *ad nauseam*,[4] that the Jews would be exterminated like bedbugs (i.e., with poison gas), prevented anybody from *not* believing them.

There is a great temptation to explain away the intrinsically incredible by means of liberal rationalizations. In each one of us, there lurks such a liberal, wheedling us with the voice of common sense. The road to totalitarian domination leads through many intermediate stages for which we can find numerous analogies and precedents. The extraordinarily bloody terror during the initial stage of totalitarian rule serves indeed the exclusive purpose of defeating the opponent and rendering all further opposition impossible; but total terror is launched only after this initial stage has been overcome and the regime no longer has anything to fear from the opposition. In this context it has been frequently remarked that in such a case the means have become the end, but this is after all only an admission, in paradoxical disguise, that the category "the end justifies the means" no longer applies, that terror has lost its "purpose," that it is no longer the means to frighten people. Nor does the explanation suffice that the revolution, as in the case of the French Revolution, was devouring its own children, for the terror continues even after everybody who might be described as a child of the revolution in one capacity or another — the Russian factions, the power centers of party, the army, the bureaucracy — has long since been devoured. Many things that nowadays have become the specialty of totalitarian government are only too well known from the study of history. There have almost always been wars of aggression; the massacre of hostile populations after a victory went unchecked until the Romans mitigated it by introducing the *parcere subjectis*;[5] through centuries the extermination of native peoples went hand in hand with the colonization of the Americas, Australia, and Africa; slavery is one of the oldest institutions of mankind and all empires of antiquity were based on the labor of state-owned slaves who erected their public buildings. Not even concentration

7

---

[4] *ad nauseam* To the point of sickness.
[5] *parcere subjectis* A Roman policy of lenience and mercy toward those they defeated.

camps are an invention of totalitarian movements. They emerge for the first time during the Boer War,[6] at the beginning of the century, and continued to be used in South Africa as well as India for "undesirable elements"; here, too, we first find the term "protective custody" which was later adopted by the Third Reich. These camps correspond in many respects to the concentration camps at the beginning of totalitarian rule; they were used for "suspects" whose offenses could not be proved and who could not be sentenced by ordinary process of law. All this clearly points to totalitarian methods of domination; all these are elements they utilize, develop, and crystallize on the basis of the nihilistic principle that "everything is permitted," which they inherited and already take for granted. But wherever these new forms of domination assume their authentically totalitarian structure they transcend this principle, which is still tied to the utilitarian motives and self-interest of the rulers, and try their hand in a realm that up to now has been completely unknown to us: the realm where "everything is possible." And, characteristically enough, this is precisely the realm that cannot be limited by either utilitarian motives or self-interest, regardless of the latter's content.

What runs counter to common sense is not the nihilistic principle that "everything is permitted," which was already contained in the nineteenth-century utilitarian conception[7] of common sense. What common sense and "normal people" refuse to believe is that everything is possible. We attempt to understand elements in present or recollected experience that simply surpass our powers of understanding. We attempt to classify as criminal a thing which, as we all feel, no such category was ever intended to cover. What meaning has the concept of murder when we are confronted with the mass production of corpses? We attempt to understand the behavior of concentration-camp inmates and SS-men psychologically, when the very thing that must be realized is that the psyche *can* be destroyed even without the destruction of the physical man; that, indeed, psyche, character, and individuality seem under certain circumstances to express themselves only through the rapidity or slowness with which they disintegrate. The end result in any case is inanimate men, i.e., men who can no longer be psychologically understood, whose return to the psychologically or otherwise

---

[6] **Boer War (1899–1902)** The British established concentration camps in which some forty thousand people died during their war against the Transvaal and the Orange Free State—which were then controlled by the Boers, who were descended from earlier Dutch settlers—in what is now South Africa.

[7] **utilitarian conception** Utilitarianism, often known for its doctrine of the greatest good for the greatest number, was a nineteenth-century philosophy rooted in what people felt was essentially common sense.

intelligibly human world closely resembles the resurrection of Lazarus.[8] All statements of common sense, whether of a psychological or sociological nature, serve only to encourage those who think it "superficial" to "dwell on horrors."

　　If it is true that the concentration camps are the most consequential　9 institution of totalitarian rule, "dwelling on horrors" would seem to be indispensable for the understanding of totalitarianism. But recollection can no more do this than can the uncommunicative eyewitness report. In both these genres there is an inherent tendency to run away from the experience; instinctively or rationally, both types of writer are so much aware of the terrible abyss that separates the world of the living from that of the living dead, that they cannot supply anything more than a series of remembered occurrences that must seem just as incredible to those who relate them as to their audience. Only the fearful imagination of those who have been aroused by such reports but have not actually been smitten in their own flesh, of those who are consequently free from the bestial, desperate terror which, when confronted by real, present horror, inexorably paralyzes everything that is not mere reaction, can afford to keep thinking about horrors. Such thoughts are useful only for the perception of political contexts and the mobilization of political passions. A change of personality of any sort whatever can no more be induced by thinking about horrors than by the real experience of horror. The reduction of a man to a bundle of reactions separates him as radically as mental disease from everything within him that is personality or character. When, like Lazarus, he rises from the dead, he finds his personality or character unchanged, just as he had left it.

　　Just as the horror, or the dwelling on it, cannot affect a change　10 of character in him, cannot make men better or worse, thus it cannot become the basis of a political community or party in a narrower sense. The attempts to build up a European elite with a program of intra-European understanding based on the common European experience of the concentration camps have foundered in much the same manner as the attempts following the First World War to draw political conclusions from the international experience of the front generation.[9] In both cases it turned out that the experiences themselves can communicate no more than nihilistic banalities. Political consequences such as postwar pacifism, for example, derived from the general fear of war, not from the experiences in war. Instead of

---

　　[8]**Lazarus** From the Bible (John 11:18–48). Jesus, urged by Martha, resurrected Lazarus, who had been dead for four days.
　　[9]**the front generation** The generation that fought or experienced the fighting in World War I (1914–1918).

producing a pacifism devoid of reality, the insight into the structure of modern wars, guided and mobilized by fear, might have led to the realization that the only standard for a necessary war is the fight against conditions under which people no longer wish to live—and our experiences with the tormenting hell of the totalitarian camps have enlightened us only too well about the possibility of such conditions. Thus the fear of concentration camps and the resulting insight into the nature of total domination might serve to invalidate all obsolete political differentiations from right to left and to introduce beside and above them the politically most important yardstick for judging events in our time, namely: whether they serve totalitarian domination or not.

In any event, the fearful imagination has the great advantage to dissolve the sophistic-dialectical[10] interpretations of politics which are all based on the superstition that something good might result from evil. Such dialectical acrobatics had at least a semblance of justification so long as the worst that man could inflict upon man was murder. But, as we know today, murder is only a limited evil. The murderer who kills a man—a man who has to die anyway—still moves within the realm of life and death familiar to us; both have indeed a necessary connection on which the dialectic is founded, even if it is not always conscious of it. The murderer leaves a corpse behind and does not pretend that his victim has never existed; if he wipes out any traces, they are those of his own identity, and not the memory and grief of the persons who loved his victim; he destroys a life, but he does not destroy the fact of existence itself.

The Nazis, with the precision peculiar to them, used to register their operations in the concentration camps under the heading "under cover of the night (*Nacht und Nebel*)." The radicalism of measures to treat people as if they had never existed and to make them disappear in the literal sense of the word is frequently not apparent at first glance, because both the German and the Russian system are not uniform but consist of a series of categories in which people are treated very differently. In the case of Germany, these different categories used to exist in the same camp, but without coming into contact with each other; frequently, the isolation between the categories was even stricter than the isolation from the outside world. Thus, out of racial considerations, Scandinavian nationals during the war were quite differently treated by the Germans than the members of other peoples, although the former were outspoken enemies of the Nazis. The latter

11

12

---

[10] **sophistic-dialectical** Arendt seems to be referring to Marxist communist views that pit two mighty historical forces—like good and evil—against one another. Her point is that such a dialectic is artificial and dangerous.

in turn were divided into those whose "extermination" was immediately on the agenda, as in the case of the Jews, or could be expected in the predictable future, as in the case of the Poles, Russians, and Ukrainians, and into those who were not yet covered by instructions about such an overall "final solution," as in the case of the French and Belgians. In Russia, on the other hand, we must distinguish three more or less independent systems. First, there are the authentic forced-labor groups that live in relative freedom and are sentenced for limited periods. Secondly, there are the concentration camps in which the human material is ruthlessly exploited and the mortality rate is extremely high, but which are essentially organized for labor purposes. And, thirdly, there are the annihilation camps in which the inmates are systematically wiped out through starvation and neglect.

13   The real horror of the concentration and extermination camps lies in the fact that the inmates, even if they happen to keep alive, are more effectively cut off from the world of the living than if they had died, because terror enforces oblivion. Here, murder is as impersonal as the squashing of a gnat. Someone may die as the result of systematic torture or starvation, or because the camp is overcrowded and superfluous human material must be liquidated. Conversely, it may happen that due to a shortage of new human shipments the danger arises that the camps become depopulated and that the order is now given to reduce the death rate at any price. David Rousset called his report on the period in a German concentration camp *"Les Jours de Notre Mort,"*[11] and it is indeed as if there were a possibility to give permanence to the process of dying itself and to enforce a condition in which both death and life are obstructed equally effectively.

14   It is the appearance of some radical evil, previously unknown to us, that puts an end to the notion of developments and transformations of qualities. Here, there are neither political nor historical nor simply moral standards but, at the most, the realization that something seems to be involved in modern politics that actually should never be involved in politics as we used to understand it, namely all or nothing—all, and that is an undetermined infinity of forms of human living-together, or nothing, for a victory of the concentration-camp system would mean the same inexorable doom for human beings as the use of the hydrogen bomb would mean the doom of the human race.

15   There are no parallels to the life in the concentration camps. Its horror can never be fully embraced by the imagination for the very reason that it stands outside of life and death. It can never be fully

---

[11] ***Les Jours . . . Mort*** Literally, the days of our death.

reported for the very reason that the survivor returns to the world of the living, which makes it impossible for him to believe fully in his own past experiences. It is as though he had a story to tell of another planet, for the status of the inmates in the world of the living, where nobody is supposed to know if they are alive or dead, is such that it is as though they had never been born. Therefore all parallels create confusion and distract attention from what is essential. Forced labor in prisons and penal colonies, banishment, slavery, all seem for a moment to offer helpful comparisons, but on closer examination lead nowhere.

Forced labor as a punishment is limited as to time and intensity. 16 The convict retains his rights over his body; he is not absolutely tortured and he is not absolutely dominated. Banishment banishes only from one part of the world to another part of the world, also inhabited by human beings; it does not exclude from the human world altogether. Throughout history slavery has been an institution within a social order; slaves were not, like concentration-camp inmates, withdrawn from the sight and hence the protection of their fellow men; as instruments of labor they had a definite price and as property a definite value. The concentration-camp inmate has no price, because he can always be replaced; nobody knows to whom he belongs, because he is never seen. From the point of view of normal society he is absolutely superfluous, although in times of acute labor shortage, as in Russia and in Germany during the war, he is used for work.

The concentration camp as an institution was not established 17 for the sake of any possible labor yield; the only permanent economic function of the camps has been the financing of their own supervisory apparatus; thus from the economic point of view the concentration camps exist mostly for their own sake. Any work that has been performed could have been done much better and more cheaply under different conditions. Especially Russia, whose concentration camps are mostly described as forced-labor camps because Soviet bureaucracy has chosen to dignify them with this name, reveals most clearly that forced labor is not the primary issue; forced labor is the normal condition of all Russian workers, who have no freedom of movement and can be arbitrarily drafted for work to any place at any time. The incredibility of the horrors is closely bound up with their economic uselessness. The Nazis carried this uselessness to the point of open anti-utility when in the midst of the war, despite the shortage of building material and rolling stock, they set up enormous, costly extermination factories and transported millions of people back and forth. In the eyes of a strictly utilitarian world the obvious contradiction between these acts and military expediency gave the whole enterprise an air of mad unreality.

This atmosphere of madness and unreality, created by an apparent lack of purpose, is the real iron curtain which hides all forms of concentration camps from the eyes of the world. Seen from outside, they and the things that happen in them can be described only in images drawn from a life after death, that is, a life removed from earthly purposes. Concentration camps can very aptly be divided into three types corresponding to three basic Western conceptions of a life after death: Hades, Purgatory, and Hell. To Hades correspond those relatively mild forms, once popular even in nontotalitarian countries, for getting undesirable elements of all sorts—refugees, stateless persons, the asocial, and the unemployed—out of the way; as DP camps,[12] which are nothing other than camps for persons who have become superfluous and bothersome, they have survived the war. Purgatory is represented by the Soviet Union's labor camps, where neglect is combined with chaotic forced labor. Hell in the most literal sense was embodied by those types of camp perfected by the Nazis, in which the whole of life was thoroughly and systematically organized with a view to the greatest possible torment.   18

All three types have one thing in common: the human masses sealed off in them are treated as if they no longer existed, as if what happened to them were no longer of any interest to anybody, as if they were already dead and some evil spirit gone mad were amusing himself by stopping them for a while between life and death before admitting them to eternal peace.   19

----

[12] **DP camps** Displaced Persons camps. These camps were common in Europe after World War II.

QUESTIONS FOR CRITICAL READING

1. Why are concentration camps described as "laboratories" for the totalitarian regime?

2. What is the importance of the concentration camps' goal of removing human spontaneity?

3. In what sense are the concentration camps "the true central institution of totalitarian organizational power" (para. 4)?

4. Arendt implies that the experience of the concentration camp has the effect of "a mental disease." Why would that be so?

5. How is murder different from the mass death that characterizes the concentration camps?

6. Why is the concentration camp "useful" to the totalitarian government?

SUGGESTIONS FOR CRITICAL WRITING

1. Examine the economic issues Arendt raises that are involved in the establishment and operation of concentration camps in a totalitarian state. Decide whether a totalitarian state, whose goal is to achieve total domination, would be able to derive economic advantage from concentration camps. Why would this be an important issue? If there were a considerable economic advantage to maintaining concentration camps, would that fact make them any less terrifying?

2. Arendt reflected the fears of her own time in this essay. For her the most terrifying and immediate totalitarian governments were those of Nazi Germany and the Soviet Union. What evidence do you see in our contemporary world that might suggest totalitarianism is not completely "dead"? Do you perceive any threatening totalitarian governments anywhere in the world today? How do they seem to function and to interact with other nations?

3. Should you establish that a government is functioning as a totalitarian state today, do you feel it is a moral imperative that you do everything possible to overthrow that state? Would it be ethical and moral to go to war against such a state even if it did not immediately threaten you? Would it be ethical and moral for you to turn your back on a totalitarian state and ignore its operation so that it could achieve the kind of total domination Arendt describes?

4. **CONNECTIONS** How would Machiavelli interpret Arendt's discussion of ends and means in paragraph 8? Would Machiavelli have recommended concentration camps to his prince as a means of maintaining power? If a prince believed that concentration camps would be the means by which a state could achieve stability and power, would he be right in assuming that the stability and power thus achieved were worthwhile ends? Do you think Machiavelli would have accepted a totalitarian prince?

5. **CONNECTIONS** Cicero is ironic in proposing a defense of injustice (**bedfordstmartins.com/worldofideas/epages**) because he did not expect his audience to take him seriously. However, it is not always easy for people to detect irony, so it is altogether possible that some readers assumed Philus's argument was also Cicero's. Which features of Philus's argument would the governments described by Arendt have accepted as sound and reasonable? How do governments behave when they treat injustice as necessary and reasonable? John Milton said "necessity is the tyrant's plea." Why do tyrants feel injustice is sometimes necessary?

6. **SEEING CONNECTIONS** What would Arendt's position be regarding Delacroix's *Liberty Leading the People* (p. 204)? Would she have applauded the revolutionary action of the painting or would she have ridiculed it as being naive and insufficient to cope with a totalitarian state? Consider her position regarding the use of violence. A number

of governments have been recently overthrown, and others threatened, because of the people's perception that they were oppressive and moving toward totalitarianism. Choose among the following recently overthrown leaders and research their career in order to decide how closely they satisfy Arendt's conditions of total domination: Muammar Gadaffi, in Libya; Hosni Mubarak, in Egypt; Saddam Hussein, in Iraq. You may also wish to examine the governments of states whose leaders are still in power: Democratic Peoples Republic of Korea (North Korea); Myanmar; Yemen; Syria. Do any of those countries qualify as totalitarian?

PART THREE

ETHICS AND MORALITY

Henry David Thoreau
Frederick Douglass
Friedrich Nietzsche
Iris Murdoch
Martin Luther King Jr.
Kwame Anthony Appiah
Michael Gazzaniga
Aristotle

INTRODUCTION

A system of morality which is based on relative emotional values
is a mere illusion, a thoroughly vulgar conception which has
nothing sound in it and nothing true.

> — SOCRATES (469–399 B.C.E.)

God considered not action, but the spirit of the action. It is the
intention, not the deed, wherein the merit or praise of the doer
consists.

> — PETER ABELARD (1079–1142)

If men were born free, they would, so long as they remained free,
form no conception of good and evil.

> — BARUCH SPINOZA (1632–1677)

All morality depends upon our sentiments; and when any action
or quality of the mind pleases us after a certain manner we say
it is virtuous; and when the neglect or nonperformance of it
displeases us after a like manner, we say that we lie under an
obligation to perform it.

> — DAVID HUME (1711–1776)

There are no whole truths; all truths are half-truths. It is trying to
treat them as whole truths that plays the devil.

> —ALFRED NORTH WHITEHEAD (1861–1947)

To set up as a standard of public morality a notion which can
neither be defined nor conceived is to open the door to every kind
of tyranny.

> — SIMONE WEIL (1909–1943)

The establishment of ethical principles that translate into moral
behavior constitutes a major step forward for civilization. To be sure,
ancient civilizations maintained rules and laws governing behavior,
and in some cases those rules were written down and adhered to
by the majority of citizens. But the move that major religions made
was to go beyond simple rules or laws—to penetrate deeper layers
of emotion to make people want to behave well toward each other.
The writers and writings in this section have all examined the nature of
morality and have come to some interesting conclusions, focusing on
various aspects of the ethical nature of humankind.

Henry David Thoreau was among the New Englanders who
stood firm against slavery and demanded its abolition. Thoreau felt
his ethical position threatened by the government's demanding a tax
that would go toward supporting laws that he regarded as immoral.
But the Fugitive Slave Law of 1850, which was passed a year after

Thoreau's "Civil Disobedience" was first published, had grown even fiercer in demanding that every citizen turn in runaway slaves or face punishment. Thoreau influenced many later thinkers and activists who also struggled against injustice and a social failure of ethics, such as Mohandas Gandhi and Martin Luther King Jr.

One victim of what we now think of as immoral behavior was Frederick Douglass, who escaped from slavery by using a deception that his owners considered unethical. Douglass's life was filled with moral conundrums that even now give us pause. But he was a remarkable man who fled slavery and became one of the most famous Americans of his age. When he amassed enough money, he actually bought his freedom from the family who had owned him. While that seems like an ethical act, some people felt that it was not at all ethical—that since he was not a piece of property he should not have paid his "owners" for a right all should unequivocally enjoy: freedom.

Friedrich Nietzsche, a nineteenth-century philosopher and critic of all social institutions, approaches the question of ethics from a completely unexpected angle. In "Morality as Anti-Nature" he argues that the moral and ethical views of traditional religions are "anti-life." He believes religious injunctions stifle individuals' natural behaviors and promote values of death rather than of life. He speculates that religion condemns certain behaviors in order to protect those who are too weak to protect themselves, and that the strong, whom Nietzsche calls "Supermen," are condemned to obey commandments that rob them of the vitality of existence. His complaint is that religions punish everyone for the sins of the few because the few are weak and unable to control themselves. Nietzsche's views have been very influential in modern thought, especially during the last decades of the nineteenth and the whole of the twentieth century.

Iris Murdoch, one of the twentieth century's most distinguished writers, spent part of her life as an Oxford don teaching philosophy. Her major interests were ethics and morals; in "Morality and Religion" she addresses the question, Can there be morality without religion? Murdoch explores the issues of virtue and duty, both of which she sees as aspects of what we think of as moral behavior, and connects them with the ideals of institutional religion. She then goes on to examine guilt, usually thought of as a religious concept, and the question of sin. That leads her to consider how religion conceives of the struggle of good and evil, aiming as it does to conquer evil through moral behavior. But a paradox arises: If evil can be totally conquered, can there still be a system of morals or a behavior that needs to be called ethical? Murdoch's method is to keep us questioning basic issues until we begin to grasp their significance.

Like Thoreau, Martin Luther King Jr. was also imprisoned for breaking a law his conscience deemed immoral and unjust. In his struggle against the Jim Crow laws enforcing segregation in the South, King acted on his belief that the individual can and should fight against laws that are immoral. King's "Letter from Birmingham Jail" provides a masterful and moving definition of what makes laws immoral and unjust. Furthermore, King develops the concept of nonviolent demonstration as a method by which people can protest unjust laws.

Kwame Anthony Appiah examines the nature of ethics itself. His excursion into virtue theory tries to work out the relationship between the agent of a good act and the act itself. Is an act virtuous because it is performed by a virtuous character, or is it virtuous in and of itself? The question of character is at the root of his "The Case against Character," but in the process of presenting his argument, Appiah examines evidence from many thinkers on the relationship between a person's character and the virtue of that person's actions. As he examines this relationship, he demonstrates how complex the issue is and how important it is not to take the question of virtue for granted.

When Michael Gazzaniga begins his examination of the nature of ethical behavior in "Toward a Universal Ethics," he brings to bear his extensive experience in brain physiology. He has not only dissected brains but has also written extensively about their various features, especially the nature of the separate left and right hemispheres and their special adaptations. Gazzaniga consults a number of evolutionary neuroscientists who study the brain to see which predilections are inherent. We take the inborn talents of geniuses as examples of brains being "hardwired" to start with, but Gazzaniga ponders the possibility that there may be a moral center in the brain and that, if he is right, there could be a universal ethics that applies to all people regardless of culture or upbringing. In his view, before neuroscience developed a significant knowledge of the functions of the brain, all we knew about ethical and moral philosophy came from people telling "stories." These stories are religious and ethical in import, but they have no scientific basis. Gazzaniga brings science to bear on ethics.

This chapter also contains a selection in e-Pages (available online at **bedfordstmartins.com/worldofideas/epages**) from Aristotle. In the fourth century B.C.E., Aristotle wrote a treatise on ethics aimed at instructing his son Nichomachus. The *Nichomachean Ethics* is the single most famous ancient document that attempts to clarify the nature of ethical behavior and its effect on the individual. In the selection from the *Ethics* included in the e-Pages, Aristotle focuses on defining the good in life, not in the abstract, but in terms of the individual's obligation to participate in statecraft—what we might call politics. Aristotle also felt that in a democracy it is everyone's duty to understand the principles by which people can live happily and well. Once he has defined it as the ultimate good he proceeds to examine the nature of human happiness, and eventually he connects it to virtuous conduct (para. 23). In the process, he examines virtuous conduct in an effort to enlighten his son on the kind of behavior that is likely to reward him with the most happiness and the best life.

Each of these selections offers insights into the ethical underpinnings of modern culture. They clarify the nature of the good and the moral. If our ultimate goal is happiness, then the path to that goal must go through the precincts of ethical and moral behavior.

VISUALIZING ETHICS AND MORALITY

Joseph Wright of Derby (1734–1797) was born and raised in Derby (pronounced "darby"), England, and after a few years in Italy centered himself as an artist there and in Liverpool, England. He is thought to be the first great painter of the industrial revolution, painting the portraits of the important industrialists based in Liverpool. He also painted scenes from a variety of industrial and commercial sites, always looking for a moment of drama in the scene. He was particularly adept at chiaroscuro — the technique of balancing strongly contrasting lights and darks — often using a single light source to highlight profound juxtapositions between the action, usually at the center of the canvas, and the inaction, at the periphery.

Originally, the philosophical disciplines of aesthetics and ethics were closely related and considered together because they both involve the question of choice. Art involves making judgments and decisions about beauty and pleasure, while ethics involves making choices about behavior, moral or otherwise. Chiaroscuro in a narrative painting can be used to imply an impending ethical decision because the sharp representation of light and dark stands as an emblem for the choice between moral and immoral behavior.

Wright's paintings of blacksmiths' shops, iron forges, and other industrial sites often featured brilliant fires illuminating workers whose postures were reminiscent of Greek and Roman deities in classical paintings. Even the furnaces were suggestive of the furnace of Vulcan in Roman myth. But at the same time he was painting these pictures, Wright also painted *The Hermit Studying Anatomy* (1771–73) and *The Alchymist* (1771), depicting the title figure trying to change base metal into gold but instead discovering phosphorous, which produces the brilliant light in the scene. Alchemy was long discredited by this time, but it remained as a reminder that science was born from such practices and progressed slowly and through unexpected paths.

JOSEPH WRIGHT OF DERBY, *AN EXPERIMENT ON A BIRD
IN THE AIR PUMP.* 1768.
Oil on canvas, 6' × 8'. The National Gallery of London.

These paintings seem to be connected with Wright's occasional
attendance at the Lunar Society in Birmingham, which tried to reconcile the religious and ethical resistance to the birth of science. His
physician, Erasmus Darwin (1731–1802), of whom Wright painted a
noted portrait, was one of the principal organizers of the society. The
Lunar Society, which met regularly from 1765 to 1813, convened for
dinner on the night of the full moon because the extra light made it
easier for people to get home.

Commentators on Wright's work have speculated on the depth of
his interest in either industrial progress or the development of science.
They suggest that, while he may have been interested in both, he was
also paying attention to the developments in the world in which he
lived. In a sense, he was keeping up with the times.

Wright's most famous painting is *An Experiment on a Bird in the Air
Pump* (1768), in the National Gallery in London (to see the painting
in color, go to **bedfordstmartins.com/worldofideas/epages**). It portrays
a traveling scientist who performs experiments in the homes of wealthy
patrons who are interested in seeing what the latest scientific developments are. The air pump was still a novelty in Wright's time, but it is
clear that this scientist is a showman, almost like a traveling magician,

and therefore something of an entertainer. The experiment involves taking the air out of the glass bowl in which a white cockatoo has been placed. The process creates a vacuum, which will kill the bird, thus demonstrating that oxygen is essential to life.

The audience is the homeowner and his family members, all of whom have a distinct reaction to what is happening. The scientist apparently does not permit the bird to die, but stops the experiment just short of death. The scientist's assistant, the boy in the far right of the painting, seems about to lower a birdcage in which to place the revived cockatoo, whose wing is outstretched to show that it is animate again. The moon outside the window is an allusion to the Lunar Society, which promoted public education in the development of science.

The range of psychological responses to the experiment is wide. The older man at the lower right adopts the posture of a thoughtful philosopher pondering the circumstances of the scene. The young woman next to him cannot look because she cannot abide the death of the bird, while the man in front of her calls her attention to it with his pointing hand, as if saying everything is all right. The small girl near the center, in the brightest light, looks upward with a fearful expression. The man seated to the left is simply curious and dispassionate; perhaps he is the pragmatic homeowner. Next to him is a small boy who watches with intent expectation. The two young people to the far left are often described as lovers and are clearly much more interested in each other than in the experiment.

The light source comes from a lamp behind a beaker with a portion of a human skull in it, suggesting that the scientist has performed an earlier demonstration, perhaps of anatomy. Of course, like Yorick's skull in *Hamlet,* this detail implies the mortality of those in the room. The scientist seems to be staring directly out at us. His left hand is in the process of restoring the air to the bowl, while his right arm halts the action of the pump. The circular, gemlike composition of the lit portion is reminiscent of similarly lit religious paintings, perhaps commenting on the ultimate compatibility of religion and science.

In the selections that follow, think about how Joseph Wright of Derby's painting, with its curious range of responses to the dove's situation, sheds light on the moral and ethical positions of each of the authors in this section. Following each selection a Seeing Connections question asks you to compare the writer's ideas with Wright's painting.

HENRY DAVID THOREAU
Civil Disobedience

HENRY DAVID THOREAU (1817–1862) began keeping a journal when he graduated from Harvard in 1837. The journal was preserved and published, and it shows us the seriousness, determination, and elevation of moral values characteristic of all his work. He is best known for *Walden* (1854), a record of his departure from the warm congeniality of Concord, Massachusetts, and the home of his close friend Ralph Waldo Emerson (1803–1882), for the comparative "wilds" of Walden Pond, where he built a cabin, planted a garden, and lived simply. In *Walden,* Thoreau describes the deadening influence of ownership and extols the vitality and spiritual uplift that come from living close to nature. He also argues that civilization's comforts sometimes rob a person of independence, integrity, and even conscience.

Thoreau and Emerson were prominent among the group of writers and thinkers who were referred to as the Transcendentalists. They believed in something that transcended the limits of sensory experience—in other words, something that transcended materialism. Their philosophy was based on the works of Immanuel Kant (1724–1804), the German idealist philosopher; Samuel Taylor Coleridge (1772–1834), the English poet; and Johann Wolfgang von Goethe (1749–1832), the German dramatist and thinker. These writers praised human intuition and the capacity to see beyond the limits of common experience.

The Transcendentalists' philosophical idealism carried over into the social concerns of the day, expressing itself in works such as *Walden* and "Civil Disobedience," which was published with the title "Resistance to Civil Government" in 1849, a year after the publication of Karl Marx's *The Communist Manifesto* (p. 453). Although Thoreau all but denies his idealism in "Civil Disobedience,"

Originally published as "Resistance to Civil Government," 1849.

it is obvious that after spending a night in the Concord jail, he realizes he cannot quietly accept his government's behavior in regard
to slavery. He begins to feel that it is not only appropriate but
imperative to disobey unjust laws.

In Thoreau's time the most flagrantly unjust laws were those
that supported slavery. The Transcendentalists strongly opposed
slavery and spoke out against it. Abolitionists in Massachusetts har-
bored escaped slaves and helped them move to Canada and freedom.
The Fugitive Slave Act, enacted in 1850, the year after "Civil Disobedience" was published, made Thoreau a criminal because he refused
to comply with Massachusetts civil authorities when in 1851 they
began returning escaped slaves to the South as the law required.

"Civil Disobedience" was much more influential in the twentieth
century than it was in the nineteenth. Mohandas Gandhi (1869–
1948) claimed that while he was editor of an Indian newspaper in
South Africa, it helped to inspire his theories of nonviolent resistance. Gandhi eventually implemented these theories against the
British Empire and helped win independence for India. In the 1960s,
Martin Luther King Jr. applied the same theories in the fight for
racial equality in the United States. Thoreau's essay once again
found widespread adherents among the many young men who
resisted being drafted into the military to fight in Vietnam because
they believed that the war was unjust.

"Civil Disobedience" was written after the Walden experience
(which began on July 4, 1845, and ended on September 6, 1847).
Thoreau quietly returned to Emerson's home and "civilization." His
refusal in 1846 to pay the Massachusetts poll tax—a "per head" tax
imposed on all citizens to help support what he considered an unjust
war against Mexico—landed him in the Concord jail. He spent just one
day and one night there—his aunt paid the tax for him—but the experience was so extraordinary that he began examining it in his journal.

Thoreau's Rhetoric

Thoreau maintained his journal throughout his life and eventually became convinced that writing was one of the few professions
by which he could earn a living. He made more money, however,
from lecturing on the lyceum circuit. The lyceum, a New England
institution, was a town adult education program, featuring important
speakers such as the very successful Emerson and foreign lecturers.
Admission fees were very reasonable, and in the absence of other
popular entertainment, the lyceum was a major proving ground for
speakers interested in promoting their ideas.

"Civil Disobedience" was first outlined in rough-hewn form in the journal, where the main ideas appear and where experiments in phrasing began. (Thoreau was a constant reviser.) Then in February 1848, Thoreau delivered a lecture on "Civil Disobedience" at the Concord Lyceum urging people of conscience to actively resist a government that acted badly. Finally, the piece was prepared for publication in *Aesthetic Papers*, an intellectual journal edited by Elizabeth Peabody (1804–1894), the sister-in-law of another important New England writer, Nathaniel Hawthorne (1804–1864). There it was refined again, and certain important details were added.

"Civil Disobedience" bears many of the hallmarks of the spoken lecture. For one thing, it is written in the first person and addresses an audience that Thoreau expects will share many of his sentiments but certainly not all his conclusions. His message is to some extent anarchistic, virtually denying an unjust government any authority or respect.

Modern political conservatives generally take his opening quote—"That government is best which governs least"—as a rallying cry against governmental interference in everyday affairs. Such conservatives usually propose reducing government interference by reducing the government's capacity to tax wealth for unpopular causes. In fact, what Thoreau opposes is simply any government that is not totally just, totally moral, and totally respectful of the individual.

The easiness of the pace of the essay also derives from its original form as a speech. Even such locutions as "But to speak practically and as a citizen" (para. 3) connect the essay with its origins. Although Thoreau was not an overwhelming orator—he was short and somewhat homely, an unprepossessing figure—he ensured that his writing achieved what some speakers might have accomplished by means of gesture and theatrics.

Thoreau's language is marked by clarity. He speaks directly to every issue, stating his own position and recommending the position he feels his audience, as reasonable and moral people, should accept. One impressive achievement in this selection is Thoreau's capacity to shape memorable, virtually aphoristic statements that remain "quotable" generations later, beginning with his own quotation from the words of John L. O'Sullivan: "That government is best which governs least." Thoreau calls it a motto, as if it belonged on the great seal of a government or on a coin. It contains an interesting and impressive rhetorical flourish—the device of repeating "govern" and the near rhyme of "best" with "least."

His most memorable statements show considerable attention to the rhetorical qualities of balance, repetition, and pattern. "The only obligation which I have a right to assume is to do at any time what

I think right" (para. 4) uses the word *right* in two senses: first, as a matter of personal volition; second, as a matter of moral rectitude. One's right, in other words, becomes the opportunity to do right. "For it matters not how small the beginning may seem to be: what is once well done is done forever" (para. 21) also relies on repetition for its effect and balances the concept of a beginning with its capacity to reach out into the future. The use of the rhetorical device of *chiasmus*, a criss-cross relationship between key words, marks "Under a government which imprisons any unjustly, the true place for a just man is also a prison" (para. 22). Here is the pattern:

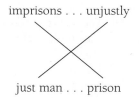

Such attention to phrasing is typical of speakers whose expressions must catch and retain the attention of listeners. Audiences do not have the advantage of referring to a text, so the words they hear must be forceful.

Thoreau relies also on analogy—comparing men with machines, people with plants, even the citizen with states considering secession from the Union. His analogies are effective and thus worth examining in some detail. He draws on the analysis of circumstance throughout the essay, carefully examining government actions to determine their qualities and their results. His questions include comments on politics (para. 1), on the Bible (para. 23), on Confucius (para. 24), and finally on his contemporary Daniel Webster (1782–1852) (para. 42), demonstrating a wide range of influences but avoiding the pedantic tone that can come from using quotations too liberally or from citing obscure sources. This essay is simple, direct, and uncluttered. Its enduring influence is in part due to the clarity and grace that characterize Thoreau's writing at its best. Its power derives from Thoreau's demand that citizens act on the basis of conscience.

PREREADING QUESTIONS: WHAT TO READ FOR

The following prereading questions may help you anticipate key issues in the discussion of Henry David Thoreau's "Civil Disobedience." Keeping them in mind during your first reading of the selection should help focus your attention.

- What kind of government does Thoreau think would be most ethical and moral?
- What is the individual's ethical responsibility regarding supporting the government when it is wrong?
- How does Thoreau deal with unjust laws that seem immoral?

Civil Disobedience

I heartily accept the motto—"That government is best which governs least,"[1] and I should like to see it acted up to more rapidly and systematically. Carried out, it finally amounts to this, which also I believe—"That government is best which governs not at all"; and when men are prepared for it, that will be the kind of government which they will have. Government is at best but an expedient; but most governments are usually, and all governments are sometimes, inexpedient. The objections which have been brought against a standing army, and they are many and weighty, and deserve to prevail, may also at last be brought against a standing government. The standing army is only an arm of the standing government. The government itself, which is only the mode which the people have chosen to execute their will, is equally liable to be abused and perverted before the people can act through it. Witness the present Mexican war,[2] the work of comparatively a few individuals using the standing government as their tool; for in the outset the people would not have consented to this measure.

This American government—what is it but a tradition, a recent one, endeavoring to transmit itself unimpaired to posterity but each instant losing some of its integrity? It has not the vitality and force of a single living man; for a single man can bend it to his will. It is a sort of wooden gun to the people themselves. But it is not the less necessary for this; for the people must have some complicated machinery or other, and hear its din, to satisfy that idea of government which they

---

[1]**". . . governs least"** John L. O'Sullivan (1813–1895) wrote in the *United States Magazine and Democratic Review* (1837) that "all government is evil, and the parents of evil. . . . The best government is that which governs least." Thomas Jefferson wrote, "That government is best which governs the least, because its people discipline themselves." Both comments echo the *Tao-te Ching*.

[2]**the present Mexican war (1846–1848)** The war was extremely unpopular in New England because it was an act of a bullying government anxious to grab land from a weaker nation. The United States had annexed Texas in 1845, precipitating a retaliation from Mexico.

have. Governments show thus how successfully men can be imposed on, even impose on themselves, for their own advantage. It is excellent, we must all allow. Yet this government never of itself furthered any enterprise but by the alacrity with which it got out of its way. *It does not keep the country free. It does not settle the West. It does not educate.* The character inherent in the American people has done all that has been accomplished; and it would have done somewhat more if the government had not sometimes got in its way. For government is an expedient by which men would fain succeed in letting one another alone; and, as has been said, when it is most expedient the governed are most let alone by it. Trade and commerce, if they were not made of India-rubber, would never manage to bounce over the obstacles which legislators are continually putting in their way; and, if one were to judge these men wholly by the effects of their actions and not partly by their intentions, they would deserve to be classed and punished with those mischievous persons who put obstructions on the railroads.

But to speak practically and as a citizen, unlike those who call themselves no-government men, I ask for, not at once no government, but *at once* a better government. Let every man make known what kind of government would command his respect, and that will be one step toward obtaining it.   3

After all, the practical reason why, when the power is once in the hands of the people, a majority are permitted, and for a long period continue, to rule is not because they are most likely to be in the right, nor because this seems fairest to the minority but because they are physically the strongest. But a government in which the majority rule in all cases cannot be based on justice, even as far as men understand it. Can there not be a government in which majorities do not virtually decide right and wrong but conscience?—in which majorities decide only those questions to which the rule of expediency is applicable? Must the citizen ever for a moment, or in the least degree, resign his conscience to the legislator? Why has every man a conscience then? I think that we should be men first and subjects afterward. It is not desirable to cultivate a respect for the law, so much as for the right. The only obligation which I have a right to assume is to do at any time what I think right. It is truly enough said that a corporation has no conscience; but a corporation of conscientious men is a corporation *with* a conscience. Law never made men a whit more just; and, by means of their respect for it, even the well-disposed are daily made the agents of injustice. A common and natural result of an undue respect for law is that you may see a file of soldiers, colonel, captain, corporal, privates, powder-monkeys,[3] and all, marching in admirable order   4

---

[3] **powder-monkeys** The boys who delivered gunpowder to cannons.

over hill and dale to the wars, against their wills, ay, against their common sense and consciences, which makes it very steep marching indeed and produces a palpitation of the heart. They have no doubt that it is a damnable business in which they are concerned; they are all peaceably inclined. Now, what are they? Men at all? or small movable forts and magazines at the service of some unscrupulous man in power? Visit the Navy-Yard,[4] and behold a marine, such a man as an American government can make, or such as it can make a man with its black arts — a mere shadow and reminiscence of humanity, a man laid out alive and standing, and already, as one may say, buried under arms with funeral accompaniments, though it may be —

> Not a drum was heard, not a funeral note,
> As his corse to the rampart we hurried;
> Not a soldier discharged his farewell shot
> O'er the grave where our hero we buried.[5]

The mass of men serve the state thus, not as men mainly, but as 5 machines, with their bodies. They are the standing army, and the militia, jailers, constables, posse comitatus,[6] &c. In most cases there is no free exercise whatever of the judgment or of the moral sense; but they put themselves on a level with wood and earth and stones; and wooden men can perhaps be manufactured that will serve the purpose as well. Such command no more respect than men of straw or a lump of dirt. They have the same sort of worth only as horses and dogs. Yet such as these even are commonly esteemed good citizens. Others — as most legislators, politicians, lawyers, ministers, and office-holders — serve the state chiefly with their heads; and, as they rarely make any moral distinctions, they are as likely to serve the Devil, without *intending* it, as God. A very few, as heroes, patriots, martyrs, reformers in the great sense, and *men*, serve the state with their consciences also and so necessarily resist it for the most part; and they are commonly treated as enemies by it. A wise man will only be useful as a man and will not submit to be "clay" and "stop a hole to keep the wind away," but leave that office to his dust at least:

> I am too high-born to be propertied,
> To be a secondary at control,
> Or useful serving-man and instrument
> To any sovereign state throughout the world.[7]

---

[4] **Navy-Yard** This is apparently the U.S. naval yard at Boston.

[5] These lines are from "Burial of Sir John Moore at Corunna" (1817) by the Irish poet Charles Wolfe (1791–1823).

[6] **posse comitatus** Literally, the power of the county; the term means a law-enforcement group made up of ordinary citizens.

[7] **"clay," "stop a hole . . . wind away," I am too high-born . . .** These lines are from Shakespeare; the first is from *Hamlet*, V.i.226–27. The verse is from *King John*, V.ii.79–82.

He who gives himself entirely to his fellow-men appears to them   6
useless and selfish; but he who gives himself partially to them is pronounced a benefactor and philanthropist.

How does it become a man to behave toward this American gov-   7
ernment today? I answer, that he cannot without disgrace be associated
with it. I cannot for an instant recognize that political organization as
my government which is the *slave's* government also.

All men recognize the right of revolution; that is, the right to   8
refuse allegiance to, and to resist the government when its tyranny
or its inefficiency are great and unendurable. But almost all say that
such is not the case now. But such was the case, they think, in the
Revolution of '75. If one were to tell me that this was a bad government because it taxed certain foreign commodities brought to its
ports, it is most probable that I should not make an ado about it, for
I can do without them. All machines have their friction; and possibly
this does enough good to counterbalance the evil. At any rate, it is a
great evil to make a stir about it. But when the friction comes to have
its machine, and oppression and robbery are organized, I say let us
not have such a machine any longer. In other words, when a sixth of
the population of a nation which has undertaken to be the refuge of
liberty are slaves, and a whole country is unjustly overrun and conquered by a foreign army and subjected to military law, I think that
it is not too soon for honest men to rebel and revolutionize. What
makes this duty the more urgent is the fact that the country so overrun is not our own, but ours is the invading army.

Paley,[8] a common authority with many on moral questions, in his   9
chapter on the "Duty of Submission to Civil Government," resolves all
civil obligation into expediency; and he proceeds to say, "that so long
as the interest of the whole society requires it, that is, so long as the
established government cannot be resisted or charged without public
inconveniency, it is the will of God that the established government
be obeyed, and no longer. . . . This principle being admitted, the justice of every particular case of resistance is reduced to a computation
of the quantity of the danger and grievance on the one side, and of
the probability and expense of redressing it on the other." Of this, he
says, every man shall judge for himself. But Paley appears never to
have contemplated those cases to which the rule of expediency does
not apply, in which a people, as well as an individual, must do justice,
cost what it may. If I have unjustly wrested a plank from a drowning

---

[8]**William Paley (1743–1805)** English theologian who lectured widely on moral
philosophy. Paley is famous for *A View of the Evidences of Christianity* (1794). "Duty of
Submission to Civil Government Explained" is Chapter 3 of Book 6 of *The Principles of
Moral and Political Philosophy* (1785).

man, I must restore it to him though I drown myself. This, according to Paley, would be inconvenient. But he that would save his life, in such a case, shall lose it. This people must cease to hold slaves and to make war on Mexico, though it cost them their existence as a people.

In their practice, nations agree with Paley; but does anyone think   10
that Massachusetts does exactly what is right at the present crisis?

> A drab of state, a cloth-o'-silver slut,
> To have her train borne up, and her soul trail in the dirt.[9]

Practically speaking, the opponents to a reform in Massachusetts are not a hundred thousand politicians at the South but a hundred thousand merchants and farmers here, who are more interested in commerce and agriculture than they are in humanity, and are not prepared to do justice to the slave and to Mexico, cost what it may. I quarrel not with far-off foes but with those who, near at home, co-operate with, and do the bidding of, those far away, and without whom the latter would be harmless. We are accustomed to say that the mass of men are unprepared; but improvement is slow because the few are not materially wiser or better than the many. It is not so important that many should be as good as you as that there be some absolute goodness somewhere; for that will leaven the whole lump. There are thousands who are in opinion opposed to slavery and to the war who yet in effect do nothing to put an end to them; who, esteeming themselves children of Washington and Franklin, sit down with their hands in their pockets and say that they know not what to do, and do nothing; who even postpone the question of freedom to the question of free trade, and quietly read the prices-current along with the latest advices from Mexico after dinner and, it may be, fall asleep over them both. What is the price-current of an honest man and patriot today? They hesitate and they regret and sometimes they petition; but they do nothing in earnest and with effect. They will wait, well disposed, for others to remedy the evil, that they may no longer have it to regret. At most, they give only a cheap vote, and a feeble countenance and God-speed, to the right, as it goes by them. There are nine hundred and ninety-nine patrons of virtue to one virtuous man. But it is easier to deal with the real possessor of a thing than with the temporary guardian of it.

All voting is a sort of gaming, like checkers or backgammon, with a   11
slight moral tinge to it, a playing with right and wrong, with moral questions; and betting naturally accompanies it. The character of the voters is not staked. I cast my vote, perchance, as I think right; but I am not vitally

---

[9]**A drab . . .**   From Cyril Tourneur (1575?–1626), *Revenger's Tragedy* (1607), IV.iv.70–72. "Drab" is an obsolete term for a prostitute. Thoreau quotes the lines to imply that Massachusetts is a "painted lady" with a defiled soul.

concerned that that right should prevail. I am willing to leave it to the
majority. Its obligation, therefore, never exceeds that of expediency. Even
voting *for the right* is *doing* nothing for it. It is only expressing to men feebly
your desire that it should prevail. A wise man will not leave the right to the
mercy of chance, nor wish it to prevail through the power of the majority.
There is but little virtue in the action of masses of men. When the majority
shall at length vote for the abolition of slavery, it will be because they are
indifferent to slavery, or because there is but little slavery left to be abolished by their vote. *They* will then be the only slaves. Only *his* vote can
hasten the abolition of slavery who asserts his own freedom by his vote.

I hear of a convention to be held at Baltimore,[10] or elsewhere, for   12
the selection of a candidate for the Presidency, made up chiefly of editors, and men who are politicians by profession; but I think, what is
it to any independent, intelligent, and respectable man what decision
they may come to? Shall we not have the advantage of his wisdom and
honesty nevertheless? Can we not count upon some independent votes?
Are there not many individuals in the country who do not attend conventions? But no: I find that the responsible man, so called, has immediately drifted from his position, and despairs of his country when his
country has more reason to despair of him. He forthwith adopts one of
the candidates thus selected as the only *available* one, thus proving that
he is himself *available* for any purposes of the demagogue. His vote is of
no more worth than that of any unprincipled foreigner or hireling native
who may have been bought. O for a man who is a *man* and, as my
neighbor says has a bone in his back which you cannot pass your hand
through! Our statistics are at fault: the population has been returned too
large. How many *men* are there to a square thousand miles in this country? Hardly one. Does not America offer any inducement for men to settle here? The American has dwindled into an Odd Fellow[11] — one who
may be known by the development of his organ of gregariousness and a
manifest lack of intellect and cheerful self-reliance; whose first and chief
concern, on coming into the world, is to see that the Almshouses are in
good repair; and, before yet he has lawfully donned the virile garb, to
collect a fund for the support of the widows and orphans that may be;
who, in short, ventures to live only by the aid of the Mutual Insurance
Company, which has promised to bury him decently.

It is not a man's duty, as a matter of course, to devote himself to the   13
eradication of any, even the most enormous wrong; he may still properly

---

[10] **Baltimore** In 1848, the political environment was particularly intense; it
was a seedbed for theoreticians of the Confederacy, which was only beginning to be
contemplated seriously.

[11] **Odd Fellow** The Independent Order of Odd Fellows, a fraternal and benevolent secret society, founded in England in the eighteenth century and first established in the United States in 1819 in Baltimore.

have other concerns to engage him; but it is his duty, at least, to wash his hands of it and, if he gives it no thought longer, not to give it practically his support. If I devote myself to other pursuits and contemplations, I must first see, at least, that I do not pursue them sitting upon another man's shoulders. I must get off him first, that he may pursue his contemplations too. See what gross inconsistency is tolerated. I have heard some of my townsmen say, "I should like to have them order me out to help put down an insurrection of the slaves, or to march to Mexico—see if I would go"; and yet these very men have each directly by their allegiance and so indirectly, at least, by their money, furnished a substitute. The soldier is applauded who refuses to serve in an unjust war by those who do not refuse to sustain the unjust government which makes the war; is applauded by those whose own act and authority he disregards and sets at naught; as if the State were penitent to that degree that it hired one to scourge it while it sinned, but not to that degree that it left off sinning for a moment. Thus, under the name of Order and Civil Government, we are all made at last to pay homage to and support our own meanness. After the first blush of sin comes its indifference; and from immoral it becomes, as it were, *un*moral, and not quite unnecessary to that life which we have made.

The broadest and most prevalent error requires the most disin- 14
terested virtue to sustain it. The slight reproach to which the virtue of patriotism is commonly liable, the noble are most likely to incur. Those who, while they disapprove of the character and measures of a government, yield to it their allegiance and support, are undoubtedly its most conscientious supporters, and so frequently the most serious obstacles to reform. Some are petitioning the State to dissolve the Union, to disregard the requisitions of the President. Why do they not dissolve it themselves—the union between themselves and the State—and refuse to pay their quota into its treasury? Do not they stand in the same relation to the State that the State does to the Union? And have not the same reasons prevented the State from resisting the Union which have prevented them from resisting the State?

How can a man be satisfied to entertain an opinion merely, and 15
enjoy *it*? Is there any enjoyment in it if his opinion is that he is aggrieved? If you are cheated out of a single dollar by your neighbor, you do not rest satisfied with knowing that you are cheated, or with saying that you are cheated, or even with petitioning him to pay you your due; but you take effectual steps at once to obtain the full amount and see that you are never cheated again. Action from principle, the perception and the performance of right, changes things and relations; it is essentially revolutionary and does not consist wholly with anything which was. It not only divides states and churches, it divides families; ay, it divides the *individual*, separating the diabolical in him from the divine.

Unjust laws exist: shall we be content to obey them, or shall we 16
endeavor to amend them and obey them until we have succeeded,

or shall we transgress them at once? Men generally, under such a government as this, think that they ought to wait until they have persuaded the majority to alter them. They think that if they should resist the remedy would be worse than the evil. *It* makes it worse. Why is it not more apt to anticipate and provide for reform? Why does it not cherish its wise minority? Why does it cry and resist before it is hurt? Why does it not encourage its citizens to be on the alert to point out its faults and *do* better than it would have them? Why does it always crucify Christ and excommunicate Copernicus and Luther[12] and pronounce Washington and Franklin rebels?

One would think that a deliberate and practical denial of its authority was the only offense never contemplated by government; else why has it not assigned its definite, its suitable and proportionate penalty? If a man who has no property refuses but once to earn nine shillings for the State, he is put in prison for a period unlimited by any law that I know, and determined only by the discretion of those who placed him there; but if he should steal ninety times nine shillings from the State, he is soon permitted to go at large again.   17

If the injustice is part of the necessary friction of the machine of government, let it go, let it go: perchance it will wear smooth — certainly the machine will wear out. If the injustice has a spring or a pulley or a rope or a crank exclusively for itself, then perhaps you may consider whether the remedy will not be worse than the evil; but if it is of such a nature that it requires you to be the agent of injustice to another, then I say break the law. Let your life be a counter friction to stop the machine. What I have to do is to see, at any rate, that I do not lend myself to the wrong which I condemn.   18

As for adopting the ways which the State has provided for remedying the evil, I know not of such ways. They take too much time, and a man's life will be gone. I have other affairs to attend to. I came into this world, not chiefly to make this a good place to live in, but to live in it, be it good or bad. A man has not everything to do, but something; and because he cannot do *everything*, it is not necessary that he should do *something* wrong. It is not my business to be petitioning the Governor or the Legislature any more than it is theirs to petition me; and if they should not hear my petition what should I do then? But in this case the State has provided no way: its very Constitution is the evil. This may seem to be harsh and stubborn and unconciliatory; but it is to treat with the utmost kindness and consideration the only spirit that can   19

---

[12] **Nicolaus Copernicus (1473–1543)** and **Martin Luther (1483–1546)** Copernicus revolutionized astronomy and the way humankind perceives the universe; Luther was a religious revolutionary who began the Reformation and created the first Protestant faith.

appreciate or deserves it. So is all change for the better, like birth and death, which convulse the body.

I do not hesitate to say that those who call themselves Abolition-   20
ists should at once effectually withdraw their support, both in person and property, from the government of Massachusetts, and not wait till they constitute a majority of one before they suffer the right to prevail through them. I think that it is enough if they have God on their side, without waiting for that other one. Moreover, any man more right than his neighbors constitutes a majority of one already.

I meet this American government or its representative, the State   21
government, directly and face to face once a year—no more—in the person of its tax-gatherer; this is the only mode in which a man situated as I am necessarily meets it; and it then says distinctly, Recognize me; and the simplest, the most effectual and, in the present posture of affairs, the indispensablest mode of treating with it on this head, of expressing your little satisfaction with and love for it, is to deny it then. My civil neighbor, the tax-gatherer, is the very man I have to deal with—for it is, after all, with men and not with parchment that I quarrel—and he has voluntarily chosen to be an agent of the government. How shall he ever know well what he is and does as an officer of the government, or as a man, until he is obliged to consider whether he shall treat me, his neighbor, for whom he has respect, as a neighbor and well-disposed man, or as a maniac and disturber of the peace, and see if he can get over this obstruction to his neighborliness without a ruder and more impetuous thought or speech corresponding with his action. I know this well, that if one thousand, if one hundred, if ten men whom I could name—if ten *honest* men only—ay, if *one* HONEST man in this State of Massachusetts, *ceasing to hold slaves*, were actually to withdraw from this copartnership and be locked up in the county jail therefor, it would be the abolition of slavery in America. For it matters not how small the beginning may seem to be: what is once well done is done forever. But we love better to talk about it: that we say is our mission. Reform keeps many scores of newspapers in its service but not one man. If my esteemed neighbor,[13] the State's ambassador, who will devote his days to the settlement of the question of human rights in the Council Chamber, instead of being threatened with the prisons of Carolina, were to sit down the prisoner of Massachusetts, that State which is so anxious to foist the sin of slavery upon her

---

[13] **esteemed neighbor** Thoreau refers to Samuel Hoar (1778–1856), a Massachusetts congressman, who went to South Carolina to protest that state's practice of seizing black seamen from Massachusetts ships and enslaving them. South Carolina threatened Hoar and drove him out of the state. He did not secure the justice he demanded.

sister—though at present she can discover only an act of inhospitality to be the ground of a quarrel with her—the Legislature would not wholly waive the subject the following winter.

Under a government which imprisons any unjustly, the true place   22
for a just man is also a prison. The proper place today, the only place which Massachusetts has provided for her freer and less desponding spirits is in her prisons, to be put out and locked out of the State by her own act, as they have already put themselves out by their principles. It is there that the fugitive slave and the Mexican prisoner on parole and the Indian come to plead the wrongs of his race should find them; on that separate but more free and honorable ground where the State places those who are not *with* her but *against* her—the only house in a slave State in which a free man can abide with honor. If any think that their influence would be lost there, and their voices no longer afflict the ear of the State, that they would not be as an enemy within its walls, they do not know by how much truth is stronger than error, nor how much more eloquently and effectively he can combat injustice who has experienced a little in his own person. Cast your whole vote, not a strip of paper merely, but your whole influence. A minority is powerless while it conforms to the majority; it is not even a minority then; but it is irresistible when it clogs by its whole weight. If the alternative is to keep all just men in prison or give up war and slavery, the State will not hesitate which to choose. If a thousand men were not to pay their tax-bills this year, that would not be a violent bloody measure, as it would be to pay them, and enable the State to commit violence and shed innocent blood. This is, in fact, the definition of a peaceable revolution, if any such is possible. If the tax-gatherer or any other public officer asks me, as one has done, "But what shall I do?" my answer is, "If you really wish to do anything, resign your office." When the subject has refused allegiance and the officer has resigned his office, then the revolution is accomplished. But even suppose blood should flow. Is there not a sort of blood shed when the conscience is wounded? Through this wound a man's real manhood and immortality flow out, and he bleeds to an everlasting death. I see this blood flowing now.

I have contemplated the imprisonment of the offender rather than   23
the seizure of his goods—though both will serve the same purpose—because they who assert the purest right, and consequently are most dangerous to a corrupt State, commonly have not spent much time in accumulating property. To such the State renders comparatively small service, and a slight tax is wont to appear exorbitant, particularly if they are obliged to earn it by special labor with their hands. If there were one who lived wholly without the use of money, the State itself would hesitate to demand it of him. But the rich man—not to make any invidious comparison—is always sold to the institution which makes him

rich. Absolutely speaking, the more money, the less virtue; for money comes between a man and his objects and obtains them for him; and it was certainly no great virtue to obtain it. It puts to rest many questions which he would otherwise be taxed to answer; while the only new question which it puts is the hard but superfluous one, how to spend it. Thus his moral ground is taken from under his feet. The opportunities of living are diminished in proportion as what are called the "means" are increased. The best thing a man can do for his culture when he is rich is to endeavor to carry out those schemes which he entertained when he was poor. Christ answered the Herodians[14] according to their condition. "Show me the tribute-money," said he—and one took a penny out of his pocket—if you use money which has the image of Caesar on it, and which he has made current and valuable, that is, if *you are men of the State* and gladly enjoy the advantages of Caesar's government, then pay him back some of his own when he demands it; "Render therefore to Caesar that which is Caesar's, and to God those things which are God's"—leaving them no wiser than before as to which was which; for they did not wish to know.

When I converse with the freest of my neighbors, I perceive that whatever they may say about the magnitude and seriousness of the question, and their regard for the public tranquillity, the long and the short of the matter is that they cannot spare the protection of the existing government, and they dread the consequences to their property and families of disobedience to it. For my own part, I should not like to think that I ever rely on the protection of the State. But if I deny the authority of the State when it presents its tax-bill, it will soon take and waste all my property and so harass me and my children without end. This is hard. This makes it impossible for a man to live honestly, and at the same time comfortably, in outward respects. It will not be worth the while to accumulate property; that would be sure to go again. You must hire or squat somewhere and raise but a small crop and eat that soon. You must live within yourself and depend upon yourself always tucked up and ready for a start, and not have many affairs. A man may grow rich in Turkey even, if he will be in all respects a good subject of the Turkish government. Confucius[15] said: "If a state is governed by the principles of reason, poverty and misery are subjects of shame; if a state is not governed by the principles of reason, riches and honors are the subjects of shame." No; until

24

---

[14] **Herodians** Followers of King Herod who were opposed to Jesus Christ (see Matt. 22:16).

[15] **Confucius (551–479 B.C.E.)** The most important Chinese religious leader. His *Analects* (collection) treated not only religious but moral and political matters as well.

I want the protection of Massachusetts to be extended to me in some distant Southern port, where my liberty is endangered, or until I am bent solely on building up an estate at home by peaceful enterprise, I can afford to refuse allegiance to Massachusetts and her right to my property and life. It costs me less in every sense to incur the penalty of disobedience to the State than it would to obey. I should feel as if I were worth less in that case.

Some years ago the State met me in behalf of the Church and   25
commanded me to pay a certain sum toward the support of a clergyman whose preaching my father attended, but never I myself. "Pay," it said, "or be locked up in the jail." I declined to pay. But, unfortunately, another man saw fit to pay it. I did not see why the schoolmaster should be taxed to support the priest, and not the priest the schoolmaster; for I was not the State's schoolmaster, but I supported myself by voluntary subscription. I did not see why the lyceum should not present its tax-bill and have the State to back its demand, as well as the Church. However, at the request of the selectmen, I condescended to make some such statement as this in writing: — "Know all men by these presents, that I, Henry Thoreau, do not wish to be regarded as a member of any incorporated society which I have not joined." This I gave to the town clerk; and he has it. The State, having thus learned that I did not wish to be regarded as a member of that church, has never made a like demand on me since; though it said that it must adhere to its original presumption that time. If I had known how to name them, I should then have signed off in detail from all the societies which I never signed on to; but I did not know where to find a complete list.

I have paid no poll-tax[16] for six years. I was put into a jail once   26
on this account, for one night; and, as I stood considering the walls of solid stone, two or three feet thick, the door of wood and iron, a foot thick, and the iron grating which strained the light, I could not help being struck with the foolishness of that institution which treated me as if I were mere flesh and blood and bones, to be locked up. I wondered that it should have concluded at length that this was the best use it could put me to and had never thought to avail itself of my services in some way. I saw that if there was a wall of stone between me and my townsmen, there was a still more difficult one to climb or break through before they could get to be as free as I was. I did not for a moment feel confined, and the walls seemed a great waste of stone and mortar. I felt as if I alone of all my townsmen had

---

[16]**poll-tax** A tax levied on every citizen living in a given area; *poll* means "head," so it is a tax per head. The tax Thoreau refers to, about $2, was used to support the Mexican War.

paid my tax. They plainly did not know how to treat me but behaved like persons who are underbred. In every threat and in every compliment there was a blunder; for they thought that my chief desire was to stand on the other side of that stone wall. I could not but smile to see how industriously they locked the door on my meditations, which followed them out again without let or hindrance, and *they* were really all that was dangerous. As they could not reach me, they had resolved to punish my body; just as boys, if they cannot come at some person against whom they have a spite, will abuse his dog. I saw that the State was half-witted, that it was timid as a lone woman with her silver spoons, and that it did not know its friends from its foes, and I lost all my remaining respect for it and pitied it.

Thus the State never intentionally confronts a man's sense, intellec- 27
tual or moral, but only his body, his senses. It is not armed with superior wit or honesty but with superior physical strength. I was not born to be forced. I will breathe after my own fashion. Let us see who is the strongest. What force has a multitude? They only can force me who obey a higher law than I. They force me to become like themselves. I do not hear of *men* being *forced* to live this way or that by masses of men. What sort of life were that to live? When I meet a government which says to me, "Your money or your life," why should I be in haste to give it my money? It may be in a great strait and not know what to do: I cannot help that. It must help itself; do as I do. It is not worth the while to snivel about it. I am not responsible for the successful working of the machinery of society. I am not the son of the engineer. I perceive that, when an acorn and a chestnut fall side by side, the one does not remain inert to make way for the other, but both obey their own laws and spring and grow and flourish as best they can till one, perchance, overshadows and destroys the other. If a plant cannot live according to its nature, it dies; and so a man.

The night in prison was novel and interesting enough. The prison- 28
ers in their shirt-sleeves were enjoying a chat and the evening air in the doorway when I entered. But the jailer said, "Come, boys, it is time to lock up"; and so they dispersed, and I heard the sound of their steps returning into the hollow apartments. My room-mate was introduced to me by the jailer as "a first-rate fellow and a clever man." When the door was locked, he showed me where to hang my hat and how he managed matters there. The rooms were whitewashed once a month; and this one, at least, was the whitest, most simply furnished, and probably the neatest apartment in the town. He naturally wanted to know where I came from and what brought me there; and when I had told him, I asked him in my turn how he came there, presuming him to be an honest man, of course; and, as the world goes, I believe he was. "Why," said he, "they accuse me of burning a barn; but I never did it." As near as I could discover, he had probably gone to bed in a barn when drunk

and smoked his pipe there; and so a barn burnt. He had the reputation of being a clever man, had been there some three months waiting for his trial to come on, and would have to wait as much longer; but he was quite domesticated and contented, since he got his board for nothing and thought that he was well treated.

He occupied one window, and I the other; and I saw that if one   29
stayed there long, his principal business would be to look out the window. I had soon read all the tracts that were left there and examined where former prisoners had broken out and where a grate had been sawed off and heard the history of the various occupants of that room; for I found that even here there was a history and a gossip which never circulated beyond the walls of the jail. Probably this is the only house in the town where verses are composed, which afterward printed in a circular form but not published. I was shown quite a long list of verses which were composed by some young men who had been detected in an attempt to escape, who avenged themselves by signing them.

I pumped my fellow-prisoner as dry as I could, for fear I should   30
never see him again; but at length he showed me which was my bed and left me to blow out the lamp.

It was like travelling into a far country, such as I had never   31
expected to behold, to lie there for one night. It seemed to me that I never had heard the town-clock strike before, nor the evening sounds of the village; for we slept with the windows open, which were inside the grating. It was to see my native village in the light of the Middle Ages, and our Concord was turned into a Rhine stream, and visions of knights and castles passed before me. They were the voices of old burghers that I heard in the streets. I was an involuntary spectator and auditor of whatever was done and said in the kitchen of the adjacent village-inn — a wholly new and rare experience to me. It was a closer view of my native town. I was fairly inside of it. I never had seen its institutions before. This is one of its peculiar institutions; for it is a shire town.[17] I began to comprehend what its inhabitants were about.

In the morning our breakfasts were put through the hole in the   32
door, in small oblong-square tin pans, made to fit, and holding a pint of chocolate, with brown bread and an iron spoon. When they called for the vessels again, I was green enough to return what bread I had left; but my comrade seized it and said that I should lay that up for lunch or dinner. Soon after he was let out to work at haying in a neighboring field, whither he went every day, and would not be back till noon; so he bade me good-day, saying that he doubted if he should see me again.

When I came out of prison — for someone interfered and paid   33
that tax — I did not perceive that great changes had taken place on

---

[17]**shire town** A county seat, which means the town had a court, county offices, and jails.

the common, such as he observed who went in a youth and emerged a tottering and gray-headed man; and yet a change had to my eyes come over the scene — the town and State and country — greater than any that mere time could effect. I saw yet more distinctly the State in which I lived. I saw to what extent the people among whom I lived could be trusted as good neighbors and friends; that their friendship was for summer weather only; that they did not greatly propose to do right; that they were a distinct race from me by their prejudices and superstitions, as the Chinamen and Malays are; that, in their sacrifices to humanity, they ran no risks, not even to their property; that, after all, they were not so noble but they treated the thief as he had treated them and hoped, by a certain outward observance and a few prayers, and by walking in a particular straight though useless path from time to time, to save their souls. This may be to judge my neighbors harshly; for I believe that many of them are not aware that they have such an institution as the jail in their village.

It was formerly the custom in our village, when a poor debtor   34
came out of jail, for his acquaintances to salute him, looking through their fingers, which were crossed to represent the grating of a jail window, "How do ye do?" My neighbors did not thus salute me but first looked at me and then at one another as if I had returned from a long journey. I was put into jail as I was going to the shoemaker's to get a shoe which was mended. When I was let out the next morning I proceeded to finish my errand, and having put on my mended shoe, joined a huckleberry party who were impatient to put themselves under my conduct; and in half an hour — for the horse was soon tackled — was in the midst of a huckleberry field on one of our highest hills two miles off, and then the State was nowhere to be seen.

This is the whole history of "My Prisons."   35

I have never declined paying the highway tax, because I am as   36
desirous of being a good neighbor as I am of being a bad subject; and as for supporting schools I am doing my part to educate my fellow countrymen now. It is for no particular item in the tax-bill that I refuse to pay it. I simply wish to refuse allegiance to the State, to withdraw and stand aloof from it effectually. I do not care to trace the course of my dollar, if I could, till it buys a man or a musket to shoot one with — the dollar is innocent — but I am concerned to trace the effects of my allegiance. In fact, I quietly declare war with the State, after my fashion, though I will still make what use and get what advantage of her I can, as is usual in such cases.

If others pay the tax which is demanded of me from a sympathy   37
with the State, they do but what they have already done in their own case, or rather they abet injustice to a greater extent than the State requires. If they pay the tax from a mistaken interest in the individual taxed, to save his property, or prevent his going to jail, it is because

they have not considered wisely how far they let their private feelings interfere with the public good.

This, then, is my position at present. But one cannot be too much 38 on his guard in such a case, lest his action be biased by obstinacy or an undue regard for the opinions of men. Let him see that he does only what belongs to himself and to the hour.

I think sometimes, Why, this people mean well; they are only 39 ignorant; they would do better if they knew how: why give your neighbors this pain to treat you as they are not inclined to? But I think again, this is no reason why I should do as they do or permit others to suffer much greater pain of a different kind. Again, I sometimes say to myself, When many millions of men, without heat, without ill will, without personal feeling of any kind, demand of you a few shillings only, without the possibility, such is their constitution, of retracting or altering their present demand, and without the possibility, on your side, of appeal to any other millions, why expose yourself to this over-whelming brute force? You do not resist cold and hunger, the winds and the waves, thus obstinately; you quietly submit to a thousand similar necessities. You do not put your head into the fire. But just in proportion as I regard this as not wholly a brute force but partly a human force, and consider that I have relations to those millions as to so many millions of men, and not of mere brute or inanimate things, I see that appeal is possible, first and instantaneously, from them to the Maker of them, and secondly, from them to themselves. But if I put my head deliberately into the fire, there is no appeal to fire or to the Maker of fire, and I have only myself to blame. If I could convince myself that I have any right to be satisfied with men as they are, and to treat them accordingly, and not according, in some respects, to my requisitions and expectations of what they and I ought to be, then, like a good Mussulman[18] and fatalist, I should endeavor to be satisfied with things as they are and say it is the will of God. And, above all, there is this difference between resisting this and a purely brute or natural force, that I can resist this with some effect; but I cannot expect, like Orpheus,[19] to change the nature of the rocks and trees and beasts.

I do not wish to quarrel with any man or nation. I do not wish to 40 split hairs, to make fine distinctions, or set myself up as better than my neighbors. I seek rather, I may say, even an excuse for conforming to the laws of the land. I am but too ready to conform to them. Indeed, I have reason to suspect myself on this head; and each year, as the tax-gatherer comes round, I find myself disposed to review the acts

---

[18] **Mussulman** Muslim; a follower of the religion of Islam.

[19] **Orpheus** In Greek mythology, Orpheus was a poet whose songs were so plaintive that they affected animals, trees, and even stones.

and position of the general and State governments, and the spirit of the people, to discover a pretext for conformity.

> We must affect our country as our parents;
> And if at any time we alienate
> Our love or industry from doing it honor,
> We must respect effects and teach the soul
> Matter of conscience and religion,
> And not desire of rule or benefit.[20]

I believe that the State will soon be able to take all my work of this sort out of my hands, and then I shall be no better a patriot than my fellow-countrymen. Seen from a lower point of view, the Constitution, with all its faults, is very good; the law and the courts are very respectable; even this State and this American government are, in many respects, very admirable and rare things, to be thankful for, such as a great many have described them; but seen from a point of view a little higher, they are what I have described them; seen from a higher still, and the highest, who shall say what they are, or that they are worth looking at or thinking of at all?

However, the government does not concern me much, and I shall 41
bestow the fewest possible thoughts on it. It is not many moments that I live under a government, even in this world. If a man is thought-free, fancy-free, imagination-free, that which *is not* never for a long time appearing *to be* to him, unwise rulers or reformers cannot fatally interrupt him.

I know that most men think differently from myself; but those 42
whose lives are by profession devoted to the study of these or kindred subjects content me as little as any. Statesmen and legislators, standing so completely within the institution, never distinctly and nakedly behold it. They speak of moving society but have no resting-place without it. They may be men of a certain experience and discrimination and have no doubt invented ingenious and even useful systems, for which we sincerely thank them; but all their wit and usefulness lie within certain not very wide limits. They are wont to forget that the world is not governed by policy and expediency. Webster[21] never goes

---

[20] **We must affect . . .** From George Peele (1556–1596), *The Battle of Alcazar* (acted 1588–1589, printed 1594), II.ii. Thoreau added these lines in a later printing of the essay. They emphasize the fact that one is disobedient to the state as one is to a parent—with love and affection and from a cause of conscience. Disobedience is not taken lightly.

[21] **Daniel Webster (1782–1852)** One of the most brilliant orators of his time. He was secretary of state from 1841 to 1843, which is why Thoreau thinks he cannot be a satisfactory critic of government.

behind government and so cannot speak with authority about it. His words are wisdom to those legislators who contemplate no essential reform in the existing government; but for thinkers, and those who legislate for all time, he never once glances at the subject. I know of those whose serene and wise speculations on this theme would soon reveal the limits of his mind's range and hospitality. Yet, compared with the cheap professions of most reformers, and the still cheaper wisdom and eloquence of politicians in general, his are almost the only sensible and valuable words, and we thank Heaven for him. Comparatively, he is always strong, original, and, above all, practical. Still his quality is not wisdom but prudence. The lawyer's truth is not Truth but consistency, or a consistent expediency. Truth is always in harmony with herself and is not concerned chiefly to reveal the justice that may consist with wrong-doing. He well deserves to be called, as he has been called, the Defender of the Constitution. There are really no blows to be given by him but defensive ones. He is not a leader but a follower. His leaders are the men of '87.[22] "I have never made an effort," he says, "and never propose to make an effort; I have never countenanced an effort, and never mean to countenance an effort, to disturb the arrangement as originally made, by which the various States came into the Union." Still thinking of the sanction which the Constitution gives to slavery, he says, "Because it was a part of the original compact—let it stand." Notwithstanding his special acuteness and ability, he is unable to take a fact out of its merely political relations and behold it as it lies absolutely to be disposed of by the intellect—what, for instance, it behooves a man to do here in America today with regard to slavery but ventures, or is driven, to make some such desperate answer as the following, while professing to speak absolutely, and as a private man—from which what new and singular code of social duties might be inferred? "The manner," says he, "in which the governments of those States where slavery exists are to regulate it, is for their own consideration, under their responsibility to their constituents, to the general laws of propriety, humanity, and justice, and to God. Associations formed elsewhere, springing from a feeling of humanity, or any other cause, have nothing whatever to do with it. They have never received any encouragement from me, and they never will."[23]

They who know of no purer sources of truth, who have traced   43
up its stream no higher, stand, and wisely stand, by the Bible and the Constitution, and drink at it there with reverence and humility; but

---

[22] **men of '87** The men who framed the Constitution in 1787.

[23] These extracts have been inserted since the Lecture was read. [Thoreau's note]

they who behold where it comes trickling into this lake or that pool gird up their loins once more and continue their pilgrimage toward its fountain-head.

No man with a genius for legislation has appeared in America. They are rare in the history of the world. There are orators, politicians, and eloquent men by the thousand; but the speaker has not yet opened his mouth to speak who is capable of settling the much-vexed questions of the day. We love eloquence for its own sake and not for any truth which it may utter or any heroism it may inspire. Our legislators have not yet learned the comparative value of free-trade and of freedom, of union, and of rectitude, to a nation. They have no genius or talent for comparatively humble questions of taxation and finance, commerce and manufacturers and agriculture. If we were left solely to the wordy wit of legislators in Congress for our guidance, uncorrected by the seasonable experience and the effectual complaints of the people, America would not long retain her rank among the nations. For eighteen hundred years, though perchance I have no right to say it, the New Testament has been written; yet where is the legislator who has wisdom and practical talent enough to avail himself of the light which it sheds on the science of legislation? 44

The authority of government, even such as I am willing to submit to — for I will cheerfully obey those who know and can do better than I, and in many things even those who neither know nor can do so well — is still an impure one: to be strictly just, it must have the sanction and consent of the governed. It can have no pure right over my person and property but what I concede to it. The progress from an absolute to a limited monarchy, from a limited monarchy to a democracy, is a progress toward a true respect for the individual. Even the Chinese philosopher[24] was wise enough to regard the individual as the basis of the empire. Is a democracy such as we know it the last improvement possible in government? Is it not possible to take a step further towards recognizing and organizing the rights of man? There will never be a really free and enlightened State until the State comes to recognize the individual as a higher and independent power, from which all its own power and authority are derived, and treats him accordingly. I please myself with imagining a State at last which can afford to be just to all men and to treat the individual with respect as a neighbor; which even would not think it inconsistent with its own repose if a few were to live aloof from it, not meddling with it, nor embraced by it, who fulfilled all the duties of neighbors and fellow-men. A State which bore this kind of fruit and suffered 45

---

[24] **Chinese philosopher** Thoreau probably means Confucius.

it to drop off as fast as it ripened would prepare the way for a still more perfect and glorious State, which also I have imagined but not yet anywhere seen.

QUESTIONS FOR CRITICAL READING

1. To what extent do you think Thoreau's intended audience agreed with him?

2. What is the relation of justice to the moral view that Thoreau maintains?

3. Thoreau provides us with a detailed account of his imprisonment (paras. 28–35). What is the ethical lesson that Thoreau learned in prison?

4. One example of Thoreau's use of irony is in paragraph 25. What other examples of irony seem effective in his argument?

5. In Thoreau's view, what is the ethical responsibility of a government to a minority population?

6. How clear is Thoreau's position on ethics and morality? What is most convincing to you?

7. It is possible that Thoreau's "Chinese philosopher" is Lao-tzu. How likely is it that Thoreau had read Lao-tzu and agreed with him?

SUGGESTIONS FOR CRITICAL WRITING

1. Thoreau refers to conscience as a monitor of government, yet he says, "Law never made men a whit more just" (para. 4). How does Thoreau's conscience help him establish the ethical principles that he acts by? To what extent do principles of ethics and morality operate in the law of Thoreau's time?

2. Thoreau tells us that the laws of the land were established by the majority population and that if he were to disobey them, he would be in a minority. What are the ethical principles that help Thoreau feel that it is just and right to disobey the laws that the majority population of the country has established?

3. Thoreau's anger is partly directed at proponents of the then-recent Mexican War (1846–1848), which resulted in Mexico's secession from New Mexico and California and which redrew the national border on the Rio Grande, giving Texas to the United States. He felt it was not an ethical war, for after its end, the nation had to decide whether to permit slavery in the acquired lands. The ensuing debate set the stage for the Civil War. If Thoreau thought the Mexican War was not ethical, what would he have thought about the Civil War?

4. Do some research on the Mexican War and decide whether or not there were any significant ethical concerns that warranted Thoreau's

reaction. Who was fighting? Who started the war? What were President Polk's intentions, and were those intentions ethical?

5. Examine quotations from Thoreau that focus on the individual and the question of justice and ethical treatment of the individual by government. What are the values of the government that Thoreau describes, and how might that government see its moral obligations to the governed? How would it treat matters of justice, ethics, and morality? To what extent does the government of Thoreau's time resemble the government of our time?

6. **CONNECTIONS**   Thoreau was especially sympathetic to the plight of African American slaves and would likely have shared the views of Martin Luther King Jr. What advice might Thoreau have given King? Apply the basic ideas of "Civil Disobedience" to the circumstances in which King found himself. What did each of these men learn about themselves while in prison? What did prison mean to them?

7. Slavery in the United States in 1849 was protected by national laws that had to be observed even by states that had abolished slavery. These were federal laws largely created by the slave states for the protection of "property." The Fugitive Slave Laws of 1793 and 1850 were enacted by Congress. Thoreau knew these laws and resisted them. Research these laws and explain how Congress could have imagined them to be ethical and just. Do you think enough attention is paid to ethical issues when Congress enacts such wide-ranging laws?

8. **CONNECTIONS**   One conflict between Aristotle (**bedfordstmartins .com/worldofideas/epages**) and Thoreau concerns their attitudes toward the state. Thoreau's view suggests that the individual's values are foremost and that the individual must resist the state when he or she thinks the state is in the wrong. Aristotle reveres the state and says that the highest good for humankind is likely to be found in statecraft; therefore, values other than those of the state always come second. Write an essay that attempts to resolve the conflict between these two authors. Which of their arguments can you most effectively support?

9. **SEEING CONNECTIONS**   The people in the household featured in Joseph Wright's *An Experiment on a Bird in the Air Pump* (p. 298) seem to represent a wide variety of emotional responses to the experiment. How would Thoreau have read the symbolism in this painting? Might he have seen the plight of the bird as similar to the plight of the American slaves? Would he have seen the hand of government symbolically at work in this painting? Would he have seen important ethical and moral issues revealed in the painting?

FREDERICK DOUGLASS
From *Narrative of the Life of Frederick Douglass, an American Slave*

FREDERICK DOUGLASS (1817–1895) was born into slavery in Maryland; he died not only a free man but also a man who commanded the respect of his country, his government, and hosts of supporters. Ironically, it was his owner's wife, Mrs. Hugh Auld, a Northerner, who helped Douglass learn to read and write. Until her husband forcefully convinced her that teaching slaves was "unlawful, as well as unsafe," Mrs. Auld taught Douglass enough so that he could begin his own education—and escape to freedom. Mrs. Auld eventually surpassed her husband in her vehement opposition to having Douglass read, leading Douglass to conclude that slavery had a negative effect on slave and slaveholder alike: both suffered the consequences of a political system that was inherently immoral.

The *Narrative* is filled with examples of the injustice of slavery. Douglass had little connection with his family. Separated from his mother, Harriet Bailey, Douglass never knew who his father was. In his *Narrative*, he records the beatings he witnessed as a slave, the conditions under which he lived, and the struggles he felt within himself to be a free man. Douglass himself survived brutal beatings and torture by a professional slave "breaker."

The laws of the time codified the injustices that Douglass and all American slaves suffered. The Fugitive Slave Act of 1793 tightened the hold on all slaves who had gone north in search of freedom. Federal marshals were enjoined to return slaves to their owners. The Underground Railroad helped so many runaway slaves find their way to Canada that a second Fugitive Slave

First published 1845; revised 1892.

Act was enacted in 1850 with stiff penalties for those who did not obey the law. In retaliation, many northern states enacted personal freedom laws to counter the Fugitive Slave Act. Eventually, these laws became central to the South's decision to secede. However, Douglass's fate, when he eventually escaped in 1838 by impersonating an African American seaman (using his papers to board ship), was not secure. Abolitionists in New York helped him find work in shipyards in New Bedford, Massachusetts. He changed his name from Auld to Douglass to protect himself, and he began his career as an orator in 1841 at an antislavery meeting in Nantucket.

To avoid capture after publication of an early version of his autobiography, Douglass spent two years on a speaking tour of Great Britain and Ireland (1845–1847). He then returned to the United States, bought his freedom, and rose to national fame as the founder and editor of the *North Star*, an abolitionist paper published in Rochester, New York. One of his chief concerns was for the welfare of the slaves who had managed to secure their freedom. When the Civil War began, there were no plans to free the slaves, but Douglass managed to convince President Lincoln that it would further the war effort to free them; in 1863, the president delivered the Emancipation Proclamation.

However, the years after the war and Lincoln's death were not good for freed slaves. Terrorist groups in both the North and the South worked to keep them from enjoying freedom, and training programs for former slaves that might have been effective were never fully instituted. During this time, Douglass worked in various capacities for the government—as assistant secretary of the Santo Domingo Commission, as an official in Washington, D.C., and as U.S. minister to Haiti (1889–1891). He was the first African American to become a national figure and to have influence with the government.

Douglass's Rhetoric

Douglass was basically self-taught, but he knew enough to read the powerful writers of his day. He was a commanding speaker in an age in which eloquence was valued and speakers were rewarded handsomely. This excerpt from the *Narrative*—Chapters 6, 7, and 8—is notable for its clear and direct style. The use of the first-person narrative is as simple as one could wish, yet the feelings projected are sincere and moving.

Douglass's structure is the chronological narrative, relating events in the order in which they occurred. He begins his story at the point of meeting a new mistress, a woman from whom he expected harsh treatment. Because she was new to the concept of slavery, how-ever, she behaved in ways that were unusual, and Douglass remarks on her initially kind attitude. Douglass does not interrupt himself with flashbacks or leaps forward in time but tells the story as it hap-pened. At critical moments, he slows the narrative to describe people or incidents in unusual detail and lets the reader infer from these details the extent of the injustice he suffered.

By today's standards, Douglass's style may seem formal. His sentences are often longer than those of modern writers, although they are always carefully balanced and punctuated by briefer sen-tences. Despite his long paragraphs, heavy with example and description, after a century and a half his work remains immediate and moving. No modern reader will have difficulty responding to what Frederick Douglass has to say. His views on education are as accessible and as powerful now as when they were written.

PREREADING QUESTIONS:
WHAT TO READ FOR

The following prereading questions may help you anticipate key issues in the discussion of the excerpt that follows from *Narrative of the Life of Frederick Douglass, an American Slave*. Keeping them in mind during your first reading of the selection should help focus your attention.

- What were the ethical issues involved in Mrs. Auld's helping Douglass learn to read?

- In what ways was Douglass treated immorally? Was he immoral in his behavior toward others?

- What was the ethical position of slave owners toward their slaves? Why did they think of themselves as ethical in their behavior?

From *Narrative of the Life of Frederick Douglass, an American Slave*

My new mistress proved to be all she appeared when I first met her at the door,—a woman of the kindest heart and finest feelings. She had never had a slave under her control previously to myself, and prior to her marriage she had been dependent upon her own indus-try for a living. She was by trade a weaver; and by constant applica-tion to her business, she had been in a good degree preserved from the blighting and dehumanizing effects of slavery. I was utterly astonished at her goodness. I scarcely knew how to behave towards her. She was entirely unlike any other white woman I had ever seen. I could not approach her as I was accustomed to approach other white ladies. My early instruction was all out of place. The crouching servility, usually so acceptable a quality in a slave, did not answer when manifested toward her. Her favor was not gained by it; she seemed to be disturbed by it. She did not deem it impudent or unmannerly for a slave to look her in the face. The meanest slave was put fully at ease in her presence, and none left without feeling better for having seen her. Her face was made of heavenly smiles, and her voice of tranquil music.

But, alas! this kind heart had but a short time to remain such. The fatal poison of irresponsible power was already in her hands, and soon commenced its infernal work. That cheerful eye, under the influence of slavery, soon became red with rage; that voice, made all of sweet accord, changed to one of harsh and horrid discord; and that angelic face gave place to that of a demon.

Very soon after I went to live with Mr. and Mrs. Auld, she very kindly commenced to teach me the A, B, C. After I had learned this, she assisted me in learning to spell words of three or four letters. Just at this point of my progress, Mr. Auld found out what was going on, and at once forbade Mrs. Auld to instruct me further, telling her, among other things, that it was unlawful, as well as unsafe, to teach a slave to read. To use his own words, further, he said, "If you give a nigger an inch, he will take an ell.[1] A nigger should know nothing but to obey his master—to do as he is told to do. Learning would *spoil* the best nigger in the world. Now," said he, "if you teach that nigger (speaking of myself) how to read, there would be no keeping him. It would forever unfit him to be a slave. He would at once become unmanageable, and of no value to his master. As to himself, it could do him no good, but a great deal of harm. It would make him discontented and unhappy." These words sank deep into my heart, stirred up sentiments within that lay slumbering, and called into existence an entirely new train of thought. It was a new and special revelation, explaining dark and mysterious things, with which my youthful understanding had struggled, but struggled in vain. I now understood what had been to me a most perplexing difficulty—to wit, the white man's power to enslave the black man. It was a grand achievement, and I prized it highly. From that moment, I understood the pathway from slavery to freedom. It was just what I wanted, and I got it at a time when I the least expected it. Whilst I was saddened by

2

3

---

[1] **ell** A measure about a yard in length.

the thought of losing the aid of my kind mistress, I was gladdened by the invaluable instruction which, by the merest accident, I had gained from my master. Though conscious of the difficulty of learning without a teacher, I set out with high hope, and a fixed purpose, at whatever cost of trouble, to learn how to read. The very decided manner with which he spoke, and strove to impress his wife with the evil consequences of giving me instruction, served to convince me that he was deeply sensible of the truths he was uttering. It gave me the best assurance that I might rely with the utmost confidence on the results which, he said, would flow from teaching me to read. What he most dreaded, that I most desired. What he most loved, that I most hated. That which to him was a great evil, to be carefully shunned, was to me a great good, to be diligently sought; and the argument which he so warmly urged, against my learning to read, only served to inspire me with a desire and determination to learn. In learning to read, I owe almost as much to the bitter opposition of my master, as to the kindly aid of my mistress. I acknowledge the benefit of both.

I had resided but a short time in Baltimore before I observed a 4 marked difference, in the treatment of slaves, from that which I had witnessed in the country. A city slave is almost a freeman, compared with a slave on the plantation. He is much better fed and clothed, and enjoys privileges altogether unknown to the slave on the plantation. There is a vestige of decency, a sense of shame, that does much to curb and check those outbreaks of atrocious cruelty so commonly enacted upon the plantation. He is a desperate slaveholder, who will shock the humanity of his nonslaveholding neighbors with the cries of his lacerated slave. Few are willing to incur the odium attaching to the reputation of being a cruel master; and above all things, they would not be known as not giving a slave enough to eat. Every city slaveholder is anxious to have it known of him, that he feeds his slaves well; and it is due to them to say, that most of them do give their slaves enough to eat. There are, however, some painful exceptions to this rule. Directly opposite to us, on Philpot Street, lived Mr. Thomas Hamilton. He owned two slaves. Their names were Henrietta and Mary. Henrietta was about twenty-two years of age, Mary was about fourteen; and of all the mangled and emaciated creatures I ever looked upon, these two were the most so. His heart must be harder than stone, that could look upon these unmoved. The head, neck, and shoulders of Mary were literally cut to pieces. I have frequently felt her head, and found it nearly covered with festering sores, caused by the lash of her cruel mistress. I do not know that her master ever whipped her, but I have been an eyewitness to the cruelty of Mrs. Hamilton. I used to be in Mr. Hamilton's house nearly every day. Mrs. Hamilton used to sit in a large chair in the middle of the room, with a heavy cowskin always by her side, and scarce an hour passed during the day but was marked by the blood of one of these slaves. The girls seldom passed her without her saying, "Move faster, you *black gip!*" at the same time giving them a blow with the cowskin over the head or shoulders, often drawing the blood. She would then say, "Take that, you *black gip!*"—continuing, "If you don't move faster, I'll move you!" Added to the cruel lashings to which these slaves were subjected, they were kept nearly half-starved. They seldom knew what it was to eat a full meal. I have seen Mary contending with the pigs for the offal thrown into the street. So much was Mary kicked and cut to pieces, that she was oftener called "*pecked*" than by her name.

I lived in Master Hugh's family about seven years. During this time,   5 I succeeded in learning to read and write. In accomplishing this, I was compelled to resort to various stratagems. I had no regular teacher. My mistress, who had kindly commenced to instruct me, had, in compliance with the advice and direction of her husband, not only ceased to instruct, but had set her face against my being instructed by any one else. It is due, however, to my mistress to say of her, that she did not adopt this course of treatment immediately. She at first lacked the depravity indispensable to shutting me up in mental darkness. It was at least necessary for her to have some training in the exercise of irresponsible power, to make her equal to the task of treating me as though I were a brute.

My mistress was, as I have said, a kind and tender-hearted woman;   6 and in the simplicity of her soul she commenced, when I first went to live with her, to treat me as she supposed one human being ought to treat another. In entering upon the duties of a slave-holder, she did not seem to perceive that I sustained to her the relation of a mere chattel, and that for her to treat me as a human being was not only wrong, but dangerously so. Slavery proved as injurious to her as it did to me. When I went there, she was a pious, warm, and tender-hearted woman. There was no sorrow or suffering for which she had not a tear. She had bread for the hungry, clothes for the naked, and comfort for every mourner that came within her reach. Slavery soon proved its ability to divest her of these heavenly qualities. Under its influence, the tender heart became stone, and the lamb-like disposition gave way to one of tiger-like fierceness. The first step in her downward course was in her ceasing to instruct me. She now commenced to practice her husband's precepts. She finally became even more violent in her opposition than her husband himself. She was not satisfied with simply doing as well as he had commanded; she seemed anxious to do better. Nothing seemed to make her more angry than to see me with a newspaper. She seemed to think that here lay the danger. I have had her rush at me with a face made all up of fury, and snatch from me a newspaper, in a manner that fully revealed her apprehension. She was an apt woman; and a little experience soon demonstrated, to her satisfaction, that education and slavery were incompatible with each other.

From this time I was most narrowly watched. If I was in a sepa-   7
rate room any considerable length of time, I was sure to be suspected of having a book, and was at once called to give an account of myself. All this, however, was too late. The first step had been taken. Mistress, in teaching me the alphabet, had given me the *inch*, and no precaution could prevent me from taking the *ell*.

The plan which I adopted, and the one by which I was most suc-   8
cessful, was that of making friends of all the little white boys whom I met in the street. As many of these as I could, I converted into teachers. With their kindly aid, obtained at different times and in different places, I finally succeeded in learning to read. When I was sent to errands, I always took my book with me, and by going one part of my errand quickly, I found time to get a lesson before my return. I used also to carry bread with me, enough of which was always in the house, and to which I was always welcome; for I was much better off in this regard than many of the poor white children in our neighborhood. This bread I used to bestow upon the hungry little urchins, who, in return, would give me that more valuable bread of knowledge. I am strongly tempted to give the names of two or three of those little boys, as a testimonial of the gratitude and affection I bear them; but prudence forbids;—not that it would injure me, but it might embarrass them; for it is almost an unpardonable offense to teach slaves to read in this Christian country. It is enough to say of the dear little fellows, that they lived on Philpot Street, very near Durgin and Bailey's ship-yard. I used to talk this matter of slavery over with them. I would sometimes say to them, I wished I could be as free as they would be when they got to be men. "You will be free as soon as you are twenty-one, *but I am a slave for life!* Have not I as good a right to be free as you have?" These words used to trouble them; they would express for me the liveliest sympathy, and console me with the hope that something would occur by which I might be free.

I was now about twelve years old, and the thought of being *a*   9
slave for life began to bear heavily upon my heart. Just about this time, I got hold of a book entitled "The Columbian Orator." Every opportunity I got, I used to read this book. Among much of other interesting matter, I found in it a dialogue between a master and his slave. The slave was represented as having run away from his master three times. The dialogue represented the conversation which took place between them, when the slave was retaken the third time. In this dialogue, the whole argument in behalf of slavery was brought forward by the master, all of which was disposed of by the slave. The slave was made to say some very smart as well as impressive things in reply to

his master—things which had the desired though unexpected effect; for the conversation resulted in the voluntary emancipation of the slave on the part of the master.

In the same book, I met with one of Sheridan's[2] mighty speeches on and in behalf of Catholic emancipation. These were choice documents to me. I read them over and over again with unabated interest. They gave tongue to interesting thoughts of my own soul, which had frequently flashed through my mind, and died away for want of utterance. The moral which I gained from the dialogue was the power of truth over the conscience of even a slaveholder. What I got from Sheridan was a bold denunciation of slavery, and a powerful vindication of human rights. The reading of these documents enabled me to utter my thoughts, and to meet the arguments brought forward to sustain slavery; but while they relieved me of one difficulty, they brought on another even more painful than the one of which I was relieved. The more I read, the more I was led to abhor and detest my enslavers. I could regard them in no other light than a band of successful robbers, who had left their homes, and gone to Africa, and stolen us from our homes, and in a strange land reduced us to slavery. I loathed them as being the meanest as well as the most wicked of men. As I read and contemplated the subject, behold! that very discontentment which Master Hugh had predicted would follow my learning to read had already come, to torment and sting my soul to unutterable anguish. As I writhed under it, I would at times feel that learning to read had been a curse rather than a blessing. It had given me a view of my wretched condition, without the remedy. It opened my eyes to the horrible pit, but to no ladder upon which to get out. In moments of agony, I envied my fellow-slaves for their stupidity. I have often wished myself a beast. I preferred the condition of the meanest reptile to my own. Any thing, no matter what, to get rid of thinking! It was this everlasting thinking of my condition that tormented me. There was no getting rid of it. It was pressed upon me by every object within sight or hearing, animate or inanimate. The silver trump of freedom had roused my soul to eternal wakefulness. Freedom now appeared, to disappear no more forever. It was heard in every sound, and seen in every thing. It was ever present to torment me with a sense of my wretched condition. I saw nothing without seeing it, I heard nothing without hearing it, and felt nothing without feeling it. It looked from every star, it smiled in every calm, breathed in every wind, and moved in every storm.

I often found myself regretting my own existence, and wishing myself dead; and but for the hope of being free, I have no doubt

10

11

---

[2] **Richard Brinsley Sheridan (1751–1816)** Irish dramatist and orator. However, Douglass really refers to a speech by Daniel O'Connell (1775–1847) in favor of Irish Catholic emancipation.

but that I should have killed myself, or done something for which I should have been killed. While in this state of mind, I was eager to hear any one speak of slavery. I was a ready listener. Every little while, I could hear something about the abolitionists.[3] It was some time before I found what the word meant. It was always used in such connections as to make it an interesting word to me. If a slave ran away and succeeded in getting clear, or if a slave killed his master, set fire to a barn, or did any thing very wrong in the mind of a slaveholder, it was spoken of as the fruit of *abolition*. Hearing the word in this connection very often, I set about learning what it meant. The dictionary afforded me little or no help. I found it was "the act of abolishing"; but then I did not know what was to be abolished. Here I was perplexed. I did not dare to ask any one about its meaning, for I was satisfied that it was something they wanted me to know very little about. After a patient waiting, I got one of our city papers, containing an account of the number of petitions from the north, praying for the abolition of slavery in the District of Columbia, and of the slave trade between the States. From this time I understood the words *abolition* and *abolitionist*, and always drew near when that word was spoken, expecting to hear something of importance to myself and fellow-slaves. The light broke in upon me by degrees. I went one day down on the wharf of Mr. Waters; and seeing two Irishmen unloading a scow of stone, I went, unasked, and helped them. When we had finished, one of them came to me and asked me if I were a slave. I told him I was. He asked, "Are ye a slave for life?" I told him that I was. The good Irishman seemed to be deeply affected by the statement. He said to the other that it was a pity so fine a little fellow as myself should be a slave for life. He said it was a shame to hold me. They both advised me to run away to the north; that I should find friends there, and that I should be free. I pretended not to be interested in what they said, and treated them as if I did not understand them; for I feared they might be treacherous. White men have been known to encourage slaves to escape, and then, to get the reward, catch them and return them to their masters. I was afraid that these seemingly good men might use me so; but I nevertheless remembered their advice, and from that time I resolved to run away. I looked forward to a time at which it would be safe for me to escape. I was too young to think of doing so immediately; besides, I wished to learn how to write, as I might have occasion to write my own pass. I consoled myself with the hope that I should one day find a good chance. Meanwhile, I would learn to write.

    The idea as to how I might learn to write was suggested to me by being in Durgin and Bailey's ship-yard, and frequently seeing the ship 12

---

[3] **abolitionists** Those who actively opposed slavery.

carpenters, after hewing, and getting a piece of timber ready for use, write on the timber the name of that part of the ship for which it was intended. When a piece of timber was intended for the larboard side, it would be marked thus—"L." When a piece was for the starboard side, it would be marked thus—"S." A piece for the larboard side forward, would be marked thus—"L.F." When a piece was for starboard side forward, it would be marked thus—"S.F." For larboard aft, it would be marked thus—"L.A." For starboard aft, it would be marked thus—"S.A." I soon learned the names of these letters, and for what they were intended when placed upon a piece of timber in the ship-yard. I immediately commenced copying them, and in a short time was able to make the four letters named. After that, when I met with any boy who I knew could write, I would tell him I could write as well as he. The next word would be, "I don't believe you. Let me see you try it." I would then make the letters which I had been so fortunate as to learn, and ask him to beat that. In this way I got a good many lessons in writing, which it is quite possible I should never have gotten in any other way. During this time, my copy-book was the board fence, brick wall, and pavement; my pen and ink was a lump of chalk. With these, I learned mainly how to write. I then commenced and continued copying the Italics in Webster's Spelling Book, until I could make them all without looking on the book. By this time, my little Master Thomas had gone to school, and learned how to write, and had written over a number of copy-books. These had been brought home, and shown to some of our near neighbors, and then laid aside. My mistress used to go to class meeting at the Wilk Street meeting-house every Monday afternoon, and leave me to take care of the house. When left thus, I used to spend the time in writing in the spaces left in Master Thomas's copy-book, copying what he had written. I continued to do this until I could write a hand very similar to that of Master Thomas. Thus, after a long, tedious effort for years, I finally succeeded in learning how to write.

In a very short time after I went to live at Baltimore, my old master's youngest son Richard died; and in about three years and six months after his death, my old master, Captain Anthony, died, leaving only his son, Andrew, and daughter, Lucretia, to share his estate. He died while on a visit to see his daughter at Hillsborough. Cut off thus unexpectedly, he left no will as to the disposal of his property. It was therefore necessary to have a valuation of the property, that it might be equally divided between Mrs. Lucretia and Master Andrew. I was immediately sent for, to be valued with the other property. Here again my feelings rose up in detestation of slavery. I had now a new conception of my degraded condition. Prior to this, I had become, if not insensible to my lot, at least partly so. I left Baltimore with a young heart overborne with sadness, and a soul full of apprehension. I took passage with Captain Rowe, in the schooner *Wild Cat*, and, after a sail of about twenty-four hours, I found myself near the place of my birth. I had now been absent from it almost, if not quite, five years. I, however, remembered the place very well. I was only about five years old when I left it, to go and live with my old master on Colonel Lloyd's plantation; so that I was now between ten and eleven years old.

We were all ranked together at the valuation. Men and women, old   14
and young, married and single, were ranked with horses, sheep, and swine. There were horses and men, cattle and women, pigs and children, all holding the same rank in the scale of being, and were all subjected to the same narrow examination. Silvery-headed age and sprightly youth, maids and matrons, had to undergo the same indelicate inspection. At this moment, I saw more clearly than ever the brutalizing effects of slavery upon both slave and slaveholder.

After the valuation, then came the division. I have no language   15
to express the high excitement and deep anxiety which were felt among us poor slaves during this time. Our fate for life was now to be decided. We had no more voice in that decision than the brutes among whom we were ranked. A single word from the white men was enough—against all our wishes, prayers, and entreaties—to sunder forever the dearest friends, dearest kindred, and strongest ties known to human beings. In addition to the pain of separation, there was the horrid dread of falling into the hands of Master Andrew. He was known to us all as being a most cruel wretch,—a common drunkard, who had, by his reckless mismanagement and profligate dissipation, already wasted a large portion of his father's property. We all felt that we might as well be sold at once to the Georgia traders, as to pass into his hands; for we knew that that would be our inevitable condition,— a condition held by us all in the utmost horror and dread.

I suffered more anxiety than most of my fellow-slaves. I had   16
known what it was to be kindly treated; they had known nothing of the kind. They had seen little or nothing of the world. They were in very deed men and women of sorrow, and acquainted with grief. Their backs had been made familiar with the bloody lash, so that they had become callous; mine was yet tender; for while at Baltimore I got few whippings, and few slaves could boast of a kinder master and mistress than myself; and the thought of passing out of their hands into those of Master Andrew—a man who, but a few days before, to give me a sample of his bloody disposition, took my little brother by the throat, threw him on the ground, and with the heel of his boot stamped upon his head till the blood gushed from his nose and ears—was well calculated to make me anxious as to my fate. After he had committed this savage outrage upon my brother, he turned

to me, and said that was the way he meant to serve me one of these days,—meaning, I suppose, when I came into his possession.

Thanks to a kind Providence, I fell to the portion of Mrs. Lucretia, 17 and was sent immediately back to Baltimore, to live again in the family of Master Hugh. Their joy at my return equalled their sorrow at my departure. It was a glad day to me. I had escaped a worse fate than lion's jaws. I was absent from Baltimore, for the purpose of valuation and division, just about one month, and it seemed to have been six.

Very soon after my return to Baltimore, my mistress, Lucretia, died, 18 leaving her husband and child, Amanda; and in a very short time after her death, Master Andrew died. Now all the property of my old master, slaves included, was in the hands of strangers,—strangers who had had nothing to do with accumulating it. Not a slave was left free. All remained slaves, from the youngest to the oldest. If any one thing in my experience, more than another, served to deepen my conviction of the infernal character of slavery, and to fill me with unutterable loathing of slaveholders, it was their base ingratitude to my poor old grandmother. She had served my old master faithfully from youth to old age. She had been the source of all his wealth; she had peopled his plantation with slaves; she had become a great grandmother in his service. She had rocked him in infancy, attended him in childhood, served him through life, and at his death wiped from his icy brow the cold death-sweat, and closed his eyes forever. She was nevertheless left a slave—a slave for life—a slave in the hands of strangers; and in their hands she saw her children, her grandchildren, and her great-grandchildren, divided, like so many sheep, without being gratified with the small privilege of a single word, as to their or her own destiny. And, to cap the climax of their base ingratitude and fiendish barbarity, my grandmother, who was now very old, having outlived my old master and all his children, having seen the beginning and end of all of them, and her present owners finding she was of but little value, her frame already racked with the pains of old age, and complete helplessness fast stealing over her once active limbs, they took her to the woods, built her a little hut, put up a little mud-chimney, and then made her welcome to the privilege of supporting herself there in perfect loneliness; thus virtually turning her out to die! If my poor old grandmother now lives, she lives to suffer in utter loneliness; she lives to remember and mourn over the loss of children, the loss of grandchildren, and the loss of great-grandchildren. They are, in the language of the slave's poet, Whittier,[4]—

> Gone, gone, sold and gone
> To the rice swamp dank and lone,

---

[4]**John Greenleaf Whittier (1807–1892)** New England abolitionist, journalist, and poet. The poem Douglass cites is "The Farewell" (1835).

Where the slave-whip ceaseless swings,
Where the noisome insect stings,
Where the fever-demon strews
Poison with the falling dews,
Where the sickly sunbeams glare
Through the hot and misty air: —
Gone, gone, sold and gone
To the rice swamp dank and lone,
From Virginia hills and waters —
Woe is me, my stolen daughters!

The hearth is desolate. The children, the unconscious children,   19
who once sang and danced in her presence, are gone. She gropes
her way, in the darkness of age, for a drink of water. Instead of the
voices of her children, she hears by day the moans of the dove, and
by night the screams of the hideous owl. All is gloom. The grave is at
the door. And now, when weighed down by the pains and aches of
old age, when the head inclines to the feet, when the beginning and
ending of human existence meet, and helpless infancy and painful old
age combine together—at this time, this most needful time, the time
for the exercise of that tenderness and affection which children only
can exercise towards a declining parent—my poor old grandmother,
the devoted mother of twelve children, is left all alone, in yonder
little hut, before a few dim embers. She stands—she sits—she stag-
gers—she falls—she groans—she dies—and there are none of her
children or grandchildren present, to wipe from her wrinkled brow
the cold sweat of death, or to place beneath the sod her fallen remains.
Will not a righteous God visit for these things?

In about two years after the death of Mrs. Lucretia, Master Tho-   20
mas married his second wife. Her name was Rowena Hamilton. She
was the eldest daughter of Mr. William Hamilton. Master now lived in
St. Michael's. Not long after his marriage, a misunderstanding took
place between himself and Master Hugh; and as a means of punishing
his brother, he took me from him to live with himself at St. Michael's.
Here I underwent another most painful separation. It, however, was not
so severe as the one I dreaded at the division of property; for, during
this interval, a great change had taken place in Master Hugh and his
once kind and affectionate wife. The influence of brandy upon him,
and of slavery upon her, had effected a disastrous change in the characters of both; so that, as far as they were concerned, I thought I had
little to lose by the change. But it was not to them that I was attached.
It was to those little Baltimore boys that I felt the strongest attachment. I had received many good lessons from them, and was still
receiving them, and the thought of leaving them was painful indeed.
I was leaving, too, without the hope of ever being allowed to return.

Master Thomas had said he would never let me return again. The barrier betwixt himself and brother he considered impassable.

I then had to regret that I did not at least make the attempt to   21
carry out my resolution to run away; for the chances of success are tenfold greater from the city than from the country.

I sailed from Baltimore for St. Michael's in the sloop *Amanda*,   22
Captain Edward Dodson. On my passage, I paid particular attention to the direction which the steamboats took to go to Philadelphia. I found, instead of going down, on reaching North Point they went up the bay, in a north-easterly direction. I deemed this knowledge of the utmost importance. My determination to run away was again revived. I resolved to wait only so long as the offering of a favorable opportunity. When that came, I was determined to be off.

QUESTIONS FOR CRITICAL READING

1. In paragraph 2, Douglass describes Mrs. Auld as possessing "the fatal poison of irresponsible power." What are the ethical responsibilities of power in her relationship with Douglass?

2. In what sense were the laws of Douglass's time immoral? How can a law be immoral?

3. Did slave owners think it immoral to teach slaves to read and write?

4. Was it immoral for Douglass to learn to read and write even though he knew it was prohibited for him to do so?

5. How does an ethical contract between slave and slaveholder function? What were the responsibilities of each to the other?

SUGGESTIONS FOR CRITICAL WRITING

1. The society in which Douglass lived was governed by laws established by elected officials who had benefited from the authors of the Constitution of the United States, which set itself as the law of the land. How could slaveholders in Maryland have considered it ethical to hold other human beings as slaves? What ethical loopholes were apparent in the Constitution?

2. What is the most important political issue raised in the essay? Douglass never talks about the law, but he implies a great deal about justice and morality. How do justice and morality intersect in Douglass's story of his life as a slave? How aware does he seem to have been that he was being dealt with in an unethical fashion?

3. The vast number of slaveholders during Douglass's time were church-goers and passionate Christians. We often think of religion as a bulwark of morality and ethics, so how could avid religious citizens behave in a way that we now think of as immoral and unethical? Is it possible that there was a

disconnect between religion and morality in the slave states? Is it possible that there is no relationship between morality and religion to start with?

4. What, on the whole, is Douglass's attitude toward white people? Examine his statements about them and establish as far as possible his feelings regarding their character. Is he bitter about his slavery experiences? Does he condemn the society that supported slavery as having been immoral?

5. How effective is the detailed description in this selection? Choose the best descriptive passages and analyze them for their effectiveness in context. What does Douglass hope to achieve by giving so much attention to such descriptions? How does his description help you better understand the concept of ethical behavior?

6. **CONNECTIONS**   Which writer would Douglass have expected to understand his views on the ethics of slavery: Henry David Thoreau, James Madison, Thomas Jefferson, or Jean-Jacques Rousseau? How do each of their views of ethics intersect with Douglass's? Which of these writers do you think would have most enjoyed being able to discuss slavery with Douglass?

7. **CONNECTIONS**   Aristotle is clear in saying that happiness is the greatest good for man. Yet in Aristotle's Athens, slavery was a simple, accepted fact of everyday life, and Aristotle likely did not have slaves' interests in mind when he wrote "The Aim of Man" (**bedfordstmartins .com/worldofideas/epages**). How might Frederick Douglass have responded to the way Aristotle connected virtue and happiness? How would Douglass's having been a slave affect his views of Aristotle's respect for the state? Did Douglass consider virtue as a means to happiness? How might Douglass have critiqued Aristotle's views of the ultimate good? For Douglass, what constituted the ultimate good?

8. One of the most constant defenses of the ethics of slavery—even after the Civil War—was that it was for the good of the slaves. Even some of the freed slaves told interviewers in the 1930s that things had been better for them under slavery than they were during the Great Depression. Is the view that slavery was good for the slaves in any way an ethical view? Is it a moral view? What's wrong with it?

9. Douglass escaped from slavery by deceiving the authorities into thinking he was an able-bodied seaman with the right to travel. He broke the law at that time, and he broke it again when he remained free. Why should we not condemn him for immoral behavior and an ethical lapse? The Aulds certainly regarded him as a criminal and as someone who acted immorally. Why should we not agree with them? What would Thoreau have said about his behavior?

10. **SEEING CONNECTIONS**   Which painting, Wright's *An Experiment on a Bird in the Air Pump* (p. 298) or Henry Chandler Christy's *Scene at the Signing of the Constitution of the United States* (p. 57), would Frederick Douglass point to as an illustration that raises the primary ethical questions involved in maintaining slavery as a matter of the law of the land in the United States? Which painting would give him the most ethical material for condemning slavery?

FRIEDRICH NIETZSCHE
Morality as Anti-Nature

FRIEDRICH NIETZSCHE (1844–1900), one of the most influential German philosophers, is the man who declared that God is
dead (in *The Gay Science*, 1882). The statement came from his conviction that science had altered the balance between humans and
nature, that psychology had begun to explain the unconscious mind,
and that the commitment to religious belief of earlier times would
give way. The result would be to leave people without a sense of
hope or purpose unless they could create it for themselves. Like
many historians and philosophers of the day, he feared that modern civilization itself was somehow hanging in the balance, and
that unless people refashioned the spiritual energy that brought
progress and prosperity, the foundations of society would collapse.

In some of his writing he characterized power as the driving force
for most people. Two late works that have been influential in modern
thought, *Daybreak: Reflections on Moral Prejudices* (1881) and *Thus
Spoke Zarathustra* (1883–1885), begin to develop some of his most
important thinking regarding what he called "the will to power." His
solution to the problem of modernity was self-mastery, which he felt
was the key to transcending the confusion of modern thought. Realizing that self-mastery was not an easy state to achieve, he called the
man who could create his own moral and ethical values instead of
blindly following conventional or societal standards "superman."

Nietzsche's personal life was difficult. Both his grandfathers
were Lutheran ministers, and his paternal grandfather was a theological scholar whose book *Gamaliel* (1796) declared the perma-
nency of Christianity. His father was also a Lutheran minister, but
he died when Friedrich was four years old. He and his younger
sister had to leave their family home in the Prussian province of

---

From *The Twilight of the Idols* (1888) in *The Portable Nietzsche*. Translated by Walter
Kaufmann.

Saxony and live with relatives in Naumberg. When he was four-teen, he went to boarding school and prepared for the University of Bonn (1864), then the University of Leipzig (1865). His studies were in theology and philology — the study of the interpretation of primarily biblical and classical texts. He was also deeply fascinated by music — which he both played and composed — and eventually grew to love the music of Richard Wagner (1813–1883), which he felt expressed the spiritual realities of modern life.

Nietzsche's father died of an unspecified brain ailment. Nietzsche himself was ill much of his life. When he joined the army after university, he experienced a bad accident on a horse that left him weak and impaired. In 1870 during the Franco-Prussian War (1870–1871), Nietzsche served in a hospital unit and witnessed the carnage of war. He contracted illnesses in the wards that stayed with him for the rest of his life. He may have contracted syphilis either during this period or earlier, and in 1889 he began to show signs of brain sickness that made it necessary for him to be in a sanatorium. His mother and later his sister Elizabeth cared for him until his death.

Despite his short life, Nietzsche achieved much. In 1868, at the age of twenty-four, he became a professor of classical philology at the University of Basel in Switzerland. He published a consider-able number of important and widely regarded books. *The Birth of Tragedy from the Spirit of Music* (1872), his first book, caught the eye of Wagner and helped establish Nietzsche's reputation. That book was an attempt to clarify the two basic religious forces in humankind: Apollonian intellectuality and Dionysian passion. Apollo was a god of conscience devoted to the arts and music. Dionysius, patron of Greek tragedy, was associated with vegetation, plentiful-ness, passion, and especially wine — and therefore inspiration. In 1873 Nietzsche published *Unfashionable Observations*, a critique of cultural critics. Before illness forced him to resign his profes-sorship at the University of Basel in 1879, he published *Human, All-Too-Human* (1878), a collection of aphorisms — brief statements ranging from a single line to a page of text. This style, repeated in *Thus Spoke Zarathustra* and other works, became one of the hall-marks of his rhetorical approach. It gave him the appearance of a sage uttering wise sayings.

His production after leaving the university was not dimin-ished. In 1882 he published one of his most impressive books, *The Gay Science*, which postulated an alternative to the Christian view that another world exists after death. His suggestion was known as "eternal recurrence," a view that says we are destined to live this life over and over again down to the slightest detail. The point of this observation was to make people take this life seriously enough to live it so well that they would not mind living it again. The concept of eternal recurrence influenced twentieth-century existentialists, who agreed that the way one lived life was the way one defined oneself.

The Genealogy of Morals (1887) was a critique of contemporary religion, especially Christianity. It emphasized his views about moral and ethical values and rejected the conventional views as being essentially based on an attack on our natural feelings and motives. A section of that book, "Beyond Good and Evil," attempts to neutralize those terms, which he sees as props of conventional religious thought.

The Twilight of the Idols: Or How One Philosophizes with a Hammer (1888), from which this selection is taken and one of his last books, is a careful attack on contemporary religious beliefs and an analysis of important philosophers such as Socrates and Plato as well as of more modern thinkers. Its title is a play on an opera by Wagner called *The Twilight of the Gods* and reveals his essential attitudes toward ethical values as maintained by most religions. Some of his basic views on ethics and morality are in evidence in the selection that follows.

Nietzsche's Rhetoric

"Morality as Anti-Nature" is a careful argument that attempts to prove that moral pronouncements by major religions are designed to stifle people's natural behaviors. According to Nietzsche, people give in to their natural, often destructive impulses because they are weak. Consequently, religions seek to enforce a moral code of conduct by threatening all people—even those who could easily control themselves—with damnation in the next world for any infraction of that code. Nietzsche regards passion as a good thing, but as he states in paragraph 1, "all the old moral monsters" agree that we must kill the passions. He opens by critiquing the Sermon on the Mount, reminding us that "it is said, for example, with particular reference to sexuality: 'If thy eye offend thee, pluck it out.' Fortunately, no Christian acts in accordance with this precept" (para. 1). This is a rhetorical salvo against many of his readers' standard views of religion.

He continues by demonstrating that religions prohibit various forms of sensuality in an effort to promote spirituality, stating, "The spiritualization of sensuality is called *love*: it represents a great triumph over Christianity" (para. 5). This is an explosive statement, much like others he makes as he develops his argument. He then addresses another passion: hostility. This becomes an interesting political concept when he asserts that the success of the then German government, the Second Reich, depends on having enemies. As he states somewhat ironically in paragraph 5, "Another triumph is our spiritualization of *hostility*. It consists in a profound appreciation of the value of having enemies: in short, it means acting and thinking in the opposite way from that which has been the rule. The church always wanted the destruction of its enemies; we, we immoralists and Antichristians, find our advantage in this, that the church exists." His own writing in this selection demonstrates his position: he is opposed to conventional views of morals, and in order to clarify his own thoughts he needs to have the opposition of the church's views.

One of his rhetorical devices — in addition to the bald oppositional stance he takes in the opening of the selection — is the aphorism. He looks for opportunities to make a clear statement that capsulizes his views. The last sentence in paragraph 8 is an example: "Life has come to an end where the 'kingdom of God' begins." He describes himself as an immoralist — by which he means one who does not subscribe to conventional morals (but not one who acts immorally) — and states, "But we ourselves, we immoralists, are the answer" (para. 12). His most inflammatory aphorism is his last sentence: "Christianity is a metaphysics of the hangman" (para. 28). All this is rather shocking today; imagine what its effect was in 1888.

Among his less sensational rhetorical strategies is his careful enumeration of the elements of his argument. The first six sections examine specific details concerning the moral prohibitions of modern religions. His purpose here is to clarify his title, which he does in paragraph 8 when he states, "*Anti-natural* morality — that is, almost every morality which has so far been taught, revered, and preached — turns, conversely, *against* the instincts of life: it is *condemnation* of these instincts, now secret, now outspoken and impudent."

He then goes on to enumerate what he calls "The Four Great Errors": 1. the error of confusing cause and effect (paras. 13–15); 2. the error of false causality (paras. 16–18); 3. the error of imaginary causes (paras. 19–25); and 4. the error of free will (paras. 26–28). Each of these is treated carefully, sometimes with an example, but always with a clearly developed analysis.

Nietzsche offers modern readers a way of thinking that helps us avoid taking the views of Moses, Aristotle, Jesus, or Muhammad for granted. He provides modern thinkers with a challenge that many have gladly accepted.

PREREADING QUESTIONS:
WHAT TO READ FOR

The following prereading questions may help you anticipate key issues in the discussion of Friedrich Nietzsche's "Morality as Anti-Nature." Keeping them in mind during your first reading of the selection should help focus your attention.

- What traditional moral views does Nietzsche attack?
- Why does Nietzsche think religious morals are anti-nature?
- What does Nietzsche say about the confusion of cause and effect?

Morality as Anti-Nature

1

All passions have a phase when they are merely disastrous, when   1
they drag down their victim with the weight of stupidity—and a later, very much later phase when they wed the spirit, when they "spiritualize" themselves. Formerly, in view of the element of stupidity in passion, war was declared on passion itself, its destruction was plotted; all the old moral monsters are agreed on this: *il faut tuer les passions.*[1] The most famous formula for this is to be found in the New Testament, in that Sermon on the Mount, where, incidentally, things are by no means looked at from a height. There it is said, for example, with particular reference to sexuality: "If thy eye offend thee, pluck it out." Fortunately, no Christian acts in accordance with this precept. *Destroying* the passions and cravings, merely as a preventive measure against their stupidity and the unpleasant consequences of this stupidity—today this itself strikes us as merely another acute form of stupidity. We no longer admire dentists who "pluck out" teeth so that they will not hurt any more.

To be fair, it should be admitted, however, that on the ground   2
out of which Christianity grew, the concept of the "*spiritualization* of passion" could never have been formed. After all the first church, as is well known, fought *against* the "intelligent" in favor of the "poor in spirit." How could one expect from it an intelligent war against passion? The church fights passion with excision in every sense: its practice, its "cure," is *castratism.*[2] It never asks: "How can one spiritualize, beautify,

---

[1] *il faut tuer les passions* One must kill the passions.
[2] **castratism** Cutting off.

deify a craving?" It has at all times laid the stress of discipline on extir-pation[3] (of sensuality, of pride, of the lust to rule, of avarice, of venge-fulness). But an attack on the roots of passion means an attack on the roots of life: the practice of the church is *hostile to life*.

2

The same means in the fight against a craving—castration, 3 extirpation—is instinctively chosen by those who are too weak-willed, too degenerate, to be able to impose moderation on themselves; by those who are so constituted that they require *La Trappe*,[4] to use a figure of speech, or (without any figure of speech) some kind of definitive declaration of hostility, a *cleft* between themselves and the passion. Radical means are indispensable only for the degenerate; the weakness of the will—or, to speak more definitely, the inability *not* to respond to a stimulus—is itself merely another form of degeneration. The radical hostility, the deadly hostility against sensuality, is always a symptom to reflect on: it entitles us to suppositions concerning the total state of one who is excessive in this manner.

This hostility, this hatred, by the way, reaches its climax only 4 when such types lack even the firmness for this radical cure, for this renunciation of their "devil." One should survey the whole history of the priests and philosophers, including the artists: the most poisonous things against the senses have been said not by the impotent, nor by ascetics,[5] but by the impossible ascetics, by those who really were in dire need of being ascetics.

3

The spiritualization of sensuality is called *love*: it represents a 5 great triumph over Christianity. Another triumph is our spiritualiza-tion of *hostility*. It consists in a profound appreciation of the value of having enemies: in short, it means acting and thinking in the opposite way from that which has been the rule. The church always wanted the destruction of its enemies; we, we immoralists and Antichristians, find our advantage in this, that the church exists. In the political realm too, hostility has now become more spiritual—much more sensible, much more thoughtful, much more *considerate*. Almost every party under-stands how it is in the interest of its own self-preservation that the oppo-sition should not lose all strength; the same is true of power politics.

---

[3] **extirpation** Rooting out.
[4] *La Trappe* The Trappist order of monks. They do not speak.
[5] **ascetics** Those practicing extreme self-discipline, often hermits.

A new creation in particular—the new *Reich*,[6] for example—needs enemies more than friends: in opposition alone does it *feel* itself necessary, in opposition alone does it *become* necessary.

Our attitude to the "internal enemy" is no different: here too we　6 have spiritualized hostility; here too we have come to appreciate its value. The price of fruitfulness is to be rich in internal opposition; one remains young only as long as the soul does not stretch itself and desire peace. Nothing has become more alien to us than that desideratum[7] of former times, "peace of soul," the *Christian* desideratum; there is nothing we envy less than the moralistic cow and the fat happiness of the good conscience. One has renounced the *great* life when one renounces war.

In many cases, to be sure, "peace of soul" is merely a misunderstanding—　7 something else, which lacks only a more honest name. Without further ado or prejudice, a few examples. "Peace of soul" can be, for one, the gentle radiation of a rich animality into the moral (or religious) sphere. Or the beginning of weariness, the first shadow of evening, of any kind of evening. Or a sign that the air is humid, that south winds are approaching. Or unrecognized gratitude for a good digestion (sometimes called "love of man"). Or the attainment of calm by a convalescent who feels a new relish in all things and waits. Or the state which follows a thorough satisfaction of our dominant passion, the well-being of a rare repletion. Or the senile weakness of our will, our cravings, our vices. Or laziness, persuaded by vanity to give itself moral airs. Or the emergence of certainty, even a dreadful certainty, after long tension and torture by uncertainty. Or the expression of maturity and mastery in the midst of doing, creating, working, and willing—calm breathing, *attained* "freedom of the will." *Twilight of the Idols*—who knows? perhaps also only a kind of "peace of soul."

4

I reduce a principle to a formula. Every naturalism in morality—　8 that is, every healthy morality—is dominated by an instinct of life; some commandment of life is fulfilled by a determinate canon of "shalt" and "shalt not"; some inhibition and hostile element on the path of life is thus removed. *Anti-natural* morality—that is, almost every morality which has so far been taught, revered, and preached—turns, conversely, *against* the instincts of life: it is *condemnation* of these instincts, now secret, now outspoken and impudent. When it says, "God looks at the heart," it says No to both the lowest

---

[6] **Reich** The Second Reich, 1871, founded by Wilhelm I as the German Empire.
[7] **desideratum** The thing that is desired.

and the highest desires of life, and posits God as the *enemy of life*. The saint in whom God delights is the ideal eunuch. Life has come to an end where the "kingdom of God" begins.

5

Once one has comprehended the outrage of such a revolt against life as has become almost sacrosanct in Christian morality, one has, fortunately, also comprehended something else: the futility, apparentness, absurdity, and *mendaciousness* of such a revolt. A condemnation of life by the living remains in the end a mere symptom of a certain kind of life: the question whether it is justified or unjustified is not even raised thereby. One would require a position *outside* of life, and yet have to know it as well as one, as many, as all who have lived it, in order to be permitted even to touch the problem of the *value* of life: reasons enough to comprehend that this problem is for us an unapproachable problem. When we speak of values, we speak with the inspiration, with the way of looking at things, which is part of life: life itself forces us to posit values; life itself values through us when we posit values. From this it follows that even that anti-natural morality which conceives of God as the counter-concept and condemnation of life is only a value judgment of life—but of what life? of what kind of life? I have already given the answer: of declining, weakened, weary, condemned life. Morality, as it has so far been understood—as it has in the end been formulated once more by Schopenhauer,[8] as "negation of the will to life"—is the very *instinct of decadence*, which makes an imperative of itself. It says: *"Perish!"* It is a condemnation pronounced by the condemned.

6

Let us finally consider how naive it is altogether to say: "Man *ought* to be such and such!" Reality shows us an enchanting wealth of types, the abundance of a lavish play and change of forms—and some wretched loafer of a moralist comments: "No! Man ought to be different." He even knows what man should be like, this wretched bigot and prig: he paints himself on the wall and comments, *"Ecce homo!"*[9] But even when the moralist addresses himself only to the single human being and says to him, "You ought to be such and such!" he does not cease to make himself ridiculous. The single human being is a piece of *fatum*[10] from the front and from the rear, one law more, one necessity

---

[8] **Arthur Schopenhauer (1788–1860)** German philosopher who believed reality was nothing but senseless will, having no divine origin.

[9] *Ecce homo!* Behold this man!

[10] *fatum* Prophecy, declaration.

more for all that is yet to come and to be. To say to him, "Change your-self!" is to demand that everything be changed, even retroactively. And indeed there have been consistent moralists who wanted man to be different, that is, virtuous—they wanted him remade in their own image, as a prig: to that end, they *negated* the world! No small madness! No modest kind of immodesty!

Morality, insofar as it *condemns* for its own sake, and *not* out of regard for the concerns, considerations, and contrivances of life, is a specific error with which one ought to have no pity—an *idiosyncrasy of degenerates* which has caused immeasurable harm. 11

We others, we immoralists, have, conversely, made room in our hearts for every kind of understanding, comprehending, and *approving*. We do not easily negate; we make it a point of honor to be *affirmers*. More and more, our eyes have opened to that economy which needs and knows how to utilize all that the holy witlessness of the priest, of the *diseased* reason in the priest, rejects—that economy in the law of life which finds an advantage even in the disgusting species of the prigs, the priests, the virtuous. *What* advantage? But we ourselves, we immoralists, are the answer. 12

The Four Great Errors

1

The error of confusing cause and effect. There is no more dangerous error than that of mistaking the effect for the cause: I call it the real corruption of reason. Yet this error belongs among the most ancient and recent habits of mankind: it is even hallowed among us and goes by the name of "religion" or "morality." Every single sentence which religion and morality formulate contains it; priests and legislators of moral codes are the originators of this corruption of reason. 13

I give an example. Everybody knows the book of the famous Cornaro[11] in which he recommends his slender diet as a recipe for a long and happy life—a virtuous one too. Few books have been read so much; even now thousands of copies are sold in England every year. I do not doubt that scarcely any book (except the Bible, as is meet) has done as much harm, has *shortened* as many lives, as this well-intentioned *curiosum*. The reason: the mistaking of the effect for the cause. The worthy Italian thought his diet was the *cause* of his long life, whereas the precondition for a long life, the extraordinary slowness 14

---

[11] **Luigi Cornaro (1467–1566)** Venetian who lived on a restricted diet. *The Sure and Certain Method of Attaining a Long and Healthful Life* (1550) was published when he was eighty-three.

of his metabolism, the consumption of so little, was the cause of his slender diet. He was not free to eat little *or* much; his frugality was not a matter of "free will": he became sick when he ate more. But whoever is no carp not only does well to eat properly, but needs to. A scholar in our time, with his rapid consumption of nervous energy, would simply destroy himself with Cornaro's diet. *Crede experto.*[12]

2

The most general formula on which every religion and morality   15
is founded is: "Do this and that, refrain from this and that—then you will be happy! Otherwise . . ." Every morality, every religion, *is* this imperative; I call it the great original sin of reason, the *immortal unreason*. In my mouth, this formula is changed into its opposite—first example of my "revaluation of all values": a well-turned-out human being, a "happy one," *must* perform certain actions and shrinks instinctively from other actions; he carries the order, which he represents physiologically, into his relations with other human beings and things. In a formula: his virtue is the *effect* of his happiness. A long life, many descendants—this is not the wages of virtue; rather virtue itself is that slowing down of the metabolism which leads, among other things, also to a long life, many descendants—in short, to *Cornarism.* . . .

3

The error of a false causality. People have believed at all times that they   16
knew what a cause is; but whence did we take our knowledge—or more precisely, our faith that we had such knowledge? From the realm of the famous "inner facts," of which not a single one has so far proved to be factual. We believed ourselves to be causal in the act of willing: we thought that here at least we caught causality in the act. Nor did one doubt that all the antecedents of an act, its causes, were to be sought in consciousness and would be found there once sought—as "motives": else one would not have been free and responsible for it. Finally, who would have denied that a thought is caused? that the ego causes the thought?

Of these three "inward facts" which seem to guarantee causality,   17
the first and most persuasive is that of the will as cause. The conception of a consciousness ("spirit") as a cause, and later also that of the ego as cause (the "subject"), are only afterbirths: first the causality of the will was firmly accepted as given, as *empirical.*

Meanwhile we have thought better of it. Today we no longer   18
believe a word of all this. The "inner world" is full of phantoms and

---

[12] **Crede experto** Believe him who has tried!

will-o'-the-wisps: the will is one of them. The will no longer moves anything, hence does not explain anything either—it merely accompanies events; it can also be absent. The so-called *motive:* another error. Merely a surface phenomenon of consciousness, something alongside the deed that is more likely to cover up the antecedents of the deeds than to represent them. And as for the *ego!* That has become a fable, a fiction, a play on words: it has altogether ceased to think, feel, or will! . . .

4

The error of imaginary causes. To begin with dreams: *ex post facto,*[13] a cause is slipped under a particular sensation (for example, one following a far-off cannon shot)—often a whole little novel in which the dreamer turns up as the protagonist. The sensation endures meanwhile in a kind of resonance: it waits, as it were, until the causal instinct permits it to step into the foreground—now no longer as a chance occurrence, but as "meaning." The cannon shot appears in a *causal* mode, in an apparent reversal of time. What is really later, the motivation, is experienced first—often with a hundred details which pass like lightning—and the shot *follows.* What has happened? The representations which were *produced* by a certain state have been misunderstood as its causes.

In fact, we do the same thing when awake. Most of our general feelings—every kind of inhibition, pressure, tension, and explosion in the play and counterplay of our organs, and particularly the state of the *nervus sympathicus*[14]—excite our causal instinct: we want to have a reason for feeling this way or that—for feeling bad or for feeling good. We are never satisfied merely to state the fact that we feel this way or that: we admit this fact only—become conscious of it only—when we have furnished some kind of motivation. Memory, which swings into action in such cases, unknown to us, brings up earlier states of the same kind, together with the causal interpretations associated with them—not their real causes. The faith, to be sure, that such representations, such accompanying conscious processes, are the causes, is also brought forth by memory. Thus originates a habitual acceptance of a particular causal interpretation, which, as a matter of fact, inhibits any investigation into the real cause—even precludes it.

5

The psychological explanation of this. To derive something unknown from something familiar relieves, comforts, and satisfies, besides giving a feeling of power. With the unknown, one is confronted with danger,

19

20

21

---

[13] **ex post facto** After the fact.
[14] **nervus sympathicus** System of sympathetic nerves that gives us a "gut feeling."

discomfort, and care; the first instinct is to abolish these painful states. First principle: any explanation is better than none. Since at bottom it is merely a matter of wishing to be rid of oppressive representations, one is not too particular about the means of getting rid of them: the first representation that explains the unknown as familiar feels so good that one "considers it true." The proof of pleasure ("of strength") as a criterion of truth.

The causal instinct is thus conditional upon, and excited by, the feeling of fear. The "why?" shall, if at all possible, not give the cause for its own sake so much as for *a particular kind of cause*—a cause that is comforting, liberating, and relieving. That it is something already familiar, experienced, and inscribed in the memory, which is posited as a cause, that is the first consequence of this need. That which is new and strange and has not been experienced before, is excluded as a cause. Thus one searches not only for some kind of explanation to serve as a cause, but for a particularly selected and preferred kind of explanation—that which has most quickly and most frequently abolished the feeling of the strange, new, and hitherto unexperienced: the *most habitual* explanations. Consequence: one kind of positing of causes predominates more and more, is concentrated into a system, and finally emerges as *dominant*, that is, as simply precluding other causes and explanations. The banker immediately thinks of "business," the Christian of "sin," and the girl of her love.

22

6

The whole realm of morality and religion belongs under this concept of imaginary causes. The "explanation" of *disagreeable* general feelings. They are produced by beings that are hostile to us (evil spirits: the most famous case—the misunderstanding of the hysterical as witches). They are produced by acts which cannot be approved (the feeling of "sin," of "sinfulness," is slipped under a physiological discomfort; one always finds reasons for being dissatisfied with oneself). They are produced as punishments, as payment for something we should not have done, for what we should not have *been* (impudently generalized by Schopenhauer into a principle in which morality appears as what it really is—as the very poisoner and slanderer of life: "Every great pain, whether physical or spiritual, declares what we deserve; for it could not come to us if we did not deserve it." *World as Will and Representation* II, 666). They are produced as effects of ill-considered actions that turn out badly. (Here the affects, the senses, are posited as causes, as "guilty"; and physiological calamities are interpreted with the help of other calamities as "deserved.")

23

The "explanation" of *agreeable* general feelings. They are produced by trust in God. They are produced by the consciousness of

24

good deeds (the so-called "good conscience"—a physiological state which at times looks so much like good digestion that it is hard to tell them apart). They are produced by the successful termination of some enterprise (a naive fallacy: the successful termination of some enterprise does not by any means give a hypochondriac or a Pascal[15] agreeable general feelings). They are produced by faith, charity, and hope—the Christian virtues.

In truth, all these supposed explanations are resultant states and, as   25
it were, translations of pleasurable or unpleasurable feelings into a false dialect: one is in a state of hope *because* the basic physiological feeling is once again strong and rich; one trusts in God *because* the feeling of fullness and strength gives a sense of rest. Morality and religion belong altogether to the *psychology of error*: in every single case, cause and effect are confused; or truth is confused with the effects of *believing* something to be true; or a state of consciousness is confused with its causes.

7

The error of free will. Today we no longer have any pity for the con-   26
cept of "free will": we know only too well what it really is—the foulest of all theologians' artifices, aimed at making mankind "responsible" in their sense, that is, *dependent upon them.* Here I simply supply the psychology of all "making responsible."

Wherever responsibilities are sought, it is usually the instinct of   27
wanting to judge and punish which is at work. Becoming has been deprived of its innocence when any being-such-and-such is traced back to will, to purposes, to acts of responsibility: the doctrine of the will has been invented essentially for the purpose of punishment, that is, because one wanted to impute guilt. The entire old psychology, the psychology of will, was conditioned by the fact that its originators, the priests at the head of ancient communities, wanted to create for themselves the right to punish—or wanted to create this right for God. Men were considered "free" so that they might be judged and punished—so that they might become *guilty:* consequently, every act had to be considered as willed, and the origin of every act had to be considered as lying within the consciousness (and thus the most fundamental counterfeit *in psychologicis* was made the principle of psychology itself).

Today, as we have entered into the reverse movement and we   28
immoralists are trying with all our strength to take the concept of guilt and the concept of punishment out of the world again, and to cleanse psychology, history, nature, and social institutions and sanctions of them, there is in our eyes no more radical opposition than

---

[15]**Blaise Pascal (1623–1662)** French mathematician and scientist.

that of the theologians, who continue with the concept of a "moral world-order" to infect the innocence of becoming by means of "punishment" and "guilt." Christianity is a metaphysics of the hangman.

QUESTIONS FOR CRITICAL READING

1. What does Nietzsche mean when he says that passions "drag down their victim" (para. 1)?
2. Why does he claim there is a war on the passions?
3. Why does Nietzsche make several references to stupidity in the opening paragraph?
4. Is there such a thing as a spiritualization of passion?
5. Why does Nietzsche consider moderation an important quality?
6. In what sense is love a spiritualization of sensuality?
7. What is "the internal enemy" (para. 6)?
8. Is there such a thing as "healthy morality" (para. 8)?
9. What is Nietzsche's view of the Ten Commandments?

SUGGESTIONS FOR CRITICAL WRITING

1. Assume you are writing for an audience that knows a bit about Nietzsche but has not read this selection. Write an essay in which you clarify Nietzsche's attitudes toward conventional morality and explain why he feels it is anti-nature. Also explain his attitude toward people who, because they have no self-control, cannot keep themselves from acting in degenerate ways.
2. Do you think Nietzsche is correct in assuming that morality is anti-nature? Use other texts from this section of the book in your argument to help you convince your readers. Be sure to define the term *anti-nature* as carefully as possible.
3. What might Nietzsche's moral views be? It is clear that he does not intend to behave unethically as a result of his analysis of the moral views he condemns. But he does not go into detail about the moral position he might take. He talks about affirming life. How would this translate into an ethical position and thus into a clear moral purpose in life? Do you think he plans to live a moral life, or will he just do as he pleases? Explain.
4. Assuming that Nietzsche is correct that conventional morality is against our natural expression of passions, argue a case that suggests that while he is correct, the truth is that people must be restricted in their natural expression. Which moral statements clearly recognize dangerous natural

inclinations and restrict them? What benefits do these restrictions provide to the individual as well as to society as a whole? How might Nietzsche react to your argument?

5. Do you believe Nietzsche is accurate when he declares in paragraph 15 that "every religion and morality" is founded on a general principle of "Do this and that, refrain from this and that—then you will be happy!"? Is he simply misreading the teachings of religion? Write an essay in which you take issue with or agree with Nietzsche's premise and conclusions.

6. In paragraphs 19 and 20, Nietzsche discusses the "error of imaginary causes." Are there instances in your own life when you made the mistake of assigning imaginary causes to effects you observed? If your examples have a moral implication, be sure to clarify the nature of the error and decide whether or not your experience helps to reinforce Nietzsche's argument or weaken it.

7. **CONNECTIONS** Both Nietzsche and Aristotle (**bedfordstmartins .com/worldofideas/epages**) pay little attention to religion as a guide to ethical or moral behavior. To what extent do they agree on the need for self-control to achieve happiness? To what extent are both interested in the spiritual inner life of the individual? Write a brief essay that examines the similarities in their attitudes toward morality and happiness as expressed in their essays, and examine also their differences. Nietzsche most definitely read Aristotle, but do you think he generally agreed with him? What in Nietzsche's essay might have most delighted Aristotle?

8. **CONNECTIONS** How would Niccolò Machiavelli (p. 219) respond to Nietzsche's argument? Would he agree or disagree with Nietzsche about morals promoted by the church? What might Machiavelli, in light of reading Nietzsche, recommend as a moral path for the Prince? What would Nietzsche have to say about Machiavelli's Prince? Would he approve or disapprove of him? Why?

9. **SEEING CONNECTIONS** Taking several of the individuals who appear in Wright's painting *An Experiment on a Bird in the Air Pump* (p. 298), determine what you think their view of the moral situation in the experiment might be. Would any of them be concerned with whether or not the experiment was "anti-nature"? When Nietzsche talks about "the spiritualization of sensuality" do you think he would include the experience of watching this experiment run its course? To what extent would he think the experiment was a sensual activity? Would the characters in the painting think so?

IRIS MURDOCH
Morality and Religion

IRIS MURDOCH (1919–1999) was born in Dublin, Ireland, but her family soon moved to London, where she grew up. Most people know Murdoch as one of the most important novelists in English in the twentieth century. She wrote twenty-six novels that explore interesting aspects of philosophy and psychology. She once said that while she distrusted psychoanalysis, she felt that she was analyzing herself in her novels. Critics have considered her one of the most important literary figures of her time.

Her early schooling prepared her for a degree in Oxford in classics and philosophy. In the 1930s, she became a member of the Communist Party, but she soon rejected its principles and resigned from the party before World War II. During the war, she worked in the British Treasury offices, and afterward she spent time in Belgium and Austria working with the United Nations Relief organization. Murdoch then spent a year trying to sort her life out. She had been given a scholarship to study at Vassar College but could not get a visa because of her Communist past. Eventually, in 1947, she accepted a studentship at Newnham College, Cambridge, to study philosophy under Ludwig Wittgenstein (1889–1951), one of the age's most influential philosophers. The next year she was elected Fellow of St. Anne's College, Oxford, and remained as a tutor (essentially a professor) until she retired in 1963 to write full time.

She won a number of important prizes for her literary work. Her novel *The Sea, The Sea* won Britain's most prestigious literary award, the Booker Prize, in 1978. The Divinity School at the University of Chicago honored her for "the religious depth of her novels" in 1992. Among the most important and interesting of her

From *Metaphysics as a Guide to Morals*.

novels are *The Flight from the Enchanter* (1956), *The Red and the Green* (1956), *The Black Prince* (1973), *The Sacred and Profane Love Machine* (1974), *The Book and the Brotherhood* (1987), and *The Green Knight* (1993).

In addition to novels, Murdoch also wrote a number of influential philosophical studies. Her first book, *Sartre, Romantic Rationalist* (1953), resulted from her meeting Jean-Paul Sartre (1905–1980) in the 1940s and her interest in existentialism. *The Sovereignty of Good and Other Concepts* (1967) is considered a work of first importance in moral studies. *Metaphysics as a Guide to Morals* (1992) developed from the Gifford Lectures she gave at the University of Edinburgh in 1981–82. Her last book, *Existentialists and Mystics: Writings on Philosophy and Literature* (1997), was published near the end of her life when she was suffering from the final stages of Alzheimer's disease.

Murdoch's impressive work *Metaphysics as a Guide to Morals*, from which the following selection is taken, deals with how we interpret and understand the nature of morals. One of the questions she addresses is whether there can be a true moral position outside the confines of religion. Murdoch weighs the arguments on both sides of the issue and lets her readers decide how to resolve them. She herself thrived on contradictions and saw them as energy for understanding.

Murdoch's Rhetoric

The first thing one notices about Murdoch's writing is that she relies on very long paragraphs. Each paragraph addresses a position on how religion and morality are related. She does not pose an overarching argument, but how religion affects what we think of as moral behavior is one of the issues she pursues.

Another aspect of her writing is her many references to philosophers such as Kant, Plato, Bentham, and Wittgenstein, and to historical events such as the Cultural Revolution in Mao's China and the murder of kulaks — wealthy farmers — in Stalin's Soviet Union. But these are not essential to our understanding of the issues she discusses.

She begins in paragraph 2 with a consideration of the nature of virtue, which she sees as "[t]he most evident bridge between morality and religion." Yet there are problems with the very idea of virtue, as she points out. For some people in the modern world, the word *virtue* has lost its positive meaning and is related to rigidity and priggishness. Moreover, it is not capable of being applied universally to people because "fear, misery, deprivation" (para. 2) will alter the nature of virtue in people who experience those conditions. Those who suffer from hunger or political oppression may not have much interest in conventional bourgeois theories of virtue. Therefore, Murdoch suggests, virtue may be a relative concept rather than a fixed idea.

In paragraph 3, she continues her discussion of virtue but adds the concept of duty, a sense of obligation that is understood in a social context. According to Murdoch, "Dutifulness could be an account of a morality with no hint of religion" (para. 3). In this extensive paragraph, Murdoch explores the idea of duty, connecting it to eighteenth-century principles of reason, showing that duty and reason fit together rather well. One understands one's duty to others, institutions, and nations, and one performs one's duty without religious intervention. Is that then a virtuous action? Is the performance of duty then irrelevant to the moral views of religion? As she says at the end of the paragraph, after exploring the issue it may be time to refer back to the "clear, rigid rules" of religions to find answers to these questions.

In paragraph 4, Murdoch contrasts secular idealism with religious belief. The question is whether one of these is more likely to produce moral good than the other. Is morality, she continually asks, dependent on religion, or can it be achieved outside religion? She points out a conundrum that continues in modern life: the criminal who constantly breaks the law and yet has a deep religious conviction. She criticizes religion indirectly by examining its nonrational elements, those of pure faith. But near the end of the paragraph she says, "Religion symbolizes high moral ideas which then travel with us and are more intimately and accessibly effective than the unadorned promptings of reason" (para. 4).

In paragraph 5, she begins to discuss the diary of Francis Kilvert (1840–1879), a simple clergyman who found in his rural community moments of intense beauty and moral uprightness. Kilvert is likened to another cleric, Julian of Norwich, who arrives at a deeply philosophical understanding when she holds a "little thing, the size of a hazel nut, which seemed to lie in the palm of my hand; and it was as round as any ball" (para. 5), and in it she saw a metaphor for the wholeness of creation, a sense that was at root a deep religious experience. Murdoch interprets this as a way of exhibiting "God's love for the world" (para. 5).

In paragraph 6, Murdoch proceeds to include religious philosophers such as Søren Kierkegaard (1813–1855), whose views on religion and morality are complex and not easily untangled.

Her discussion reaches into the question of whether God exists and the Ontological Proof, a proof of God's existence that dates to the Middle Ages. The proof asserts that we can imagine a perfect being, God, and that because we can imagine it, it must exist because perfection is consistent only with actual existence. Murdoch puts it this way: "Guilt, especially deep apparently incurable guilt, can be one of the worst of human pains. To cure such an ill, because of human sin, God *must* exist" (para. 6).

In her final paragraph, Murdoch explores mysticism, which implies having a direct spiritual experience of God, achieved through prayer, religious discipline, fasting, or a variety of ascetic practices similar to meditation. As she says in her opening sentence, "Religion (even if 'primitive') is generally assumed to be in some sense moral. Mysticism is also assumed to be, by definition, moral" (para. 7). However, despite this assurance, she also points out that in some ages, such as the eighteenth-century Enlightenment period, "institutionalized religion [was] an enemy of morality, an enemy of freedom and free thought, guilty of cruelty and repression" (para. 7). In the remainder of this paragraph she attempts to work out some of the obvious conflicts inherent in these statements.

She ends with an interesting discussion of the relationship of two contradictory forces in the universe: good and evil. As she states in a rather paradoxical fashion: "Discord is essential to goodness" (para. 7). In other words, there can only be a concept of morality in an environment in which there is evil *and* goodness. Murdoch points out that "both morality and religion face the same insuperable difficulty": that if the goal of eradicating evil is achieved "the struggle, the need for devotion, would cease to be real. . . . If there is to be morality, there cannot altogether be an end to evil" (para. 7).

PREREADING QUESTIONS:
WHAT TO READ FOR

The following prereading questions may help you anticipate key issues in the discussion of Iris Murdoch's "Morality and Religion." Keeping them in mind during your first reading of the selection should help focus your attention.

- How is the idea of virtue a bridge between religion and morality?

- In what senses do religion and morality seem to be different?

- Is morality impossible without religion?

Morality and Religion

In the background of many of these arguments lies a question   1
about the relation of morality to religion, the difference between them,
and the definition of religion. I have already suggested that my whole
argument can be read as moral philosophy. In any case moral philosophy must include this dimension whether we call it religion or not.
Someone may say that there is only one way to "acquire" religion and
that is through being taught it as a small child. You have to breathe it
in. It is an ineffable attitude to the world which cannot really be discussed. People who take up religion as adults are merely playing at it,
it remains at a level of illusion. So someone could speak, being either
a believer or an unbeliever. The unbeliever might add that religion
is imbibed in childhood, when it forms part of the infantile child–
parent relationship now well-known to psychology; only religion,
being a soothing drug, is less easy to give up in later life.

The most evident bridge between morality and religion is the idea   2
of virtue. Virtue is still treated in some quarters as something precious to be positively pursued; yet the concept has also faded, even
tending to fall apart between "idealism" and "priggishness." It may be
seen as a self-indulgent luxury. It has, perhaps has always had, many
enemies. Fear of a perverted ideology or of a too fervent "enthusiasm"
may prevent a positive conception of virtue. Cynicism and materialism
and *dolce vita*[1] can occlude it, also fear, misery, deprivation, and loss
of concepts. Even in a religious context "personal spirituality" may be
something that has to be argued for. A utilitarian morality[2] may treat a
concern with becoming virtuous as a waste of energy which should be
transmitted directly to the alleviation of suffering. Of course numerous
people are virtuous without thinking about it, and sages may say that,
if thought about, it may *ipso facto*[3] diminish. A saint may perhaps be
good by instinct and nature, though saintly figures are also revered as
reformed sinners. Perhaps the word itself begins to seem pretentious
and old-fashioned.

An idea (concept) of virtue which need not be formally reflec-   3
tive or clarified bears some resemblance to religion, so that one might
say either that it is a shadow of religion, or religion is a shadow of
it. The demand that we should be virtuous or try to become good is

---

[1] *dolce vita* The sweet life; the irresponsible life.
[2] **utilitarian morality** Utilitarianism professed a creed of the greatest good for
the greatest number and would insist that any moral principle produce the greatest
happiness and the least pain for all involved.
[3] *ipso facto* By the very fact itself.

something that goes beyond explicit calls of duty. One can of course extend the idea of duty into the area of generalized goodness (virtuous living) by making it a duty always to have pure thoughts and good motives. For reasons I have suggested I would rather keep the concept of duty nearer to its ordinary sense as something fairly strict, recognizable, intermittent, so that we can say that there may be time off from the call of duty, but no time off from the demand of good. These are conceptual problems which are important in the building up of a picture; that is, an overall extension of the idea of duty would blur a valuable distinction, and undermine the particular function of the concept. Duty then I take to be formal obligation, relating to occasions where it can be to some extent clarified. ("Why go?" "I promised." "Why go?" "He's an old friend." "Why go?" "Well, it's somehow that sort of situation.") Duty may be easily performed without strain or reflection, but may also prompt the well-known experience of the frustration of desire together with a sense of necessity to act, wherein there is a proper place for the concept of *will*. Dutifulness could be an account of a morality with no hint of religion. The rational formality of moral maxims made to govern particular situations might make them seem like separated interrupted points of insight rather than like a light which always shines. This could be a picture of human life. Yet Kant[4] also portrays us as *belonging* at every second to the noumenal world of rationality and freedom, the separated pure source. We are orderly because duty is duty, yet also behind the exercise of it we might (surely, after all) glimpse the inspiring light of pure goodness which Kant calls Reason, and sometimes even God. Beyond all this we may picture a struggle in Kant's religious soul over the concept of Reason, so essential, yet so awkward. The rationality (Pure Reason) which enables us to deal with objects and causes *must* be related to that (Practical Reason) which enables us to deal with right and wrong. Well, the concept of truth can relate them. . . . Perhaps Kant felt no awkwardness—it is we who feel awkward, when we connect morality with love and desire. Certainly it does seem possible to set up a contrast between the dutiful man and the virtuous man which is different from the contrast between the dutiful man and the religious man. Here we may think of Christ saying render unto Caesar what is Caesar's. Duty as order, relating morals to politics. Good decent men lead orderly lives. It might also be said in this context that given the abysmal sinfulness of humans, only a strict list of rules can keep them from mutual destruction! The moral (or spiritual) life

---

[4]**Immanuel Kant (1724–1804)** German philosopher who linked pure reason and experiential knowledge. *Noumenal* is a Kantian term that refers to the unknowable world as it is in itself. According to Kant, we can only know the world as it appears to us, as a phenomenon. We can never know it as it is in itself, as a noumenon.

is both one and not one. There is the idea of a sovereign good, but there are also compartments, obligations, rules, aims, whose identity may have to be respected. These separate aspects or modes of behavior occasion some of the most difficult kinds of moral problems, as if we have to move between *styles*, or to change gear. We have to live a single moral existence, and also to retain the separate force of various kinds of moral vision. Jeanie Deans in Scott's novel[5] loves her sister, but cannot lie to save her life. Isabella in *Measure for Measure* will not save her brother by yielding her chastity to Angelo. Duty is one thing, love is another. These are dramatic examples; one can invent many more homely ones of the conflict of moral requirements of entirely different kinds, wherein one seems to have to choose between being two different kinds of person. This may be a choice between two paths in life, or it may be some everyday matter demanding an instant response. We tend to feel that these dissimilar demands and states of mind must somehow connect, there must be a deep connection, it must all somehow make a unified sense; this is a religious craving, God sees it all. What I earlier called axioms[6] are moral entities whose force must not be overcome by, or dissolved into, other moral streams: a requirement in liberal politics. Axioms may not "win" but must remain in consideration, a Benthamite[7] utilitarian conception of happiness must not, as a frequently relevant feature, be eroded by high-minded considerations about quality of happiness or by theories which make happiness invisible, or of course by political objectives. (The Cultural Revolution, the liquidation of the kulaks.[8]) Equally of course, degraded or evil pleasure cannot count as simple or silly happiness. Such complexities, involving conflicts of moral discernment and moral style, are with us always. So, "keeping everything in mind" is not an easy matter in morals. This may be an argument for clear rigid rules. Modern clerics who do not feel able to tell newly married couples to be virtuous, tell them to have a sense of humor. This shift is a telling case of a change of style.

Religious belief may be a stronger motive to good conduct   4 than non-religious idealism. Corrupt immoral persons (for instance

---

[5] **Scott's novel** *The Heart of Mid-Lothian* (1818) by Sir Walter Scott (1771–1832).

[6] **axioms** Statements of truth, as in geometry.

[7] **Benthamite: Jeremy Bentham (1748–1832)** proposed a scheme of "private ethics" in which the aim of one's actions should be to cause the greatest pleasure and least pain. He was influential in developing English utilitarianism.

[8] **The Cultural Revolution . . . kulaks** The Cultural Revolution (1966–1976), begun by Mao Zedong (1893–1976), chairman of the Chinese Communist Party, was a period of political zealotry characterized by purges of intellectuals and anticommunists. The kulaks were relatively wealthy farmers who opposed Soviet collectivization of their land. Soviet leader Joseph Stalin (1879–1953) sought to execute or deport the kulaks, whom he maligned as "exploiters."

hardened criminals) who cheerfully break all the "moral rules," may retain the religious images of their childhood which can, at some juncture, affect their conduct. This idea has been (not unsentimentally) dealt with in various novels and films. Indeed, this retention of images, and sensibility to images, might suggest the importance of a religious childhood. (Is it easier to get out of religion, or to get in?) Parents who have had such a childhood themselves, but have "given up religion," may often think along these lines. A kind of sensible well-meaning tolerance is involved here. But, a sterner breed may say, what about *truth*? Religion just *isn't true*. A religious man, even a goodish one, is spoilt and flawed by irrational superstitious convictions; and it is held to be ridiculous for lapsed parents to let their innocent children be tainted with beliefs which the parents know to be false. It is no use talking of a "good atmosphere," what is fundamentally at stake is *truth*. Such arguments come near to familiar problems of today. Is the non-religious good man so like the religious good man that it is merely some point of terminology or superficial style which is at issue? Orthodoxly religious people often tolerantly compliment the unbeliever by saying, "He is *really* a true Christian"; which may well annoy the unbeliever. More positively attempting a distinction to form part of a definition, it might be suggested that religion is a form of heightened consciousness (Matthew Arnold[9] said it was "morality touched by emotion"), it is intense and highly toned, it is about what is deep, what is holy, what is absolute, the emotional imaginative image-making faculties are engaged, the whole man is engaged. Every moment matters, there is no time off. High morality without religion is too abstract, high morality craves for religion. Religion symbolizes high moral ideas which then travel with us and are more intimately and accessibly effective than the unadorned promptings of reason. Religion suits the image-making human animal. Think what the image of Christ has done for us through centuries. Can such images *lie*? Do we not indeed adjust our attitudes to them, as time passes, so as to "make them true"? This continuous adjustment is an aspect of the history of religion.

I intended here, thinking about holiness and reverence, not the   5 exclusive property of believers, to quote from Francis Kilvert's[10] Diary (begun in 1870). Kilvert was a parson in country parishes on the

---

[9]**Matthew Arnold (1822–1888)** Prominent English poet and social commentator.

[10]**Francis Kilvert (1840–1879)** English clergyman and diarist. Although after his death his widow destroyed many of his notebooks, the remainder were discovered by William Plomer (1903–1973), a South African writer, and published in 1938 and 1940.

Welsh border, a religious good man of simple faith. However, it is difficult to quote from the Diary because of the transparent artless lucidity of Kilvert's account of his days. Any particular quotation can sound naive, or sentimental. "I went to see my dear little lover Mary Tavener, the deaf and half dumb child. When I opened the door of the poor crazy old cottage in the yard the girl uttered a passionate inarticulate cry of joy and running to me flung her arms about my neck and covered me with kisses." (12 June 1875.) "Old William Price sat in his filthy den, unkempt, unshaven, shaggy and grey like a wild beast, and if possible filthier than the den. I read to him Faber's hymn of the Good Shepherd. He was much struck with it. 'That's what He has been telling me,' said the old man." (26 January 1872.) "The road was very still. No one seemed to be passing and the birds sang late and joyfully in the calm mild evening as if they thought it must be spring. A white mist gathered in the valley and hung low along the winding course of the river mingled with the rushing of the brooks, the distant voices of children at play came floating at intervals across the river and near at hand a pheasant screeched now and then and clapped its wings or changed his roost from tree to tree like a man turning in bed before he falls asleep." (27 January 1872.) Kilvert spent his days walking all over his territory, visiting everyone, noticing everything (people, animals, birds, flowers) and describing it all in simple humble extremely readable detail. "How delightful on these sweet summer evenings to wander from cottage to cottage and farm to farm." It may be said that Kilvert was lucky, but also that he deserved his luck. There is a serene light and a natural kindly selfless love of people and of nature in what he writes. He felt secure. He had faith. Wittgenstein[11] was struck by a character in a play who seemed to him to feel safe, nothing that happened could harm him. Wittgenstein's "Ontological Proof" or "statement" (*Tractatus* 6.41) places the sense of the world outside the world, outside *all* of the contingent facts. Thinking of Wittgenstein's picture of the world (all the facts) as a self-contained sphere, a sort of steel ball, outside which ineffable value roams, we might look at something similar but different. "He showed me a little thing, the size of a hazel nut, which seemed to lie in the palm of my hand; and it was as round as any ball. I looked upon it with my eye of understanding, and thought 'What may this be?' I was answered in a general way thus: 'It is all that is made.' I wondered how long it could

---

[11] **Ludwig Wittgenstein (1889–1951)** Murdoch's philosophy professor. His *Tractatus* approaches problems of language in describing philosophical ideas. His concept of the "world outside the world" implies that we imaginatively observe the world outside itself, much as we observe ourselves. Thus the "little thing" becomes an observable metaphor for a little world.

last, for it seemed as though it might suddenly fade away to nothing, it was so small. And I was answered in my understanding: 'It lasts and ever shall last, for God loveth it. And even so hath everything being, by the love of God.'" (Julian of Norwich,[12] *Revelations of Divine Love*, chapter 5.) Julian's showing, besides exhibiting God's love for the world, also indicates our absolute dependence as created things. We are nothing, we owe our being to something not ourselves. We are enlivened from a higher source.

Kierkegaard[13] would object to a moral–religious continuum. 6
We, existing individuals, therefore sinners, feel guilt, feel in need of salvation, to be reborn into a new being. "If any man be in Christ he is a new creature: old things are passed away, behold all things are become new." (2 Corinthians 5:17.) In Kierkegaard's version of Hegelian dialectic[14] it is not endlessly evolving toward totality, but is a picture of levels in the soul, or of different kinds of people, or of the pilgrimage of a particular person. The aesthetic individual is private, the ethical man, including the tragic hero, is public, the religious individual, the man of faith, is once more private. This dramatic triad also suggests the dangerous link between the two private stages, the aesthetic and the religious, so deeply unlike, so easily confused. The idea of repentance and leading a better cleansed and renewed life is a generally understood moral idea; and the, however presented, granting of absolution, God's forgiveness, keeps many people inside religion, or invites them to enter. Guilt, especially deep apparently incurable guilt, can be one of the worst of human pains. To cure such an ill, because of human sin, God *must* exist. (As Norman Malcolm[15] suggested when discussing the Ontological Proof.) The condition of being changed and made anew is a general religious idea, sometimes appearing as magical instant salvation (as in suddenly "taking Christ as Saviour") or as the result of some lengthy ascesis.[16] Here salvation as spiritual change often goes with the conception of a *place* of

---

[12]**Julian of Norwich (1332–1416?)** English mystic and writer. Her book *Revelations of Divine Love* recounts her mystical religious experiences.

[13]**Søren Kierkegaard (1813–1855)** Danish philosopher whose concept of "Either/Or" explored the choice between an ethical life or one that ignored ethics.

[14]**Hegelian dialectic** Postulates that the conflict of two opposites ultimately resolves itself through synthesis (a third option). Georg Wilhelm Friedrich Hegel (1770–1831), a German philosopher, has been enormously influential on all modern philosophers. He felt that humans experience a constant and irreconcilable conflict of reason and emotion.

[15]**Norman Malcolm (1911–1990)** American philosopher whose book *Ludwig Wittgenstein: A Memoir* is referenced in Murdoch's text.

[16]**ascesis** Ascetic behavior, such as fasting, celibacy, or becoming a hermit.

purification and healing. (We light candles, we bring flowers, we go somewhere and kneel down.) This sense of a safe place is characteristic of religious imagery. Here the outer images the inner, and the inner images the outer. There is a literal place, the place of pilgrimage, the place of worship, the shrine, the sacred grove, there is also a psychological or spiritual place, a part of the soul. "Do not seek for God outside your soul." Religion provides a well-known well-tried procedure of rescue. Particularly in relation to guilt and remorse or the obsessions which can be bred from these, the *mystery* of religion (respected, intuited) is a source of spiritual energy. An orientation toward the good involves a reorientation of desire. Here a meeting with a good person may bring about a change of direction. If Plato had never met Socrates and experienced his death perhaps Western thinking might have been different. The mystical Christ too can be "met" with. (The idea of redemptive suffering is repugnant to some; but such suffering is everywhere around us, where the innocent suffers through love of the guilty.) Of course it may well be argued that there are sound unmysterious secular equivalents to these devices, there are many resources for the afflicted who may use their enlightened common sense, or go to their friends, doctors, therapists, psychoanalysts, social workers, take refuge in art or nature, or say (as the religious too may say) to hell with it all. Many people hate religion, with its terrible history and its irrationality, and would regard resort to religious rituals as a false substitute for real morals and genuine amendment of life. Judaism and Islam, who have avoided the path of image-making, and have revered the name of [God], avoid many of the problems which now beset Christianity. Buddhists live with the mystical Buddha in the soul. (Like Eckhart's[17] God and Christ in the soul.) The Hindu religion also has its philosophical mysticism above its numerous gods. Religion has been fundamentally mystical, and this becomes, in this age, more evident. So will the theologians invent new modes of speech, and will the churches fill with people who realize they do not need to believe in the supernatural?

Religion (even if "primitive") is generally assumed to be in some   7
sense moral. Mysticism is also assumed to be, by definition, moral. Thinkers of the Enlightenment however, and many since, have held, often rightly, that organized, institutionalized religion is an enemy of morality, an enemy of freedom and free thought, guilty of cruelty and repression. This has been so and in many quarters is so. Therefore the whole institution may be rationally considered to be discredited

---

[17]**Johannes Eckhart (1260?–1327?)** German theologian who saw a unity in the soul and God: "the core of the soul and the core of God are one."

or outmoded. Many other influences from the past support such a line of thought. Kierkegaard saw Hegel as the enemy of religion and of, *ipso facto*, the existing individual. The vast force of Hegel's thinking, followed up by Marx, is inimical to both. The Romantic Movement and the liberal political thinking which went with it have tended to look after the individual, and we associate high morality (idealism, selflessness, goodness) with many people in this century and the last who assumed that religion was *finished*. It must be agreed that, in very many ways, Western society has improved, become more tolerant, more free, more decently happy, in this period. It may also be agreed that with the decline of religious observance and religious "consciousness" (the practice of prayer and the fear of God for instance), some aspects of moral conduct may decline also. (Of course this decline can have other causes.) However that may be, Hegel and Marx, Nietzsche and Freud, have had influence. Virtues and values may give way to a more relaxed sense of determinism. There is a more "reasonable," ordinary, *available* relativism and "naturalism" about. Hegel's *Geist*[18] is the energy which perpetually urges the ever-unsatisfied intellect (and so the whole of being) onward toward Absolute reality. Everything is relative, incomplete, not yet fully real, not yet fully true, dialectic is a continual reformulation. Such is the history of thought, of civilization, or of the "person" who, immersed in the process, is carried on toward some postulated self-consistent totality. Vaguely, such an image as something plausible may linger in the mind. I shall not discuss Hegel here, but look for a moment at a milder form of quasi-Hegelianism in F. H. Bradley's[19] *Appearance and Reality*. According to Bradley both morality and religion demand an unattainable unity. "Every separate aspect of the universe goes on to demand something higher than itself." This is the dialectic, the overcoming of the incomplete, of appearance and illusion, the progress toward what is more true, more real, more harmoniously integrated. "And, like every other appearance, goodness implies that which, when carried out, must absorb it." Religion is higher than morality, being more unified, more expressive of a perfect wholeness. But both morality and religion face the same insuperable difficulty. Morality–religion believes in the reality of perfect good, and in the demand that good be victorious and evil destroyed. The postulated whole (good) is at once actually to be good, and at the same time to make itself good. Neither its perfect

---

[18] **Geist** The reference is to Hegel's concept of the spirit/mind (geist). Hegel had three categories of spirit/mind: subjective, objective, and absolute. The absolute was reserved for contemplation of religion, fine arts, and philosophy.
[19] **F. H. Bradley (1846–1924)** English philosopher influenced by Hegel who emphasized the force of the mind over the physical world.

goodness nor its struggle may be degraded to an appearance (something incomplete and imperfect). But to unite these two aspects consistently is impossible. If the desired end were reached, the struggle, the need for devotion, would have ceased to be real. If there is to be morality, there cannot altogether be an end to evil. Discord is essential to goodness. Moral evil exists only in moral experience and that experience is essentially inconsistent. Morality desires unconsciously, with the suppression of evil, to become non-moral. It shrinks from this, yet it unknowingly desires the existence and perpetuity of evil. Morality, which makes evil, desires in evil to remove a condition of its own being; it labors to pass into a super-moral and therefore non-moral sphere. Moral–religious faith is make-believe: be sure that opposition to the good is overcome, but act as if it (the opposition) persists. "The religious consciousness rests on the felt unity of unreduced opposites."

QUESTIONS FOR CRITICAL READING

1. Can there be only one concept of virtue?
2. Why is virtue different from duty?
3. How is dutiful behavior different from religious behavior?
4. Does religion foster good behavior more than nonreligious idealism does?
5. How does guilt relate to morality?
6. Is religion essentially moral in nature?
7. Is high morality (idealism, selflessness, goodness) essentially religious?

SUGGESTIONS FOR CRITICAL WRITING

1. One question that underlies Murdoch's views is whether or not a high morality could ever be produced in a completely nonreligious environment. What is your view on this issue? What are the arguments in defense of religion as the essential producer of the high morality Murdoch points to in paragraph 7? Why might it be difficult for such a high morality to be produced by secular means? In a nonreligious context, what would ultimately support high morality?

2. One of Murdoch's assertions is that moral–religious views depend on the existence of evil, otherwise there can be no good behavior. This assertion is commonly made by those who insist on a Hegelian dialectic—a condition in which two opposites collide and a third force emerges. What would the world be like if there were no evil? Would moral behavior then be possible? Would immoral behavior be possible? Would all behavior be morally neutral? Explain.

3. What effects do poverty and the absence of opportunity have on individuals' senses of virtue? Do you agree with Murdoch that virtue "may be seen as a self-indulgent luxury" (para. 2)? Why or why not? Should bourgeois concepts of morality be applied to those without hope of change in their lives? Is morality dependent on social condition? Explain.

4. In paragraph 3 Murdoch states, "Dutifulness could be an account of a morality with no hint of religion." Do you agree? She is obviously tentative in her statement. Examine your own sense of duty and that of someone you know and decide how much duty—as well as the expression of dutiful acts—satisfies our concept of a true morality.

5. Murdoch implies at the end of paragraph 3 that certain political complexities suggest there might be a need to have "clear rigid rules" of behavior in order to establish a morality. She implies that even clerics are viewing contemporary moral standards as flexible, perhaps alterable in some circumstances. How do you feel? Should morality follow the "rules" approach of the Ten Commandments? Or is there a more flexible, "realistic" alternative? Explain.

6. What do you consider virtuous behavior? Try to be as specific as possible. Do you find it difficult to apply your virtues in everyday life? Why or why not? To what extent do you feel an individual's religious beliefs dictate his or her virtuousness? Is religious faith an accurate indicator of virtue? Why or why not? What is Murdoch's view of this issue?

7. **CONNECTIONS**   Aristotle's disregard for religious issues in his position on ethics and morality (**bedfordstmartins.com/worldofideas /epages**) might disappoint Murdoch. However, as a professional philosopher, Murdoch knew Aristotle's work thoroughly and respected it; she considered the *Nichomachean Ethics* to be a major statement guiding modern ethicists. Therefore, though she found much to agree with him in this essay, she naturally disagreed with him on religion. How can you reconcile these authors' disagreement using the principles that Murdoch defends in her essay? How might she have amended Aristotle's essay to make it more compatible with her views?

8. **CONNECTIONS**   How would Friedrich Nietzsche (p. 343) approach a critique of the views that Murdoch explores in this essay? Where would his sympathies lie in relation to her discussion of the relationship of virtue to duty? Where would he stand on the controversies that suggest that organized religion inhibits rather than fosters morality? What points in Murdoch's argument would he most take issue with?

9. **CONNECTIONS**   Which of the selections in this section would most satisfy Murdoch's sense of the nature of morality and the relation of morality to religion? Who among these writers is most sympathetic to her views? Is she sympathetic to Martin Luther King Jr.'s ideas in "Letter from Birmingham Jail" (p. 375)? Does she share anything in common with Nietzsche in his "Morality as Anti-Nature" (p. 343)? Choose one and compare their views.

10. **SEEING CONNECTIONS**   Science and religion were somewhat at odds with each other when Wright painted *An Experiment on a Bird in the Air Pump* (p. 298). His association with Lunar Society members, who tried to reconcile the two, led him to employ a visual composition often used in baroque religious paintings. What connection between science and morality seems to be implied in the painting? Does it seem similar to the connection Murdoch sees between morality and religion? Is it possible that the white bird in the bell jar is not a cockatoo but rather a dove and, therefore, conceivably a symbol for Christ? If that were the case, what would Murdoch be likely to say about the moral circumstance of the painting?

MARTIN LUTHER KING JR.
Letter from Birmingham Jail

MARTIN LUTHER KING JR. (1929–1968) was the most influential civil rights leader in America for a period of more than fifteen years. He was an ordained minister with a doctorate in theology from Boston University. He worked primarily in the South, where he labored steadily to overthrow laws that promoted segregation and to increase the number of black voters registered in southern communities.

From 1958 to 1968, demonstrations and actions opened up opportunities for African Americans who in the South hitherto had been prohibited from sitting in certain sections of buses, using facilities such as water fountains in bus stations, and sitting at luncheon counters with whites. Such laws—unjust and insulting, not to mention unconstitutional—were not challenged by local authorities. Martin Luther King Jr., who became famous for supporting a program to integrate buses in Montgomery, Alabama, was asked by the Southern Christian Leadership Conference (SCLC) to assist in the fight for civil rights in Birmingham, Alabama, where an SCLC meeting was to be held.

King was arrested as the result of a program of sit-ins at luncheon counters and wrote the letter printed here to a group of clergymen who had criticized his position. King had been arrested before and would be arrested again—resembling Henry David Thoreau somewhat in his attitude toward laws that did not conform to moral justice.

King, like Thoreau, was willing to suffer for his views, especially when he found himself faced with punitive laws denying civil rights to all citizens. His is a classic case in which the officers of the government pled that they were dedicated to maintaining a stable civil society, even as they restricted King's individual rights. In 1963, many of the good people to whom King addressed this letter firmly believed that peace and order might be threatened by granting African Americans the true independence and freedom that King insisted were their rights and indeed were guaranteed under the Constitution. This is why King's letter objects to an injustice that was rampant in Frederick Douglass's time but inexcusable in the time of John F. Kennedy.

Eventually the causes King promoted were victorious. His efforts helped change attitudes in the South and spur legislation that has benefited all Americans. His views concerning nonviolence spread throughout the world, and by the early 1960s he had become famous as a man who stood for human rights and human dignity virtually everywhere. He won the Nobel Peace Prize in 1964.

Although King himself was nonviolent, his program left both him and his followers open to the threat of violence. The sit-ins and voter registration programs spurred countless bombings, threats, and murders by members of the white community. King's life was often threatened, his home bombed, his followers harassed. He was assassinated at the Lorraine Motel in Memphis, Tennessee, on April 4, 1968. But before he died he saw—largely through his own efforts, influence, and example—the face of America change.

King's Rhetoric

The most obvious rhetorical tradition King assumes in this important work is that of the books of the Bible that were originally letters, such as Paul's Epistle to the Ephesians and his several letters to the Corinthians. Many of Paul's letters were written while he was in prison in Rome, and he established a moral position that could inspire the citizens who received the letters. At the same time, Paul carried out the most important work of the early Christian church—spreading the word of Jesus to those who wished to be Christians but who needed clarification and encouragement.

It is not clear that the clergymen who received King's letter fully appreciated the rhetorical tradition he drew on—but they were men who preached from the Bible and certainly should have understood it. The text itself alludes to the mission of Paul and to his communications to his people. King works with this rhetorical tradition not only because it is effective but also because it resonates with the deepest aspect of his calling—spreading the Gospel of Christ. Brotherhood and justice were his message.

King's tone is one of utmost patience with his critics. He seems bent on winning them over to his point of view, just as he seems confident that—because they are, like him, clergymen—their goodwill should help them see the justice of his views.

His method is that of careful reasoning, focusing on the substance of their criticism, particularly on their complaints that his actions were "unwise and untimely" (para. 1). King takes each of those charges in turn, carefully analyzes it against his position, and then follows with the clearest possible statement of his own views and why he feels they are worth adhering to. "Letter from Birmingham Jail" is a model of close and reasonable analysis of a very complex situation. It succeeds largely because it remains concrete, treating one issue after another carefully, refusing to be caught up in passion or posturing. Above all, King remains grounded in logic, convinced that his arguments will in turn convince his audience.

PREREADING QUESTIONS: WHAT TO READ FOR

The following prereading questions may help you anticipate key issues in the discussion of Martin Luther King's "Letter from Birmingham Jail." Keeping them in mind during your first reading of the selection should help focus your attention.

- What kind of injustice did Martin Luther King find in Birmingham?
- Why was Martin Luther King disappointed in the white churches?

Letter from Birmingham Jail

April 16, 1963

MY DEAR FELLOW CLERGYMEN:[1]

While confined here in the Birmingham city jail, I came across your   1
recent statement calling my present activities "unwise and untimely." Seldom do I pause to answer criticism of my work and ideas. If I sought to answer all the criticisms that cross my desk, my secretaries would have

---

[1] This response to a published statement by eight fellow clergymen from Alabama (Bishop C. C. J. Carpenter, Bishop Joseph A. Durick, Rabbi Hilton L. Grafman, Bishop Paul Hardin, Bishop Holan B. Harmon, the Reverend George M. Murray, the Reverend Edward V. Ramage, and the Reverend Earl Stallings) was composed under somewhat constricting circumstances. Begun on the margins of the newspaper in which the statement appeared while I was in jail, the letter was continued on scraps of writing paper supplied by a friendly Negro trusty, and concluded on a pad my attorneys were eventually permitted to leave me. Although the text remains in substance unaltered, I have indulged in the author's prerogative of polishing it for publication. [King's note]

little time for anything other than such correspondence in the course of the day, and I would have no time for constructive work. But since I feel that you are men of genuine good will and that your criticisms are sincerely set forth, I want to try to answer your statement in what I hope will be patient and reasonable terms.

I think I should indicate why I am here in Birmingham, since you   2 have been influenced by the view which argues against "outsiders coming in." I have the honor of serving as president of the Southern Christian Leadership Conference, an organization operating in every southern state, with headquarters in Atlanta, Georgia. We have some eighty-five affiliated organizations across the South, and one of them is the Alabama Christian Movement for Human Rights. Frequently we share staff, educational, and financial resources with our affiliates. Several months ago the affiliate here in Birmingham asked us to be on call to engage in a nonviolent direct-action program if such were deemed necessary. We readily consented, and when the hour came we lived up to our promise. So I, along with several members of my staff, am here because I was invited here. I am here because I have organizational ties here.

But more basically, I am in Birmingham because injustice is here.   3 Just as the prophets of the eighth century B.C. left their villages and carried their "thus saith the Lord" far beyond the boundaries of their home towns, and just as the Apostle Paul left his village of Tarsus[2] and carried the gospel of Jesus Christ to the far corners of the Greco-Roman world, so am I compelled to carry the gospel of freedom beyond my own hometown. Like Paul, I must constantly respond to the Macedonian call for aid.[3]

Moreover, I am cognizant of the interrelatedness of all communities   4 and states. I cannot sit idly by in Atlanta and not be concerned about what happens in Birmingham. Injustice anywhere is a threat to justice everywhere. We are caught in an inescapable network of mutuality, tied in a single garment of destiny. Whatever affects one directly, affects all indirectly. Never again can we afford to live with the narrow, provincial, "outside agitator" idea. Anyone who lives inside the United States can never be considered an outsider anywhere within its bounds.

You deplore the demonstrations taking place in Birmingham. But   5 your statement, I am sorry to say, fails to express a similar concern for the conditions that brought about the demonstrations. I am sure that

---

[2] **village of Tarsus** Birthplace of St. Paul (?–67 C.E.), in Asia Minor, present-day Turkey, close to Syria.

[3] **the Macedonian call for aid** The citizens of Philippi, in Macedonia (northern Greece), were among the staunchest Christians. Paul went to their aid frequently; he also had to resolve occasional bitter disputes within the Christian community there (see Phil. 2:2–14).

none of you would want to rest content with the superficial kind of social analysis that deals merely with effects and does not grapple with underlying causes. It is unfortunate that demonstrations are taking place in Birmingham, but it is even more unfortunate that the city's white power structure left the Negro community with no alternative.

In any nonviolent campaign there are four basic steps: collec- 6 tion of the facts to determine whether injustices exist; negotiation; self-purification; and direct action. We have gone through all these steps in Birmingham. There can be no gainsaying the fact that racial injustice engulfs this community. Birmingham is probably the most thoroughly segregated city in the United States. Its ugly record of brutality is widely known. Negroes have experienced grossly unjust treatment in the courts. There have been more unsolved bombings of Negro homes and churches in Birmingham than in any other city in the nation. These are the hard brutal facts of the case. On the basis of these conditions, Negro leaders sought to negotiate with the city fathers. But the latter consistently refused to engage in good-faith negotiation.

Then, last September, came the opportunity to talk with leaders 7 of Birmingham's economic community. In the course of the negotiations, certain promises were made by the merchants—for example, to remove the stores' humiliating racial signs. On the basis of these promises, the Reverend Fred Shuttlesworth and the leaders of the Alabama Christian Movement for Human Rights agreed to a moratorium on all demonstrations. As the weeks and months went by, we realized that we were the victims of a broken promise. A few signs, briefly removed, returned; the others remained.

As in so many past experiences, our hopes had been blasted, and 8 the shadow of deep disappointment settled upon us. We had no alternative except to prepare for direct action, whereby we would present our very bodies as a means of laying our case before the conscience of the local and the national community. Mindful of the difficulties involved, we decided to undertake a process of self-purification. We began a series of workshops on nonviolence, and we repeatedly asked ourselves: "Are you able to accept blows without retaliating?" "Are you able to endure the ordeal of jail?" We decided to schedule our direct-action program for the Easter season, realizing that except for Christmas, this is the main shopping period of the year. Knowing that a strong economic-withdrawal program would be the by-product of direct action, we felt that this would be the best time to bring pressure to bear on the merchants for the needed change.

Then it occurred to us that Birmingham's mayoral election was 9 coming up in March, and we speedily decided to postpone action until after election day. When we discovered that the Commissioner of Public Safety, Eugene "Bull" Connor, had piled up enough votes to be in the run-off, we decided again to postpone action until the day after the run-off so that the demonstrations could not be used to cloud the issues. Like many others, we waited to see Mr. Connor defeated, and to this end we endured postponement after postponement. Having aided in this community need, we felt that our direct-action program could be delayed no longer.

You may well ask, "Why direct action? Why sit-ins, marches, and   10 so forth? Isn't negotiation a better path?" You are quite right in calling for negotiation. Indeed, this is the very purpose of direct action. Nonviolent direct action seeks to create such a crisis and foster such a tension that a community which has constantly refused to negotiate is forced to confront the issue. It seeks so to dramatize the issue that it can no longer be ignored. My citing the creation of tension as part of the work of the nonviolent resister may sound rather shocking. But I must confess that I am not afraid of the word "tension." I have earnestly opposed violent tension, but there is a type of constructive, nonviolent tension which is necessary for growth. Just as Socrates[4] felt that it was necessary to create a tension in the mind so that individuals could rise from the bondage of myths and half truths to the unfettered realm of creative analysis and objective appraisal, so must we see the need for nonviolent gadflies to create the kind of tension in society that will help men rise from the dark depths of prejudice and racism to the majestic heights of understanding and brotherhood.

The purpose of our direct-action program is to create a situation   11 so crisis-packed that it will inevitably open the door to negotiation. I therefore concur with you in your call for negotiation. Too long has our beloved Southland been bogged down in a tragic effort to live in monologue rather than dialogue.

One of the basic points in your statement is that the action that I   12 and my associates have taken in Birmingham is untimely. Some have asked: "Why didn't you give the new city administration time to act?" The only answer that I can give to this query is that the new Birmingham administration must be prodded about as much as the outgoing one, before it will act. We are sadly mistaken if we feel that the election of Albert Boutwell as mayor will bring the millennium[5] to Birmingham.

---

[4]**Socrates (470?–399 B.C.E.)** The "tension in the mind" King refers to is created by the question-answer technique known as the Socratic method. By posing questions at the beginning of the paragraph, King shows his willingness to share Socrates' rhetorical techniques. Socrates was imprisoned and killed for his civil disobedience (see paras. 21 and 25). He was the greatest of the Greek philosophers.

[5]**the millennium** A reference to Revelation 20, according to which the second coming of Christ will be followed by one thousand years of peace, when the devil will be incapacitated. After this will come a final battle between good and evil, followed by the Last Judgment.

While Mr. Boutwell is a much more gentle person than Mr. Connor, they are both segregationists, dedicated to maintenance of the status quo. I have hoped that Mr. Boutwell will be reasonable enough to see the futility of massive resistance to desegregation. But he will not see this without pressure from devotees of civil rights. My friends, I must say to you that we have not made a single gain in civil rights without determined legal and nonviolent pressure. Lamentably, it is an historical fact that privileged groups seldom give up their privileges voluntarily. Individuals may see the moral light and voluntarily give up their unjust posture; but, as Reinhold Niebuhr[6] has reminded us, groups tend to be more immoral than individuals.

We know through painful experience that freedom is never   13
voluntarily given by the oppressor; it must be demanded by the oppressed. Frankly, I have yet to engage in a direct-action campaign that was "well timed" in the view of those who have not suffered unduly from the disease of segregation. For years now I have heard the word "Wait!" It rings in the ear of every Negro with piercing familiarity. This "Wait" has almost always meant "Never." We must come to see, with one of our distinguished jurists, that "justice too long delayed is justice denied."[7]

We have waited for more than 340 years for our constitutional   14
and God-given rights. The nations of Asia and Africa are moving with jet-like speed toward gaining political independence, but we still creep at horse-and-buggy pace toward gaining a cup of coffee at a lunch counter. Perhaps it is easy for those who have never felt the stinging darts of segregation to say, "Wait." But when you have seen vicious mobs lynch your mothers and fathers at will and drown your sisters and brothers at whim; when you have seen hate-filled policemen curse, kick, and even kill your black brothers and sisters; when you see the vast majority of your twenty million Negro brothers smothering in an airtight cage of poverty in the midst of an affluent society; when you suddenly find your tongue twisted and your speech stammering as you seek to explain to your six-year-old daughter why she can't go to the public amusement park that has just been advertised on television, and see tears welling up in her eyes when she is told that Funtown is closed to colored children, and see ominous clouds

---

[6] **Reinhold Niebuhr (1892–1971)** Protestant American philosopher who urged church members to put their beliefs into action against social injustice. He urged Protestantism to develop and practice a code of social ethics and wrote in *Moral Man and Immoral Society* (1932) of the point King mentions here.

[7] **"justice too long delayed is justice denied"** Chief Justice Earl Warren's expression in 1954 was adapted from English writer Walter Savage Landor's phrase "Justice delayed is justice denied."

of inferiority beginning to form in her little mental sky, and see her beginning to distort her personality by developing an unconscious bitterness toward white people; when you have to concoct an answer for a five-year-old son who is asking, "Daddy, why do white people treat colored people so mean?"; when you take a cross-country drive and find it necessary to sleep night after night in the uncomfortable corners of your automobile because no motel will accept you; when you are humiliated day in and day out by nagging signs reading "white" and "colored"; when your first name becomes "nigger," your middle name becomes "boy" (however old you are) and your last name becomes "John," and your wife and mother are never given the respected title "Mrs."; when you are harried by day and haunted by night by the fact that you are a Negro, living constantly at tiptoe stance, never quite knowing what to expect next, and are plagued with inner fears and outer resentments; when you are forever fighting a degenerating sense of "nobodiness" — then you will understand why we find it difficult to wait. There comes a time when the cup of endurance runs over, and men are no longer willing to be plunged into the abyss of despair. I hope, sirs, you can understand our legitimate and unavoidable impatience.

You express a great deal of anxiety over our willingness to break   15
laws. This is certainly a legitimate concern. Since we so diligently urge people to obey the Supreme Court's decision of 1954 outlawing segregation in the public schools, at first glance it may seem rather paradoxical for us consciously to break laws. One may well ask: "How can you advocate breaking some laws and obeying others?" The answer lies in the fact that there are two types of laws: just and unjust. I would be the first to advocate obeying just laws. One has not only a legal but a moral responsibility to obey just laws. Conversely, one has a moral responsibility to disobey unjust laws. I would agree with St. Augustine[8] that "an unjust law is no law at all."

Now, what is the difference between the two? How does one   16
determine whether a law is just or unjust? A just law is a manmade code that squares with the moral law or the law of God. An unjust law is a code that is out of harmony with the moral law. To put it in the terms of St. Thomas Aquinas:[9] An unjust law is a human law that is not rooted in eternal law and natural law. Any law that uplifts human personality is just. Any law that degrades human personality is unjust. All segregation statutes are unjust because segregation

---

[8] **St. Augustine (354–430)** Early bishop of the Christian Church who deeply influenced the spirit of Christianity for many centuries.

[9] **St. Thomas Aquinas (1225–1274)** The greatest of the medieval Christian philosophers and one of the greatest church authorities.

distorts the soul and damages the personality. It gives the segregator a false sense of superiority and the segregated a false sense of inferiority. Segregation, to use the terminology of the Jewish philosopher Martin Buber,[10] substitutes an "I-it" relationship for an "I-thou" relationship and ends up relegating persons to the status of things. Hence segregation is not only politically, economically, and sociologically unsound, it is morally wrong and sinful. Paul Tillich[11] has said that sin is separation. Is not segregation an existential expression of man's tragic separation, his awful estrangement, his terrible sinfulness? Thus it is that I can urge men to obey the 1954 decision of the Supreme Court, for it is morally right; and I can urge them to disobey segregation ordinances, for they are morally wrong.

17   Let us consider a more concrete example of just and unjust laws. An unjust law is a code that a numerical or power majority group compels a minority group to obey but does not make binding on itself. This is *difference* made legal. By the same token, a just law is a code that a majority compels a minority to follow and that it is willing to follow itself. This is *sameness* made legal.

18   Let me give another explanation. A law is unjust if it is inflicted on a minority that, as a result of being denied the right to vote, had no part in enacting or devising the law. Who can say that the legislature of Alabama which set up that state's segregation laws was democratically elected? Throughout Alabama all sorts of devious methods are used to prevent Negroes from becoming registered voters, and there are some counties in which, even though Negroes constitute a majority of the population, not a single Negro is registered. Can any law enacted under such circumstances be considered democratically structured?

19   Sometimes a law is just on its face and unjust in its application. For instance, I have been arrested on a charge of parading without a permit. Now, there is nothing wrong in having an ordinance which requires a permit for a parade. But such an ordinance becomes unjust when it is used to maintain segregation and to deny citizens the First Amendment privilege of peaceful assembly and protest.

20   I hope you are able to see the distinction I am trying to point out. In no sense do I advocate evading or defying the law, as would the

---

[10]**Martin Buber (1878–1965)** Jewish theologian. *I and Thou* (1923) is his most famous book.

[11]**Paul Tillich (1886–1965)** An important twentieth-century Protestant theologian who held that Christianity was reasonable and effective in modern life. Tillich saw sin as an expression of man's separation from God, from himself, and from his fellow man. King sees the separation of the races as a further manifestation of man's sinfulness. Tillich, who was driven out of Germany by the Nazis, stresses the need for activism and the importance of action in determining moral vitality, just as King does.

rabid segregationist. That would lead to anarchy. One who breaks
an unjust law must do so openly, lovingly, and with a willingness to
accept the penalty. I submit that an individual who breaks a law that
conscience tells him is unjust, and who willingly accepts the penalty
of imprisonment in order to arouse the conscience of the community
over its injustice, is in reality expressing the highest respect for law.

Of course, there is nothing new about this kind of civil disobe-   21
dience. It was evidenced subliminally in the refusal of Shadrach,
Meshach, and Abednego to obey the laws of Nebuchadnezzar,[12] on the
ground that a higher moral law was at stake. It was practiced superbly
by the early Christians, who were willing to face hungry lions and the
excruciating pain of chopping blocks rather than submit to certain
unjust laws of the Roman Empire. To a degree, academic freedom is
a reality today because Socrates practiced civil disobedience. In our
own nation, the Boston Tea Party represented a massive act of civil
disobedience.

We should never forget that everything Adolf Hitler did in Ger-   22
many was "legal" and everything the Hungarian freedom fighters[13] did
in Hungary was "illegal." It was "illegal" to aid and comfort a Jew in
Hitler's Germany. Even so, I am sure that, had I lived in Germany at
the time, I would have aided and comforted my Jewish brothers. If
today I lived in a Communist country where certain principles dear to
the Christian faith are suppressed, I would openly advocate disobey-
ing that country's antireligious laws.

I must make two honest confessions to you, my Christian and   23
Jewish brothers. First, I must confess that over the past few years I
have been gravely disappointed with the white moderate. I have
almost reached the regrettable conclusion that the Negro's great stumbling block in his stride toward freedom is not the White Citizen's
Counciler[14] or the Ku Klux Klanner, but the white moderate, who is
more devoted to "order" than to justice; who prefers a negative peace
which is the absence of tension to a positive peace which is the
presence of justice; who constantly says, "I agree with you in the goal

---

[12] **Nebuchadnezzar (c. 630–562 B.C.E.)** Chaldean king who twice attacked
Jerusalem. He ordered Shadrach, Meshach, and Abednego to worship a golden
image. They refused, were cast into a roaring furnace, and were saved by God (see
Dan. 1:7–3:30).

[13] **Hungarian freedom fighters** The Hungarians rose in revolt against Soviet
rule in 1956. Soviet forces put down the uprising with great force, which shocked
the world. Many freedom fighters died, and many others escaped to the West.

[14] **White Citizen's Counciler** White Citizen's Councils organized in southern
states in 1954 to fight school desegregation as ordered by the Supreme Court in
May 1954. The councils were not as secret or violent as the Klan; they were also
ineffective.

you seek, but I cannot agree with your methods of direct action"; who paternalistically believes he can set the timetable for another man's freedom; who lives by a mythical concept of time and who constantly advises the Negro to wait for a "more convenient season." Shallow understanding from people of good will is more frustrating than absolute misunderstanding from people of ill will. Lukewarm acceptance is much more bewildering than outright rejection.

I had hoped that the white moderate would understand that law 24 and order exist for the purpose of establishing justice and that when they fail in this purpose they become the dangerously structured dams that block the flow of social progress. I had hoped that the white moderate would understand that the present tension in the South is a necessary phase of the transition from an obnoxious negative peace, in which the Negro passively accepted his unjust plight, to a substantive and positive peace, in which all men will respect the dignity and worth of human personality. Actually, we who engage in nonviolent direct action are not the creators of tension. We merely bring to the surface the hidden tension that is already alive. We bring it out in the open, where it can be seen and dealt with. Like a boil that can never be cured so long as it is covered up but must be opened with all its ugliness to the natural medicines of air and light, injustice must be exposed, with all the tension its exposure creates, to the light of human conscience and the air of national opinion, before it can be cured.

In your statement you assert that our actions, even though peace- 25 ful, must be condemned because they precipitate violence. But is this a logical assertion? Isn't this like condemning a robbed man because his possession of money precipitated the evil act of robbery? Isn't this like condemning Socrates because his unswerving commitment to truth and his philosophical inquiries precipitated the act by the misguided populace in which they made him drink hemlock? Isn't this like condemning Jesus because his unique God-consciousness and never-ceasing devotion to God's will precipitated the evil act of crucifixion? We must come to see that, as the federal courts have consistently affirmed, it is wrong to urge an individual to cease his efforts to gain his basic constitutional rights because the quest may precipitate violence. Society must protect the robbed and punish the robber.

I had also hoped that the white moderate would reject the myth 26 concerning time in relation to the struggle for freedom. I have just received a letter from a white brother in Texas. He writes: "All Christians know that the colored people will receive equal rights eventually, but it is possible that you are in too great a religious hurry. It has taken Christianity almost two thousand years to accomplish what it has. The teachings of Christ take time to come to earth." Such an attitude stems from a tragic misconception of time, from the strangely irrational notion that there is something in the very flow of time that will inevitably cure all ills. Actually, time itself is neutral; it can be used either destructively or constructively. More and more I feel that the people of ill will have used time much more effectively than have the people of good will. We will have to repent in this generation not merely for the hateful words and actions of the bad people, but for the appalling silence of the good people. Human progress never rolls in on wheels of inevitability; it comes through the tireless efforts of men willing to be co-workers with God, and without this hard work, time itself becomes an ally of the forces of social stagnation. We must use time creatively, in the knowledge that the time is always ripe to do right. Now is the time to make real the promise of democracy and transform our pending national elegy into a creative psalm of brotherhood. Now is the time to lift our national policy from the quicksand of racial injustice to the solid rock of human dignity.

You speak of our activity in Birmingham as extreme. At first I was   27
rather disappointed that fellow clergymen would see my nonviolent efforts as those of an extremist. I began thinking about the fact that I stand in the middle of two opposing forces in the Negro community. One is a force of complacency, made up in part of Negroes who, as a result of long years of oppression, are so drained of self-respect and a sense of "somebodiness" that they have adjusted to segregation; and in part of a few middle-class Negroes who, because of a degree of academic and economic security and because in some ways they profit by segregation, have become insensitive to the problems of the masses. The other force is one of bitterness and hatred, and it comes perilously close to advocating violence. It is expressed in the various black nationalist groups that are springing up across the nation, the largest and best known being Elijah Muhammad's Muslim movement.[15] Nourished by the Negro's frustration over the continued existence of racial discrimination, this movement is made up of people who have lost faith in America, who have absolutely repudiated Christianity, and who have concluded that the white man is an incorrigible "devil."

I have tried to stand between these two forces, saying that we   28
need emulate neither the "do-nothingism" of the complacent nor the hatred and despair of the black nationalist. For there is the more

---

[15] **Elijah Muhammad's Muslim movement** The Black Muslim movement, which began in the 1920s but flourished in the 1960s under its leader, Elijah Muhammad (1897–1975). Among notable figures who became Black Muslims were the poet Amiri Baraka (b. 1934), the world champion prizefighter Muhammad Ali (b. 1942), and the controversial reformer and religious leader Malcolm X (1925–1965). King saw their rejection of white society (and consequently brotherhood) as a threat.

excellent way of love and nonviolent protest. I am grateful to God that, through the influence of the Negro church, the way of nonviolence became an integral part of our struggle.

If this philosophy had not emerged, by now many streets of the   29
South would, I am convinced, be flowing with blood. And I am further convinced that if our white brothers dismiss as "rabble-rousers" and "outside agitators" those of us who employ nonviolent direct action, and if they refuse to support our nonviolent efforts, millions of Negroes will, out of frustration and despair, seek solace and security in black nationalist ideologies—a development that would inevitably lead to a frightening racial nightmare.[16]

Oppressed people cannot remain oppressed forever. The yearn-   30
ing for freedom eventually manifests itself, and that is what has happened to the American Negro. Something within has reminded him of his birthright of freedom, and something without has reminded him that it can be gained. Consciously or unconsciously, he has been caught up by the *Zeitgeist*,[17] and with his black brothers of Africa and his brown and yellow brothers of Asia, South America, and the Caribbean, the United States Negro is moving with a sense of great urgency toward the promised land of racial justice. If one recognizes this vital urge that has engulfed the Negro community, one should readily understand why public demonstrations are taking place. The Negro has many pent-up resentments and latent frustrations, and he must release them. So let him march; let him make prayer pilgrimages to the city hall; let him go on freedom rides[18]—and try to understand why he must do so. If his repressed emotions are not released in nonviolent ways, they will seek expression through violence; this is not a threat but a fact of history. So I have not said to my people, "Get rid of your discontent." Rather, I have tried to say that this normal and healthy discontent can be channeled into the creative outlet of nonviolent direct action. And now this approach is being termed extremist.

But though I was initially disappointed at being categorized as an   31
extremist, as I continued to think about the matter I gradually gained a measure of satisfaction from the label. Was not Jesus an extremist for love: "Love your enemies, bless them that curse you, do good to them

---

[16]**a frightening racial nightmare** The black uprisings of the 1960s in all major American cities, and the conditions that led to them, were indeed a racial nightmare. King's prophecy was quick to come true.

[17]***Zeitgeist*** German word for the intellectual, moral, and cultural spirit of the times.

[18]**freedom rides** In 1961, the Congress of Racial Equality (CORE) organized rides of whites and blacks to test segregation in southern buses and bus terminals with interstate passengers. More than 600 federal marshals were needed to protect the riders, most of whom were arrested.

that hate you, and pray for them which despitefully use you, and perse-
cute you." Was not Amos an extremist for justice: "Let justice roll down
like waters and righteousness like an ever-flowing stream." Was not
Paul an extremist for the Christian gospel: "I bear in my body the marks
of the Lord Jesus." Was not Martin Luther an extremist: "Here I stand;
I cannot do otherwise, so help me God." And John Bunyan: "I will
stay in jail to the end of my days before I make a butchery of my conscience." And Abraham Lincoln: "This nation cannot survive half slave
and half free." And Thomas Jefferson: "We hold these truths to be
self-evident, that all men are created equal . . ."[19] So the question is not
whether we will be extremists, but what kind of extremists we will be.
Will we be extremists for hate or for love? Will we be extremists for the
preservation of injustice or for the extension of justice? In that dramatic
scene on Calvary's hill three men were crucified. We must never forget
that all three were crucified for the same crime — the crime of extremism. Two were extremists for immorality, and thus fell below their environment. The other, Jesus Christ, was an extremist for love, truth, and
goodness, and thereby rose above his environment. Perhaps the South,
the nation, and the world are in dire need of creative extremists.

I had hoped that the white moderate would see this need. Perhaps   32
I was too optimistic; perhaps I expected too much. I suppose I should
have realized that few members of the oppressor race can understand
the deep groans and passionate yearnings of the oppressed race, and still
fewer have the vision to see that injustice must be rooted out by strong,
persistent, and determined action. I am thankful, however, that some of
our white brothers in the South have grasped the meaning of this social
revolution and committed themselves to it. They are still all too few
in quantity, but they are big in quality. Some — such as Ralph McGill,
Lillian Smith, Harry Golden, James McBride Dabbs, Ann Braden, and
Sarah Patton Boyle — have written about our struggle[20] in eloquent and
prophetic terms. Others have marched with us down nameless streets of
the South. They have languished in filthy, roach-infested jails, suffering

---

[19] **Amos, Old Testament prophet (eighth century B.C.E.); Paul (?–C.E. 67);
Martin Luther (1483–1546); John Bunyan (1628–1688); Abraham Lincoln
(1809–1865); and Thomas Jefferson (1743–1826)** These figures are all noted
for religious, moral, or political innovations that changed the world. Amos was a
prophet who favored social justice; Paul argued against Roman law; Luther began
the Reformation of the Christian Church; Bunyan was imprisoned for preaching the
gospel according to his own understanding; Lincoln freed America's slaves; Jefferson
drafted the Declaration of Independence.

[20] **written about our struggle** These are all prominent southern writers who
expressed their feelings regarding segregation in the South. Some of them, like Smith
and Golden, wrote very popular books with a wide influence. Some, like McGill and
Smith, were severely rebuked by white southerners.

the abuse and brutality of policemen who view them as "dirty nigger-lovers." Unlike so many of their moderate brothers and sisters, they have recognized the urgency of the moment and sensed the need for powerful "action" antidotes to combat the disease of segregation.

Let me take note of my other major disappointment. I have been 33 so greatly disappointed with the white church and its leadership. Of course, there are some notable exceptions. I am not unmindful of the fact that each of you has taken some significant stands on this issue. I commend you, Reverend Stallings, for your Christian stand on this past Sunday, in welcoming Negroes to your worship service on a non-segregated basis. I commend the Catholic leaders of this state for integrating Spring Hill College several years ago.

But despite these notable exceptions, I must honestly reiterate 34 that I have been disappointed with the church. I do not say this as one of those negative critics who can always find something wrong with the church. I say this as a minister of the gospel, who loves the church; who was nurtured in its bosom; who has been sustained by its spiritual blessings and who will remain true to it as long as the cord of life shall lengthen.

When I was suddenly catapulted into the leadership of the bus 35 protest in Montgomery, Alabama, a few years ago, I felt we would be supported by the white church. I felt that the white ministers, priests, and rabbis of the South would be among our strongest allies. Instead, some have been outright opponents, refusing to understand the freedom movement and misrepresenting its leaders; all too many others have been more cautious than courageous and have remained silent behind the anesthetizing security of stained-glass windows.

In spite of my shattered dreams, I came to Birmingham with the 36 hope that the white religious leadership of this community would see the justice of our cause and, with deep moral concern, would serve as the channel through which our just grievances could reach the power structure. I had hoped that each of you would understand. But again I have been disappointed. . . .

There was a time when the church was very powerful—in the 37 time when the early Christians rejoiced at being deemed worthy to suffer for what they believed. In those days the church was not merely a thermometer that recorded the ideas and principles of popular opinion; it was a thermostat that transformed the mores of society. Whenever the early Christians entered a town, the people in power became disturbed and immediately sought to convict the Christians for being "disturbers of the peace" and "outside agitators." But the Christians pressed on, in the conviction that they were "a colony of heaven," called to obey God rather than man. Small in number, they were big in commitment. They were too God-intoxicated to be "astronomically intimidated." By their effort and example they brought an end to such ancient evils as infanticide and gladiatorial contests.

Things are different now. So often the contemporary church is 38 a weak, ineffectual voice with an uncertain sound. So often it is an archdefender of the status quo. Far from being disturbed by the presence of the church, the powerful structure of the average community is consoled by the church's silent—and often even vocal—sanction of things as they are.

But the judgment of God is upon the church as never before. If 39 today's church does not recapture the sacrificial spirit of the early church, it will lose its authenticity, forfeit the loyalty of millions, and be dismissed as an irrelevant social club with no meaning for the twentieth century. Every day I meet young people whose disappointment with the church has turned into outright disgust.

Perhaps I have once again been too optimistic. Is organized religion 40 too inextricably bound to the status quo to save our nation and the world? Perhaps I must turn my faith to the inner spiritual church, the church within the church, as the true *ekklesia*[21] and the hope of the world. But again I am thankful to God that some noble souls from the ranks of organized religion have broken loose from the paralyzing chains of conformity and joined us as active partners in the struggle for freedom. They have left their secure congregations and walked the streets of Albany, Georgia, with us. They have gone down the highways of the South on torturous rides for freedom. Yes, they have gone to jail with us. Some have been dismissed from their churches, have lost the support of their bishops and fellow ministers. But they have acted in the faith that right defeated is stronger than evil triumphant. Their witness has been the spiritual salt that has preserved the true meaning of the gospel in these troubled times. They have carved a tunnel of hope through the dark mountain of disappointment.

I hope the church as a whole will meet the challenge of this deci- 41 sive hour. But even if the church does not come to the aid of justice, I have no despair about the future. I have no fear about the outcome of our struggle in Birmingham, even if our motives are at present misunderstood. We will reach the goal of freedom in Birmingham and all over the nation, because the goal of America is freedom. Abused and scorned though we may be, our destiny is tied up with America's destiny. Before the pilgrims landed at Plymouth, we were here. Before the pen of Jefferson etched the majestic words of the Declaration of Independence across the pages of history, we were here. For more than two centuries

---

[21] **ekklesia** Greek word for "church" meaning not just the institution but the spirit of the church.

our forebears labored in this country without wages; they made cotton king; they built the homes of their masters while suffering gross injustice and shameful humiliation—and yet out of a bottomless vitality they continued to thrive and develop. If the inexpressible cruelties of slavery could not stop us, the opposition we now face will surely fail. We will win our freedom because the sacred heritage of our nation and the eternal will of God are embodied in our echoing demands.

Before closing I feel impelled to mention one other point in your   42 statement that has troubled me profoundly. You warmly commended the Birmingham police force for keeping "order" and "preventing violence." I doubt that you would have so warmly commended the police force if you had seen its dogs sinking their teeth into unarmed, nonviolent Negroes. I doubt that you would so quickly commend the policemen if you were to observe their ugly and inhumane treatment of Negroes here in the city jail; if you were to watch them push and curse old Negro women and young Negro girls; if you were to see them slap and kick old Negro men and young boys; if you were to observe them, as they did on two occasions, refuse to give us food because we wanted to sing our grace together. I cannot join you in your praise of the Birmingham police department.

It is true that the police have exercised a degree of discipline in han-   43 dling the demonstrators. In this sense they have conducted themselves rather "nonviolently" in public. But for what purpose? To preserve the evil system of segregation. Over the past few years I have consistently preached that nonviolence demands that the means we use must be as pure as the ends we seek. I have tried to make clear that it is wrong to use immoral means to attain moral ends. But now I must affirm that it is just as wrong, or perhaps even more so, to use moral means to preserve immoral ends. Perhaps Mr. Connor and his policemen have been rather nonviolent in public, as was Chief Pritchett in Albany, Georgia, but they have used the moral means of nonviolence to maintain the immoral end of racial injustice. As T. S. Eliot[22] has said, "The last temptation is the greatest treason: To do the right deed for the wrong reason."

I wish you had commended the Negro sit-inners and demonstrators   44 of Birmingham for their sublime courage, their willingness to suffer, and their amazing discipline in the midst of great provocation. One day the

---

[22] **Thomas Stearns Eliot (1888–1965)** Renowned as one of the twentieth century's major poets, Eliot was born in the United States but in 1927 became a British subject and a member of the Church of England. Many of his poems focused on religious and moral themes. These lines are from Eliot's play *Murder in the Cathedral*, about Saint Thomas à Becket (1118–1170), the archbishop of Canterbury, who was martyred for his opposition to King Henry II.

South will recognize its real heroes. They will be the James Merediths,[23] with the noble sense of purpose that enables them to face jeering and hostile mobs, and with the agonizing loneliness that characterizes the life of the pioneer. They will be old, oppressed, battered Negro women, symbolized in a seventy-two-year-old woman in Montgomery, Alabama, who rose up with a sense of dignity and with her people decided not to ride segregated buses, and who responded with ungrammatical profundity to one who inquired about her weariness: "My feets is tired, but my soul is at rest." They will be the young high school and college students, the young ministers of the gospel and a host of their elders, courageously and nonviolently sitting in at lunch counters and willingly going to jail for conscience's sake. One day the South will know that when these disinherited children of God sat down at lunch counters, they were in reality standing up for what is best in the American dream and for the most sacred values in our Judaeo-Christian heritage, thereby bringing our nation back to those great wells of democracy which were dug deep by the founding fathers in their formulation of the Constitution and the Declaration of Independence.

45   Never before have I written so long a letter. I'm afraid it is much too long to take your precious time. I can assure you that it would have been much shorter if I had been writing from a comfortable desk, but what else can one do when he is alone in a narrow jail cell, other than write long letters, think long thoughts, and pray long prayers?

46   If I have said anything in this letter that overstates the truth and indicates an unreasonable impatience, I beg you to forgive me. If I have said anything that understates the truth and indicates my having a patience that allows me to settle for anything less than brotherhood, I beg God to forgive me.

47   I hope this letter finds you strong in the faith. I also hope that circumstances will soon make it possible for me to meet each of you, not as an integrationist or a civil rights leader but as a fellow clergyman and a Christian brother. Let us all hope that the dark clouds of racial prejudice will soon pass away and the deep fog of misunderstanding will be lifted from our fear-drenched communities, and in some not too distant tomorrow the radiant stars of love and brotherhood will shine over our great nation with all their scintillating beauty.

> Yours in the cause of
> Peace and Brotherhood,
> MARTIN LUTHER KING, JR.

---

[23] **the James Merediths** James Meredith (b. 1933) was the first black to become a student at the University of Mississippi. His attempt to register for classes in 1962 created the first important confrontation between federal and state authorities, when Governor Ross Barnett personally blocked Meredith's entry to the university. Meredith graduated in 1963 and went on to study law at Columbia University.

QUESTIONS FOR CRITICAL READING

1. Define "nonviolent direct action" (para. 2). In what areas of human experience is it best implemented? Is politics its best area of application? What are the four steps in a nonviolent campaign?

2. Do you agree that "law and order exist for the purpose of establishing justice" (para. 24)? Why? Describe how law and order either do or do not establish justice in your community. Compare notes with your peers.

3. King describes an unjust law as "a code that a numerical or power majority group compels a minority group to obey but does not make binding on itself" (para. 17). Devise one or two other definitions of an unjust law. What unjust laws currently on the books do you disagree with?

4. What do you think is the best-written paragraph in the essay? Why?

5. King cites "tension" in paragraph 10 and elsewhere as a beneficial force. Do you agree? What kind of tension does he mean?

6. In what ways was King an extremist (paras. 30–31)?

7. In his letter, to what extent does King consider the needs of women? Would he feel that issues of women's rights are unrelated to issues of racial equality?

8. According to King, how should a government function in relation to the needs of the individual? Does he feel, like Thoreau's "Chinese philosopher," that the empire is built on the individual?

SUGGESTIONS FOR CRITICAL WRITING

1. Write a brief letter protesting an injustice that you feel may not be entirely understood by people you respect. Clarify the nature of the injustice, the reasons that people hold an unjust view, and the reasons your views should be accepted. Consult King's letter, and use his techniques. How are injustice and immorality related?

2. In paragraph 43, King says, "I have consistently preached that nonviolence demands that the means we use must be as pure as the ends we seek." What does he mean by this? Define the ends he seeks and the means he approves. Do you agree with him on this point? If you have read the selection from Machiavelli, contrast their respective views. Which view seems more reasonable to you?

3. The first part of the letter defends King's journey to Birmingham as a Christian to help his fellows gain justice. He challenges the view that he is an outsider, using such expressions as "network of mutuality" and "garment of destiny" (para. 4). How effective is his argument? Examine the letter for other expressions that justify King's intervention on behalf of his brothers and sisters. Using his logic, describe other social areas where you might be justified in acting on your own

views on behalf of humanity. Do you expect your endeavors would be welcomed? Are there any areas where you think it would be wrong to intervene?

4. In paragraphs 15–22, King discusses two kinds of laws—those that are morally right and those that are morally wrong. Which laws did King regard as morally right? Which laws did he consider morally wrong? Analyze one or two current laws that you feel are morally wrong. Be sure to be fair in describing the laws and establishing their nature. Then explain why you feel they are morally wrong. Would you feel justified in breaking these laws? Would you feel prepared, as King was, to pay the penalties demanded of one who breaks the law?

5. Compare King's letter with sections of Paul's letters to the faithful in the New Testament. Either choose a single letter, such as the Epistle to the Romans, or select passages from Romans, the two letters to the Corinthians, the Galatians, the Ephesians, the Thessalonians, or the Philippians. How did Paul and King agree and disagree about brotherly love, the mission of Christ, the mission of the church, concern for the law, and the duties of the faithful? Inventory the New Testament letters and King's letter carefully for concrete evidence of similar or contrary positions.

6. **CONNECTIONS**   How would King define "the aim of man"? Would he agree with Aristotle (**bedfordstmartins.com/worldofideas/epages**) that "No one would call a man just who did not take pleasure in doing justice" (para. 21)? Would he agree with Aristotle that to "'live well' and 'do well' are the same as to be 'happy'" (para. 8)? Write a brief essay that defends the view that King, because of the nobility of his actions, is happy while he is in Birmingham Jail. Would King agree with Aristotle that happiness is "the highest of all realizable goods" (para. 8)?

7. **CONNECTIONS**   To what extent do Martin Luther King Jr.'s views about government coincide with those of Lao-tzu? Is there a legitimate comparison to be made between King's policy of nonviolent resistance and Lao-tzu's judicious inactivity? To what extent would King have agreed with Lao-tzu's views? Would Lao-tzu have supported King's position in his letter, or would he have interpreted events differently?

8. **CONNECTIONS**   King cites conscience as a guide to obeying just laws and defying unjust laws. How close is his position to that of Henry David Thoreau? Do you think that King had read Thoreau's "Civil Disobedience" as an important document regarding morality and immorality? Compare and contrast the positions of these two writers.

9. Throughout "Letter from Birmingham Jail," Martin Luther King Jr. stresses the question of justice. In paragraphs 15–22, he raises the question of moral laws and immoral laws. If justice depends on moral laws, can we say that justice is a form of morality or ethical behavior? Are justice and morality the same? Is there a religious issue connected to justice? Is that why King, a minister of the church, constantly refers to justice? How are morality and justice connected? What do they have in common?

10. **SEEING CONNECTIONS**   Imagine yourself to be writing a letter from jail. Appeal for justice and ethics using Wright's *An Experiment on a Bird in the Air Pump* (p. 298) in an argument supporting your cause. What issues of ethics and of morality implicit in the painting would be of most value to you in clarifying your argument? Do you think Martin Luther King Jr. would have found this painting useful to allude to in his own letter from Birmingham Jail? How do the values of justice and morality intersect in the painting?

KWAME ANTHONY APPIAH
The Case against Character

KWAME ANTHONY APPIAH was born in London in 1954 and is currently the Laurance S. Rockefeller University Professor of Philosophy at the University Center for Human Values at Princeton University. As a child he was raised in Ghana, the home of his father, Joe Emmanuel Appiah, a lawyer and politician, but he also spent time in England at the family home of his mother, Enid Margaret Appiah. Appiah's grandfather was Sir Stafford Cripps, a noted modern British statesman. Appiah's schooling eventually led him to go to Cambridge University for his Ph.D. in philosophy. His cosmopolitan experience of being raised in Africa and Europe and then having a career in the United States has given him a unique view of international politics and the position of nations both rich and poor in the world today.

Appiah is somewhat skeptical of the ability of well-meaning social groups to help those less fortunate in other nations. He is not opposed to charity, but he sees that the virtuous organizations that try to help the poor have a limited scope and ability to make substantial change. His view is that the responsibility for the well-being of people in Africa, for example, lies in the hands of the governments in Africa. Only local governments can make the changes necessary to improve the lot of their citizens. This view has not met with approval from some Africanists, particularly those who are Afrocentric. For Appiah, Afrocentrism is similar to nineteenth-century Eurocentrism and thus represents a limited view of the world.

Appiah is a philosopher but also a novelist. His work is wide-ranging and remarkable for the variety of interests covered. Among the books that concern themselves with racial issues is *In My Father's House: Africa in the Philosophy of Culture* (1992), which explores the question of African identity, a subject that he has considered deeply. In *Color Conscious: The Political Morality*

From *Experiments in Ethics.*

of Race (1998), he examines the entire question of race: what it is, how it is expressed, and how it has affected different cultures. The moral issues involved in racism are among his chief concerns. In *The Ethics of Identity* (2007), Appiah examines the ways in which people regard their own identity in relation to their religion, their nationality, their race, and the groups to which they choose to belong. He examines the constraints that are imposed on individuals by the choices they make in terms of the organizations and institutions to which they attach themselves.

In *Experiments in Ethics* (2008), from which the following selection is taken, Appiah aims to bring philosophy and the social sciences together in a tradition he sees as tracing back to Aristotle. The book derives from an invitation for him to give the Flexner Lectures at Bryn Mawr College in 2005. The term *experiments* in the title implies much the same as the term *essays*, in that they refer to the writer trying out ideas in ways that help the reader come to a new understanding of the issues at hand.

Appiah's Rhetoric

Because Appiah began teaching the philosophy of language and the uses of semantics, or the study of meaning, his care in the use of words is obvious from the start. Yet, his style is direct because his purpose in "The Case against Character" is to reach the general reader, not the specialist in the field of philosophical ethics.

He begins this selection with a story by Lydia Davis, a rhetorical device that acts as an introduction to the question of character and how it is expressed. In that short story, Davis portrays a serious man, a playful man, an angry man, and a patient man—who are all the same man. This fictional description of the complexity of personality is central to Appiah's investigation because he is trying to distinguish between the act of virtue and the agent of virtue in order to understand how virtuous behavior relates to a virtuous person. He is trying to work out the details of the virtue theory and its relation to ethics. In this sense, the story is a good beginning because it shows that people behave in different ways at different times and can be inconsistent despite our feeling that their character is defined by what we think we know about them.

Appiah also relies on a good number of sources by people who write about virtue and ethics. For example, he discusses at length the work of Rosalind Hursthouse, whose book *On Virtue Ethics* (1997) supports the virtue theorists, especially when she says, "To possess a virtue is to be a certain sort of person with a certain complex mindset" (para. 3). Appiah then goes on to discuss Aristotle's concept of *eudaimonia,* which translates as "happiness" or " flourishing," and connects it to the concept of living a virtuous life. For Aristotle, a virtuous life is a better life, a happy life, the life worth living. The point of discussing Hursthouse and Aristotle is to give Appiah the opportunity to analyze their ideas in relation to the issues at hand: the act and agency of virtue.

Definition is also one of Appiah's rhetorical techniques. He defines ethics as "what it means for a life to be well lived" (para. 8), in line with Aristotle's view that virtue is necessary for a happy life. He then defines morality as "the constraints that govern how we should and should not treat other people." His definitions provide the groundwork to deal with the issues that follow and to cope with what he sees as the limits of virtue ethics and the complexities of situationist ethics.

Appiah's reliance on data gathered by social scientists to help shed light on the question of virtue is another important rhetorical technique. For example, take his discussion of situationist ethics, a view that assumes we will act virtuously in some situations, but not in others. He points out studies that show people are helpful to someone who drops a bunch of papers in front of a public telephone if those same people just found a dime in the telephone slot. He also reviews evidence that people will offer change for a dollar if they are enjoying the aromas in front of a bakery. In other words, there are some unconscious situations that affect virtuous behavior.

Appiah also uses an example from popular culture, the protagonist from *Schindler's List*, a film based on the life of a German businessman who saved one thousand Jews in Germany during World War II. Appiah points out that Oskar Schindler's character was marked by both virtuous and vicious behavior and implies that it may be difficult to consider Schindler a virtuous man simply on the basis of his having performed some virtuous acts, despite their magnitude. Underlying this is the question: Does the virtuous act make the agent virtuous, or does the virtuous agent make the act virtuous?

Relating personality traits, such as those manifest in Oskar Schindler, to the likelihood of virtuous behavior was the subject of a psychology experiment performed in the 1920s that gave schoolchildren the opportunity to cheat on tests. The outcome of the experiment demonstrated that there was no way to tell if a child who cheated on one test would cheat on all of them—or any of them. "Knowing that a child cheated on a spelling test didn't even tell you whether he would cheat on a math test" (para. 14). Even seminarians, whom one might expect to put virtuous behavior first, were not consistent in their behavior when offered the opportunity to be "good Samaritans."

In examining the "situationist challenge," Appiah begins to raise interesting questions about motive and intention. If a virtuous act is what a virtuous person does, then how do we interpret that person's intention? Is it important that a virtuous act be considered virtuous only if the person committing that act intended it to be virtuous? Must we do the right thing for the right reason for that act to be virtuous and ethically significant? Is a moral act moral only if we intend it to be so? Is it not possible to commit a moral act accidentally and still have it be considered moral?

PREREADING QUESTIONS:
WHAT TO READ FOR

The following prereading questions may help you anticipate key issues in the discussion of Kwame Anthony Appiah's "The Case against Character." Keeping them in mind during your first reading should help focus your attention.

- What is virtue ethics?
- What is situationist ethics?
- What traits of character do we need to live well?

The Case against Character

Les circonstances sont bien peu de chose, le caractère est tout; c'est en vain qu'on brise avec les objets et les êtres extérieurs; on ne saurait briser avec soi-même.

(Circumstances don't amount to much, character is everything; there's no point breaking with exterior objects and things; you cannot break with yourself.)

         —BENJAMIN CONSTANT, *Adolphe*

The Virtue Revival

Lydia Davis,[1] the fiction writer, once published a short story   1
entitled, significantly, "Trying to Learn"—and if you know her work, you

---

[1]**Lydia Davis (b. 1947)** Professor of creative writing at the State University of New York at Albany. She is noted for her very short stories and is also a renowned translator of Marcel Proust.

won't be surprised to learn that it's a *very* short story indeed. Here's
how it goes, in its entirety:

> I am trying to learn that this playful man who teases me is the
> same as that serious man talking money to me so seriously he
> does not even see me anymore and that patient man offering me
> advice in times of trouble and that angry man slamming the door
> as he leaves the house. I have often wanted the playful man to
> be more serious, and the serious man to be less serious, and the
> patient man to be more playful. As for the angry man, he is a
> stranger to me and I do not feel it is wrong to hate him. Now I am
> learning that if I say bitter words to the angry man as he leaves the
> house, I am at the same time wounding the others, the ones I do
> not want to wound, the playful man teasing, the serious man talk-
> ing money, and the patient man offering advice. Yet I look at the
> patient man, for instance, whom I would want above all to protect
> from such bitter words as mine, and though I tell myself he is the
> same man as the others, I can only believe I said those words, not
> to him, but to another, my enemy, who deserved all my anger.

That's the story. It's also the story, more or less, of a growing   2
body of research in the social sciences: we have met that man, many
social scientists say, and he is us. In this chapter, then, I'd like to focus
on the seeming clash between two different pictures of character and
conduct: the picture that seems to underlie much virtue ethics, on the
one hand, and the picture that has emerged from work in experimental psychology, on the other.

What does the first picture look like? The power core of virtue   3
ethics is the idea of the virtuous person. A virtuous act is one that
a virtuous person would do, done for the reasons a virtuous person
would do it. Character is primary; virtues are more than simple dispositions to do the right thing. Those who draw on Aristotle's ideas
are likely to stress, with Rosalind Hursthouse, author of a recent
book entitled *On Virtue Ethics,* that the dispositions in question are
deep, stable, and enmeshed in yet other traits and dispositions. The
character trait of honesty, for instance, is "a disposition which is well
entrenched in its possessor, something that, as we say, 'goes all the
way down,'" and "far from being a single track disposition to do honest actions, or even honest actions for certain reasons, it is multi-
track." For the disposition "is concerned with many other actions as
well, with emotions and emotional reactions, choices, values, desires,
perceptions, attitudes, interests, expectations, and sensibilities. To
possess a virtue is to be a certain sort of person with a certain complex
mindset."

How complex? Well, Hursthouse explains, an honest person   4
"chooses, where possible, to work with honest people, to have

honest friends, to bring up her children to be honest. She disapproves of, dislikes, deplores dishonesty, is not amused by certain tales of chicanery, despises or pities those who succeed by dishonest means rather than thinking they have been clever, is unsurprised or pleased (as appropriate) when honesty triumphs, is shocked or distressed when those near and dear to her do what is dishonest and so on."

Virtue ethicists also claim that having a virtue, which is something that comes by degrees, contributes to making one's life a good one—to what Aristotle called *eudaimonia*,[2] or flourishing. A life that exhibits the virtues is for that very reason a better life: not because the acts of the virtuous have good consequences (though they may); not because they lead to satisfaction or give pleasure to the agent (though, for Aristotle at least, learning to take pleasure in what is virtuous is one component of moral development). Virtues are intrinsically worth having. Being virtuous is part, at least, of what makes a life worthwhile.   5

Corresponding to the virtues, as their antitheses, are the vices. They are to be shunned, just as the virtues are to be developed. And their presence in a life makes that life correspondingly less worthwhile. Vices, too, are seen as multi-track, deeper than mere habits. They are certainly multifarious; more so, it seems, than the virtues. Hursthouse, our stalking horse, offers a list of dispositions to avoid; we should not be "irresponsible, feckless, lazy, inconsiderate, uncooperative, harsh, intolerant, selfish, mercenary, indiscreet, tactless, arrogant, unsympathetic, cold, incautious, unenterprising, pusillanimous, feeble, presumptuous, rude, hypocritical, self-indulgent, materialistic, grasping, short-sighted, vindictive, calculating, ungrateful, grudging, brutal, profligate, disloyal, and on and on."   6

Virtue ethics, to be sure, comes in a Baskin-Robbins array of flavors; I take Hursthouse's avowedly neo-Aristotelian account to be representative, because it succeeds in capturing elements that are shared by many of the doctrinal variants in circulation: the basic cream, sugar, and eggs, so to speak. The core of the basic theory, as she formulates it, lies in three claims.   7

1. The right thing to do is what a virtuous agent would do in the circumstances.

2. A virtuous person is one who has and exercises the virtues.

3. A virtue is a character trait that a person needs in order to have *eudaimonia*—that is, in order to live a good life.

---

[2]**eudaimonia** Aristotle's idea of highest good, usually translated as "happiness," "welfare," or "flourishing."

The task of ethics, then, will be to discover what traits of character we need to live well.

This will be as convenient a place as any to announce a termino- 8
logical convention. Here and elsewhere, I'll generally follow Aristotle in using *ethics* to refer to questions about human flourishing, about what it means for a life to be well lived. I'll use *morality* to designate something narrower, the constraints that govern how we should and should not treat other people. Terminological stipulations of this sort are useful only if they allow us to track distinctions that matter. There are crucial issues that come into view only if we keep in mind the distinction between two general questions, "What is it for a life to go well?" and "What do we owe to other people?" Using the words *ethics* and *morality* in this way will help illuminate the connections between the answers to these two questions. So in making this distinction I wish emphatically to avoid the impression that I think these questions are unconnected.

This may seem obvious enough in virtue ethics, where the right- 9
ness of actions is conceptually dependent upon the goodness of lives; and where the goodness of one's life consists, at least in part, in having certain complex traits of character. Its modern practitioners urge us to determine, first, what we must be like to live well (for someone like that is virtuous), and then decide what to do on any particular occasion by deciding what a virtuous person would do. Aristotle wrote that, while everyone agrees that *eudaimonia* is the "highest of all the goods," there is no such agreement as to what it requires; the "popular account of it is not the same as that given by the philosophers." Virtue ethics aims at the wisest answer to the question of what *eudaimonia* requires. Its first answer is: the development of a virtuous character.

Wrongful Attributions

Anscombe,[3] recall, wanted us to become better acquainted with 10
psychology before resuming our moral philosophizing. What sort of psychological findings might prove relevant to the virtue ethics she helped resurrect? The underpinning conception of character shared by most virtue ethicists, including Aristotle, is what the philosopher John Doris[4] calls "globalist," which is to say, it involves consistent dispositions to respond across contexts under the guidance of a certain value; and many philosophers have also held some version of Aristotle's thesis of the unity of the virtues, according to which you fully possess

---

[3]**G. Elizabeth Anscombe (1919–1982)** Professor of philosophy at Cambridge University and one of England's most distinguished philosophers.

[4]**John Doris (b. 1944)** Professor of philosophy at Washington University, St. Louis, and author of *Lack of Character* (2002).

one virtue only if you have them all. But just as modern moral philosophers were rediscovering the virtues, social psychologists were uncovering evidence that most actual people (including people ordinarily thought to be, say, honest) don't exhibit virtues of this sort. The reason wasn't the one that most moralists would have suspected: that vice far exceeds virtue. The reason was that most people simply didn't display such multi-track, context-independent dispositions at all, let alone in a unified ensemble.

It's not so surprising to find the unity-of-virtues thesis, in its stronger forms, called into question. Oskar Schindler—as portrayed in the film *Schindler's List*—is mercenary, arrogant, hypocritical, and calculating; but he is also courageous and compassionate. How many of Jane Austen's young women[5] are kind but a little bit vain, too? We all know that such traits aren't served up in a fixed combination like a characterological Happy Meal. (Indeed, a reader of ecclesiastical hagiography might conclude that the virtues of the saints are sometimes less spectacular than their vices.) At the same time, there are *some* reasons for thinking that the virtues would have to be integrated in a virtuous person: for compassion without courage, say, will too often leave you not doing the compassionate thing. So there may be, at least in this straightforward way, something to be said for Aristotle's view. (As there usually is for Aristotle's views.)

No, the surprising challenge is to the core claim: that character, conceived of in terms of the virtues we ordinarily speak about, is consistent. Yet that is exactly what many social psychologists today would deny. They find that character traits simply don't exhibit (in the current argot) cross-situational stability. These psychologists are not globalists but "situationists": they claim—this is a first stab at a definition—that a lot of what people do is best explained not by traits of character but by systematic human tendencies to respond to features of their situations that nobody previously thought to be crucial at all. They think that someone who is, say, reliably honest in one kind of situation will often be reliably dishonest in another. They'd predict that Oskar Schindler was mercenary, arrogant, hypocritical, and calculating sometimes . . . but not always; and that his courage and compassion could be elicited in some contexts but not in others. The playful man, the serious man, the patient man, and the angry man: same fellow, different circumstances.

Now, to ascribe a virtue to someone is, among other things, to say that she tends to do what the virtue requires in contexts where it is

[5] **Jane Austen's young women** The reference is to characters in Jane Austen's (1775–1817) novels: Elizabeth Bennett in *Pride and Prejudice* (1813); Emma Woodhouse in *Emma* (1815); and Anna Elliot in *Persuasion* (1818).

appropriate. An honest person, for example, will resist the temptations to dishonesty posed by situations where, say, a lie will bring advantage, or where failing to return a lost wallet will allow one to buy something one needs. Indeed, our natural inclination, faced with someone who does something helpful or kind—or, for that matter, something hostile or thoughtless—is to suppose that these acts flow from their character, where character is understood in the way that "globalism" suggests: as a trait that is consistent across situations and, therefore, insensitive to differences in the agent's environment, especially small ones. But situationists cite experiments suggesting that small—and morally irrelevant—changes in the situation will lead a person who acted honestly in one context to do what is dishonest in another.

This result has been known since the earliest days of modern personality psychology. In the late 1920s, the Yale psychologists Hugh Hartshorne and Mark May[6] studied some ten thousand American schoolchildren, giving them opportunities to lie, cheat, and steal in various academic and athletic situations. What they found is that deceit was, to a surprising extent, a function of situations. It didn't track at all with measurable personality traits or assessments of moral reasoning, and the data gave little support to cross-situational predictions; the child who wouldn't break the rules at home, even when it seemed nobody was looking, was no less likely to cheat on an exam at school. Knowing that a child cheated on a spelling test didn't even tell you whether he would cheat on a math test, let alone in a sporting event.

In the past thirty years or so, broader psychological evidence against globalism has been accumulating. Back in 1972, Alice M. Isen[7] and Paula Levin found that when you dropped your papers outside a phone booth in a shopping mall, you were far more likely to be helped by people if they had just had the good fortune of finding a dime in the phone's coin-return slot. A year later, John Darley[8] and Daniel Batson discovered that Princeton seminary students, even those who had just been reflecting on the Gospel account of the Good Samaritan, were much less likely to stop to help someone "slumped in a doorway, apparently in some sort of distress," if they'd been told that they were late for an appointment. In a 1975 study, people were much less likely to help someone who "accidentally" dropped a pile of papers when the ambient noise level was 85 decibels than when it was

14

15

---

[6] **Hartshorne and May** Hugh Hartshorne (1885–1967) taught at Union Theological Seminary and the Yale Divinity School. Mark A. May was a professor of psychology at Syracuse University. They coauthored *Studies in Deceit* (1928).

[7] **Alice M. Isen** Professor of psychology at Cornell University.

[8] **John Darley (b. 1938)** Professor of psychology at Princeton University and mentor to Daniel Batson (b. 1943), who taught at the University of Kansas.

65 decibels. More recently, Robert Baron and Jill Thomley[9] showed that you were more likely to get change for a dollar outside a fragrant bakery shop than standing near a "neutral-smelling dry-goods store."

Many of these effects are extremely powerful: huge differences   16
in behavior flow from differences in circumstances that seem of little normative consequence. Putting the dime in the slot in that shopping-mall phone raised the proportion of those who helped pick up the papers from 1 out of 25 to 6 out of 7 — that is, from almost no one to almost everyone. Seminarians in a hurry are one-sixth as likely to stop and act like a Good Samaritan. Knowing what I've just told you, you should surely be a little less confident that "she's helpful" is a good explanation next time someone stops to assist you in picking up your papers (especially if you're outside a bakery!).

But, the research also suggests, you will probably go on ascribing   17
good characters to people who do good things and bad ones to those who do bad things, anyway. (Lydia Davis, recall, entitled her story *"Trying* to Learn"—not "I Have Learned.") Experimental research into what psychologists call "attribution theory" shows that people are inclined to suppose that what someone does reflects her underlying character even when you explain to them that she is just putting on a performance. In one classic study, which dates from 1967, subjects were asked to read essays that were either pro- or anti-Castro and decide whether their authors favored or opposed Fidel Castro's regime. People supposed that the writer was pro-Castro if the piece was pro-Castro (and anti-Castro if the essay was anti-Castro, too), even when they had been told both that the authors had been *instructed* to write pro or con, and that whether they were assigned to write for or against Castro was decided by flipping a coin. This tendency to ignore the role of context in determining behavior and to suppose that what people do is best explained by their traits rather than their circumstances is known, in the social-psychology literature, as Correspondence Bias (the supposed correspondence, here, is between conduct and character), or sometimes, more disparagingly, as the Fundamental Attribution Error.

Nor do we go wrong only when we're explaining the actions of   18
other people; our self-accounting is often untrustworthy. Remember those helpful people who picked up your papers after getting a free dime, or who made change outside the fragrant bakery. Who—buoyed

---

[9] **Baron and Thomley** Robert A. Baron is a professor of management at Oklahoma State University. Jill E. Thomley is a professor of mathematics at Appalachian State University. Together they authored "A Whiff of Reality: Empirical Evidence Concerning the Effects of Pleasant Fragrances on Work-Related Behavior" (1994).

by that dime, cheered by that fragrance—would explain what they themselves had just done by saying, "I helped him because I was feeling cheerful because I got a dime," or by thinking, "Hey, I did that mostly because I was in a terrific mood brought on by the wafting smell of croissants"? And, indeed, when experimenters asked people why they did what they did, they seldom mentioned these critical variables . . . just as you would have expected.

Now, one rationale for not mentioning these facts is that they don't seem relevant: ask people *why* they do something and they'll expect that you want not a causal explanation of what they did, but their *reason* for doing it—that is, what it was about the choice that made it seem a good thing to do. The fact that there's a splendid aroma of croissants in the air doesn't make offering change more reasonable; so it wouldn't do as an answer, especially if you're one of those philosophers who take moral theory to be centrally concerned with offering justifications for action. But, of course, you fail to mention it not because it seems like the wrong sort of answer; you fail to mention it because you have no idea that the aroma is having this effect on you. The researchers, faced with these data, may hypothesize that when you're cheerful, you're more inclined to do what you think is helpful; that is, the fact that offering change is helpful will strike you as a particularly strong reason for doing it when you're feeling particularly cheerful. But this is not something that the agent herself will notice in the ordinary course of things. So, even though she's doing what's helpful, and even though she might give that as her explanation—"He needed help," she might say—there remains another sense in which she doesn't understand why she's doing what she's doing.

And that, as we've seen, seems consistent with our broader explanatory habits—with the observation that much of what we say when we're explaining what we've done is confabulation: stories we've made up (though quite sincerely) for ourselves and in response to others. In short—to overstate the point only slightly—because people don't really know why they do what they do, they give explanations of their own behavior that are about as reliable as anyone else's, and in many circumstances actually less so.

The Situationist Challenge

I am not, for the moment, going to worry about whether all these psychological claims are true or whether we can give an account of the results that better comports with our common sense about why people, ourselves included, do what they do. The question I want to ask is: Why should ethical theory care about these claims at all?

Suppose I give you change because (in part) I just got a whiff   22
of my favorite perfume. Of course, if I had a settled policy of never giving change, even that pleasant aroma wouldn't help. So there are other things about me—the sorts of things we would normally assess morally—that are clearly relevant to what I have done. But let's suppose that, other things being equal, if I hadn't had the whiff, I'd have ignored your plaintive plea to stop and change your dollar for the parking meter. I had, in these circumstances, an inclination to do what, according to the virtue theorist, a kind or helpful or thoughtful person—a virtuous person—would do; and I acted on that inclination. A typical virtue theorist will think I have done the right thing because it is the kind thing (and there are no countervailing moral demands on me). But, on the situationist account, I don't act out of the virtue of kindness, and therefore this act doesn't accrue to my ethical credit. Well now, do I deserve praise in this circumstance or not? Have I or haven't I made my life better by doing a good thing?

A situationist might well say that, as a prudential matter, we should,   23
in fact, praise someone who does what is right or good—what a virtuous person would do—whether or not she did it out of a virtuous disposition. After all, psychological theory also suggests that praise, which is a form of reward, is likely to reinforce the behavior. (What behavior? Presumably not helpfulness, but being helpful when you're in a good mood.) For we tend to think that helping people in these circumstances, whatever the reason, is a good thing. But the virtue ethicist cannot be content that one acts *as if* virtue ethics is true. And we can all agree that the more evidence there is that a person's conduct is responsive to a morally irrelevant feature of the situation, the less praiseworthy it is.

If these psychological claims are right, very often when we credit   24
people with compassion, as a character trait, we're wrong. They're just in a good mood. And if hardly anyone is virtuous in the way that virtue ethics conceives of it, isn't the doctrine's appeal eroded? Given that we are so sensitive to circumstances and so unaware of the fact, isn't it going to be wondrously difficult to develop compassion, say, as a character trait? We just can't keep track of all the cues and variables that may prove critical to our compassionate responses: the presence or absence of the smell of baking is surely just one among thousands of contextual factors that will have their way with us. How, if this is so, can I make myself disposed to do or to feel the right thing? I have no voluntary control on how aromas affect me. I cannot be sure that I will have a free dime show up whenever it would be a fine thing to be helpful.

There are some philosophers—among them the aforementioned   25
John Doris (author of *Lack of Character*) and, even more strenuously,

my colleague Gilbert Harman[10]—who take the social-science literature about character and conduct to pose a serious and perhaps lethal challenge to the virtue ethicist's worldview. Talk all you like about virtuous dispositions, the challenge goes: we're just not built that way. Owen Flanagan,[11] who has long worked at the crossroads of psychology and moral theory, once proposed this maxim: "Make sure when constructing a moral theory or projecting a moral ideal that the character, decision processing, and behavior described are possible, or are perceived to be possible, for creatures like us." Plainly, there are costs for those who fail to clear this hurdle.

For one thing, our virtue theorist faces an epistemological difficulty   26
if there are no actually virtuous people. As in all spheres of thought, so in moral deliberation: we sometimes need to think not only about what the right answer is but also about how we discover what the right answers are. Hursthouse, remember, claims that:

1. The right thing to do is what a virtuous agent would do in the circumstances.

2. A virtuous person is one who has and exercises the virtues.

3. A virtue is a character trait that a person needs in order to have *eudaimonia*, in order to live a good life.

No interesting version of virtue ethics holds that doing the right thing is all that matters; we should want to be the kind of person who does the right thing for the right reasons. Still, Hursthouse and others insist that virtue ethics isn't *entirely* "agent-centered," rather than "act-centered"; it can also specify what the right thing to do is—namely, what a virtuous person would do. How are we to follow that advice? If we were fully virtuous, we would find ourselves disposed to think and act and feel the right things. But we are not. If we knew someone who was virtuous, we could see what she would do, I suppose. But, given the depressing situationist reality, maybe no actual human being really is (fully) virtuous. And even if a few people did get to be virtuous against all the odds, we would have to have some way of identifying them, before we could see what they would do. So we would need, first, to know what a good life looks like and then we would need, second, to be able to tell, presumably by reflecting on actual and imaginary cases, whether having a certain disposition is required for a life to be good; and required not in some

---

[10] **Gilbert Harman (b. 1938)** Professor of philosophy at Princeton University.
[11] **Owen Flanagan** Professor of neurobiology at Duke University.

instrumental way—as nourishment is required for any life at all—
but intrinsically.

If experimental psychology shows that people cannot have   27
the sorts of character traits that the virtue theorist has identified as
required for *eudaimonia,* there are only two possibilities: she has identified the wrong character traits or we cannot have worthwhile lives.
Virtue theory now faces a dilemma.

The problem for the idea that we have gotten the wrong virtues is a   28
problem of method. For virtue theory of the sort inspired by Anscombe,
we must discover what the virtues are by reflection on concepts.
We can, in principle, reflect on which of the stable dispositions
that psychology suggests might be possible—being helpful when
we are in a good mood, say—are constitutive of a worthwhile life;
or which—being unhelpful when we aren't buoyed up by pleasant
aromas—detract from a life's value. But to concede *that* is to accept
that we'll need to do the experimental moral psychology before we
can ask the right normative questions. On this horn of the dilemma,
virtue theory will find itself required to take up with the very empirical psychology it so often disdains.

On the other horn of the dilemma, the prospect that we cannot   29
have worthwhile lives makes normative ethics motivationally irrelevant. What is the point of *doing* what a virtuous person would do if
I can't *be* virtuous? Once more, whether I can be virtuous is obviously
an empirical question. Once more, then, psychology seems clearly
apropos.

Still, we should not overstate the threat that situationism poses.   30
The situationist account doesn't, for example, undermine the claim
that it would be better if we *were* compassionate people, with a persistent, multi-track disposition to acts of kindness. Philosophical
accounts of the character ideal or compassion, the conception of it as
a virtue, need make no special assumptions about how easy or widespread this deep disposition is. Acquiring virtue, Aristotle already
knew, is hard; it is something that takes many years, and most people
don't make it. These experiments might confirm the suspicion that
compassionate men and women are rare, in part because becoming
compassionate is difficult. But difficult is not the same as impossible;
and perhaps we can ascend the gradient of these virtues only through
aspiring to the full-fledged ideal. Nor would the ideal be defeated by a
situationist who busily set about showing that people whom we take
to exemplify compassion—the Buddha, Christ, Mother Teresa—
were creatures of environments that were particularly rich in the conditions that (according to situationists) elicit kindly acts.

Finally, we could easily imagine a person who, on the virtue eth-   31
icists' view, was in some measure compassionate, and who actually

welcomed the psychologists' research. Reading about these experiments will only remind her that she will often be tempted to avoid doing what she ought to do. So these results may help her realize the virtue of compassion. Each time she sees someone who needs help when she's hurrying to a meeting, she'll remember those Princeton seminarians and tell herself that, after all, she's not in *that* much of a hurry—that the others can wait. The research, for her, provides a sort of perceptual correction akin to the legend you see burned onto your car's rear-view mirror: *objects may be closer than they appear.* Thanks for the tip, she says. To think that these psychological claims by themselves undermine the normative idea that compassion is a virtue is just a mistake.

We might also notice what the situationist research *doesn't* show. It doesn't tell us anything about those seminarians (a healthy 10 percent) who were helpful even when rushing to an appointment; perhaps that subpopulation really did have a stable tendency to be helpful—or, for all we know, to be heedless of the time and careless about appointments. (Nor can we yet say how the seminarians would have compared with, say, members of the local Ayn Rand Society.[12]) There could, consistent with the evidence, be a sprinkling of saints among us. Some will dispute whether the dispositions interrogated by social psychology can be identified with the normative conception of character traits elaborated by the classical virtue theorists. And, of course, the situationist hypothesis is only that, in explaining behavior, we're inclined to overestimate disposition and underestimate situation. It doesn't claim that dispositions don't exist; it hardly could, since one stable disposition it reports is the tendency to commit the Fundamental Attribution Error.   32

None of these caveats wholly blunts the situationist point that the virtues, as the virtue ethicists conceive them, seem exceedingly hard to develop—a circumstance that must leave most of us bereft of *eudaimonia*. But virtue ethics is hardly alone in assigning a role to elusive ideals. Our models of rationality are also shot through with such norms. In the previous chapter, I mentioned the nineteenth-century hope that, as one formula had it, logic might be reduced to a "physics of thought." What succeeded that project was an approach captured in another formula according to which logic is, in effect, an "ethics of thought." It tells us not how we do reason but how we ought to reason. And it points toward one way of responding to the question we have posed to the virtue ethicist: How might we human beings take seriously an ideal that human beings must fall so far short of attaining?   33

---

[12] **Ayn Rand Society** Ayn Rand (1905–1982) was a Russian American novelist and philosopher. Her teachers regarded altruism as a form of weakness.

QUESTIONS FOR CRITICAL READING

1. What is a virtue? What virtues are very important?

2. Are virtues intrinsically worth having?

3. Which virtues do you most respect?

4. Why should one avoid vices? Is it difficult to avoid vices even if you wish to?

5. What are traits and dispositions? (See para. 3.)

6. Appiah mentions globalism in paragraph 13. What is globalism?

7. What are the problems with having compassion as a character trait? (See para. 24.)

SUGGESTIONS FOR CRITICAL WRITING

1. Look up the word *eudaimonia* and establish what you think Appiah means by the term. What would *flourishing* mean in relation to achieving a happy life? What is the relationship of eudaimonia to the concept of ethics? How would an ethical life be conducive to eudaimonia? Why does Aristotle call it the highest good and declare that it is the most desired thing in one's life? Do you feel that you could achieve eudaimonia? If so, how?

2. Explain why you think a virtuous life is likely to be a happy life. If you think that Aristotle and Appiah are correct that virtue produces happiness, why do you think so many people permit themselves to practice various vices? If people enjoy vices, does that mean that vices make people happy? Are vices universally undesirable and bad? What are the complications involved in relating virtues to vices in the way we live today? Can we measure our life in terms of virtue and vice?

3. Examine Rosalind Hursthouse's three claims (para. 7). According to Hursthouse, what is a virtuous agent? When she says that a virtuous person "exercises the virtues," what does she mean? Do you agree? Do examples from your own experience support that view? Finally, she says that a "virtue is a character trait." Do you agree? How do we define character traits? Is a virtuous character trait essential "to live a good life"?

4. In paragraph 9, Appiah suggests that Hursthouse believes eudaimonia requires "the development of a virtuous character." What is a virtuous character? If the implication is that a virtuous character can be developed, does that suggest that we do not naturally possess one? Does it suggest that there may be a procedure by which we can achieve a virtuous character? Do you have evidence from your observations of people that it is possible to develop a virtuous character? Do you wish to develop a virtuous character?

5. **CONNECTIONS** Appiah is obviously influenced by the position on virtue that Aristotle expressed in the *Nichomachean Ethics* (**bedfordstmartins .com/worldofideas/epages**). Appiah mentions Aristotle several times and indicates specific agreement with his views, and he also quotes other writers who refer to Aristotle's work. How does Aristotle's position on virtue ethics differ from the positions Appiah and other philosophers hold? Would Aristotle defend the view that virtuous behavior stems from virtuous character? Does Aristotle take character into consideration? Does Aristotle make any allowances for situationist ethics? How does Aristotle help clarify Appiah's thoughts, and how do Appiah's thoughts help clarify those of Aristotle?

6. **CONNECTIONS** Examine Appiah's definition of *ethics* and his definition of *morality* in paragraph 8. Do Appiah's definitions satisfy you with regard to the relationship of ethics to morality? Do you think Iris Murdoch (p. 359) would agree with his definitions and find them acceptable in relation to her views of religion? Define *ethics* and *morality* in terms that your peers would understand, using examples to bolster your definitions.

7. Write an essay for an audience that has not read this selection and is unaware of the concept of eudaimonia. Explain what situationist ethics is and how it works. Suggest some situations—either genuine ones you have experienced or hypothetical ones that are likely or possible among your peers. What situations might incite a nonvirtuous person to act virtuously? Why would the situation, rather than the character of the actor, control the virtue of the action? What is necessary for a situation ethicist to call an action virtuous?

8. One authority says that the virtues are love, kindness, justice, and service. The Greeks, Aristotle and Plato, say they are temperance, wisdom, justice, and courage. The seven heavenly virtues are chastity, temperance, charity, diligence, patience, kindness, and humility. Research the virtues and explain what they entail, how they are expressed, and why they are important. Decide how many true virtues there are. At the end of your essay, identify which virtues you most value and why.

9. **SEEING CONNECTIONS** Choose one of the paintings in this book and explain why Appiah would likely see some of his theories about ethics at work in the painting. Especially applicable paintings include the following: Henry O. Tanner's *The Thankful Poor* (p. 438) and Joseph Wright of Derby's *An Experiment on a Bird in the Air Pump* (p. 298). Do you think Appiah would have made any judgments about virtue in relation to character or to situations in either of these paintings?

MICHAEL GAZZANIGA
Toward a Universal Ethics

MICHAEL GAZZANIGA (b. 1939) is professor of psychology at the University of California at Santa Barbara. He is among the most distinguished scientists currently studying the relationship of the mind to the brain. When he was a student at the California Institute of Technology, Gazzaniga's mentor was Roger Sperry, who pioneered important research into the split-brain phenomenon. Sperry relieved severely impaired sufferers of epilepsy by severing the corpus callosum, the informational tissues connecting the left hemisphere to the right hemisphere of the brain. Resultant research at first seemed to indicate that the two hemispheres were so distinct as to almost represent different personalities. Ultimately, research demonstrated that the left hemisphere is usually specialized to deal with language, writing, reading, and math skills, while the right hemisphere is usually specialized to deal with spatial relations and visual, musical, and artistic skills. Gazzaniga's early book *The Bisected Brain* (1970) was among the first general explanations of the implications of this body of brain research.

Since then, various kinds of brain analysis using electromagnetic imaging and other techniques have broadened our understanding of the function of the brain. Research has found with some precision the locations in the brain that govern memory and the acquisition of memories, the areas excited by certain emotions, and the rate of development of important areas of the brain, such as the prefrontal lobe, which governs social and antisocial behavior. The fact that the prefrontal lobe does not develop fully until about twenty-one years of age has been taken as an indication that youthful irrationality is to some extent a matter of immature brain development, not just a matter of character failure.

From *The Ethical Brain*

Gazzaniga is prominent as a cognitive neuroscientist, which is to say as a student of the interaction of the brain and the mind it supports. He has served on the President's Council for Bioethics, advising the government on a wide variety of ethical issues arising from brain research. One ethical issue, for example, has to do with the concern that there may be people who are "hardwired" to be antisocial and potentially criminal. Some scientists contend that evolutionary forces made some brains naturally prone to violence as a means of survival. Such a characteristic may be helpful in the wild, but in a complex social system that behavior is a deficit. The result is that philosophers and scientists are continually debating the question of how ethically responsible a person who is naturally violent can be.

In his research, Gazzaniga has concluded that even such evolutionary traits do not mean that we are deprived of free will. He feels that people are socialized in ways that may make them prone to violence, but that the very act of socialization implies that people can control themselves if they wish to. One's will is not overridden by one's inclinations. Of course, this is a very hotly contested opinion, particularly in court, where the temporary insanity defense is often used as an excuse for violent behavior. Brain lesions are sometimes blamed for irrational behavior, too, but Gazzaniga has determined that not even lesions can excuse criminal behavior. Yet there are documented instances of patients with brain tumors whose growing masses resulted in changed behavior and personality.

Gazzaniga has written widely on the interconnected subjects of the mind, the brain, and the will. His book *Mind Matters: How Mind and Brain Interact to Create Our Conscious Lives* (1988) addresses many of the problems that have attracted and baffled neuroscientists concerned with consciousness, one of the most intractable puzzles of contemporary science. He reviews the research and the resultant understanding of the nature of the brain as a result of studies of split-brain patients as well as studies of the effects of brain chemistry on behavior. His recent book, *Who's in Charge? Free Will and the Science of the Brain* (2011), examines current research that demonstrates that the brain is a complex of many subsystems that operate at times independently and automatically. As a result, Gazzaniga asks how all of these separately functioning systems can aggregate into a single person who can imagine a freedom of will. Like in much of his earlier work, he is pursuing the issue of how the brain functions to produce a sense of self that we feel is unique and independent.

The following selection is from *The Ethical Brain* (2005), which approaches the issues raised by psychologists who have appropriated neuroscience and tend to connect psychological disorders with anomalies in the physiology of the brain. Some research implies a form of determinism, a concept that has stimulated legal debate over whether humans really have a free will. A number of important studies imply that the brain, rather than a person's will, can determine a person's action, at least to some extent. Gazzaniga reviews the research and cannot give credence to such a view. In his book, he explores the way the brain develops and ages. He takes on the legal issues centered on genetics and on brain enhancement. Finally, he addresses the question of an ethics that takes into consideration what we know about the physiology of the brain.

Gazzaniga's Rhetoric

Gazzaniga is exploring a question that may have no absolute answer—yet. He is asking a serious question: Is ethical behavior hardwired in the brain through years of evolution? To begin answering, he has to take into consideration the moral questions raised and answered over the centuries by philosophers and religious leaders who created what he calls "stories" about the way we should behave. These early thinkers were working in what Gazzaniga might consider "the dark" because they knew nothing about the science of brain development and brain systems. Gazzaniga explains that modern observations of the brain indicate that specific responses and resulting behavior can be tracked with some clarity by brain scans. Moreover, specific areas of brain function seem to be responsible for various kinds of actions that all people perform. The seat of personality and the areas involved in moral choice are usually centered in the prefrontal lobe of the brain, while other areas are supportive and functional in decision making. Indeed, Gazzaniga refers to the brain as a "decision-making device" (para. 12).

In the beginning of his essay, Gazzaniga explores the question of evolution and our inheritance of genes from the earliest human population, when there were a mere ten thousand people on the planet. We have inherited their genes, and our genes are virtually the same as theirs. That raises the question, How much of our response when we make moral judgments is built into our brains as a matter of survival? In the process of considering this question, Gazzaniga refers to a great many authorities in the world of neuroscience. This is a key part of his rhetorical strategy, and it is effective because, as a scientist, he feels it is his responsibility to represent the work of other scientists who may or may not agree with him (most are working in similar scientific areas, but some are not). In any event, his rhetorical stance demands that he refer to the testimony of experts and not just tell a "story."

The value of moral empathy, the ability to respond to the distress of others, and the willingness to come to the aid of others are useful to evolutionary survival in the long run. As social animals, we survive when we help others survive. Gazzaniga refers to this as social neuroscience, tying the urge to behave ethically to the evolutionary power of our genes and the physiology of the brain. He devotes quite a bit of time at the end of the passage to the issue of "reading minds." By that, he means our ability to interact with others by imagining what they are possibly thinking, what they are doing, and what they may do. This is a skill that makes social intercourse possible and at the same time helps us be secure in our environment. Without that skill, he implies, we would self-destruct and the species itself would not survive. Gazzaniga goes as far as to refer to mirror neurons that are "believed to be responsible for 'action understanding'—that is, understanding the actions of others" (para. 30).

Gazzaniga also explores the question of whether our moral decisions are more rational than they are intuitive. He points to gut instincts that propel people to make moral judgments and ethical decisions that are almost instantaneous. He also refers to some common ethical dilemmas, such as the "trolley problem" (para. 16), which involve making a decision that would influence the fate of either a small number of people or a large number of people. The rational issues in such problems are such that solving them involves thinking more than feeling. But Gazzaniga also establishes that there are emotional issues that combine with rational decisions to behave ethically. His point is that moral decisions have an emotional quotient that is measurable in brain scans.

His central concern is to decide whether on the basis of our evolution and the physiology of our brain there can be a universal ethics that transcends the limitations of our individual cultures. He hopes that scientific discoveries and scientific understandings will either replace or augment our dependence on "tales from the past."

PREREADING QUESTIONS:
WHAT TO READ FOR

The following prereading questions may help you anticipate key issues in the discussion of Michael Gazzaniga's "Toward a Universal Ethics." Keeping them in mind during your first reading should help focus your attention.

- What is the relationship of ethics to the survival of the species?
- What do studies of the physiology of the brain reveal about moral behavior?
- Do people have an innate moral sense?

Toward a Universal Ethics

Ever-advancing human knowledge seeps into the assumptions of 1
everyone on earth whether they like it or not. From Harvard Square to a
remote village in Sri Lanka, people have concepts of a gene, a brain, the
Internet, the good life. Affluent cultures and democracies gain from all
this knowledge, even though the lessons of modern knowledge about
the nature of the world may produce conflicts with some traditional
beliefs. That is what is happening on the surface. Underneath these
material gains is another, psychological reality. Modern knowledge is
on a collision course with the ubiquitous personal spiritual belief systems of one kind or another that are held by billions of people. Putting
it in secular terms, no one has told the kids yet there is no Santa Claus.

We are big animals, and only five thousand generations ago there 2
were just ten thousand of us roaming the world. Our genes stem from
those ten thousand people and are 99.9 percent the same. Ever since that
time, we have been busy cooking up cultures and stumbling forward.
Anyone who does not appreciate this fundamental fact of modern life is
either clinging to heartfelt beliefs about the nature of life and the history
of the world, or is quite simply out of the loop. This is the single most disturbing reality of modern-day citizenship and our notion of shared values.

Received wisdom—the thoughts of the giants of human history—is 3
stunning, captivating, and intelligent. But for the most part it is based
on first guesses, as we know from current scientific and historical information. Aristotle, Socrates, Hume, Locke, Descartes, Aquinas, Darwin,
Hobbes[1]—all put forward explanations of human nature that still reso-
nate today. Their thinking about approaches to life are brilliant schemas
for how the world must be, based on the information made available to
them at the time, and are the products of clear-thinking people. Religious movements throughout human history produced moral codes and
interpretations and stories about what it means to be human—indeed,
what it means to exist at all. All are part of our rich past. The harsh, cold
fact, however, is that these rich, metaphoric, engaging ideas—whether
philosophical or religious—are stories, although some are based on
more evidence than others. Even if you do not believe or accept this as
a given, you should be aware that this is what every modern-day secular
university is teaching, either implicitly or explicitly.

What is more fascinating to me is that even though new data 4
provide scientific and historical bases for new views about nature

---

[1]**Aristotle . . . Hobbes** Philosophers ranging from early Greeks to nineteenth-
century thinkers who posited theories of human behavior and also expressed or implied
moral theories.

and our past, people can still disagree about whether there even *is* a human nature. As Steven Pinker[2] recently remarked before the President's Council on Bioethics, "In much of the 20th Century, there was a widespread denial of the existence of human nature in Western intellectual life, and I will just present three representative quotations. 'Man has no nature,' from the philosopher José Ortega y Gasset. 'Man has no instincts,' from the anthropologist and public intellectual Ashley Montagu. 'The human brain is capable of a full range of behaviors and predisposed to none,' from the evolutionary biologist Stephen Jay Gould."[3]

Yet we know there *is* something we call human nature, with fixed   5 qualities and inevitable expression in any number of situations. We know that some fixed properties of mind come with us from the baby factory, that all humans possess certain skills and abilities other animals don't have, and that all of this makes up the human condition. And we now know that we are the products of an evolutionary process that has shaped our species, for better or for worse. We are big animals. The rest of our stories about our origins are just that, stories that comfort, cajole, and even motivate—but stories nonetheless.

This leaves us in a quandary and with a task. The quandary is   6 daunting: to understand that most of our current beliefs and moral systems derive from theories, perhaps based on the logic of what our species' best minds through the ages, reacting to life's events, could posit about the nature of reality. For those who realize and believe this, the task and the challenge of modern humans is to try to discern whether our highly evolved human nature and culture benefit from an underlying universal ethics, a moral response to life's challenges that has been a feature of our species from the beginning. The question is, Do we have an innate moral sense as a species, and if so, can we recognize and accept it on its own terms? It is not a good idea to kill because it is not a good idea to kill, not because God or Allah or Buddha said it was not a good idea to kill.

Guessing about Our Moral Sense

Until recently, the possibility that our species has a built-in moral   7 sense, a basic human capacity to make judgments about right and wrong, has been argued more by assertion and analysis of human behavior

---

[2]**Steven Pinker (b. 1954)** Professor of psychology at Harvard University and a student of the evolutionary nature of the language instinct.

[3]**Ortega y Gasset . . . Gould** José Ortega y Gasset (1883–1955) was one of Spain's greatest modern philosophers; Ashley Montagu (1905–1999) was a prominent anthropologist; Stephen Jay Gould (1941–2002) was professor of zoology at Harvard University and author of books studying evidence relating to Darwin's evolutionary theories.

than by demonstrated biological fact. Especially rare, if not missing entirely from the argument, has been the fact that we could not draw upon how the brain works in morally challenging situations. Modern social scientists can get only so far in their efforts to understand human behavior. James Q. Wilson[4] used analysis of social science research in his classic 1993 book, *The Moral Sense,* but admitted, "The truth, if it exists, is in the details . . . I am not trying to discover 'facts' that will prove 'values'; I am endeavoring to uncover the evolutionary, developmental, and cultural origins of our moral habits and our moral sense. But in discovering these origins, I suspect that we will encounter uniformities; and by revealing uniformities, I think that we can better appreciate what is general, nonarbitrary, and emotionally compelling about human nature."[5] Wilson, the distinguished political scientist from Harvard and now UCLA, suggested, "However much the scientific method is thought to be the enemy of morality, scientific findings provide substantial support for its existence and power."[6] Wilson cast an astonishingly wide net to make his case for an innate human moral sense. He reviewed not only the history of philosophy but also evolutionary theory, anthropology, criminology, psychology, and sociology. He concluded that no matter what intellectuals argue, there are certain universal, guiding moral instincts. In fact, they are so instinctual that they often get overlooked: "Much of the dispute over the existence of human universals has taken the form of a search for laws and stated practices. But what is most likely to be universal are those impulses that, because they are so common, scarcely need to be stated in the form of a rule . . ."[7] Highest among these are that all societies believe that murder and incest are wrong, that children are to be cared for and not abandoned, that we should not tell lies or break promises, and that we should be loyal to family.

Wilson rejected the idea that morality is purely a social construct—that we are constrained by the need to behave a certain way because of external factors: "For there to be a contract, whether to create a state or manage and exchange, there must first be a willingness to obey contracts; there must be in Durkheim's[8] phrase, some noncontractual elements of contract."   8

Wilson may have been prescient. A series of studies suggesting   9 that there *is* a brain-based account of moral reasoning have burst onto

---

[4]**James Q. Wilson (b. 1931)** Political scientist and professor of government at UCLA.

[5]Wilson, J. Q. (1993). *The Moral Sense* (New York: Free Press), p. 26. [Gazzaniga's note]

[6]Ibid., p. xii. [Gazzaniga's note]

[7]Ibid., p. 18. [Gazzaniga's note]

[8]**Emile Durkheim (1858–1917)** Considered the father of modern sociology.

the scientific scene. It has been found that regions of the brain normally active in emotional processing are activated with one kind of moral judgment but not another. Arguments that have raged for centuries about the nature of moral decisions and their sameness or difference are now quickly and distinctly resolved with modern brain imaging. The short form of the new results suggests that when someone is willing to *act* on a moral belief, it is because the emotional part of his or her brain has become active when considering the moral question at hand. Similarly, when a morally equivalent problem is presented that he or she decides not to act on, it is because the emotional part of the brain does not become active. This is a stunning development in human knowledge because it points the way toward figuring out how the brain's automatic response may predict our moral response.

Scanning for Moral Reasoning

First, to be able to assess moral reasoning, scientists have analyzed the psychology of different moral theories. In other words, they have asked what kinds of decisions or judgments a person needs to make in order to decide what actions to take. This careful assessment of moral reasoning is obviously tricky, and in a laboratory setting, ascertaining what kinds of decisions trigger what kinds of brain reactions is even trickier; but some clever researchers are doing just that.   10

Evolutionary psychology points out that moral reasoning is good for human survival—the ability to recognize a certain norm for behaving in society and to apply it to others and oneself helps one to survive and thrive. As William D. Casebeer,[9] a young philosopher at the Air Force Academy, has written, "We are social creatures, and if we are to flourish in our social environments, we must learn how to reason well about what we should do."[10] The question, then, is whether this skill might be built in to the brain, hardwired by evolution.   11

To me, these kinds of issues may be where the true secrets about the uniqueness of the human brain, the human condition, lie. Research long ago recognized that the essential function of the human brain is to make decisions; it is a decision-making device. On no dimension of human consciousness are more decisions made than on social issues, the second-by-second, minute-by-minute judgments we   12

---

[9]**William D. Casebeer** Former professor of philosophy at the Air Force Academy and current intelligence officer for the U.S. Air Force. His book is *Natural Ethical Facts: Evolution, Connectionism, and Moral Cognition* (2003).

[10]Casebeer, W. D. (2003). "Moral Cognition and Its Neural Constituents," *Nature Reviews Neuroscience* 4: 840–847. [Gazzaniga's note]

make all day long about our standing and situation in a social group. The enormous cerebral cortex—the huge expansion of capacity in the human brain—may be there for social processes such as our relentless need for social comparison. Could it be that these decisions are influenced by some kind of universal moral compass we all possess? This issue, along with others, is why the new field of social neuroscience is so exciting and potentially enlightening.

When a scientist wants to design experiments to see what brain 13
centers become active during moral reasoning, he or she needs to examine moral reasoning itself. This is difficult, given how many different moral philosophies exist. Nonetheless, a good place to begin is with the three main Western philosophies: utilitarianism, deontology, and virtue theory—represented by the philosophers John Stuart Mill, Immanuel Kant, and Aristotle, respectively. Utilitarians believe in actions that produce the most happiness for the most people; in other words, they look to the bottom line. Deontologists don't worry about the outcome of an action but focus on the intention that produced it—it's more important not to violate another person's rights than to have an ideal outcome. Virtue theorists look to cultivate virtue and avoid vices.[11]

Casebeer reviewed this trio of philosophies and concluded, "Jok- 14
ingly, then, it could be said that these approaches emphasize different brain regions: frontal (Kant); prefrontal, limbic, and sensory (Mill); the properly coordinated action of all (Aristotle)."[12] That goes to the heart of the question: Are there moral reasoning centers in the brain? It's surely not as simple as that, but it may well be that intricate and distributed neural networks are active when a person is making certain moral decisions. Can they be captured with modern brain-imaging technologies?

Research on moral cognition studies three main topics: moral emo- 15
tions, theory of mind, and abstract moral reasoning. Moral emotions— those that motivate behavior—are driven mostly by the brain stem and limbic axis, which regulate basic drives such as sex, food, thirst, and so on. *Theory of mind* is the term for our ability to judge what others are thinking so that we can behave appropriately in response to them—an essential in moral reasoning because it guides our social

---

[11] Ibid. [Gazzaniga's note]

[12] **frontal . . . all** The frontal lobe of the brain is the large portion of both hemispheres located behind the forehead; the prefrontal cortex is beneath the forehead and responsible for actions involving moral decisions; the limbic system is responsible for emotional behavior; the sensory is a group of lobes that parse sight, sound, and so on. Casebeer connects each to the philosopher whose "stories" most clearly relate to those portions of the brain.

behavior. The "mirror neurons" I discussed [earlier], the orbital frontal cortex, the medial structures of the amygdala, and the superior temporal sulcus are believed to be responsible for theory-of-mind processes. Finally, abstract moral reasoning, brain imaging is showing us, uses many brain systems.

The dilemma in abstract moral reasoning studies most often presented by researchers to volunteers is the trolley problem, one version of which I described [earlier]. In this version, a trolley is hurtling down a track, headed straight for five people. You have to decide whether to let it hit the five people or, up close and personal, throw a person standing next to you onto the tracks to stop the trolley from hitting the other five.   16

Most people claim they won't throw the nearby person in front of the trolley. At the same time, they will pull a switch and divert the train to another track, which will spare the five people even though the switched train will run into and kill a single person. So the question is, Where do these gut reactions come from? Is there a neural basis for these two prevalent responses? Have they been honed through evolution?   17

Joshua Greene,[13] a neurophilosopher from Princeton, raises two additional commonly used examples. Say you are driving along in your new car and you see a man on the side of the road. He has been in an accident and is bloody. You could take him to the hospital and save his life; however, you would get blood all over your new car. Is it morally okay to leave him there? Or take another scenario. You receive a request in the mail saying that if you send in $100, you will save the lives of ten starving children. Is it okay to not send in the money?   18

In analyzing these kinds of dilemmas, Greene and his colleagues found that while the choices are the same on the surface — do nothing and preserve your self-interest, or save lives at little cost to yourself — the difference is that the first scenario is personal whereas the second is impersonal. As already mentioned, Greene's studies found that judgments of personal dilemmas such as those seen in the trolley problem involve more brain activity in areas associated with emotion and moral cognition. Why is this? From an evolutionary perspective the theory is that the neural structures that tie altruistic instincts to emotion may have been selected for over time because helping people immediately is beneficial. Gut instinct, or morality, is a result of processes selected for over the evolutionary process. We have cognitive processes that allow us to make quick moral decisions that will   19

---

[13]**Joshua Greene** Professor of psychology at Harvard University and author of *The Moral Brain and How to Use It* (2012).

increase our likelihood of survival. If we are wired to save a guy right in front of us, we all survive better. In the case of the money contribution, long-distance altruism just isn't as necessary; out of sight, out of mind. There is no dire need.

This brings us back to the central issue of whether moral   20 truths are really universal truths, or whether they are merely opinions, individual gut instincts. When making moral judgments, are we perceiving external truths or expressing internal attitudes? The new brain imaging results are highly suggestive that our brains are responding to the great underlying moral dilemmas. It is as if all the social data of the moment, the personal survival interests we each possess, the cultural experience we have undergone, and the basic temperament of our species all feed into the subconscious mechanisms we all possess and out comes a response, an urging for either action or inaction. This is the moral spark Wilson was talking about. This is the glue that keeps our species, over the long haul, from destroying itself.

Marc Hauser[14] has addressed this issue, as we saw [earlier]. He   21 reasoned that if moral judgments were derived from rational processes, one would predict that people from different cultures, of different ages and sexes, would respond differently to a common challenge. He also reasoned that they would have readily available and articulate justifications for their decisions. Hauser showed that irrespective of sex, age, and culture, most subjects responded in a similar fashion, making similar moral choices. Further, and most important, none could articulate or justify their responses. In short, there seem to be common subconscious mechanisms that are activated in all members of our species in response to moral challenges. When the participants in Hauser's research were challenged to explain their decision, none of them were particularly rational or logical. Their explanations seemed to be the product of personal interpreters spinning out some theory or other that seemed right to them on the spot.

Most moral judgments are intuitive, as I've noted throughout this   22 book. We have a reaction to a situation, or an opinion, and we form a theory as to why we feel the way we do. In short, we have an automatic reaction to a situation—a brain-derived response. Upon feeling that response, we come to believe we are reacting to absolute truths. What I am suggesting is that these moral ideas are generated by our interpreter, by our brains, yet we form a theory about their absolute "rightness." Characterizing the formation of a moral code in this way

---

[14] **Marc Hauser (b. 1959)** Professor of psychology at Harvard University until 2011, where he focused on evolutionary biology and cognitive neuroscience.

puts the challenge directly on us. As Greene points out, "It is one thing to care about the plight of the poor, and another to think that one's caring is objectively correct."[15] It looks like it may be correct after all.

Somehow our brains are cued to be alert to the mental states of others as we struggle to play a productive role in developing a moral code in a social group. Somehow it would seem the universally recognized mechanisms of self-survival have been co-opted and are used to work in more social settings. Evolution is saving the group, not just the person, because it would seem that saving the group saves the person. To do this, we have somehow become mind readers, reflexively.   23

How We Read Minds

There are two major theories about how we "read minds"— that is, how we attribute certain mental or emotional states to others in order to explain or predict their behavior. The first is simulation theory (ST), whereby, very simply, we put ourselves in another person's shoes and figure out what we'd do in his or her situation. This requires us to use our imaginations to feed in "fake" data and to be able to hold the fake data separate from real life so that we don't act on it but only imagine what we would do, given the circumstances.[16]   24

Rivaling ST is the redundant-sounding theory-theory, or TT. "TT maintains that the mental terms and concepts used in understanding human behavior get their predictive and explanatory credentials by being embedded in a folk theory of mind."[17] This folk psychology, the theory goes, is a set of rules that we use to judge and gauge others' behavior. We need not be conscious of this set of rules, or even of using them; they are just there. But where does the theory come from? Here is where TT comes up against the same problem that Greene raises about where moral truths come from, the nature-nurture dilemma. Are we born with the knowledge, or do the rules exist in the ether, available for us to learn? TT adherents differ on whether the theory is innate or learned, as well as on whether we use   25

---

[15] **Greene, Joshua (2003).** "From Neural 'Is' to Moral 'Ought': What Are the Moral Implications of Neuroscientific Moral Psychology?," *Nature Reviews Neuroscience* 4: 847–850. [Gazzaniga's note]

[16] **Gallese, V., and A. Goldman (1998).** "Mirror Neurons and the Simulation Theory of Mind-Reading," *Trends in Cognitive Sciences* 2: 493–501; Goldman, A. (1989). "Interpretation Psychologized," *Mind and Language* 4: 104–119. [Gazzaniga's note]

[17] Ibid. [Gazzaniga's note]

a distinct "theory of mind" module in the brain or some more continuous system of representations that produce the same effect. What theory-theorists agree on is that we are in fact using knowledge that is encoded in a theory to judge behavior.

ST, on the other hand, denies that we are using a theory or body   26
of knowledge or rules to judge behavior; "rather our own mental processes are treated as a manipulable model of other minds." Even though we may make generalizations that, say, people tend to do X in circumstances like Y, simulation theorists believe this approach is process driven rather than being based strictly on preexisting knowledge. "The basic idea is that if the resources our own brain uses to guide our own behavior can be put to work as a model of other people, then we have no need to store general information about what makes people tick: We just do the ticking for them."[18]

A long and rich history of psychological research has outlined   27
what is called the empathy altruism hypothesis, which seeks to explain the pro-social behavior we engage in when we watch another human being in distress. We automatically and unconsciously simulate this distress in our minds, which in turn makes us feel bad—not in an abstract way, but literally bad. We become infected by the other person's negative feelings, and in order to alleviate this state in ourselves, we are motivated to action. A number of studies support this idea—that manipulating feelings toward an individual increases helping behavior. Looking at expressions of distress, for example, enhances helping behavior.[19]

Indeed, Adam Smith[20] was onto aspects of this thinking about   28
social contagion. In 1759 he wrote, "When we see a stroke aimed and just ready to fall upon the leg or arm of another person, we naturally shrink and draw back our leg or our own arm; and when it does fall, we feel it in some measure, and are hurt by it as well as the sufferer . . . Persons of delicate fibres and weak constitution of body complain, that in looking at the sores and ulcers which are exposed by beggars

---

[18] Gordon, R. See www.umsl.edu/~philo/Mind_Seminar/New%20Pages/subject .html. [Gazzaniga's note]

[19] Batson, C. D., and J. S. Coke (1981). "Empathy: A Souce of Altruistic Motivation for Helping," in *Altruism and Helping Behavior: Social Personality and Developmental Perspectives,* J. P. Rushton and R. M. Sorrentino, eds. (Hillsdale, N.J.: Erlbaum), pp. 167–211. Also, Cialdini, R. B., S. L. Brown, B. P. Lewis, C. Luce, and S. L. Neuberg (1997). "Reinterpreting the Empathy-Altruism Relationship: When One into One Equals Oneness," *Journal of Personality and Social Psychology* 73: 481–494; and Hoffman, M. L. (2000). *Empathy and Moral Development: Implications for Caring and Justice* (New York: Cambridge University Press). [Gazzaniga's note]

[20] **Adam Smith (1723–1790)** Professor of moral philosophy at Glasgow University and author of *Wealth of Nations* (1776).

on the streets, they are apt to feel an itching or uneasy sensation in the correspondent part of their own bodies."[21]

Countless experiments have been carried out to support this general idea. My former colleague at Dartmouth, John Lanzetta,[22] and his colleagues demonstrated repeatedly that people tend to respond to the sense of touch, taste, pain, fear, joy, and excitement of others with analogous physiological activation patterns of their own. They literally feel the emotional states of others as their own.[23] This tendency to react to the distress of others appears to be innate: it has been demonstrated in newborn infants, who cry in response to the distress of other infants within the first days of life.[24]

In considering all these arguments, I believe the STs have it right. From a neuroscience perspective, the mirror neuron could support the ST view of how this works. Mirror neurons are believed to be responsible for "action understanding"—that is, understanding the actions of others. While we can't ethically do single-cell recording of mirror neurons in humans, some neurophysiological and brain imaging experiments suggest that mirror neurons do exist in humans and that they function to help with action understanding as well as action imitation.[25]

The neurophysiology of what might be called social process started in 1954, when Henri Gastaut[26] and his colleagues in Marseille noted in EEG studies that human subjects have a brain wave response not only when performing actions themselves but when watching others perform actions. Gastaut's research has since been confirmed by many studies using both additional brain measurement techniques, such as the more advanced magnetoencephalographic technique, and stimulation techniques, such as transcranial magnetic stimulation (TMS), a noninvasive technique for electrical stimulation of the nervous system. Another important finding of the more recent studies has been that the spinal cord inhibits the

29

30

31

---

[21] **Hatfield, E., J. T. Caccioppo, and R. L. Rapson (1994).** *Emotional Contagion* (New York: Cambridge University Press), p. 17. [Gazzaniga's note]

[22] **John T. Lanzetta (1926–1989)** Former professor of psychology at Dartmouth College.

[23] **Lanzetta, J. T., and B. G. Englis (1989).** "Expectations of Cooperation and Competition and Their Effects on Observers' Vicarious Emotional Responses," *Journal of Personality and Social Psychology* 56: 543–554. [Gazzaniga's note]

[24] **Simner, M. L. (1971).** "Newborn's Response to the Cry of Another Infant," *Developmental Psychology* 5: 136–150. [Gazzaniga's note]

[25] **Rizzolatti, G., and L. Craighero (2004).** "The Mirror Neuron System," *Annual Reviews in Neuroscience* 27: 169–192. [Gazzaniga's note]

[26] **Henri Gastaut (1915–1995)** French neurologist and specialist in epilepsy.

execution of the observed action, "leaving the cortical motor system free to 'react' to that action without the risk of every movement generation."[27] Rizzolatti[28] and his colleagues point out that, in total, the TMS studies indicate that the human mirror system not only exists, but differs from the monkey system in a key way: it seems to recognize meaningless movements, such as vague gestures, as well as goal-directed movements.

Why is that important? Because these are the skills needed to imitate movements. This could suggest that the human mirror neuronal system is the basis for learning by imitation.   32

Human imaging studies are seeking to identify the complex network that is activated by the human mirror system. This is important to the search for the biology of moral reasoning. If we know what part of the brain is activated when observing an action, we can start to understand what mechanisms the brain uses to understand the world. For instance, if observing a barking dog activates my motor and visual areas, but seeing a picture of a barking dog activates only my visual area, this suggests not only that we process the information from these two situations differently, but that this different processing may evoke a different psychological experience of the observation. Observing a dog barking activates my motor system and therefore creates a deeper resonance with the observed action; seeing a picture of a barking dog just doesn't get "in my bones" in the same way.   33

Rizzolatti suggests that when we learn new motor patterns, it is possible we break them down into basic movements, via the mirror mechanism, and that once the mirror system activates these basic motor representations, they are recombined into the action. He goes on to argue, as did Robin Allott[29] before him, that the mirror system, with its role in imitation and action understanding, may be the evolutionary precursor to language.[30] In other words, we went from understanding others' gestures, to understanding abstract representations   34

---

[27] **Rizzolatti and Craighero** "Mirror Neuron System," citing Baldissera, F., P. Cavallari, L. Craighero, and L. Fadiga (2001). "Modulation of Spinal Excitability During Observation of Hand Actions in Humans," *European Journal of Neuroscience* 13: 190–194. [Gazzaniga's note]

[28] **Giacomo Rizzolatti (b. 1937)** Italian neurophysiologist at the University of Parma.

[29] **Robin Allott** Author of *Motor Theory of Language* (1987) who describes himself as a "higher education professional."

[30] **Allott, R. (1991)** "The Motor Theory of Language," in *Studies in Language Origins*, vol. 2, W. von Raffler-Enel, J. Wind, and A. Jonker, eds. (Amsterdam: John Benjamins), pp. 123–157. [Gazzaniga's note]

of meaning—speech. This idea is supported by research suggesting hand and mouth gestures are linked in humans.

V. S. Ramachandran's[31] work on anosognosia patients—the stroke patients who deny their paralysis—indicates another crucial role mirror neurons may play in humans. Ramachandran found that some patients deny not only their own paralysis but the obvious paralysis of others—something he suggests may be due to damage to mirror neurons. "It's as if anytime you want to make a judgment about someone else's movements, you have to run a VR [virtual reality] simulation of the corresponding movements in your own brain, and without mirror neurons you cannot do this."[32] If this is so, it would seem that mirror neurons support the simulation theorists' view that the brain is built to feel not only our own experiences but those of others.

The tension between ST and TT gets us back to the universal ethics dilemma. Are the moral truths we seem to live by a set of rules that exist independently of us, rules that we learn and live by? Or are these rules the result of our brains using built-in systems to empathize and thereby predict behavior and act accordingly? Whatever the answer, one thing is clear: the rules exist.

I believe, therefore, that we should look not for a universal ethics comprising hard-and-fast truths, but for the universal ethics that arises from being human, which is clearly contextual, emotion-influenced, and designed to increase our survival. This is why it is hard to arrive at absolute rules to live by that we can all agree on. But knowing that morals are contextual and social, and based on neural mechanisms, can help us determine certain ways to deal with ethical issues. This is the mandate for neuroethics: to use our understanding that the brain reacts to things on the basis of its hardwiring to contextualize and debate the gut instincts that serve the greatest good—or the most logical solutions—given specific contexts.

I am convinced that we must commit ourselves to the view that a universal ethics is possible, and that we ought to seek to understand it and define it. It is a staggering idea, and one that on casual thought seems preposterous. Yet there is no way out. We now understand how tendentious our beliefs about the world and the nature of human experience truly are, and how dependent we have become on tales from the past. At some level we all know this. At the same time, our species wants to believe in something, some natural order, and it is

35

36

37

38

---

[31] **V. S. Ramachandran (b. 1951)** Professor of psychology at the University of California at San Diego. Among his books is *The Emerging Mind* (2003).

[32] Ramachandran, V. S. "Mirror Neurons and Imitation Learning as the Driving Force Behind 'the Great Leap Forward' in Human Evolution," *Third Edge*. See www .edge.org/3rd_culture/ramachandran/ramachandran_p1.html. [Gazzaniga's note]

the job of modern science to help figure out how that order should be characterized.

QUESTIONS FOR CRITICAL READING

1. What does Gazzaniga mean when he says that modern knowledge is on a collision course with traditional beliefs (para. 1)? Do you agree?

2. How important is it for Gazzaniga's discussion that we think of ourselves as "big animals" (para. 2)?

3. What is the significance of "theory of mind," our ability to judge what other people are thinking and so respond to them (para. 15)?

4. In paragraph 4, the question of human nature is broached. Is there such a thing as human nature?

5. Is morality specifically a social construct? What evidence informs your answer?

6. Do humans have an innate moral sense? What is Gazzaniga's view regarding an innate moral sense?

7. What are the limitations of the philosophical views of human nature described in paragraph 3?

SUGGESTIONS FOR CRITICAL WRITING

1. In paragraph 2, Gazzaniga says, "This is the single most disturbing reality of modern-day citizenship and our notion of shared values." What is he referring to, and how well does the remainder of the essay address the issues that he raises in this and the preceding paragraph? Do you agree that the rise of scientific understanding of brain functions will conflict with the "stories" that constitute much of what we think we know about human nature?

2. Early in the essay, Gazzaniga considers whether human nature exists. He quotes authorities who deny that there are instincts or anything like a human nature and assert that the brain has no predisposition but is adaptable to "a full range of behaviors" (para. 4). Argue the case either for or against the existence of human nature. Consider what role the recent studies of brain physiology might play in this debate. Why is whether or not human nature exists an important question to answer?

3. Review the "trolley problem" (para. 16). If you were in a situation in which you could control the outcome of an event that would kill either one innocent person or five people who may or may not be innocent, what would you do? Construct a different "trolley problem" and explore the possibilities that would face someone making a moral decision in response to that problem. Why are such decisions difficult? Is it possible to have an intuitive response to such problems? Can a gut instinct inform one when dealing with such problems?

4. When considering the question of "an underlying universal ethics," Gazzaniga says, "The question is, Do we have an innate moral sense as a species, and if so, can we recognize and accept it on its own terms?" (para. 6). He then declares, "It is not a good idea to kill because it is not a good idea to kill, not because God or Allah or Buddha said it was not a good idea to kill." What he does he mean? How does this line of reasoning lead us to consider a universal ethics?

5. In paragraph 11, Gazzaniga says that evolutionary psychology supports the view that moral behavior is good for human survival. That leads him to ask "whether this skill might be built in to the brain, hardwired by evolution." What is your view on this possibility? What, in addition to a moral sense, might be hardwired into the brain? Are talents, such as those possessed by musical prodigies, examples of hardwiring in the brain? What about intelligence, athletic skill, or risk taking? If such hardwiring exists, could it be a result of evolution?

6. To what extent do you agree that the emotional parts of the brain control moral behavior? Observe your own emotional reaction to events that demand a moral response and interview others to see if they have similar emotional reactions to morally complex situations. How much are you informed by your emotional responses to immoral behavior or unethical practices? Are your emotions good moral guides? Do you think it is universally true that emotions inform moral decisions?

7. **CONNECTIONS** For Gazzaniga, Aristotle's "The Aim of Man" (**bedfordstmartins.com/worldofideas/epages**) is essentially just a "story" because it is not rooted in scientific study and does not take into account what we in the modern world know about brain development and evolution. Yet Aristotle's discussion of ethics still guides the thinking of many modern philosophers and ethicists. Given Gazzaniga's views, how much of Aristotle would he think is still meaningful and relevant to modern society? What would Gazzaniga reject, and what would he accept? On what basis might Gazzaniga disregard entirely the views that Aristotle holds most dear?

8. **CONNECTIONS** Which of the authors in Part Three would have the most problem with Gazzaniga's views that there might be a universal ethics based on evolutionary developments in the human brain? Consider closely the work of Iris Murdoch in "Morality and Religion" (p. 359) and of Kwame Anthony Appiah in "The Case against Character" (p. 397). Which of these authors would be most opposed to Gazzaniga and which would be most in agreement?

9. **SEEING CONNECTIONS** What would Gazzaniga say in response to seeing Joseph Wright of Derby's *An Experiment on a Bird in the Air Pump* (p. 298)? Would he see this primarily as a scientific experiment or as a moral dilemma? How would he validate the emotional expressions of the people surrounding the experiment? What contribution would an analysis of this painting make to Gazzaniga's fundamental theories of the brain's role in making ethical decisions?

PART FOUR

WEALTH AND POVERTY

Adam Smith
Karl Marx
Andrew Carnegie
John Kenneth Galbraith
Robert B. Reich
Milton and Rose Friedman

INTRODUCTION

Wealth and poverty: the one is the parent of luxury and indolence, and the other of meanness and viciousness, and both of
discontent.

> — PLATO (428–347 B.C.E.)

What difference does it make how much you have? What you do
not have amounts to much more.

> — SENECA (4 B.C.E.–65 C.E.)

Great eagerness in the pursuit of wealth, pleasure, or honor, cannot
exist without sin.

> — DESIDERIUS ERASMUS (1466–1536)

In any country where talent and virtue produce no advancement,
money will be the national god. Its inhabitants will either have to
possess money or make others believe that they do. Wealth will
be the highest virtue, poverty the greatest vice.

> — DENIS DIDEROT (1713–1784)

Poverty in itself does not make men into a rabble; a rabble is created only when there is joined to poverty a disposition of mind,
an inner indignation against the rich, against society, against the
government.

> — GEORG WILHELM FRIEDRICH HEGEL (1770–1831)

Animals struggle with each other for food or for leadership, but
they do not, like human beings, struggle with each other for
that that stands for food or leadership: such things as our paper
symbols of wealth (money, bonds, titles), badges of rank to wear
on our clothes, or low-number license plates, supposed by some
people to stand for social precedence.

> — S. I. HAYAKAWA (1906–1992)

Ancient writers talk about wealth in terms of a surplus of necessary
or desirable goods and products. After the invention of coins—which
historians attribute to the Lydians, whose civilization flourished in the
eastern Mediterranean region from 800 to 200 B.C.E.—wealth also
became associated with money. However, the relationship of wealth to
money has long been debated. According to Aristotle, people misunderstand wealth when they think of it as "only a quantity of coin." For him,
money was useful primarily as a means of representing and purchasing
goods but was not sustaining in and of itself.

Writers like Aristotle have argued that wealth benefits the state
by ensuring stability, growth, security, and cultural innovations and
that it benefits the individual by providing leisure time, mobility, and
luxury. Most societies, however, have struggled with the problems

caused by unequal distribution of wealth, either among individuals or between citizens and the state. The Spartan leader Lycurgus is said to have tackled the problem in the ninth century B.C.E. by convincing the inhabitants of the Greek city-state of Sparta that they needed to redistribute their wealth. Land and household goods were redistributed among the citizens, and Lycurgus was hailed as a hero. However, Lycurgus's model has not been the norm in subsequent civilizations, and questions about the nature of wealth and its role and distribution in society have persisted.

The selections in this section present ideas on wealth and poverty from a variety of perspectives. Adam Smith begins by tracing the natural evolution of wealth from farming to trade. Karl Marx expounds on what he feels are the corrosive effects of excessive wealth on the individual and on the problems caused by unequal distribution of wealth between laborers and business owners. Andrew Carnegie, himself an extremely wealthy business owner, John Kenneth Galbraith, and Robert B. Reich further investigate the problems that an unequal distribution of wealth poses for society as a whole.

Adam Smith was known originally as a moral philosopher with a professorship at Glasgow, but he wrote at a time of extraordinary expansion in Great Britain. As industrial power grew in the late eighteenth century, England became more wealthy and began to dominate trade in important areas of commerce. In his own mind, Smith's interest in wealth may have been connected with his studies in morality, or it may have grown from his considerable curiosity about a broad range of subjects. Regardless, he produced one of the century's most important and extensive books on economics, *The Wealth of Nations*. It is still consulted by economists today.

Smith's "Of the Natural Progress of Opulence" is an attempt to understand the "natural" steps to wealth. Smith posits an interesting relationship between the country, where food and plants, such as cotton and flax, supply the necessities of life, and the city, which produces no food but takes the surplus from the country and turns it into manufactured goods. Smith's ideas concerning this process center on surplus. The farmers produce more than they can consume, and therefore they can market their goods to the city. The city takes some of the goods from the farmers and turns them into manufactured products, which can be sold back to the people in the country. When there is a surplus of manufactured goods, they can be sold abroad. That process can produce wealth—on a grand scale.

Karl Marx's *Communist Manifesto* clarifies the relationship between a people's condition and the economic system in which they live. Marx saw that capitalism provided opportunities for the wealthy and powerful to take advantage of labor. He argued that because labor cannot efficiently sell its product, management can keep labor in perpetual economic bondage.

Marx knew poverty firsthand, but one of his close associates, Friedrich Engels, who collaborated on portions of the *Manifesto*, was the son of a factory owner and so was able to observe closely how the rich can oppress the poor. For both of them, the economic system of capitalism produced a class struggle between the rich (bourgeoisie) and the laboring classes (proletariat).

In an effort to avoid anything like a class struggle between the rich and the poor, Andrew Carnegie wrote *The Gospel of Wealth*, defending not only the economic system that permitted a few people to amass great wealth but also praising it for being the highest expression of civilization. Carnegie dismisses communism as a failed system and cites Darwinian theories as supporting the laws of competition and accumulation that permitted men like him to possess vast fortunes. His proposal is that such men should give their wealth back to the community for its benefit in the form of institutions that would contribute to "the improvement of the race." Moreover, the rich should give their money away while they are living so that they can clearly guide their gifts in the directions they feel are most important. Carnegie, for example, concentrated on building public libraries throughout the United States and Canada, while founding a university and supporting others rather generously.

John Kenneth Galbraith's selection, "The Position of Poverty," dates from the middle of the twentieth century and addresses an issue that earlier thinkers avoided: the question of poverty. It is not that earlier writers were unaware that poverty existed—most mention it in passing—but their main concern was the accumulation and preservation of wealth. Galbraith, in his study of the economics of contemporary America, also focuses on wealth; the title of his most famous book is *The Affluent Society* (1958; rev. 1998). He, however, points toward something greater than the issue of attaining affluence. His concern is with the allocation of the wealth that American society has produced. His fears that selfishness and waste will dominate the affluent society have led him to write about what he considers the most important social issue related to economics: poverty and its effects. If Smith was correct in seeing wealth as appropriate subject matter for economic study, then Galbraith has pointed to the opposite of wealth as being equally worthy of close examination.

Robert B. Reich, a lecturer at Harvard University until he was appointed secretary of labor in the first Clinton administration, has taught courses in economics and published widely. His 1991 book, *The Work of Nations,* echoes the title of Adam Smith's eighteenth-century masterpiece of capitalist theory, *The Wealth of Nations*. Although Reich's views on labor are distinct from Smith's, his essay focuses on labor with the same intensity Smith brings to money. His views consider how worldwide economic developments will affect labor in the next decades. According to Reich, labor falls into three groups—routine workers, in-person servers, and symbolic analysts—each of which will fare differently in the coming years.

This chapter also contains a selection in e-Pages (available online at **bedfordstmartins.com/worldofideas/epages**) from Milton and Rose Friedman. The Friedmans are unconcerned with the distinctions of wealth or poverty—at least in the sense that neither economic condition commands their attention. Instead, they focus on the efforts of government that aim to produce what they call equality of outcome. They are fierce believers in equality of opportunity, but they assert that any effort to guarantee an equality of outcome will restrict the freedom of the high achievers in a society. For them, equality of outcome means guaranteeing the economic well-being of people who may not have earned it, while restricting the economic well-being of those who have. Indirectly, the Friedmans offer an argument that would help preserve the wealth of those with unusual talents for business. They see their position as completely opposed to Marx's.

Most of these theorists agree that a healthy economy can relieve the misery and suffering of a population. Most agree that wealth and plenty are preferable to impoverishment and want. But some are also concerned with the effects of materialism and greed on the spiritual life of a nation. Galbraith sees a society with enormous power to bring about positive social change and the capacity to make positive moral decisions. But, for all his optimism, Galbraith reminds us that we have made very little progress in an area of social concern that has been a focus of thought and action for a generation.

VISUALIZING WEALTH AND POVERTY

Some of the most famous images associated with wealth are portraits, often photographs of great industrialists and financiers such as Andrew Carnegie and J. P. Morgan. They are imposing figures in their business attire, staring straight at the viewer as if daring us to say a single word to them. In some renderings the subjects seem aware of their own mightiness. Others affect a brotherly kindness, allowing their wealth to reveal itself through the Renaissance furniture, rich Oriental rugs, and art masterpieces depicted with them.

Newspaper images of wealthy individuals usually include one or more possessions associated with their opulent lifestyles. Movie stars stand beside their Bentleys, real-estate tycoons are profiled next to their grandest buildings, playboys show up on their yachts, and inventors pose near their jet planes. Wealth has many faces, communicated by just as many images, and we see them constantly in magazines aimed at both the rich and the less rich. Lifestyles of the rich are visible on television shows, in films, and even on YouTube.

HENRY O. TANNER, *THE THANKFUL POOR*. 1894.
Oil on canvas. Collection of William H. and Camille O. Cosby.

Images of the poor, on the other hand, are different. Very few
are images that attempt to maintain the dignity of the poor. Usually images of poverty show suffering people from remote parts of
the globe; such imagery often accompanies requests for money to
relieve that poverty. In the 1890s, the vast majority of Americans
lived on farms and were what we would today describe as poor.
Yet the poor maintained a sense of dignity that was recognized by
all. Families stood by one another and helped relieve any sense of
desperation caused by impoverishment. Poverty in the cities took a
different form. The photographs by Jacob Riis (1849–1914) of the
tenements on the Lower East Side of New York were among the most
powerful images of genuine poverty that Americans might see in the
early years of the twentieth century. Some of the neighborhoods
he photographed were so crime ridden that even police would not
venture in.

One of the most remarkable portraits of the poor dates to the era
of Andrew Carnegie. It portrays an older man and a young boy, who
appears to be his grandson, preparing to have dinner. The only source
of light in the room seems to come from the window, which brings the
wall alive with color. The two figures are poised, apparently saying grace

before eating. (To see this painting in color, go to **bedfordstmartins .com/worldofideas/epages**.)

Henry Osawa Tanner (1859–1937) was born in Pittsburgh, Pennsylvania, where his father was a minister in the African Methodist Episcopal Church. When he was seven, his family moved to Philadelphia. He decided on his profession after watching an artist painting in a nearby park when he was thirteen. Tanner, a clearly talented painter, enrolled in the prestigious Pennsylvania Academy of Fine Arts in 1880 where he was a student of one of America's greatest painters, Thomas Eakins (1844–1916). Eakins recognized Tanner's ability and encouraged him. He also painted Tanner's portrait around the turn of the century, something he did for very few of his students.

Tanner often went to the Philadelphia Zoo to sketch animals to use in his early paintings. Professionals told him that he could sell animal paintings, so he painted several. But his primary subject matter was religious scenes, often from the Bible. Paintings such as *The Resurrection of Lazarus* and *The Good Shepherd* made his reputation. However, racism in Philadelphia, heightened by the northern migration of freed African Americans from the Carolinas, was such that Tanner felt pained and dismayed. He decided in 1891 to live in Paris and study there. In France, his race was of little or no concern and he found it more and more difficult to return to the United States.

In 1893, while back in the United States for a short time, he painted his most famous work, *The Banjo Lesson*. It portrays a man carefully instructing what seems to be his grandson on how to play the instrument. The two figures in that painting may have been the same that appear in *The Thankful Poor*. Tanner died on May 25, 1937, in Paris.

The Thankful Poor shows a small family at dinner, with sparkling plates, a stoneware water pitcher, and a plate with a fish and what seems to be a portion of chicken. Tanner did not paint this family in a fashion that evokes a sense of pity for their poverty—in part because, while they may be poor, they are not impoverished. They have a home, they have furniture and food, and they have each other. The reverence with which they approach their meal is such that one cannot help but respect their dignity and wonder what their conversation was while they ate together. The structure of the painting weights the action to the lower left diagonal half of the composition. If one were to draw a line from the upper left corner to the lower right, all the important information regarding the older man appears to the left, while the image of the young boy appears to the right. General darkness is more powerful near the older man, while the light reflecting from the wall illuminates the young boy, as if to suggest that life may be brighter for him than for the older man. In this sense it is visually a hopeful painting.

ADAM SMITH
Of the Natural Progress
of Opulence

ADAM SMITH (1723–1790) was born in Kirkcaldy on the eastern coast of Scotland. He attended Glasgow University and received a degree from Oxford, after which he gave a successful series of lectures on rhetoric in his hometown. This resulted in his appointment as professor of logic at Glasgow in 1751. A year later, he moved to a professorship in moral philosophy that had been vacated by Thomas Craggie, one of his former teachers. He held this position for twelve years. Smith's early reputation was built entirely on his work in moral philosophy, which included theology, ethics, justice, and political economy.

In many ways Adam Smith's views are striking in their modernity; in fact, his work continues to inform our understanding of current economic trends. His classic and best-known book, *An Inquiry into the Nature and Causes of the Wealth of Nations* (1776), examines the economic system of the modern nation that has reached, as England had, the commercial level of progress. According to Smith, a nation has to pass through a number of levels of culture—from hunter-gatherer to modern commercial—on its way to becoming modern. In this sense, he was something of an evolutionist in economics.

Wealth of Nations is quite different in both tone and concept from Smith's earlier success, *Theory of Moral Sentiments* (1759). The earlier work postulates a social order based, in part, on altruism—an order in which individuals aid one another—whereas *Wealth of Nations* asserts that the best economic results are obtained when individuals work for their own interests and their own gain. This kind of effort, Smith assures us, results in the general improvement of a society because the industry of the

---

From *An Inquiry into the Nature and Causes of the Wealth of Nations.*

individual benefits everyone in the nation by producing more wealth; the greater the wealth of the nation, the better the lot of every individual in the nation.

There is no question that Smith was an ardent capitalist who felt an almost messianic need to spread the doctrine of capitalism. He maintained throughout his life that *Wealth of Nations* was one with his writings on moral and social issues and that when his work was complete it would encompass the basic elements of any society.

In "Of the Natural Progress of Opulence," Smith outlines a microcosm of the progress of capitalism as he understood it. His purpose is to establish the steps by which a nation creates its wealth and the steps by which a region becomes wealthy. For the most part, he is interested in the development of capitalism in Great Britain, including his native Scotland. His perspective includes the natural developments that he observed in his own time in the late eighteenth century as well as developments that he could imagine from earlier times. Because he wrote and published his book just before the American Revolution and the subsequent industrial revolution, his primary concerns are farming and agriculture. In earlier sections of *Wealth of Nations*, Smith focused on metal—silver and gold—as a measure of wealth, then later on corn (by which he usually meant wheat or barley) as a measure of wealth. In this selection, he is more emphatic about land as a convenient instrument of wealth.

His primary point is related to what he sees as a natural progression. People in the country have land on which they plant crops, which they sell, in part, to people in the town. The people in the town, lacking land but possessing skills such as weaving, building, and the like, create a market for the goods from the country. They take the product of the land and, with the surplus beyond their daily needs for food and sustenance, manufacture useful goods. In turn, they sell the desirable goods to people in the country, and both manage to accumulate wealth in the process. In this view the manufactures of the town are important but by no means as essential as the food that sustains the nation. Indeed, Smith regards surplus production as the key to the move toward wealth, which accumulates into opulence.

It is interesting that Smith does not emphasize the trade of goods among nations. He does emphasize the fact that the interchange between the country and the town in England also has a counterpart in international trade. However, Smith seems a bit uneasy in contemplating the usefulness of international trade as a means to accumulate wealth. Land, he reminds the reader, is secure, controllable, and not likely to yield to the whimsy of foul winds, leaky ships, or dishonest foreign merchants. One realizes that regardless of what he might say in praise of other possibilities, Smith himself would likely prefer a life in the country on a spread of his own land, collecting rent from tenants who produce food and flax and other goods that help him accumulate wealth.

Smith's Rhetoric

Adam Smith is widely regarded as one of the most influential economic thinkers of the eighteenth century. His *Wealth of Nations* is a gigantic book with many complex arguments regarding the nature of money and the role of capital in trade. This selection is a relatively straightforward statement regarding what he feels is the usual progress that all nations experience in the creation and accumulation of wealth. However, the normal eighteenth-century paragraph is much longer than those of today. By the same token, the normal eighteenth-century sentence is more complex in structure than we are used to today. For that reason, many readers will pause for reflection as they read Smith's work.

Still, his sentences are ultimately clear and direct. His opening sentence, for example, is a mighty declaration: "The great commerce of every civilized society, is that carried on between the inhabitants of the town and those of the country." In this sentence Smith makes a clear pronouncement, a statement about *every* society. Such a sweeping generalization is likely to invite attack and skepticism, but he feels totally secure in his assertion and proceeds to argue his position point by point.

On a more modest note, when Smith says, "Upon equal, or nearly equal profits, most men will choose to employ their capitals rather in the improvement and cultivation of land, than either in manufactures or in foreign trade" (para. 3), he expects the reader to see the simple wisdom of trusting the land and distrusting instruments of trade. However, many readers — even in his own time — would see this sentence as revealing a personal preference rather than a general rule. Even in the eighteenth century, many merchants were growing rich by ignoring land and trusting trade on the high seas.

Smith's view on this issue reflects an aspect of his conservatism, a stance that remains recognizably conservative even by today's standards. Nevertheless, his principles have guided traders as well as farmers for more than two hundred years. In his time, the workers in agriculture outnumbered workers in manufactures by a factor of eighty or ninety. But today, workers in agriculture have decreased progressively since the industrial revolution. Now, as a result of more efficient farming methods, only two or three people out of a hundred work on farms producing food and other goods. It would be interesting to know how Smith might react to this dramatic shift in occupations.

In helping the reader to work through his argument, Smith includes inset "summaries" of the content of each paragraph. For paragraph 2, he includes two insets. The first—"*The cultivation of the country must be prior to the increase of the town*"—alerts the reader to look for his explanation of why this claim is true. The second inset—"*though the town may sometimes be distant from the country from which it derives its subsistence*"—helps readers focus on the implications of distances from agriculture and manufacture for the local population. Those who grow corn nearest the city will make more money than those who live at a distance and must pay for its transportation to market. It is interesting to note that later ages developed relatively inexpensive means of transport—such as canals and railroads—to even out the cost of carriage in relation to fixed prices.

Smith depends on the clear, step-by-step argument to hold the attention of his reader. He establishes and examines each major point, clarifies his own position, then moves on to the next related point. For example, he talks about nations with uncultivated land, or large areas of land, and how the procedure he outlines works. Then he introduces the situation of a nation that has no uncultivated land available or land available only at very high cost. Under such circumstances, people will turn to manufacture but not rely on selling their products locally. In those conditions, they will risk foreign sales.

It is also worth noting that when Smith talks about the American colonies, he reminds the reader that there is plenty of land for people to work. As a result, little or no manufacture is produced for sale abroad. He sees this as an indication that the Americans are fiercely independent, demanding land of their own so as to guarantee that they will have adequate sustenance in the future. Throughout the selection Smith establishes a clear sense of the progress of nations toward the accumulation of wealth, and he provides the reader with a blueprint for financial success.

PREREADING QUESTIONS:
WHAT TO READ FOR

The following prereading questions may help you anticipate key issues in the discussion of Adam Smith's "Of the Natural Progress of Opulence."

Keeping them in mind during your first reading of the selection should help focus your attention.

- What is the nature of the commerce between the country and the town?
- What does Smith think is the natural order of things in the development of commerce?

Of the Natural Progress of Opulence

The great commerce is that between town and country, which is obviously advantageous to both.

The great commerce of every civilized society, is 1 that carried on between the inhabitants of the town and those of the country. It consists in the exchange of rude for manufactured produce, either immediately, or by the intervention of money, or of some sort of paper which represents money. The country supplies the town with the means of subsistence, and the materials of manufacture. The town repays this supply by sending back a part of the manufactured produce to the inhabitants of the country. The town, in which there neither is nor can be any reproduction of substances, may very properly be said to gain its whole wealth and subsistence from the country. We must not, however, upon this account, imagine that the gain of the town is the loss of the country. The gains of both are mutual and reciprocal, and the division of labor is in this, as in all other cases, advantageous to all the different persons employed in the various occupations into which it is subdivided. The inhabitants of the country purchase of the town a greater quantity of manufactured goods, with the produce of a much smaller quantity of their own labor, than they must have employed had they attempted to prepare them themselves. The town affords a market for the surplus produce of the country, or what is over and above the maintenance of the cultivators, and it is there that the inhabitants of the country exchange it for something else which is in demand among them. The greater the number and revenue of the inhabitants of the town, the more extensive is the market which it affords to those of the country; and the more extensive that market, it is always the more advantageous to a great number. The corn which grows within a mile of the town, sells there for the same price with that which comes from twenty miles distance. But the price of the latter must, generally, not only pay the expence of raising and bringing it to market, but afford too the ordinary profits of agriculture to the farmer. The proprietors and cultivators of the country, therefore, which lies in the neighborhood of the town, over and above the ordinary profits of agriculture, gain, in the price of what they sell, the whole value of the carriage of the like produce that is brought from more distant parts, and they save, besides, the whole value of this carriage in the price of what they buy. Compare the cultivation of the lands in the neighborhood of any considerable town, with that of those which lie at some distance from it, and you will easily satisfy yourself how much the country is benefited by the commerce of the town. Among all the absurd speculations that have been propagated concerning the balance of trade, it has never been pretended that either the country loses by its commerce with the town, or the town by that with the country which maintains it.

The cultivation of the country must be prior to the increase of the town,

As subsistence is, in the nature of things, prior 2 to conveniency and luxury, so the industry which procures the former, must necessarily be prior to that which ministers to the latter. The cultivation and improvement of the country, therefore, which affords subsistence, must, necessarily, be prior to the increase of the town, which furnishes only the means of conveniency and luxury. It is the surplus produce of the country only, or what is over and above the maintenance of the cultivators, that constitutes the subsistence of the town, which can therefore increase only with the increase of this surplus produce. The town, indeed, may not always derive its whole subsistence from the country in its neighborhood, or even from the territory to which it belongs, but from very distant countries; and this, though it forms no exception from the general rule, has occasioned considerable variations in the progress of opulence in different ages and nations.

though the town may sometimes be distant from the country from which it derives its subsistence.

That order of things which necessity imposes in 3 general, though not in every particular country, is,

This order of things is favored by the natural preference of man for agriculture.

in every particular country, promoted by the natural inclinations of man. If human institutions had never thwarted those natural inclinations, the towns could no-where have increased beyond what the improvement and cultivation of the territory in which they were situated could support; till such time, at least, as the whole of that territory was completely cultivated and improved. Upon equal, or nearly equal profits, most men will choose to employ their capitals rather in the improvement and cultivation of land, than either in manufactures or in foreign trade. The man who employs his capital in land, has it more under his view and command, and his fortune is much less liable to accidents, than that of the trader, who is obliged frequently to commit it, not only to the winds and the waves, but to the more uncertain elements of human folly and injustice, by giving great credits in distant countries to men, with whose character and situation he can seldom be thoroughly acquainted. The capital of the landlord, on the contrary, which is fixed in the improvement of his land, seems to be as well secured as the nature of human affairs can admit of. The beauty of the country besides, the pleasures of a country life, the tranquillity of mind which it promises, and wherever the injustice of human laws does not disturb it, the independency which it really affords, have charms that more or less attract every body; and as to cultivate the ground was the original destination of man, so in every stage of his existence he seems to retain a predilection for this primitive employment.

Cultivators require the assistance of artificers, who settle together and form a village, and their employment augments with the improvement of the country.

Without the assistance of some artificers, indeed, 4 the cultivation of land cannot be carried on, but with great inconveniency and continual interruption. Smiths, carpenters, wheel-wrights, and plough-wrights, masons, and bricklayers, tanners, shoemakers, and tailors, are people, whose service the farmer has frequent occasion for. Such artificers too stand, occasionally, in need of the assistance of one another; and as their residence is not, like that of the farmer, necessarily tied down to a precise spot, they naturally settle in the neighborhood of one another, and thus form a small town or village. The butcher, the brewer, and the baker, soon join them, together with many other artificers and retailers, necessary or useful for supplying their occasional wants, and who contribute still further to augment the town. The inhabitants of the town and those of the country are mutually the servants of one another. The town is a continual fair or market, to which the inhabitants of the country resort in order to exchange their rude for manufactured produce. It is this commerce which supplies the inhabitants of the town both with the materials of their work, and the means of their subsistence. The quantity of the finished work which they sell to the inhabitants of the country, necessarily regulates the quantity of the materials and provisions which they buy. Neither their employment nor subsistence, therefore, can augment, but in proportion to the augmentation of the demand from the country for finished work; and this demand can augment only in proportion to the extension of improvement and cultivation. Had human institutions, therefore, never disturbed the natural course of things, the progressive wealth and increase of the towns would, in every political society, be consequential, and in proportion to the improvement and cultivation of the territory or country.

In the American colonies an artificer who has acquired sufficient stock becomes a planter instead of manufacturing for distant sale,

In our North American colonies, where unculti- 5 vated land is still to be had upon easy terms, no manufactures for distant sale have ever yet been established in any of their towns. When an artificer has acquired a little more stock than is necessary for carrying on his own business in supplying the neighboring country, he does not, in North America, attempt to establish with it a manufacture for more distant sale, but employs it in the purchase and improvement of uncultivated land. From artificer he becomes planter, and neither the large wages nor the easy subsistence which that country affords to artificers, can bribe him rather to work for other people than for himself. He feels that an artificer is the servant of his customers, from whom he derives his subsistence; but that a planter who cultivates his own land, and derives his necessary subsistence from the labor of his own family, is really a master, and independent of all the world.

as in countries where no uncultivated land can be procured.

In countries, on the contrary, where there is 6 either no uncultivated land, or none that can be had upon easy terms, every artificer who has acquired more stock than he can employ in the occasional jobs of the neighborhood, endeavors to prepare work for more distant sale. The smith erects some sort of iron, the weaver some sort of linen or woollen manufactory. Those different manufactures come, in process of time, to be gradually subdivided, and thereby improved and refined in a great variety of ways, which may easily be conceived, and which it is therefore unnecessary to explain any further.

Manufactures are naturally preferred to foreign commerce.

In seeking for employment to a capital, manufactures are, upon equal or nearly equal profits, naturally preferred to foreign commerce, for the same reason that agriculture is naturally preferred to manufactures. As the capital of the landlord or farmer is more secure than that of the manufacturer, so the capital of the manufacturer, being at all times more within his view and command, is more secure than that of the foreign merchant. In every period, indeed, of every society, the surplus part both of the rude and manufactured produce, or that for which there is no demand at home, must be sent abroad in order to be exchanged for something for which there is some demand at home. But whether the capital, which carries this surplus produce abroad, be a foreign or a domestic one, is of very little importance. If the society has not acquired sufficient capital both to cultivate all its lands, and to manufacture in the completest manner the whole of its rude produce, there is even a considerable advantage that that rude produce should be exported by a foreign capital, in order that the whole stock of the society may be employed in more useful purposes. The wealth of ancient Egypt, that of China and Indostan, sufficiently demonstrate that a nation may attain a very high degree of opulence, though the greater part of its exportation trade be carried on by foreigners. The progress of our North American and West Indian colonies would have been much less rapid, had no capital but what belonged to themselves been employed in exporting their surplus produce. 7

So the natural course of things is first agriculture,

According to the natural course of things, therefore, the greater part of the capital of every growing society is, first, directed to agriculture, afterwards to manufactures, and last of all to foreign commerce. 8

*then
manufactures,
and finally
foreign
commerce.*

This order of things is so very natural, that in every society that had any territory, it has always, I believe, been in some degree observed. Some of their lands must have been cultivated before any considerable towns could be established, and some sort of coarse industry of the manufacturing kind must have been carried on in those towns, before they could well think of employing themselves in foreign commerce.

*But this order
has been in
many respects
inverted.*

But though this natural order of things must have   9
taken place in some degree in every such society, it has, in all the modern states of Europe, been, in many respects, entirely inverted. The foreign commerce of some of their cities has introduced all their finer manufactures, or such as were fit for distant sale; and manufactures and foreign commerce together, have given birth to the principal improvements of agriculture. The manners and customs which the nature of their original government introduced, and which remained after that government was greatly altered, necessarily forced them into this unnatural and retrograde order.

QUESTIONS FOR CRITICAL READING

1. How does manufacture eventually help agriculture?
2. Why is it more important to cultivate land than foreign trade?
3. What is special about the civilizations of Egypt, China, and Indostan?
4. Why did the American and West Indian colonies grow so rapidly?
5. In unpopulated countries, what is the natural way people treat the land?
6. How do the town manufactures profit from the country's surplus goods?
7. What is an artificer?

SUGGESTIONS FOR CRITICAL WRITING

1. Explain how you know that Smith favors country living over town life. What seems to be his opinion of each way of living?
2. Explain what Smith means by "subsistence is, in the nature of things, prior to conveniency and luxury, so the industry which procures the former, must necessarily be prior to that which ministers to the latter" (para. 2). Smith makes this claim several times. Is he correct even today?
3. Examine Smith's discussion and write an essay that takes issue with his conclusions. Base your argument on the changes that have occurred in

world economy since Smith's time. How have things changed economically to render his arguments less valid or less applicable?

4. In paragraph 3, Smith talks about the "natural inclinations of man." What are they? What relevance do they have to Smith's argument? Have man's "natural inclinations" changed substantially since Smith wrote *Wealth of Nations*?

5. Smith says, "The town affords a market for the surplus produce of the country" (para. 1). What does he mean by this statement? Is it still true today? What are the implications of this statement for the theories that Smith attempts to establish? Why is a surplus essential for his theory on the natural progress of opulence to be persuasive?

6. **CONNECTIONS**   Examine Thomas Jefferson's Declaration of Independence (p. 259) for issues that relate well to the questions that Smith raises. What are the economic and capitalist underpinnings of Jefferson's statements? In what ways does Jefferson agree or disagree with Smith's concepts of the development of opulence?

7. **CONNECTIONS**   Smith is the most important theorist of capitalism prior to the twentieth century. How do his ideas contrast with Karl Marx's views (p. 453) about capitalism and how capitalists work? What would Marx take issue with in Smith's argument? What can you tell about the nature of capitalism in the worlds of Adam Smith in 1776 and of Karl Marx in 1850?

8. **CONNECTIONS**   How does Adam Smith's concept of a natural progress of opulence agree with Milton and Rose Friedman's ideas about the equality of opportunity in the marketplace (**bedfordstmartins .com/worldofideas/epages**)? Do both agree that some people in a society will naturally become wealthy while others will naturally become poor? To what extent do the authors agree that a distinction between the wealthy and the poor is a natural outcome of any society? How comfortable do you think Smith would be in accepting the Friedmans' arguments? Which arguments might he reject?

9. **CONNECTIONS**   How does Robert B. Reich's analysis of the "new economy" (p. 513) alter the basic wisdom of Smith's views on the natural progress of an economy's development from agriculture to manufactures to foreign trade? What novelties in the "new economy" alter your view of Smith's theory?

10. **SEEING CONNECTIONS**   Smith talks extensively about land, agriculture, and manufacturing. Were he to see *The Thankful Poor* (p. 438), what would he have imagined the people in Tanner's painting did for a living? Would he have thought they owned land? Would he have thought they worked in agriculture? Or would he have thought they worked in manufacturing? What evidence in the painting might suggest one or another of these possibilities? Smith is concerned with the production of wealth and tries to help people understand how to do it. What would his advice to the old man and the young boy be? What would he have said about the likelihood of these people achieving wealth?

KARL MARX
The Communist Manifesto

KARL MARX (1818–1883) was born in Germany to Jewish parents who converted to Lutheranism. A scholarly man, Marx studied literature and philosophy, ultimately earning a doctorate in philosophy at the University of Jena. After being denied a university position, however, he turned to journalism to earn a living.

Soon after beginning his journalistic career, Marx came into conflict with Prussian authorities because of his radical social views, and after a period of exile in Paris he moved to Brussels. After several more moves, Marx found his way to London, where he finally settled in absolute poverty; his friend Friedrich Engels (1820–1895) contributed money to prevent Marx and his family from starving. During this time in London, Marx wrote the books for which he is famous while also writing for and editing newspapers. His contributions to the *New York Daily Tribune* number over three hundred items between the years 1851 and 1862.

Marx is best known for his theories of socialism, as expressed in *The Communist Manifesto* (1848) — which, like much of his important work, was written with Engels's help — and in the three-volume *Das Kapital* (*Capital*), the first volume of which was published in 1867. In his own lifetime, he was not well known, nor were his ideas widely debated. Yet he was part of an ongoing movement composed mainly of intellectuals. Vladimir Lenin (1870–1924) was a disciple whose triumph in the Russian Revolution of 1917 catapulted Marx to the forefront of world thought. Since 1917, Marx's thinking has been scrupulously analyzed, debated, and argued. Capitalist thinkers have found him unconvincing, whereas Communist thinkers have found him a prophet and keen analyst of social structures.

Translated by Samuel Moore. Part III of *The Communist Manifesto*, "Socialist and Communist Literature," is omitted here.

In England, Marx's studies centered on the concept of an ongoing class struggle between those who owned property—the bourgeoisie—and those who owned nothing but whose work produced wealth—the proletariat. Marx was concerned with the forces of history, and his view of history was that it is progressive and, to an extent, inevitable. This view is prominent in *The Communist Manifesto*, particularly in Marx's review of the overthrow of feudal forms of government by the bourgeoisie. He thought it inevitable that the bourgeoisie and the proletariat would engage in a class struggle, from which the proletariat would emerge victorious. In essence, Marx took a materialist position. He denied the providence of God in the affairs of humans and defended the view that economic institutions evolve naturally and that, in their evolution, they control the social order. Thus, communism was an inevitable part of the process, and in the *Manifesto* he worked to clarify the reasons for its inevitability.

One of Marx's primary contentions was that capital is "not a personal, it is a social power" (para. 78). Thus, according to Marx, the "past dominates the present" (para. 83) because the accumulation of past capital determines how people will live in the present society. Capitalist economists, however, see capital as a personal power, but a power that, as John Kenneth Galbraith might say, should be used in a socially responsible way.

Marx's Rhetoric

The selection included here omits one section, the least important for the modern reader. The first section has a relatively simple rhetorical structure that depends on comparison. The title, "Bourgeois and Proletarians," tells us that the section will clarify the nature of each class and then go on to make some comparisons and contrasts. These concepts were by no means as widely discussed or thought about in 1848 as they are today, so Marx is careful to define his terms. At the same time, he establishes his theories regarding history by making further comparisons with class struggles in earlier ages.

Marx's style is simple and direct. He moves steadily from point to point, establishing his views on the nature of classes, on the nature of bourgeois society, and on the questions of industrialism and its effects on modern society. He considers wealth, worth, nationality, production, agriculture, and machinery. Each point is addressed in turn, usually in its own paragraph.

The organization of the next section, "Proletarians and Communists" (paras. 60–133), is not, despite its title, comparative in nature. Rather, with the proletariat defined as the class of the future, Marx tries to show that the Communist cause is the proletarian cause. In the process, Marx uses a clever rhetorical strategy. He assumes that he is addressed by an antagonist—presumably a bourgeois or a proletarian who is in sympathy with the bourgeoisie. He then proceeds to answer each popular complaint against communism. He shows that it is not a party separate from other workers' parties (para. 61). He clarifies the question of abolishing existing property relations (paras. 68–93). He emphasizes the antagonism between capital and wage labor (para. 76); he discusses the disappearance of culture (para. 94); he clarifies the questions of the family (paras. 98–100) and of the exploitation of children (para. 101). He brings up the new system of public education (paras. 102–4). He raises the touchy issue of the "community of women" (paras. 105–10), as well as the charge that Communists want to abolish nations (paras. 111–15). He brushes aside religion (para. 116). When he is done with the complaints, he gives us a rhetorical signal: "But let us have done with the bourgeois objections to Communism" (para. 126).

The rest of the second section contains a brief summary, and then Marx presents his ten-point program (para. 131). The structure is simple, direct, and effective. In the process of answering the charges against communism, Marx is able to clarify exactly what it is and what it promises. In contrast to his earlier arguments, the ten points of his Communist program seem clear, easy, and (again by contrast) almost acceptable. Although the style is not dashing (despite a few memorable lines), the rhetorical structure is extraordinarily effective for the purposes at hand.

In the last section (paras. 135–45), in which Marx compares the Communists with other reform groups such as those agitating for redistribution of land and other agrarian reforms, he indicates that the Communists are everywhere fighting alongside existing groups for the rights of people who are oppressed by their societies. As Marx says, "In short, the Communists everywhere support every revolutionary movement against the existing social and political order of things" (para. 141). Nothing could be a more plain and direct declaration of sympathies.

PREREADING QUESTIONS: WHAT TO READ FOR

The following prereading questions may help you anticipate key issues in the discussion of Karl Marx's *Communist Manifesto*. Keeping them in mind during your first reading of the selection should help focus your attention.

- What is the economic condition of the bourgeoisie? What is the economic condition of the proletariat?

- How does the expanding world market for goods affect national identity?
- What benefits does Marx expect communism to provide the proletariat?

The Communist Manifesto

A specter is haunting Europe—the specter of Communism. All [1] the Powers of old Europe have entered into a holy alliance to exorcise this specter; Pope and Czar, Metternich[1] and Guizot,[2] French Radicals[3] and German police-spies.

Where is the party in opposition that has not been decried as [2] communistic by its opponents in power? Where is the opposition that has not hurled back the branding reproach of Communism against the more advanced opposition parties, as well as against its reactionary adversaries?

Two things result from this fact. [3]

I. Communism is already acknowledged by all European Powers [4] to be itself a Power.

II. It is high time that Communists should openly, in the face of [5] the whole world, publish their views, their aims, their tendencies, and meet this nursery tale of the specter of Communism with a Manifesto of the party itself.

To this end, Communists of various nationalities have assembled [6] in London and sketched the following Manifesto, to be published in the English, French, German, Italian, Flemish, and Danish languages.

Bourgeois and Proletarians[4]

The history of all hitherto existing society is the history of class [7] struggles.

---

[1]**Prince Klemens von Metternich (1773–1859)** Foreign minister of Austria (1809–1848), who had a hand in establishing the peace after the final defeat in 1815 of Napoleon (1769–1821); Metternich was highly influential in the crucial Congress of Vienna (1814–1815).

[2]**François Pierre Guizot (1787–1874)** Conservative French statesman, author, and philosopher. Like Metternich, he was opposed to communism.

[3]**French Radicals** Actually middle-class liberals who wanted a return to a republic in 1848 after the eighteen-year reign of Louis-Philippe (1773–1850), the "citizen king."

[4]By bourgeois is meant the class of modern Capitalists, owners of the means of social production and employers of wage labor. By proletarians, the class of modern wage laborers who, having no means of production of their own, are reduced to selling their labor-power in order to live. [Engels's note]

Freeman and slave, patrician and plebeian, lord and serf, guild- 8
master and journeyman, in a word, oppressor and oppressed, stood in
constant opposition to one another, carried on uninterrupted, now hidden, now open fight, a fight that each time ended, either in a revolutionary
re-constitution of society at large, or in the common ruin of the contending classes.

In the earlier epochs of history we find almost everywhere a 9
complicated arrangement of society into various orders, a mani-
fold gradation of social rank. In ancient Rome we have patricians,
knights, plebeians, slaves; in the Middle Ages, feudal lords, vassals,
guild-masters, journeymen, apprentices, serfs; in almost all of these
classes, again, subordinate gradations.

The modern bourgeois society that has sprouted from the ruins of 10
feudal society, has not done away with class antagonisms. It has but
established new classes, new conditions of oppression, new forms of
struggle in place of the old ones.

Our epoch, the epoch of the bourgeoisie, possesses, however, this 11
distinctive feature; it has simplified the class antagonisms. Society as a
whole is more and more splitting up into two great hostile camps, into
two great classes directly facing each other: Bourgeoisie and Proletariat.

From the serfs of the Middle Ages sprang the chartered burghers 12
of the earliest towns. From these burgesses the first elements of the
bourgeoisie were developed.

The discovery of America, the rounding of the Cape,[5] opened up 13
fresh ground for the rising bourgeoisie. The East Indian and Chinese
markets, the colonization of America, trade with the colonies, the
increase in the means of exchange and in commodities generally,
gave to commerce, to navigation, to industry, an impulse never before
known, and thereby, to the revolutionary element in the tottering feudal society, a rapid development.

The feudal system of industry, under which industrial produc- 14
tion was monopolized by closed guilds, now no longer sufficed for
the growing wants of the new market. The manufacturing system took
its place. The guild-masters were pushed on one side by the manufacturing middle-class: division of labor between the different corporate
guilds vanished in the face of division of labor in each single workshop.

Meantime the markets kept ever growing, the demand ever rising. 15
Even manufacture no longer sufficed. Thereupon, steam and machinery
revolutionized industrial production. The place of manufacture was
taken by the giant, Modern Industry, the place of the industrial

---

[5] **the Cape** The Cape of Good Hope, at the southern tip of Africa. This was a
main sea route for trade with India and the Orient. Europe profited immensely from
the opening up of these new markets in the sixteenth century.

middle-class, by industrial millionaires, the leaders of whole industrial armies, the modern bourgeois.

Modern industry has established the world-market, for which   16
the discovery of America paved the way. This market has given an immense development to commerce, to navigation, to communication by land. This development has, in its turn, reacted on the extension of industry; and in proportion as industry, commerce, navigation, railways extended, in the same proportion the bourgeoisie developed, increased its capital, and pushed into the background every class handed down from the Middle Ages.

We see, therefore, how the modern bourgeoisie is itself the prod-   17
uct of a long course of development, of a series of revolutions in the modes of production and of exchange.

Each step in the development of the bourgeoisie was accompanied   18
by a corresponding political advance of that class. An oppressed class under the sway of the feudal nobility, an armed and self-governing association in the medieval commune,[6] here independent urban repub-lic (as in Italy and Germany), there taxable "third estate"[7] of the mon-archy (as in France), afterwards, in the period of manufacture proper, serving either the semi-feudal or the absolute monarchy as a counter-poise against nobility, and, in fact, corner stone of the great monar-chies in general, the bourgeoisie has at last, since the establishment of Modern Industry and of the world-market, conquered for itself, in the modern representative State, exclusive political sway. The executive of the modern State is but a committee for managing the common affairs of the whole bourgeoisie.

The bourgeoisie, historically, has played a most revolutionary part.   19

The bourgeoisie, wherever it has got the upper hand, has put an   20
end to all feudal, patriarchal, idyllic relations. It has pitilessly torn asunder the motley feudal ties that bound man to his "natural supe-riors," and has left no other nexus between man and man than naked self-interest, than callous "cash payment." It has drowned the most heavenly ecstasies of religious fervor,[8] of chivalrous enthusiasm, of

---

[6] **the medieval commune** Refers to the growth in the eleventh century of towns whose economy was highly regulated by mutual interest and agreement.

[7] **"third estate"** The clergy was the first estate, the aristocracy the second estate, and the bourgeoisie the third estate.

[8] **religious fervor** This and other terms in this sentence contain a compressed historical observation. "Religious fervor" refers to the Middle Ages; "chivalrous enthusiasm" refers to the rise of the secular state and to the military power of knights; "Philistine sentimentalism" refers to the development of popular arts and literature in the sixteenth, seventeenth, and eighteenth centuries. "Philistine" refers to those who were generally uncultured, that is, the general public. "Sentimentalism" is a code word for the encouragement of emotional response rather than rational thought.

Philistine sentimentalism, in the icy water of egotistical calculation. It has resolved personal worth into exchange value, and in place of the numberless indefeasible chartered freedoms, has set up that single, unconscionable freedom—Free Trade. In one word, for exploitation, veiled by religious and political illusions, it has substituted naked, shameless, direct, brutal exploitation.

21   The bourgeoisie has stripped of its halo every occupation hitherto honored and looked up to with reverent awe. It has converted the physician, the lawyer, the priest, the poet, the man of science, into its paid wage laborers.

22   The bourgeoisie has torn away from the family its sentimental veil, and has reduced the family relation to a mere money relation.

23   The bourgeoisie has disclosed how it came to pass that the brutal display of vigor in the Middle Ages, which reactionists so much admire, found its fitting complement in the most slothful indolence. It has been the first to show what man's activity can bring about. It has accomplished wonders far surpassing Egyptian pyramids, Roman aqueducts, and Gothic cathedrals; it has conducted expeditions that put in the shade all former Exoduses of nations and crusades.

24   The bourgeoisie cannot exist without constantly revolutionizing the instruments of production, and thereby the relations of production, and with them the whole relations of society. Conservation of the old modes of production in unaltered form was, on the contrary, the first condition of existence for all earlier industrial classes. Constant revolutionizing of production, uninterrupted disturbance of all social conditions, everlasting uncertainty and agitation distinguish the bourgeois epoch from all earlier ones. All fixed, fast frozen relations, with their train of ancient and venerable prejudices and opinions, are swept away, all new formed ones become antiquated before they can ossify. All that is solid melts into the air, all that is holy is profaned, and man is at last compelled to face with sober senses, his real conditions of life, and his relations with his kind.

25   The need of a constantly expanding market for its products chases the bourgeoisie over the whole surface of the globe. It must nestle everywhere, settle everywhere, establish connections everywhere.

26   The bourgeoisie has through its exploitation of the world-market given a cosmopolitan character to production and consumption in every country. To the great chagrin of reactionists, it has drawn from under the feet of industry the national ground on which it stood. All old-established national industries have been destroyed or are daily being destroyed. They are dislodged by new industries, whose introduction becomes a life and death question for all civilized nations, by industries that no longer work up indigenous raw material, but raw

material drawn from the remotest zones; industries whose products are consumed, not only at home, but in every quarter of the globe. In place of the old wants, satisfied by the productions of the country, we find new wants, requiring for their satisfaction the products of distant lands and climes. In place of the old local and national seclusion and self-sufficiency, we have intercourse in every direction, universal interdependence of nations. And as in material, so also in intellectual production. The intellectual creations of individual nations become common property. National onesidedness and narrowmindedness become more and more impossible, and from the numerous national and local literatures there arises a world-literature.

The bourgeoisie, by the rapid improvement of all instruments   27 of production, by the immensely facilitated means of communication, draws all, even the most barbarian nations into civilization. The cheap prices of its commodities are the heavy artillery with which it batters down all Chinese walls, with which it forces the barbarians' intensely obstinate hatred of foreigners to capitulate. It compels all nations, on pain of extinction, to adopt the bourgeois mode of production; it compels them to introduce what it calls civilization into their midst, i.e., to become bourgeois themselves. In a word, it creates a world after its own image.

The bourgeoisie has subjected the country to the rule of the   28 towns. It has created enormous cities, has greatly increased the urban population as compared with the rural and has thus rescued a considerable part of the population from the idiocy of rural life. Just as it has made the country dependent on the towns, so it has made barbarian and semi-barbarian countries dependent on civilized ones, nations of peasants on nations of bourgeois, the East on the West.

The bourgeoisie keeps more and more doing away with the scat-   29 tered state of the population, of the means of production, and of property. It has agglomerated population, centralized means of production, and has concentrated property in a few hands. The necessary consequence of this was political centralization. Independent, or but loosely connected provinces, with separate interests, laws, governments, and systems of taxation, became lumped together in one nation, with one government, one code of laws, one national class interest, one frontier, and one customs tariff.

The bourgeoisie, during its rule of scarce one hundred years,   30 has created more massive and more colossal productive forces than have all preceding generations together. Subjection of Nature's forces to man, machinery, application of chemistry to industry and agriculture, steam-navigation, railways, electric telegraphs, clearing of whole continents for cultivation, canalization of rivers, whole populations conjured out of the ground — what earlier century had even a presentiment that such productive forces slumbered in the lap of social labor?

We see then: the means of production and of exchange on whose foundation the bourgeoisie built itself up, were generated in feudal society. At a certain stage in the development of these means of production and of exchange, the conditions under which feudal society produced and exchanged, the feudal organization of agriculture and manufacturing industry, in one word, the feudal relations of property became no longer compatible with the already developed productive forces; they became so many fetters. They had to burst asunder; they were burst asunder.

Into their place stepped free competition, accompanied by a social and political constitution adapted to it, and by the economical and political sway of the bourgeois class.

A similar movement is going on before our own eyes. Modern bourgeois society with its relations of production, of exchange and of property, a society that has conjured up such gigantic means of production and of exchange, is like the sorcerer, who is no longer able to control the powers of the nether world whom he has called up by his spells. For many a decade past, the history of industry and commerce is but the history of the revolt of modern productive forces against modern conditions of production, against the property relations that are the conditions for the existence of the bourgeoisie and of its rule. It is enough to mention the commercial crises that by their periodical return put on its trial, each time more threateningly, the existence of the entire bourgeois society. In these crises a great part not only of the existing products, but also of the previously created productive forces, are periodically destroyed. In these crises there breaks out an epidemic that, in all earlier epochs, would have seemed an absurdity—the epidemic of overproduction. Society suddenly finds itself put back into a state of momentary barbarism; it appears as if a famine, a universal war of devastation, had cut off the supply of every means of subsistence; industry and commerce seem to be destroyed; and why? Because there is too much civilization, too much means of subsistence, too much industry, too much commerce. The productive forces at the disposal of society no longer tend to further the development of the conditions of the bourgeois property; on the contrary, they have become too powerful for these conditions by which they are fettered, and as soon as they overcome these fetters they bring disorder into the whole of bourgeois society, endanger the existence of bourgeois property. The conditions of bourgeois society are too narrow to comprise the wealth created by them. And how does the bourgeoisie get over these crises? On the one hand by enforced destruction of a mass of productive forces; on the other, by the conquest of new markets, and by the more thorough exploitation of the old ones. That is to say, by paving the way for more extensive and more destructive crises, and by diminishing the means whereby crises are prevented.

The weapons with which the bourgeoisie felled feudalism to the ground are now turned against the bourgeoisie itself.   34

But not only has the bourgeoisie forged the weapons that bring death to itself; it has also called into existence the men who are to wield those weapons — the modern working class — the proletarians.   35

In proportion as the bourgeoisie, i.e., capital, is developed, in the same proportion is the proletariat, the modern working class, developed, a class of laborers who live only so long as they find work, and who find work only so long as their labor increases capital. These laborers, who must sell themselves piecemeal, are a commodity, like every other article of commerce, and are consequently exposed to all the vicissitudes of competition, to all the fluctuations of the market.   36

Owing to the extensive use of machinery and to division of labor, the work of the proletarians has lost all individual character, and, consequently, all charm for the workman. He becomes an appendage of the machine, and it is only the most simple, most monotonous, and most easily acquired knack that is required of him. Hence, the cost of production of a workman is restricted almost entirely to the means of subsistence that he requires for his maintenance, and for the propagation of his race. But the price of a commodity, and also of labor, is equal to its cost of production. In proportion, therefore, as the repulsiveness of the work increases the wage decreases. Nay more, in proportion as the use of machinery and division of labor increases, in the same proportion the burden of toil increases, whether by prolongation of the working hours, by increase of the work enacted in a given time, or by increased speed of the machinery, etc.   37

Modern industry has converted the little workshop of the patriarchal master into the great factory of the industrial capitalist. Masses of laborers, crowded into factories, are organized like soldiers. As privates of the industrial army they are placed under the command of a perfect hierarchy of officers and sergeants. Not only are they the slaves of the bourgeois class and of the bourgeois state, they are daily and hourly enslaved by the machine, by the overlooker, and, above all, by the individual bourgeois manufacturer himself. The more openly this despotism proclaims gain to be its end and aim, the more petty, the more hateful and the more embittering it is.   38

The less the skill and exertion or strength implied in manual labor, in other words, the more modern industry becomes developed,   39 the more is the labor of men superseded by that of women. Differences of age and sex have no longer any distinctive social validity for the working class. All are instruments of labor, more or less expensive to use, according to their age and sex.

No sooner is the exploitation of the laborer by the manufacturer, so far at an end, that he receives his wages in cash, than he is set upon by the other portions of the bourgeoisie, the landlord, the shopkeeper, the pawnbroker, etc.   40

The lower strata of the middle class—the small trades-people, shopkeepers and retired tradesmen generally, the handicraftsmen, and peasants—all these sink gradually into the proletariat, partly because their diminutive capital does not suffice for the scale on which Modern Industry is carried on, and is swamped in the competition with the large capitalists, partly because their specialized skill is rendered worthless by new methods of production. Thus the proletariat is recruited from all classes of the population.   41

The proletariat goes through various stages of development. With its birth begins its struggle with the bourgeoisie. At first the contest is carried on by individual laborers, then by the workpeople of a factory, then by the operatives of one trade, in one locality, against the individual bourgeois who directly exploits them. They direct their attacks not against the bourgeois conditions of production, but against the instruments of production themselves; they destroy imported wares that compete with their labor, they smash to pieces machinery, they set factories ablaze, they seek to restore by force the vanished status of the workman of the Middle Ages.   42

At this stage the laborers still form an incoherent mass scattered over the whole country, and broken up by their mutual competition. If anywhere they unite to form more compact bodies, this is not yet the consequence of their own active union, but of the union of the bourgeoisie, which class, in order to attain its own political ends, is compelled to set the whole proletariat in motion, and is moreover yet, for a time, able to do so. At this stage, therefore, the proletarians do not fight their enemies, but the enemies of their enemies, the remnants of absolute monarchy, the landowners, the non-industrial bourgeois, the petty bourgeoisie. Thus the whole historical movement is concentrated in the hands of the bourgeoisie, every victory so obtained is a victory for the bourgeoisie.   43

But with the development of industry the proletariat not only increases in number; it becomes concentrated in greater masses, its strength grows and it feels that strength more. The various interests and conditions of life within the ranks of the proletariat are more and more equalized, in proportion as machinery obliterates all distinctions of labor, and nearly everywhere reduces wages to the same low level.   44

The growing competition among the bourgeois, and the resulting commercial crisis, make the wages of the workers even more fluctuating. The unceasing improvement of machinery, ever more rapidly developing, makes their livelihood more and more precarious; the collisions between individual workmen and individual bourgeois take more and more the character of collisions between two classes. Thereupon the workers begin to form combinations (Trades' Unions)[9] against the bourgeois; they club together in order to keep up the rate of wages; they found permanent associations in order to make provision beforehand for these occasional revolts. Here and there the contest breaks out into riots.

Now and then the workers are victorious, but only for a time.   45
The real fruit of their battle lies not in the immediate result but in the ever-expanding union of workers. This union is helped on by the improved means of communication that are created by modern industry, and that places the workers of different localities in contact with one another. It was just this contact that was needed to centralize the numerous local struggles, all of the same character, into one national struggle between classes. But every class struggle is a political struggle. And that union, to attain which the burghers of the Middle Ages with their miserable highways, required centuries, the modern proletarians, thanks to railways, achieve in a few years.

This organization of the proletarians into a class, and conse-   46
quently into a political party, is continually being upset again by the competition between the workers themselves. But it ever rises up again, stronger, firmer, mightier. It compels legislative recognition of particular interests of the workers by taking advantage of the divisions among the bourgeoisie itself. Thus the ten hours' bill in England[10] was carried.

Altogether collisions between the classes of the old society fur-   47
ther, in many ways, the course of development of the proletariat. The bourgeoisie finds itself involved in a constant battle. At first with the aristocracy; later on, with those portions of the bourgeoisie itself whose interests have become antagonistic to the progress of industry; at all times, with the bourgeoisie of foreign countries. In all these

---

[9] **combinations (Trades' Unions)** The labor movement was only beginning in 1848. It consisted of trades' unions that started as social clubs but soon began agitating for labor reform. They represented an important step in the growth of socialism in Europe.
[10] **the ten hours' bill in England** This bill (1847) was an important labor reform. It limited the working day for women and children in factories to only ten hours, at a time when it was common for some people to work sixteen hours a day. The bill's passage was a result of political division, not of benevolence on the managers' part.

battles it sees itself compelled to appeal to the proletariat, to ask for its help, and thus, to drag it into the political arena. The bourgeoisie itself, therefore, supplies the proletariat with its own elements of political and general education; in other words, it furnishes the proletariat with weapons for fighting the bourgeoisie.

Further, as we have already seen, entire sections of the ruling   48
classes are, by the advance of industry, precipitated into the proletariat, or are at least threatened in their conditions of existence. These also supply the proletariat with fresh elements of enlightenment and progress.

Finally, in times when the class struggle nears the decisive   49
hour, the process of dissolution going on within the ruling class — in fact, within the whole range of an old society — assumes such a violent, glaring character that a small section of the ruling class cuts itself adrift and joins the revolutionary class, the class that holds the future in its hands. Just as, therefore, at an earlier period, a section of the nobility went over to the bourgeoisie, so now a portion of the bourgeoisie goes over to the proletariat, and in particular, a portion of the bourgeois ideologists, who have raised themselves to the level of comprehending theoretically the historical movements as a whole.

Of all the classes that stand face to face with the bourgeoisie today   50
the proletariat alone is a really revolutionary class. The other classes decay and finally disappear in the face of Modern Industry; the proletariat is its special and essential product.

The lower middle class, the small manufacturer, the shopkeeper,   51
the artisan, the peasant, all these fight against the bourgeoisie, to save from extinction their existence as fractions of the middle class. They are therefore not revolutionary, but conservative. Nay, more; they are reactionary, for they try to roll back the wheel of history. If by chance they are revolutionary, they are so only in view of their impending transfer into the proletariat; they thus defend not their present, but their future interests; they desert their own standpoint to place themselves at that of the proletariat.

The "dangerous class," the social scum, that passively rotting mass   52
thrown off by the lowest layers of old society, may, here and there, be swept into the movement by a proletarian revolution; its conditions of life, however, prepare it far more for the part of a bribed tool of reactionary intrigue.

In the conditions of the proletariat, those of the old society at large   53
are already virtually swamped. The proletarian is without property; his relation to his wife and children has no longer anything in common with the bourgeois family relations; modern industrial labor, modern subjection to capital, the same in England as in France, in America as

in Germany, has stripped him of every trace of national character. Law, morality, religion, are to him so many bourgeois prejudices, behind which lurk in ambush just as many bourgeois interests.

All the preceding classes that got the upper hand sought to for- 54 tify their already acquired status by subjecting society at large to their conditions of appropriation. The proletarians cannot become masters of the productive forces of society, except by abolishing their own previous mode of appropriation, and thereby also every other previous mode of appropriation. They have nothing of their own to secure and to fortify; their mission is to destroy all previous securities for and insurances of individual property.

All previous historical movements were movements of minori- 55 ties, or in the interest of minorities. The proletarian movement is the self-conscious, independent movement of the immense majority. The proletariat, the lowest stratum of our present society, cannot stir, cannot raise itself up without the whole superincumbent strata of official society being sprung into the air.

Though not in substance, yet in form, the struggle of the prole- 56 tariat with the bourgeoisie is at first a national struggle. The proletariat of each country must, of course, first of all settle matters with its own bourgeoisie.

In depicting the most general phases of the development of the 57 proletariat, we traced the more or less veiled civil war, raging within existing society, up to the point where that war breaks out into open revolution, and where the violent overthrow of the bourgeoisie, lays the foundations for the sway of the proletariat.

Hitherto every form of society has been based, as we have 58 already seen, on the antagonism of oppressing and oppressed classes. But in order to oppress a class, certain conditions must be assured to it under which it can, at least, continue its slavish existence. The serf, in the period of serfdom, raised himself to membership in the commune, just as the petty bourgeois, under the yoke of feudal absolutism, managed to develop into a bourgeois. The modern laborer, on the contrary, instead of rising with the progress of industry, sinks deeper and deeper below the conditions of existence of his own class. He becomes a pauper, and pauperism develops more rapidly than population and wealth. And here it becomes evident that the bourgeoisie is unfit any longer to be the ruling class in society, and to impose its conditions of existence upon society as an over-riding law. It is unfit to rule, because it is incompetent to assure an existence to its slave within his slavery, because it cannot help letting him sink into such a state that it has to feed him, instead of being fed by him. Society can no longer live under this bourgeoisie; in other words, its existence is no longer compatible with society.

The essential condition for the existence, and for the sway of the 59 bourgeois class, is the formation and augmentation of capital; the condition for capital is wage labor. Wage labor rests exclusively on competition between the laborers. The advance of industry, whose involuntary promoter is the bourgeoisie, replaces the isolation of the laborers, due to competition, by their involuntary combination, due to association. The development of Modern Industry, therefore, cuts from under its feet the very foundation on which the bourgeoisie produces and appropriates products. What the bourgeoisie therefore produces, above all, are its own grave diggers. Its fall and the victory of the proletariat are equally inevitable.

Proletarians and Communists

In what relation do the Communists stand to the proletarians as 60 a whole?

The Communists do not form a separate party opposed to other 61 working class parties.

They have no interests separate and apart from those of the prole- 62 tariat as a whole.

They do not set up any sectarian principles of their own, by 63 which to shape and mold the proletarian movement.

The Communists are distinguished from the other working class 64 parties by this only: 1. In the national struggles of the proletarians of the different countries, they point out and bring to the front the common interests of the entire proletariat, independently of all nationality. 2. In the various stages of development which the struggle of the working class against the bourgeoisie has to pass through, they always and everywhere represent the interests of the movement as a whole.

The Communists, therefore, are on the one hand practically the 65 most advanced and resolute section of the working class parties of every country, that section which pushes forward all others; on the other hand, theoretically, they have over the great mass of the proletariat the advantage of clearly understanding the line of march, the conditions, and the ultimate general results of the proletarian movement.

The immediate aim of the Communists is the same as that of all 66 the other proletarian parties: formation of the proletariat into a class, overthrow of the bourgeois of supremacy, conquest of political power by the proletariat.

The theoretical conclusions of the Communists are in no way 67 based on ideas or principles that have been invented or discovered by this or that would-be universal reformer.

They merely express, in general terms, actual relations springing 68 from an existing class struggle, from a historical movement going on under our very eyes. The abolition of existing property relations is not at all a distinctive feature of Communism.

All property relations in the past have continually been sub- 69 ject to historical change consequent upon the change in historical conditions.

The French Revolution, for example, abolished feudal property in 70 favor of bourgeois property.

The distinguishing feature of Communism is not the abolition 71 of property generally, but the abolition of bourgeois property. But modern bourgeois private property is the final and most complete expression of the system of producing and appropriating products, that is based on class antagonism, on the exploitation of the many by the few.

In this sense, the theory of the Communists may be summed up 72 in the single sentence: abolition of private property.

We Communists have been reproached with the desire of abol- 73 ishing the right of personally acquiring property as the fruit of a man's own labor, which property is alleged to be the groundwork of all personal freedom, activity, and independence.

Hard won, self-acquired, self-earned property! Do you mean 74 the property of the petty artisan and of the small peasant, a form of property that preceded the bourgeois form? There is no need to abolish that; the development of industry has to a great extent already destroyed it, and is still destroying it daily.

Or do you mean modern bourgeois private property? 75

But does wage labor create any property for the laborer? Not a bit. 76 It creates capital, i.e., that kind of property which exploits wage labor, and which cannot increase except upon condition of getting a new supply of wage labor for fresh exploitation. Property, in its present form, is based on the antagonism of capital and wage labor. Let us examine both sides of this antagonism.

To be a capitalist is to have not only a purely personal, but 77 a social status in production. Capital is a collective product, and only by the united action of many members, nay, in the last resort, only by the united action of all members of society, can it be set in motion.

Capital is therefore not a personal, it is a social power. 78

When, therefore, capital is converted into common property, 79 into the property of all members of society, personal property is not thereby transformed into social property. It is only the social character of the property that is changed. It loses its class character.

Let us now take wage labor. 80

The average price of wage labor is the minimum wage, i.e., that 81 quantum of the means of subsistence which is absolutely requisite to keep the laborer in bare existence as a laborer. What, therefore, the wage laborer appropriates by means of his labor, merely suffices to prolong and reproduce a bare existence. We by no means intend to abolish this personal appropriation of the products of labor, an appropriation that is made for the maintenance and reproduction of human life, and that leaves no surplus wherewith to command the labor of others. All that we want to do away with is the miserable character of this appropriation, under which the laborer lives merely to increase capital and is allowed to live only insofar as the interests of the ruling class require it.

In bourgeois society, living labor is but a means to increase 82 accumulated labor. In Communist society accumulated labor is but a means to widen, to enrich, to promote the existence of the laborer.

In bourgeois society, therefore, the past dominates the present; 83 in Communist society the present dominates the past. In bourgeois society, capital is independent and has individuality, while the living person is dependent and has no individuality.

And the abolition of this state of things is called by the bourgeois 84 abolition of individuality and freedom! And rightly so. The abolition of bourgeois individuality, bourgeois independence, and bourgeois freedom is undoubtedly aimed at.

By freedom is meant, under the present bourgeois conditions of 85 production, free trade, free selling and buying.

But if selling and buying disappears, free selling and buying 86 disappears also. This talk about free selling and buying, and all the other "brave words" of our bourgeoisie about freedom in general have a meaning, if any, only in contrast with restricted selling and buying, with the fettered traders of the Middle Ages, but have no meaning when opposed to the Communistic abolition of buying and selling, of the bourgeois conditions of production, and of the bourgeoisie itself.

You are horrified at our intending to do away with private property. But in your existing society private property is already done away with for nine-tenths of the population; its existence for the few is solely due to its nonexistence in the hands of those nine-tenths. You reproach us, therefore, with intending to do away with a form of property, the necessary condition for whose existence is the nonexistence of any property for the immense majority of society.

In one word, you reproach us with intending to do away with 88
your property. Precisely so: that is just what we intend.

From the moment when labor can no longer be converted into 89
capital, money, or rent, into a social power capable of being monopolized, i.e., from the moment when individual property can no longer
be transformed into bourgeois property, into capital, from that moment,
you say, individuality vanishes.

You must, therefore, confess that by "individual" you mean no 90
other person than the bourgeois, than the middle-class owner of
property. This person must, indeed, be swept out of the way and
made impossible.

Communism deprives no man of the power to appropriate the 91
products of society: all that it does is to deprive him of the power to
subjugate the labor of others by means of such appropriation.

It has been objected that upon the abolition of private property 92
all work will cease and universal laziness will overtake us.

According to this, bourgeois society ought long ago to have 93
gone to the dogs through sheer idleness; for those of its members
who work acquire nothing, and those who acquire anything do not
work. The whole of this objection is but another expression of the
tautology:[11] that there can no longer be any wage labor when there is
no longer any capital.

All objections urged against the Communistic mode of produc- 94
ing and appropriating material products have, in the same way, been
urged against the Communistic modes of producing and appropriating intellectual products. Just as, to the bourgeois, the disappearance
of class property is the disappearance of production itself, so the disappearance of class culture is to him identical with the disappearance
of all culture.

That culture, the loss of which he laments, is, for the enormous 95
majority, a mere training to act as a machine.

But don't wrangle with us so long as you apply, to our intended 96
abolition of bourgeois property, the standard of your bourgeois
notions of freedom, culture, law, etc. Your very ideas are but the outgrowth of the conditions of your bourgeois production and bourgeois
property, just as your jurisprudence is but the will of your class made
into a law for all, a will whose essential character and direction are
determined by the economical conditions of existence of your class.

The selfish misconception that induces you to transform into 97
eternal laws of nature and of reason the social forms springing from

---

[11] **tautology** A statement whose two parts say essentially the same thing. The
second half of the previous sentence is a tautology.

your present mode of production and form of property—historical relations that rise and disappear in the progress of production—this misconception you share with every ruling class that has preceded you. What you see clearly in the case of ancient property, what you admit in the case of feudal property, you are of course forbidden to admit in the case of your own bourgeois form of property.

Abolition of the family! Even the most radical flare up at this infamous proposal of the Communists. 98

On what foundation is the present family, the bourgeois family, based? On capital, on private gain. In its completely developed form this family exists only among the bourgeoisie. But this state of things finds its complement in the practical absence of the family among the proletarians, and in public prostitution. 99

The bourgeois family will vanish as a matter of course when its complement vanishes, and both will vanish with the vanishing of capital. 100

Do you charge us with wanting to stop the exploitation of children by their parents? To this crime we plead guilty. 101

But, you will say, we destroy the most hallowed of relations when we replace home education by social. 102

And your education! Is not that also social, and determined by the social conditions under which you educate; by the intervention, direct or indirect, of society by means of schools, etc.? The Communists have not invented the intervention of society in education; they do but seek to alter the character of that intervention, and to rescue education from the influence of the ruling class. 103

The bourgeois clap-trap about the family and education, about the hallowed correlation of parent and child, become all the more disgusting, the more, by the action of Modern Industry, all family ties among the proletarians are torn asunder and their children transformed into simple articles of commerce and instruments of labor. 104

But you Communists would introduce community of women, screams the whole bourgeoisie chorus. 105

The bourgeois sees in his wife a mere instrument of production. He hears that the instruments of production are to be exploited in common, and, naturally, can come to no other conclusion, than that the lot of being common to all will likewise fall to the women. 106

He has not even a suspicion that the real point aimed at is to do away with the status of women as mere instruments of production. 107

For the rest, nothing is more ridiculous than the virtuous indignation of our bourgeois at the community of women which, they pretend, is to be openly and officially established by the Communists. The Communists have no need to introduce community of women, it has existed almost from time immemorial. 108

Our bourgeois, not content with having the wives and daugh- 109
ters of their proletarians at their disposal, not to speak of common prostitutes, take the greatest pleasure in seducing each others'
wives.

Bourgeois marriage is in reality a system of wives in common, and 110
thus, at the most, what the Communists might possibly be reproached
with, is that they desire to introduce, in substitution for a hypocritically
concealed, an openly legalized community of women. For the rest, it is
self-evident that the abolition of the present system of production must
bring with it the abolition of the community of women springing from
that system, i.e., of prostitution both public and private.

The Communists are further reproached with desiring to abolish 111
countries and nationalities.

The working men have no country. We cannot take from them 112
what they don't possess. Since the proletariat must first of all acquire
political supremacy, must rise to be the leading class of the nation,
must constitute itself the nation, it is, so far, itself national, though not
in the bourgeois sense of the word.

National differences and antagonisms between peoples are daily 113
more and more vanishing, owing to the development of the bourgeoisie, to freedom of commerce, to the world-market, to uniformity in
the mode of production and in the conditions of life corresponding
thereto.

The supremacy of the proletariat will cause them to vanish still 114
faster. United action, of the leading civilized countries at least, is one
of the first conditions for the emancipation of the proletariat.

In proportion as the exploitation of one individual by another is 115
put an end to, the exploitation of one nation by another will also be
put an end to. In proportion as the antagonism between classes within
the nation vanishes, the hostility of one nation to another will come to
an end.

The charges against Communism made from a religious, a phil- 116
osophical, and generally, from an ideological standpoint, are not
deserving of serious examination.

Does it require deep intuition to comprehend that man's ideas, 117
views, and conceptions, in one word, man's consciousness, changes
with every change in the conditions of his material existence, in his
social relations, and in his social life?

What else does the history of ideas prove than that intellectual 118
production changes in character in proportion as material production
is changed? The ruling ideas of each age have ever been the ideas of its
ruling class.

When people speak of ideas that revolutionize society they 119
do but express the fact that within the old society the elements of

a new one have been created, and that the dissolution of the old ideas keeps even pace with the dissolution of the old conditions of existence.

When the ancient world was in its last throes the ancient religions 120 were overcome by Christianity. When Christian ideas succumbed in the eighteenth century to rationalist ideas, feudal society fought its death battle with the then revolutionary bourgeoisie. The ideas of religious liberty and freedom of conscience merely gave expression to the sway of free competition within the domain of knowledge.

"Undoubtedly," it will be said, "religious, moral, philosophi- 121 cal, and judicial ideas have been modified in the course of historical development. But religion, morality, philosophy, political science, and law, constantly survived this change.

"There are, besides, eternal truths such as Freedom, Justice, etc., 122 that are common to all states of society. But Communism abolishes eternal truths, it abolishes all religion and all morality, instead of constituting them on a new basis; it therefore acts in contradiction to all past historical experience."

What does this accusation reduce itself to? The history of all past 123 society has consisted in the development of class antagonisms, antagonisms that assumed different forms at different epochs.

But whatever form they may have taken, one fact is common to 124 all past ages, viz., the exploitation of one part of society by the other. No wonder, then, that the social consciousness of past ages, despite all the multiplicity and variety it displays, moves within certain common forms, or general ideas, which cannot completely vanish except with the total disappearance of class antagonisms.

The Communist revolution is the most radical rupture with tradi- 125 tional property relations; no wonder that its development involves the most radical rupture with traditional ideas.

But let us have done with the bourgeois objections to Communism. 126

We have seen above that the first step in the revolution by the 127 working class is to raise the proletariat to the position of ruling class, to win the battle of democracy.

The proletariat will use its political supremacy to wrest, by 128 degrees, all capital from the bourgeoisie, to centralize all instruments of production in the hands of the State, i.e., of the proletariat organized as a ruling class; and to increase the total productive forces as rapidly as possible.

Of course, in the beginning, this cannot be effected except by 129 means of despotic inroads on the rights of property, and on the conditions of bourgeois production; by means of measures, therefore, which appear economically insufficient and untenable, but which in the course of the movement outstrip themselves, necessitate further inroads upon the old social order, and are unavoidable as a means of entirely revolutionizing the mode of production.

These measures will of course be different in different countries.   130

Nevertheless in the most advanced countries the following will be   131
pretty generally applicable:

1. Abolition of property in land and application of all rents of land to public purposes.

2. A heavy progressive or graduated income tax.

3. Abolition of all right of inheritance.

4. Confiscation of the property of all emigrants and rebels.

5. Centralization of credit in the hands of the State, by means of a national bank with State capital and an exclusive monopoly.

6. Centralization of the means of communication and transport in the hands of the State.

7. Extension of factories and instruments of production owned by the State; the bringing into cultivation of waste lands, and the improvement of the soil generally in accordance with a common plan.

8. Equal liability of all to labor. Establishment of industrial armies, especially for agriculture.

9. Combination of agriculture with manufacturing industries; gradual abolition of the distinction between town and country by a more equable distribution of the population over the country.

10. Free education for all children in public schools. Abolition of children's factory labor in its present form. Combination of education with industrial production, etc., etc.

When, in the course of development, class distinctions have dis-   132
appeared, and all production has been concentrated in the hands of a vast association of the whole nation, the public power will lose its political character. Political power, properly so called, is merely the organized power of one class for oppressing another. If the proletariat during its contest with the bourgeoisie is compelled, by the force of circumstances, to organize itself as a class, if, by means of a revolution, it makes itself the ruling class, and, as such, sweeps away by force the old conditions of production, then it will, along with these conditions, have swept away the conditions for the existence of class antagonism, and of classes generally, and will thereby have abolished its own supremacy as a class.

In place of the old bourgeois society, with its classes and class 133
antagonisms, we shall have an association in which the free development of each is the condition for the free development of all. . . .

Position of the Communists in Relation to the
Various Existing Opposition Parties

[The preceding section] has made clear the relations of the Com- 134
munists to the existing working class parties, such as the Chartists in
England and the Agrarian Reforms[12] in America.

The Communists fight for the attainment of the immediate aims, 135
for the enforcement of the momentary interests of the working class;
but in the movement of the present they also represent and take
care of the future of that movement. In France the Communists ally
themselves with the Social-Democrats[13] against the conservative and
radical bourgeoisie, reserving, however, the right to take up a critical position in regard to phrases and illusions traditionally handed
down from the great Revolution.

In Switzerland they support the Radicals,[14] without losing sight of 136
the fact that this party consists of antagonistic elements, partly of Democratic Socialists, in the French sense, partly of radical bourgeois.

In Poland they support the party that insists on an agrarian revo- 137
lution, as the prime condition for national emancipation, that party
which fomented the insurrection of Cracow in 1846.[15]

In Germany they fight with the bourgeoisie whenever it acts in a 138
revolutionary way, against the absolute monarchy, the feudal squire-
archy, and the petty bourgeoisie.

But they never cease for a single instant to instill into the work- 139
ing class the clearest possible recognition of the hostile antagonism

---

[12] **Agrarian Reforms** Agrarian reform was a very important issue in America
after the Revolution. The Chartists were a radical English group established in 1838;
they demanded political and social reforms. They were among the more violent revolutionaries of the day. Agrarian reform, or redistribution of the land, was slow to
come, and the issue often sparked violence between social classes.

[13] **Social-Democrats** In France in the 1840s, a group that proposed the ideal
of labor reform through the establishment of workshops supplied with government
capital.

[14] **Radicals** By 1848, European Radicals, taking their name from the violent
revolutionaries of the French Revolution (1789–1799), were a nonviolent group
content to wait for change.

[15] **the insurrection of Cracow in 1846** Cracow was an independent city
in 1846. The insurrection was designed to join Cracow with Poland and to further
large-scale social reforms.

between bourgeoisie and proletariat, in order that the German workers may straightway use, as so many weapons against the bourgeoisie, the social and political conditions that the bourgeoisie must necessarily introduce along with its supremacy, and in order that, after the fall of the reactionary classes in Germany, the fight against the bourgeoisie itself may immediately begin.

The Communists turn their attention chiefly to Germany, because   140 that country is on the eve of a bourgeois revolution,[16] that is bound to be carried out under more advanced conditions of European civilization, and with a more developed proletariat, than that of England was in the seventeenth and of France in the eighteenth century, and because the bourgeois revolution in Germany will be but the prelude to an immediately following proletarian revolution.

In short, the Communists everywhere support every revolutionary   141 movement against the existing social and political order of things.

In all these movements they bring to the front, as the leading   142 question in each, the property question, no matter what its degree of development at the time.

Finally, they labor everywhere for the union and agreement of the   143 democratic parties of all countries.

The Communists disdain to conceal their views and aims. They   144 openly declare that their ends can be attained only by the forcible overthrow of all existing social conditions. Let the ruling classes tremble at a Communistic revolution. The proletarians have nothing to lose but their chains. They have a world to win.

Working men of all countries, unite!   145

QUESTIONS FOR CRITICAL READING

1. Begin by establishing your understanding of the terms *bourgeois* and *proletarian*. Does Marx make a clear distinction between the terms? Are such terms applicable to American society today? Which of these groups, if any, do you feel that you belong to?

2. Marx makes the concept of social class fundamental to his theories. Can "social class" be easily defined? Are social classes evident in our society? Are they engaged in a struggle of the sort Marx assumes to be inevitable?

---

[16]**on the eve of a bourgeois revolution** Ferdinand Lassalle (1825–1864) developed the German labor movement and was in basic agreement with Marx, who was nevertheless convinced that Lassalle's approach was wrong. The environment in Germany seemed appropriate for revolution, in part because of its fragmented political structure and in part because no major revolution had yet occurred there.

3. What are Marx's views about the value of work in the society he describes? What is his attitude toward wealth?

4. Marx says that every class struggle is a political struggle. Do you agree?

5. Examine the first part. Which class gets more paragraphs—the bourgeoisie or the proletariat? Why?

6. Is the modern proletariat a revolutionary class?

7. Is Marx's analysis of history clear? Try to summarize his views on the progress of history.

8. Is capital a social force, or is it a personal force? Do you think of your savings (either now or in the future) as belonging to you alone or as in some way belonging to your society?

9. What, in Marx's view, is the responsibility of wealthy citizens?

SUGGESTIONS FOR CRITICAL WRITING

1. Defend or attack Marx's statement: "The executive of the modern State is but a committee for managing the common affairs of the whole bourgeoisie" (para. 18). Is this generally true? Take three "affairs of the whole bourgeoisie" and test each one in turn.

2. Examine Marx's statements regarding women. Refer especially to paragraphs 39, 98, 105, and 110. Does he imply that his views are in conflict with those of his general society? After you have a list of his statements, see if you can establish exactly what he is recommending. Do you approve of his recommendations?

3. Marx's program of ten points is listed in paragraph 131. Using the technique that Marx himself uses—taking each point in its turn, clarifying the problems with the point, and finally deciding for or against the point—evaluate his program. Which points do you feel are most beneficial to society? Which are detrimental to society? What is your overall view of the general worth of the program? Do you think it would be possible to put such a program into effect?

4. All Marx's views are predicated on the present nature of property ownership and the changes that communism will institute. He claims, for example, that a rupture with property relations "involves the most radical rupture with traditional ideas" (para. 125). And he discusses in depth his proposal for the rupture of property relations (paras. 68–93). Clarify traditional property relations—what can be owned and by whom—and then contrast with these the proposals Marx makes. Establish your own views as you go along. Include your reasons for taking issue or expressing agreement with Marx. What kinds of property relations do you see around you? What kinds are most desirable for a healthy society?

5. What is the responsibility of the state toward the individual in the kind of economic circumstances that Marx describes? How can the independence of individuals who have amassed great wealth and wish to operate freely be balanced against the independence of those who are poor and have no wealth to manipulate? What kinds of abuse are possible in such circumstances, and what remedies can a state achieve through altering the economic system? What specific remedies does Marx suggest? Are they workable?

6. Do you feel that Marx's suggestions are desirable? Or that they are likely to produce the effects he desires? Critics sometimes complain about Marx's misunderstanding of human nature. Do you feel he has an adequate understanding of human nature? What do you see as impediments to the full success of his program?

7. How accurate is Marx's view of the bourgeoisie? He identifies the bourgeoisie with capital and capitalists. He also complains that the bourgeoisie has established a world market for goods and by doing so has destroyed national and regional identities. Examine his analysis in paragraphs 22–36 in terms of what you see happening in the economic world today and decide whether or not his ideas about how the bourgeoisie functions still apply and ring true. Did Marx foresee the problems of globalization that incited protests and riots such as those aimed at the World Bank, the World Trade Organization, and the International Monetary Fund during the last years of the twentieth century into the early part of the twenty-first century?

8. **CONNECTIONS**   Examine Marx's ten points (para. 131) and determine how the Friedmans argue against each of the points (**bedfordstmartins.com/worldofideas/epages**). Which of Marx's points do the Friedmans attack most forcefully, and why? What is your position regarding the arguments between Marx and the Friedmans? Which of these authors is most concerned with equality? Which is most concerned about the welfare of the individual? Which of these authors is the more significant champion of personal freedom? How can you tell that the Friedmans have definitely read Marx carefully and disagree with him?

9. **CONNECTIONS**   Marx's philosophy differs from that of Robert B. Reich. How would Marx respond to Reich's analysis (p. 513) of the future of labor in the next few decades? Would Marx see signs of a coming class struggle in the distinctions Reich draws between the routine workers, the in-person servers, and the symbolic analysts? Does Reich's essay take any of Marx's theories into account?

10. **CONNECTIONS**   For Marx, there is no more antagonistic figure of capitalism than Andrew Carnegie. Carnegie himself condemns communism as a failed system, while Marx condemns capitalism as a system designed to keep the rich rich and the poor poor. Imagine that Marx read Carnegie's *The Gospel of Wealth* (p. 481) and decided to

counter it with an argument written as a letter to the editor of a major newspaper. What would be the basis of his attack, and how might he structure his letter? Consider Marx's own techniques in defending communism against the bourgeoisie (paras. 60 onward) as you go about constructing the argument against Carnegie.

11. **SEEING CONNECTIONS** Marx would obviously have seen the old man and the young boy in Tanner's *The Thankful Poor* (p. 438) as belonging to the proletariat. To what extent would this painting have alarmed and annoyed Marx? What evidence would it have given him to support his views about the evils of capitalism? What evidence in the painting might have weakened his views? How would he have reacted to the implied piety in the painting and the thankfulness in the title? Would Marx have approved of the figures being thankful? To whom would he say they are thankful—and why would he think they express thanks, given their economic situation? Would Marx have praised Tanner for painting this scene, or would he have condemned him?

ANDREW CARNEGIE
The Gospel of Wealth

ANDREW CARNEGIE (1835–1919) was a truly self-made man. Born in Scotland, he immigrated with his family to Allegheny, Pennsylvania, when he was thirteen. He went right to work in a cotton mill where he labored twelve hours a day, six days a week, for $1.20. Three years later, he became a messenger boy for $2.20 a week for the local telegraph company in Pittsburgh. His connection with the telegraph company and his self-taught mastery of telegraphy proved fortuitous. This was a cutting-edge technology at the time and it intersected another cutting-edge industry next to which the telegraph wires were strung, the railroads. In 1853, Thomas A. Scott, the president of the Pennsylvania Railroad, employed him as his assistant for $35 per month. His rise through the company was rapid after that.

Through the help of Scott, Carnegie invested money successfully then reinvested his profits in sleeping cars for the railroad. That led to his buying out part of the company that made the cars. Because his investments were so successful, he was able to move into the iron and iron products industry, manufacturing components for bridges and railroad tracks. By the time the Civil War began, Carnegie had amassed a considerable amount of capital: the key to his later success. During the war, Scott appointed Carnegie superintendent of military transport and the Union telegraph lines, which had to be kept up to speed for communication between Washington and the field commanders.

Late in the war, Carnegie invested $40,000 in property in Pennsylvania that yielded petroleum, and profits from that venture led him to move into the steel business in response to the need for cannon, shells, armor, and other military products. Because he

Originally published as "Wealth" in the *North American Review*, June 1889.

had put some of his investment money into iron companies before the war, he was positioned to make considerable profits. After the end of the war, Carnegie saw an opportunity to expand his business by replacing older wooden railroad bridges with steel and iron bridges, further building his fortune. It was then, in the 1870s, that he began to conceive of what was to become in 1892 the Carnegie Steel Company, one of the largest companies in the nation. Before that, however, he had purchased huge fields of iron ore around Lake Superior, so he was positioned as a supplier as well as a manufacturer of steel and iron.

Carnegie was a published author and expressed interest in improving his education and in meeting important literary and philosophical people such as Matthew Arnold (1822–1888), whom he admired, and Herbert Spencer (1820–1903), who became a very important influence on his thinking. Spencer was a utilitarian philosopher who was known as a social Darwinist. Spencer coined the phrase "the survival of the fittest" and applied it to the social sphere. Carnegie found Spencer's views totally congenial since he felt that there were superior people (he said "men") who were indeed the fittest in any economy and who deserved to profit from a laissez-faire economy and to rise in society. He was one of those men.

Carnegie was a serious reader and a lover of music. Late in life, he built and named Carnegie Hall in New York, which he designed specifically for concerts. Moreover, part of his success was due to his personal charm and grace, qualities that permitted him to travel in the highest social circles of his day. He also expressed a strong concern in helping working people educate themselves and enjoy the pleasures of art and music. Even in his thirties, he began to conceive his ultimate plan of giving away his fortune and had already begun giving some of his money away to public programs.

His operations in the steel industry, however, were not as obviously benevolent as his programs to benefit the public. He ruthlessly cut wages for skilled and unskilled workers because he thought that the greater his profits the more money he would have to give away and that he could do more good with that money than his workers could. His purpose was to serve the greatest good for the greatest number. In 1892, his workers held a strike at Homestead Steel that lasted 143 days. Carnegie was in Scotland most of this time, and his next in command, Henry Clay Frick, ordered Pinkerton guards to drive out the workers, who were then replaced with immigrants. There was violence and ten men were killed. After that incident, Carnegie's reputation was never the same.

He sold his holdings in 1901 to the banker J. P. Morgan for $480 million, which in today's money would be about $10.6 billion.

Morgan told Carnegie that he was probably the richest man in the world, which may have been true. The only other man at that time who could claim that title was John D. Rockefeller. Carnegie retired at sixty-six and began giving his money away in earnest, a sum ultimately amounting to $350 million. He founded Carnegie Mellon University in Pittsburgh, gave considerable sums to Scottish universities and to his hometown in Scotland, and established pension funds for his workers at Homestead and at universities. In small towns and cities throughout the United States and Canada, he is remembered for having built free public libraries, very few of which existed before he began his program. He built 2,509 libraries in all before he ended his project in 1917. Carnegie was not a religious man, preferring to think of himself as more influenced by science and learning, but he did commission a large number of pipe organs to be installed in churches, ostensibly because he approved of the music they would play.

Interestingly, Carnegie challenged the great holders of fortunes in his day to give their money away while they were still living, as he was planning to do. However, other than John D. Rockefeller, few of them followed his lead. Many established philanthropies after their deaths, but they did not have the pleasure of seeing their wealth perform public service.

Carnegie's Rhetoric

One of the first rhetorical notes is the use of the word *Gospel* in the title. Originally the essay was titled "Wealth," but when it was quickly reprinted to be distributed more widely *Gospel* was added. The effect is to impart an almost divine authority to the text because it echoes the gospels of the New Testament and seems then to connect to the teachings of Jesus. Originally, *gospel* meant "good news," and Carnegie certainly thought his concepts here were the best news he could provide.

The organization of the essay is clear enough. Carnegie begins by posing a problem: "The problem of our age is the proper administration of wealth." This profound declaration focuses our attention, but in 1889 we might have felt that it was not the only, nor the most important, problem of the age. Being hyperbolic in that fashion simply forces us to put aside other considerations and attend to the problem of the "contrast between the palace of the millionaire and the cottage of the laborer" (para. 1). We might expect Carnegie to be critical of this unequal distinction, but instead he says that this is the natural result of civilization. By contrast, the home of the leader of the Sioux is much the same as the most ordinary Indian, and thus Carnegie tacitly implies that the Sioux are not civilized. Hidden in his discussion is the assumption that there is a form of Darwinian evolution at work that has produced a "progress of the race," a theme he touches on constantly, and that the modern industrial leader, such as Carnegie himself, is an example of the "fittest" in society.

Carnegie's Darwinism derives from the teaching of Herbert Spencer and was enthusiastically adopted by other leaders who amassed astonishing fortunes in the years during and after the Civil War. It surfaces in specific rhetorical flourishes that center on the idea of laws of nature that are inevitable and, for Carnegie, desirable. In paragraph 6, Carnegie introduces the "law of competition" and sees it as one of the most beneficial laws because it concentrates wealth into the hands of the few. The few then create capital and capital is what makes civilization the beautiful thing it is in his eyes. In paragraph 7, Carnegie talks about "the Law of Accumulation of Wealth, and the Law of Competition" and admits that, although the laws may be imperfect in some ways, "they are, nevertheless, like the highest type of man, the best and most valuable of all that humanity has yet accomplished." In the next paragraph, he refers to these as "the laws upon which civilization is founded," leaving the reader no other option than to accept his view.

Another crucial issue that Carnegie treats and develops throughout the essay is his concept of individualism. He contrasts the individualism of capitalism with the collectivism of communism, a movement that had been discussed throughout the second half of the nineteenth century. Individualism produced the wealth of the nation, according to Carnegie. It was responsible for the achievements of men like him. He treats it as a sacred principle in itself, although he does not declare it a law, as he does the laws of accumulation and distribution.

After praising the system that has produced so much wealth, he then condemns those who would make a religion of wealth. His main point is that fortunes such as his are only in trust, to be disbursed for the public good. Of course, he is the person to decide what the public should have: parks, works of art, public institutions, and other benefits "in the forms best calculated to do them lasting good" (para. 22). The community gets the benefit, but the philanthropist administers "it for the community far better than it could or would have done for itself" (para. 23).

Carnegie praises wealth but condemns charity. He cites an example of a wealthy man who gave a handout to a stranger on the street and claims that what that man did was "probably one of the most selfish and very worst actions of his life" (para. 20).

"Indiscriminate charity" is to be condemned because "[o]f every thousand dollars spent in so-called charity to-day, it is probable that $950 is unwisely spent." Charity only goes to those who can help themselves, and as he says, those who can help themselves rarely need assistance. Charity, he fears, only encourages "the slothful, the drunken, the unworthy."

Among the remarkable experiences Carnegie had in his philanthropic years was his singular effort to help support the Tuskegee Institute, a traditionally African American college in Alabama associated with its founder, Booker T. Washington (1856–1915). Carnegie and Washington worked together on a number of projects, among them the founding of the National Negro Business League. Carnegie was a major contributor to the early development of Tuskegee and an enthusiastic friend of Washington, whose views regarding self-improvement much resembled his own.

Carnegie died in Lenox, Massachusetts, in 1919, and the bulk of his remaining wealth went to the Carnegie Corporation and continued his program of public funding.

PREREADING QUESTIONS: WHAT TO READ FOR

The following prereading questions may help you anticipate key issues in the discussion of Andrew Carnegie's *The Gospel of Wealth*. Keeping them in mind during your first reading of the selection should help focus your attention.

- What does Carnegie see as the problem of "our age"?
- Why does Carnegie accept the great gap between the wealth of the millionaire and the relative poverty of the laborer?
- What laws does Carnegie feel are at work in society to help produce great wealth?
- What is the highest obligation of the person who has amassed a great fortune?

The Gospel of Wealth

The problem of our age is the proper administration of wealth, so   1
that the ties of brotherhood may still bind together the rich and poor in harmonious relationship. The conditions of human life have not

only been changed, but revolutionized, within the past few hundred years. In former days there was little difference between the dwelling, dress, food, and environment of the chief and those of his retainers. The Indians are to-day where civilized man then was. When visiting the Sioux, I was led to the wigwam of the chief. It was just like the others in external appearance, and, even within, the difference was trifling between it and those of the poorest of his braves. The contrast between the palace of the millionaire and the cottage of the laborer with us to-day measures the change which has come with civilization.

This change, however, is not to be deplored, but welcomed 2 as highly beneficial. It is well, nay, essential for the progress of the race, that the houses of some should be homes for all that is highest and best in literature and the arts, and for all the refinements of civilization, rather than that none should be so. Much better this great irregularity than universal squalor. Without wealth there can be no Maecenas.[1] The "good old times" were not good old times. Neither master nor servant was as well situated then as to-day. A relapse to old conditions would be disastrous to both—not the least so to him who serves—and would sweep away civilization with it. But whether the change be for good or ill, it is upon us, beyond our power to alter, and therefore to be accepted and made the best of. It is a waste of time to criticize the inevitable.

It is easy to see how the change has come. One illustration will 3 serve for almost every phase of the cause. In the manufacture of products we have the whole story. It applies to all combinations of human industry, as stimulated and enlarged by the inventions of this scientific age. Formerly articles were manufactured at the domestic hearth or in small shops which formed part of the household. The master and his apprentices worked side by side, the latter living with the master, and therefore subject to the same conditions. When these apprentices rose to be masters, there was little or no change in their mode of life, and they, in turn, educated in the same routine succeeding apprentices. There was, substantially, social equality, and even political equality, for those engaged in industrial pursuits had then little or no political voice in the State.

But the inevitable result of such a mode of manufacture was crude 4 articles at high prices. To-day the world obtains commodities of excellent quality at prices which even the generation preceding this would have deemed incredible. In the commercial world similar causes have produced similar results, and the race is benefited thereby. The poor enjoy what the rich could not before afford. What were the luxuries

---

[1] **Gaius Maecenas (c. 74–8 B.C.E.)** Wealthy patron to great Roman authors.

have become the necessaries of life. The laborer has now more comforts than the farmer had a few generations ago. The farmer has more luxuries than the landlord had, and is more richly clad and better housed. The landlord has books and pictures rarer, and appointments more artistic, than the King could then obtain.

The price we pay for this salutary change is, no doubt, great. We 5 assemble thousands of operatives in the factory, in the mine, and in the counting-house, of whom the employer can know little or nothing, and to whom the employer is little better than a myth. All intercourse between them is at an end. Rigid Castes are formed, and, as usual, mutual ignorance breeds mutual distrust. Each Caste is without sympathy for the other, and ready to credit anything disparaging in regard to it. Under the law of competition, the employer of thousands is forced into the strictest economies, among which the rates paid to labor figure prominently, and often there is friction between the employer and the employed, between capital and labor, between rich and poor. Human society loses homogeneity.

The price which society pays for the law of competition, like the 6 price it pays for cheap comforts and luxuries, is also great; but the advantages of this law are also greater still, for it is to this law that we owe our wonderful material development, which brings improved conditions in its train. But, whether the law be benign or not, we must say of it, as we say of the change in the conditions of men to which we have referred: it is here; we cannot evade it; no substitutes for it have been found; and while the law may be sometimes hard for the individual, it is best for the race, because it insures the survival of the fittest in every department. We accept and welcome, therefore, as conditions to which we must accommodate ourselves, great inequality of environment, the concentration of business, industrial and commercial, in the hands of a few, and the law of competition between these, as being not only beneficial, but essential for the future progress of the race. Having accepted these, it follows that there must be great scope for the exercise of special ability in the merchant and in the manufacturer who has to conduct affairs upon a great scale. That this talent for organization and management is rare among men is proved by the fact that it invariably secures for its possessor enormous rewards, no matter where or under what laws or conditions. The experienced in affairs always rate the MAN whose services can be obtained as a partner as not only the first consideration, but such as to render the question of his capital scarcely worth considering, for such men soon create capital; while, without the special talent required, capital soon takes wings. Such men become interested in firms or corporations using millions; and estimating only simple interest to be made upon the capital invested, it is inevitable that their income must exceed their expenditures, and that they must accumulate wealth. Nor is there any middle ground which such men can occupy, because the great manufacturing or commercial concern which does not earn at least interest upon its capital soon becomes bankrupt. It must either go forward or fall behind: to stand still is impossible. It is a condition essential for its successful operation that it should be thus far profitable, and even that, in addition to interest on capital, it should make profit. It is a law that men possessed of this peculiar talent for affairs, under the free play of economic forces, must of necessity soon be in receipt of more revenue than can be judiciously expended upon themselves; and this law is as beneficial for the race as the others.

Objections to the foundations upon which society is based are not   7
in order, because the condition of the race is better with these than it has been with any others which have been tried. Of the effect of any new substitutes proposed we cannot be sure. The Socialist or Anarchist who seeks to overturn present conditions is to be regarded as attacking the foundation upon which civilization itself rests, for civilization took its start from the day that the capable, industrious workman said to his incompetent and lazy fellow, "If thou dost not sow, thou shalt not reap," and thus ended primitive Communism by separating the drones from the bees. One who studies this subject will soon be brought face to face with the conclusion that upon the sacredness of property civilization itself depends—the right of the laborer to his hundred dollars in the savings-bank, and equally the legal right of the millionaire to his millions. To those who propose to substitute Communism for this intense Individualism the answer, therefore, is: the race has tried that. All progress from that barbarous day to the present time has resulted from its displacement. Not evil, but good, has come to the race from the accumulation of wealth by those who have the ability and energy that produce it. But even if we admit for a moment that it might be better for the race to discard its present foundation, Individualism—that it is a nobler ideal that man should labor, not for himself alone, but in and for a brotherhood of his fellows, and share with them all in common, realizing Swedenborg's[2] idea of Heaven, where, as he says, the angels derive their happiness, not from laboring for self, but for each other—even admit all this, and a sufficient answer is, This is not evolution, but revolution. It necessitates the changing of human nature itself—a work of aeons, even if it were good to change it, which we cannot know. It is not practicable in our day or in our age. Even if desirable theoretically, it belongs to another and long-succeeding

---

[2]**Emanuel Swedenborg (1688–1771)** A spiritual awakening late in life made him believe he could speak with angels and visit heaven and hell. His book *Heaven and Hell* (1758) was widely read in the nineteenth century and is still influential.

sociological stratum. Our duty is with what is practicable now; with the next step possible in our day and generation. It is criminal to waste our energies in endeavoring to uproot, when all we can profitably or possibly accomplish is to bend the universal tree of humanity a little in the direction most favorable to the production of good fruit under existing circumstances. We might as well urge the destruction of the highest existing type of man because he failed to reach our ideal as to favor the destruction of Individualism, Private Property, the Law of Accumulation of Wealth, and the Law of Competition; for these are the highest results of human experience, the soil in which society so far has produced the best fruit. Unequally or unjustly, perhaps, as these laws sometimes operate, and imperfect as they appear to the Idealist, they are, nevertheless, like the highest type of man, the best and most valuable of all that humanity has yet accomplished.

We start, then, with a condition of affairs under which the best 8 interests of the race are promoted, but which inevitably gives wealth to the few. Thus far, accepting conditions as they exist, the situation can be surveyed and pronounced good. The question then arises—and, if the foregoing be correct, it is the only question with which we have to deal—What is the proper mode of administering wealth after the laws upon which civilization is founded have thrown it into the hands of the few? And it is of this great question that I believe I offer the true solution. It will be understood that *fortunes* are here spoken of, not moderate sums saved by many years of effort, the returns from which are required for the comfortable maintenance and education of families. This is not *wealth,* but only *competence,* which it should be the aim of all to acquire.

There are but three modes in which surplus wealth can be dis- 9 posed of. It can be left to the families of the decedents; or it can be bequeathed for public purposes; or, finally, it can be administered during their lives by its possessors. Under the first and second modes most of the wealth of the world that has reached the few has hitherto been applied. Let us in turn consider each of these modes. The first is the most injudicious. In monarchical countries, the estates and the greatest portion of the wealth are left to the first son, that the vanity of the parent may be gratified by the thought that his name and title are to descend to succeeding generations unimpaired. The condition of this class in Europe to-day teaches the futility of such hopes or ambitions. The successors have become impoverished through their follies or from the fall in the value of land. Even in Great Britain the strict law of entail[3] has been found inadequate to maintain the

---

[3] **Law of entail** A law designed to restrict inheritance to only the heirs of the family who owns the property.

status of an hereditary class. Its soil is rapidly passing into the hands
of the stranger. Under republican institutions the division of property
among the children is much fairer, but the question which forces itself
upon thoughtful men in all lands is: Why should men leave great fortunes to their children? If this is done from affection, is it not misguided affection? Observation teaches that, generally speaking, it is
not well for the children that they should be so burdened. Neither is it
well for the state. Beyond providing for the wife and daughters moderate sources of income, and very moderate allowances indeed, if any,
for the sons, men may well hesitate, for it is no longer questionable
that great sums bequeathed oftener work more for the injury than for
the good of the recipients. Wise men will soon conclude that, for the
best interests of the members of their families and of the state, such
bequests are an improper use of their means.

It is not suggested that men who have failed to educate their sons   10
to earn a livelihood shall cast them adrift in poverty. If any man has
seen fit to rear his sons with a view to their living idle lives, or, what
is highly commendable, has instilled in them the sentiment that they
are in a position to labor for public ends without reference to pecuniary considerations, then, of course, the duty of the parent is to see that
such are provided for *in moderation*. There are instances of millionaires'
sons unspoiled by wealth, who, being rich, still perform great services
in the community. Such are the very salt of the earth, as valuable as,
unfortunately, they are rare; still it is not the exception, but the rule,
that men must regard, and, looking at the usual result of enormous
sums conferred upon legatees, the thoughtful man must shortly say,
"I would as soon leave to my son a curse as the almighty dollar," and
admit to himself that it is not the welfare of the children, but family
pride, which inspires these enormous legacies.

As to the second mode, that of leaving wealth at death for pub-   11
lic uses, it may be said that this is only a means for the disposal of
wealth, provided a man is content to wait until he is dead before it
becomes of much good in the world. Knowledge of the results of legacies bequeathed is not calculated to inspire the brightest hopes of
much posthumous good being accomplished. The cases are not few in
which the real object sought by the testator is not attained, nor are
they few in which his real wishes are thwarted. In many cases the
bequests are so used as to become only monuments of his folly. It is
well to remember that it requires the exercise of not less ability than
that which acquired the wealth to use it so as to be really beneficial to
the community. Besides this, it may fairly be said that no man is to be
extolled for doing what he cannot help doing, nor is he to be thanked
by the community to which he only leaves wealth at death. Men who
leave vast sums in this way may fairly be thought men who would not

have left it at all had they been able to take it with them. The memories of such cannot be held in grateful remembrance, for there is no grace in their gifts. It is not to be wondered at that such bequests seem so generally to lack the blessing.

The growing disposition to tax more and more heavily large   12
estates left at death is a cheering indication of the growth of a salutary change in public opinion. The State of Pennsylvania now takes—subject to some exceptions—one-tenth of the property left by its citizens. The budget presented in the British Parliament the other day proposes to increase the death-duties; and, most significant of all, the new tax is to be a graduated one. Of all forms of taxation, this seems the wisest. Men who continue hoarding great sums all their lives, the proper use of which for public ends would work good to the community, should be made to feel that the community, in the form of the state, cannot thus be deprived of its proper share. By taxing estates heavily at death the state marks its condemnation of the selfish millionaire's unworthy life.

It is desirable that nations should go much further in this direc-   13
tion. Indeed, it is difficult to set bounds to the share of a rich man's estate which should go at his death to the public through the agency of the state, and by all means such taxes should be graduated, beginning at nothing upon moderate sums to dependents, and increasing rapidly as the amounts swell, until of the millionaire's hoard, as of Shylock's,[4] at least

> —The other half
> Comes to the privy coffer of the state.

This policy would work powerfully to induce the rich man to attend to the administration of wealth during his life, which is the end that society should always have in view, as being that by far most fruitful for the people. Nor need it be feared that this policy would sap the root of enterprise and render men less anxious to accumulate, for to the class whose ambition it is to leave great fortunes and be talked about after their death, it will attract even more attention, and, indeed, be a somewhat nobler ambition to have enormous sums paid over to the state from their fortunes.

There remains, then, only one mode of using great fortunes; but   14
in this we have the true antidote for the temporary unequal distribution of wealth, the reconciliation of the rich and the poor—a reign of harmony—another ideal, differing, indeed, from that of the Communist in requiring only the further evolution of existing conditions, not the

---

[4] **Shylock** The moneylender and title character in Shakespeare's *The Merchant of Venice.*

total overthrow of our civilization. It is founded upon the present most intense individualism, and the race is prepared to put it in practice by degrees whenever it pleases. Under its sway we shall have an ideal state, in which the surplus wealth of the few will become, in the best sense, the property of the many, because administered for the common good, and this wealth, passing through the hands of the few, can be made a much more potent force for the elevation of our race than if it had been distributed in small sums to the people themselves. Even the poorest can be made to see this, and to agree that great sums gathered by some of their fellow-citizens and spent for public purposes, from which the masses reap the principal benefit, are more valuable to them than if scattered among them through the course of many years in trifling amounts.

If we consider what results flow from the Cooper Institute,[5] for instance, to the best portion of the race in New York not possessed of means, and compare these with those which would have arisen for the good of the masses from an equal sum distributed by Mr. Cooper in his lifetime in the form of wages, which is the highest form of distribution, being for work done and not for charity, we can form some estimate of the possibilities for the improvement of the race which lie embedded in the present law of the accumulation of wealth. Much of this sum, if distributed in small quantities among the people, would have been wasted in the indulgence of appetite, some of it in excess, and it may be doubted whether even the part put to the best use, that of adding to the comforts of the home, would have yielded results for the race, as a race, at all comparable to those which are flowing and are to flow from the Cooper Institute from generation to generation. Let the advocate of violent or radical change ponder well this thought.

We might even go so far as to take another instance, that of Mr. Tilden's bequest of five millions of dollars for a free library in the city of New York, but in referring to this one cannot help saying involuntarily, How much better if Mr. Tilden[6] had devoted the last years of his own life to the proper administration of this immense sum; in which case neither legal contest nor any other cause of delay could have interfered with his aims. But let us assume that Mr. Tilden's millions finally become the means of giving to New York a noble public library, where the treasures of the world contained in books will be open to all forever, without money and without price. Considering

---

[5] **Cooper Institute** Now Cooper Union, founded in 1858 by Peter Cooper as a free school for the sciences and the arts.
[6] **Samuel Tilden (1814–1886)** He bequeathed $4 million to found the New York Public Library after he died. His will was contested and only $3 million was given to found the library.

the good of that part of the race which congregates in and around Manhattan Island, would its permanent benefit have been better promoted had these millions been allowed to circulate in small sums through the hands of the masses? Even the most strenuous advocate of Communism must entertain a doubt upon this subject. Most of those who think will probably entertain no doubt whatever.

17   Poor and restricted are our opportunities in this life; narrow our horizon; our best work most imperfect; but rich men should be thankful for one inestimable boon. They have it in their power during their lives to busy themselves in organizing benefactions from which the masses of their fellows will derive lasting advantage, and thus dignify their own lives. The highest life is probably to be reached, not by such imitation of the life of Christ as Count Tolstoi[7] gives us, but, while animated by Christ's spirit, by recognizing the changed conditions of this age, and adopting modes of expressing this spirit suitable to the changed conditions under which we live; still laboring for the good of our fellows, which was the essence of his life and teaching, but laboring in a different manner.

18   This, then, is held to be the duty of the man of Wealth: first, to set an example of modest, unostentatious living, shunning display or extravagance; to provide moderately for the legitimate wants of those dependent upon him; and after doing so to consider all surplus revenues which come to him simply as trust funds, which he is called upon to administer, and strictly bound as a matter of duty to administer in the manner which, in his judgment, is best calculated to produce the most beneficial results for the community—the man of wealth thus becoming the mere agent and trustee for his poorer brethren, bringing to their service his superior wisdom, experience, and ability to administer, doing for them better than they would or could do for themselves.

19   We are met here with the difficulty of determining what are moderate sums to leave to members of the family; what is modest, unostentatious living; what is the test of extravagance. There must be different standards for different conditions. The answer is that it is as impossible to name exact amounts or actions as it is to define good manners, good taste, or the rules of propriety; but, nevertheless, these are verities, well known although undefinable. Public sentiment is quick to know and to feel what offends these. So in the case of wealth. The rule in regard to good taste in the dress of men or women applies here. Whatever makes one conspicuous offends the canon. If any family be chiefly known for display, for extravagance in home,

---

[7] **Leo Tolstoy (1828–1910)** Author of *War and Peace* and *Anna Karenina*. Tolstoy lived a spare and simple life in his old age.

table, equipage, for enormous sums ostentatiously spent in any form upon itself—if these be its chief distinctions, we have no difficulty in estimating its nature or culture. So likewise in regard to the use or abuse of its surplus wealth, or to generous, free-handed cooperation in good public uses, or to unabated efforts to accumulate and hoard to the last, whether they administer or bequeath. The verdict rests with the best and most enlightened public sentiment. The community will surely judge, and its judgments will not often be wrong.

The best uses to which surplus wealth can be put have already been indicated. Those who would administer wisely must, indeed, be wise, for one of the serious obstacles to the improvement of our race is indiscriminate charity. It were better for mankind that the millions of the rich were thrown into the sea than so spent as to encourage the slothful, the drunken, the unworthy. Of every thousand dollars spent in so-called charity to-day, it is probable that $950 is unwisely spent; so spent, indeed, as to produce the very evils which it proposes to mitigate or cure. A well-known writer of philosophic books admitted the other day that he had given a quarter of a dollar to a man who approached him as he was coming to visit the house of his friend. He knew nothing of the habits of this beggar; knew not the use that would be made of this money, although he had every reason to suspect that it would be spent improperly. This man professed to be a disciple of Herbert Spencer;[8] yet the quarter-dollar given that night will probably work more injury than all the money which its thoughtless donor will ever be able to give in true charity will do good. He only gratified his own feelings, saved himself from annoyance—and this was probably one of the most selfish and very worst actions of his life, for in all respects he is most worthy. 20

In bestowing charity, the main consideration should be to help those who will help themselves; to provide part of the means by which those who desire to improve may do so; to give those who desire to rise the aids by which they may rise; to assist, but rarely or never to do all. Neither the individual nor the race is improved by alms-giving. Those worthy of assistance, except in rare cases, seldom require assistance. The really valuable men of the race never do, except in cases of accident or sudden change. Every one has, of course, cases of individuals brought to his own knowledge where temporary assistance can do genuine good, and these he will not overlook. But the amount which can be wisely given by the individual for individuals is necessarily limited by his lack of knowledge of the circumstances connected with each. He is the only true reformer who is as careful and as anxious not to aid the unworthy as he is to aid the worthy, and, 21

---

[8] **Herbert Spencer (1820–1903)** British philosopher who applied Darwinian theories of evolution to the social sciences.

perhaps, even more so, for in alms-giving more injury is probably done by rewarding vice than by relieving virtue.

The rich man is thus almost restricted to following the examples of Peter Cooper, Enoch Pratt of Baltimore, Mr. Pratt of Brooklyn, Senator Stanford,[9] and others, who know that the best means of benefiting the community is to place within its reach the ladders upon which the aspiring can rise — parks, and means of recreation, by which men are helped in body and mind; works of art, certain to give pleasure and improve the public taste; and public institutions of various kinds, which will improve the general condition of the people — in this manner returning their surplus wealth to the mass of their fellows in the forms best calculated to do them lasting good.

Thus is the problem of Rich and Poor to be solved. The laws of accumulation will be left free; the laws of distribution free. Individualism will continue, but the millionaire will be but a trustee for the poor; intrusted for a season with a great part of the increased wealth of the community, but administering it for the community far better than it could or would have done for itself. The best minds will thus have reached a stage in the development of the race in which it is clearly seen that there is no mode of disposing of surplus wealth creditable to thoughtful and earnest men into whose hands it flows save by using it year by year for the general good. This day already dawns. But a little while, and although, without incurring the pity of their fellows, men may die sharers in great business enterprises from which their capital cannot be or has not been withdrawn, and is left chiefly at death for public uses, yet the man who dies leaving behind him millions of available wealth, which was his to administer during life, will pass away "unwept, unhonored, and unsung," no matter to what uses he leaves the dross which he cannot take with him. Of such as these the public verdict will then be: "The man who dies thus rich dies disgraced."

Such, in my opinion, is the true Gospel concerning Wealth, obedience to which is destined some day to solve the problem of the Rich and the Poor, and to bring "Peace on earth, among men Good-Will."

---

[9] **Peter Cooper (1791–1883), Enoch Pratt (1808–1896), Charles Pratt (1830–1891), Leland Stanford (1824–1893)** All were prominent millionaires and eventual philanthropists, three of whom founded universities.

QUESTIONS FOR CRITICAL READING

1. What do you see as the problem of wealth in this age?
2. What were the conditions of production in the age prior to Carnegie's (para. 3)?

3. What was wrong with the products of the age prior to Carnegie's?

4. What is the law of competition? Is it still at work today? Is it a law?

5. Is conformity an important issue for Carnegie? Is he for or against it?

6. How great are the inequalities of wealth in this country today?

7. Why does Carnegie take a hard line on charity? What is your view on charity today?

8. In paragraph 7, Carnegie refers to the "highest existing type of man." Whom do you think he is referring to? Whom would you mean if you used that term?

SUGGESTIONS FOR CRITICAL WRITING

1. Is it true that today the "poor enjoy what the rich could not before afford" (para. 4)? What do the poor enjoy today that the rich could not have enjoyed in 1889? To what extent are the things and conditions the poor enjoy now the result of the laws of competition and accumulation that Carnegie says operate in our civilization and make such enjoyment possible? If you feel that Carnegie is right in his contention about the production of benefits for the poor, do you then feel yourself inclined to agree with Carnegie in general?

2. What would Carnegie say about the great inequalities of wealth in this country today? In his time, about 1 percent of the population controlled half the wealth. Today it is about 3 percent. One person in the United States whose wealth could compare with Carnegie's is Bill Gates, and his fortune is about half of Carnegie's in today's dollars. Would Carnegie feel things are getting better or that conditions are so different that there is no comparison with his age? What would his advice be to those with great wealth today?

3. One of Carnegie's important ideas is that societies evolve in the manner that life on earth evolves. He uses the term "survival of the fittest" (para. 6) and lauds the system in economics that permits competition to weed out the weak and reward the strong. Social Darwinism, which is the theory Carnegie talks about, was very popular in the late 1800s. Learn what you can about the idea and determine whether or not Carnegie is following the main line of social Darwinism or if he is changing the idea to suit himself. After you have done some research, answer this question: Is Carnegie right in what he proposes for the progress of civilization?

4. In paragraphs 6 and 7, Carnegie explains what kind of person will rise to great wealth, enumerating that person's qualities and establishing that such persons are rare enough to be worthy of great reward. He also argues against any criticism of his point of view by talking about how communism would be detrimental to society. He says, "Not evil, but good, has come to the race from the accumulation of wealth by

those who have the ability and energy that produce it" (para. 7). Examine his arguments in these paragraphs and decide whether or not he is correct and explain why.

5. Carnegie gave away most of his wealth to support projects he felt would benefit the community. He built over 2,500 libraries, endowed many parks, and gave money to universities and other foundations that he thought would "improve the race." Assuming that you had unlimited wealth to give away, what would your priorities be? Do you approve of Carnegie's priorities, or do you feel they are not appropriate for today's communities? What would you want your wealth to achieve in our world?

6. **CONNECTIONS** By using the word *Gospel* in his title, Carnegie implies that he follows an ethical and moral pattern in his life and in his attitude toward society. With which of the authors in Part Three, "Ethics and Morality," would Carnegie most sympathize? Which authors(s) would question his recommendations regarding the use of wealth? Imagine one of these writers writing to Carnegie about *The Gospel of Wealth*. What would that author praise and what would he or she condemn? Would that author be likely to regard Carnegie as a hero or as a misguided do-gooder? Is Carnegie really interested in questions of morality and ethical behavior?

7. **CONNECTIONS** Andrew Carnegie's essay exemplifies the laissez-faire economic policies of his era. The Friedmans might have held Carnegie up as proof that their theories work, and work well (**bedfordstmartins.com/worldofideas/epages**). Assuming that you choose to defend the arguments of the Friedmans for a free and open economic system, write an essay that establishes Carnegie's career and achievements as the best model for their economic views. What benefits to the individual and what benefits to the general society would the Friedmans say Carnegie has produced? What would Carnegie most appreciate about the Friedmans' arguments for equality and liberty? How convinced are you that the Friedmans and Carnegie have the right ideas about how society should manage economic opportunity?

8. **SEEING CONNECTIONS** Imagine that Carnegie saw Tanner's *The Thankful Poor* (p. 438) in a museum. What would have been his reaction to the man and boy portrayed in the painting? How would they fit into his thinking about charity and individualism? Would he have felt these people deserved support? To whom would he think they owe thanks, and for what? Considering Carnegie's connection with the Tuskegee Institute, how might he have regarded the simplicity and the reverence with which the older man and the young boy approach the basic act of sharing a meal? Would he have seen this as having a religious subtext, or would he have seen it simply as an economic statement? In another essay, "The Advantages of Poverty," Carnegie complains that the wealthy are estranged from their children because of tutors, nannies, and boarding schools. What "advantages of poverty" would he see in this painting?

JOHN KENNETH GALBRAITH
The Position of Poverty

JOHN KENNETH GALBRAITH (1908–2006) was born in Canada but became an American citizen in 1937. He grew up on a farm in Ontario and received his first university degree in agricultural science. This background may have contributed to the success of his many books on subjects such as economics, the State Department, Indian art, and government, which have always explained complex concepts with a clarity easily grasped by laypeople. Sometimes he has been criticized for oversimplifying issues, but on the whole, he has made a brilliant success of writing with wit and humor about perplexing and sometimes troubling issues.

Galbraith was a professor of economics at Harvard University for many years. During the presidential campaigns of Adlai Stevenson in 1952 and 1956, he assisted the Democrats as a speechwriter and economics adviser. He performed the same tasks for John F. Kennedy in 1960. Kennedy appointed Galbraith ambassador to India, a post that he maintained for a little over two years, including the period during which India and China fought a border war. His experiences in India resulted in *Ambassador's Journal: A Personal Account of the Kennedy Years* (1969). Kennedy called Galbraith his finest ambassadorial appointment.

Galbraith's involvement with politics was somewhat unusual for an academic economist at that time. It seems to have stemmed from strongly held personal views on the social issues of his time. One of the most important contributions of his best-known and probably most significant book, *The Affluent Society* (1958; rev. eds. 1969, 1976, 1998), was its analysis of America's economic ambitions. He pointed out that at that time the economy was entirely focused on the measurement and growth of the gross national product. Economists and government officials concentrated on boosting output, a goal that he felt

From *The Affluent Society*.

was misdirected because it would result in products that people really did not need and that would not benefit them. Creating artificial needs for things that had no ultimate value, and building in a "planned obsolescence," seemed to him to be wasteful and ultimately destructive.

Galbraith suggested that America concentrate on genuine needs and satisfy them immediately. He was deeply concerned about the environment and suggested that clean air was a priority that should take precedence over industry. He supported development of the arts and stressed the importance of improving housing across the nation. His effort was directed at trying to help Americans change certain basic values by giving up the pursuit of useless consumer novelties and substituting a program of genuine social development. The commitment to consumer products as the basis of the economy naturally argued against a redirection of effort toward the solution of social problems.

Galbraith is so exceptionally clear in his essay that little commentary is needed to establish its importance. He is insightful in clarifying two kinds of poverty: case poverty and insular poverty. Case poverty is restricted to an individual and his or her family and often seems to be caused by alcoholism, ignorance, mental deficiency, discrimination, or specific disabilities. It is an individual, not a group, disorder. Insular poverty affects a group in a given area—an "island" within the larger society. He points to poverty in Appalachia and in the slums of major cities, where most of the people in those "islands" are at or below the poverty level. Insular poverty is linked to the environment, and its causes are somehow derived from that environment.

Galbraith's analysis is perceptive and influential, and although little or no progress has been made in solving the problem of poverty since 1959, he assures us that there are steps that can be taken to help eradicate it. Such steps demand the nation's will, however, and he warns that the nation may lack the will. He also reasons that because the poor are a minority, few politicians make their plight a campaign issue. Actually, in this belief he is wrong. Kennedy in 1960, Lyndon Johnson in 1964, and Jimmy Carter in 1976 made programs for the poor central among their governmental concerns. Because of the war in Vietnam and other governmental policies, however, the 1960s and early 1970s were a time of staggering inflation, wiping out any of the advances the poor had made.

Galbraith's Rhetoric

The most important rhetorical achievement of the piece is its style. This is an example of the elevated plain style: a clear, direct, and basically simple approach to language that only occasionally admits a somewhat learned vocabulary—as in the use of a very few words such as *opulent, unremunerative,* and *ineluctable.* Most of the words he uses are ordinary ones.

He breaks the essay into five carefully numbered sections. In this way he highlights its basic structure and informs us that he has clearly separated its elements into related groups so that he can speak directly to aspects of his subject rather than to the entire topic. This rhetorical technique of division contributes to clarity and confers a sense of authority on the writer.

Galbraith relies on statistical information that the reader can examine if necessary. This information is treated in the early stages of the piece as a prologue. Once such information has been given, Galbraith proceeds in the manner of a logician establishing premises and deriving the necessary conclusions. The subject is sober and sobering, involving issues that are complex, uncertain, and difficult, but the style is direct, confident, and essentially simple. This is the secret of the success of the book from which this selection comes. *The Affluent Society* has been translated into well over a dozen languages and has been a best-seller around the globe, and more than fifty years after its first publication it remains an influential book. Its fundamental insights are such that it is likely to be relevant to the economy of the United States for generations to come.

PREREADING QUESTIONS:
WHAT TO READ FOR

The following prereading questions may help you anticipate key issues in the discussion of John Kenneth Galbraith's "The Position of Poverty." Keeping them in mind during your first reading of the selection should help focus your attention.

- Why is modern poverty different from that of a century ago?
- What is case poverty?
- What is insular poverty?

The Position of Poverty

"The study of the causes of poverty," Alfred Marshall observed at   1
the turn of the century, "is the study of the causes of the degradation of a large part of mankind." He spoke of contemporary England as well

as of the world beyond. A vast number of people both in town and country, he noted, had insufficient food, clothing, and house-room; they were: "Overworked and undertaught, weary and careworn, without quiet and without leisure." The chance of their succor, he concluded, gave to economic studies "their chief and their highest interest."[1]

No contemporary economist would be likely to make such an observation about the United States. Conventional economic discourse makes obeisance to the continued existence of some poverty. "We must remember that we still have a great many poor people." In the nineteen-sixties, poverty promised, for a time, to become a subject of serious political concern. Then the Vietnam war came and the concern evaporated or was displaced. For economists of conventional mood, the reminders that the poor still exist are a useful way of allaying uneasiness about the relevance of conventional economic goals. For some people, wants must be synthesized. Hence, the importance of the goods to them is not *per se* very high. So much may be conceded. But others are far closer to physical need. And hence we must not be cavalier about the urgency of providing them with the most for the least. The sales tax may have merit for the opulent, but it still bears heavily on the poor. The poor get jobs more easily when the economy is expanding. Thus poverty survives in economic discourse partly as a buttress to the conventional economic wisdom.

The privation of which Marshall spoke was, going on to a century ago, the common lot at least of all who worked without special skill. As a general affliction, it was ended by increased output which, however imperfectly it may have been distributed, nevertheless accrued in substantial amount to those who worked for a living. The result was to reduce poverty from the problem of a majority to that of a minority. It ceased to be a general case and became a special case. It is this which has put the problem of poverty into its peculiar modern form.

II

For poverty does survive. In part, it is a physical matter; those afflicted have such limited and insufficient food, such poor clothing, such crowded, cold, and dirty shelter that life is painful as well as comparatively brief. But just as it is far too tempting to say that, in matters of living standards, everything is relative, so it is wrong to rest everything

---

[1] *Principles of Economics,* 8th ed. (London: Macmillan, 1927), pp. 2–4. [Galbraith's note] Alfred Marshall (1842–1924) was an English economist whose *Principles of Economics* (1890) was long a standard text and is still relied on by some economists for its theories of costs, values, and distribution.

on absolutes. People are poverty-stricken when their income, even if adequate for survival, falls radically behind that of the community. Then they cannot have what the larger community regards as the minimum necessary for decency; and they cannot wholly escape, therefore, the judgment of the larger community that they are indecent. They are degraded for, in the literal sense, they live outside the grades or categories which the community regards as acceptable.

Since the first edition of this book appeared, and one hopes however slightly as a consequence, the character and dimension of this degradation have become better understood. There have also been fulsome promises that poverty would be eliminated. The performance on these promises has been less eloquent.

The degree of privation depends on the size of the family, the place of residence—it will be less with given income in rural areas than in the cities—and will, of course, be affected by changes in living costs. One can usefully think of deprivation as falling into two broad categories. First, there is what may be called *case* poverty. This one encounters in every community, rural or urban, however prosperous that community or the times. Case poverty is the poor farm family with the junk-filled yard and the dirty children playing in the bare dirt. Or it is the gray-black hovel beside the railroad tracks. Or it is the basement dwelling in the alley.

Case poverty is commonly and properly related to some characteristic of the individuals so afflicted. Nearly everyone else has mastered his or her environment; this proves that it is not intractable. But some quality peculiar to the individual or family involved—mental deficiency, bad health, inability to adapt to the discipline of industrial life, uncontrollable procreation, alcohol, discrimination involving a very limited minority, some educational handicap unrelated to community shortcoming, or perhaps a combination of several of these handicaps—has kept these individuals from participating in the general well-being.

Second, there is what may be called *insular* poverty—that which manifests itself as an "island" of poverty. In the island, everyone or nearly everyone is poor. Here, evidently, it is not easy to explain matters by individual inadequacy. We may mark individuals down as intrinsically deficient in social performance; it is not proper or even wise so to characterize an entire community. The people of the island have been frustrated by some factor common to their environment.

Case poverty exists. It has also been useful to those who have needed a formula for keeping the suffering of others from causing suffering to themselves. Since this poverty is the result of the deficiencies, including the moral shortcomings, of the persons concerned, it is possible to shift the responsibility to them. They are worthless and, as a simple manifestation of social justice, they suffer for it. Or, at a somewhat higher level of social perception and compassion, it means that the problem of poverty is sufficiently solved by private and public charity. This rescues those afflicted from the worst consequences of their inadequacy or misfortune; no larger social change or reorganization is suggested. Except as it may be insufficient in its generosity, the society is not at fault.

Insular poverty yields to no such formulas. In earlier times, when 10 agriculture and extractive industries were the dominant sources of livelihood, something could be accomplished by shifting the responsibility for low income to a poor natural endowment and thus, in effect, to God. The soil was thin and stony, other natural resources absent and hence the people were poor. And, since it is the undoubted preference of many to remain in the vicinity of the place of their birth, a homing instinct that operates for people as well as pigeons, the people remained in the poverty which heaven had decreed for them. It is an explanation that is nearly devoid of empirical application. Connecticut is very barren and stony and incomes are very high. Similarly Wyoming. West Virginia is well watered with rich mines and forests and the people are very poor. The South is much favored in soil and climate and similarly poor and the very richest parts of the South, such as the Mississippi-Yazoo Delta, have long had a well-earned reputation for the greatest deprivation. Yet so strong is the tendency to associate poverty with natural causes that even individuals of some modest intelligence will still be heard, in explanation of insular poverty, to say, "It's basically a poor country." "It's a pretty barren region."

Most modern poverty is insular in character and the islands are 11 the rural and urban slums. From the former, mainly in the South, the southern Appalachians and Puerto Rico, there has been until recent times a steady flow of migrants, some white but more black, to the latter. Grim as life is in the urban ghetto, it still offers more hope, income, and interest than in the rural slum.

The most important characteristic of insular poverty is forces, 12 common to all members of the community, that restrain or prevent participation in economic life at going rates of return. These restraints are several. Race, which acts to locate people by their color rather than by the proximity to employment, is obviously one. So are poor educational facilities. (And this effect is further exaggerated when the poorly educated, endemically a drug on the labor market, are brought together in dense clusters by the common inadequacy of the schools available to blacks and the poor.) So is the disintegration of family life in the slum which leaves households in the hands of women. Family life itself is in some measure a manifestation of affluence. And so, without doubt, is the shared sense of helplessness and rejection and the resulting demoralization which is the product of the common misfortune.

The most certain thing about this poverty is that it is not remedied   13
by a general advance in income. Case poverty is not remedied because the specific individual inadequacy precludes employment and participation in the general advance. Insular poverty is not directly alleviated because the advance does not remove the specific frustrations of environment to which the people of these areas are subject. This is not to say that it is without effect. If there are jobs outside the ghetto or away from the rural slum, those who are qualified, and not otherwise constrained, can take them and escape. If there are no such jobs, none can escape. But it remains that advance cannot improve the position of those who, by virtue of self or environment, cannot participate.

III

With the transition of the very poor from a majority to a com-   14
parative minority position, there has been a change in their political position. Any tendency of a politician to identify himself with those of the lowest estate usually brought the reproaches of the well-to-do. Political pandering and demagoguery were naturally suspected. But, for the man so reproached, there was the compensating advantage of alignment with a large majority. Now any politician who speaks for the very poor is speaking for a small and generally inarticulate minority. As a result, the modern liberal politician regularly aligns himself not with the poverty-ridden members of the community but with the far more numerous people who enjoy the far more affluent income of (say) the modern trade union member or the intellectual. Ambrose Bierce, in *The Devil's Dictionary,* called poverty "a file provided for the teeth of the rats of reform."[2] It is so no longer. Reform now concerns itself with the needs of people who are relatively well-to-do— whether the comparison be with their own past or with those who are really at the bottom of the income ladder.

In consequence, a notable feature of efforts to help the very poor is   15
their absence of any very great political appeal.[3] Politicians have found it possible to be indifferent where they could not be derisory. And very few have been under a strong compulsion to support these efforts.

The concern for inequality and deprivation had vitality only   16
so long as the many suffered while a few had much. It did not survive

---

[2] **Ambrose Bierce (1842–1914)** A southern American writer noted for satirical writings such as the one quoted.

[3] This was true of the Office of Economic Opportunity—the so-called poverty program—and was ultimately the reason for its effective demise. [Galbraith's note]

as a decisive political issue in a time when the many had much even though others had much more. It is our misfortune that when inequality declined as an issue, the slate was not left clean. A residual and in some ways rather more hopeless problem remained.

IV

An affluent society that is also both compassionate and rational   17
would, no doubt, secure to all who needed it the minimum income essential for decency and comfort. The corrupting effect on the human spirit of unearned revenue has unquestionably been exaggerated as, indeed, have the character-building values of hunger and privation. To secure to each family a minimum income, as a normal function of the society, would help ensure that the misfortunes of parents, deserved or otherwise, were not visited on their children. It would help ensure that poverty was not self-perpetuating. Most of the reaction, which no doubt would be adverse, is based on obsolete attitudes. When poverty was a majority phenomenon, such action could not be afforded. A poor society, as this essay has previously shown, had to enforce the rule that the person who did not work could not eat. And possibly it was justified in the added cruelty of applying the rule to those who could not work or whose efficiency was far below par. An affluent society has no similar excuse for such rigor. It can use the forthright remedy of providing income for those without. Nothing requires such a society to be compassionate. But it no longer has a high philosophical justification for callousness.

The notion that income is a remedy for indigency has a cer-   18
tain forthright appeal.[4] It would also ease the problems of economic management by reducing the reliance on production as a source of income. The provision of such a basic source of income must henceforth be the first and the strategic step in the attack on poverty.

But it is only one step. In the past, we have suffered from the sup-   19
position that the only remedy for poverty lies in remedies that allow people to look after themselves—to participate in the economy. Nothing has better served the conscience of people who wished to avoid inconvenient or expensive action than an appeal, on this issue, to Calvinist precept—"The only sound way to solve the problem of poverty is to help people help themselves." But this does not mean that steps to allow participation and to keep poverty from being self-perpetuating are unimportant. On the contrary. It requires that the investment in children from families presently afflicted be as little below normal

---

[4] As earlier noted, in the first edition the provision of a guaranteed income was discussed but dismissed as "beyond reasonable hope." [Galbraith's note]

as possible. If the children of poor families have first-rate schools and school attendance is properly enforced; if the children, though badly fed at home, are well nourished at school; if the community has sound health services, and the physical well-being of the children is vigilantly watched; if there is opportunity for advanced education for those who qualify regardless of means; and if, especially in the case of urban communities, housing is ample and housing standards are enforced, the streets are clean, the laws are kept, and recreation is adequate—then there is a chance that the children of the very poor will come to maturity without inhibiting disadvantage. In the case of insular poverty, this remedy requires that the services of the community be assisted from outside. Poverty is self-perpetuating partly because the poorest communities are poorest in the services which would eliminate it. To eliminate poverty efficiently, we must, indeed, invest more than proportionately in the children of the poor community. It is there that high-quality schools, strong health services, special provision for nutrition and recreation are most needed to compensate for the very low investment which families are able to make in their own offspring.

The effect of education and related investment in individuals is to   20 help them overcome the restraints that are imposed by their environment. These need also to be attacked even more directly—by giving the mobility that is associated with plentiful, good, and readily available housing, by provision of comfortable, efficient, and economical mass transport, by making the environment pleasant and safe, and by eliminating the special health handicaps that afflict the poor.

Nor is case poverty entirely resistant to such remedies. Much can   21 be done to treat those characteristics which cause people to reject or be rejected by the modern industrial society. Educational deficiencies can be overcome. Mental deficiencies can be treated. Physical handicaps can be remedied. The limiting factor is not a lack of knowledge of what can be done. Overwhelmingly, it is a shortage of money.

V

It will be clear that, to a remarkable extent, the remedy for poverty   22 leads to the same requirements as those for social balance. The restraints that confine people to the ghetto are those that result from insufficient investment in the public sector. And the means to escape from these constraints and to break their hold on subsequent generations just mentioned—better nutrition and health, better education, more and better housing, better mass transport, an environment more conducive to effective social participation—all, with rare exceptions, call for massively greater investment in the public sector. In recent years, the problems of the urban ghetto have been greatly discussed but with little resultant effect. To a certain extent, the search for deeper social explanations of its troubles has been motivated by the hope that these (together with more police) might lead to solutions that would somehow elide the problem of cost. It is an idle hope. The modern urban household is an extremely expensive thing. We have not yet taken the measure of the resources that must be allocated to its public tasks if it is to be agreeable or even tolerable. And first among the symptoms of an insufficient allocation is the teeming discontent of the modern ghetto.

A further feature of these remedies is to be observed. Their consequence is to allow of participation in the economic life of the larger community—to make people and the children of people who are now idle productive. This means that they will add to the total output of goods and services. We see once again that even by its own terms the present preoccupation with the private sector of the economy as compared with the whole spectrum of human needs is inefficient. The parallel with investment in the supply of trained and educated manpower discussed above will be apparent.   23

But increased output of goods is not the main point. Even to the most intellectually reluctant reader, it will now be evident that enhanced productive efficiency is not the motif of this volume. The very fact that increased output offers itself as a by-product of the effort to eliminate poverty is one of the reasons. No one would be called upon to write at such length on a problem so easily solved as that of increasing production. The main point lies elsewhere. Poverty—grim, degrading, and ineluctable—is not remarkable in India. For relatively few, the fate is otherwise. But in the United States, the survival of poverty is remarkable. We ignore it because we share with all societies at all times the capacity for not seeing what we do not wish to see. Anciently this has enabled the nobleman to enjoy his dinner while remaining oblivious to the beggars around his door. In our own day, it enables us to travel in comfort through the South Bronx and into the lush precincts of midtown Manhattan. But while our failure to notice can be explained, it cannot be excused. "Poverty," Pitt[5] exclaimed, "is no disgrace but it is damned annoying." In the contemporary United States, it is not annoying but it is a disgrace.   24

---

[5]**William Pitt, the Younger (1759–1806)** British prime minister from 1783 to 1801 and, briefly, again in 1804 and 1805.

QUESTIONS FOR CRITICAL READING

1. What is the fundamental difference between the attitude Alfred Marshall held toward the poor (para. 1) and the attitude contemporary economists hold?

2. Galbraith avoids a specific definition of poverty because he says it changes from society to society. How would you define poverty as it exists in our society? What are its major indicators?

3. According to Galbraith, what is the relationship of politics to poverty?

4. What, according to this essay, seem to be the causes of poverty?

5. Clarify the distinctions Galbraith makes between case poverty and insular poverty. Are they reasonable distinctions?

6. Does Galbraith oversimplify the issues of poverty in America?

7. Galbraith first published this piece in 1958. How much have attitudes toward poverty changed since then? What kinds of progress seem to have been made toward eradicating poverty?

SUGGESTIONS FOR CRITICAL WRITING

1. In paragraph 4, Galbraith says, "People are poverty-stricken when their income, even if adequate for survival, falls radically behind that of the community. Then they cannot have what the larger community regards as the minimum necessary for decency; and they cannot wholly escape, therefore, the judgment of the larger community that they are indecent. They are degraded for, in the literal sense, they live outside the grades or categories which the community regards as acceptable." Examine what he says here, and explain what he means. Is this an accurate description of poverty? How would you amend it? If you accept his description of poverty, what public policy would you recommend to deal with it? What would be the consequences of accepting Galbraith's description?

2. Galbraith points out some anomalies of poverty and place. For example, he notes that West Virginia is rich in resources but that its people have been notable for their poverty. Connecticut, on the other hand, is poor in resources, with stony, untillable land, yet its people have been notable for their wealth. Some economists have also pointed out that when the Americas were settled, South America had gold, was home to lush tropics that yielded food and fruit for the asking, and held the promise of immense wealth. North America had a harsh climate, stubborn soil conditions, and dense forests that needed clearing. Yet North America has less poverty now than does South America. Write a brief essay in which you consider whether what is said above is too simplified to be useful. If it is not, what do you think is the reason for the economic distinctions that Galbraith and others point out?

3. What personal experiences have you had with poverty? Are you familiar with examples of case poverty? If so, describe them in such a way as to help others understand them. What causes produced the poverty? What is the social situation of the people in your examples? How might they increase their wealth?

4. Examine the newspapers for the last several days, and look through back issues of magazines such as *Time, Newsweek,* the *New Republic,* the *New Leader,* or *U.S. News & World Report.* How many stories does each devote to the question of poverty? Present a survey of the views you find, and compare them with Galbraith's. How much agreement or disagreement is there? Would the level of the nation's concern with poverty please Galbraith?

5. Write a brief essay about current political attitudes toward poverty. If possible, gather some recent statements made by politicians. Analyze them to see how closely they tally with Galbraith's concerns and views. Do any specific politicians act as spokespeople for the poor?

6. Galbraith says that poverty has undergone a dramatic change in our society: once most people were poor and only a few were affluent, and now most people are affluent and only a few are poor. Is Galbraith correct in this assessment? Interview your parents and grandparents and their friends to establish or disprove the validity of Galbraith's claim, and then explain what you feel are the problems the poor face as a result of their minority status. If possible, during your interviews ask what feelings your parents and their friends have about the poor. What feelings do you have? Are they shared by your friends?

7. **CONNECTIONS**   What might Karl Marx (p. 453) say in reaction to Galbraith's definition of poverty and his terms for case poverty and insular poverty? Should Galbraith have examined the role of the bourgeoisie in creating, maintaining, or ignoring poverty? Galbraith wrote the original version of this piece during the 1950s, while world communism was at its height. How might he have accommodated the issues that Marx felt were most important for the working person?

8. **CONNECTIONS**   The Friedmans have a great deal to say about wealth but very little to say about poverty (**bedfordstmartins.com /worldofideas/epages**). How would they react to the basic principles that John Kenneth Galbraith seems to support in his essay? Is Galbraith any less committed to principles of liberty and equality of opportunity than the Friedmans? Both Galbraith and the Friedmans are renowned economists. Why does it seem that Galbraith primarily discusses poverty and the Friedmans primarily discuss wealth? What basic economic or political commitments seem to direct the authors' attention in their respective arguments?

9. **CONNECTIONS**   Galbraith certainly read Andrew Carnegie's *The Gospel of Wealth* (p. 481). What do you think his criticisms of Carnegie might be? Would he have agreed with Carnegie's praise of the laws of competition and accumulation? What alternatives or modifications might Galbraith have suggested to Carnegie? Would Galbraith have approved Carnegie's views on the proper distribution of wealth? How would Galbraith have responded to Carnegie's assurances that his program of philanthropy would heal the rift between the rich and the poor classes? Argue Galbraith's case either in praise of Carnegie's ideas

and theories or in condemnation of them. Use specific points from Carnegie and critique them using Galbraith's principles.

10. **SEEING CONNECTIONS**   Tanner's *The Thankful Poor* (p. 438) is not a painting Galbraith was likely to have seen in his lifetime, but if he had, would he think of the people depicted as examples of case poverty or of insular poverty? What evidence within the painting points to one or the other of these causes? Would Galbraith have had more or less sympathy than Carnegie for the condition of the older man and the young boy? How would Galbraith have reacted to the thankfulness expressed in the title of the painting? What would he have thought the chances were of the young boy growing up and out of poverty? Is it possible that Galbraith would not have thought of these people as examples of poverty? If not, what would his view be?

ROBERT B. REICH
Why the Rich Are Getting Richer and the Poor, Poorer

ROBERT B. REICH (b. 1946), professor of public policy at the Goldman School of Public Policy at the University of California at Berkeley, who served as secretary of labor in the first Clinton administration, holds a graduate degree from Yale Law School, and, unlike his former colleagues in the John F. Kennedy School of Government at Harvard, he does not hold a Ph.D. in economics. Nonetheless, he has written numerous books on economics and has been a prominent lecturer for more than a dozen years. Reich's books include *The Future of Success: Working and Living in the New Economy* (2000); *Reason: Why Liberals Will Win the Battle for America* (2004); and *Supercapitalism: The Transformation of Business, Democracy, and Everyday Life* (2007). All of these have been best-sellers, something unusual for the work of an academic concerned with economics. *Locked in the Cabinet* (1997) is a memoir of his four years as secretary of labor. *The Work of Nations* (1991), from which this essay comes, is the distillation of many years' analysis of modern economic trends.

As a college student, Reich was an activist but not a radical. In 1968, he was a Rhodes scholar, studying at Oxford University with Bill Clinton and a number of others who became influential American policy makers. Reich is a specialist in policy studies — that is, the relationship of governmental policy to the economic health of the nation. Unlike those who champion free trade and unlimited expansion, Reich questions the existence of free trade by pointing to the effect of government taxation on business enterprise. Taxation — like many governmental policies regarding immigration, tariffs, and money supply — directly shapes the behavior of most

From *The Work of Nations*.

513

companies. Reich feels that government must establish and execute an industrial policy that will benefit the nation.

Even though organized labor groups, such as industrial unions, have rejected much of his theorizing about labor, Reich has developed a reputation as a conciliator who can see opposite sides of a question and resolve them. He is known for his denunciation of mergers, lawsuits, takeovers, and other deals that he believes simply churn money around rather than produce wealth. He feels that such maneuvers enrich a few predatory people but do not benefit labor in general — and, indeed, that the debt created by such deals harms labor in the long run.

In *The Next American Frontier* (1983), Reich insists that government, unions, and businesses must cooperate to create a workable program designed to improve the economy. Trusting to chance and free trade, he argues, will not work in the current economy. He also has said that the old assembly-line methods must give way to what he calls "flexible production," involving smaller, customized runs of products for specific markets.

Reich's *The Work of Nations* (1991), whose title draws on Adam Smith's classic *The Wealth of Nations* (1776), examines the borderless nature of contemporary corporations. Multinational corporations are a reality, and as he points out in the following essay, their flexibility makes it possible for them to thrive by moving manufacturing plants from nation to nation. The reasons for moving are sometimes connected to lower wages but more often are connected to the infrastructure of a given nation. Reliable roads, plentiful electricity, well-educated workers, low crime rates, and political stability are all elements that make a location attractive to a multinational corporation.

Reich's Rhetoric

The structure of "Why the Rich Are Getting Richer and the Poor, Poorer" is built on a metaphor: that of boats rising or falling with the tide. As Reich notes, "All Americans used to be in roughly the same economic boat" (para. 2), and when the economic tide rose, most people rose along with it. However, today "national borders no longer define our economic fates"; Reich therefore views Americans today as being in different boats, depending on their role in the economy, and his essay follows the fates of three distinct kinds of workers.

Examining the routine worker, he observes, "The boat containing routine producers is sinking rapidly" (para. 3). As he demonstrates, the need for routine production has declined in part because of improvements in production facilities. Much labor-intensive work has been replaced by machines. Modern factories often scramble to locate in places where production costs are lowest. People in other nations work at a fraction of the hourly rate of American workers, and because factories are relatively cheap to establish, they can be easily moved.

Reich continues the boat metaphor with "in-person servers." The boat that carries these workers, he says, "is sinking as well, but somewhat more slowly and unevenly" (para. 20). Workers in restaurants, retail outlets, car washes, and other personal service industries often work part-time and have few health or other benefits. Their jobs are imperiled by machines as well, although not as much as manufacturing jobs are. Although the outlook for such workers is buoyed by a declining population, which will reduce competition for their jobs, increased immigration may cancel this benefit.

Finally, Reich argues that the "vessel containing America's symbolic analysts is rising" (para. 28). This third group contains the population that identifies and solves problems and brokers ideas. "Almost everyone around the world is buying the skills and insights of Americans who manipulate oral and visual symbols" (para. 33). Engineers, consultants, marketing experts, publicists, and those in entertainment fields all manage to cross national boundaries and prosper at a rate that is perhaps startling. As a result of an expanding world market, symbolic analysts do not depend only on the purchasing power of routine and in-service workers. Instead, they rely on the same global web that dominates the pattern of corporate structure.

Reich's essay follows the fate of these three groups in turn to establish the pattern of change and expectation that will shape America's economic future. His metaphor is deftly handled, and he includes details, examples, facts, and careful references to support his position.

PREREADING QUESTIONS:
WHAT TO READ FOR

The following prereading questions may help you anticipate key issues in the discussion of Robert B. Reich's "Why the Rich Are Getting Richer and the Poor, Poorer." Keeping them in mind during your first reading of the selection should help focus your attention.

- Why and how does an individual's position in the world economy depend on the function he/she performs in it?

- Who are the "routine producers"? What will be their fate in the future?

- Who are the "symbolic analysts" in our economy? How does one become a symbolic analyst?

Why the Rich Are Getting Richer
and the Poor, Poorer

The division of labor is limited by the extent of the market.
—ADAM SMITH
An Inquiry into the Nature
and Causes of the Wealth of Nations (1776)

Regardless of how your job is officially classified (manufacturing, 1
service, managerial, technical, secretarial, and so on), or the industry
in which you work (automotive, steel, computer, advertising, finance,
food processing), your real competitive position in the world economy is coming to depend on the function you perform in it. Herein
lies the basic reason why incomes are diverging. The fortunes of routine producers are declining. In-person servers are also becoming
poorer, although their fates are less clear-cut. But symbolic analysts—
who solve, identify, and broker new problems—are, by and large,
succeeding in the world economy.

All Americans used to be in roughly the same economic boat. 2
Most rose or fell together as the corporations in which they were
employed, the industries comprising such corporations, and the
national economy as a whole became more productive—or languished. But national borders no longer define our economic fates.
We are now in different boats, one sinking rapidly, one sinking more
slowly, and the third rising steadily.

The boat containing routine producers is sinking rapidly. Recall 3
that by midcentury routine production workers in the United States
were paid relatively well. The giant pyramidlike organizations at the
core of each major industry coordinated their prices and investments—
avoiding the harsh winds of competition and thus maintaining healthy
earnings. Some of these earnings, in turn, were reinvested in new plant
and equipment (yielding ever-larger-scale economies); another portion
went to top managers and investors. But a large and increasing portion
went to middle managers and production workers. Work stoppages
posed such a threat to high-volume production that organized labor
was able to exact an ever-larger premium for its cooperation. And the
pattern of wages established within the core corporations influenced the
pattern throughout the national economy. Thus the growth of a relatively affluent middle class, able to purchase all the wondrous things
produced in high volume by the core corporations.

But, as has been observed, the core is rapidly breaking down 4
into global webs which earn their largest profits from clever

problem-solving, -identifying, and brokering. As the costs of transporting standard things and of communicating information about them
continue to drop, profit margins on high-volume, standardized production are thinning, because there are few barriers to entry. Modern
factories and state-of-the-art machinery can be installed almost anywhere on the globe. Routine producers in the United States, then,
are in direct competition with millions of routine producers in other
nations. Twelve thousand people are added to the world's population
every hour, most of whom, eventually, will happily work for a small
fraction of the wages of routine producers in America.[1]

The consequence is clearest in older, heavy industries, where   5
high-volume, standardized production continues its ineluctable move
to where labor is cheapest and most accessible around the world. Thus,
for example, the Maquiladora factories cluttered along the Mexican
side of the U.S. border in the sprawling shanty towns of Tijuana, Mex-
icali, Nogales, Agua Prieta, and Ciudad Juárez—factories owned mostly
by Americans, but increasingly by Japanese—in which more than a
half million routine producers assemble parts into finished goods to
be shipped into the United States.

The same story is unfolding worldwide. Until the late 1970s,   6
AT&T had depended on routine producers in Shreveport, Louisiana,
to assemble standard telephones. It then discovered that routine producers in Singapore would perform the same tasks at a far lower cost.
Facing intense competition from other global webs, AT&T's strategic
brokers felt compelled to switch. So in the early 1980s they stopped
hiring routine producers in Shreveport and began hiring cheaper
routine producers in Singapore. But under this kind of pressure for
ever-lower high-volume production costs, today's Singaporean can
easily end up as yesterday's Louisianan. By the late 1980s, AT&T's
strategic brokers found that routine producers in Thailand were eager
to assemble telephones for a small fraction of the wages of routine
producers in Singapore. Thus, in 1989, AT&T stopped hiring Singa-
poreans to make telephones and began hiring even cheaper routine
producers in Thailand.

The search for ever-lower wages has not been confined to heavy   7
industry. Routine data processing is equally footloose. Keypunch operators located anywhere around the world can enter data into computers,

---

[1] The reader should note, of course, that lower wages in other areas of the
world are of no particular attraction to global capital unless workers there are sufficiently productive to make the labor cost of producing *each unit* lower there than
in higher-wage regions. Productivity in many low-wage areas of the world has
improved due to the ease with which state-of-the-art factories and equipment can be
installed there. [Reich's note]

linked by satellite or transoceanic fiber-optic cable, and take it out again. As the rates charged by satellite networks continue to drop, and as more satellites and fiber-optic cables become available (reducing communication costs still further), routine data processors in the United States find themselves in ever more direct competition with their counterparts abroad, who are often eager to work for far less.

By 1990, keypunch operators in the United States were earning,   8
at most, $6.50 per hour. But keypunch operators throughout the rest of the world were willing to work for a fraction of this. Thus, many potential American data-processing jobs were disappearing, and the wages and benefits of the remaining ones were in decline. Typical was Saztec International, a $20-million-a-year data-processing firm head-quartered in Kansas City, whose American strategic brokers contracted with routine data processors in Manila and with American-owned firms that needed such data-processing services. Compared with the average Philippine income of $1,700 per year, data-entry operators working for Saztec earn the princely sum of $2,650. The remainder of Saztec's employees were American problem-solvers and -identifiers, searching for ways to improve the worldwide system and find new uses to which it could be put.[2]

By 1990, American Airlines was employing over 1,000 data pro-   9
cessors in Barbados and the Dominican Republic to enter names and flight numbers from used airline tickets (flown daily to Barbados from airports around the United States) into a giant computer bank located in Dallas. Chicago publisher R. R. Donnelley was sending entire manuscripts to Barbados for entry into computers in preparation for printing. The New York Life Insurance Company was dispatching insurance claims to Castleisland, Ireland, where routine producers, guided by simple directions, entered the claims and determined the amounts due, then instantly transmitted the computations back to the United States. (When the firm advertised in Ireland for twenty-five data-processing jobs, it received six hundred applications.) And McGraw-Hill was processing subscription renewal and marketing information for its magazines in nearby Galway. Indeed, literally millions of routine workers around the world were receiving information, converting it into computer-readable form, and then sending it back—at the speed of electronic impulses—whence it came.

The simple coding of computer software has also entered into   10
world commerce. India, with a large English-speaking population of technicians happy to do routine programming cheaply, is proving

---

[2] John Maxwell Hamilton, "A Bit Player Buys into the Computer Age," *New York Times Business World,* December 3, 1989, p. 14. [Reich's note]

to be particularly attractive to global webs in need of this service. By 1990, Texas Instruments maintained a software development facility in Bangalore, linking fifty Indian programmers by satellite to TI's Dallas headquarters. Spurred by this and similar ventures, the Indian government was building a teleport in Poona, intended to make it easier and less expensive for many other firms to send their routine software design specifications for coding.[3]

11   This shift of routine production jobs from advanced to developing nations is a great boon to many workers in such nations who otherwise would be jobless or working for much lower wages. These workers, in turn, now have more money with which to purchase symbolic-analytic services from advanced nations (often embedded within all sorts of complex products). The trend is also beneficial to everyone around the world who can now obtain high-volume, standardized products (including information and software) more cheaply than before.

12   But these benefits do not come without certain costs. In particular the burden is borne by those who no longer have good-paying routine production jobs within advanced economies like the United States. Many of these people used to belong to unions or at least benefited from prevailing wage rates established in collective bargaining agreements. But as the old corporate bureaucracies have flattened into global webs, bargaining leverage has been lost. Indeed, the tacit national bargain is no more.

13   Despite the growth in the number of new jobs in the United States, union membership has withered. In 1960, 35 percent of all nonagricultural workers in America belonged to a union. But by 1980 that portion had fallen to just under a quarter, and by 1989 to about 17 percent. Excluding government employees, union membership was down to 13.4 percent.[4] This was a smaller proportion even than in the early 1930s, before the National Labor Relations Act created a legally protected right to labor representation. The drop in membership has been accompanied by a growing number of collective bargaining agreements to freeze wages at current levels, reduce wage levels of entering workers, or reduce wages overall. This is an important reason why the long economic recovery that began in 1982 produced a smaller rise in unit labor costs than any of the eight recoveries since

---

[3] Udayan Gupta, "U.S.-Indian Satellite Link Stands to Cut Software Costs," *Wall Street Journal*, March 6, 1989, p. B2. [Reich's note]

[4] *Statistical Abstract of the United States* (Washington, D.C.: U.S. Government Printing Office, 1989), p. 416, table 684. [Reich's note]

World War II—the low rate of unemployment during its course not-withstanding.

Routine production jobs have vanished fastest in traditional   14
unionized industries (autos, steel, and rubber, for example), where average wages have kept up with inflation. This is because the jobs of older workers in such industries are protected by seniority; the youngest workers are the first to be laid off. Faced with a choice of cutting wages or cutting the number of jobs, a majority of union members (secure in the knowledge that there are many who are junior to them who will be laid off first) often have voted for the latter.

Thus the decline in union membership has been most striking   15
among young men entering the workforce without a college education. In the early 1950s, more than 40 percent of this group joined unions; by the late 1980s, less than 20 percent (if public employees are excluded, less than 10 percent).[5] In steelmaking, for example, although many older workers remained employed, almost half of all routine steelmaking jobs in America vanished between 1974 and 1988 (from 480,000 to 260,000). Similarly with automobiles: during the 1980s, the United Auto Workers lost 500,000 members— one-third of their total at the start of the decade. General Motors alone cut 150,000 American production jobs during the 1980s (even as it added employment abroad). Another consequence of the same phenomenon: the gap between the average wages of unionized and non-unionized workers widened dramatically—from 14.6 percent in 1973 to 20.4 percent by end of the 1980s.[6] The lesson is clear. If you drop out of high school or have no more than a high school diploma, do not expect a good routine production job to be awaiting you.

Also vanishing are lower- and middle-level management jobs   16
involving routine production. Between 1981 and 1986, more than 780,000 foremen, supervisors, and section chiefs lost their jobs through plant closings and layoffs.[7] Large numbers of assistant division heads, assistant directors, assistant managers, and vice presidents also found themselves jobless. GM shed more than 40,000 white-collar employees and planned to eliminate another 25,000 by the mid-1990s.[8] As America's core pyramids metamorphosed into

---

[5] Calculations from Current Population Surveys by L. Katz and A. Revenga, "Changes in the Structure of Wages: U.S. and Japan," National Bureau of Economic Research, September 1989. [Reich's note]

[6] U.S. Department of Commerce, Bureau of Labor Statistics, "Wages of Unionized and Non-Unionized Workers," various issues. [Reich's note]

[7] U.S. Department of Labor, Bureau of Labor Statistics, "Reemployment Increases Among Displaced Workers," *BLS News*, USDL 86–414, October 14, 1986, table 6. [Reich's note]

[8] *Wall Street Journal*, February 16, 1990, p. A5. [Reich's note]

global webs, many middle-level routine producers were as obsolete as routine workers on the line.

As has been noted, foreign-owned webs are hiring some Americans to do routine production in the United States. Philips, Sony, and Toyota factories are popping up all over—to the self-congratulatory applause of the nation's governors and mayors, who have lured them with promises of tax abatements and new sewers, among other amenities. But as these ebullient politicians will soon discover, the foreign-owned factories are highly automated and will become far more so in years to come. Routine production jobs account for a small fraction of the cost of producing most items in the United States and other advanced nations, and this fraction will continue to decline sharply as computer-integrated robots take over. In 1977 it took routine producers thirty-five hours to assemble an automobile in the United States; it is estimated that by the mid-1990s, Japanese-owned factories in America will be producing finished automobiles using only eight hours of a routine producer's time.[9]   17

The productivity and resulting wages of American workers who run such robotic machinery may be relatively high, but there may not be many such jobs to go around. A case in point: in the late 1980s, Nippon Steel joined with America's ailing Inland Steel to build a new $400 million cold-rolling mill fifty miles west of Gary, Indiana. The mill was celebrated for its state-of-the-art technology, which cut the time to produce a coil of steel from twelve days to about one hour. In fact, the entire plant could be run by a small team of technicians, which became clear when Inland subsequently closed two of its old cold-rolling mills, laying off hundreds of routine workers. Governors and mayors take note: your much-ballyhooed foreign factories may end up employing distressingly few of your constituents.   18

Overall, the decline in routine jobs has hurt men more than women. This is because the routine production jobs held by men in high-volume metal-bending manufacturing industries had paid higher wages than the routine production jobs held by women in textiles and data processing. As both sets of jobs have been lost, American women in routine production have gained more equal footing with American men—equally poor footing, that is. This is a major reason why the gender gap between male and female wages began to close during the 1980s.   19

The second of the three boats, carrying in-person servers, is sinking as well, but somewhat more slowly and unevenly. Most   20

---

[9] Figures from the International Motor Vehicles Program, Massachusetts Institute of Technology, 1989. [Reich's note]

in-person servers are paid at or just slightly above the minimum wage and many work only part-time, with the result that their take-home pay is modest, to say the least. Nor do they typically receive all the benefits (health care, life insurance, disability, and so forth) garnered by routine producers in large manufacturing corporations or by symbolic analysts affiliated with the more affluent threads of global webs.[10] In-person servers are sheltered from the direct effects of global competition and, like everyone else, benefit from access to lower-cost products from around the world. But they are not immune to its indirect effects.

For one thing, in-person servers increasingly compete with   21
former routine production workers, who, no longer able to find well-paying routine production jobs, have few alternatives but to seek in-person service jobs. The Bureau of Labor Statistics estimates that of the 2.8 million manufacturing workers who lost their jobs during the early 1980s, fully one-third were rehired in service jobs paying at least 20 percent less.[11] In-person servers must also compete with high school graduates and dropouts who years before had moved easily into routine production jobs but no longer can. And if demographic predictions about the American workforce in the first decades of the twenty-first century are correct (and they are likely to be, since most of the people who will comprise the workforce are already identifiable), most new entrants into the job market will be black or Hispanic men, or women—groups that in years past have possessed relatively weak technical skills. This will result in an even larger number of people crowding into in-person services. Finally, in-person servers will be competing with growing numbers of immigrants, both legal and illegal, for whom in-person services will comprise the most accessible jobs. (It is estimated that between the mid-1980s and the end of the century, about a quarter of all workers entering the American labor force will be immigrants.[12])

Perhaps the fiercest competition that in-person servers face   22
comes from labor-saving machinery (much of it invented, designed, fabricated, or assembled in other nations, of course). Automated tellers, computerized cashiers, automatic car washes, robotized vending

---

[10] The growing portion of the American labor force engaged in in-person services, relative to routine production, thus helps explain why the number of Americans lacking health insurance increased by at least 6 million during the 1980s. [Reich's note]

[11] U.S. Department of Labor, Bureau of Labor Statistics, "Reemployment Increases Among Disabled Workers," October 14, 1986. [Reich's note]

[12] Federal Immigration and Naturalization Service, *Statistical Yearbook* (Washington, D.C.: U.S. Government Printing Office, 1986, 1987). [Reich's note]

machines, self-service gasoline pumps, and all similar gadgets substitute for the human beings that customers once encountered. Even telephone operators are fast disappearing, as electronic sensors and voice simulators become capable of carrying on conversations that are reasonably intelligent and always polite. Retail sales workers — among the largest groups of in-person servers — are similarly imperiled. Through personal computers linked to television screens, tomorrow's consumers will be able to buy furniture, appliances, and all sorts of electronic toys from their living rooms — examining the merchandise from all angles, selecting whatever color, size, special features, and price seem most appealing, and then transmitting the order instantly to warehouses from which the selections will be shipped directly to their homes. So, too, with financial transactions, airline and hotel reservations, rental car agreements, and similar contracts, which will be executed between consumers in their homes and computer banks somewhere else on the globe.[13]

Advanced economies like the United States will continue to generate sizable numbers of new in-person service jobs, of course, the automation of older ones notwithstanding. For every bank teller who loses her job to an automated teller, three new jobs open for aerobics instructors. Human beings, it seems, have an almost insatiable desire for personal attention. But the intense competition nevertheless ensures that the wages of in-person servers will remain relatively low. In-person servers — working on their own, or else dispersed widely amid many small establishments, filling all sorts of personal-care niches — cannot readily organize themselves into labor unions or create powerful lobbies to limit the impact of such competition.   23

In two respects, demographics will work in favor of in-person servers, buoying their collective boat slightly. First, as has been noted, the rate of growth of the American workforce is slowing. In particular, the number of young workers is shrinking. Between 1985 and 1995, the number of eighteen- to twenty-four-year-olds will have declined by 17.5 percent. Thus, employers will have more incentive to hire and train in-person servers whom they might previously have avoided. But this demographic relief from the competitive pressures will be only temporary. The cumulative procreative energies of the postwar baby-boomers (born between 1946 and 1964) will result in a new surge of workers by 2010 or thereabouts.[14]   24

---

[13] See Claudia H. Deutsch, "The Powerful Push for Self-Service," *New York Times*, April 9, 1989, section 3, p. 1. [Reich's note]

[14] U.S. Bureau of the Census, Current Population Reports, Series P-23, no. 138, tables 2-1, 4-6. See W. Johnson, A. Packer, et al., *Workforce 2000: Work and Workers for the 21st Century* (Indianapolis: Hudson Institute, 1987). [Reich's note]

And immigration—both legal and illegal—shows every sign of increasing in years to come.

Next, by the second decade of the twenty-first century, the 25 number of Americans aged sixty-five and over will be rising precipitously, as the baby-boomers reach retirement age and live longer. Their life expectancies will lengthen not just because fewer of them will have smoked their way to their graves and more will have eaten better than their parents, but also because they will receive all sorts of expensive drugs and therapies designed to keep them alive—barely. By 2035, twice as many Americans will be elderly as in 1988, and the number of octogenarians is expected to triple. As these decaying baby-boomers ingest all the chemicals and receive all the treatments, they will need a great deal of personal attention. Millions of deteriorating bodies will require nurses, nursing-home operators, hospital administrators, orderlies, home-care providers, hospice aides, and technicians to operate and maintain all the expensive machinery that will monitor and temporarily stave off final disintegration. There might even be a booming market for euthanasia specialists. In-person servers catering to the old and ailing will be in strong demand.[15]

One small problem: the decaying baby-boomers will not have 26 enough money to pay for these services. They will have used up their personal savings years before. Their Social Security payments will, of course, have been used by the government to pay for the previous generation's retirement and to finance much of the budget deficits of the 1980s. Moreover, with relatively fewer young Americans in the population, the supply of housing will likely exceed the demand, with the result that the boomers' major investments—their homes—will be worth less (in inflation-adjusted dollars) when they retire than they planned for. In consequence, the huge cost of caring for the graying boomers will fall on many of the same people who will be paid to care for them. It will be like a great sump pump: in-person servers of the twenty-first century will have an abundance of health-care jobs, but a large portion of their earnings will be devoted to Social Security payments and income taxes, which will in turn be used to pay their salaries. The net result: no real improvement in their standard of living.

The standard of living of in-person servers also depends, indi- 27 rectly, on the standard of living of the Americans they serve who are engaged in world commerce. To the extent that these Americans are richly rewarded by the rest of the world for what they contribute, they will have more money to lavish upon in-person services. Here we

---

[15] The Census Bureau estimates that by the year 2000, at least 12 million Americans will work in health services—well over 6 percent of the total workforce. [Reich's note]

find the only form of "trickle-down" economics that has a basis in reality. A waitress in a town whose major factory has just been closed is unlikely to earn a high wage or enjoy much job security; in a swank resort populated by film producers and banking moguls, she is apt to do reasonably well. So, too, with nations. In-person servers in Bangladesh may spend their days performing roughly the same tasks as in-person servers in the United States, but have a far lower standard of living for their efforts. The difference comes in the value that their customers add to the world economy.

Unlike the boats of routine producers and in-person servers, however, the vessel containing America's symbolic analysts is rising. Worldwide demand for their insights is growing as the ease and speed of communicating them steadily increases. Not every symbolic analyst is rising as quickly or as dramatically as every other, of course; symbolic analysts at the low end are barely holding their own in the world economy. But symbolic analysts at the top are in such great demand worldwide that they have difficulty keeping track of all their earnings. Never before in history has opulence on such a scale been gained by people who have earned it, and done so legally.   28

Among symbolic analysts in the middle range are American scientists and researchers who are busily selling their discoveries to global enterprise webs. They are not limited to American customers. If the strategic brokers in General Motors' headquarters refuse to pay a high price for a new means of making high-strength ceramic engines dreamed up by a team of engineers affiliated with Carnegie Mellon University in Pittsburgh, the strategic brokers of Honda or Mercedes-Benz are likely to be more than willing.   29

So, too, with the insights of America's ubiquitous management consultants, which are being sold for large sums to eager entrepreneurs in Europe and Latin America. Also, the insights of America's energy consultants, sold for even larger sums to Arab sheikhs. American design engineers are providing insights to Olivetti, Mazda, Siemens, and other global webs; American marketers, techniques for learning what worldwide consumers will buy; American advertisers, ploys for ensuring that they actually do. American architects are issuing designs and blueprints for opera houses, art galleries, museums, luxury hotels, and residential complexes in the world's major cities; American commercial property developers, marketing these properties to worldwide investors and purchasers.   30

Americans who specialize in the gentle art of public relations are in demand by corporations, governments, and politicians in virtually every nation. So, too, are American political consultants, some of whom, at this writing, are advising the Hungarian Socialist Party, the remnant of Hungary's ruling Communists, on how to salvage a few   31 parliamentary seats in the nation's first free election in more than forty years. Also at this writing, a team of American agricultural consultants is advising the managers of a Soviet farm collective employing 1,700 Russians eighty miles outside Moscow. As noted, American investment bankers and lawyers specializing in financial circumnavigations are selling their insights to Asians and Europeans who are eager to discover how to make large amounts of money by moving large amounts of money.

Developing nations, meanwhile, are hiring American civil engineers 32 to advise on building roads and dams. The present thaw in the Cold War will no doubt expand these opportunities. American engineers from Bechtel (a global firm notable for having employed both Caspar Weinberger and George Shultz for much larger sums than either earned in the Reagan administration) have begun helping the Soviets design and install a new generation of nuclear reactors. Nations also are hiring American bankers and lawyers to help them renegotiate the terms of their loans with global banks, and Washington lobbyists to help them with Congress, the Treasury, the World Bank, the IMF, and other politically sensitive institutions. In fits of obvious desperation, several nations emerging from communism have even hired American economists to teach them about capitalism.

Almost everyone around the world is buying the skills and 33 insights of Americans who manipulate oral and visual symbols— musicians, sound engineers, film producers, makeup artists, directors, cinematographers, actors and actresses, boxers, scriptwriters, songwriters, and set designers. Among the wealthiest of symbolic analysts are Steven Spielberg, Bill Cosby, Charles Schulz, Eddie Murphy, Sylvester Stallone, Madonna, and other star directors and performers—who are almost as well known on the streets of Dresden and Tokyo as in the Back Bay of Boston. Less well rewarded but no less renowned are the unctuous anchors on Turner Broadcasting's Cable News, who appear daily, via satellite, in places ranging from Vietnam to Nigeria. Vanna White is the world's most-watched game-show hostess. Behind each of these familiar faces is a collection of American problem-solvers, -identifiers, and brokers who train, coach, advise, promote, amplify, direct, groom, represent, and otherwise add value to their talents.[16]

There are also the insights of senior American executives who 34 occupy the world headquarters of global "American" corporations and

---

[16] In 1989, the entertainment business summoned to the United States $5.5 billion in foreign earnings — making it among the nation's largest export industries, just behind aerospace. U.S. Department of Commerce, International Trade Commission, "Composition of U.S. Exports," various issues. [Reich's note]

the national or regional headquarters of global "foreign" corporations. Their insights are duly exported to the rest of the world through the webs of global enterprise. IBM does not export many machines from the United States, for example. Big Blue makes machines all over the globe and services them on the spot. Its prime American exports are symbolic and analytic. From IBM's world headquarters in Armonk, New York, emanate strategic brokerage and related management services bound for the rest of the world. In return, IBM's top executives are generously rewarded.

The most important reason for this expanding world market and   35 increasing global demand for the symbolic and analytic insights of Americans has been the dramatic improvement in worldwide communication and transportation technologies. Designs, instructions, advice, and visual and audio symbols can be communicated more and more rapidly around the globe, with ever-greater precision and at ever-lower cost. Madonna's voice can be transported to billions of listeners, with perfect clarity, on digital compact discs. A new invention emanating from engineers in Battelle's laboratory in Columbus, Ohio, can be sent almost anywhere via modem, in a form that will allow others to examine it in three dimensions through enhanced computer graphics. When face-to-face meetings are still required — and videoconferencing will not suffice — it is relatively easy for designers, consultants, advisers, artists, and executives to board supersonic jets and, in a matter of hours, meet directly with their worldwide clients, customers, audiences, and employees.

With rising demand comes rising compensation. Whether in the   36 form of licensing fees, fees for service, salaries, or shares in final profits, the economic result is much the same. There are also nonpecuniary rewards. One of the best-kept secrets among symbolic analysts is that so many of them enjoy their work. In fact, much of it does not count as work at all, in the traditional sense. The work of routine producers and in-person servers is typically monotonous; it causes muscles to tire or weaken and involves little independence or discretion. The "work" of symbolic analysts, by contrast, often involves puzzles, experiments, games, a significant amount of chatter, and substantial discretion over what to do next. Few routine producers or in-person servers would "work" if they did not need to earn the money. Many symbolic analysts would "work" even if money were no object.

At midcentury, when America was a national market dominated by   37 core pyramid-shaped corporations, there were constraints on the earnings of people at the highest rungs. First and most obviously, the market for their services was largely limited to the borders of the nation.

In addition, whatever conceptual value they might contribute was small relative to the value gleaned from large scale—and it was dependent on large scale for whatever income it was to summon. Most of the problems to be identified and solved had to do with enhancing the efficiency of production and improving the flow of materials, parts, assembly, and distribution. Inventors searched for the rare breakthrough revealing an entirely new product to be made in high volume; management consultants, executives, and engineers thereafter tried to speed and synchronize its manufacture, to better achieve scale efficiencies; advertisers and marketers sought then to whet the public's appetite for the standard item that emerged. Since white-collar earnings increased with larger scale, there was considerable incentive to expand the firm; indeed, many of America's core corporations grew far larger than scale economies would appear to have justified.

By the 1990s, in contrast, the earnings of symbolic analysts were   38
limited neither by the size of the national market nor by the volume of production of the firms with which they were affiliated. The marketplace was worldwide, and conceptual value was high relative to value added from scale efficiencies.

There had been another constraint on high earnings, which also   39
gave way by the 1990s. At midcentury, the compensation awarded to top executives and advisers of the largest of America's core corporations could not be grossly out of proportion to that of low-level production workers. It would be unseemly for executives who engaged in highly visible rounds of bargaining with labor unions, and who routinely responded to government requests to moderate prices, to take home wages and benefits wildly in excess of what other Americans earned. Unless white-collar executives restrained themselves, moreover, blue-collar production workers could not be expected to restrain their own demands for higher wages. Unless both groups exercised restraint, the government could not be expected to forbear from imposing direct controls and regulations.

At the same time, the wages of production workers could not be   40
allowed to sink too low, lest there be insufficient purchasing power in the economy. After all, who would buy all the goods flowing out of American factories if not American workers? This, too, was part of the tacit bargain struck between American managers and their workers.

Recall the oft-repeated corporate platitude of the era about the   41
chief executive's responsibility to carefully weigh and balance the interests of the corporation's disparate stakeholders. Under the stewardship of the corporate statesman, no set of stakeholders—least of all white-collar executives—was to gain a disproportionately large share of the benefits of corporate activity; nor was any stakeholder—especially the average worker—to be left with a share that was

disproportionately small. Banal though it was, this idea helped to maintain the legitimacy of the core American corporation in the eyes of most Americans, and to ensure continued economic growth.

But by the 1990s, these informal norms were evaporating,   42
just as (and largely because) the core American corporation was vanishing. The links between top executives and the American production worker were fading: an ever-increasing number of subordinates and contractees were foreign, and a steadily grow-ing number of American routine producers were working for foreign-owned firms. An entire cohort of middle-level managers, who had once been deemed "white collar," had disappeared; and, increasingly, American executives were exporting their insights to global enterprise webs.

As the American corporation itself became a global web almost   43
indistinguishable from any other, its stakeholders were turning into a large and diffuse group, spread over the world. Such global stakehold-ers were less visible, and far less noisy, than national stakeholders. And as the American corporation sold its goods and services all over the world, the purchasing power of American workers became far less relevant to its economic survival.

Thus have the inhibitions been removed. The salaries and   44
benefits of America's top executives, and many of their advisers and consultants, have soared to what years before would have been unimaginable heights, even as those of other Americans have declined.

QUESTIONS FOR CRITICAL READING

1. What are symbolic analysts? Give some examples from your own experience.

2. What is the apparent relationship between higher education and an educated worker's prospects for wealth?

3. To what extent do you agree or disagree with Reich's description and analysis of routine workers and in-service workers?

4. If Reich's analysis is correct, which gender or social groups are likely to be most harmed by modern economic circumstances in America? Which are most likely to become wealthy? Why?

5. Are symbolic analysts inherently more valuable to our society than routine or in-service workers? Why do symbolic analysts command so much more wealth?

6. Which of the three groups Reich mentions do you see as having the greatest potential for growth in the next thirty years?

SUGGESTIONS FOR CRITICAL WRITING

1. Judging from the views that Reich holds about decreasing job opportunities for all three groups of workers, how will increased immigration affect the American economy? Is immigration a hopeful sign? Is it
   a danger to the economy? How do most people seem to perceive the
   effect of increased immigration?

2. To what extent do you think Reich is correct about the growing wealth
   of symbolic analysts? He says, "Never before in history has opulence
   on such a scale been gained by people who have earned it, and done
   so legally" (para. 28). Do you see yourself as a symbolic analyst? How
   do you see your future in relation to the three economic groups Reich
   describes?

3. Reich says, "Few routine producers or in-person servers would 'work'
   if they did not need to earn the money. Many symbolic analysts would
   'work' even if money were no object" (para. 36). Is this true? Examine your own experience—along with the experience of others you
   know —and defend or attack this view. How accurate do you consider
   Reich to be in his analysis of the way various workers view their work?

4. Describe the changes that have taken place in the American economy
   since 1960, according to this essay. How have they affected the way
   Americans work and the work that Americans can expect to find? How
   have your personal opportunities been broadened or narrowed by the
   changes? Do you feel the changes have been good for the country or
   not? Why?

5. Reich's view of the great success of Japanese corporations and of their
   presence as manufacturing giants in the United States and elsewhere
   is largely positive. He has pointed out elsewhere that Honda and
   other manufacturers in the United States provide jobs and municipal
   income that would otherwise go to other nations. What is your view
   of the presence of large Japanese corporations in the United States?
   What is your view of other nations' manufacturing facilities in the
   United States?

6. Why are the rich getting richer and the poor, poorer? Examine the kinds
   of differences between the rich and the poor that Reich describes. Is the
   process of increasing riches for the rich and increasing poverty for the
   poor inevitable, or will it begin to change in the near future?

7. **CONNECTIONS**   Karl Marx (p. 453) warns against globalism in the
   economy in part because it harms local industry and damages local
   styles and customs. How would Reich counter those fears? Is it clear
   that Reich approves of the new economy he describes, or does he
   accept globalism as a form of economic evolution? Would he be likely
   to agree with Andrew Carnegie (p. 481) that the laws of competition
   and accumulation operate in the new economy at least as forcefully
   as they did in Carnegie's time? Does he in any way seem approving of
   Marx's theories?

8. **CONNECTIONS**   Robert Reich makes a distinction between symbolic analysts and routine workers. According to the Friedmans (**bedfordstmartins.com/worldofideas/epages**), which of these are more likely to achieve great wealth? Why? If both have freedom of opportunity, why should there be a difference? Reich approves of the increase of opulence (para. 28); should he not agree with the Friedmans' views about the equality of opportunity and its natural outcome of an inequity of wealth in any nation? What arguments might Reich make against the Friedmans? What arguments might he most fervently support?

9. **CONNECTIONS**   Reich examines what seems to be a new form for the economy now that free trade is essentially a reality and major foreign nations—like Japan, China, and India—are creating enormous wealth while Western industrial nations are losing industries and jobs to those countries. How would Reich respond to Adam Smith's (p. 441) concepts of how a nation produces wealth? What are the differences Reich sees in the current economy as compared with that of Smith's time? Would he feel that any of Smith's principles regarding land, agriculture, and manufactures applies to our new economy? Establish Reich's position regarding Smith's basic theories.

10. **SEEING CONNECTIONS**   Where do the two people in Tanner's *The Thankful Poor* (p. 438) fit in Reich's concept of the new economy? What would Reich say about them if he were to include them in his discussion? What details in the painting might Reich point to as significant of the new economy? Keeping in mind that the painting was made in 1894, is it possible that Reich would simply say that these people have nothing to do with current economic conditions? Or would he say that the painting represents what will happen to many of the working poor in the United States? What evidence from the painting and from your understanding of the principles of wealth and poverty helps you draw your conclusions?

INTRODUCTION

Knowledge without education is but armed injustice.
— HORACE (65–8 B.C.E.)

The ink of the scholar is more sacred than the blood of the martyr.
— MUHAMMAD (570–632)

You cannot teach a man anything; you can only help him to find it within himself.
— GALILEO GALILEI (1564–1642)

There is less flogging in our great schools than formerly — but then less is learned there; so what the boys get at one end they lose at the other.
— SAMUEL JOHNSON (1709–1784)

In large states public education will always be mediocre, for the same reason that in large kitchens the cooking is usually bad.
— FRIEDRICH NIETZSCHE (1844–1900)

Education makes machines which act like men and produces men who act like machines.
— ERICH FROMM (1900–1980)

In classical times, when education was largely conducted at home or in schools that served the privileged few, education was rarely a matter of general philosophical discussion. In ancient Rome the schools taught Greek literature and modeled themselves on Greek schools. In Arab societies the traditions of the Platonic Greek academies were maintained until late in the Renaissance, and as a result Europe rediscovered the great Greek texts of Plato and Aristotle that those societies had preserved. However, in all these cases education was reserved for the privileged classes. The average person learned what was needed on the job and often could not read or write.

Among the early writings on the subject is John Milton's *Of Education* (1644), written as a public letter to Samuel Hartlib, who had written on education after having been influenced by Johann Comenius, a religious reformer in Europe. Milton was himself a schoolmaster for a few years, primarily teaching his sister's children. One of his famous statements concerns the learning of Latin and Greek, which was expected of all schoolchildren: "We do amiss to spend seven or eight years merely in scraping together so much miserable Latin and Greek as might be learned otherwise easily and delightfully in one year." Milton may have been a good teacher, but it is clear that he was working with a very select kind of student.

However, things were changing in the seventeenth century. For example, in America the Puritans declared in 1642 that every boy who did not train for a trade must go to school. The tradition of public schooling began in 1635 in Massachusetts and spread to the rest of the nation. The first schools were grammar schools in which Latin was usually emphasized. Most of these schools were for boys only; girls went to private "dame" schools conducted by women in their own homes. Public high schools were not created in the United States until 1821. On the other hand, a grammar school education was quite extensive and would in some cases prepare students for college study. The earliest college was Harvard, founded in 1639. Harvard's initial purpose was to train ministers for the church, but it rapidly expanded to include more secular studies.

Universal education was the law in the United States in the early part of the nineteenth century, and other nations soon followed, with modifications. Theoreticians of education developed a number of views on how to educate the masses. The selections that comprise this part of the book represent an international group of well-known educators and writers, all of whom had a personal stake in the success or failure of education in their time. They also understood the political implications of widespread free public education.

The Confucian philosopher Hsün Tzu, also known as Xunzi, was an ardent proponent for education, though his reasons were somewhat unorthodox during his time. Hsün Tzu lived during the period of the Warring States (453–221 B.C.E.), a time of frequent wars and social turmoil in China. He held the fundamental Confucian belief that humans could make a difference in the world, but in a far cry from other Confucians, he also believed that human nature was fundamentally evil rather than good and that following one's own instincts would lead to an unfulfilling life. According to Hsün Tzu, the only way that humans' evil nature could be overcome was by studying the classic writings and wisdom of the Way (the Tao), which required a lifelong commitment to education and understanding.

The most influential American educator of the twentieth century was John Dewey, a philosopher who had many skills and many interests. He began his career as a philosopher writing about philosophers, but he moved into the field of pedagogy and quickly joined one of the early schools of education at Columbia University, where he became world famous. Dewey's focus in the selection included here is on thought and thinking in education.

This subject may seem self-evident, but Dewey's emphasis is on critical thinking—the kind of thinking a skeptical and inquiring student would develop if given the opportunity. Dewey wanted students to be involved in activities that were interesting and educational and to have the opportunity to test their conclusions and validate their insights.

Another influential educator, Maria Montessori devoted her life to the education of the young, with an emphasis on preschool children. She was a physician, an anthropologist, a professor, and a sociologist. Her great experiment in education took place in the worst slum in Rome at the turn of the twentieth century. While the slum was being torn down and rebuilt with clean, modern buildings, she was given the opportunity to build a school that would accommodate the neighborhood's youngest children. Against great odds, Montessori used what she called "scientific pedagogy" to help students find themselves and make discoveries about the world in an environment designed for learning. The results of her experiment were far more impressive than anyone could have expected. In this school for impoverished students, she had three- and four-year-old children learning to read and write. They were excited by opportunities to learn about science and mathematics. Her approach to teaching, known as "The Montessori Method," was introduced in a number of Italian cities. Eventually Montessori traveled the world training teachers to use her methods and establish Montessori Schools. Those schools still flourish today, their principles based on the successes Montessori achieved beginning in 1906.

Carter G. Woodson, the "father of black history," was one of the first African Americans to receive a Ph.D. in history at Harvard University. He taught in the public schools in Washington, D.C., before eventually becoming dean of the College of Arts and Sciences at Howard University. He left teaching to devote himself to writing and to promoting educational programs for African Americans who he felt were not being told the truth about their own history. He wrote many important historical works that examined patterns of education in the early part of the nineteenth century. He also wrote a number of history textbooks designed for primary schools to correct the errors he found in the standard textbooks of the time, many of which were prejudiced against African Americans; some texts actually went as far as to blame the Civil War solely on the pressure from abolitionists to end slavery in the United States. The steps that Woodson took to amend the history being taught to America's youth and to support education for disenfranchised African Americans were pioneering and unprecedented.

Inspired by the lives of young students in poor neighborhoods, Jonathan Kozol found himself stymied by the public-school system in Boston when he deviated from accepted curriculum by reading a poem by Harlem Renaissance poet Langston Hughes in class. He was fired for doing so because Hughes was not officially on the curriculum for his grade. Kozol wrote *Death at an Early Age* (1967) about his experiences working in a Roxbury school. Because the book was a success and made him famous, he left teaching to research public schools in the inner cities across the United States. He devoted himself to exposing what he felt were injustices and failures, focusing in the selection in this book on what he feels is the myth of diversity in the schools. The selection is a letter he wrote to a teacher who, at a conference on diversity, made a presentation that called attention to the fact that there is very little diversity in American schools since 1954, when they were officially desegregated.

Howard Gardner, professor at Harvard's Graduate School of Education, is famous for his book promoting the idea that the kinds of intelligence commonly addressed on IQ tests are limited and that there are many other kinds of intelligence that need to be recognized. He also agrees with Montessori in demanding that education focus not on facts and figures alone but on a deeper understanding of the principles involved in mathematics, science, the arts, and history. He feels that studying a few things in depth, rather than a multitude of things superficially to ensure "coverage," will benefit students and help guarantee comprehension. Gardner's concern is for education designed to help students learn how to live a serious life. His entire program centers on the goals of imparting an awareness of truth, beauty, and goodness to students in primary and secondary schools.

This chapter also contains a selection in e-Pages (available online at **bedfordstmartins.com/worldofideas/epages**) from Ralph Waldo Emerson. Emerson was a teacher for a short time, but eventually became famous as a speaker and essayist. He is still widely read and valued for his observations on important ideas of his own time. His speech "On Education," a favorite of his, was delivered many times at commencement ceremonies. It was not published until after his death. Emerson includes a great deal of simple wisdom in this speech, as in his statement, "The secret of a good Education lies in respecting the pupil." He was also a champion of nature in the classroom, by which he meant that one must pay attention to human nature and the natural desire of students to learn and teachers to teach. His advice, while general and applicable to several levels of education, is still valid and important in today's schools.

The writers in this section on education are innovators looking for ways to improve education at all levels. They may have different perspectives and individual approaches to solving the problems they see before them, but they all know that education is of supreme importance to humanity and that improvement is always possible, no matter how advanced the schools may become.

VISUALIZING EDUCATION

For many of us, the classical painting that represents education is *The School of Athens* by Raphael, featuring Plato, Aristotle, and other Greek geniuses in discussion of their world of ideas. But much more telling for a modern audience is Norman Rockwell's (1894–1978) *The Problem We All Live With* (1964). (To see Rockwell's painting in color, go to **bedfordstmartins.com/worldofideas/epages**.) This painting shows Ruby Bridges Hall, an African American kindergarten student on her first day of school on November 14, 1960, walking determinedly and with great anticipation into William Frantz Public School in New Orleans, Louisiana, with two federal marshals in front of her and two behind her. On her first two days of school, Ruby's mother walked by her side, but eventually she had to go back to work and look after her other children. The white bystanders shouted epithets at Ruby; she spent her first day sitting in the principal's office. When she finally got to her classroom, there were no other students there because the white parents had taken their children out of the school in protest. No white teacher from the school would work with Ruby, either.

Eventually, Barbara Henry, a teacher from Massachusetts, was hired, and Ruby sat in the classroom alone with Mrs. Henry, learning the alphabet and then to read. She had never had a white teacher before, and after her uncertainty, she found that each day she came to school through the mob of people shouting at her, she was grateful to get a hug from her teacher and to feel somewhat secure.

The image that Rockwell created shows the marshals walking in step as if they are part of a military escort. The marshals are represented from the shoulder down in the painting because they are "faceless" officials who represent authority—not individuals in the drama, like the little girl with her schoolbook and ruler. However, apart from the visual effectiveness of leaving their faces out, Rockwell also apparently had been told that the marshals had received death threats,

NORMAN ROCKWELL, *THE PROBLEM WE ALL LIVE WITH* (1964).

which made using their portraits in the painting untenable. For the same reason, the schoolgirl in the image is probably not an accurate portrait of Ruby either. The wall has an epithet written on it, indicating the feelings of the community members who are throwing tomatoes at the child. The lead marshal has a letter in his pocket, which must be taken to represent the direct orders of the court to permit the girl to go to this school.

In reality, there were six African American students chosen by a testing system to be integrated into the all-white schools in New Orleans. Two decided to stay in segregated schools, and the others went to different schools from the one Ruby Bridges Hall was to attend. Her parents were divided on whether to let her go. Her father was afraid there would be an incident and that their lives would be made more difficult. Ruby's mother thought that it was important to take a stand and try to change the system. Indeed, Ruby's father lost his job and their lives were made painful. However, authorities did not reveal Ruby's name to the press, and it is unlikely that Norman Rockwell knew who she truly was.

In a fortunate coincidence, John Steinbeck was traveling across America with his dog Charley when Ruby was integrating her new school. He eventually wrote a best-seller called *Travels with Charley* in which he included his observations on Ruby's experience. He was in New Orleans and managed to get through the mob of women and teenagers who were cursing the girl with language that even Steinbeck found abusive and shocking.

According to the Norman Rockwell Museum in Stockbridge, Massachusetts, this painting is the most requested reproduction in the entire museum collection. Rockwell was known best for his portraits of white middle America celebrating values of faith, family, and hard work. His portraits of small-town heroes, returning veterans, and local pharmacists and doctors were on the cover of the *Saturday Evening Post* for decades. But this painting is completely different from his earlier work because it has a political message that has been embraced by many people around the world as a symbol of courage and a call for change. It is worthwhile to note that while this painting was never featured on the cover of the *Saturday Evening Post*, for which Rockwell had stopped painting in 1963, it was a centerfold for the January 14, 1964, issue of *Look* magazine. Rockwell painted for *Look* for ten years following his departure from the *Post*. Much of Rockwell's work for *Look* centered on social issues and the problem of racism, about which he did a special series for the magazine. His subjects for these ten years were more serious than for the 321 covers he had done for the *Post*. *Look* was famous for its photographs, and for this painting, like many of Rockwell's, he used photographs to work from, and the result—although an oil painting—is quite photographic.

The Problem We All Live With has been analyzed extensively. The painting's title has been interpreted in many ways, but it is clear from the dignity with which Rockwell imbues the little girl that the problem is hatred—and how easily hatred and intolerance can threaten and disenfranchise an entire group of people, even when their rights are protected legally. The presence of federal marshals reminds us of James Madison's "Federalist No. 51" (p. 109) because, until the federal government stepped in with orders from the Supreme Court, segregation laws were both local and statewide. The Court interpreted the "equal protection" clause of the Fourteenth Amendment of the Constitution as applying to the integration of schools in order to override the existing laws of the state of Louisiana and, at that time, the laws of all other states that maintained segregated schools. For that reason, beyond the painting's obvious message about the dangers of hatred and racism, any of the educators represented in Part Five would appreciate that the painting also depicts how equal education should not be reserved for just one group of privileged people within any society.

For a careful analysis of the background of the painting, go to Ken Laird's Web site at http://kenlairdstudios.hubpages.com/hub /The-Problem-We-All-Live-With---Norman-Rockwell-the-truth-about-his-famous-painting. For comments by Ruby Bridges Hall, go to http://www.rubybridges.com/story.htm. For a visual analysis of the painting, go to Scott McDaniel's Web site at http://www.scottmcd.net /artanalysis/?p=818.

HSÜN TZU
Encouraging Learning

HSÜN TZU (310–c. 220 B.C.E.), also known as Xunzi, was
born in interesting and tumultuous times to a moderately aristo-
cratic family in the small state of Chao in the northeast of China.
Hsün Tzu means "Master Hsün," and at birth his family name was
Hsün K'uang. His education centered on the writings of the sages
of ancient China and a study of Confucian doctrine. The era in
China from 453 to 221 B.C.E. is known as the period of the Warring
States, during which frequent conflicts arose between competing states. China was not unified until 221 B.C.E., when one of
Hsün Tzu's former students, Li Ssu, aided the first emperor of the
authoritarian Ch'in dynasty, ironically enough by using oppressive
methods that Hsün Tzu would have opposed.

Hsün Tzu is first mentioned by early biographers at age fifty,
when he was living in the state of Ch'i where, because of the policies of its governor, a good many of China's great early philosophers practiced. In terms of the era and the collection of thinkers,
the state of Ch'i was comparable to ancient Athens. The doctrines
of Confucius (551–479 B.C.E.) had taken root and were interpreted
by major figures such as Mencius (372–289 B.C.E.), who became
chief interpreter. Like Confucius, Mencius held that human nature
was fundamentally good, and he credited a deity with power over
the world with a positive moral drive.

Hsün Tzu, however, took a very different stance. He felt that
the forces of heaven that Mencius promoted were actually the
forces of nature and that there was no divine force operating within
nature. He did not credit prayer with any coincidental outcome
(such as the sun coming out after one prayed for sunshine). Further, Hsün Tzu became famous for declaring that human nature

---

From *Hsün Tzu: Basic Writings*. Translated by Burton Watson.

was evil, somewhat in line with the Christian religion's concept
of original sin. The result of his dissension was a bitter disagreement with Mencius, who held the reigning philosophical view of
the period. Hsün Tzu came to be considered unorthodox, and his
work was widely neglected during his life. He seems to have spent
time in the three major states of the period—Ch'i, Ch'in, and
Ch'u—but late in life, when he returned to Ch'i after having lived
in its rival state Ch'in, he found himself unwelcome and ultimately
retired to Ch'u, where he died.

Despite his philosophy being out of favor, Hsün Tzu's works
were exceptionally well preserved. They were edited in 818 C.E.
by a court scholar who collected all the individual writings and
gathered them into thirty-two sections—an edition that survives
today. It is not known whether every one of the sections was written by Hsün Tzu himself, but twenty-five sections are unquestionably authentic. His view that human nature was evil was based on
his conviction that following one's natural instincts would almost
certainly lead one to an unhappy life. Yet, he also maintained that
we are born without any moral leanings or moral knowledge. As a
result, Hsün Tzu insisted that we must study the writings of the
classics and the sages, that we must follow the Way (the Tao),
the path that leads to peace and understanding, and that we use
the rituals of the ancients as aids in self-perfection. As a result,
Hsün Tzu is well known for placing great emphasis on education as
a lifelong pursuit.

Hsün Tzu's Rhetoric

Hsün Tzu is a very careful writer who understands language
and the principles of rhetoric. He relies on analogy and simile to
a much greater extent than the other authors in this book. For
example, his first paragraph begins with a simple statement:
"Learning should never cease." He then goes on to use analogies from flowers, water, ice, wood, and perspective. He relies
on masses of examples from nature chosen to illustrate his point.
Verses of poetry are interjected to reinforce his primary points.
He also uses a number of aphorisms, such as "he who serves two
masters will please neither," "[a]chievement consists of never giving up," and "the flying squirrel has many talents but finds itself
hard pressed" (para. 5).

He considers three stages of learning. First, there is the
scholar, or the man of breeding, which means simply the prepared
student. Then there is the gentleman, who is deep in learning,

such as the gentleman in the first line of the essay. Finally, there is
the sage, the man who has found the right path, thought the right
thoughts, and learned the right lessons and who continues to follow the path—the Way, as Lao-tzu describes it—to the end of his
life. These three stages are considered by Hsün's translator, Burton
Watson, to be "three grades in the moral hierarchy of men." The
important point is that Hsün Tzu links education to the achievement of moral perfection. Since he feels that our natural inclinations may lead us astray, we need the rituals of discipline—in the
case of education, going to school—to help us achieve moral perfection. Otherwise, we may lose our way. He is insistent on making
us aware that the process of learning is not just amassing facts and
information but rather pursuing a path that leads to wisdom. Like
Aristotle, he associates wisdom with virtue and living the good life,
with pursuing good rather than evil.

Most of the Confucian doctrines and teachers in Hsün Tzu's
time were optimistic because they assumed that people are born
with a moral character that will lead them to a virtuous life. But
Hsün Tzu thought that the sensory life of nature would veer toward
immorality and evil behavior resulting from pride, envy, lust, and
fear. Education, then, is the antidote to his pessimistic prediction
for an unschooled life. Hsün Tzu recommends that we follow educational ritual and, in the process, accrue learning and wisdom:
"Do good and see if it does not pile up" (para. 6), which is another
way of saying to learn a little at a time and see if your learning—
and the wisdom to understand what you have learned—does
not grow. He insists on a lifetime of learning and says flatly,
"To pursue it is to be a man, to give it up is to become a beast"
(para. 7). By his own reckoning, the man who has no learning
is not much different from a beast of the fields because that man,
like all animals, gives over to his natural inclinations, which
Hsün Tzu sees as leading to degradation and moral destruction.
For Hsün Tzu, education is the means of becoming truly human,
of becoming a moral person bent on achieving wisdom and true
happiness.

For a modern student, what Hsün Tzu says can be difficult to
understand at first. The connection between education and moral
behavior was once very fundamental in Western schools but is no
longer central to today's educational schemes. The author who
said that everything he needed to know he learned in kindergarten
was not entirely facetious; learning to curb questionable behavior is more likely to take place in the early grades. But secondary
education and college classes rarely introduce the question of how
one should live one's life. Nonetheless, using one's learning in a

morally responsible way is still as central to our time as it was to
Hsün Tzu's. Likewise, the culmination of learning is to become a
full person, a person who understands the meaning of truth and
the responsibilities of citizenship. For the modern student, the
Way is the path one follows to achievement and one's goals, and
the ritual is following the steps necessary to develop new knowledge in any chosen field of study—with the expectation that
doing so will make one competent and prepared to continue learning throughout life.

PREREADING QUESTIONS:
WHAT TO READ FOR

The following prereading questions may help you anticipate key issues
in the discussion of Hsün Tzu's "Encouraging Learning." Keeping them in
mind during your first reading should help focus your attention.

- Where does learning begin and where does it end?
- What does Hsün Tzu consider to be the connection between conduct
  and learning?
- Why does Hsün Tzu encourage us to learn?

Encouraging Learning

The gentleman says: Learning should never cease. Blue comes   1
from the indigo plant but is bluer than the plant itself. Ice is made
of water but is colder than water ever is. A piece of wood as straight
as a plumb line may be bent into a circle as true as any drawn with
a compass and, even after the wood has dried, it will not straighten
out again. The bending process has made it that way. Thus, if wood
is pressed against a straightening board, it can be made straight; if
metal is put to the grindstone, it can be sharpened; and if the gentleman studies widely and each day examines himself, his wisdom will
become clear and his conduct be without fault. If you do not climb a
high mountain, you will not comprehend the highness of the heavens;
if you do not look down into a deep valley, you will not know the
depth of the earth; and if you do not hear the words handed down
from the ancient kings, you will not understand the greatness of
learning. Children born among the Han or Yüeh people of the south
and among the Mo barbarians of the north cry with the same voice at

birth, but as they grow older they follow different customs. Education causes them to differ. The *Odes* says:

> Oh, you gentlemen,
> Do not be constantly at ease and rest!
> Quietly respectful in your posts,
> Love those who are correct and upright
> And the gods will hearken to you
> And aid you with great blessing.[1]

There is no greater godliness[2] than to transform yourself with the Way, no greater blessing than to escape misfortune.

I once tried spending the whole day in thought, but I found it of less value than a moment of study.[3] I once tried standing on tiptoe and gazing into the distance, but I found I could see much farther by climbing to a high place. If you climb to a high place and wave to someone, it is not as though your arm were any longer than usual, and yet people can see you from much farther away. If you shout down the wind, it is not as though your voice were any stronger than usual, and yet people can hear you much more clearly. Those who make use of carriages or horses may not be any faster walkers than anyone else, and yet they are able to travel a thousand *li*. Those who make use of boats may not know how to swim, and yet they manage to get across rivers. The gentleman is by birth no different from any other man; it is just that he is good at making use of things.

In the south there is a bird called the *meng* dove. It makes a nest out of feathers woven together with hair and suspends it from the tips of the reeds. But when the wind comes, the reeds break, the eggs are smashed, and the baby birds killed. It is not that the nest itself is faulty; the fault is in the thing it is attached to. In the west there is a tree called the *yeh-kan*. Its trunk is no more than four inches tall and it grows on top of the high mountains, from whence it looks down into valleys a hundred fathoms deep. It is not a long trunk which affords the tree such a view, but simply the place where it stands. If pigweed grows up in the midst of hemp, it will stand up straight without propping. If white sand is mixed with mud, it too will turn black.[4] The root

---

[1] "Lesser Odes," *Hsiao-ming*, Mao text no. 207. Here and elsewhere in quotations from the *Odes* and *Documents* I have for the most part followed the interpretations of Karlgren. [Translator's note]

[2] Hsün Tzu repeats the word *shen* (gods) from the ode, but gives it a humanistic interpretation, making it a moral quality of the good man; I have therefore translated it as "godliness." [Translator's note]

[3] A paraphrase of Confucius's remark in *Analects* XV, 30. [Translator's note]

[4] This sentence has been restored from quotations of *Hsün Tzu* preserved in other texts. [Translator's note]

of a certain orchid is the source of the perfume called *chih*; but if the root were to be soaked in urine, then no gentleman would go near it and no commoner would consent to wear it. It is not that the root itself is of an unpleasant quality; it is the fault of the thing it has been soaked in. Therefore a gentleman will take care in selecting the community he intends to live in, and will choose men of breeding for his companions. In this way he wards off evil and meanness, and draws close to fairness and right.

Every phenomenon that appears must have a cause. The glory or shame that come to a man are no more than the image of his virtue. Meat when it rots breeds worms; fish that is old and dry brings forth maggots. When a man is careless and lazy and forgets himself, that is when disaster occurs. The strong naturally bear up under weight; the weak naturally end up bound.[5] Evil and corruption in oneself invite the anger of others. If you lay sticks of identical shape on a fire, the flames will seek out the driest ones; if you level the ground to an equal smoothness, water will still seek out the dampest spot. Trees of the same species grow together; birds and beasts gather in herds; for all things follow after their own kind. Where a target is hung up, arrows will find their way to it; where the forest trees grow thickest, the axes will enter. When a tree is tall and shady, birds will flock to roost in it; when vinegar turns sour, gnats will collect around it. So there are words that invite disaster and actions that call down shame. A gentleman must be careful where he takes his stand.

Pile up earth to make a mountain and wind and rain will rise up from it. Pile up water to make a deep pool and dragons will appear. Pile up good deeds to create virtue and godlike understanding will come of itself; there the mind of the sage will find completion. But unless you pile up little steps, you can never journey a thousand *li*; unless you pile up tiny streams, you can never make a river or a sea. The finest thoroughbred cannot travel ten paces in one leap, but the sorriest nag can go a ten days' journey. Achievement consists of never giving up. If you start carving and then give up, you cannot even cut through a piece of rotten wood; but if you persist without stopping, you can carve and inlay metal or stone. Earthworms have no sharp claws or teeth, no strong muscles or bones, and yet above ground they feast on the mud, and below they drink at the yellow springs. This is because they keep their minds on one thing. Crabs have six legs and two pincers, but unless they can find an empty hole dug by a snake or a water serpent, they have no place to lodge. This is because they allow their minds to go off in all directions. Thus if there is no dark

---

[5] Following the interpretation of Liu Shih-p'ei. [Translator's note]

and dogged will, there will be no shining accomplishment; if there is no dull and determined effort, there will be no brilliant achievement. He who tries to travel two roads at once will arrive nowhere; he who serves two masters will please neither. The wingless dragon has no limbs and yet it can soar; the flying squirrel has many talents but finds itself hard pressed. The *Odes* says:

> Ringdove in the mulberry,
> Its children are seven.
> The good man, the gentleman,
> His forms are one.
> His forms are one,
> His heart is as though bound.[6]

Thus does the gentleman bind himself to oneness.

In ancient times, when Hu Pa played the zither, the fish in the streams came forth to listen; when Po Ya played the lute, the six horses of the emperor's carriage looked up from their feed trough. No sound is too faint to be heard, no action too well concealed to be known. When there are precious stones under the mountain, the grass and trees have a special sheen; where pearls grow in a pool, the banks are never parched. Do good and see if it does not pile up. If it does, how can it fail to be heard of?

Where does learning begin and where does it end? I say that as to program, learning begins with the recitation of the Classics and ends with the reading of the ritual texts; and as to objective, it begins with learning to be a man of breeding, and ends with learning to be a sage.[7] If you truly pile up effort over a long period of time, you will enter into the highest realm. Learning continues until death and only then does it cease. Therefore we may speak of an end to the program of learning, but the objective of learning must never for an instant be given up. To pursue it is to be a man, to give it up is to become a beast. The *Book of Documents* is the record of government affairs, the *Odes* the repository of correct sounds, and the rituals are the great basis of law and the foundation of precedents. Therefore learning reaches its completion with the rituals, for they may be said to represent the highest point of the Way and its power. The reverence and order of the rituals, the fitness and harmony of music, the breadth of the *Odes* and *Documents*,

---

[6] "Airs of Ts'ao," *Shih-chiu*, Mao text no. 152. The last line I have interpreted differently from Karlgren in order to make it fit Hsün Tzu's comment. [Translator's note]

[7] Hsün Tzu customarily distinguishes three grades in the moral hierarchy of men: *shih*, *chün-tzu*, and *sheng-jen*, which I have translated as "man of breeding," "gentleman," and "sage" respectively, though at times he uses the first two terms more or less interchangeably. [Translator's note]

the subtlety of the *Spring and Autumn Annals*—these encompass all that is between heaven and earth.

The learning of the gentleman enters his ear, clings to his mind, 8 spreads through his four limbs, and manifests itself in his actions. His smallest word, his slightest movement can serve as a model. The learning of the petty man enters his ear and comes out his mouth. With only four inches between ear and mouth, how can he have possession of it long enough to ennoble a seven-foot body? In old times men studied for their own sake; nowadays men study with an eye to others.[8] The gentleman uses learning to ennoble himself; the petty man uses learning as a bribe to win attention from others. To volunteer information when you have not been asked is called officiousness; to answer two questions when you have been asked only one is garrulity. Both officiousness and garrulity are to be condemned. The gentleman should be like an echo.

In learning, nothing is more profitable than to associate with those 9 who are learned. Ritual and music present us with models but no explanations; the *Odes* and *Documents* deal with ancient matters and are not always pertinent; the *Spring and Autumn Annals*[9] is terse and cannot be quickly understood. But if you make use of the erudition of others and the explanations of gentlemen, then you will become honored and may make your way anywhere in the world. Therefore I say that in learning nothing is more profitable than to associate with those who are learned, and of the roads to learning, none is quicker than to love such men. Second only to this is to honor ritual. If you are first of all unable to love such men and secondly are incapable of honoring ritual, then you will only be learning a mass of jumbled facts, blindly following the *Odes* and *Documents*, and nothing more. In such a case you may study to the end of your days and you will never be anything but a vulgar pedant.[10] If you want to become like the former kings and seek out benevolence and righteousness, then ritual is the very road by which you must travel. It is like picking up a fur coat by the collar: grasp it with all five fingers and the whole coat can easily be lifted. To lay aside the rules of ritual and try to attain your objective with the *Odes* and *Documents* alone is like trying to measure the depth of a river with your finger, to pound millet with a spear point, or to eat a pot of stew with an awl. You will get nowhere. Therefore one who honors ritual, though he may not

---

[8] This sentence is quoted from *Analects* XIV, 25, where it is attributed to Confucius. [Translator's note]

[9] The *Odes* and *Documents* are ancient Chinese books. The *Spring and Autumn Annals* are traditionally attributed to Confucius and are the record of state activities from 722 to 481 B.C.E. They are among the earliest historical documents of China.

[10] Literally, "vulgar Confucian," but here and below Hsün Tzu uses the word *ju* in the older and broader sense of a scholar. [Translator's note]

yet have full understanding, can be called a model man of breeding; while one who does not honor ritual, though he may have keen perception, is no more than a desultory pedant.

Do not answer a man whose questions are gross. Do not question a   10 man whose answers are gross. Do not listen to a man whose theories are gross. Do not argue with a contentious man. Only if a man has arrived where he is by the proper way should you have dealings with him; if not, avoid him. If he is respectful in his person,[11] then you may discuss with him the approach to the Way. If his words are reasonable, you may discuss with him the principles of the Way. If his looks are gentle, you may discuss with him the highest aspects of the Way. To speak to someone you ought not to is called officiousness; to fail to speak to someone you ought to is called secretiveness; to speak to someone without first observing his temper and looks is called blindness.[12] The gentleman is neither officious, secretive, nor blind, but cautious and circumspect in his manner. This is what the *Odes* means when it says:

> Neither overbearing nor lax,
> They are rewarded by the Son of Heaven.[13]

He who misses one shot in a hundred cannot be called a really   11 good archer; he who sets out on a thousand-mile journey and breaks down half a pace from his destination cannot be called a really good carriage driver; he who does not comprehend moral relationships and categories and who does not make himself one with benevolence and righteousness cannot be called a good scholar. Learning basically means learning to achieve this oneness. He who starts off in this direction one time and that direction another is only a commoner of the roads and alleys, while he who does a little that is good and much that is not good is no better than the tyrants Chieh and Chou or Robber Chih.

The gentleman knows that what lacks completeness and purity   12 does not deserve to be called beautiful. Therefore he reads and listens to explanations in order to penetrate the Way, ponders in order to understand it, associates with men who embody it in order to make it part of himself, and shuns those who impede it in order to sustain and nourish it. He trains his eyes so that they desire only to see what is right, his ears so that they desire to hear only what is right, his mind so that it desires to think only what is right. When he has truly

---

[11] Reading *t'i* instead of *li* in order to complete the parallelism with "words" and "looks." [Translator's note]

[12] This sentence is a paraphrase of *Analects* XVI, 6, where the saying is attributed to Confucius. [Translator's note]

[13] "Lesser Odes," *Ts'ai-shu*, Mao text no. 222. But Hsün Tzu quotes from the Lu version, which differs slightly from the Mao text. [Translator's note]

learned to love what is right, his eyes will take greater pleasure in it than in the five colors; his ears will take greater pleasure than in the five sounds; his mouth will take greater pleasure than in the five flavors; and his mind will feel keener delight than in the possession of the world. When he has reached this stage, he cannot be subverted by power or the love of profit; he cannot be swayed by the masses; he cannot be moved by the world. He follows this one thing in life; he follows it in death. This is what is called constancy of virtue. He who has such constancy of virtue can order himself, and, having ordered himself, he can then respond to others. He who can order himself and respond to others—this is what is called the complete man. It is the characteristic of heaven to manifest brightness, of earth to manifest breadth, and of the gentleman to value completeness.

QUESTIONS FOR CRITICAL READING

1. What is the significance of the verses at the end of paragraph 1?
2. What is the connection between learning and moral behavior?
3. Why does Hsün Tzu use the image of the orchid root in paragraph 3?
4. How would a petty man use learning as a bribe (para. 8)?
5. What is the effect of the mass of analogies in paragraph 4? What is Hsün Tzu's point?
6. Is it true that "[a]chievement consists of never giving up" (para. 5)?
7. What does Hsün Tzu mean by one should not "answer a man whose questions are gross" (para. 10)?

SUGGESTIONS FOR CRITICAL WRITING

1. Hsün Tzu says more than once that there is nothing more profitable than to associate with those who are learned. What do you think he means by this statement? How important is his recommendation today? Based on your experience, how do you profit from your association with those who are learned? What are the moral implications of this statement?

2. The basis of Hsün Tzu's essay is that learning is fundamentally moral because it trains us to know the truth and to restrict the kind of behavior that is typical of ignorant people. Is this true? What argument can you develop that would explore the basis of this essay and come to a conclusion that takes into account the question of moral development in an individual? If Hsün Tzu is correct about how we would behave without proper education, is it then true that education will make us better people?

3. In paragraph 12, Hsün Tzu talks about "constancy of virtue." Examine the context in which this statement is made and explain what it ultimately means. Why would the learned man not be "subverted by power or the love of profit"? How would learning produce this kind of virtue? Do you think Hsün Tzu is correct, or do you think things in our time are so different from what they were in his that what he says no longer applies?

4. **CONNECTIONS** Examine this essay from the point of view of the argument for virtue ethics in the essay by Kwame Anthony Appiah, "The Case against Character" (p. 397). How would Appiah be likely to regard what Hsün Tzu says about virtue? What would Hsün Tzu say about the connection between virtue and character?

5. **CONNECTIONS** Hsün Tzu is deeply concerned with education's capacity to produce moral perfection. To what extent does Ralph Waldo Emerson's emphasis on nature, genius, and drill (**bedfordstmartins .com/worldofideas/epages**) help develop the moral nature of students? Is Emerson as concerned with moral perfection in education as Hsün Tzu? Should he be? Is moral perfection an important issue in education?

6. In paragraph 12, Hsün Tzu says that the gentleman "reads and listens to explanations in order to penetrate the Way, ponders in order to understand it, associates with men who embody it in order to make it part of himself, and shuns those who impede it in order to sustain and nourish it." Is this in any way a description of your approach to education at your institution? Is this an ideal or is it a procedure that you can aspire to or actually achieve? Explore this statement in terms of the behavior you witness in yourself and in your peers.

7. At the end of the essay, Hsün Tzu comments on the "complete man." What does he see as constituting a complete man? How can such a state be achieved? Do you aspire to the kind of completeness that Hsün Tzu proposes? Do you think that education as you know it is aimed at producing the complete person? Is your own sense of purpose to make yourself a complete person? Will your education help you do so?

8. Obviously, Hsün Tzu imagined the prospect of education for men only. Even in the West, higher education for women was not available until the nineteenth century. Today, however, there are more women than men in higher education. Are the precepts that Hsün Tzu recommends just as appropriate for modern women as they are for men?

9. **SEEING CONNECTIONS** What issues central to the fundamental theories of education in Hsün Tzu's essay are evident in Norman Rockwell's *The Problem We All Live With* (p. 539)? How do concepts like the Way and the path become realized in Rockwell's painting? What ritual has been attended to in this painting? Would Hsün Tzu have felt that this painting was appropriate for connecting the sense of moral purpose to the principles of education?

JOHN DEWEY
Thinking in Education

JOHN DEWEY (1859–1952) was arguably the most influential voice in twentieth-century American education. He was born,
raised, and educated in Vermont, having graduated from the University of Vermont at age nineteen. He went on to teach high school
in Pennsylvania for two years, eventually moving on to graduate
work at Johns Hopkins University. He studied philosophy, particularly the works of idealist German philosophers Immanuel Kant
(1724–1804) and Georg Wilhelm Friedrich Hegel (1770–1831),
both of whom felt that freedom was connected with reason, and
that the end goal of history was to produce freedom. Dewey wrote
a dissertation on the psychology of Kant; however, it has been lost.

Dewey was deeply interested in the connection between psychology and philosophy at a time when the discipline of philosophy was
closely tied to principles of Christian theology. When he went to teach
at the University of Michigan from 1884 to 1894 (with a year teaching
at the University of Minnesota), he was fortunate to have a department
chair who valued Dewey's work in relation to what was then the study
of modern German philosophers. Eventually, Dewey moved to the
University of Chicago, which was only four years old and dedicated
to graduate studies and serious original research. The new department
Dewey joined combined studies of psychology, philosophy, and pedagogy. Eventually, Dewey managed to establish pedagogy as a separate
department, making it one of the first schools of education.

Because of differences of opinion, Dewey left Chicago in 1904
and moved to Columbia University, with appointments in the
department of philosophy and at Teachers College. He spent the rest
of his professional career there. In these years his own philosophical views underwent a change. He embraced the then-modern tenets

From *Democracy in Education.*

of pragmatism, a philosophy that values ideas in terms of their use-fulness and their ultimate effectiveness. Pragmatists emphasized the practical over the ideal. They placed a high value on experience as a way of knowing. Ideas were valued for what they actually effected in terms of behavior or change. In education the pragmatists were interested in results and in usefulness of instruction.

Dewey published more than forty books during his career. His first book was *Psychology* (1887). He also published *The School and Society* (1899), which revealed his lifelong interest in the social implications of educational programs. His *Ethical Principles Under-lying Education* was published in 1908, and his enormously influ-ential *Democracy and Education* (1916) developed some of his most important ideas about teaching and learning. In later books, such as *Human Nature and Conduct* (1922), *Experience and Nature* (1925), *Philosophy and Civilization* (1931), and *Freedom and Culture* (1939), Dewey continued to develop his ideas on issues of philosophic and social importance. All these books reveal the practical nature that was a hallmark of his most important work.

Dewey's Rhetoric

One of the first things one notices about "Thinking in Education" is that it is divided into sections announced with, first, an Arabic number 1, then by subsequent Roman numerals. Roman numeral I appears at paragraph 2; II at paragraph 9; III at paragraph 12; IV at paragraph 16. The final paragraph is a summary of all that precedes it, thus acting as a kind of review of what we just read.

Clearly, this indicates a pedagogic motive. Each basic issue is presented, defined, discussed, and analyzed to the extent neces-sary, and a conclusion is drawn. Considering the nature of this selec-tion, one must conclude that the audience addressed is primarily the teacher. Given Dewey's concerns for the involvement of the student in an experiential activity that would result in ideas put into action, this structure, while clear and effective, would be less likely to appeal to a young student than to a more mature teacher or teacher-to-be.

In paragraph 1, Dewey explains that "thinking is the method of intelligent learning," which he realizes is a statement that might seem too obvious. But by thinking he means the process of dealing with experiential activities that deeply involve the student in such a way that the problems the student is to solve are really the student's and not just artificial problems set by the teacher. As he explains in paragraph 2, thinking must be connected with experience, with hands-on activity, an example of which is the activity of children making discoveries on their own with common materials such as blocks. He makes an important distinction between "genuine or simulated or mock problems" (para. 6) in the classroom.

Part of Dewey's rhetorical approach derives from the technique of dialectic, particularly as developed by one of his favorite philosophers, Hegel. Dialectic proceeds by opposing two concepts or truths and examining them to see which is preferable. As he sets genuine problems that truly involve students against simulated problems that are those only of the curriculum or the teacher, it is clear that he prefers problems that are "real" and produce enthusiasm in children. The dialectic is continued in terms of problems that relate to life experience and those that are limited to the classroom. As Dewey states, when the latter case is dominant, "A pupil has a problem, but it is the problem of meeting the peculiar requirements set by the teacher. His problem becomes that of finding out what the teacher wants" (para. 8).

The four parts of the selection emphasize first experience, then data, then ideas, and finally the testing of ideas. Each section begins with an appropriate definition of terms, then proceeds to a discussion of the practical application of the terms, and then connects the subject of the section with the method of thinking that Dewey feels is the key to education. Dewey's ideas about thinking and education constitute a form of critical thinking if only because he is anxious to challenge pupils to examine their ideas critically. He condemns the classroom that makes pupils feel that the problems they are to solve are not connected to their experiences. Moreover, he hopes that ideas eventually will be translated into action in the life of the child.

He also has the rhetorical gift of making pithy statements that contain a great deal of meaning in a few words. For example, "The initial stage of that developing experience which is called thinking is *experience*" (para. 2). This innocent-sounding sentence contains much of his basic theory of education, which implies working from concrete experience toward ideas that can then be converted back into a new concrete experience. When speaking of a shared activity between teacher and pupil, he tells us: "In such shared activity, the teacher is a learner, and the learner is, without knowing it, a teacher" (para. 15). This judicious use of the rhetorical scheme called chiasmus is effective in part because Dewey uses very few such devices.

Dewey summarizes his material cogently in the final paragraph, thus tying all the elements of his argument together. The student must

a. be involved in an activity that's important on its own
b. be presented with a genuine problem to solve
c. be given information (data) that is necessary to solve the problem

d. develop reasonable solutions to the problem
e. be given the opportunity to test out his solutions in action.

Dewey was a careful thinker who could also communicate with a broad audience. He felt that in the interest of presenting important ideas, such as those in *Democracy and Education*, he would emphasize the organization and development of his ideas rather than aim for a smooth and poetic style. Dewey is pragmatic. He is simple and direct, although his ideas—especially for 1916—were radically different from those of most other educators.

PREREADING QUESTIONS: WHAT TO READ FOR

The following prereading questions may help you anticipate key issues in the discussion of John Dewey's "Thinking in Education." Keeping them in mind during your first reading of the selection should help focus your attention.

- What does Dewey seem to mean by the expression "thinking in education"?

- What conditions must exist for the student to use thinking in education?

- What seems to be the best process of education, according to Dewey?

Thinking in Education

1. The Essentials of Method

No one doubts, theoretically, the importance of fostering in school good habits of thinking. But apart from the fact that the acknowledgement is not so great in practice as in theory, there is not adequate theoretical recognition that all which the school can or need do for pupils, so far as their *minds* are concerned (that is, leaving out certain specialized muscular abilities), is to develop their ability to think. The parceling out of instruction among various ends such as acquisition of skill (in reading, spelling, writing, drawing, reciting); acquiring information (in history and geography); *and* training of thinking is a measure of the ineffective way in which we accomplish all three. Thinking which is not connected with increase of efficiency in action, and with learning more about ourselves and the world in which we live, has something the matter with it just as thought. And skill obtained apart from thinking is not connected with any sense of the purposes for which it is to be used. It consequently leaves a man at the mercy of his routine habits and of the authoritative control of others, who know what they are about and who are not especially scrupulous as to their means of achievement. And information severed from thoughtful action is dead, a mind-crushing load. Since it simulates knowledge and thereby develops the poison of conceit, it is a most powerful obstacle to further growth in the grace of intelligence. The sole direct path to enduring improvement in the methods of instruction and learning consists in centering upon the conditions which exact, promote, and test thinking. Thinking *is* the method of intelligent learning, of learning that employs and rewards mind. We speak, legitimately enough, about the method of thinking, but the important thing to bear in mind about method is that thinking is method, the method of intelligent experience in the course which it takes.

I.   The initial stage of that developing experience which is called   2 thinking is *experience*. This remark may sound like a silly truism. It ought to be one; but unfortunately it is not. On the contrary, thinking is often regarded both in philosophic theory and in educational practice as something cut off from experience, and capable of being cultivated in isolation. In fact, the inherent limitations of experience are often urged as the sufficient ground for attention to thinking. Experience is then thought to be confined to the senses and appetites; to a mere material world, while thinking proceeds from a higher faculty (of reason), and is occupied with spiritual or at least literary things. So, oftentimes, a sharp distinction is made between pure mathematics as a peculiarly fit subject matter of thought (since it has nothing to do with physical existences) and applied mathematics, which has utilitarian but not mental value.

Speaking generally, the fundamental fallacy in methods of instruc-   3 tion lies in supposing that experience on the part of pupils may be assumed. What is here insisted upon is the necessity of an actual empirical situation as the initiating phase of thought. Experience is here taken as previously defined: trying to do something and having the thing perceptibly do something to one in return. The fallacy consists in supposing that we can begin with ready-made subject matter of arithmetic, or geography, or whatever, irrespective of some direct personal experience of a situation. Even the kindergarten and Montessori techniques are so anxious to get at intellectual distinctions, without "waste of time," that they tend to ignore—or reduce—the immediate crude handling of the familiar material of experience, and to introduce pupils at once to material which expresses the intellectual distinctions which adults have made. But the first stage of contact with any new material, at whatever age of maturity, must inevitably be of the trial and error sort. An individual must actually try, in play or work, to do something with material in carrying out his own impulsive activity, and then note the interaction of his energy and that of the material employed. This is what happens when a child at first begins to build with blocks, and it is equally what happens when a scientific man in his laboratory begins to experiment with unfamiliar objects.

Hence the first approach to any subject in school, if thought is   4
to be aroused and not words acquired, should be as unscholastic as possible. To realize what an experience, or empirical situation, means, we have to call to mind the sort of situation that presents itself outside of school; the sort of occupations that interest and engage activity in ordinary life. And careful inspection of methods which are permanently successful in formal education, whether in arithmetic or learning to read, or studying geography, or learning physics or a foreign language, will reveal that they depend for their efficiency upon the fact that they go back to the type of the situation which causes reflection out of school in ordinary life. They give the pupils something to do, not something to learn; and the doing is of such a nature as to demand thinking, or the intentional noting of connections; learning naturally results.

That the situation should be of such a nature as to arouse think-   5
ing means of course that it should suggest something to do which is not either routine or capricious—something, in other words, presenting what is new (and hence uncertain or problematic) and yet sufficiently connected with existing habits to call out an effective response. An effective response means one which accomplishes a perceptible result, in distinction from a purely haphazard activity, where the consequences cannot be mentally connected with what is done. The most significant question which can be asked, accordingly, about any situation or experience proposed to induce learning is what quality of problem it involves.

At first thought, it might seem as if usual school methods mea-   6
sured well up to the standard here set. The giving of problems, the putting of questions, the assigning of tasks, the magnifying of difficulties, is a large part of school work. But it is indispensable to discriminate between genuine and simulated or mock problems. The following questions may aid in making such discrimination. (*a*) Is there anything but a problem? Does the question naturally suggest itself within some situation or personal experience? Or is it an aloof thing, a problem only for the purposes of conveying instruction in some school topic? Is it the sort of trying that would arouse observation and engage experimentation outside of school? (*b*) Is it the pupil's own problem, or is it the teacher's or textbook's problem, made a problem for the pupil

only because he cannot get the required mark or be promoted or win the teacher's approval, unless he deals with it? Obviously, these two questions overlap. They are two ways of getting at the same point: Is the experience a personal thing of such a nature as inherently to stimulate and direct observation of the connections involved, and to lead to inference and its testing? Or is it imposed from without, and is the pupil's problem simply to meet the external requirement?

Such questions may give us pause in deciding upon the extent to 7 which current practices are adapted to develop reflective habits. The physical equipment and arrangements of the average schoolroom are hostile to the existence of real situations of experience. What is there similar to the conditions of everyday life which will generate difficulties? Almost everything testifies to the great premium put upon listening, reading, and the reproduction of what is told and read. It is hardly possible to overstate the contrast between such conditions and the situations of active contact with things and persons in the home, on the playground, in fulfilling of ordinary responsibilities of life. Much of it is not even comparable with the questions which may arise in the mind of a boy or girl in conversing with others or in reading books outside of the school. No one has ever explained why children are so full of questions outside of the school (so that they pester grown-up persons if they get any encouragement), and the conspicuous absence of display of curiosity about the subject matter of school lessons. Reflection on this striking contrast will throw light upon the question of how far customary school conditions supply a context of experience in which problems naturally suggest themselves. No amount of improvement in the personal technique of the instructor will wholly remedy this state of things. There must be more actual material, more *stuff*, more appliances, and more opportunities for doing things, before the gap can be overcome. And where children are engaged in doing things and in discussing what arises in the course of their doing, it is found, even with comparatively indifferent modes of instruction, that children's inquiries are spontaneous and numerous, and the proposals of solution advanced, varied, and ingenious.

As a consequence of the absence of the materials and occupa- 8 tions which generate real problems, the pupil's problems are not his; or, rather, they are his *only as* a pupil, not as a human being. Hence the lamentable waste in carrying over such expertness as is achieved in dealing with them to the affairs of life beyond the schoolroom. A pupil has a problem, but it is the problem of meeting the peculiar requirements set by the teacher. His problem becomes that of finding out what the teacher wants, what will satisfy the teacher in recitation and examination and outward deportment. Relationship to subject matter is no longer direct. The occasions and material of thought are not found in the arithmetic or the history or geography itself, but in skillfully adapting that material to the teacher's requirements. The pupil studies, but unconsciously to himself the objects of his study are the conventions and standards of the school system and school authority, not the nominal "studies." The thinking thus evoked is artificially one-sided at the best. At its worst, the problem of the pupil is not how to meet the requirements of school life, but how to *seem* to meet them—or, how to come near enough to meeting them to slide along without an undue amount of friction. The type of judgment formed by these devices is not a desirable addition to character. If these statements give too highly colored a picture of usual school methods, the exaggeration may at least serve to illustrate the point: the need of active pursuits, involving the use of material to accomplish purposes, if there are to be situations which normally generate problems occasioning thoughtful inquiry.

II.   There must be *data* at command to supply the considerations   9 required in dealing with the specific difficulty which has presented itself. Teachers following a "developing" method sometimes tell children to think things out for themselves as if they could spin them out of their own heads. The material of thinking is not thoughts, but actions, facts, events, and the relations of things. In other words, to think effectively one must have had, or now have, experiences which will furnish him resources for coping with the difficulty at hand. A difficulty is an indispensable stimulus to thinking, but not all difficulties call out thinking. Sometimes they overwhelm and submerge and discourage. The perplexing situation must be sufficiently like situations which have already been dealt with so that pupils will have some control of the means of handling it. A large part of the art of instruction lies in making the difficulty of new problems large enough to challenge thought, and small enough so that, in addition to the confusion naturally attending the novel elements, there shall be luminous familiar spots from which helpful suggestions may spring.

In one sense, it is a matter of indifference by what psychological   10 means the subject matter for reflection is provided. Memory, observation, reading, communication, are all avenues for supplying data. The relative proportion to be obtained from each is a matter of the specific features of the particular problem in hand. It is foolish to insist upon observation of objects presented to the senses if the student is so familiar with the objects that he could just as well recall the facts independently. It is possible to induce undue and crippling dependence upon sense-presentations. No one can carry around with him a museum of all the things whose properties will assist the conduct of thought. A well-trained mind is one that has a maximum of resources behind it, so to speak, and that is accustomed to go over its past experiences to see what they yield. On the other hand, a quality or relation of even a familiar object may previously have been passed over, and be just the fact that is helpful in dealing with the question. In this case direct observation is called for. The same principle applies to the use to be made of observation on one hand and of reading and "telling" on the other. Direct observation is naturally more vivid and vital. But it has its limitations; and in any case it is a necessary part of education that one should acquire the ability to supplement the narrowness of his immediately personal experiences by utilizing the experiences of others. Excessive reliance upon others for data (whether got from reading or listening) is to be depreciated. Most objectionable of all is the probability that others, the book or the teacher, will supply solutions ready-made, instead of giving material that the student has to adapt and apply to the question in hand for himself.

There is no inconsistency in saying that in schools there is usu- 11
ally both too much and too little information supplied by others. The accumulation and acquisition of information for purposes of reproduction in recitation and examination is made too much of. "Knowledge," in the sense of information, means the working capital, the indispensable resources, of further inquiry; of finding out, or learning, more things. Frequently it is treated as an end itself, and then the goal becomes to heap it up and display it when called for. This static, cold-storage ideal of knowledge is inimical to educative development. It not only lets occasions for thinking go unused, but it swamps thinking. No one could construct a house on ground cluttered with miscellaneous junk. Pupils who have stored their "minds" with all kinds of material which they have never put to intellectual uses are sure to be hampered when they try to think. They have no practice in selecting what is appropriate, and no criterion to go by; everything is on the same dead static level. On the other hand, it is quite open to question whether, if information actually functioned in experience through use in application to the student's own purposes, there would not be need of more varied resources in books, pictures, and talks than are usually at command.

III.   The correlate in thinking of facts, data, knowledge already 12
acquired, is suggestions, inferences, conjectured meanings, suppositions, tentative explanations: —*ideas*, in short. Careful observation and recollection determine what is given, what is already there, and hence assured. They cannot furnish what is lacking. They define, clarify, and locate the question; they cannot supply its answer. Projection, invention, ingenuity, devising come in for that purpose. The data *arouse* suggestions, and only by reference to the specific data can we pass upon the appropriateness of the suggestions. But the suggestions run beyond what is, as yet, actually *given* in experience. They forecast possible

results, things *to* do, not facts (things already done). Inference is always an invasion of the unknown, a leap from the known.

In this sense, a thought (what a thing suggests but is not as it is presented) is creative,—an incursion into the novel. It involves some inventiveness. What is suggested must, indeed, be familiar in *some* context; the novelty, the inventive devising, clings to the new light in which it is seen, the different use to which it is put. When Newton[1] thought of his theory of gravitation, the creative aspect of his thought was not found in its materials. They were familiar; many of them commonplaces—sun, moon, planets, weight, distance, mass, square of numbers. These were not original ideas; they were established facts. His originality lay in the *use* to which these familiar acquaintances were put by introduction into an unfamiliar context. The same is true of every striking scientific discovery, every great invention, every admirable artistic production. Only silly folk identify creative originality with the extraordinary and fanciful; others recognize that its measure lies in putting everyday things to uses which had not occurred to others. The operation is novel, not the materials out of which it is constructed.

The educational conclusion which follows is that *all* thinking is original in a projection of considerations which have not been previously apprehended. The child of three who discovers what can be done with blocks, or of six who finds out what he can make by putting five cents and five cents together, is really a discoverer, even though everybody else in the world knows it. There is a genuine increment of experience; not another item mechanically added on, but enrichment by a new quality. The charm which the spontaneity of little children has for sympathetic observers is due to perception of this intellectual originality. The joy which children themselves experience is the joy of intellectual constructiveness—of creativeness, if the word may be used without misunderstanding.

The educational moral I am chiefly concerned to draw is not, however, that teachers would find their own work less of a grind and strain if school conditions favored learning in the sense of discovery and not in that of storing away what others pour into them; nor that it would be possible to give even children and youth the delights of personal intellectual productiveness—true and important as are these things. It is that no thought, no idea, can possibly be conveyed as an idea from one person to another. When it is told, it is, to the one to whom it is told, another given fact, not an idea. The communication may stimulate the other person to realize the question for himself and to think

13

14

15

---

[1] **Isaac Newton (1642–1727)** English scientist and mathematician who discovered the universal law of gravity and also invented calculus.

out a like idea, or it may smother his intellectual interest and suppress his dawning effort at thought. But what he *directly* gets cannot be an idea. Only by wrestling with the conditions of the problem at first hand, seeking and finding his own way out, does he think. When the parent or teacher has provided the conditions which stimulate thinking and has taken a sympathetic attitude toward the activities of the learner by entering into a common or conjoint experience, all has been done which a second party can do to instigate learning. The rest lies with the one directly concerned. If he cannot devise his own solution (not of course in isolation, but in correspondence with the teacher and other pupils) and find his own way out he will not learn, not even if he can recite some correct answer with one hundred per cent accuracy. We can and do supply ready-made "ideas" by the thousand; we do not usually take much pains to see that the one learning engages in significant situations where his own activities generate, support, and clinch ideas—that is, perceived meanings or connections. This does not mean that the teacher is to stand off and look on; the alternative to furnishing ready-made subject matter and listening to the accuracy with which it is reproduced is not quiescence, but participation, sharing, in an activity. In such shared activity, the teacher is a learner, and the learner is, without knowing it, a teacher—and upon the whole, the less consciousness there is, on either side, of either giving or receiving instruction, the better.

IV.   Ideas, as we have seen, whether they be humble guesses or 16
dignified theories, are anticipations of possible solutions. They are anticipations of some continuity or connection of an activity and a consequence which has not as yet shown itself. They are therefore tested by the operation of acting upon them. They are to guide and organize further observations, recollections, and experiments. They are intermediate in learning, not final. All educational reformers, as we have had occasion to remark, are given to attacking the passivity of traditional education. They have opposed pouring in from without, and absorbing like a sponge; they have attacked drilling in material as into hard and resisting rock. But it is not easy to secure conditions which will make the getting of an idea identical with having an experience which widens and makes more precise our contact with the environment. Activity, even self-activity, is too easily thought of as something merely mental, cooped up within the head, or finding expression only through the vocal organs.

While the need of application of ideas gained in study is 17
acknowledged by all the more sucessful methods of instruction, the exercises in application are sometimes treated as devices for *fixing* what has already been learned and for getting greater practical skill in its manipulation. These results are genuine and not to be despised. But practice in applying what has been gained in study ought primarily to have an intellectual quality. As we have already seen, thoughts just as

thoughts are incomplete. At best they are tentative; they are suggestions, indications. They are standpoints and methods for dealing with situations of experience. Till they are applied in these situations they lack full point and reality. Only application tests them, and only testing confers full meaning and a sense of their reality. Short of use made of them, they tend to segregate into a peculiar world of their own. It may be seriously questioned whether the philosophies which isolate mind and set it over against the world did not have their origin in the fact that the reflective or theoretical class of men elaborated a large stock of ideas which social conditions did not allow them to act upon and test. Consequently men were thrown back into their own thoughts as ends in themselves.

However this may be, there can be no doubt that a peculiar arti- 18 ficiality attaches to much of what is learned in schools. It can hardly be said that many students consciously think of the subject matter as unreal; but it assuredly does not possess for them the kind of reality which the subject matter of their vital experiences possesses. They learn not to expect that sort of reality of it; they become habituated to treating it as having reality for the purposes of recitations, lessons, and examinations. That it should remain inert for the experiences of daily life is more or less a matter of course. The bad effects are twofold. Ordinary experience does not receive the enrichment which it should; it is not fertilized by school learning. And the attitudes which spring from getting used to and accepting half-understood and ill-digested material weaken vigor and efficiency of thought.

If we have dwelt especially on the negative side, it is for the sake 19 of suggesting positive measures adapted to the effectual development of thought. Where schools are equipped with laboratories, shops, and gardens, where dramatizations, plays, and games are freely used, opportunities exist for reproducing situations of life, and for acquiring and applying information and ideas in the carrying forward of progressive experiences. Ideas are not segregated, they do not form an isolated island. They animate and enrich the ordinary course of life. Information is vitalized by its function; by the place it occupies in direction of action.

The phrase "opportunities exist" is used purposely. They may not 20 be taken advantage of; it is possible to employ manual and constructive activities in a physical way, as means of getting just bodily skill; or they may be used almost exclusively for "utilitarian," *i.e.,* pecuniary, ends. But the disposition on the part of upholders of "cultural" education to assume that such activities are merely physical or professional in quality, is itself a product of the philosophies which isolate mind from direction of the course of experience and hence from action upon and with things. When the "mental" is regarded as a self-contained separate realm, a counterpart fate befalls bodily activity and movements. They are regarded as at the best mere external annexes to mind. They may be necessary for the satisfaction of bodily needs and the attainment of external decency and comfort, but they do not occupy a necessary place in mind nor enact an indispensable rôle in the completion of thought. Hence they have no place in a liberal education— *i.e.,* one which is concerned with the interests of intelligence. If they come in at all, it is as a concession to the material needs of the masses. That they should be allowed to invade the education of the élite is unspeakable. This conclusion follows irresistibly from the isolated conception of mind, but by the same logic it disappears when we perceive what mind really is—namely, the purposive and directive factor in the development of experience.

While it is desirable that all educational institutions should be 21 equipped so as to give students an opportunity for acquiring and testing ideas and information in active pursuits typifying important social situations, it will, doubtless, be a long time before all of them are thus furnished. But this state of affairs does not afford instructors an excuse for folding their hands and persisting in methods which segregate school knowledge. Every recitation in every subject gives an opportunity for establishing cross connections between the subject matter of the lesson and the wider and more direct experiences of everyday life. Classroom instruction falls into three kinds. The least desirable treats each lesson as an independent whole. It does not put upon the student the responsibility of finding points of contact between it and other lessons in the same subject, or other subjects of study. Wiser teachers see to it that the student is systematically led to utilize his earlier lessons to help understand the present one, and also to use the present to throw additional light upon what has already been acquired. Results are better, but school subject matter is still isolated. Save by accident, out-of-school experience is left in its crude and comparatively irreflective state. It is not subject to the refining and expanding influences of the more accurate and comprehensive material of direct instruction. The latter is not motivated and impregnated with a sense of reality by being intermingled with the realities of everyday life. The best type of teaching bears in mind the desirability of affecting this interconnection. It puts the student in the habitual attitude of finding points of contact and mutual bearings.

Summary

Processes of instruction are unified in the degree in which 22 they center in the production of good habits of thinking. While we may speak, without error, of the method of thought, the important thing is that thinking is the method of an educative experience. The essentials of method are therefore identical with the essentials of reflection. They are first that the pupil have a genuine situation of experience—that there be a continuous activity in which he is interested for its own sake; secondly, that a genuine problem develop within this situation as a stimulus to thought; third, that he possess the information and make the observations needed to deal with it; fourth, that suggested solutions occur to him which he shall be responsible for developing in an orderly way; fifth, that he have opportunity and occasion to test his ideas by application, to make their meaning clear and to discover for himself their validity.

QUESTIONS FOR CRITICAL READING

1. What is the relationship of experience to thought? Why does experience precede thought?

2. Why is "learning more about ourselves and the world" (para. 1) crucial to thought and education?

3. In what ways does Dewey concern himself with nature in the classroom?

4. Dewey states that for some people thinking is cut off from experience. How could this be true? What are its consequences?

5. What is the relationship between a student being given something to do and being given something to learn?

6. What is the difference between genuine and mock problems in a classroom?

7. What is the importance of data in the classroom?

8. How does Dewey define creative originality?

SUGGESTIONS FOR CRITICAL WRITING

1. In paragraphs 2 and 3, Dewey discusses the question of experience in mathematics, reminding us that "it has nothing to do with physical existences." If you were teaching in an elementary school classroom, how could you introduce experiences that would help children learn mathematics as part of a practical, real-life experience? How would your methods relate to children's personal experiences?

2. In paragraph 3 Dewey makes some important comments on the nature of the child's experience in the classroom. He says that in the classroom "[w]hat is here insisted upon is the necessity of an actual empirical situation as the initiating phase of thought." This is a fundamental idea in his essay. What does he mean by it? How can a teacher help produce such a situation? How well would it help develop real thought in the classroom?

3. In paragraph 8 Dewey addresses the circumstances of the classroom in which the student "has a problem, but it is the problem of meeting the peculiar requirements set by the teacher. His problem becomes that of finding out what the teacher wants, what will satisfy the teacher in recitation and examination and outward deportment." Judging from your own experience, is this situation still common in the early grades? Is it common in later grades? What has been your experience with this "problem"? Does it extend to the college level too?

4. The kind of education Dewey advocated was called progressive, and among its tenets were the questioning of authority and an emphasis on independence of thought on the part of the student. Throughout the twentieth century, schools of education at universities around the world were influenced by Dewey's ideas about education. Is it possible they are responsible for the current breakdown in respect for authority on the part of young people? Is it possible that Dewey can be held responsible for the permissiveness that is common in society today? Is this the ultimate empirical result of his educational ideas?

5. What examples do you have from your own learning experience that help validate Dewey's concepts of how learning should occur in a classroom? Since Dewey's theories are still extant (like Montessori's), it is reasonable that some of your teachers would have used his techniques. Describe any such techniques that you recall having been used in your classroom and from which you feel you profited.

6. In paragraph 11 Dewey states, "The accumulation and acquisition of information for purposes of reproduction in recitation and examination is made too much of." Under what conditions is this statement true of education? Under what conditions is it not true? Do you think that the process he describes is still common in education, or have Dewey's theories tended to make it rare in the classroom? What are its effects, either for good or for bad?

7. **CONNECTIONS** Dewey comments briefly on the Montessori method, which he feels moves too quickly from the child's sensory experiences to the transformation of those experiences into intellectual activity. Apart from that quibble, what ideas about education do Montessori and Dewey have that seem compatible? Assuming that Dewey may have read Montessori's book or visited her schools, in what particular ways does he seem to take account of her recommendations? Does he improve upon Montessori's ideas, or does he strike out in a different direction?

8. **CONNECTIONS** Both Ralph Waldo Emerson (**bedfordstmartins.com /worldofideas/epages**) and Maria Montessori write about respecting nature in the educational process. While Dewey does not invoke that term specifically, is it possible that he is also developing their thoughts on this point? What would be considered natural about the processes Dewey describes? What would be a natural situation in a Dewey-led classroom?

9. **SEEING CONNECTIONS** John Dewey emphasizes four major issues in his essay: experience, data, ideas, and the testing of ideas. Referring to Norman Rockwell's *The Problem We All Live With* (p. 539), write an essay that incorporates all his issues in response to this painting. What do you as a student gather from the experience of looking at the painting? What data does the painting contain that informs your experience? What ideas that Dewey might consider important to all students are represented in the painting? How can you as a student test the ideas represented in the painting? Would Dewey think this painting would be important to show to young students? Would Dewey think this painting would be important to show to college students?

MARIA MONTESSORI
The Montessori Method

MARIA MONTESSORI (1870–1952) was born in Chiaravelle, Ancona, Italy. When she was twelve, her family moved to Rome so that she could receive a better education. At the age of fourteen, despite her father's misgivings and traditional views, Montessori enrolled in a technical college and studied engineering. Her interest in biology, however, led her to study medicine instead, and with Pope Leo XIII's help, Montessori was admitted to the University of Rome's medical school. In 1894 she graduated and became Italy's first female doctor, a feat that reinforced her commitment to women's rights.

Her appointment working with mentally challenged children in a hospital in Rome in 1897 catalyzed her interest in education. Montessori's work with these children convinced her that their problems were more connected with their education than with any perceived mental defects. She hypothesized that a change in education would make a large difference in the lives of these children, and she decided to devote her life to improving education for all children, not just those with mental handicaps.

In 1898 Montessori, unwed and devoutly Catholic, gave birth to a son, Mario. Guiseppe Montesano, the child's father, was a fellow educator who later became the director of an organization that trained Montessori-method teachers.

Montessori returned to the University of Rome in 1901 to study psychology and philosophy. When she completed her degree in 1904, she was made professor of anthropology, a position she held until 1906, when she began the experiment that altered her career forever. In 1907 she founded the *Casa dei Bambini* (Children's House) in one of Rome's worst slums. She helped design the building because she felt that the environment in which children studied should be conducive to their learning. In the beginning, her school was essentially a preschool

From *The Montessori Method*. Translated by Anne E. George.

daycare program. Her approach was based on her observations of how children naturally learn and teach each other. Her purpose was to avoid blunting children's natural impulse to learn what interests them.

Her methods differed in several ways from those then in use. She respected all her students, regardless of their background. She insisted on providing them with moveable child-sized furniture, and she maintained a quiet, clean, and safe environment at all times. Montessori's teaching methods showed results immediately. Although the children entered school as unruly as one might expect, it was not long before they began to reveal remarkable skills; in fact, some of the three- and four-year-olds had learned to read and were beginning to write. As Montessori observed elsewhere, "then we saw them 'absorb' far more than reading and writing . . . it was botany, zoology, mathematics, geography, and all with the same ease, spontaneously."

Montessori spent almost three decades helping to establish schools based on her education model in Europe and North America. Because of the rise of Mussolini and Italian fascism, she left Italy in 1934, but found herself in the midst of the Spanish Civil War in Barcelona. A British cruiser rescued her in 1936. She then went to Holland and opened a training center for her methods, which she had introduced in Amsterdam in 1929. She was in India in 1940 when that country entered World War II, and being Italian nationals, she and her son were interned as enemy aliens. After the war, she established Montessori schools in India and Sri Lanka. She died in Holland in 1952, still involved in her work.

The Montessori method is child-centered, aimed at letting the child determine solutions to the problems developed in the classroom. Montessori thought it important that a task involve the child's whole personality and that the teacher's role was to prepare the child to approach that task. For example, the senses had to be addressed, so there was a great deal of emphasis on seeing, hearing, and touching, which prepared children for intellectual processes that depend on those skills — as, for instance, reading depends on seeing. Parents were expected to be part of the process, and room was made for their visits to the school. Essentially, Montessori established an environment that freed children to learn spontaneously. Educators around the world still use the methods Montessori developed more than a hundred years ago.

Montessori's Rhetoric

In the selection that follows, which is excerpted from the opening chapter of the book *The Montessori Method*, Montessori crafts a subtle argument for a new kind of "scientific pedagogy" (a scientific method of instruction) that emphasizes the freedom of the student. Montessori eventually moves to the adult life of people who have gone through traditional schools to point out that the restrictions they have in their daily office or work lives resemble the restrictions that characterized the environment in which they were taught as children. She argues in the early part of her discussion (para. 9) that stationary desks, benches, and chairs are proof that "the principle of slavery still pervades pedagogy."

Scientific approaches to teaching had been in vogue in the early years of the twentieth century, but they had been restricted to various quantifiable measures, such as the circumference of heads and upper bodies, general height and weight, or results of various psychological tests. These, Montessori argues, are scientifically irrelevant to the teaching of children. Her science depends on careful observation of the ways in which children pursue their own learning. Once those ways are understood, Montessori argues, better teaching and learning will result.

One of her rhetorical methods is comparison. She describes the zoologist who studies butterflies that have been killed and stuck on pins, "their outspread wings motionless" (para. 5). A teacher who behaves like the zoologist would teach in a school "where the children are repressed in the spontaneous expression of their personality till they are almost like dead beings. In such a school the children, like butterflies mounted on pins, are fastened each to his place, the desk, spreading the useless wings of barren and meaningless knowledge which they have acquired" (para. 6). In this paragraph she argues for life in the classroom and for freedom of the individual.

Montessori further develops her argument by referencing a concrete situation: the architecture of the classroom, with a close examination of the stationary desks and chairs. She spends quite a bit of time with this material (paras. 9–20) because she wants us to realize that people have thought out this unworkable system in a scientific fashion. She introduces a personal anecdote when she describes the woman who presented her with a brace or harness in which to place children in the classroom, thus absolutely immobilizing them in a manner similar to zoologists pinning butterflies. As she states, this approach perfects the "immobility" of the child and his or her repression.

The conflict between methods that produce "an instrument of slavery" in the classroom and the "movement of social liberation" that is growing throughout the modern world is central to much of the rest of her argument. Her example of the use of braces for spinal curvature is almost an absurd argument, but its absurdity makes all the more intense the insight Montessori has into educational practices that must be overturned. They look scientific, but they ignore the study of the child.

In paragraphs 37–40 Montessori addresses the inner spirit of the child. In this section, as in the opening paragraphs, some of her own religious views peek out in her emphasis on the freedom of the spirit. As she points out, the death of the spirit occurs in slavery, and her argument against slavery takes its shape in a reminder that "[a]ll forms of slavery tend little by little to weaken and disappear, even the sexual slavery of woman" (para. 28). Montessori ends her essay with an emphasis on the inner life of the child and a warning concerning criminality, which she considers a form of slavery. But criminals are a small portion of society and their punishment is exact. "The real punishment of normal man is the loss of the consciousness of that individual power and greatness which are the sources of his inner life" (para. 41). By respecting children, observing their natural behaviors, and permitting them to pursue tasks freely in an environment that is conducive to real learning, Montessori believes educators can bring out the best qualities in every individual.

PREREADING QUESTIONS: WHAT TO READ FOR

The following prereading questions may help you anticipate key issues in the discussion of Maria Montessori's "The Montessori Method." Keeping them in mind during your first reading of the selection should help focus your attention.

- What is the basis of scientific pedagogy for Montessori?
- How does school furniture affect the education of the child?
- What effect does freedom have on the education of the child?

The Montessori Method

The interest in humanity to which we wish to educate the teacher   1 must be characterised by the intimate relationship between the observer and the individual to be observed; a relationship which does not exist between the student of zoology or botany and that form of nature which he studies. Man cannot love the insect or the chemical reaction which he studies, without sacrificing a part of himself.

This self-sacrifice seems to one who looks at it from the standpoint of the world, a veritable renunciation of life itself, almost a martyrdom.

But the love of man for man is a far more tender thing, and so   2
simple that it is universal. To love in this way is not the privilege of any especially prepared intellectual class, but lies within the reach of all men.

To give an idea of this second form of preparation, that of the   3
spirit, let us try to enter into the minds and hearts of those first followers of Christ Jesus as they heard Him speak of a Kingdom not of this world, greater far than any earthly kingdom, no matter how royally conceived. In their simplicity they asked of Him, "Master, tell us who shall be greatest in the Kingdom of Heaven?" To which Christ, caressing the head of a little child who, with reverent, wondering eyes, looked into His face, replied, "Whosoever shall become as one of these little ones, he shall be greatest in the Kingdom of Heaven." Now let us picture among those to whom these words were spoken, an ardent, worshipping soul, who takes them into his heart. With a mixture of respect and love, of sacred curiosity and of a desire to achieve this spiritual greatness, he sets himself to observe every manifestation of this little child. Even such an observer placed in a classroom filled with little children will not be the new educator whom we wish to form. But let us seek to implant in the soul the self-sacrificing spirit of the scientist with the reverent love of the disciple of Christ, and we shall have prepared the *spirit* of the teacher. From the child itself he will learn how to perfect himself as an educator.

Let us consider the attitude of the teacher in the light of another   4
example. Picture to yourself one of our botanists or zoologists experienced in the technique of observation and experimentation; one who has traveled in order to study "certain fungi" in their native environment. This scientist has made his observations in open country and, then, by the aid of his microscope and of all his laboratory appliances, has carried on the later research work in the most minute way possible. He is, in fact, a scientist who understands what it is to study nature, and who is conversant with all the means which modern experimental science offers for this study.

Now let us imagine such a man appointed, by reason of the original   5
work he has done, to a chair of science in some university, with the task before him of doing further original research work with hymenoptera.[1] Let us suppose that, arrived at his post, he is shown a glass-covered

---

[1] **hymenoptera** A class of insects including wasps, bees, and ants.

case containing a number of beautiful butterflies, mounted by means of pins, their outspread wings motionless. The student will say that this is some child's play, not material for scientific study, that these specimens in the box are more fitly a part of the game which the little boys play, chasing butterflies and catching them in a net. With such material as this the experimental scientist can do nothing.

The situation would be very much the same if we should place 6 a teacher who, according to our conception of the term, is scientifically prepared, in one of the public schools where the children are repressed in the spontaneous expression of their personality till they are almost like dead beings. In such a school the children, like butterflies mounted on pins, are fastened each to his place, the desk, spreading the useless wings of barren and meaningless knowledge which they have acquired.

It is not enough, then, to prepare in our Masters the scientific 7 spirit. We must also make ready the *school* for their observation. The school must permit the *free, natural manifestations* of the *child* if in the school scientific pedagogy is to be born. This is the essential reform.

No one may affirm that such a principle already exists in pedagogy 8 and in the school. It is true that some pedagogues, led by Rousseau,[2] have given voice to impracticable principles and vague aspirations for the liberty of the child, but the true concept of liberty is practically unknown to educators. They often have the same concept of liberty which animates a people in the hour of rebellion from slavery, or perhaps, the conception of *social liberty*, which although it is a more elevated idea is still invariably restricted. "Social liberty" signifies always one more round of Jacob's ladder. In other words it signifies a partial liberation, the liberation of a country, of a class, or of thought.

That concept of liberty which must inspire pedagogy is, instead, 9 universal. The biological sciences of the nineteenth century have shown it to us when they have offered us the means for studying life. If, therefore, the old-time pedagogy foresaw or vaguely expressed the principle of studying the pupil before educating him, and of leaving him free in his spontaneous manifestations, such an intuition, indefinite and barely expressed, was made possible of practical attainment only after the contribution of the experimental sciences during the last century. This is not a case for sophistry or discussion, it is enough that we state our point. He who would say that the principle of liberty informs the pedagogy of today, would make us smile as at a child who, before the box of mounted butterflies, should insist that they

---

[2] **Jean-Jacques Rousseau (1712–1778)** Philosopher who wrote the novel *Emile or On Education.*

were alive and could fly. The principle of slavery still pervades pedagogy, and, therefore, the same principle pervades the school. I need
only give one proof—the stationary desks and chairs. Here we have,
for example, a striking evidence of the errors of the early materialistic scientific pedagogy which, with mistaken zeal and energy, carried
the barren stones of science to the rebuilding of the crumbling walls
of the school. The schools were at first furnished with the long, narrow benches upon which the children were crowded together. Then
came science and perfected the bench. In this work much attention
was paid to the recent contributions of anthropology. The age of the
child and the length of his limbs were considered in placing the seat
at the right height. The distance between the seat and the desk was
calculated with infinite care, in order that the child's back should not
become deformed, and, finally, the seats were separated and the width
so closely calculated that the child could barely seat himself upon it,
while to stretch himself by making any lateral movements was impossible. This was done in order that he might be separated from his neighbor. These desks are constructed in such a way as to render the child
visible in all his immobility. One of the ends sought through this separation is the prevention of immoral acts in the schoolroom. What shall
we say of such prudence in a state of society where it would be considered scandalous to give voice to principles of sex morality in education, for fear we might thus contaminate innocence? And, yet, here we
have science lending itself to this hypocrisy, fabricating machines! Not
only this; obliging science goes farther still, perfecting the benches in
such a way as to permit to the greatest possible extent the immobility
of the child, or, if you wish, to repress every movement of the child.

It is all so arranged that, when the child is well-fitted into his 10
place, the desk and chair themselves force him to assume the position
considered to be hygienically comfortable. The seat, the footrest, the
desks are arranged in such a way that the child can never stand at
his work. He is allotted only sufficient space for sitting in an erect
position. It is in such ways that schoolroom desks and benches have
advanced toward perfection. Every cult of the so-called scientific pedagogy has designed a model scientific desk. Not a few nations have
become proud of their "national desk,"—and in the struggle of competition these various machines have been patented.

Undoubtedly there is much that is scientific underlying the con- 11
struction of these benches. Anthropology has been drawn upon in
the measuring of the body and the diagnosis of the age; physiology,
in the study of muscular movements; psychology, in regard to perversion of instincts; and, above all, hygiene, in the effort to prevent
curvature of the spine. These desks were indeed scientific, following
in their construction the anthropological study of the child. We have

here, as I have said, an example of the literal application of science to the schools.

I believe that before very long we shall all be struck with great surprise by this attitude. It will seem incomprehensible that the fundamental error of the desk should not have been revealed earlier through the attention given to the study of infant hygiene, anthropology, and sociology, and through the general progress of thought. The marvel is greater when we consider that during the past years there has been stirring in almost every nation a movement toward the protection of the child.

I believe that it will not be many years before the public, scarcely believing the descriptions of these scientific benches, will come to touch with wondering hands the amazing seats that were constructed for the purpose of preventing among our school children curvature of the spine!

The development of these scientific benches means that the pupils were subjected to a régime, which, even though they were born strong and straight, made it possible for them to become humpbacked! The vertebral column, biologically the most primitive, fundamental, and oldest part of the skeleton, the most fixed portion of our body, since the skeleton is the most solid portion of the organism—the vertebral column, which resisted and was strong through the desperate struggles of primitive man when he fought against the desert-lion, when he conquered the mammoth, when he quarried the solid rock and shaped the iron to his uses, bends, and cannot resist, under the yoke of the school.

It is incomprehensible that so-called *science* should have worked to perfect an instrument of slavery in the school without being enlightened by one ray from the movement of social liberation, growing and developing throughout the world. For the age of scientific benches was also the age of the redemption of the working classes from the yoke of unjust labor.

The tendency toward social liberty is most evident, and manifests itself on every hand. The leaders of the people make it their slogan, the laboring masses repeat the cry, scientific and socialistic publications voice the same movement, our journals are full of it. The underfed workman does not ask for a tonic, but for better economic conditions which shall prevent malnutrition. The miner who, through the stooping position maintained during many hours of the day, is subject to inguinal rupture, does not ask for an abdominal support, but demands shorter hours and better working conditions, in order that he may be able to lead a healthy life like other men.

And when, during this same social epoch, we find that the children in our schoolrooms are working amid unhygienic conditions, so poorly adapted to normal development that even the skeleton becomes deformed, our response to this terrible revelation is an orthopedic bench.

It is much as if we offered to the miner the abdominal brace, or arsenic to the underfed workman.

Some time ago a woman, believing me to be in sympathy with all 18 scientific innovations concerning the school, showed me with evident satisfaction *a corset or brace for pupils.* She had invented this and felt that it would complete the work of the bench.

Surgery has still other means for the treatment of spinal curva- 19 ture. I might mention orthopedic instruments, braces, and a method of periodically suspending the child, by the head or shoulders, in such a fashion that the weight of the body stretches and thus straightens the vertebral column. In the school, the orthopedic instrument in the shape of the desk is in great favor today; someone proposes the brace—one step farther and it will be suggested that we give the scholars a systematic course in the suspension method!

All this is the logical consequence of a material application of 20 the methods of science to the decadent school. Evidently the rational method of combating spinal curvature in the pupils, is to change the form of their work—so that they shall no longer be obliged to remain for so many hours a day in a harmful position. It is a conquest of liberty which the school needs, not the mechanism of a bench.

Even were the stationary seat helpful to the child's body, it would 21 still be a dangerous and unhygienic feature of the environment, through the difficulty of cleaning the room perfectly when the furniture cannot be moved. The footrests, which cannot be removed, accumulate the dirt carried in daily from the street by the many little feet. Today there is a general transformation in the matter of house furnishings. They are made lighter and simpler so that they may be easily moved, dusted, and even washed. But the school seems blind to the transformation of the social environment.

It behooves us to think of what may happen to the *spirit* of the 22 child who is condemned to grow in conditions so artificial that his very bones may become deformed. When we speak of the redemption of the workingman, it is always understood that beneath the most apparent form of suffering, such as poverty of the blood, or ruptures, there exists that other wound from which the soul of the man who is subjected to any form of slavery must suffer. It is at this deeper wrong that we aim when we say that the workman must be redeemed through liberty. We know only too well that when a man's very blood has been consumed or his intestines wasted away through his work, his soul must have lain oppressed in darkness, rendered insensible, or, it may be, killed within him. The *moral* degradation of the slave is, above all things, the weight that opposes the progress of humanity—humanity striving to rise and held back by this great burden. The cry of redemption speaks far more clearly for the souls of men than for their bodies.

What shall we say then, when the question before us is that of *educating children?*   23

We know only too well the sorry spectacle of the teacher who, in the ordinary schoolroom, must pour certain cut and dried facts into the heads of the scholars. In order to succeed in this barren task, she finds it necessary to discipline her pupils into immobility and to force their attention. Prizes and punishments are ever-ready and efficient aids to the master who must force into a given attitude of mind and body those who are condemned to be his listeners.   24

It is true that today it is deemed expedient to abolish official whippings and habitual blows, just as the awarding of prizes has become less ceremonious. These partial reforms are another prop approved of by science, and offered to the support of the decadent school. Such prizes and punishments are, if I may be allowed the expression, the *bench* of the soul, the instrument of slavery for the spirit. Here, however, these are not applied to lessen deformities, but to provoke them. The prize and the punishment are incentives toward unnatural or forced effort, and, therefore we certainly cannot speak of the natural development of the child in connection with them. The jockey offers a piece of sugar to his horse before jumping into the saddle, the coachman beats his horse that he may respond to the signs given by the reins; and, yet, neither of these runs so superbly as the free horse of the plains.   25

And here, in the case of education, shall man place the yoke upon man?   26

True, we say that social man is natural man yoked to society. But if we give a comprehensive glance to the moral progress of society, we shall see that little by little, the yoke is being made easier, in other words, we shall see that nature, or life, moves gradually toward triumph. The yoke of the slave yields to that of the servant, and the yoke of the servant to that of the workman.   27

All forms of slavery tend little by little to weaken and disappear, even the sexual slavery of woman. The history of civilization is a history of conquest and of liberation. We should ask in what stage of civilization we find ourselves and if, in truth, the good of prizes and of punishments be necessary to our advancement. If we have indeed gone beyond this point, then to apply such a form of education would be to draw the new generation back to a lower level, not to lead them into their true heritage of progress.   28

Something very like this condition of the school exists in society, in the relation between the government and the great numbers of the men employed in its administrative departments. These clerks work day after day for the general national good, yet they do not feel or see the advantage of their work in any immediate reward. That is, they do not realize   29 that the state carries on its great business through their daily tasks, and that the whole nation is benefited by their work. For them the immediate good is promotion, as passing to a higher class is for the child in school. The man who loses sight of the really big aim of his work is like a child who has been placed in a class below his real standing: like a slave, he is cheated of something which is his right. His dignity as a man is reduced to the limits of the dignity of a machine which must be oiled if it is to be kept going, because it does not have within itself the impulse of life. All those petty things such as the desire for decorations or medals, are but artificial stimuli, lightening for the moment the dark, barren path in which he treads.

In the same way we give prizes to schoolchildren. And the fear of not 30 achieving promotion, withholds the clerk from running away, and binds him to his monotonous work, even as the fear of not passing into the next class drives the pupil to his book. The reproof of the superior is in every way similar to the scolding of the teacher. The correction of badly executed clerical work is equivalent to the bad mark placed by the teacher upon the scholar's poor composition. The parallel is almost perfect.

But if the administrative departments are not carried on in a way 31 which would seem suitable to a nation's greatness; if corruption too easily finds a place; it is the result of having extinguished the true greatness of man in the mind of the employee, and of having restricted his vision to those petty, immediate facts, which he has come to look upon as prizes and punishments. The country stands, because the rectitude of the greater number of its employees is such that they resist the corruption of the prizes and punishments, and follow an irresistible current of honesty. Even as life in the social environment triumphs against every cause of poverty and death, and proceeds to new conquests, so the instinct of liberty conquers all obstacles, going from victory to victory.

It is this personal and yet universal force of life, a force often 32 latent within the soul, that sends the world forward.

But he who accomplishes a truly human work, he who does some- 33 thing really great and victorious, is never spurred to his task by those trifling attractions called by the name of "prizes," nor by the fear of those petty ills which we call "punishments." If in a war a great army of giants should fight with no inspiration beyond the desire to win promotion, epaulets, or medals, or through fear of being shot, if these men were to oppose a handful of pygmies who were inflamed by love of country, the victory would go to the latter. When real heroism has died within an army, prizes and punishments cannot do more than finish the work of deterioration, bringing in corruption and cowardice.

All human victories, all human progress, stand upon the inner force. 34

Thus a young student may become a great doctor if he is spurred 35 to his study by an interest which makes medicine his real vocation.

But if he works in the hope of an inheritance, or of making a desirable marriage, or if indeed he is inspired by any material advantage, he will never become a true master or a great doctor, and the world will never make one step forward because of his work. He to whom such stimuli are necessary, had far better never become a physician. Everyone has a special tendency, a special vocation, modest, perhaps, but certainly useful. The system of prizes may turn an individual aside from this vocation, may make him choose a false road, for him a vain one, and forced to follow it, the natural activity of a human being may be warped, lessened, even annihilated.

We repeat always that the world *progresses* and that we must urge   36
men forward to obtain progress. But progress comes from the *new things that are born,* and these, not being foreseen, are not rewarded with prizes: rather, they often carry the leader to martyrdom. God forbid that poems should ever be born of the desire to be crowned in the Capitol! Such a vision need only come into the heart of the poet and the muse will vanish. The poem must spring from the soul of the poet, when he thinks neither of himself nor of the prize. And if he does win the laurel, he will feel the vanity of such a prize. The true reward lies in the revelation through the poem of his own triumphant inner force.

There does exist, however, an external prize for man; when, for   37
example, the orator sees the faces of his listeners change with the emotions he has awakened, he experiences something so great that it can only be likened to the intense joy with which one discovers that he is loved. Our joy is to touch, and conquer souls, and this is the one prize which can bring us a true compensation.

Sometimes there is given to us a moment when we fancy ourselves   38
to be among the great ones of the world. These are moments of happiness given to man that he may continue his existence in peace. It may be through love attained or because of the gift of a son, through a glorious discovery or the publication of a book; in some such moment we feel that there exists no man who is above us. If, in such a moment, someone vested with authority comes forward to offer us a medal or a prize, he is the important destroyer of our real reward—"And who are you?" our vanished illusion shall cry, "Who are you that recalls me to the fact that I am not the first among men? Who stands so far above me that he may give me a prize?" The prize of such a man in such a moment can only be Divine.

As for punishments, the soul of the normal man grows perfect   39
through expanding, and punishment as commonly understood is always a form of *repression*. It may bring results with those inferior natures who grow in evil, but these are very few, and social progress is not affected by them. The penal code threatens us with punishment if we are dishonest within the limits indicated by the laws. But we are

not honest through fear of the laws; if we do not rob, if we do not kill, it is because we love peace, because the natural trend of our lives leads us forward, leading us ever farther and more definitely away from the peril of low and evil acts.

Without going into the ethical or metaphysical aspects of the question, we may safely affirm that the delinquent before he transgresses the law, has, *if he knows of the existence of a punishment*, felt the threatening weight of the criminal code upon him. He has defied it, or he has been lured into the crime, deluding himself with the idea that he would be able to avoid the punishment of the law. But there has occurred within his mind, *a struggle between the crime and the punishment*. Whether it be efficacious in hindering crime or not, this penal code is undoubtedly made for a very limited class of individuals; namely, criminals. The enormous majority of citizens are honest without any regard whatever to the threats of the law.   40

The real punishment of normal man is the loss of the consciousness of that individual power and greatness which are the sources of his inner life. Such a punishment often falls upon men in the fullness of success. A man whom we would consider crowned by happiness and fortune may be suffering from this form of punishment. Far too often man does not see the real punishment which threatens him.   41

And it is just here that education may help.   42

Today we hold the pupils in school, restricted by those instruments so degrading to body and spirit, the desk—and material prizes and punishments. Our aim in all this is to reduce them to the discipline of immobility and silence,—to lead them,—where? Far too often toward no definite end.   43

Often the education of children consists in pouring into their intelligence the intellectual contents of school programs. And often these programs have been compiled in the official department of education, and their use is imposed by law upon the teacher and the child.   44

Ah, before such dense and willful disregard of the life which is growing within these children, we should hide our heads in shame and cover our guilty faces with our hands!   45

Sergi[3] says truly: "Today an urgent need imposes itself upon society: the reconstruction of methods in education and instruction, and he who fights for this cause, fights for human regeneration."   46

---

[3] **Giuseppe Sergi (1841–1936)** A professor of anthropology who worked with Montessori at the University of Rome.

QUESTIONS FOR CRITICAL READING

1. Why does Montessori emphasize love of the child in regard to scientific pedagogy?

2. What is the point of the reference to Jesus in paragraph 3?

3. How effective, in terms of argument, is the comparison of the pinned butterflies with the children penned in by their desks? Is the comparison valid?

4. Why is there so much emphasis on the example of the desks and chairs that have been scientifically provided for schoolchildren?

5. What does it mean to study the pupils before educating them?

6. Montessori says the principle of slavery still pervades pedagogy. Is that true even today?

7. Comment on Montessori's use of irony in paragraph 19.

8. How does Montessori connect the educational environment of the child with the working environment of the adult?

SUGGESTIONS FOR CRITICAL WRITING

1. In paragraph 3 Montessori asserts, "From the child itself he will learn how to perfect himself as an educator." In practical terms, how useful do you think this statement is in teaching preschool children? How valuable would it be in teaching children in the early grades? Is it less valuable or more valuable in teaching college students?

2. If you have had experience in a Montessori school, describe the ways in which learning occurred. Review your own experience and compare it with the principles that Montessori outlines in her selection. How many of her values were present in the school you attended? How effective was that early education for you? Did you feel that your inner spirit was developed as you learned?

3. Montessori states, "The school must permit the *free, natural manifestations* of the *child* if in the school scientific pedagogy is to be born" (para. 7). In terms of your experience, do you feel this statement is valid? How can scientific pedagogy be put into effect while also educating the child? What conditions need to be met?

4. Beginning in paragraph 24, Montessori writes extensively about school prizes and punishments. Examine her argument and either defend it on the basis of your observations, or attack it. Explain what the nature of her argument is and how it applies to the education of the child as Montessori understands it. What is your view on the usefulness of prizes and punishments in the education of children?

5. Montessori's great experiment took place in the San Lorenzo quarter of Rome, one of the toughest slums in the city. It was being rebuilt when

Montessori got the opportunity to construct her "Children's House." Do some research on *Casa dei Bambini* and write an essay that clarifies exactly what she did there and what kind of results she eventually got. How successful was her experiment? What criticisms of the experiment seem valid to you?

6. Montessori states, "Everyone has a special tendency, a special vocation, modest, perhaps, but certainly useful" (para. 35). Explain what this statement means. Do you see evidence for Montessori's assertion in your friends? In yourself? Why is her statement important to consider in the education of a child? How has your education affected your sense of vocation?

7. **CONNECTIONS** Montessori and Emerson (**bedfordstmartins.com /worldofideas/epages**) agree on several points. What are those points? How complete is their agreement? What are the principal issues on which they seem either to disagree or ignore one another? What basic values most importantly connect their views on education? Does Montessori agree with Emerson's views on nature, genius, and drill?

8. **CONNECTIONS** To what extent is the "education" of Frederick Douglass (p. 327) evidence that Montessori's theories are sound? What does he do that validates her ideas concerning slavery and freedom? Consider Douglass's narrative of how he learned to read when he was a child. How were the conditions under which he learned similar to those Montessori describes?

9. **SEEING CONNECTIONS** If you were to assume that the young student portrayed in Norman Rockwell's *The Problem We All Live With*, 1964, on page 539, went to a Montessori School before being escorted into a Southern public school, how would you expect her to respond to a situation in which she is likely to be rejected by her classmates? What training in terms of self-education and self-development would have been most helpful to her in dealing with a lack of "communitivity"? What would the Montessori Method give her that would make her strong enough not only to survive her environment, but to learn in it? What would she most miss in a standard classroom situation?

CARTER G. WOODSON
The Mis-Education of the Negro

CARTER G. WOODSON (1875–1950) is known as the "father of black history." It was through his efforts that Black History Week began in February 1926 and then grew into Black History Month in 1976. Woodson was a distinguished historian throughout his life, writing more than a dozen books and editing several more. His first book, *The Education of the Negro before 1861* (1915), established his dedication to the question of education, which led to his most famous book, *The Mis-Education of the Negro* (1933), which is still in print. His position as a historian was strengthened by his interdisciplinary concerns. His books *A Century of Negro Migration* (1918) and *A History of the Negro Church* (1921) demonstrate a wide range of learning and research and help explain why he became a leading scholar in African American studies.

Woodson's parents were freed slaves in Canton, Virginia. His father had helped the Union troops during the Civil War, and after the war, Woodson's father moved the family to West Virginia because he knew that Huntington was building a high school that would take African Americans. Woodson, unable to go to school at first, taught himself the essentials of grade school and then went to work in the mines in West Virginia to help his family economically. He was twenty years old when he entered Douglass High School in Huntington, and he was able to complete all his course work in two years. Woodson then earned a degree in literature at Berea College, which had been established in Kentucky by abolitionists to further the education of both blacks and whites. From 1903 to 1908, he was a school supervisor in the Philippines.

After teaching, Woodson went to the University of Chicago for his master's degree in European history and then continued his work at Harvard University, where he was awarded his Ph.D. in

From *The Mis-Education of the Negro.*

history in 1912. He was the second African American to be awarded a doctorate in history at Harvard. (W. E. B. DuBois was the first.) He taught high school history in Washington, D.C., while researching in the Library of Congress and finishing his dissertation. He eventually accepted an appointment at Howard University and became dean of the College of Arts and Sciences. However, as a result of a dispute with the president of Howard, Woodson moved to the West Virginia Collegiate Institute (now West Virginia State University) to become its dean.

Woodson left teaching in 1922 and devoted himself to historical research. He was active in the Washington, D.C., branch of the National Association for the Advancement of Colored People (NAACP) for several years, but he later severed ties with the organization because he felt it was too moderate and not active enough to truly benefit African Americans. Central to Woodson's activities in the 1920s and 1930s was his gathering of original research material from Europe and the United States on the history and achievements of African Americans, and he added many important documents to the manuscript collection of the Library of Congress. His purpose in conducting this research was to overhaul the textbooks that students of all colors used, both in the North and the South. Some textbooks used in the South implied that the slaves were treated very well before the Civil War and that the war itself was largely the result of tensions brought on the South by Northern abolitionists. Textbooks at that time had also distorted the history of the Reconstruction period, the years after the slaves were given their freedom. Woodson wrote five textbooks to try to help undo the misconceptions and damage that contemporary texts had wrought.

Woodson founded the *Journal of Negro History* in 1915, which continues today as the *Journal of African American History*. He also founded the Association for the Study of African American Life and History, which still exists. Woodson clearly earned his epithet, father of black history, because of his devotion to research on and publication of books about African American history, such as the one from which the following selection is taken.

Woodson's Rhetoric

Woodson wrote this selection in 1933, during the Great Depression. He was a careful historian of the African American experience in the United States and abroad. When he wrote, segregation was a fact of American life, and it would continue for another thirty years. Segregated schools in the South were strictly run on the basis of "separate but equal" but were rarely equal in actuality, and schools in the North were nominally integrated but segregated by neighborhood. Opportunities for African Americans pursuing higher education in the 1920s and 1930s were limited; few were able to receive the high school preparation necessary for college, and even among those who were, few were accepted into universities because colleges restricted their admission. Woodson himself overcame incredible odds to achieve his own education, and he knew what difficulties other African Americans faced.

Rhetorically, Woodson positions himself to give us an overview of the condition of contemporary African Americans in 1930s society in relation to the kinds of education available at that time. He relies on a historical survey of the kind of education available to African Americans in the past as well as the present to make his argument. But he also scrutinizes the psychology of "the educated Negroes," suggesting that their "white" education makes it difficult for them to properly educate other African Americans; he also includes a review of ways in which society makes African Americans feel inferior. His rhetorical strategy is that of the teacher, giving us a general picture of the situation as he sees it.

What Woodson does not do is offer specific examples, refer to other scholars on related subjects, or provide testimony from the educated or miseducated individuals he may know. He does not refer to data, statistics, or evidence. The result is that Woodson gives us what is essentially an argument based on his opinion, which he tells us is in turn based on his understanding of history. Such arguments can be very powerful, and in Woodson's case we sense that his argument is bolstered by what we all know about the mistreatment of African Americans both before and after the Civil War. Segregation was a fact of life, and it is not unreasonable to think that Woodson's understanding of the ways in which African Americans were educated may have had the results he says.

When Woodson uses a categorical approach to his writing, he takes a teacherly strategy and devotes a paragraph each to the essential educational issues: "science or mathematics" (para. 7); "schools of theology" (para. 8); "schools of business administration" (para. 9); and "schools of journalism" (para. 10). He uses the same technique later in the essay: teaching "science" (para. 30); "study of language" (para. 31); "literature" (para. 32); "fine arts" (para. 33); "law" (para. 34); "medical schools" (para. 35); and "history" (para. 36). In each of these paragraphs, Woodson reviews the range of education available to the African American. He then explains why each type of education offers special problems that makes it unsatisfying.

What makes Woodson's argument relevant today is that most
educators, particularly at the secondary level, agree with Woodson
and have made an effort to include materials on African American
culture and African American achievements in the sciences, art,
industry, and culture. Black History Month, which was initiated by
Woodson, has made important inroads by providing a vehicle for
informing students of African and African American contributions
to modern Western culture. Moreover, just as Woodson regarded
African Americans as a minority group in the United States, other
contemporary minorities can claim similar ignorance of their
cultural achievements in the schools. Asian Americans, Latino
Americans, and Native Americans as well as other minorities — such
as people who are gay, lesbian, transgender, or feminist — may
all read Woodson and see themselves in place of the "Negroes" for
whom he had such concern. Indeed, many such groups have followed Woodson's lead and celebrate their achievements and culture during similar monthlong tributes on college campuses and in
communities.

PREREADING QUESTIONS:
WHAT TO READ FOR

The following prereading questions may help you anticipate key
issues in the discussion of Carter G. Woodson's "The Mis-Education of the
Negro." Keeping them in mind during your first reading should help focus
your attention.

- What does Woodson mean by *mis-education*?
- What is the difference between a classical and an industrial education?
- Why does Woodson feel the Negro has been "mis-educated"?

The Mis-Education of the Negro

The Seat of the Trouble

The "educated Negroes" have the attitude of contempt toward   1
their own people because in their own as well as in their mixed schools
Negroes are taught to admire the Hebrew, the Greek, the Latin, and
the Teuton and to despise the African. Of the hundreds of Negro high
schools recently examined by an expert in the United States Bureau of

Education only eighteen offer a course taking up the history of the Negro, and in most of the Negro colleges and universities where the Negro is thought of, the race is studied only as a problem or dismissed as of little consequence. For example, an officer of a Negro university, thinking that an additional course on the Negro should be given there, called upon a Negro Doctor of Philosophy of the faculty to offer such work. He promptly informed the officer that he knew nothing about the Negro. He did not go to school to waste his time that way. He went to be educated in a system which dismissed the Negro as a nonentity.

2   At a Negro summer school two years ago, a white instructor gave a course on the Negro, using for his text a work which teaches that whites are superior to the blacks. When asked by one of the students why he used such a textbook the instructor replied that he wanted them to get that point of view. Even schools for Negroes, then, are places where they must be convinced of their inferiority.

3   The thought of the inferiority of the Negro is drilled into him in almost every class he enters and in almost every book he studies. If he happens to leave school after he masters the fundamentals, before he finishes high school or reaches college, he will naturally escape some of this bias and may recover in time to be of service to his people.

4   Practically all of the successful Negroes in this country are of the uneducated type or of that type of Negroes who have had no formal education at all. The large majority of the Negroes who have put on the finishing touches of our best colleges are all but worthless in the development of their people. If after leaving school they have the opportunity to give out to Negroes what traducers of the race would like to have it learn such persons may thereby earn a living at teaching or preaching what they have been taught but they never become a constructive force in the development of the race. The so-called school, then, becomes a questionable factor in the life of this despised people.

5   As another has well said, to handicap a student by teaching him that his black face is a curse and that his struggle to change his condition is hopeless is the worst sort of lynching. It kills one's aspirations and dooms him to vagabondage and crime. It is strange, then, that the friends of truth and the promoters of freedom have not risen up against the present propaganda in the schools and crushed it. This crusade is much more important than the antilynching movement, because there would no lynching if it did not start in the schoolroom. Why not exploit, enslave, or exterminate a class that everybody is taught to regard as inferior?

6   To be more explicit we may go to the seat of the trouble. Our most widely known scholars have been trained in universities outside of the South. Northern and Western institutions, however, have had no time

to deal with matters which concern the Negro especially. They must direct their attention to the problems of the majority of their constituents, and too often they have stimulated their prejudices by referring to the Negro as unworthy of consideration. Most of what these universities have offered as language, mathematics, and science may have served a good purpose, but much of what they have taught as economics, history, literature, religion, and philosophy is propaganda and cant that involved a waste of time and misdirected the Negroes thus trained.

And even in the certitude of science or mathematics it has been 7 unfortunate that the approach to the Negro has been borrowed from a "foreign" method. For example, the teaching of arithmetic in the fifth grade in a backward county in Mississippi should mean one thing in the Negro school and a decidedly different thing in the white school. The Negro children, as a rule, come from the homes of tenants and peons who have to migrate annually from plantation to plantation, looking for light which they have never seen. The children from the homes of white planters and merchants live permanently in the midst of calculations, family budgets, and the like, which enable them sometimes to learn more by contact than the Negro can acquire in school. Instead of teaching such Negro children less arithmetic, they should be taught much more of it than the white children, for the latter attend a graded school consolidated by free transportation when the Negroes go to one-room rented hovels to be taught without equipment and by incompetent teachers educated scarcely beyond the eighth grade.

In schools of theology Negroes are taught the interpretation 8 of the Bible worked out by those who have justified segregation and winked at the economic debasement of the Negro sometimes almost to the point of starvation. Deriving their sense of right from this teaching, graduates of such schools can have no message to grip the people whom they have been ill trained to serve. Most of such mis-educated ministers, therefore, preach to benches while illiterate Negro preachers do the best they can in supplying the spiritual needs of the masses.

In the schools of business administration Negroes are trained exclu- 9 sively in the psychology and economics of Wall Street and are, therefore, made to despise the opportunities to run ice wagons, push banana carts, and sell peanuts among their own people. Foreigners, who have not studied economics but have studied Negroes, take up this business and grow rich.

In schools of journalism Negroes are being taught how to edit 10 such metropolitan dailies as the *Chicago Tribune* and the *New York Times*, which would hardly hire a Negro as a janitor; and when these graduates come to the Negro weeklies for employment they are not prepared to function in such establishments, which, to be successful, must be built upon accurate knowledge of the psychology and philosophy of the Negro.

When a Negro has finished his education in our schools, then, he has been equipped to begin the life of an Americanized or Europeanized white man, but before the steps from the threshold of his alma mater he is told by his teachers that he must go back to his own people from whom he has been estranged by a vision of ideals which in his disillusionment he will realize that he cannot attain. He goes forth to play his part in life, but he must be both social and bisocial at the same time. While he is a part of the body politic, he is in addition to this a member of a particular race to which he must restrict himself in all matters social. While serving his country he must serve within a special group. While being a good American, he must above all things be a "good Negro"; and to perform this definite function he must learn to stay in a "Negro's place." 11

For the arduous task of serving a race thus handicapped, however, the Negro graduate has had little or no training at all. The people whom he has been ordered to serve have been belittled by his teachers to the extent that he can hardly find delight in undertaking what his education has led him to think is impossible. Considering his race as blank in achievement, then, he sets out to stimulate their imitation of others. The performance is kept up a while; but, like any other effort at meaningless imitation, it results in failure. 12

Facing this undesirable result, the highly educated Negro often grows sour. He becomes too pessimistic to be a constructive force and usually develops into a chronic faultfinder or a complainant at the bar of public opinion. Often when he sees that the fault lies at the door of the white oppressor whom he is afraid to attack, he turns upon the pioneering Negro who is at work doing the best he can to extricate himself from an uncomfortable predicament. 13

In this effort to imitate, however, these "educated people" are sincere. They hope to make the Negro conform quickly to the standard of the whites and thus remove the pretext for the barriers between the races. They do not realize, however, that even if the Negroes do successfully imitate the whites, nothing new has thereby been accomplished. You simply have a larger number of persons doing what others have been doing. The unusual gifts of the race have not thereby been developed, and an unwilling world, therefore, continues to wonder what the Negro is good for. 14

These "educated" people, however, decry any such thing as race consciousness; and in some respects they are right. They do not like to hear such expressions as "Negro literature," "Negro poetry," "African art," or "thinking black"; and, roughly speaking, we must concede that such things do not exist. These things did not figure in the courses which 15 they pursued in school, and why should they? "Aren't we all Americans? Then, whatever is American is as much the heritage of the Negro as of any other group in this country."

The "highly educated" contend, however, that when the Negro   16
emphasizes these things he invites racial discrimination by recognizing such differentness of the races. The thought that the Negro is one thing and the white man another is the stock-in-trade argument of the Caucasian to justify segregation. Why, then, should the Negro blame the white man for doing what he himself does?

These "highly educated" Negroes, however, fail to see that it is not   17
the Negro who takes this position. The white man forces him to it, and to extricate himself therefrom the Negro leader must so deal with the situation as to develop in the segregated group the power with which they can elevate themselves. The differentness of races, moreover, is no evidence of superiority or of inferiority. This merely indicates that each race has certain gifts which the others do not possess. It is by the development of these gifts that every race must justify its right to exist.

How We Missed the Mark

How we have arrived at the present state of affairs can be under-   18
stood only by studying the forces effective in the development of Negro education since it was systematically undertaken immediately after Emancipation. To point out merely the defects as they appear today will be of little benefit to the present and future generations. These things must be viewed in their historic setting. The conditions of today have been determined by what has taken place in the past, and in a careful study of this history we may see more clearly the great theater of events in which the Negro has played a part. We may understand better what his role has been and how well he has functioned in it.

The idea of educating the Negroes after the Civil War was largely a   19
prompting of philanthropy. Their white neighbors failed to assume this responsibility. These black people had been liberated as a result of a sectional conflict out of which their former owners had emerged as victims. From this class, then, the freedmen could not expect much sympathy or cooperation in the effort to prepare themselves to figure as citizens of a modern republic.

From functionaries of the United States government itself and from   20
those who participated in the conquest of the secessionists early came the plan of teaching these freedmen the simple duties of life as worked out by the Freedmen's Bureau and philanthropic agencies. When systematized this effort became a program for the organization of churches and schools and the direction of them along lines which had

been considered most conducive to the progress of people otherwise cir-
cumstanced. Here and there some variation was made in this program in
view of the fact that the status of the freedmen in no way paralleled that
of their friends and teachers, but such thought was not general. When
the Negroes in some way would learn to perform the duties which
other elements of the population had prepared themselves to discharge
they would be duly qualified, it was believed, to function as citizens of
the country.

Inasmuch as most Negroes lived in the agricultural South, more-   21
over, and only a few of them at first acquired small farms there was little
in their life which any one of thought could not have easily understood.
The poverty which afflicted them for a generation after Emancipation held them down to the lowest order of society, nominally free but
economically enslaved. The participation of the freedmen in government for a few years during the period known as the Reconstruction
had little bearing on their situation except that they did join with the
uneducated poor whites in bringing about certain much-desired social
reforms, especially in giving the South its first plan of democratic education in providing for a school system at public expense.

Neither this inadequately supported school system nor the strug-   22
gling higher institutions of a classical order established about the same
time, however, connected the Negroes very closely with life as it was.
These institutions were concerned rather with life as they hoped to make
it. When the Negro found himself deprived of influence in politics,
therefore, and at the same time unprepared to participate in the higher
functions in the industrial development which this country began to
undergo, it soon became evident to him that he was losing ground in
the basic things of life. He was spending his time studying about the
things which had been or might be, but he was learning little to help
him to do better the tasks at hand. Since the Negroes believed that the
causes of this untoward condition lay without the race, migration was
attempted, and emigration to Africa was again urged. At this psychological moment came the wave of industrial education which swept the
country by storm. The educational authorities in the cities and States
throughout the Black Belt began to change the course of study to make
the training of the Negro conform to this policy.

The missionary teachers from the North in defense of their idea of   23
more liberal training, however, fearlessly attacked this new educational
policy; and the Negroes participating in the same dispute arrayed themselves respectively on one side or the other. For a generation thereafter the quarrel as to whether the Negro should be given a classical or
a practical education was the dominant topic in Negro schools and
churches throughout the United States. Labor was the most important
thing of life, it was argued; practical education counted in reaching

that end; and the Negro worker must be taught to solve this problem of efficiency before directing attention to other things.

Others more narrow-minded than the advocates of industrial education, seized upon the idea, feeling that, although the Negro must have some semblance of education, it would be a fine stroke to be able to make a distinction between the training given the Negro and that provided for the whites. Inasmuch as the industrial educational idea rapidly gained ground, too, many Negroes for political purposes began to espouse it; and schools and colleges hoping thereby to obtain money worked out accordingly makeshift provisions for such instruction, although they could not satisfactorily offer it. A few real industrial schools actually equipped themselves for this work and turned out a number of graduates with such preparation. 24

Unfortunately, however, the affair developed into a sort of battle of words, for in spite of all they said and did the majority of the Negroes, those who did make some effort to obtain an education, did not actually receive either the industrial or the classical education. Negroes attended industrial schools, took such training as was prescribed, and received their diplomas; but few of them developed adequate efficiency to be able to do what they were supposedly trained to do. The schools in which they were educated could not provide for all the experience with machinery which white apprentices trained in factories had. Such industrial education as these Negroes received, then, was merely to master a technique already discarded in progressive centers; and even in less complicated operations of industry these schools had no such facilities as to parallel the numerous processes of factories conducted on the plan of the division of labor. Except what value such training might have in the development of the mind by making practical applications of mathematics and science, then, it was a failure. 25

The majority of Negro graduates of industrial schools, therefore, have gone into other avenues, and too often into those for which they have had no preparation whatever. Some few who actually prepared for the industrial sphere by self-improvement likewise sought other occupations for the reason that Negroes were generally barred from higher pursuits by trades unions; and, being unable to develop captains of industry to increase the demand for persons in these lines, the Negroes have not opened up many such opportunities for themselves. 26

During these years, too, the schools for the classical education for Negroes have not done any better. They have proceeded on the basis that every ambitious person needs a liberal education when as a matter of fact this does not necessarily follow. The Negro trained in the advanced phases of literature, philosophy, and politics had been unable to develop far in using his knowledge because of having to function in the lower spheres of the social order. Advanced knowledge of science, 27

mathematics, and languages, moreover, has not been much more useful except for mental disciplines because of the dearth of opportunity
to apply such knowledge among people who were largely common
laborers in towns or peons on the plantations. The extent to which such
higher education has been successful in leading the Negro to think,
which above all is the chief purpose of education, has merely made him
more of a malcontent when he can sense the drift of things and appreciate the impossibility of success in visioning conditions as they really are.

It is very clear, therefore, that we do not have in the life of the   28
Negro today a large number of persons who have been benefited by
either of the systems about which we have quarreled so long. The
number of Negro mechanics and artisans have comparatively declined
during the last two generations. The Negroes do not proportionately
represent as many skilled laborers as they did before the Civil War. If
the practical education which the Negroes received helped to improve
the situation so that it is today no worse than what it is, certainly it
did not solve the problem as was expected of it.

· · ·

The description of the various parts of the world was worked   29
out according to the same plan. The parts inhabited by the Caucasian
were treated in detail. Less attention was given to the yellow people,
still less to the red, very little to the brown, and practically none to the
black race. Those people who are far removed from the physical characteristics of the Caucasians or who do not materially assist them in
the domination or exploitation of others were not mentioned except
to be belittled or decried.

From the teaching of science the Negro was likewise eliminated.   30
The beginnings of science in various parts of the Orient were mentioned, but the Africans' early advancement in this field was omitted.
Students were not told that ancient Africans of the interior knew sufficient science to concoct poisons for arrowheads, to mix durable colors
for paintings, to extract metals from nature and refine them for development in the industrial arts. Very little was said about the chemistry
in the method of Egyptian embalming which was the product of the
mixed breeds of Northern Africa, now known in the modern world as
"colored people."

In the study of language in school pupils were made to scoff at   31
the Negro dialect as some peculiar possession of the Negro which they
should despise rather than directed to study the background of this
language as a broken-down African tongue—in short to understand
their own linguistic history, which is certainly more important for

them than the study of French Phonetics or Historical Spanish Grammar. To the African language as such no attention was given except in case of the preparation of traders, missionaries, and public functionaries to exploit the natives. This number of persons thus trained, of course, constituted a small fraction hardly deserving attention.

From literature the African was excluded altogether. He was not 32 supposed to have expressed any thought worth knowing. The philosophy in the African proverbs and in the rich folklore of that continent was ignored to give preference to that developed on the distant shores of the Mediterranean. Most missionary teachers of the freedmen, like most men of our time, had never read the interesting books of travel in Africa, and had never heard of the *Tarikh Es-Soudan*.[1]

In the teaching of fine arts these instructors usually started with 33 Greece by showing how that art was influenced from without, but they omitted the African influence which scientists now regard as significant and dominant in early Hellas. They failed to teach the student the Mediterranean Melting Pot with the Negroes from Africa bringing their wares, their ideas, and their blood therein to influence the history of Greece, Carthage, and Rome. Making desire father to the thought, our teachers either ignored these influences or endeavored to belittle them by working out theories to the contrary.

The bias did not stop at this point, for it invaded the teaching 34 of the professions. Negro law students were told that they belonged to the most criminal element in the country; and an effort was made to justify the procedure in the seats of injustice where law was interpreted as being one thing for the white man and a different thing for the Negro. In constitutional law the spinelessness of the United States Supreme Court in permitting the judicial nullification of the Fourteenth and Fifteenth Amendments was and still is boldly upheld in our few law schools.

In medical schools Negroes were likewise convinced of their infe- 35 riority in being reminded of their role as germ carriers. The prevalence of syphilis and tuberculosis among Negroes was especially emphasized without showing that these maladies are more deadly among the Negroes for the reason that they are Caucasian diseases; and since these plagues are new to Negroes, these sufferers have not had time to develop against them the immunity which time has permitted in the Caucasian. Other diseases to which Negroes easily fall prey were mentioned to point out the race as an undesirable element when this condition was due to the Negroes' economic and social status. Little

---

[1] ***Tarikh Es-Soudan*** *The History of the Sudan* by Abd al-Sadi, written in 1655. It is a history of the Songhay Empire, centering on the Moroccan invasion of Timbuktu.

emphasis was placed upon the immunity of the Negro from diseases like yellow fever and influenza which are so disastrous to whites. Yet, the whites were not considered inferior because of this differential resistance to these plagues.

In history, of course, the Negro had no place in this curriculum. He 36 was pictured as a human being of the lower order, unable to subject passion to reason, and therefore useful only when made the hewer of wood and the drawer of water for others. No thought was given to the history of Africa except so far as it had been a field of exploitation for the Caucasian. You might study the history as it was offered in our system from the elementary school throughout the university, and you would never hear Africa mentioned except in the negative. You would never thereby learn that Africans first domesticated the sheep, goat, and cow, developed the idea of trial by jury, produced the first stringed instruments, and gave the world its greatest boon in the discovery of iron. You would never know that prior to the Mohammedan invasion about 1000 A.D. these natives in the heart of Africa had developed powerful kingdoms which were later organized as the Songhay Empire[2] on the order of that of the Romans and boasting of similar grandeur.

Unlike other people, then, the Negro, according to this point of 37 view, was an exception to the natural plan of things, and he had no such mission as that of an outstanding contribution to culture. The status of the Negro, then, was justly fixed as that of an inferior. Teachers of Negroes in their first schools after Emancipation did not proclaim any such doctrine, but the content of their curricula justified these inferences.

An observer from outside of the situation naturally inquires why the 38 Negroes, many of whom serve their race as teachers, have not changed this program. These teachers, however, are powerless. Negroes have no control over their education and have little voice in their other affairs pertaining thereto. In a few cases Negroes have been chosen as members of public boards of education, and some have been appointed members of private boards, but these Negroes are always such a small minority that they do not figure in the final working out of the educational program. The education of the Negroes, then, the most important thing in the uplift of the Negroes, is almost entirely in the hands of those who have enslaved them and now segregate them.

With "mis-educated Negroes" in control themselves, however, it 39 is doubtful that the system would be very much different from what it is or that it would rapidly undergo change. The Negroes thus placed

---

[2] **Songhay Empire** A region of almost a half-million square miles in western Africa, it was one of the largest of Islamic empires in the fifteenth and sixteenth centuries. Gao and Timbuktu were its major cities.

in charge would be the products of the same system and would show no more conception of the task at hand than do the whites who have educated them and shaped their minds as they would have them function. Negro educators of today may have more sympathy and interest in the race than the whites now exploiting Negro institutions as educators, but the former have no more vision than their competitors. Taught from books of the same bias, trained by Caucasians of the same prejudices or by Negroes of enslaved minds, one generation of Negro teachers after another have served for no higher purpose than to do what they are told to do. In other words, a Negro teacher instructing Negro children is in many respects a white teacher thus engaged, for the program in each case is about the same.

There can be no reasonable objection to the Negro's doing what   40
the white man tells him to do, if the white man tells him to do what is right; but right is pure relative. The present system under the control of the whites trains the Negro to be white and at the same time convinces him of the impropriety or the impossibility of his becoming white. It compels the Negro to become a good Negro for the performance of which his education is ill-suited. For the white man's exploitation of the Negro through economic restriction and segregation the present system is sound and will doubtless continue until this gives place to the saner policy of actual interracial cooperation—not the present farce of racial manipulation in which the Negro is a figurehead. History does not furnish a case of the elevation of a people by ignoring the thought and aspiration of the people thus served.

This is slightly dangerous ground here, however, for the Negro's   41
mind has been all but perfectly enslaved in that he has been trained to think what is desired of him. The "highly educated" Negroes do not like to hear anything uttered against this procedure because they make their living in this way, and they feel that they must defend the system. Few mis-educated Negroes ever act otherwise; and, if they so express themselves, they are easily crushed by the large majority to the contrary so that the procession may move on without interruption.

The result, then, is that the Negroes thus mis-educated are of   42
no service to themselves and none to the white man. The white man does not need the Negroes' professional, commercial, or industrial assistance; and as a result of the multiplication of mechanical appliances he no longer needs them in drudgery or menial service. The "highly educated" Negroes, moreover, do not need the Negro professional or commercial classes because Negroes have been taught that whites can serve them more efficiently in these spheres. Reduced, then, to teaching and preaching, the Negroes will have no outlet but

to go down a blind alley, if the sort of education which they are now receiving is to enable them to find the way out of their present difficulties.

QUESTIONS FOR CRITICAL READING

1. Why does Woodson think the schools "miseducated" African Americans?

2. Have secondary schools made enough progress in promoting the cultural awareness that Woodson had hoped for?

3. Which of the descriptions of "educated Negroes" seem no longer relevant to you? How have things changed since Woodson's time?

4. How much of what Woodson complains about in terms of the education of "the Negro" applies to other minorities today?

5. How much of what Woodson complains about regarding the education of "the Negro" still applies and is still relevant in our schools and colleges?

6. Which kind of education do you think is best for you: classical or industrial? Which do you think is best for any minority group? Which is best for our country?

7. Which of Woodson's statements about education strikes you as most significant for us to consider?

SUGGESTIONS FOR CRITICAL WRITING

1. To what extent do programs in African American studies in contemporary colleges satisfy the needs that Woodson saw in the 1930s for properly educating African American students? Do such programs seem to have been affected by Woodson's arguments in favor of instilling cultural awareness in students? Have they helped in educating people of all races?

2. Considering the positive effects of Black History Month in promoting cultural awareness and the understanding of cultural achievement, would you support a national move to develop a Latino History Month in secondary schools? Would you support a Gay and Lesbian History Month? Would all these possibilities raise awareness of culture and achievement? What other history month would you support?

3. Write an essay that establishes a secondary school curriculum in English, science, history, or sociology that would please Woodson and be the opposite of a "mis-education." Construct a curriculum that could actually be put into action and explain why your suggestions would please Woodson. At the same time, defend your curriculum as being preferable to the curriculum you experienced in your own secondary education.

4. Woodson also discusses industrial education, by which he means developing a mastery of the machinery and skills needed to work in industry. When he discusses this option (para. 23), he suggests that northern teachers originally thought that "[l]abor was the most important thing of life." Today many people feel higher education should aim to prepare students for the workplace. Yet Woodson also says that "the chief purpose of education" is leading the student to think (para. 27). Which kind of education do you think fulfills "the chief purpose of education"?

5. **CONNECTIONS** Woodson makes a reference to "Negro dialect" when he discusses literature and language. He says, "In the study of language in school pupils were made to scoff at the Negro dialect as some peculiar possession of the Negro which they should despise" (para. 31). How would Woodson have responded to James Baldwin's "If Black English Isn't a Language, Then Tell Me, What Is?" (p. 795)? How much does Baldwin sympathize with Woodson and to what extent do you think Baldwin would have been in agreement with Woodson's overall argument?

6. **CONNECTIONS**   Like Woodson, Emerson (**bedfordstmartins.com /worldofideas/epages**) was an abolitionist and refused to obey the Fugitive Slave Law. To what extent do their styles reflect the fact that Woodson and Emerson were both teachers? To what extent do they both share the concept of respect for the student? Woodson would undoubtedly have read Emerson; to what extent does Woodson agree with Emerson in many of his views on education? Which of Emerson's principles of education would Woodson have disagreed with? Which of these writers' suggestions about education sound more modern to you?

7. Write an essay that takes Woodson's argument and applies it to another minority group. What other group has been as much disregarded as Woodson says African American students were in his time? To what extent does the pattern of contemporary education do this minority group as much a disservice as Woodson describes in his essay? What suggestions do you have for changing the current pattern of education in a way that would be more of a service to this group?

8. **SEEING CONNECTIONS**   If Woodson had stood before Norman
   Rockwell's *The Problem We All Live With* (p. 539), would he have considered the prospects for the young student in the painting to be better in 1964 than they were in 1933? How would he have responded
   to the need for U.S. marshals to march in front of and behind her?
   What would he have made of the fact that the only face in the painting is that of the student? Would he have thought it significant that
   the only student in the painting is a young girl, not a boy? Would
   Woodson have thought that Rockwell might have read his book
   The Mis-Education of the Negro?

JONATHAN KOZOL
The Uses of "Diversity"

JONATHAN KOZOL (b. 1936), a passionate defender of children's right to a good education, grew up in Newton, Massachusetts, and attended Harvard University, from where he graduated summa cum laude and was named a Rhodes Scholar. After his time at Magdalen College, Oxford, he spent a few years in Paris. Back home, he became a tutor for students in Roxbury, Massachusetts, a largely black neighborhood, and learned how underprivileged children coped with bureaucratic institutions and nondiversified schools. He took a job as a teacher in the Boston public schools but was fired in 1965 for reading from a book of poems by Langston Hughes, which was not part of the curriculum for the grade level of his students. Shortly thereafter, Kozol became a teacher in Newton, Massachusetts, in his own childhood school system. He taught for several years before he gave up teaching and devoted himself to writing and becoming a public figure fighting for better schools.

His first book, *Death at an Early Age* (1967), won the National Book Award in 1968 and sold more than two million copies. It was the story of his year teaching in the Boston public school system. It touched off a national debate on the state of the public schools in the major cities of the nation. Kozol lamented the decrepit atmosphere, the inadequate classroom furniture, and the lack of instruction in the arts and music as well as the fact that the curriculum was uninspired and unexciting. The building resembled a mental hospital more than it did a school. But with a minimum of effort, Kozol was able to introduce new material — including poetry — and managed to drastically improve his students' mathematics and reading skills by helping them become motivated and excited to learn.

From *Letters to a Young Teacher.*

After leaving the teaching profession, Kozol became involved in the civil rights movement of the 1960s. He received two Guggenheim awards and many other accolades that permitted him to lecture and continue his work trying to improve education in the United States. Among his books are *Rachel and Her Children: Homeless Families in America* (1988), which won several major awards; *Savage Inequalities: Children in America's Schools* (1992), which was a *New York Times* best seller; and *Amazing Grace: The Lives of Children and the Conscience of a Nation* (1995), which describes his work in the South Bronx, where he felt children were living in a kind of hell of neglect. Kozol has said that this book touched him most deeply because he witnessed firsthand how children in the Bronx coped and survived in what he felt was a profoundly hostile environment.

Kozol's more recent book *The Shame of the Nation: The Restoration of Apartheid Schooling in America* (2005) is possibly his most controversial work. By using the word *apartheid,* Kozol implies that large cities have systematically condoned segregated schools for decades after the United States Supreme Court decision, *Brown v. Board of Education* (1954), which overturned the Supreme Court's earlier 1896 decision, *Plessy v. Ferguson* permitting states to maintain separate but equal school systems. *Brown v. Board of Education* declared that separate schools for black and white students were unconstitutional and a violation of the equal rights clause of the Fourteenth Amendment. In *The Shame of the Nation,* Kozol argues that the years since the 1954 ruling have produced even more segregated schools than had existed earlier in large cities. He quotes a number of statistics concerning the amount of money spent per pupil in inner-city schools at the time: approximately $11,000 in New York City, but in the wealthy suburb of Manhasset, $22,000. These figures were echoed in Chicago, Boston, Los Angeles, and other major cities across the nation. He cites numerous schools in these cities that are 98 percent black and Hispanic, illustrating that not only is there virtually no diversity in these schools but they are almost as segregated as they were in the early 1950s South.

Not everyone has been convinced that minority-only city schools are necessarily inferior to schools with a racial balance. But Kozol has pointed to the records of undersupported inner-city schools with 90 percent or greater minority population and has shown that they rarely graduate more than 60 percent of their students. Kozol's critics question his emphasis on the amount of money spent on each student in urban and suburban schools because they cannot see that per-student expenditure translates into student success. Kozol counters by insisting that the conditions of poverty, often a mark of inner-city schools, warrant greater expenditure in money and services if any real changes are to be made in "apartheid" schools.

Kozol's Rhetoric

This selection from Kozol's 2007 book, *Letters to a Young Teacher*, is a letter in the tradition of the epistolary writers of earlier centuries. Today, such letters are rarely written because so much of our correspondence is electronic and usually very brief. In effect, Kozol is resurrecting a literary tradition for the purpose of permitting us to eavesdrop on an intimate communication. The style of the letter is informal to the point of being almost conversational. He says, for instance, that Francesca's presentation was "pretty damn amazing" (para. 1). The tone is easy, frank, and apparently guileless. All this is typical of a casual letter between good friends.

But the difference here is that the subject matter of the letter is much more serious than one would expect in a friendly letter. Kozol was in the audience when Francesca gave a presentation to teachers about diversity, the subject of the conference. But by using quotation marks around the word *diversity*, he calls the term into question, implying that it "has been adulterated to the point where it can only mock reality instead of openly describing it" (para. 2). It is clear from the context that Kozol and Francesca agree that there is little or no diversity in most of the schools that actually have diversity curricula.

One of Kozol's rhetorical approaches is to translate words such as *diversity* into more inflammatory terms like *racial segregation*. The point he is trying to make is that people writing about the schools "have learned to do semantic somersaults" so as to avoid calling things by their right names, which might harm "civic pride" (para. 4). The use of the word *apartheid* in the title of one of his books is an example of his efforts to shock his audience into seeing things the way he sees them.

In order to back up his claim of widespread educational segregation, Kozol depends on recording his own experiences visiting schools. These visits, along with the data gathered about populations in city schools, are important sources of his evidence. Because he is known for having traveled across the country to visit schools and because he has actually spent time living in communities like the South Bronx and being in the local schools, his authority on the issues is such that it warrants the readers's attention. He records several conversations with school administrators who try to deny that their schools are not diverse despite data demonstrating otherwise.

He also complains that the lesson plans including information on "civil rights" and the stories of the struggles in Selma and elsewhere have done little more than pacify students by permitting them to think that the hopes of the 1960s have been realized. Kozol says the "victories they celebrate" have been "canceled out by more polite but no less implacable arrangements" (para. 8). He states this very directly in his claim that the "percentage of black children who now go to integrated public schools has fallen to its lowest level since the death of Dr. King in 1968" (para. 13).

Kozol seemed most surprised when he talked with ninth-grade students in a school named for Martin Luther King Jr. and suggested that the school was segregated only to hear the students say that was not so, " 'because white students are allowed to come here' " (para. 20). That may have been true, but another student said flatly, " 'This school is a segregated school' " (para. 23), and ended the discussion with a thank you. Even the teachers in this school began to confront the facts that Kozol presented to them.

PREREADING QUESTIONS:
WHAT TO READ FOR

The following prereading questions may help you anticipate key issues in the discussion of Jonathan Kozol's "The Uses of 'Diversity.'" Keeping them in mind during your first reading should help focus your attention.

- What is diversity in the schools?
- What "ugly little secret" was Francesca protesting at the Vermont conference?
- Why does Kozol feel diversity is essential in the schools?

The Uses of "Diversity"

Dear Francesca,

I thought the presentation that you made during the conference in 1 Vermont about "diversity" last week was pretty damn amazing. I was glad you had a chance to speak. Too many of those education conferences never give real teachers any opportunity to voice their own beliefs.

I also agree with you entirely that the way the subject of diver- 2 sity is introduced to children in most public schools has come to be a very bland and boring ritual in which the word itself, "diversity," has been adulterated to the point where it can only mock reality instead of openly describing it.

"The ugly little secret," as you put it, is that there is almost no 3 diversity at all in most of the schools in which diversity curricula are generally used. The word, you said, has come to be a cover-up for situations to which it can't possibly apply.

As you've noticed, this is right in keeping with the way the word 4 is used in education journals and the media. There is a seemingly agreed-upon convention, in the written press especially, never to use a plain, unvarnished term like "racial segregation"—not, at least, in reference to the city where the newspaper is published—if there's any way the term can be avoided. This is the case even in a narrative description of a segregated school, where journalists have learned to do semantic somersaults in order not to use a word that may do injury to civic pride. High schools that enroll as few as six or seven white or Asian students in a total population of as many as 3,000, and where every other child in the building is black or Hispanic, are commonly referred to, in the parlance of reporters, as "diverse."

School systems employ this euphemism too. In a school I visited 5 last fall in Kansas City, for example, I was provided with a document that said the school's curriculum "addresses the needs of children from diverse backgrounds." But as I went from class to class I didn't see a single child who was white or Asian—or Hispanic, for that matter. The principal, when I pressed her on the demographics of the school, said that 99.6 percent of students there were black.

In a similar document, the school board of a district in New York 6 referred to "the diversity" and "rich variations" in the "ethnic backgrounds" of its student population. But when I looked at the racial numbers that the district had provided to the state, I learned that there were 2,800 black and Hispanic children in the system, one Asian child, and three whites. If school boards cannot bring themselves to call things by their right names, it's not surprising that the same misleading use of language infiltrates instructional materials as well.

The pattern carries through to many of those so-called civil rights 7 curricula which tend to function, as you said, not as challenges to critical analysis of present-day realities, and even less as provocations to take action on those challenges, but instead, to use your words, as "soporific pacifiers" that provide a feel-good resolution to the contradictions school officials do not dare to name.

Many deeply segregated public schools pay tribute, for example, 8 to the history of civil rights by introducing children to a set of lesson plans about the struggles of the past while steering clear of any reference to the struggles of a comparable order that remain before their generation now. Typically, these lesson plans rely upon heroic stories about children in the South during the 1950s and the early 1960s who had the courage to walk into previously all-white schools, guarded at times by federal marshals or police, and who defied the jeers and cat-calls of white students and adults, overcame their own anxieties, and at length achieved what are presented to our students as enduring victories. These may be uplifting stories but they also fail to give our kids the slightest indication that most of the victories they celebrate have, since that time, been canceled out by more polite but no less implacable arrangements for the isolation of black children like themselves.

I think you were being very honest when you said you feel as   9
if you're lying to your children if you leave these false impressions uncorrected and allow the class, essentially, to swallow the idea that segregation is a shameful piece of distant history for which our nation has absolved itself, rather than an ever-present aspect of the lives they lead and education they receive today.

"Here we are in a public school with not a single white child in   10
our class and only three white children in the school's entire population. Hooray for Ruby Bridges and for Linda Brown[1] and all the other brave black children of the South for having left us with a legacy of social justice in our public schools, even if this legacy has been completely, and intentionally, ripped apart and shredded and abandoned in the years since all the kids we teach today were born!"

I thought you were brave to say that to an audience of influential   11
educators who have built their own careers around "diversity instruction." I hope you made them thoroughly uncomfortable.

I also think that you were right on target when you said the way   12
to honor heroes of the past isn't to embalm their courage in a lesson plan of arm's-length admiration but to *emulate* that courage by empowering our students to see clearly and speak openly about the schools that they attend and neighborhoods in which they live right now. Otherwise, we place them in the strange position of believing that the unmistakable realities they see in school each day are somehow not to be believed and must be an incorrect perception or, if not a false perception, must be something that deserves a different name that carries no dishonor and bears no resemblance to the situation children of their race and age encountered fifty years ago.

The percentage of black children who now go to integrated pub-   13
lic schools has fallen to its lowest level since the death of Dr. King

---

[1] **Ruby Bridges . . . Linda Brown** Ruby Bridges (b. 1954) integrated in to a white school in New Orleans in 1960. She was the inspiration for the little girl in Norman Rockwell's *The Problem We All Live With* (p. 539). Linda Brown (b. 1943) was selected by the NAACP to integrate the schools in Topeka, Kansas. The resulting legal battle produced the landmark ruling *Brown v. Board of Education* (1954), forcing states to integrate their schools.

in 1968. In New York and California, seven out of every eight black students presently attend a segregated school. In your school, as you have pointed out, as in almost every inner-city school I visit, white children make up only 1 or 2 percent of the enrollment.

Once, when I was in a class at P.S. 65, which was Pineapple's 14 elementary school, I was surprised to see a white boy sitting in the second row, since I'd almost never seen another white child in the school. I asked the teacher how many white kids she had taught over the years. "I've been at this school for eighteen years," she said. "This is the first white student I have ever had!" It turned out he was an immigrant from Germany who had been assigned there by mistake. He had left the school before I visited again. The only other white child I had ever noticed in the school's enrollment of 800 students happened to be an immigrant as well. He was a kind and thoughtful Russian boy but he, too, departed rapidly.

In the elementary district that encompassed P.S. 65, there were 15 only 26 white children in an overall enrollment of 11,000 students, which, according to my long division, comes out to a segregation rate of 99.8 percent—an improvement, if you want to call it that, of two-tenths of one percentage point on the segregation rate in southern states a century ago.

The same scenario is seen in schools that serve black and Hispanic 16 neighborhoods even in middle-sized and smaller cities. If I took a photo of the children that I meet in almost any of these schools, it would be indistinguishable from photos taken of the children in the all-black schools in Mississippi back in 1925 or 1930—precisely the same photos that are reproduced in textbooks now in order to convince our children of the moral progress that our nation has made since. Teachers "are participating in deception of their students," as you said up in Vermont, if these myths are not confronted and the truths that counter them are not presented to our children as a part of any course of study on "diversity."

Most of these inner-city schools, as you also pointed out, "don't 17 simply make a mockery of *Brown v. Board of Education*." They don't even live up to the promises of *Plessy v. Ferguson,* which stipulated back in 1896, as you said you felt you needed to remind your audience, that if our public schools were to be separate, "they must at very least be equal." It's a tribute to the awkward game that must be played in many school departments now that it takes a first-grade teacher to spell out, and hammer out, the obvious to people who design curricula in history.

Admittedly, there are limits as to how far teachers ought to delve 18 into these matters with a class of children who are only six years old. But even while employing wise discretion and while making full allowance for the fragile sensibilities of children who are still in the first grade, I think you're correct in saying that our teachers need to introduce a good big helping of political and intellectual irreverence into any lesson that might otherwise suggest to children in a class-room of contemporary racial isolation that they must discredit what they see before their eyes, with the result of teaching them to live with a peculiarly destructive lie.

At a New York City high school named for Dr. Martin Luther King,   19
a classic segregated institution (96 percent black and Hispanic) in the middle of an affluent white section of Manhattan, students who appar-ently had thoroughly imbibed the lessons of their elementary grades went into the most remarkable contortions when I asked them if they thought it accurate to say that they were pupils in a "segregated" school. Indeed, the very introduction of that word seemed to surprise a number of the students in the ninth-grade class that I was visiting. It was as if they'd never been invited by a teacher to consider this idea before.

"I don't think this is a segregated school," one student said,   20
"because white students are allowed to come here. At least, if they want. . . ."

"Why don't they come here then?" I asked, noting that the neigh-   21
borhood immediately around the school was home to thousands of white children.

"This school is *named* for Dr. Martin Luther King," another stu-   22
dent said, wrestling oddly with the paradox this might present. But she seemed to work around that paradox in a surprising way. "I don't see how you could say this is a segregated school. Dr. King believed that every race is equal."

A few of the students launched into a heated disagreement with   23
the students who had spoken first. "Hey!" said a tall black boy whose head was shaven and who told me that he once had been a student briefly at an integrated elementary school. "This right here"—he ges-tured to the students sitting all around him—"*this is it!* This is what it's all about." He wore an army jacket and he had a look of shrewd impatience in his eyes. "This school is a segregated school. I don't think we need to dance around something so obvious."

A boy sitting next to him slapped his hand. "Thank you!" said a tall   24
Hispanic girl who turned around to nod at him from the front row.

But some of the other students seemed affronted by his words   25
and, oddly enough, appeared to be concerned that I might be offended somehow, even though I'd asked the question, by the slightly cutting way that he'd replied. I also had the clear impression that a number of the students felt it would be disrespectful of their school if they were to let themselves concede that what he said was true.

At that point, one of the older teachers in the room jumped into   26
the argument and asked the students what exactly they believed

Dr. King had been "about." All but a few of the answers she received were very vague—"we need to learn to get along with one another" and "respect our differences," "he was a man of peace," and other accurate but imprecise assertions that suggested they had never read a book on Dr. King, or one that presented an unsanitized account of his beliefs.

Later, in the hallway after class, the teacher vented her frustration   27
that so many of these students had arrived in the ninth grade with virtually no knowledge of our nation's recent history. "If I'm teaching in a school named Martin Luther King," she told me, "I'm not going to come in and sugarcoat the things that he believed in. This is exactly the kind of institution he regarded as a moral wrong. Students who come here have a right to know this."

Some of my white friends in New York City take it as an act of   28
incivility when I confront them with an angry statement like the one this teacher made or with the flat-out accusation that the student in the army jacket voiced. Several of these friends of mine are liberals or, more accurately, former liberals who participated in some of the protests and the marches in the South during the 1960s but who now reject the practicality or, it seems, even the moral value of pursuing integration in the schools their own children attend.

Instead of conceding—even wistfully, regretfully—that racial seg-   29
regation or, if they can't bear to bring themselves to speak those words, at very least near-total racial isolation is an accurate description of the status of most children in the education system in the city where they live, they bristle at this implication and appear to grant themselves some sort of ethical exemption by reminding me of all the decent things they did to help the cause of civil rights when they were young.

"I was at the March on Washington with Dr. King" is a familiar   30
answer that I hear. Protest marches deeper in the South are also commonly recalled. Some recollect with pride that they were in the march across the fabled bridge in Selma, Alabama, which took place in 1965. I'm often struck by the nostalgia and authentic pride they seem to feel about those idealistic years in their own lives, which coincided with an idealistic era in our history. What is disturbing, nonetheless, is the apparent ease with which they use these memories to blind them to the more sophisticated system of apartheid in which they are, willingly or not, participating now.

Many black educators have expressed the same frustration you   31
did when you spoke about the uses of the past as something like a piece of "meaningful but old and tattered cloth" that we have placed upon a shelf within a cupboard that we briefly open and then carefully lock up again. I'd like to introduce you someday to an African American teacher in New York who told me once, during the time

when I was working on my book *Amazing Grace*, that he'd gotten to the point where he confessed he couldn't "stand to hear about the bridge at Selma, Alabama, anymore" and refused to give his kids a set of lesson plans he'd been assigned for what he called "The Famous March Curriculum." Instead, he said he'd posted on his classroom walls all the stuff that he could find about the racist education system in which he was working now.

"You see," he said, "to the very poor black children that I teach . . . ,   32
it doesn't matter much what bridge you might have stood on thirty years ago. They want to know what bridge you stand on now."

He was teaching older kids than you do. I'm not sure what grade   33
they were, but I thought of what he said when you let me read the notes you typed up for your presentation in Vermont. It seemed that all the irritation you had felt exploded suddenly. In that moment, you weren't speaking merely as a teacher who's been working her heart out every day to do the best job that she can to serve the children in her class. You were also speaking as a witness. I don't know if I would say this to you if I didn't recognize how strongly you believe it, but I think *all* teachers ought to feel the right and have the courage to speak out as witnesses to the injustices they see their children undergo. If we won't speak out on these seemingly forbidden matters, then who will?

But I also liked the fact that, even in the midst of all the indig-   34
nation that you voiced, you did not leave out the sweetness and the many, many hours of sheer happiness you've known this year, as well as certain of the funny details you tucked in about the real life of a teacher in the elementary grades. I tried to imagine the reaction of the audience when you said that six-year-olds are "leaky little people" because of the many "accidents" they have. I wonder how many presentations made at education conferences ever mention matters quite so interesting as the great importance of the distance of the nearest bathroom from the classroom door. ("First graders leak!" as you explained this to me later, "either from their eyes" when they have painful quarrels with each other "or from their dribbly noses" when they're coming down with colds—or, as you put it, "from the other end more frequently.")

One of the reasons why I've found our conversations and our cor-   35
respondence so refreshing is that you enjoy so much the small realities and daily misadventures, even the wet and messy ones, that take place in the classroom with your children. Even when you're speaking of school system policies that might leave another person sounding wilted by frustration, I notice that your voice still has that energetic sound of somebody who never lets herself be beaten down but keeps on coming back with a nice sense of lively combat, usually intermixed

with pleasant bits of irony about the contradictions that you have to deal with.

I hope you won't mind this, but I told some teachers in New York 36 the anecdote you shared with me when you were working on the first report cards for your students. You said there was a box you had to check off that was labeled, "STUDENT IS RESPECTFUL OF DIVERSITY." The teachers very much enjoyed your speculations about how to answer this.

First, you said, you toyed with the idea of filling in "Not Appli- 37 cable." You said there was no way that you could honestly report that they had proven they might be respectful to another race of children whom they'd never had a chance to know. Then you said you thought of writing you were sure, because they're sensitive children, that they would respect the children of another race if Boston's schools "should someday figure out that it would be a good idea to let them meet such children" by allowing them to go to school together. I knew that in the end you wouldn't yield to the temptation to write either of these things, because you knew they might cause problems for your principal and certainly would make a few waves higher up in the administration if somebody in the school department happened to be told that you had done this. Teachers learn to choose which battles are worth fighting. This one obviously wasn't worth it.

Besides, I think that your impatience with the misuse of that 38 word, "diversity," and the whole surrounding repertoire of watered-down discussion about civil rights, comes across to children in a number of more subtle ways. The intonations of your voice, a passing glance within your eyes in reaction to a passage in a story that you may be reading to the class, have their effect as well. The secret curriculum in almost any class, in my belief, is not the message that is written in a lesson plan or a specific book but the message of implicit skepticism or, conversely, of passivity or acquiescence that is written in the teacher's eyes and in the multitude of other ways in which her critical intelligence, her reservations about given truths, or else the absence of these inclinations and these capabilities, are quietly revealed.

Education, no matter what the rule books say, is never absolutely 39 neutral. We either teach our children it's okay to write and talk about the things they think to be the truth or else we teach them that it's more acceptable to silence their beliefs, or even not to *have* beliefs but to settle for official truths that someone else has carefully prepared for them. A lot of those kids with whom I spoke at Martin Luther King School in New York had learned the second of these lessons far too well and long before they ever got to the ninth grade. The results were manifested in that muzzled consciousness in which they seemed to be

entombed, that inability to scrutinize or speak about their own reality
in thoughts or words that were their own.

I think we need to find the will to shatter this rock of silence	40
starting at the earliest age possible. I wanted to cheer for you for having had the nerve to stand before an audience and say so!

QUESTIONS FOR CRITICAL READING

1. Was there diversity in your secondary school?
2. Kozol mentions diversity curricula. What would that be?
3. Do you think it appropriate to use the term *racial segregation* to describe present-day schools?
4. Why does Kozol think school teachers and administrators sometimes use language that obscures the truth?
5. Why are there so few white students in the inner-city schools?
6. If having white students in school classrooms increases diversity, what percentage would be needed to actually achieve diversity?
7. What is the ideal diversity desirable in the schools?

SUGGESTIONS FOR CRITICAL WRITING

1. Based on this selection, write a short essay that describes what you think Francesca believes first-grade education should be like. Kozol gives us a number of clues as to what her beliefs are and what her approach to speaking out to other teachers would be. What do you learn about her from reading this letter? Do you think she would be a good teacher? Defend your view.

2. Write a letter that begins "Dear Jonathan Kozol" and tells him about your own experience in primary and secondary school. How much of what he describes is true of your experience? How much of it is untrue? Be sure to suggest whether you are in general agreement with him or whether you feel he is being too severe or too one-sided. Be sure to give things their proper names and be very direct in writing to him, in the same manner that he wrote to Francesca.

3. In paragraph 12, Kozol talks about "the unmistakable realities [children] see in school each day." What were the unmistakable realities to which he refers? What unmistakable realities did you observe in your school? Do they have an important bearing on the argument that Kozol is presenting? Did people ignore those realities in the manner that Kozol says they might?

4. Kozol's entire focus is on racial diversity in the schools. What other kinds of diversity should be taken into consideration when planning

for diversity in the schools? Write a brief essay defending the view that racial diversity is only one form of diversity necessary in a well-balanced school. Would Kozol be supportive of your argument?

5. Kozol talks about "diversity curricula" several times in his letter to Francesca. What diversity curricula does he point to? Write a brief essay that lays out a diversity curriculum that you think would benefit students in the fourth through the sixth grades. What should students that age learn about diversity that would help them do well in school and in their later studies?

6. If you think the issue of diversity in the schools is exaggerated, write an essay that defends the absence of diversity in the primary or the secondary grades. If you have visited schools or classrooms other than your own, use that experience to defend your case. If you experienced education in schools without diversity, use that experience to defend your view. Why has diversity gotten so much attention if its value is overstated?

7. **CONNECTIONS**   Kozol talks mostly about the structure of education rather than the facts of education, but he is familiar with Emerson's writings (**bedfordstmartins.com/worldofideas/epages**). Which of Emerson's principles would Kozol most likely accept as useful in educating primary or secondary school students? Does he sympathize with Emerson's views on common sense in education? Does Kozol put as much weight on moral development as Emerson or Hsün Tzu? What, for Kozol and Emerson, are the overriding moral issues in education?

8. **CONNECTIONS**   Carter G. Woodson and Maria Montessori talk about the educational needs of the poor. Which of these authors would take issue with Jonathan Kozol? Which would reinforce his observations? Imagine Woodson or Montessori writing a letter to Kozol, bringing to bear his or her point of view and explaining his or her position in such a way as to convince Kozol of the importance of accepting it in the modern school.

9. **SEEING CONNECTIONS**   The young student in Norman Rockwell's *The Problem We All Live With* (p. 539) represents Ruby Bridges Hall on her way to her first day of kindergarten in 1960. She was integrating into the school on federal orders and was protected by federal marshals. White parents took their children out of kindergarten, leaving her the only student. Write a letter to Ruby Bridges Hall that explains the significance of her act for you. Explain what the meaning of her victory over racism signifies and what, in the more than fifty years since her entrance into school, the primary educational system is like in terms of diversity.

HOWARD GARDNER
Designing Education for Understanding

HOWARD GARDNER (b. 1943), Hobbs Professor of Cognition and Education at the Harvard Graduate School of Education, served for nearly thirty years as codirector of Harvard's Project Zero, a program dedicated to improving education in schools by emphasizing creativity in thinking and problem solving. By emphasizing the arts and the newer electronic technologies associated with learning, the program cultivates a "culture of thinking" in the classroom as opposed to a culture of rote learning. Gardner received a MacArthur Foundation Award (1981), which supported his research for five years, and has won a number of other important awards, including the Grawemeyer Award in Education (1990), given for the first time to an American. In 2000 he won a Guggenheim Fellowship. Among his many books are *Leading Minds: An Anatomy of Leadership* (1995); *Extraordinary Minds: Portraits of Exceptional Individuals and an Examination of Our Extraordinariness* (1997); and *Truth, Beauty, and Goodness Reframed: Educating for the Virtues in the Twenty-first Century* (2011).

Perhaps the most important and best-known product of Project Zero is the theory of multiple intelligences, which Gardner first published in *Frames of Mind* (1983). (His *Intelligence Reframed: Multiple Intelligence for the Twenty-first Century* [1999] offers a revisitation and more detailed elaboration on multiple intelligence theory and its application.) In *Frames of Mind,* he notes that the general attitude toward intelligence centers on the IQ (intelligence quotient) test that Alfred Binet (1857–1911) devised. Binet believed that intelligence is measurable and that IQ tests result in numerical

From *The Disciplined Mind: Beyond Facts and Standardized Tests, the K–12 Education That Every Child Deserves.*

scores that are reliable indicators of a more or less permanent basic intelligence. Gardner offers several objections to that view. One is that IQ predictors might point to achievement in schools and colleges but not necessarily to achievement in life. For example, students with middling scores performed at extraordinary levels in business, politics, and other walks of life, whereas high-achieving students often settled for middling careers. The reports on high-performing executives indicated a considerable intelligence at work, but it was not necessarily the kind of intelligence that could be measured on Binet tests. Gardner's theories about multiple intelligences have not had a strong effect on psychologists, but they have been embraced warmly in the field of education.

Gardner's research efforts are directed at trying to help improve education not only in this country but also abroad. In the 1980s, he spent a great deal of time working with Chinese schools and Chinese students and returned to the United States with many new ideas for his courses of instruction. His purposes, as revealed in this selection from his book *The Disciplined Mind: Beyond Facts and Standardized Tests, the K–12 Education That Every Child Deserves* (1999), are to go beyond rote learning and reliance on facts that do not stay with students after they leave the classroom. His focus is on students in primary and secondary schools and more specifically on their experiences with learning that will produce understanding as well as awareness of the significance of learning. He is less interested in a mastery of tests than in a mastery of ways of thinking.

Gardner's Rhetoric

Gardner's most obvious rhetorical technique is the opening comparison between for-profit colleges—like Phoenix University, which ignores liberal arts and concentrates on training for specific jobs—and colleges that aim to give students a model for living. Clearly, Gardner champions schools that prepare students to live fully and well, not schools that train people to fit a specific job profile. He does, however, see that once a student has an education based on mastery of the basic disciplines of mathematics, science, arts, and history (para. 12) job training may be desirable. Gardner also uses a few metaphoric turns of phrase, such as his reference to the world of learning as "the ever-expanding knowledge waterfront" (para. 8) and referring to understanding as "coin of the realm" (para. 55). His analogy of the "engraving" of early ways of thinking into the student's mind (para. 26) is useful because, as he says, it is difficult to alter ways of thinking that are deeply incised within the mind.

Several times, Gardner relies on enumeration as a means to make clear the range and depth of his suggestions for education. His "Four Approaches to Understanding" comes deep in the essay, after he has examined difficulties that sometimes make the kind of approach he recommends problematic. After offering problems, he then offers solutions. The first of the four approaches that will help develop understanding in education is learning from institutions. He cites the institution of apprenticeship, learning with someone who is a master of the discipline, as a basic approach to learning (para. 44). He also praises institutions such as museums that promote an interactive environment. The second approach is "Direct Confrontations of Erroneous Conceptions" (para. 47). In this approach, the student has the chance to make mistakes and learn from them. If the student is incorrect in a basic understanding, there should be a means by which that understanding can be detected, such as through experimentation, as Gardner suggests. Learning from one's errors can be profound.

The third approach is extremely important: "A Framework That Facilitates Understanding" (para. 52). In this extensive section, Gardner describes a "performance of understanding" (para. 53), which means simply the chance to show what one has learned by talking about the material, writing about it, and engaging with both students and teachers with regard to what has been learned. In other words, the student must be given the chance to demonstrate competence and learn from both praise and criticism. Gardner uses another analogy by likening "performance of understanding" to the art student who shows paintings or sculptures or the music student who performs a piece that has just been learned. "Novices see older students and teachers engaged in the performances which they ultimately must carry out—writing essays, mounting oral arguments, debating with one another, explaining scientific phenomena, carrying out experiments, creating and critiquing works of art" (para. 55). It is this level of engagement that produces understanding that goes far beyond the simple grasp of facts.

In the following paragraphs, Gardner offers what he calls "understanding goals," the kind of educational goals that will produce understanding. He offers such goals for a science class, an arts class, and a history class, along with a few other examples that help explain his principles.

His fourth approach to understanding, "Multiple Entry Points to Understanding" (para. 70), introduces his theory that there are several kinds of intelligence. In another of his books, he cites linguistic, logical-mathematical, spatial, musical, bodily-kinesthetic, interpersonal, and intrapersonal intelligences. In this fourth approach, Gardner hopes that students will bring these other kinds of intelligence to bear on the disciplinary issues that most interest him: mathematics, science, arts, and history.

PREREADING QUESTIONS:
WHAT TO READ FOR

The following prereading questions may help you anticipate key issues in the discussion of Howard Gardner's "Designing Education for Understanding." Keeping them in mind during your first reading should help focus your attention.

- What is the value of an education designed for understanding?
- Why is a fact-based education limited?
- How would a teacher educate students for understanding?

Designing Education for Understanding

A Classroom Perspective

Over the last twenty years, a new kind of educational institution has arisen in the United States. It is aimed primarily at young adults who wish to secure particular skills that will help them to advance in the world. While it calls itself a university, in many ways it runs completely counter to the traditional vision of what a university is—or should be—like.

The prototypical example is the University of Phoenix. In the late 1990s, this franchised profit-making operation has spread to forty-seven sites in a dozen states, and with over 40,000 students, it has become the largest private university in the United States. Students can earn degrees in a variety of fields, including nursing, education, information technology, and business. Unlike most American universities, the University of Phoenix features neither a campus, nor a library, nor a permanent faculty. Rather than consisting of academics, the faculty is composed of individuals who are practiced in the fields being taught.

It is fair to say that there is no intellectual life at the university, in any meaningful sense of that term; ideas have value only if they can be put to immediate commercial use. Rather, the university offers students an opportunity to gain desired skills as efficiently as possible. Classes take place in the late afternoon or early evening. Students (who must be twenty-three or older) can park right near the class building, take the course, and drive home again. Much of the work can be done at one's home computer. Convenience of delivery is the hallmark. William Gibbs, the president of the company, declares: "The people who are our students don't really want the education. They want what the education provides for them—better jobs, moving up in their career, the ability to speak up in meetings, that kind of stuff. They want it to *do* something for them." And, like the customers of the most successful fast-food chains, students seem satisfied with what the university delivers.

In the preceding chapter, I described a number of precollegiate   4
educational models and indicated how each emerged from its cultural environment. It would be easy to do the same things with the University of Phoenix—to show how institutions like this meet the needs of busy young working American adults who want to gain new skills and expertise. And I could even indicate how the university prizes the capacity to make use of what one has learned—in my terms, the capacity to demonstrate one's understanding.

My goal, however, is neither to bury nor praise the experiment   5
occurring in Phoenix and all over the United States, in large corporations and in for-profit educational institutions. Rather, I want simply to stipulate in the clearest possible way a set of educational goals that are the *opposite* of those I cherish. The Phoenix mission is completely utilitarian; at least until this point, there is not the slightest intellectual interest in truth, beauty, or goodness—or, for that matter, in falsity, ugliness, or immorality. Nor is there interest in how these virtues might relate to one another or how they might be drawn on to help create a better community. As if to confirm this characterization, the firm recently dropped its requirement that students have some background in the liberal arts.

So much for a contrast case. Let me now shift attention to the   6
kind of education that I personally favor.

False Starts

A sensible way to think about education is to "plan backward":   7
to determine the kind of a person one would like to see emerge at the end of an educational regime—for example, at graduation from secondary school. The challenge then becomes to sculpt an educational approach that is most likely to achieve that vision.

It is easy to see why so many educational systems have foun-   8
dered. Designers survey knowledge and skills that seem important and decide to cover them all. But time is short and there is far too

much material. Thus, the fatal weakness of an approach that strives to cover the ever-expanding knowledge waterfront.

Another flawed approach is to paper over the differences within a   9
community and try to please all interest groups: a little bit of this, a little bit of that. This solution is particularly appealing in cases when various cultures, or warring camps, all clamor for recognition. Since no one wants to come down too hard on anyone else, the evident solution—though it ends up being patchwork at best—is to make sure that every interest group is represented, either equally or proportionally.

This studied ecumenicism proves devastating in the curricular   10
area. We must teach science, and there are so many sciences (biology, physics, chemistry, astronomy, geology, not to mention the social sciences and information sciences) that we must make sure to touch on. We must teach the arts, and since there are so many artistic interest groups, we must be sure to include the visual arts, the dramatic arts, instrumental music, vocal music, classical ballet, and modern dance—and of course, we must be sensitive to different cultural embodiments of these several art forms.

Another solution, one all too often followed in America, is to pay   11
lip service to the formal curriculum and bow to the standardized tests, but thereafter to shut the classroom door and to do one's own thing. Sometimes, teachers' "own things" are meritorious—after all, there are many great teachers—but the lack of coordination among classes and the absence of accountability to those "outside the door" is lamentable. It is for this reason that American students study the Pilgrims at Thanksgiving almost every year, with unjustifiable redundancy; or that, in a case I recently observed, the same information about the Wampanoag Indians is taught over and over in a Massachusetts elementary curriculum, while large parts of world and American history receive no mention at all. The lack of coordination and accountability regularly results in cases where students who move from one school to another discover almost no overlap between the two institutions' offerings.

Teaching for Understanding:
A Formal Introduction

I call for an education that inculcates in students an understand-   12
ing of major disciplinary ways of thinking. The disciplines that I have singled out are science, mathematics, the arts, and history.[1] Within those disciplinary families, it is important that students study substantial

---

[1] Mathematics should be part of every precollegiate curriculum. I mention it here as part of my generic discussion of curriculum, but touch on it only tangentially in my treatment of evolution, the music of Mozart, and the Holocaust. [Gardner's note]

topics in depth. However, it is not important *which* disciplines or topics are featured. I do not consider it essential that students survey the entire range of sciences listed above; in mathematics, it is not essential that they master all of Euclid's proofs or every algebraic or trigonometric formula; they need not study every art form nor every historical event.

Instead, students should probe with sufficient depth *a manageable*   13 *set of examples* so that they come to see how one thinks and acts in the manner of a scientist, a geometer, an artist, a historian. This goal can be achieved even if each student investigates only one art, science, or historical era. The purpose of such immersion is *not*—I must stress—to make students miniature experts in a given discipline, but to enable them to draw on these modes of thinking in coming to understand their world. Later, if they want to range more widely in these disciplines or pursue a career in one of them, they will find the time and the tools to do so.

It is not easy to bite the bullet and to cast aside many disciplines,   14 not to mention the numerous aspects of a given discipline that also clamor for attention. And that is why so few educators the world over do so. Cultural literacy—with its promise of five minutes on every topic—seems more inviting than in-depth knowledge of a necessarily idiosyncratic set of topics. However, in the absence of disciplinary ways of thinking, cultural literacy lacks an epistemological home; it amounts to a hodgepodge of concepts and facts ("Well, students, that's enough on the Holocaust. Let's move on to holograms") waiting to be used somehow, somewhere, sometime. Moreover, absent such disciplinary texture and glue, the facts are likely to be soon forgotten. Anyone who doubts this state of affairs is welcome to test students a few years later on the factual material of any subject they may once have studied and see how well they do; or, being especially diabolical, to test those policy makers who insist on stuffing the curriculum with vast numbers of isolated facts and concepts . . . and then publish the scores attained by these officials!

Let me introduce my alternative educational vision—one firmly   15 centered on understanding. An individual understands a concept, skill, theory, or domain of knowledge to the extent that he or she can apply it appropriately in a new situation. An individual with a keen memory might well understand a topic; however, it is also plausible that he or she merely remembers the information and has not a clue about how to use it appropriately in an unfamiliar circumstance.

This formulation entails an acid test for understanding: posing   16 to students a topic or theme or demonstration that they have never before encountered, and determining what sense they can make of those phenomena. An individual who possesses relevant understanding will be able to draw on appropriate concepts, while not activating ones irrelevant to the issue at hand. An individual with emerging understanding will at least be able to draw on concepts that bear some relevance to the topic at hand; or will indicate which information or resources are needed in order to elucidate the phenomenon. In contrast, an individual with little or no understanding will be stymied or will invoke information bearing only a superficial or tangential relationship to the theme under consideration.

Consider someone who understands the rationale underlying the   17
program at Reggio Emilia.[2] If he visits a new "Reggio-inspired" school that enrolls eight- to ten-year-olds, he will be able to assess whether the students' projects are sustained and coherent, whether they lead to enhanced understanding of the phenomena being investigated, and whether the documentation of those activities is accurate and useful. Should the school involve the students themselves in documentation, perhaps as the final phase of a project, that innovation might count as an appropriate adaptation of the Reggio approach with older children.

In contrast, an individual with partial but flawed understanding   18
will more likely draw up a checklist of desired features and simply tally how many are present at the new site. Children's participation as full-fledged documentarians will probably be considered inappropriate and will result in a lower "grade" for the school. An individual devoid of understanding will either throw up his hands or will look to see whether the new site has implemented a rainbow project in precisely the way it was originally done at a Reggio school.

Note that the University of Phoenix may well succeed in inculcat-   19
ing mastery of certain practical disciplines. What is lacking is any concern with, or understanding of, the broader themes of life—indeed, with the questions of why the world is as it is and how life can and should be lived.

Difficulties of Understanding

Would that understanding were easy! In my book *The Unschooled*   20
Mind, I survey a vast body of research documenting that, by and large, even the best students in our best schools do not understand very much of the curricular content. The "smoking gun" is found among physics students at excellent universities—for example, MIT and

---

[2] **Reggio Emilia** A city in northern Italy in which preschool children study in the kind of physical environment championed by Maria Montessori and in which the teachers document the creative activities of the students. From their documentation, the teachers create constantly growing curricula that reflect the interests and achievements of the students. *Newsweek*, in the early 1990s, declared that the preschools of Reggio Emilia were the best in the world.

Johns Hopkins. These students perform credibly in classroom exercises and end-of-term tests. But consider what happens outside class, when they are asked to explain relatively simple phenomena, such as the forces operating on a tossed coin, or the trajectory of a pellet after it has been propelled through a curved tube. Not only do a significant proportion of students (often more than half) fail to give the appropriate explanation; even worse, they tend to give the same kind of answers as peers and younger children who have never studied mechanics. Despite years of schooling, the minds of these college students remain fundamentally unschooled.

One might hope that the problem occurs just in physics departments. But, alas, that is not the case. Similar difficulties appear across the sciences. Students who have studied evolution continue to think of the process as guided by an unseen hand—though in fact evolution results from random genetic mutations, a few of which manage to survive long enough to be passed on to succeeding generations. Students who have studied astronomy insist that the earth is warmer in the summer than it is in the winter because it is closer to the sun in the summer. If that were true, of course, Southern Hemisphere lands like Australia and Argentina would also be warmer in July. 21

When one examines other parts of the curriculum, similar limitations arise. In mathematics, the problem encountered by students can be described as "rigidly applied algorithms." Students memorize formulas and can then plug numbers appropriately into those formulas. But in the absence of some trigger that a particular formula is wanted, they prove unable to marshal it. And if they forget the formula, there is little chance that they will be able to derive it from scratch, because they never actually understood it. The formula was just a syntactic string that had been committed to memory. 22

Finally, in the traditional humanistic parts of the curriculum—history, literature, and the arts—students are sustained by scripts or stereotypes. All human beings distill experience in order to arrive at typical regularities; nearly every youngster in our society has constructed scripts about birthday parties, trips to a fast-food restaurant, a visit to a shopping mall. Having constructed such scripts, we—of any age—then interpret and remember new events, with reference to those already familiar patterns. This tack proves adequate when the new event follows the internalized scripts in important particulars. However, one cannot always count on that familiar state of affairs. 23

Let me give an example. Most five-year-olds have developed a *Star Wars* script. Life consists of a struggle between Good and Bad forces, with the Good generally triumphant. Many movies and television programs, and a few events in real life, can adequately be described in terms of such a script. Most historical events or works of 24 literature, however, prove far more complex; to understand the causes of World War I or the U.S. Civil War, or to grasp the thrust of a novel by Hawthorne or Austen, one must weigh and integrate multiple factors and nuances. Students learn in class to give more complex explanations for such historical or literary events. Yet, when they are confronted with new and unfamiliar materials—say, a story from another culture, or a war in an unfamiliar part of the world—even capable students lapse to an elemental way of thinking. The *Star Wars* "good guy–bad guy" script is often invoked in such situations, even when it is manifestly inappropriate.

Obstacles to Understanding

A chief obstacle to understanding stems from the theories children develop in early life. Children do not require formal tutelage in order to develop representations or theories about inanimate objects, animate objects, their own minds, or the minds of others. Usually, these theories develop quite naturally, seemingly automatically, from the flow of experiences. | 25

As I mentioned earlier, there is a serious problem. Some of these theories feature misconceptions that prove very robust. The misconceived theories can be thought of as powerful engravings that have been incised upon the mind-brain of the child during the opening years of life. The facts learned in school may seem to obscure this engraving; indeed, an observer may be impressed by how much information the child seems to be learning, if one weighs only the mastery of individual numbers, facts, definitions. However, all along, the initial erroneous engraving remains largely unaffected. And then a lamentable event happens. Formal schooling ends, the facts gradually fade away, and the same misconceptions—the same flawed engraving—remains unaltered. | 26

In the case of biology, for example, the mistaken belief that evolution is a teleological process, leading inevitably to the crowning achievement of *Homo sapiens sapiens,* survives despite years of tutelage, as does the Lamarckian[3] belief that important adaptations in one generation will be passed on to the succeeding ones. In history, despite numerous counterexamples, many students continue to believe that the world is divided into good guys and bad guys, with the strug- | 27

---

[3]**Lamarckian** Jean-Baptiste Lamarck (1744–1829) was a French naturalist who believed animals could genetically transmit to later generations the adaptations they developed to aid their survival. His theories were wrong, but his assistants faked some experiments, thus giving him false hope.

gle between these Manichaean[4] forces constituting a staple of life. And they suffer as well from the opposed fallacies of presentism—the notion that all times are just like our own—and atemporality—the inability to differentiate events of a generation ago from those of an earlier century or millennium. For such reasons students have difficulties appreciating important aspects of the Holocaust: that it actually occurred within the lifetimes of their parents or grandparents; that it involved human beings like themselves, most partially flawed, some unexpectedly compassionate; and that attempts at genocide continue to this day, for example in Bosnia and Rwanda.

Unwittingly, teachers are complicit in the survival of early, inadequate representations and misconceptions. The villains include a text-test context, in which students are simply examined on the content of texts or lectures, without being challenged to use the information in new ways; short-answer tests, which offer a set of choices, rather than requiring students to create the choices and select among them; and the uneasy but prevalent compromise by which teachers tacitly agree not to push students too hard, as long as students return the favor. And, above all, there is that old devil "coverage." So long as one is determined to get through the book no matter what, it is virtually guaranteed that most students will not advance toward genuine understanding of the subject at hand.   28

This state of affairs constitutes the strongest set of arguments in favor of a curriculum that examines a limited number of topics in depth. For only rich, probing, and multifaceted investigation of significant topics is likely to make clear the inadequacy of early misconceptions, and only further exploration of those topics, under the guidance of individuals capable of disciplinary thinking, makes it reasonably likely that more sophisticated understandings will emerge. To revisit our analogy, first one must smooth out the initial misleading engraving; and then, preferably with judicious instruction, one must fashion a new and more adequate engraving.   29

Consideration of the obstacles to understanding provides an excellent illustration of why—as I earlier argued—education must take into account both cognitive and cultural factors. To understand the power of early misconceptions, one must adopt the lens of the psychologist and the biologist. That is, one must appreciate how such misconceptions arise early in life and why, absent aggressive interventions,   30

---

[4] **Manichaean** Manichaeism is a religion founded by the Persian Mani (215–276 C.E.), whose teachings stated that the forces of good and of light are in a constant struggle with the forces of evil and of darkness. Adherents were to devote themselves to fighting darkness because God alone could not overcome evil. Because Christians believe God is all-powerful, Manichaeism was declared a heresy.

they prove so resistant to change. At the same time, one must see how certain cultural inventions—the test, the textbook, the conventional superficial interactions between teacher and student—all serve to reinforce misunderstandings.

To move toward enhanced understanding, one must again adopt   31
both cognitive and cultural perspectives. One must identify those internal representations in need of alteration; construct cultural practices that confront, rather than overlook, the obstacles to deeper understanding; and devise measures to determine whether the "corrective cognitive surgery" has been effective.

Disciplinary Expertise

In contrast to the naive student or the information-crammed but   32
still ignorant adult, an expert is a person who really does think differently about his or her specialty. The expert has successfully achieved the desired set of engravings. Expertise generally arises as a result of several years of sustained work within a domain, discipline, or craft, often courtesy of a traditional apprenticeship. Part of that training involves the elimination of habits and concepts that, however attractive to the naive person, are actually inimical to the skilled practice of a discipline or craft. And the remaining part of that training involves the construction of habits and concepts that reflect the best contemporary thinking and practices of the domain.

For example, a crucial scientific understanding is that correlation   33
does not mean causation. The fact that two events co-occur does not mean that one causes another, even though it may appear so to common sense. We discover, for example, that individuals who smoke over a number of years are more likely to get lung cancer, and we are tempted (perhaps correctly!) to assume that smoking causes cancer.

However, it may also turn out that poorly nourished people are   34
more likely to get lung cancer; so perhaps malnutrition causes cancer. But because this link seems intuitively less plausible, one is inclined to consider possible intervening variables. Perhaps people who smoke are less well educated than people who don't; undereducated people are more likely to be poor; indigent people are less likely to be able to afford a balanced diet and good medical treatment. Hence, it makes more sense to see malnutrition as a correlate of poverty than as a primary cause of cancer.

Another chain of possibilities arises. Perhaps the underlying cause   35
of both smoking and cancer is stress. People who are under stress are more likely to smoke; and people who are under stress are more likely to develop cancer. Perhaps, indeed, stress increases the likelihood that

one will smoke and decreases the likelihood that one will be able to stop smoking; taken together, these two factors increase the likelihood that one will contract cancer. Now one has identified a primary variable that may be the underlying trigger of cancer—at least in the sense that its elimination might significantly reduce the incidence of the disease.

Finally, it might turn out that people whose names begin with 36 letters in the first half of the alphabet are more likely to suffer from cancer than those whose names begin with letters in the last half of the alphabet. Perhaps there is a causal link here, but it seems probable that this is mere coincidence.

My point, here, is not to unravel the causes of lung cancer or 37 other cancers but rather to demonstrate a certain kind of systematic and skeptical thinking that lies at the heart of the scientific enterprise. Superficially, of course, the logic of "Smoking causes cancer" and "The spelling of one's last name causes cancer" is identical. Only our common sense leads us to favor the first hypothesis over the second. But someone who has learned to think like a scientist will realize that neither statement, on its own, can be substantiated. One needs to initiate a research program, with proper control groups, to discover whether both of these hypothetical causal chains, one of them, or neither of them stands up in the face of scientific investigation.

I propose that individuals are more likely to learn to think like 38 scientists if they probe deeply into an area (such as the causes of cancer or poverty or stress) than if they jet by a hundred different examples drawn from a dozen sciences.

Let us consider, as a contrast, the pitfalls that may undermine histor- 39 ical thinking. For instance, suppose that a document is discovered that purports to provide new information about the biblical king Solomon. One person unschooled in historical thinking is likely to assume that the document is authentic, and that it describes a person who is much like ourselves. Another unschooled person might conclude the opposite: that the document must be a fake, since so little writing from the time has survived; and that Solomon, being world famous and from a remote historical era, represents an entirely different species of human being.

Neither set of assumptions is justified, of course; and the his- 40 torically informed individual would think about the issues in a quite different way. She would first of all attempt to discover the conditions under which the document was found, and she might use carbon dating (or, if more humanistically inclined, linguistic analysis) to test its age. If she found evidence to suggest that the document was authentic, she would then turn to the issue of whether the picture of Solomon it presented was consistent with historical and contemporary notions of the Hebrew leader, or whether it contradicted them.

This investigation might include revisiting other texts of the era, as well as commentaries from succeeding centuries. Finally, knowing that Solomon once lived, but that he represented a civilization in many ways quite unlike our own, she would try to characterize the new Solomon in a way that suffered neither from presentism ("All people are just like us") nor from exoticism ("Anyone who lived before my grandparents is as remote as an alien from another planet").

Again, such habits of mind are not arrived at easily, nor are they likely to result from a course of study that blitzes, in thirty-five breathless weeks, from Plato to NATO or from Cleopatra to Clinton. But it is the ways of thinking that are crucial here: only if armed with some notion of how historians work will a student be able to make sense of the various claims made about, say, the causes of the Vietnam War or the character of Martin Luther King Jr. Only if equipped with some understanding of how scientists proceed will a student be able to evaluate claims about the causes of AIDS or the advisability of taking a certain hormone to increase fertility or prevent baldness or osteoporosis.   41

It should now be clear why a "fact-based" approach will make even less sense in the future. One can never attain a disciplined mind simply by mastering facts—one must immerse onself deeply in the specifics of cases and develop one's disciplinary muscles from such immersion. Moreover, in the future, desired facts, definitions, lists, and details will literally be at one's fingertips: Either one will be able to type out a brief command on a handheld computer or one may even be able simply to blurt aloud, "What is the capital of Estonia?" or, "Just where is Ecuador situated?" Sheer memorization will be anachronistic; it will be necessary only to show students their way around the current version of Encarta. Increasingly, the art of teaching will inhere in aiding students to acquire the moves and the insights of major disciplinary fields.   42

Four Approaches to Understanding

There is, alas, no royal road to understanding; or, to put it positively, many clues suggest how best to enhance understanding. I'll mention four that have seemed particularly promising to me and my colleagues at Harvard Project Zero.   43

1. *Learning from Suggestive Institutions.*   Some ancient institutions, such as the apprenticeship, harbor instructive clues. In an apprenticeship, a novice spends a great deal of time in the company of a master. The master tackles new problems as they arise, drawing the novice into   44

problem-solving (and troubleshooting) at a level appropriate to his current skills and understandings. The rising journeyman thus receives much healthy exposure to examples of understanding, as well as many opportunities to exhibit incipient understanding and receive apt feedback.

Clues may emerge from new institutions as well. My favorite 45 examples here are science museums, as well as other hands-on museums, in which children are encouraged to explore exhibits at a comfortable pace. Of course, such an opportunity does not in itself compel understanding. Effective museum exhibitions encourage youngsters to try out their own theories and to see for themselves what works and what does not. For example, students can shoot balls through various kinds of tubes and predict how the balls will fall and where they will land. The balls can be dotted with lights to make their trajectories easier to follow. The exhibit can also include simulations or virtual realities, by means of which, again, the course of the ball can be observed, predictions checked, theories (and their underlying "engravings") revised in the light of often surprising new data.

Such hands-on experiences often reveal ways in which the chil- 46 dren's current thinking is inadequate. And given spirited conversation, proper guidance and scaffolding, or an ingenious and reflective child, a more appropriate theory can arise. That freshly minted engraving can in turn be checked and revised in the light of new observations.

2. *Direct Confrontations of Erroneous Conceptions.*   Going one step 47 further, one can actually confront students with ways in which their current conceptions are inadequate. Consider a child who believes that one feels warm when wearing a sweater because the sweater itself generates warmth. Once this explanation has been offered, a parent or teacher can suggest that the sweater be left outside each evening. If the sweater itself is a heat generator, then it ought to be warm on the following morning (or at least warmer than neighboring rocks or other items of clothing). If, however, the temperature of the sweater (as measured by a thermometer) proves identical to that of surrounding entities, one has challenged the child's theory that the sweater itself generates heat.

When it comes to the rigid algorithms activated by many students 48 of mathematics, it makes sense to create a situation in which students must think like the mathematician who developed the formula, and see whether they can themselves progress toward an appropriate formula. Consider, for example, how long it takes a vehicle to traverse a certain distance. Students can be equipped with a whole range of vehicles, a stopwatch, and a room with various racecourses and barriers. They can then be asked to predict how quickly various vehicles will cover specific distances, and what might be done to change the speed of a particular vehicle or make it more competitive.

Engaged in such an activity, many students will discover the irrel-   49
evant variables—for example, the size, shape, and color of the vehicle, the barriers, the room's dimensions—as well as the relevant one—the average speed (rate) of the vehicle. Some will move toward a formulation that approximates the classroom staple: distance covered = rate × time. And even those who do not arrive at that formula on their own will at least be more likely to understand it once it has been introduced. They have now had considerable experience in manipulating variables that are (or are not) relevant to the problem at hand.

Finally, in the case of scripts and stereotypes, the proper anti-   50
dote is regular assumption of multiple perspectives. Scripts and stereotypes reflect a certain perspective at a certain moment in time. If, however, students accumulate considerable experience in thinking about a situation or event from a number of points of view, they are less likely to embrace a simplistic, one-dimensional explanation. And so, for example, students come to possess a much richer view of the American Revolutionary War if they learn about the struggle from diverse angles: the point of view of the British, who were dealing with rebellious colonies; from the perspective of the French, who had little interest in the colonies per se, but much interest in thwarting their British rivals; and from the vantage point of colonial Tories, who sought to remain loyal to their motherland.

As the educational psychologist Lauren Resnick[5] has pointed out,   51
disconfirming experiences do not always suffice to dissolve faulty conceptions and enhance understanding. Misconceptions can be quite robust, and they sometimes prove as insensitive to disproof as the belief system of a religious fundamentalist is to incontrovertible scientific evidence or disconfirmed predictions. Yet, for most individuals, a challenge to a deeply held belief at least compels attention; and efforts to defend that belief, or to discover a better belief, line the most promising routes toward enhanced understanding.

3. *A Framework That Facilitates Understanding.*   With my Harvard   52
colleagues David Perkins, Vito Perrone, Rebecca Simmons, and Stone Wiske, I have developed an approach that places understanding front and center. The key idea is that understanding should be construed as a performance, a public exhibition of what one knows and is able to do. Students ought to be exposed from the start to

---

[5] **Lauren Resnick** Distinguished Professor of Psychology and Cognitive Studies at the University of Pittsburgh. She has made important contributions to cognitive studies in learning.

examples of understanding, and should be given ample opportunities to practice and perform their own understandings. Indeed, only if they have multiple opportunities to apply their knowledge in new ways are they likely to advance toward enhanced understandings in their schoolwork and in their lives beyond the schoolhouse walls.

Talk of a "performance of understanding" may seem a bit oxymoronic, since we usually think of understanding as an internal event, one that occurs in mental representations, between the ears. And we have no reason to doubt that much *is* occurring between the ears, as inadequate representations are being challenged and—should teaching and learning prove successful—more adequate ones are being constructed. Still, the focus on understanding as a performance proves salutary. 53

A helpful analogy can be drawn from the arts and athletics. People would smirk, rightly, if the mastery of a young art student, musician, or athlete were assessed in an examination hall on a Saturday morning, with a standardized paper-and-pencil or computerized test. Rather, what typically happens in these realms is illuminating. From the start of their training, youngsters observe more proficient (usually older) individuals performing the required actions and understandings: playing new pieces of music, practicing dance steps, engaged in scrimmages or in games against tough and wily opponents. The youngsters can see the moves that must be mastered; they can try them out; they can monitor their improvement and compare it with that of peers; and they can benefit from timely coaching. 54

In an "understanding" class or school, a similar ambience is created. Novices see older students and teachers engaged in the performances which they ultimately must carry out—writing essays, mounting oral arguments, debating with one another, explaining scientific phenomena, carrying out experiments, creating and critiquing works of art. They see which kinds of performances are valued and why; which criteria are imposed and why; how performances improve and how they do not; the intellectual and social consequences of enhanced understandings. Some of the mandated performances will be enactments of models already observed; but a healthy proportion will require students to stretch. "Milieu is all" in education; these students are reared in surroundings where performances of understanding have become the coin of the realm. 55

Our work on understanding does not simply present a vision. It also features a particular pedagogical approach, which can be applied throughout the curriculum and can be used with students of different ages and approaches to learning. This approach to understanding was not merely worked out by a group of ivy-covered professors seated in their offices. On the contrary, it emerged from a several-year-long collaborative project involving dozens of teachers in New England. In the 56 intervening years, it has been tried out in many schools all over the United States and in Latin America.

First comes a delineation of "understanding goals." These are simple 57
statements about the understandings that one wishes to achieve over the course of a unit. There should not be too many understanding goals; a few suffice. Let me draw on the examples elaborated on in this [selection]:

- An understanding goal for a biology unit might read: "A student will understand the way that evolutionary forces affect individuals, groups, and entire species."

- An understanding goal for a music course might read: "Students will understand how Mozart and his librettist Da Ponte worked together to create a powerful and lovely score that captured the social conflicts of the era."

- An understanding goal for a modern-history course might read: "Students will understand the ways in which the Holocaust resembled and differed from other attempted genocides of this century."

Other examples from a range of disciplines might include what it 58
means to be alive, the role of the Civil War in American history, how to discover the philosophical themes in the poetry of Keats, why we have negative numbers and how they differ from positive ones.

Second, one identifies "generative topics" or "essential questions." 59
These are initial lessons or provocations that satisfy two main criteria. First of all, they must be central to the topic, with its stated understanding goals. School life is short and there is scant time for lessons or examples that are peripheral. Second of all, the generative topics must engage students. If it proves too difficult to convey a topic's interest and relevance, then one should probably seek another entry point. Of course, the better the teacher and the more trusting the students, the more likely that almost any topic or question can arouse and sustain the curiosity of the bulk of a class.

For our three chosen areas of investigation—there is no paucity of 60
generative topics. Students in a biology class might be asked to explain why there are so many different species in the rain forest; students in an arts class might be challenged to figure out what is happening in a scene during which each of three people is singing a different phrase to himself or herself in a foreign language; students in a history class might ponder why the leaders of what many regarded as the most civilized country in the world would decide to eradicate an entire population.

Third, and most fundamental, is the identification and promulga- 61
tion of "performances of understanding." To put it crisply, students must know what they have to do: they must be familiarized with the

ways in which they will be asked to perform their understandings; and they must appreciate the criteria by which their performances will be judged. Far from being subjected to mysterious exams (no tests under lock and key), students should be exposed from the beginning to performances reflecting various degrees of competence; they should be assured that they will have plenty of opportunities to practice the required performances and to secure helpful feedback; and they should be confident that the culminating performances will typically be occasions for pride, rather than for apprehension or shame.

With respect to the above examples, "performances of understanding" might include a prediction of what will happen to a species given a radical shift in the local ecology; the creation of a song with lyrics that captures the generation gap in contemporary American society; and an analysis of a current virulent struggle between two ethnic groups, in terms of its similarities to, and differences from, the Holocaust.   62

The fourth and final component of our "understanding approach" is ongoing assessment. Most assessment in most schools comes down to a single test given at the end of a unit and kept secret until then. Students often do not know or care about the particulars of their performance; they just want to know their final grade. In contrast, in a milieu that stresses understanding, students receive continual feedback from teachers and others about the quality of their performances, along with concrete suggestions about how these performances might be improved. The criteria for evaluation are public, and students are welcome to discuss or to contest them. They have time to reflect on their performances, to practice, to receive help.   63

Optimally, over time, assessment no longer lies primarily with others. Rather, like seasoned professionals or experts, students gradually internalize the criteria by which they are assessed, becoming able to judge how well their performances stack up against an ideal and in comparison with performances by more and less skilled peers. That is why, incidentally, the culminating performances should be occasions of pleasure. If (like practiced artists or athletes) the students have come to understand well, then these public exhibitions should produce a state of "flow."   64

At first blush, our approach may seem behavioristic. Our focus is primarily on the quality of student behaviors. And, in keeping with classical behaviorist terminology, our provision of unfamiliar materials as a test of understanding may seem like a measure of the degree to which a skill has been "transferred."   65

But the "understanding approach" is behavioristic only in the sense that all assessments must ultimately examine behaviors; one cannot directly examine mental representations. Viewed up close, this approach reveals its cognitivist assumptions and affinities through and through. To begin with, my colleagues and I were stimulated to tackle   66 understanding precisely because of the discovery that early mental representations are both robust and misleading; only a full court press is likely to undo them and to construct better ones.

Next, the coaching techniques that we favor are ones that point up 67 inadequate conceptions and that encourage students to confront and revise conceptions that stand in the way of adequate understandings. Talk about assumptions is quite explicit; how students think about their own learning is a topic that fits comfortably into our understanding framework.

Finally, students are unlikely to be able to succeed regularly in 68 responding to new and unfamiliar challenges unless they have actually altered their initial, flawed representations of the key notions in a domain. The acid test of a performance view of understanding is the development of more adequate and more flexible representations; such a test could not be conceived of in behaviorist terms.

Like any new approach, "teaching for understanding" cannot imme- 69 diately be implemented perfectly; indeed, this view of understanding is itself deceptively simple and requires time to be mastered. At first, the elements are dealt with quite separately; neither students nor teachers are sure precisely why they are doing what they are doing when they attempt to put the framework into place. In contrast, expert implementation features a smooth meshing of the four component parts, so that a unit encompasses the goals, performances, and assessments as part of a seamless whole. Best of all, teachers at various levels find the framework useful and are motivated to keep using it. And so do its creators, including me.

4. *Multiple Entry Points to Understanding.*   My fourth and final 70 approach to understanding takes advantage of the fact that individuals possess different kinds of minds, featuring different blends of mental representations. People will, consequently, approach and master curricular materials in quite idiosyncratic ways. To put it formulaically, the fourth approach weds the theory of multiple intelligences to the goal of enhanced performances of understanding. Here, I believe, lies the best way for us to enable all students to achieve enhanced understanding. And, accordingly, the multiple approaches to understanding are the primary focus of the next several chapters.

Other Players

Goals must come first; and they must be kept in mind. But there 71 are also important "other players." Let me now introduce the other members of the ideal cast.

Well-trained, Enthusiastic Teachers.   To teach for understand- 72 ing, the teachers themselves must be comfortable with and understand the material. Teachers need to feel expert, and they need to embody expertise in the eyes of their students. They must also believe that understanding is important and be prepared to embody that understanding in their own lives. Nothing more impresses students than the opportunity to see informed adults make apt use of the material being introduced. That is why young musicians love to watch their teachers perform, and tennis students want to play with their instructors. And that is why students soon become disenchanted with teachers who fail to "walk the talk."

As the educator Lee Shulman has insisted, knowledge of one's 73 subject is necessary, but it does not suffice. Of two individuals who know their subject equally well, only one may know how to present it to naive students in ways that engage them, dissolve prominent misconceptions, and build up firmer and more flexible understandings. Teachers of teachers must help their students to gain such pedagogical knowledge and to draw on it regularly in their future classroom preparations. Teachers must be ever on the lookout for the most appropriate projects, lessons, questions, and forms of assessment, ones that dovetail with a curriculum of understanding and that help monitor students' evolving understandings.

Moreover, it is not sufficient for teachers to rest on the laurels 74 of their own training. All disciplines evolve—some, like the natural sciences, with daunting speed. The boundaries of disciplines change, and opportunities for interdisciplinary work arise both predictably and unpredictably. Teachers need to keep up; optimally, they should desire ardently to keep up. Again, students take note when teachers are themselves continuing to learn, and when they appear to be excited by new discoveries.

Of course, many teachers lack deep understanding of their topic, 75 and some are not motivated to enhance their understandings. Education for understanding is difficult to pursue without a cohort of teachers who are committed to understanding for themselves, as well as for their charges. The good news is that there are many ways for motivated teachers to delve more deeply into their discipline and to practice their own understandings. But the motivation to do so can only come from the teacher.

Students Prepared and Motivated to Learn.   A teacher's work is 76 half done when students arrive at school healthy, secure, and eager to learn. It hardly needs to be said that many students around the world, and many in the affluent United States, do not come so equipped. It is harder to admit that even students who are healthy and secure often display little interest in what school has to offer.

Faced with students who are not excited by school, it is easy and 77 tempting to blame parents, the students themselves, or last year's teachers. And, indeed, sometimes the job of keeping students healthy, safe, and motivated proves too difficult for any one teacher or team of teachers to accomplish. But this is a conclusion that can only be reached after the fact. From day one, teachers must seek to motivate their students, even against the odds. And their own belief in the importance and the rightness of what they are doing can be a pivotal motivator.

Master principal Deborah Meier recalls how she and her brother   78 used to go to Yankee Stadium in the 1940s to watch the great out-fielder Joe DiMaggio. Meier admired his beauty and grace, while her brother wanted to play ball like Joltin' Joe. Meier looks back nostalgi-cally to the way so many of her generation were enchanted by DiMaggio and eager to follow his lead. She then pointedly adds, with reference to our students today, "We've got to be their Joe DiMaggios."

With knowledge changing so rapidly, students must become   79 able—eager—to assume responsibility for their learning. To the extent that students can craft their own goals, keep track of their own accomplishments, reflect on their own thinking and learning— where it has improved, where it continues to fall short—they become partners in their own education. Even more crucially, once formal schooling has concluded, it should have become second nature for adults to keep on learning—sometimes alone, sometimes in groups—for as long as they choose; indeed, one hopes, for the rest of their lives.

Technology as Helper.   In itself, technology is neither helpful   80 nor harmful; it is simply a tool. The most advanced and speediest computers in the world will be of little help in our mission if the software is mindless and fails to engage understanding. Conversely, armed only with their minds, a few books, chalk, and a pencil, well-informed and motivated teachers can lead their students trium-phantly down the road to understanding. Indeed, Socrates had not so much as a blackboard; he stimulated understanding simply by the shrewd questions that he asked, the order in which he posed them, and his often pointed reactions to the responses of those for whom he served as gadfly.

Still, we would be ill-advised to ignore the opportunities afforded   81 us by the sophisticated technologies of today. Videodiscs can draw stu-dents vividly into mathematical problem-solving or the art treasures of the past. Databases allow them to collect and manipulate all kinds of information about their world, their community, and their own lives. Electronic linkages allow them to share their interests with oth-ers from around the world. Networked personal computers and scan-ners enable them to write, make diagrams, draw, and compose music, revise their works as much as they wish, share them with peers, and make them available to experts anywhere—or indeed, to the students' own subsequent review and critique.

Note that technology does not dictate these beneficent uses. 82 Rather, skilled educators must examine goals and determine, on a case-by-case basis, which technologies, and which uses thereof, can help them meet those goals. The search must proceed in an empirical way. Perhaps, before too long, intelligent systems will themselves be able to judge how they have been successful with students, where they have failed, and how they might be reconfigured.

A Supportive Community.   Even when all the necessary com- 83 ponents are present at school, effective education is not guaranteed. Other stakeholders have a powerful voice in what happens, what is supported, what is thwarted.

The identities of stakeholders differ widely across educational 84 contexts. Parents, school-board members, key citizens of the community, the local, state/provincial, and national ministries of education, and the general public are all factors in the equation that yields a curriculum, a means of assessment, and a cohort of graduates who do or don't possess significant understandings.

Needless to say, education cannot proceed successfully if these 85 stakeholders are ignorant of what is going on in the classroom, if they disagree vociferously with one another, or if they collectively find themselves at odds with a goal, be it the acquisition of core knowledge or the achievement of deep understanding. Moreover, even well-intentioned policies can wreck an educational program. What is the likely fate of a program that educates for understanding, if the graduating or college admissions examinations sample coverage of routine factual material rather than probing the intellectual power of the curriculum and the students' depth of understanding?

Learning need not occur only within the four walls of the class- 86 room. Technology can take us all over the world, and back again. Support at home is crucial. A community's citizens and institutions can make significant contributions to the education of its children. These contributions may start with field trips, but they need not and should not end there. Students ought to have available mentors, apprenticeships, work-study positions in community institutions; and experts from these institutions ought to visit schools, in reality or virtually. Workplaces are changing rapidly; many people now work from home, often by participating in electronic networks and virtual offices. Precollegiate education needs to assume the multifaceted cast and contours of the emerging new world.

QUESTIONS FOR CRITICAL READING

1. Why does Gardner begin by discussing the University of Phoenix?
2. Which grade levels seem to be most important to Gardner?
3. What is the *Star Wars* script? Why is it important?
4. How does apprenticeship affect someone's learning experiences?
5. Why do physics students sometimes fail to understand some basic principles of physics?
6. How does teaching for understanding benefit the student?
7. Why do people's misconceptions about basic phenomena persist even after they learn truths that contradict them?

SUGGESTIONS FOR CRITICAL WRITING

1. In what ways have "erroneous conceptions" (para. 47) been part of your life-learning experiences? Are they more likely to fit into the disciplines of mathematics, science, the arts, or history? How have you profited from being given the chance to explore these misconceptions? How did you manage to exchange these misconceptions for conceptions that were not erroneous? Do you agree that this is a good way to help educate students in the schools?

2. Write a brief essay that outlines a program for education that does not educate for understanding. Have you had any personal experience with such a program? What are the virtues of a program that does not stress understanding? In what academic disciplines would such a program work best? Why? In which discipline would it work least well? For which students is this the better method of education? Should curricula for the primary grades be based on education for understanding? Why or why not?

3. In paragraph 32, Gardner says an expert differs from others in his or her ways of thinking. If you feel you have expertise in some area of study, school, or life, discuss the differences between the way you think about that subject and the ways other nonexperts think about it. You may consider for your area of expertise games — such as chess, basketball, baseball — that you play; sports, movies, or music videos that you watch and critique; music, acting, or stand-up comedy that you perform; or book genres that you read.

4. In paragraph 24, Gardner says, "Most five-year-olds have developed a *Star Wars* script. Life consists of a struggle between Good and Bad forces, with the Good generally triumphant." Is this statement true in your experience? What is the point Gardner is trying to make with this example? How does it relate to the realities of literature and films? Why is adherence to this script a problem for people interested in literature? In what senses might it promote "erroneous conceptions"? How would a teacher help a young student get beyond the simplicity of this script?

5. Beginning with paragraph 72, Gardner goes into detail concerning what he calls "other players," the people and procedures needed to help support the work of the student in school. He mentions well-trained, inspiring teachers; motivated students; helpful technology; and a supportive community. Which of these is most difficult to achieve? Which do you feel is most essential to a good school? Were you aware of the presence of these "other players" when you were in school? Examine the possible effect of each of these four elements on the potential success of the educational system that would produce understanding rather than simple rote memorization.

6. **CONNECTIONS** It is a virtual certainty that Gardner has read the work of Francis Bacon. How does Gardner's attitude toward how we know what we know seem in sympathy with Bacon's precepts in his essay "The Four Idols" (p. 879)? How sympathetic are these authors toward each other's concepts of the way experts ought to think? What rhetorical devices do they seem most to enjoy in common? Do you think Bacon would have made a good schoolteacher? Would Gardner?

7. **CONNECTIONS** What basic views on education does Emerson (**bedfordstmartins.com/worldofideas/epages**) have to add to Gardner's concept of educating students for understanding? Does Gardner take the concept of respecting the student into account in enough ways to satisfy Emerson? These two writers refer to educational systems in two very different centuries in the United States. What evidence do you see in their essays that suggests critical differences in their views of how the society works, how students are educated, and what they expect their education to do for them? Which of these writers seems closest to your own concepts of education? Which would you have wanted to have as a teacher? Why?

8. Gardner says, "A chief obstacle to understanding stems from the theories children develop in early life" (para. 25). What theories do most children seem to have before they head off to school? What are their theories about the animals, the earth, the sun, or adults? What are their theories about other children? What did you happily accept as truths when you were very young? Do you hold those theories as truth today, or have you changed your mind? What are the silliest things you may have believed? What helped you change your thinking?

9. **SEEING CONNECTIONS** The kindergarten student in Norman Rockwell's *The Problem We All Live With* (p. 539) is based on Ruby Bridges Hall, on her way to the first day of school in 1960, when she became the first black child to integrate a school in the South. Using Gardner's methods to educate for understanding, practice the discipline of history by researching Ruby Bridges Hall and her historic experience in Louisiana. If possible, read psychologist Robert Coles's book *The Story of Ruby Bridges* (1995). Coles volunteered to act as a psychologist for Ruby and met with her weekly while she was in school. Apart from the facts, what is the most important understanding that you need to impart with regard to this history?

PART SIX

GENDER AND CULTURE

Mary Wollstonecraft
John Stuart Mill
Virginia Woolf
Margaret Mead
Germaine Greer
Judith Butler
Karen Horney

INTRODUCTION

Male and female represent the two sides of the great radical dual-
ism. But in fact they are perpetually passing into one another.
Fluid hardens to solid, solid rushes to fluid. There is no wholly
masculine man, no purely feminine woman.

— MARGARET FULLER (1810–1850)

Class, race, sexuality, gender, and all other categories by which
we categorize and dismiss each other need to be excavated from
the inside.

— DOROTHY ALLISON (b. 1949)

Male and female citizens, being equal in the eyes of the law,
must be equally admitted to all honors, positions, and public
employment according to their capacity and without other
distinctions besides those of their virtues and talents.

— OLYMPE DE GOUGES (1748–1793)

Every time we liberate a woman, we liberate a man.

— MARGARET MEAD (1901–1978)

Gender equality is more than a goal in itself. It is a precondition
for meeting the challenge of reducing poverty, promoting sustain-
able development, and building good governance.

— KOFI ANNAN (b. 1938)

Gender consciousness has become involved in almost every intellectual field: history, literature, science, anthropology. There's
been an extraordinary advance.

— CLIFFORD GEERTZ (1926–2006)

For a long period of time, the question of gender appeared to be a
simple matter of society's assigning appropriate roles for men and women,
thus defining them in an important way in terms of their gender. However, modern studies in anthropology over the last 150 years have altered
our view by demonstrating that gender is largely a variable, cultural invention. Men and women are, these studies tell us, shaped by the cultural
environment into which they are born. Their gender expectations may differ widely from what we currently think of as appropriate in our culture.

The political unrest of the eighteenth century in the West instigated profound changes in the way people thought about conventional
sex roles. Men like William Godwin (1756–1836) wrote extensively
about women's rights, beginning a movement that continues to this
day. Some nineteenth-century plays, such as Henrik Ibsen's *A Doll's
House,* simply reflected social changes and deep-seated concerns that
involved examining gender assumptions. The authors represented
here, from philosophers to anthropologists to literary critics, examine

the question of gender from a wide range of viewpoints spanning considerations that include women's rights, homosexual patterns in American Indian culture, and masculinity in our own culture.

Mary Wollstonecraft wrote in a time of extreme political change: when revolution was erupting in the American colonies in 1776 and in France in 1789. Kings and aristocrats were losing their heads, literally. Monarchies were giving way to republics. During this period democracy in its modern forms began to grace the lives of some, whereas tyranny oppressed others. Even though radical changes took place in some areas, a conservative backlash in England and elsewhere threatened to heighten oppression rather than expand freedom. Although Wollstonecraft is known today chiefly for her feminist works, she was also engaged in the radical political thought of the time. For example, her defense of the ideals of the French Revolution in *A Vindication of the Rights of Men* (1790) brought her work to the attention of other radical thinkers such as William Godwin (whom she later married), Thomas Paine, William Blake, and William Wordsworth.

Still, Wollstonecraft's name remains a keystone in the history of feminism. She went on to write one of the most important books of the late eighteenth century, *Vindication of the Rights of Woman* (1792), and is remembered most for her careful analysis of a society that did not value the gifts and talents of women. Her complaint is based on a theory of efficiency and economics: it is a waste to limit the opportunities of women. By making her appeal in this fashion she may have expected to gain the attention of the men who held power in late-eighteenth-century England. Some of them did listen. By the 1830s, at the height of the industrial revolution, women were often employed outside the home. However, they were frequently given the most wretched jobs (such as in mining) and were not accorded the kind of respect and opportunity that Wollstonecraft envisioned. They often became drudges in a process of industrial development that demeaned their humanity.

John Stuart Mill, born nine years after Wollstonecraft's death, was one of those men who began to take seriously the economic issues involved in the suppression of women in English and European societies. His prestige as a leading utilitarian philosopher gave him an audience of men who may have been more sympathetic to his views than they might have been to the views of a woman. As it was, Mill himself was deeply moved by the ideas of Harriet Taylor, an ardent champion of women's rights, whom he eventually married. Mill saw not only the waste to the productivity of the human race but also the moral incorrectness of treating half of that race as if it were not worthy, restricting its advancement by withholding higher education and economic opportunity.

In 1929, the novelist and essayist Virginia Woolf considered the question of how gifted women could hope to achieve important works if the current and historical patterns of oppression were to continue.

Her book *A Room of One's Own* was addressed originally to a group of women studying at Cambridge in the two colleges reserved for them at the time. Woolf regarded these women appropriately as gifted, but she worried for their future because their opportunities in postwar England were quite limited. In a stroke of brilliance, Woolf demonstrates the pattern that oppresses gifted women by imagining for William Shakespeare an equally gifted sister named Judith and then tracing her probable development in sixteenth-century England. What chance would Judith have had to be a world-famous figure like her brother? Woolf's discussion is so lifelike and so well realized that it stands as a classic in modern feminist literature.

Margaret Mead brings a very different kind of authority to the gender question because it was one of her primary research topics when she lived among various tribal groups in Papua New Guinea. She is famous for having studied closely the sexual development of women in societies that had not been totally altered by contact with modern Europeans. She discovered that the roles thought appropriate to men and women in our society were not always the same in the Mundugumor (now Biwat) society, which demonstrated a considerable capacity for change. Mead warns against societies that standardize genders and adhere to rigid expectations. She cautions that individuals who do not have the temperaments that their society thinks gender appropriate will suffer great pain and frustration. She points to the berdache, the "men-women" of the Plains Indians who were valued for their all-encompassing skills, which transcended sex roles.

Germaine Greer, a noted feminist, examines the modern vision of masculinity and carefully regards arguments that propose gender qualities as being natural and biological rather than cultural constructs. She questions the "scientific" basis of the role of biology and comes up with some surprising facts. More importantly, the bulk of her study examines the nature of masculinity as it is regarded in our culture. Then Greer proposes the ways masculinity is developed in the male starting from birth. Her views may be controversial, but they are verifiable by simple observation of our own experiences. The feminine role in creating masculinity is one of her last concerns, since she sees women as playing an uneasy part in producing and promoting the masculine ideal.

Judith Butler analyzes the topics of gender identification and gender essentialism. Her selection, from *Undoing Gender* (2004), is an examination of a remarkable narrative of a young boy's mutilation in infancy that resulted in his being raised as a girl. The problems that this young child faced were complicated by other children's ridicule as well as by the constant examination by doctors who were supervising the transgender experiment. Butler's essay is essentially an analysis of the narrative of the boy's experiences. She questions the reliability of the boy's narrative and asks us to examine it in depth to reach an understanding of the boy's true experience. The issues of gender dimorphism and society's limiting view of gender are of concern in Butler's selection.

The e-Pages for this chapter (available online at **bedfordstmartins .com/worldofideas/epages**) feature a selection from Karen Horney, a contemporary of philosophers and psychologists such as Sigmund Freud and Carl Jung. Horney incorporates ideas from both these thinkers while advancing her own theories on the relations between men and women. "The Distrust between the Sexes" describes certain habits of mind that may be thought of as culturally induced but that may also reflect genuine differences in individual minds. Like Jung, Horney argues that if culture has produced an archetypal male and an archetypal female, no matter what the experiences of the individual, the unconscious registers those archetypes. Horney also talks about culturally induced behavior that begins in one's "formative years." Because she is a follower of Freud, however, she does not propose that the archetypal distinctions are as clearly gender-linked as Jung insists that archetypes are culturally linked. However, some of her theories about how one sex views the other imply that gender plays a significant role in forming attitudes.

These essays represent a number of ways of looking at issues of gender. The stereotypical views that most people have in the modern industrialized world are brought into question by authors who work from a wide range of disciplines, bringing a considerable body of research and observation into the discussion. The one thing they have in common is that they urge us to rethink concepts of gender and to examine the role of societies in establishing gender expectations in all of us.

VISUALIZING GENDER AND CULTURE

When Mary Stevenson Cassatt (1844–1926) was born, society had few uncertainties regarding gender, relegating women to the home and family. But during and after the First World War, women began to follow Cassatt's example in choosing a career over a household. During Cassatt's lifetime, women fought for the vote in many countries: it was granted in Finland in 1906; in the United Kingdom, Canada, and Germany in 1918; and in the United States in 1920. Cassatt was a trendsetter and a gender rebel, although a gentle one.

She is known for having shocked her well-to-do parents by refusing to follow the ordinary path set for her as a young Philadelphia society woman. Instead of marriage or even a "sensible" career, she chose to be a painter. Her father was a wealthy banker of French ancestry, and for part of Cassatt's childhood the family lived in France and Germany. She visited London, Paris, and Berlin before she was ten years old, so at a young age, she had a broad understanding of the world. She had seen great art and great architecture. In Philadelphia, she studied art at the Pennsylvania Academy of Fine Arts from 1861 to 1865, learning the academic style of the day, which focused mainly on mythic and historic subject matter. When the American Civil War ended, she returned to

MARY STEVENSON CASSATT, *IN THE LOGE.* 1878.
Oil on canvas, 32" × 26". Museum of Fine Arts, Boston.
The Hayden Collection—Charles Henry Hayden Fund. Photograph © Museum of Fine Arts, Boston.

Europe, traveling—usually by herself—from 1865 to 1870, some-thing that women rarely did at that time. Her work was first shown at the Salon, France's annual art showcase, in 1868, but she returned to the United States during the Franco-Prussian War of 1870. She went back to Europe the next year and settled permanently in Paris in 1873.

Her career in painting put her in the company of the best of the French impressionists, who, like her, grew tired of the restrictions of the standard academic subject matter and style. She met Edgar Degas (1834–1917) in 1874 and found his approach to painting much more congenial. He introduced her to Édouard Manet, Claude Monet, Berthe Morisot,

Camille Pissarro, Pierre-Auguste Renoir, and many more of the "new" painters. She showed with the impressionists four times between 1879 and 1886 and was one of only three women painters in the impressionist movement. She had her brother Alexander buy many important impressionist paintings and show them in the United States, where they were a great success. Her own work had a good reception in the United States as well, and she became known as the American impressionist painter.

Her style and subject matter varied from her early to her later work. After 1880, her signature subject matter was portraits of mothers and children, a subject that very few male painters explored. She admired the French impressionists' willingness to paint everyday scenes of ordinary people at work or at leisure. Her own work centered on people—often women engaged in daily activities in their homes. In a way, she was paying tribute to them. She rarely produced formal portraits and painted few landscapes.

In the Loge was the first of Cassatt's paintings to be shown in the United States. (To see Cassatt's painting in color, go to **bedfordstmartins .com/worldofideas/epages**.) Because the critics had not yet seen and developed an understanding of impressionist paintings, they praised it as being a sketch rather than a finished work. But her painting was nonetheless a great success with the American public.

In the Loge is dominated by a black-garbed woman at the theater, looking through her opera glasses at someone or something we cannot see. To the upper left of the painting, a man leans from his box, looking through his opera glasses at the woman in the loge. They are at the Français theater, doing what people in public often do, looking to see who is there or contemplating a meeting of some kind. The woman's dress style reveals that they are at an afternoon performance.

One of the most subtle aspects of this painting is implied rather than specifically indicated. The two figures with the opera glasses are only part of an incomplete triangulation. The viewer wonders if the woman is looking critically at another woman to see if she is well dressed and attractive or if she is looking romantically at a man or another woman, contemplating a meeting. The man looking at her is straightforward: he's interested in the woman. But Cassatt has made the woman's situation purposely complex and ambiguous.

Modern French critics have proposed a theory of the gaze that places the power in a sexual relationship with the gazer, not the object of the gaze. Given the respective sizes of the gentleman and the woman, it is clear which of these gazers has the greater power in the composition of the painting. But there is yet another level to the concept of the gaze because, as we look at the painting and the figures within in it, we become part of the triangulation ourselves. We do not need opera glasses, so we are in a much more intimate relationship to these figures than they are to the ones they watch. How, then, are we to look at this woman? This man? What is our power relationship in viewing this painting?

MARY WOLLSTONECRAFT
Of the Pernicious Effects Which Arise from the Unnatural Distinctions Established in Society

MARY WOLLSTONECRAFT (1759–1797) was born into relatively modest circumstances, with a father whose heavy drinking
and spending eventually ruined the family and left her and her sisters to support themselves. She became a governess, a teacher, and
eventually a writer. Her views were among the most enlightened of
her day, particularly regarding women and women's rights, giving
her the reputation of being a very forward-looking feminist for her
time, and even for ours. Her thinking, however, is comprehensive
and not limited to a single issue.

She was known to the American patriot Thomas Paine (1737–
1809), to Dr. Samuel Johnson (1709–1783), and to the English
philosopher William Godwin (1756–1836), whom she eventually
married. Her views on marriage were remarkable for her time;
among other beliefs, she felt it unnecessary to marry a man in order
to live happily with him. Her first liaison, with an American, Gilbert
Imlay, gave her the opportunity to travel and learn something
about commerce and capitalism at first hand. Her second liaison,
with Godwin, brought her into the intellectual circles of her day.
She married Godwin when she was pregnant, and died in child-
birth. Her daughter, Mary, married the poet Percy Bysshe Shelley
and wrote the novel *Frankenstein* (1818).

The excitement generated by the French Revolution (1789–
1799) caused Wollstonecraft to react against the very conservative

From *Vindication of the Rights of Woman.*

view put forward by the philosopher Edmund Burke. Her pamphlet *A Vindication of the Rights of Men* (1790) was well received. She followed it with *Vindication of the Rights of Woman* (1792), which was translated into French.

She saw feminism in political terms. The chapter reprinted here concentrates on questions of property, class, and law. As a person committed to the revolutionary principles of liberty, equality, and fraternity, Wollstonecraft linked the condition of women to the political and social structure of her society. Her aim was to point out the inequities in the treatment of women—which her society simply did not perceive—and to attempt to rectify them.

Wollstonecraft's Rhetoric

Mary Wollstonecraft wrote for an audience that did not necessarily appreciate brief, exact expression. Rather, they appreciated a more luxuriant and leisurely style than we use today. As a result, her prose can sometimes seem wordy to a modern audience. However, she handles imagery carefully (especially in the first paragraph) without overburdening her prose. She uses an approach that she calls "episodical observations" (para. 12). These are anecdotes—personal stories—and apparently casual cataloguings of thoughts on a number of related issues. She was aware that her structure was not tight, that it did not develop a specific argument, and that it did not force the reader to accept or reject her position. She also considered this a wise approach because it was obvious to her that her audience was completely prejudiced against her view. To attempt to convince them of her views was to invite total defeat.

Instead, she simply puts forward several observations that stand by themselves as examples of the evils she condemns. Even those who stand against her will see that there is validity to her claims; and they will not be so threatened by her argument as to become defensive before they have learned something new. She appeals always to the higher intellectual capacities of both men and women, directing her complaints, too, against both men and women. This balance of opinion, coupled with a range of thought-provoking examples, makes her views clear and convincing.

Also distinctive in this passage is the use of metaphor. The second sentence of paragraph 1 is particularly heavy with metaphor: "For it is in the most polished society that noisome reptiles and venomous serpents lurk under the rank herbage; and there is voluptuousness pampered by the still sultry air, which relaxes every good disposition before it ripens into virtue." The metaphor presents society as a garden in which the grass is decaying and dangerous serpents are lurking. Good disposition—character—is a plant that might ripen, but—continuing the metaphor—it ripens into virtue. A favorite source of metaphors for Wollstonecraft is drapery (dressmaking). When she uses one of these metaphors she is usually reminding the reader that drapery gives a new shape to things, that it sometimes hides the truth, and that it ought not to put a false appearance on what it covers.

One of her rhetorical techniques is that of literary allusion. By alluding to important literary sources—such as Greek mythology, William Shakespeare, Jean-Jacques Rousseau, and Samuel Johnson— she not only demonstrates her knowledge but also shows that she respects her audience, which she presumes shares the same knowledge. She does not show off by overquoting or by referring to very obscure writers. She balances her allusions perfectly, even transforming folk aphorisms into "homely proverbs" such as "whoever the devil finds idle he will employ."

Wollstonecraft's experiences with her difficult father gave her knowledge of gambling tables and card games, another source of allusions. She draws further on personal experience—shared by some of her audience—when she talks about the degradation felt by a woman of intelligence forced to act as a governess—a glorified servant—in a well-to-do family. Wollstonecraft makes excellent uses of these allusions, never overdoing them, always giving them just the right touch.

PREREADING QUESTIONS: WHAT TO READ FOR

The following prereading questions may help you anticipate key issues in the discussion of Mary Wollstonecraft's "Of the Pernicious Effects Which Arise from the Unnatural Distinctions Established in Society." Keeping them in mind during your first reading of the selection should help focus your attention.

- What are some of the pernicious effects that Wollstonecraft decries?

- What kinds of work are women fit for, in Wollstonecraft's view?

- What happens to people who are born to wealth and have nothing to do?

Of the Pernicious Effects Which Arise from the Unnatural Distinctions Established in Society

From the respect paid to property flow, as from a poisoned foun-   1
tain, most of the evils and vices which render this world such a dreary
scene to the contemplative mind. For it is in the most polished society that noisome reptiles and venomous serpents lurk under the rank
herbage; and there is voluptuousness pampered by the still sultry air,
which relaxes every good disposition before it ripens into virtue.

One class presses on another; for all are aiming to procure respect   2
on account of their property: and property, once gained, will procure the respect due only to talents and virtue. Men neglect the duties
incumbent on man, yet are treated like demi-gods; religion is also
separated from morality by a ceremonial veil, yet men wonder that the
world is almost, literally speaking, a den of sharpers or oppressors.

There is a homely proverb, which speaks a shrewd truth, that who-   3
ever the devil finds idle he will employ. And what but habitual idleness can hereditary wealth and titles produce? For man is so constituted
that he can only attain a proper use of his faculties by exercising them,
and will not exercise them unless necessity of some kind first set the
wheels in motion. Virtue likewise can only be acquired by the discharge
of relative duties; but the importance of these sacred duties will scarcely
be felt by the being who is cajoled out of his humanity by the flattery
of sycophants.[1] There must be more equality established in society,
or morality will never gain ground, and this virtuous equality will not
rest firmly even when founded on a rock, if one half of mankind be
chained to its bottom by fate, for they will be continually undermining
it through ignorance or pride.

It is vain to expect virtue from women till they are in some degree   4
independent of men; nay, it is vain to expect that strength of natural
affection which would make them good wives and mothers. Whilst
they are absolutely dependent on their husbands they will be cunning,
mean, and selfish, and the men who can be gratified by the fawning
fondness of spaniel-like affection have not much delicacy, for love
is not to be bought, in any sense of the words; its silken wings are
instantly shrivelled up when anything beside a return in kind is sought.

---

[1] **sycophants** Toadies or false flatterers.

Yet whilst wealth enervates men, and women live, as it were, by their personal charms, how can we expect them to discharge those ennobling duties which equally require exertion and self-denial? Hereditary property sophisticates[2] the mind, and the unfortunate victims to it, if I may so express myself, swathed from their birth, seldom exert the locomotive faculty of body or mind; and, thus viewing everything through one medium, and that a false one, they are unable to discern in what true merit and happiness consist. False, indeed, must be the light when the drapery of situation hides the man, and makes him stalk in masquerade, dragging from one scene of dissipation to another the nerveless limbs that hang with stupid listlessness, and rolling round the vacant eye which plainly tells us that there is no mind at home.

I mean, therefore, to infer[3] that the society is not properly organized   5 which does not compel men and women to discharge their respective duties, by making it the only way to acquire that countenance from their fellow-creatures which every human being wishes some way to attain. The respect, consequently, which is paid to wealth and mere personal charms, is a true north-east blast that blights the tender blossoms of affection and virtue. Nature has wisely attached affections to duties to sweeten toil, and to give that vigor to the exertions of reason which only the heart can give. But the affection which is put on merely because it is the appropriated insignia of a certain character, when its duties are not fulfilled, is one of the empty compliments which vice and folly are obliged to pay to virtue and the real nature of things.

To illustrate my opinion, I need only observe that when a woman   6 is admired for her beauty, and suffers herself to be so far intoxicated by the admiration she receives as to neglect to discharge the indispensable duty of a mother, she sins against herself by neglecting to cultivate an affection that would equally tend to make her useful and happy. True happiness, I mean all the contentment and virtuous satisfaction that can be snatched in this imperfect state, must arise from well regulated affections; and an affection includes a duty. Men are not aware of the misery they cause and the vicious weakness they cherish by only inciting women to render themselves pleasing; they do not consider that they thus make natural and artificial duties clash by sacrificing the comfort and respectability of a woman's life to voluptuous notions of beauty when in nature they all harmonize.

Cold would be the heart of a husband, were he not rendered   7 unnatural by early debauchery, who did not feel more delight at seeing his child suckled by its mother, than the most artful wanton tricks

---

[2] **sophisticates** Ruins or corrupts.
[3] **infer** Imply.

could ever raise; yet this natural way of cementing the matrimonial tie and twisting esteem with fonder recollections, wealth leads women to spurn. To preserve their beauty and wear the flowery crown of the day, which gives them a kind of right to reign for a short time over the sex, they neglect to stamp impressions on their husbands' hearts that would be remembered with more tenderness when the snow on the head began to chill the bosom than even their virgin charms. The maternal solicitude of a reasonable affectionate woman is very interesting, and the chastened dignity with which a mother returns the caresses that she and her child receive from a father who has been fulfilling the serious duties of his station, is not only a respectable but a beautiful sight. So singular indeed are my feelings, and I have endeavored not to catch factitious[4] ones, that after having been fatigued with the sight of insipid grandeur and the slavish ceremonies that with cumbrous pomp supplied the place of domestic affections, I have turned to some other scene to relieve my eye by resting it on the refreshing green everywhere scattered by nature. I have then viewed with pleasure a woman nursing her children, and discharging the duties of her station with, perhaps, merely a servant maid to take off her hands the servile part of the household business. I have seen her prepare herself and children, with only the luxury of cleanliness, to receive her husband, who returning weary home in the evening found smiling babes and a clean hearth. My heart has loitered in the midst of the group, and has even throbbed with sympathetic emotion, when the scraping of the well known foot has raised a pleasing tumult.

Whilst my benevolence has been gratified by contemplating this 8 artless picture, I have thought that a couple of this description, equally necessary and independent of each other, because each fulfilled the respective duties of their station, possessed all that life could give. Raised sufficiently above abject poverty not to be obliged to weigh the consequence of every farthing they spend, and having sufficient to prevent their attending to a frigid system of economy, which narrows both heart and mind, I declare, so vulgar[5] are my conceptions, that I know not what is wanted to render this the happiest as well as the most respectable situation in the world, but a taste for literature, to throw a little variety and interest into social converse, and some superfluous money to give to the needy and to buy books. For it is not pleasant when the heart is opened by compassion and the head active in arranging plans of usefulness, to have a prim urchin continually twitching back the elbow to prevent the hand from drawing out an almost empty

---

[4] **factitious** False.
[5] **vulgar** Common.

purse, whispering at the same time some prudential maxim about the priority of justice.

Destructive, however, as riches and inherited honors are to the human character, women are more debased and cramped, if possible, by them than men, because men may still, in some degree, unfold their faculties by becoming soldiers and statesmen. 9

As soldiers, I grant, they can now only gather, for the most part, vainglorious laurels, whilst they adjust to a hair the European balance, taking especial care that no bleak northern nook or sound incline the beam.[6] But the days of true heroism are over, when a citizen fought for his country like a Fabricius[7] or a Washington, and then returned to his farm to let his virtuous fervor run in a more placid, but not a less salutary, stream. No, our British heroes are oftener sent from the gaming table than from the plough[8] and their passions have been rather inflamed by hanging with dumb suspense on the turn of a die, than sublimated by panting after the adventurous march of virtue in the historic page. 10

The statesman, it is true, might with more propriety quit the faro bank, or card table, to guide the helm, for he has still but to shuffle and trick.[9] The whole system of British politics, if system it may courteously be called, consisting in multiplying dependents and contriving taxes which grind the poor to pamper the rich; thus a war, or any wild goose chase, is, as the vulgar use the phrase, a lucky turn-up of patronage for the minister, whose chief merit is the art of keeping himself in place. It is not necessary then that he should have bowels for[10] the poor, so he can secure for his family the odd trick. Or should some show of respect, for what is termed with ignorant ostentation an Englishman's birthright, be expedient to bubble the gruff mastiff[11] that he has to lead by the nose, he can make an empty show very safely by giving his single voice and suffering his light squadron to file off to the other side. And when a 11

---

[6] **incline the beam** The metaphor is of the balance — the scale that representations of blind justice hold up. Wollstonecraft's point is that in her time soldiers fought to prevent changes in a balance of power that grew ever more delicate, not in heroic wars with heroic consequences.

[7] **Fabricius (fl. 282 B.C.E.)** Gaius Fabricius, a worthy Roman general and statesman known for resistance to corruption.

[8] **from the plough** Worthy Roman heroes were humble farmers, not gamblers.

[9] **shuffle and trick** The upper class spent much of its time gambling: faro is a high-stakes card game. Wollstonecraft is ironic when she says the statesman has "still but to shuffle and trick," but she connects the "training" of faro with the practice of politics in a deft, sardonic fashion. She is punning on the multiple meanings of *shuffle* — to mix up a deck of cards and to move oneself or one's papers about slowly and aimlessly — and *trick* — to win one turn of a card game and to do a devious deed.

[10] **bowels for** Feelings for; sense of pity.

[11] **to bubble the gruff mastiff** To fool even a guard dog.

question of humanity is agitated he may dip a sop in the milk of human kindness to silence Cerberus,[12] and talk of the interest which his heart takes in an attempt to make the earth no longer cry for vengeance as it sucks in its children's blood, though his cold hand may at the very moment rivet their chains by sanctioning the abominable traffic. A minister is no longer a minister than while he can carry a point which he is determined to carry. Yet it is not necessary that a minister should feel like a man, when a bold push might shake his seat.

But, to have done with these episodical observations, let me return to the more specious slavery which chains the very soul of woman, keeping her forever under the bondage of ignorance.   12

The preposterous distinctions of rank, which render civilization a curse by dividing the world between voluptuous tyrants and cunning envious dependents, corrupt, almost equally, every class of people, because respectability is not attached to the discharge of the relative duties of life, but to the station, and when the duties are not fulfilled the affections cannot gain sufficient strength to fortify the virtue of which they are the natural reward. Still there are some loopholes out of which a man may creep, and dare to think and act for himself; but for a woman it is a herculean task, because she has difficulties peculiar to her sex to overcome which require almost superhuman powers.   13

A truly benevolent legislator always endeavors to make it the interest of each individual to be virtuous; and thus private virtue becoming the cement of public happiness, an orderly whole is consolidated by the tendency of all the parts towards a common center. But, the private or public virtue of woman is very problematical; for Rousseau, and a numerous list of male writers, insist that she should all her life be subjected to a severe restraint, that of propriety. Why subject her to propriety—blind propriety, if she be capable of acting from a nobler spring, if she be an heir of immortality? Is sugar always to be produced by vital blood? Is one half of the human species, like the poor African slaves, to be subject to prejudices that brutalize them, when principles would be a surer guard, only to sweeten the cup of man? Is not this indirectly to deny woman reason? For a gift is a mockery, if it be unfit for use.   14

Women are, in common with men, rendered weak and luxurious by the relaxing pleasures which wealth procures; but added to this they are made slaves to their persons, and must render them alluring that man may lend them his reason to guide their tottering steps aright. Or should they be ambitious, they must govern their tyrants by sinister tricks, for without rights there cannot be any incumbent duties. The laws respecting woman, which I mean to discuss in a   15

---

[12] **Cerberus** The guard dog of Hades, the Greek hell or underworld.

future part, make an absurd unit of a man and his wife,[13] and then, by the easy transition of only considering him as responsible, she is reduced to a mere cypher.[14]

The being who discharges the duties of its station is independent;   16
and, speaking of women at large, their first duty is to themselves as rational creatures, and the next in point of importance, as citizens, is that which includes so many, of a mother. The rank in life which dispenses with their fulfilling this duty necessarily degrades them by making them mere dolls. Or, should they turn to something more important than merely fitting drapery upon a smooth block, their minds are only occupied by some soft platonic attachment; or, the actual management of an intrigue may keep their thoughts in motion; for when they neglect domestic duties, they have it not in their own power to take the field and march and counter-march like soldiers, or wrangle in the senate to keep their faculties from rusting.

I know that, as a proof of the inferiority of the sex, Rousseau has   17
exultingly exclaimed, How can they leave the nursery for the camp![15] And the camp has by some moralists been termed the school of the most heroic virtues; though, I think, it would puzzle a keen casuist[16] to prove the reasonableness of the greater number of wars that have dubbed heroes. I do not mean to consider this question critically; because, having frequently viewed these freaks of ambition as the first natural mode of civilization, when the ground must be torn up, and the woods cleared by fire and sword, I do not choose to call them pests; but surely the present system of war has little connection with virtue of any denomination, being rather the school of *finesse* and effeminacy than of fortitude.

Yet if defensive war, the only justifiable war, in the present   18
advanced state of society, where virtue can show its face and ripen amidst the rigors which purify the air on the mountain's top, were alone to be adopted as just and glorious, the true heroism of antiquity might again animate female bosoms. But fair and softly, gentle reader, male or female, do not alarm thyself, for though I have compared the character of a modern soldier with that of a civilized woman, I am not going to advise them to turn their distaff[17] into a musket, though I sincerely wish to see the bayonet converted into a pruning-hook.

---

[13] **absurd unit of a man and his wife** In English law man and wife were legally one; the man spoke for both.

[14] **cypher** Zero.

[15] **leave the nursery for the camp!** Rousseau's Émile complains that women cannot leave a nursery to go to war.

[16] **casuist** One who argues closely, persistently, and sometimes unfairly.

[17] **distaff** Instrument to wind wool in the act of spinning, notoriously a job only "fit for women."

I only recreated an imagination, fatigued by contemplating the vices and follies which all proceed from a feculent[18] stream of wealth that has muddied the pure rills of natural affection, by supposing that society will some time or other be so constituted, that man must necessarily fulfill the duties of a citizen or be despised, and that while he was employed in any of the departments of civil life, his wife, also an active citizen, should be equally intent to manage her family, educate her children, and assist her neighbors.

But, to render her really virtuous and useful, she must not, if she   19
discharge her civil duties, want, individually, the protection of civil laws; she must not be dependent on her husband's bounty for her subsistence during his life or support after his death—for how can a being be generous who has nothing of its own? or virtuous, who is not free?

The wife, in the present state of things, who is faithful to her hus-   20
band, and neither suckles nor educates her children, scarcely deserves the name of a wife, and has no right to that of a citizen. But take away natural rights, and duties become null.

Women then must be considered as only the wanton solace of men   21
when they become so weak in mind and body that they cannot exert themselves, unless to pursue some frothy pleasure or to invent some frivolous fashion. What can be a more melancholy sight to a thinking mind than to look into the numerous carriages that drive helter-skelter about this metropolis in a morning full of pale-faced creatures who are flying from themselves. I have often wished, with Dr. Johnson,[19] to place some of them in a little shop with half a dozen children looking up to their languid countenances for support. I am much mistaken if some latent vigor would not soon give health and spirit to their eyes, and some lines drawn by the exercise of reason on the blank cheeks, which before were only undulated by dimples, might restore lost dignity to the character, or rather enable it to attain the true dignity of its nature. Virtue is not to be acquired even by speculation, much less by the negative supineness that wealth naturally generates.

Besides, when poverty is more disgraceful than even vice, is not   22
morality cut to the quick? Still to avoid misconstruction, though I consider that women in the common walks of life are called to fulfill the duties of wives and mothers, by religion and reason, I cannot help lamenting that women of a superior cast have not a road open by which they can pursue more extensive plans of usefulness and independence.

---

[18] **feculent** Filthy, polluted; related to *feces*.

[19] **Dr. Samuel Johnson (1709–1784)** The greatest lexicographer and one of the most respected authors of England's eighteenth century. He was known to Mary Wollstonecraft and to her sister, Eliza, a teacher. The reference is to an item published in his *Rambler*, essay 85.

I may excite laughter by dropping a hint which I mean to pursue some future time, for I really think that women ought to have representatives, instead of being arbitrarily governed without having any direct share allowed them in the deliberations of government.

But, as the whole system of representation is now in this country only a convenient handle for despotism, they need not complain, for they are as well represented as a numerous class of hard-working mechanics, who pay for the support of royalty when they can scarcely stop their children's mouths with bread. How are they represented whose very sweat supports the splendid stud of an heir apparent, or varnishes the chariot of some female favorite who looks down on shame? Taxes on the very necessaries of life enable an endless tribe of idle princes and princesses to pass with stupid pomp before a gaping crowd, who almost worship the very parade which costs them so dear. This is mere gothic grandeur, something like the barbarous useless parade of having sentinels on horseback at Whitehall,[20] which I could never view without a mixture of contempt and indignation.

How strangely must the mind be sophisticated when this sort of state impresses it! But, till these monuments of folly are levelled by virtue, similar follies will leaven the whole mass. For the same character, in some degree, will prevail in the aggregate of society; and the refinements of luxury, or the vicious repinings,[21] of envious poverty, will equally banish virtue from society, considered as the characteristic of that society, or only allow it to appear as one of the stripes of the harlequin coat worn by the civilized man.

In the superior ranks of life every duty is done by deputies, as if duties could ever be waived, and the vain pleasures which consequent idleness forces the rich to pursue appear so enticing to the next rank that the numerous scramblers for wealth sacrifice everything to tread on their heels. The most sacred trusts are then considered as sinecures,[22] because they were procured by interest, and only sought to enable a man to keep *good company.* Women, in particular, all want to be ladies. Which is simply to have nothing to do, but listlessly to go they scarcely care where, for they cannot tell what.

But what have women to do in society? I may be asked, but to loiter with easy grace; surely you would not condemn them all to suckle

---

[20] **sentinels on horseback at Whitehall** This is a reference to the expensive demonstration of showmanship that continues to our day: the changing of the guard at Whitehall.

[21] **repinings** Discontent, fretting.

[22] **sinecures** Jobs with few duties but good pay.

fools and chronicle small beer![23] No. Women might certainly study the art of healing, and be physicians as well as nurses. And midwifery, decency seems to allot to them, though I am afraid the word midwife in our dictionaries will soon give place to *accoucheur*,[24] and one proof of the former delicacy of the sex be effaced from the language.

They might also study politics, and settle their benevolence on 27 the broadest basis; for the reading of history will scarcely be more useful than the perusal of romances, if read as mere biography; if the character of the times, the political improvements, arts, &c., be not observed. In short, if it be not considered as the history of man; and not of particular men, who filled a niche in the temple of fame, and dropped into the black rolling stream of time, that silently sweeps all before it, into the shapeless void called—eternity. For shape, can it be called, "that shape hath none"?[25]

Business of various kinds they might likewise pursue, if they were 28 educated in a more orderly manner, which might save many from common and legal prostitution. Women would not then marry for a support, as men accept of places under government, and neglect the implied duties; nor would an attempt to earn their own subsistence—a most laudable one!—sink them almost to the level of those poor abandoned creatures who live by prostitution. For are not milliners and mantua-makers[26] reckoned the next class? The few employments open to women, so far from being liberal, are menial; and when a superior education enables them to take charge of the education of children as governesses, they are not treated like the tutors of sons, though even clerical tutors are not always treated in a manner calculated to render them respectable in the eyes of their pupils, to say nothing of the private comfort of the individual. But as women educated like gentlewomen are never designed for the humiliating situation which necessity sometimes forces them to fill, these situations are considered in the light of a degradation; and they know little of the human heart, who need to be told that nothing so painfully sharpens sensibility as such a fall in life.

Some of these women might be restrained from marrying by a 29 proper spirit or delicacy, and others may not have had it in their power to escape in this pitiful way from servitude; is not that government then very defective, and very unmindful of the happiness of one half of its members, that does not provide for honest, independent women,

---

[23]**chronicle small beer!** *Othello* (II.i.158). This means to keep the household accounts.

[24]*accoucheur* Male version of the female midwife.

[25]**"that shape hath none"** The reference is to *Paradise Lost* (II.667) by John Milton (1608–1674); it is an allusion to death.

[26]**milliners and mantua-makers** Dressmakers, usually women (whereas tailors were usually men).

by encouraging them to fill respectable stations? But in order to render their private virtue a public benefit, they must have a civil existence in the state, married or single; else we shall continually see some worthy woman, whose sensibility has been rendered painfully acute by undeserved contempt, droop like "the lily broken down by a plowshare."

It is a melancholy truth—yet such is the blessed effect of   30 civilization!—the most respectable women are the most oppressed; and, unless they have understandings far superior to the common run of understandings, taking in both sexes, they must, from being treated like contemptible beings, become contemptible. How many women thus waste life away the prey of discontent, who might have practiced as physicians, regulated a farm, managed a shop, and stood erect, supported by their own industry, instead of hanging their heads surcharged with the dew of sensibility, that consumes the beauty to which it at first gave lustre; nay, I doubt whether pity and love are so near akin as poets feign, for I have seldom seen much compassion excited by the helplessness of females, unless they were fair; then, perhaps pity was the soft handmaid of love, or the harbinger of lust.

How much more respectable is the woman who earns her   31 own bread by fulfilling any duty, than the most accomplished beauty!—beauty did I say?—so sensible am I of the beauty of moral loveliness, or the harmonious propriety that attunes the passions of a well regulated mind, that I blush at making the comparison; yet I sigh to think how few women aim at attaining this respectability by withdrawing from the giddy whirl of pleasure, or the indolent calm that stupefies the good sort of women it sucks in.

Proud of their weakness, however, they must always be protected,   32 guarded from care, and all the rough toils that dignify the mind. If this be the fiat of fate, if they will make themselves insignificant and contemptible, sweetly to waste "life away," let them not expect to be valued when their beauty fades, for it is the fate of the fairest flowers to be admired and pulled to pieces by the careless hand that plucked them. In how many ways do I wish, from the purest benevolence, to impress this truth on my sex; yet I fear that they will not listen to a truth that dear-bought experience has brought home to many an agitated bosom, nor willingly resign the privileges of rank and sex for the privileges of humanity, to which those have no claim who do not discharge its duties.

Those writers are particularly useful, in my opinion, who make   33 man feel for man, independent of the station he fills, or the drapery of factitious sentiments. I then would fain[27] convince reasonable men of the importance of some of my remarks; and prevail on them to weigh dispassionately the whole tenor of my observations. I appeal to

---

[27] **fain** Happily, gladly.

their understandings; and, as a fellow-creature, claim, in the name of my sex, some interest in their hearts. I entreat them to assist to emancipate their companion, to make her a *help meet*[28] for them!

Would men but generously snap our chains, and be content with   34
rational fellowship instead of slavish obedience, they would find us more observant daughters, more affectionate sisters, more faithful wives, more reasonable mothers—in a word, better citizens. We should then love them with true affection, because we should learn to respect ourselves; and, the peace of mind of a worthy man would not be interrupted by the idle vanity of his wife, nor the babes sent to nestle in a strange bosom, having never found a home in their mother's.

-----

[28]***help meet*** Helper, helpmate.

QUESTIONS FOR CRITICAL READING

1. Who is the audience for Wollstonecraft's writing? Is she writing more for men than for women? Is it clear from what she says that she addresses an explicit audience with specific qualities?

2. Analyze paragraph 1 carefully for the use of imagery, especially metaphor. What are the effects of these images? Are they overdone?

3. Wollstonecraft begins by attacking property, or the respect paid to it. What does she mean? Does she sustain that line of thought throughout the piece?

4. In paragraph 12, Wollstonecraft speaks of the "bondage of ignorance" in which women are held. Clarify precisely what she means by that expression.

5. In paragraph 30, Wollstonecraft says that people who are treated as if they were contemptible will become contemptible. Is this a political or a psychological judgment?

6. What is the substance of Wollstonecraft's complaint concerning the admiration of women for their beauty?

SUGGESTIONS FOR CRITICAL WRITING

1. Throughout the piece Wollstonecraft attacks the unnatural distinctions made between men and women. Establish carefully what those unnatural distinctions are, why they are unnatural, and whether such distinctions persist to the present day. By contrast, establish what some natural distinctions between men and women are and whether Wollstonecraft has taken them into consideration.

2. References are made throughout the piece to prostitution and to the debaucheries of men. Paragraph 7 specifically refers to the "wanton tricks" of prostitutes. What is Wollstonecraft's attitude toward men in regard to sexuality and their attitudes toward women—both the women

of the brothels and the women with whom men live? Find passages in the piece that you can quote and analyze in an effort to examine her views.

3. In paragraph 2, Wollstonecraft complains that "the respect due only to talents and virtue" is instead being given to people on account of their property. Further, she says in paragraph 9 that riches are "destructive . . . to the human character." Determine carefully, by means of reference to and analysis of specific passages, just what Wollstonecraft means by such statements. Then, use your own anecdotes or "episodical observations" to take a stand on whether these are views you yourself can hold for our time. Are riches destructive to character? Is too much respect paid to those who possess property? If possible, use metaphor or allusion—literary or personal.

4. In paragraph 4, Wollstonecraft speaks of "men who can be gratified by the fawning fondness of spaniel-like affection" from their women. Search through the essay for other instances of similar views and analyze them carefully. Establish exactly what the men she describes want their women to be like. Have today's men changed very much in their expectations? Why? Why not? Use personal observations where possible in answering this question.

5. The question of what roles women ought to have in society is addressed in paragraphs 26, 27, and 28. What are those roles? Why are they defined in terms of work? Do you agree that they are, indeed, the roles that women should assume? Would you include more roles? Do women in our time have greater access to those roles? Consider what women actually did in Wollstonecraft's time and what they do today.

6. **CONNECTIONS** Mary Wollstonecraft wrote more than a century and a half before Karen Horney (**bedfordstmartins.com/worldofideas/epages**). Examine the assumptions each writer makes about the role and nature of each sex in her historical situation. How much has changed since Wollstonecraft wrote her book? How much does each of these writers agree about the position of power of men and women in their society? How much of what each writer describes about the relationship between men and women do you observe in your own environment?

7. **CONNECTIONS** Compare Wollstonecraft's views on the ways in which women are victims of prejudice with the views of Martin Luther King Jr. How much do women of Wollstonecraft's time have in common with the conditions of African Americans as described by King? What political issues are central to the efforts of both groups to achieve justice and equal opportunity? Might Wollstonecraft see herself in the same kind of struggle as King, or would she draw sharp distinctions?

8. **SEEING CONNECTIONS** Write a commentary on Cassatt's *In the Loge* (p. 650), assuming the views of Wollstonecraft. What would Wollstonecraft say about Cassatt's decision to become a professional painter and earn money through her work? How might she defend the choice of a career as a painter over other possible careers for Cassatt? How might Wollstonecraft interpret the scene presented in *In the Loge*? Would she see it as possibly sexual? Would she see the woman in the foreground as assuming a specific role in society? If so, would the role be one that would satisfy Wollstonecraft's view of how women should behave and be treated?

JOHN STUART MILL
The Subjection of Women

THE SON OF JAMES MILL, a distinguished philosopher and proponent of utilitarianism, John Stuart Mill (1806–1873) was educated by his father at home and restricted from associating with other children his age, except for those in his family. His education was remarkable. He was introduced to Greek when he was three and by the age of eight had read all of Herodotus and some of Plato in the original language. He went on to read the great Latin classics as a teenager. He praised his system of education in part because his father made him solve intellectual problems on his own, even if they were very difficult. The purpose of this education was to produce a philosopher who would carry on the work of utilitarians, like his father and Jeremy Bentham (1748–1832), whose views John Stuart Mill revised and elaborated on throughout his life.

Unfortunately, Mill suffered a nervous breakdown when he was twenty, essentially as a result of his not having had a relatively normal upbringing in a social circle larger than his family. But he recovered and went on to be a man of action as a member of Parliament, as a member of the British East India Company, and as one of the most influential thinkers of his time. He contributed important ideas in the area of logic and argument as well as in politics. His landmark work, *On Liberty* (1859), established a liberal position based on the "no harm" principle: people were free to do as they wished as long as they did no harm to anyone else. "The only part of the conduct of anyone, for which he is amenable to society, is that which concerns others. In the part which merely concerns himself, his independence is, of right, absolute. Over himself, over his own body and mind, the individual is sovereign." Mill established the priority of the individual over the collective, propounding a libertarian view that is still respected today.

Mill's views in *Utilitarianism* (1863) modified the principles of his father and Bentham. Bentham's ideal was to achieve the greatest happiness for the greatest number of people. Mill's emphasis on individual freedom modified these views in several ways. One was that he advised wariness of a tyranny of the majority in which society could

From *The Subjection of Women.*

command behavior on the basis of what most people thought was right and proper action, thus restricting the happiness of some individuals. In another modification he qualified the kinds of happiness that should be sought after in life. Bentham treated all kinds of happiness as equal, while Mill gave priority to intellectual and spiritual happiness over physical happiness. As he wrote, "It is better to be a human being dissatisfied than a pig satisfied; better to be Socrates dissatisfied than a fool satisfied. And if the fool, or the pig, are of a different opinion, it is because they only know their own side of the question."

Another of his views, derived from his father's thinking, was called *associationism*. He felt that people were altered by their associations with ideas and others and that given the proper associations ordinary people could do unusual things. In modern terms, this would translate to the influence of the environment that shapes the intellectual, social, and familial values of the individual. The significance of this view was basic to his concerns regarding the subjection of women in nineteenth-century society. The prevalent male view was that women were innately unequal to men and, therefore, did not deserve to be given the rights and privileges of men. Mill knew that women were provided with an inferior education and an environment designed to prevent them from competing equally with men.

His views on the subjection of women were a natural outgrowth of his personal philosophy and that of his father, but they were reinforced by a long relationship with Harriet Taylor, a prominent feminist whom he married in 1851 while he was working for the British East India Company. She was clearly influential in his writing *On Liberty*, which was published the year after her death. Taylor was an extraordinary person in that her education was superior to most men and her arguments sharp and clear. They were friends for many years before they married.

The Subjection of Women (1869) was greeted with enormous controversy. Until 1870, a wife's property was owned by her husband; a wife had few grounds for divorce, while a husband had many; the children of a marriage belonged exclusively to the husband; a wife had no legal status independent of her husband; and no husband could be guilty of raping his wife. Mill wrote out of a sense of outrage for the obvious inequality that was tolerated by the majority and protected by the male legislative establishment.

Mill's Rhetoric

The section of *The Subjection of Women* that follows is less an argument than it is an examination of a simple question: "Would mankind be at all better off if women were free?" By and large Mill's focus here is on married women. He considers the question from several points of view. The consideration of justice illuminates the wife's perspective because the demands of justice clearly take her rights into account and suggest that since slavery has been abolished entirely it only follows that a wife should not be a slave in her own home. His exploration of this point is subtle, but thorough, in part because his audience knew the details of a wife's situation. The intended audience for his book seems to have been primarily educated men, which we surmise from the often quoted Latin—and even Greek—phrases, and thus Mill limited his influence to the privileged males of the "easy classes" and to a small number of atypically educated women.

One of his first concerns relates clearly to his views in *On Liberty* when he talks about the abuse of power. When one person has absolute power over another, he asks, what is the likely outcome? He points to the institution of slavery as an example of the tyranny of the individual and the complete abuse of power often visited upon slaves. The same situation exists in the institution of marriage in the Victorian period in which Mill lived. And it has not entirely been altered except in terms of the laws and the protection they sometimes give married women.

Another concern is more utilitarian and clearly an appeal to male readers who can see the advantages for their own economic interests and, perhaps, to men who can see the potential for the general advancement of learning: equal education for women. The effect of such education, combined with the opportunities of useful employment and advancement, would be to tap into the potential of that half of society that had influence only in the home. It is a terrible thing, he implies, to shut women away from free choice of employment. "Mental superiority of any kind is at present everywhere so much below the demand; there is such a deficiency of persons competent to do excellently anything which it requires any considerable amount of ability to do: that the loss to the world, by refusing to make use of one-half of the whole quantity of talent it possesses, is extremely serious" (para. 6). Among the advantages of giving women equal opportunity is "the stimulus that would be given to the intellect of men by the competition." It is interesting to see that he feels men would be improved by such competition instead of threatened by it.

A good deal of the essay is devoted to the topic of comparison: examining the differences between men and women. Mill describes the quality husbands have that tends toward the abuse of power: self-worship. "The self-worship of the monarch, or of the feudal superior, is matched by the self-worship of the male" (para. 4). For the self-worshiping male, his wife is merely a vassal, only a notch above a slave.

He describes women as having different interests from men, thus offering society an enlargement of understanding and influence.

Mill praises the effect of "women's opinions" on men especially in his discussion of chivalry, which he describes as "the acme of the influence of women's sentiments on the moral cultivation of mankind" (para. 9). And, at the same time, he laments that chivalry has passed away, especially now that fighting as a primary activity for men has given way to business. The modern world has no room for the virtues of chivalry.

Mill's primary complaint about the behavior of women is that they pay much too much attention to charity. He feels that women's tendency to give money and services to the poor comes from their own unfree upbringing, when they were themselves given charity in anticipation of their marrying, rather than their becoming independent. Charity, Mill says, induces dependence and stifles the willingness and ability to do for oneself. It does more harm than good. However, apart from this warning, Mill supports the independence and freedom of women at a time when such an idea was virtually freakish.

PREREADING QUESTIONS:
WHAT TO READ FOR

The following prereading questions may help you anticipate key issues in the discussion of John Stuart Mill's "The Subjection of Women." Keeping them in mind during your first reading of the selection should help focus your attention.

- What was the nature of the subjection of women in marriage? Who benefited from women's subjection?
- What are the primary effects of women on the character of males?
- What basic differences does Mill see between men and women?
- What are the primary reasons for demanding the end of the subjection of women?

The Subjection of Women

There remains a question, not of less importance than those already discussed, and which will be asked the most importunately by those opponents whose conviction is somewhat shaken on the main point. What good are we to expect from the changes proposed in our customs and institutions? Would mankind be at all better off if women were free? If not, why disturb their minds, and attempt to make a social revolution in the name of an abstract right?   1

It is hardly to be expected that this question will be asked in respect to the change proposed in the condition of women in marriage.   2

The sufferings, immoralities, evils of all sorts, produced in innumerable cases by the subjection of individual women to individual men, are far too terrible to be overlooked. Unthinking or uncandid persons, counting those cases alone which are extreme, or which attain publicity, may say that the evils are exceptional; but no one can be blind to their existence, nor, in many cases, to their intensity. And it is perfectly obvious that the abuse of the power cannot be very much checked while the power remains. It is a power given, or offered, not to good men, or to decently respectable men, but to all men; the most brutal, and the most criminal. There is no check but that of opinion, and such men are in general within the reach of no opinion but that of men like themselves. If such men did not brutally tyrannize over the one human being whom the law compels to bear everything from them, society must already have reached a paradisiacal state. There could be no need any longer of laws to curb men's vicious propensities. Astraea[1] must not only have returned to earth, but the heart of the worst man must have become her temple. The law of servitude in marriage is a monstrous contradiction to all the principles of the modern world, and to all the experience through which those principles have been slowly and painfully worked out. It is the sole case, now that negro slavery has been abolished, in which a human being in the plenitude of every faculty is delivered up to the tender mercies of another human being, in the hope forsooth that this other will use the power solely for the good of the person subjected to it. Marriage is the only actual bondage known to our law. There remain no legal slaves, except the mistress of every house.

It is not, therefore, on this part of the subject, that the question   3
is likely to be asked, *Cui bono?*[2] We may be told that the evil would outweigh the good, but the reality of the good admits of no dispute. In regard, however, to the larger question, the removal of women's disabilities—their recognition as the equals of men in all that belongs to citizenship—the opening to them of all honorable employments, and of the training and education which qualifies for those employments—there are many persons for whom it is not enough that the inequality has no just or legitimate defense; they require to be told what express advantage would be obtained by abolishing it.

To which let me first answer, the advantage of having the most   4
universal and pervading of all human relations regulated by justice instead of injustice. The vast amount of this gain to human nature, it is hardly possible, by any explanation or illustration, to place in a stronger light than it is placed by the bare statement, to any one who attaches a moral meaning to words. All the selfish propensities,

---

[1] **Astraea** The first Greek goddess of justice, innocence, and purity; she left earth at the end of the Golden Age due to man's evilness.

[2] **Cui bono?** Latin, "Who benefits from it?"

the self-worship, the unjust self-preference, which exist among mankind, have their source and root in, and derive their principal nourishment from, the present constitution of the relation between men and women. Think what it is to a boy, to grow up to manhood in the belief that without any merit or any exertion of his own, though he may be the most frivolous and empty or the most ignorant and stolid of mankind, by the mere fact of being born a male he is by right the superior of all and every one of an entire half of the human race: including probably some whose real superiority to himself he has daily or hourly occasion to feel; but even if in his whole conduct he habitually follows a woman's guidance, still, if he is a fool, she thinks that of course she is not, and cannot be, equal in ability and judgment to himself; and if he is not a fool, he does worse — he sees that she is superior to him, and believes that, notwithstanding her superiority, he is entitled to command and she is bound to obey. What must be the effect on his character, of this lesson? And men of the cultivated classes are often not aware how deeply it sinks into the immense majority of male minds. For, among right-feeling and well-bred people, the inequality is kept as much as possible out of sight; above all, out of sight of the children. As much obedience is required from boys to their mother as to their father: they are not permitted to domineer over their sisters, nor are they accustomed to see these postponed to them, but the contrary; the compensations of the chivalrous feeling being made prominent, while the servitude which requires them is kept in the background. Well brought-up youths in the higher classes thus often escape the bad influences of the situation in their early years, and only experience them when, arrived at manhood, they fall under the dominion of facts as they really exist. Such people are little aware, when a boy is differently brought up, how early the notion of his inherent superiority to a girl arises in his mind; how it grows with his growth and strengthens with his strength; how it is inoculated by one schoolboy upon another; how early the youth thinks himself superior to his mother, owing her perhaps forbearance, but no real respect; and how sublime and sultan-like a sense of superiority he feels, above all, over the woman whom he honors by admitting her to a partnership of his life. Is it imagined that all this does not pervert the whole manner of existence of the man, both as an individual and as a social being? It is an exact parallel to the feeling of a hereditary king that he is excellent above others by being born a king, or a noble by being born a noble. The relation between husband and wife is very like that between lord and vassal, except that the wife is held to more unlimited obedience than the vassal was. However the vassal's character may have been affected, for better and for worse, by his subordination, who can help seeing that the lord's was affected greatly for the worse? Whether he was led to believe that his vassals were really superior to himself, or to feel that he was placed in command over people as good as himself, for no merits or labors of his own, but merely for having, as Figaro[3] says, taken the trouble to be born. The self-worship of the monarch, or of the feudal superior, is matched by the self-worship of the male. Human beings do not grow up from childhood in the possession of unearned distinctions, without pluming themselves upon them. Those whom privileges not acquired by their merit, and which they feel to be disproportioned to it, inspire with additional humility, are always the few, and the best few. The rest are only inspired with pride, and the worst sort of pride, that which values itself upon accidental advantages, not of its own achieving. Above all, when the feeling of being raised above the whole of the other sex is combined with personal authority over one individual among them; the situation, if a school of conscientious and affectionate forbearance to those whose strongest points of character are conscience and affection, is to men of another quality a regularly constituted Academy or Gymnasium for training them in arrogance and overbearingness; which vices, if curbed by the certainty of resistance in their intercourse with other men, their equals, break out towards all who are in a position to be obliged to tolerate them, and often revenge themselves upon the unfortunate wife for the involuntary restraint which they are obliged to submit to elsewhere.

The example afforded, and the education given to the sentiments,   5 by laying the foundation of domestic existence upon a relation contradictory to the first principles of social justice, must, from the very nature of man, have a perverting influence of such magnitude, that it is hardly possible with our present experience to raise our imaginations to the conception of so great a change for the better as would be made by its removal. All that education and civilization are doing to efface the influences on character of the law of force, and replace them by those of justice, remains merely on the surface, as long as the citadel of the enemy is not attacked. The principle of the modern movement in morals and politics, is that conduct, and conduct alone, entitles to respect: that not what men are, but what they do, constitutes their claim to deference; that, above all, merit, and not birth, is the only rightful claim to power and authority. If no authority, not in its nature temporary, were allowed to one human being over another, society would not be employed in building up propensities with one hand which it has to curb with the other. The child would

---

[3] **Figaro** Character critical of the aristocracy in Pierre-Augustin Caron de Beaumarchais's (1732–1799) plays *The Barber of Seville* and *The Marriage of Figaro*. Both were turned into operas.

really, for the first time in man's existence on earth, be trained in the way he should go, and when he was old there would be a chance that he would not depart from it. But so long as the right of the strong to power over the weak rules in the very heart of society, the attempt to make the equal right of the weak the principle of its outward actions will always be an uphill struggle; for the law of justice, which is also that of Christianity, will never get possession of men's inmost sentiments; they will be working against it, even when bending to it.

The second benefit to be expected from giving to women the free 6 use of their faculties, by leaving them the free choice of their employments, and opening to them the same field of occupation and the same prizes and encouragements as to other human beings, would be that of doubling the mass of mental faculties available for the higher service of humanity. Where there is now one person qualified to benefit mankind and promote the general improvement, as a public teacher, or an administrator of some branch of public or social affairs, there would then be a chance of two. Mental superiority of any kind is at present everywhere so much below the demand; there is such a deficiency of persons competent to do excellently anything which it requires any considerable amount of ability to do; that the loss to the world, by refusing to make use of one-half of the whole quantity of talent it possesses, is extremely serious. It is true that this amount of mental power is not totally lost. Much of it is employed, and would in any case be employed, in domestic management, and in the few other occupations open to women; and from the remainder indirect benefit is in many individual cases obtained, through the personal influence of individual women over individual men. But these benefits are partial; their range is extremely circumscribed; and if they must be admitted, on the one hand, as a deduction from the amount of fresh social power that would be acquired by giving freedom to one-half of the whole sum of human intellect, there must be added, on the other, the benefit of the stimulus that would be given to the intellect of men by the competition; or (to use a more true expression) by the necessity that would be imposed on them of deserving precedency before they could expect to obtain it.

This great accession to the intellectual power of the species, and to 7 the amount of intellect available for the good management of its affairs, would be obtained, partly, through the better and more complete intellectual education of women, which would then improve *pari passu*[4] with that of men. Women in general would be brought up equally capable of understanding business, public affairs, and the higher matters

---

[4] *pari passu* Latin, "in the same place."

of speculation, with men in the same class of society; and the select few of the one as well as of the other sex, who were qualified not only to comprehend what is done or thought by others, but to think or do something considerable themselves, would meet with the same facilities for improving and training their capacities in the one sex as in the other. In this way, the widening of the sphere of action for women would operate for good, by raising their education to the level of that of men, and making the one participate in all improvements made in the other. But independently of this, the mere breaking down of the barrier would of itself have an educational virtue of the highest worth. The mere getting rid of the idea that all the wider subjects of thought and action, all the things which are of general and not solely of private interest, are men's business, from which women are to be warned off—positively interdicted from most of it, coldly tolerated in the little which is allowed them—the mere consciousness a woman would then have of being a human being like any other, entitled to choose her pursuits, urged or invited by the same inducements as any one else to interest herself in whatever is interesting to human beings, entitled to exert the share of influence on all human concerns which belongs to an individual opinion, whether she attempted actual participation in them or not—this alone would effect an immense expansion of the faculties of women, as well as enlargement of the range of their moral sentiments.

Besides the addition to the amount of individual talent available 8 for the conduct of human affairs, which certainly are not at present so abundantly provided in that respect that they can afford to dispense with one-half of what nature proffers; the opinion of women would then possess a more beneficial, rather than a greater, influence upon the general mass of human belief and sentiment. I say a more beneficial, rather than a greater influence; for the influence of women over the general tone of opinion has always, or at least from the earliest known period, been very considerable. The influence of mothers on the early character of their sons, and the desire of young men to recommend themselves to young women, have in all recorded times been important agencies in the formation of character, and have determined some of the chief steps in the progress of civilization. Even in the Homeric age, αἰδώς towards the Τρωάδας ἑλκεσιπέπλους is an acknowledged and powerful motive of action in the great Hector.[5] The moral influence of women has had two modes of operation. First, it has been a softening influence. Those who were most liable to be the victims of

---

[5] **Hector** Hector in *The Iliad* is concerned with what the women will think of him. The quote is from book 6, lines 441–43. Translated from the Greek, the first part of the quote means "a sense of shame," while the second part means "wearing long, flowing robes."

violence, have naturally tended as much as they could towards limiting its sphere and mitigating its excesses. Those who were not taught to fight, have naturally inclined in favor of any other mode of settling differences rather than that of fighting. In general, those who have been the greatest sufferers by the indulgence of selfish passion, have been the most earnest supporters of any moral law which offered a means of bridling passion. Women were powerfully instrumental in inducing the northern conquerors to adopt the creed of Christianity, a creed so much more favorable to women than any that preceded it. The conversion of the Anglo-Saxons and of the Franks may be said to have been begun by the wives of Ethelbert and Clovis.[6] The other mode in which the effect of women's opinion has been conspicuous, is by giving a powerful stimulus to those qualities in men, which, not being themselves trained in, it was necessary for them that they should find in their protectors. Courage, and the military virtues generally, have at all times been greatly indebted to the desire which men felt of being admired by women: and the stimulus reaches far beyond this one class of eminent qualities, since, by a very natural effect of their position, the best passport to the admiration and favor of women has always been to be thought highly of by men. From the combination of the two kinds of moral influence thus exercised by women, arose the spirit of chivalry: the peculiarity of which is, to aim at combining the highest standard of the warlike qualities with the cultivation of a totally different class of virtues—those of gentleness, generosity, and self-abnegation, towards the non-military and defenseless classes generally, and a special submission and worship directed towards women; who were distinguished from the other defenseless classes by the high rewards which they had it in their power voluntarily to bestow on those who endeavored to earn their favor, instead of extorting their subjection. Though the practice of chivalry fell even more sadly short of its theoretic standard than practice generally falls below theory, it remains one of the most precious monuments of the moral history of our race; as a remarkable instance of a concerted and organized attempt by a most disorganized and distracted society, to raise up and carry into practice a moral ideal greatly in advance of its social condition and institutions; so much so as to have been completely frustrated in the main object, yet never entirely inefficacious, and which has left a most sensible, and for the most part a highly valuable impress on the ideas and feelings of all subsequent times.

The chivalrous ideal is the acme of the influence of women's sentiments on the moral cultivation of mankind: and if women are to   9

---

[6]**Ethelbert and Clovis** Pagan English kings who married Christian women and were converted.

remain in their subordinate situation, it were greatly to be lamented that the chivalrous standard should have passed away, for it is the only one at all capable of mitigating the demoralizing influences of that position. But the changes in the general state of the species rendered inevitable the substitution of a totally different ideal of morality for the chivalrous one. Chivalry was the attempt to infuse moral elements into a state of society in which everything depended for good or evil on individual prowess, under the softening influences of individual delicacy and generosity. In modern societies, all things, even in the military department of affairs, are decided, not by individual effort, but by the combined operations of numbers; while the main occupation of society has changed from fighting to business, from military to industrial life. The exigencies of the new life are no more exclusive of the virtues of generosity than those of the old, but it no longer entirely depends on them. The main foundations of the moral life of modern times must be justice and prudence; the respect of each for the rights of every other, and the ability of each to take care of himself. Chivalry left without legal check all forms of wrong which reigned unpunished throughout society; it only encouraged a few to do right in preference to wrong, by the direction it gave to the instruments of praise and admiration. But the real dependence of morality must always be upon its penal sanctions—its power to deter from evil. The security of society cannot rest on merely rendering honor to right, a motive so comparatively weak in all but a few, and which on very many does not operate at all. Modern society is able to repress wrong through all departments of life, by a fit exertion of the superior strength which civilization has given it, and thus to render the existence of the weaker members of society (no longer defenseless but protected by law) tolerable to them, without reliance on the chivalrous feelings of those who are in a position to tyrannize. The beauties and graces of the chivalrous character are still what they were, but the rights of the weak, and the general comfort of human life, now rest on a far surer and steadier support; or rather, they do so in every relation of life except the conjugal.

At present the moral influence of women is no less real, but it is 　10 no longer of so marked and definite a character: it has more nearly merged in the general influence of public opinion. Both through the contagion of sympathy, and through the desire of men to shine in the eyes of women, their feelings have great effect in keeping alive what remains of the chivalrous ideal—in fostering the sentiments and continuing the traditions of spirit and generosity. In these points of character, their standard is higher than that of men; in the quality of justice, somewhat lower. As regards the relations of private life it may be said generally, that their influence is, on the whole, encouraging to the softer virtues, discouraging to the sterner: though the statement must be taken with all the modifications dependent on individual character. In the chief of the greater trials to which virtue is subject in the concerns of life—the conflict between interest and principle—the tendency of women's influence is of a very mixed character. When the principle involved happens to be one of the very few which the course of their religious or moral education has strongly impressed upon themselves, they are potent auxiliaries to virtue: and their husbands and sons are often prompted by them to acts of abnegation which they never would have been capable of without that stimulus. But, with the present education and position of women, the moral principles which have been impressed on them cover but a comparatively small part of the field of virtue, and are, moreover, principally negative; forbidding particular acts, but having little to do with the general direction of the thoughts and purposes. I am afraid it must be said, that disinterestedness in the general conduct of life—the devotion of the energies to purposes which hold out no promise of private advantages to the family—is very seldom encouraged or supported by women's influence. It is small blame to them that they discourage objects of which they have not learnt to see the advantage, and which withdraw their men from them, and from the interests of the family. But the consequence is that women's influence is often anything but favorable to public virtue.

Women have, however, some share of influence in giving the tone 11 to public moralities since their sphere of action has been a little widened, and since a considerable number of them have occupied themselves practically in the promotion of objects reaching beyond their own family and household. The influence of women counts for a great deal in two of the most marked features of modern European life—its aversion to war, and its addiction to philanthropy. Excellent characteristics both; but unhappily, if the influence of women is valuable in the encouragement it gives to these feelings in general, in the particular applications the direction it gives to them is at least as often mischievous as useful. In the philanthropic department more particularly, the two provinces chiefly cultivated by women are religious proselytism and charity. Religious proselytism at home, is but another word for embittering of religious animosities: abroad, it is usually a blind running at an object, without either knowing or heeding the fatal mischiefs—fatal to the religious object itself as well as to all other desirable objects—which may be produced by the means employed. As for charity, it is a matter in which the immediate effect on the persons directly concerned, and the ultimate consequence to the general good, are apt to be at complete war with one another: while the education given to women—an education of the sentiments rather than of the understanding—and the habit inculcated by their whole life, of looking to immediate effects on persons, and not to remote effects on classes of persons—make them both unable to see, and unwilling to admit, the ultimate evil tendency of any form of charity or philanthropy which commends itself to their sympathetic feelings. The great and continually increasing mass of unenlightened and shortsighted benevolence, which, taking the care of people's lives out of their own hands, and relieving them from the disagreeable consequences of their own acts, saps the very foundations of the self-respect, self-help, and self-control which are the essential conditions both of individual prosperity and of social virtue—this waste of resources and of benevolent feelings in doing harm instead of good, is immensely swelled by women's contributions, and stimulated by their influence. Not that this is a mistake likely to be made by women, where they have actually the practical management of schemes of beneficence. It sometimes happens that women who administer public charities—with that insight into present fact, and especially into the minds and feelings of those with whom they are in immediate contact, in which women generally excel men—recognize in the clearest manner the demoralizing influence of the alms given or the help afforded, and could give lessons on the subject to many a male political economist. But women who only give their money, and are not brought face to face with the effects it produces, how can they be expected to foresee them? A woman born to the present lot of women, and content with it, how should she appreciate the value of self-dependence? She is not self-dependent; she is not taught self-dependence; her destiny is to receive everything from others, and why should what is good enough for her be bad for the poor? Her familiar notions of good are of blessings descending from a superior. She forgets that she is not free, and that the poor are; that if what they need is given to them unearned, they cannot be compelled to earn it: that everybody cannot be taken care of by everybody, but there must be some motive to induce people to take care of themselves; and that to be helped to help themselves, if they are physically capable of it, is the only charity which proves to be charity in the end.

These considerations show how usefully the part which women 12 take in the formation of general opinion, would be modified for the better by that more enlarged instruction, and practical conversancy with the things which their opinions influence, that would necessarily arise from their social and political emancipation. But the improvement it would work through the influence they exercise, each in her own family, would be still more remarkable.

It is often said that in the classes most exposed to temptation, a 13 man's wife and children tend to keep him honest and respectable, both by the wife's direct influence, and by the concern he feels for their future welfare. This may be so, and no doubt often is so, with those who are more weak than wicked; and this beneficial influence would be preserved and strengthened under equal laws; it does not depend on the woman's servitude, but is, on the contrary, diminished by the disrespect which the inferior class of men always at heart feel towards those who are subject to their power. But when we ascend higher in the scale, we come among a totally different set of moving forces. The wife's influence tends, as far as it goes, to prevent the husband from falling below the common standard of approbation of the country. It tends quite as strongly to hinder him from rising above it. The wife is the auxiliary of the common public opinion. A man who is married to a woman his inferior in intelligence, finds her a perpetual dead weight, or, worse than a dead weight, a drag, upon every aspiration of his to be better than public opinion requires him to be. It is hardly possible for one who is in these bonds, to attain exalted virtue. If he differs in his opinion from the mass—if he sees truths which have not yet dawned upon them, or if, feeling in his heart truths which they nominally recognize, he would like to act up to those truths more conscientiously than the generality of mankind—to all such thoughts and desires, marriage is the heaviest of drawbacks, unless he be so fortunate as to have a wife as much above the common level as he himself is.

For, in the first place, there is always some sacrifice of personal 14 interest required; either of social consequence, or of pecuniary means; perhaps the risk of even the means of subsistence. These sacrifices and risks he may be willing to encounter for himself; but he will pause before he imposes them on his family. And his family in this case means his wife and daughters; for he always hopes that his sons will feel as he feels himself, and that what he can do without, they will do without, willingly, in the same cause. But his daughters—their marriage may depend upon it: and his wife, who is unable to enter into or understand the objects for which these sacrifices are made—who, if she thought them worth any sacrifice, would think so on trust, and solely for his sake—who can participate in none of the enthusiasm or the self-approbation he himself may feel, while the things which he is disposed to sacrifice are all in all to her; will not the best and most unselfish man hesitate the longest before bringing on her this consequence? If it be not the comforts of life, but only social consideration, that is at stake, the burthen upon his conscience and feelings is still very severe. Whoever has a wife and children has given hostages to Mrs. Grundy.[7] The approbation of that potentate may be a matter of indifference to him, but it is of great importance to his wife. The man himself may be above opinion,

---

[7]**Mrs. Grundy** Character in an eighteenth-century play who became the stereotype for a prude.

or may find sufficient compensation in the opinion of those of his own way of thinking. But to the women connected with him, he can offer no compensation. The almost invariable tendency of the wife to place her influence in the same scale with social consideration, is sometimes made a reproach to women, and represented as a peculiar trait of feebleness and childishness of character in them: surely with great injustice. Society makes the whole life of a woman, in the easy classes, a continued self-sacrifice; it exacts from her an unremitting restraint of the whole of her natural inclinations, and the sole return it makes to her for what often deserves the name of a martyrdom, is consideration. Her consideration is inseparably connected with that of her husband, and after paying the full price for it, she finds that she is to lose it, for no reason of which she can feel the cogency. She has sacrificed her whole life to it, and her husband will not sacrifice to it a whim, a freak, an eccentricity; something not recognized or allowed for by the world, and which the world will agree with her in thinking a folly, if it thinks no worse! The dilemma is hardest upon that very meritorious class of men, who, without possessing talents which qualify them to make a figure among those with whom they agree in opinion, hold their opinion from conviction, and feel bound in honor and conscience to serve it, by making profession of their belief, and giving their time, labor, and means, to anything undertaken in its behalf. The worst case of all is when such men happen to be of a rank and position which of itself neither gives them, nor excludes them from, what is considered the best society; when their admission to it depends mainly on what is thought of them personally—and however unexceptionable their breeding and habits, their being identified with opinions and public conduct unacceptable to those who give the tone to society would operate as an effectual exclusion. Many a woman flatters herself (nine times out of ten quite erroneously) that nothing prevents her and her husband from moving in the highest society of her neighborhood—society in which others well known to her, and in the same class of life, mix freely—except that her husband is unfortunately a Dissenter, or has the reputation of mingling in low radical politics. That it is, she thinks, which hinders George from getting a commission or a place, Caroline from making an advantageous match, and prevents her and her husband from obtaining invitations, perhaps honors, which, for aught she sees, they are as well entitled to as some folks. With such an influence in every house, either exerted actively, or operating all the more powerfully for not being asserted, is it any wonder that people in general are kept down in that mediocrity of respectability which is becoming a marked characteristic of modern times?

There is another very injurious aspect in which the effect, not of women's disabilities directly, but of the broad line of difference which those disabilities create between the education and character of a woman 15 and that of a man, requires to be considered. Nothing can be more unfavorable to that union of thoughts and inclinations which is the ideal of married life. Intimate society between people radically dissimilar to one another, is an idle dream. Unlikeness may attract, but it is likeness which retains; and in proportion to the likeness is the suitability of the individuals to give each other a happy life. While women are so unlike men, it is not wonderful that selfish men should feel the need of arbitrary power in their own hands, to arrest *in limine*[8] the lifelong conflict of inclinations, by deciding every question on the side of their own preference. When people are extremely unlike, there can be no real identity of interest. Very often there is conscientious difference of opinion between married people, on the highest points of duty. Is there any reality in the marriage union where this takes place? Yet it is not uncommon anywhere, when the woman has any earnestness of character; and it is a very general case indeed in Catholic countries, when she is supported in her dissent by the only other authority to which she is taught to bow, the priest. With the usual barefacedness of power not accustomed to find itself disputed, the influence of priests over women is attacked by Protestant and Liberal writers, less for being bad in itself, than because it is a rival authority to the husband, and raises up a revolt against his infallibility. In England, similar differences occasionally exist when an Evangelical wife has allied herself with a husband of a different quality; but in general this source at least of dissension is got rid of, by reducing the minds of women to such a nullity, that they have no opinions but those of Mrs. Grundy, or those which the husband tells them to have. When there is no difference of opinion, differences merely of taste may be sufficient to detract greatly from the happiness of married life. And though it may stimulate the amatory propensities of men, it does not conduce to married happiness, to exaggerate by differences of education whatever may be the native differences of the sexes. If the married pair are well-bred and well-behaved people, they tolerate each other's tastes; but is mutual toleration what people look forward to, when they enter into marriage? These differences of inclination will naturally make their wishes different, if not restrained by affection or duty, as to almost all domestic questions which arise. What a difference there must be in the society which the two persons will wish to frequent, or be frequented by! Each will desire associates who share their own tastes: the persons agreeable to one, will be indifferent or positively disagreeable to the other; yet there can be none who are not common to both, for married people do not now live in different parts of the house and have totally different visiting lists, as in the reign of Louis XV.[9] They cannot help having different wishes as to the

---

[8] *in limine* Latin, "at the outset."
[9] **Louis XV (1710–1774)** King of France from 1715 until his death.

bringing up of the children: each will wish to see reproduced in them their own tastes and sentiments: and there is either a compromise, and only a half-satisfaction to either, or the wife has to yield—often with bitter suffering; and, with or without intention, her occult influence continues to counterwork the husband's purposes.

It would of course be extreme folly to suppose that these dif-   16
ferences of feeling and inclination only exist because women are brought up differently from men, and that there would not be differences of taste under any imaginable circumstances. But there is nothing beyond the mark in saying that the distinction in bringing-up immensely aggravates those differences, and renders them wholly inevitable. While women are brought up as they are, a man and a woman will but rarely find in one another real agreement of tastes and wishes as to daily life. They will generally have to give it up as hopeless, and renounce the attempt to have, in the intimate associate of their daily life, that *idem velle, idem nolle,*[10] which is the recognized bond of any society that is really such: or if the man succeeds in obtaining it, he does so by choosing a woman who is so complete a nullity that she has no *velle* or *nolle* at all, and is as ready to comply with one thing as another if anybody tells her to do so. Even this calculation is apt to fail; dullness and want of spirit are not always a guarantee of the submission which is so confidently expected from them. But if they were, is this the ideal of marriage? What, in this case, does the man obtain by it, except an upper servant, a nurse, or a mistress? On the contrary, when each of two persons, instead of being a nothing, is a something; when they are attached to one another, and are not too much unlike to begin with; the constant partaking in the same things, assisted by their sympathy, draws out the latent capacities of each for being interested in the things which were at first interesting only to the other; and works a gradual assimilation of the tastes and characters to one another, partly by the insensible modification of each, but more by a real enriching of the two natures, each acquiring the tastes and capacities of the other in addition to its own. This often happens between two friends of the same sex, who are much associated in their daily life: and it would be a common, if not the commonest, case in marriage, did not the totally different bringing-up of the two sexes make it next to an impossibility to form a really well-assorted union. Were this remedied, whatever differences there might still be in individual tastes, there would at least be, as a general rule, complete unity and unanimity as to the great objects of life. When the two persons both care for great objects, and are a help and encouragement to each other in whatever regards these, the minor matters on which their tastes may differ

---

[10] **idem velle, idem nolle** Latin for "same likes, same dislikes."

are not all-important to them; and there is a foundation for solid friendship, of an enduring character, more likely than anything else to make it, through the whole of life, a greater pleasure to each to give pleasure to the other, than to receive it.

QUESTIONS FOR CRITICAL READING

1. Has modern society put an end to the subjection of women?
2. Do young men today grow up with the sense of their "inherent superiority to a girl"?
3. Do you agree that the rightful claim to power and authority should be given to merit, not to birth? How does gender figure into that equation?
4. What is the best argument for freeing women to compete with men for important jobs?
5. How does Mill seem conscious of class differences between people?
6. How would women be changed by the proposals Mill makes here?
7. What was the chivalrous ideal? Is it still in effect in your society?
8. Are you sympathetic to Mill's position regarding charity in paragraph 11?

SUGGESTIONS FOR CRITICAL WRITING

1. Mill says, "The main foundations of the moral life of modern times must be justice and prudence . . ." (para. 9). What is the relation of the moral life of modern times to the argument in favor of releasing women from subjection? How much progress do you see in your immediate environment in relation to freeing women? How do women and men seem to differ today from the descriptions of them in Mill's essay of 1869?

2. Research the chivalrous ideal and comment on Mill's understanding of it. Do you agree that the chivalrous ideal "is the acme of the influence of women's sentiments on the moral cultivation of mankind" (para. 9)? Describe the positive and negative influences of that ideal, and then examine your own relationship with members of the opposite sex and determine whether or not that ideal is, however weakened, still in effect in modern times.

3. In paragraph 11, Mill says that women are not taught to be independent: "[s]he is not self-dependent; she is not taught self-dependence; her destiny is to receive everything from others. . . ." To what extent does that description still apply to women in our society or in other societies you know about? What are the impediments in modern life to women's development of self-dependence?

4. Examine the social implications of Mill's comments about an unequal marriage and its effect on a husband: "marriage is the heaviest of

drawbacks, unless he be so fortunate as to have a wife as much above the common level as he himself is" (para. 13). What is the "common level," and what does his concern for level imply about his perception of society itself? Given his description of conditions in the Victorian era, what were the chances of an equal marriage taking place? What might be the results of a seriously unequal marriage?

5. Mill declares in paragraph 15 that "[i]ntimate society between people radically dissimilar to one another, is an idle dream. Unlikeness may attract, but it is likeness which retains. . . ." How realistic is this view? Does it seem to hold in modern life as much as Mill felt it held in his time? Has society changed so much that his view is now no longer reasonable, or have things essentially remained the same in this regard?

6. If you disagree with Mill on the question of women's subjugation, write an essay arguing against his key positions. You'll notice that Mill does not use example to bolster his argument. He uses probability and likelihood: men with power will abuse it, he says. Take the key points of his argument and turn them back on him using reason, example, and testimony. Be sure to avoid reducing his arguments to absurdity before you address them. Try to be as concrete and effective in your argument as possible. Then, see how many people you can convince.

7. **CONNECTIONS** Mill talks about marriage and raises the question of power in a marriage. Karen Horney discusses distrust between men and women (**bedfordstmartins.com/worldofideas/epages**). What common ground do these authors have in talking about the ways that men and women interact both in and out of marriage? Would Mill have a point of view that might alarm Horney? Or would Mill's point of view tend to reinforce Horney's suspicions about distrust between the sexes?

8. **CONNECTIONS** Write an essay comparing Mill's position on charity and philanthropy with the views of Andrew Carnegie (p. 481). Which views seem stronger? Which seem most compelling to you? Once you have clarified those views, decide exactly how John Kenneth Galbraith (p. 499) would argue either for or against Mill's position on charity. Would he have found Mill or Carnegie sympathetic, or would he have proposed counterarguments to their positions?

9. **SEEING CONNECTIONS** Cassatt painted *In the Loge* (p. 650) less than ten years after Mill published *The Subjection of Women*. Imagine that Mill saw this painting in Cassatt's studio and offered his interpretation of the woman with the opera glasses to us in terms of her being in subjection or being free. What would he have said about this painting and the people who are represented in it? Would he have assumed that the woman was married or single or widowed? Would he have praised her for appearing at the theater alone, or would he have felt she was going beyond the bounds of polite society? What would he have said about her class and the class of people represented in the painting? How would that have affected his attitude toward the woman or toward Cassatt, who—like him—lived independently in France?

VIRGINIA WOOLF
Shakespeare's Sister

Virginia Woolf (1882–1941), one of the most gifted of the modernist writers, was a prolific essayist and novelist in what came to be known as the Bloomsbury group, named after a section of London near the British Museum. Most members of the group were writers, such as E. M. Forster, Lytton Strachey, and the critic Clive Bell, and some were artists, such as Duncan Grant and Virginia Woolf's sister, Vanessa Bell. The eminent economist John Maynard Keynes was part of the group as well, along with a variety of other accomplished intellectuals.

Virginia Woolf published some of the most important works of the early twentieth century, including the novels *Jacob's Room* (1922), *Mrs. Dalloway* (1925), *To the Lighthouse* (1927), *Orlando* (1928), and *The Waves* (1931). Among her many volumes of nonfiction prose is *A Room of One's Own* (1929). In this book Woolf speculates on what life would have been like for an imaginary gifted sister of William Shakespeare.

In discussing the imaginary Judith Shakespeare, Woolf examines the circumstances common to women's lives during the Renaissance. For example, women had little or no say in their future. Unlike their male counterparts, they were not educated in grammar schools and did not learn trades that would enable them to make a living for themselves. Instead, they were expected to marry as soon as possible, even as young as thirteen or fourteen years of age, and begin raising a family of their own. When they did marry, their husbands were men selected by their parents; the wives essentially became the property of those men. Under English law a married couple was regarded as one entity, and that entity was spoken for only by the man. Similarly, the women of the period had few civil rights.

From *A Room of One's Own*.

As Woolf points out, the history books do not mention women very often, and when they do, it is usually to relate that wife beating was common and generally approved of in all classes of society.

As Woolf comments on the opportunities that women were denied during the Renaissance, she agrees with an unnamed bishop who said that no woman could have written Shakespeare's plays. Woolf explains that no woman could have had enough contact with the theater in those days to be received with anything but disdain and discourtesy. Women could not even act on stage in Shakespeare's time, much less write for it.

It would be all but impossible in a society of this sort to imagine a woman as a successful literary figure, much less as a popular playwright. After all, society excluded women, marginalizing them as insignificant—at least in the eyes of historians. Certainly women were mothers; as such, they bore the male children who went on to become accomplished and famous. However, without a trade or an education, women in Shakespeare's time were all but chattel slaves in a household.

In this setting, Woolf places a brilliant girl named Judith Shakespeare, a fictional character who, in Woolf's imaginative construction, had the same literary fire as her famous brother. How would she have tried to express herself? How would she have followed her talent? Woolf suggests the results would have been depressing, and for good reason. No one would have listened to Judith; in all likelihood her life would have ended badly.

The women of Shakespeare's time mentioned in the history books are generally Elizabeths and Marys, queens and princesses whose power was inherent in their positions. Little is known, Woolf says, about the lives of ordinary middle-class women. In Woolf's time, historians were uninterested in such information. However, many recent books have included detailed research into the lives of people in the Elizabethan period. Studying journals, day-books (including budgets and planning), and family records, modern historians have found much more information than English historian George Trevelyan (to whom Woolf refers in her essay) drew on. In fact, it is now known that women's lives were more varied than even Woolf implies, but women still had precious few opportunities compared to men of the period.

Woolf's Rhetoric

This selection is the third chapter from *A Room of One's Own*; thus, it begins with a sentence that implies continuity with an earlier section. The context for the essay's opening is as follows: a male dinner guest has said something insulting to women at a dinner party, and Woolf wishes she could come back with some hard fact to contradict the insult. However, she has no hard fact, so her strategy is to construct a situation that is as plausible and as accurate as her knowledge of history permits. Lacking fact, the novelist Virginia Woolf relies on imagination.

As it turned out, Woolf's portrait of Judith Shakespeare is so vivid that many readers actually believed William Shakespeare had such a sister. Judith Shakespeare did not exist, however. Her fictional character enables Woolf to speculate on how the life of any talented woman would have developed given the circumstances and limitations imposed on all women at the time. In the process, Woolf tries to reconstruct the world of Elizabethan England and place Judith in it.

Woolf goes about this act of imagination with extraordinary deliberateness. Her tone is cool and detached, almost as if she were a historian herself. She rarely reveals contempt for the opinions of men who are dismissive of women, such as the unnamed bishop. Yet, we catch an edgy tone when she discusses his views on women in literature. On the other hand, when she turns to Mr. Oscar Browning, a professor who believed the best women in Oxford were inferior to the worst men, we see another side of Woolf. She reveals that after making his high-minded pronouncements, Mr. Browning returned to his quarters for an assignation with an illiterate stable boy. This detail is meant to reveal the true intellectual level of Mr. Browning, as well as his attitude toward women.

Woolf makes careful use of simile in such statements as "for fiction, imaginative work that is, is not dropped like a pebble upon the ground, as science may be; fiction is like a spider's web, attached ever so lightly perhaps, but still attached to life at all four corners" (para. 2). Later, she shows a highly efficient use of language: "to write a work of genius is almost always a feat of prodigious difficulty. . . . Dogs will bark; people will interrupt; money must be made; health will break down" (para. 11). For a woman—who would not even have had a room of her own in an Elizabethan household—the impediments to creating "a work of genius" were insurmountable.

One reason for Woolf's controlled and cool tone is that she wrote with the knowledge that most men were very conservative. In 1929, people would not read what she wrote if she became enraged on paper. They would turn the page and ignore her argument. Thus, her tone seems inviting and cautious, almost as if Woolf is portraying herself as conservative on women's issues and in agreement with men like the historian Trevelyan and the unnamed bishop. However, nothing could be further from the truth. Woolf's anger may seethe and rage beneath the surface, but she keeps the surface smooth enough for those who disagree with her to be lured on to read.

One of the interesting details of Woolf's style is her allusiveness. She alludes to the work of many writers—male writers such as John Keats; Alfred, Lord Tennyson; and Robert Burns; and women writers such as Jane Austen, Emily Brontë, and George Eliot. Woolf's range of reference is that of the highly literary person—which she was; yet the way in which she makes reference to other important writers is designed not to offend the reader. If the reader knows the references, then Woolf will communicate on a special shared level of understanding. If the reader does not know the references, there is nothing in Woolf's manner that makes it difficult for the reader to continue and understand her main points.

Woolf's rhetoric in this piece is singularly polite. She makes her points without rancor and alarm. They are detailed, specific, and in many ways irrefutable. What she feels she has done is nothing less than tell the truth.

PREREADING QUESTIONS:
WHAT TO READ FOR

The following prereading questions may help you anticipate key issues in the discussion of Virginia Woolf's "Shakespeare's Sister." Keeping them in mind during your first reading of the selection should help focus your attention.

- What was the expected role of women in Shakespeare's time?
- By what means could Shakespeare's imaginary sister have become a dramatist?

Shakespeare's Sister

It was disappointing not to have brought back in the evening some important statement, some authentic fact. Women are poorer than men because—this or that. Perhaps now it would be better to give up seeking for the truth, and receiving on one's head an avalanche of opinion hot as lava, discolored as dish-water. It would be better to draw the curtains; to shut out distractions; to light the lamp; to narrow the enquiry and to ask the historian, who records not opinions but facts, to describe under what conditions women lived, not throughout the ages, but in England, say in the time of Elizabeth.

For it is a perennial puzzle why no woman wrote a word of that extraordinary literature when every other man, it seemed, was capable of song or sonnet. What were the conditions in which women lived, I asked myself; for fiction, imaginative work that is, is not dropped like a pebble upon the ground, as science may be; fiction is like a spider's web, attached ever so lightly perhaps, but still attached to life at all four corners. Often the attachment is scarcely perceptible; Shakespeare's plays, for instance, seem to hang there complete by themselves. But when the web is pulled askew, hooked up at the edge, torn in the middle, one remembers that these webs are not spun in midair by incorporeal creatures, but are the work of suffering human beings, and are attached to grossly material things, like health and money and the houses we live in.

2

I went, therefore, to the shelf where the histories stand and took down one of the latest, Professor Trevelyan's[1] *History of England.* Once more I looked up Women, found "position of," and turned to the pages indicated. "Wife-beating," I read, "was a recognized right of man, and was practiced without shame by high as well as low. . . . Similarly," the historian goes on, "the daughter who refused to marry the gentleman of her parents' choice was liable to be locked up, beaten, and flung about the room, without any shock being inflicted on public opinion. Marriage was not an affair of personal affection, but of family avarice, particularly in the 'chivalrous' upper classes. . . . Betrothal often took place while one or both of the parties was in the cradle, and marriage when they were scarcely out of the nurses' charge." That was about 1470, soon after Chaucer's time. The next reference to the position of women is some two hundred years later, in the time of the Stuarts. "It was still the exception for women of the upper and middle class to choose their own husbands, and when the husband had been assigned, he was lord and master, so far at least as law and custom could make him. Yet even so," Professor Trevelyan concludes, "neither Shakespeare's women nor those of authentic seventeenth-century memoirs, like the Verneys and the Hutchinsons, seem wanting in personality and character." Certainly, if we consider it, Cleopatra must have had a way with her; Lady Macbeth, one would suppose, had a will of her own; Rosalind, one might conclude, was an attractive girl. Professor Trevelyan is speaking no more than the truth when he remarks that Shakespeare's women do not seem wanting in personality

3

---

[1] **Trevelyan: George Macaulay (1876–1962)** One of England's great historians. [Woolf's note]

and character. Not being a historian, one might go even further and say that women have burnt like beacons in all the works of all the poets from the beginning of time—Clytemnestra, Antigone, Cleopatra, Lady Macbeth, Phèdre, Cressida, Rosalind, Desdemona, the Duchess of Malfi, among the dramatists; then among the prose writers: Millamant, Clarissa, Becky Sharp, Anna Karenina, Emma Bovary, Madame de Guermantes—the names flock to mind, nor do they recall women "lacking in personality and character." Indeed, if woman had no existence save in the fiction written by men, one would imagine her a person of the utmost importance; very various; heroic and mean; splendid and sordid; infinitely beautiful and hideous in the extreme; as great as a man, some think even greater.[2] But this is woman in fiction. In fact, as Professor Trevelyan points out, she was locked up, beaten, and flung about the room.

A very queer, composite being thus emerges. Imaginatively she is   4
of the highest importance; practically she is completely insignificant. She pervades poetry from cover to cover; she is all but absent from history. She dominates the lives of kings and conquerors in fiction; in fact she was the slave of any boy whose parents forced a ring upon her finger. Some of the most inspired words, some of the most profound thoughts in literature fall from her lips; in real life she could hardly read, could scarcely spell, and was the property of her husband.

It was certainly an odd monster that one made up by reading the   5
historians first and the poets afterwards—a worm winged like an eagle; the spirit of life and beauty in a kitchen chopping up suet. But these monsters, however amusing to the imagination, have no existence in fact. What one must do to bring her to life was to think poetically and prosaically at one and the same moment, thus keeping in touch with fact—that she is Mrs. Martin, aged thirty-six, dressed in blue, wearing a black hat and brown shoes; but not losing sight of fiction either—that

---

[2] **even greater** "It remains a strange and almost inexplicable fact that in Athena's city, where women were kept in almost Oriental suppression as odalisques or drudges, the stage should yet have produced figures like Clytemnestra and Cassandra, Atossa and Antigone, Phèdre and Medea, and all the other heroines who dominate play after play of the 'misogynist' Euripides. But the paradox of this world where in real life a respectable woman could hardly show her face alone in the street, and yet on the stage a woman equals or surpasses a man, has never been satisfactorily explained. In modern tragedy the same predominance exists. At all events, a very cursory survey of Shakespeare's work (similarly with Webster, though not with Marlowe or Jonson) suffices to reveal how this dominance, this initiative of women, persists from Rosalind to Lady Macbeth. So too in Racine; six of his tragedies bear their heroines' names; and what male characters of his shall we set against Hermione and Andromaque, Bérénice and Roxane, Phèdre and Athalie? So again with Ibsen; what men shall we match with Solveig and Nora, Hedda and Hilda Wangel and Rebecca West?"—F. L. Lucas, *Tragedy*, pp. 114–15. [Woolf's note]

she is a vessel in which all sorts of spirits and forces are coursing and flashing perpetually. The moment, however, that one tries this method with the Elizabethan woman, one branch of illumination fails; one is held up by the scarcity of facts. One knows nothing detailed, nothing perfectly true and substantial about her. History scarcely mentions her. And I turned to Professor Trevelyan again to see what history meant to him. I found by looking at his chapter headings that it meant—

"The Manor Court and the Methods of Open-field Agriculture . . .   6
The Cistercians and Sheep-farming . . . The Crusades . . . The University . . . The House of Commons . . . The Hundred Years' War . . . The Wars of the Roses . . . The Renaissance Scholars . . . The Dissolution of the Monasteries . . . Agrarian and Religious Strife . . . The Origin of English Sea-power . . . The Armada . . ." and so on. Occasionally an individual woman is mentioned, an Elizabeth, or a Mary; a queen or a great lady. But by no possible means could middle-class women with nothing but brains and character at their command have taken part in any one of the great movements which, brought together, constitute the historian's view of the past. Nor shall we find her in any collection of anecdotes. Aubrey[3] hardly mentions her. She never writes her own life and scarcely keeps a diary; there are only a handful of her letters in existence. She left no plays or poems by which we can judge her. What one wants, I thought—and why does not some brilliant student at Newnham or Girton[4] supply it?—is a mass of information; at what age did she marry; how many children had she as a rule; what was her house like; had she a room to herself; did she do the cooking; would she be likely to have a servant? All these facts lie somewhere, presumably, in parish registers and account books; the life of the average Elizabethan woman must be scattered about somewhere, could one collect it and make a book of it. It would be ambitious beyond my daring, I thought, looking about the shelves for books that were not there, to suggest to the students of those famous colleges that they should rewrite history, though I own that it often seems a little queer as it is, unreal, lopsided; but why should they not add a supplement to history? calling it, of course, by some inconspicuous name so that women might figure there without impropriety? For one often catches a glimpse of them in the lives of the great, whisking away into the background, concealing, I sometimes think, a wink, a laugh, perhaps

---

[3]**John Aubrey (1626–1697)** English antiquarian noted for his *Brief Lives,* biographical sketches of famous men.

[4]**Newnham or Girton** Two women's colleges founded at Cambridge in the 1870s. [Woolf's note] Newnham (1871) and Girton (1869) were the first women's colleges at Cambridge University.

a tear. And, after all, we have lives enough of Jane Austen; it scarcely seems necessary to consider again the influence of the tragedies of Joanna Baillie upon the poetry of Edgar Allan Poe; as for myself, I should not mind if the homes and haunts of Mary Russell Mitford were closed to the public for a century at least. But what I find deplorable, I continued, looking about the bookshelves again, is that nothing is known about women before the eighteenth century. I have no model in my mind to turn about this way and that. Here am I asking why women did not write poetry in the Elizabethan age, and I am not sure how they were educated; whether they were taught to write; whether they had sitting-rooms to themselves; how many women had children before they were twenty-one; what, in short, they did from eight in the morning till eight at night. They had no money evidently; according to Professor Trevelyan they were married whether they liked it or not before they were out of the nursery, at fifteen or sixteen very likely. It would have been extremely odd, even upon this showing, had one of them suddenly written the plays of Shakespeare, I concluded, and I thought of that old gentleman, who is dead now, but was a bishop, I think, who declared that it was impossible for any woman, past, present, or to come, to have the genius of Shakespeare. He wrote to the papers about it. He also told a lady who applied to him for information that cats do not as a matter of fact go to heaven, though they have, he added, souls of a sort. How much thinking those old gentlemen used to save one! How the borders of ignorance shrank back at their approach! Cats do not go to heaven. Women cannot write the plays of Shakespeare.

Be that as it may, I could not help thinking, as I looked at the works of Shakespeare on the shelf, that the bishop was right at least in this; it would have been impossible, completely and entirely, for any woman to have written the plays of Shakespeare in the age of Shake- speare. Let me imagine, since facts are so hard to come by, what would have happened had Shakespeare had a wonderfully gifted sister, called Judith, let us say. Shakespeare himself went, very probably—his mother was an heiress—to the grammar school, where he may have learnt Latin—Ovid, Virgil, and Horace—and the elements of gram- mar and logic. He was, it is well known, a wild boy who poached rab- bits, perhaps shot a deer, and had, rather sooner than he should have done, to marry a woman in the neighborhood, who bore him a child rather quicker than was right. That escapade sent him to seek his for- tune in London. He had, it seemed, a taste for the theatre; he began by holding horses at the stage door. Very soon he got work in the theatre, became a successful actor, and lived at the hub of the universe, meet- ing everybody, knowing everybody, practicing his art on the boards, exercising his wits in the streets, and even getting access to the palace of the queen. Meanwhile his extraordinarily gifted sister, let us suppose, remained at home. She was as adventurous, as imaginative, as agog to see the world as he was. But she was not sent to school. She had no chance of learning grammar and logic, let alone of reading Horace and Virgil. She picked up a book now and then, one of her brother's perhaps, and read a few pages. But then her parents came in and told her to mend the stockings or mind the stew and not moon about with books and papers. They would have spoken sharply but kindly, for they were substantial people who knew the conditions of life for a woman and loved their daughter—indeed, more likely than not she was the apple of her father's eye. Perhaps she scribbled some pages up in an apple loft on the sly, but was careful to hide them or set fire to them. Soon, however, before she was out of her teens, she was to be betrothed to the son of a neighboring wool-stapler. She cried out that marriage was hateful to her, and for that she was severely beaten by her father. Then he ceased to scold her. He begged her instead not to hurt him, not to shame him in this matter of her marriage. He would give her a chain of beads or a fine petticoat, he said; and there were tears in his eyes. How could she disobey him? How could she break his heart? The force of her own gift alone drove her to it. She made up a small parcel of her belongings, let herself down by a rope one summer's night and took the road to London. She was not seventeen. The birds that sang in the hedge were not more musical than she was. She had the quickest fancy, a gift like her brother's, for the tune of words. Like him, she had a taste for the theatre. She stood at the stage door; she wanted to act, she said. Men laughed in her face. The manager—a fat, loose-lipped man—guffawed. He bellowed something about poodles dancing and women acting—no woman, he said, could possibly be an actress. He hinted—you can imagine what. She could get no training in her craft. Could she even seek her dinner in a tavern or roam the streets at midnight? Yet her genius was for fiction and lusted to feed abundantly upon the lives of men and women and the study of their ways. At last—for she was very young, oddly like Shakespeare the poet in her face, with the same grey eyes and rounded brows—at last Nick Greene, the actor-manager took pity on her; she found herself with child by that gentleman and so—who shall measure the heat and violence of the poet's heart when caught and tangled in a woman's body?—killed herself one winter's night and lies buried at some cross-roads where the omnibuses now stop outside the Elephant and Castle.[5]

That, more or less, is how the story would run, I think, if a woman in Shakespeare's day had had Shakespeare's genius. But for my 8

---

[5] **Elephant and Castle** A bus stop in London. The name came from a local pub.

part, I agree with the deceased bishop, if such he was—it is unthinkable that any woman in Shakespeare's day should have had Shakespeare's genius. For genius like Shakespeare's is not born among laboring, uneducated, servile people. It was not born in England among the Saxons and the Britons. It is not born today among the working classes. How, then, could it have been born among women whose work began, according to Professor Trevelyan, almost before they were out of the nursery, who were forced to it by their parents and held to it by all the power of law and custom? Yet genius of a sort must have existed among women as it must have existed among the working classes. Now and again an Emily Brontë or a Robert Burns[6] blazes out and proves its presence. But certainly it never got itself on to paper. When, however, one reads of a witch being ducked, of a woman possessed by devils, of a wise woman selling herbs, or even of a very remarkable man who had a mother, then, I think we are on the track of a lost novelist, a suppressed poet, of some mute and inglorious Jane Austen, some Emily Brontë who dashed her brains out on the moor or mopped and mowed about the highways crazed with the torture that her gift had put her to. Indeed, I would venture to guess that Anon, who wrote so many poems without signing them, was often a woman. It was a woman Edward Fitzgerald,[7] I think, suggested who made the ballads and the folk-songs, crooning them to her children, beguiling her spinning with them, or the length of the winter's night.

This may be true or it may be false—who can say?—but what is true in it, so it seemed to me, reviewing the story of Shakespeare's sister as I had made it, is that any woman born with a great gift in the sixteenth century would certainly have gone crazed, shot herself, or ended her days in some lonely cottage outside the village, half witch, half wizard, feared and mocked at. For it needs little skill in psychology to be sure that a highly gifted girl who had tried to use her gift for poetry would have been so thwarted and hindered by other people, so tortured and pulled asunder by her own contrary instincts, that she must have lost her health and sanity to a certainty. No girl could have walked to London and stood at a stage door and forced her way into the presence of actor-managers without doing herself a violence and suffering an anguish which may have been irrational—for chastity may be a fetish invented by certain societies for unknown reasons—but were none the less inevitable. Chastity had then, it has even now,

9

[6] **Emily Brontë (1818–1848)** wrote *Wuthering Heights;* **Robert Burns (1759–1796)** was a Scots poet; **Jane Austen (1775–1817)** wrote *Pride and Prejudice* and many other novels. All three wrote against very great odds.
[7] **Edward Fitzgerald (1809–1883)** British scholar, poet, and translator who wrote *The Rubaiyat of Omar Khayyam.*

a religious importance in a woman's life, and has so wrapped itself round with nerves and instincts that to cut it free and bring it to the light of day demands courage of the rarest. To have lived a free life in London in the sixteenth century would have meant for a woman who was poet and playwright a nervous stress and dilemma which might well have killed her. Had she survived, whatever she had written would have been twisted and deformed, issuing from a strained and morbid imagination. And undoubtedly, I thought, looking at the shelf where there are no plays by women, her work would have gone unsigned. That refuge she would have sought certainly. It was the relic of the sense of chastity that dictated anonymity to women even so late as the nineteenth century. Currer Bell, George Eliot, George Sand,[8] all the victims of inner strife as their writings prove, sought ineffectively to veil themselves by using the name of a man. Thus they did homage to the convention, which if not implanted by the other sex was liberally encouraged by them (the chief glory of a woman is not to be talked of, said Pericles, himself a much-talked-of man), that publicity in women is detestable. Anonymity runs in their blood. The desire to be veiled still possesses them. They are not even now as concerned about the health of their fame as men are, and, speaking generally, will pass a tombstone or a signpost without feeling an irresistible desire to cut their names on it, as Alf, Bert, or Chas. must do in obedience to their instinct, which murmurs if it sees a fine woman go by, or even a dog, *Ce chien est à moi.*[9] And, of course, it may not be a dog, I thought, remembering Parliament Square, the Sieges Allee and other avenues; it may be a piece of land or a man with curly black hair. It is one of the great advantages of being a woman that one can pass even a very fine negress without wishing to make an Englishwoman of her.

That woman, then, who was born with a gift of poetry in the six-   10 teenth century, was an unhappy woman, a woman at strife against herself. All the conditions of her life, all her own instincts, were hostile to the state of mind which is needed to set free whatever is in the brain. But what is the state of mind that is most propitious to the act of creation, I asked. Can one come by any notion of the state that furthers and makes possible that strange activity? Here I opened the volume containing the Tragedies of Shakespeare. What was Shakespeare's state of mind, for instance, when he wrote *Lear* and *Antony and Cleopatra*? It was certainly the state of mind most favorable to poetry that there has ever existed. But Shakespeare himself said nothing about it. We only know

---

[8] **Currer Bell (1816–1855), George Eliot (1819–1880), and George Sand (1804–1876)** Masculine pen names for Charlotte Brontë, Mary Ann Evans, and Amandine-Aurore-Lucille Dudevant, three major novelists of the nineteenth century.

[9] **Ce chien est à moi** That's my dog.

casually and by chance that he "never blotted a line." Nothing indeed
was ever said by the artist himself about his state of mind until the
eighteenth century perhaps. Rousseau perhaps began it. At any rate,
by the nineteenth century self-consciousness had developed so far that
it was the habit for men of letters to describe their minds in confessions and autobiographies. Their lives also were written, and their
letters were printed after their deaths. Thus, though we do not know
what Shakespeare went through when he wrote *Lear,* we do know
what Carlyle went through when he wrote the *French Revolution;* what
Flaubert went through when he wrote *Madame Bovary;* what Keats[10]
was going through when he tried to write poetry against the coming of
death and the indifference of the world.

     And one gathers from this enormous modern literature of confes-   11
sion and self-analysis that to write a work of genius is almost always
a feat of prodigious difficulty. Everything is against the likelihood that
it will come from the writer's mind whole and entire. Generally material circumstances are against it. Dogs will bark; people will interrupt;
money must be made; health will break down. Further, accentuating all
these difficulties and making them harder to bear is the world's notorious indifference. It does not ask people to write poems and novels
and histories; it does not need them. It does not care whether Flaubert
finds the right word or whether Carlyle scrupulously verifies this or
that fact. Naturally, it will not pay for what it does not want. And
so the writer, Keats, Flaubert, Carlyle, suffers, especially in the creative years of youth, every form of distraction and discouragement. A
curse, a cry of agony, rises from those books of analysis and confession. "Mighty poets in their misery dead" — that is the burden of their
song. If anything comes through in spite of all this, it is a miracle, and
probably no book is born entire and uncrippled as it was conceived.

     But for women, I thought, looking at the empty shelves, these dif-   12
ficulties were infinitely more formidable. In the first place, to have a
room of her own, let alone a quiet room or a sound-proof room, was
out of the question, unless her parents were exceptionally rich or very
noble, even up to the beginning of the nineteenth century. Since her
pin money, which depended on the goodwill of her father, was only
enough to keep her clothed, she was debarred from such alleviations
as came even to Keats or Tennyson or Carlyle, all poor men, from
a walking tour, a little journey to France, from the separate lodging
which, even if it were miserable enough, sheltered them from the
claims and tyrannies of their families. Such material difficulties were

---

[10] **Thomas Carlyle (1795–1881), Gustave Flaubert (1821–1880),** and **John
Keats (1795–1821)** Important nineteenth-century writers, all men.

formidable; but much worse were the immaterial. The indifference of the world which Keats and Flaubert and other men of genius have found so hard to bear was in her case not indifference but hostility. The world did not say to her as it said to them, Write if you choose; it makes no difference to me. The world said with a guffaw, Write? What's the good of your writing? Here the psychologists of Newnham and Girton might come to our help, I thought, looking again at the blank spaces on the shelves. For surely it is time that the effect of discouragement upon the mind of the artist should be measured, as I have seen a dairy company measure the effect of ordinary milk and Grade A milk upon the body of the rat. They set two rats in cages side by side, and of the two one was furtive, timid, and small, and the other was glossy, bold, and big. Now what food do we feed women as artists upon? I asked, remembering, I suppose, that dinner of prunes and custard. To answer that question I had only to open the evening paper and to read that Lord Birkenhead is of opinion—but really I am not going to trouble to copy our Lord Birkenhead's opinion upon the writing of women. What Dean Inge says I will leave in peace. The Harley Street specialist may be allowed to rouse the echoes of Harley Street with his vociferations without raising a hair on my head. I will quote, however, Mr. Oscar Browning, because Mr. Oscar Browning was a great figure in Cambridge at one time, and used to examine the students at Girton and Newnham. Mr. Oscar Browning was wont to declare "that the impression left on his mind, after looking over any set of examination papers, was that, irrespective of the marks he might give, the best woman was intellectually the inferior of the worst man." After saying that Mr. Browning went back to his rooms—and it is this sequel that endears him and makes him a human figure of some bulk and majesty—he went back to his rooms and found a stable-boy lying on the sofa—"a mere skeleton, his cheeks were cavernous and sallow, his teeth were black, and he did not appear to have the full use of his limbs. . . . 'That's Arthur' [said Mr. Browning]. 'He's a dear boy really and most high-minded.'" The two pictures always seem to me to complete each other. And happily in this age of biography the two pictures often do complete each other, so that we are able to interpret the opinions of great men not only by what they say, but by what they do.

But though this is possible now, such opinions coming from the   13
lips of important people must have been formidable enough even fifty years ago. Let us suppose that a father from the highest motives did not wish his daughter to leave home and become writer, painter, or scholar. "See what Mr. Oscar Browning says," he would say; and there was not only Mr. Oscar Browning; there was the *Saturday Review;* there was Mr. Greg—the "essentials of a woman's being," said Mr. Greg emphatically, "are that *they are supported by, and they minister*

to, men"—there was an enormous body of masculine opinion to the effect that nothing could be expected of women intellectually. Even if her father did not read out loud these opinions, any girl could read them for herself; and the reading, even in the nineteenth century, must have lowered her vitality, and told profoundly upon her work. There would always have been that assertion—you cannot do this, you are incapable of doing that—to protest against, to overcome. Probably for a novelist this germ is no longer of much effect; for there have been women novelists of merit. But for painters it must still have some sting in it; and for musicians, I imagine, is even now active and poisonous in the extreme. The woman composer stands where the actress stood in the time of Shakespeare. Nick Greene, I thought, remembering the story I had made about Shakespeare's sister, said that a woman acting put him in mind of a dog dancing. Johnson repeated the phrase two hundred years later of women preaching. And here, I said, opening a book about music, we have the very words used again in this year of grace, 1928, of women who try to write music. "Of Mlle. Germaine Tailleferre one can only repeat Dr. Johnson's dictum concerning a woman preacher, transposed into terms of music. 'Sir, a woman's composing is like a dog's walking on his hind legs. It is not done well, but you are surprised to find it done at all.'"[11] So accurately does history repeat itself.

Thus, I concluded, shutting Mr. Oscar Browning's life and push-   14
ing away the rest, it is fairly evident that even in the nineteenth century a woman was not encouraged to be an artist. On the contrary, she was snubbed, slapped, lectured, and exhorted. Her mind must have been strained and her vitality lowered by the need of opposing this, of disproving that. For here again we come within range of that very interesting and obscure masculine complex which has had so much influence upon the woman's movement; that deep-seated desire, not so much that *she* shall be inferior as that *he* shall be superior, which plants him wherever one looks, not only in front of the arts, but barring the way to politics too, even when the risk to himself seems infinitesimal and the suppliant humble and devoted. Even Lady Bessborough, I remembered, with all her passion for politics, must humbly bow herself and write to Lord Granville Leveson-Gower: ". . . notwithstanding all my violence in politics and talking so much on that subject, I perfectly agree with you that no woman has any business to meddle with that or any other serious business, farther than giving her opinion (if she is ask'd)." And so she goes on to spend her enthusiasm where it meets with no obstacle whatsoever upon that immensely important subject, Lord Granville's maiden speech in the House of Commons. The spectacle

---

[11] *A Survey of Contemporary Music*, Cecil Gray, p. 246. [Woolf's note]

is certainly a strange one, I thought. The history of men's opposition to women's emancipation is more interesting perhaps than the story of that emancipation itself. An amusing book might be made of it if some young student at Girton or Newnham would collect examples and deduce a theory—but she would need thick gloves on her hands, and bars to protect her of solid gold.

But what is amusing now, I recollected, shutting Lady Bessborough, had to be taken in desperate earnest once. Opinions that one now pastes in a book labelled cock-a-doodle-dum and keeps for reading to select audiences on summer nights once drew tears, I can assure you. Among your grandmothers and great-grandmothers there were many that wept their eyes out. Florence Nightingale shrieked aloud in her agony.[12] Moreover, it is all very well for you, who have got yourselves to college and enjoy sitting-rooms—or is it only bed-sitting-rooms?—of your own to say that genius should disregard such opinions; that genius should be above caring what is said of it. Unfortunately, it is precisely the men or women of genius who mind most what is said of them. Remember Keats. Remember the words he had cut on his tombstone.[13] Think of Tennyson; think—but I need hardly multiply instances of the undeniable, if very unfortunate, fact that it is the nature of the artist to mind excessively what is said about him. Literature is strewn with the wreckage of men who have minded beyond reason the opinions of others.

And this susceptibility of theirs is doubly unfortunate, I thought, returning again to my original enquiry into what state of mind is most propitious for creative work, because the mind of an artist, in order to achieve the prodigious effort of freeing whole and entire the work that is in him, must be incandescent, like Shakespeare's mind, I conjectured, looking at the book which lay open at *Antony and Cleopatra*. There must be no obstacle in it, no foreign matter unconsumed.

For though we say that we know nothing about Shakespeare's state of mind, even as we say that, we are saying something about Shakespeare's state of mind. The reason perhaps why we know so little of Shakespeare—compared with Donne or Ben Jonson or Milton[14]—is that his grudges and spites and antipathies are hidden from us. We are not held up by some "revelation" which reminds us of the writer. All desire to protest, to preach, to proclaim an injury, to pay off a score, to make the world the witness of some hardship or

15

16

17

---

[12] *See Cassandra* by Florence Nightingale, printed in *The Cause*, by R. Strachey. [Woolf's note]

[13] **words . . . tombstone** "Here lies one whose name is writ on water." [Woolf's note]

[14] **John Donne (1572–1631), Ben Jonson (1572/3–1637), John Milton (1608–1674)** Three of the most important seventeenth-century poets.

grievance was fired out of him and consumed. Therefore his poetry flows from him free and unimpeded. If ever a human being got his work expressed completely, it was Shakespeare. If ever a mind was incandescent, unimpeded, I thought, turning again to the bookcase, it was Shakespeare's mind.

QUESTIONS FOR CRITICAL READING

1. How did Elizabethan gender roles limit opportunities for women in the literary arts?

2. Why does Woolf begin by referring to an eminent historian?

3. Why does history treat sixteenth- and seventeenth-century women with so little notice?

4. What is Woolf's point regarding the behavior of Oscar Browning?

5. Why does Woolf worry over the relation of opinions to facts?

6. What is the difference between the way women are represented in history and the way they are depicted in fiction?

7. Why does Woolf have Judith Shakespeare become pregnant?

SUGGESTIONS FOR CRITICAL WRITING

1. Woolf says that a woman "born with a gift of poetry in the sixteenth century, was an unhappy woman, a woman at strife against herself" (para. 10). What does it mean for a woman to be "at strife against herself"? What are the characteristics of such a strife, and what are its implications for the woman? In what ways would she be aware of such inner strife?

2. Look up brief biographies of the women writers who took men's names. Woolf lists three together: Currer Bell, George Eliot, and George Sand. What did they have in common? Why did they feel the need to use a man's name for their pseudonym? What did they do to avoid being stigmatized as women writers? Were they equally successful? Are they now considered feminist writers?

3. Woolf's view is that biology determines one's fate. She is explicitly speaking of the biology of the female in our culture, but how much do you feel she attends to the entire range of gender? Margaret Mead (p. 707) talks about gender deviance and its effect on the individual in a standardized society. Woolf's society was standardized, but she belonged to a subculture of intellectuals, the Bloomsbury group, that practiced many forms of deviant gender behavior. Would she have argued as strongly in support of deviant sexual behavior as she does for equal opportunities for Shakespeare's "sister"? What would her argument be? Present your case, using some of Woolf's rhetorical techniques.

4. Read the book from which this essay comes, *A Room of One's Own*. The last chapter discusses androgyny, the quality of possessing characteristics of both sexes. Woolf argues that perhaps a writer should not be exclusively male or female in outlook, but should combine both. How effective is her argument in that chapter? How much of an impact did the book have on your own views of feminism?

5. Explain why it is so important for a woman to have "a room of one's own." Obviously, the use of the word *room* stands for much more than a simple room with four walls and a door. What is implied in the way Woolf uses this term? Do you think this point is still valid for women in the twenty-first century? Why are so many women in any age denied the right to have "a room of one's own"?

6. Woolf says that "even in the nineteenth century a woman was not encouraged to be an artist. On the contrary, she was snubbed, slapped, lectured, and exhorted. Her mind must have been strained and her vitality lowered by the need of opposing this, of disproving that" (para. 14). Explain the implications of this statement, and decide whether it still describes the situation of many or most women. Use your personal experience where relevant, but consider the situations of any women you find interesting.

7. **CONNECTIONS**   Karen Horney (**bedfordstmartins.com/worldofideas /epages**) and Woolf both take analytical approaches to their subject matter, despite the fact that Horney is a psychologist and Woolf is a literary figure. What methods of analysis does Woolf use that are also characteristic of Horney? Does Horney's psychological approach to analyzing the relationship between men and women match Woolf's? How does each author make use of narrative techniques in her analytic approach?

8. **CONNECTIONS**   In what ways are Mary Wollstonecraft (p. 653) and Woolf in agreement about the waste of women's talents in any age? As you comment on this, consider, too, the ways in which these writers differ in their approach to discussing women and the ways in which women sometimes cooperate in accepting their own restrictions. Which of these writers is more obviously a modern feminist in your mind? Which of them is more convincing? Why?

9. **CONNECTIONS**   Based on Woolf's attitudes in this essay, which of the male writers in this collection comes closest to supporting feminist views? Consider especially the work of Karl Marx, Martin Luther King Jr., and Henry David Thoreau. Which of their views seems most sympathetic to the problems Woolf considers here?

10. **SEEING CONNECTIONS**   Woolf says that women artists were snubbed and ignored even in the nineteenth century. How would Woolf react to seeing Cassatt's *In the Loge* (p. 650) and learning that she was accepted by an important group of mostly male painters? Do some research on Cassatt, especially on her progress as a painter and her success in selling her work. Does Woolf's generalization hold true for Cassatt? Would Woolf have felt that the woman portrayed in Cassatt's painting was "in strife with herself" as a nineteenth-century woman?

MARGARET MEAD
Sex and Temperament

MARGARET MEAD (1901–1978) received her Ph.D. in anthropology from Columbia University in 1929. She is renowned for her extensive fieldwork in the South Pacific, especially for her work on Manus, one of the Admiralty Islands, northwest of New Guinea. The fieldwork that she did in 1925 led to her doctoral dissertation and to the book that established her as one of the most visible and readable modern anthropologists, *Coming of Age in Samoa: A Psychological Study of Primitive Youth for Western Civilization* (1928). She learned seven indigenous languages and always used them with the people she studied and lived with so that she could think in their vernacular. Her experiences with the Manus spanned twenty-five years, some of which included a disastrous world war. She first lived with them in 1928, when she began the work that led her to write *Growing Up in New Guinea: A Comparative Study of Primitive Education* (1930).

Mead was married three times, as she tells us in her autobiography, *Blackberry Winter* (1972), which focuses on her early years. All three of her husbands were also anthropologists. With Gregory Bateson, to whom she was married from 1936 to 1950, she had her only child, a daughter. Later, Mead was romantically involved with yet another anthropologist, Rhoda Metraux, with whom she lived from 1955 until her death. She taught as an adjunct professor at Columbia University from 1954 to 1978 and took two years off to found the anthropology department at Fordham University in Lincoln Center, New York. Throughout these years, she was also involved with work in museums, particularly the American Museum of Natural History.

Her primary research interests were the patterns of education of the young and the patterns of socialization of women and women's sexuality, particularly early sexual development. Mead asserted that

From *Sex and Temperament in Three Primitive Societies*.

cultural mores are relative and that there are many ways of working out the details of courtship, sex, marriage, and love. She consistently argued that there is no right way, suggesting rather that there are many ways, all of which are right within an individual culture.

Mead emphasizes the psychological model of cultures. To the dismay of some anthropologists, Mead also emphasizes the social, traditional, and historical aspects of a culture while concerning herself less with the biological or genetic. Recent critics have faulted Mead for this emphasis and have charged her with ignoring biological determinism in her research.

Near the end of her life, Mead was the most famous anthropologist in the United States. She wrote columns for popular magazines, published more than twenty books, and lectured widely to various audiences. Mead was popular, but she was also a careful and devoted scientist. Her work in the South Pacific still stands as a major contribution to our knowledge of how different cultures deal with basic social issues.

Mead's Rhetoric

Mead has the advantage of writing clearly and with a journalist's skill, focusing on the most interesting details. "Sex and Temperament" explores society's expectations regarding temperament rather than trying to convince the reader that one or another of the points of view is accurate. As she says in her opening paragraph, she is not interested in determining if there are "actual and universal differences between the sexes." Instead, she is concerned with the range of temperaments—"dominance, bravery, aggressiveness, objectivity, malleability" (para. 6)—that human beings can have and all the other temperamental qualities individuals can possess. Then, she goes on to explore whether any specific group of temperaments is explicitly limited to one sex or the other.

She admits that, at the beginning of her study, "[she] too had been accustomed to use in [her] thinking such concepts as 'mixed type,' to think of some men as having 'feminine' temperaments, of some women as having 'masculine' minds" (para. 6). In other words, she originally felt that there was a natural disposition of temperaments that was inbuilt depending on sex. Then, with her work among other cultures, her thinking began to change. Ultimately, she realized that each culture begins shaping individuals at birth to fit the patterns that it has determined as most desirable. As she says, there are several courses of action available to a society. One is to emphasize contrasting temperaments in boys and girls.

Another is to de-emphasize differences and concentrate on individual talent and natural temperament in determining occupation and behavior, a condition that Mead seems to imply is in place in her own time. However, she is worried that we may "return to a strict regimentation of women" (para. 9) in the future. Society can also "admit that men and women are capable of being molded to a single pattern as easily as to a diverse one" (para. 11).

Interestingly, Mead offers a view that may not be a counterargument so much as a personal lament. She sees in societies in which men and women dress differently, behave differently, and are given different occupations a beautiful diversity that is lost when those distinctions are lost. She is careful to point out that standard biologically relevant distinctions—the difference in male strength and male height—are rendered vastly less significant in leveling the relationship of men and women today because the law has some of the same force that strength in battle had ages ago. Mead is balanced in her view, pointing to the behavior of societies as being responsible for the shaping of male and female standard temperaments.

Two of her rhetorical techniques are comparison and example. She frequently turns to her experience in the Arapesh or Mundugumor societies. She points to an instance in which the "sacrifice of sex-differences has meant a loss in complexity to the society" (para. 13) of the Mundugumor, and by implication, she seems to say that similar results either have happened or will happen in our own culture. Her discussion of the stereotyping of women and priests as always opposed to war demonstrates that this attitude has no basis in any "natural" endowments of either group. However, in any society in which such rigid temperamental qualities are educated into either sex, there will be a considerable number of rebels. She says that the greater the standardization of temperament, the greater will be the tendency to produce rebels.

She also exhibits considerable concern for individuals in a society that places great emphasis on gender-related temperaments when those individuals do not themselves have the "proper" temperaments. These are people who do not fit the mold, who are not naturally disposed to the roles that society has established for them. When society is inflexible and makes it difficult for such individuals to express themselves, they endure a lifetime of frustration. Her concern extends even to those who are victims of birth, by which she means those born into nobility or into peasantry, with temperaments opposite to those that their society demands. She uses India, with its former caste system, as a specific example.

Mead proposes an experiment in which the temperamental distinctions that our society assumes are natural to men and women were linked to eye color instead of gender. She suggests attributing gentleness, nurturance, and submissiveness to blue-eyed people and arrogance, domination, and purposiveness to brown-eyed people. Thus, these qualities would not be gender linked. Interestingly, in some grade schools similar experiments with eye color were put into place to help young people understand the effect of sanctioned distinctions on people who did not fit the requirements of the group.

Mead's final suggestion is to avoid standardizing society or removing all of society's expectations. Instead, she suggests that society might learn to tolerate and accept the natural diversity within a population of many individuals with differing temperaments, some of whom fit society's expectations and some of whom do not. In any event, she celebrates diversity and sees that societies all have different ways of establishing desired temperaments but that they must make room for people who do not easily fit into sanctioned roles.

PREREADING QUESTIONS: WHAT TO READ FOR

The following prereading questions may help you anticipate key issues in the discussion of Margaret Mead's "Sex and Temperament." Keeping them in mind during your first reading of the selection should help focus your attention.

- What does Mead mean by *temperament*?
- What is a "standardized" society?
- What alternatives are there to a standardized society?
- Do all societies regard men and women as different in temperament?

Sex and Temperament

This study is not concerned with whether there are or are not actual   1 and universal differences between the sexes, either quantitative or qualitative. It is not concerned with whether women are more variable than men, which was claimed before the doctrine of evolution exalted variability, or less variable, which was claimed afterwards. It is not a treatise on the rights of women, nor an inquiry into the basis of feminism. It is, very simply, an account of how three primitive societies have grouped their social attitudes towards temperament about the very obvious facts of sex-difference. I studied this problem in simple societies because here we have the drama of civilization writ small, a social microcosm alike in kind, but different in size and magnitude, from the complex social structures of peoples who, like our own, depend upon a written tradition and upon the integration of a great number of conflicting historical traditions. Among the gentle mountain-dwelling Arapesh, the fierce cannibalistic Mundugumor, and the graceful head-hunters of Tchambuli, I studied this question. Each of these tribes had, as has every human society, the point of sex-difference to use as one theme in the plot of social life, and each of these three peoples has developed that theme differently. In comparing the way in which they have dramatized sex-difference, it is possible to gain a greater insight into what elements are social constructs, originally irrelevant to the biological facts of sex-gender.

Our own society makes great use of this plot. It assigns different   2 roles to the two sexes, surrounds them from birth with an expectation of different behavior, plays out the whole drama of courtship, marriage, and parenthood in terms of types of behavior believed to be innate and therefore appropriate for one sex or for the other. We know dimly that these roles have changed even within our history. Studies like Mrs. Putnam's *The Lady*[1] depict woman as an infinitely malleable lay figure upon which mankind has draped ever varying period-costumes, in keeping with which she wilted or waxed imperious, flirted or fled. But all discussions have emphasized not the relative social personalities assigned to the two sexes, but rather the superficial behavior-patterns assigned to women, often not even to all women, but only to women of the upper class. A sophisticated recognition that upper-class women were puppets of a changing tradition blurred rather than clarified the issue. It left untouched the roles assigned to men, who were conceived as proceeding along a special masculine road, shaping women to their fads and whims in womanliness. All discussion of the position of women, of the character and temperament of women, the enslavement or the emancipation of women, obscures the basic issue—the recognition that the cultural plot behind human relations is the way in which the roles of the two sexes are conceived, and that the growing boy is shaped to a local and special emphasis as inexorably as is the growing girl. . . .

. . . We know that human cultures do not all fall into one side   3 or the other of a single scale and that it is possible for one society to ignore completely an issue which two other societies have solved in contrasting ways. Because a people honor the old may mean that they hold children in slight esteem, but a people may also, like the Ba Thonga of South Africa, honor neither old people nor children; or,

---

[1] ***The Lady: Studies of Certain Phases of Her History*** Book by Emily James Putnam (1865–1944), the first woman dean of Barnard College, in New York City.

like the Plains Indians, dignify the little child and the grandfather; or, again, like the Manus and parts of modern America, regard children as the most important group in society. In expecting simple reversals—that if an aspect of social life is not specifically sacred, it must be specifically secular; that if men are strong, women must be weak—we ignore the fact that cultures exercise far greater license than this in selecting the possible aspects of human life which they will minimize, overemphasize, or ignore. And while every culture has in some way institutionalized the roles of men and women, it has not necessarily been in terms of contrast between the prescribed personalities of the two sexes, nor in terms of dominance or submission. With the paucity of material for elaboration, no culture has failed to seize upon the conspicuous facts of age and sex in some way, whether it be the convention of one Philippine tribe that no man can keep a secret, the Manus assumption that only men enjoy playing with babies, the Toda prescription of almost all domestic work as too sacred for women, or the Arapesh insistence that women's heads are stronger than men's. In the division of labor, in dress, in manners, in social and religious functioning—sometimes in only a few of these respects, sometimes in all—men and women are socially differentiated, and each sex, as a sex, forced to conform to the role assigned to it. In some societies, these socially defined roles are mainly expressed in dress or occupation, with no insistence upon innate temperamental differences. Women wear long hair and men wear short hair, or men wear curls and women shave their heads; women wear skirts and men wear trousers, or women wear trousers, and men wear skirts. Women weave and men do not, or men weave and women do not. Such simple tie-ups as these between dress and occupation and sex are easily taught to every child and make no assumptions to which a given child cannot easily conform.

It is otherwise in societies that sharply differentiate the behav- 4
ior of men and of women in terms which assume a genuine difference in temperament. Among the Dakota Indians of the Plains, the importance of an ability to stand any degree of danger or hardship was frantically insisted upon as a masculine characteristic. From the time that a boy was five or six, all the conscious educational effort of the household was bent towards shaping him into an indubitable male. Every tear, every timidity, every clinging to a protective hand or desire to continue to play with younger children or with girls, was obsessively interpreted as proof that he was not going to develop into a real man. In such a society it is not surprising to find the *berdache*,[2]

---

[2] **berdache** American Indian term for a man who dresses as a woman and does a woman's work.

the man who had voluntarily given up the struggle to conform to the masculine role and who wore female attire and followed the occupations of a woman. The institution of the *berdache* in turn served as a warning to every father; the fear that the son might become a *berdache* informed the parental efforts with an extra desperation, and the very pressure which helped to drive a boy to that choice was redoubled. The invert who lacks any discernible physical basis for his inversion has long puzzled students of sex, who when they can find no observable glandular abnormality turn to theories of early conditioning or identification with a parent of opposite sex. In the course of this investigation, we shall have occasion to examine the "masculine" woman and the "feminine" man as they occur in these different tribes, to inquire whether it is always a woman of dominating nature who is conceived as masculine, or a man who is gentle, submissive, or fond of children or embroidery who is conceived as feminine.

. . . [W]e shall be concerned with the patterning of sex-behavior 5 from the standpoint of temperament, with the cultural assumptions that certain temperamental attitudes are "naturally" masculine and others "naturally" feminine. In this matter, primitive people seem to be, on the surface, more sophisticated than we are. Just as they know that the gods, the food habits, and the marriage customs of the next tribe differ from those of their own people, and do not insist that one form is true or natural while the other is false or unnatural, so they often know that the temperamental proclivities which they regard as natural for men or for women differ from the natural temperaments of the men and women among their neighbors. Nevertheless, within a narrower range and with less of a claim for the biological or divine validity of their social forms than we often advance, each tribe has certain definite attitudes towards temperament, a theory of what human beings, either men or women or both, are naturally like, a norm in terms of which to judge and condemn those individuals who deviate from it.

Two of these tribes have no idea that men and women are dif- 6 ferent in temperament. They allow them different economic and religious roles, different skills, different vulnerabilities to evil magic and supernatural influences. The Arapesh believe that painting in color is appropriate only to men, and the Mundugumor consider fishing an essentially feminine task. But any idea that temperamental traits of the order of dominance, bravery, aggressiveness, objectivity, malleability, are inalienably associated with one sex (as opposed to the other) is entirely lacking. This may seem strange to a civilization which in its sociology, its medicine, its slang, its poetry, and its obscenity accepts the socially defined differences between the sexes as having an innate basis in temperament and explains any deviation from the socially determined role as abnormality of native endowment or early maturation. It came as a surprise to me because I too had been accustomed to use in my thinking such concepts as "mixed type," to think of some men as having "feminine" temperaments, of some women as having "masculine" minds. I set as my problem a study of the conditioning of the social personalities of the two sexes, in the hope that such an investigation would throw some light upon sex-differences. I shared the general belief of our society that there was a natural sex-temperament which could at the most only be distorted or diverted from normal expression. I was innocent of any suspicion that the temperaments which we regard as native to one sex might instead be mere variations of human temperament, to which the members of either or both sexes may, with more or less success in the case of different individuals, be educated to approximate.

·   ·   ·

7   The knowledge that the personalities of the two sexes are socially produced is congenial to every program that looks forward towards a planned order of society. It is a two-edged sword that can be used to hew a more flexible, more varied society than the human race has ever built, or merely to cut a narrow path down which one sex or both sexes will be forced to march, regimented, looking neither to the right nor to the left. . . .

8   There are at least three courses open to a society that has realized the extent to which male and female personality are socially produced. Two of these courses have been tried before, over and over again, at different times in the long, irregular, repetitious history of the race. The first is to standardize the personality of men and women as clearly contrasting, complementary, and antithetical, and to make every institution in the society congruent with this standardization. If the society declared that woman's sole function was motherhood and the teaching and care of young children, it could so arrange matters that every woman who was not physiologically debarred should become a mother and be supported in the exercise of this function. It could abolish the discrepancy between the doctrine that women's place is the home and the number of homes that were offered to them. It could abolish the discrepancy between training women for marriage and then forcing them to become the spinster supports of their parents.

9   Such a system would be wasteful of the gifts of many women who could exercise other functions far better than their ability to bear children in an already overpopulated world. It would be wasteful of the gifts of many men who could exercise their special personality gifts far better in the home than in the market-place. It would be wasteful, but it would be clear. It could attempt to guarantee to each individual the

role for which society insisted upon training him or her, and such a system would penalize only those individuals who, in spite of all the training, did not display the approved personalities. There are millions of persons who would gladly return to such a standardized method of treating the relationship between the sexes, and we must bear in mind the possibility that the greater opportunities open in the twentieth century to women may be quite withdrawn, and that we may return to a strict regimentation of women.

The waste, if this occurs, will be not only of many women, but also   10
of as many men, because regimentation of one sex carries with it, to greater or less degree, the regimentation of the other also. Every parental behest that defines a way of sitting, a response to a rebuke or a threat, a game, or an attempt to draw or sing or dance or paint, as feminine, is molding the personality of each little girl's brother as well as molding the personality of the sister. There can be no society which insists that women follow one special personality-pattern, defined as feminine, which does not do violence also to the individuality of many men.

Alternatively, society can take the course that has become espe-   11
cially associated with the plans of most radical groups: admit that men and women are capable of being molded to a single pattern as easily as to a diverse one, and cease to make any distinction in the approved personality of both sexes. Girls can be trained exactly as boys are trained, taught the same code, the same forms of expression, the same occupations. This course might seem to be the logic which follows from the conviction that the potentialities which different societies label as either masculine or feminine are really potentialities of some members of each sex, and not sex-linked at all. If this is accepted, is it not reasonable to abandon the kind of artificial standardizations of sex-differences that have been so long characteristic of European society, and admit that they are social fictions for which we have no longer any use? In the world today, contraceptives make it possible for women not to bear children against their will. The most conspicuous actual difference between the sexes, the difference in strength, is progressively less significant. Just as the difference in height between males is no longer a realistic issue, now that lawsuits have been substituted for hand-to-hand encounters, so the difference in strength between men and women is no longer worth elaboration in cultural institutions.

In evaluating such a program as this, however, it is necessary to   12
keep in mind the nature of the gains that society has achieved in its most complex forms. A sacrifice of distinctions in sex-personality may mean a sacrifice in complexity. The Arapesh recognize a minimum of distinction in personality between old and young, between men and women, and they lack categories of rank or status. We have seen that such a society at the best condemns to personal frustration, and at the worst to

maladjustment, all of those men and women who do not conform to its simple emphases. The violent person among the Arapesh cannot find, either in the literature, or in the art, or in the ceremonial, or in the history of his people, any expression of the internal drives that are shattering his peace of mind. Nor is the loser only the individual whose own type of personality is nowhere recognized in his society. The imaginative, highly intelligent person who is essentially in tune with the values of his society may also suffer by the lack of range and depth characteristic of too great simplicity. The active mind and intensity of one Arapesh boy whom I knew well was unsatisfied by the laissez-faire solutions, the lack of drama in his culture. Searching for some material upon which to exercise his imagination, his longing for a life in which stronger emotions would be possible, he could find nothing with which to feed his imagination but tales of the passionate outbursts of the maladjusted, outbursts characterized by a violent hostility to others that he himself lacked.

Nor is it the individual alone who suffers. Society is equally the   13
loser, and we have seen such an attenuation in the dramatic representations of the Mundugumor. By phrasing the exclusion of women as a protective measure congenial to both sexes, the Arapesh kept their *tamberan*[3] cult, with the necessary audiences of women. But the Mundugumor developed a kind of personality for both men and women to which exclusion from any part of life was interpreted as a deadly insult. And as more and more Mundugumor women have demanded and been given the right of initiation, it is not surprising that the Mundugumor ceremonial life has dwindled, the actors have lost their audience, and one vivid artistic element in the life of the Mundugumor community is vanishing. The sacrifice of sex-differences has meant a loss in complexity to the society.

So in our own society. To insist that there are no sex-differences in a   14
society that has always believed in them and depended upon them may be as subtle a form of standardizing personality as to insist that there are many sex-differences. This is particularly so in a changing tradition, when a group in control is attempting to develop a new social personality, as is the case today in many European countries. Take, for instance, the current assumption that women are more opposed to war than men, that any outspoken approval of war is more horrible, more revolting, in women than in men. Behind this assumption women can work for peace without encountering social criticism in communities that would immediately criticize their brothers or husbands if they took a similarly active part in peace propaganda. This belief that women are naturally more

---

[3] ***tamberan*** A noise-making device such as a bullhorn used by the Arapesh in rituals that assert male solidarity and masculinity.

interested in peace is undoubtedly artificial, part of the whole mythology that considers women to be gentler than men. But in contrast let us consider the possibility of a powerful minority that wished to turn a whole society whole-heartedly towards war. One way of doing this would be to insist that women's motives, women's interests, were identical with men's, that women should take as bloodthirsty a delight in preparing for war as ever men do. The insistence upon the opposite point of view, that the woman as a mother prevails over the woman as a citizen at least puts a slight drag upon agitation for war, prevents a blanket enthusiasm for war from being thrust upon the entire younger generation. The same kind of result follows if the clergy are professionally committed to a belief in peace. The relative bellicosity of different individual clerics may be either offended or gratified by the prescribed pacific role, but a certain protest, a certain dissenting note, will be sounded in society. The dangerous standardization of attitudes that disallows every type of deviation is greatly reinforced if neither age nor sex nor religious belief is regarded as automatically predisposing certain individuals to hold minority attitudes. The removal of all legal and economic barriers against women's participating in the world on an equal footing with men may be in itself a standardizing move towards the wholesale stamping-out of the diversity of attitudes that is such a dearly bought product of civilization.

15 Such a standardized society, in which men, women, children, priests, and soldiers were all trained to an undifferentiated and coherent set of values, must of necessity create the kind of deviant that we found among the Arapesh and the Mundugumor, the individual who, regardless of sex or occupation, rebels because he is temperamentally unable to accept the one-sided emphasis of his culture. The individuals who were specifically unadjusted in terms of their psycho-sexual role would, it is true, vanish, but with them would vanish the knowledge that there is more than one set of possible values.

16 To the extent that abolishing the differences in the approved personalities of men and women means abolishing any expression of the type of personality once called exclusively feminine, or once called exclusively masculine, such a course involves a social loss. Just as a festive occasion is the gayer and more charming if the two sexes are dressed differently, so it is in less material matters. If the clothing is in itself a symbol, and a woman's shawl corresponds to a recognized softness in her character, the whole plot of personal relations is made more elaborate, and in many ways more rewarding. The poet of such a society will praise virtues, albeit feminine virtues, which might never have any part in a social Utopia that allowed no differences between the personalities of men and women.

17 To the extent that a society insists upon different kinds of personality so that one age-group or class or sex-group may follow purposes

disallowed or neglected in another, each individual participant in that society is the richer. The arbitrary assignment of set clothing, set manners, set social responses, to individuals born in a certain class, of a certain sex, or of a certain color, to those born on a certain day of the week, to those born with a certain complexion, does violence to the individual endowment of individuals, but permits the building of a rich culture. The most extreme development of a society that has attained great complexity at the expense of the individual is historical India, based, as it was, upon the uncompromising association of a thousand attributes of behavior, attitude, and occupation with an accident of birth. To each individual there was given the security, although it might be the security of despair, of a set role, and the reward of being born into a highly complex society.

Furthermore, when we consider the position of the deviant individual in historical cultures, those who are born into a complex society in the wrong sex or class for their personalities to have full sway are in a better position than those who are born into a simple society which does not use in any way their special temperamental gifts. The violent women in a society that permits violence to men only, the strongly emotional member of an aristocracy in a culture that permits downright emotional expression only in the peasantry, the ritualistically inclined individual who is bred a Protestant in a country which has also Catholic institutions—each one of these can find expressed in some other group in the society the emotions that he or she is forbidden to manifest. He is given a certain kind of support by the mere existence of these values, values so congenial to him and so inaccessible because of an accident of birth. For those who are content with a vicarious spectator-role, or with materials upon which to feast the creative imagination, this may be almost enough. They may be content to experience from the sidewalks during a parade, from the audience of a theatre or from the nave of a church, those emotions the direct expression of which is denied to them. The crude compensations offered by the moving pictures to those whose lives are emotionally starved are offered in subtler forms by the art and literature of a complex society to the individual who is out of place in his sex or his class or his occupational group. 18

Sex-adjustments, however, are not a matter of spectatorship, but a situation in which the most passive individual must play some part if he or she is to participate fully in life. And while we may recognize the virtues of complexity, the interesting and charming plots that cultures can evolve upon the basis of accidents of birth, we may well ask: Is not the price too high? Could not the beauty that lies in contrast and complexity be obtained in some other way? If the social insistence upon different personalities for the two sexes results in so much confusion, so many unhappy deviants, so much disorientation, can we imagine a 19 society that abandons these distinctions without abandoning the values that are at present dependent upon them?

Let us suppose that, instead of the classification laid down on the "natural" bases of sex and race, a society had classified personality on the basis of eye-color. It had decreed that all blue-eyed people were gentle, submissive, and responsive to the needs of others, and all brown-eyed people were arrogant, dominating, self-centered, and purposive. In this case two complementary social themes would be woven together—the culture, in its art, its religion, its formal personal relations, would have two threads instead of one. There would be blue-eyed men, and blue-eyed women, which would mean that there were gentle, "maternal" women, and gentle, "maternal" men. A blue-eyed man might marry a woman who had been bred to the same personality as himself, or a brown-eyed woman who had been bred to the contrasting personality. One of the strong tendencies that makes for homosexuality, the tendency to love the similar rather than the antithetical persons, would be eliminated. Hostility between the two sexes as groups would be minimized, since the individual interests of members of each sex could be woven together in different ways, and marriages of similarity and friendships of contrast need carry no necessary handicap of possible psycho-sexual maladjustment. The individual would still suffer a mutilation of his temperamental preferences, for it would be the unrelated fact of eye-color that would determine the attitudes which he was educated to show. Every blue-eyed person would be forced into submissiveness and declared maladjusted if he or she showed any traits that it had been decided were only appropriate to the brown-eyed. The greatest social loss, however, in the classification of personality on the basis of sex would not be present in this society which based its classification on eye-color. Human relations, and especially those which involve sex, would not be artificially distorted. 20

But such a course, the substitution of eye-color for sex as a basis upon which to educate children into groups showing contrasting personalities, while it would be a definite advance upon a classification by sex, remains a parody of all the attempts that society has made through history to define an individual's role in terms of sex, or color, or date of birth, or shape of head. 21

However, the only solution of the problem does not lie between an acceptance of standardization of sex-differences with the resulting cost in individual happiness and adjustment, and the abolition of these differences with the consequent loss in social values. A civilization might take its cues not from such categories as age or sex, race or hereditary position in a family line, but instead of specializing personality along such simple lines recognize, train, and make a place for many and divergent temperamental endowments. It might build upon 22 the different potentialities that it now attempts to extirpate artificially in some children and create artificially in others.

Historically the lessening of rigidity in the classification of the   23
sexes has come about at different times, either by the creation of a new artificial category, or by the recognition of real individual differences. Sometimes the idea of social position has transcended sex-categories. In a society that recognizes gradations in wealth or rank, women of rank or women of wealth have been permitted an arrogance which was denied to both sexes among the lowly or the poor. Such a shift as this has been, it is true, a step towards the emancipation of women, but it has never been a step towards the greater freedom of the individual. A few women have shared the upper-class personality, but to balance this a great many men as well as women have been condemned to a personality characterized by subservience and fear. Such shifts as these mean only the substitution of one arbitrary standard for another. A society is equally unrealistic whether it insists that only men can be brave, or that only individuals of rank can be brave.

To break down one line of division, that between the sexes, and sub-   24
stitute another, that between classes, is no real advance. It merely shifts the irrelevancy to a different point. And meanwhile, individuals born in the upper classes are shaped inexorably to one type of personality, to an arrogance that is again uncongenial to at least some of them, while the arrogant among the poor fret and fume beneath their training for submissiveness. At one end of the scale is the mild, unaggressive young son of wealthy parents who is forced to lead, at the other the aggressive, enterprising child of the slums who is condemned to a place in the ranks. If our aim is greater expression for each individual temperament, rather than any partisan interest in one sex or its fate, we must see these historical developments which have aided in freeing some women as nevertheless a kind of development that also involved major social losses.

The second way in which categories of sex-differences have   25
become less rigid is through a recognition of genuine individual gifts as they occurred in either sex. Here a real distinction has been substituted for an artificial one, and the gains are tremendous for society and for the individual. Where writing is accepted as a profession that may be pursued by either sex with perfect suitability, individuals who have the ability to write need not be debarred from it by their sex, nor need they, if they do write, doubt their essential masculinity or femininity. An occupation that has no basis in sex-determined gifts can now recruit its ranks from twice as many potential artists. And it is here that we can find a ground-plan for building a society that would substitute real differences for arbitrary ones. We must recognize that beneath the superficial classifications of sex and race the same potentialities exist, recurring generation after generation, only

to perish because society has no place for them. Just as society now permits the practice of an art to members of either sex, so it might also permit the development of many contrasting temperamental gifts in each sex. It might abandon its various attempts to make boys fight and to make girls remain passive, or to make all children fight, and instead shape our educational institutions to develop to the full the boy who shows a capacity for maternal behavior, the girl who shows an opposite capacity that is stimulated by fighting against obstacles. No skill, no special aptitude, no vividness of imagination or precision of thinking would go unrecognized because the child who possessed it was of one sex rather than the other. No child would be relentlessly shaped to one pattern of behavior, but instead there should be many patterns, in a world that had learned to allow to each individual the pattern which was most congenial to his gifts.

Such a civilization would not sacrifice the gains of thousands of 26 years during which society has built up standards of diversity. The social gains would be conserved, and each child would be encouraged on the basis of his actual temperament. Where we now have patterns of behavior for women and patterns of behavior for men, we would then have patterns of behavior that expressed the interests of individuals with many kinds of endowment. There would be ethical codes and social symbolisms, an art and a way of life, congenial to each endowment.

Historically our own culture has relied for the creation of rich and 27 contrasting values upon many artificial distinctions, the most striking of which is sex. It will not be by the mere abolition of these distinctions that society will develop patterns in which individual gifts are given place instead of being forced into an ill-fitting mold. If we are to achieve a richer culture, rich in contrasting values, we must recognize the whole gamut of human potentialities, and so weave a less arbitrary social fabric, one in which each diverse human gift will find a fitting place.

QUESTIONS FOR CRITICAL READING

1. What temperament traits do you have? Are they gender linked?
2. What problems face a society that has established rigid gender-linked expectations?
3. How are gender-linked temperament expectations reinforced by society?
4. How much of a range of difference in gender expectation has Mead found in other cultures?
5. Does our society expect different behavior from men than from women? Are those differences visible in daily behavior?

6. Is it possible for a society to mold similar behavior in men and women?

7. Why does Mead give us all the examples she does from other societies? Do you find them convincing?

8. What problems do people with the "wrong" temperaments face in a society?

9. Do you think gender-linked temperaments are biological and natural? Why or why not?

SUGGESTIONS FOR CRITICAL WRITING

1. Mead contends that gender-linked temperaments exist because a society has promoted and reinforced those distinctions. She suggests that gender-linked distinctions are not specifically biological. In a brief essay, summarize the key points of her argument and then, using your own observations and experiences, argue a case that either defends or attacks her position.

2. Which of the societies Mead refers to seems to have the best solution to dealing with what appear to be gender-linked temperaments? If possible, research that society and clarify the nature of its treatment of men and women. How does it treat men who seem "feminine" and women who seem "masculine" in temperament?

3. As best you can tell from this selection, what would Mead's ideal society be like in regard to the question of individual temperaments? Examine the passages in which she makes statements that you feel express her views and respond to them with your own analysis. Would her society satisfy the needs of our modern culture? Would it benefit a great many people, or would it benefit only the few? Is it a society in which you would be comfortable?

4. Drawing on your own experience, explain what you have observed about the way people you know treat "masculine women" and "feminine men." What has the culture done to those who mistreat such individuals? How do the individuals react? What price do they pay for the fact that their temperaments do not fit in with societal expectations? What price does the entire society pay for insisting on rigid patterns of behavior?

5. In paragraph 12, Mead begins an exploration of societies that erase sex differences between men and women. After describing those societies and the results of their decisions, Mead seems to be rethinking her position. She says, "The sacrifice of sex-differences has meant a loss in complexity to the society" (para. 13). Would our society lose complexity if sex differences were somehow erased? Or would the level of complexity remain the same or even increase?

6. **CONNECTIONS**   To what extent does John Stuart Mill in his essay "The Subjection of Women" (p. 669) agree with or differ from Mead's

concerns about gender-linked temperaments? What would he say to her suggestion that society could mold boys and girls to value whatever traits it chose? Would Mill have regarded a society that standardized temperament distinctions as representing a "tyranny of the majority"? How close are Mill's and Mead's thinking?

7. **CONNECTIONS** How does Horney's psychological discussion of the relationships of men and women in society (**bedfordstmartins .com/worldofideas/epages**) support Mead's view that people's temperaments are developed according to the needs of society? Given Horney's analysis, what predictions might Mead make about the ways in which our current society would probably tend to shape the temperaments of men and women in the future? Do you think that Horney is fearful that, as Mead says, our future culture may "return to a strict regimentation of women" (para. 9)? Could that be the basis for the sense of distrust that Horney references?

8. **SEEING CONNECTIONS** Would Mead feel that the figures in Cassatt's *In the Loge* (p. 650) were acting out in typical gender-linked fashion? Or would she have seen a shift from the expectations of Cassatt's time? What role do you think Cassatt's society would have expected of the woman in the painting? In what ways has that figure accepted that role? In what ways has she rejected it? Do you think she would be comfortable in our society? How might Mead interpret the principal female figure?

GERMAINE GREER
Masculinity

BORN IN MELBOURNE, Australia, in 1939, Germaine Greer
has long been considered a leading feminist even though she has
sometimes been critical of feminist politics. She taught English literature at the University of Sydney, where she earned an M.A. for a
thesis on the poetry of Lord Byron. Her thesis won her a Commonwealth Scholarship to get her Ph.D. in early English literature at
Cambridge, where she became a faculty member at the all-women's
Newnham College. She was controversial while at Cambridge, not
only for her outspoken feminism and racy language, but also for
her anarchist polemics and occasional pranks. After she earned
her doctorate in 1968, she married an Australian journalist, but
the marriage did not last. By the time she was thirty and her first
book, *The Female Eunuch* (1970), was published, she had become
an international celebrity. The book was a sensation and its success led her to leave behind her academic career temporarily and
become a public figure.

She traveled broadly after 1972, championing women's rights
in many countries, including Bangladesh where she wrote a story
on the women who were raped by soldiers during the war in that
country. She produced a comedy show on Granada Television
in England and wrote for a number of underground magazines.
In 1979, she accepted a professorship at the University of Tulsa
and founded the *Tulsa Studies in Women's Literature*. In 1989, she
returned to Newnham College, Cambridge, but left in 1996 over a
stand she took against offering a fellowship to Rachael Padman, a
transsexual, on the grounds that she had been born a man and that
Newnham was a college for women. The controversy was acrimo-
nious and stimulated considerable discussion in academic circles.
One attack on Greer was so disparaging that it was eventually

From *The Whole Woman*.

removed from Web sites for legal reasons. Today Greer teaches at the University of Warwick, in Coventry, England.

Greer's argument in *The Female Eunuch* centered in large part on examining the ways in which women are raised in contemporary society. She feels that they have been trained to be submissive and yielding and have grown suspicious of their sexuality and ashamed of their bodies. The nuclear family is an especially damaging environment for women, she feels. Such a position naturally drew criticism from the conservative press, but it also attracted a wide following among women who felt that Greer had awakened them from a long sleep.

Her second book, *The Obstacle Race: The Fortunes of Women Painters and Their Work* (1979), involved extensive research into art and art history. In it she examines stories of women painters whose work was attributed to men, including a number of famous paintings whose value diminished critically and financially when they were discovered to be the work of women. She explains, much as Virginia Woolf does regarding women writers, how difficult it has been for women artists to be taken seriously and to be properly rewarded for the quality of their work. One chapter discusses what she feels is the equivalent of aesthetic rape: the failure to preserve the work of women, many of whose paintings were discarded or lost to posterity.

Sex and Destiny (1984) continued her examination of sexual issues in numerous communities, especially in the developing world. Here, too, she sees the structure of the family as damaging to women and their potential for growth. *The Change: Women, Aging, and the Menopause* (1991) explored an aspect of feminism rarely discussed and at the same time attacked hormone replacement for menopausal women. Greer feels that women are bullied into accepting procedures that will do them no good and that may do them harm.

The Whole Woman (1999) supplies the selection that follows. In a sense, this book picks up where *The Female Eunuch* left off thirty years earlier. Greer sees that much has changed, but she makes something of a rallying call, fearing that today's young women may have given in to the pressures of popular culture that require them to aspire to a role that is unhealthy for them to play. As she says, women in 1970 were not starving and cutting themselves, so she is somewhat worried that the feminist movement is backsliding.

Greer's Rhetoric

"Masculinity," one of the last chapters in her book, may seem out of place in a study of the whole woman, but it is appropriate as a contrast to the body of her argument. She presents her argument almost in the form of an anthropological study, essentially reporting what she has discovered about the nature of masculinity in our culture. One of her most interesting rhetorical devices is the use of strong short statements that almost take the form of a maxim or proverb:

> "Masculinity is to maleness as femininity is to femaleness." (para. 1)
>
> "Men do not only give orders; they also take orders." (para. 8)
>
> "Masculinity requires the creation of dangerous situations, actual or symbolic." (para. 10)
>
> "Masculinity is a system." (para. 12)

Each of these requires an examination and therefore a clear focus for understanding. Her device of interweaving quotations from both men and women regarding masculine behavior interrupts the discussion but adds the weight of outside testimony on her subject, similar to the list of quotations that opens this section on gender.

Greer begins by establishing that "masculinity is the cultural construct" (para. 1) of maleness in our society. Once she has made that point, she moves on to explain how society actually goes about constructing the idea of masculinity. Her strategy is effective in that, after making her declaration, she seems aware that her readers may take immediate issue with her and feel that masculinity is not cultural but rather biological. She then begins paragraph 2 with an analysis of a scientific study that seems to be a clear counterargument to her position. Research on people with Turner's syndrome—a condition in which males do not have the usual XY chromosome in their genes but only one X and females, instead of the XX chromosome, also have only one X. The result is that people with Turner's syndrome are classified as female, even if they do not have the biological capacity to have children.

The researchers who reported on the behavior of children with Turner's syndrome determined that single-X boys seemed feminine and single-X girls seemed masculine. But when Greer examined the data and the testing of these individuals she was able to see that the criteria the researchers used were essentially cultural and that the behavior of the single-X individuals was not conspicuously different from that of XX and XY individuals given similar tests. Thus, the biological argument suffers and Greer continues with her determination of how a culture constructs masculinity.

Greer begins with the first caretaker and discovers that a widely regarded study noted that boy babies are treated quite differently from girl babies. "The boy baby learns that he can have what he wants and quickly, the girl baby that she has to learn patience" (para. 4). Then she establishes the somewhat Freudian notion that the boy baby's first love affair is with his mother and that it is a success. But the girl baby's first love affair with her father is "inevitably a failure" (para. 5). The outcome is that "boys grow up convinced that they are lovable regardless of their appearance or their behavior."

Greer then launches into the body of her essay, tracing the cultural forces at work that help shape the masculine male. Her argument, using examples and some quotations, stays at a very basic level, describing the language and activities that ordain male behavior. At one point, she uses a metaphor when she describes the behavior of a group of males in terms of primate behavior: "grooming the silverback" (para. 9). After clarifying her position regarding the cultural influences on males, she briefly discusses how those influences not only produce the masculine male but also how women fit into the groups, such as corporations, that were originally constructed by masculine males.

The strength of her arguments lies first in her ability to balance her views against opposing ones and then in her ability to present what seem to be uncontroversial observations about the behavior of men that readers can verify or deny from their own experience. Ultimately, that is the test of her position on masculinity.

PREREADING QUESTIONS: WHAT TO READ FOR

The following prereading questions may help you anticipate key issues in the discussion of Germaine Greer's "Masculinity." Keeping them in mind during your first reading of the selection should help focus your attention.

- Why is masculinity a cultural construct?
- What is the argument against masculinity being a cultural construct?
- How differently is a male baby raised from a female baby in our culture?
- How do male organizations help shape the masculine male?

Masculinity

Masculinity is to maleness as femininity is to femaleness. That is   1
to say that maleness is the natural condition, the sex if you like, and masculinity is the cultural construct, the gender. Where once feminists

talked of sex discrimination, they now usually refer to gender roles, because the cultural construct is what can and should be changed; sex, as a biological given, is less susceptible. The distinction is rather like the one to be found between the genotype, which is what is written in the DNA, and the phenotype, which is how that immense text is quoted in actuality. The potential of the genotype is enormous; the phenotype is the finite creature that is all that can be made of almost limitless possibility in a single lifespan in a single set of circumstances.

> A man feels himself more of a man when he is imposing himself
> and making others the instruments of his will.
>   —BERTRAND DE JOUVENEL, *Power*

In June 1997 a report in *Nature* argued that masculinity (as dis-   2
tinct from maleness) was genetic: David Skuse of the Institute of Child
Health and workers at the Wessex Regional Genetics Laboratory had
been studying Turner's syndrome, which is a consequence of being
born with only the X of the final pair of chromosomes. Though they
have no uteri or ovaries, these single-X individuals are classified as
female. They usually grow up to be short in stature and infertile. The
researchers found that the single-X "girls" displayed "masculine" characteristics in that they were insensitive, demanding, and obtuse. The
researchers explained this as a lack of the feminine traits of intuition
and sociability, on which girls usually score higher than boys, the
inference being that these were carried in the second X. The single-X
individuals who inherited their X from their mother had more problems of social adjustment than the ones who inherited their X from
their father. Peter McGuffin and Jane Scourfield of the University of
Wales Medical College welcomed the information.

> There has been a tendency to play down the possible role of biol-
> ogy in accounting for psychological differences between men and
> women. For the first time we have evidence about the location of
> a gene that plays a part, challenging the prevailing belief that gen-
> der differences are largely culturally determined.

If we look more closely at what the new information actually   3
amounted to, this interpretation seems rather too definite. The Skuse
team had graded eighty-eight Turner's syndrome individuals on an
unsociability questionnaire; those whose X chromosome came from
their fathers scored five out of a possible twenty-four, those whose X
came from their mothers scored nine, but this compares with scores
for a control population of four for the boys and two for the girls. The
Turner's syndrome children would appear to have rather more serious socialization problems than normal XY boys who scored closer

to XX girls. An "unsociability" test that establishes a high of twenty-four when the norm is between two and four would seem to contain a number of significant variables; did the whole group of single-X "girls" display the same or contrasting kinds of unsociability? How much of the single-X truculence could have been explained by differential treatment from carers and parents? And so on.

> He [President Clinton] embodies a masculine virility that has
> been under attack in the States for so long.
> —KATIE ROIPHE

Despite all the hoo-ha, Skuse and his team had not proved that   4
masculine men are born. They had certainly not done nearly enough
to counter the vast amount of research on how they are made. That
process begins when the carer who thinks a child a boy readily offers
it food when it cries; the same carer, thinking a child a girl, will allow
it to cry longer and will soothe rather than feed it. This sounds preposterous but it has been proved in a famous series of experiments,
in which subjects were given wrapped-up infants and randomly told
that the infants were male or female. When told that female babies
were male, the subjects treated them as male, responding quickly to
their vociferations and interpreting them as demands for food. When
told that male babies were female, they let them cry longer and were
comparatively reluctant to offer them food. Observers of breast-feeding
have likewise observed that male babies are fed more often and for
longer at a time than female babies. Mothers perceive boy babies as
hungrier and as better feeders than girls; what this means is probably
that they enjoy feeding their boy babies more than they enjoy feeding
their girls, for whatever reason. We know less about these mechanisms
than we should because as little work has been done on the psychology
of breast-feeding as on every other aspect of the well woman's function. The boy baby learns that he can have what he wants and quickly,
the girl baby that she has to learn patience. Boy babies are cooed to on
a different note. They are potty-trained later. The sociability and intui-
tiveness that Skuse valued in XX girls is simply biddability by another
name, and there is a distinct possibility that it has its roots in the insecurity that the little girl feels in her relationship with both her parents.

> Do you think that men are any good for anything? It seems to me
> that men are ruining the world.
> —NINA SIMONE, 1997

Then there is the vexed question of father-love versus mother-   5
love. Daughters will develop more self-confidence if their fathers are

encouraging and appreciative of their efforts, but fathers seldom give such matters much attention and, if they do, usually demand objective verification of a daughter's merit before giving encouragement. The self-confidence of boys, on the other hand, is reinforced by mothers' attention which is abundant and rarely conditional. Whether it be because a girl's first love affair (with her father) is inevitably a failure compared to a boy's effortless conquest of his mother, or the outcome of interaction of more complex and mysterious causes, boys grow up convinced that they are lovable regardless of their appearance or their behavior. The saddest, smelliest, most shambling male individual still imagines that women will find him attractive and is prepared to act on the assumption. And he considers himself entitled to criticize any and all aspects of a women's appearance as harshly as any other male.

Until comparatively recently both boys and girls were dressed alike   6
and looked alike until a boy was breeched and his hair cut into a manly style. As long as his mother's milk was in him a boy was expected to be girlish, a milksop; his tears were no shame to him. The age at which induction into masculinity was to commence was indeterminate and unstable, especially as mothers wept and railed at the mere thought of giving their babies up to the brutality of schoolmasters, who were expected to teach them to bear pain without flinching as a condition of teaching them anything else. Elizabeth Barrett Browning[1] is thought to have exaggerated a tad in keeping her son's blond curls trailing over his shoulders until he was almost in his teens, by which time it was thought too late to make a man of him. Though we might hope that schoolmaster brutality is a thing of the past, comparatively young men have experienced extreme brutalization at the hands of schoolmasters. An article in *Loaded* magazine described teachers who punched boys in the stomach and hit them with sticks. This is one of them:

> A brick shithouse with a ruddy face and unusually thick eyebrows, he was an ex-army man with the morals of a housefly and a temper meaner than the Moscow winter. A man who might have been put on earth for the singular purpose of terrorizing each and every adolescent male under his charge.

The persistence of the expression "to make a man of [someone]"   7
is the best possible evidence of the deliberateness of the streamlining of the male person into the masculine man. Repeatedly the boy is told that he is about to be made a man of, especially when he joins some

---

[1] **Elizabeth Barrett Browning (1806–1861)** Author of *Sonnets from the Portuguese*.

paramilitary organization, the scout movement, the cadets, the school officer training corps. At a slightly less belligerent level, he is encouraged to take part in team sports, to get used to rough and tumble and learn to take his punishment "like a man." If at all possible he will usually take as his model his father, present or absent, alive or dead. The primary virtue of masculinity for the young man is courage, manifested as stoicism in everyday vicissitudes and as belligerence

> My uncles would take me out just to learn how to fight and the lesson was, don't lose the fight or else your uncles are going to give you a hiding.   — JONAH LOMU

when threatened. A man is supposed to be unflinching, hard in every sense. So he is taught to control his gestures, to keep his hands and arms still and his face expressionless. His body outline is to be contained and impermeable. Real men do not fuss or scurry. It is not women who have foisted this requirement upon men but other men, who prove their own hardness by constantly challenging other men to repeated trials of physical and mental strength. Women often connive at the process; some mothers will taunt their sons if they think them cowardly; some wives and sweethearts will incite their men to attack other men in their defense. Generally, however, though women make boys out of babies it is men who make men out of boys. Though in these enlightened times schoolteachers may encourage boys to express softer feelings, even to weep, in the schoolyard, on the playing field, and in the street, compensation for this erosion of masculinity is exacted with interest. Young males form groups behind dominant individuals and prove themselves by conflict with rival groups; at the same time they jockey for power and seniority within the group. The group may be nothing more macho than a cricket team but, even when the game is played in the correct sportsmanlike fashion, individuals are caught up in the drama of acquiring and losing prestige.

Men do not only give orders; they also take orders. A masculine man's attention is focused upon his role in the various groups to which he belongs and from which he gains verification of self-worth. If he spends time with women it is partly or even mostly because he wants to demonstrate his prowess to his mates; he owes no loyalty to the women whatsoever. If it might improve his status he will surrender a woman with whom he has been intimate to another man and feel no qualm of jealousy. Young women are slow to grasp their irrelevance to the emotional center of a masculine man's life, mainly because young men are the emotional center of young women's lives. To be successful young men have to achieve a measure of respect from other men; this is the spring of all their behaviors, in the workplace and at play. They have to acquire a vast amount of lore, principally about sport, but also about cars and other boys' toys, subjects upon which girls are uninformed and stupid, and they have to keep it up to date, which requires attention. For a man who is not imposing physically there is the resort of humor; if he is amusing enough he will be caressed by the hard men he cannot emulate.

Wherever men are gathered together, in the pool hall, at a restaurant, you can see the wannabes waiting on the dominant males, studying their reactions, gauging when to defer and when to challenge. There 9

> Despite advances towards sexual equality, many men still feel embarrassed when they have to buy nappies. They fear people will think them henpecked husbands ordered by their wives to buy the nappies. Proudly placing a six-pack [of beer] alongside the nappies sends out the message that the man is really a he-man.
> — NICK GREEN, Tesco Clubcard manager

will always be one man who can silence the others with a look; most will defer, one may challenge or mock challenge, giving the leader a chance to strut his stuff, and there will be the junior males, who seek to ingratiate themselves by stepping and fetching, and grooming the silverback. The presence of women in such groups distracts the men from the work in hand—if they acknowledge women's presence; which they usually don't. The conversation is between males; when women make a contribution the men ignore it and respond to the last utterance by a male. Often the only woman present is the silent, smiling consort of the dominant male, who is gratified if his subordinates pay her an appropriate measure of attention. The kind of consort who is exhibited in this way is usually particularly decorative; the top honcho is pleased to see his henchmen afraid to catch her eye or speak to her, even as they dream of such executive totty for themselves.

Masculinity requires the creation of dangerous situations, actual 10 or symbolic. The myth that feeds masculinity is that every boy should become a strong and resolute warrior capable of defending his women and children from attack by other males. In stature he should be bigger than a woman, and more heavily muscled. As a U.S. Navy officer wrote in the *Navy Times* in July 1989:

> Warriors kill. If someone cannot kill, regardless of the reason, that individual is not a warrior. Men make the best warriors in comparison to women because men are better at killing in war.
>
> Women cannot compete in a battlefield as they cannot compete in professional sports against men. Women do not hold even one Olympic record for strength or speed. Women are weaker and slower on average as well. Strength, not weakness, wins battles and wars.

As a typical masculinist statement this deserves analysis. "Killing   11
in war" is here represented as a gendered activity, with the unstated
inference that any man who is not good at "killing in war" is less of a
man. The role of modern technology which, being inanimate, must be
gender-free, is transferred to a mythical supermale who is good at killing not because he is equipped with devastatingly effective weaponry
but because he is some kind of an athlete. Only a minute proportion
of males will ever come within reach of an Olympic record, but the
achievements of male record-holders empower all men. The implication that the weakest man must be stronger and faster than any woman
whatsoever is obviously absurd. The ultimate effect of the myth of
masculinity is to generate anxiety in the vast majority of men who
cannot live up to it. The cult of masculinity drives many a man who
knows himself to be unaggressive and timid to opt out of conventional
manhood altogether. Masculinity run riot creates the situation it most
dreads, the wholesale effeminization of men who cannot play its game.

Masculinity is a system. It is the complex of learned behaviors   12
and subtly coded interactions that forms the connective tissue of
corporate society. Women who are inducted into masculinist hierarchies are exported tissue, in constant danger of provoking an inflammatory response and summary rejection. The brokers of Wall Street
are typical of a self-selecting masculinist elite in that they bond by
sharing intensely transgressive experiences. Juniors will recommend
themselves to the alpha males by persecuting underlings, and in particular, women. The men of one Wall Street brokerage firm used to
hold drinking parties in the "boom-boom" room from which women
were excluded. Any woman who dared to make a complaint about
the incessant verbal abuse and physical harassment she was subjected
to would be dealt with after hours in the boom-boom room, where a
lavatory bowl hung from the ceiling. Fifty-year-old stockbroker Pamela
Martens described Wall Street as "an old boy network where that bar-
baric aggressive behavior has to be cloned if you want to advance." The
British Stock Exchange is no more civilized: a successful trader used
to be known as a "big swinging dick" and women as either "babes,"
"mums" or, if they were thought to be at all feminist, "lesbians."

Female interlopers are often quite unaware of the intensity   13
of the inter-male negotiation and consolidation going on around
them. When push comes to shove the guys repair to the men's room
and plot their strategy. The woman who thinks her male colleagues
are dealing with the case on its merits rather than as a pawn in a
long-term power play will only remain in her position of eminence

> The time has come for all guys to come out of the locker room.
> Don't be ashamed of that fetid jockstrap and those toxic

sweat socks. Leave that toilet seat up proudly! The time has come
not only to live openly guy but to embrace the whole guy lifestyle.
— "Guy Pride," *Maxim* Manifesto, March 1997

as long as she serves their purposes. It is no accident that women
inducted into male hierarchies so seldom identify with other women
or advance the interests of other women. They wouldn't have risen
so far in the organization if they did. The most obvious case of this
mechanism at work was Margaret Thatcher,[2] imported into the Tory
hierarchy as an irritant, only to prove strangely successful and so
extend the men's tolerance to an unprecedented degree, and ultimately to be unceremoniously, ageistly, sexistly dumped.

According to Ken Auletta,[3] writing in the *New Yorker,* women exec-   14
utives in the American entertainment business believe that "women
are better managers—more nurturing, more collegial, more commu-
nicative, more instinctual—and that these strengths mesh better with
the corporate culture of teamwork and partnering which is emblematic
of the information age. And as women gain authority, most of them
believe, our movies, our music, our television, our software, and our
other communications will improve." The accompanying photograph
showed twenty-four utterly conformist apparently pre-menopausal
females; none wore glasses; almost all were smiling, decorously
rather than broadly; all wore lipstick, suits, and heels; all were carefully coifed; more than half were blonde. If we have them to thank
for the current state of entertainment, rotten as it is with the crudest
misogyny, drunk as it is on extravagant and trivialized violence, they
must be a very curious bunch of women. The old rule probably still
holds good; if women are running the front office, power must have
taken refuge somewhere else. Insisting on women's management style
as fundamentally softer and more accommodating is a very good way
of ensuring that power stays where it is, in the men's room.

---

[2]**Margaret Thatcher (b. 1925)** Prime minister of Great Britain 1979–1990.
[3]**Ken Auletta (b. 1942)** Author of eight books and a columnist for the
New Yorker magazine.

QUESTIONS FOR CRITICAL READING

1. At what age does induction into masculinity begin?
2. Do organizations like the Boy Scouts and the army try to make men
   out of boys? How?
3. To what extent do you think it is true that boy babies are raised differently than girl babies?

4. What is a good definition of *masculinity*?

5. How do women survive in a masculine organization?

6. What is the significance of courage in the formation of the masculine male?

7. What does Greer mean when she says, "Real men do not fuss or scurry" (para. 7)?

8. Why is killing in war no longer a gendered activity?

SUGGESTIONS FOR CRITICAL WRITING

1. Greer says that as a result of the way he has been raised since babyhood, "The saddest, smelliest, most shambling male individual still imagines that women will find him attractive and is prepared to act on the assumption" (para. 5). Write an essay in which you verify this statement—primarily from experience but possibly from news magazines, biographies, or a study of popular films or TV. If you disagree with Greer on this point, argue your own view carefully, using examples or observations.

2. In paragraph 12, Greer says, "Masculinity is a system. It is the complex of learned behaviors and subtly coded interactions that forms the connective tissue of corporate society." Interpreting "corporate society" to include any structured organization—gangs, fraternities, sororities, or student organizations—establish what you think the "learned behaviors and coded interactions" are that represent and produce the system and how that then produces masculinity. Are you in agreement with Greer, or do you feel you must argue against her?

3. To what extent do you feel that Greer thinks masculinity is a desirable quality in our society? Her statement about "[m]asculinity run riot" (para. 11) implies that there is a form of masculinity that does not run riot and that therefore may be acceptable behavior. Taking your cue from Greer, write a short essay that establishes exactly what qualities of masculinity you think are essential in your immediate society—and perhaps in society at large—for it to function properly. Would an absence of masculinity do our society irreparable harm?

4. Greer makes a great deal out of the expression "to make a man" of a boy. If you are male, describe your experiences with people or organizations that have tried to make a man of you. Do you value their efforts or do you find that they did you a disservice? If you are female, what have you observed in your male acquaintances regarding the effort people have made to make men of them? Did your acquaintances seem to change for the better or for the worse? What do you think it means to make a man of a boy? From your point of view, is it a good thing?

5. In paragraph 11, Greer says, "Masculinity run riot creates the situation it most dreads, the wholesale effeminization of men who cannot play

its game." Does this observation seem true to you? Describe what you think Greer means by "[m]asculinity run riot." Is it possible to overdo masculinity? Can a man be too masculine? Why would masculinity "run riot" effeminize men? Would the "junior males" who "step and fetch it" in the "pool hall" or "restaurant" be effeminized men? What does Greer seem to mean by "effeminization"?

6. **CONNECTIONS** In paragraph 5, Greer discusses issues that sound particularly close to the Freudian view on the oedipal complex. How much in agreement with Freud does Greer seem to be? Compare her views with those of Freud in his essay "The Oedipus Complex" (p. 915). Although Freud insists that oedipal drives are totally unconscious for the individual, you may have witnessed either in literature or in your own experience the complex in action. Do you think it works the way Greer says it does? Is Greer being Freudian? Explain your reasoning on this point.

7. **CONNECTIONS** Germaine Greer focuses on the ways in which boys are raised in their families, arguing that they derive considerable ego strength from the strength of their relationships with their mothers. However, the opposite may be true of girls. To what extent does Horney (**bedfordstmartins.com/worldofideas/epages**) seem to take into account the socialization of boys and girls? Would she find Greer's theories substantial enough to bolster her own views? Which of these writers seems to have a more profound grip on evidence in their positions on masculinity and femininity? Are their arguments equally convincing?

8. **SEEING CONNECTIONS** Greer's book on female painters, *The Obstacle Race*, is more concerned with women who were disregarded and whose work was lost than it is with painters, such as Cassatt, who were successful in a man's world. Greer says women pay a price for being successful, as she describes in her final paragraphs. Research Cassatt's background and decide whether or not she fits the pattern Greer establishes for female painters. Then examine *In the Loge* (p. 650) with an eye to expressions of masculinity and femininity. Has Cassatt portrayed the woman in the loge as being more masculine than feminine in behavior? What details or visual structures in the painting seem classifiable as masculine or feminine? Are they all cultural constructs?

JUDITH BUTLER
From *Undoing Gender*

JUDITH BUTLER (b. 1956) is Maxine Eliot Professor of Rhetoric and Comparative Literature at the University of California, Berkeley. Currently, she is a visiting professor at Columbia University in New York City. She was originally trained in philosophy, and much of her work has been wide-ranging, considering gender studies and political and psychoanalytic issues, as well as concerns for how language shapes our understanding of not just the world, but ourselves.

Her work is often theoretical and influenced by the modern European theoreticians who have sometimes been described as post-structuralist. As a result, her writing has been criticized for being too indirect, abstract, and obscure. However, her book *Undoing Gender* (2004), from which the following selection is taken, is written in a style marked by clarity and directness, unlike many of her articles and other books. She has done a great deal of work focused on gender identity and on the nature of sexuality and argues that both are largely the result of socialization and the force of language in our society. She admits that this idea seems inherently contrary to common sense, but it is for that very reason that she asks us to listen closely to her reasoning. Given the power of language to shape ideas, and given the fluidity of the concept of gender, her argument is taken very seriously by psychologists and philosophers concerned with how individuals view their own nature.

Gender Trouble: Feminism and the Subversion of Identity (1990) was an immediately influential book, its powerful critique of the feminist movement resounding with both academic and popular audiences alike. In it, Butler argues against a "binary view of gender," or a view that limits the definition of gender to a male body and a female body. Butler's argument is that gender is flexible, a continuum from one pole to another of desire. Feminism in 1990, she felt, limited itself to two absolute categories—women and men—with the subsequent view that the focus of sexual desire was also limited to one of these two categories. However, as a lesbian herself and a researcher into gender issues, she knew that desire takes many forms and that feminists holding to their binary view limited the movement as well as themselves. If feminists rejected the doctrine that biology is destiny on the basis of a male-female model, then it was necessary for them to explore their views of the nature of biology and the demands of society with more vigor.

Current research has shown that rigid categories of sexuality have been impossible to maintain. Transgender operations have proliferated enough that public figures have had national recognition in their efforts to change their perceived gender status. Queer studies has become a valid academic discipline in many major universities, especially now that efforts have been made to remove any stigma from homosexual and lesbian lifestyles. Same-sex marriage has become, if not common, more greatly recognized by state laws. Butler has been in the forefront of trying to change society's awareness of how limitations in attitudes affect the perceptions of all of us.

Butler's Rhetoric

As a professor of rhetoric, Butler is deeply concerned with the ways in which language defines people and things. She points out that in some cases it is only through language that we understand the nature of reality—and at that, we cannot totally trust language to give us the complete truth about things. As a result of her concerns for language, she uses it very carefully and performs complex analyses at crucial points in her argument so as to guarantee us as clear a sense of understanding as possible.

The opening pages of her selection establish the general circumstances that she is interested in treating. She explains that she will focus on the human, on "the conditions of intelligibility by which the human emerges" (para. 1). She points to her subjects as "human love," "norms," and "ways of knowing, modes of truth, that forcibly define intelligibility." Her point is that there may be ways of understanding norms and what it is to be human from a careful consideration of what is said and that what we say stands for the truth about humanity.

Once she has established her focus, she introduces us to a narrative of great interest and some complexity. She tells us the case story of David Reimer, a boy who accidentally had his penis burned and subsequently amputated at the age of eight months. The accident was the result of a doctor's mismanagement of an electrocautery needle that he was unfamiliar with. What should have been a risk-free operation totally changed David. His parents, hoping to find a way for him to have a heterosexual life, took him to Dr. John Money at Johns Hopkins University to consult about what should be done. Money was famous for his sex transformation cases involving infants with anomalous sexual organs (often described as hermaphrodites). Money convinced the parents that David could be raised as a girl with great success. He explained that socialization, along with hormones, would establish gender and that David, renamed Brenda, would grow up as a girl and achieve a sense of female identity and feel normal. Money had a reputation for success in cases similar to this, and Brenda was raised as a girl never knowing about the medical mutilation during his infancy.

But the story was complicated by several things. One was that Brenda, as the subject of Dr. Money's scientific studies, was being studied by others to see how the gender change was working: she was frequently asked to disrobe and was examined by other doctors; she was questioned routinely about her feelings and her progress. Brenda became a medical subject and therefore did not experience what others might have considered a normal upbringing. By age two, Brenda began to show signs of gender-assignment discomfort, rejecting clothes chosen for her and choosing what were thought to be inappropriate toys, such as machine guns. Ultimately, Brenda rejected her female assignment and, at age fourteen, became David once again. He underwent another surgery to return himself to something close to the physical male norm.

Butler comments on all the phases of this narrative and ends her essay with a detailed analysis of the narrative that she presents of David's development. She also analyzes David's own account of his circumstances as it is told in the literature. The story has subtleties that Butler unravels in her quest to answer certain questions about what she calls "gender essentialism" and the relationship of gender and gender assignments to the body itself. The question of what constitutes a norm is also central to her interests in understanding the significance of David's experiences moving from gender to gender. Butler's analysis is detailed and thorough, but she admits that there are many aspects of this case that cannot be easily understood, especially by examining the narratives in which the case is presented. As readers of her narrative and her analysis, we are brought to an understanding of our own limitations in the face of narratives that limit our intelligence of what really happened. That is a major part of Butler's central point. Language comes between us and the reality, but that does not prevent us from trying to understand the reality of David's experiences.

Unfortunately, while Butler was preparing her book for press, David Reimer killed himself. She appends that information in a post-script at the end of the selection, but there is much more to the story that should be known. For example, David's was the first experiment by John Money on a child not born a hermaphrodite or with inde-terminate genitals. Moreover, David was never told he was born a boy until he was fourteen years old. Once he was told, he said he knew why he had the feelings he had had when he was young and that now he did not feel like a freak. He had his breasts removed and then insisted on being given the FTM (female-to-male) surgery that restored him to his original gender. John Colapinto, who wrote a best-selling book about David, was not entirely surprised that David killed himself. Colapinto said that David had been taunted relent-lessly as a child and that those experiences haunted him. In addi-tion, his mother and brother had been clinically depressed. His twin brother Brian overdosed on antidepressants two years before David took his own life at the age of thirty-eight.

Butler focuses on David as an example of someone who struggled with gender issues while in the care of doctors who held to some fundamental decisions regarding the truth about gender and what it should look like. Butler makes us aware that such decisions are not easily reached nor are they easily defended.

PREREADING QUESTIONS:
WHAT TO READ FOR

The following prereading questions may help you anticipate key issues in the discussion of this excerpt from Judith Butler's *Undoing Gender*. Keeping them in mind during your first reading should help focus your attention.

- What is the relation of gender to personhood?
- Is there an essential gender core (see para. 9)?
- What was David Reimer's experience with gender reassignment?

From *Undoing Gender*

I would like to take my point of departure from a question of   1
power, the power of regulation, a power that determines, more or less, what we are, what we can be. I am not speaking of power only in a juridical or positive sense, but I am referring to the workings of a certain

regulatory regime, one that informs the law, and also exceeds the law. When we ask, what are the conditions of intelligibility by which the human emerges, by which the human is recognized, by which some subject becomes the subject of human love, we are asking about conditions of intelligibility composed of norms, of practices, that have become presuppositional, without which we cannot think the human at all. So I propose to broach the relationship between variable orders of intelligibility and the genesis and knowability of the human. And it is not just that there are laws that govern our intelligibility, but ways of knowing, modes of truth, that forcibly define intelligibility.

This is what Foucault[1] describes as the politics of truth, a politics   2 that pertains to those relations of power that circumscribe in advance what will and will not count as truth, which order the world in certain regular and regulatable ways, and which we come to accept as the given field of knowledge. We can understand the salience of this point when we begin to ask: What counts as a person? What counts as a coherent gender? What qualifies as a citizen? Whose world is legitimated as real? Subjectively, we ask: Who can I become in such a world where the meanings and limits of the subject are set out in advance for me? By what norms am I constrained as I begin to ask what I may become? And what happens when I begin to become that for which there is no place within the given regime of truth? This is what Foucault describes as the desubjugation of the subject in the play of . . . the politics of truth."

Another way of putting this is the following: "What, given the   3 contemporary order of being, can I be?" This question does not quite broach the question of what it is not to be, or what it is to occupy the place of not-being within the field of being. What it is to live, breathe, attempt to love neither as fully negated nor as fully acknowledged as being. This relationship, between intelligibility and the human is an urgent one; it carries a certain theoretical urgency, precisely at those points where the human is encountered at the limits of intelligibility itself. I would like to suggest that this interrogation has something important to do with justice. Justice is not only or exclusively a matter of how persons are treated or how societies are constituted. It also concerns consequential decisions about what a person is, and what social norms must be honored and expressed for "personhood" to become allocated, how we do or do not recognize animate others as persons depending on whether or not we recognize a certain norm manifested in and by the body of that other. The very criterion by which we judge a person to be a gendered being, a criterion that posits

---

[1] **Michel Foucault (1926–1984)** Important French historian of ideas.

coherent gender as a presupposition of humanness, is not only one which, justly or unjustly, governs the recognizability of the human, but one that informs the ways we do or do not recognize ourselves at the level of feeling, desire, and the body, at the moments before the mirror, in the moments before the window, in the times that one turns to psychologists, to psychiatrists, to medical and legal professionals to negotiate what may well feel like the unrecognizability of one's gender and, hence, the unrecognizability of one's personhood.

I want to consider a legal and psychiatric case of a person who   4
was determined without difficulty to be a boy at the time of birth, then determined again within a few months to be a girl, who decided in his teenage years to become a man. This is the story of David Reimer, whose situation is referred to as "the Joan/John case," one that was brought to public attention by the BBC and in various popular, psychological, and medical journals. I base my analysis on several documents: an article written by Dr. Milton Diamond, an endocrinologist, and the popular book *As Nature Made Him,* written by John Colapinto, a journalist for *Rolling Stone,* as well as several publications by John Money, and critical commentaries offered by Anne Fausto-Sterling and Suzanne Kessler in their important recent books.[2] David Reimer has now talked openly to the media and has chosen to live outside the pseudonym reserved for him by Milton Diamond and his colleagues. David became "Brenda" at a certain point in his childhood which I discuss below, and so instead of referring to him as Joan and John, neither of which is his name, I will use the name he uses.

David was born with XY chromosomes and at the age of eight   5
months, his penis was accidentally burned and severed in the course of a surgical operation to rectify phimosis, a condition in which the foreskin thwarts urination. This is a relatively risk-free procedure, but the doctor who performed it on David was using a new machine, apparently one that he hadn't used before, one that his colleagues declared was unnecessary for the job. He had trouble making the machine work, so he increased the power to the machine to the point that it effectively burned away a major portion of the penis. The parents were, of course, appalled and shocked, and they were, according to their own description, unclear how to proceed. Then one evening, about a year after this event, they were watching television, and there they encountered John Money, talking about transsexual and intersexual surgery, offering the view that if a child underwent surgery and started socialization

---

[2]**John Money (1921–2006)** Controversial psychologist and sex researcher; **Anne Fausto-Sterling (b. 1944)**, author of "The Five Sexes: Why Male and Female Are Not Enough" (2000); **Suzanne Kessler (b. 1946)**, author of *Lessons from the Intersexed* (2000). All three are important experts in gender studies.

as a gender different from the one originally assigned at birth, the child could develop normally, adapt perfectly well to the new gender, and live a happy life. The parents wrote to Money and he invited them to Baltimore, and so David was subsequently seen at Johns Hopkins University, at which point the strong recommendation was made by Dr. John Money that David be raised as a girl. The parents agreed, and the doctors removed the testicles, made some preliminary preparation for surgery to create a vagina, but decided to wait until Brenda, the newly named child, was older to complete the task. So Brenda grew up as a girl, and was monitored often, given over on a periodic basis to John Money's Gender Identity Institute for the purposes of fostering adaptation to being a girl. Then between the ages of eight and nine, Brenda found herself developing the desire to buy a toy machine gun. Between the ages of nine and eleven, she started to make the realization that she was not a girl. This realization seems to coincide with the desire to buy certain kinds of toys: more guns, apparently, and some trucks. Although there was no penis, Brenda liked to stand to urinate. And she was caught in this position once, at school, and the other girls threatened to "kill" her if she continued.

At this point, the psychiatric teams that were intermittently moni- 6 toring Brenda's adaptation offered her estrogen, and she refused this. Money tried to talk to her about getting a real vagina, and she refused; in fact, she went screaming from the room. Money had her view sexually graphic pictures of vaginas. Money even went so far as to show Brenda pictures of women giving birth, holding out the promise that Brenda might be able to give birth if she acquired a vagina. And in a scene that could have been the model for the recent film *But I'm a Cheerleader!* she and her brother were required to perform mock coital exercises with one another, on command. They both later reported being very frightened and disoriented by this demand and did not tell their parents at the time. Brenda is said to have preferred male activities and not to have liked developing breasts. And all of these attributions to Brenda are made by another set of doctors, this time a team of psychiatrists at Brenda's local hospital. The local psychiatrists and medical professionals intervened in the case, believing that a mistake had been made in sex reassignment here, and eventually the case was reviewed by Milton Diamond, a sex researcher who believes in the hormonal basis of gender identity and who has been battling Money for several years. This new set of psychiatrists and doctors offered her the choice of changing paths, which she accepted. She started living as a boy, named David, at the age of fourteen. At this point, David started requesting, and receiving, male hormone shots, and also had his breasts removed. A phallus, so it was called by Diamond, was constructed for him between the age of fifteen and sixteen. David, it is reported, does not ejaculate, although he feels some sexual pleasure there; he urinates from its base. It is a phallus that only approximates some of its expected functions and, as we shall see, enters David only ambivalently into the norm.

During the time that David was Brenda, Money continued to pub-   7
lish papers extolling the success of this sex reassignment case. The case was enormously consequential because Brenda had a brother for an identical twin, and so Money could track the development of both siblings and assume an identical genetic makeup for both of them. He insisted that both were developing normally and happily into their different genders. But his own recorded interviews, mainly unpublished, and subsequent research, have called his honesty into question. Brenda was hardly happy, refused to adapt to many so-called girl behaviors, and was appalled and angered by Money's invasive and constant interrogations. And yet, the published records from Johns Hopkins claim that Brenda's adaptation to girlhood was "successful," and immediately certain ideological conclusions followed. John Money's Gender Identity Clinic, which monitored Brenda often, concluded that Brenda's successful development as a girl "offers convincing evidence that the gender identity gate is open at birth for a normal child no less than for one born with unfinished sex organs or one who was prenatally over or underexposed to androgen, and that it stays open at least for something over a year at birth." Indeed, the case was used by the public media to make the case that what is feminine and what is masculine can be altered, that these cultural terms have no fixed meaning or internal destiny, and that they are more malleable than previously thought. Even Kate Millett[3] cited the case in making the argument that biology is not destiny. And Suzanne Kessler also cowrote with Money essays in favor of the social constructionist thesis. Later Kessler would disavow the alliance and write one of the most important books on the ethical and medical dimensions of sex assignment, *Lessons from the Intersexed,* which includes a trenchant critique of Money himself.

Money's approach to Brenda was to recruit male to female trans-   8
sexuals to talk to Brenda about the advantages of being a girl. Brenda was subjected to myriad interviews, asked again and again whether she felt like a girl, what her desires were, what her image of the future was, whether it included marriage to a man. Brenda was also asked to strip and show her genitals to medical practitioners who were either interested in the case or monitoring the case for its adaptational success.

When this case was discussed in the press, and when psychia-   9
trists and medical practitioners have referred to it, they have done

---

[3] **Kate Millett (b. 1934)** Important feminist and author of *Sexual Politics* (1990).

so in order to criticize the role that John Money's institute played in the case and, in particular, how quickly that institute sought to use Brenda as an example of its own theoretical beliefs, beliefs about the gender neutrality of early childhood, about the malleability of gender, of the primary role of socialization in the production of gender identity. In fact, this is not exactly everything that Money believes, but I will not probe that question here. Those who have become critical of this case believe that it shows us something very different. When we consider, they argue, that David found himself deeply moved to become a boy, and found it unbearable to continue to live as a girl, we have to consider as well that there was some deep-seated sense of gender that David experienced, one that is linked to his original set of genitals, one that seems to be there, as an internal truth and necessity, which no amount of socialization could reverse. This is the view of Colapinto and of Milton Diamond as well. So now the case of Brenda/David is being used to make a revision and reversal in developmental gender theory, providing evidence this time for the reversal of Money's thesis, supporting the notion of an essential gender core, one that is tied in some irreversible way to anatomy and to a deterministic sense of biology. Indeed, Colapinto clearly links Money's cruelty to Brenda to the "cruelty" of social construction as a theory, remarking that Money's refusal to identify a biological or anatomical basis for gender difference in the early 1970s "was not lost on the then-burgeoning women's movement, which had been arguing against a biological basis for sex differences for decades." He claims that Money's published essays "had already been used as one of the main foundations of modern feminism." He quotes *Time* magazine as engaging in a similarly misguided appropriation of Money's views when they argued that this case "provides strong support for a major contention of women's liberationists: that conventional patterns of masculine and feminine behavior can be altered. . . ." Indeed, Colapinto proceeds to talk about the failure of surgically reassigned individuals to live as "normal" and "typical" women or men, arguing that normality is never achieved and, hence, assuming throughout the inarguable value of normalcy itself.

When Natalie Angier[4] reported on the refutation of Money's theory in the *New York Times* (14 March 1997), she claimed that the story of David had "the force of allegory." But which force was that? And is this an allegory with closure? In that article, Angier reports that Diamond used the case to make an argument about intersexual surgery   10

---

[4]**Natalie Angier (b. 1958)** A science correspondent for the *New York Times* and author of *Natural Obsessions* (1988), a study of cancer research.

and, by implication, the relative success of transsexual surgery. Diamond argued, for instance, that intersexed infants, that is, those born with mixed genital attributes, generally have a Y chromosome, and the possession of the Y is an adequate basis for concluding that the child ought to be raised as a boy. As it is, the vast majority of intersexed infants are subjected to surgery that seeks to assign them to a female sex, since, as Cheryl Chase, points out, it is simply considered easier to produce a provisional vaginal tract than it is to construct a phallus. Diamond argues that these children should be assigned to the male sex, since the presence of the Y is sufficient grounds for the presumption of social masculinity.

In fact, Chase, the founder and director of the Intersexed Society of North America, voiced skepticism about Diamond's recommendations. Her view, defended by Anne Fausto-Sterling as well, is that although a child should be given a sex assignment for the purposes of establishing a stable social identity, it does not follow that society should engage in coercive surgery to remake the body in the social image of that gender. Such efforts at "correction" not only violate the child but lend support to the idea that gender has to be borne out in singular and normative ways at the level of anatomy. Gender is a different sort of identity, and its relation to anatomy is complex. According to Chase, a child upon maturing may choose to change genders or, indeed, elect for hormonal or surgical intervention, but such decisions are justified because they are based on knowing choice. Indeed, research has shown that such surgical operations have been performed without parents knowing, that such surgical operations have been performed without the children themselves ever having been truthfully told, and without waiting until the child is old enough to offer his or her consent. Most astonishing, in a way, is the mutilated state that these bodies are left in, mutilations performed and then paradoxically rationalized in the name of "looking normal," the rationale used by medical practitioners to justify these surgeries. They often say to parents that the child will not look normal, that the child will be ashamed in the locker room, the locker room, that site of prepubescent anxiety about impending gender developments, and that it would be better for the child to look normal, even when such surgery may deprive the person permanently of sexual function and pleasure. So, as some experts, such as Money, claim that the absence of the full phallus makes the social case for rearing the child as a girl, others such as Diamond argue that the presence of the Y is the most compelling evidence, that it is what is being indexed in persistent feelings of masculinity, and that it cannot be constructed away.

Thus, in the one case, how anatomy looks, how it appears to others, and to myself, as I see others looking at me—this is the basis of

11

12

a social identity as woman or man. In the other case, how the genetic presence of the "Y" works in tacit ways to structure feeling and self-understanding as a sexed person is the basis. Money thus argues for the ease with which a female body can be surgically constructed, as if femininity was always little more or less than a surgical construction, an elimination, a cutting away. Diamond argues for the invisible and necessary persistence of maleness, one that does not need to "appear" in order to operate as the key feature of gender identity itself. When Angier asks Chase whether she agrees with Diamond's recommendations on intersexual surgery, Chase replies: "They can't conceive of leaving someone alone." Indeed, is the surgery performed in order to create a "normal-looking" body after all? The mutilations and scars that remain hardly offer compelling evidence that this is what the surgeries actually accomplish. Or are these bodies, precisely because they are "inconceivable," subjected to medical machinery that marks them for life?

Another paradox emerges here—one that I hope to write about 13 further on another occasion—namely, the place of sharp machines, of the technology of the knife, in debates on intersexuality and trans-sexuality alike. If the David/Brenda case is an allegory, or has the force of allegory, it seems to be the site where debates on intersexuality (David is not an intersexual) and transsexuality (David is not a trans-sexual) converge. This body becomes a point of reference for a narra-tive that is not about this body, but which seizes upon the body, as it were, in order to inaugurate a narrative that interrogates the limits of the conceivably human. What is inconceivable is conceived again and again, through narrative means, but something remains outside the narrative, a resistant moment that signals a persisting inconceivability.

Despite Diamond's recommendations, the intersex movement has 14 been galvanized by the Brenda/David case, able now to bring to public attention the brutality, coerciveness, and lasting harm of the unwanted surgeries performed on intersexed infants. The point is to try to imag-ine a world in which individuals with mixed genital attributes might be accepted and loved without having to transform them into a more socially coherent or normative version of gender. In this sense, the intersex movement has sought to question why society maintains the ideal of gender dimorphism[5] when a significant percentage of children are chromosomally various, and a continuum exists between male and female that suggests the arbitrariness and falsity of the gen-der dimorphism as a prerequisite of human development. There are humans, in other words, who live and breathe in the interstices of this

---

[5]**gender dimorphism** Theory that the only genders are male and female, based on the male and female bodies.

binary relation, showing that it is not exhaustive; it is not necessary. Although the transsexual movement, which is internally various, has called for rights to surgical means by which sex might be transformed, it is also clear—and Chase underscores this—that there is also a serious and increasingly popular critique of idealized gender dimorphism within the transsexuality movement itself. One can see it in the work of Riki Wilchins,[6] whose gender theory makes room for transsexuality as a transformative exercise, but one can see it perhaps most dramatically in Kate Bornstein, who argues that to go from F to M, or from M to F, is not necessarily to stay within the binary frame of gender, but to engage transformation itself as the meaning of gender. In some ways, it is Kate Bornstein who is now carrying the legacy of Simone de Beauvoir:[7] if one is not born a woman, but rather becomes one, then becoming is the vehicle for gender itself. But why, we might ask, has David become the occasion for a reflection on transsexuality?

Although David comes to claim that he would prefer to be a man,   15 it is not clear whether David himself believes in the primary causal force of the Y chromosome. Diamond finds support for his theory in David, but it is not clear that David agrees with Diamond. David clearly knows about the world of hormones, asked for them and takes them. David has learned about phallic construction from transsexual contexts, wants a phallus, has it made, and so allegorizes a certain transsexual transformation without precisely exemplifying it. He is, in his view, a man born a man, castrated by the medical establishment, feminized by the psychiatric world, and then enabled to return to who he is. But in order to return to who he is, he requires—and wants, and gets—a subjection to hormones and surgery. He allegorizes transsexuality in order to achieve a sense of naturalness. And this transformation is applauded by the endocrinologists on the case since they understand his appearance now to be in accord with an inner truth. Whereas the Money Institute enlists transsexuals to instruct Brenda in the ways of women, and *in the name of normalization,* the endocrinologists prescribe the sex change protocol of transsexuality to David for him to reassume his genetic destiny, *in the name of nature.*

And though the Money Institute enlists transsexuals to allegorize   16 Brenda's full transformation into a woman, the endocrinologists propose to appropriate transsexual surgery in order to build the phallus that will make David a more legible man. Importantly, it seems, the

---

[6] **Riki Wilchins (b. 1952)** An activist who focuses on gender norms but who is best known for bringing transgender people into public acceptance.

[7] **Kate Bornstein (b. 1948)** A transsexual and author of *Gender Outlaw* (1994). **Simone de Beauvoir (1908–1986)** was a celebrated French writer and philosopher and author of *The Second Sex* (1953).

norms [that] govern intelligible gender for Money are those that can be forcibly imposed and behaviorally appropriated, so the malleability of gender construction, which is part of his thesis, turns out to require a forceful application. And the "nature" that the endocrinologists defend also needs a certain assistance through surgical and hormonal means, at which point a certain nonnatural intervention in anatomy and biology is precisely what is mandated by nature. So in each case, the primary premise is in some ways refuted by the means by which it is implemented. *Malleability is, as it were, violently imposed. And naturalness is artificially induced.* There are ways of arguing social construction that have nothing to do with Money's project, but that is not my aim here. And there are no doubt ways of seeking recourse to genetic determinants that do not lead to the same kind of interventionist conclusions that are arrived at by Diamond and Sigmundsen. But that is also not precisely my point. For the record, though, the prescriptions arrived at by these purveyors of natural and normative gender in no way follow necessarily from the premises from which they begin, and that the premises with which they begin have no necessity of itself. (One might well disjoin the theory of gender construction, for instance, from the hypothesis of gender normativity and have a very different account of social construction than that offered by Money; one might allow from genetic factors without assuming that they are the only aspect of "nature" that one might consult to understand the sexed characteristics of a human: Why is the "Y" considered the exclusive and primary determinant of maleness, exercising preemptive rights over any and all other factors?)

But my point in recounting this story to you and its appropriation for the purposes of gender theory is to suggest that the story as we have it does not actually supply evidence for either thesis, and to suggest that there may be another way of reading this story, one that neither confirms nor denies the theory of social construction, one that neither affirms nor denies gender essentialism. Indeed, what I hope to underscore here is the disciplinary framework within which Brenda/David develops a discourse of self-reporting and self-understanding, since it constitutes the grid of intelligibility by which his own humanness is both questioned and asserted. It seems crucial to remember, as one considers what might count as the evidence of the truth of gender, that Brenda/David was intensely monitored by psychological teams through childhood and adolescence, that teams of doctors observed her behavior, that teams of doctors asked her and her brother to disrobe in front of them so that genital development could be gauged, that there was the doctor who asked her to engage in mock coital exercises with her brother, to view the pictures, to know and want the so-called normalcy of unambiguous genitalia. There was an apparatus of knowledge applied to the person and body of Brenda/David that is

17

rarely, if ever, taken into account as part of what David is responding to when he reports on his feelings of true gender.

The act of self-reporting and the act of self-observation take place   18
in relation to a certain audience, with a certain audience as the imagined recipient, before a certain audience for whom a verbal and visual picture of selfhood is being produced. These are speech acts that are very often delivered to those who have been scrutinizing, brutally, the truth of Brenda's gender for years. And even though Diamond and Sigmundsen and even Colapinto are in the position of defending David against Money's various intrusions, they are still asking David how he feels and who he is, trying to ascertain the truth of his sex through the discourse he provides. Because Brenda was subjected to such scrutiny and, most importantly, constantly and repeatedly subjected to a norm, a normalizing ideal that was conveyed through a plurality of gazes, a norm applied to the body, a question is constantly posed: Is this person feminine enough? Has this person made it to femininity? Is femininity being properly embodied here? Is the embodiment working? What evidence can be marshalled in order to know? And surely we must have knowledge here. We must be able to say that we know, and to communicate that in the professional journals, and justify our decision, our act. In other words, these exercises interrogate whether the gender norm that establishes coherent personhood has been successfully accomplished. The inquiries and inspections can be understood, along these lines, as the violent attempt to implement the norm, and the institutionalization of that power of implementation.

The pediatricians and psychiatrists who have revisited the case in   19
recent years cite David's own self-description to support their point. David's narrative about his own sense of being male that supports the theory that David is really male, and that he was, even when he was Brenda, always male.

David tells his interviewers the following about himself: 20

> There were little things from early on. I began to see how different I felt and was, from what I was supposed to be. But I didn't know what it meant. I thought I was a freak or something . . . I looked at myself and said I don't like this type of clothing, I don't like the types of toys I was always being given. I like hanging around with the guys and climbing trees and stuff like that and girls don't like any of that stuff. I looked in the mirror and [saw] my shoulders [were] so wide, I mean there [was] nothing feminine about me. I [was] skinny, but other than that, nothing. But that [was] how I figured it out. [I figured I was a guy] but didn't want to admit it. I figured I didn't want to wind up opening a can of worms.

So now you read how David describes himself. And so, if part of   21
my task here is to do justice, not only to my topic, but to the person

I am sketching for you, the person around whom so much has been said, the person whose self-description and whose decisions have become the basis for so much gender theorizing, I must be careful in presenting these words. For these words can give you only something of the person I am trying to understand, some part of that person's verbal instance. Since I cannot truly understand this person, since I do not know this person, and have no access to this person, I am left to be a reader of a selected number of words, words that I did not fully select, ones that were selected for me, recorded from interviews and then chosen by those who decided to write their articles on this person for journals such as the *Archives of Pediatric Adolescent Medicine.* So we might say that I am given fragments of the person, linguistic fragments of something called a person; what might it mean to do justice to someone under these circumstances? Can we?

On the one hand, we have a self-description, and that is to be   22
honored. These are the words by which this individual gives himself to be understood. On the other hand, we have a description of a self that takes place in a language that is already going on, that is already saturated with norms, that predisposes us as we seek to speak of ourselves. Moreover, we have words that are delivered in the context of an interview, an interview which is part of the long and intrusive observational process that has accompanied Brenda's formation from the start. To do justice to David is, certainly, to take him at his word, and to call him by his chosen name, but how are we to understand his word and his name? Is this the word that he creates? Is this the word that he receives? Are these the words that circulate prior to his emergence as an "I" who might only gain a certain authorization to begin a self-description within the norms of this language? So that when one speaks, one speaks a language that is already speaking, even if one speaks it in a way that is not precisely how it has been spoken before. So what and who is speaking here, when David reports: "There were little things from early on. I began to see how different I felt and was, from what I was supposed to be."

This claim tells us minimally that David understands that there   23
is a norm, a norm of how he was supposed to be, and that he has fallen short of the norm. The implicit claim here is that the norm is femininity, and he has failed to live up to that norm. And there is the norm, and it is externally imposed, communicated through a set of expectations that others have; and then there is the world of feeling and being, and these realms are, for him, distinct. What he feels is not in any way produced by the norm, and the norm is other, elsewhere, not part of who he is, who he has become, what he feels.

But given what we know about how David has been addressed,   24
I might, in an effort to do justice to David, ask, what did Brenda see

as Brenda looks at himself, feels as he feels himself, and please excuse my mixing of pronouns here, but matters are becoming changeable. When Brenda looks in the mirror and sees something nameless, freakish, something between the norms, is she not at that moment in question as a human, is she not the spectre of the freak against which and through which the norm installs itself? What is the problem with Brenda such that people are always asking to see her naked, asking her questions about what she is, how she feels, whether this is or is not the same as what is normatively true? Is that self-seeing distinct from the way s/he is seen? He seems clear that the norms are external to him, but what if the norms have become the means by which he sees, the frame for his own seeing, his way of seeing himself? What if the action of the norm is to be found not merely in the ideal that it posits, but in the sense of aberration and of freakishness that it conveys? Consider where precisely the norm operates when David claims, "I looked at myself and said I don't like this type of clothing." To whom is David speaking? And in what world, under what conditions, does not liking that type of clothing provide evidence for being the wrong gender? For whom would that be true? And under what conditions?

Brenda reports, "I didn't like the toys I was being given," and Brenda is speaking here as someone who understands that such a dislike can function as evidence. And it seems reasonable to assume that the reason Brenda understands this "dislike" as evidence of gender dystopia, to use the technical term, is that Brenda has been addressed time and again by those who make use of every utterance that Brenda makes about her experience as evidence for or against a true gender. That Brenda happens not to like certain toys, certain dolls, certain games, may be significant in relation to the question of how and with what Brenda likes to play. But in what world, precisely, do such dislikes count as clear or unequivocal evidence for or against being a given gender? Do parents regularly rush off to gender identity clinics when their boys play with yarn, or their girls play with trucks? Or must there already be a rather enormous anxiety at play, an anxiety about the truth of gender which seizes on this or that toy, this or that proclivity of dress, the size of the shoulder, the leanness of the body, to conclude that something like a clear gender identity can or cannot be built from these scattered desires, these variable and invariable features of the body, of bone structure, of proclivity, of attire? 25

So what does my analysis imply? Does it tell us whether the gender here is true or false? No. And does this have implications for whether David should have been surgically transformed into Brenda, or Brenda surgically transformed into David? No, it does not. I do not know how to judge that question here, and I am not sure it can be mine to judge. Does justice demand that I decide? Or does justice demand that I wait 26 to decide, that I practice a certain deferral in the face of a situation in which too many have rushed to judgment? Might it not be useful, important, even just, to consider a few matters before we decide, before we ascertain whether it is, in fact, ours to decide.

Consider in this spirit, then, that it is for the most part the gender essentialist position that must be voiced for transsexual surgery to take place, and that someone who comes in with a sense of the gender as changeable will have a more difficult time convincing psychiatrists and doctors to perform the surgery. In San Francisco, FTM[8] candidates actually practice the narrative of gender essentialism that they are required to perform before they go in to see the doctors, and there are now coaches to help them, dramaturgs[9] of transsexuality who will help you make the case for no fee. Indeed, we might say that Brenda/David together went through two transsexual surgeries: the first based on a hypothetical argument about what gender should be, given the ablated[10] nature of the penis; the second based on what the gender should be, based on the behavioral and verbal indications of the person in question. In both cases, certain inferences are made, ones that suggest that a body must be a certain way for a gender to work, another which says that a body must feel a certain way for a gender to work. David clearly came to disrespect and abhor the views of the first set of doctors and developed, we might say, a lay critique of the phallus to support his resistance: 27

> Doctor said "it's gonna be tough, you're gonna be picked on, you're gonna be very alone, you're not gonna find anybody (unless you have vaginal surgery and live as a female)." And I thought to myself, you know I wasn't very old at the time, but it dawned on me that these people gotta be pretty shallow if that's the only thing they think I've got going for me; that the only reason why people get married and have children and have a productive life is because of what they have between their legs. . . . If that's all they think of me, that they justify my worth by what I have between my legs, then I gotta be a complete loser.

Here David makes a distinction between the "I" that he is, the person that he is, and the value that is conferred upon his personhood by virtue of what is or is not between his legs. He was wagering that he will be loved for something other than this or, at least, that his penis will not be the reason he is loved. He was holding out, implicitly, for something called "depth" over and against the "shallowness" of the doctors. 28

---

[8] **FTM** Female-to-male surgical transformation.
[9] **dramaturgs** Those who supplement the dramatic production of a play through research.
[10] **ablated** Amputated; making a portion of the body nonfunctional.

And so although David asked for and received his new status as male, has asked for and received his new phallus, he is also something other than what he now has, and though he has undergone this transformation, he refuses to be reduced to the body part that he has acquired. "If that's all they think of me," he begins his sentence, offering a knowing and critical rejoinder to the work of the norm. There is something of me that exceeds this part, though I want this part, though it is part of me. He does not want his "worth justified" by what he has between his legs, and what this means is that he has another sense of how the worth of the person might be justified. So we might say that he is living his desire, acquiring the anatomy that he wants in order to live his desire, but that his desire is complex, and his worth is complex. And this is why, no doubt, in response to many of the questions that Money posed: Do you want to have a penis? Do you want to marry a girl? David often refused to answer the question, refused to stay in the room where Money was, refused to visit Baltimore at all after a while.

David does not trade in one gender norm for another, not exactly.   29
It would be as wrong to say that he has simply internalized a gendered norm (from a critical position) as it would be to say that he has failed to live up to a gendered norm (from a normalizing, medical position), since he has already established that what will justify his worth will be the invocation of an "I" which is not reducible to the compatibility of his anatomy with the norm. He thinks something more of himself than what others think, he does not fully justify his worth through recourse to what he has between his legs, and he does not think of himself as a complete loser. Something exceeds the norm, and he recognizes its unrecognizability. It is, in a sense, his distance from the knowably human that operates as a condition of critical speech, the source of his worth, as the justification for his worth. He says that if what those doctors believe were true, he would be a complete loser, and he implies that he is not a complete loser, that something in him is winning.

But he is also saying something more—he is cautioning us   30
against the absolutism of distinction itself, for his phallus does not constitute the entirety of his worth. There is an incommensurability between who he is and what he has, an incommensurability between the phallus he has and what it is expected to be (and in this way no different from anyone with a phallus), which means that he has not become one with the norm, and yet he is still someone, speaking, insisting, even referring to himself. And it is from this gap, this incommensurability, between the norm that is supposed to inaugurate his humanness and the spoken insistence on himself that he performs that he derives his worth, that he speaks his worth. And we cannot precisely give content to this person at the very moment that he speaks

his worth, which means that it is precisely the ways in which he is not fully recognizable, fully disposable, fully categorizable, that his humanness emerges. And this is important because we might ask that he enter into intelligibility in order to speak and to be known, but what he does instead, through his speech, is to offer a critical perspective on the norms that confer intelligibility itself. He shows, we might say, that there is an understanding to be had that exceeds the norms of intelligibility itself. And he achieves this "outside," we might speculate, by refusing the interrogations that besiege him, reversing their terms, and learning the ways in which he might escape. If he renders himself unintelligible to those who seek to know and capture his identity, this means that something about him is intelligible outside of the framework of accepted intelligibility. We might be tempted to say that there is some core of a person, and so some presumption of humanism, that emerges here, that is supervenient to the particular discourses on sexed and gendered intelligibility that constrain him. But that would mean only that he is denounced by one discourse only to be carried by another discourse, the discourse of humanism. Or we might say that there is some core of the subject who speaks, who speaks beyond what is sayable, and that it is this ineffability that marks David's speech, the ineffability of the other who is not disclosed through speech, but leaves a portentious shard of itself in its saying, a self that is beyond discourse itself.

But what I would prefer is that we might consider carefully that when David invokes the "I" in this quite hopeful and unexpected way, he is speaking about a certain conviction he has about his own lovability; he says that "they" must think he is a real loser if the only reason anyone is going to love him is because of what he has between his legs. The "they" is telling him that he will not be loved, or that he will not be loved unless he takes what they have for him, and that they have what he needs in order to get love, that he will be loveless without what they have. But he refuses to accept that what they are offering in their discourse is love. He refuses their offering of love, understanding it as a bribe, as a seduction to subjection. He will be and he is, he tells us, loved for some other reason, a reason they do not understand, and it is not a reason we are given. It is clearly a reason that is beyond the regime of reason established by the norms of sexology itself. We know only that he holds out for another reason, and that in this sense, we no longer know what kind of reason this is, what reason can be; he establishes the limits of what they know, disrupting the politics of truth, making use of his desubjugation within that order of being to establish the possibility of love beyond the grasp of that norm. He positions himself, knowingly, in relation to the norm, but he does not comply with its requirements. He risks a certain "desubjugation"—is he a subject? How will we know? And in this sense, David's discourse puts into play the operation of critique itself, critique which, defined by Foucault, is precisely the desubjugation of the subject within the politics of truth. This does not mean that David becomes unintelligible and, therefore, without value to politics; rather, he emerges at the limits of intelligibility, offering a perspective on the variable ways in which norms circumscribe the human. It is precisely because we understand, without quite grasping, that he has another reason, that he *is*, as it were, another reason, that we see the limits to the discourse of intelligibility that would decide his fate. David does not precisely occupy a new world, since he is still, even within the syntax which brings about his "I," still positioned somewhere between the norm and its failure. And he is, finally, neither one; he is the human in its anonymity, as that which we do not yet know how to name or that which sets a limits on all naming. And in that sense, he is the anonymous — and critical — condition of the human as it speaks itself at the limits of what we think we know.

> Postscript: As this book was going to press in June of 2004, I was saddened to learn that David Reimer took his life at the age of 38. The *New York Times* obituary (5/12/04) mentions that his brother died two years earlier and that he was now separated from his wife. It is difficult to know what, in the end, made his life unlivable or why this life was one he felt was time to end. It seems clear, however, that there was always a question posed for him, and by him, whether life in his gender would be survivable. It is unclear whether it was his gender that was the problem, or the "treatment" that brought about an enduring suffering for him. The norms governing what it is to be a worthy, recognizable, and sustainable human life clearly did not support his life in any continuous or solid way. Life for him was always a wager and a risk, a courageous and fragile accomplishment.

QUESTIONS FOR CRITICAL READING

1. What is most shocking about David Reimer's childhood experiences?
2. What are some of the problems inherent in establishing gender norms?
3. Butler talks about gender essentialism. What does she mean by that term?
4. What seems to be the basis of Dr. John Money's assurance that gender identity is largely socialized?
5. What does David Reimer's experience seem to say about the nature/nurture debate?
6. To what extent do you think a child's choice of toys defines his or her gender?

7. Why did children treat Brenda so badly when she was a child? What motivates children to taunt someone like Brenda when she behaved differently from what they thought was normal?

SUGGESTIONS FOR CRITICAL WRITING

1. In paragraph 14, Butler talks about gender dimorphism. Explain what she means by the term and use the narrative about David Reimer to clarify what you think about the limits of gender identification based on the dimorphism of a male body and a female body. If you feel there are no limits, then explain how David Reimer's story clarifies your position.

2. Judging by the way people behave in your environment, what do you feel the markers of gender difference are? How are they expressed in social situations? How do you think Butler might describe gender differences in our society? How are they expressed in terms of clothing, attitudes, interests, language, and appearance? What are your views on gender-appropriate clothing, attitudes, interests, language, and appearance? Do most of your friends agree or disagree with you?

3. In his narrative, David denies that his value as a human being is limited to "what he has between his legs" (para. 29). Examine his narrative and decide whether you agree with Butler's analysis of this statement and her declaration that in deciding for a sex change he "does not trade in one gender norm for another." How much does "what he has between his legs" define him as a human being? Butler agrees with David on this issue. Do you? How do you think your peers generally feel about how genitalia define them in the estimation of others? How do you respond to their views on this issue?

4. In paragraph 30, Butler talks about David's sense of worth. She says, "We might be tempted to say that there is some core of a person . . . that emerges here." Reflecting on David's own narrative about himself, defend or attack the view that there is a basic core to a person that may or may not be altered or affected by gender or gender choice. Does David's story shed light on the concept that people have a basic core? What seems to be Butler's view on this issue?

5. Is the feminist movement aided by the story of Dr. Money's treatment of David Reimer? Is Butler correct in feeling that feminists limit themselves by assuming that there are only two genders and that they are based entirely on anatomy? Feminists reject the idea that anatomy is destiny, so would they not agree with Butler on this issue? If gender is not based on anatomy, what might it be based on? Does Butler give you any hints?

6. **CONNECTIONS** How do the questions of trust and distrust help clarify the principles that Butler develops in her argument? What in Karen Horney's essay (**bedfordstmartins.com/worldofideas/epages**)

helps Butler make her case? How might Horney, as a psychologist, react to the story of David Reimer and his experiences in sex change? To what extent would Butler be likely to be suspicious of the categories that Horney establishes?

7. **CONNECTIONS**   How could Butler use the findings about the behavior of the tribes Margaret Mead studied in "Sex and Temperament" (p. 707)? Mead reviews the ways in which our society "assigns different roles to the two sexes" and then goes on to examine the tribal groups that she lived with. Why would the study of a tribal society shed light on the question of gender difference or sameness in our society? How would Mead analyze Butler's narrative of gender behavior? What would she find to agree with and what would she question? How does reading Mead help you better understand the concerns of Butler? How does reading Mead affect your understanding of what David Reimer experienced at the hands of the medical community?

8. **SEEING CONNECTIONS**   What might Butler say in an analysis of the painting *In the Loge* by Mary Cassatt (p. 650)? What gender issues might she raise relative to the posture of the main figure in the painting, the action of the figure, her environment, her clothing, or her jewelry? Are the gender definitions in the painting socially constructed, or are they somehow anatomically essential? How feminine is this figure? How feminine would you think Butler would say she wishes to appear? Butler puts great emphasis on appearance as a way of identifying oneself. Given that the figure in the painting is "making an appearance," how does she wish to identify herself?

PART SEVEN

LANGUAGE

Susanne K. Langer
Mario Pei
James Baldwin
Bill Bryson
Neil Postman
Noam Chomsky
Alexander Pope

INTRODUCTION

Language is the dress of thought.
— SAMUEL JOHNSON (1709–1784)

The only language men ever speak perfectly is the one they learn
in babyhood, when no one can teach them anything!
— MARIA MONTESSORI (1870–1952)

Language is wine upon the lips.
— VIRGINIA WOOLF (1882–1941)

The communication of the dead is tongued with fire beyond the
language of the living.
— T. S. ELIOT (1888–1965)

The limits of my language means the limits of my world.
— LUDWIG WITTGENSTEIN (1889–1951)

A different language is a different vision of life.
— FEDERICO FELLINI (1920–1993)

Every legend, moreover, contains its residuum of truth, and the
root function of language is to control the universe by describing it.
— JAMES BALDWIN (1924–1987)

A riot is the language of the unheard.
— MARTIN LUTHER KING JR. (1929–1968)

War is what happens when language fails.
— MARGARET ATWOOD (b. 1939)

The study of language has recently gained considerable importance as a result of new research and discoveries in linguistics. But language has been a subject of wonder and science for centuries because
it has often been seen as a unique principle limited to human beings.
Early commentators made much of the fact that animals do not speak,
nor do they participate in language except on the lowest level—such
as when pets learn to respond to commands and calls. The how and
the why of language have always been a mystery that tempts many
different thinkers to postulate theories of origination and operation.

During the Renaissance, René Descartes (1596–1650), in what
Noam Chomsky calls the first cognitive revolution, proposed that the
mind was the source of human identity and that reason was the key to
comprehending the material world. John Locke (1632–1704), influenced by Descartes, developed a theory of the mind as a tabula rasa,
or blank slate, that began with no content and was shaped entirely
by environment and experience. The mind is still the focus of language studies and the center of research into language activity, but the

concept of the blank slate has been seriously questioned. One current theory proposes that the human mind brings with it at birth a hard-wired system designed explicitly to produce language and that this language faculty exists only in the brains of our species, *Homo sapiens.*

The first selection in this section, by Susanne K. Langer, is a study of the origins of language, focusing especially on the vocalizations of early mankind and the ways in which those vocalizations took on meaning. Langer concerns herself with the infant's instincts toward babbling, or lalling, making sounds that seem to have no meaning in the moment but which eventually transform themselves into words. Her view is that the babbling period in a baby's life is the ideal period for an infant to learn language. Once that period passes, acquiring language is extremely difficult, as she points out in her discussion of Victor, the "Savage of Aveyron," who was discovered wandering near a forest in France in 1797 when he was around twelve years old. Victor was unable to talk because he had grown up without human contact. He was never able to form more than a few basic words and could not communicate complex ideas, despite careful instruction. Langer's basic concern, beyond language acquisition, is to establish that using language is a symbolic action. As she says in *Philosophy in a New Key,* "The development of language is the history of the gradual accumulation and elaboration of verbal symbols." Her point is that the symbolic nature of language allowed people to think in completely different ways from other animals. Language changed the nature of the human mind.

The distinguished modern linguist Mario Pei developed some important popular books on language and was reportedly himself a master of over thirty languages. He had a powerful interest in words in part because he knew so many in so many different languages; he was aware of their origins and their interrelationships. His selection, "Theories of Language Beginning," concerns the origin of language in general. How did it start? And when? He admits that those questions will probably never be answered satisfactorily but are nonetheless important to ask. He reviews a number of colorful theories of origins, such as the "bow-wow" theory, which involves imitating animals, and the "pooh-pooh" theory, which suggests that language originates in reactions to shocks and vocalizations in response to pleasure or pain, fear or delight, and so on. The "yo-he-ho" theory suggests that language began as a result of the vocalizations of people at work, grunting, groaning, shouting, and moaning. All these theories are interesting, and Pei goes on to explore those and many more issues that relate to the beginnings of language and language acquisition.

James Baldwin, one of the United States' most gifted writers, wrote at a time when being African American often made life in his native country unpleasant. He was also a homosexual writer, which sometimes caused tension with the people around him. He resolved these issues by living much of his life in southern France, where he was given more freedom and independence than he might have had in his native Harlem. When he wrote the selection reprinted in this book, he was reacting to controversial arguments that condemned black English as a dialect rather than crediting it as a language. Baldwin comes to the rescue with a powerful polemic that is clearly an emotional outburst as well as a brilliant performance in language.

First a journalist and now a freelance writer, Bill Bryson is known for brilliant books on travel as well as for science books that have won some of the most important major prizes in Great Britain. His several books on language reveal a powerful affection for words. He explores the ways in which words develop in our language and how they differ from other related languages. Words are sometimes created by simple mistakes—people hear a sound and think it is a word; they see a misprint and unknowingly or sportingly accept it as a word. Many words come from other languages, like *ketchup* and *slogan*, and become English by adoption. Some words, like *dog* and *fun*, are simple inventions. No one knows where they came from. Bryson is entertaining while he educates readers to the many ways in which words have entered and continue to enter the English language.

Neil Postman's essay is somewhat more serious. He focuses on the ways in which language shapes our understanding of the world we live in. Words, he tells us, help us map our environment and in some ways both limit and expand our awareness of our world. He is concerned with making us aware that language creates our understanding of just about everything. One of his most important observations points us to the power of metaphor to control meaning and to convince the reader. He is also a devotee of semantics, the science of the meaning of words. He introduces us to the thinking of Alfred Korzybski, the scholar who most helped define the study of semantics. Postman was fearful that television and other electronic sources of entertainment would rob children of their childhood by introducing them to adult subject matter too early in life. He had thought that television would be a great aid in education, but he changed his mind when he realized that what children need more is early exposure to texts in order to develop their language faculties more fully.

"New Horizons in the Study of Language" by Noam Chomsky—who is among the world's best-known contemporary linguists—is a challenging piece that lays out a theory of language and language acquisition based on Chomsky's premise that the brain is specialized to learn language. Because a child can learn any language in the world, Chomsky argues, there must be an "initial state" of language already in the brain from which all languages develop. Chomsky depends on metaphor for much of his argument. He describes, for example, the initial state as something like a switch box in which, depending on experience and what the child hears, switches are turned on one way to produce Japanese, another way to produce Spanish, another way to produce Swahili, and yet another way to produce English. His theory has had a very broad influence on modern linguistics, but it has not been accepted by all contemporary language experts. The question of culture is still a deep concern to all linguisticians and Chomsky also credits experience as having its force in language acquisition.

The e-Pages for this chapter (available online at **bedfordstmartins .com/worldofideas/epages**) feature a selection from Alexander Pope. Rather than taking a scientific stance, Pope discusses language as it was applied for poetic purposes during his time—and uses a poetic form to do so. Pope was a neoclassicist in eighteenth-century England and therefore respected both the Aristotelian and Platonic positions in literature. But he was, like most poets of his time, influenced more by the Roman than the Greek poets. Roman experts in poetic language were Virgil, Horace, Catullus, and Cicero. Their concerns often centered on moral issues and the obligations of the individual to live an upstanding life and contribute to the body politic. In his *Essay on Criticism*, Pope praises poetry that has a strong moral center balanced by temperate qualities and the avoidance of excess. His advice to critics also recommends that they take a holistic view of poetry and not praise or disparage a specific part, such as its language or its metrical patterns. Pope echoes Roman moralists by favoring a middle path and by relying on aphorisms such as: "Be not first by whom we are now tried / Nor yet the last to lay the old aside" (l. 135–136).

VISUALIZING LANGUAGE

Since language is both aural and textual, it is something of a challenge to present a visual image that can embody its complexity. Wosene Worke Kosrof's painting *The Color of Words IX* on page 766 uses Ethiopian Amharic script (a language of ancient Africa) as a way of exploring language in an almost abstract fashion. (To see *The Color of Words IX* in full color, go to **bedfordstmartins.com/worldofideas /epages**.) Wosene—as he signs his work—was born in Ethiopia in 1950 and received his B.F.A. from the School of Fine Arts at Addis Ababa and his M.F.A. from Howard University. His work is in the National Museum at Addis Ababa, the Smithsonian Museum of African Art, the Fowler Museum at UCLA, the Newark Museum in New Jersey, and many more. He exhibits throughout the United States and has his studio in Oakland, California. He says on his Web site, "Applying the

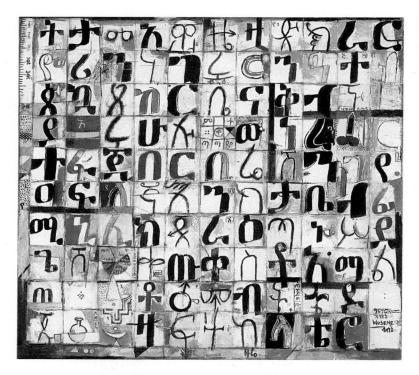

WOSENE WORKE KOSROF, *THE COLOR OF WORDS IX*,
from *WordPlay*. 2002. Acrylic on linen, 31 7/64" × 34". Private collection.

symbols in my paintings, I relieve words of conventional meanings
and, instead, explore their aesthetic, sensual, and visual content."

For thirty years Wosene has been working on an extended series
of paintings called *WordPlay* that rely on the script of Amharic.
Wosene plays with the alphabetic characters and sometimes distorts
them, breaks them, and reassembles them. He has said, "My painting
process is an intense interplay of intention and accident, curiosity and
discovery." He knows that the characters he works with would have
meaning if organized in a specific way, a fact that helps him sense
a potential depth of meaning in his paintings. He is also intent on
exploring the abstract values in the individual elements of the script
itself, which is why he distorts, breaks, and plays with the figures of
the script.

In *The Color of Words IX*, Wosene uses color, but he also says his
painting works in black and white, in part because most of the script
elements are black on a white background. But Wosene also includes

a number of figures in the patterning of the painting that seem drawn from graffiti or natural forms. His project permits him to be both creative and playful with his images and the exploration of the dissection and combination of the Amharic script as well as the other images he is able to combine with the script. The painting is created with language and demonstrates the inexhaustible nature of the combinations of alphabetic script. That is one of the pleasures Wosene draws from his work, knowing that his creations are infinite in their possibilities, just like language.

SUSANNE K. LANGER
Language

SUSANNE K. LANGER (1895–1985) was raised in Manhattan
and developed a youthful interest in philosophy. At Radcliffe College of Harvard University, she studied with Alfred North Whitehead and a host of other distinguished philosophers. Whitehead
was her advisor when she earned her doctorate in philosophy in
1926. Since there were no openings for female philosophy professors at Harvard at that time, she was appointed as a tutor there from
1927 to 1942. Thereafter, she taught at the University of Delaware,
Wellesley College, Smith College, and Columbia University. From
1952 to 1962, Langer taught at Connecticut College, which in
those years was a women's college. The Edgar J. Kaufmann Fund
awarded her a grant that permitted her to continue her research
and writing until her death in 1985.

Langer's career as a teacher was distinguished, and her influence as a philosopher in studies of the mind and of the arts has
been widespread. Her *Philosophy in a New Key: A Study in the Symbolism of Reason, Rite, and Art* (1942) is probably her most widely
read book. It deals with the fundamental issues involved in the
human disposition to use symbolism as a means of communication
on many levels. Her views established the relationship of symbol
to language and language formation as well as developed an understanding of other kinds of symbols by which we shape our lives. As
she says in *Philosophy in a New Key*, "The development of language
is the history of the gradual accumulation and elaboration of verbal symbols. By means of this phenomenon, man's whole behavior-
pattern has undergone an immense change from the simple biological
scheme, and his mentality has expanded to such a degree that it is no
longer comparable to the minds of animals." Langer's concentration

From *Philosophy in a New Key: A Study in the Symbolism of Reason, Rite, and Art.*

on the uses of symbols led her to see how our cultures developed and how our arts flourished.

Feeling and Form: A Theory of Art (1953) continued her studies of symbolic development by demonstrating how we use symbols in the arts to express our feelings. Among the interesting ideas Langer championed was her assurance that the arts are the only things that truly educate our emotions. She continued and deepened her studies in *Problems of Art: Ten Philosophical Lectures* (1957), another major contribution to the study of symbols in the arts. Her final work was a three-volume study called *Mind: An Essay on Human Feeling* that was published between 1967 and 1982.

Langer's Rhetoric

Langer's interest is in the acquisition of language by humans, so one of her strategies is to contrast how infants learn language with what we know about experiments with primates and the success experimenters have had trying to teach them language. Her focus is on vocalization rather than on signing. In experiments conducted several decades after Langer wrote, some primates were taught to use signs as a means of communication, and some of them, such as the famous Washoe, seem to have been able to express complex thoughts. But Langer's emphasis on vocalization separates her concerns from those of later researchers.

Because she is speaking to an audience with a deep interest in language, another of her rhetorical strategies is to reference experts in the field whose research helps her establish her own understanding of how humans develop the ability to communicate through language. She refers to several primary experts and quotes a few of them fully enough for us to understand how they relate to her argument. Additionally, when quoting from some of these authorities, she also relies on narrative, such as her references to Victor, the "Savage of Aveyron," who was discovered in the wilderness of France when he was twelve. He seemed to have been abandoned as an extremely young child and never to have lived with another human nor to have been exposed to language. He was studied very carefully, especially by Dr. Jean Marc Gaspard Itard, who spent several years trying to teach him language. The experiment was a failure despite very arduous efforts to try to make Victor understand the relationship between a word's sound and the object it represented. Langer takes this experiment seriously and offers a complex set of analyses to try to explain why Victor could not use language and why he lacked the intellectual capacity to determine vocalizations as indicators of meaning.

Her main point concerns the relationship between a word and its conceptualization as a symbol of meaning rather than a word as a sign of an object. She begins the essay with what seems like a difficult concept, but as she continues, her meaning becomes clear. She says, "The notion that the essence of language is the formulation and expression of conceptions rather than the communication of natural wants . . . opens a new vista upon the mysterious problem of origins" (para. 1). As she goes on to demonstrate, Victor does not say *eau*, French for *water*, when he wants water. If he says it at all, it is only because he is amused at its sound. Language, Langer says, does not develop because people want something and then vocalize the word that correlates with that want, but instead language develops when infants conceptualize the sound that they hear with a meaning of some kind. They may discover it associatively, as when the vocalization *ma-ma* is responded to by a mother, or they may discover it by the sensory means by which Helen Keller, who went blind and deaf at age 19 months, discovered the meaning of the word *water* when it was flowing over her hand.

Langer's interest in language centers on its symbolic virtues. She sees the human mind as distinct from the minds of other animals because of the human ability to think symbolically and therefore to elevate vocalizations to the status of language designed to interpret symbols and therefore communicate complex and subtle ideas. In one of her more unexpected observations, she suspects that there is a connection between certain human activities that she feels must have preceded our use of language, such as dance and rituals. Such activities, she suggests, may have hastened and shaped our urge to speak and communicate.

PREREADING QUESTIONS: WHAT TO READ FOR

The following prereading questions may help you anticipate key issues in the discussion of Susanne K. Langer's "Language." Keeping them in mind during your first reading should help focus your attention.

- What is the value of lalling in the infant stage of development?
- What is the optimum period of learning for language?
- Why does Langer emphasize the point that language is conceptual?

Language

The notion that the essence of language is the formulation and expression of conceptions rather than the communication of natural wants (the essence of pantomime) opens a new vista upon the mysterious problem of origins. For its beginnings are not natural adjustments, ways to means; they are purposeless lalling-instincts, primitive aesthetic reactions, and dreamlike associations of ideas that fasten on such material. The preparations for language are much lower in the rational scale than word-uses; they can be found below the evolutionary level of any communication by sounds.

Moreover, this originally impractical, or better, *conceptual,* use of speech is borne out by the fact that all attempts to teach apes or the speechless "wild children" to talk, by the method of making them ask for something, have failed; whereas all cases where the use of language has dawned on an individual, simian or human, under such difficult circumstances, have been independent of the practical use of the word at the moment. Helen Keller's[1] testimony has already been cited; after all her teacher's efforts in formal daily lessons to make the child *use* words like "cup" and "doll" to obtain the denoted objects, the significance of the word "water" suddenly burst upon her, not when she needed water, but when the stream gushed over her hand! Likewise, Yerkes'[2] efforts to make Chim use an articulate syllable to ask for a piece of banana all failed; he articulated no "word" resembling the speech of man, nor did he seem to establish a relation between the sound and any particular object. Furness,[3] on the other hand, carefully kept all practical interests out of his experiment. He tried only to associate an impression, a visual experience, with a word, so that by constant association the two should fuse, not as sign and result, but as name and image; and he has had the greatest success on record so far as I know.

But the most decisive and, at the same time, pathetic evidence that the utilitarian view of language is a mistake, may be found in the story of Victor, the Savage of Aveyron,[4] written by the young doctor who undertook to study and educate him. Since the boy always took notice when anyone exclaimed "Oh!" and even imitated the sound, Dr. Itard undertook to make him use the word *"eau"* as a *sign* when he

---

[1] **Helen Keller (1880–1968)** Born deaf and blind, she learned language after a struggle with and because of the persistence of her teacher, Anne Sullivan.

[2] **Robert Yerkes (1876–1956)** Worked with primates to see if they could learn language.

[3] **William Furness (1867–1920)** Tried to teach an orangutan the word *cup*.

[4] **Savage of Aveyron** Victor, a young boy discovered in the forest near Aveyron. He had lived without human contact for most of his life and had little ability to learn language.

wanted water; but this attempt failed because he used every sign *but* the vocal one, and water could not be indefinitely withheld to force the issue. So a second attempt was made with the word *"lait,"*[5] of which Itard gives the following account:

"The fourth day of this, my second experiment, I succeeded to the 4 utmost of my wishes; I heard Victor pronounce distinctly, in a manner, it must be confessed, rather harsh, the word *lait*, which he repeated almost incessantly; it was the first time that an articulate sound had escaped his lips, and of course I did not hear it without the most lively satisfaction. I nevertheless made afterwards an observation, which deduced very much from the advantage which it was reasonable to expect from the first instance of success. It was not till the moment, when, despairing of a happy result, I actually poured the milk into the cup which he presented to me, the word *lait* escaped him again, with evident demonstrations of joy; and it was not till after I had poured it out a second time, by way of reward, that he repeated the expression. It is evident from hence, that the result of the experiment was far from accomplishing my intentions; the word pronounced, instead of being the sign of a want, it appeared, from the time in which it was articulated, to be merely an exclamation of joy. If this word had been uttered before the thing that he desired had been granted, my object would have been nearly accomplished: then the true sense of speech would have been soon acquired by Victor; a point of communication would have been established between him and me, and the most rapid progress must necessarily have ensued. Instead of this I had obtained only an expression of the pleasure which he felt, insignificant as it related to himself, and useless to us both. . . . It was generally only during the enjoyment of the thing, that the word *lait* was pronounced. Sometimes he happened to utter it before, and at other times a little after, but always without having any view in the use of it. I do not attach any more importance to his spontaneous repetition of it, when he happens to wake during the course of the night."[6]

Another word which Victor acquired quite spontaneously was 5 "Li," which Itard identifies as the name of a young girl, Julie, who stayed at the house for several weeks, to Victor's great delight; but this word he uttered to himself, all the time, and "even during the night, at those moments when there is reason to believe that he is in a profound sleep," so no importance was attached to it as a sign of reason.

Unfortunately, the young doctor was such a faithful disciple of 6 Locke and Condillac[7] that after his "failure" with the word *"lait"* he

---

[5] **lait** French for "milk."

[6] *The Savage of Aveyron*, pp. 93–96. [Langer's note]

[7] **Locke and Condillac** John **Locke** (1632–1704) and Etienne Bonnot de Condillac (1715–1780) were both important philosophers of the mind who had observations about the acquisition of language.

gave up the attempt to teach the Wild Boy spoken language, and tried to instruct him in the deaf-mutes' alphabet instead. Victor picked up a few spoken words, subsequently, by himself; but as he merely said them when he contemplated their objects with joy or sorrow, not when he *lacked* anything, no one paid much attention to these "mere exclamations" or made response to them.

Young children learn to speak, after the fashion of Victor, by constantly using words to bring things *into their minds,* not *into their hands.* They learn it fully whether their parents consciously teach them by wrong methods or right or not at all. Why did Victor not defy the doctor's utilitarian theories and learn language by the babbling method?   7

Because he was already about twelve years old, and the lalling-impulse of early childhood was all but completely outgrown. The tendency to constant vocalization seems to be a passing phase of our instinctive life. If language is not developed during this period, the individual is handicapped—like the apes—by a lack of *spontaneous phonetic material* to facilitate his speech experiments. The production of sounds is conscious then, and is used economically instead of prodigally. Victor did not articulate to amuse himself; his first word had to be stimulated. Wild Peter, we are told, never babbled to himself, though he sang a great deal; Kamala,[8] the surviving little "wolf-girl" found at Midnapur, had learned about forty words at the end of six years in human surroundings, and formed sentences of two or three words; but even with this vocabulary, which would serve a three-year-old to carry on incessant conversations, Kamala *never talked unless she was spoken to.* The impulse to chatter had been outgrown without being exploited for the acquisition of language.   8

In a social environment, the vocalizing and articulating instinct of babyhood is fostered by response, and as the sounds become symbols their use becomes a dominant habit. Yet the passing of the *instinctive phase* is marked by the fact that a great many phonemes[9] which do not meet with response are completely lost. Undoubtedly that is why children, who have not entirely lost the impulse to make random sounds which their mother tongue does not require, can so easily learn a foreign language and even master several at once, like many English youngsters born in India, who learn not only one vernacular, but speak with every native servant in whatever happens to be   9

---

[8] **Kamala** In 1920 in Mindapore, India, Kamala and her sister, Amala, were found after having been raised by a wolf. They were feral and looked and acted like wolves. Amala died, but Kamala was helped by a minister's wife to learn a few words and begin acclimating to civilized life.

[9] **phonemes** The smallest distinctive sounds in a language.

his dialect. A British psychologist, J. W. Tomb,[10] has called attention
to this phenomenon and concluded from it that children have a *linguistic intuition* which is lost later in life.

But *intuition* is a slippery word, which has to cover, in this case,   10
understanding, reproduction, and use—i.e., independent, analogous application—of words. It is hard to imagine any "intuition" that
would bestow so many powers. It is better, perhaps, to say that there
is an *optimum period of learning,* and this is a stage of mental development in which several impulses and interests happen to coincide: the
lalling instinct, the imitative impulse, a natural interest in distinctive
sounds, *and a great sensitivity to "expressiveness" of any sort.* Where any
one of these characteristics is absent or is not synchronized with the
others, the "linguistic intuition" miscarries.

The last requirement here mentioned is really the "higher func-   11
tion" of the mind that shines forth so conspicuously in human intercourse; yet it is the one that linguists and psychologists either overlook
entirely, or certainly do not credit to early childhood. The peculiar
impressionability of childhood is usually treated under the rubric of
attention to exact colors, sounds, etc.; but what is much more important, I think, is the child's tendency to read a vague sort of *meaning*
into pure visual and auditory forms. Childhood is the great period
of synesthesia;[11] sounds and colors and temperatures, forms and feelings, may have certain characters in common, by which a vowel may
"be" of a certain color, a tone may "be" large or small, low or high,
bright or dark, etc. There is a strong tendency to form associations
among sensa that are not practically fixed in the world, even to confuse such random impressions. Most of all, the overactive feelings fasten upon such flotsam material. Fear lives in pure *Gestalten,*[12] warning
or friendliness emanates from objects that have no faces and no voices,
no heads or hands; for they all have "expression" for the child, though
not—as adults often suppose—anthropomorphic form. One of my
earliest recollections is that chairs and tables *always kept the same look,*
in a way that people did not, and that I was awed by the sameness of
that appearance. They *symbolized* such-and-such a mood; even as a little child I would not have judged that they *felt* it (if any one had raised

---

[10]**J. W. Tomb (fl. 1925)** Psychologist who wrote an article on the "intuitive
capacity of children to learn language."

[11]**synesthesia** Neurological condition in which one sensory experience generates another, as in perceiving different numbers as being different colors or connecting a visual stimulus with a smell.

[12]***Gestalten*** German term meaning a collection of elements—psychological, physical, or environmental—that work together to form a whole, or a pattern. In this sense,
Langer means that fear is a perception of a pattern that is incompletely understood.

such a silly question). There was just such-and-such a look — dignity, indifference, or ominousness — about them. They continued to convey that silent message no matter what you did to them.

A mind to which the stern character of an armchair is more   12
immediately apparent than its use or its position in the room, is oversensitive to expressive forms. It grasps analogies that a riper experience would reject as absurd. It fuses sensa that practical thinking must keep apart. Yet it is just this crazy play of associations, this uncritical fusion of impressions, that exercises the powers of symbolic transformation. To project feelings into outer objects is the first way of symbolizing, and thus of *conceiving* those feelings. This activity belongs to about the earliest period of childhood that memory can recover. The conception of "self," which is usually thought to mark the beginning of actual memory, may possibly depend on this process of symbolically epitomizing our feelings.

From this dawn of memory, where we needs must begin any   13
firsthand record, to adolescence, there is a constant decrease in such dreamlike experience, a growing shift from subjective, symbolic, to practical associations. Sense-data now keep to their categories, and signify further events. Percepts become less weighted with irrelevant feeling and fantasy, and are more readily ranged in an objective order. But if in theory we count backward over the span which none of us recollect, and which covers the period of learning language — is it likely that the mind was realistic in its earlier phase? Is it not probable that association was even more trivial, more ready, and that the senses fused more completely in yielding impressions? No experience belongs to any class as yet, in this primitive phase. Consider, now, that the vocal play of the infant fills his world with *audible actions,* the nearest and most completely absorbing stimuli, because they are both inner and outer, autonomously produced yet unexpected, inviting that *repetition* of accidental motions which William James[13] deemed the source of all voluntary acts; intriguing, endlessly variable noises mysteriously connected with the child himself! For a while, at least, his idle experiments in vocalization probably fill his world.

If, now, his audible acts wake echoes in his surroundings — that   14
is to say, if his elders reply to them — there is a growth of experience; for the baby appears to recognize, gradually, that the sound which happens there and comes to him, is the *same* as his lalling. This is a rudimentary abstraction; by that sameness he becomes aware of the tone, the product of his activity, which absorbs his interest. He repeats that sound rather than another. His ear has made its first judgment.

---

[13]**William James (1842–1910)** One of America's most important psychologists.

A sound (such as "da-da," or "ma-ma," probably) has been *conceived,* and his diffuse awareness of vocalizing gives way to an apparently delightful awareness of a vocable.

It is doubtful whether a child who never heard any articulate 15 sounds but his own would ever become conscious of different phonemes. Voice and uttered syllable and the feeling of utterance would probably remain one experience to him; the babbling period might come and go without his recognizing any *product* of his own activity. If this guess is correct, it is easy to understand why Victor and Wild Peter did not invent language, and were nearly, if not entirely, past the hope of acquiring it when they were socialized.

A new vocable is an outstanding *Gestalt.* It is a possession, too, 16 because it may be had at will, and this itself makes it very interesting. Itard tells us that when Victor pronounced his first word he repeated it "almost incessantly"; as does every baby who has learned a new syllable. Moreover, an articulate sound is an entirely *unattached* item, a purely phenomenal experience without externally fixed relations; it lies wide open to imaginative and emotional uses, synesthetic identifications, chance associations. It is the readiest thing in the world to become a symbol when a symbol is wanted. The next sharp and emotional arrest of consciousness, the next deeply interesting experience that coincides with hearing or uttering the vocable, becomes fixed by association with that one already distinct item; it may be the personality of the mother, the concrete character of the bottle, or what not, that becomes thus identified with the recognizable, producible sound; whatever it is, the baby's mind has hold of it through the word, and can invoke a conception of it by uttering the word, which has thus become the *name* of the thing.

For a considerable time, playing with conceptions seems to be the 17 main interest and aim in speaking. To name things is a thrilling experience, a tremendous satisfaction. Helen Keller bears witness to the sense of power it bestows. Word and conception become fused in that early period wherein both grow up together, so that even in later life they are hard to separate. In a sense, language is conception, and conception is the frame of perception; or, as Sapir[14] has put it, "Language is heuristic . . . in that its forms predetermine for us certain modes of observation and interpretation. . . . While it may be looked upon as a symbolic system which reports or refers or otherwise substitutes for direct experience, it does not as a matter of actual behavior stand apart from or run parallel to direct experience but completely interpenetrates with it. This is indicated by the widespread feeling, particularly

---

[14]**Edward Sapir (1884–1939)** One of the most important early American linguists.

among primitive people, of that virtual identity or close correspondence of word and thing which leads to the magic of spells. . . . Many
lovers of nature, for instance, do not feel that they are truly in touch
with it until they have mastered the names of a great many flowers
and trees, as though the primary world of reality were a verbal one
and as though one could not get close to nature unless one first mastered the terminology which somehow magically expresses it."[15]

The fact is that our primary world of reality *is* a verbal one. With- 18
out words our imagination cannot retain distinct objects and their
relations, but out of sight is out of mind. Perhaps that is why Köhler's[16]
apes could use a stick to reach a banana outside the cage so long as
the banana and the stick could be seen in one glance, but not if they
had to turn their eyes away from the banana to see the stick. Apparently they could not look at the one and *think of* the other. A child
who had as much practical initiative as the apes, turning away from
the coveted object, yet still murmuring "banana," would have seen the
stick in its instrumental capacity at once.

The transformation of experience into concepts, not the elabora- 19
tion of signals and symptoms, is the motive of language. Speech is
through and through symbolic; and only sometimes signific. Any
attempt to trace it back entirely to the need of communication,
neglecting the formulative, abstractive experience at the root of it,
must land us in the sort of enigma that the problem of linguistic origins has long presented. I have tried, instead, to trace it to the characteristic human activity, symbolic transformation and abstraction, of
which prehuman beginnings may perhaps be attributed to the highest apes. Yet we have not found the commencement of language anywhere between their state and ours. Even in man, who has all its pre-
requisites, it depends on education not only for its full development,
but for its very inception. How, then, did it ever arise? And why do all
men possess it?

It could only have arisen in a race in which the lower forms of sym- 20
bolistic thinking—dream, ritual, superstitious fancy—were already
highly developed, i.e., where the process of symbolization, though
primitive, was very active. Communal life in such a group would be
characterized by vigorous indulgence in purely expressive acts, in ritual gestures, dances, etc., and probably by a strong tendency to fantastic terrors and joys. The liberation from practical interests that is
already marked in the apes would make rapid progress in a species
with a definitely symbolistic turn of mind; conventional meanings

---

[15] From Sapir, Article "Language." [Langer's note]
[16] **Wolfgang Köhler (1887–1967)** Studied primates and wrote *The Mentality of Apes* (1917).

would gradually imbue every originally random act, so that the group life as a whole would have an exciting, vaguely transcendental tinge, without any definable or communicable body of ideas to cling to. A wealth of dance forms and antics, poses and maneuvers might flourish in a society that was somewhat above the apes' in nonpractical interests, and rested on a slightly higher development of the symbolific brain functions. There are quite articulated play forms, verging on dance forms, in the natural repertoire of the chimpanzees; with but a little further elaboration, these would become most obvious material for symbolic expression. It is not at all impossible that *ritual*, solemn and significant, antedates the evolution of language.

QUESTIONS FOR CRITICAL READING

1. What does the experiment with Victor tell us about the optimum period for learning language?
2. When do sounds become symbols? (See para. 9.)
3. Do you agree that lalling by infants is as crucial to developing language as Langer says it is?
4. Why is expressiveness important when talking about language acquisition (para. 10)?
5. In paragraph 8, Langer refers to "*spontaneous phonetic material.*" What is she referring to and why is it important?
6. Langer points out that Victor did not vocalize when he needed something. She says this is true of infants as well. Does your experience bear her out?
7. Langer says very young children articulate sounds to amuse themselves. Is this true?

SUGGESTIONS FOR CRITICAL WRITING

1. If you have observed very young children beginning to use language, how much of what they do is similar to what Langer says they do? She speaks about the chattering instinct as being one of the most crucial forms of behavior for young children learning language. Have you observed the chattering instinct? Do young children repeat the same sound over and over as Langer says they do? How does that seem to help young children master language? Do your experiences validate Langer's views?
2. In one of Langer's most striking observations, she says, "Young children learn to speak, after the fashion of Victor, by constantly using words to bring things *into their minds*, not *into their hands*" (para. 7).

What does she mean by this statement, and what are the implications for her theory of language acquisition by children? Do you agree with her, or is there another theory that you feel might explain the beginnings of language acquisition just as well?

3. Victor was discovered living in a forest in France and regarded as a feral (wild) boy. Beginning in 1800, Doctor Jean Marc Gaspard Itard worked with him for five years to see how much Victor could learn. Itard's memoir is available as *The Wild Boy of Aveyron* (1962). There are other accounts as well, some of which are fictional. Read Itard's book and write an account of his experiments with Victor and connect them with Langer's concerns with symbolic understanding and conceptualization. Itard was credited with developing methods for teaching children with mental disabilities. Do his methods respect Langer's theories?

4. What does Langer seem to mean by the term *intuition* (para. 10)? Once you have clarified her meaning, add to it what you think the term means. Do you sense that you have intuition about events in your life? Was your intuition more active when you were a child than it is now? Write a short essay that defines *intuition* and connects it to your understanding of your use of language and your awareness of the world around you.

5. In paragraph 11, Langer says that "[c]hildhood is the great period of synesthesia." Do you agree? As a child, were you aware of imparting feelings to colors? Of imparting feelings to specific vowels or consonants? Examine her observations in that paragraph, and ask yourself what it means to interconnect sensory information from one intellectual area to another. Some people feel the days of the week have different colors, different personalities, or different moods. Research synesthesia and comment on your own experiences with the phenomenon. Do you know people who may be synesthetes?

6. Recently some chimpanzees were said to have learned language. Look up the research on the chimpanzee named Washoe, who learned American Sign Language. Her vocabulary was as much as 350 words and she was herself able to teach an adopted chimpanzee as many as 150 words. Find out the methods used to teach Washoe and compare them to the concepts that Langer discusses. Langer emphasizes vocalization, but since Washoe and other chimpanzees cannot vocalize words, researchers felt sign language was a good substitute. What is your view on this point? Do you feel that Washoe understood language conceptually, or did she merely understand signs and signals?

7. **CONNECTIONS** Dr. Itard has been credited with developing methods of instruction that may have affected the techniques that Maria Montessori (p. 571) used to teach preschool children. What similarities in attitude and understanding do Susanne K. Langer and Maria Montessori have in their analyses of the education of very young children? What would Montessori have found reassuring about Langer's

MARIO PEI
Theories of Language Beginning

BORN IN ROME, Mario Andrew Pei (1901–1978) came to the United States after his father's drugstore business failed in 1908. He was seven years old and spoke Italian, but he quickly acclimated to English while attending a parochial school in New York City. At Francis Xavier High School, Pei learned Latin and Greek and added a modern language, French, to his repertoire. He went on to City College, graduating cum laude in 1925. He taught at City College while earning his Ph.D. at Columbia University in 1932. Pei taught briefly at Rutgers, the University of Pittsburgh, Brigham Young University, and Seton Hall University. In 1937, he returned to teach at Columbia and stayed on as a professor for thirty-three years. He became an eminent linguist and penned more than fifty books covering a wide range of subjects from language to politics, and because he was a great cook, even to Italian cuisine. Pei was extraordinary in that, though he was a ranking linguistic scholar, he was also a gifted, popular writer who could make the study of language intelligible to the interested reader.

Esperanto, a synthetic language, has been connected with Pei because in 1958 he published *One Language for the World and How to Achieve It* and then sent a free copy to every head of state in the world. Pei advocated that world leaders choose a single language to be taught as a second language to every child in every school in every country. That way, people would be able to communicate with each other with much greater understanding than was then possible. Teachers of Esperanto viewed it as universal because it contained elements of most modern languages, which is why Pei became associated with it and ultimately supported those who wished to make it a worldwide phenomenon. He knew that any child

From *The Story of Language.*

was capable of learning several languages from infancy on, and
thus his suggestion would prove no hardship for children.

Pei himself was fluent in many languages. Italian, English,
French, and Spanish were his primary languages, but he was said to
be conversant in over thirty others. He wrote several books on languages, including *The Italian Language* (1941), *The Story of Language*
(1949), and *The Story of English* (1952), the latter two of which were
both best-sellers and named to the Book of the Month Club. After
the publication of these books, his articles discussing language were
frequently published in newspapers and popular magazines.

Pei's Rhetoric

Because Pei imagined his audience to be people interested in
language but not to be specialists or linguists, he adopted a very
direct and fundamentally simple style. His sentences are brief and
compact, his paragraphs are relatively short, and his approach is
very straightforward. He begins with a number of theories of language's beginning, using an essentially comic approach in naming his categories: the "bow-wow" theory, the "ding-dong" theory,
the "pooh-pooh" theory, and so on. His use of these terms alerts
us right away that he is avoiding the technical language used by
advanced researchers.

Apart from relying on categories to organize his essay, Pei
depends heavily on enumeration. He has four kinds of theories
of language origins, two ancient sources of theories, two theories
of how language devolves into dialects, and two ways language
sounds change.

Once he has dealt with his proposed categories of theories,
he moves on to reference examples of thinkers who mused on the
origins of language. He begins with discussing the ancients—the
Stoic and the Epicurean philosophers—then jumps to the eighteenth century and modern-language specialists. He even remarks
on modern experiments with children who had been isolated
before they began to speak. Pei uses the technique of contrast when
he cites animal sounds as a potential origin of speech, remarking
on their sameness over generations as opposed to the variety of
human speech over the same time span.

The changeability of languages over time is another topic that
he treats with some care; then he moves on to changes in sound
and dialects. He refers to very ancient languages, such as Sanskrit,
Sumerian, Akkadian, and even to Native American languages. His
contrast among the oldest records of Sanskrit, Greek, and Latin

introduces important texts, such as the Vedic hymns and the Homeric epics. Finally, Pei talks not about the origin of language but about the origin and development of words themselves, such as *wine*, *mules*, and *gum*.

Pei's essay introduces us to some of the complexities of language that any researcher must face in trying to imagine language's origins.

PREREADING QUESTIONS: WHAT TO READ FOR

The following prereading questions may help you anticipate key issues in the discussion of Mario Pei's "Theories of Language Beginning." Keeping them in mind during your first reading should help focus your attention.

- What is the "bow-wow" theory?
- Why are we unlikely to develop an adequate theory of language's beginnings?
- How do words change?

Theories of Language Beginning

God, that all-powerful Creator of nature and architect of the world, has impressed man with no character so proper to distinguish him from other animals, as by the faculty of speech.

—QUINTILIAN

Language,—human language,—after all, is but little better than the croak and cackle of fowls, and other utterances of brute nature,— sometimes not so adequate.

—HAWTHORNE

If there is one thing on which all linguists are fully agreed, it is   1
that the problem of the origin of human speech is still unsolved.

Theories have not been wanting. Some are traditional and mysti-   2
cal, like the legends current among many primitive groups that language was a gift from the gods. Even as late as the seventeenth century, a Swedish philologist seriously maintained that in the Garden of Eden God spoke Swedish, Adam Danish, and the serpent French, while at a Turkish linguistic congress held in 1934 it was as seriously argued that Turkish is at the root of all languages, all words being

derived from *günes,* the Turkish word for "sun," the first object to strike the human fancy and demand a name.

Other theories may be described as quasi-scientific. One hypoth-   3
esis, originally sponsored by Darwin, is to the effect that speech was in origin nothing but mouth-pantomime, in which the vocal organs unconsciously attempted to mimic gestures by the hands.

Several theories are current among linguists today, but with the dis-   4
tinct understanding that they are as yet unproved and, in the nature of things, probably unprovable. They have been given picturesque names, which proves that linguists, too, can be imaginative on occasion.

The "bow-wow" theory holds that language arose in imitation   5
of the sounds occurring in nature. A dog barks; his bark sounds like "bow-wow" to a human hearer. Therefore he designates the dog as "bow-wow." The trouble with this theory is that the same natural noise is, apparently, differently heard by different people. What is "cock-a-doodle-doo" to an Englishman is *cocorico* to a Frenchman and *chicchirichì* to an Italian.

The "ding-dong" theory sustains that there is a mystic correlation   6
between sound and meaning. Like everything mystical, it is best discarded in a serious scientific discussion.

The "pooh-pooh" theory is to the effect that language at first con-   7
sisted of ejaculations of surprise, fear, pleasure, pain, etc. It is often paired with the "yo-he-ho" theory to the effect that language arose from grunts of physical exertion, and even with the "sing-song" theory, that language arose from primitive inarticulate chants.

The "ta-ta" theory that language comes from imitation of bodily move-   8
ments is further exemplified in the Darwinian belief described above.

The ancient Greek philosophers, who gave some attention to the   9
problem of the origin of language, allowed themselves to be led afield by their speculative leanings. Pythagoras, Plato, and the Stoics[1] held that language had come into being out of "inherent necessity" or "nature," which is begging the question, while Democritus, Aristotle, and the Epicureans[2] believed it had arisen by "convention" or "agreement." How this agreement had been reached by people who had no previous means of mutual understanding they did not trouble to explain.

Leibniz,[3] at the dawn of the eighteenth century, first advanced   10
the theory that all languages come not from a historically recorded

---

[1] **Stoics** Greek philosophers who felt a life of virtue and public service produced happiness.

[2] **Epicureans** Greek philosophers who felt the pursuit of comfort and pleasure brought the greatest happiness.

[3] **Gottfried William Leibniz (1646–1716)** Philosopher who examined language as well as the mind/body relationship.

source, but from a proto-speech. In some respects he was a precursor of the Italian twentieth-century linguist Trombetti,[4] who boldly asserted that the biblical account of the Tower of Babel is at least figuratively true, and that all languages have a common origin. A contemporary linguist, E. H. Sturtevant,[5] presents a novel theory which, though slightly paradoxical, has its merits. Since all real intentions and emotions, he says, get themselves involuntarily expressed by gesture, look, or sound, voluntary communication, such as language, must have been invented for the purpose of lying or deceiving. People forced to listen to diplomatic jargon and political double-talk will be tempted to agree.

On at least three recorded occasions attempts were made to iso-   11
late children before they began talking to see whether they would evolve a language of their own. One such attempt was made by the Egyptian king Psammetichos, the second by Frederick II of Sicily about 1200, the third by King James IV[6] of Scotland around 1500. These attempts, lacking scientific controls, proved inconclusive. More recent cases of children who had allegedly grown up among wolves, dogs, monkeys, or gazelles have added little to our knowledge, save that the human child, though ignorant of human language when found, takes to it readily and with seeming pleasure, something that his animal playmates are incapable of doing.

Animal cries, whether we choose to describe them as "language"   12
or not, are characterized by invariability and monotony. Dogs have been barking, cats meowing, lions roaring, and donkeys braying in the same fashion since time immemorial. The ancient Greek comic poets indicated a sheep's cry by Greek letters having the value of "beh"; in modern Greek, those letters have changed their value to "vee." The sheep's cry has not changed in two thousand years, but the Greek language has.

Human language, in contrast with animal cries, displays infinite   13
variability, both in time and in space. Activity and change may be described as the essence of all living language. Even so-called dead languages partake of this changeability, as evidenced by the ingenious combination devised by the Vatican to express the ultramodern

---

[4]**Alfredo Trombetti (1866–1929)** Linguist and member of the Italian Academy who believed all languages went back to a single source.

[5]**Edgar Howard Sturtevant (1875–1952)** Linguist who wrote on the origins of language. He also wrote a study of the Hittite language, one of the world's oldest.

[6]**Psammetichos . . . James IV** Psammeticus (fl. 400 B.C.E.) experimented by depriving two boys of human contact to see what their first natural word would be (it was "Becos"); Frederick II (1194–1250) knew many languages and promoted a court that produced the first sonnet; King James IV of Scotland (1473–1513) spoke six languages and promoted culture.

concept of "motorcycle" in Latin—*birota ignifero latice incita* ("two-wheeled vehicle driven by fire-bearing juice").

In one sense, the reason for the changeability of language is as   14
mysterious as the origin of language itself. In another sense, it is crystal clear. Language is an expression of human activity, and as human activity is forever changing, language changes with it. It seems at least partly established that language changes least rapidly when its speakers are isolated from other communities, most rapidly when they find themselves, so to speak, at the crossroads of the world. Among the Romance languages, a tongue like Sardinian, comparatively sheltered from the rest of the world, has changed little from the original Latin, while French, exposed to all inroads, invasions, and crosscurrents from the rest of Europe, has diverged the most. Arabic, long confined to the relative isolation of the Arabian peninsula, preserves the original Semitic structure far better than Hebrew, located in much-visited Palestine.

Many linguists hold that agricultural and sedentary pursuits tend   15
to give stability to language, warlike and nomadic life to hasten its change. Lithuanian, the tongue of a population of peaceful farmers, has changed little during the last two thousand years, while Scandinavian evolved very rapidly during the Viking era. An influence exerted on language by climate has often been claimed, but never fully substantiated.

Whether much or little, all languages change in due course of   16
time. A modern English speaker encounters some difficulty with the English of Shakespeare, far more with the English of Chaucer, and has to handle the English of King Alfred as a foreign tongue. A French speaker finds the fourteenth-century language of François Villon[7] a little difficult, has considerable trouble with the twelfth-century *Chanson de Roland*, barely recognizes the tongue of the ninth-century Oaths of Strasbourg, and if he *goes* further back has to handle the documents he finds from the Latin rather than from the French standpoint; yet there was never a break in the continuity of the spoken tongue of France or its speakers.

Two main theories have been advanced concerning the breaking-   17
up of an original tongue into separate languages or dialects, and here again there is evidence of secret imaginative, even poetic leanings on the part of supposedly unemotional linguistic scientists. One is the "tree-stem" theory, whereby the parent language is supposed to act as a tree trunk, while new languages are branches or offshoots. The other

---

[7] **François Villon (1431–1463)** Important French poet; he got in trouble for brawling and theft and was sentenced to death but had his sentence commuted to ten years' banishment from Paris in 1463. He was never heard from again.

is the "wave" theory, in accordance with which new languages and dialects arise and spread like ripples when you throw a stone into the water.

Two different modes of change in language sounds are recognized: the change may arise very gradually, almost imperceptibly, and be as gradually and unconsciously adopted by the speakers; or it may arise suddenly, as the result of an innovation made by one speaker who has prestige in the community and is therefore widely imitated. 18

It is estimated by scientists that some tens of thousands of years elapsed between the beginning of society and art (and, probably, speech) and the first appearance of writing. During these long centuries language continued to evolve, but we unfortunately have no record of that evolution. Linguistic records properly described as such are almost exclusively in writing. The oldest such records at our disposal are those of Sumerian, a language spoken in the Mesopotamian valley between about 4000 B.C. and 300 B.C., when it became extinct. The affiliations of Sumerian are undetermined, but it seems unrelated to the Semitic Akkadian spoken by the Babylonians and Assyrians, who invaded the Sumerian territory about 3000 B.C. 19

Sumerian and Akkadian lived side by side for a long period. Almost contemporaneous with Akkadian are written records of ancient Egypt and China, both of which go back to almost 2000 B.C. 20

After this beginning, language records come thick and fast. Many languages of antiquity have disappeared, leaving few and scanty remains. Etruscan, Cretan, Iberian, and Gaulish, to cite a few better-known examples, are among the fallen. Other languages, like those of the North American Indians, are similarly disappearing today. For some dead languages our only records are a few inscriptions on coins or tombstones, or names of people, rivers, and mountains that have come down to us, like the Delaware Indian "Manhattan" and the Iroquois "Adirondack," which survive their originators. Hesychius,[8] a Greek lexicographer of the fifth century A.D., cites words from many ancient languages, including Egyptian, Akkadian, Galatian, Lydian, Phrygian, Phoenician, Scythian, and Parthian. It is a favorite pastime among comparative linguists to reconstruct extinct languages from a few words or inscriptions, in much the same fashion that paleontologists reconstruct extinct animals from a few fossil bones. 21

No document of the original parent language of our Western tongues, Indo-European, has ever been found or is likely to be found, since the language probably broke up into separate Indo-European 22

---

[8]**Hesychius** Greek philosopher of the fifth century B.C.E. who compiled a lexicon—which remains a valuable resource to this day—of words and their meanings.

languages before the invention of writing. By a comparison of the known daughter tongues, however, linguists are able to present a hypothetical but quite plausible facsimile of this unknown tongue.

The oldest languages of our Indo-European family of which   23
we have records are Sanskrit, Greek, and Latin, in the order given. The approximate dates for each are 2000, 800, and 500 B.C. The original homeland of the Indo-European speakers is unknown, but the Iranian plateau and the shores of the Baltic are the places most favored. From a study of words common to all the Indo-European languages, it can be argued that the original Indo-Europeans knew snow, the birch, willow, and pine, the horse, bear, hare, and wolf, copper and iron. This would place them in the Copper-Stone Age, about 2500 B.C.

The oldest Sanskrit records are the Vedic hymns, a series of reli-   24
gious poems. The Homeric poems, *Iliad* and *Odyssey,* mark the beginning of Greek, while for Latin we have a series of inscriptions, the oldest of which, appearing on a belt buckle from the city of Praeneste, reads: "Manius made me for Nummerius."

Among all the world's languages, the Latin-Romance group   25
is the one of which we have the most complete unbroken history. Latin records run from 500 B.C. to the end of the Roman Empire and beyond, merging with nascent French in A.D. 842 and with nascent Spanish and Italian in 950 and 960, respectively.

Anglo-Saxon and Old English are synonymous terms. The Anglo-   26
Saxon period lasted until the middle of the twelfth century, when the Middle English period began. Modern English begins about 1400. Approximately the same periods apply to Old, Middle, and Modern German. It is perhaps of interest to note that as late as the sixteenth century English, today the tongue of 230 million people, had less than five million speakers, being surpassed in point of numbers by German, French, Spanish, and Italian.

Words in our modern languages that can be traced directly back   27
to the pre-Classical tongues of antiquity are relatively few. Our "wine" comes from the Latin *vinum* which Latin seems to have borrowed previously from Etruscan; the word *vinum* appears frequently in Etruscan inscriptions. "Mules" for "house slippers" may go back to Sumerian, which called such slippers *mulus.* Our word "gum" comes from the Greek *kommi,* but Greek appears to have borrowed it from ancient Egyptian, where it appears in the form *qmit;* Coptic, Egyptian's closest modern descendant, has *komi.* "Cream" may have originally come from the Gaulish or Aquitanian *krama,* though some authorities ascribe its origin to Greek *chrisma.* The "eena meena mina mo" used in childish games goes back to numerals used by the ancient Welsh tribes, and the Indo-European word which gives rise to our "ten" is

said to have been originally a compound of "two" and "hand," while "five" seems connected with "finger."

English "dad" is a word from baby talk, but the baby talk must   28
have started early, since similar forms appear in many Indo-European languages; Gaulish has *tatula,* Gothic has *atta,* Welsh has *tad,* Russian has *otyets,* and some Italian dialects have *tata.*

Animal call words have a long and interesting history. *Dil,* which   29
was originally a call word for geese, became in Irish the word for "dear." "Hog," originally a pet name for a pig, which in sections of England is used for pet lambs and bullocks, gave rise in Irish to *og* ("young" or "little"). The use of "puss" or some very similar word or sound (*bis, pss,* etc.) to call a cat is common to the British Isles, Arabia, North Africa, Spain, Brittany, Italy, Scandinavia, Germany, and Holland. Such forms as *pusei* in the Tamil of southern India, *pisa* in Rumanian, *piso* in Albanian testify to the widespread use of the form.

What are the chances that modern linguists, equipped with the   30
powerful aids of present-day science, may one day break down the veil of mystery that enshrouds the origin of language? Frankly, very slight. The mightiest searchlight cannot cast a beam on what is not there. When man first began to speak, he left no material records, as he did when he first began to write. Hence, the truly scientific study of the origin of language can properly begin only with the beginning of written-language records.

All that the scientist in the linguistic field can do in connection with   31
the beginning of speech is to observe what is observable around him (the speech of infants, the language of primitive groups, etc.), compare his observations with the earliest records and known historical and anthropological facts, and, basing himself upon those observations and comparisons, make surmises, which will be more or less plausible, more or less complete, but never scientific in the true, full sense of the word.

QUESTIONS FOR CRITICAL READING

1. Which of the four theories of language origination seems most plausible to you?

2. What are some of the reasons languages change?

3. What are Darwin's theories of the origin of language?

4. Why are the theories of the Stoics and the Epicureans inadequate?

5. Is language a gift of the gods?

6. What does Leibniz mean when he says all language comes "from a proto-speech" (para. 10)? Do babies create a proto-speech?

7. What gives a language stability (para. 15)?

SUGGESTIONS FOR CRITICAL WRITING

1. Pei refers to the linguist Trombetti who postulated that all languages have a common origin. How likely do you think that theory is? Is it reasonable to think that all languages derived from a single source in some distant era? What kind of evidence might you propose for such a theory? What evidence would you need that may not be available to you at this time? Even if there is not enough evidence now to support such a theory, do you think it possible that evidence might show up in the future that would prove it so?

2. Even though Pei discounts the four theories of language beginning, it may be that one of them is as good a theory as we are ever to derive. Take one of those theories and defend it with your own examples and arguments. Why is it a better theory than the others? Why do you think it has a good chance of truly answering the question of how language began?

3. What role does war have in stimulating language growth? Research a recent war and search for new terms that have been introduced into the language as a result of the conflict. Why would war be a stimulant to language growth?

4. Pei says that language change is all but inevitable. He also says that language specialists can only observe what is observable. What unusual uses of language do you observe in your immediate surroundings? As your surroundings change, how does the language used change? What words have you heard used in novel ways? How do different groups of your friends use language differently from one another? Do young people use many different words from those used by older people?

5. In paragraph 8, Pei refers to the fact that one speaker with considerable prestige can affect the way large numbers of people use language. Which person in today's world has the kind of prestige that people respond to by adopting that person's speech habits? Is such a person likely to be a politician, an entertainer, a sports figure, a criminal, a teacher, or a military person? Is a speaker with enough prestige to affect the way we use language more likely to be female or male?

6. **CONNECTIONS**   Which of the ideas in Pei's essay are most likely to be illuminated by Charles Darwin's "Natural Selection" (p. 897)? Which are most likely to be illuminated by reference to Plato's "The Allegory of the Cave" (p. 865)? Which other writer in this book seems likely to be sympathetic to Pei's theories of language change?

7. **CONNECTIONS**   Alexander Pope was aware that the English language was in flux during the eighteenth century. Two centuries later, Mario Pei discussed the way in which words come into a language. Write a brief essay that examines the unusual uses of words in Pope's *An Essay on Criticism* (**bedfordstmartins.com/worldofideas/epages**). Which uses surprise you, and which do you have trouble understanding? The English language has changed considerably since Pope's time. Which

words or expressions do you find so original that you could imagine Pei referring to them as "new" to the language?

8. **SEEING CONNECTIONS**   Wosene Worke Kosrof's painting *The Color of Words IX* (p. 766) is a record of sorts of an ancient language spoken by people in a less than optimal environment. The script is ancient, but many people still speak Amharic. Research the geography and climate of Ethiopia and defend or attack the thesis that Amharic is spoken much the same way today as it was a thousand years ago. Consider what Pei says about the reasons for change in languages and what conditions are needed for a language to remain largely unchanged.

JAMES BALDWIN
If Black English Isn't a Language, Then Tell Me, What Is?

By THE TIME James Baldwin (1924–1987) wrote this essay in 1979, he was known as one of America's foremost African American writers, despite the fact that he refused to refer to himself as a "black writer," preferring instead to regard himself as simply an American writer. He had already become famous for *Go Tell It on the Mountain* (1953), an autobiographical novel about a single day in a church in Harlem. The book drew on Baldwin's personal experiences as a preacher between the ages of fourteen and sixteen. Indeed, he has said that the rhythms of the gospel church were one of his great resources as a writer.

Baldwin's childhood was spent as one of nine children in a family in Harlem. His father was a preacher whose hatred of whites distorted his personality. As a result, Baldwin grew acutely aware of how damaging hatred can be to an individual. His early essays explore the damage that racism and hatred did to his family, and many of his novels, stories, and essays center on these same themes and issues—as well as on the damage hatred does to America as a whole. Interestingly, although Baldwin is regarded as a uniquely American writer, he lived primarily in France from 1948 on, returning to the United States occasionally to lecture and teach. (He had gone to France in part to avoid American racism and in part to be near Richard Wright [1908–1960], author of *Native Son* [1940].)

Baldwin's novel *Giovanni's Room* (1956) moved away from racial subject matter and involved an exploration of gender and romance. The main character is torn between love for a man and love for a woman. Again, the subject matter is somewhat auto-biographical; Baldwin refused to identify himself as a gay writer

From *Collected Essays*.

primarily because he felt the important issue was to be able to love whomever he chose, man or woman. In many ways, his professional career was spent trying to avoid being labeled as one kind of writer or another.

Baldwin was equally adept at writing in multiple forms — plays, novels, short stories (*Going to Meet the Man,* 1965), and essays — making it all the more difficult for people to categorize him. After writing the play *The Amen Corner* (1955; published 1968), which centers on a woman evangelist married to a jazz musician, he won a Guggenheim Fellowship. His essay collection *Nobody Knows My Name: More Notes of a Native Son* (1961) established him as one of the finest writers of expository prose in America. *Another Country* (1962), addressing interracial and sexual themes, raised his stature to a novelist of distinction. One of his most famous essays, "The Fire Next Time" (1963), long enough to virtually fill an issue of the *New Yorker*, established him as a spokesperson for civil rights and black rage. The essay begins with an exploration of his encounter with Black Muslim separatists and then speaks loudly and clearly about the anger and sense of futility experienced by millions of black Americans.

Baldwin was known throughout his adulthood as a sparkling talent and a witty and fascinating person. However, he was also an alcoholic and grew increasingly unreliable in his later years. He rarely showed up anywhere on time and often failed to meet publishing deadlines. Some critics have suggested that his personal habits contributed to the falling off of his later work.

When the essay that follows was written in 1979, however, Baldwin was at the top of his game. He saw America with clear eyes, and while he had hopes for the civil rights movement, he did not think there were serious chances of significant change in American life. He was living in the south of France in a very small town that seemed almost unchanged since the late Renaissance. In France, he felt much freer than he did in the United States — something he wrote about in the essay "Stranger in the Village," which appeared in his *Notes of a Native Son* (1955). It was in the 1960s that Baldwin styled himself a transatlantic commuter, living part of the time in St. Paul de Vence or other places in southern France, as well as in New York and New England.

Baldwin's Rhetoric

As a young man Baldwin began preaching in his father's church. Some of that preacherly style is reflected in his writing, especially when, as in this essay, he feels he has a moral mission to convey. To some extent, his writing rises to polemic, a defense against an insult that he cannot let pass. He refers to the question of the legitimacy of black English as "the present skirmish." Shortly before he wrote this essay, a black teacher introduced the term *Ebonics* to describe the special language of black Americans. This raised a furor that Baldwin seems to be responding to. Baldwin was deeply concerned with the question of black English in the 1970s and 1980s in part because he was angry at writers working with him on a film project who had rejected his use of language. Moreover, when he wrote the essay below, he was aware that the South was still unfriendly toward black liberation. An interview he gave in early 1980 was titled "James Baldwin Finds the New South Is a Myth."

Baldwin's concern for language was based on his fear that language could control people. He thought that how whites use language essentially defines black people, and he protested that African Americans must define themselves through their own language.

Because his byline is France, Baldwin begins by referencing a number of places where French is spoken yet whose speakers have trouble understanding the French of the other places. As he says, a Parisian in northern France will have trouble understanding someone from Marseilles, which is in southern France, and they both may have trouble understanding people from Quebec, Martinique, or Guadeloupe. His point is that their experiences all define them in ways that are reflected in their language, and the fact that their language is nominally French does not mean that it is totally the same language.

He insists that "language is also a political instrument" that "reveals the private identity" and either links or separates one from a public community (para. 4). The question of how American English would sound if there were no "black people in the United States" (para. 5) is something he can hardly imagine. He knows it would be vastly different from what it is, which is one of the main ideas in his essay. In order to impress us with the magnitude of his subject and the seriousness of the issue, he makes the claim that how blacks use language "permits the nation its only glimpse of reality" (para. 6). If white society creates an illusory vision of black society, then black English will reveal the truth, and it will reveal the truth about America itself.

After a few lines of historical background in paragraph 7, he maintains that "[a] *language comes into existence by means of brutal necessity* [Baldwin's italics]," by which he means that slaves who had different languages had to create their own common one in order to communicate. When he tells us at the end of the essay that "[t]he brutal truth is that the bulk of the white people in America never had any interest in educating black people," he implies that black people had to educate themselves. They created their own language as a way of speaking truths that the white people could not understand because they disavowed black language. Language, he implies, can be an instrument of oppression. In the America that Baldwin lived in and "emigrated" from, there were more than a few examples of efforts at and results of oppression, including assassinations and uprisings. Language, as he implies, is a force to be understood in all its power.

PREREADING QUESTIONS:
WHAT TO READ FOR

The following prereading questions may help you anticipate key issues in the discussion of James Baldwin's "If Black English Isn't a Language, Then Tell Me, What Is?" Keeping them in mind during your first reading should help focus your attention.

- How can language define the "other"?
- Why does black English permit our society "its only glimpse of reality" (paras. 5 and 6)?
- Why did black English develop?

If Black English Isn't a Language, Then Tell Me, What Is?

St. Paul de Vence, France — The argument concerning the use, or 1 the status, or the reality, of black English is rooted in American history and has absolutely nothing to do with the question the argument supposes itself to be posing. The argument has nothing to do with language itself but with the *role* of language. Language, incontestably, reveals the speaker. Language, also, far more dubiously, is meant to define the other — and, in this case, the other is refusing to be defined by a language that has never been able to recognize him.

People evolve a language in order to describe and thus control 2 their circumstances, or in order not to be submerged by a reality that they cannot articulate. (And, if they cannot articulate it, they *are* submerged.) A Frenchman living in Paris speaks a subtly and crucially different language from that of the man living in Marseilles; neither sounds very much like a man living in Quebec; and they would all have great difficulty in apprehending what the man from Guadeloupe, or Martinique, is saying, to say nothing of the man from Senegal — although the "common" language of all these areas is French. But each has paid, and is paying, a different price for this "common" language, in which, as it turns out, they are not saying, and cannot be saying, the same things: they each have very different realities to articulate, or control.

What joins all languages, and all men, is the necessity to confront 3 life, in order, not inconceivably, to outwit death: the price for this is the acceptance, and achievement, of one's temporal identity. So that, for example, though it is not taught in the schools (and this has the potential of becoming a political issue) the south of France still clings to its ancient and musical Provençal,[1] which resists being described as a "dialect." And much of the tension in the Basque countries, and in Wales, is due to the Basque and Welsh determination not to allow their languages to be destroyed. This determination also feeds the flames in Ireland for among the many indignities the Irish have been forced to undergo at English hands is the English contempt for their language.

It goes without saying, then, that language is also a political instru- 4 ment, means, and proof of power. It is the most vivid and crucial key to identity: it reveals the private identity, and connects one with, or divorces one from, the larger, public, or communal identity. There have been, and are, times, and places, when to speak a certain language could be dangerous, even fatal. Or, one may speak the same language, but in such a way that one's antecedents are revealed, or (one hopes) hidden. This is true in France, and is absolutely true in England: the range (and reign) of accents on that damp little island make England coherent for the English and totally incomprehensible for everyone else. To open your mouth in England is (if I may use black English) to "put your business in the street": you have confessed your parents, your youth, your school, your salary, your self-esteem, and, alas, your future.

Now, I do not know what white Americans would sound like if 5 there had never been any black people in the United States, but they would not sound the way they sound. *Jazz,* for example, is a very specific sexual term, as in *jazz me, baby,* but white people purified it into the Jazz Age. *Sock it to me,* which means, roughly, the same thing, has been adopted by Nathaniel Hawthorne's[2] descendants with no qualms or hesitations at all, along with *let it all hang out* and *right on! Beat to*

---

[1] **Provençal** The Occitan language, spoken in southern France and parts of Spain.
[2] **Nathaniel Hawthorne (1804–1864)** One of America's greatest novelists.

his socks, which was once the black's most total and despairing image of poverty, was transformed into a thing called the Beat Generation, which phenomenon was, largely, composed of *uptight,* middle-class white people, imitating poverty, trying to *get down,* to get *with it,* doing their *thing,* doing their despairing best to be *funky,* which we, the blacks, never dreamed of doing—we *were* funky, baby, like *funk* was going out of style.

Now, no one can eat his cake, and have it, too, and it is late in the   6
day to attempt to penalize black people for having created a language that permits the nation its only glimpse of reality, a language without which the nation would be even more *whipped* than it is.

I say that the present skirmish is rooted in American history,   7
and it is. Black English is the creation of the black diaspora. Blacks came to the United States chained to each other, but from different tribes: neither could speak the other's language. If two black people, at that bitter hour of the world's history, had been able to speak to each other, the institution of chattel slavery could never have lasted as long as it did. Subsequently, the slave was given, under the eye, and the gun, of his master, Congo Square,[3] and the Bible—or, in other words, and under these conditions, the slave began the formation of the black church, and it is within this unprecedented tabernacle that black English began to be formed. This was not, merely, as in the European example, the adoption of a foreign tongue, but an alchemy that transformed ancient elements into a new language: *A language comes into existence by means of brutal necessity, and the rules of the language are dictated by what the language must convey.*

There was a moment, in time, and in this place, when my brother,   8
or my mother, or my father, or my sister, had to convey to me, for example, the danger in which I was standing from the white man standing just behind me, and to convey this with a speed, and in a language, that the white man could not possibly understand, and that, indeed, he cannot understand, until today. He cannot afford to understand it. This understanding would reveal to him too much about himself, and smash that mirror before which he has been frozen for so long.

Now, if this passion, this skill, this (to quote Toni Morrison)[4]   9
"sheer intelligence," this incredible music, the mighty achievement of having brought a people utterly unknown to, or despised by "history"—to have brought this people to their present, troubled, troubling, and unassailable and unanswerable place—if this absolutely

---

[3]**Congo Square** In parts of eighteenth-century Louisiana, slaves were given Sunday as a free day. They often met, sang, played music, and danced in places reserved for them. One such place, Congo Square, survives today in New Orleans.

[4]**Toni Morrison (b. 1931)** African American novelist and Nobel Prize winner.

unprecedented journey does not indicate that black English is a language, I am curious to know what definition of language is to be trusted.

A people at the center of the Western world, and in the midst of   10
so hostile a population, has not endured and transcended by means of what is patronizingly called a "dialect." We, the blacks, are in trouble, certainly, but we are not doomed, and we are not inarticulate because we are not compelled to defend a morality that we know to be a lie.

The brutal truth is that the bulk of the white people in America   11
never had any interest in educating black people, except as this could serve white purposes. It is not the black child's language that is in question, it is not his language that is despised: it is his experience. A child cannot be taught by anyone who despises him, and a child cannot afford to be fooled. A child cannot be taught by anyone whose demand, essentially, is that the child repudiate his experience, and all that gives him sustenance, and enter a limbo in which he will no longer be black, and in which he knows that he can never become white. Black people have lost too many black children that way.

And, after all, finally, in a country with standards so untrust-   12
worthy, a country that makes heroes of so many criminal mediocrities, a country unable to face why so many of the nonwhite are in prison, or on the needle, or standing, futureless, in the streets—it may very well be that both the child, and his elder, have concluded that they have nothing whatever to learn from the people of a country that has managed to learn so little.

QUESTIONS FOR CRITICAL READING

1. What does Baldwin mean by "black English"?
2. How is black English a "creation of the black diaspora"?
3. What effect did the black church have in developing black English?
4. How would you describe Baldwin's relationship with white America?
5. Has Baldwin convinced you that black English is a language?
6. What is society's current view, more than thirty-five years after this essay was written, on the subject of black English as a language?

SUGGESTIONS FOR CRITICAL WRITING

1. Examine the terms Baldwin refers to in paragraph 5. Why does he choose these terms to help define black English? He refers to the concept of reality in this and the next paragraph. What kind of

reality is he referring to? How does the language help the nation "glimpse" reality? Do you think the nation has done so? Is the nation glimpsing reality through black English today? Have other Englishes joined the reality refrain?

2. How can language be an instrument of oppression? What groups or individuals are currently oppressed by the use of language in popular media, such as in films, in speeches, or in books? What seems to be the motivation for the oppression of that group or individual? How successful has it been? What are its results?

3. Rap music developed from the black urban community. Is it an example of black English? Examine some lyrics of the rap music you find most interesting and explain to Baldwin's ghost what, on the basis of that music, black English is today. If you feel rap is black English, what is the reality that it is holding up to white society?

4. What changes in society's attitude toward the use of language by any minority group have been wrought by the more than thirty-five years that have passed since this essay was written? Have Latino Americans used language in special ways to achieve a Latino language similar to what Baldwin describes? Would Baldwin think Spanglish a good candidate for being deemed a language? Who might argue against such a view? Who would support it? Would there be political or cultural motives on the part of those who support or do not support such a view?

5. **CONNECTIONS**   In paragraph 11, Baldwin says, "The brutal truth is that the bulk of the white people in America never had any interest in educating black people, except as this could serve white purposes." What evidence in Jonathan Kozol's essay (p. 605) supports Baldwin's statement? Have the bulk of white people in America changed their attitudes in the more than thirty-five years since Baldwin wrote his essay? How does the question of education affect the ideas about language that Baldwin raises? If you wish, you may reference Frederick Douglass's experiences with education during his early life as a slave. Is what Baldwin says true according to your own experiences?

6. **CONNECTIONS**   James Baldwin presents a powerful and emotional argument against those who deny that black English is not a language. In his argument, which is in many ways a criticism of those who disagree with him, which of Pope's principles of good criticism (**bedfordstmartins.com/worldofideas/epages**) does Baldwin use? Which principles of bad criticism does he use? Does Pope give evidence that language can oppress people? Does he give evidence that criticism can help liberate them? Does Baldwin feel criticism can liberate people? Does Baldwin agree with Pope on the central issues of criticism?

7. **SEEING CONNECTIONS**   Wosene Worke Kosrof's painting *The Color of Words IX* (p. 766) contains the script of an ancient language of

Ethiopian people, a language called Amharic. It is still spoken today. What do you think Baldwin would have said about this painting? Would he have felt it to be a liberating language? Or would he have regarded it as potentially oppressive to minority groups within Ethiopia? Does there seem to be political content in this painting? What is the ultimate effect of displaying such an alphabet in a painting? Could the same effect be achieved with our alphabet? What advantage does an unrecognizable alphabet have in a painting? Does the painting, like language, communicate meaning?

BILL BRYSON
Where Words Come From

WILLIAM MCGUIRE BRYSON (b. 1951) was born in Des
Moines, Iowa, but spent several years touring Europe starting in
1973. He worked for a time in a psychiatric hospital in England,
which is where he met his future wife—a nurse named Cynthia.
The couple lived for two decades in Great Britain and had four children, eventually moving to the United States in 1995 and living
for several years in Hanover, New Hampshire. (Bryson has since
returned to Great Britain.) Bryson began a career in newspaper
journalism, which eventually led him to become a freelance writer.
This new career involved a considerable amount of research and
travel and has resulted in Bryson's writing a remarkable number
of books on many subjects. His travel writing is especially notable
and includes *A Walk in the Woods* (1998), about his walking the
Appalachian Trail, and *I'm a Stranger Here Myself* (1999), about his
experience living in New Hampshire.

In addition to writing about travel, Bryson is known for his
books on science, such as *A Short History of Nearly Everything*
(2003), for which he won the Aventis Prize for best science writing.
A few years later he won the Descartes Prize, the "Prize of Prizes,"
for best science communication. He gave the €50,000 prize
($65,600) to the Royal Society. One of his more recent books is
*Seeing Further: The Story of Science, Discovery, and the Genius of the
Royal Society* (2010).

Bryson's curiosity about language has resulted in several
important books designed to stimulate general interest in how language works and what its characteristics are, especially in terms
of regional usage. His first book was the *Penguin Book of Troublesome Words* (1984), written while he was a young copyeditor on
the *London Times*. The book grew out of Bryson's realization that

From *The Mother Tongue: English and How It Got That Way*.

there were many words — and many usages of words — that were unclear in his own mind, and he set about trying to clarify them for others. For example, should the phrase be "fewer than 10 percent of voters" or "less than 10 percent of voters"? Addressing questions about punctuation was only part of his efforts; he also tackled issues such as when "lie" or "lay," "further" or "farther," and "infer" or "imply" should be used and thousands of other similar problems. His book was eventually a best-seller and reprinted much enlarged in 2002 as *Bryson's Book of Troublesome Words*.

In 1994, Bryson wrote *Made in America: An Informal History of the English Language in the United States*. His subject centers on the differences between the ways in which the British use English and the ways in which Americans use it. Bryson discusses some regional differences in the United States and in one place begins a search for the origin of the expression *okay*. Does it come from Andrew Jackson, who is said to have signed some papers with "oll korrect," or from Martin Van Buren's nickname, "Old Kinderhook"? Bryson uses the study of American English to explore some of the delights of American popular culture, which in some ways has its own manner of speech.

The Mother Tongue: English and How It Got That Way (1994), the book from which the following passage is taken, was also a best-seller. It includes chapters on swearing, spelling, pronunciation, and the future of English, which is spoken by 500 million people today. The *New York Times* praised the book as a "motherlode of delectable trivia," and the *Los Angeles Times* described it as "a scholarly and fascinating book."

Bryson's Rhetoric

Bryson relies on our curiosity in this selection. Most of us are curious about words that we will probably never use, such as *properispomenon*, and we find some of them comical, such as *muliebrity*. Bryson piques our interest by introducing such exotic words, but he is careful not to go too far. He tells of words that once were common but now are rare or lost to us almost entirely. Then he goes on to tell about some of the peculiarities of languages, such as the remarkable number of meanings of the English word *set*. We all use most of the words he describes in the body of the essay, and in the process of telling us about them he reminds us how difficult the English language must be for adults trying to learn it. As he points out, other languages do not have some of the important properties that distinguish English.

Once he has our attention, Bryson relies on two very simple but effective rhetorical strategies. The first is an organizational strategy.

Because he has a great deal to say about many words, he adopts a categorical approach, somewhat like that used by Aristotle. His subject is "Where Words Come From," so he sets up a series of five categories that he feels cover the range of word origins:

1. Words are created by error. People mistake a sound for a new word, or they assume a misspelling is in fact a new word, as in the example "D or d," which was misapprehended as "dord."

2. Words are adopted. English is known for accepting foreign words as if they were English to start with, such as *ketchup* from China and *potato* from Haiti.

3. Words are created. Remarkably, the word *dog* seems to have been created from no Latin or Greek nor from any other root language. Other such words, like *big, fun, bad,* and *put,* are in the same category as *dog.* No one knows how they got into the language, but they are securely part of our vocabulary.

4. Words change by doing nothing. Ironically, some words over time come to mean almost the opposite of what they once meant. This is true of *brave, crafty, nice,* and *notorious.* No one quite knows why these changes occur.

5. Words are created by adding or subtracting something. Adding a prefix, such as *anti-* or *pro-,* can totally change the meaning of a word like *Federalist.* Suffixes, such as *-ship* or *-less,* can totally change the meaning of words like *kin* or *father.*

Once the categories are established, Bryson brings to bear his second most important rhetorical strategy: the use of many examples. Each of these categories is illustrated by dozens of examples of words that have been created by the method he establishes. As he introduces new words, he comments on their qualities and points particularly to the aspects of the words that make them unusual or strange. In that way, he continues to involve our curiosity and maintain our attention. These techniques are basic and reliable, while also being available to virtually any writer on any subject for which there are different kinds of examples.

PREREADING QUESTIONS: WHAT TO READ FOR

The following prereading questions may help you anticipate key issues in the discussion of Bill Bryson's "Where Words Come From." Keeping them in mind during your first reading should help focus your attention.

• What are the five categories Bryson sets up?
• How do words change their meaning?

Where Words Come From

If you have a morbid fear of peanut butter sticking to the roof 1
of your mouth, there is a word for it: *arachibutyrophobia*. There is a
word to describe the state of being a woman: *muliebrity*. And there's
a word for describing a sudden breaking off of thought: *aposiopesis*.
If you harbor an urge to look through the windows of the homes you
pass, there is a word for the condition: *crytoscopophilia*. When you are
just dropping off to sleep and you experience that sudden sensation
of falling, there is a word for it: it's a *myoclonic jerk*. If you want to
say that a word has a circumflex on its penultimate syllable, without
saying flat out that is has a circumflex there, there is a word for it:
properispomenon. There is even a word for a figure of speech in which
two connotative words linked by a conjunction express a complex
notion that would normally be conveyed by an adjective and a substantive working together. It is a *hendiadys*. (But of course.) In English,
in short, there are words for almost everything.

Some of these words deserve to be better known. Take *velleity*, 2
which describes a mild desire, a wish or urge too slight to lead to
action. Doesn't that seem a useful term? Or how about *slubberdegullion*,
a seventeenth-century word signifying a worthless or slovenly fellow? Or *ugsome*, a late medieval word meaning loathsome or disgusting? It has lasted half a millennium in English, was a common synonym for *horrid* until well into the last century, and can still be found
tucked away forgotten at the back of most unabridged dictionaries.
Isn't it a shame to let it slip away? Our dictionaries are full of such
words—words describing the most specific of conditions, the most
improbable of contingencies, the most arcane of distinctions.

And yet there are odd gaps. We have no word for coolness 3
corresponding to warmth. We are strangely lacking in middling
terms—words to describe with some precision the middle ground
between hard and soft, near and far, big and little. We have a posses-
sive impersonal pronoun *its* to place alongside *his, her,* and *their,* but
no equivalent impersonal pronoun to contrast with the personal *whose.*
Thus we have to rely on inelegant constructions such as "The house
whose roof" or resort to periphrasis. We have a word to describe all
the work you find waiting for you when you return from vacation,
backlog, but none to describe all the work you have to do before you
go. Why not *forelog*? And we have a large number of negative words—
inept, disheveled, incorrigible, ruthless, unkempt—for which the positive
form is missing. English would be richer if we could say admiringly
of a tidy person, "She's *so* sheveled," or praise a capable person for
being full of ept or an energetic one for having heaps of ert. Many of

these words did once have positive forms. *Ruthless* was companioned by *ruth,* meaning compassion. One of Milton's poems contains the well-known line "Look homeward, Angel, now, and melt with ruth." But, as with many such words, one form died and another lived. Why this should be is beyond explanation. Why should we have lost *demit* (send away) but saved *commit*? Why should *impede* have survived while the once equally common and seemingly just as useful *expede* expired? No one can say.

Despite these gaps and casualties, English retains probably the richest vocabulary, and most diverse shading of meanings, of any language. We can distinguish between house and home (as, for instance, the French cannot), between continual and continuous, sensual and sensuous, forceful and forcible, childish and childlike, masterful and masterly, assignment and assignation, informant and informer. For almost every word we have a multiplicity of synonyms. Something is not just big, it is large, immense, vast, capacious, bulky, massive, whopping, humongous. No other language has so many words all saying the same thing. It has been said that English is unique in possessing a synonym for each level of our culture: popular, literary, and scholarly—so that we can, according to our background and cerebral attainments, rise, mount, or ascend a stairway, shrink in fear, terror, or trepidation, and think, ponder, or cogitate upon a problem. This abundance of terms is often cited as a virtue. And yet a critic could equally argue that English is an untidy and acquisitive language, cluttered with a plethora of needless words. After all, do we really need *fictile* as a synonym for *moldable, glabrous* for *hairless, sternutation* for *sneezing*? Jules Feiffer[1] once drew a strip cartoon in which the down-at-heel character observed that first he was called poor, then needy, then deprived, then underprivileged, and then disadvantaged, and concluded that although he still didn't have a dime he sure had acquired a fine vocabulary. There is something in that. A rich vocabulary carries with it a concomitant danger of verbosity, as evidenced by our peculiar affection for redundant phrases, expressions that say the same thing twice: *beck and call, law and order, assault and battery, null and void, safe and sound, first and foremost, trials and tribulations, hem and haw, spick-and-span, kith and kin, dig and delve, hale and hearty, peace and quiet, vim and vigor, pots and pans, cease and desist, rack and ruin, without let or hindrance, to all intents and purposes, various different.* 4

Despite this bounty of terms, we have a strange—and to foreigners it must seem maddening—tendency to load a single word with a 5

---

[1]**Jules Feiffer (b. 1929)** American cartoonist.

whole galaxy of meanings. *Fine,* for instance, has fourteen definitions as an adjective, six as a noun, and two as an adverb. In the *Oxford English Dictionary* it fills two full pages and takes 5,000 words of description. We can talk about fine art, fine gold, a fine edge, feeling fine, fine hair, and a court fine and mean quite separate things. The condition of having many meanings is known as *polysemy,* and it is very common. *Sound* is another polysemic word. Its vast repertory of meanings can suggest an audible noise, a state of healthiness (sound mind), an outburst (sound off), an inquiry (sound out), a body of water (Puget Sound), or financial stability (sound economy), among many others. And then there's *round.* In the *OED, round* alone (that is without variants like *rounded* and *roundup*) takes 7 1/2 pages to define or about 15,000 words of text—about as much as is contained in the first hundred pages of this book. Even when you strip out its obsolete senses, *round* still has twelve uses as an adjective, nineteen as a noun, seven as a transitive verb, five as an intransitive verb, one as an adverb, and two as a preposition. But the polysemic champion must be *set.* Superficially it looks a wholly unseeming monosyllable, the verbal equivalent of the single-celled organism. Yet it has 58 uses as a noun, 126 as a verb, and 10 as a participial adjective. Its meanings are so various and scattered that it takes the *OED* 60,000 words—the length of a short novel—to discuss them all. A foreigner could be excused for thinking that to know *set* is to know English.

Generally polysemy happens because one word sprouts a variety   6
of meanings, but sometimes it is the other way around—similar but quite separate words evolve identical spellings. *Boil* in the sense of heating a pan of water and *boil* in the sense of an irruption of the skin are two unrelated words that simply happen to be spelled the same way. So are *policy* in the sense of a strategy or plan and the *policy* in a life insurance policy. *Excise,* meaning "to cut," is quite distinct in origin from *excise* in the sense of a customs duty.

Sometimes, just to heighten the confusion, the same word ends up   7
with contradictory meanings. This kind of word is called a *contronym.* *Sanction,* for instance, can either signify permission to do something or a measure forbidding it to be done. *Cleave* can mean cut in half or stick together. A sanguine person is either hotheaded and bloodthirsty or calm and cheerful. Something that is fast is either stuck firmly or moving quickly. A door that is bolted is secure, but a horse that has bolted has taken off. If you wind up a meeting, you finish it; if you wind up a watch, you start it. To ravish means to rape or to enrapture. *Quinquennial* describes something that lasts for five years or happens only once in five years. Trying one's best is a good thing, but trying one's patience is a bad thing. A blunt instrument is dull, but a blunt remark is pointed. Occasionally when this happens the dictionary

makers give us different spellings to differentiate the two meanings—as with *flour* and *flower, discrete* and *discreet*—but such ortho-
logical thoughtfulness is rare.

So where do all these words come from? According to the great 8
Danish linguist Otto Jespersen[2] words are for the most part formed
in one of four ways: by adding to them, by subtracting from them,
by making them up, and by doing nothing to them. Neat as that formula is, I would venture to suggest that it overlooks two other prolific
sources of new words: borrowing them from other languages and creating them by mistake. Let us look at each in turn.

1. WORDS ARE CREATED BY ERROR. One kind of these is 9
called ghost words. The most famous of these perhaps is *dord,* which
appeared in the 1934 *Merriam-Webster International Dictionary* as
another word for density. In fact, it was a misreading of the scribbled
"D or d," meaning that "density" could be abbreviated either to a
capital or lowercase letter. The people at Merriam-Webster quickly
removed it, but not before it found its way into other dictionaries.
Such occurrences are more common than you might suppose. According to the First Supplement of the *OED,* there are at least 350 words
in English dictionaries that owe their existence to typographical errors
or other misrenderings. For the most part they are fairly obscure. One
such is *messuage,* a legal term used to describe a house, its land, and
buildings. It is thought to be simply a careless transcription of the
French *ménage.*

Many other words owe their existence to mishearings. *Buttonhole* 10
was once *buttonhold. Sweetheart* was originally *sweetard,* as in *dullard*
and *dotard. Bridegroom* was in Old English *bryd-guma,* but the context
made people think of groom and an *r* was added. By a similar process an
l found its way into *belfrey. Asparagus* was for 200 years called *sparrow-
grass. Pentice* became *penthouse. Shamefaced* was originally *shamefast*
(*fast* here having the sense of lodged firmly, as in "stuck fast"). The
process can still be seen today in the tendency among many people to
turn *catercorner* into *catty-corner* and *chaise longue* into *chaise lounge.*

Sometimes words are created by false analogy or back-formation. 11
One example of this is the word *pea.* Originally the word was *pease,* as
in the nursery rhyme "pease porridge hot, pease porridge cold." But
this was mistakenly thought to signify a plural and the word *pea* was
back-formed to denote singularity. A similar misunderstanding gave us
cherry (from *cerise*). Etymologically *cherries* ought to be both singular

---

[2] **Otto Jespersen (1860–1943)** Prominent Danish linguist who studied English grammar and authored *Language: Its Nature, Development, and Origin* (1922).

and plural—and indeed it once was. The words *grovel* and *sidle* similarly came into English because the original adverbs, *groveling* and *sideling,* were assumed to contain the participle *-ing,* as in walking and seeing. In fact, it was the suffix *-ling,* but this did not stop people from adding a pair of useful verbs to the language. Other back-formations are *laze* (from *lazy*), *rove, burgle, greed* (from *greedy*), *beg* (from *beggar*), and *difficult* (from *difficulty*). Given the handiness and venerability of the process, it is curious to note that language authorities still generally squirm at the addition of new ones to the language. Among those that still attract occasional opprobrium are *enthuse* and *donate.*

Finally, erroneous words are sometimes introduced by respected   12
users of the language who simply make a mistake. Shakespeare thought *illustrious* was the opposite of *lustrous* and thus for a time gave it a sense that wasn't called for. Rather more alarmingly, the poet Robert Browning[3] caused considerable consternation by including the word *twat* in one of his poems, thinking it an innocent term. The work was *Pippa Passes,* written in 1841 and now remembered for the line "God's in His heaven, all's right with the world." But it also contains this disconcerting passage:

> Then owls and bats,
> Cowls and twats,
> Monks and nuns in a cloister's moods,
> Adjourn to the oak-stump pantry!

Browning had apparently somewhere come across the word   13
twat—which meant precisely the same then as it does now—but pronounced it with a flat *a* and somehow took it to mean a piece of headgear for nuns. The verse became a source of twittering amusement for generations of schoolboys and a perennial embarrassment to their elders, but the word was never altered and Browning was allowed to live out his life in wholesome ignorance because no one could think of a suitably delicate way of explaining his mistake to him.

2. WORDS ARE ADOPTED.   This is of course one of the glories   14
of English—its willingness to take in words from abroad, rather as if they were refugees. We take words from almost anywhere—*shampoo* from India, *chaparral* from the Basques, *caucus* from the Algonquin Indians, *ketchup* from China, *potato* from Haiti, *sofa* from Arabia, *boondocks* from the Tagalog language of the Philippines, *slogan* from Gaelic. You can't get much more eclectic than that. And we have

---

[3] **Robert Browning (1812–1899)** One of the most important English poets of the Victorian age.

been doing it for centuries. According to Baugh and Cable[4] as long ago as the sixteenth century English had already adopted words from more than fifty other languages—a phenomenal number for the age. Sometimes the route these words take is highly circuitous. Many Greek words became Latin words, which became French words, which became English words. *Garbage,* which has had its present meaning of food waste since the Middle Ages, was brought to England by the Normans, who had adapted it from an Italian dialectal word, *garbuzo,* which in turn had been taken from the Old Italian *garbuglio* (a mess), which ultimately had come from the Latin *bullire* (to boil or bubble).

Sometimes the same word reaches us at different times, having   15
undergone various degrees of filtering, and thus can exist in English in two or more related forms, as with *canal* and *channel, regard* and *reward, poor* and *pauper, catch* and *chase, cave* and *cage, amiable* and *amicable.* Often these words have been so modified in their travels that their kinship is all but invisible. Who would guess that *coy* and *quiet* both have the same grandparent in the Latin *quietus,* or that *sordid* and *swarthy* come jointly from the Latin *sordere* (to be soiled or dirty), or that *entirety* and *integrity* come from the Latin *integritus* (complete and pure)?

Occasionally a single root gave birth to triplets, as with *cattle,*   16
chattel, and *capital, hotel, hostel,* and *hospital,* and *strait, straight,* and *strict.* There is at least one quadruplet—*jaunty, gentle, gentile,* and *genteel,* all from the Latin *gentilis*—though there may be more. But the record holder is almost certainly the Latin *discus,* which has given us *disk, disc, dish, desk, dais,* and, of course, *discus.* (But having said that, one native Anglo-Saxon root, *bear,* has given birth to more than forty words, from *birth* to *born* to *burden.*)

Often words change meanings dramatically as they pass from one   17
nation to another. The Latin *bestia* has become variously *biscia* (snake) in Italy, *bitch* (female dog) in England, *biche* (female deer) in France, and *bicho* (insect) in Portugal. [Cited by Pei.[5]]

We in the English-speaking world are actually sometimes better   18
at looking after our borrowed words than the parents were. Quite a number of words that we've absorbed no longer exist in their place of birth. For instance, the French do not use *nom de plume, double entendre, panache, bon viveur, legerdemain* (literally "light of hand"), or *R.S.V.P.* for *répondez s'il vous plaît.* (Instead they write: "Prière de

---

[4]**Baugh and Cable** Albert C. Baugh (1891–1981) and Thomas Cable (b. 1942) authored *History of the English Language* (1957), a standard reference book.
[5]**Mario Pei** See his selection on page 783.

répondre.") The Italians do not use *brio* and although they do use *al fresco*, to them it signifies not being outside but being in prison.

Many of the words we take in are so artfully anglicized that it can   19
be a surprise to learn they are not native. Who would guess that our word *puny* was once the Anglo-Norman *puis né* or that *curmudgeon* may once have been the French *coeur méchant* (evil heart), or that *breeze*, so English-sounding, was taken from the Spanish *briza*, or that the distress signal *mayday* was lifted from the French cry *m'aidez* (meaning "help me") or that *poppycock* comes from the Dutch *pappekak*, meaning "soft dung"? *Chowder* came directly from the French *chaudière* (cauldron), while *bankrupt* was taken literally from the Italian expression *banca rotta*, meaning "broken bench." In the late Middle Ages, when banking was evolving in Italy, transactions were conducted in open-air markets. When a banker became insolvent his bench was broken up. Sometimes the foreign words came quietly, but other times they needed a good pummeling before they assumed anything like a native shape, as when the Gaelic *sionnachuighim* was knocked into *shenanigan* and the Amerind *raugroughcan* became *raccoon*.

This tendency to turn foreign sounds into native speech is com-   20
mon. In New York, Flatbush was originally Vlacht Bos and Gramercy Park was originally De Kromme Zee. British soldiers in World War I called Ypres Wipers and in the 1950s, American soldiers in Japan converted the song "Shi-i-Na-Na Ya-Ru" into "She Ain't Got No Yo-Yo."

One of our more inexplicable habits is the tendency to keep the   21
Anglo-Saxon noun but to adopt a foreign form for the adjectival form. Thus fingers are not fingerish; they are digital. Eyes are not eyeish; they are ocular. English is unique in this tendency to marry a native noun to an adopted adjective. Among other such pairs are *mouth/oral, book/literary, water/aquatic, house/domestic, moon/lunar, son/filial, sun/solar, town/urban*. This is yet another perennial source of puzzlement for anyone learning English. Sometimes, a Latinate adjective was adopted but the native one kept as well, so that we can choose between, say, *earthly* and *terrestrial, motherly* and *maternal, timely* and *temporal*.

Although English is one of the great borrowing tongues—deriving   22
at least half of its common words from non-Anglo-Saxon stock—others have been even more enthusiastic in adopting foreign terms. In Armenian, only 23 percent of the words are of native origin, while in Albanian the proportion is just 8 percent. A final curious fact is that although English is a Germanic tongue and the Germans clearly were one of the main founding groups of America, there is almost no language from which we have borrowed fewer words than German. Among the very few are *kindergarten* and *hinterland*. We have borrowed far more words from every other European language, and

probably as many from several smaller and more obscure languages such as Inuit. No one has yet come up with a plausible explanation for why this should be.

3. WORDS ARE CREATED. Often they spring seemingly from 23 nowhere. Take *dog*. For centuries the word in English was *hound* (or *hund*). Then suddenly in the late Middle Ages, *dog*—a word etymologically unrelated to any other known word—displaced it. No one has any idea why. This sudden arising of words happens more often than you might think. Among others without known pedigree are *jaw, jam, bad, big, gloat, fun, crease, pour, put, niblick* (the golf club), *noisome, numskull, jalopy,* and countless others. *Blizzard* suddenly appeared in the nineteenth century in America (the earliest use is attributed to Davy Crockett) and *rowdy* appeared at about the same time. Recent examples of this phenomenon are *yuppie* and *sound bites,* which seem to have burst forth spontaneously and spread with remarkable rapidity throughout the English-speaking world.

Other words exist in the language for hundreds of years, either 24 as dialect words or as mainstream words that have fallen out of use, before suddenly leaping to prominence—again quite mysteriously. *Scrounge* and *seep* are both of this type. They have been around for centuries and yet neither, according to Robert Burchfield[6] [*The English Language*], came into general use before 1900.

Many words are made up by writers. According to apparently 25 careful calculations, Shakespeare used 17,677 words in his writings, of which at least one-tenth had never been used before. Imagine if every tenth word you wrote were original. It is a staggering display of ingenuity. But then Shakespeare lived in an age when words and ideas burst upon the world as never before or since. For a century and a half, from 1500 to 1650, English flowed with new words. Between 10,000 and 12,000 words were coined, of which about half still exist. Not until modern times would this number be exceeded, but even then there is no comparison. The new words of today represent an explosion of technology—words like *lunar module* and *myocardial infarction*—rather than of poetry and feeling. Consider the words that Shakespeare alone gave us, *barefaced, critical, leapfrog, monumental, castigate, majestic, obscene, frugal, radiance, dwindle, countless, submerged, excellent, fretful, gust, hint, hurry, lonely, summit, pedant,* and some 1,685 others. How would we manage without them? He might well have created even more except that he had to bear in mind the practicalities

---

[6]**Robert Burchfield (1923–2004)** Lexicographer born in New Zealand who edited the supplement to the *Oxford English Dictionary*.

of being instantly apprehended by an audience. Shakespeare's vocabulary changed considerably as he aged. Jespersen notes that there are some 200 to 300 words to be found in the early plays that are never repeated. Many of these were provincialisms that he later shed, but which independently made their way into the language later—among them *cranny, beautified, homicide, aggravate,* and *forefathers*. It has also been observed by scholars that the new terms of his younger years appeal directly to the senses (*snow-white, fragrant, brittle*) while the coinages of the later years are more often concerned with psychological considerations.

Shakespeare was at the center of this remarkable verbal outburst but not alone in it. Ben Jonson gave us *damp, defunct, clumsy,* and *strenuous* among many other useful terms. Isaac Newton coined *centrifugal* and *centripetal*. Sir Thomas More came up with *absurdity, acceptance, exact, explain,* and *exaggerate*. The classical scholar Sir Thomas Elyot fathered, among others, *animate, exhaust,* and *modesty*. Coleridge produced *intensify*. Jeremy Bentham produced *international* (and apologized for its inelegance). Thomas Carlyle gave us *decadent* and *environment*. George Bernard Shaw thought up *superman*. 26

Many new coinages didn't last—often for obvious reasons. Jonson's less inspired efforts included *ventositous* and *obstupefact*. Shakespeare gave us the useful *gloomy,* but failed with *barky* and *brisky* (formed after the same pattern but somehow never catching on) and failed equally with *conflux, vastidity,* and *tortive*. Milton found no takers for *inquisiturient,* while, later still, Dickens tried to give the world *vocular*. The world didn't want it. 27

Sometimes words are made up for a specific purpose. The U.S. Army in 1974 devised a food called *funistrada* as a test word during a survey of soldiers' dietary preferences. Although no such food existed, funistrada ranked higher in the survey than lima beans and eggplant (which seems about right to me, at least as far as the lima beans go). 28

According to Mary Helen Dohan,[7] in her absorbing book *Our Own Words,* the military vehicle the tank got its name because during its secretive experimental phase people were encouraged to think it was a storage receptacle—hence a tank. The curiously nautical terminology for its various features—*hatch, turret, hull, deck*—arises from the fact that it was developed by the British admiralty rather than the army. 29

4. WORDS CHANGE BY DOING NOTHING. That is, the word stays the same but the meaning changes. Surprisingly often the meaning 30

---

[7]**Mary Helen Dohan (1914–2011)** American writer who wrote a book about Eleanor Roosevelt as well as a book about words.

becomes its opposite or something very like it. *Counterfeit* once meant a legitimate copy. *Brave* once implied cowardice—as indeed *bravado* still does. (Both come from the same source as *depraved*.) *Crafty,* now a disparaging term, originally was a word of praise, while *enthusiasm,* which is now a word of praise, was once a term of mild abuse. *Zeal* has lost its original pejorative sense, but *zealot* curiously has not. *Garble* once meant to sort out, not to mix up. A *harlot* was once a boy, and a *girl* in Chaucer's day was any young person, whether male or female. *Manufacture,* from the Latin root for hand, once signified something made by hand; it now means virtually the opposite. *Politician* was originally a sinister word (perhaps, on second thought, it still is), while *obsequious* and *notorious* simply meant flexible and famous. Simeon Potter[8] notes that when James II first saw St. Paul's Cathedral he called it amusing, awful, and artificial, and meant that it was pleasing to look at, deserving of awe, and full of skillful artifice.

This drift of meaning, technically called *catachresis,* is as widespread as it is curious. *Egregious* once meant eminent or admirable. In the sixteenth century, for no reason we know of, it began to take on the opposite sense of badness and unworthiness (it is in this sense that Shakespeare employs it in *Cymbeline*) and has retained that sense since. Now, however, it seems that people are increasingly using it in the sense not of bad or shocking, but of simply being pointless and unconstructive.
31

According to Mario Pei, more than half of all words adopted into English from Latin now have meanings quite different from their original ones. A word that shows just how wide-ranging these changes can be is *nice,* which was first recorded in 1290 with the meaning of stupid and foolish. Seventy-five years later Chaucer was using it to mean lascivious and wanton. Then at various times over the next four hundred years it came to mean extravagant, elegant, strange, slothful, unmanly, luxurious, modest, slight, precise, thin, shy, discriminating, dainty, and—by 1769—pleasant and agreeable. The meaning shifted so frequently and radically that it is now often impossible to tell in what sense it was intended, as when Jane Austen wrote to a friend, "You scold me so much in a nice long letter . . . which I have received from you."
32

Sometimes the changing connotations of a word can give a new and startling sense to literary passages, as in *The Mayor of Casterbridge* where Thomas Hardy[9] has one of his characters gaze upon "the unattractive
33

---

[8] **Simeon Potter (1898–c. 1976)** English author of many books on language.

[9] **Thomas Hardy (1840–1928)** One of England's most important novelists and author of *Jude the Obscure* (1895).

exterior of Farfrae's erection" or in *Bleak House* where Dickens writes that "Sir Leicester leans back in his chair, and breathlessly ejaculates." [Taken from "Red Pants," by Robert M. Sebastian, in the Winter 1989 issue of *Verbatim*.]

This drift of meaning can happen with almost anything, even our   34 clothes. There is a curious but not often noted tendency for the names of articles of apparel to drift around the body. This is particularly apparent to Americans in Britain (and vice versa) who discover that the names for clothes have moved around at different rates and now often signify quite separate things. An American going into a London department store with a shopping list consisting of vest, knickers, suspenders, jumper, and pants would in each instance be given something dramatically different from what he expected. (To wit, a British vest is an American undershirt. Our vest is their waistcoat. Their knickers are our panties. To them a jumper is a sweater, while what we call a jumper is to them a pinafore dress. Our suspenders are their braces. They don't need suspenders to hold up their pants because to them pants are underwear and clearly you don't need suspenders for that, so instead they employ suspenders to hold up their stockings. Is that clear?)

Sometimes an old meaning is preserved in a phrase or expres-   35 sion. *Neck* was once widely used to describe a parcel of land, but that meaning has died out except in the expression "neck of the woods." *Tell* once meant to count. This meaning died out but is preserved in the expression *bank teller* and in the term for people who count votes. When this happens, the word is called a *fossil*. Other examples of fossils are the italicized words in the following list:

> short *shrift*
> *hem* and *haw*
> *rank* and *file*
> *raring* to go
> not a *whit*
> out of *kilter*
> new*fangled*
> at *bay*
> *spick-and-span*
> to and *fro*
> *kith* and kin

Occasionally, because the sense of the word has changed, fossil   36 expressions are misleading. Consider the oft-quoted statement "the exception proves the rule." "Most people take this to mean that the exception confirms the rule, though when you ask them to explain the logic in that statement, they usually cannot. After all, how *can* an exception prove a rule? It can't. The answer is that an earlier meaning of *prove* was to test (a meaning preserved in *proving ground*) and with that meaning the statement suddenly becomes sensible—the exception tests the rule. A similar misapprehension is often attached to the statement "the proof of the pudding is in the eating."

Sometimes words change by becoming more specific. *Starve* originally meant to die before it took on the more particular sense of to die by hunger. A deer was once any animal (it still is in the German *tier*) and meat was any food (the sense is preserved in "meat and drink" and in the English food mincemeat, which contains various fruits but no meat in the sense that we now use it). A forest was any area of countryside set aside for hunting, whether or not it was covered with trees. (In England to this day, the Forest of Bowland in Lancashire is largely treeless, as are large stretches of the New Forest in Hampshire.) And *worm* was a term for any crawling creature, including snakes.

5. WORDS ARE CREATED BY ADDING OR SUBTRACTING SOMETHING. English has more than a hundred common prefixes and suffixes— *-able, -ness, -ment, pre-, dis-, anti-,* and so on—and with these it can form and reform words with a facility that yet again sets it apart from other tongues. For example, we can take the French word *mutin* (rebellion) and turn it into *mutiny, mutinous, mutinously, mutineer,* and many others, while the French have still just the one form, *mutin.*

We are astonishingly indiscriminate in how we form our compounds, sometimes adding an Anglo-Saxon prefix or suffix to a Greek or Latin root *(plainness, sympathizer)*, and sometimes vice versa *(readable, disbelieve)*. [Examples cited by Burchfield, *The English Language*.] This inclination to use affixes and infixes provides gratifying flexibility in creating or modifying words to fit new uses, as strikingly demonstrated in the word *incomprehensibility*, which consists of the root *-hen-* and eight affixes and infixes: *in-, -com-, -pre-, -s-, -ib-, -il-, -it-,* and *-y.* Even more melodic is the musical term *quasihemidemisemiquaver,* which describes a note that is equal to 128th of a semibreve.

As well as showing flexibility it also promotes confusion. We have six ways of making *labyrinth* into an adjective: *labyrinthian, labyrinthean, labyrinthal, labyrinthine, labyrinthic,* and *labyrinthical.* We have at least six ways of expressing negation with prefixes: *a-, anti-, in-, il-, im-, ir-, un-,* and *non-.* It is arguable whether this is a sign of admirable variety or just untidiness. It must be exasperating for foreigners to have to learn that a thing unseen is not unvisible, but invisible, while something that cannot be reversed is not inreversible but irreversible and that a thing not possible is not nonpossible or antipossible but impossible. Furthermore, they must learn not to make the elementary mistake of assuming that because a word contains a negative suffix or prefix it is necessarily a negative word. *In-,* for instance, almost always implies negation but not with *invaluable,*

37

38

39

40

while *-less* is equally negative, as a rule, but not with *priceless*. Things are so confusing that even native users have shown signs of mental fatigue and left us with two forms meaning the same thing: *flammable* and *inflammable, iterate* and *reiterate, ebriate* and *inebriate, habitable* and *inhabitable, durable* and *perdurable, fervid* and *perfervid, gather* and *forgather, ravel* and *unravel.*

Some of our word endings are surprisingly rare. If you think of   41
angry and *hungry,* you might conclude that *-gry* is a common ending, but in fact it occurs in no other common words in English. Similarly *-dous* appears in only *stupendous, horrendous, tremendous, hazardous,* and *jeopardous,* while *-lock* survives only in *wedlock* and *warlock* and *-red* only in *hatred* and *kindred. Forgiveness* is the only example of a verb + *-ness* form. Equally some common-seeming prefixes are actually more rare than superficial thought might lead us to conclude. If you think of *forgive, forget, forgo, forbid, forbear, forlorn, forsake,* and *forswear,* you might think that *for-* is a common prefix, but in fact it appears in no other common words, though once it appeared in scores of others. Why certain forms like *-ish, -ness, -ful,* and *-some* should continue to thrive while others like *-lock* and *-gry* that were once equally popular should fall into disuse is a question without a good answer.

Fashion clearly has something to do with it. The suffix *-dom* was   42
long in danger of disappearing, except in a few established words like *kingdom,* but it underwent a resurgence (largely instigated in America) in the last century, giving us such useful locutions as *officialdom* and *boredom* and later more contrived forms like *best-sellerdom.* The ending *-en* is today one of the most versatile ways we have of forming verbs from adjectives (*harden, loosen, sweeten,* etc.) and yet almost all such words are less than three hundred years old.

Nor is there any discernible pattern to help explain why a par-   43
ticular affix attaches itself to a particular word or why some creations have thrived while others have died of neglect. Why, for instance, should we have kept *disagree* but lost *disadorn,* retained *impede* but banished *expede,* kept *inhibit* but rejected *cohibit?*

The process is still perhaps the most prolific way of forming new   44
words and often the simplest. For centuries we had the word *political,* but by loading the single letter *a* onto the front of it, a new word, *apolitical,* joined the language in 1952.

Still other words are formed by lopping off their ends. *Mob,* for   45
example, is a shortened form of *mobile vulgus* (fickle crowd). *Exam, gym,* and *lab* are similar truncations, all of them dating only from the last century when syllabic amputations were the rage. Yet the impulse to shorten words is an ancient one.

Finally, but no less importantly, English possesses the ability to   46
make new words by fusing compounds—*airport, seashore, footwear,*

wristwatch, landmark, flowerpot, and so on almost endlessly. All Indo-European languages have the capacity to form compounds. Indeed, German and Dutch do it, one might say, to excess. But English does it more neatly than most other languages, eschewing the choking word chains that bedevil other Germanic languages and employing the nifty refinement of making the elements reversible, so that we can distinguish between a houseboat and a boathouse, between basketwork and a workbasket, between a casebook and a bookcase. Other languages lack this facility.

QUESTIONS FOR CRITICAL READING

1. What makes English difficult for non-English-speaking people to learn?

2. Which example of word change is most striking to you?

3. Is "But of course" a hendiadys (para. 1)?

4. What is the meaning of *polysemy* (para. 5)?

5. What is odd about English words borrowed from the German language?

6. How does one "back-form" a word (para. 11)?

7. What effects do suffixes and prefixes have on words?

SUGGESTIONS FOR CRITICAL WRITING

1. Which words used in everyday speech are borrowed from sports? Which sports seem to contribute the most words and which the fewest? What is the effect of using sports words to describe actions, places, people, and events? What rhetorical strategy seems to be at work when a person uses sports terms rather than neutral terms to describe events of considerable political importance? Are there parts of the country where terms borrowed from football are more prevalent than terms borrowed from baseball? Is there a class distinction implied in borrowing terms from golf or tennis rather than from contact sports?

2. Examine newspaper or magazine articles on politicians or political events and comment on the use of language, particularly words that may be interpreted in different ways. Polysemy is an example of words that can have two or more meanings. How many such words are present in the articles? How many of the words Bryson describes are present in the articles? Would a non-English speaker have trouble learning English by reading these articles?

3. Your peer group uses language and words in ways that are different from those of your parents and grandparents. Write an essay that describes some of the meanings that you give to words that your parents would not give to them. How often do you find it difficult to explain to your parents what you mean by these terms? Which terms would you never use in the presence of your grandparents (or parents) because you fear they would misunderstand? Categorize those words, such as (1) words of praise, (2) words of dispraise, and (3) swear words.

4. Examine a textbook on economics, computer science, psychology, or general science. Categorize the terms specific to that discipline that (1) likely will never be part of your general vocabulary; (2) were already part of your vocabulary, even before you began reading; (3) are definitely becoming part of your general vocabulary; and (4) will likely become part of the general vocabulary of most people. How have discipline-specific terms affected the way people think? How have any of these terms affected your own thinking patterns?

5. What effect has rock music, hip-hop, or your favorite form of popular music had on expanding the vocabulary of English? Which groups of musicians have added words to the language? Research the lyrics of popular songs and decide whether those texts have made a contribution to the language we currently speak. Why would popular music affect everyday speech?

6. **CONNECTIONS**   Mario Pei (p. 783) is referred to in Bryson's essay. Does Pei seem to be sympathetic to Bryson's views on the origins of words? What does Pei have to add to Bryson's discussion? Does Pei introduce a new category of word development that Bryson does not consider? Does Bryson's analysis of the ways in which words originate support James Baldwin's defense of black English (p. 795)?

7. **CONNECTIONS**   Bill Bryson is interested in where words come from. If he was interested in where ideas come from, which of Pope's (**bedfordstmartins.com/worldofideas/epages**) most memorable lines would he offer as examples of new ideas expressed in words? How many of Pope's couplets can you find that, by being joined in rhyme, add weight to the ideas that underlie the words? Which would Bryson most happily take notice of? How concerned is Pope with finding new words or giving new meanings to old words? Why would Bryson take special interest in *An Essay on Criticism*?

8. **SEEING CONNECTIONS**   If Bryson saw Wosene Worke Kosrof's painting *The Color of Words IX* (p. 766) and studied it, how would he fit it into his ideas of word invention and word categorization? Can you categorize the letters and symbols in the painting? For example,

do the numbers 3, 5, 8, and 9 on the topmost line of the painting suggest the human form? How many of these symbols appear in the painting? Can you divine any meaning from them or use them in combination to suggest new words? Do any of the letters imply an animal form? Which letters seem completely abstract (like the letters in our alphabet)? Which seem to be in a category of their own? How many of these characters seem to definitely be characters in an alphabet?

NEIL POSTMAN
The Word Weavers/The World Makers

NEIL POSTMAN (1931–2003) was a student of the word. In 1958, while a graduate student at Columbia University, he taught at San Francisco State University, which was then at the center of original work in semantics, the science of the study of meaning in words. S. I. Hayakawa (1906–1992) was a leader in the field and a colleague of Postman's at San Francisco State. Both were influenced by the work of Alfred Korzybski (1879–1950), who had founded the Institute for Semantics and had been a highly influential lecturer and writer on meaning in language. Korzybski had taught a course called Language and Human Behavior in the Continuing Education School at New York University. It was, Postman said, the first course given in semantics at a major university. And in 1959, when Postman accepted a position at NYU, he was delighted to be able to continue the tradition, teach that same course there for more than forty years.

While Postman was teaching at NYU, the Canadian rhetorician and professor of English Marshall McLuhan (1911–1980) was becoming famous for his work in media and language; his slogan "the medium is the message" was influential on media scholars, especially during the explosion of television broadcasting and the beginning of the computer revolution. McLuhan promoted the idea that the media shape culture. Postman was influenced by McLuhan and other semanticists and developed his own views of the media and the influence of electronic forms of communication.

In 1961, Postman published his first book, *Television and the Teaching of English,* in which he applied the theories of linguistics and semantics to teaching English in primary and secondary schools. He followed this book with a series of related texts called *The New English* for grades 7 to 12, which also focused on English education. Postman was quick to see the power of television and its usefulness in teaching. In these books, he reviews the effects of

From *The End of Education: Redefining the Value of School.*

various media on language and words and describes the power of television to deliver meaning and shape language (though he would later come to reverse this stance). *Teaching as a Subversive Activity* (1969), which he wrote with Charles Weingartner, was another highly influential book that questioned many of the assumptions about education across the board, not just those regarding English education. Postman and Weingartner pressed the issue of how language not only carries meaning but also shapes it. Postman's point was that language competence was of enormous importance to K–12 students because it actually shaped the way they perceived and understood the world they lived in. He argued for greater language competence at all levels and for a child-centered curriculum that did away with textbooks and permitted students to make discoveries in a controlled environment.

In the late 1970s, Postman began work on a trilogy of books designed to alert educators to the problems involved with the use of media not only in education but in the public sphere. The first, *Teaching as a Conserving Activity* (1979), announced that his earlier work, which had praised the power of television and electronic media, needed a total revision. He had become aware that children did not need much special training to adapt to television. Instead, they needed much more training to deal with basic texts, such as books and printed material. His second book in the series was *The Disappearance of Childhood* (1982), which discussed the entire idea of childhood, a concept that he felt was essentially recent. In the ancient world, children were not treated in a special way. But, Postman argued, by the middle of the nineteenth century through the beginning of the twentieth century a special place had been created in society specifically to accommodate children. In this book, he points to the power of television to influence children by inundating them with adult content that emphasizes consumerism, materialism, and adult hedonism. The worlds of children and adults were conflated on television, and he thought that as a result TV viewers were stunting their intellectual development. Much of Postman's later work was aimed at revealing the ways in which electronic media hindered the growth of those passively immersed in it.

His third book was *Amusing Ourselves to Death: Public Discourse in the Age of Show Business* (1985). In this volume, Postman deals with the question of the effects on children of constant entertainment as a primary source of knowledge of the world. In addition, he points out that the public in general depends on entertainment to satisfy their intellectual needs. Postman became well-known for his positions on the damage he said is done to the intellectual capacity of those who depend on television and other electronic media to describe and represent the world around them. His complaint is in some ways quite simple: television, he said, treats serious subjects with indifference and shallow presentation because it is entirely devoted to light entertainment rather than thoughtful instruction. Postman, as a dedicated and gifted teacher, could not sit back and ignore television's effects on his students and his world.

Postman's Rhetoric

One of Postman's constant suggestions to writers is that they stress clarity while writing. He made this suggestion at a time when some academic disciplines were becoming more theoretical and the writing produced was often unclear. Postman follows his own advice in this selection and maintains perfect clarity throughout. His subject is the ways in which the control of language affects our perception of the world. He makes it clear that the world is complex and that we need a means to bring what we observe under control and make the complexities of experience manageable. When he talks about a cup, for instance, he reminds us that no one can really perceive a cup in its entirety and that, even more importantly, no one can perceive the reality of a cup because it is a collection of molecules and atoms in constant motion. And even if we could perceive that, we may not be perceiving reality. We use, he tells us, a process of abstraction to create a concept of a cup, just as we do for other physical objects. Such concepts make it possible for us to maintain some control over our environment.

Because Postman was a lifelong educator, his focus throughout the selection is on the ways in which we learn and develop ideas and concepts of the world. His views on semantics are central to the entire essay. He realizes as he writes that the fashion in English and language studies does not currently favor studies in semantics (which was wildly popular from the 1960s through the 1980s). Semantics, he says, should not be limited to study in graduate school but should in fact be introduced in the lower grades, as he did repeatedly while teaching. As he says, we learn by asking questions and we need to know where the questions come from and how they are phrased—and we hope that the best questions will produce even better questions to help clarify areas of study. In fact, Postman would like schools to pay special attention just to the idea of questions.

The essay has a simple three-part structure, which helps Postman achieve the kind of clarity he respects. The first part of the discussion focuses on three verbal issues: definition, questions, and metaphor. The fact that a word has a definition is interesting, he says, but it is important to know who gave it that definition and what other definitions of the word may be relevant. This is part of the process of understanding the meaning of words. He contends that questions shape the way we understand everything, and he states, "Everything we know has its origins in questions" (para. 3). Finally, he discusses metaphor: a comparison between two different things, the result of which is that one of those things is understood in a new way. He illustrates this concept with "Is the human mind, for example, like a dark cavern (needing illumination)? A muscle (needing exercise)? A vessel (needing filling)?" and continues with more examples. The point is that if we liken the human mind to anything else metaphorically, then we reshape the way we understand the concept of the mind.

The second part of the essay focuses on the work of Alfred Korzybski, the "father" of semantics and an inspiration to Postman. Postman provides a brief biography, then talks about Korzybski's major publications and makes an appeal for better understanding of semantics by clarifying Korzybski's original motivations in studying language. Korzybski's war experience made him wonder why so much progress had been made in science and such little progress in social sciences up to his time. Science was successful, but social sciences failed to prevent World War I—in which Korzybski fought and was wounded. Korzybski and Postman are both convinced that a better education in language would help people have better control over their world and help them avoid the rush to war that characterized much of the twentieth century.

The final part of the essay returns to the three issues that are central to the opening pages: concepts of definition, questions, and metaphor, now developed in light of the ideas suggested by Korzybski's work. This three-part structure makes the most difficult ideas in the selection more intelligible. It is similar to the classic structure of the sonata in music: theme, variation and development, restatement of theme. Postman understands how this three-part structure in an essay can help produce and maintain clarity.

PREREADING QUESTIONS:
WHAT TO READ FOR

The following prereading questions may help you anticipate key issues in the discussion of Neil Postman's "The Word Weavers/The World Makers." Keeping them in mind during your first reading should help focus your attention.

- What is a metaphor and how does it shape meaning?
- How does language shape our understanding of the world?
- What is the definition of *semantics*?

The Word Weavers/The World Makers

In an effort to clear up confusion (or ignorance) about the mean-   1
ing of a word, does anyone ask, What is *a* definition of this word? Just
about always, the way of putting the question is, What is *the* definition
of this word? The difference between *a* and *the* in this context is vast,
and I have no choice but to blame the schools for the mischief created by an inadequate understanding of what a definition is. From the
earliest grades through graduate school, students are given definitions
and, with few exceptions, are not told whose definitions they are, for
what purposes they were invented, and what alternative definitions
might serve equally as well. The result is that students come to believe
that definitions are *not* invented; that they are not even human creations; that, in fact, they are — how shall I say it? — part of the natural
world, like clouds, trees, and stars.

In a thousand examinations on scores of subjects, students are asked   2
to give definitions of hundreds of things, words, concepts, procedures. It
is to be doubted that there are more than a few classrooms in which there
has been any discussion of what a definition is. How is that possible?

Let us take the equally strange case of questions. There will be no   3
disagreement, I think, to my saying that all the answers given to students are the end products of questions. Everything we know has its
origin in questions. Questions, we might say, are the principal intellectual instruments available to human beings. Then how is it possible that no more than one in one hundred students has ever been
exposed to an extended and systematic study of the art and science
of question-asking? How come Alan Bloom didn't mention this, or
E. D. Hirsch Jr.,[1] or so many others who have written books on how
to improve our schools? Did they simply fail to notice that *the principal
intellectual instrument available to human beings is not examined in school*?

We are beginning to border on absurdity here. And we cross the   4
line when we consider what happens in most schools on the subject of metaphor. Metaphor does, in fact, come up in school, usually introduced by an English teacher wanting to show how it is
employed by poets. The result is that most students come to believe
metaphor has a decorative function and only a decorative function.
It gives color and texture to poetry, as jewelry does to clothing. The
poet wants us to see, smell, hear, or feel something concretely, and so
resorts to metaphor. I remember a discussion, when I was in college,
of Robert Burns's lines: "O, my love is like a red, red rose/That's newly

---

[1] **Bloom . . . Hirsch** Alan Bloom (1930–1992) and E. D. Hirsch Jr. (b. 1928)
both wrote books critical of American culture.

sprung in June./O my love is like the melodie/That's sweetly play'd in tune."

The first questions on the test were: "Is Burns using metaphors or similes? Define each term. Why did Burns choose to use metaphors instead of similes, or similes instead of metaphors?"

I didn't object to these questions at the time except for the last one, to which I gave a defiant but honest answer: How the hell should I know? I have the same answer today. But today, I have some other things to say on the matter. Yes, poets use metaphors to help us see and feel. But so do biologists, physicists, historians, linguists, and everyone else who is trying to say something about the world. A metaphor is not an ornament. It is an organ of perception. Through metaphors, we see the world as one thing or another. Is light a wave or a particle? Are molecules like billiard balls or force fields? Is history unfolding according to some instructions of nature or a divine plan? Are our genes like information codes? Is a literary work like an architect's blueprint or a mystery to be solved?

Questions like these preoccupy scholars in every field. Do I exaggerate in saying that a student cannot understand what a subject is about without some understanding of the metaphors that are its foundation? I don't think so. In fact, it has always astonished me that those who write about the subject of education do not pay sufficient attention to the role of metaphor in giving form to the subject. In failing to do so, they deprive those studying the subject of the opportunity to confront its basic assumptions. Is the human mind, for example, like a dark cavern (needing illumination)? A muscle (needing exercise)? A vessel (needing filling)? A lump of clay (needing shaping)? A garden (needing cultivation)? Or, as so many say today, is it like a computer that processes data? And what of students? Are they patients to be cared for? Troops to be disciplined? Sons and daughters to be nurtured? Personnel to be trained? Resources to be developed?

There was a time when those who wrote on the subject of education, such as Plato, Comenius, Locke, and Rousseau,[2] made their metaphors explicit and in doing so revealed how their metaphors controlled their thinking. "Plants are improved by cultivation," Rousseau wrote in *Emile,* "and man by education." And his entire philosophy rests upon this comparison of plants and children. Even in such ancient texts as the Mishnah,[3] we find that there are four kinds of students:

---

[2]**Plato . . . Rousseau** Plato (429–347 B.C.E.), John Amos Comenius (1592–1670), John Locke (1632–1704), and Jean-Jacques Rousseau (1712–1778) were philosophers of language who wrote widely.

[3]**Mishnah** An important rabbinic collection of Jewish oral tradition collected in 220 C.E.

the sponge, the funnel, the strainer, and the sieve. It will surprise you to know which one is preferred. The sponge, we are told, absorbs all; the funnel receives at one end and spills out at the other; the strainer lets the wine drain through it and retains the dregs; but the sieve— that is the best, for it lets out the flour dust and retains the fine flour. The difference in educational philosophy between Rousseau and the compilers of the Mishnah is precisely reflected in the difference between a wild plant and a sieve.

Definitions, questions, metaphors—these are three of the most   9
potent elements with which human language constructs a worldview. And in urging, as I do, that the study of these elements be given the highest priority in school, I am suggesting that world making through language is a narrative of power, durability, and inspiration. It is the story of how we make the world known to ourselves, and how we make ourselves known to the world. It is different from other narratives because it is about nouns and verbs, about grammar and inferences, about metaphors and definitions, but it is a story of creation, nonetheless. Even further, it is a story that plays a role in all other narratives. For whatever we believe in, or don't believe in, is to a considerable extent a function of how our language addresses the world. Here is a small example:

Let us suppose you have just finished being examined by a doc-   10
tor. In pronouncing his verdict, he says somewhat accusingly, "Well, you've done a very nice case of arthritis here." You would undoubtedly think this is a strange diagnosis, or more likely, a strange doctor. People do not "do" arthritis. They "have" it, or "get" it, and it is a little insulting for the doctor to imply that you have produced or manufactured an illness of this kind, especially since arthritis will release you from certain obligations and, at the same time, elicit sympathy from other people. It is also painful. So the idea that you have done arthritis to yourself suggests a kind of self-serving masochism.

Now, let us suppose a judge is about to pass sentence on a man   11
convicted of robbing three banks. The judge advises him to go to a hospital for treatment, saying with an air of resignation, "You certainly have a bad case of criminality." On the face of it, this is another strange remark. People do not "have" criminality. They "do" crimes, and we are usually outraged, not saddened, by their doings. At least that is the way we are accustomed to thinking about the matter.

The point I am trying to make is that such simple verbs as *is* or *does*   12
are, in fact, powerful metaphors that express some of our most fundamental conceptions of the way things are. We believe there are certain things people "have," certain things people "do," even certain things people "are." These beliefs do not necessarily reflect the structure of reality. They simply reflect a habitual way of talking about reality.

In his book *Erewhon,* Samuel Butler[4] depicted a society that lives according to the metaphors of my strange doctor and strange judge. There, illness is something people "do" and therefore have moral responsibility for; criminality is something you "have" and therefore is quite beyond your control. Every legal system and every moral code is based on a set of assumptions about what people are, have, or do. And, I might add, any significant changes in law or morality are preceded by a reordering of how such metaphors are employed.

I am not, incidentally, recommending the culture of the people of   13
Erewhon. I am trying to highlight the fact that our language habits are at the core of how we imagine the world. And to the degree that we are unaware of how our ways of talking put such ideas in our heads, we are not in full control of our situation. It needs hardly to be said that one of the purposes of an education is to give us greater control of our situation.

School does not always help. In schools, for instance, we find   14
that tests are given to determine how smart someone *is* or, more precisely, how much smartness someone *has.* If, on an IQ test, one child scores a 138 and another a 106, the first is thought to *have* more smartness than the other. But this seems to me a strange conception—every bit as strange as "doing" arthritis or "having" criminality. I do not know anyone who *has* smartness. The people I know sometimes *do* smart things (as far as I can judge) and sometimes *do* dumb things—depending on what circumstances they are in, how much they know about a situation, and how interested they are. Smartness, so it seems to me, is a specific performance, done in a particular set of circumstances. It is not something you *are* or *have* in measurable quantities. In fact, the assumption that smartness is something you *have* has led to such nonsensical terms as *over-* and *underachievers.* As I understand it, an overachiever is someone who doesn't *have* much smartness but does a lot of smart things. An underachiever is someone who *has* a lot of smartness but does a lot of dumb things.

The ways in which language creates a worldview are not usually   15
part of the schooling of our young. There are several reasons for this. Chief among them is that in the education of teachers, the subject is not usually brought up, and if it is, it is introduced in a cavalier and fragmentary fashion. Another reason is that it is generally believed that the subject is too complex for schoolchildren to understand, with the unfortunate result that language education is mostly confined to the study of rules governing grammar, punctuation, and usage. A third reason is that the study of language as "world-maker" is, inescapably, of

---

[4] **Samuel Butler (1835–1902)** His utopian novel *Erewhon* (an anagram of *Nowhere*) is still considered an important cultural statement.

an interdisciplinary nature, so that teachers are not clear about which subject ought to undertake it.

As to the first reason, I have no good idea why prospective teachers are denied knowledge of this matter. (Actually, I have *some* ideas, but a few of them are snotty and all are unkind.) But if it were up to me, the study of the subject would be at the center of teachers' professional education and would remain there until they were done—that is, until they retire. This would require that they become well acquainted with the writings of Aristotle and Plato (among the ancients), Locke and Kant (among recent "ancients"), and (among the moderns) I. A. Richards, Benjamin Lee Whorf,[5] and, especially, Alfred Korzybski. 16

A few paragraphs about Korzybski are in order here, since his work offers the most systematic means of introducing the subject, deepening it, and staying with it. Another reason is that academics at the university level either do not know about Korzybski's work or, if they do, do not understand it (which does not mean, by the way, that fifth graders cannot). If they do understand it, they hate it. The result is that an exceedingly valuable means of exploring the relationship between language and reality goes unused. 17

Korzybski was born in Poland in 1879. He claimed to be of royal ancestry, referring to himself as Count Alfred Korzybski—another reason why academics have kept him at arm's length. He was trained in mathematics and engineering, and served as an artillery officer in World War I. The carnage and horror he witnessed left him haunted by a question of singular importance. He wondered why scientists could have such astonishing successes in discovering the mysteries of nature while, at the same time, the nonscientific community experienced appalling failure in its efforts to solve psychological, social, and political problems. Scientists signify their triumphs by almost daily announcements of new theories, new discoveries, new pathways to knowledge. The rest of us announce our failures by warring against ourselves and others. Korzybski began to publish his answer to this enigma in 1921 in his book *Manhood of Humanity: The Science and Art of Human Engineering.* This was followed in 1926 by *Time-Binding: The General Theory,* and finally by his magnum opus, *Science and Sanity,* in 1933. 18

In formulating his answer, Korzybski was at all times concerned that his ideas should have practical applications. He conceived of himself as an educator who would offer to humanity both a theory and a method by which it might find some release from the poignant yet 19

---

[5]**I. A. Richards (1893–1979)** A British critic and teacher famous for introducing techniques of close reading of literary texts. One of his books is *How to Read a Page.* **Benjamin Lee Whorf (1897–1941)** An American linguist who advocated the principle of "linguistic relativity."

catastrophic ignorance whose consequences were to be witnessed in all the historic forms of human degradation. This, too, was held against him by many academics, who accused him of grandiosity and hubris.[6] Perhaps if Korzybski had thought *smaller,* his name would now appear more frequently in university catalogues.

Korzybski began his quest to discover the roots of human   20 achievement and failure by identifying a critical functional difference between humans and other forms of life. We are, to use his phrase, "time-binders," while plants are "chemistry-binders," and animals are "space-binders." Chemistry-binding is the capacity to transform sunlight into organic chemical energy; space binding, the capacity to move about and control a physical environment. Humans have these capacities, too, but are unique in their ability to transport their experience through time. As time-binders, we can accumulate knowledge from the past and communicate what we know to the future. Science-fiction writers need not strain invention in their search for interesting time-transporting machinery: *we* are the universe's time machines.

Our principal means of accomplishing the binding of time is the   21 symbol. But our capacity to symbolize is dependent upon and integral to another process, which Korzybski called "abstracting." Abstracting is the continuous activity of selecting, omitting, and organizing the details of reality so that we experience the world as patterned and coherent. Korzybski shared with Heraclitus[7] the assumption that the world is undergoing continuous change and that no two events are identical. We give stability to our world only through our capacity to re-create it by ignoring differences and attending to similarities. Although we know that we cannot step into the "same" river twice, abstracting allows us to act as if we can. We abstract at the neurological level, at the physiological level, at the perceptual level, at the verbal level; all of our systems of interaction with the world are engaged in selecting data from the world, organizing data, generalizing data. An abstraction, to put it simply, is a kind of summary of what the world is like, a generalization about its structure.

Korzybski might explain the process in the following way: let us   22 suppose we are confronted by the phenomenon we call a "cup." We must understand, first of all, that a cup is not a thing, but an event; modern physics tells us that a cup is made of billions of electrons in constant movement, undergoing continuous change. Although none of this activity is perceptible to us, it is important to acknowledge it, because by so doing, we may grasp the idea that *the world is not*

---

[6]**hubris** Overweening pride.
[7]**Heraclitus (c. 535–c. 475 B.C.E.)** Early Greek philosopher who claimed that everything was in change and said, famously, that "no one steps in the same river twice."

the way we see it. What we see is a summary—an abstraction, if you will—of electronic activity. But even what we *can* see is not what we *do* see. No one has ever seen a cup in its entirety, all at once in space-time. We see only parts of wholes. But usually we see enough to allow us to reconstruct the whole and to act as if we know what we are dealing with. Sometimes, such a reconstruction betrays us, as when we lift a cup to sip our coffee and find that the coffee has settled in our lap rather than on our palate. But most of the time, our assumptions about a cup will work, and we carry those assumptions forward in a useful way by the act of naming. Thus we are assisted immeasurably in our evaluations of the world by our language, which provides us with names for the events that confront us and, by our naming them, tells us what to expect and how to prepare ourselves for action.

The naming of things, of course, is an abstraction of a very high   23
order and of crucial importance. By naming an event and categorizing it as a "thing," we create a vivid and more or less permanent map of what the world is like. But it is a curious map indeed. The word *cup,* for example, *does not in fact denote anything that actually exists in the world.* It is a concept, a summary of millions of particular things that have a similar look and function. The word *tableware* is at a still higher level of abstraction, since it includes not only all the things we normally call cups but also millions of things that look nothing like cups but have a vaguely similar function.

The critical point about our mapping of the world through lan-   24
guage is that the symbols we use, whether *patriotism* and *love* or *cups* and *spoons,* are always at a considerable remove from the reality of the world itself. Although these symbols become part of ourselves— Korzybski believed they become imbedded in our neurological and perceptual systems—we must never take them completely for granted. As Korzybski once remarked, "Whatever we say something *is,* it is not."

Thus, we may conclude that humans live in two worlds—the world   25
of events and things, and the world of *words* about events and things. In considering the relationship between these two worlds, we must keep in mind that language does much more than construct concepts about the events and things in the world; it tells us what sorts of concepts we ought to construct. For we do not have a name for everything that occurs in the world. Languages differ not only in their names for things but in what things they choose to name. Each language, as Edward Sapir[8] observed, constructs reality differently from all the others.

This, then, is what Korzybski meant by what he called general   26
semantics: the study of the relationship between the world of words

---

[8] **Edward Sapir (1884–1939)** Prominent American linguist also trained as an anthropologist.

and the world of "not words," the study of the territory we call reality and how, through abstracting and symbolizing, we map the territory. In focusing on this process, Korzybski believed he had discovered why scientists are more effective than the rest of us in solving problems. Scientists tend to be more conscious of the abstracting process; more aware of the distortions in their verbal maps; more flexible in altering their symbolic maps to fit the world. His main educational objective was to foster the idea that by making our ordinary uses of language more like the scientific uses of language, we may avoid misunderstanding, superstition, prejudice, and just plain nonsense. Some of his followers, S. I. Hayakawa, Irving Lee, and Wendell Johnson,[9] wrote readable texts for use in schools, but their material is not much in fashion these days. I wrote some texts along these lines myself, mostly to find out if these ideas are suitable for younger students, and discovered that they are. (I remember with delight the easy success we had with them in Arlington, Virginia, at the Fort Myer Elementary School.) But, of course, not all of the ideas are useful, and not all of them are good. General semantics, like any other system, has to be applied with a considerable degree of selectivity. Assuming teachers know something about the subject, they will discover what works and what doesn't. It is, in any case, a mistake to assume that profound ideas about language, from general semantics or any other place, cannot be introduced until graduate school.

Of course, there are plenty of "other places" from which profound   27
ideas about language may come. The work of I. A. Richards (generally) and what he says, specifically, on definition and metaphor are good introductions to language as world-maker. On definition (from his *Interpretation in Teaching*):

> I have said something at several places . . . about the peculiar paralysis which the mention of definitions and, still more, the discussion of them induces. It can be prevented, I believe, by stressing the purposive aspect of definitions. We want to do something and a definition is a means of doing it. If we want certain results, then we must use certain meanings (or definitions). But no definition has any authority apart from a purpose, or to bar us from other purposes. And yet they endlessly do so. Who can doubt that we are often deprived of very useful thoughts merely because the words which might express them are being temporarily preempted by other meanings? Or that a development is often frustrated merely because we are sticking to a former definition of no service to the new purpose?

What Richards is talking about here is how to free our minds from the   28
tyranny of definitions, and I can think of no better way of doing this than to provide students, as a matter of course, with alternative definitions of

---

[9]**Hayakawa . . . Johnson** S. I. Hayakawa (1906–1992), Irving Lee (1909–1955), and Wendell Johnson (1906–1965) were all important theoreticians of semantics.

the important concepts with which they must deal in a subject. Whether it be molecule, fact, law, art, wealth, genes, or whatever, it is essential that students understand that definitions are instruments designed to achieve certain purposes, that the fundamental question to ask of them is not, Is this the real definition? or Is this the correct definition? but What purpose does the definition serve? That is, Who made it up and why?

I have had some great fun, and so have students, considering the question of definition in a curious federal law. I refer to what you may not say when being frisked or otherwise examined before boarding an airplane. You may not, of course, give false or misleading information about yourself. But beyond that, you are also expressly forbidden to joke about any of the procedures being used. This is the only case I know of where a joke is prohibited by law (although there are many situations in which it is prohibited by custom).   29

Why joking is illegal when you are being searched is not entirely clear to me, but that is only one of several mysteries surrounding this law. Does the law distinguish, for example, between good jokes and bad jokes? (Six months for a good one, two years for a bad one?) I don't know. But even more important, how would one know when something is a joke at all? Is there a legal definition of a joke? Suppose, while being searched, I mention that my middle name is Milton (which it is) and that I come from Flushing (which I do). I can tell you from experience that people of questionable intelligence sometimes find those names extremely funny, and it is not impossible that a few of them are airport employees. If that were the case, what would be my legal status? I have said something that has induced laughter in another. Have I, therefore, told a joke? Or look at it from the opposite view: suppose that, upon being searched, I launch into a story about a funny thing that happened to me while boarding a plane in Chicago, concluding by saying, "And then the pilot said, 'That was no stewardess. That was my wife.'" Being of questionable intelligence myself, I think it is a hilarious story, but the guard does not. If he does not laugh, have I told a joke? Can a joke be a story that does *not* make people laugh?   30

It can, of course, if someone of authority says so. For the point is that in every situation, including this one, someone (or some group) has a decisive power of definition. In fact, to have power means to be able to define and to make it stick. As between the guard at the airport and me, he will have the power, not me, to define what a joke is. If his definition places me in jeopardy, I can, of course, argue my case at a trial, at which either a judge or a jury will then have the decisive authority to define whether or not my words qualified as a joke. But it is also worth noting that even if I confine my joke-telling to dinner parties, I do not escape the authority of definition. For at parties, popular opinion will decide whether or not my jokes are good ones, or even jokes at all. If opinion runs against me, the penalty is that I   31 am not invited to many parties. There is, in short, no escaping the jurisdiction of definitions. Social order requires that there be authoritative definitions, and though you may search from now to doomsday, you will find no system without official definitions and authoritative sources to enforce them. And so we must add to the questions we ask of definition, What is the source of power that enforces the definition? And we may add further the question of what happens when those with the power to enforce definitions go mad. Here is an example that came from the Prague government several years ago. I have not made this up and produce it without further comment:

> Because Christmas Eve falls on a Thursday, the day has been designated a Saturday for work purposes. Factories will close all day, with stores open a half day only. Friday, December 25, has been designated a Sunday, with both factories and stores open all day. Monday, December 28, will be a Wednesday for work purposes. Wednesday, December 30, will be a business Friday. Saturday, January 2, will be a Sunday, and Sunday, January 3, will be a Monday.

As for metaphor, I pass along a small assignment which I. A. Richards used on an occasion when I attended a seminar he conducted. (It is but one of a hundred ways to introduce the subject.) Richards divided the class into three groups. Each group was asked to write a paragraph describing language. However, Richards provided each group with its first sentence. Group A had to begin with "Language is like a tree"; Group B with "Language is like a river"; Group C with "Language is like a building." You can imagine, I'm sure, what happened. The paragraphs were strikingly different, with one group writing of roots and branches and organic growth; another of tributaries, streams, and even floods; another of foundations, rooms, and sturdy structures. In the subsequent discussion, we did not bother with the question, Which is the "correct" description? Our discussion centered on how metaphors control what we say, and to what extent what we say controls what we see.   32

As I have said, there are hundreds of ways to study the relationship between language and reality, and I could go on at interminable length with ideas on how to get into it. Instead, I will confine myself to three further suggestions. The first is, simply, that the best book I know for arousing interest in the subject is Helen Keller's *The Story of My Life*.[10] It is certainly the best account we have—from the inside, as it were—of how symbols and the abstracting process work to create a world.   33

Second, I would propose that in every subject—from history to biology to mathematics—students be taught, explicitly and   34

---

[10] ***The Story of My Life*** Autobiography written by Helen Keller (1880–1968) who went deaf and blind at 19 months of age but still learned language.

systematically, the universe of discourse that comprises the subject. Each teacher would deal with the structure of questions, the process of definition, and the role of metaphor as these matters are relevant to his or her particular subject. Here I mean, of course, not merely what are the questions, definitions, and metaphors of a subject but also *how* these are formed and how they have been formed in the past.

Of special importance are the ways in which the forms of ques- 35 tions have changed over time and how these forms vary from subject to subject. The idea is for students to learn that the terminology of a question determines the terminology of its answer; that a question cannot be answered unless there are procedures by which reliable answers can be obtained; and that the value of a question is determined not only by the specificity and richness of the answers it produces but also by the quantity and quality of the new questions it raises.

Once this topic is opened, it follows that some attention must be 36 given to how such terms as *right, wrong, truth,* and *falsehood* are used in a subject, as well as what assumptions they are based upon. This is particularly important, since words of this type cause far more trouble in students' attempts to understand a field of knowledge than do highly technical words. It is peculiar, I think, that of all the examinations I have ever seen, I have never come across one in which students were asked to say what is the basis of "correctness" or "falsehood" in a particular subject. Perhaps this is because teachers believe the issue is too obvious for discussion or testing. If so, they are wrong. I have found that students at all levels rarely have thought about the meaning of such terms in relation to a subject they are studying. They simply do not know in what sense a historical fact is different from a biological fact, or a mathematical "truth" is different from the "truth" of a literary work. Equally astonishing is that students, particularly those in elementary and secondary schools, rarely can express an intelligible sentence on the uses of the word *theory.* Since most subjects studied in school consist largely of theories, it is difficult to imagine exactly what students are in fact studying when they do their history, biology, economics, physics, or whatever. It is obvious, then, that language education must include not only the serious study of what truth and falsehood mean in the context of a subject but also what is meant by a theory, a fact, an inference, an assumption, a judgment, a generalization.

QUESTIONS FOR CRITICAL READING

1. What is a metaphor and how does it affect our understanding?
2. What is Postman's concern about the questions we ask and their effect on the answers we get?

3. Who defines words? What word do you define differently than other people do?

4. Are definitions invented?

5. What does Postman mean by the term *abstraction* (para. 21)?

6. In what ways are we "time-binders"? Why is that metaphor important?

7. What does Postman mean by "world making through language" (para. 9)?

SUGGESTIONS FOR CRITICAL WRITING

1. When Postman says, "Everything we know has its origin in questions," he directs us to consider how we come to an understanding of disciplines such as biology, physics, English, psychology, and sociology. Choose a half-dozen questions that are central to one area of study and explore the ways in which these questions help shape your understanding of that area. What new questions arise when you try to provide answers to those questions?

2. One of Postman's fundamental claims is that "our language habits are at the core of how we imagine the world" (para. 13). Write a brief essay for someone who has not read this selection and explain to that audience what Postman means and then defend or attack Postman's position. How can Postman think that our language habits shape our sense of the world? What evidence does he develop to bolster his position? What observations have you made that help explain Postman's idea?

3. Postman says that "one of the purposes of our education is to give us greater control of our situation" (para. 13). If you feel this is true, examine the details of your own education up to this point and explain how it has given you more control over your situation. Then look to the future and discuss how you think your education will contribute to your gaining more control of your situation. What do you think Postman means by the term *situation*? Is *situation* a metaphor?

4. In paragraph 25, Postman says, "we may conclude that humans live in two worlds—the world of events and things, and the world of *words* about events and things." Explain what Postman means by this statement and then examine your own experience with the world of events and things and the world of words about those events and things. How do the words you use actually "map" the world of your personal experience? You may limit yourself to talking about a single event and the things that are part of that event. For instance, how do you map your first hours of the day when you wake up and have breakfast? How do you map a first romantic encounter? Explain the richness of the word *map* used as a metaphor.

5. Find two different newspapers' accounts of a major national event and examine the use of metaphor in each. Do the same for the questions asked or implied and the definitions stated or implied. Is it possible to see that each newspaper "slants" the story somewhat differently by means of the metaphors used and the language choices made? Which

story is the most trustable? Does either newspaper give you a sense of confidence in its general truthfulness? Try to avoid accounts that are "fed" to newspapers through an agency such as the Associated Press or Reuters because the accounts will be essentially the same.

6. Try I. A. Richards's experiment and write a brief three-part essay that uses each of the following opening sentences:

   (a) Language is like a tree.   (b) Language is like a river.

   (c) Language is like a building.

   Are you convinced that any one of the three parts of your essay is a more accurate and convincing description of language than the others are?

7. Respond to Postman's complaints about the effects of television on children. Consider your childhood experience or the experiences of young children you know. Did you or the children grow up too fast and miss the pleasures of early childhood? Do you think television programming today emphasizes entertainment over information? Do you think it encourages young people to be consumers, to be materialistic, and to develop adult desires? Do you think television stunts the intellectual growth of people who watch it?

8. **CONNECTIONS**   When Postman tells us that the world is not the way we see it, he seems to invoke the selection known as Plato's Cave—which appears in this book as "The Allegory of the Cave" (p. 865). How much in agreement are Postman and Plato about the question of perception of the world? Examine Plato's metaphors and decide how they help shape the meaning of his selection. In what sense is the cave a metaphor? How convincing is Plato's metaphor? Comment on his definitions and the questions he asks.

9. **CONNECTIONS**   Neil Postman was concerned with the ways in which language use affects the world we live in. Alexander Pope (**bedfordstmartins.com/worldofideas/epages**) was deeply aware of the same issues and in writing about good criticism he became more than a "word weaver." Write a brief essay that establishes how Pope's "word weaving" continues to shape modern attitudes toward good and bad criticism. In what senses would Postman see Pope as a "world maker"? How would he see Pope as having made the world of criticism what it is today? Which of Pope's principles of criticism would most please Postman if he were to expect his own work to be the object of a good critic?

10. **SEEING CONNECTIONS**   In what sense would Postman say Wosene Worke Kosrof's painting *The Color of Words IX* (p. 766) is a metaphor for language? Some of the symbols are part of the alphabet for Amharic, an Ethiopian language, but some seem to be playful images rather than alphabetic details. What questions does the painting imply about the nature of language? What questions do you ask of this painting? To what extent has the painter anticipated your questions? What is the relationship between the playful and the obviously alphabetic images in the painting? What does that relationship have to do with the idea of language?

NOAM CHOMSKY
New Horizons
in the Study of Language

NOAM CHOMSKY (b. 1928) is probably the most famous linguist living today. He is known for his work in language studies,
philosophy, and cognitive studies and for his political activism.
Born to Jewish parents who spoke English, Russian, Yiddish, and
Hebrew, Chomsky grew up in a Philadelphia neighborhood where
he was often threatened by anti-Semitism. He was aware of the evils
of the Fascist government of Spain during the Spanish Civil War
in the late 1930s, and he began thinking and writing about anti-
Fascist politics when he was in grade school. Chomsky is famous
today in the popular press for championing libertarian Socialist
principles and for taking radical positions that have sometimes
proven dangerous. A professor at the Massachusetts Institute of
Technology since 1955, when he gives lectures he is often under
police protection because of the threats he receives. When Theodore
Kaczynski, "the Unabomber," was at large and sent bombs in the
mail to important scientists engaged in computer and cognitive
studies, Chomsky was one of his targets. For years Chomsky did
not open any of his mail himself.

Chomsky completed his undergraduate and graduate work at
the University of Pennsylvania, moving early into linguistic studies.
He began to develop some of his basic theories about language in
his doctoral dissertation, published as *Syntactic Structures* (1957).
He concerned himself, not with the surface features of language,
but with what he thought of as its deep structure. Chomsky's most
important contribution to the study of linguistics is sometimes
called generative or transformational grammar. The concept is
that all languages differ on the surface but that they are essentially

From *New Horizons in the Study of Language and Mind.*

alike in their deep structure. One of his key points is that while the words and the order of the words may change profoundly, all languages can express the same idea, such as "the sun rises in the east," in many ways. The semantic level is the same no matter how diverse the lexical qualities of the statements are.

Ultimately, this led Chomsky to postulate a language faculty in the brain that is found in people but not in animals. The fact that no animals possess language has led Chomsky's followers to suggest that evolution has somehow produced a "linguistic organ" that permits children to learn whatever language or languages are common to their environment. This, in turn, implies that people are not born with tabula rasa—with brains that have no content—but that they are hardwired in advance to acquire language. Chomsky's theory suggests a proposed single universal grammar that human brains begin with and by which they form individual languages. The deep structure is the same, but the surfaces—the words and the specific grammar of the given language—are diverse. All languages follow complex rules that originate in a universal grammar.

Chomsky's theories have been studied widely and with considerable interest, but not every linguistician accepts them. Most linguists feel that it is true that only people possess language but believe that this has to do with the various cognitive capacities of different portions of the brain combined with biological structures that permit humans to utter, hear, and distinguish meaning in distinctive sounds. In other words, some linguists see that the various systems in the human brain and body, which may have developed through evolution for other purposes, are uniquely appropriate for language also. There is no special language organ; rather there is a system of faculties that adapt to the production of language.

Chomsky's Rhetoric

The purpose of this piece is as a brief introduction to what Chomsky considers the most important current thinking in linguistics. Naturally, it focuses essentially on his theories and the researchers who have made progress working out the details. The structure of the piece is basic. It begins with a historic overview telling us that the study of language has been of concern for many centuries and that the result has been to declare it a "true 'species property'" (para. 2), which is to say that it is common to all in our species, *Homo sapiens*. As he says, quoting René Descartes (1596–1650), it marks "the true distinction between man and animal" (para. 2).

Chomsky introduces a technical term, the property of "discrete infinity" (para. 4), by which he means the process by which a limited number of discrete linguistic elements can be combined in infinite ways. The same property is true of our number system, which has discrete numbers that can be combined in infinite ways. Chomsky says this language property is "biologically isolated," which means it is not learned by children but rather it is something that "the mind already possesses" (para. 4).

One of the key rhetorical strategies Chomsky uses is metaphor, itself a high-level linguistic device. For example, he tells us that the "faculty of language can reasonably be regarded as a 'language organ' in the sense in which scientists speak of the visual system, or immune system, or circulatory system, as organs of the body" (para. 6). The power of this metaphor, comparing the ability to acquire language with the ability of organs to function in the body, is meant to be rhetorically convincing. Chomsky's basic claim is that language is acquired because the individual is uniquely equipped with a built-in biological mental faculty residing in the brain, there even before the baby-babble stage. Thus, the metaphor is not just a description of the faculty of language; it is also designed to convince us that the faculty exists.

Having established the language faculty, Chomsky connects it to our genes, which control all our organs and are the product of evolution. Interestingly, our genes also possess the quality of discrete infinity since they can rearrange themselves in infinite patterns, which is one reason DNA testing can identify individuals accurately. This part of his argument implies that evolution somehow produced the language faculty in us but not in other animals.

By paragraph 7, Chomsky is able to become more technical in his description and to suggest there are many ways to "investigate the genetically determined 'initial state' of the language faculty" (para. 7). He admits that it will take time and a great deal of research to clarify how genes create or modify the "initial state," but he explains that language is acquired by individuals as a result of the "initial state" (the language organ) in contact with experience. In this case, experience may consist of the actual language being spoken in the presence of the individual, whether it is Japanese, Chinese, English, or Spanish. If the deep structure of language is the same for all humans—the genetic "organ" must be universal—then all humans should be able to grow up learning any language. And Chomsky admits that his own children, were they to grow up in Japan, would speak Japanese. This, he suggests, proves "there is strong reason to believe that the initial state is common to the species" (para. 8).

The essay up to this point is clearly an argument structured to convince us of the truth of his research that establishes an inborn faculty in the brain produced by evolution that all healthy individuals possess at birth. That claim is bolstered by the analysis of the faculty of language as we know it in its expression. The fact that a child will learn any language just by growing up in an environment in which it is spoken is a powerful piece of evidence supporting the claim.

Once he feels this point is established, Chomsky introduces new terms. The phrase *infinite use of finite means* was first used by Wilhelm von Humboldt (1767–1835), and it connects with *discrete infinity*. Von Humboldt used the term in relation to language, noting that with a finite number of terms one could create an infinite number of combinations. Children, for example, can create an infinite number of sentences from even a limited number of words. They do not need to be taught to do so; they have a natural grasp of the grammar of their language that permits them to create sentences that may never have been uttered by anyone before. Chomsky takes this fact as further evidence of an inborn language faculty. He calls this ability generative grammar because a child can generate sentences without having been taught how. That child is not working from rote, or from memory, but from a creative ability that is inborn. Explaining how this is so in every language is a job for researchers.

It is in paragraph 19, however, that Chomsky introduces one of his most striking metaphors. It seems to be related to the computer and it echoes the idea of a hardwired system in the brain. He describes the "initial state" of language (with no words, no surface details) as a "fixed network connected to a switch box." Once that idea is clear, then it is just a matter of turning on the switches that will produce Japanese or Swahili or any other language. This is a proposal that Chomsky says will need a great deal of research to clarify, but he feels it is one of the most profitable directions of study.

Chomsky's views have been equally controversial and equally influential. He has tried to examine a human faculty that has fascinated us for millennia, and he has forced us to focus on our biology and our evolutionary development in order to begin to understand the issue.

PREREADING QUESTIONS:
WHAT TO READ FOR

The following prereading questions may help you anticipate key issues in the discussion of Noam Chomsky's "New Horizons in the Study of Language." Keeping them in mind during your first reading should help focus your attention.

- What is discrete infinity?
- What is the initial state of language?
- Why is generative grammar important?

New Horizons
in the Study of Language

The study of language is one of the oldest branches of systematic   1
inquiry, tracing back to classical India and Greece, with a rich and fruitful history of achievement. From a different point of view, it is quite young. The major research enterprises of today took shape only about forty years ago, when some of the leading ideas of the tradition were revived and reconstructed, opening the way to what has proven to be very productive inquiry.

That language should have exercised such fascination over the   2
years is not surprising. The human faculty of language seems to be a true "species property," varying little among humans and without significant analogue elsewhere. Probably the closest analogues are found in insects, at an evolutionary distance of a billion years. There is no serious reason today to challenge the Cartesian[1] view that the ability to use linguistic signs to express freely formed thoughts marks "the true distinction between man and animal" or machine, whether by "machine" we mean the automata that captured the imagination of the seventeenth and eighteenth century, or those that are providing a stimulus to thought and imagination today.

Furthermore, the faculty of language enters crucially into every   3
aspect of human life, thought, and interaction. It is largely responsible for the fact that alone in the biological world, humans have a history, cultural evolution and diversity of any complexity and richness, even biological success in the technical sense that their numbers are huge. A Martian scientist observing the strange doings on Earth could hardly fail to be struck by the emergence and significance of this apparently unique form of intellectual organization. It is even more natural that

---

[1] **Cartesian** A reference to the theories of René Descartes (1596–1650). *Discourse on the Method* (1637) is his most well-known work. He was early to discuss natural phenomena in mechanical terms.

the topic, with its many mysteries, should have stimulated the curiosity of those who seek to understand their own nature and their place within the wider world.

Human language is based on an elementary property that also seems to be biologically isolated: the property of discrete infinity, which is exhibited in its purest form by the natural numbers 1, 2, 3, . . . Children do not learn this property; unless the mind already possessces the basic principles, no amount of evidence could provide them. Similarly, no child has to learn that there are three and four word sentences, but no three-and-an half word sentences, and that they go on forever; it is always possible to construct a more complex one, with a definite form and meaning. Such knowledge must come to us from "the original hand of nature," in David Hume's[2] phrase, as part of our biological endowment.

This property intrigued Galileo,[3] who regarded the discovery of a means to communicate our "most secret thoughts to any other person with 24 little characters" as the greatest of all human inventions. The invention succeeds because it reflects the discrete infinity of the language that these characters are used to represent. Shortly after, the authors of the Port Royal Grammar[4] were struck by the "marvellous invention" of a means to construct from a few dozen sounds an infinity of expressions that enable us to reveal to others what we think and imagine and feel—from a contemporary standpoint, not an "invention" but no less "marvelous" as a product of biological evolution, about which virtually nothing is known, in this case.

The faculty of language can reasonably be regarded as a "language organ" in the sense in which scientists speak of the visual system, or immune system, or circulatory system, as organs of the body. Understood in this way, an organ is not something that can be removed from the body, leaving the rest intact. It is a subsystem of a more complex structure. We hope to understand the full complexity by investigating parts that have distinctive characteristics, and their interactions. Study of the faculty of language proceeds in the same way.

We assume further that the language organ is like others in that its basic character is an expression of the genes. How that happens remains

---

[2] **David Hume (1711–1776)** One of the most influential English philosophers; his *A Treatise on Human Nature* (1739) has been credited by the philosopher Jerry Fodor as a "founding document" of cognitive science.

[3] **Galileo Galilei (1564–1642)** Astronomer, mathematician, and philosopher of wide-ranging influence. Chomsky refers to his book *Dialogue Concerning the Two Chief World Systems* (1632). The two systems are the Copernican, which said the earth went around the sun, and the Ptolemaic, which said all heavenly objects circled the earth. Galileo's book was banned.

[4] **The Port Royal Grammar (1660)** Book that held that grammar was universal because it was a natural property of the mind.

a distant prospect for inquiry, but we can investigate the genetically determined "initial state" of the language faculty in other ways. Evidently, each language is the result of the interplay of two factors: the initial state and the course of experience. We can think of the initial state as a "language acquisition device" that takes experience as "input" and gives the language as an "output"—an "output" that is internally represented in the mind/brain. The input and the output are both open to examination: we can study the course of experience and the properties of the languages that are acquired. What is learned in this way can tell us quite a lot about the initial state that mediates between them.

Furthermore, there is strong reason to believe that the initial state   8 is common to the species: if my children had grown up in Tokyo, they would speak Japanese, like other children there. That means that evidence about Japanese bears directly on the assumptions concerning the initial state for English. In such ways, it is possible to establish strong empirical conditions that the theory of the initial state must satisfy, and also to pose several problems for the biology of language: How do the genes determine the initial state, and what are the brain mechanisms involved in the initial state and the later states it assumes? These are extremely hard problems, even for much simpler systems where direct experiment is possible, but some may be at the horizons of inquiry.

The approach I have been outlining is concerned with the faculty   9 of language: its initial state, and the states it assumes. Suppose that Peter's language organ is in state L. We can think of L as Peter's "internalized language." When I speak of a language here, that is what I mean. So understood, a language is something like "the way we speak and understand," one traditional conception of language.

Adapting a traditional term to a new framework, we call the the-   10 ory of Peter's language the "grammar" of his language. Peter's language determines an infinite array of expressions, each with its sound and meaning. In technical terms, Peter's language "generates" the expressions of his language. The theory of his language is therefore called a generative grammar. Each expression is a complex of properties, which provide "instructions" for Peter's performance systems: his articulatory apparatus, his modes of organizing his thoughts, and so on. With his language and the associated performance systems in place, Peter has a vast amount of knowledge about the sound and meaning of expressions, and a corresponding capacity to interpret what he hears, express his thoughts, and use his language in a variety of other ways.

Generative grammar arose in the context of what is often called   11 "the cognitive revolution" of the 1950s, and was an important factor in its development. Whether or not the term "revolution" is appropriate, there was an important change of perspective: from the study of behavior and its products (such as texts), to the inner mechanisms that enter into thought and action. The cognitive perspective regards behavior and its products not as the object of inquiry, but as data that may provide evidence about the inner mechanisms of mind and the ways these mechanisms operate in executing actions and interpreting experience. The properties and patterns that were the focus of attention in structural linguistics find their place, but as phenomena to be explained along with innumerable others, in terms of the inner mechanisms that generate expressions. The approach is "mentalistic," but in what should be an uncontroversial sense. It is concerned with "mental aspects of the world," which stand alongside its mechanical, chemical, optical, and other aspects. It undertakes to study a real object in the natural world—the brain, its states, and its functions—and thus to move the study of the mind towards eventual integration with the biological sciences.

The "cognitive revolution" renewed and reshaped many of the insights, achievements, and quandaries of what we might call "the first cognitive revolution" of the seventeenth and eighteenth century, which was part of the scientific revolution that so radically modified our understanding of the world. It was recognized at the time that language involves "the infinite use of finite means," in Wilhelm von Humboldt's[5] phrase; but the insight could be developed only in limited ways, because the basic ideas remained vague and obscure. By the middle of the twentieth century, advances in the formal sciences had provided appropriate concepts in a very sharp and clear form, making it possible to give a precise account of the computational principles that generate the expressions of a language, and thus to capture, at least partially, the idea of "infinite use of finite means." Other advances also opened the way to investigation of traditional questions with greater hope of success. The study of language change had registered major achievements. Anthropological linguistics provided a far richer understanding of the nature and variety of languages, also undermining many stereotypes. And certain topics, notably the study of sound systems, had been much advanced by the structural linguistics of the twentieth century.   12

The earliest attempts to carry out the program of generative grammar quickly revealed that even in the best studied languages, elementary properties had passed unrecognized, that the most comprehensive traditional grammars and dictionaries only skim the surface. The basic properties of languages are presupposed throughout, unrecognized   13

---

[5] **Wilhelm von Humboldt (1767–1835)** German linguist who studied the Basque language and wrote about language in Java. He was among the first linguists to realize that languages had careful rules governing their structure and expression.

and unexpressed. That is quite appropriate if the goal is to help people to learn a second language, to find the conventional meaning and pronunciation of words, or to have some general idea of how languages differ. But if our goal is to understand the language faculty and the states it can assume, we cannot tacitly presuppose "the intelligence of the reader." Rather, this is the object of inquiry.

The study of language acquisition leads to the same conclu-   14
sion. A careful look at the interpretation of expressions reveals very quickly that from the earliest stages, the child knows vastly more than experience has provided. That is true even of simple words. At peak periods of language growth, a child is acquiring words at a rate of about one an hour, with extremely limited exposure under highly ambiguous conditions. The words are understood in delicate and intricate ways that are far beyond the reach of any dictionary, and are only beginning to be investigated. When we move beyond single words, the conclusion becomes even more dramatic. Language acquisition seems much like the growth of organs generally; it is something that happens to a child, not that the child does. And while the environment plainly matters, the general course of development and the basic features of what emerges are predetermined by the initial state. But the initial state is a common human possession. It must be, then, that in their essential properties and even down to fine detail, languages are cast to the same mold. The Martian scientist might reasonably conclude that there is a single human language, with differences only at the margins.

As languages were more carefully investigated from the point of   15
view of generative grammar, it became clear that their diversity had been underestimated as radically as their complexity and the extent to which they are determined by the initial state of the faculty of language. At the same time, we know that the diversity and complexity can be no more than superficial appearance.

These were surprising conclusions, paradoxical but undeniable.   16
They pose in a stark form what has become the central problem of the modern study of language: How can we show that all languages are variations on a single theme, while at the same time recording faithfully their intricate properties of sound and meaning, superficially diverse? A genuine theory of human language has to satisfy two conditions: "descriptive adequacy" and "explanatory adequacy." The grammar of a particular language satisfies the condition of descriptive adequacy insofar as it gives a full and accurate account of the properties of the language, of what the speaker of the language knows. To satisfy the condition of explanatory adequacy, a theory of language must show how each particular language can be derived from a uniform initial state under the "boundary conditions" set by experience.

In this way, it provides an explanation of the properties of languages at a deeper level.

There is a serious tension between these two research tasks. The 17 search for descriptive adequacy seems to lead to ever greater complexity and variety of rule systems, while the search for explanatory adequacy requires that language structure must be invariant, except at the margins. It is this tension that has largely set the guidelines for research. The natural way to resolve the tension is to challenge the traditional assumption, carried over to early generative grammar, that a language is a complex system of rules, each specific to particular languages and particular grammatical constructions: rules for forming relative clauses in Hindi, verb phrases in Swahili, passives in Japanese, and so on. Considerations of explanatory adequacy indicate that this cannot be correct.

The central problem was to find general properties of rule systems 18 that can be attributed to the faculty of language itself, in the hope that the residue will prove to be more simple and uniform. About fifteen years ago, these efforts crystallized in an approach to language that was a much more radical departure from the tradition than earlier generative grammar had been. This "Principles and Parameters" approach, as it has been called, rejected the concept of rule and grammatical construction entirely: there are no rules for forming relative clauses in Hindi, verb phrases in Swahili, passives in Japanese, and so on. The familiar grammatical constructions are taken to be taxonomic artifacts, useful for informal description perhaps but with no theoretical standing. They have something like the status of "terrestrial mammal" or "household pet." And the rules are decomposed into general principles of the faculty of language, which interact to yield the properties of expressions.

We can think of the initial state of the faculty of language as a fixed 19 network connected to a switch box; the network is constituted of the principles of language, while the switches are the options to be determined by experience. When the switches are set one way, we have Swahili; when they are set another way, we have Japanese. Each possible human language is identified as a particular setting of the switches—a setting of parameters, in technical terminology. If the research program succeeds, we should be able literally to deduce Swahili from one choice of settings, Japanese from another, and so on through the languages that humans can acquire. The empirical conditions of language acquisition require that the switches can be set on the basis of the very limited information that is available to the child. Notice that small changes in switch settings can lead to great apparent variety in output, as the effects proliferate through the system. These are the general properties of language that any genuine theory must capture somehow.

This is, of course, a program, and it is far from a finished prod- 20 uct. The conclusions tentatively reached are unlikely to stand in their present form; and, needless to say, one can have no certainty that the whole approach is on the right track. As a research program, however, it has been highly successful, leading to a real explosion of empirical inquiry into languages of a very broad typological range, to new questions that could never even have been formulated before, and to many intriguing answers. Questions of acquisition, processing, pathology, and others also took new forms, which have proven very productive as well. Furthermore, whatever its fate, the program suggests how the theory of language might satisfy the conflicting conditions of descriptive and explanatory adequacy. It gives at least an outline of a genuine theory of language, really for the first time.

21 Within this research program, the main task is to discover and clarify the principles and parameters and the manner of their interaction, and to extend the framework to include other aspects of language and its use. While a great deal remains obscure, there has been enough progress to at least consider, perhaps to pursue, some new and more far-reaching questions about the design of language. In particular, we can ask how good the design is. How close does language come to what some superengineer would construct, given the conditions that the language faculty must satisfy?

22 The questions have to be sharpened, and there are ways to proceed. The faculty of language is embedded within the broader architecture of the mind/brain. It interacts with other systems, which impose conditions that language must satisfy if it is to be usable at all. We might think of these as "legibility conditions," in the sense that other systems must be able to "read" the expressions of the language and use them as "instructions" for thought and action. The sensorimotor systems, for example, have to be able to read the instructions having to do with sound, that is the "phonetic representations" generated by the language. The articulatory and perceptual apparatus have specific design that enables them to interpret certain phonetic properties, not others. These systems thus impose legibility conditions on the generative processes of the faculty of language, which must provide expressions with the proper phonetic form. The same is true of conceptual and other systems that make use of the resources of the faculty of language: they have their intrinsic properties, which require that the expressions generated by the language have certain kinds of "semantic representations," not others. We may therefore ask to what extent language is a "good solution" to the legibility conditions imposed by the external systems with which it interacts. Until quite recently this question could not seriously be posed, even formulated sensibly. Now it seems that it can, and there are even indications that the language faculty may be close to "perfect" in this sense; if true, this is a surprising conclusion.

QUESTIONS FOR CRITICAL READING

1. What is a species property (para. 2)?
2. Why is discrete infinity important in the study of language?
3. How convincing is Chomsky's view that the language faculty is inborn?
4. In what ways other than for language might the mind be "hardwired"?
5. What might all languages have in common?
6. Which of Chomsky's metaphors seems most convincing to you?
7. What kind of research might be necessary for Chomsky to prove his basic claim?

SUGGESTIONS FOR CRITICAL WRITING

1. Explain some of Chomsky's theories of language to a friend who has not read this selection. While doing so, comment on Chomsky's use of metaphor and his linking of language acquisition to biology rather than to culture. You may also comment on the degree to which you are convinced of his theories.

2. What other human qualities may be "species specific"? What is the likelihood that any one of those qualities may be "hardwired" in the same way Chomsky describes the "language organ" as being? Is talent one of those qualities? Or is it just a chance association of mental qualities that evolution produced for other survival purposes? Do animals have talent?

3. Go through the selection carefully looking for all its metaphors. How many are biological, electronic, mechanical, agricultural, recreational, or from other sources? Which class of metaphors is most convincing of the truth of Chomsky's claims? Which is most questionable? Does any one metaphor stand out as being the most imaginative and most demanding of attention?

4. If you have access to young children, either in your family, a friend's family, or in a preschool setting, test Chomsky's theory that they can generate language features not taught by rote or instruction. Write down their statements over a period of time and see how many variations in language details you can discover. Consider the differences in word placement. The word pattern subject, verb, object is common, but children may vary this order at times. Consider their use of the tenses: present, future, past, conditional, and so on. How linguistically creative are the children you observe?

5. Not every linguist is convinced that Chomsky is correct in his theoretical assumptions. On which points do you most seriously disagree with him? If possible, research the writings of other current linguists, such as John McWhorter or Daniel L. Everett, to see how professionals respond to Chomsky's work.

6. **CONNECTIONS** Chomsky may or may not know the work of Susanne K. Langer (p. 769) on language. She, on the other hand, may have read his early work. Examine both writers for their similar conclusions about language. Or, examine their work looking for ways in which they seem to contradict each other. Does the story of the Wild Boy of Aveyron shed light on the question of the brain's possessing a "language organ" that makes it possible to learn a language?

7. **CONNECTIONS** Read Alexander Pope's *An Essay on Criticism* (**bedfordstmartins.com/worldofideas/epages**). Chomsky defends the view that people are "hardwired" for language. Is there a possibility that people are also "hardwired" for the talent to write rhymed poetry? Take any major topic in Chomsky's essay (discrete infinity, species specificity, generative grammar, or any other idea you find interesting) and write a poem inspired by that subject. Use Pope's form: rhymed iambic couplets. Aim to write a poem of at least fourteen lines. Then answer the question of whether you think that, because some people are much better at this task than others, our brains may be hardwired to write couplets. As an alternative, you may try writing a rap poem on a Chomsky subject. How much is it like Pope's poetry?

8. **SEEING CONNECTIONS** Refer to Wosene Worke Kosrof's painting *The Color of Words IX* (p. 766). Most of the characters represented in the painting are alphabetic items that are part of the Amharic language script of early Ethiopia. Copy the most distinctly alphabetic forms and decide whether, like our twenty-six-character alphabet, these characters represent a discrete infinity. Is it possible that the "language organ" is also designed to accommodate alphabetic characters such as these and those of other languages? Could this painting be interpreted metaphorically by Chomsky and help him in his argument?

PART EIGHT

DISCOVERIES AND THE MIND

Plato
Francis Bacon
Charles Darwin
Sigmund Freud
Carl Jung
René Descartes

INTRODUCTION

We are shaped by our thoughts; we become what we think.
When the mind is pure, joy follows like a shadow that never
leaves.
> — Siddhārtha Gautama, the Buddha (563–483 b.c.e.)

That in the soul which is called the mind is, before it thinks, not
actually any real thing.
> — Aristotle (384–322 b.c.e.)

Distinctions drawn by the mind are not necessarily equivalent to
distinctions in reality.
> — St. Thomas Aquinas (1225–1274)

Consciousness is the perception of what passes in a man's own
mind. Can another man perceive that I am conscious of any
thing, when I perceive it not myself? No man's knowledge here
can go beyond his experience.
> — John Locke (1632–1704)

The difference in mind between man and the higher animals,
great as it is, is one of degree and not of kind.
> — Charles Darwin (1809–1882)

The computer takes up where psychoanalysis left off. It takes the
ideas of a decentered self and makes it more concrete by mod-
eling mind as a multiprocessing machine.
> — Sherry Turkle (b. 1948)

Ideas about the nature of the human mind have abounded
throughout history. Philosophers and scientists have sought to discern the mind's components and functions and have distinguished
humans from other animals according to the qualities associated with
the mind, such as reason and self-awareness. The ancient Greeks formulated the concept of the psyche (from which we derive the term
psychology) as the center of consciousness and reason as well as emotions. During the Renaissance, René Descartes (1596–1650) concluded *Cogito ergo sum* ("I think, therefore I am") and proposed that
the mind was the source of human identity and that reason was the
key to comprehending the material world. Influenced by Descartes,
John Locke (1632–1704) developed a theory of the mind as a tabula
rasa, or blank slate, that was shaped entirely by external experiences.
The selections in this section further explore these questions about
the nature of the mind and its relationship to consciousness, knowledge, intellect, and the other means by which we work to understand
ourselves and our world.

The first selection, by Plato, contains one of the seminal ideas about the nature of the mind. Plato posited that the world of sensory experience is not the real world and that our senses are in fact incapable of experiencing reality. In Plato's view, reality is an ideal that exists only in an environment that is somewhat akin to the concept of heaven. He suggested that people are born with knowledge of that reality. The infant, in other words, possesses the ideas of reality to start with, having gained them from heaven and retaining them in memory. For Plato, education was the process by which students regained such "lost" memories and made them part of their conscious understanding. Although he never uses the terms *conscious* and *unconscious* in describing the mind, Plato's views foreshadow the later theories of psychologists such as William James (1842–1910), Sigmund Freud, and Carl Jung.

By the Renaissance, education had become more sophisticated than in Plato's day. At the time Francis Bacon (1561–1626) wrote, before the advent of complex scientific instruments, most scientists relied on their five senses and their theoretical preconceptions to investigate the workings of the world around them. In "The Four Idols," Bacon raises questions about these modes of scientific inquiry by asking, What casts of mind are essential to gaining knowledge? What prevents us from understanding nature clearly? By critiquing traditional presumptions and methods of investigation, Bacon challenges his readers to examine nature with new mental tools.

Such a challenge is evident in "Natural Selection," in which Charles Darwin (1809–1882) proposes a theory that is still controversial today. While on a voyage around South America on HMS *Beagle*, Darwin observed remarkable similarities in the structures of various animals. He approached these discoveries with the advantages of a good education, a deep knowledge of the Bible and theology (he was trained as a minister), and a systematic and inquiring mind. Ultimately, he developed his theories of evolution to explain the significance of resemblances he detected among his scientific samples of insects and flowers and other forms of life. Explaining the nature of nature forms the underpinnings of Darwin's work.

Explaining the nature of the human mind on the other hand is the province of Sigmund Freud (1856–1939). One of the best-known results of Freud's study of dreams is his conclusion that all people suffer from an Oedipus complex when they are extremely young. Freud explains that Oedipus, thinking he was escaping his fate, killed his father and married his mother, both of whom were strangers to him. Freud takes this familiar Greek myth and explores its significance in the lives of very young children, showing that it is common for them to wish to do away with their parent of the same sex and have their opposite-sex parent all to themselves. As people grow older, both the memory and the desire to follow through on this feeling are repressed and forgotten. They become part of our unconscious and, in some cases, may resurface in the form of guilt. As adults we know that such feelings are completely unacceptable, and the guilt that results can create psychological illness.

Carl Jung began his studies with Freud's views of the content of the unconscious, but one of his analyses led him in a novel direction. He concluded that some of the content of the unconscious mind could not have begun in the conscious mind because it was not the product of the individual's conscious experience. Jung reasoned that certain images present in the unconscious were common to all members of a culture. He called these images *archetypal* because they seemed fundamental and universal, such as the archetype of the father and the archetype of the mother. He then hypothesized that part of the mind's content is derived from cultural history. Unlike Freud, Jung saw the unconscious as containing images that represent deep instinctual longings belonging to an entire culture, not just to the individual.

The e-Pages for this chapter (available online at **bedfordstmartins .com/worldofideas/epages**) feature a selection from René Descartes. Descartes wrote in an age that was influenced by a revival of attention to Greek philosophers. His views were consistent in some ways with those of Plato and Aristotle, especially in the quest for a form of certainty in knowledge on which all thought could be based. His primary motive was to prove the existence of God, which he felt he could do if he could establish one absolute truth on which to build a clear argument. His solution was *Cogito ergo sum*, which translates as "I think, therefore I am." Having established his own existence without a doubt, he was able to move toward a defensible proof of the existence of God. However, in the process of developing his argument, he introduced a long-lasting idea that influenced thought for many years: that the mind and the body are separate entities. The mind/body split had been apparent in the work of earlier writers, but it never had such a forceful champion as in Descartes. His influence has continued to modern times despite the current view that the mind and body are much more closely integrated than earlier investigators had assumed.

These essays approach the issues of discovery and the mind from different positions and are concerned with various questions of consciousness, scientific inquiry, and the nature of man and of nature. They raise some of the most basic questions concerning the mind, such as, What can it know? What should we most value in its function? In answering these questions, each essay provides us with ideas that provoke more thought and still more questions.

SALVADOR DALÍ, THE PERSISTENCE OF MEMORY. 1931.
Oil on canvas, 9 1/2" × 13". Museum of Modern Art, New York.

VISUALIZING DISCOVERIES AND THE MIND

Among the many art movements of the early twentieth century, surrealism is one of the most interesting and persistent in its effect on the mind of the viewer. The movement began in France in the 1920s and produced a good number of lasting works. Part of the inspiration for the artists was the work of Sigmund Freud, whose concept of the unconscious was a novelty early in the century and created wide-ranging controversy. William James had proposed the existence of the unconscious mind in the late nineteenth century, but Freud's work, with its emphasis on sexual urges that he insisted were present in everyone—even in those who did not know they possessed the urges—proposed that much of what we do and much of what we dream comes from the unconscious mind.

Even writers, such as James Joyce, were influenced by the theories of psychoanalysis and experimented with mixing reality with unreality in the manner of our dreams. Dreams became a source for considerable experimentation in the arts. Ideally, these works were created as a means of connecting us with our unconscious mind. Surrealism is powerful even today in part because our understanding of the intersection of psychology and everyday behavior is even stronger than it was in the 1910s. The technique of many of the surrealist painters is based on visual distortion, particularly of the kind that people experience when using powerful hallucinogenic drugs. Art produces the distortion without reliance on mind-changing substances.

Salvador Dalí (1904–1989) was an outrageous showman who constantly flaunted his eccentric sexual behavior and who promoted himself as the "bad boy" of art. His self-promotion worked extremely well and he remained a famous artist until his death. And while *The Persistence of Memory* is a very small painting, hardly larger than a piece of 8" × 11" paper, its impact has been significant both in the popular imagination and in the writings of authorities on art. (To see this painting in color, go to **bedfordstmartins.com/worldofideas/epages**.)

The painting shows a barren landscape with a bay, said to be Port Lligat in northeastern Spain, near where Dalí was born. The landscape is populated by watches that drape over a tree limb, over a rectangular object, and over a mysterious figure with long eyelashes resembling Dalí's own. A great many explanations for the painting have surfaced and doubtless many more will be proposed. Dalí himself said that he had been inspired by a dream, as he had been inspired in many of his other works. As he said, his dream paintings were designed to "stamp themselves indelibly on the mind." *The Persistence of Memory* has indeed achieved that end by becoming one of the most iconic images of the first part of the twentieth century.

The clocks in the painting all have different times on their faces; the one more or less "normal" clock is infested with ants. Some commentators have seen the clock imagery as the result of the influence of the theory of relativity of Albert Einstein (1879–1955), who won the Nobel Prize in 1921. Like Freud's theories, Einstein's quickly caught the imagination of the artistic community. They were struck by his theory that time is not absolute but varies according to the space/time plane on which it is measured. The idea of relativity was adopted by artists, although hardly understood in detail, in part because it was an alternative to thinking that the laws of the universe were absolutes, like the law of gravity. It gave artists room to maneuver imaginatively.

The figure in the center has been described as a self-portrait, a mass of brain cells, and as a representation of Dalí as a fetus. This interpretation depends on the idea that the fetus could take many shapes or forms and is thus surreal in this environment, but it also relies on Dalí's comment that he had a memory not only of having been in his mother's womb but also of having the classic Freudian Oedipus complex in loving his mother. That may be the persistence of memory to which he alludes. Whether it is intended to represent a fetus or not, it seems to be intended as a self-portrait of sorts, but one that is intensely distorted.

An art historian, Mariel Jean drew a connection between the painting and a child being told to stick out his tongue in a doctor's office. The French word *montrer* means "to show" and it is extremely close to *montre*, which means watch, while the word for tongue, *langue*, is cognate to *langueur* or *languid*, as in drooping, tired, exhausted. The watches in the painting are drooping, exhausted, and because none of them are in agreement, they are essentially timeless. The idea of timelessness is reinforced by the massive stone cliffs, themselves the product of eons, jutting out into the bay. The tree appears to be dead, which implies that time stops for living things. By playing with Einstein's assurance that time is relative, Dalí's painting may imply that timelessness means there is no time, that it has become extinct, or that time is only part of our imagination and can be stretched much the way the watches are stretched. Whatever the painting implies, it has been seen as a powerful dream vision ever since it was first shown.

PLATO
The Allegory of the Cave

PLATO (428–347 B.C.E.) was born into an aristocratic, probably Athenian, family and educated according to the best precepts available. He eventually became a student of Socrates and later involved himself closely with Socrates' work and teaching. Plato was not only Socrates' finest student but also the one who immortalized Socrates in his works. Most of Plato's works are philosophical essays in which Socrates speaks as a character in a dialogue with one or more students or listeners.

Both Socrates and Plato lived in turbulent times. In 404 B.C.E. Athens was defeated by Sparta, and its government was taken over by tyrants. Political life in Athens became dangerous. Plato felt, however, that he could effect positive change in Athenian politics — until Socrates was tried unjustly for corrupting the youth of Athens and sentenced to death in 399 B.C.E. After that, Plato withdrew from public life and devoted himself to writing and to the academy he founded in an olive grove in Athens. The academy endured for almost a thousand years, which tells us how greatly Plato's thought was valued.

Although it is not easy to condense Plato's views, he may be said to have held the world of sense perception to be inferior to the world of ideal entities that exist only in a pure spiritual realm. These ideals, or forms, Plato argued, are perceived directly by everyone before birth and then dimly remembered here on earth. But the memory, dim as it is, enables people to understand what the senses perceive, despite the fact that the senses are unreliable and their perceptions imperfect.

This view of reality has long been important to philosophers because it gives a philosophical basis to antimaterialistic thought.

From *The Republic*. Translated and glossed by Benjamin Jowett.

It values the spirit first and frees people from the tyranny of sensory perception and sensory reward. In the case of love, Plato held that Eros leads individuals to revere the body and its pleasures; but the thrust of his teaching is that the body is a metaphor for spiritual delights. Plato maintains that the body is only a starting point, which eventually can lead to both spiritual fulfillment and the appreciation of true beauty.

On the one hand, "The Allegory of the Cave" is a discussion of politics: *The Republic*, from which it is taken, is a treatise on justice and the ideal government. On the other hand, it has long stood as an example of the notion that if we rely on our perceptions to know the truth about the world, then we will know very little about it. In order to live ethically, it is essential to know what is true and, therefore, what is important beyond the world of sensory perception.

Plato's allegory has been persuasive for centuries and remains at the center of thought that attempts to counter the pleasures of the sensual life. Most religions aim for spiritual enlightenment and praise the qualities of the soul, which lies beyond perception. Thus, it comes as no surprise that Christianity and other religions have developed systems of thought that bear a close resemblance to Plato's. Later refinements of his thought, usually called Neo-Platonism, have been influential even into modern times.

Plato's Rhetoric

Two important rhetorical techniques are at work in the following selection. The first and more obvious—at least on one level—is the device of the allegory, a story in which the characters and situations actually represent people and situations in another context. It is a difficult technique to sustain, although Aesop's fables were certainly successful in using animals to represent people and their foibles. The advantage of the technique is that a complex and sometimes unpopular argument can be fought and won before the audience realizes that an argument is under way. The disadvantage of the technique is that the terms of the allegory may only approximate the situation it represents; thus, the argument may fail to be convincing.

The second rhetorical technique Plato uses is the dialogue. In fact, this device is a hallmark of Plato's work; indeed, most of his writings are called dialogues. The *Symposium*, *Apology*, *Phaedo*, *Crito*, *Meno*, and most of his famous works are written in dialogue form. Usually in these works Socrates is speaking to a student or a friend about highly abstract issues, asking questions that require simple answers. Slowly, the questioning proceeds to elucidate the answers to complex issues.

This question-and-answer technique basically constitutes the Socratic method. Socrates analyzes the answer to each question, examines its implications, and then asserts the truth. The method works partly because Plato believes that people do not learn things but remember them. That is, people originate from heaven, where they knew the truth; they already possess knowledge and must recover it by means of the dialogue. Socrates' method is ideally suited to that purpose.

Beyond these techniques, however, we must look at Plato's style. It is true that he is working with difficult ideas, but his style is so clear, simple, and direct that few people would have trouble understanding what he is saying. Considering the influence this work has had on world thought, and the reputation Plato had earned by the time he wrote *The Republic*, its style is remarkably plain and accessible. Plato's respect for rhetoric and its proper uses is part of the reason he can express himself with such impressive clarity.

PREREADING QUESTIONS:
WHAT TO READ FOR

The following prereading questions may help you anticipate key issues in the discussion of Plato's "The Allegory of the Cave." Keeping them in mind during your first reading of the selection should help focus your attention.

- In what ways are we like the people in the cave looking at shadows?
- Why is the world of sensory perception somewhat illusory?
- For Plato, what is the difference between the upper world and the lower world?

The Allegory of the Cave

SOCRATES, GLAUCON. *The den, the prisoners: the light at a distance;*

And now, I said, let me show in a figure how far our nature is enlightened or unenlightened:—Behold! human beings living in an underground den, which has a mouth open towards the light and reaching all along the den; here they have been from their childhood, and have their legs and necks chained so that they cannot move, and can only see before them, being prevented by the chains from turning round their heads. Above and behind them a fire is blazing at a distance, and between the fire and the prisoners there is a raised way; and you will see, if you look, a low wall built along the way, like the screen which marionette players have in front of them, over which they show the puppets.

I see.   2

the low wall, and the moving figures of which the shadows are seen on the opposite wall of the den.

And do you see, I said, men passing along the   3
wall carrying all sorts of vessels, and statues and figures of animals made of wood and stone and various
materials, which appear over the wall? Some of them
are talking, others silent.

You have shown me a strange image, and they   4
are strange prisoners.

Like ourselves, I replied; and they see only their   5
own shadows, or the shadows of one another, which
the fire throws on the opposite wall of the cave?

True, he said; how could they see anything but   6
the shadows if they were never allowed to move
their heads?

And of the objects which are being carried in   7
like manner they would only see the shadows?

Yes, he said.   8

And if they were able to converse with one   9
another, would they not suppose that they were
naming what was actually before them?

Very true.   10

The prisoners would mistake the shadows for realities.

And suppose further that the prison had an   11
echo which came from the other side, would they
not be sure to fancy when one of the passers-by
spoke that the voice which they heard came from
the passing shadow?

No question, he replied.   12

To them, I said, the truth would be literally   13
nothing but the shadows of the images.

That is certain.   14

And now look again, and see what will naturally   15
follow if the prisoners are released and disabused
of their error. At first, when any of them is liberated
and compelled suddenly to stand up and turn his
neck round and walk and look towards the light, he
will suffer sharp pains; the glare will distress him, and

And when released, they would still persist in maintaining the superior truth of the shadows.

he will be unable to see the realities of which in his former state he had seen the shadows; and then conceive someone saying to him, that what he saw before was an illusion, but that now, when he is approaching nearer to being and his eye is turned towards more real existence, he has a clearer vision—what will be his reply? And you may further imagine that his instructor is pointing to the objects as they pass and requiring him to name them,—will he not be perplexed? Will he not fancy that the shadows which he formerly saw are truer than the objects which are now shown to him?

Far truer. 16

And if he is compelled to look straight at the 17 light, will he not have a pain in his eyes which will make him turn away to take refuge in the objects of vision which he can see, and which he will conceive to be in reality clearer than the things which are now being shown to him?

True, he said. 18

When dragged upwards, they would be dazzled by excess of light.

And suppose once more, that he is reluctantly 19 dragged up a steep and rugged ascent, and held fast until he is forced into the presence of the sun himself, is he not likely to be pained and irritated? When he approaches the light his eyes will be dazzled, and he will not be able to see anything at all of what are now called realities.

Not all in a moment, he said. 20

He will require to grow accustomed to the sight 21 of the upper world. And first he will see the shadows best, next the reflections of men and other objects in the water, and then the objects themselves; then he will gaze upon the light of the moon and the stars and the spangled heaven; and he will see the sky and the stars by night better than the sun or the light of the sun by day?

Certainly. 22

At length they will see the sun and understand his nature.

Last of all he will be able to see the sun, and 23 not mere reflections of him in the water, but he will see him in his own proper place, and not in another; and he will contemplate him as he is.

Certainly. 24

He will then proceed to argue that this is 25 he who gives the season and the years, and is the guardian of all that is in the visible world, and in a

certain way the cause of all things which he and his
fellows have been accustomed to behold?

Clearly, he said, he would first see the sun and   26
then reason about him.

And when he remembered his old habitation,   27
and the wisdom of the den and his fellow prisoners,
do you not suppose that he would felicitate himself
on the change, and pity them?

*They would then
pity their old
companions
of the den.*

Certainly, he would.   28

And if they were in the habit of conferring hon-   29
ors among themselves on those who were quickest to observe the passing shadows and to remark
which of them went before, and which followed
after, and which were together; and who were therefore best able to draw conclusions as to the future,
do you think that he would care for such honors
and glories, or envy the possessors of them? Would
he not say with Homer,

Better to be the poor servant of a poor master,

and to endure anything, rather than think as they do
and live after their manner?

Yes, he said, I think that he would rather suffer   30
anything than entertain these false notions and live
in this miserable manner.

Imagine once more, I said, such an one coming   31
suddenly out of the sun to be replaced in his old situation; would he not be certain to have his eyes full
of darkness?

To be sure, he said.   32

*But when they
returned to the
den, they would
see much worse
than those
who had never
left it.*

And if there were a contest, and he had to com-   33
pete in measuring the shadows with the prisoners who had never moved out of the den, while his
sight was still weak, and before his eyes had become
steady (and the time which would be needed to
acquire this new habit of sight might be very considerable), would he not be ridiculous? Men would
say of him that up he went and down he came without his eyes; and that it was better not even to think
of ascending; and if any one tried to loose another
and lead him up to the light, let them only catch the
offender, and they would put him to death.

No question, he said.   34

This entire allegory, I said, you may now   35
append, dear Glaucon, to the previous argument;

The prison is the world of sight, the light of the fire is the sun.

the prison house is the world of sight, the light of the fire is the sun, and you will not misapprehend me if you interpret the journey upwards to be the ascent of the soul into the intellectual world according to my poor belief, which, at your desire, I have expressed — whether rightly or wrongly God knows. But, whether true or false, my opinion is that in the world of knowledge the idea of good appears last of all, and is seen only with an effort; and, when seen, is also inferred to be the universal author of all things beautiful and right, parent of light and of the lord of light in this visible world, and the immediate source of reason and truth in the intellectual; and that this is the power upon which he who would act rationally either in public or private life must have his eye fixed.

I agree, he said, as far as I am able to understand you.

Moreover, I said, you must not wonder that those who attain to this beatific vision are unwilling to descend to human affairs; for their souls are ever hastening into the upper world where they desire to dwell; which desire of theirs is very natural, if our allegory may be trusted.

Yes, very natural.

Nothing extraordinary in the philosopher being unable to see in the dark.

And is there anything surprising in one who passes from divine contemplations to the evil state of man, misbehaving himself in a ridiculous manner; if, while his eyes are blinking and before he has become accustomed to the surrounding darkness, he is compelled to fight in courts of law, or in other places, about the images or the shadows of images of justice, and is endeavoring to meet the conceptions of those who have never yet seen absolute justice?

Anything but surprising, he replied.

The eyes may be blinded in two ways, by excess or by defect of light.

Anyone who has common sense will remember that the bewilderments of the eyes are of two kinds, and arise from two causes, either from coming out of the light or from going into the light, which is true of the mind's eye, quite as much as of the bodily eye; and he who remembers this when he sees anyone whose vision is perplexed and weak, will not be too ready to laugh; he will first ask whether that soul of man has come out of the brighter life, and is unable to see because unaccustomed to the dark, or having turned from darkness to the day

36

37

38

39

40

41

is dazzled by excess of light. And he will count the one happy in his condition and state of being, and he will pity the other; or, if he have a mind to laugh at the soul which comes from below into the light, there will be more reason in this than in the laugh which greets him who returns from above out of the light into the den.

That, he said, is a very just distinction.   42

The conversion of the soul is the turning round the eye from darkness to light.

But then, if I am right, certain professors of edu-   43
cation must be wrong when they say that they can put a knowledge into the soul which was not there before, like sight into blind eyes.

They undoubtedly say this, he replied.   44

Whereas, our argument shows that the power   45
and capacity of learning exists in the soul already; and that just as the eye was unable to turn from darkness to light without the whole body, so too the instrument of knowledge can only by the move-ment of the whole soul be turned from the world of becoming into that of being, and learn by degrees to endure the sight of being, and of the brightest and best of being, or in other words, of the good.

Very true.   46

And must there not be some art which will   47
effect conversion in the easiest and quickest manner; not implanting the faculty of sight, for that exists already, but has been turned in the wrong direction, and is looking away from the truth?

Yes, he said, such an art may be presumed.   48

And whereas the other so-called virtues of the   49
soul seem to be akin to bodily qualities, for even when they are not originally innate they can be

The virtue of wisdom has a divine power which may be turned either towards good or towards evil.

implanted later by habit and exercise, the virtue of wisdom more than anything else contains a divine element which always remains, and by this conver-sion is rendered useful and profitable; or, on the other hand, hurtful and useless. Did you never observe the narrow intelligence flashing from the keen eye of a clever rogue—how eager he is, how clearly his paltry soul sees the way to his end; he is the reverse of blind, but his keen eyesight is forced into the service of evil, and he is mischievous in proportion to his cleverness?

Very true, he said.   50

But what if there had been a circumcision of   51
such natures in the days of their youth; and they

had been severed from those sensual pleasures, such as eating and drinking, which, like leaden weights, were attached to them at their birth, and which drag them down and turn the vision of their souls upon the things that are below—if, I say, they had been released from these impediments and turned in the opposite direction, the very same faculty in them would have seen the truth as keenly as they see what their eyes are turned to now.

Very likely.   52

Neither the uneducated nor the over-educated will be good servants of the State.

Yes, I said; and there is another thing which is   53 likely, or rather a necessary inference from what has preceded, that neither the uneducated and unin-formed of the truth, nor yet those who never make an end of their education, will be able ministers of State; not the former, because they have no single aim of duty which is the rule of all their actions, pri-vate as well as public; nor the latter, because they will not act at all except upon compulsion, fancying that they are already dwelling apart in the islands of the blessed.

Very true, he replied.   54

Then, I said, the business of us who are the   55 founders of the State will be to compel the best minds to attain that knowledge which we have already shown to be the greatest of all—they must continue to ascend until they arrive at the good; but when they have ascended and seen enough we must not allow them to do as they do now.

What do you mean?   56

Men should ascend to the upper world, but they should also return to the lower.

I mean that they remain in the upper world: 57 but this must not be allowed; they must be made to descend again among the prisoners in the den, and partake of their labors and honors, whether they are worth having or not.

But is not this unjust? he said; ought we to give   58 them a worse life, when they might have a better?

You have again forgotten, my friend, I said,   59 the intention of the legislator, who did not aim at making any one class in the State happy above the rest; the happiness was to be in the whole State, and he held the citizens together by persuasion and necessity, making them benefactors of the

State, and therefore benefactors of one another; to this end he created them, not to please themselves, but to be his instruments in binding up the State.

True, he said, I had forgotten.   60

The duties of philosophers.

Observe, Glaucon, that there will be no injus-   61
tice in compelling our philosophers to have a care and providence of others; we shall explain to them that in other States, men of their class are not obliged to share in the toils of politics: and this is reasonable, for they grow up at their own sweet will, and the government would rather not have them. Being self-taught, they cannot be expected to show any gratitude for a culture which they have never received. But we have brought you into the world to be rulers of the hive, kings of yourselves and of the other citizens, and have educated you far better and more perfectly than they have been educated, and you are better able to share in the double duty. Wherefore each of you, when his turn comes, must go down to the general underground abode, and get the habit of seeing in the dark.

Their obligations to their country will induce them to take part in her government.

When you have acquired the habit, you will see ten thousand times better than the inhabitants of the den, and you will know what the several images are, and what they represent, because you have seen the beautiful and just and good in their truth. And thus our State, which is also yours, will be a reality, and not a dream only, and will be administered in a spirit unlike that of other States, in which men fight with one another about shadows only and are distracted in the struggle for power, which in their eyes is a great good. Whereas the truth is that the State in which the rulers are most reluctant to govern is always the best and most quietly governed, and the State in which they are most eager, the worst.

Quite true, he replied.   62

And will our pupils, when they hear this, refuse   63
to take their turn at the toils of State, when they are allowed to spend the greater part of their time with one another in the heavenly light?

They will be willing but not anxious to rule.

Impossible, he answered; for they are just   64
men, and the commands which we impose upon

them are just; there can be no doubt that every one of them will take office as a stern necessity, and not after the fashion of our present rulers of State.

The statesman must be provided with a better life than that of a ruler; and then he will not covet office.

Yes, my friend, I said; and there lies the point. You must contrive for your future rulers another and a better life than that of a ruler, and then you may have a well-ordered State; for only in the State which offers this, will they rule who are truly rich, not in silver and gold, but in virtue and wisdom, which are the true blessings of life. Whereas if they go to the administration of public affairs, poor and hungering after their own private advantage, thinking that hence they are to snatch the chief good, order there can never be; for they will be fighting about office, and the civil and domestic broils which thus arise will be the ruin of the rulers themselves and of the whole State. 65

Most true, he replied. 66

And the only life which looks down upon the life of political ambition is that of true philosophy. Do you know of any other? 67

Indeed, I do not, he said. 68

QUESTIONS FOR CRITICAL READING

1. What is the relationship between Socrates and Glaucon? Are they equal in intellectual authority? Are they concerned with the same issues?

2. How does the allegory of the prisoners in the cave watching shadows on a wall relate to us today? What shadows do we see, and how do they distort our sense of what is real?

3. Are we prisoners in the same sense that Plato's characters are?

4. If Plato is right that the material world is an illusion, how would too great a reliance on materialism affect ethical decisions?

5. What ethical issues, if any, are raised by Plato's allegory?

6. In paragraph 49, Plato states that the virtue of wisdom "contains a divine element." What is "a divine element"? What does this statement seem to mean? Do you agree with Plato?

7. What distinctions does Plato make between the public and the private? Would you make the same distinctions (see paras. 53–55)?

SUGGESTIONS FOR CRITICAL WRITING

1. Analyze the allegory of the cave for its strengths and weaknesses. Consider what the allegory implies for people living in a world of the senses and for what might lie behind that world. To what extent are people like (or unlike) the figures in the cave? To what extent is the world we know like the cave?

2. Socrates ends the dialogue by saying that rulers of the state must be able to look forward to a better life than that of being rulers. He and Glaucon agree that only one life "looks down upon the life of political ambition"—"that of true philosophy" (para. 67). What is the life of true philosophy? Is it superior to that of governing (or anything else)? How would you define its superiority? What would its qualities be? What would its concerns be? Would you be happy leading such a life?

3. In what ways would depending on the material world for one's highest moral values affect ethical behavior? What is the connection between ethics and materialism? Write a brief essay that defends or attacks materialism as a basis for ethical action. How can people aspire to the good if they root their greatest pleasures in the senses? What alternatives do modern people have if they choose to base their actions on nonmaterialistic, or spiritual, values? What are those values? How can they guide our ethical behavior? Do you think they should?

4. In paragraph 61, Socrates outlines a program that would assure Athens of having good rulers and good government. Clarify exactly what the program is, what its problems and benefits are, and how it could be put into action. Then decide whether the program would work. You may consider whether it would work for our time, for Socrates' time, or both. If possible, use examples (hypothetical or real) to bolster your argument.

5. Socrates states unequivocally that Athens should compel the best and the most intelligent young men to be rulers of the state. Review his reasons for saying so, consider what his concept of the state is, and then take a stand on the issue. Is it right to compel the best and most intelligent young people to become rulers? If so, would it be equally proper to compel those well suited for the professions of law, medicine, teaching, or religion to follow those respective callings? Would an ideal society result if all people were forced to practice the calling for which they had the best aptitude?

6. **CONNECTIONS** Plato has a great deal to say about goodness as it relates to government. Compare his views with those of Lao-tzu (p. 203) and Niccolò Machiavelli (p. 219). Which of these thinkers would Plato have agreed with most? In comparing these three writers and their political views, consider the nature of goodness they required in a ruler. Do you think that we hold similar attitudes today in our expectations for the goodness of our government?

7. **CONNECTIONS** Plato is concerned with the question of how we know what we know. Francis Bacon in "The Four Idols" (p. 879) is

concerned with the same question, although he poses it in different terms. Examine the fundamental issues each author raises. How well do these thinkers agree on basic issues? To what extent, for example, does Bacon warn us to beware the evidence of our senses? To what extent is Bacon concerned about getting to the truth as Plato is?

8. **CONNECTIONS**   How does Plato illustrate the basic principles that Descartes (**bedfordstmartins.com/worldofideas/epages**) defends when he decides not to rely upon sensory evidence to explain complex ideas? Since Plato was known and venerated in seventeenth-century France, why is it evident that Descartes read "The Allegory of the Cave" and incorporated it in his work? What fault might Plato find in Descartes' argument for the existence of God? What do both writers share regarding the "cause of falsity and error"?

9. **SEEING CONNECTIONS**   How would Plato have used Salvador Dalí's *The Persistence of Memory* (p. 861) to help defend his view that what we perceive through our senses is not a form of reality? Would he have felt the images in the painting belong to the upper world or the lower world? If he were to interpret the images in the painting as a portrait of a dream experience, would he then have felt the world of dreams was similar to the world of those chained in the cave? Or would he have felt the painting itself was a record of yet another "reality" that was illusory?

FRANCIS BACON
The Four Idols

FRANCIS BACON, Lord Verulam (1561–1626), lived during one of the most exciting times in history. Among his contemporaries were the essayist Michel Eyquem de Montaigne; the playwrights Christopher Marlowe and William Shakespeare; the adventurer Sir Francis Drake; and Queen Elizabeth I, in whose reign Bacon held several high offices. He became lord high chancellor of England in 1618 but fell from power in 1621 through a complicated series of events, among which was his complicity in a bribery scheme. His so-called crimes were minor, but he paid dearly for them. His book *Essayes* (1597) was exceptionally popular during his lifetime, and when he found himself without a proper job, he devoted himself to what he declared to be his own true work: writing about philosophy and science.

His purpose in *Novum Organum* (The new organon), published in 1620, was to replace the old organon, or instrument of thought, Aristotle's treatises on logic and thought. Despite Aristotle's pervasive influence on sixteenth- and seventeenth-century thought—his texts were used in virtually all schools and colleges—Bacon assumed that Aristotelian deductive logic produced error. In *Novum Organum* he tried to set the stage for a new attitude toward logic and scientific inquiry. He proposed a system of reasoning usually referred to as induction. This quasi-scientific method involves collecting and listing observations from nature. Once a mass of observations is gathered and organized, Bacon believed, the truth about what is observed will become apparent.

Bacon is often mistakenly credited with having invented the scientific method of inquiring into nature; but although he was right about the need for collecting and observing, he was wrong

---

From *Novum Organum*. Translated by Francis Headlam and R. L. Ellis.

about the outcome of such endeavors. After all, one could watch an infinite number of apples (and oranges, too) fall to the ground without ever having the slightest sense of why they do so. What Bacon failed to realize—and he died before he could become scientific enough to realize it—is the creative function of the scientist as expressed in the hypothesis. The hypothesis—an educated guess about why something happens—must be tested by the kinds of observations Bacon recommended.

Nonetheless, "The Four Idols" is a brilliant work. It does establish the requirements for the kind of observation that produces true scientific knowledge. Bacon despaired of any thoroughly objective inquiry in his own day, in part because no one paid attention to the ways in which the idols, limiting preconceptions, strangled thought, observation, and imagination. He realized that the would-be natural philosopher was foiled even before he began. Bacon was a farsighted man. He was correct about the failures of science in his time; and he was correct, moreover, in his assessment that advancement would depend on sensory perception and on aids to perception, such as microscopes and telescopes. The real brilliance of "The Four Idols" lies in Bacon's focus not on what is observed but on the instrument of observation—the human mind. Only when the instrument is freed of error can we rely on its observations to reveal the truth.

Bacon's Rhetoric

Bacon was trained during the great age of rhetoric, and his prose (even though in this case it is translated from Latin) shows the clarity, balance, and organization that characterize the prose writing of seventeenth-century England. The most basic device Bacon uses is enumeration: stating clearly that there are four idols and implying that he will treat each one in turn.

Enumeration is one of the most common and most reliable rhetorical devices. The listener hears a speaker say "I have only three things I want to say today" and is alerted to listen for all three, while feeling secretly grateful that there are only three. When encountering complex material, the reader is always happy to have such "road signs" as "The second aspect of this question is . . ."

"The Four Idols," after a three-paragraph introduction, proceeds with a single paragraph devoted to each idol, so that we have an early definition of each and a sense of what to look for. Paragraphs 8–16 cover only the issues related to the Idols of the Tribe: the problems all people have simply because they are people. Paragraphs 17–22 consider the Idols of the Cave: those particular fixations individuals have because of their special backgrounds or limitations. Paragraphs 23–26 address the questions related to Idols of the Marketplace, particularly those that deal with the way people misuse words and abuse definitions. The remainder of the selection treats the Idols of the Theater, which relate entirely to philosophic systems and preconceptions—all of which tend to narrow the scope of research and understanding.

Enumeration is used within each of these groups of paragraphs as well. Bacon often begins a paragraph with such statements as "There is one principal . . . distinction between different minds" (para. 19). Or he says, "The idols imposed by words on the understanding are of two kinds" (para. 24). The effect is to ensure clarity where confusion could easily reign.

As an added means of achieving clarity, Bacon sets aside a single paragraph—the last—to summarize the main points that he has made, in the order in which they were made.

Within any section of this selection, Bacon depends on observation, example, and reason to make his points. When he speaks of a given idol, he defines it, gives several examples to make it clearer, discusses its effects on thought, and then dismisses it as dangerous. He then goes on to the next idol. Where appropriate, in some cases he names those who are victims of a specific idol. In each case he tries to be thorough, explanatory, and convincing.

Not only is this work a landmark in thought, it is also, because of its absolute clarity, a beacon. We can still benefit from its light.

PREREADING QUESTIONS: WHAT TO READ FOR

The following prereading questions may help you anticipate key issues in the discussion of Francis Bacon's "The Four Idols." Keeping them in mind during your first reading of the selection should help focus your attention.

- What are the four idols?
- Why do the four idols make it difficult for us to see the truth?
- What are some chief characteristics of human understanding?

The Four Idols

The idols[1] and false notions which are now in possession of the human understanding, and have taken deep root therein, not only so beset men's minds that truth can hardly find entrance, but even after entrance obtained, they will again in the very instauration[2] of the sciences meet and trouble us, unless men being forewarned of the danger fortify themselves as far as may be against their assaults.   1

There are four classes of idols which beset men's minds. To these for distinction's sake I have assigned names—calling the first class *Idols of the Tribe;* the second, *Idols of the Cave;* the third, *Idols of the Market-place;* the fourth, *Idols of the Theater.*   2

The formation of ideas and axioms by true induction[3] is no doubt the proper remedy to be applied for the keeping off and clearing away of idols. To point them out, however, is of great use; for the doctrine of idols is to the interpretation of nature what the doctrine of the refutation of sophisms[4] is to common logic.   3

The *Idols of the Tribe* have their foundation in human nature itself, and in the tribe or race of men. For it is a false assertion that the sense of man is the measure of things. On the contrary, all perceptions as well of the sense as of the mind are according to the measure of the individual and not according to the measure of the universe. And the human understanding is like a false mirror, which, receiving rays irregularly, distorts and discolors the nature of things by mingling its own nature with it.   4

The *Idols of the Cave* are the idols of the individual man. For everyone (besides the errors common to human nature in general) has a cave or den of his own, which refracts[5] and discolors the light of nature; owing either to his own proper and peculiar nature; or to his education and conversation with others; or to the reading of books, and the authority of those whom he esteems and admires; or to the differences   5

---

[1] **idols** By this term Bacon means phantoms or illusions. The Greek philosopher Democritus spoke of *eidola*, tiny representations of things that impressed themselves on the mind (see note 21).

[2] **instauration** Institution.

[3] **induction** Bacon championed induction as the method by which new knowledge is developed. As he saw it, induction involved a patient gathering and categorizing facts in the hope that a large number of them would point to the truth. As a process of gathering evidence from which inferences are drawn, induction is contrasted with Aristotle's method, *deduction*, according to which a theory is established and the truth deduced. Deduction places the stress on the authority of the expert; induction places the stress on the facts themselves.

[4] **sophisms** Apparently intelligent statements that are wrong; false wisdom.

[5] **refracts** Deflects, bends back, alters.

of impressions, accordingly as they take place in a mind preoccupied and predisposed or in a mind indifferent and settled; or the like. So that the spirit of man (according as it is meted out to different individuals) is in fact a thing variable and full of perturbation,[6] and governed as it were by chance. Whence it was well observed by Heraclitus[7] that men look for sciences in their own lesser worlds, and not in the greater or common world.

There are also idols formed by the intercourse and association of 6
men with each other, which I call *Idols of the Marketplace,* on account of the commerce and consort of men there. For it is by discourse that men associate; and words are imposed according to the apprehension of the vulgar.[8] And therefore the ill and unfit choice of words wonderfully obstructs the understanding. Nor do the definitions or explanations wherewith in some things learned men are wont[9] to guard and defend themselves, by any means set the matter right. But words plainly force and overrule the understanding, and throw all into confusion and lead men away into numberless empty controversies and idle fancies.

Lastly, there are idols which have immigrated into men's minds 7
from the various dogmas of philosophies, and also from wrong laws of demonstration.[10] These I call *Idols of the Theater;* because in my judgment all the received systems[11] are but so many stage-plays, representing worlds of their own creation after an unreal and scenic fashion. Nor is it only of the systems now in vogue, or only of the ancient sects and philosophies, that I speak; for many more plays of the same kind may yet be composed and in like artificial manner set forth; seeing that errors the most widely different have nevertheless causes for the most part alike. Neither again do I mean this only of entire systems, but also of many principles and axioms in science, which by tradition, credulity, and negligence, have come to be received.

But of these several kinds of idols I must speak more largely and 8
exactly, that the understanding may be duly cautioned.

The human understanding is of its own nature prone to suppose the existence of more order and regularity in the world than 9
it finds. And though there be many things in nature which are singular

---

[6]**perturbation** Uncertainty, disturbance. In astronomy, the motion caused by the gravity of nearby planets.

[7]**Heraclitus (535?–475? B.C.E.)** Greek philosopher who believed that there was no reality except in change; all else was illusion. He also believed that fire was the basis of all the world and that everything we see is a transformation of it.

[8]**vulgar** Common people.

[9]**wont** Accustomed.

[10]**laws of demonstration** Bacon may be referring to Aristotle's logical system of syllogism and deduction.

[11]**received systems** Official or authorized views of scientific truth.

and unmatched, yet it devises for them parallels and conjugates and relatives[12] which do not exist. Hence the fiction that all celestial bodies move in perfect circles; spirals and dragons being (except in name) utterly rejected. Hence too the element of fire with its orb is brought in, to make up the square with the other three which the sense perceives. Hence also the ratio of density[13] of the so-called elements is arbitrarily fixed at ten to one. And so on of other dreams. And these fancies affect not dogmas only, but simple notions also.

The human understanding when it has once adopted an opinion   10 (either as being the received opinion or as being agreeable to itself) draws all things else to support and agree with it. And though there be a greater number and weight of instances to be found on the other side, yet these it either neglects and despises, or else by some distinction sets aside and rejects; in order that by this great and pernicious predetermination the authority of its former conclusions may remain inviolate. And therefore it was a good answer that was made by one who when they showed him hanging in a temple a picture of those who had paid their vows as having escaped shipwreck, and would have him say whether he did not now acknowledge the power of the gods—"Ay," asked he again, "but where are they painted that were drowned after their vows?" And such is the way of all superstition, whether in astrology, dreams, omens, divine judgments, or the like; wherein men having a delight in such vanities, mark the events where they are fulfilled, but where they fail, though this happen much oftener, neglect and pass them by. But with far more subtlety does this mischief insinuate itself into philosophy and the sciences; in which the first conclusion colors and brings into conformity with itself all that come after, though far sounder and better. Besides, independently of that delight and vanity which I have described, it is the peculiar and perpetual error of the human intellect to be more moved and excited by affirmatives than by negatives; whereas it ought properly to hold itself indifferently disposed towards both alike. Indeed, in the establishment of any true axiom, the negative instance is the more forcible of the two.

The human understanding is moved by those things most which   11 strike and enter the mind simultaneously and suddenly, and so fill the imagination; and then it feigns and supposes all other things to be somehow, though it cannot see how, similar to those few things by

---

[12] **parallels and conjugates and relatives** A reference to the habit of assuming that phenomena are regular and ordered, consisting of squares, triangles, circles, and other regular shapes.

[13] **ratio of density** The false assumption that the relationship of mass or weight to volume was ten to one. This is another example of Bacon's complaint, establishing a convenient regular "relative," or relationship.

which it is surrounded. But for that going to and fro to remote and heterogeneous instances, by which axioms are tried as in the fire,[14] the intellect is altogether slow and unfit, unless it be forced thereto by severe laws and overruling authority.

The human understanding is unquiet; it cannot stop or rest, and still presses onward, but in vain. Therefore it is that we cannot conceive of any end or limit to the world, but always as of necessity it occurs to us that there is something beyond. Neither again can it be conceived how eternity has flowed down to the present day; for that distinction which is commonly received of infinity in time past and in time to come can by no means hold; for it would thence follow that one infinity is greater than another, and that infinity is wasting away and tending to become finite. The like subtlety arises touching the infinite divisibility of lines,[15] from the same inability of thought to stop. But this inability interferes more mischievously in the discovery of causes:[16] for although the most general principles in nature ought to be held merely positive, as they are discovered, and cannot with truth be referred to a cause; nevertheless, the human understanding being unable to rest still seeks something prior in the order of nature. And then it is that in struggling towards that which is further off, it falls back upon that which is more nigh at hand; namely, on final causes: which have relation clearly to the nature of man rather than to the nature of the universe, and from this source have strangely defiled philosophy. But he is no less an unskilled and shallow philosopher who seeks causes of that which is most general, than he who in things subordinate and subaltern[17] omits to do so. 12

The human understanding is no dry light, but receives an infusion from the will and affections;[18] whence proceed sciences which may 13

---

[14] **tried as in the fire** Trial by fire is a figure of speech representing thorough, rigorous testing even to the point of risking what is tested. An axiom is a statement of apparent truth that has not yet been put to the test of examination and investigation.

[15] **infinite divisibility of lines** This gave rise to the paradox of Zeno, the Greek philosopher of the fifth century B.C.E. who showed that it was impossible to get from one point to another because one had to pass the midpoint of the line determined by the two original points, and then the midpoint of the remaining distance, and then of that remaining distance, down to an infinite number of points. By using accepted truths to "prove" an absurdity about motion, Zeno actually hoped to prove that motion itself did not exist. This is the "subtlety," or confusion, Bacon says is produced by the "inability of thought to stop."

[16] **discovery of causes** Knowledge of the world was based on four causes: efficient (who made it?), material (what is it made of?), formal (what is its shape?), and final (what is its purpose?). The scholastics concentrated their thinking on the first and last, whereas the "middle causes," related to matter and shape, were the proper subject matter of science because they alone yielded to observation. (See para. 34.)

[17] **subaltern** Lower in status.

[18] **will and affections** Human free will and emotional needs and responses.

be called "sciences as one would." For what a man had rather were true he more readily believes. Therefore he rejects difficult things from impatience of research; sober things, because they narrow hope; the deeper things of nature, from superstition; the light of experience, from arrogance and pride, lest his mind should seem to be occupied with things mean and transitory; things not commonly believed, out of deference to the opinion of the vulgar. Numberless in short are the ways, and sometimes imperceptible, in which the affections color and infect the understanding.

But by far the greatest hindrance and aberration of the human understanding proceeds from the dullness, incompetency, and deceptions of the senses; in that things which strike the sense outweigh things which do not immediately strike it, though they be more important. Hence it is that speculation commonly ceases where sight ceases; insomuch that of things invisible there is little or no observation. Hence all the working of the spirits[19] enclosed in tangible bodies lies hid and unobserved of men. So also all the more subtle changes of form in the parts of coarser substances (which they commonly call alteration, though it is in truth local motion through exceedingly small spaces) is in like manner unobserved. And yet unless these two things just mentioned be searched out and brought to light, nothing great can be achieved in nature, as far as the production of works is concerned. So again the essential nature of our common air, and of all bodies less dense than air (which are very many) is almost unknown. For the sense by itself is a thing infirm and erring; neither can instruments for enlarging or sharpening the senses do much; but all the truer kind of interpretation of nature is effected by instances and experiments fit and apposite;[20] wherein the sense decides touching the experiment only, and the experiment touching the point in nature and the thing itself.

The human understanding is of its own nature prone to abstractions and gives a substance and reality to things which are fleeting. But to resolve nature into abstractions is less to our purpose than to dissect her into parts; as did the school of Democritus,[21] which went further into nature than the rest. Matter rather than forms should be the object of our attention, its configurations and changes of configuration, and simple action, and law of action or motion; for forms are

14

15

---

[19] **spirits** The soul or animating force.

[20] **apposite** Appropriate; well related.

[21] **Democritus (460?–370? B.C.E.)** Greek philosopher who thought the world was composed of atoms. Bacon felt such "dissection" to be useless because it was impractical. Yet Democritus's concept of the *eidola*, the mind's impressions of things, may have contributed to Bacon's idea of "the idol."

figments of the human mind, unless you will call those laws of action forms.

Such then are the idols which I call *Idols of the Tribe;* and which   16
take their rise either from the homogeneity of the substance of the human spirit,[22] or from its preoccupation, or from its narrowness, or from its restless motion, or from an infusion of the affections, or from the incompetency of the senses, or from the mode of impression.

The *Idols of the Cave* take their rise in the peculiar constitution,   17
mental or bodily, of each individual; and also in education, habit, and accident. Of this kind there is a great number and variety; but I will instance those the pointing out of which contains the most important caution, and which have most effect in disturbing the clearness of the understanding.

Men become attached to certain particular sciences and specu-   18
lations, either because they fancy themselves the authors and inventors thereof, or because they have bestowed the greatest pains upon them and become most habituated to them. But men of this kind, if they betake themselves to philosophy and contemplations of a general character, distort and color them in obedience to their former fancies; a thing especially to be noticed in Aristotle,[23] who made his natural philosophy[24] a mere bondservant to his logic, thereby rendering it contentious and well nigh useless. The race of chemists[25] again out of a few experiments of the furnace have built up a fantastic philosophy, framed with reference to a few things; and Gilbert[26] also, after he had employed himself most laboriously in the study and observation of the loadstone, proceeded at once to construct an entire system in accordance with his favorite subject.

There is one principal and, as it were, radical distinction between   19
different minds, in respect of philosophy and the sciences, which is this: that some minds are stronger and apter to mark the differences of things, others to mark their resemblances. The steady and acute mind can fix its contemplations and dwell and fasten on the subtlest distinctions: the lofty and discursive mind recognizes and puts together

---

[22] **human spirit** Human nature.

[23] **Aristotle (384–322 B.C.E.)** Greek philosopher whose *Organon* (system of logic) dominated the thought of Bacon's time. Bacon sought to overthrow Aristotle's hold on science and thought.

[24] **natural philosophy** The scientific study of nature in general—biology, zoology, geology, and so on.

[25] **chemists** Alchemists had developed a "fantastic philosophy" from their experimental attempts to transmute lead into gold.

[26] **William Gilbert (1544–1603)** English scientist who studied magnetism and codified many laws related to magnetic fields. He was particularly ridiculed by Bacon for being too narrow in his researches.

the finest and most general resemblances. Both kinds however easily err in excess, by catching the one at gradations, the other at shadows.

There are found some minds given to an extreme admiration of antiquity, others to an extreme love and appetite for novelty; but few so duly tempered that they can hold the mean, neither carping at what has been well laid down by the ancients, nor despising what is well introduced by the moderns. This however turns to the great injury of the sciences and philosophy; since these affectations of antiquity and novelty are the humors[27] of partisans rather than judgments; and truth is to be sought for not in the felicity of any age, which is an unstable thing, but in the light of nature and experience, which is eternal. These factions therefore must be abjured,[28] and care must be taken that the intellect be not hurried by them into assent.   20

Contemplations of nature and of bodies in their simple form break up and distract the understanding, while contemplations of nature and bodies in their composition and configuration overpower and dissolve the understanding: a distinction well seen in the school of Leucippus[29] and Democritus as compared with the other philosophies. For that school is so busied with the particles that it hardly attends to the structure; while the others are so lost in admiration of the structure that they do not penetrate to the simplicity of nature. These kinds of contemplation should therefore be alternated and taken by turns; that so the understanding may be rendered at once penetrating and comprehensive, and the inconveniences above mentioned, with the idols which proceed from them, may be avoided.   21

Let such then be our provision and contemplative prudence for keeping off and dislodging the *Idols of the Cave*, which grow for the most part either out of the predominance of a favorite subject, or out of an excessive tendency to compare or to distinguish, or out of partiality for particular ages, or out of the largeness or minuteness of the objects contemplated. And generally let every student of nature take this as a rule — that whatever his mind seizes and dwells upon with peculiar satisfaction is to be held in suspicion, and that so much the more care is to be taken in dealing with such questions to keep the understanding even and clear.   22

But the *Idols of the Marketplace* are the most troublesome of all: idols which have crept into the understanding through the alliances of words and names. For men believe that their reason governs words; but it is also true that words react on the understanding; and this it is   23

---

[27] **humors** Used in a medical sense to mean a distortion caused by imbalance.
[28] **abjured** Renounced, sworn off, repudiated.
[29] **Leucippus (fifth century B.C.E.)** Greek philosopher; teacher of Democritus and inventor of the atomistic theory. His works survive only in fragments.

that has rendered philosophy and the sciences sophistical and inactive. Now words, being commonly framed and applied according to the capacity of the vulgar, follow those lines of division which are most obvious to the vulgar understanding. And whenever an understanding of greater acuteness or a more diligent observation would alter those lines to suit the true divisions of nature, words stand in the way and resist the change. Whence it comes to pass that the high and formal discussions of learned men end oftentimes in disputes about words and names; with which (according to the use and wisdom of the mathematicians) it would be more prudent to begin, and so by means of definitions reduce them to order. Yet even definitions cannot cure this evil in dealing with natural and material things; since the definitions themselves consist of words, and those words beget others: so that it is necessary to recur to individual instances, and those in due series and order; as I shall say presently when I come to the method and scheme for the formation of notions and axioms.[30]

The idols imposed by words on the understanding are of two   24
kinds. They are either names of things which do not exist (for as there are things left unnamed through lack of observation, so likewise are there names which result from fantastic suppositions and to which nothing in reality responds), or they are names of things which exist, but yet confused and ill-defined, and hastily and irregularly derived from realities. Of the former kind are Fortune, the Prime Mover, Planetary Orbits, Element of Fire, and like fictions which owe their origin to false and idle theories.[31] And this class of idols is more easily expelled, because to get rid of them it is only necessary that all theories should be steadily rejected and dismissed as obsolete.

But the other class, which springs out of a faulty and unskillful   25
abstraction, is intricate and deeply rooted. Let us take for example such a word as *humid,* and see how far the several things which the word is used to signify agree with each other; and we shall find the word *humid* to be nothing else than a mark loosely and confusedly applied to denote a variety of actions which will not bear to be reduced to any constant meaning. For it both signifies that which easily spreads itself round any other body; and that which in itself is indeterminate and cannot solidize; and that which readily yields in every direction; and that which easily divides and scatters itself;

---

[30] **notions and axioms** Conceptions and definitive statements of truth.

[31] **idle theories** These are things that cannot be observed and thus do not exist. Fortune is fate; the Prime Mover is God or some "first" force; the notion that planets orbited the sun was considered as "fantastic" as these others or as the idea that everything was made up of fire and its many permutations.

and that which easily unites and collects itself; and that which readily flows and is put in motion; and that which readily clings to another body and wets it; and that which is easily reduced to a liquid, or being solid easily melts. Accordingly when you come to apply the word—if you take it in one sense, flame is humid; if in another, air is not humid; if in another, fine dust is humid; if in another, glass is humid. So that it is easy to see that the notion is taken by abstraction only from water and common and ordinary liquids, without any due verification.

There are however in words certain degrees of distortion and error. One of the least faulty kinds is that of names of substances, especially of lowest species and well-deduced (for the notion of *chalk* and of *mud* is good, of *earth* bad);[32] a more faulty kind is that of actions, as *to generate, to corrupt, to alter;* the most faulty is of qualities (except such as are the immediate objects of the sense), as *heavy, light, rare, dense,* and the like. Yet in all these cases some notions are of necessity a little better than others, in proportion to the greater variety of subjects that fall within the range of the human sense.   26

But the *Idols of the Theater* are not innate, nor do they steal into the understanding secretly, but are plainly impressed and received into the mind from the play-books of philosophical systems and the perverted rules of demonstration.[33] To attempt refutations in this case would be merely inconsistent with what I have already said: for since we agree neither upon principles nor upon demonstrations, there is no place for argument. And this is so far well, inasmuch as it leaves the honor of the ancients untouched. For they are no wise disparaged—the question between them and me being only as to the way. For as the saying is, the lame man who keeps the right road outstrips the runner who takes a wrong one. Nay, it is obvious that when a man runs the wrong way, the more active and swift he is the further he will go astray.   27

But the course I propose for the discovery of sciences is such as leaves but little to the acuteness and strength of wits, but places all wits[34] and understandings nearly on a level. For as in the drawing of a straight line or perfect circle, much depends on the steadiness and practice of the hand, if it be done by aim of hand only, but if with the aid of rule or compass, little or nothing; so is it exactly with my plan.   28

---

[32] *earth* **bad** Chalk and mud were useful in manufacture; hence they were terms of approval. *Earth* is used here in the sense we use *dirt*, as in "digging in the dirt."

[33] **perverted rules of demonstration** Another complaint against Aristotle's logic as misapplied in Bacon's day.

[34] **wits** Intelligence, powers of reasoning.

But though particular confutations[35] would be of no avail, yet touching the sects and general divisions of such systems I must say something; something also touching the external signs which show that they are unsound; and finally something touching the causes of such great infelicity and of such lasting and general agreement in error; that so the access to truth may be made less difficult, and the human understanding may the more willingly submit to its purgation and dismiss its idols.

Idols of the Theater, or of systems, are many, and there can be and 29
perhaps will be yet many more. For were it not that now for many ages men's minds have been busied with religion and theology; and were it not that civil governments, especially monarchies, have been averse to such novelties, even in matters speculative; so that men labor therein to the peril and harming of their fortunes—not only unrewarded, but exposed also to contempt and envy; doubtless there would have arisen many other philosophical sects like to those which in great variety flourished once among the Greeks. For as on the phenomena of the heavens many hypotheses may be constructed, so likewise (and more also) many various dogmas may be set up and established on the phenomena of philosophy. And in the plays of this philosophical theater you may observe the same thing which is found in the theater of the poets, that stories invented for the stage are more compact and elegant, and more as one would wish them to be, than true stories out of history.

In general, however, there is taken for the material of philosophy 30
either a great deal out of a few things, or a very little out of many things; so that on both sides philosophy is based on too narrow a foundation of experiment and natural history, and decides on the authority of too few cases. For the rational school of philosophers[36] snatches from experience a variety of common instances, neither duly ascertained nor diligently examined and weighed, and leaves all the rest to meditation and agitation of wit.

There is also another class of philosophers,[37] who having 31
bestowed much diligent and careful labor on a few experiments, have

---

[35] **confutations** Specific counterarguments. Bacon means that he cannot offer particular arguments against each scientific sect; thus he offers a general warning.

[36] **rational school of philosophers** Platonists who felt that human reason alone could discover the truth and that experiment was unnecessary. Their observation of experience produced only a "variety of common instances" from which they reasoned.

[37] **another class of philosophers** William Gilbert (1544–1603) experimented tirelessly with magnetism, from which he derived numerous odd theories. Though Gilbert was a true scientist, Bacon thought of him as limited and on the wrong track.

thence made bold to educe and construct systems; wresting all other facts in a strange fashion to conformity therewith.

And there is yet a third class,[38] consisting of those who out of   32 faith and veneration mix their philosophy with theology and traditions; among whom the vanity of some has gone so far aside as to seek the origin of sciences among spirits and genii.[39] So that this parent stock of errors—this false philosophy—is of three kinds: the sophistical, the empirical, and the superstitious. . . .

But the corruption of philosophy by superstition and an admix-   33 ture of theology is far more widely spread, and does the greatest harm, whether to entire systems or to their parts. For the human understanding is obnoxious to the influence of the imagination no less than to the influence of common notions. For the contentious and sophistical kind of philosophy ensnares the understanding; but this kind, being fanciful and tumid[40] and half poetical, misleads it more by flattery. For there is in man an ambition of the understanding, no less than of the will, especially in high and lofty spirits.

Of this kind we have among the Greeks a striking example in   34 Pythagoras, though he united with it a coarser and more cumbrous superstition; another in Plato and his school,[41] more dangerous and subtle. It shows itself likewise in parts of other philosophies, in the introduction of abstract forms and final causes and first causes, with the omission in most cases of causes intermediate, and the like. Upon this point the greatest caution should be used. For nothing is so mischievous as the apotheosis of error; and it is a very plague of the understanding for vanity to become the object of veneration. Yet in this vanity some of the moderns have with extreme levity indulged so far as to attempt to found a system of natural philosophy on the first chapter of Genesis, on the book of Job, and other parts of the sacred writings; seeking for the dead among the living: which also makes the inhibition and repression of it the more important, because from this unwholesome mixture of things human and divine there arises not only a fantastic philosophy but also an heretical religion. Very meet

---

[38] **a third class** Pythagoras (c. 580–500 B.C.E.) was a Greek philosopher who experimented rigorously with mathematics and a tuned string. He is said to have developed the musical scale. His theory of reincarnation, or the transmigration of souls, was somehow based on his travels in India and his work with scales. The superstitious belief in the movement of souls is what Bacon complains of.

[39] **genii** Oriental demons or spirits; a slap at Pythagoras, who traveled in the Orient.

[40] **tumid** Overblown, swollen.

[41] **Plato and his school** Plato's religious bent was further developed by Plotinus (205–270 C.E.) in his *Enneads*. Although Plotinus was not a Christian, his Neo-Platonism was welcomed as a philosophy compatible with Christianity.

it is therefore that we be sober-minded, and give to faith that only which is faith's. . . .

So much concerning the several classes of Idols, and their equipage: all of which must be renounced and put away with a fixed and solemn determination, and the understanding thoroughly freed and cleansed; the entrance into the kingdom of man, founded on the sciences, being not much other than the entrance into the kingdom of heaven, whereunto none may enter except as a little child.

35

QUESTIONS FOR CRITICAL READING

1. Which of Bacon's idols is the most difficult to understand? Do your best to define it.

2. Which of these idols do we still need to worry about? Why? What dangers does it present?

3. What does Bacon mean by implying that our senses are weak (para. 14)? In what ways do you agree or disagree with that opinion?

4. Occasionally Bacon says something that seems a bit like an aphorism (see the introduction to Machiavelli, p. 219). Find at least one such expression in this selection. On examination, does the expression have as much meaning as it seems to have?

5. What kind of readers did Bacon expect for this piece? What clues does his way of communicating provide regarding the nature of his anticipated readers?

SUGGESTIONS FOR CRITICAL WRITING

1. Which of Bacon's idols most seriously affects the way you as a person observe nature? Using enumeration, arrange the idols in order of their effect on your own judgment. If you prefer, you may write about the idol you believe is most effective in slowing investigation into nature.

2. Is it true, as Bacon says in paragraph 10, that people are in general "more moved and excited by affirmatives than by negatives"? Do we really stress the positive and de-emphasize the negative in the conduct of our general affairs? Find at least three instances in which people seem to gravitate toward the positive or the negative in everyday situations. Try to establish whether Bacon has, in fact, described what is a habit of mind.

3. In paragraph 13, Bacon states that the "will and affections" enter into matters of thought. By this he means that our understanding of what we observe is conditioned by what we want and what we feel. Thus, when he says, "For what a man had rather were true he more readily believes," he tells us that people tend to believe what they want to believe. Test this statement by means of observation. Find out, for example, how many older people are convinced that the world is deteriorating, how many younger people feel that there is a plot on the part of older people to hold them back, how many women feel that men consciously oppress women, and how many men feel that feminists are not as feminine as they should be. What other beliefs can you discover that seem to have their origin in what people want to believe rather than in what is true?

4. Bacon's views on religion have always been difficult to define. He grew up in a very religious time, but his writings rarely discuss religion positively. In this work, he talks about giving "to faith that only which is faith's" (para. 34). He seems to feel that scientific investigation is something quite separate from religion. Examine the selection carefully to determine what you think Bacon's view on this question is. Then take a stand on the issue of the relationship between religion and science. Should science be totally independent of religious concerns? Should religious issues control scientific experimentation? What does Bacon mean when he complains about the vanity of founding "a system of natural philosophy on the first chapter of Genesis, on the book of Job, and other parts of the sacred writings" (para. 34)? "Natural philosophy" means biology, chemistry, physics, and science in general. Are Bacon's complaints justified? Would his complaints be relevant today?

5. **CONNECTIONS** How has the reception of Charles Darwin's work been affected by a general inability of the public to see beyond Bacon's four idols? Read both Darwin's essay (p. 897) and that of Germaine Greer (p. 725). Which of these two writers is more concerned with the lingering effects of the four idols? Do you feel that the effects have seriously affected people's beliefs regarding Darwinian theory?

6. **CONNECTIONS** How does Descartes (**bedfordstmartins.com /worldofideas/epages**) rate in dealing with the four idols? Which of these idols is most important to avoid if one, like Descartes, wishes to avoid reasoning based on sensory evidence? Bacon was not interested in avoiding sensory evidence; which of Descartes' positions would Bacon most take issue with? How would he advise him in constructing his method of finding the truth? Does Bacon, like Descartes, try to find a single unassailable idea or principle from which to argue his position? Were they to converse, would Bacon and Descartes be likely to mostly agree or mostly disagree with each other?

7. **SEEING CONNECTIONS** Salvador Dalí's *The Persistence of Memory* (p. 861) is purposely unrealistic. What would Bacon have said about how we perceive the objects in the painting? What in our mental processes prevents us from believing what we see? Why is surrealism a threat to our fundamental way of understanding? Which visual elements of the painting would Bacon say are the "affirmatives" and which the "negatives"? Would Bacon be excited at the possibility of this painting illustrating the basic principles of his theory of the idols? In what sense are the objects in the painting susceptible to Bacon's four idols? Which idol is most important as a test for responding to this painting? Which is most important for helping us understand the painting?

CHARLES DARWIN
Natural Selection

CHARLES DARWIN (1809–1882) was trained as a minister
in the Church of England, but he was also the grandson of one of
England's greatest horticulturists, Erasmus Darwin. Partly as a way of
putting off ordination in the church and partly because of his natural
curiosity, Darwin found himself performing the functions of a naturalist on HMS *Beagle*, which was engaged in scientific explorations
around South America during the years 1831 to 1836. Darwin's book
*Journal of Researches into the Geology and Natural History of the Var-
ious Countries Visited by H. M. S. Beagle, 1832–36* (1839) details the
experiences he had and offers some views of his self-education as a
naturalist.

His journeys on the *Beagle* led him to note variations in species of animals he found in various separate locales, particularly
between remote islands and the mainland. Varieties—his term for
any visible (or invisible) differences in markings, coloration, size,
or shape of appendages, organs, or bodies—were of some peculiar
use, he believed, for animals in the environment in which he found
them. He was not certain about the use of these varieties, and he
did not know whether the changes that created the varieties resulted
from the environment or from some chance operation of nature.
Ultimately, he concluded that varieties in nature were caused by
three forces: (1) natural selection, in which varieties occur spontaneously by chance but are then "selected for" because they are aids

From *On the Origin of Species by Means of Natural Selection*. This text is from
the first edition, published in 1859. In the five subsequent editions, Darwin hedged
more and more on his theory, often introducing material in defense against objections. The first edition is vigorous and direct; this edition jolted the worlds of science and religion out of their complacence. In later editions, this chapter was titled
"Natural Selection; or, Survival of the Fittest."

to survival; (2) direct action of the environment, in which non-adaptive varieties do not survive because of climate, food conditions, or the like; and (3) the effects of use or disuse of a variation (for example, the short beak of a bird mentioned in para. 9). Darwin later regarded sexual selection, which figures prominently in this work, as less significant.

The idea of evolution—the gradual change of species through some kind of modification of varieties—had been in the air for many years when Darwin began his work. The English scientists W. C. Wells in 1813 and Patrick Matthew in 1831 had both proposed theories of natural selection, although Darwin was unaware of their work. Alfred Russel Wallace (1823–1913), a younger English scientist, revealed in 1858 that he was about to propose the same theory of evolution as was Darwin. They jointly published brief versions of their theories in 1858, and the next year Darwin rushed the final version of his book *On the Origin of Species by Means of Natural Selection* to press.

Darwin did not mention human beings as part of the evolutionary process in *On the Origin of Species*; because he was particularly concerned about the probable adverse reactions of theologians, he merely promised later discussion of that subject. It came in *The Descent of Man and Selection in Relation to Sex* (1871), the companion to *On the Origin of Species*.

When Darwin returned to England after completing his research on the *Beagle*, he supplemented his knowledge with information gathered from breeders of pigeons, livestock, dogs, and horses. This research, it must be noted, involved relatively few samples and was conducted according to comparatively unscientific practices. Yet although limited, it corresponded with his observations of nature. Humans could and did cause changes in species; Darwin's task was to show that nature—through the process of natural selection—could do the same thing.

The Descent of Man stirred up a great deal of controversy between the church and Darwin's supporters. Not since the Roman Catholic Church denied the fact that the earth went around the sun, which Galileo proved scientifically by 1632 (and was placed under house arrest for his pains), had there been a more serious confrontation between science and religion. Darwin was ridiculed by ministers and doubted by older scientists; but his views were stoutly defended by younger scientists, many of whom had arrived at similar conclusions. In the end, Darwin's views were accepted by the Church of England, and when he died in 1882 he was lionized and buried at Westminster Abbey in London. Only recently has controversy concerning his work arisen again.

Darwin's Rhetoric

Despite the complexity of the material it deals with, Darwin's writing is fluent, smooth, and stylistically sophisticated and keeps the reader engaged. Darwin's rhetorical method depends entirely on the yoking of thesis and demonstration. He uses definition frequently, but most often he uses testimony, gathering information and instances, both real and imaginary, from many different sources.

Interestingly enough, Darwin claimed that he used Francis Bacon's method of induction in his research, gathering evidence of many instances of a given phenomenon, from which the truth—or a natural law—emerges. In fact, Darwin did not quite follow this path. Like most modern scientists, he established a hypothesis after a period of observation, and then he looked for evidence that confirmed or refuted the hypothesis. He was careful to include examples that argued against his view, but like most scientists, he emphasized the importance of the supportive samples.

Induction plays a part in the rhetoric of this selection in that it is dominated by examples from bird breeding, birds in nature, domestic farm animals and their breeding, and botany, including the breeding of plants and the interdependence of certain insects and certain plants. Erasmus Darwin was famous for his work with plants, and it is natural that such observations would play an important part in his grandson's thinking.

The process of natural selection is carefully discussed, particularly in paragraph 8 and thereafter. Darwin emphasizes its positive nature and its differences from selection by human breeders. The use of comparison, which appears frequently in the selection, is most conspicuous in these paragraphs. He postulates a nature in which the fittest survive because they are best adapted for survival, but he does not dwell on the fate of those who are unfit individuals. It was left to later writers, often misapplying his theories, to do that.

PREREADING QUESTIONS:
WHAT TO READ FOR

The following prereading questions may help you anticipate key issues in the discussion of Charles Darwin's "Natural Selection." Keeping them in mind during your first reading of the selection should help focus your attention.

- What is the basic principle of natural selection?
- How does "human" selection differ from nature's selection?

Natural Selection

How will the struggle for existence . . . act in regard to variation?   1
Can the principle of selection, which we have seen is so potent in the
hands of man, apply in nature? I think we shall see that it can act
most effectually. Let it be borne in mind in what an endless number of
strange peculiarities our domestic productions, and, in a lesser degree,
those under nature, vary; and how strong the hereditary tendency is.
Under domestication, it may be truly said that the whole organization
becomes in some degree plastic.[1] Let it be borne in mind how infinitely complex and close-fitting are the mutual relations of all organic
beings to each other and to their physical conditions of life. Can it,
then, be thought improbable, seeing that variations useful to man have
undoubtedly occurred, that other variations useful in some way to
each being in the great and complex battle of life, should sometimes
occur in the course of thousands of generations? If such do occur, can
we doubt (remembering that many more individuals are born than
can possibly survive) that individuals having any advantage, however
slight, over others, would have the best chance of surviving and or
procreating their kind? On the other hand, we may feel sure that any
variation in the least degree injurious would be rigidly destroyed. This
preservation of favorable variations and the rejection of injurious variations, I call Natural Selection. Variations neither useful nor injurious
would not be affected by natural selection, and would be left a fluctuating element, as perhaps we see in the species called polymorphic.[2]

We shall best understand the probable course of natural selec-   2
tion by taking the case of a country undergoing some physical change,
for instance, of climate. The proportional numbers of its inhabitants
would almost immediately undergo a change, and some species might
become extinct. We may conclude, from what we have seen of the intimate and complex manner in which the inhabitants of each country
are bound together, that any change in the numerical proportions of
some of the inhabitants, independently of the change of climate itself,
would most seriously affect many of the others. If the country were
open on its borders, new forms would certainly immigrate, and this
also would seriously disturb the relations of some of the former inhabitants. Let it be remembered how powerful the influence of a single
introduced tree or mammal has been shown to be. But in the case of an
island, or of a country partly surrounded by barriers, into which new

---

[1] **plastic** Capable of being shaped and changed.
[2] **species called polymorphic** Species that have more than one form over the
course of their lives, such as butterflies.

and better adapted forms could not freely enter, we should then have places in the economy of nature which would assuredly be better filled up, if some of the original inhabitants were in some manner modified; for, had the area been open to immigration, these same places would have been seized on by intruders. In such case, every slight modification, which in the course of ages chanced to arise, and which in any way favored the individuals of any of the species, by better adapting them to their altered conditions, would tend to be preserved; and natural selection would thus have free scope for the work of improvement.

We have reason to believe . . . that a change in the conditions **3** of life, by specially acting on the reproductive system, causes or increases variability; and in the foregoing case the conditions of life are supposed to have undergone a change, and this would manifestly be favorable to natural selection, by giving a better chance of profitable variations occurring; and unless profitable variations do occur, natural selection can do nothing. Not that, as I believe, any extreme amount of variability is necessary; as man can certainly produce great results by adding up in any given direction mere individual differences, so could Nature, but far more easily, from having incomparably longer time at her disposal. Nor do I believe that any great physical change, as of climate, or any unusual degree of isolation to check immigration, is actually necessary to produce new and unoccupied places for natural selection to fill up by modifying and improving some of the varying inhabitants. For as all the inhabitants of each country are struggling together with nicely balanced forces, extremely slight modifications in the structure or habits of one inhabitant would often give it an advantage over others; and still further modifications of the same kind would often still further increase the advantage. No country can be named in which all the native inhabitants are now so perfectly adapted to each other and to the physical conditions under which they live, that none of them could anyhow be improved; for in all countries, the natives have been so far conquered by naturalized productions, that they have allowed foreigners to take firm possession of the land. And as foreigners have thus everywhere beaten some of the natives, we may safely conclude that the natives might have been modified with advantage, so as to have better resisted such intruders.

As man can produce and certainly has produced a great result **4** by his methodical and unconscious means of selection, what may not nature effect? Man can act only on external and visible characters; nature cares nothing for appearances, except in so far as they may be useful to any being. She can act on every internal organ, on every shade of constitutional difference, on the whole machinery of life. Man selects only for his own good; Nature only for that of the being which she tends. Every selected character is fully exercised by her; and the being is placed under well-suited conditions of life. Man keeps the natives of many climates in the same country; he seldom exercises each selected character in some peculiar and fitting manner; he feeds a long and a short beaked pigeon on the same food; he does not exercise a long-backed or long-legged quadruped in any peculiar manner; he exposes sheep with long and short wool to the same climate. He does not allow the most vigorous males to struggle for the females. He does not rigidly destroy all inferior animals, but protects during each varying season, as far as lies in his power, all his productions. He often begins his selection by some half-monstrous form; or at least by some modification prominent enough to catch the eye, or to be plainly useful to him. Under nature, the slightest difference of structure or constitution may well turn the nicely balanced scale in the struggle for life, and so be preserved. How fleeting are the wishes and efforts of man! how short his time! and consequently how poor will his products be, compared with those accumulated by nature during whole geological periods. Can we wonder, then, that nature's productions should be far "truer" in character than man's productions; that they should be infinitely better adapted to the most complex conditions of life, and should plainly bear the stamp of far higher workmanship?

It may be said that natural selection is daily and hourly scrutinizing, throughout the world, every variation, even the slightest; rejecting that which is bad, preserving and adding up all that is good; silently and insensibly working, whenever and wherever opportunity offers, at the improvement of each organic being in relation to its organic and inorganic conditions of life. We see nothing of these slow changes in progress, until the hand of time has marked the long lapse of ages, and then so imperfect is our view into long past geological ages, that we only see that the forms of life are now different from what they formerly were.

Although natural selection can act only through and for the good of each being, yet characters and structures, which we are apt to consider as of very trifling importance, may thus be acted on. When we see leaf-eating insects green, and bark-feeders mottled-grey; the alpine ptarmigan white in winter, the red-grouse the color of heather, and the black-grouse that of peaty earth, we must believe that these tints are of service to these birds and insects in preserving them from danger. Grouse, if not destroyed at some period of their lives, would increase in countless numbers; they are known to suffer largely from birds of prey; and hawks are guided by eyesight to their prey—so much so that on parts of the Continent[3] persons are warned not to keep

---

[3] **Continent** European continent; the contiguous landmass of Europe, which excludes the British Isles.

white pigeons, as being the most liable to destruction. Hence I can see no reason to doubt that natural selection might be most effective in giving the proper color to each kind of grouse, and in keeping that color, when once acquired, true and constant. Nor ought we to think that the occasional destruction of an animal of any particular color would produce little effect; we should remember how essential it is in a flock of white sheep to destroy every lamb with the faintest trace of black. In plants, the down on the fruit and the color of the flesh are considered by botanists as characters of the most trifling importance; yet we hear from an excellent horticulturist, Downing,[4] that in the United States, smooth-skinned fruits suffer far more from a beetle, a curculio,[5] than those with down; that purple plums suffer far more from a certain disease than yellow plums; whereas another disease attacks yellow-fleshed peaches far more than those with other colored flesh. If, with all the aids of art, these slight differences make a great difference in cultivating the several varieties, assuredly, in a state of nature, where the trees would have to struggle with other trees and with a host of enemies, such differences would effectually settle which variety, whether a smooth or downy, a yellow or purple fleshed fruit, should succeed.

In looking at many small points of difference between species, which, as far as our ignorance permits us to judge, seem to be quite unimportant, we must not forget that climate, food, etc., probably produce some slight and direct effect. It is, however, far more necessary to bear in mind that there are many unknown laws of correlation[6] of growth, which, when one part of the organization is modified through variation and the modifications are accumulated by natural selection for the good of the being, will cause other modifications, often of the most unexpected nature. 7

As we see that those variations which under domestication appear at any particular period of life, tend to reappear in the offspring at the same period—for instance, in the seeds of the many varieties of our culinary and agricultural plants; in the caterpillar and cocoon stages of the varieties of the silkworm; in the eggs of poultry, and in the color of the down of their chickens; in the horns of our sheep and cattle when nearly adult—so in a state of nature, natural selection will be enabled to act on and modify organic beings at any age, by the accumulation of profitable variations at that age, and by their inheritance at a corresponding age. If it profit a plant to have its seeds more and more widely disseminated by the wind, I can see no greater difficulty in this 8

---

[4] **Andrew Jackson Downing (1815–1852)** American horticulturist and specialist in fruit and fruit trees.

[5] **curculio** A weevil.

[6] **laws of correlation** In certain plants and animals, one condition relates to another, as in the case of blue-eyed white cats, which are often deaf; the reasons are not clear but have to do with genes and their locations.

being effected through natural selection than in the cotton-planter increasing and improving by selection the down in the pods on his cotton-trees. Natural selection may modify and adapt the larva of an insect to a score of contingencies, wholly different from those which concern the mature insect. These modifications will no doubt effect, through the laws of correlation, the structure of the adult; and probably in the case of those insects which live only for a few hours, and which never feed, a large part of their structure is merely the correlated result of successive changes in the structure of their larvae. So, conversely, modifications in the adult will probably often affect the structure of the larva; but in all cases natural selection will ensure that modifications consequent on other modifications at a different period of life, shall not be in the least degree injurious: for if they became so, they would cause the extinction of the species.

Natural selection will modify the structure of the young in relation to the parent, and of the parent in relation to the young. In social animals it will adapt the structure of each individual for the benefit of the community, if each in consequence profits by the selected change. What natural selection cannot do is to modify the structure of one species, without giving it any advantage, for the good of another species; and though statements to this effect may be found in works of natural history, I cannot find one case which will bear investigation. A structure used only once in an animal's whole life, if of high importance to it, might be modified to any extent by natural selection; for instance, the great jaws possessed by certain insects, and used exclusively for opening the cocoon—or the hard tip to the beak of nestling birds, used for breaking the egg. It has been asserted that of the best short-beaked tumbler-pigeons, more perish in the egg than are able to get out of it; so that fanciers[7] assist in the act of hatching. Now, if nature had to make the beak of a full-grown pigeon very short for the bird's own advantage, the process of modification would be very slow, and there would be simultaneously the most rigorous selection of the young birds within the egg, which had the most powerful and hardest beaks, for all with weak beaks would inevitably perish; or, more delicate and more easily broken shells might be selected, the thickness of the shell being known to vary like every other structure. 9

Sexual Selection

Inasmuch as peculiarities often appear under domestication in one sex and become hereditarily attached to that sex, the same fact 10

---

[7]**fanciers** Amateurs who raise and race pigeons.

probably occurs under nature, and if so, natural selection will be able to modify one sex in its functional relations to the other sex, or in relation to wholly different habits of life in the two sexes, as is sometimes the case with insects. And this leads me to say a few words on what I call Sexual Selection. This depends, not on a struggle for existence, but on a struggle between the males for possession of the females; the result is not death to the unsuccessful competitor, but few or no offspring. Sexual selection is, therefore, less rigorous than natural selection. Generally, the most vigorous males, those which are best fitted for their places in nature, will leave most progeny. But in many cases, victory will depend not on general vigor, but on having special weapons, confined to the male sex. A hornless stag or spurless cock would have a poor chance of leaving offspring. Sexual selection by always allowing the victor to breed might surely give indomitable courage, length to the spur, and strength to the wing to strike in the spurred leg, as well as the brutal cock fighter,[8] who knows well that he can improve his breed by careful selection of the best cocks. How low in the scale of nature this law of battle descends, I know not; male alligators have been described as fighting, bellowing, and whirling round, like Indians in a wardance, for the possession of the females; male salmons have been seen fighting all day long; male stag-beetles often bear wounds from the huge mandibles[9] of other males. The war is, perhaps, severest between the males of polygamous animals,[10] and these seem oftenest provided with special weapons. The males of carnivorous animals are already well armed; though to them and to others, special means of defense may be given through means of sexual selection, as the mane to the lion, the shoulder-pad to the boar, and the hooked jaw to the male salmon; for the shield may be as important for victory as the sword or spear.

Among birds, the contest is often of a more peaceful character. All those who have attended to the subject believe that there is the severest rivalry between the males of many species to attract, by singing, the females. The rock-thrush of Guiana,[11] birds of paradise, and some others, congregate; and successive males display their gorgeous plumage and perform strange antics before the females, which standing by as spectators, at last choose the most attractive partner. Those who

11

---

[8] **brutal cock fighter** Cockfights were a popular spectator sport in England, especially for gamblers, but many people considered them a horrible brutality.

[9] **mandibles** Jaws.

[10] **polygamous animals** Animals that typically have more than one mate.

[11] **Guiana** Formerly British Guiana, now Guyana, on the northeast coast of South America.

have closely attended to birds in confinement well know that they often take individual preferences and dislikes: thus Sir R. Heron[12] has described how one pied peacock was eminently attractive to all his hen birds. It may appear childish to attribute any effect to such apparently weak means: I cannot here enter on the details necessary to support this view; but if man can in a short time give elegant carriage and beauty to his bantams,[13] according to his standard of beauty, I can see no good reason to doubt that female birds, by selecting, during thousands of generations, the most melodious or beautiful males, according to their standard of beauty, might produce a marked effect. I strongly suspect that some well-known laws with respect to the plumage of male and female birds, in comparison with the plumage of the young, can be explained on the view of plumage having been chiefly modified by sexual selection, acting when the birds have come to the breeding age or during the breeding season; the modifications thus produced being inherited at corresponding ages or seasons, either by the males alone, or by the males and females; but I have not space here to enter on this subject.

Thus it is, as I believe, that when the males and females of any animal have the same general habits of life, but differ in structure, color, or ornament, such differences have been mainly caused by sexual selection; that is, individual males have had, in successive generations, some slight advantage over other males, in their weapons, means of defense, or charms; and have transmitted these advantages to their male offspring. Yet, I would not wish to attribute all such sexual differences to this agency: for we see peculiarities arising and becoming attached to the male sex in our domestic animals (as the wattle in male carriers, horn-like protuberances in the cocks of certain fowls, etc.), which we cannot believe to be either useful to the males in battle, or attractive to the females. We see analogous cases under nature, for instance, the tuft of hair on the breast of the turkey-cock, which can hardly be either useful or ornamental to this bird; indeed, had the tuft appeared under domestication, it would have been called a monstrosity.

Illustrations of the Action of Natural Selection

In order to make it clear how, as I believe, natural selection acts, I must beg permission to give one or two imaginary illustrations. Let us

---

[12] **Sir Robert Heron (1765–1854)** English politician who maintained a menagerie of animals.

[13] **bantams** Cocks bred for fighting.

take the case of a wolf, which preys on various animals, securing some by craft, some by strength, and some by fleetness; and let us suppose that the fleetest prey, a deer for instance, had from any change in the country increased in numbers, or that other prey had decreased in numbers, during that season of the year when the wolf is hardest pressed for food. I can under such circumstances see no reason to doubt that the swiftest and slimmest wolves would have the best chance of surviving, and so be preserved or selected, provided always that they retained strength to master their prey at this or at some other period of the year, when they might be compelled to prey on other animals. I can see no more reason to doubt this, than that man can improve the fleetness of his greyhounds by careful and methodical selection, or by that unconscious selection which results from each man trying to keep the best dogs without any thought of modifying the breed.

Even without any change in the proportional numbers of the animals on which our wolf preyed, a cub might be born with an innate tendency to pursue certain kinds of prey. Nor can this be thought very improbable; for we often observe great differences in the natural tendencies of our domestic animals; one cat, for instance, taking to catch rats, another mice; one cat, according to Mr. St. John,[14] bringing home winged game, another hares or rabbits, and another hunting on marshy ground and almost nightly catching woodcocks or snipes. The tendency to catch rats rather than mice is known to be inherited. Now, if any slight innate change of habit or of structure benefited an individual wolf, it would have the best chance of surviving and of leaving offspring. Some of its young would probably inherit the same habits or structure, and by the repetition of this process, a new variety might be formed which would either supplant or coexist with the parent-form of wolf. Or, again, the wolves inhabiting a mountainous district, and those frequenting the lowlands, would naturally be forced to hunt different prey; and from the continued preservation of the individuals best fitted for the two sites, two varieties might slowly be formed. These varieties would cross and blend where they met; but to this subject of intercrossing we shall soon have to return. I may add, that, according to Mr. Pierce,[15] there are two varieties of the wolf inhabiting the Catskill Mountains in the United States, one with a light greyhound-like form, which pursues deer, and the other more

14

---

[14] **Charles George William St. John (1809–1856)** English naturalist whose book *Wild Sports and Natural History of the Highlands* was published in 1846.
[15] **Mr. Pierce** Unidentified.

bulky, with shorter legs, which more frequently attacks the shepherd's flocks.

Let us now take a more complex case. Certain plants excrete a [15] sweet juice, apparently for the sake of eliminating something injurious from their sap; this is effected by glands at the base of the stipules[16] in some Leguminosae, and at the back of the leaf of the common laurel. This juice, though small in quantity, is greedily sought by insects. Let us now suppose a little sweet juice or nectar to be excreted by the inner bases of the petals of a flower. In this case insects in seeking the nectar would get dusted with pollen, and would certainly often transport the pollen from one flower to the stigma of another flower. The flowers of two distinct individuals of the same species would thus get crossed; and the act of crossing, we have good reason to believe (as will hereafter be more fully alluded to), would produce very vigorous seedlings, which consequently would have the best chance of flourishing and surviving. Some of these seedlings would probably inherit the nectar-excreting power. Those individual flowers which had the largest glands or nectaries, and which excreted most nectar, would be oftenest visited by insects, and would be oftenest crossed; and so in the long-run would gain the upper hand. Those flowers, also, which had their stamens and pistils[17] placed, in relation to the size and habits of the particular insects which visited them, so as to favor in any degree the transportal of their pollen from flower to flower, would likewise be favored or selected. We might have taken the case of insects visiting flowers for the sake of collecting pollen instead of nectar; and as pollen is formed for the sole object of fertilization, its destruction appears a simple loss to the plant; yet if a little pollen were carried, at first occasionally and then habitually, by the pollen-devouring insects from flower to flower, and a cross thus effected, although nine-tenths of the pollen were destroyed, it might still be a great gain to the plant; and those individuals which produced more and more pollen, and had larger and larger anthers,[18] would be selected.

When our plant, by this process of the continued preservation or [16] natural selection of more and more attractive flowers, had been rendered highly attractive to insects, they would, unintentionally on their part, regularly carry pollen from flower to flower; and that they can most effectually do this, I could easily show by many striking instances.

---

[16] **stipules** Spines at the base of a leaf.

[17] **stamens and pistils** Sexual organs of plants. The male and female organs appear together in the same flower.

[18] **anthers** That part of the stamen that contains pollen.

I will give only one—not as a very striking case, but as likewise illustrating one step in the separation of the sexes of plants, presently to be alluded to. Some holly-trees bear only male flowers, which have four stamens producing rather a small quantity of pollen, and a rudimentary pistil; other holly-trees bear only female flowers; these have a full-sized pistil, and four stamens with shrivelled anthers, in which not a grain of pollen can be detected. Having found a female tree exactly sixty yards from a male tree, I put the stigmas[19] of twenty flowers, taken from different branches, under the microscope, and on all, without exception, there were pollen-grains, and on some a profusion of pollen. As the wind had set for several days from the female to the male tree, the pollen could not thus have been carried. The weather had been cold and boisterous, and therefore not favorable to bees; nevertheless every female flower which I examined had been effectually fertilized by the bees, accidentally dusted with pollen, having flown from tree to tree in search of nectar. But to return to our imaginary case: as soon as the plant had been rendered so highly attractive to insects that pollen was regularly carried from flower to flower, another process might commence. No naturalist doubts the advantage of what has been called the "physiological division of labor"; hence we may believe that it would be advantageous to a plant to produce stamens alone in one flower or on one whole plant, and pistils alone in another flower or on another plant. In plants under culture and placed under new conditions of life, sometimes the male organs and sometimes the female organs become more or less impotent; now if we suppose this to occur in ever so slight a degree under nature, then as pollen is already carried regularly from flower to flower, and as a more complete separation of the sexes of our plant would be advantageous on the principle of the division of labor, individuals with this tendency more and more increased, would be continually favored or selected, until at last a complete separation of the sexes would be effected.

Let us now turn to the nectar-feeding insects in our imagi-   17
nary case: we may suppose the plant of which we have been slowly increasing the nectar by continued selection, to be a common plant; and that certain insects depended in main part on its nectar for food. I could give many facts, showing how anxious bees are to save time; for instance, their habit of cutting holes and sucking the nectar at the bases of certain flowers, which they can, with a very little more trouble, enter by the mouth. Bearing such facts in mind, I can see no reason to doubt that an accidental deviation in the size and

---

[19]**stigmas** Where the plant's pollen develops.

form of the body, or in the curvature and length of the proboscis,[20] etc., far too slight to be appreciated by us, might profit a bee or other insect, so that an individual so characterized would be able to obtain its food more quickly, and so have a better chance of living and leaving descendants. Its descendants would probably inherit a tendency to a similar slight deviation of structure. The tubes of the corollas[21] of the common red and incarnate clovers (Trifolium pratense and incarnatum) do not on a hasty glance appear to differ in length; yet the hive-bee can easily suck the nectar out of the incarnate clover, but not out of the common red clover, which is visited by humble-bees[22] alone; so that whole fields of the red clover offer in vain an abundant supply of precious nectar to the hive-bee. Thus it might be a great advantage to the hive-bee to have a slightly longer or differently constructed proboscis. On the other hand, I have found by experiment that the fertility of clover greatly depends on bees visiting and moving parts of the corolla, so as to push the pollen on to the stigmatic surface. Hence, again, if humble-bees were to become rare in any country, it might be a great advantage to the red clover to have a shorter or more deeply divided tube to its corolla, so that the hive-bee could visit its flowers. Thus I can understand how a flower and a bee might slowly become, either simultaneously or one after the other, modified and adapted in the most perfect manner to each other, by the continued preservation of individuals presenting mutual and slightly favorable deviations of structure.

I am well aware that this doctrine of natural selection, exemplified in the above imaginary instances, is open to the same objections which were at first urged against Sir Charles Lyell's noble views[23] on "the modern changes of the earth, as illustrative of geology"; but we now very seldom hear the action, for instance, of the coast-waves, called a trifling and insignificant cause, when applied to the excavation of gigantic valleys or to the formation of the longest lines of inland cliffs. Natural selection can act only by the preservation and accumulation of infinitesimally small inherited modifications, each profitable to the preserved being; and as modern geology has almost banished such views as the excavation of a

18

---

[20] **proboscis** Snout.
[21] **corollas** Inner set of floral petals.
[22] **humble-bees** Bumblebees.
[23] **Sir Charles Lyell's noble views** Lyell (1797–1875) was an English geologist whose landmark work, *Principles of Geology* (1830–1833), Darwin read while on the *Beagle*. The book inspired Darwin, and the two scientists became friends. Lyell was shown portions of *On the Origin of Species* while Darwin was writing it.

great valley by a single diluvial[24] wave, so will natural selection, if it be a true principle, banish the belief of the continued creation of new organic beings, or of any great and sudden modification in their structure.

---

[24] **diluvial** Pertaining to a flood. Darwin means that geological changes, such as those that caused the Grand Canyon, were no longer thought of as occurring instantly by flood (or other catastrophes) but were considered to have developed over a long period of time, as he imagines happened in the evolution of the species.

QUESTIONS FOR CRITICAL READING

1. Darwin's metaphor "battle of life" (para. 1) introduces issues that might be thought extraneous to a scientific inquiry. What is the danger of using such a metaphor? What is the advantage of doing so?

2. Many religious groups reject Darwin's concept of natural selection, but they heartily accept human selection in the form of controlled breeding. Why would there be such a difference between the two?

3. Do you feel that the theory of natural selection is a positive force? Could it be directed by divine power?

4. In this work, there is no reference to human beings in terms of the process of selection. How might the principles at work on animals also work on people? Do you think that Darwin assumes this?

5. When this chapter was published in a later edition, Darwin added to its title "Survival of the Fittest." What issues or emotions does that new title raise that "Natural Selection" does not?

SUGGESTIONS FOR CRITICAL WRITING

1. In paragraph 13, Darwin uses imaginary examples. Compare the value of his genuine examples and these imaginary ones. How effective is the use of imaginary examples in an argument? What requirements should an imaginary example meet to be forceful in an argument? Do you find Darwin's imaginary examples to be strong or weak?

2. From paragraph 14 on, Darwin discusses the process of modification of a species through its beginning in the modification of an individual. Explain, insofar as you understand the concept, how a species could be modified by a variation occurring in just one individual. In your explanation, use Darwin's rhetorical technique of the imaginary example.

3. Write an essay that takes as its thesis statement the following sentence from paragraph 18: "Natural selection can act only by the preservation and accumulation of infinitesimally small inherited modifications, each profitable to the preserved being." Be sure to examine the work carefully for other statements by Darwin that add strength, clarity, and meaning to this one. You may also employ the Darwinian device of presenting imaginary instances in your essay.

4. A controversy exists concerning the Darwinian theory of evolution. Explore the *Readers' Guide to Periodical Literature* (a reference you can find at your local or college library) and the Internet for up-to-date information on the creationist-evolutionist conflict in schools. Look up either or both terms to see what articles you can find. Define the controversy and take a stand on it. Use your knowledge of natural selection gained from this piece. Remember, too, that Darwin was trained as a minister of the church and was concerned about religious opinion.

5. When Darwin wrote this piece, he believed that sexual selection was of great importance in evolutionary changes in species. Assuming that this belief is true, establish the similarities between sexual selection in plants and animals and sexual selection, as you have observed it, in people. Paragraphs 10–12 discuss this issue. Darwin does not discuss selection in human beings, but it is clear that physical and stylistic distinctions between the sexes have some bearing on selection. Assuming that to be true, what qualities in people (physical and mental) are likely to survive? Why?

6. **CONNECTIONS**　Which of Francis Bacon's four idols (p. 879) would have made it most difficult for Darwin's contemporaries to accept the theory of evolution, despite the mass of evidence he presented? Do the idols interfere with people's ability to evaluate evidence?

7. **CONNECTIONS**　To what extent are Darwin's theories a threat to public morality? Consider Iris Murdoch's "Morality and Religion" (p. 359) and Friedrich Nietzsche's "Morality as Anti-Nature" (p. 343) in Part Three. How do their ideas on morality relate to Darwin's ideas on the survival of the fittest? Some people in the mid-nineteenth century feared that Darwin's theories could undermine religion and therefore religious codes of ethics and morality. Why do you think some people felt that way? Explain. Do you think such fears were legitimate? Why or why not?

8. **CONNECTIONS**　Write a brief essay explaining how Descartes (**bedfordstmartins.com/worldofideas/epages**) would criticize Darwin's methods of inquiry. Would Descartes be more annoyed by Darwin's conclusions or by the fact that he depends so much on observation of nature? Given that Descartes ends his piece by referencing God, would he have been more forgiving of Darwin if he had done the same? Darwin was trained as a clergyman, but he does not discuss God in his essay.

Why does he avoid such a discussion? Does Darwin's method of inquiry prevent him from introducing God into his discussion, or is God implicit in his discoveries?

9. **SEEING CONNECTIONS**   Salvador Dalí's *The Persistence of Memory* (p. 861) places mechanical objects in a natural environment. Given the concepts that Darwin introduces in "Natural Selection," how might a modern thinker interpret the evolution of time as symbolized in the painting? Do instruments such as clocks and watches evolve in the modern world in a manner similar to the way nature evolves? Is it possible that Dalí's flexible timepieces imply that the world of mechano-electric objects will at some future point merge with living people? How does the idea of evolution affect the world of our time? How might Darwin have interpreted this painting?

SIGMUND FREUD
The Oedipus Complex

SIGMUND FREUD (1856–1939) is, in the minds of many, the founder of modern psychiatry. He developed the psychoanalytic method: the examination of the mind using dream analysis, the analysis of the unconscious through free association, and the correlation of findings with attitudes toward sexuality and sexual development. His theories changed the way people treated neurosis and most other mental disorders. Today we use terms he either invented or championed, such as *psychoanalysis, penis envy, Oedipus complex,* and *wish fulfillment.*

Freud was born in Freiberg, Moravia (now Pribor in the Czech Republic), and moved to Vienna, Austria, when he was four. He pursued a medical career and soon began exploring neurology, which stimulated him to begin his psychoanalytic methods. *The Interpretation of Dreams* (1899) is one of his first important books. It was followed in rapid succession by a number of groundbreaking studies: *The Psychopathology of Everyday Life* (1904), *Three Essays on the Theory of Sexuality* (1905), *Totem and Taboo* (1913), *Beyond the Pleasure Principle* (1920), and *Civilization and Its Discontents* (1930). Freud's personal life in Vienna was essentially uneventful until he was put under house arrest by the Nazis in 1938 because he was Jewish. He was released and then moved to London, where he died the following year.

As a movement, psychoanalysis shocked most of the world by postulating a superego, which establishes high standards of personal behavior; an ego, which corresponds to the apparent personality; an id, which includes the deepest primitive forces of life; and an unconscious, into which thoughts and memories we cannot face are repressed or sublimated. The origin of much mental illness, the

From *The Interpretation of Dreams*. Translated by James Strachey.

theory presumes, lies in the inability of the mind to find a way to sublimate—to express in harmless and creative ways—the painful thoughts that have been repressed. Dreams and unconscious actions sometimes act as releases or harmless expressions of these thoughts and memories.

As Freud states in *The Interpretation of Dreams*, the unconscious works in complex ways to help us cope with feelings and desires that our superego deems unacceptable. Dreams are mental events, not necessarily connected to physical events. The repression of important emotions, a constant process, often results in dreams that express repressed feelings in a harmless and sometimes symbolic way. In a sense, dreams help us maintain our mental health.

Further, dreams are a primary subject matter of psychoanalysis because they reveal a great deal about the unconscious mind, especially the material that we repress from our consciousness. His discussion of the Oedipus complex, which follows, is a classic case in point. Most people found Freud's theory of the Oedipus complex very compelling once they began to understand the details of its expression. Freud assumed that when we are infants we love our opposite-sex parent and hate our same-sex parent. These feelings of love and hate change as we grow, but they can still linger and cause neurotic behavior. Because these feelings are repressed into the unconscious, we are not aware of them as adults.

Freud's Rhetoric

This selection comes from a section of *The Interpretation of Dreams* in which Freud discusses what he calls "typical dreams." It is here that he speaks directly about his theory of the Oedipus complex and links it specifically with two major pieces of Western literature. *Oedipus Rex* by Sophocles (496–406 B.C.E.) and *Hamlet* by William Shakespeare (1564–1616) are tragedies in which some of the unconscious desires of the hero to marry his mother are either carried out, as in *Oedipus Rex*, or strongly hinted at, as in *Hamlet*.

Freud realizes that many readers will not be convinced that such a compulsion exists. He explains, however, that because most young people outgrow the compulsion and thereafter repress it, most adults are unaware of their own oedipal feelings.

The rhetorical strategy of introducing two classic dramatic works that are centuries apart and demonstrating what they have in common is effective in helping the reader understand that the psychological condition Freud refers to is not unknown to Western culture. His analysis of his patients' dreams has helped dredge up the original content and the connection with the oedipal urge, thus freeing them of a sense of guilt and a need for self-punishment. Paragraphs 2–6 detail the story of King Oedipus and the strange way in which he eventually married his mother and thus brought a plague upon his land. Freud's point is that this ancient text reveals an aspect of the inner nature of the human mind that has not changed for many thousands of years.

As he tells us, his patients have dreams of intercourse with parents and then feel such torrents of guilt and shame that they sometimes become neurotic. The fact that Oedipus severely punishes himself at the end of the play corresponds with the sense of guilt that Freud's patients experience. Hamlet is even more severely punished and suffers even more psychological anguish throughout the play, even though he never commits incest with his mother. The power of thought is enough. Hamlet is described as "a pathologically irresolute character which might be classed as neurasthenic" (para. 7). In other words, he could have benefited from Freud's psychoanalysis.

Freud uses these two great plays as examples of his theories because he sees them as imaginative constructs that work out the repressed feelings people have always had. They are similar to dreams in that they are written by poets; and poets who rely on inspiration have traditionally drawn on the unconscious. Because these two tragedies are so important to Western literature, they have a special value that no minor literature could have. Consequently, they have been enormously convincing to those interested in the way the mind works. What Freud has done with these works is to hold them up as a mirror. In that mirror one can see quite clearly the evidence for the Oedipus complex that would be totally invisible in any self-examination. It is one of Freud's great rhetorical achievements.

In paragraph 8, Freud makes some other observations about the dreams some of his patients have had in which they imagined themselves killing their parents. This is such a horrible idea for most people that Freud is surprised that our internal censor permits such dreams to occur. His theory is that the thought is so monstrous that the dream censor "is not armed to meet" it (para. 8). His analysis suggests that worry about a parent may disguise the unconscious wish that the parent should die. Freud mentions "our explanation of dreams in general" (para. 8), by which he means that dreams are wish fulfillments. If that is true, those who dream about killing a parent are likely to be deeply upset and may make themselves neurotic by their own sense of guilt.

Though most people go through an infantile oedipal stage, they usually grow out of it early in life. Freud suggests, however, that those who do not grow out of it may need psychoanalytic help.

PREREADING QUESTIONS: WHAT TO READ FOR

The following prereading questions may help you anticipate key issues in the discussion of Sigmund Freud's "The Oedipus Complex." Keeping them in mind during your first reading of the selection should help focus your attention.

- What, exactly, is the Oedipus complex?
- How does the Oedipus complex express itself in dreams?
- How do *Oedipus Rex* and *Hamlet* illustrate the Oedipus complex?

The Oedipus Complex

In my experience, which is already extensive, the chief part in the mental lives of all children who later become psychoneurotics is played by their parents. Being in love with the one parent and hating the other are among the essential constituents of the stock of psychical impulses which is formed at that time and which is of such importance in determining the symptoms of the later neurosis. It is not my belief, however, that psychoneurotics differ sharply in this respect from other human beings who remain normal—that they are able, that is, to create something absolutely new and peculiar to themselves. It is far more probable—and this is confirmed by occasional observations on normal children—that they are only distinguished by exhibiting on a magnified scale feelings of love and hatred to their parents which occur less obviously and less intensely in the minds of most children.

This discovery is confirmed by a legend that has come down to us from classical antiquity: a legend whose profound and universal power to move can only be understood if the hypothesis I have put forward in regard to the psychology of children has an equally universal validity. What I have in mind is the legend of King Oedipus and Sophocles' drama which bears his name.

Oedipus, son of Laïus, King of Thebes, and of Jocasta, was exposed as an infant because an oracle had warned Laïus that the still unborn child would be his father's murderer. The child was rescued, and grew up as a prince in an alien court, until, in doubts as to his origin, he too questioned the oracle and was warned to avoid his home since he was destined to murder his father and take his mother in marriage. On the road leading away from what he believed was his home, he met King Laïus and slew him in a sudden quarrel. He came next to Thebes and solved the riddle set him by the Sphinx who barred his way. Out of gratitude the Thebans made him their king and gave him Jocasta's hand in marriage. He reigned long in peace and honor, and she who, unknown to him, was his mother bore him two sons and two daughters. Then at last a plague broke out and the Thebans made enquiry once more of the oracle. It is at this point that Sophocles' tragedy opens. The messengers bring back the reply that the plague will cease when the murderer of Laïus has been driven from the land.

> But he, where is he? Where shall now be read
> The fading record of this ancient guilt?

The action of the play consists in nothing other than the process of revealing, with cunning delays and ever-mounting excitement—a process that can be likened to the work of a psychoanalysis—that Oedipus himself is the murderer of Laïus, but further that he is the son of the murdered man and of Jocasta. Appalled at the abomination which he has unwittingly perpetrated, Oedipus blinds himself and forsakes his home. The oracle has been fulfilled.

Oedipus Rex is what is known as a tragedy of destiny. Its tragic   4
effect is said to lie in the contrast between the supreme will of the gods and the vain attempts of mankind to escape the evil that threatens them. The lesson which, it is said, the deeply moved spectator should learn from the tragedy is submission to the divine will and realization of his own impotence. Modern dramatists have accordingly tried to achieve a similar tragic effect by weaving the same contrast into a plot invented by themselves. But the spectators have looked on unmoved while a curse or an oracle was fulfilled in spite of all the efforts of some innocent man: later tragedies of destiny have failed in their effect.

If *Oedipus Rex* moves a modern audience no less than it did the con-   5
temporary Greek one, the explanation can only be that its effect does not lie in the contrast between destiny and human will, but is to be looked for in the particular nature of the material on which that contrast is exemplified. There must be something which makes a voice within us ready to recognize the compelling force of destiny in the *Oedipus*, while we can dismiss as merely arbitrary such dispositions as are laid down in *Die Ahnfrau*[1] or other modern tragedies of destiny. And a factor of this kind is in fact involved in the story of King Oedipus. His destiny moves us only because it might have been ours—because the oracle laid the same curse upon us before our birth as upon him. It is the fate of all of us, perhaps, to direct our first sexual impulse towards our mother and our first hatred and our first murderous wish against our father.

---

[1] **Die Ahnfrau** Franz Grillparzer (1791–1872) wrote *Die Ahnfrau* (The Ancestress).

Our dreams convince us that that is so. King Oedipus, who slew his father Laïus and married his mother Jocasta, merely shows us the fulfillment of our own childhood wishes. But, more fortunate than he, we have meanwhile succeeded, insofar as we have not become psychoneurotics, in detaching our sexual impulses from our mothers and in forgetting our jealousy of our fathers. Here is one in whom these primeval wishes of our childhood have been fulfilled, and we shrink back from him with the whole force of the repression by which those wishes have since that time been held down within us. While the poet, as he unravels the past, brings to light the guilt of Oedipus, he is at the same time compelling us to recognize our own inner minds, in which those same impulses, though suppressed, are still to be found. The contrast with which the closing Chorus leaves us confronted—

> . . . Fix on Oedipus your eyes,
> Who resolved the dark enigma, noblest champion and most wise.
> Like a star his envied fortune mounted beaming far and wide:
> Now he sinks in seas of anguish, whelmed beneath a raging tide . . .

—strikes as a warning at ourselves and our pride, at us who since our childhood have grown so wise and so mighty in our own eyes. Like Oedipus, we live in ignorance of these wishes, repugnant to morality, which have been forced upon us by Nature, and after their revelation we may all of us well seek to close our eyes to the scenes of our childhood.[2]

There is an unmistakable indication in the text of Sophocles' tragedy itself that the legend of Oedipus sprang from some primeval dream material which had as its content the distressing disturbance of a child's relation to his parents owing to the first stirrings of sexuality. At a point when Oedipus, though he is not yet enlightened, has begun to feel troubled by his recollection of the oracle, Jocasta consoles him by referring to a dream which many people dream, though, as she thinks, it has no meaning:

> Many a man ere now in dreams hath lain
> With her who bare him. He hath least annoy
> Who with such omens troubleth not his mind.

---

[2] [*Footnote added* 1914:] None of the findings of psychoanalytic research has provoked such embittered denials, such fierce opposition—or such amusing contortions—on the part of critics as this indication of the childhood impulses towards incest which persist in the unconscious. An attempt has even been made recently to make out, in the face of all experience, that the incest should only be taken as "symbolic."—Ferenczi (1912) has proposed an ingenious "over-interpretation" of the Oedipus myth, based on a passage in one of Schopenhauer's letters.—[*Added* 1919:] Later studies have shown that the "Oedipus complex," which was touched upon for the first time in the above paragraphs in the *Interpretation of Dreams*, throws a light of undreamt-of importance on the history of the human race and the evolution of religion and morality. (See my *Totem and Taboo*, 1912–13.) [Freud's notes]

Today, just as then, many men dream of having sexual relations with their mothers, and speak of the fact with indignation and astonishment. It is clearly the key to the tragedy and the complement to the dream of the dreamer's father being dead. The story of Oedipus is the reaction of the imagination to these two typical dreams. And just as these dreams, when dreamt by adults, are accompanied by feelings of repulsion, so too the legend must include horror and self-punishment. Its further modification originates once again in a misconceived secondary revision of the material, which has sought to exploit it for theological purposes. The attempt to harmonize divine omnipotence with human responsibility must naturally fail in connection with this subject matter just as with any other.

Another of the great creations of tragic poetry, Shakespeare's *Hamlet*, has its roots in the same soil as *Oedipus Rex*. But the changed treatment of the same material reveals the whole difference in the mental life of these two widely separated epochs of civilization: the secular advance of repression in the emotional life of mankind. In the *Oedipus* the child's wishful fantasy that underlies it is brought into the open and realized as it would be in a dream. In *Hamlet* it remains repressed; and —just as in the case of a neurosis—we only learn of its existence from its inhibiting consequences. Strangely enough, the overwhelming effect produced by the more modern tragedy has turned out to be compatible with the fact that people have remained completely in the dark as to the hero's character. The play is built up on Hamlet's hesitations over fulfilling the task of revenge that is assigned to him; but its text offers no reasons or motives for these hesitations and an immense variety of attempts at interpreting them have failed to produce a result. According to the view which was originated by Goethe[3] and is still the prevailing one today, Hamlet represents the type of man whose power of direct action is paralyzed by an excessive development of his intellect. (He is "sicklied o'er with the pale cast of thought.") According to another view, the dramatist has tried to portray a pathologically irresolute character which might be classed as neurasthenic. The plot of the drama shows us, however, that Hamlet is far from being represented as a person incapable of taking any action. We see him doing so on two occasions: first in a sudden outburst of temper, when he runs his sword through the eavesdropper behind the arras, and secondly in a premeditated and even crafty fashion, when, with all the callousness of a Renaissance prince, he sends the two courtiers to the death that had been planned for himself. What is it, then, that inhibits him in fulfilling the task set him by his father's ghost? The answer,

[3]**Johann Wolfgang von Goethe (1749–1832)** One of Germany's greatest writers.

once again, is that it is the peculiar nature of the task. Hamlet is able to do anything—except take vengeance on the man who did away with his father and took that father's place with his mother, the man who shows him the repressed wishes of his own childhood realized. Thus the loathing which should drive him on to revenge is replaced in him by self-reproaches, by scruples of conscience, which remind him that he himself is literally no better than the sinner whom he is to punish. Here I have translated into conscious terms what was bound to remain unconscious in Hamlet's mind; and if anyone is inclined to call him a hysteric, I can only accept the fact as one that is implied by my interpretation. The distaste for sexuality expressed by Hamlet in his conversation with Ophelia fits in very well with this: the same distaste which was destined to take possession of the poet's mind more and more during the years that followed, and which reached its extreme expression in *Timon of Athens*. For it can of course only be the poet's own mind which confronts us in Hamlet. I observe in a book on Shakespeare by Georg Brandes (1896) a statement that *Hamlet* was written immediately after the death of Shakespeare's father (in 1601), that is, under the immediate impact of his bereavement and, as we may well assume, while his childhood feelings about his father had been freshly revived. It is known, too, that Shakespeare's own son who died at an early age bore the name of "Hamnet," which is identical with "Hamlet." Just as *Hamlet* deals with the relation of a son to his parents, so *Macbeth* (written at approximately the same period) is concerned with the subject of childlessness. But just as all neurotic symptoms, and, for that matter, dreams, are capable of being "over-interpreted" and indeed need to be, if they are to be fully understood, so all genuinely creative writings are the product of more than a single motive and more than a single impulse in the poet's mind, and are open to more than a single interpretation. In what I have written I have only attempted to interpret the deepest layer of impulses in the mind of the creative writer.[4]

I cannot leave the subject of typical dreams of the death of loved 8 relatives, without adding a few more words to throw light on their significance for the theory of dreams in general. In these dreams we find the highly unusual condition realized of a dream-thought formed by a repressed wish entirely eluding censorship and passing into the dream without modification. There must be special factors

---

[4] [*Footnote added* 1919:] The above indications of a psychoanalytic explanation of *Hamlet* have since been amplified by Ernest Jones and defended against the alternative views put forward in the literature of the subject. [*Added* 1930:] Incidentally, I have in the meantime ceased to believe that the author of Shakespeare's works was the man from Stratford. [*Added* 1919:] Further attempts at an analysis of *Macbeth* will be found in a paper of mine [Freud, 1916d] and in one by Jekels (1917). [Freud's notes]

at work to make this event possible, and I believe that the occurrence of these dreams is facilitated by two such factors. Firstly, there is no wish that seems more remote from us than this one: "we couldn't even *dream*"—so we believe—of wishing such a thing. For this reason the dream-censorship is not armed to meet such a monstrosity, just as Solon's[5] penal code contained no punishment for parricide. Secondly, in this case the repressed and unsuspected wish is particularly often met halfway by a residue from the previous day in the form of a *worry* about the safety of the person concerned. This worry can only make its way into the dream by availing itself of the corresponding wish; while the wish can disguise itself behind the worry that has become active during the day. We may feel inclined to think that things are simpler than this and that one merely carries on during the night and in dreams with what one has been turning over in one's mind during the day; but if so we shall be leaving dreams of the death of people of whom the dreamer is fond completely in the air and without any connection with our explanation of dreams in general, and we shall thus be clinging quite unnecessarily to a riddle which is perfectly capable of solution.

It is also instructive to consider the relation of these dreams to anxiety-dreams. In the dreams we have been discussing, a repressed wish has found a means of evading censorship—and the distortion which censorship involves. The invariable concomitant is that painful feelings are experienced in the dream. In just the same way anxiety-dreams only occur if the censorship has been wholly or partly overpowered; and, on the other hand, the overpowering of the censorship is facilitated if anxiety has already been produced as an immediate sensation arising from somatic[6] sources. We can thus plainly see the purpose for which the censorship exercises its office and brings about the distortion of dreams: it does so *in order to prevent the generation of anxiety or other forms of distressing affect*.

9

---

[5] **Solon (638–558 B.C.E.)** Greek known as the law giver. His ideas on law continue to influence us today.

[6] **somatic** Having to do with the physical body.

QUESTIONS FOR CRITICAL READING

1. What role do parents play in the lives of those who become neurotics?
2. Do psychoneurotics differ substantially from normal people?
3. What does Freud expect his example of *Oedipus Rex* to call up in the mind of the reader?

4. What is a tragedy of destiny?

5. In what ways are all of us like Oedipus?

6. How is literature related to dreams, according to Freud?

7. Why do dreams sometimes need to be overinterpreted?

8. How does censorship operate in dreams?

SUGGESTIONS FOR CRITICAL WRITING

1. Most adults have absolutely no awareness of having had an oedipal period in their infancy. However, you may have observed oedipal behavior in young children. If so, describe how the children behaved and if possible describe how they have grown up and whether they have left the oedipal stage behind. Do your observations help bolster Freud's views, or do they help weaken them?

2. Describe in as much detail as possible any anxiety dreams you may have had. Often anxiety dreams are repetitive and recurrent. What are the circumstances in which you find yourself in your dream? What worries you most in the dream? What threatens you most? How does the dream resolve itself? Does the dream provoke guilt or shame? How would you interpret the dream in the light of what you have read here?

3. If you find yourself unable to remember your dreams, interview some friends and "collect" dreams from them. Ask them for dreams that make them feel uneasy—anxiety dreams. Have them write down their dreams and then ask them to talk about events in their waking life that preceded the dreams. See if there are contributing events or anticipations in the mind of the dreamers that would lead them to have anxiety dreams. See, too, if there are any patterns to dreams of different people. Are there any "typical dreams" shared by your friends?

4. What are your typical dreams? Try to write them out as if they were plays. Identify characters, setting, and time, and then write the dialogue and stage directions that would give a good approximation of the content of the dreams. Do not censor your dreams or try to "overanalyze" them (despite Freud's recommendation). Do your best to make the dreams clear in their expression. Does this approach make your dreams any more meaningful to you? Explain.

5. Does your reading of *Hamlet* help bear out Freud's theory that suggests Hamlet is suffering from an Oedipus complex? What is his relationship to his mother? How does she regard him? Is his killing of King Claudius an act of parricide? Is Hamlet's punishment warranted? Argue for or against Freud's view of the play.

6. In paragraph 6, Freud states, "There is an unmistakable indication in the text of Sophocles' tragedy itself that the legend of Oedipus sprang from some primeval dream material." Examine his evidence for this claim and decide yourself whether this seems a reasonable conclusion.

7. Most horror films involve monstrous actions and severe punishment. Is it possible that one of the functions of horror films is to reveal some of the inner nature of our minds somewhat the way *Oedipus Rex* and *Hamlet* do? Choose a favorite film and analyze it in terms of its revealing hidden desires that might trouble us if we felt them consciously and acted on them in life.

8. **CONNECTIONS** Plato's concerns in "The Allegory of the Cave" (p. 865) point to a level of reality that humans cannot reach because of the limitations of sensory apprehension. Is it also true that the dream world represents a level of reality that is impossible to reach because of the limitations of the conscious waking mind? Which part of the mind — the conscious or the unconscious — does Freud seem to regard as primary in his discussion of the Oedipus complex? Is there the sense that he regards one or the other as possessing a greater "reality"? How do his views fit with those of Plato?

9. **CONNECTIONS** Describe Freud's method of inquiry and compare it with that of Descartes (**bedfordstmartins.com/worldofideas/epages**). Freud begins with basic ideas from classic Greek texts. Descartes does not refer to texts, but reasons from ideas he knows are true. Freud's method is not scientific, nor is Descartes' method scientific. Both, however, are forceful instruments in presenting truths about the human mind. What does Freud do that Descartes does not do in constructing his argument? What would Descartes take issue with in Freud's analysis of the Oedipus complex? Would Descartes have considered dreams sensory evidence?

10. **SEEING CONNECTIONS** Dalí explicitly called attention to his personal Oedipus complex, describing his love for his mother and implying that the fetal figure in the center of *The Persistence of Memory* (p. 861) was a self-portrait. Dalí may never have experienced psychoanalysis, "the talking cure," but he did express himself very openly in his painting. Would Freud have thought this painting might have helped Dalí achieve some kind of cure, or approach some kind of resolution, of his oedipal fixations? Freud was much more influenced by words than by visual art, but with an obvious connection to his own theories, could the painting have been an important factor in psychoanalysis? How might Freud have interpreted it?

CARL JUNG
The Personal and the Collective Unconscious

CARL GUSTAV JUNG (1875–1961), Freud's most famous disciple, was a Swiss physician who collaborated with Freud from 1907 to 1912, when the two argued about the nature of the unconscious. Jung's *Psychology of the Unconscious* (1912) posits an unconscious that is composed of more than the ego, superego, and id. According to Jung, an additional aspect of the unconscious is a collection of archetypal images that can be inherited by members of the same group. Experience clarifies these images, but the images in turn direct experience.

In one of his essays on the collective unconscious, Jung asserts that the great myths express the archetypes of actions and heroes stored in the unconscious by elucidating them for the individual and society. These archetypes represent themselves in mythic literature in images, such as the great father or the great mother, or in patterns of action, such as disobedience and self-sacrifice. They transcend social barriers and exemplify themselves similarly in most people in any given cultural group. For Jung, the individual must adapt to the archetypes that reveal themselves in the myths in order to be psychically healthy.

Like Freud, Jung postulates a specific model of the way the mind works: he claims the existence not only of a conscious mind—which all of us can attest to from experience and common sense—but also of an unconscious component to the mind. He argues that we are unaware of the content of our unconscious mind except, perhaps, in dreams (which occur when we are unconscious), which Freud and others insist speak to us in symbols rather than in direct language.

From *The Basic Writings of C. G. Jung*. Translated by Cary F. Baynes.

Jung also acknowledges the symbolic nature of the unconscious but disagrees with the source of the content of the unconscious mind.

In "The Personal and the Collective Unconscious" (1916), Jung describes the pattern of psychological transference that most psychoanalysts experience with their patients. In the case presented here, the patient's problems were associated with her father, and the transference was the normal one of conceiving of the doctor—in this case, Jung—in terms of the father. When this transference occurs, the patient often is cured of the problems that brought her to the psychoanalyst, but in this case the transference was incomplete. Jung offers a detailed analysis of the dreams that revealed the problems with the transference and describes the intellectual state of the woman whose dreams form the basis of the discussion. She is intelligent, conscious of the mechanism of transference, and careful about her own inner life. Yet the dream that Jung analyzes had a content that he could not relate to her personal life.

In an attempt to explain his inability to analyze the woman's dream strictly in terms of her personal life, Jung reexamines Freud's definition of the unconscious. As Jung explains Freud's view, the unconscious is a repository for material that is produced by the conscious mind and later repressed so as not to interfere with the function of the conscious mind. Thus, painful memories and unpleasant fears are often repressed and rarely become problems because they are sublimated—transformed into harmless activity, often dreams—and released. According to Freud, the material in the unconscious mind develops solely from personal experience.

Jung, however, argues that personal experiences form only part of the individual's unconscious, what he calls the "personal unconscious" (para. 17). For the patient in this essay, the images in the dream that he and the patient at first classified as a transference dream (in which the doctor became the father/lover figure) had qualities that could not be explained fully by transference. Instead, the dream seemed to represent a primordial figure, a god. From this, Jung develops the view that such a figure is cultural in nature and not personal. Nothing in the patient's life pointed to her concern for a god of the kind that developed in her dream. Jung proposes that the images that constituted the content of her dream were not a result of personal experience or education but, instead, were inherited. Jung defines this portion of the unconscious as the "collective unconscious" (para. 19).

Jung's theories proved unacceptable to Freud. After their collaboration ended, Jung studied the world's myths and mythic systems, including alchemy and occult literature. In them he saw many of the archetypal symbols that he felt were revealed in dreams— including symbolic quests, sudden transformations, dramatic or threatening landscapes, and images of God. His conclusions were that this literature, most or all of which was suppressed or rejected by modern religions such as Christianity, was a repository for the symbols of the collective unconscious—at least of Western civilization and perhaps of other civilizations.

Jung's Rhetoric

Like Freud, Jung tells a story. His selection is a narrative beginning with a recapitulation of Freud's view of the unconscious. Jung tells us that according to the conventional view, the contents of the unconscious have passed "the threshold of consciousness" (para. 2): in other words, they were once in the conscious mind of the individual. However, Jung also asserts that "the unconscious also contains components that have *not yet* reached the threshold of consciousness" (para. 3). At least two questions arise from this assertion: What is that content, and where did it come from?

Jung then provides the "example" (para. 5) of the woman whose therapy he was conducting. He tells us, as one would tell a story, about the woman's treatment and how such treatment works in a general sense. He explains the phenomenon of transference, claiming that "a successful transference can . . . cause the whole neurosis to disappear" (para. 5). Near the end of this patient's treatment he analyzed her dreams and found something he did not expect. He relates the narrative of the dream (para. 10), which includes the image of a superhuman father figure in a field of wheat swaying in the wind. From this he concludes that the image of the dream is not the doctor/father/lover figure that is common to transference—and that the patient was thoroughly aware of—but something of an entirely different order. He connects it to an archetype of God and proceeds to an analysis that explains the dream in terms of a collective unconscious whose content is shared by groups of people rather than created by the individual alone.

Jung's rhetorical strategy here is an argument proceeding from both example and analysis. The example is given in detail, along with enough background to make it useful to the reader. Then the example is narrated carefully, and its content is examined through a process of analysis familiar to those in psychiatry.

Some of the material in this selection is relatively challenging because Jung uses technical language and occasionally obscure references. However, the simplicity of the technique of narrative, telling a story of what happened, makes the selection intelligible, even though it deals with highly complex and controversial ideas.

The following prereading questions may help you anticipate key issues in the discussion of Carl Jung's "The Personal and the Collective Unconscious." Keeping them in mind during your first reading of the selection should help focus your attention.

- What are some of the contents of the unconscious?
- What is the difference between the personal and the collective unconscious?

The Personal and
the Collective Unconscious

In Freud's view, as most people know, the contents of the unconscious are limited to infantile tendencies which are repressed because of their incompatible character. Repression is a process that begins in early childhood under the moral influence of the environment and lasts throughout life. Through analysis the repressions are removed and the repressed wishes made conscious.

According to this theory, the unconscious contains only those parts of the personality which could just as well be conscious and are in fact suppressed only through upbringing. Although from one point of view the infantile tendencies of the unconscious are the most conspicuous, it would nonetheless be incorrect to define or evaluate the unconscious entirely in these terms. The unconscious has still another side to it: it includes not only repressed contents, but also all psychic material that lies below the threshold of consciousness. It is impossible to explain the subliminal nature of all this material on the principle of repression; otherwise, through the removal of repressions, a man would acquire a phenomenal memory which would thenceforth forget nothing.

We therefore emphatically say that in addition to the repressed material the unconscious contains all those psychic components that have fallen below the threshold, including subliminal sense perceptions. Moreover we know, from abundant experience as well as for theoretical reasons, that the unconscious also contains components that have *not yet* reached the threshold of consciousness. These are the seeds of future conscious contents. Equally we have reason to suppose that the unconscious is never at rest in the sense of being inactive, but is continually engaged in grouping and regrouping its contents. Only in pathological cases can this activity be regarded as completely autonomous; normally it is coordinated with the conscious mind in a compensatory relationship.

It is to be assumed that all these contents are personal insofar as 4
they are acquired during the individual's life. Since this life is limited, the number of acquired contents in the unconscious must also be limited. This being so, it might be thought possible to empty the unconscious either by analysis or by making a complete inventory of unconscious contents, on the ground that the unconscious cannot produce anything more than is already known and accepted in the conscious mind. We should also have to infer, as already indicated, that if one could stop the descent of conscious contents into the unconscious by doing away with repression, unconscious productivity would be paralyzed. This is possible only to a very limited extent, as we know from experience. We urge our patients to hold fast to repressed contents that have been re-associated with consciousness, and to assimilate them into their plan of life. But this procedure, as we may daily convince ourselves, makes no impression on the unconscious, since it calmly continues to produce dreams and fantasies which, according to Freud's original theory, must arise from personal repressions. If in such cases we pursue our observations systematically and without prejudice, we shall find material which, although similar in form to the previous personal contents, yet seems to contain allusions that go far beyond the personal sphere.

Casting about in my mind for an example to illustrate what I have 5
just said, I have a particularly vivid memory of a woman patient with a mild hysterical neurosis which, as we expressed it in those days, had its principal cause in a "father complex." By this we wanted to denote the fact that the patient's peculiar relationship to her father stood in her way. She had been on very good terms with her father, who had since died. It was a relationship chiefly of feeling. In such cases it is usually the intellectual function that is developed, and this later becomes the bridge to the world. Accordingly our patient became a student of philosophy. Her energetic pursuit of knowledge was motivated by her need to extricate herself from the emotional entanglement with her father. This operation may succeed if her feelings can find an outlet on the new intellectual level, perhaps in the formation of an emotional tie with a suitable man, equivalent to the former tie. In this particular case, however, the transition refused to take place, because the patient's feelings remained suspended, oscillating between her father and a man who was not altogether suitable. The progress of her life was thus held up, and that inner disunity so characteristic of a neurosis promptly made its appearance. The so-called normal person would probably be able to break the emotional bond in one or the other direction by a

powerful act of will, or else—and this is perhaps the more usual thing—
he would come through the difficulty unconsciously, on the smooth
path of instinct, without ever being aware of the sort of conflict that lay
behind his headaches or other physical discomforts. But any weakness
of instinct (which may have many causes) is enough to hinder a smooth
unconscious transition. Then all progress is delayed by conflict, and the
resulting stasis of life is equivalent to a neurosis. In consequence of the
standstill, psychic energy flows off in every conceivable direction, apparently quite uselessly. For instance, there are excessive innervations of
the sympathetic system, which lead to nervous disorders of the stomach
and intestines; or the vagus (and consequently the heart) is stimulated;
or fantasies and memories, uninteresting enough in themselves, become
overvalued and prey on the conscious mind (mountains out of mole-
hills). In this state a new motive is needed to put an end to the morbid
suspension. Nature herself paves the way for this, unconsciously and
indirectly, through the phenomenon of the transference (Freud). In the
course of treatment the patient transfers the father imago[1] to the doctor,
thus making him, in a sense, the father, and in the sense that he is *not* the
father, also making him a substitute for the man she cannot reach. The
doctor therefore becomes both a father and a kind of lover—in other
words, the object of conflict. In him the opposites are united, and for
this reason he stands for a quasi-ideal solution of the conflict. Without
in the least wishing it, he draws upon himself an overvaluation that is
almost incredible to the outsider, for to the patient he seems like a savior or a god. This way of speaking is not altogether so laughable as it
sounds. It is indeed a bit much to be a father and lover at once. Nobody
could possibly stand up to it in the long run, precisely because it is too
much of a good thing. One would have to be a demigod at least to sustain such a role without a break, for all the time one would have to
be the giver. To the patient in the state of transference, this provisional
solution naturally seems ideal, but only at first; in the end she comes to
a standstill that is just as bad as the neurotic conflict was. Fundamentally, nothing has yet happened that might lead to a real solution. The
conflict has merely been transferred. Nevertheless a successful transference can—at least temporarily—cause the whole neurosis to disappear, and for this reason it has been very rightly recognized by Freud
as a healing factor of first-rate importance, but, at the same time, as a
provisional state only, for although it holds out the possibility of a cure,
it is far from being the cure itself.

This somewhat lengthy discussion seemed to me essential if my
example was to be understood, for my patient had arrived at the state

6

---

[1] **imago** Idealized image of a person.

of transference and had already reached the upper limit where the standstill begins to make itself disagreeable. The question now arose: What next? I had of course become the complete savior, and the thought of having to give me up was not only exceedingly distasteful to the patient, but positively terrifying. In such a situation "sound common sense" generally comes out with a whole repertory of admonitions: "you simply must," "you really ought," "you just cannot," etc. So far as sound common sense is, happily, not too rare and not entirely without effect (pessimists, I know, exist), a rational motive can, in the exuberant feeling of health you get from transference, release so much enthusiasm that a painful sacrifice can be risked with a mighty effort of will. If successful—and these things sometimes are—the sacrifice bears blessed fruit, and the erstwhile patient leaps at one bound into the state of being practically cured. The doctor is generally so delighted that he fails to tackle the theoretical difficulties connected with this little miracle.

If the leap does not succeed—and it did not succeed with 7 my patient—one is then faced with the problem of severing the transference. Here "psychoanalytic" theory shrouds itself in a thick darkness. Apparently we are to fall back on some nebulous trust in fate: somehow or other the matter will settle itself. "The transference stops automatically when the patient runs out of money," as a slightly cynical colleague once remarked to me. Or the ineluctable demands of life make it impossible for the patient to linger on in the transference—demands which compel the involuntary sacrifice, sometimes with a more or less complete relapse as a result. (One may look in vain for accounts of such cases in the books that sing the praises of psychoanalysis!)

To be sure, there are hopeless cases where nothing helps; but 8 there are also cases that do not get stuck and do not inevitably leave the transference situation with bitter hearts and sore heads. I told myself, at this juncture with my patient, that there must be a clear and respectable way out of the impasse. My patient had long since run out of money—if indeed she ever possessed any—but I was curious to know what means nature would devise for a satisfactory way out of the transference deadlock. Since I never imagined that I was blessed with that "sound common sense" which always knows exactly what to do in every tangled situation, and since my patient knew as little as I, I suggested to her that we could at least keep an eye open for any movements coming from a sphere of the psyche uncontaminated by our superior wisdom and our conscious plannings. That meant first and foremost her dreams.

Dreams contain images and thought associations which we do 9 not create with conscious intent. They arise spontaneously without our assistance and are representatives of a psychic activity withdrawn from our arbitrary will. Therefore the dream is, properly speaking, a highly objective, natural product of the psyche, from which we might expect indications, or at least hints, about certain basic trends in the psychic process. Now, since the psychic process, like any other life process, is not just a causal sequence, but is also a process with a teleological orientation,[2] we might expect dreams to give us certain indicia about the objective causality as well as about the objective tendencies, because they are nothing less than self-portraits of the psychic life process.

On the basis of these reflections, then, we subjected the dreams to a careful examination. It would lead too far to quote word for word all the dreams that now followed. Let it suffice to sketch their main character: the majority referred to the person of the doctor, that is to say, the actors were unmistakably the dreamer herself and her doctor. The latter, however, seldom appeared in this natural shape, but was generally distorted in a remarkable way. Sometimes his figure was of supernatural size, sometimes he seemed to be extremely aged, then again he resembled her father, but was at the same time curiously woven into nature, as in the following dream: *Her father (who in reality was of small stature) was standing with her on a hill that was covered with wheat fields. She was quite tiny beside him, and he seemed to her like a giant. He lifted her up from the ground and held her in his arms like a little child. The wind swept over the wheat fields, and as the wheat swayed in the wind, he rocked her in his arms.*

From this dream and from others like it I could discern various things. Above all I got the impression that her unconscious was holding unshakably to the idea of my being the father-lover, so that the fatal tie we were trying to undo appeared to be doubly strengthened. Moreover one could hardly avoid seeing that the unconscious placed a special emphasis on the supernatural, almost "divine" nature of the father-lover, thus accentuating still further the overvaluation occasioned by the transference. I therefore asked myself whether the patient had still not understood the wholly fantastic character of her transference, or whether perhaps the unconscious could never be reached by understanding at all, but must blindly and idiotically pursue some nonsensical chimera. Freud's idea that the unconscious can "do nothing but wish," Schopenhauer's[3] blind and aimless Will, the gnostic demi-urge who in his vanity deems himself perfect and then in the blindness of his limitation creates something lamentably imperfect—all these pessimistic suspicions of an essentially negative background to the world and the soul came threateningly near.

10

11

---

[2] **teleological orientation** Possessing a sense of design; directed toward an end or a purpose.

[3] **Arthur Schopenhauer (1788–1860)** German pessimistic philosopher.

And indeed there would be nothing to set against this except a well-meaning "you ought," reinforced by a stroke of the ax that would cut down the whole phantasmagoria for good and all.

But as I turned the dreams over and over in my mind, there dawned   12
on me another possibility. I said to myself: it cannot be denied that the dreams continue to speak in the same old metaphors with which our conversations have made both doctor and patient sickeningly familiar. But the patient has an undoubted understanding of her transference fantasy. She knows that I appear to her as a semidivine father-lover, and she can, at least intellectually, distinguish this from my factual reality. Therefore the dreams are obviously reiterating the conscious standpoint minus the conscious criticism, which they completely ignore. They reiterate the conscious contents, not *in toto*, but insist on the fantastic standpoint as opposed to "sound common sense."

I naturally asked myself what was the source of this obstinacy and   13
what was its purpose? That it must have some purposive meaning I was convinced, for there is no truly living thing that does not have a final meaning, that can in other words be explained as a mere leftover from antecedent facts. But the energy of the transference is so strong that it gives one the impression of a vital instinct. That being so, what is the purpose of such fantasies? A careful examination and analysis of the dreams, especially of the one just quoted, revealed a very marked tendency—in contrast to conscious criticism, which always seeks to reduce things to human proportions—to endow the person of the doctor with superhuman attributes. He had to be gigantic, primordial, huger than the father, like the wind that sweeps over the earth—was he then to be made into a god? Or, I said to myself, was it rather the case that the unconscious was trying to *create* a god out of the person of the doctor, as it were to free a vision of God from the veils of the personal, so that the transference to the person of the doctor was no more than a misunderstanding on the part of the conscious mind, a stupid trick played by "sound common sense"? Was the urge of the unconscious perhaps only apparently reaching out towards the person, but in a deeper sense towards a god? Could the longing for a god be a *passion* welling up from our darkest, instinctual nature, a passion unswayed by any outside influences, deeper and stronger perhaps than the love for a human person? Or was it perhaps the highest and truest meaning of that inappropriate love we call transference, a little bit of real *Gottesminne*,[4] that has been lost to consciousness ever since the fifteenth century?

No one will doubt the reality of a passionate longing for a human   14
person; but that a fragment of religious psychology, a historical

---

[4] **Gottesminne** Love of God.

anachronism, indeed something of a medieval curiosity—we are reminded of Mechtild of Magdeburg[5]—should come to light as an immediate living reality in the middle of the consulting room, and be expressed in the prosaic figure of the doctor, seems almost too fantastic to be taken seriously.

A genuinely scientific attitude must be unprejudiced. The sole   15 criterion for the validity of a hypothesis is whether or not it possesses a heuristic—i.e., explanatory—value. The question now is, can we regard the possibilities set forth above as a valid hypothesis? There is no a priori[6] reason why it should not be just as possible that the unconscious tendencies have a goal beyond the human person, as that the unconscious can "do nothing but wish." Experience alone can decide which is the more suitable hypothesis.

This new hypothesis was not entirely plausible to my very critical   16 patient. The earlier view that I was the father-lover, and as such presented an ideal solution of the conflict, was incomparably more attractive to her way of feeling. Nevertheless her intellect was sufficiently clear to appreciate the theoretical possibility of the new hypothesis. Meanwhile the dreams continued to disintegrate the person of the doctor and swell them to ever vaster proportions. Concurrently with this there now occurred something which at first I alone perceived, and with the utmost astonishment, namely a kind of subterranean undermining of the transference. Her relations with a certain friend deepened perceptibly, notwithstanding the fact that consciously she still clung to the transference. So that when the time came for leaving me, it was no catastrophe, but a perfectly reasonable parting. I had the privilege of being the only witness during the process of severance. I saw how the transpersonal control point developed—I cannot call it anything else—a *guiding function* and step by step gathered to itself all the former personal overvaluations; how, with this afflux of energy, it gained influence over the resisting conscious mind without the patient's consciously noticing what was happening. From this I realized that the dreams were not just fantasies, but self-representations of unconscious developments which allowed the psyche of the patient gradually to grow out of the pointless personal tie.

This change took place, as I showed, through the unconscious   17 development of a transpersonal control point; a virtual goal, as it were, that expressed itself symbolically in a form which can only be described as a vision of God. The dreams swelled the human person of the doctor to superhuman proportions, making him a gigantic

---

[5]**Mechtild of Magdeburg (1207–1282)** Thirteenth-century German mystic, writer, and saint.

[6]**a priori** Based on theory rather than on experiment or evidence.

primordial father who is at the same time the wind, and in whose protecting arms the dreamer rests like an infant. If we try to make the patient's conscious, and traditionally Christian, idea of God responsible for the divine image in the dreams, we would still have to lay stress on the distortion. In religious matters the patient had a critical and agnostic attitude, and her idea of a possible deity had long since passed into the realm of the inconceivable, i.e., had dwindled into a complete abstraction. In contrast to this, the god-image of the dreams corresponded to the archaic conception of a nature demon, something like Wotan.[7] *Theos to pneûma*, "God is spirit," is here translated back into its original form where *pneûma* means "wind": God is the wind, stronger and mightier than man, an invisible breath-spirit. As in the Hebrew *ruach*, so in Arabic *ruh* means breath and spirit. Out of the purely personal form the dreams developed an archaic god-image that is infinitely far from the conscious idea of God. It might be objected that this is simply an infantile image, a childhood memory. I would have no quarrel with this assumption if we were dealing with an old man sitting on a golden throne in heaven. But there is no trace of any sentimentality of that kind; instead, we have a primitive conception that can correspond only to an archaic mentality. These primitive conceptions, of which I have given a large number of examples in my *Symbols of Transformation*, tempt one to make, in regard to unconscious material, a distinction very different from that between "preconscious" and "unconscious" or "subconscious" and "unconscious." The justification for these distinctions need not be discussed here. They have a definite value and are worth refining further as points of view. The fundamental distinction which experience has forced upon me merely claims the value of a further point of view. From what has been said it is clear that we have to distinguish in the unconscious a layer which we may call the *personal unconscious*. The materials contained in this layer are of a personal nature insofar as they have the character partly of acquisitions derived from the individual's life and partly of psychological factors which could just as well be conscious. It is readily understandable that incompatible psychological elements are liable to repression and therefore become unconscious; but on the other hand we also have the possibility of making and keeping the repressed contents conscious, once they have been recognized. We recognize them as personal contents because we can discover their effects, or their partial manifestation, or their specific origin in our personal past. They are the integral components of the personality, they belong to its inventory, and their loss to consciousness produces an inferiority in one or the

---

[7]**Wotan** Supreme God; character in Richard Wagner's *Ring* cycle of operas.

other respect—an inferiority, moreover, that has the psychological character not so much of an organic mutilation or an inborn defect as of a want which gives rise to a feeling of moral resentment. The sense of moral inferiority always indicates that the missing element is something which, one feels, should not be missing, or which could be made conscious if only one took enough trouble. The feeling of moral inferiority does not come from a collision with the generally accepted and, in a sense, arbitrary moral law, but from the conflict with one's own self which, for reasons of psychic equilibrium, demands that the deficit be redressed. Whenever a sense of moral inferiority appears, it shows that there is not only the demand to assimilate an unconscious component, but also the possibility of assimilating it. In the last resort it is a man's moral qualities which force him, either through direct recognition of the necessity to do so, or indirectly through a painful neurosis, to assimilate his unconscious self and to keep himself fully conscious. Whoever progresses along this road of realizing the unconscious self must inevitably bring into consciousness the contents of the personal unconscious, thus widening the scope of his personality. I should add at once that this "widening" primarily concerns the moral consciousness, one's self-knowledge, for the unconscious contents that are released and brought into consciousness by analysis are usually unpleasant—which is precisely why these wishes, memories, tendencies, plans, etc. were repressed. These are the contents that are brought to light in much the same way by a thorough confession, though to a much more limited extent. The rest comes out as a rule in dream analysis. It is often very interesting to watch how the dreams fetch up the essential points, bit by bit and with the nicest choice. The total material that is added to consciousness causes a considerable widening of the horizon, a deepened self-knowledge which, more than anything else, is calculated to humanize a man and make him modest. But even self-knowledge, assumed by all wise men to be the best and most efficacious, has different effects on different characters. We make very remarkable discoveries in this respect in practical analysis, . . .

As my example of the archaic idea of God shows, the unconscious seems to contain other things besides personal acquisitions and belongings. My patient was quite unconscious of the derivation of "spirit" from "wind," or of the parallelism between the two. This content was not the product of her thinking, nor had she ever been taught it. The critical passage in the New Testament was inaccessible to her—*to pneûma pneî hopou thelei*[8]—since she knew no Greek. If we must take it as a wholly personal acquisition, it might be a case

18

---

[8] *to pneûma pneî hopou thelei* The wind blows where it wishes (John 3:8).

of so-called cryptomnesia,[9] the unconscious recollection of a thought which the dreamer had once read somewhere. I have nothing against such a possibility in this particular case; but I have seen a sufficient number of other cases—many of them are to be found in the book mentioned above—where cryptomnesia can be excluded with certainty. Even if it were a case of cryptomnesia, which seems to me very improbable, we should still have to explain what the predisposition was that caused just this image to be retained and later, as Semon puts it, "ecphorated" (*ekphoreîn*, Latin *efferre*, "to produce"). In any case, cryptomnesia or no cryptomnesia, we are dealing with a genuine and thoroughly primitive god image that grew up in the unconscious of a civilized person and produced a living effect—an effect which might well give the psychologist of religion food for reflection. There is nothing about this image that could be called personal: it is a wholly collective image, the ethnic origin of which has long been known to us. Here is a historical image of worldwide distribution that has come into existence again through a natural psychic function. This is not so very surprising, since my patient was born into the world with a human brain which presumably still functions today much as it did of old. We are dealing with a reactivated archetype, as I have elsewhere called these primordial images. These ancient images are restored to life by the primitive, analogical mode of thinking peculiar to dreams. It is not a question of inherited ideas, but of inherited thought patterns.

In view of these facts we must assume that the unconscious contains not only personal, but also impersonal, collective components in the form of inherited categories or archetypes. I have therefore advanced the hypothesis that at its deeper levels the unconscious possesses collective contents in a relatively active state. That is why I speak of the collective unconscious.

19

---

[9] Cf. Théodore Flournoy, *Des Indes à la planète Mars: Étude sur un cas de somnambulisme avec glossolalie* (Paris and Geneva, 1900; trans. by D. B. Vermilye as *From India to the Planet Mars*, New York, 1900), and Jung, "Psychology and Pathology of So-called Occult Phenomena," *Coll. Works*, Vol. 1, pp. 81ff. [Jung's note]

QUESTIONS FOR CRITICAL READING

1. What is Jung's view of the relationship of the unconscious mind to the conscious mind? How does it compare to Freud's?

2. What is repression? Why does repression work as it does?

3. How does transference work in psychoanalytic treatment? Is it a good thing or not?

4. What is unusual about Jung's patient's dream? What about it can he not fit into a normal pattern of transference?

5. What is the distinction between the personal unconscious and the collective unconscious?

6. Do you agree that "Dreams contain images and thought associations which we do not create with conscious intent" (para. 9)? Why or why not?

SUGGESTIONS FOR CRITICAL WRITING

1. Jung talks about common sense and its limitations. For some people, common sense denies the existence of an unconscious mind. Relying on Jung, your own personal experiences, and any other sources you choose, defend the existence of an unconscious mind. At the same time, do your best to explain the content of the unconscious and why it is important to the individual.

2. With reference to your own dreams, argue for or against the belief that dreams are products of the conscious mind. Have you had dreams whose content did not pass the "threshold" of your conscious mind?

3. Although the adult Jung was not religious, as the son of a Swiss pastor he was well acquainted with religion. In paragraph 13, Jung asserts that his patient's dream reveals a fundamental human longing for God. As he puts it, "Could the longing for a god be a *passion* welling up from our darkest, instinctual nature?" Examine the possibility that such a psychological phenomenon has affected your attitude toward religion and religious belief.

4. Jung suggests that mythic literature maintains some of the images that make up the collective unconscious of a group of people. Select a myth (consult Ovid's *Metamorphosis*, Grimm's fairy tales, or the Greek myths, or choose a pattern of mythic behavior repeated in popular films) and analyze the instinctual longing it represents for us. What does the myth reveal about our culture?

5. **CONNECTIONS** Jung was a follower of Freud until he eventually broke from him. The break was not altogether friendly, and the feelings between the two—on professional matters—were often strained. Compare Jung's approach to the subject of the unconscious with Freud's. In what respects do they differ? In what ways are their methods either compatible or incompatible with each other? Do you find Jung's methods more or less useful than Freud's? Explain why.

6. **CONNECTIONS** In "Natural Selection" (p. 897), Charles Darwin suggests that as humans developed over a long period of time they may have continued many traditions that began early in history. How would Darwin's ideas help reinforce the concept of an unconscious that might transcend the ages and thus become part of our collective "memory"

gathered through eons of evolution? Would Jung have found Darwin's ideas congenial, or would he have discounted them? Does he show any evidence of having been influenced by Darwin? Explain.

7. **CONNECTIONS** Jung reasons from his unconscious mind, the mind that produces dreams. Descartes began his method of inquiry in his own mind, establishing that he existed because he was thinking (**bedfordstmartins.com/worldofideas/epages**), which is another way of saying that he reasoned from his conscious mind. Since neither Jung nor Descartes resort to sensory evidence for their arguments, can you confidently say that their methods are compatible? Compare the two writers in the manner in which they argue their case. Which is more convincing? How similar are their approaches to reality?

8. **SEEING CONNECTIONS** Would Jung consider Dalí's *The Persistence of Memory* (p. 861) to be an example of the personal or of the collective "memory"? Given what Jung says of the collective unconscious, and considering that Dalí stated the painting developed from a dream, do you feel this painting validates or invalidates Jung's theories? What elements in the painting most satisfy Jung's requirements for understanding the collective unconscious? Is it likely that Dalí somehow represented the collective unconscious in this painting and that as a result the painting quickly became world famous? Or is the collective unconscious irrelevant to the painting?

Acknowledgments

Text Credits

Hannah Arendt, "Total Domination" from *The Origins of Totalitarianism*. Copyright © 1973, 1968, 1966, 1958, 1951, 1948 by Hannah Arendt and renewed 2001, 1996, 1994, 1988 by Lotte Kohler. Copyright © renewed 1979 by Mary McCarthy West. Copyright © renewed 1976 by Hannah Arendt. Reprinted with permission of Houghton Mifflin Harcourt Publishing Company and Georges Borchardt, Inc. on behalf of the Hannah Arendt Bluecher Literary Trust. All rights reserved.

Aristotle, "Democracy and Oligarchy" from *The Oxford Translation of Aristotle*, Volume 10, translated by B. Jowett, edited by W. D. Ross. Copyright © 1921 by Oxford University Press. Reprinted with permission of Oxford University Press. All rights Reserved.

James Baldwin, "If Black English Isn't a Language, Then Tell Me, What Is?" originally published in *The New York Times*. Collected in *James Baldwin: Collected Essays*, published by Library of America. Copyright © 1979 by James Baldwin. Reprinted with permission of the James Baldwin Estate. All rights reserved.

Carl L. Becker, "The Ideal" and "Afterthoughts on Constitutions" from *Modern Democracy* and from *Yale Review*, XXVII, 455. 1941. Copyright © 1941 by Carl L. Becker. Reprinted with permission of Blackwell Publishing Ltd.

Benazir Bhutto, "Islam and Democracy: History and Practice" from *Reconciliation: Islam, Democracy, and the West*. Copyright © 2008 by Benazir Bhutto. Reprinted with permission of HarperCollins Publishers. All rights reserved.

Bill Bryson, "Where Words Come From" from *The Mother Tongue*. Copyright © 1990 by Bill Bryson. Reprinted with permission of HarperCollins Publishers. All rights reserved.

Judith Butler, "Doing Justice to Someone: Sex Reassignment and Allegories of Transsexuality" from *Undoing Gender*. Copyright © 2004 by Routledge. Reprinted with permission of Taylor Francis Group, LLC, via Copyright Clearance Center. All rights reserved.

Stephen L. Carter, "The Separation of Church and State" from *The Culture of Disbelief: How American Law and Politics Trivialize Religious Devotion*. Copyright © 1993 by Stephen L. Carter. Reprinted with permission of the author. [e-Pages selection]

Marcus Tullius Cicero, translated by Michael Grant, "The Defense of Injustice" from *On Government*. Copyright © 1993 by Michael Grant. Reprinted with permission of Penguin Books Limited. All rights reserved. [e-Pages selection]

Noam Chomsky, "New Horizons in the Study of Language" from *New Horizons in the Study of Language and Mind*. Copyright © 2000 by Noam Chomsky. Reprinted with permission of Cambridge University Press. All rights reserved.

Lydia Davis, "Trying to Learn" from *Almost No Memory*. Copyright © 1997 by Lydia Davis. Reprinted with permission of Farrar, Straus and Giroux, LLC. All rights reserved.

Sigmund Freud, translated and edited by James Strachey "The Oedipus Complex" from *The Interpretation of Dreams, The Standard Edition of the Complete Psychological Works of Sigmund Freud,* Volume IV. Copyright © 1953 by Sigmund Freud. Copyright © 2010 by Sigmund Freud, James Strachey. Reprinted with permission of The Marsh Agency Ltd on behalf of Sigmund Freud Copyrights, Basic Books, a member of the Perseus Books Group, and The Random House Group Limited. All rights reserved.

Milton and Rose D. Friedman, "Created Equal" from *Free to Choose: A Personal Statement*. Copyright © 1980 by Milton Friedman and Rose D. Friedman. Reprinted with permission of Houghton Mifflin Harcourt Publishing Company. All rights reserved.[e-Pages selection]

John Kenneth Galbraith, "The Position of Poverty" from *The Affluent Society*, 4th Edition. Copyright © 1958, 1969, 1976, 1984 by John Kenneth Galbraith. Reprinted with permission of Houghton Mifflin Harcourt Publishing Company. All rights reserved.

Howard Gardner, "Designing Education for Understanding" from *The Disciplined Mind: What All Students Should Understand*. Copyright © 1999 by Howard Gardner. Reprinted with permission of Simon & Schuster, Inc. All rights reserved.

Michael S. Gazzaniga, "Toward a Universal Ethics" from *The Ethical Brain*. Copyright © 2005 by Michael S. Gazzaniga. Published by Dana Press, New York. Reprinted with permission. All rights reserved.

Germaine Greer, "Masculinity" from *The Whole Woman*. Copyright © 1996 by Germaine Greer. Reprinted with permission of Alfred A. Knopf, a division of Random House, Inc. and Aitken Alexander Associates, Ltd. All rights reserved.

Karen Horney, "The Distrust between the Sexes." Speech read before the Berlin-Brandenburg Branch of the German Women's Medical Association, November 20, 1930, as "Das Misstrauen zwischen den Geschlechtern," *Die Ärztin*, VII. Copyright © 1930 by the Estate of Karen Horney. Reprinted with permission. [e-Pages selection]

C. G. Jung, excerpt from *Psyche and Symbol*. Copyright © 1991 by Princeton University Press. Reprinted with permission of Princeton University Press. All rights reserved.

Martin Luther King Jr., "Letter from Birmingham Jail." Copyright © 1963 by Dr. Martin Luther King Jr.; copyright © renewed 1991 by Coretta Scott King. Reprinted with permission. All rights reserved.

Jonathan Kozol, "The Uses of Diversity" from *Letters to a Young Teacher*. Copyright © 2007 by Jonathan Kozol. Reprinted with permission of Crown Publishers, a division of Random House, Inc. All rights reserved.

Susanne K. Langer, "Language" from *Philosophy in a New Key: A Study in the Symbolism of Reason, Rite, and Art*, 3rd Edition, pp. 118–128, Cambridge, Mass.: Harvard University Press. Copyright © 1942, 1951, 1957 by the President and Fellows of Harvard College. Copyright © renewed 1970, 1979 by Susanne Knauth Langer, 1985 by Leonard C. R. Langer. Reprinted with permission. All rights reserved.

Niccolò di Bernardo Machiavelli, translated by Mark Musa and Peter Bondanella, edited by Peter Bondanella and Mark Musa, "The Prince" from *The Portable Machiavelli*. Translation copyright © 1979 by The Viking Press, Inc. Reprinted with permission of Penguin Group (USA) Inc. All rights reserved.

Margaret Mead, "Sex and Temperament" from *Sex and Temperament: Three Primitive Societies*. Copyright © 1935 by Margaret Mead. Published by William Morrow & Co. Reprinted with permission of the American Anthropological Association. Not for sale or further reproduction. All rights reserved.

Stephen Mitchell, selections from *Tao Te Ching: A New English Version, with Foreword and Notes*. Translation copyright © 1988 by Stephen Mitchell. Reprinted with permission of HarperCollins Publishers. All rights reserved.

Iris Murdoch, "Morality and Religion" from *Metaphysics as a Guide to Morals*. Copyright © 1992 by Iris Murdoch. Published by Chatto & Windus. Reprinted with permission of The Random House Group Limited, Penguin Group (USA) Inc., and Ed Victor Ltd. All rights reserved.

Friedrich Nietzsche, edited and translated by Walter Kaufmann, "Morality as Anti-Nature" from *The Portable Nietzsche*. Translation copyright © 1954 by The Viking Press, renewed © 1982 by Viking Press Penguin, Inc. Reprinted with permission of Penguin Group (USA) Inc. All rights reserved.

Julius K. Nyerere, "One-Party Government" as appeared in *African Intellectual Heritage: A Book of Sources*, originally published in *Transition: A Journal of the Arts, Culture, and Society*, Vol. 1, No. 2, December 1961. Copyright © 1961 by Julius K. Nyerere. Reprinted with permission of the publisher, Indiana University Press. All rights reserved.

Mario Pei, "Theories of Language Beginning" from *The Story of Language*. Copyright © 1949, 1965 by Mario Pei. Reprinted with permission of HarperCollins Publishers. All rights reserved.

Image Credits

[8.3] Page 878. Francis Bacon. © ARPL/HIP/The Image Works.

[8.4] Page 896. Charles Darwin. © Mansell/Time Life Pictures/Getty Images.

[8.5] Page 914. Sigmund Freud. © ARPL/HIP/The Image Works.

[8.6] Page 926. Photograph of Carl Jung. © Hulton Archive/Getty Images.

Photo/Art Credits: e-Pages

[e.1.2] Photo of Stephen L. Carter. © Kathy deWitt/Alamy.

[e.2.2] Bust of Marcus Tullius Cicero. Alfredo Dagli Orti / The Art Archive at Art Resource, NY.

[e.3.2] Bust of Artistotle. Museo Nazionale Romano Rome /Collection Dagli Orti/The Art Archive at Art Resource, NY.

[e.4.2] Photo of Milton and Rose Friedman. © Alex Wong/Getty Images.

[e.5.2] Photo of Ralph Waldo Emerson. © Hulton Archive /Getty Images.

[e.6.2] Photo of Karen Horney. © Photo Researchers/Getty Images.

[e.7.2] Portrait of Alexander Pope. © Hulton Archive /Getty Images.

[e.8.2] Etching of Rene Descartes. © Bettmann/CORBIS.

INDEX OF
RHETORICAL TERMS

Missing something? To access the e-Pages that accompany this text, visit **bedfordstmartins.com/worldofideas/epages**. Students who do not buy a new print book can purchase access to e-Pages at this site.

Inside the e-Pages for *A World of Ideas*

PART ONE: DEMOCRACY
Howard Chandler Christy, *Scene at the Signing of the Constitution of the United States* [Color image]
Stephen L. Carter, *The Separation of Church and State*

PART TWO: GOVERNMENT
Eugéne Delacroix, *Liberty Leading the People* [Color image]
Marcus Tullius Cicero, *The Defense of Injustice*

PART THREE: ETHICS AND MORALITY
Joseph Wright of Derby, *An Experiment on a Bird in the Air Pump* [Color image]
Aristotle, *The Aim of Man*

PART FOUR: WEALTH AND POVERTY
Henry Ossawa Tanner, *The Thankful Poor* [Color image]
Milton and Rose Friedman, *Created Equal*

PART FIVE: EDUCATION
Norman Rockwell, *The Problem We All Live With* [Color image]
Ralph Waldo Emerson, *On Education*

PART SIX: GENDER AND CULTURE
Mary Cassatt, *In the Loge* [Color image]
Karen Horney, *The Distrust between the Sexes*

PART SEVEN: LANGUAGE
Wosene Worke Kosrof, *The Color of Words IX* [Color image]
Alexander Pope, from *An Essay on Criticism*

PART EIGHT: DISCOVERIES AND THE MIND
Salvador Dalí, *The Persistence of Memory* [Color image]
René Descartes, *Fourth Meditation: Of Truth and Error*